Encyclopedia of Sociology

Second Edition

Editorial Board

Encyclopedia of Sociology

Second Edition

VOLUME 4

Edgar F. Borgatta
Editor-in-Chief
University of Washington, Seattle

Rhonda J. V. Montgomery
Managing Editor
University of Kansas, Lawrence

Macmillan Reference USA
an imprint of the Gale Group
New York • Detroit • San Francisco • London • Boston • Woodbridge, CT

Encyclopedia of Sociology
Second Edition

Macmillan Reference USA
an imprint of The Gale Group
1633 Broadway
New York, NY 10019

Library of Congress Catalog in Publication Data

Encyclopedia of Sociology / Edgar F. Borgatta, editor-in-chief, Rhonda Montgomery, managing editor.—2nd ed.
    p. cm.
    Includes bibliographical references and index.
    ISBN 0-02-864853-6 (set: alk paper)—ISBN 0-02-864849-8 (v. 1: alk. paper)—0-02-864850-1 (v. 2)—0-02-864851-X (v. 3)—0-02-864852-8 (v. 4)—0-02-865581-8 (v. 5)
    1. Sociology—Encyclopedias. I. Borgatta, Edgar F., 1924- II. Montgomery, Rhonda J. V.

HM425 .E5 2000
301'.03—dc21   00-028402
                                                               CIP

Printed in the United States of America by the Gale Group
Gale Group and Design is a trademark used herein under license.

Q

QUALITATIVE METHODS

The term *qualitative methods* refers to a variety of research techniques and procedures associated with the goal of trying to understand the complexities of the social world in which we live and how we go about thinking, acting, and making meaning in our lives. These research practices, which emphasize getting close to participants and trying to understand how they (and we) view the world, include, among others, participant observation, interviews, life histories, and focus groups; autoethnographic, phenomenological, narrative, and most ethnomethodological and feminist approaches; particular forms of documentary, content, discourse, and conversational analysis research; and some action research.

Qualitative researchers may be placed along a broad continuum ranging from an orientation akin to positivist science to one more akin to art and literature. In between is a vast middle ground where elements of both orientations are present. Moving along the qualitative continuum from science to art and literature, one finds practitioners who see social life as something out there to be discovered independently of the researcher, those who view social life as something constructed through interaction and engagement with the world, and those who focus more closely on the person describing social life and the modes and practices of description (see Crotty 1998; Denzin 1997). Across the continuum, the focus changes from studying others who are assumed to be uniquely separate from the researcher, to examining interactions between the researcher and others, to including the positionality, politics, and story of the researcher who interacts with others.

Currently qualitative work enjoys a burgeoning interest across social science disciplines including anthropology, sociology, communication, education, social work, and nursing. The result is a growing sense of a qualitative community unconstrained by disciplinary boundaries. As this community grows and forms its identity, the spectrum of possibilities broadens, creating new alternatives for qualitative research and, in the process, raising vexing and controversial questions (see Denzin and Lincoln 1995; Snow and Morrill 1995). Given the interpretive turn (Rabinow and Sullivan 1987) in social science, more and more researchers are applying art-based criteria to their work; at the same time, new computer programs, such as NVivo, allow for more systematic and rigorous coding of qualitative data. We view these differences and ensuing conversations as strengthening qualitative research and representing a coming of age for qualitative work (Bochner and Ellis in press).

We organize our discussion of qualitative methods according to three ideal types representing points on the qualitative continuum from the science/causal pole through the middle ground to the artful/interpretive pole. These categories are intended as a useful means of dividing the territory, but they are also arbitrary and should not be taken as a literal map of the field. Rather, we encourage readers to envision a wide expanse of methodological approaches and to view the boundaries we have constructed as permeable, flexible, and fleeting, with many qualitative researchers likely to position themselves in more than one category. As the authors, both of us have engaged in middle ground and artful/interpretive qualitative work; our current allegiance lies primarily in the artful/interpretive region of the continuum.

QUALITATIVE RESEARCH AS SCIENCE

At one end of the qualitative spectrum, researchers approach qualitative research as an extension of quantitative inquiry. Their goal is to produce propositional knowledge about human behavior generalizable to specific populations. They see truth as something "out there" to be discovered and explained by the researcher. Positioning themselves as neutral, disinterested parties in the research process, they want to be able to control and predict subsequent behavior of samples within the population being investigated. These researchers follow the building-block, foundational model of scientific knowledge, viewing inquiry as a linear progression, with each new discovery adding on to available explanations. Qualitative researchers in this tradition express many of the same concerns as their quantitative counterparts, including an interest in random sampling, reliability, validity, and ethical issues. The language they use to present and discuss results applies many of the familiar lines of the hypothetico-deductive model.

Random sampling of the studied population (regardless of specific research tools to be used) provides assurance that the qualitative researcher has obtained a representative and unbiased sample of research subjects (Lindlof 1995, p. 121). Since researchers want to claim that their findings can be generalized to the selected population, it is critical that the demographic characteristics of the sample match those of the population defined in the study. For example, Lowry and Towles (1989), in their study of the portrayal of sex and its consequences in afternoon soap operas, randomly sampled episodes of soap operas from each TV network in order to be able to draw conclusions about soap opera content in general.

Using an approach similar to that of quantitative research, qualitative researchers in this tradition examine variables that relate to specific behaviors, traits, or characteristics that are narrowly defined in as specific a manner as possible. They manipulate the independent variables and measure the outcome of the experiment in terms of dependent variables, those defined behaviors, traits, or characteristics thought to exist in relationship to the independent variables. Before they conduct experiments, researchers form a hypothesis about the relationship between the variables. Data interpretation then centers on determining whether the hypotheses are negated by the results; researchers do not generally examine data for themes or issues unrelated to the predetermined focuses of the study. Based on a review of relevant literature, Chavez (1985), for example, hypothesized that writers treat men and women differently in comic strips. She then collected a sample of comic strips, coded the gender, settings, and activities of the characters, and concluded that her hypothesis was supported.

This process of hypothesis formation and testing often is less formal, however, even among those striving to maintain a scientific approach to their research, and it can take many different forms. In the study of the realism of aggression on television by Potter et al. (1995), for example, the authors laid out a set of premises about what would constitute a realistic (similar to the real world levels of violence in numbers and context) portrayal of aggression. They then collected a sample of television programming, coded the various acts of aggression, and compared the numbers and types of aggression in their sample to the premises they had developed.

Even those researchers who do not convert their data into numerical form often go to great lengths to assure that their findings are valid and reliable. For researchers at this end of the qualitative continuum, validity means that the concepts they examine are those intended to be examined and not confounded or overlapping with other concepts not intended to be included. A study is reliable if researchers find, or could expect to find, the same, or very similar, results when they conduct the study again For example, Waitzkin (1990) provides criteria to establish reliability and validity of qualitative data: (1) discourse should be selected through a sampling procedure, preferably a randomized technique; (2) recordings of sampled discourse should be available for review by other observers; (3) standardized rules of transcription should be used; (4) the reliability of transcription should be assessed by multiple observers; (5) procedures of interpretation should be decided in advance, should be validated in relation to theory, and should address both content and structure of texts; (6) the reliability of applying interpretive procedures should be assessed by multiple observers; (7) a summary and excerpts from transcripts should accompany the interpretation, but full transcripts should also be available for review; and (8) texts and interpretations should convey the variability of content and structure across sampled texts (pp. 480–482).

Waitzkin's criteria (1990) emphasize three specific concerns associated with reliability and validity from a scientific perspective. First, the collective decisions and interpretations of multiple researchers would be closer to an "objective" reality than a presumably more biased perspective of a single individual. Second, it is important to consider the whole body of available data as the basis for interpretation to avoid making general statements that reflect only a subset of the data; the emphasis is on what is common throughout the data, not on that which is unusual, distinctive, or unique. Third, written transcripts must be publicly available for verification.

Qualitative researchers working in this tradition use a system of coding to categorize videotaped or observed behaviors, written responses to survey questions, verbal responses to an interviewer, or other data (Wimmer and Dominick 1997). Once labeled, the observed behaviors can be counted, sorted, and analyzed statistically. Coding schema can be standardized typologies that are used by other researchers, or they can be developed in light of a specific research question or body of data. Chavez (1985), mentioned above, developed a typology of settings and activities (e.g., child care or working in an office) for the cartoon characters based on what she found in her comic strip data set. To aid in the analysis of transcript data, specialized computer software programs, such as NUD*IST, Ethnograph, or NVivo (a new program that integrates text, image, sound, and video data sets), are available. A critical component to coding is establishing intercoder agreement; that is, a measure to ensure that the coding schema can be consistently applied to the same set of data by different coders and the same or very similar results obtained (Wimmer and Dominick 1997).

Ethical issues at this end of the continuum, similar to those in quantitative research, focus on methodological procedures, in particular honesty and thoroughness in data collection and analysis. Authors often elaborately spell out their research procedures in their publications, making the procedures and data available for scrutiny in order to justify claims or conclusions they draw. In science-oriented qualitative research, authors stay behind the scenes, portraying themselves as trustworthy and credible through their disembodied discussion of methods without showing in their texts their own involvement or self-interest.

Those engaging in scientific approaches to qualitative research usually adhere closely to the writing style used by quantitative researchers. A passive voice shadows the presence of the author and obscures the "I" of the researcher (Gergen 1994). Statements such as "It was found that . . ." and "The data revealed that . . ." reinforce the notion of neutral authors who have discovered preexisting ideas, and who, without contaminating the material with their own perspectives, then pass it along for readers to receive as knowledge. Of course, researchers who see their work as scientific often acknowledge that the author is not a blank slate without values and beliefs, but their use of a disinterested, passive voice remains a sign of how important they view the ideal of distance and objectivity, even if it is not fully attainable.

MIDDLE-GROUND APPROACHES TO RESEARCH

Between science and art, one finds a sprawling middle ground of qualitative researchers, who seek to analyze events, find patterns, and create models from their data (Neuman 1997). Here, researchers do not adhere rigidly to the rules of empiricism; but they are not likely to experiment with narrative, poetic, or literary forms of writing either. In the middle, researchers seek some combination of scientific rigor and artistic imagination. How these two goals intersect differs for various researchers and often connects to the author's specific location relative to art and science on the qualitative continuum.

Middle-ground researchers use a variety of methodologies to gather data for analysis, including unstructured or semistructured interviewing (Fontana and Frey 1994; Mishler 1986), focus groups (Kitzinger 1994), participant observation or fieldwork (Lincoln and Guba 1985; Lofland and Lofland 1995), textual analysis (Reinharz 1992), and analysis of narrative (M. M. Gergen 1992; Riessman 1993). While there are many ways to go about selecting a sample, those in the middle ground of qualitative research often use purposeful sampling (Miles and Huberman 1984), in which they try to obtain cases that are information rich, or a "snowball" approach (Reinharz 1992), in which they ask current participants to identify other possible participants.

One of the most useful and widely applied strategies associated with the middle ground is an approach, developed by Glaser and Strauss (1967), called *grounded theory*. In this approach, researchers emphasize the generation of categories and theory from systematic coding and analysis of qualitative data (often transcripts) (Charmaz 1990; Glaser and Strauss 1967; Janesick 1994). This method of inductive reasoning differs from traditional social science in which researchers use previously established theory and test it deductively with data to see whether the theory can be sustained.

Methodological concerns are very important to grounded theory researchers, who often hold to the belief that if you apply a valid and systematic methodological approach, you'll get closer to an accurate representation of what's actually going on. In analyzing the data, some adhere rigidly to formal steps in grounded theory research—data notes, sort and classify, open coding, axial coding, selective coding, with memo writing occurring throughout the process (Charmaz 1990; Neuman 1997; Strauss and Corbin 1994). The more the researcher adheres to systematic analysis, the greater the likelihood of using computer programs to assist in coding. Other theorists, in the middle of the continuum, who think of themselves as grounded theorists, "eyeball" the data in less systematic ways, perhaps not even completely transcribing or coding data into categories. Yet they too seek patterns among the data they have collected, though they view the process as more subjective and intuitive than scientific and objective.

While some middle-ground researchers may place less emphasis on scientific precision, they usually adhere to criteria or guidelines concerning the processes of data analysis, though these rules may vary widely (see, for example, Charmaz 1997; Glaser 1978; Strauss and Corbin 1997). Tompkins (1994), for example, refers to representativeness,

consistency (for public and private texts), and recalcitrance (sanction by research participants or a similar group) as standards for evaluating data used in qualitative research (see also Fitch 1994). Working closer to the interpretive pole, Lather (1986) argues that validity in openly ideological research can be established through four guidelines: *triangulation* of multiple data sources, methods, and theoretical perspective; *assessment* of construct validity through use of systematized reflexivity between the daily experiences of people and the theoretical constructs being developed; *establishment* of face validity through sharing analysis with respondents and refining analysis with their input; and *determination* of catalytic validity, that is the potential for bringing about positive change and social transformation (p. 67). These different criteria are similar insofar as they provide standards for bridging researcher and participant perspectives, so that findings reflect the meanings of the people whose lives were examined.

Ethical issues for those in the middle group focus on research practices such as covert research, deception, informed consent, anonymity, confidentiality, and revealing knowledge about the less powerful. These issues then lead to ethical questions about what should be studied, how, and by whom (see Lofland and Lofland 1995).

Most middle-ground researchers note the positionality of participants, such as race, class, and sexual orientation, in order to avoid obscuring these factors. For example, Ellingson and Buzzanell (1999) studied a group of white, middle-class, heterosexual breast cancer survivors in a small Midwestern city. They acknowledged that these demographic characteristics impacted the results of the study; a more racially mixed group, or a group composed of lesbians, for instance, most likely would have produced a different set of findings.

Just as those in the middle ground acknowledge the positionality of participants, they also sometimes acknowledge their standpoint, personal background, politics, and interests in the topic (Collins 1991). Insofar as they see knowledge as "constructed" rather than discovered, middle-ground researchers discuss their personal perspectives or political commitments as an acknowledgment that all knowledge is generated from a specific social position and reflects the perspectives of the researchers involved. Researchers in the middle ground may try to decrease the power disparity between themselves and the people they study (DeVault 1990; Ellingson and Buzzanell 1999). They generally refer to those in the study as research participants or informants rather than subjects, indicating a degree of respect for the people whose lives are being studied (Reinharz 1992).

In the middle ground, researchers study a variety of topics, including complex issues that are difficult or impossible to address with quantitative methodology, such as understanding hierarchy in groups (Whyte [1943] 1993) or awareness contexts in death (Glaser and Strauss 1964). Some seek to make visible previously invisible aspects of the lives of women and other groups underrepresented in traditional social scientific research such as ethnic and racial minorities, gays and lesbians, and people with disabilities (Spitzack and Carter 1989). Others examine groups that are hidden, unknown, or inaccessible to most people, such as mushroom gatherers (Fine 1992) or white supremists (Mitchell 1998). As the topics get more complex and oriented toward meanings, subjectivity, and emotionality, it becomes more difficult to invoke older, more traditional, systematic "scientific methods" and apply them.

Writers in this tradition alter some of the conventions of scientific writing. They may include standpoint statements within the introductory section of articles, indicating their personal interest in the topic. They may use a conventional format but preface the article with vignettes or include excerpts from participant narratives in the discussion of findings or in an appendix to add texture and authenticity to the work. To acknowledge their presence in the work, authors may write in the first person. Nevertheless, researchers in this tradition usually privilege theory generation, typicality, and generalization to a wider world over evocative storytelling, concrete experience, and multiple perspectives that include participants' voices and interpretations. They tend to write realist tales in an authorial, omnipotent voice. Snippets of fieldwork data then represent participants' stories, primarily valued for illustrating general concepts, patterns, and themes (see Van Maanen 1988).

RESEARCH AS ARTISTIC ENDEAVOR

During the last two decades, many qualitative researchers have moved toward an emphasis on the artistic aspects of qualitative work (Wolcott 1995). Working from an orientation that blends the practices and emphases of social science with the aesthetic sensibility and expressive forms of art, these researchers seek to tell stories that show experience as lived in all its bodily, cognitive, emotional, and spiritual aspects. The goal is to practice an artful, poetic, and empathic social science in which readers can keep in their minds and feel in their bodies the complexities of concrete moments of lived experience. These writers want readers to be able to put themselves in the place of others, within a culture of experience that enlarges their social awareness and empathy. Their goals include: evoking emotional experience in readers (Ellis 1997); giving voice to stories and groups of people traditionally left out of social scientific inquiry (DeVault 1990); producing writing of high literary/artistic quality (Richardson in press); and improving readers', participants', and authors' lives (see Denzin 1997; Fine 1994).

According to Bochner, Ellis, and their colleagues (Bochner 1994; Bochner et al. 1998; Ellis 1997), the interpretive, narrative, autoethnographic project has the following distinguishing features: the author usually writes in the first person, making herself or himself the object of research (Jackson 1989; Tedlock 1991); the narrative text focuses on generalization within a single case extended over time (Geertz 1973); the text is presented as a story replete with a narrator, characterization, and plot line, akin to forms of writing associated with the novel or biography; the story often discloses hidden details of private life and highlights emotional experience; the ebb and flow of relationship experience is depicted in an episodic form that dramatizes the motion of connected lives across the curve of time; a reflexive connection exists between the lives of participants and researchers that must be explored; and the relationships between writers and readers of the texts is one of involvement and participation.

Rather than believing in the presence of an external, unconstructed truth, researchers on this end of the continuum embrace narrative truth (Spence 1982), which means that the experience as described is believable, lifelike, and possible.

Through narrative we learn to understand the meanings and significance of the past as incomplete, tentative, and revisable according to contingencies of present life circumstances (Crites 1971). In this research, authors are concerned about issues of validity, reliability, and generalizability, but these issues may be redefined to meet the goals of the research.

Ellis and Bochner (in press), for example, define *validity* to mean that the work resonates with readers and evokes in them a feeling that the experience has verisimilitude. A story is valid if it stimulates readers to enter the experience described or to feel and think about their own, whether in memory, anticipated, or lived. Validity might be judged by whether it offers readers assistance in communicating with others different from themselves, or a way to improve the lives of participants and readers or even the author's own. Since writers always create their personal narrative from a situated location, trying to make their present, imagined future, and remembered past cohere, orthodox *reliability* does not exist in narrative research. But reliability checks are still important. Researchers often take their work back to participants and give them a chance to comment, add materials, change their minds, and offer their interpretations. Since we all participate in a limited number of cultures and institutions, lives are typical and generalizable, as well as particular. A story's *generalizability* is constantly being tested by readers as they determine whether the story speaks to them about their own experiences or about the experiences of others they know. Likewise, does it tell them about people or lives about which they are unfamiliar? Does a work bring "felt" news from one world to another and provide opportunities for the reader to have vicarious experience of the things told (Stake 1994)?

Interpretive research reflects the messiness of lived experience and emotions. Unlike researchers at the scientific end and in the middle ground, artful or interpretive researchers do not look for common denominators and generalities, but instead examine experience that is unique, particular, moving, and possible. They embrace their own subjectivity not to acknowledge bias but to celebrate positionality and their particular construction of the world. While some of these writers employ traditional analysis in their work, examining stories for concepts, patterns, and themes,

others argue for the importance of thinking *with* a story, not just about a story. Thinking *with* a story means to allow yourself to resonate with the story, reflect on it, become a part of it (see Frank 1995b). Others argue that theory is embedded in the story (Ellis 1995b), that all good stories make a theoretical point.

Arguments about methods are not nearly as prevalent here as in the other two groups. Methods articles are much more likely to emphasize flexibility and emergence than to offer strict rules for how to proceed (Ellis et al. 1997). One of the most discussed methodological issues is whether researchers should attempt to follow the rules of traditional ethnographic methods or whether narrative research should be approached more like writing fiction. One's position on that question most likely intersects with one's stance regarding the role of criteria in evaluating narrative writing. In the former, traditional ethnographic criteria might be more commonplace; in the latter, narratives might be judged by their usefulness, the compassion they encourage, and the dialogue they promote (Ellis and Bochner in press). Seeking to position interpretive texts as an intersection of social science and art form, Richardson (in press) discusses five criteria she uses to evaluate interpretive ethnography: (1) *Substantive contribution*: Does the work contribute to an understanding of the text? (2) *Aesthetic merit*: Is the text artistically shaped, complex, and satisfying? (3) *Reflexivity*: Does the writer reflect on the production of the text so that the reader can make judgments about the point of view employed in the text? (4) *Impactfulness*: Does this work affect me and move me to respond or act? (5) *Expression of Reality*: Does this work seem a credible account of the real?

Rather than method and criteria, most articles about interpretive/artful ethnography grapple with issues of writing. For narrative researchers, writing (the form) is inseparable from the process of data interpretation (the content). As Richardson (in press) phrases it, writing in interpretive qualitative research is not a "mopping-up" activity at the end of a research project but an integral part of data analysis; authors write to find out what they have to say about their data and their experiences. The voice of the author is as central to the text as the voices of those "being studied." Writers experiment with approaches and writing conventions to dislodge assumptions about science and incorporate the artistic into representations of data.

Interpretive research embraces a range of processes and approaches, including biographical method (Denzin 1989), observation of participation (Tedlock 1991), ethnography (Van Maanen 1988), autoethnography (Ellingson 1998; Reed-Danahay 1997), interactive interviewing (Ellis et al. 1997), systematic sociological introspection (Ellis 1991), co-constructed methods (Bochner and Ellis 1992), personal experience methods (Clandinin and Connelly 1994), narrative analysis (Bochner 1994), and feminist methods (Reinharz 1992).

Examples of creative representation include layered accounts (Ronai 1995), ethnographic fiction (Angrosino 1998), personal essays (Krieger 1991), impressionist tales (Van Maanen 1988), co-constructed narratives (Bochner and Ellis 1992), poetic representation of data (Austin 1996; Glesne 1997; Richardson 1992, 1994), writing stories (Richardson 1997), ethnographic performance or ethnodrama (Jones 1998; Mienczakowski 1996), and polyvocal texts (Lather and Smithies 1997).

A particularly controversial narrative writing practice and form is autoethnography, which is an autobiographical genre of writing and research that displays multiple layers of consciousness as it connects the personal to the cultural. Several autoethnographic genres currently exist side by side (Ellis and Bochner in press): (1) Reflexive ethnographies focus on a culture or subculture, but authors use their own experiences in the culture reflexively to bend back on self and look more deeply at self-other interactions. Reflexive ethnographers ideally use all their senses, their bodies, moment, feeling, and their whole being to learn about the other (Jackson 1989). (2) In native ethnographies, researchers who are natives of cultures that have been marginalized or exoticized by others write about and interpret their own cultures for others. (3) In personal narratives, social scientists take on the dual identities of academic and personal selves to tell autobiographical stories about some aspect of their daily life.

In all these forms of qualitative writing, narrative researchers use fiction-writing techniques such as dramatic recall, dialogue, flashback, strong imagery, scene setting, character development, interior monologue, suspense, and a dramatic plot line that is developed through the specific actions of specific characters with specific bodies doing specific things. They ask readers to relive the events with the writer and then to reflect on their emotional responses and life experiences, and on the moral questions and concerns that arise. Yet, the work differs from fiction in that the writing and publishing conventions used arise out of social science traditions, and in that the work often, though not always, has more of an overt analytic purpose and more of an analytic frame than fiction has.

Ethical concerns include matters of how we go about doing our research and what we owe those who become characters in and readers of our stories (Ellis 1995a). How do we deal with issues of confidentiality when including people, such as family members, who can be easily identified? What do we do if characters in our stories disagree with our interpretations or want us to omit material about them? How do we include multiple voices and perspectives within our stories? What is the role of the traditional authorial voice of the author? How do we stay true to our participants yet not deceive our readers (Josselson 1996; see also Chase 1996)? Is there value in working from an ethic of care, empathy, and responsibility, rather than informed consent, and is that ever possible in the world of research (Collins 1991; Denzin 1997)? How do we make our projects therapeutic for ourselves as well as our participants and readers? What do we want the world to be? How can we contribute to making it that way and, in the process, become better human beings?

CONCLUSION

Qualitative methods is a rich and varied set of approaches to research. Journals such as *Qualitative Inquiry, Qualitative Sociology, Symbolic Interaction*, and the *Journal of Contemporary Ethnography*, as well as a number of research annuals such as *Studies in Symbolic Interaction* and *Cultural Studies: A Research Annual*, along with subfield-specific journals, such as *Qualitative Health Research*, showcase examples of qualitative research in sociology and provide forums for discussion of methodological issues. The joy (and sometimes the frustration!) of qualitative methods is the promotion and valuing of a wide spectrum of methods, none of which should be viewed as the only way to conduct research in sociology. It might be more comforting if there was one set of rules to follow, but that comfort would come with the tragic price of close-mindedness, silencing of voices, and narrowing of vision. We agree with Rorty (1982), who says we ought to learn to live with differences without feeling we have to resolve them.

REFERENCES

Angrosino, M. V. 1998 *Opportunity House: Ethnographic Stories of Mental Retardation*. Walnut Creek, Calif.: AltaMira.

Austin, D. A. 1996 "Kaleidoscope: The Same and Different." In C. Ellis and A. P. Bochner, eds., *Composing Ethnography: Alternative Forms of Qualitative Writing*. Walnut Creek, Calif.: AltaMira.

Bochner, A. P. 1994 "Perspectives on Inquiry II: Theories and Stories." In M. Knapp and G. R. Miller, eds., *The Handbook of Interpersonal Communication*, 2nd ed. Thousand Oaks, Calif.: Sage.

——, and C. Ellis 1992 "Personal Narrative as a Social Approach to Interpersonal Communication." *Communication Theory* 2:165–172.

—— in press "Which Way to Turn?" *Journal of Contemporary Ethnography*.

——, and L. Tillmann-Healy 1998 "Mucking Around Looking for Truth." In B. Montgomery and L. Baxter, eds., *Dialectical Approaches to Studying Personal Relationships*. Mahwah, N.J.: Lawrence Erlbaum.

Chase, S. 1996. "Personal Vulnerability and Interpretive Authority in Narrative Research." In R. Josselson, ed., *Ethics and Process in The Narrative Study of Lives*, vol. 4. Thousand Oaks, Calif.: Sage.

Charmaz, K. 1990 "'Discovering' Chronic Illness: Using Grounded Theory." *Sociology of Health and Illness* 30:1161–1172.

Chavez, D. 1985 "Perpetuation of Gender Inequality: A Content Analysis of Comic Strips." *Sex Roles* 13: 93–102.

Clandinin, D. J., and F. M. Connelly 1994 "Personal Experience Methods." In N. K. Denzin and Y. S. Lincoln, eds., *Handbook of Qualitative Research*. Thousand Oaks, Calif.: Sage.

Collins, P. H. 1991 *Black Feminist Thought*. New York: Routledge.

Crites, S. 1971 "The Narrative Quality of Experience." *Journal of the American Academy of Religion* 39:291–311.

Crotty, M. 1998 *The Foundations of Social Research*. London: Sage.

Denzin, N. 1989 *Interpretive Biography*. Newbury Park, Calif.: Sage.

—— 1997 *Interpretive Ethnography: Ethnographic Practices for the 21st Century*. Thousand Oaks, Calif.: Sage.

——, and Y. Lincoln 1995 "Transforming Qualitative Research Methods: Is It a Revolution?" *Journal of Contemporary Ethnography* 24:349–358.

DeVault, M. L. 1990 "Talking and Listening from Women's Standpoint: Feminist Strategies for Interviewing and Analysis." *Social Problems* 37:96–116.

Ellingson, L. L. 1998 "'Then You Know How I Feel': Empathy, Identification, and Reflexivity in Fieldwork." *Qualitative Inquiry* 4:492–514.

——, and P. M. Buzzanell 1999 "Listening to Women's Narratives of Breast Cancer Treatment: A Feminist Approach to Patient Satisfaction with Physician-Patient Communication." *Health Communication* 11:153–183.

Ellis, C. 1991 "Sociological Introspection and Emotional Experience." *Symbolic Interaction* 14:23–50.

—— 1995a "Emotional and Ethical Quagmires in Returning to the Field." *Journal of Contemporary Ethnography* 24:711–713.

—— 1995b *Final Negotiations: A Story of Love, Loss, and Chronic Illness*. Philadelphia: Temple University Press.

—— 1997 "Evocative Autoethnography: Writing Emotionally about Our Lives." In W. Tierney and Y. Lincoln, eds., *Representation and the Text: Reframing the Narrative Voice*. Albany, N.Y.: SUNY Press.

——, and A. Bochner in press "Autoethnography, Personal Narrative, Reflexivity: Researcher as Subject." In N. K. Denzin and Y. S. Lincoln, eds., *Handbook of Qualitative Research*, 2nd ed. Thousand Oaks, Calif.: Sage.

Ellis, C., K. E. Kiesinger, and L. M. Tillmann-Healy 1997 "Interactive Interviewing: Talking about Emotional Experience." In R. Hertz, ed., *Reflexivity and Voice*. Thousand Oaks, Calif.: Sage.

Fine, G. 1992 "Wild Life: Authenticity and the Human Experience of 'Natural' Places." In C. Ellis and M. Flaherty, eds., *Investigating Subjectivity: Research on Lived Experience*. Newbury Park, Calif.: Sage.

Fine, M. 1994 "Working the Hyphens: Reinventing Self and Other in Qualitative Research." In N. K. Denzin and Y. S. Lincoln, eds., *Handbook of Qualitative Research*. Thousand Oaks, Calif.: Sage.

Fitch, K. L. 1994 "Criteria for Evidence in Qualitative Research." *Western Journal of Communication* 58:32–38.

Fontana, A., and J. Frey 1994 "Interviewing: The Art of Science." In N. K. Denzin and Y. S. Lincoln, eds.,

Handbook of Qualitative Research. Thousand Oaks, Calif.: Sage.

Frank, A. 1995 *The Wounded Storyteller: Body, Illness, and Ethics*. Chicago: University of Chicago Press.

Geertz, C. 1973 *The Interpretation of Cultures: Selected Essays*. New York: Basic Books.

Gergen, K. J. 1994 *Realities and Relationships: Soundings in Social Construction*. Cambridge: Harvard University Press.

Gergen, M. M. 1992 "Life Stories: Pieces of a Dream." In G. C. Rosenwald and R. L. Ochberg, eds., *Storied Lives: The Cultural Politics of Self-Understanding*. New Haven, Conn.: Yale University Press.

Glaser, B. 1978 *Theoretical Sensitivity*. Mill Valley, Calif.: Sociological Press.

——, and B. Strauss 1964 *Awareness of Dying*. Chicago: Aldine.

—— 1967 *The Discovery of Grounded Theory: Strategies for Qualitative Research*. Chicago: Aldine.

Glesne, C. 1997 "That Rare Feeling: Re-Presenting Research through Poetic Transcription." *Qualitative Inquiry* 3:202–221.

Jackson, M. 1989 *Paths toward a Clearing: Radical Empiricism and Ethnographic Inquiry*. Bloomington: Indiana University Press.

Janesick, V. J. 1994 "The Dance of Qualitative Research Design: Metaphor, Methodology, and Meaning." In N. K. Denzin and Y. S. Lincoln, eds., *Handbook of Qualitative Research*. Thousand Oaks, Calif.: Sage.

Jones, S. H. 1998 *Kaleidoscope Notes: Writing Women's Music and Organizational Culture*. Walnut Creek, Calif.: AltaMira.

Josselson, R. 1996. "On Writing Other People's Lives: Self-Analytic Reflections of a Narrative Researcher." In R. Josselson, ed., *Ethics and Process in the Narrative Study of Lives*, vol. 4. Thousand Oaks, Calif.: Sage.

Kitzinger, J. 1994 "The Methodology of Focus Groups: The Importance of Interaction between Research Participants." *Sociology of Health and Illness* 16:103–121.

Krieger, S. 1991 *Social Science and the Self: Personal Essays on an Art Form*. New Brunswick, N.J.: Rutgers University Press.

Lather, P. 1986 "Research as Praxis." *Harvard Educational Review* 56:257–277.

——, and C. Smithies 1997 *Troubling the Angels: Women Living with HIV/AIDS*. Boulder, Colo.: Westview.

Lincoln, Y. S., and E. Guba 1985 *Naturalistic Inquiry*. Beverly Hills, Calif.: Sage.

Lindlof, T. R. 1995 *Qualitative Communication Research Methods*. Thousand Oaks, Calif.: Sage.

Lofland, J., and L. H. Lofland 1995 *Analyzing Social Settings: A Guide to Qualitative Observation and Analysis*, 3rd ed. Belmont, Calif.: Wadsworth.

Lowry, D. T., and D. E. Towles 1989 "Soap Opera Portrayals of Sex, Contraception, and Sexually Transmitted Diseases." *Journal of Communication* 39:76–83.

Mienczakowski, J. 1996 "An Ethnographic Act: The Construction of Consensual Theatre." In C. Ellis and A. P. Bochner, eds., *Composing Ethnography: Alternative Forms of Qualitative Writing*. Walnut Creek, Calif.: AltaMira.

Miles, M., and A. M. Huberman 1984 *Qualitative Data Analysis: A Sourcebook of New Methods*. Beverly Hills, Calif.: Sage.

Mishler, E. G. 1986 *Research Interviewing: Context and Narrative*. Cambridge, Mass.: Harvard University Press.

Mitchell, R. 1998 "Thirteen Stars and Chocolate Cake: Reasoning with Apocalypse," Paper presented to the Society for the Study of Symbolic Interaction, San Francisco.

Neuman, W. L. 1997 *Social Research Methods: Qualitative and Quantitative Approaches*, 3rd ed. Boston: Allyn and Bacon.

Potter, W. J., M. W. Vaughan, R. Warren, K. Howley, A. Land, and J. C. Hagemeyer 1995 "How Real Is the Portrayal of Aggression in Television Entertainment Programming?" *Journal of Broadcasting and Electronic Media* 39:494–516.

Rabinow, P., and W. Sullivan 1987 *Interpretive Social Science: A Second Look*. Berkeley: University of California Press.

Reed-Danahay, D. 1997 *Auto-Ethnography: Rewriting the Self and the Social*. Oxford, England: Berg.

Reinharz, S. 1992 *Feminist Methods in Social Research*. New York: Oxford University Press.

Richardson, L. 1992 "The Consequences of Poetic Representation." In C. Ellis and M. G. Flaherty, eds., *Investigating Subjectivity: Research on Lived Experience*. Newbury Park, Calif.: Sage.

—— 1994 "Nine Poems." *Journal of Contemporary Ethnography* 23:3–13.

—— 1997 *Fields of Play: Constructing an Academic Life*. New Brunswick, N.J.: Rutgers University Press.

—— in press "Writing: A Method of Inquiry." In N. Denzin and Y. Lincoln, eds., *Handbook of Qualitative Research*, 2nd ed. Thousand Oaks, Calif.: Sage.

Riessman, C. K. 1993 *Narrative Analysis. Qualitative Research Methods*, vol. 30. Newbury Park, Calif.: Sage Publications.

Ronai, C. R. 1995 "Multiple Reflections of Child Sex Abuse: An Argument for a Layered Account." *Journal of Contemporary Ethnography* 23:395–426.

Rorty, R. 1982 *Consequences of Pragmatism (Essays 1972–1980)*. Minneapolis: University of Minnesota Press.

Snow, D., and C. Morrill 1995 "A Revolutionary Handbook or a Handbook for Revolution?" *Journal of Contemporary Ethnography* 24:341–348.

Spence, D. 1982 *Narrative Truth and Historical Truth*. New York: Norton.

Spitzack, C., and K. Carter 1989 *Doing Research on Women's Communication: Perspectives on Theory and Method*. Norwood, N.J.: Ablex.

Stake, R. 1994 "Case Studies." In N. K. Denzin and Y. S. Lincoln, eds., *The Handbook of Qualitative Research*. Thousand Oaks, Calif.: Sage.

Strauss, A., and J. Corbin 1994 "Grounded Theory Methodology: An Overview." In N. K. Denzin and Y. S. Lincoln, eds., *The Handbook of Qualitative Research*. Thousand Oaks, Calif.: Sage.

Tedlock, B. 1991 "From Participant Observation to the Observation of Participation: The Emergence of Narrative Ethnography." *Journal of Anthropological Research* 41:69–94.

Tompkins, P. K. 1994 "Principles of Rigor for Assessing Evidence in 'Qualitative' Communication Research." *Western Journal of Communication* 58:44–50.

Van Maanen, J. 1988 *Tales of the Field: On Writing Ethnography*. Chicago: University of Chicago Press.

Waitzkin, H. 1990 "On Studying the Discourse of Medical Encounters: A Critique of Quantitative and Qualitative Methods and a Proposal for Reasonable Compromise. *Medical Care* 28:473–487.

Whyte, W. F. (1943) 1993 *Street Corner Society: The Social Structure of an Italian Slum*, 5th ed., Chicago: University of Chicago Press.

Wilkinson, S. 1998 "Focus Groups in Feminist Research: Power, Interaction and the Co-Construction of Meaning." *Women's Studies International Forum* 21:111–125.

Wimmer, R. D., and J. Dominick 1997 *Mass Media Research: An Introduction*, 5th ed. Belmont, Calif.: Wadsworth.

Wolcott, H. 1995 *The Art of Fieldwork*. Walnut Creek, Calif.: AltaMira.

CAROLYN ELLIS
LAURA ELLINGSON

QUALITATIVE MODELS

Qualitative models describe structure and metamorphoses among things or events or among properties of things or events. Sociologists have several ways of formulating qualitative models.

Qualitative modeling based on *logic* involves the following ideas. Propositions are simple sentences such as "All humans are mortal" and "A dictator is a human." Propositions can be true or false, and negation of a proposition transforms truth into falsity, or falsity into truth. Compound statements are formed when two or more propositions are placed in disjunction or conjunction, signified in English by the words *or* (or *nor*) and *and* (or *but*). Compound statements are true if all their component propositions are true, and compound statements are false if all their component propositions are false. Disjunction of true and false propositions yields a compound statement that is true, whereas conjunction of true and false propositions yields a compound statement that is false. These definitions are sufficient for logical analyses, but a supplementary definition is useful: the conditional "P implies Q," or "If P, then Q," means that whenever proposition P is true, proposition Q is true also, but when P is false, Q may be either true or false.

Set theory corresponds closely with logic, to the point that logic formulations can be interpreted in terms of sets, and information about the existence of elements in sets and subsets can be interpreted in terms of logic. Logic also can be translated to Boolean algebra (which operates as does ordinary algebra except that there are only two numbers, 0 and 1, and $1 + 1 = 1$), so any formulation in terms of logic can be transformed to an algebraic problem and processed mathematically.

Logic models have been used to define sociological constructs. Balzer (1990), for example, employed logic plus some additional mathematical ideas in order to construct a comprehensive definition of social institution. Logic models also can be used to compare competing sociological theories. Hannan (1998), for example, formalized different "stories" about how organizational age relates to organizational demise, and he used a computer program for automated deduction to prove that various empirical observations can be derived from different theoretical assumptions.

Znaniecki (1934) systematized *analytic induction* as a method for deriving logic models from statements known to be true as a result of sociological research. For example (alluding to a study by Becker [1953] that applied the method), field research might have disclosed a set of fourteen males who are marijuana users, all of whom were taught to enjoy the drug; a set of three females who use marijuana though they were never taught to enjoy it; and a set of six males who were taught how to enjoy marijuana, but who do not use it. Implicitly it is understood that other people were never taught to enjoy marijuana and do not use it. From this information one might conclude that for males like the ones who were studied, using marijuana implies being taught to enjoy the drug. Robinson's critique of analytic induction (1951) led to a hiatus in the development of logic models in sociology until modeling difficulties were understood better.

Ragin (1988) developed a method for constructing logic models from cross-sectional data. Empirically valid propositions about all cases in a population are conjoined into a complex compound statement, transformed into Boolean algebra format, and processed by a computer program. The result is a reduced compound statement that is empirically true for the cases and the propositions studied. The approach differs from statistical analysis of multifold tables in ignoring count information (other than whether a cell in a table has zero cases or more than zero cases), and in describing data patterns in terms of logic statements rather than in terms of the effects of variables and their interactions.

Abell (1987) and Heise (1989) developed a logic model approach for *event sequence analyses*. Logic models for sequences do not predict what will happen next but instead offer developmental accounts indicating what events must have preceded a focal event. A narrative of events is elicited from a culturally competent consultant who also defines prerequisites of the events in terms of other events within the happening. Since prerequisites define implication relations, a logic model is obtained that accounts for sequencing of events within the happening and that can be tested as a possible explanation of event sequencing in other happenings. Routines that appear to have little

surface similarity may be accountable by abstract events in a logic model; for instance, Corsaro and Heise (1990) showed that an abstract model accounted for observed play routines among children in two different cultures. Abell (1987) suggested that abstraction involves homomorphic reduction: That is, abstract events categorize concrete events that have identical logical relations with respect to events outside the category. Abbott (1995) reviewed logic models and other approaches to sequence analysis.

Careers are sequences in which the events are status transformations. Heise's logic model analysis of careers (1990) emphasized that individuals' sequences of status transformations are generated in limited patterns from institutional taxonomies of roles. *Guttman scaling* can be employed as a means of analyzing individual experiences in order to infer logic models that generate career sequences (e.g., see Wanderer 1984). Abbott and Hrycak (1990) applied *optimal matching* techniques to the problem of comparing career sequences, with the similarity of two sequences being measured as the minimum number of transformations required to change one sequence into the other; clusters of similar sequences discovered from the similarity measures are identified as genres of career patterns.

A *formal grammar* defines sequences of symbols that are acceptable in a language, being "essentially a deductive system of axioms and rules of inference, which generates the sentences of a language as its theorems" (Partee et al. 1990, p. 437). A grammar, like a logic model, is explanatory rather than predictive, interpreting why a sequence was constructed as it was or why a sequence is deviant in the sense of being unprincipled. Grammars have been applied for modeling episodes of social interaction, viewing sequences of social events as symbolic strings that are, or are not, legitimate within a language of action provided by a social institution (Skvoretz and Fararo 1980; Skvoretz 1984). The grammatical perspective on institutionalized action can be reformulated as a *production system* model in which a hierarchy of if-then rules defines how particular conditions instigate particular actions (Axten and Fararo 1977; Fararo and Skvoretz 1984).

Case frame grammar (Dirven and Radden 1987) deals with how syntactic position within a set of symbols designates function. For example, syntactic positioning in a sentence can designate an event's agent, action, object, instrument, product, beneficiary, and location (e.g., "The locksmith cut the blank with a grinder into a key for the customer in his shop"). Heise and Durig (1997) adapted case frame grammar to define an *event frame* for theoretical and empirical studies of social routines. The case-grammar perspective also informed Heise's (1979) symbolic interactionist modeling of social interaction by providing an agent-action-object-location framework for analyzing social events. Guttman's *facet mapping sentences* (see Shye 1978) implicitly employ a case grammar framework for analyzing a conceptual domain in terms of sets of concepts that fit into different syntactic slots and thereby generate a large number of propositions related to the domain. For example, Grimshaw (1989) developed a complex mapping sentence that suggested how different kinds of ambiguities arise in conversation and are resolved as a function of a variety of factors.

The mathematics of *abstract groups* provide a means for modeling some deterministic systems. Suppose a few different situations exist, and combining any two situations establishes another one of the situations; the result of a string of combinations can be computed by combining adjacent situations two at a time in any order. Also suppose that any situation can be reproduced by combining it with one particular situation, and this identity situation can be obtained from any other situation through a single combination. Then the set of situations and the scheme for combining them together constitute a group, and the group describes a completely deterministic system of transformations. Kosaka (1989) suggested a possible application of abstract groups by modeling the aesthetic theory of a Japanese philosopher in which there are sixty-four defined transformations, such as "yabo" (rusticity) combines with "hade" (flamboyance) to produce "iki" (chic urbanity).

A classic sociological application of groups involved kinship. Classificatory kinship systems (which are common in aboriginal cultures) put every pair of people in a society into a kinship relationship that may have little relation to genetic closeness, and each person implicitly is in a societywide kinship class that determines relationships with others. White (1963) showed through mathematical analysis that classificatory rules regarding marriage and parentage generate clans of people who are in the same kinship situation and that the resulting classificatory kinship system operates as an abstract group; then he demonstrated that existing kinship systems accord with analytic results.

Models of social networks sometimes employ the notion of *semigroup*—a set of situations and a scheme for combining them (i.e., a group without an identity situation). For example, Breiger and Pattison (1986) examined economic and marriage relations among elite families in fifteenth-century Florence and showed that each family's relations to other families constituted a semigroup that was part of the overall semigroup of family relations in the city; they were able to identify the allies and enemies of the famous Medici family from the structure of family relationships. Social network research, a sophisticated area of qualitative modeling in sociology, employs other algebraic and graph-theoretic notions as well (Marsden and Laumann 1984; Wasserman and Faust 1994).

In general, qualitative models describe systematic structures and processes, and developing qualitative models aids in interpretating nebulous phenomena. Creating and manipulating qualitative models confronts researchers with technical challenges, but software providing computer assistance is lessening the difficulties.

REFERENCES

Abbot, Andrew 1995 "Sequence Analysis: New Methods for Old Ideas." *Annual Review of Sociology* 21:93–113.

——, and Alexandra Hrycak 1990 "Measuring Resemblance in Sequence Data: An Optimal Matching Analysis of Musicians' Careers." *American Journal of Sociology* 96:144–185.

Abell, Peter 1987 *The Syntax of Social Life: The Theory and Method of Comparative Narratives.* New York: Oxford University Press.

Axten, N., and Thomas J. Fararo 1977 "The Information Processing Representation of Institutionalized Social Action." In P. Krishnan, ed., *Mathematical Models of Sociology*. Keele, United Kingdom: University of Keele Press.

Balzer, Wolfgang 1990 "A Basic Model for Social Institutions." *Journal of Mathematical Sociology* 16:1–29.

Becker, Howard S. 1953 "Becoming a Marijuana User." *American Journal of Sociology* 59:235–243.

Breiger, Ronald L., and Philippa E. Pattison 1986 "Cumulated Social Roles: The Duality of Persons and Their Algebras." *Social Networks* 8:215–256.

Corsaro, William, and D. Heise 1990 "Event Structure Models from Ethnographic Data." In C. Clogg, ed., *Sociological Methodology: 1990*. Cambridge, Mass.: Basil Blackwell.

Dirven, René, and Günter Radden (eds.) 1987 *Fillmore's Case Grammar: A Reader*. Heidelberg, Germany: Julius Groos Verlag.

Fararo, Thomas J., and John Skvoretz 1984 "Institutions as Production Systems." *Journal of Mathematical Sociology* 10:117–182.

Grimshaw, Allen D. 1989 *Collegial Discourse: Professional Conversation among Peers*. Norwood, N.J.: Ablex.

Hannan, Michael T. 1998 "Rethinking Age Dependence in Organizational Mortality: Logical Formalizations." *American Journal of Sociology* 104:126–164.

Heise, D. R. 1979 *Understanding Events: Affect and the Construction of Social Action*. New York: Cambridge University Press.

—— 1989 "Modeling Event Structures." *Journal of Mathematical Sociology* 14:139–169.

—— 1990 "Careers, Career Trajectories, and the Self." In J. Rodin, C. Schooler, and K. W. Schaie, eds., *Self-Directedness: Cause and Effects Throughout the Life Course*. New York: Lawrence Erlbaum.

——, and Alex Durig 1997 "A Frame for Organizational Actions and Macroactions." *Journal of Mathematical Sociology* 22:95–123.

Kosaka, Kenji 1989 "An Algebraic Reinterpretation of IKI NO KOZO (Structure of IKI)." *Journal of Mathematical Sociology* 14:293–304.

Marsden, Peter V., and Edward O. Laumann 1984 "Mathematical Ideas in Social Structure Analysis." *Journal of Mathematical Sociology* 10:271–294.

Partee, B. H., A. ter Meulen, and R. E. Wall 1990 *Mathematical Methods in Linguistics*. Boston: Kluwer Academic.

Ragin, Charles C. 1988. *Between Complexity and Generality: The Logic of Qualitative Comparison*. Berkeley: University of California Press.

Robinson, W. S. 1951 "The Logical Structure of Analytic Induction." *American Sociological Review* 16:812–818.

Shye, S. (ed.) 1978. *Theory Construction and Data Analysis in the Behavioral Sciences: A Volume in Honor of Louis Guttman*. San Francisco: Jossey-Bass.

Skvoretz, John 1984 "Languages and Grammars of Action and Interaction: Some Further Results." *Behavioral Science* 29:81–97.

——, and Thomas J. Fararo 1980 "Languages and Grammars of Action and Interaction: A Contribution to the Formal Theory of Action." *Behavioral Science* 25:9–22.

Wanderer, J. J. 1984 "Scaling Delinquent Careers Over Time." *Criminology* 22:83–95.

Wasserman, Stanley, and Katherine Faust 1994 *Social Network Analysis: Methods and Applications*. New York: Cambridge University Press.

White, Harrison C. 1963 *An Anatomy of Kinship: Mathematical Models for Structures of Cumulated Roles*. Englewood Cliffs, N.J.: Prentice Hall.

Znaniecki, Florian 1934 *The Method of Sociology*. New York: Farrar and Rinehart.

DAVID R. HEISE
ALEX DURIG

QUALITY OF LIFE

Although the concept of quality of life (QL) is not new, quality of life as an area of research and scholarship dates back only to the 1960s. Schuessler and Fisher (1985) noted that President Dwight Eisenhower's 1960 Commission on National Goals and Bauer's book on social indicators (1966) are often credited as providing the impetus for the development of QL as an area of research. Campbell (1981) suggested that the 1960s were favorable times for the development of QL research because of the emergence then of a belief that people must examine the quality of their lives and must do so in an environment that goes beyond providing material goods to foster individual happiness. Campbell quotes President Lyndon Johnson, who stated in 1964:

> *The task of the Great Society is to ensure our people the environment, the capacities, and the social structures which will give them a meaningful chance to pursue their individual happiness. Thus the Great Society is concerned not with how much, but with how good–not with the quantity of goods but with the quality of their lives.* (Campbell 1981, p. 4)

Schuessler and Fisher (1985) note that the Russell Sage Foundation promoted QL and research on social indicators in the 1960s and 1970s and that the Institute for Social Research at the University of Michigan and the National Opinion Research Center at the University of Chicago have conducted QL research since the late 1960s. Despite the high volume of QL research during the 1960s and 1970s, it was not until 1979 that "quality of life" became an index entry in *Sociological Abstracts*.

The emerging QL research in the 1970s provided a departure from previous work that focused on objective indicators, primarily economic in nature, of individual well-being. The book *The Quality of American Life: Perceptions, Evaluations, and Satisfactions*, published by Campbell and colleagues in 1976, particularly promoted the use of subjective or psychological indicators of well-being. The work reported was founded on the conviction that the relationship between objective and subjective well-being indicators was weak and poorly understood. Moreover, the rising affluence of the post–World War II era had been accompanied by steady increases in social problems afflicting American society as well as other Western societies.

The year 1976 also saw the publication of another major work focusing on subjective indicators of well-being. *Social Indicators of Well-Being: Americans' Perceptions of Life Quality* by Andrews and Withy (1976) reported findings from interviews with representative samples of more than 5,000 Americans. The interviews focused on satisfaction with the quality of various life domains. A more recent volume, titled *Research on the Quality of Life* and edited by Frank Andrews (1986), brought together a variety of papers originating at a symposium honoring the memory of Angus Campbell, one of the founders of the Institute for Social Research. Although this volume included important papers on cross-national differences in life satisfaction and papers on African-Americans and Hispanics, a number of the papers had no direct relationship to QL research. Rockwell (1989) noted that a useful focus of the field was lost in this volume, the focus on subjective indicators of the quality of life. Andrews also noted that support for large-scale, wide-ranging surveys had become increasingly difficult in the 1980s in the United States, resulting in a lack of replication of the national surveys conducted in the previous decade by the Institute for Social Research.

Parallel to the large national surveys of subjective well-being during the 1970s, there was a proliferation of studies focusing on the subjective well-being of the elderly. In a useful article, Larson (1978) reviewed three decades of research that focused on the psychological well-being of older people. Perhaps no other area of research in the emerging field of gerontology had received as much attention during the 1960s and 1970s as the area of life satisfaction, morale, mental health, and psychological well-being in general. Much of this research was spurred by the lively debate over the merits of disengagement theory (proposed by Cumming and Henry 1961) and activity theory (identified with various authors, including Havighurst et al. 1968; Maddox 1968, 1970) in predicting "successful aging." Gerontological work in the 1980s showed a marked decline in the number of articles predicting life satisfaction and morale and an increase in articles focusing on specific dimensions of psychological well-being, such as depression and psychological distress, positive and negative affect (Lawton 1996), as well as articles focusing on the prediction of physical health outcomes (Markides 1989).

An exception to the general decline of sociological studies of QL in the 1980s was a study by Thomas and Hughes of racial differences in QL in the United States (1986), in which they found significantly lower subjective well-being among African-Americans than among whites over the period 1972–1984. In their recent extension of their work to 1996 using data from the General Social Survey, Hughes and Thomas (1998) found that African-Americans continue to have a lower subjective QL than whites, as expressed in terms of happiness, life satisfaction, marital happiness, and self-rated health. This was in contrast to other recent work that challenged the notion that African-Americans had lower subjective well-being. However, much of this work had examined such indicators of QL as psychiatric disorders, including depression (Kessler et al. 1994; Williams et al. 1992). Moreover, one analysis did not find that race magnified the negative effect of socioeconomic status on psychiatric disorders (Williams et al. 1992). Hughes and Thomas conclude that their findings suggest that their measures of subjective QL capture separate dimensions of life rather than measures of psychiatric disorder and that African Americans in all social classes express lower QL of "social life experience" (1998, p. 792). This is an example of how different measures of QL can produce substantially different results.

The relative decline in research on the subjective QL of Americans in general, as well as on the subjective well-being of the elderly during the 1980s, was accompanied by a marked increase in QL research in medicine, which continued to accelerate during the 1990s, both in North America and in Europe. This development has included the publication of the massive *Quality of Life and Pharmacoeconomics in Clinical Trials* (Spilker 1996), the journal *Quality of Life Research*, the *Quality of Life Newsletter*, and the establishment of the *International Society for Quality of Life Research*. In medicine, as in the social sciences, the field of QL is conceptually weak. As Leplège and Hunt (1997) recently argued, a problem has been the overwhelming emphasis of the medical model on function and health status at the expense of attention to social and psychological aspects of QL as expressed by patients themselves.

Within medicine, there has been particular interest in studying the quality of life of cancer patients. Before 1970, cancer research focused almost exclusively on survival and life extension. With extended survival from cancer becoming the rule, research has given increasing attention to the quality of life of the surviving patients afflicted with cancer or patients treated for cancer. In 1987, for example, a volume entitled *The Quality of Life of Cancer Patients* was published. The volume, edited by Aaronson and Beckman (1987), contains papers from researchers in a number of European countries as well as the United States. More recently, Gotay and Muraoka (1998) reviewed thirty-four studies published in English language journals from 1980 to 1998 on the quality of life of long-term survivors of adult-onset cancers.

Another parallel to this work has been the focus on active life expectancy. The work has gone beyond predicting extension of life in general to investigating the extent to which recent extensions of life expectancy have been accompanied by extensions of "active" life. A recent variant of this work is the concept of health expectancy or the proportion of life expectancy that consists of healthy years (Olshansky and Wilkins 1998).

DEFINITIONS OF QUALITY OF LIFE

As seen in the previous section, there has been a movement in recent decades away from objective,

quantitative research and toward subjective, qualitative assessments of QL in sociology and other fields. Even within these broad approaches to QL, there appears to be little agreement about an appropriate definition of QL.

Some writings include under QL research the social indicators movement. Land (1971) noted that in the early years of the movement, the most popular definition of social indicators was given in *Toward a Social Report*:

> *A social indicator . . . may be defined to be a statistic of direct normative interest which facilitates concise, comprehensive and balanced judgements about the condition of a major aspect of a society. It is in all cases a direct measure of welfare and is subject to the interpretation that, if it changes, in the "right" direction, while other things remain equal, things have gotten better, or people are "better off." Thus statistics on the number of doctors or policemen could not be social indicators whereas figures on health or crime rates could be.* (U.S. DHEW 1969, p. 97)

Land criticized the above definition and proposed a broader one that treats social indicators as both "outputs" and "inputs" in "a sociological model of a social system or some segment thereof" (1971, p. 324). Thus, for example, the number of doctors is essential to understanding the health of the population, as are other factors. Land's definition has been largely accepted by the social indicators movement (Mukherjee 1989, p. 53).

This article gives only limited attention to social indicators, because a separate article is devoted to the topic. Yet the term "social indicators" is often used interchangeably with "quality of life," at least with respect to what Mukherjee calls "need-based" quality of life research (1989, p. 49). Moreover, the journal *Social Indicators Research* is subtitled *An International Journal of Quality of Life Measurement*.

In his book *The Quality of Life Valuation in Social Research*, Mukherjee notes that QL researchers employ several dichotomies, such as "quantity" and "quality," "behavior" and "perception," and "objective" and "subjective" indicators. He argues:

> *Economists and planners . . . are almost exclusively concerned with behavioral research*

on the basis of quantitative variables to improve the quality of life of the people. In that context, they ignore qualitative variations in the appraisal of a better quality of life or treat these variations as introducing a classificatory . . . distinction in the field of enquiry. They also equate the individual-wise subjective perception of reality to a group-wise "objective" perception by experts. Their appraisal of social reality in this manner leads them to formulate what the people need in order to improve their quality of life. (1989, pp. 37–38).

The dependent variables of this research tend to be items or scales measuring satisfaction or happiness. Milbrath, for example, argues: "I have come to the conclusion that the only defensible definition of quality of life is a general feeling of happiness" (1978, p. 36). Even though such global evaluations have been common, much of the research has focused on describing and explaining satisfactions with various life "domains" such as work, family, and housing.

In discussing subjective indicators of QL, Land notes the difficulties in relating them to objective indicators. He notes, for example, that while income levels tend to be associated with satisfaction and happiness within given countries and at given times, "higher per capita levels of national income do not produce higher average levels of national satisfaction over time or cross sectionally" (1983, p. 5). He goes on to suggest that from the standpoint of generating theory of social change, it is not clear that satisfaction indexes provide an unambiguous criterion for the formulation of public policy.

According to O'Boyle (1997), a more focused definition of QL favored by those in the health field has its origins in the original definition of health by the World Health Organization (WHO) that emphasized the presence of social, mental, and physical well-being instead of only focusing on the absence of disease. The WHO Quality of Life Group offered the following definition:

Quality of life is defined as the individual's perception of their position in life in the context of the culture and value systems in which they live and in relation to their goals, expectations, standards and concerns. It is a broad ranging concept affected in a complex way by a person's physical health, psychological state, and level of independence and their relationships to salient features of their environment. (WHOQoL Group 1993, p. 5)

MEASURING QUALITY OF LIFE

The broadest and most commonly employed distinction in measures of QL is between objective and subjective measures. Among the former are indicators such as per capita income, average calorie consumption, percent of adult illiteracy, quality of air, average daily temperature, crime rates, life expectancy, and a myriad of other indicators that are best seen as causes of quality of life.

Any one of the above has shortcomings. For example, gross national product (GNP) per capita has been acknowledged to suffer from many well-known limitations, including that it may not capture the spending power of the masses but rather that of a small minority (Mukherjee 1989, p. 42). To overcome the limitations of single indicators, researchers have proposed a number of composite indexes, such as the Physical Quality of Life Index (PQLI; see Morris 1977), which includes, among other variables, life expectancy at birth, infant mortality, and literacy. The purpose of the PQLI is to rank countries by physical well-being. Yet it has limitations, as its proponent acknowledges, including that "it is based on the assumption that the needs and desires of individuals initially and at the most basic level are for larger life expectancy, reduced illness, and greater opportunity" (Morris 1977, p 147).

Another composite index of objective indicators of QL is the Index of Social Progress (ISP) proposed originally by Estes (1984) and revised more recently by the same author (Estes 1988). The latest version (ISP83) consists of thirty-six indicators and is divided into ten subindexes covering "education, health status, status of women, defense effort, economic, demographic, political participation, cultural diversity and welfare effort" (Estes 1988, p. 1). A number of equally important indicators (e.g., crime rates, suicide rates, maldistribution of wealth) were not included because reliable data were not available on the 124 nations studied.

There has also been a lively interest in developing indexes consisting of objective indicators to rank quality of life of American cities on the basis of such domains of QL as economic, environmental, health, education, social, and political. Such rankings of cities elicit national attention and often surprise individuals about how high or low their community ranks. Rankings also do not often correlate with each other. For example, Berger and colleagues (1987) found that their revealed-preference rankings had a correlation of -0.075 with those proposed by Boyer and Savageau (1981) and a correlation of 0.048 with Liu's rankings (1976).

There have been numerous subjective measures of QL, with most relating to happiness or life satisfaction. Some measures are global in the sense that they aim at capturing happiness or satisfaction with life as a whole, while others pertain to happiness or satisfaction with certain life domains. The studies by Andrews and Withy (1976) and by Campbell and colleagues (1976) include measures of both domain-specific and global life satisfaction and employ the former as predictors of the latter. In general, they find that the best predictors of global satisfaction are marriage and family life, leisure activities, work and finances, housing, the community, and friendships.

Well before these landmark studies, W. Wilson (1967) reviewed prior literature on subjective well-being and concluded that the "happy person emerges as a young, healthy, well-educated, well-paid, extroverted, optimistic, worry-free, religious, married person with high self-esteem, high job morale, modest aspirations, of either sex and of a wide range of intelligence" (1967, p. 294). He also concluded that little progress had been made in understanding happiness since the time of the Greek philosophers. Diener (1984) noted that between W. Wilson's 1967 article and 1984, over seven hundred studies on subjective well-being had been published. In general, Wilson's conclusions regarding predictors of well-being appeared to be supported by the literature, including that little theoretical progress had been made in the field since the ancient Greeks.

This voluminous literature on subjective well-being has employed a variety of single-item and multiple-item measures of happiness and life satisfaction. Among the best-known single-item measures are: Cantril's "self-anchoring ladder" (1965), which asks respondents to place themselves on a nine-rung ladder ranging from "best possible for you" to "worst possible for you"; Gurin and colleagues's item (1960), "Taking all things together, how would you say things are these days?" with possible response choices being "very happy," "pretty happy," and "not too happy"; and Andrews and Withy's item (1976), "How do you feel about how happy you are?" with seven choices ranging from "delighted" to "terrible."

A problem with single-item measures is that because internal reliability estimates cannot be computed, the only way of assessing their reliability is through temporal correlation, which makes it difficult to separate measurement error from true change. However, convergence with other measures of well-being has suggested that these single-item measures enjoy moderate levels of validity. They do suffer from other limitations, however, such as positive skewness, acquiescence, and inability to capture the various dimensions of well-being (Diener 1984).

There have also been a variety of multi-item scales employed. Some of the best-known general scales include: the Affect Balance Scale (Bradburn 1969), which consists of ten items capturing positive and negative well-being. Respondents are asked whether in the past few weeks they felt: "particularly excited or interested in something," "so restless you couldn't sit long in a chair," "proud because someone complimented you on something you had done," "very lonely or remote from other people," "pleased about having accomplished something," "bored," "on top of the world," "depressed or very unhappy," "that things were going your way," and "upset because someone criticized you." Summing the positive items provides a positive score and summing the negative ones a negative score. An "affect balance score" is obtained by subtracting the negative score from the positive score. The two subscales have been found to be relatively independent of each other and are sometimes used as different scales of positive and negative affect.

Another multi-item scale is Campbell and colleagues' Index of General Affect (1976), which asks respondents to describe their present lives using semantic differential scales (miserable–enjoyable, hard–easy, boring–interesting, useless–worthwhile, lonely–friendly, discouraging–hopeful, empty–full, disappointing–rewarding, and doesn't give me a chance–brings out the best in me).

Although happiness and satisfaction are often used interchangeably, many writers believe they are distinct measures of well-being. George, for example, suggests that "happiness refers to an affective assessment of quality of life," while "life satisfaction refers to an assessment of the overall conditions of life, as derived from a comparison of one's aspirations to one's actual achievements" (1981, p. 351). Campbell and colleagues (1976) prefer satisfaction measures over happiness measures because they are more sensitive to intervention. While happiness tends to be transitory and volatile, life satisfaction changes gradually and systematically in response to changing life conditions (see also Stull 1987). Satisfaction scales have been particularly popular in gerontology.

QUALITY OF LIFE IN THE ELDERLY

An area in which lively interest has been shown in subjective indicators of QL has been the field of gerontology. As mentioned earlier, use of subjective measures of well-being was particularly high during the 1960s and 1970s, when social gerontologists were occupied with assessing the merits of disengagement and activity theories. In the late 1970s, Larson (1978) reviewed three decades of research and concluded that the most consistent predictors of subjective well-being are self-reports of health.

Although gerontological studies have employed general well-being measures (e.g., the Affect Balance Scale), they have also employed scales specifically developed for use with older people. The two best known are the Life Satisfaction Index A (Neugarten et al. 1961) and the Philadelphia Geriatric Morale Scale (Lawton 1975). The Life Satisfaction Index A consists of twenty items, with which respondents indicate agreement or disagreement. A combined life satisfaction score is obtained by summing scores on all twenty items. Twelve items are positive (e.g., "I am just as happy as when I was younger," "I expect some interesting and pleasant things to happen to me in the future," "As I look back on my life, I am fairly well satisfied") and eight items are negative (e.g., "When I think back over my life, I didn't get most of the important things I wanted," "Most of the things I do are boring and monotonous," "Compared to other people, I get down in the dumps too often").

Because the index covers a variety of areas, including happiness, satisfaction, and "activation level" (see Cherlin and Reeder 1975), the combined score confounds separate dimensions of well-being (Stull 1987).

The Philadelphia Geriatric Center Morale Scale (PGCMS) originally consisted of twenty-two items (Lawton 1972), and the revised version consisted of seventeen items (Lawton 1975). Like the Life Satisfaction Index, the PGCMS consists of positive items (e.g., "I am as happy now as I was when I was younger," "As I get older things are better than I thought they would be," "I have as much pep as I did last year") and negative items (e.g. "Things keep getting worse as I get older," "I sometimes feel life is not worth living," "I sometimes worry so much I can't sleep"). Factor analyses have produced three dimensions: agitation, attitude toward own aging, and lonely dissatisfaction. The scale has problems similar to those of the Life Satisfaction Index, such as the confounding of satisfaction and happiness. The two scales are in many ways similar (in fact, they share some items) and have been found to be highly intercorrelated ($r = 0.76$; see Lohman 1977).

Liang (1985) attempted to integrate the Life Satisfaction Index A and the Affect Balance Scale by selecting seven items from the former and eight from the latter. His analysis yielded four factors (congruence, happiness, positive affect, and negative affect) that correspond to dimensions of well-being discussed by Lawton (1983). However, Liang acknowledged a gap between the operationalization of well-being and its theoretical operationalization: "Most instruments were developed with only a general conceptual definition, and the sampling of the item domain is usually based on intuition, experience, and empirical experimentation" (Liang 1985, p. 553).

After reviewing the voluminous literature on subjective well-being among the elderly, Gubrium and Lynott (1983) concluded that it was time to "rethink life satisfaction" in old age. One of their key concerns was that the dominant measures employed tended to dwell on the earlier years of people's lives and have less relevance for their current circumstances. In addition, "current measures do not allow for co-equal dialogue between subject and researcher about the content of items and responses" (Gubrium and Lynott 1983, p. 37).

Possibly because of these and other conceptual and methodological problems in subjective well-being measures, we have seen a substantial decline in published studies in major journals aiming at predicting life satisfaction, morale, and related concepts during the 1980s and 1990s. Social gerontologists have instead concentrated on predicting more narrow dimensions of well-being, such as psychological distress and depression (Ferraro and Su 1999; Lawton et al. 1999; Lawton 1996), and are increasingly employing a life-course perspective that involves examination of main and interactive effects of stress, social support, coping styles, and related factors (e.g., George 1989). Measures of depression and psychological distress are being employed more frequently, perhaps because they are perceived as more amenable to intervention than are measures of life satisfaction and morale.

A general conclusion of the field of subjective well-being in the elderly is that most elderly people, particularly those who have reasonably good health and finances, and are socially engaged, report relatively high levels of well-being. According to some literature, elderly people may even report higher levels of subjective QL than do people in younger age groups (Lawton 1996).

STUDIES OF QUALITY OF LIFE IN MEDICINE

Perhaps the most activity in the area of quality of life is currently found in medicine, much of it conducted by behavioral and social scientists. Interest in QL after medical treatments is based on the realization that chronic diseases cannot be cured, and, therefore, the goal of much therapy becomes to limit the effects of illness so that patients may live productive, comfortable, and satisfying lives. Traditionally, success of medical treatment was evaluated in terms of lengthening lives and post-treatment complications. However, there has been a realization that medical and surgical treatments may extend survival but often reduce quality of life (Eisman 1981).

Hollandsworth (1988) reviewed studies evaluating the impact of medical treatment on QL during the period 1980 to 1984 and compared his results with those of studies conducted during 1975 to 1979 (Najman and Levine 1981). Hollandsworth's comparison (1988) revealed a marked increase between the two time periods in both quantity and quality of studies. Although recent studies tended to be more sophisticated, the majority nevertheless relied on convenience samples. One marked improvement in the recent research is the increase in use of subjective measures of quality of life, with 60 percent of the recent studies employing at least one such measure, compared to only around 10 percent in the earlier period.

Another interesting outcome of Hollandsworth's analysis (1988) was the increase over time in the proportion of studies that do not report favorable outcomes. Studies published in the late 1970s were almost unanimous in claiming favorable outcomes of treatment, but this optimism must be tempered by the many methodological limitations of these studies (Najman and Levine 1981). Of the more sophisticated studies published from 1980 to 1984, almost one-half reported either negative outcomes or at least mixed results. In fact, it appeared that the probability of reporting negative outcomes (or lack of positive results) tended to be correlated with the methodological sophistication of the studies (Hollandsworth 1988).

The impact of a variety of medical treatments have been examined, including cardiovascular therapies (e.g., Jenkins et al. 1983; Wenger et al. 1984), end-stage renal disease (e.g., Evans et al. 1985) and chronic obstructive pulmonary disease (e.g., McSweeney et al. 1982). However, by far the most frequently studied area is that relating to outcomes of cancer treatment (see Aaronson 1989; Aaronson and Beckman 1987; Cella and Cherin 1988). Aaronson noted that while "there is no universally accepted definition of the quality of life concept, in oncology it is most often used to describe such aspects of health status as physical symptoms, daily activity level, psychological well-being, and social functioning" (1989, p. 69). This increasing use of subjective QL indicators is becoming an integral part of evaluation in clinical cancer research, but a major challenge facing researchers is the development of measures capturing all dimensions of QL while meeting rigorous standards of reliability and validity (Aaronson 1989).

In a recent review, Gotay and Muraoka (1998) observed that recent studies of cancer survivors have increasingly been using standardized instruments relying primarily on self-reports to assess

QL. They identified thirty-four studies published in English-language journals during 1990 to 1998 that focused on the QL of patients surviving five or more years. A variety of standardized instruments were used measuring a variety of aspects of QL. As in other studies of patients, a popular instrument has been the Short-Form 36 Health Survey (SF-36) (Ware and Sherbourne 1992). The SF-36 is a 36-item short form of the Rand Corporation's Medical Outcomes Study. It was designed to be a general measure of health status that can be used in community studies as well as in studies of patients. It consists of multi-item scales measuring eight dimensions of health: general perceptions of health, physical functioning, activity limitations due to physical health problems, bodily pain, social functioning, psychological well-being, activity limitations due to emotional problems, and energy/vitality.

During the 1990s the SF-36 has become the instrument of choice in studies of health-related QL in both community surveys and studies of patients. Like other abbreviated instruments of general health status and QL, the SF-36 has been criticized on a number of grounds, including that it covers some areas only superficially (McDowell and Newell 1996, p. 454).

In their recent critical assessment of QL measurement in medicine, Leplège and Hunt (1997) have criticized the field for relying on instruments (like the SF-36) that have physical, emotional, and social functioning components. While these, according to the authors, are measuring health status, it is not clear that they are measuring QL. This overwhelming emphasis on function, they argue, ignores the person's perspective on the meaning and importance of functions and roles under study. They go on to cite evidence that many physically disabled people do indeed consider their QL to be high despite severe limitations (Leplège and Hunt 1997).

Leplège and Hunt (1997) are also critical of the economic model of QL as expressed in the notion of Quality Adjusted Life Years (QALYs). The concept has evolved over the years as a tool for health policy. Typically, the utility value of specific health status measures, including function and symptoms, during a given period of time is combined with survival data. This perspective usually assumes that rational human beings, if given a choice, would prefer a shorter but relatively healthy life, to a longer life with serious discomfort and handicap. Leplège and Hunt argue that:

the methods used for the valuation of health states do not encompass the fact that the same people value the same state differently at different times, while different people have different preferences that become meaningless if aggregated. The concept of utility . . . operatively addresses what people think they might (or should) do under artificial circumstances and not what they actually do in the real world. (1997, p. 48)

An overview of the literature on medical treatment outcomes does indeed reveal increasing use of subjective QL measures. As in the broader QL field, many studies tend to employ single-item global indicators capturing life satisfaction or happiness. However, an increasing number of studies are employing the general multiple-item measures discussed earlier, such as the Affect Balance Scale and the Life Satisfaction Index Z. Other scales capturing more specific and narrow dimensions of QL include measures of mood, anxiety, self-concept, and depression (Lawton 1996) as well as more comprehensive instruments that capture physical, emotional, and social functioning, such as the McMaster Health Index Questionnaire (Chambers et al. 1982) and the SF-36. A general conclusion of much of the research is that most patients, including cancer patients, demonstrate an incredible capacity to cope with and adapt to the challenges of life-threatening disease and disability. A welcome recent addition to the field has been the development of a variety of disease-specific QL measures (Bowling 1995).

CONCLUSION

This brief and selective overview of the field of quality of life indicates a variety of perspectives employed within sociology and in related fields. In fact, it may be said that there is more interest in QL outside the mainstream of sociology, as, for example, in the area of medical treatment. While much of the pioneer work and many of the large-scale national studies in the 1970s were conducted by sociologists, research on quality of life remains very much outside the mainstream of sociology. For example, Schuessler and Fisher's review (1985) uncovered only one article (Gerson 1976) explicitly on quality of life, which was published in the *American Sociological Review* way back in 1976. More recently, we noted the work of Thomas and Hughes published in 1986 and 1998.

This overview also reveals some patterns and trends in QL research in the last four decades. First, there have been two broad approaches, one focusing on objective indicators and one focusing on subjective indicators. Related dichotomies noted by Mukherjee (1989) include quantity versus quality and behavior versus perception. It is clear that there has been a trend away from relying simply on objective indicators and toward relying increasingly on people's subjective reports about the quality of their lives. Objective measures have been the domain primarily of the social indicator movement, with subjective approaches to QL increasingly perceived as the domain of QL research.

Within the subjective QL approach, we also see a trend away from single-item indicators capturing global happiness and life satisfaction and toward multiple-item scales such as the Affect Balance Scale and the Life Satisfaction Index Z. At the same time, there have been attempts to measure subjective quality of life in specific life domains, and there has been continuing interest by sociologists, economists, and others (including popular magazines) in ranking urban areas according to a variety of objective QL indicators.

During the 1960s and 1970s a great deal of subjective QL research was conducted by social and behavioral gerontologists, who used measures of life satisfaction and morale as indicators of successful aging. For a number of reasons, gerontologists began abandoning research on life satisfaction and morale in favor of measures more amenable to intervention, such as measures of psychological distress, depression, and physical health function. Perhaps the most exciting research on QL currently being conducted is in the area of medical treatment outcomes, particularly cancer treatment. In this field, as in others, there is considerable disagreement about what constitutes quality of life and how it should be measured.

It is becoming increasingly difficult to obtain funding to conduct large-scale national surveys of subjective quality of life such as those conducted during the 1970s. The future of QL research is uncertain, at least as a broad unified field of inquiry. Studies ranking urban areas are likely to continue, because of the immediate and broad appeal they elicit. It is also safe to predict that the concept of quality of life will continue to have some appeal in social gerontology. The most exciting work may well take place in the area of medical intervention outcomes. Sociologists and other behavioral scientists are increasingly conducting research related to medicine, and much of this research relates to quality of life. It is becoming apparent that medical interventions (as well as other factors) are enabling us to live longer, but it is not clear that the added years of life are "quality" years. There will be increasing interest in finding ways to improve the quality of the added years, and sociologists have an opportunity and a responsibility to help find ways of accomplishing that.

(SEE ALSO: *Social Indicators*)

REFERENCES

Aaronson, Neil K. 1989 "Quality of Life: What Is It? How Should It Be Measured?" *Oncology* 2:69–74.

——, and J. H. Beckman (eds.) 1987 *The Quality of Life of Cancer Patients*. New York: Raven.

Andrews, Frank M. (ed.) 1986 *Research on the Quality of Life*. Ann Arbor: University of Michigan, Institute for Social Research.

Andrews, Frank M., and Stephen B. Withey 1976 *Social Indicators of Well-Being: Americans' Perceptions of Life Quality*. New York: Plenum.

Bauer, Raymond A. (ed.) 1966 *Social Indicators*. Cambridge: Massachusetts Institute of Technology Press.

Berger, Mark C., Glenn C. Blomquist, and Werner Waldner 1987 "A Revealed-Preference Ranking of Quality of Life for Metropolitan Areas." *Social Science Quarterly* 68:761–778.

Bowling, Ann 1995 *Measuring Disease*. Buckingham, U.K.: Open University Press.

Boyer, Rick, and D. Savageau 1981 *Places Rated Almanac*. Chicago: Rand McNally.

Bradburn, Norman 1969 *The Structure of Psychological Well-Being*. Chicago: Aldine.

Campbell, Angus 1981 *The Sense of Well-Being in America: Recent Patterns and Trends*. New York: McGraw-Hill.

——, Phillip Converse, and Willard L. Rogers 1976 *The Quality of American Life: Perceptions, Evaluations, and Satisfactions*. New York: Russell Sage Foundation.

Cantril, Hadley 1965 *The Pattern of Human Concerns*. New Brunswick, N.J.: Rutgers University Press.

Cella, David F., and E. A. Cherin 1988 "Quality of Life during and after Cancer Treatment." *Comprehensive Therapy* 14:69–75.

Chambers, Larry W., Lorry A. MacDonald, Peter Tugwell, W. Watson Buchanan, and Gunnar Kraag 1982 "The McMaster Health Index Questionnaire as a Measure of Quality of Life for Patients with Rheumatoid Disease." *Journal of Rheumatology* 9:780–784.

Cherlin, Andy, and Leo G. Reeder 1975 "The Dimensions of Psychological Well-Being: A Critical Review." *Sociological Methods and Research* 4:189–214.

Cumming, Elaine, and William E. Henry 1961 *Growing Old: The Process of Disengagement*. New York: Basic.

Diener, Ed 1984 "Subjective Well-Being." *Psychological Bulletin* 95:542–575.

Eisman, B. 1981 "The Second Dimension." *Archives of Surgery* 116:11–13.

Estes, Richard J. 1984 *The Social Progress of Nations*. New York: Praeger.

—— 1988 *Trends in World Social Development: The Social Progress of Nations, 1970–1987*. New York: Praeger.

Evans, R. W., D. L. Manninen, L. P. Garrison, L. G. Hart, C. R. Blagg, R. A. Gutman, A. R. Hull, and E. G. Lowrie 1985 "The Quality of Life of Patients with End-State Renal Disease." *New England Journal of Medicine* 312:553–559.

Ferraro, Kenneth F., and Ya-ping Su 1999 "Financial Strain, Social Relations, and Psychological Distress among Older People: A Cross-Cultural Analysis." *Journal of Gerontology: Social Sciences* 54B:S3–S15.

George, Linda K. 1981 "Subjective Well-Being: Conceptual and Methodological Issues." *Annual Review of Gerontology and Geriatrics* 2:345–382.

—— 1989 "Stress, Social Support, and Depression over the Life Course." In Kyriakos S. Markides and Cary L. Cooper, eds., *Aging, Stress and Health*. Chichester, England: John Wiley.

Gerson, Elihu M. 1976 "On 'Quality of Life'." *American Sociological Review* 41:793–806.

Gotay, Carolyn C. and Miles Y. Muraoka 1998 "Quality of Life in Long-Term Survivors of Adult-Onset Cancers." *Journal of the National Cancer Institute* 90:656–667.

Gubrium, Jaber F., and Robert J. Lynott 1983 "Rethinking Life Satisfaction." *Human Organization* 42:30–38.

Gurin, Gerald, J. Veroff, and S. Feld 1960 *Americans View Their Mental Health*. New York: Basic.

Havighurst, Robert J., Bernice Neugarten, and Sheldon S. Tobin 1968 "Disengagement and Patterns of Aging." In Bernice L. Neugarten, ed., *Middle Age and Aging*. Chicago: University of Chicago Press.

Hollandsworth, James G. 1988 "Evaluating the Impact of Medical Treatment on the Quality of Life: A Five-Year Update." *Social Science and Medicine* 26:425–434.

Hughes, Michael, and Melvin E. Thomas 1998 "The Continuing Significance of Race Revisited: A Study of Race, Class and Quality of Life in America, 1972 to 1996." *American Sociological Review* 63:785–795.

Jenkins, C. David, Babette A. Stanton, J. A. Savageau, P. Denlinger, and M. D. Klein 1983 "Coronary Artery Bypass Surgery: Physical, Psychological, Social, and Economic Outcomes Six Months Later." *Journal of the American Medical Association* 250:782–788.

Kessler, Ronald C., Katherine A. McGonagle, Shanyang Zhao, Christopher B. Nelson, Michael Hughes, Suzann Eshleman, Hans-Ulrich Wittchen, and Kenneth S. Kendler 1994 "Lifetime and 12-Month Prevalence of DSM-III-R Psychiatric Disorders in the United States." *Archives of General Psychiatry* 51:8–19.

Land, Kenneth C. 1971 "On the Definition of Social Indicators." *American Sociologist* 6:322–325.

—— 1983 "Social Indicators." *Annual Review of Sociology* 9:1–26.

Larson, Reed 1978 "Thirty Years of Research on Subjective Well-Being of Older Americans." *Journal of Gerontology* 33:109–125.

Lawton, M. Powell 1972 "The Dimensions of Morale." In Donald Kent, Robert Kastenbaum, and Sylvia Sherwood, eds., *Research, Planning, and Action for the Elderly*. New York: Behavioral Publications.

——1975 "The Philadelphia Geriatric Center Morale Scale" A Revision." *Journal of Gerontology* 30:85–89.

——1983 "The Varieties of Well-Being." *Experimental Aging Research* 9:65–72.

—— 1996 "Quality of Life and Affect in Later Life." In C. Magai and S. McFadden, eds. *Handbook of Emotion, Adult Development, and Aging*. Orlando, Fla.: Academic.

——, Laraine Winter, Morton H. Kleban, and Katy Ruckdeschel 1999 "Affect and Quality of Life: Objective and Subjective." *Journal of Aging and Health* 11:169–198.

Leplège, Alain, and Sonia Hunt 1999 "The Problem of Quality of Life in Medicine" *Journal of the American Medical Association* 278:47–50.

Liang, Jersey 1985 "A Structural Integration of the Affect Balance Scale and the Life Satisfaction Index A." *Journal of Gerontology* 40:552–561.

Liu, Ben-Cheih 1976 *Quality of Life Indicators in U.S. Metropolitan Areas.* New York: Praeger.

Lohman, Nancy 1977 "Correlations of Life Satisfaction, Morale, and Adjustment Measures." *Journal of Gerontology* 32:73–75.

McDowell, Ian, and Claire Newell 1996 *Measuring Health: A Guide to Rating Scales and Questionnaires*, 2nd ed. New York: Oxford University Press.

McSweeney, A. J., I. Grant, R. K. Heaton, K. Adams, and R. M. Timms 1982 "Life Quality of Patients with Chronic Obstructive Pulmonary Disease." *Archives of Internal Medicine* 142:473–478.

Maddox, George L. 1968 "Persistence of Life Styles among the Elderly: A Longitudinal Study of Patterns of Social Activity in Relation to Life Satisfaction." In Bernice L. Neurgarten, ed., *Middle Age and Aging.* Chicago: University of Chicago Press.

—— 1970 "Themes and Issues in Sociological Theories of Aging." *Human Development* 13:17–27.

Markides, Kyriakos S. 1989 "Aging, Gender, Race/Ethnicity, Class, and Health: A Conceptual Overview." In K. S. Markides, ed., *Aging and Health: Perspectives on Gender, Race, Ethnicity, and Class.* Newbury Park, Calif.: Sage.

Milbrath, L. W. 1978 "Indicators of Environmental Quality." In *Indicators of Environmental Quality and Quality of Life.* UNESCO Reports and Papers in the Social Sciences, No. 38. Paris: UNESCO.

Morris, David M. 1977 "A Physical Quality of Life Index (PQLI)." In J. W. Sewell, ed., *The United States and the World Development Agenda 1977.* New York: Praeger.

Mukherjee, Ramkrishna 1989 *The Quality of Life Valuation in Social Research.* New Delhi: Sage.

Najman, J. M., and Sol Levine 1981 "Evaluating the Impact of Medical Care and Technologies on the Quality of Life: A Review and Critique." *Social Science and Medicine* 15(F):107–115.

Neugarten, Bernice L., Robert J. Havighurst, and Sheldon S. Tobin 1961 "The Measurement of Life Satisfaction." *Journal of Gerontology* 16:134–143.

O'Boyle, Ciaran A. 1997 "Measuring the Quality of Later Life." *Philosophical Transactions of the Royal Society of London B.* 352:1871–1879.

Olshansky, S. Jay, and Russell Wilkins (eds.) 1998 "Policy Implications of the Measures and Trends in Health Expectancy." *Journal of Aging and Health* 30(2).

Rockwell, R. C. 1989 "Review of Research on Quality of Life." F. M. Andrews, ed., *Social Forces* 67:824–826.

Schuessler, Karl F., and G. A. Fisher 1985 "Quality of Life Research in Sociology." *Annual Reviews of Sociology* 11:129–149.

Spilker, B. (ed.) 1996 *Quality of Life and Pharmacoeconomics in Clinical Trials.* Philadelphia: Lippincott-Raven.

Stull, Donald E. 1987 "Conceptualization and Measurement of Well-Being: Implications for Policy Evaluation." In Edgar F. Borgatta and Rhonda J. V. Montgomery, eds., *Critical Issues in Aging Policy.* Newbury Park, Calif.: Sage.

Thomas, Melvin E., and Michael Hughes 1986 "The Continuing Significance of Race: A Study of Race, Class, and Quality of Life in America, 1972–1985." *American Sociological Review* 51:830–841.

U.S. Department of Health, Education, and Welfare 1969 *Toward a Social Report.* Washington, D.C.: U.S. Government Printing Office.

Ware, Johyn E., and C. D. Sherbourne 1992 "The MOS 36-item Short-Form Health Survey (SF-36). I. Conceptual Framework and Item Selection." *Medical Care* 30:473–483.

Wenger, Nanette K., Margaret E. Mattson, Curt D. Furberg, and Jack Elinson (eds.) 1984 *Assessment of Quality of Life in Clinical Trials of Cardiovascular Therapies.* New York: Le Jacq.

WHO Qol Group 1993 *Measuring Quality of Life: The Development of the World Health Organization Quality of Life Instrument.* Geneva: World Health Organization.

Williams, David R., David T. Takeuchi, and Russell K. Adair 1992 "Socioeconomic Status and Psychiatric Disorder among Blacks and Whites." *Social Forces* 71:179–194.

Wilson, Warner 1967 "Correlates of Avowed Happiness." *Psychological Bulletin* 67:294–306.

KYRIAKOS S. MARKIDES

QUASI-EXPERIMENTAL RESEARCH DESIGNS

The goal of most social scientific research is to explain the causes of human behavior in its myriad forms. Researchers generally attempt to do this by uncovering causal associations among variables. For example, researchers may be interested in whether a causal relationship exists between income and happiness. One might expect a positive association between these two variables. That is, an increase in income, the independent variable, produces an increase in happiness, the dependent variable. Unfortunately, observing a positive correlation between these two variables does not prove that income causes happiness. In order to make a valid causal inference, three conditions must be present: (1) there must be an association between the variables (e.g., income and happiness); (2) the variable that is the presumed cause (e.g., income) must precede the effect (e.g., happiness) in time; and (3) the association between the two variables cannot be explained by the influence of some other variable (e.g., education) that may be related to both of them. The purpose of any research design is to construct a circumstance within which a researcher can achieve these three conditions and thus make valid causal inferences.

Experimental designs are one of the most efficient ways to accomplish this goal of making valid causal inferences. Four characteristics are especially desirable in designing experiments. First, researchers *manipulate* the independent variable. That is, they actively modify persons' environment (e.g., provide some people with money they otherwise would not have received)—as contrasted with passively observing the existing, "natural" environment (e.g., simply measuring the amount of income persons normally make). Second, researchers have complete control over *when* the independent variable is manipulated (e.g., when persons receive supplementary income). Third, researchers have complete control over *what* they manipulate. That is, they can specify the exact content of the different "treatment conditions" (different levels) of the independent variable to which subjects are exposed (e.g., how much supplementary income persons receive and the manner in which they receive it). Fourth, researchers have complete control over *who* is assigned to which treatment condition (e.g., who receives the supplementary income and who does not, or who receives higher versus lower amounts of income).

Of these four characteristics important in designing experiments, only manipulation of the independent variable and control over who receives the treatments are essential to classify a study as a true experimental design.

Control over who receives treatment conditions is especially powerful in enhancing valid causal inference when researchers use the technique of *random assignment*. For example, in evaluating the effect of income on happiness, investigators might randomly assign individuals who are below the poverty level to treatment groups receiving varying levels of supplementary income (e.g., none versus $1,000).

Table 1 *(a)* illustrates this example. It depicts an experimental design in which subjects are randomly assigned to one of two groups. At time 1, researchers manipulate the independent variable (*X*): Each subject in group 1 receives $1,000 in supplementary income. Conversely, no subjects in group 2 receive any supplementary income. At time 2, researchers observe (measure) the average level of happiness *(O)* for group 1 versus group 2. The diagram $X \rightarrow O$ indicates an expected increase in happiness when supplementary income increases. That is, the average happiness score should be higher for group 1 than for group 2.

By assigning each subject to a particular treatment condition based on a coin flip or some other random procedure, experimental designs ensure that each subject has an equal chance off appearing in any one of the treatment conditions (e.g., at any level of supplementary income). Therefore, as a result of random assignment, the different treatment groups depicted in Table 1 *(a)* should be approximately equivalent in all characteristics (average education, average physical health, average religiosity, etc.) except their exposure to different levels of the independent variable (i.e., different levels of supplementary income). Consequently, even though there is a large number of other variables (e.g., education, physical health, and religiosity) that might affect happiness, none of these variables can serve as a plausible alternative explanation for why the higher-income group has higher average happiness than does the lower-income group.

For example, due to random assignment, physically healthy versus unhealthy persons should be approximately equally distributed between the higher versus lower supplementary income treatment groups. Hence, a critic could not make a plausible argument that the treatment group receiving the higher amount of supplementary income (i.e., group 1) also has better health, and it is the better health and not the greater income that is producing the higher levels of happiness in that treatment

Types of Research Designs

Causal inferencee for each design: $\uparrow$ $X_{income} \longrightarrow O_{income}$ $\uparrow$

RANDOMIZED EXPERIMENTAL DESIGN:

a. Posttest-only control group

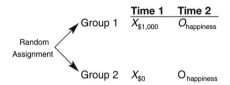

	Time 1	Time 2
Group 1	$X_{\$1,000}$	$O_{happiness}$
Group 2	$X_{\$0}$	$O_{happiness}$

Random Assignment

PREEXPERIMENTAL DESIGNS:

b. One-group pretest-posttest

	Time 1	Time 2	Time 3	Time 4
Group 1	$X_{\$0}$	$O_{happiness}$	$X_{\$1,000}$	$O_{happiness}$

c. Static-group comparison

	Time 1	Time 2
Group 1	$X_{\$1,000}$	$O_{happiness}$
Group 2	$X_{\$0}$	$O_{happiness}$

QUASI-EXPERIMENTAL DESIGNS:

d. Time series

	Time 1	Time 2	Time 3	Time 4	Time 5	Time 6	Time 7	Time 8	Time 9	Time 10
Group 1	$X_{\$0}$	$O_{happiness}$	$X_{\$0}$	$O_{happiness}$	$X_{\$1,000}$	$O_{happiness}$	$X_{\$0}$	$O_{happiness}$	$X_{\$0}$	$O_{happiness}$

e. Nonequivalent control group

	Time 1	Time 2	Time 3	Time 4
Group 1	$X_{\$0}$	$O_{happiness}$	$X_{\$1,000}$	$O_{happiness}$
Group 2	$X_{\$0}$	$O_{happiness}$	$X_{\$0}$	$O_{happiness}$

f. Multiple time series

	Time 1	Time 2	Time 3	Time 4	Time 5	Time 6	Time 7	Time 8	Time 9	Time 10
Group 1	$X_{\$0}$	$O_{happiness}$	$X_{\$0}$	$O_{happiness}$	$X_{\$1,000}$	$O_{happiness}$	$X_{\$0}$	$O_{happiness}$	$X_{\$0}$	$O_{happiness}$
Group 2	$X_{\$0}$	$O_{happiness}$	$X_{\$0}$	$O_{happiness}$	$X_{\$0}$	$O_{happiness}$	$X_{\$0}$	$O_{happiness}$	$X_{\$0}$	$O_{happiness}$

g. Regression–discontinuity

(See Figure 1.)

NONEXPERIMENTAL DESIGNS:

h. Passive static group comparison[1]

	Time 1
Group 1	$(X_{high\ income}\ O_{happiness})$
Group 2	$(X_{medium\ income}\ O_{happiness})$
Group 3	$(X_{low\ income}\ O_{happiness})$

i. Panel (passive nonequivalent control group)[2]

	Time 1	Time 2
Group 1	$X_{\$0}\ O_{happiness}$	$(X_{high\ income}\ O_{happiness})$
Group 2	$X_{\$0}\ O_{happiness}$	$(X_{medium\ income}\ O_{happiness})$
Group 3	$X_{\$0}\ O_{happiness}$	$(X_{low\ income}\ O_{happiness})$

Table 1

Table 1, continued

NOTE: O = Observed effect on the dependent variable

X = Independent variable (the cause)

[1]Parentheses around the independent and the dependent variable (*X* and *O*)indicates that the measure of *X* and *O* (income and happiness) occur at the same time.

[2]The panel design depends on statistical controls to make groups equivalent in income (and happiness) at time 1.

group. Indeed, this same logic applies no matter what other causal variables a critic might substitute for physical health as an alternative explanation for why additional income is associated with greater happiness.

In sum, strong causal inferences are possible where social scientists manipulate the independent variable and retain great control over when treatments occur, what treatments occur, and, especially, who receives the different treatments. But there are times when investigators, typically in "field" (i.e., nonlaboratory, natural, or real-world) settings, are interested in the effects of an intervention but cannot do randomized experiments. More specifically, there are times when researchers in naturally occurring settings can manipulate the independent variable and exercise at least some control over when the manipulation occurs and what it includes. But these same field researchers may have less control over who receives the treatment conditions. In other words, there are many real-world settings in which *random assignment is not possible*.

Where randomized experiments are not possible, a large number of potential threats to valid causal inference can occur. Under these less-than-optimal field conditions, investigators may resort to a number of alternative research designs that help reduce at least some of the threats to making valid causal inferences. These alternative procedures are collectively referred to as *quasi-experimental designs*. (See also Campbell and Stanley 1963; Cook and Campbell 1979; Cook and Shaddish 1994; Shaddish et al. in preparation.)

None of these designs is as powerful as a randomized experiment in establishing causal relationships, but some of the designs are able to overcome the absence of random assignment such that they approximate the power of randomized experiments. Conversely, where the designs are particularly weak in establishing causal relationships, Campbell and Stanley (1963) have described

them as *preexperimental designs*. Furthermore, social scientists describe as *nonexperimental designs* those studies in which the researcher can only measure (observe) rather than manipulate the independent variable. As we shall see, however, one type of nonexperimental design—the "panel"—may surpass preexperimental designs and approach the power of some quasi-experimental designs in overcoming threats to valid causal inference.

Below we describe common threats to "internal validity" (i.e., the making of valid causal inferences) in field settings, the conditions under which such threats are likely to occur, and representative research designs and strategies used to combat the threats. Later we briefly examine threats to "external validity," "construct validity," and "statistical conclusion validity," and strategies used to reduce these threats. As we shall see, whereas randomized experiments are the exemplary design for enhancing internal validity (causal inference), they often suffer in comparison to other research designs with regard to external validity (generalizability across persons, places, and times) and construct validity (whether one is measuring and manipulating what one intended).

THREATS TO INTERNAL VALIDITY

Where researchers are unable to assign subjects to treatment conditions randomly, a large number of threats to internal validity (causal inference) can occur. These potential threats include effects due to history, maturation, testing, instrumentation, regression to the mean, selection, mortality, and reverse causal order. (See Cook and Campbell 1979, and Shaddish et al. in preparation for more elaborate lists.)

Research designs vary greatly in *how many* and *which* of these potential threats are likely to occur—that is, are likely to serve as plausible alternative explanations for an apparent causal relationship between an independent and a dependent variable. As an example of a weak (preexperimental) research design in which most of the various threats to internal validity are plausible, consider the "one-group pretest-posttest design" (Campbell and Stanley 1963). Furthermore, assume that researchers have adapted this design to study the effect of income on happiness. As depicted in Table 1 (b), investigators observe the happiness ($O_{happiness}$) of persons at time 2 following a period (during time 1) in which subjects (all below the poverty line) receive no supplementary income ($X_{\$0}$). Subsequently, subjects receive a $1,000 "gift" ($X_{\$1,000}$) at time 3, and their happiness is remeasured ($O_{happiness}$) at time 4.

The investigators find that posttest happiness (i.e., time 4 $O_{happiness}$) is indeed substantially higher than pretest happiness (i.e., time 2 $O_{happiness}$). Accordingly, an increase in supplementary income is associated with an increase in happiness. But is this association due to supplementary income's *causing* an increase in happiness? Or is the association due to some alternative explanation?

Given this weak, preexperimental research design, there are a number of threats to internal validity that serve as plausible alternative explanations for increases in happiness other than the $1,000 gift. These plausible threats include effects due to history, maturation, testing, instrumentation, and regression to the mean, with less likely or logically impossible threats due to selection, mortality, and reverse causal order.

History effects refer to some specific event that exerts a causal influence on the dependent variable, and that occurs at roughly the same time as the manipulation of the independent variable. For instance, during the period between the pretest (time 2) and posttest (time 4) measure of happiness as outlined in Table 1 (b), Congress may have declared a national holiday. This event could have the effect of elevating everyone's happiness. Consequently, even if the $1,000 gift had no effect on happiness, researchers would observe an increase in happiness from the pretest to posttest measure. In other words, the effects of the $1,000 gifts are totally confounded with the effects of the holiday, and both remain reasonable explanations for the change in happiness from time 2 to time 4. That is, a plausible rival explanation for the increase in happiness with an increase in income is that the holiday and not the additional income made people happier.

Maturation effects are changes in subjects that result simply from the passage of time (e.g., growing hungrier, growing older, growing more tired). Simply put, "people change." To continue with our current example using a weak, preexperimental research design, assume that individuals, as they grow older, increase in happiness owing to their improved styles of coping, increasing acceptance of adverse life events, or the like. If such developmental changes appear tenable, then maturation becomes a plausible rival explanation for why subjects' happiness increased after receiving the $1,000 gift. That is, subjects would have displayed an increase in happiness over time even if they had *not* received the $1,000 gift.

Testing effects are the influences of taking a pretest on subsequent tests. In the current study of income and happiness, pretest measures of happiness allow participants to become familiar with the measures' content in a way that may have "carryover" effects on later measures of happiness. That is, familiarity with the pretest may make salient certain issues that would not be salient had subjects not been exposed to the pretest. Consequently, it is possible that exposure to the pretest could cause participants to ponder these suddenly salient issues and therefore change their opinions of themselves. For example, people may come to see themselves as happier than they otherwise would have perceived themselves. Consequently, posttest happiness scores would be higher than pretest scores, and this difference need not be due to the $1,000 gift.

Instrumentation effects are a validity threat that occurs as the result of changes in the way that a variable is measured. For instance, in evaluating the effect of income on happiness, researchers may make pretest assessments with one type of happiness measure. Then, perhaps to take advantage of a newly released measure of happiness, researchers might use a different happiness measure on the posttest. Unless the two measures have exactly parallel forms, however, scores on the pretests and posttests are likely to differ. Accordingly, any observed increase in happiness may be due to the differing tests and not to the $1,000 gift.

Regression to the mean is especially likely to occur whenever two conditions are present in combination: (1) researchers select subjects who have extreme scores on a pretest measure of the dependent variable, and (2) the dependent variable is less than perfectly measured (i.e., is less than totally reliable owing to random measurement error). It is a principle of statistics that individuals who score either especially high or low on an imperfectly measured pretest are most likely to have more moderate scores (i.e., regress toward their respective mean) on the posttest. In the social sciences, almost all variables (e.g., happiness) are less than perfectly reliable. Hence, whenever social scientists assign subjects to treatment conditions based on high or low pretest scores, regression to the mean is likely to occur. For example, researchers may believe that those persons who are most unhappy will benefit most from a $1,000 gift. Therefore, only persons with low pretest scores are allowed into the study. However, low scorers on the pretest are likely to have higher happiness scores on the posttest simply as a result of remeasurement. Under such circumstances, regression to the mean remains a plausible rival explanation for any observed increase in happiness following the $1,000 gift.

Selection effects are processes that result in different kinds of subjects being assigned to one treatment group as compared to another. If these differences (e.g., sex) affect the dependent variable (e.g., happiness), then selection effects serve as a rival explanation for the assumed effect of the hypothesized causal variable (e.g., income). Because there is not a second group in the one-group pretest-posttest design illustrated here, the design is *not* subject to validity threats due to selection. That is, because the same group receives all treatment conditions (e.g., no gift versus a $1,000 gift), the characteristics of subjects (e.g., the number of females versus the number of males) remain constant across treatment conditions. Thus, even if females tended to be happier than males, this effect could not explain why an increase in happiness occurred after subjects received the $1,000 gift.

Mortality effects refer to the greater loss of participants (e.g., due to death or disinterest) in one treatment group compared to another. For instance, in the study of the effects of income on happiness, the most unhappy people are more likely than other subjects to drop out of the study before its completion. Because these dropouts appear in the pretest but not the posttest, the average level of happiness will increase. That is, an increase in happiness would occur even if the

supplementary income had no effect whatsoever. Mortality is *not*, however, a plausible alternative explanation in the current example of a study using the one-group pretest-posttest design. Researchers can simply exclude from the study any subjects who appear in the pretest but not the posttest measure of happiness.

Reverse causal order effects are validity threats due to ambiguity about the direction of a causal relationship; that is, does X cause O, or does O cause X? The one-group pretest-posttest design is *not* subject to this internal validity threat. The manipulation of the independent variable (giving the $1,000 gift) clearly precedes observation of the dependent variable (degree of happiness). In general, where research designs manipulate rather than measure the independent variable, they greatly reduce the threat of reverse causal order.

As an overview, the reader should note that the various threats to internal validity, where plausible, violate the last two of three conditions necessary for establishing a valid causal inference. Recall that the three conditions are: (1) an association between two variables is present; (2) the presumed cause must precede the presumed effect in time; and (3) the association between the two variables cannot be explained by the influence of a "third" variable that may be related to both of them.

Only the violation of the *first* condition is *not* covered by the list of specific threats to internal validity. (But see the later discussion of threats to statistical conclusion validity.) Reverse causal order is a threat to internal validity that violates the *second* condition of causal inference. Furthermore, history, maturation, testing, instrumentation, regression to the mean, selection, and mortality are all threats to internal validity that one can broadly describe as the potential influence of a "third" variable—that is, threats that violate the *third* condition of causal inference. That is, each of these threats represents a specific type of third variable that affects the dependent variable and coincides with the manipulation of the independent variable. In other words, the third variable is *related* to both the independent and dependent variable. Because the third variable affects the dependent variable at the same time that the independent variable is manipulated, it will *appear* that the independent variable causes a change in the dependent variable. But in fact this apparent causal relation is a *spurious* (i.e., noncausal) by-product of the third variable's influence.

As an illustration, recall how validity threats due to history can produce a spurious correlation between income and happiness. In the example used earlier, Congress declared a national holiday that increased subjects' happiness and coincided with subjects receiving a $1,000 gift. Hence, the occurrence of a national holiday represents a "third" variable that is related both to income and happiness, and makes it appear (falsely) that income increases happiness.

Research, in its broadest sense, can be viewed as an investigator's attempt to convince the scientific community that a claimed causal relationship between two variables really exists. Clearly, the presence of one or more threats to internal validity challenges the researcher's claim. That is, the more likely a validity threat seems, the less convincing is the investigator's claim.

When confronted with the specific threats to internal validity in field settings, investigators can attempt to modify their research design to control one or more of these threats. The fact that a specific threat is *possible* for a given research design, however, does not mean it is *plausible*. Implausible threats do little to reduce the persuasiveness of researchers' claims. Therefore, the specific design researchers' use should be determined in large part by the specific threats to validity that are considered most plausible.

Furthermore, as noted earlier, each research design has a given number of possible threats to internal validity, and some designs have more possible threats than do other designs. But only a certain number of these threats will be plausible for *the specific set of variables under study*. That is, different sets of independent and dependent variables will carry different threats to internal validity. Thus, researchers may select weaker designs where the plausible threats for a given set of variables are relatively few and not among the possible threats for the given design. Campbell and Stanley (1963) note, for example, that the natural sciences can often use the one-group pretest-posttest design despite its long list of *possible* threats to internal validity. Given the carefully controlled laboratory conditions and focus on variables measuring nonhuman phenomena, *plausible* threats to internal validity are low.

The next section examines some common quasi-experimental designs and plausible threats to internal validity created by a given design. The discussion continues to use the concrete example of studying the relationship between income and happiness. Examples using a different set of variables might, of course, either reduce or increase the number of plausible threats for a given design.

QUASI-EXPERIMENTAL DESIGNS

When researchers have the opportunity to make more than a single pretest and posttest, some form of *time series design* becomes possible. Table 1 (*d*) illustrates the structure of this design. The *O*'s designate a series of observations (measures of happiness) on the same individuals (group 1) over time. The table shows that subjects receive no supplementary income ($X_{\$0}$) through the first two (times 2 and 4) observational periods. Then at time 5 subjects receive the $1,000 gift ($X_{\$1,000}$). Their subsequent level of happiness is then observed at three additional points (times 6, 8, and 10).

This quasi-experimental design has a number of advantages over the single-group pretest-posttest (preexperimental) design. For instance, by examining the trend yielded by multiple observations prior to providing the $1,000 gift, it is possible to rule out validity threats due to maturation, testing, and regression to the mean. In contrast, instrumentation could still be a threat to validity, if researchers changed the way they measured happiness—especially for changes occurring just before or after giving the $1,000 gift. Moreover, artifacts due to history remain uncontrolled in the time series design. For example, it is still possible that some positive event in the broader environment could occur at about the same time as the giving of the $1,000 gift. Such an event would naturally serve as a plausible alternative explanation for why happiness increased after the treatment manipulation.

In addition to eliminating some threats to internal validity found in the one-group pretest-posttest design, the time series design provides measures of how long a treatment effect will occur. That is, the multiple observations (*O*'s) following the $1,000 gift allow researchers to assess how long happiness will remain elevated after the treatment manipulation.

In some circumstances, the time series design may not be possible, owing to constraints of time or money. In such cases, other quasi-experimental designs may be more appropriate. Consequently, as an alternative strategy for dealing with some of the threats to internal validity posed by the single-group pretest-posttest (preexperimental) design, researchers may add one or more *comparison groups*.

The simplest multigroup design is the *static-group comparison* (Campbell and Stanley 1963). Table 1 (*c*) provides an illustration of this design. Here observations are taken from two different groups (G_1 and G_2) at the same point in time. The underlying assumption is that the two groups differ only in the treatment condition (a $1,000 gift versus no gift) they receive prior to the measure of happiness. In many instances, this is not a safe assumption to make.

The static-group comparison design does reduce some potential threats to internal validity found in the single-group pretest-posttest design; namely, history, testing, instrumentation, and regression to the mean. That is, each of these threats should have *equal* effects on the two experimental groups. Thus, these threats cannot explain why experimental groups differ in posttest happiness.

Conversely, the static-group comparison design adds other potential threats—selection, reverse causal order, and mortality effects—not found in the single-group pretest-posttest design. Indeed, these threats are often so serious that Stanley and Campbell (1963) refer to the static-group comparison, like the single-group pretest-posttest, as a "pre-experimental" design.

Selection effects are generally the most plausible threats to internal validity in the static-group comparison design. That is, in the absence of random assignment, the treatment groups are likely to differ in the type of people they include. For example, researchers might assign poverty-level subjects to the $1,000 gift versus no gift treatment groups based on physical health criteria. Subjects in poor health would receive the supplementary income; subjects in better health would not. Note, however, that poor health is likely to reduce happiness, and that less healthy—and therefore less happy—people appear in the $1,000 treatment condition. Hence, it is possible that this selection effect based on physical health could *obscure* the increase in happiness due to the supplementary income. In other words, even if the $1,000 gift does have a positive effect on happiness, researchers might make a false causal inference; namely, that supplementary income has *no* affect on happiness.

This result illustrates the point that threats to internal validity are not always ones that refute a claim that a causal effect occurred. Threats to internal validity can also occur that refute a claim that a causal effect did *not* happen. In other words, threats to internal validity concern possible false-negative findings as well as false-positive findings.

The preceding example showed how false-negative findings can result due to selection effects in the static-group comparison. False-*positive* findings can, of course, also occur due to selection effects in this design. Consider, for instance, a situation in which researchers assign subjects to treatment conditions based on contacts with a particular governmental agency that serves the poor. Say that the first twenty subjects who contact this agency on a specific day receive the $1,000 gift, and the next twenty contacts serve as the no-gift comparison group. Furthermore, assume that the first twenty subjects that call have extroverted personalities that made them call early in the morning. In contrast, the next twenty subjects are less extroverted and thus call later in the day. If extroverted personality also produces higher levels of happiness, then the group receiving the $1,000 gift would be happier than the no-gift comparison group even before the treatment manipulation. Accordingly, even if supplementary income has no effect on happiness, it will appear that the $1,000 gift increased happiness. In other words, extroverted personality is a "third" variable that has a positive causal effect on both level of supplementary income and happiness. That is, the more extroversion, the more supplementary income; and the more extroversion, the more happiness. These causal relationships therefore make it appear that there is a positive, causal relationship between supplementary income and happiness; but in fact this latter correlation is *spurious*.

Reverse causal order effects are another potential threat to internal validity when researchers use the static-group comparison design. Indeed, reverse causal order effects are really just a special case of selection effects. More specifically, reverse causal order effects will occur whenever the dependent variable is also the "third" variable that determines who is assigned to which treatment groups.

By substituting happiness for extroversion as the "third" variable in the preceding example, one can demonstrate how this reverse causal order effect could occur. Recall that subjects who contacted the government agency first were the most extroverted. Assume now, instead, that the earliest callers were happier people than those who called later (because unhappy people are more likely to delay completing tasks). Under these conditions, then, prior levels of happiness comprise a "third" variable that has a positive causal effect on both level of supplementary income and subsequent happiness. That is, those subjects who are initially happier are more likely to receive supplementary income; and those subjects who are initially happier are more likely to experience subsequent (posttest) happiness. These causal relationships hence make it appear that there is a positive, causal association between supplementary income and happiness. In fact, however, this correlation is spurious. Indeed, it is not supplementary income that determines happiness; it is happiness that determines supplementary income.

Mortality is another possible threat to internal validity in the static-group comparison design. Even if the treatment groups have essentially identical characteristics before the manipulation of the independent variable (i.e., no selection effects), differences between the groups can occur as a consequence of people dropping out of the study. That is, by the time researchers take posttest measures of the dependent variable, the treatment groups may no longer be the same.

For example, in the study of income and happiness, perhaps some individuals in the no-gift group hear that others are receiving a $1,000 gift. Assume that among those people, the most likely to drop out are those who have a "sour" disposition, that is, those who are likely to be the most unhappy members of the group in general. Consequently, the no-gift comparison group will display a higher posttest measure of happiness than the group would have if all members had remained in the study. Thus, even if the $1,000 gift increases happiness, the effect may be obscured by the corresponding, "artificial" increase in happiness

in the no-gift comparison group. In other words, mortality effects may lead researchers to make a false causal inference; namely, that there isn't a causal relationship between two variables, when in fact there is.

One of the most common quasi-experimental designs is the *nonequivalent control group design*. This design is an elaboration of the static-group comparison design. The former is a stronger design than the latter, however, because researchers administer pretests on all groups prior to manipulating the independent variable. Table 1 (*e*) illustrates this design.

A major advantage of the pretests is that they allow researchers to *detect the presence* of selection effects. Specifically, by comparing pretest scores for the different treatment groups before the manipulation of treatment conditions, it is possibly to discern whether the groups are initially different. If the groups differ at the time of the pretest, any observed differences at the posttest may simply be a reflection of these preexisting differences.

For instance, in the income and happiness study, if the group receiving the $1,000 gift is happier than the no-gift comparison group at the time of the pretest, it would not be surprising for this group to be happier at posttest, even if supplementary income had no causal effect. The point is that the nonequivalent control group design, unlike the static-group comparison design, can test whether this difference is present. If there is no difference, then researchers can safely argue that selection effects are not a threat to internal validity in their study.

The inclusion of pretest scores also permits the nonequivalent control group design to detect the presence or absence of other threats to internal validity not possible using the static-group comparison design—namely, mortality and reverse causal order. Recall that threats due to reverse causal order are a special subset of selection effects. Thus, the ability of the nonequivalent control group design to detect selection effects means it should also detect reverse causal order effects. Selection effects occur as a consequence of differences in pretest measures of the dependent variable. Therefore, in the present example, differences between groups in pretest happiness would indicate the possibility of reverse causal order effects. In other words, the amount of pretest happiness determined the amount of supplementary income subjects received ($1,000 gift versus no gift), rather than the converse, that the amount of supplementary income determined the amount of posttest happiness.

Furthermore, the pretest scores of the nonequivalent control group design also allow assessment of mortality effects. Regardless of which subjects drop out of which treatment condition, the researcher can examine the pretest scores for the remaining subjects to ensure that the different treatment groups have equivalent initial scores (e.g., on happiness).

In sum, the nonequivalent control group design is able to reduce all the threats to internal validity noted up to this point. Unfortunately, it is unable to detect one threat to internal validity not previously covered—*selection by maturation interactions*. (For a more complete list of interactions with selection, see Cook and Campbell 1979, and Shaddish et al. in preparation.) This threat occurs whenever the various treatment groups are maturing—growing more experienced, tired, bored, and so forth—at different rates.

For example, consider a situation in which the pretest happiness of the group receiving no gift is as high as the group receiving the $1,000 gift. Moreover, the pretest measures occur when both groups are in stimulating environments, in contrast to the boring environments for the posttest measures. Assume now that there is a greater proportion of people who become bored easily in the no-gift group as compared to the $1,000-gift group. That is, there is a selection effect operating that results in different kinds of people in one group compared to the other. But this difference doesn't manifest itself until a nonstimulating environment triggers the maturational process that generates increasingly higher levels of boredom. The differential rates at which boredom occurs in the two groups result in higher levels of boredom and corresponding unhappiness in the no-gift as compared to the $1,000-gift group. In other words, the group receiving the $1,000 gift will display higher levels of posttest happiness than the no-gift

group, even if supplementary income has no effect on happiness.

The *multiple time series design* incorporates aspects of both the nonequivalent control group and the time series designs. Table 1 (*f*) illustrates the results of this combination. By extending the number of pretest and posttest observations found in the nonequivalent control group design, the multiple time series design can detect selection-maturation interactions. For instance, if differential reactions to boredom explain why the group receiving the $1,000 gift has higher happiness than the no-gift group, then we should expect to see these differences in at least some of the additional pretest measures (assuming that some of these additional group comparisons occur in nonstimulating environments). We would also expect the differential reaction to boredom to manifest itself in the additional posttest measures of the multiple time series design. That is, whenever researchers take posttest measures in stimulating environments, they should observe no group differences. Conversely, whenever researchers take posttest measures in nonstimulating environments, they should observe higher happiness among the group receiving the $1,000 gift.

Furthermore, by adding a second group to the original, single-group time series, the multiple time series reduces the threat of history that is a major problem with the single-group design. Events (e.g., national holidays) that coincide with the manipulation of the independent variable (e.g., $1,000 gift versus no gift) should have equal impacts on each group in the analysis.

By incorporating multiple groups with pretests and posttests, the multiple time series and nonequivalent control group designs can be effective at reducing a long list of internal validity threats; but in order to actually reduce a number of these threats, researchers must assume that the different treatment groups are functionally equivalent prior to manipulating the independent variable. Pretest scores allow researchers to detect, at least in part, whether this condition of equivalence is present; but what if the groups are not initially equivalent? Under these conditions, researchers may attempt to equate the groups through "matching" or other, "statistical" adjustments or controls (e.g., analysis of covariance). However, matching is never an acceptable technique for making groups initially equivalent (see Nunnally 1975; Kidder and Judd 1986). And statistical controls are a better but still less-than-desirable procedure for equating groups at the pretest (see Lord 1967; Dwyer 1983; Rogosa 1985).

In sum, an overview of pre- and quasi-experimental designs using multiple groups indicates the importance of establishing the equivalence of the groups through pretest measures. Further, researchers should try to obtain as many additional observations as possible both before and after manipulating the treatments. When groups are nonequivalent at the outset, it is extremely difficult to discern whether treatment manipulations have a causal effect.

In certain field settings, however, ethical considerations may *mandate* that groups be nonequivalent at the outset. That is, researchers must assign subjects to certain treatment conditions based on who is most "needy" or "deserving." If the dependent variable (e.g., happiness) is associated with the criterion (e.g., physical health) that determines who is most needy or deserving, then the experimental groups will not display pretest equivalence (e.g., the people with the worst health and hence lowest pretest happiness must be assigned to the group receiving the $1,000 gift).

Fortunately, the *regression-discontinuity design* (Thistlethwaite and Campbell 1960; Cook and Campbell 1979) often allows researchers to make relatively unambiguous interpretation of treatment effects, even where groups are not initially equivalent. Indeed, evidence indicates that this design, when properly implemented, is *equivalent* to a *randomized experiment* in its ability to rule out threats to internal validity (Cook and Shadish 1994; Shaddish et al. in preparation).

To continue with the example of income and happiness, researchers may feel compelled to give the $1,000 gift to those individuals with the poorest health. The investigators would therefore begin by developing a scale of "need" in which

participants below a certain level of physical health receive the gift and those above this cutting point do not. This physical health scale constitutes the "pseudo"-pretest necessary for the regression-discontinuity design. The usual posttest measures of the dependent variable—happiness—would follow the manipulation of the no-gift versus the $1,000-gift treatment conditions. Researchers would then regress posttest happiness measures on "pretest" measures of physical health. This regression analysis would include the calculation of separate regression lines for (1) those subjects receiving the $1,000 gift and (2) those subjects not receiving it.

Figure 1 provides an illustration of the results using the regression-discontinuity design. (The structure of the design does not appear in Table 1 due to its relative complexity.) If the $1,000 gift has a discernible impact on happiness, a "discontinuity" should appear in the regression lines at the cutting point for "good" versus "poor" health. An essential requirement for the regression-discontinuity design is a clear cutting point that defines an unambiguous criterion (e.g., degree of physical health) by which researchers can assign subjects to the treatment conditions. It is the clarity of the decision criterion, not its content, that is important.

An interesting characteristic of the regression-discontinuity design is that it works even if the decision criterion has no effect on the outcome of interest (e.g., happiness). Indeed, as the variable that forms the decision criterion approaches a condition in which it is totally unrelated to the outcome, the decision criterion becomes the functional equivalent of *assigning subjects randomly* to treatment conditions (Campbell 1975). Even where the criterion is strongly related to the outcome, the regression-discontinuity design, when properly implemented, can still approximate a randomized experiment in reducing threats to internal validity.

There are, however, several threats to internal validity that can occur in using the regression-discontinuity design (hence the use of the above qualifier: "when properly implemented"). One threat emerges when the relationship between the pseudo-pretest measure (e.g., physical health) and

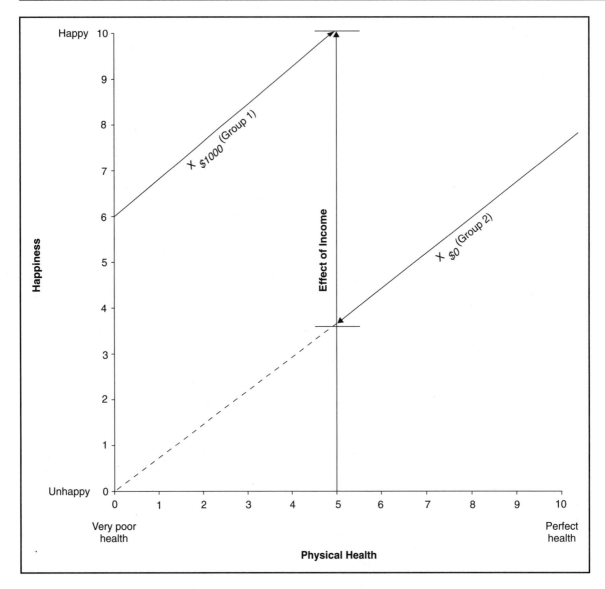

Figure 1. Regression-Discontinuity Design Showing Treatment Effect of Income on Happiness (Dashed line indicates projected happiness scores for group 1 if the $1,000 treatment had no effect on happiness.)

the posttest measure (e.g., happiness) does not form a linear pattern. In fact, a curvilinear relationship near the cutting point may be indistinguishable from the discontinuity between the separate regression lines. Moreover, another threat to internal validity arises if the investigators do not strictly adhere to the decision criterion (e.g., if they feel sorry for someone who is close to qualifying for the $1,000 and thus gives that person the "benefit of the doubt"). Additionally, if only a few people receive a given treatment condition (e.g., if

only a few $1,000 awards can be made, for financial reasons), the location of the regression line may be difficult to estimate with any degree of accuracy for that particular treatment condition. Accordingly, researchers should include relatively large numbers of subjects for all treatment conditions.

In summary, quasi-experimental designs allow researchers to maintain at least some control over how and when they manipulate the independent variable, but researchers lose much control over who receives specific treatment conditions (i.e., the designs do not permit random assignment). Quasi-experimental designs differ in how closely they approximate the power of randomized experiments to make strong causal inferences. As a general rule, the more observations quasi-experimental designs add (i.e., the more *O*'s, as depicted in the diagrams of Table 1), the more the designs are able to reduce threats to internal validity.

NONEXPERIMENTAL DESIGNS

In contrast to quasi-experimental designs, *nonexperimental designs* do *not manipulate* the independent variable. Thus, researchers have no control over who falls into which category of the independent variable when there is a change from one to another category of the independent variable, or what content the various levels of the independent variable will contain. Rather than serving as an agent that actively changes (manipulates) the independent variable, the researcher must be content to passively observe (measure) the independent variable as it naturally occurs. Hence, some social scientists also refer to nonexperimental designs as *passive-observational designs* (Cook and Campbell 1979).

When researchers can only measure rather than manipulate the independent variable, threats to internal validity increase greatly. That is, reverse causal order effects are much more likely to occur. There is also a much greater probability that some "third" variable has a causal effect on both the independent and the dependent variables, therefore producing a spurious relationship between the latter two variables.

To illustrate these points, consider the most widely used research design among sociologists; namely, the static-group comparison design with measured rather than manipulated independent variables—or what we will refer to here as the *passive static-group comparison*. Table 1 depicts the structure of this nonexperimental, cross-sectional design. Researchers generally combine this design with a "survey" format, in which subjects self-report their scores on the independent and dependent variables (e.g., report their current income and happiness).

Note that the structure of this nonexperimental design is basically the same as the static-group

comparison design found in Table 1 *(c)*. To better capture the various levels of naturally occurring income, however, the diagram in Table 1 expands the number of categories for income from two *manipulated* categories ($1,000 gift versus no gift) to three *measured* categories (high, medium, and low personal income). Furthermore, whereas the original static-group design manipulated income *before* measuring happiness, the passive static-group design measures both personal income and happiness at the *same time* (i.e., when subjects respond to the survey). Consequently, the temporal ordering of the independent and dependent variable is often uncertain.

Indeed, because researchers do not manipulate the independent variable, and because they measure the independent and dependent variables at the same time, the threat of reverse causal order effects is particularly strong in the passive static-group comparison design. In the present example, it is quite possible that the amount of happiness a person displays is a determinant of how much money that person will subsequently make. That is, happiness causes income rather than income causes happiness. What is even more likely is that both causal sequences occur.

Additionally, the passive static-group comparison design is also especially susceptible to the threat that "third" variables will produce a spurious relationship between the independent and dependent variables. For example, it is likely that subjects who fall into different income groupings (high, medium, and low) also differ on a large number of other (selection effect) variables. That is, the different income groups are almost certainly nonequivalent with regard to characteristics of subjects in addition to income. One would expect, for instance, that the higher-income groups have more education, and that education is associated with greater happiness. In other words, there is a causal link between education and income, and between education and happiness. More specifically, higher education should produce greater income, and higher education should also produce greater happiness. Hence, education could produce a spurious association between income and happiness.

As noted earlier, researchers can attempt to equate the various income groups with regard to third variables by making statistical adjustments (i.e., controlling for the effects of the third variables). But this practice is fraught with difficulties (again, see Lord 1967; Dwyer 1983; Rogosa 1985).

It is especially sobering to realize that a design as weak as the passive static-group comparison is so widely used in sociology. Note, too, that this design is a substantially weaker version of the static-group comparison design that Campbell and Stanley (1963) considered so weak that they labeled it "preexperimental." Fortunately, there are other nonexperimental, longitudinal designs that have more power to make valid causal inferences. Most popular among these designs is the *panel design*. (For additional examples of passive longitudinal designs, see Rogosa 1988; Eye 1990.)

Table 1 depicts the structure of this longitudinal survey design. It is very similar to the nonequivalent control group design in Table 1 (*e*). It differs from the quasi-experimental design, however, because the independent variable is measured rather than manipulated, and the independent and dependent variable are measured at the same time.

In its simplest, and weaker, two-wave form (shown in Table 1), the panel design can address at least some threats due to reverse causal order and third variables associated with the independent and dependent variable. (This ability to reduce threats to internal validity is strengthened where investigators include three and preferably four or more waves of measures.) The most powerful versions of the panel design include data analysis using structural equation modeling (SEM) with multiple indicators (see Kessler and Greenberg 1981; Dwyer 1983; and for a more general introduction to SEM, see Kline 1998). Simultaneous equations involve statistical adjustments for reverse causal order and causally linked third variables. Thus, the standard admonishments noted earlier about using statistical control techniques apply here too.

Finally, Cook and his associates (Cook and Shaddish 1994; Shaddish et al. in preparation) have noted a real *advantage* of nonexperimental designs over randomized experiments. Specifically, experimental designs lend themselves to studying causal linkages (i.e., "descriptions" of causal conditions) rather than the *processes* accounting for these linkages (i.e., explanations of causal effects). In contrast, nonexperimental designs lend themselves to using causal (path) modeling to study "process"—that is, intervening variables that "mediate" the effect of the independent on the dependent variable. The field of causal modeling using nonexperimental designs has developed at a tremendous pace, dominated by the very flexible and sophisticated data analytic procedure of SEM (Kline 1998).

RANDOMIZED EXPERIMENTS REVISITED

The great problems that nonexperimental designs encounter in making causal inferences help illustrate the increased power researchers obtain when they move from these passive-observational to quasi-experimental designs. But no matter how well a quasi-experimental design controls threats to internal validity, there is no quasi-experimental design that can match the ability of randomized experiments to make strong causal inferences. Indeed, threats to internal validity are greatly reduced when researchers are able to randomly assign subjects to treatment groups. Therefore, the value of this simple procedure cannot be overstated.

Consider the simplest and most widely used of all randomized experiments, the *posttest-only control group design* (Campbell and Stanley 1963), as depicted in Table 1 (*a*). Note that it is similar in structure to the very weak, preexperimental, static-group comparison design in Table 1 (*c*). These two designs differ primarily with regard to whether they do or do not use *random assignment*.

The addition of random assignment buys enormous power to make valid causal inferences. With this procedure, and the manipulation of an independent variable that temporally precedes observation of the dependent variable, reverse causal order effects are impossible. Likewise, with the addition of random assignment, other threats to internal validity present in the static-group comparison design dissipate. Specifically, selection effects are no longer a major threat to internal validity. That is, selection factors—different kinds of people—should appear approximately evenly distributed between categories of the independent variable (e.g., $1,000 gift versus no gift). In other words, the different groups forming the treatment conditions should be roughly equivalent prior to the treatment manipulation. Further, given this equivalence, threats due to selection-maturation interactions are also reduced.

Conversely, given that pretest measures of the dependent variable (e.g., happiness) are absent, mortality effects remain a potential threat to internal validity in the posttest-only control group design. Of course, for mortality effects to occur, different kinds of subjects have to drop out of one experimental group as compared to another. For example, in the study of income on happiness, if certain kinds of subjects (say, those who are unhappy types in general) realize that they are not in the group receiving the $1,000 gift they may refuse to continue. This situation could make it appear (falsely) that people receiving the $1,000 gift are less happy than those not receiving the gift.

Naturally, the probability that *any* subjects drop out is an increasing function of how much time passes between manipulation of treatment conditions and posttest measures of the dependent variable. The elapsed time is generally quite short for many studies using the posttest-only control group design. Consequently, in many cases, mortality effects are not a plausible threat.

In sum, one may conclude that random assignment removes, at least in large part, all of the major threats to internal validity. (But see Cook and Campbell 1979, Cook and Shaddish 1994, and Shaddish et. al. in preparation for some additional qualifications.)

Two more points are noteworthy with respect to random assignment. First, it is important to realize that this procedure *does not ensure* that third variables that might influence the outcome will be evenly distributed between groups in any particular experiment. For instance, random assignment does not ensure that the average level of education will be the same for the group receiving the $1,000 gift as for the group receiving no gift. Rather, random assignment allows researchers to *calculate the probability* that third variables (such as education) are a plausible alternative explanation for an apparent causal relationship (e.g., between supplementary income and happiness). Researchers are generally willing to accept that a causal relationship between two variables is real if the relationship could have occurred by chance—that is, due

to the *coincidental* operation of third variables—less than one time out of twenty.

Some researchers add pretests to the posttest-only control group design in order to evaluate the "success" of the random assignment procedure, and to add "statistical power." According to Nunnally (1975), however, the use of a pretest is generally not worth the attendant risks. That is, the pretest may sensitize subjects to the treatment conditions (i.e., create a treatment-testing interaction). In other words, the effect of the independent variable may not occur in other situations where there are no pretest measures. Thus, any gain from pretest information is likely to be offset by this threat to "construct validity." (For an example of a treatment-testing interaction, see the section on threats to construct validity, below).

Second, random *assignment* of subjects is different from random *selection* of subjects. Random assignment means that a subject has an equal probability of entry into each treatment condition. Random selection refers to the probability of entry into the study as a whole. The former issue bears on internal validity (i.e., whether observed outcomes are unambiguously due to the treatment manipulation); the latter is an issue of external validity (i.e., the extent to which the results of the study are generalizable).

THREATS TO EXTERNAL VALIDITY

Whereas internal validity refers to whether or not a treatment is effective, *external validity* refers to the conditions under which the treatment will be effective. That is, to what extent will the (internally valid) causal results of a given study apply to different people and places?

One type of threat to external validity occurs when certain treatments are likely to be most effective on certain kinds of people. For example, researchers might find that a $1,000 gift has a strong effect on happiness among a sample of young adults. Conversely, a study of extremely elderly persons might find that the $1,000 has no effect on happiness (say, because very old people are in general less stimulated by their environment than are younger age groups). Cook and Campbell (1979) label this external validity threat an *interaction between selection factors and treatment*.

Researchers sometimes mistakenly assume that they can overcome this threat to external validity by *randomly selecting* persons from the population across which they wish to generalize research findings. Random samples do not, however, provide appropriate tests of whether a given cause-effect finding applies to different kinds of people. Obtaining a random sample of, say, the U.S. population would not, for instance, reproduce the above (hypothetical) finding that a $1,000 gift increases happiness among younger but not older people. Combining younger and older persons in a representative sample would only lead to an averaging or "blending" of the strong effect for youths with the no-effect result for the elderly. In fact, the resulting finding of a "moderate" effect would not be an accurate statement of income's effect on happiness for either the younger or older population.

Including younger and older persons in a random sample would only increase external validity if the researchers *knew* to provide separate analyses for young and old—among an infinite variety of *possible* human characteristics that researchers might choose to do subsample analyses on (e.g., males and females). But if researchers suspected that the treatment might interact with age, then they could simply make sure that their nonrandomly selected, "convenience" sample contained sufficient numbers of both youths and elderly to do separate analyses on each age group.

Additionally, threats to external validity occur because certain treatments work best in certain settings. Giving $1,000 to a person at a shopping mall may increase their happiness substantially compared to the same gift given to someone stranded on a desert island with nowhere to spend the money. Cook and Campbell (1979) label this external validity threat an *interaction between treatment and setting*. Given that quasi-experimental designs are most often located in "real-life," field settings, they are somewhat less susceptible to this threat than are randomized experiments—which most often occur in "artificial," laboratory settings.

Note that threats to external validity are concerned with restricting cause-effect relationships to particular persons or places. Therefore, the best procedure for reducing these restrictions is to *replicate* the findings on different persons and in different settings—either within a single study or

across a series of studies (Cook and Campbell 1979; Cook and Shaddish 1994).

THREATS TO CONSTRUCT VALIDITY

Construct validity refers to the accuracy with which researchers manipulate or measure the construct intended rather than something else (Cook and Campbell 1979; and for updates, see Cook and Shaddish 1994; and Shaddish et al. in preparation). Thus, for example, investigators might establish that their manipulation of a variable labeled "income" does indeed have a causal effect on their measure of the outcome labeled "happiness." That is, the researchers have avoided plausible threats to internal validity and, consequently, have presented a convincing claim for a cause-and-effect relationship. Critics might question, however, whether the manipulation labeled "income" and the measure labeled "happiness" do in fact represent the concepts that the investigators claim they have manipulated and measured, respectively.

For instance, in providing supplementary income to selected subjects, researchers might also have manipulated, say, the perception that the researchers really are concerned about the welfare of the subjects. It may be subjects' perceptions of this "caring attitude," and not an increase in "economic well-being," that produced the effect the $1,000 gift had on happiness. In other words, investigators were manipulating a dimension in addition to the economic dimension they intended to manipulate.

Likewise, in asking subjects to answer a questionnaire that purportedly measures "happiness," researchers may not be measuring happiness but rather the degree to which subjects will respond in socially desirable ways (e.g., some subjects will respond honestly to questions asking how depressed they are, and other subjects will hide their depression).

Cook and Campbell (1979) provide an extensive list of threats to construct validity. The description of these threats is rather abstract and complicated. Hence, the following discussion includes only a few concrete examples of potential threats. For a more complete list and discussion of these threats, the interested reader should consult the original article by Cook and Campbell, as well as the update to their book (Shaddish et al. in preparation) and other volumes on the construct validity of measures and manipulations (e.g., Costner 1971; Nunnally and Bernstein 1994).

One type of threat to construct validity occurs in research designs that use pretests (e.g., the nonequivalent control group design). Cook and Campbell (1979) label this threat an *interaction of testing and treatment*. This threat occurs when something about the pretest makes participants more receptive to the treatment manipulation. For example, in the study of income and happiness, the pretest may make salient to participants that "they don't have much to be happy about." This realization may, in turn, make subjects more appreciative and thus especially happy when they later receive a $1,000 gift. In contrast, the $1,000 gift might have had little or no causal impact on happiness if subjects were not so sensitized, that is, were not exposed to a pretest. Accordingly, it is the combination of the pretest and $1,000 gift that produces an increase in happiness. Neither condition alone is sufficient to create the casual effect. Consequently, researchers who use pretests must be cautious in claiming that their findings would apply to situations in which pretests are not present. Because quasi-experimental designs are dependent on pretest observations to overcome threats to internal validity (i.e., to establish the initial equivalence of the experimental groups), researchers cannot safely eliminate these measures. Thus, to enhance the construct validity of the manipulation, researchers should strive to use as unobtrusive measures as possible (e.g., have trained observers or other people familiar with a given subject secretly record the subject's level of happiness).

Another set of potential threats to construct validity concerns what Campbell and Stanley (1963) describe as *reactive arrangements*. Cook and Campbell (1979) have subsequently provided more specific labels for these threats: *hypothesis-guessing within experimental conditions, evaluation apprehension*, and *experimenter expectancies* (see also Rosenthal and Rosnow 1969). Threats due to reactive arrangements result as a consequence of the participants' knowing they are in a study, and therefore behaving in a way that they might not in more natural circumstances. With regard to this phenomena, Orne (1962) used the term "demand characteristics" to refer to the totality of cues that affect a subject's response in an research setting in the sense that certain characteristics "demand" certain behaviors. For instance, subjects receiving the $1,000 gift may guess the hypothesis of the study when they are subsequently asked to respond to questions about their state of happiness. Realizing that the study may be an attempt to show that supplementary income increases happiness, participants may try to be "good subjects" and confirm the experimental hypothesis by providing high scores on the happiness questionnaire. In other words, the treatment manipulation did in fact produce an increase in the assumed *measure* of "happiness," but the measure was actually capturing participants' willingness to be "good subjects."

A classic example of reactive arrangements is the Hawthorne effect (see Lang 1992 for a more comprehensive review). The Hawthorne effect was named for a series of studies conducted between 1924 and 1932 at the Hawthorne Works of the Western Electric Company near Chicago (Mayo 1933; Roethlisberger and Dickson 1939). Researchers attempted to determine, among other things, the effects of illumination on worker productivity. The results were puzzling. There was no clear relationship between illumination and worker performance. Every change, even seemingly adverse changes in which normal lighting was reduced by 50 to 70 percent resulted in increased productivity. In addition, productivity often remained high even after workers were returned to their original working conditions. Even more confusing was the fact that not all the studies reported increased productivity. In some studies, depending upon the factors being manipulated, the effect was even reversed, with workers apparently deliberately reducing their output.

The three most common explanations for the Hawthorne effect are: (1) subjects in studies respond to special attention; (2) awareness of being in a study affects subjects' performance; and (3) subjects react to the novelty of certain aspects of the research procedures (Lang 1992). Subsequent research has not supported any of these explanations conclusively (Adair et al. 1989). Nor is there widespread evidence of the Hawthorne effect in either experimental or field settings (Cook and Campbell 1979). What is clear, however, is that employees, within organizations, are part of social systems that can affect behavior in research settings. Indeed, the Hawthorne studies provided impetus to the development of the new field of "organizational behavior," which has strong links to sociology.

No widely accepted model of the processes involved in subject reactivity presently exists. But to reduce threats to construct validity due to reactive arrangements, researchers may attempt, where feasible, to disguise the experimental hypothesis, use unobtrusive measures and manipulations, and keep both the subject and the person administering the treatments "blind" to who is receiving what treatment conditions. These disguises are generally easier to accomplish in the naturally occurring environments of quasi-experimental designs than in the artificial settings of laboratory experiments. Finally, there are additional, sophisticated structural equation modeling procedures for discerning where reactive arrangements may be present in a study, and for making "statistical adjustments" to correct for the bias that these threats would otherwise introduce (Blalock 1985).

THREATS TO STATISTICAL CONCLUSION VALIDITY

Before researchers can establish whether an independent variable has a causal effect on the dependent variable, they must first establish whether an *association* between the two variables does or does not exist. *Statistical conclusion validity* refers to the accuracy with which one makes inferences about an association between two variables—without concern for whether the association is causal or not (Cook and Campbell 1979; Shaddish et al. in preparation). The reader will recall that an association between two variables is the first of three conditions necessary to make a valid causal inference. Thus, statistical conclusion validity is closely linked to internal validity. To put it another way, statistical conclusion validity is a necessary but not sufficient condition for internal validity.

Threats to statistical conclusion validity concern either one of two types of errors: (1) inferring an association where one does not exist (described as a "Type I error," or (2) inferring no association where one does exist (described as a "Type II error"). Researchers ability to avoid Type II errors depends on the power of a research design to uncover even weak associations, that is, the power

to avoid making the mistake of claiming an association is due to "chance" (is statistically insignificant) when in fact the association really exists. Type II errors are more likely to occur the lower the probability level that researchers set for accepting an association as being statistically significant; the smaller the sample size researchers use; the less reliable their measures and manipulations; and the more random error introduced by (1) extraneous factors in the research setting that affect the dependent variable, and (2) variations among subjects on extraneous factors that affect the dependent variable (Cook and Campbell 1979).

Investigators can reduce Type II errors (false claims of no association) by: (1) setting a higher probability level for accepting an association as being statistically significant (e.g., p.05 instead of p.01); (2) increasing the sample size; (3) correcting for unreliability of measures and manipulations (see Costner 1971); (4) selecting measures that have greater reliability (e.g., using a ten-item composite measure of happiness instead of a single-item measure); (5) making treatment manipulations as consistent as possible across occasions of manipulation (e.g., giving each subject the $1,000 gift in precisely the same manner); (6) isolating subjects from extraneous (outside) influences; and (7) controlling for the influence of extraneous subject characteristics (e.g., gender, race, physical health) suspected to impact the dependent variable (Cook and Campbell 1979).

Type I errors (inferring an association where one does not exist) are more likely the higher the probability level that researchers set for accepting an association as being statistically significant, and the more associations a researcher examines in a given study. The latter error occurs because the more associations one includes in a study, the more associations one should find that are statistically significant "just by chance alone." For example, given 100 associations and a probability level of .05, one should on the average find 5 associations that are statistically significant due to chance.

Researchers can reduce threats of making Type I errors by setting a lower probability level for statistical significance, particularly when examining many associations between variables. Of course, decreasing Type I errors increases the risk of Type II errors. Hence, one should set lower probability levels in conjunction with obtaining reasonably large samples—the latter strategy to offset the risk of Type II errors.

Research designs vary greatly in their ability to implement strategies for reducing threats to statistical conclusion validity. For example, very large sample sizes (say, 500 subjects or more) are generally much easier to obtain for nonexperimental designs than for quasi-experimental or experimental designs. Moreover, experimental designs generally occur in laboratory rather than naturally occurring settings. Thus, it is easier for these designs to control for extraneous factors of the setting (i.e., random influences of the environment). Additionally, experimental designs are generally better able than quasi-experimental designs to standardize the conditions under which treatment manipulations occur.

SUMMARY AND CONCLUSIONS

Quasi-experimental designs offer valuable tools to sociologists conducting field research. This article has reviewed various threats that researchers must overcome when using such designs. In addition, to provide a context in which to evaluate the relative power of quasi-experimental designs to make valid causal inferences, this article also reviewed examples of experimental and nonexperimental designs.

It is important to note that the quasi-experimental designs described here are merely illustrative; they are representative of the types of research designs that sociologists might use in field settings. These designs are not, however, exhaustive of the wide variety of quasi-experimental designs possible. (See Campbell and Stanley 1963, Cook and Campbell 1979, and Shaddish et al. in preparation, for more extensive reviews.) In fact, great flexibility is one of the appealing features of quasi-experimental designs. It is possible literally to combine bits and pieces from different standard designs in order to evaluate validity threats in highly specific or unusual situations. This process highlights the appropriate role of research design as a *tool* in which the specific research topic dictates what design investigators should use. Unfortunately, investigators too often use a less appropriate design for a specific research topic simply because they are most familiar with that design. When thoughtfully constructed, however, quasi-experimental designs can provide researchers with the tools they need to explore the wide array of important topics in sociological study.

REFERENCES

Adair, J., D. Sharpe, and C. Huynh 1989 "Hawthorne Control Procedures in Educational Experiments: A Reconsideration of Their Use and Effectiveness." *Review of Educational Research* 59:215–228.

Blalock, H. M. (ed.) 1985 *Causal Model in Panel and Experimental Designs*. New York: Aldine.

Campbell, D. T. 1975 "Reforms as Experiments." In M. Guttentag and E. Struening, eds., *Handbook of Evaluation Research*, vol. 1. Beverly Hills, Calif.: Sage.

——, and J. C. Stanley 1963. "Experimental and Quasi-Experimental Designs for Research on Teaching." In N. I. Gage, ed., *Handbook of Research on Teaching*. Chicago: Rand McNally.

Cook, T. D., and D. T. Campbell 1979 *Quasi-Experimentation: Design and Analysis Issues for Field Settings*. Chicago: Rand McNally.

Cook, T. D., and W. R. Shaddish 1994 "Social Experiments: Some Developments over the Past Fifteen Years." In L. W. Porter and M. Rosenzweig, eds., *Annual Review of Psychology* 45:545–580.

Costner, H. L. 1971 "Utilizing Casual Models to Discover Flaws in Experiments." *Sociometry* 34:398–410.

Dwyer, J. H. 1983 *Statistical Models for the Social and Behavioral Sciences*. New York: Oxford University Press.

Eye, A. (ed.) 1990 *Statistical Methods in Longitudinal Research*, vols. I and II. San Diego, Calif.: Academic.

Kessler, R. C., and D. G. Greenberg 1981 *Linear Panel Analysis: Models of Quantitative Change*. New York: Academic.

Kidder, L. H., and J. M. Judd 1986 *Research Methods in Social Relations*, 5th ed. New York: Holt, Rhinehart, and Winston.

Kline, R. B. 1998 *Principles and Practice of Structural Equation Modeling*. New York: Guilford.

Lang, E. 1992 "Hawthorne Effect." In E. Borgatta and M. Borgatta, eds., *Encyclopedia of Sociology*, 1st ed. New York: Macmillan.

Lord, F. M. 1967 "A Paradox in the Interpretation of Group Comparisons." *Psychological Bulletin* 68:304–305.

Mayo, E. 1933 *The Human Problems of an Industrial Civilization*. New York: Macmillan.

Nunnally, J. 1975 "The Study of Change in Evaluation Research: Principles Concerning Measurement, Experimental Design, and Analysis." In M. Guttentag and R. Struening, eds., *Handbook of Evaluation Research*. Beverly Hills, Calif.: Sage.

Nunnally, J. C., and I. H. Bernstein 1994 *Psychometric Theory*, 3rd ed. New York: McGraw-Hill.

Orne, M. 1962 "On the Social Psychology of the Psychological Experiment: With Particular Reference to Demand Characteristics and Their Implications." *American Psychologist* 17:776–783.

Roethlisberger, F., and W. Dickson 1939 *Management and the Worker*. New York: John Wiley.

Rogosa, D. 1985 "Analysis of Reciprocal Effects." In T. Husen and N. Postlethwaite, eds., *International Encyclopedia of Education*. London: Pergamon Press.

——1988 "Myths about Longitudinal Research." In K. W. Schaie, R. T. Campbell, W. Meredith, and S. C.

Rawlings, eds., *Methodological Issues in Aging Research* New York: Springer.

Rosenthal, R., and R. L. Rosnow 1969 *Artifacts in Behavioral Research*. New York: Academic.

Shaddish, W. R., T. D. Cook, and D. T. Campbell in preparation "Experimental and Quasi-Experimental Designs for Generalized Causal Inference." Boston: Houghton-Mifflin

Thistlethwaite, D. L., and D. T. Campbell 1960 "Regression-Discontinuity Analysis: An Alternative to the Ex Post Facto Experiment." *Journal of Educational Psychology* 51:309–317.

KYLE KERCHER
KARL KOSLOSKI

R

RACE

The study of race and race relations has long been a central concern of sociologists. The assignment of individuals to racial categories profoundly affects the quality and even the length of their lives. These assignments are ostensibly made on the basis of biological criteria, such as skin color, hair texture, and facial features. Yet the biological meaning of race is so unclear that many social and natural scientists argue that *race*, as a biological phenomenon, does not exist. Others take the position that while different races exist, extensive interbreeding in many societies has produced large numbers of people of mixed ancestry. The assignment of these people to racial categories depends on social, rather than on biological, criteria. Thus the social consequences of biologically inherited traits is the fundamental issue of the sociological study of race.

BIOLOGICAL CONCEPTIONS OF RACE

While the terms *race* and *ethnicity* are often used interchangeably, social scientists assign them distinct meanings. Scholars differ on the precise definition of ethnicity, but these definitions usually include some or all of the following criteria. First, ethnic groups are extended kinship groups, although kinship may be defined loosely, as based on a common homeland rather than common ancestry. Second, coethnics share a distinctive culture, marked by differences ranging from language and religion to styles of dress or cooking. A

distinctive culture need not be a matter of everyday practice, however. It may be primarily symbolic, as when a group's traditional language is no longer widely used, or its religious observance is confined to holidays. Third, an ethnic group shares a common history, in which key events such as immigration, colonization, and the like form a sense of collective memory. Finally, an ethnic group is marked by self-consciousness, in that its members see themselves as a people, and are seen as such by others (Cornell and Hartmann 1998).

For most of human history, ethnic groups living in close proximity did not differ significantly in physical appearance. Thus the observable biological differences associated with *race* were not used to distinguish friend from foe, and interracial antagonisms were virtually unknown. The rapid, long-distance migration required to bring members of different racial groups together is a comparatively recent phenomenon that was accelerated by trade and the large-scale European exploration and colonial expansion of the sixteenth through the nineteenth centuries (van den Berghe 1981). It was also during this period that Western science assumed a central role in the attempt to understand the natural and social worlds. Thus, as Europeans became aware of peoples who differed from them in culture and appearance, the concept of race entered the popular and scientific vocabularies as a means of classifying previously unknown groups.

Not content merely to classify people into racial groups, nineteenth- and early-twentieth-century scientists attempted to sort these groups into a hierarchy. Darwin's theory of evolution, which holds that species are engaged in a struggle for existence in which only the fittest will survive, was gaining widespread acceptance during this period. Herbert Spencer, William Graham Sumner, and other early social theorists extended this evolutionary argument, suggesting that different social groups, including races, were at different states of evolution; the more advanced groups were destined to dominate groups less "fit." This idea, called *social Darwinism* (which Darwin himself did not support), provided justification for European imperialism and for America's treatment of its racial minorities.

Building on the notion that some races were at a more advanced stage of evolution than others, a number of scientists tried to measure differences between the races, especially in the area of intelligence. The first intelligence test was developed by Alfred Binet and Theodore Simon in 1905. Modified versions of this test were administered to approximately one million American soldiers in World War I, and the results were used to argue that there were large, genetically determined differences in intelligence between blacks and whites. Such a conclusion implied that blacks could not benefit from education to the extent that whites could; these findings were then used as a justification for the inferior education made available to blacks.

Binet himself rejected the notion that intelligence was a fixed quantity determined by heredity, or that intelligence could be measured with the kind of precision claimed by other intelligence testers, especially in the United States. Furthermore, other scholars demonstrated that the early tests were heavily biased against members of certain class, ethnic, and racial groups, including blacks. While the *average* scores of blacks have tended to fall below the average scores of whites, greater variation occurs within each group than between the two groups; that is, many blacks outscore many whites.

Charles Murray and Richard Herrnstein argue in *The Bell Curve* (1994) that much of the gap between black and white average scores can be attributed to heredity, rather than to environmental influences. These writers use an extensive array of studies on race and intelligence to support their claim. Yet their methods and conclusions have

been roundly attacked by leading scholars in the field, some of whom contend that intelligence is multidimensional, and cannot therefore be summarized in a single test score. Others point out that since intelligence tests measure academic achievement rather than innate potential, the impoverished background and substandard education of some African Americans offers a reasonable explanation for their lower average scores. Research has repeatedly failed to demonstrate that racial groups differ in terms of their innate capacity for learning. Today, therefore, the vast majority of social scientists reject the idea that any one race is superior in intelligence or any other ability, at least to the extent that such abilities are determined by heredity. (For interesting accounts of the race-intelligence controversy, see Gould 1981; Fraser 1995.)

Controversy continues also on the subject of race itself. In the nineteenth century the concept was defined quite loosely, and the idea was widely held that people of similar appearance but different nationalities constituted different races. As recently as World War II it was not uncommon to hear people speak of the "British race," the "Jewish race," and so on. Some physical anthropologists narrowed the concept to include three main racial groups: the Negroid, Caucasoid, and Mongoloid, or black, white, and Asian races.

Others argue that human populations have always exhibited some degree of interbreeding, and that this has greatly increased during the last few centuries, producing large groups of people who defy such racial classification. "Pure races" have probably never existed, and certainly do not exist now. According to this thesis, race is a cultural myth, a label that has no biological basis but is attached to groups in order to buttress invidious social distinctions. (For an interesting discussion on the biological meaning of race, see Begley 1995; the following section owes much to this work.)

IS RACE A MYTH?

At the most basic level, biologists sort organisms into species. A species is essentially a breeding boundary, in that it defines the limits within which interbreeding can occur. Thus golden retrievers can be bred with standard poodles, but not with pigs or cats. By this fairly straightforward criterion, all humans, regardless of appearance, belong to the same species. The difficulty arises when one attempts to identify subspecies, the technical equivalent of races. In some species, this is relatively simple because their distinctive traits are "concordant." That is, the same subgroups are produced using any of a number of traits: a golden retriever can be distinguished from a standard poodle on the basis of fur color and texture, ear shape, or body type. Among humans, however, identifying subspecies is not so simple, because the traits associated with human subpopulations are nonconcordant. In short, using one trait will result in one set of "racial" categories, while another trait will produce an entirely different set.

Consider the traits commonly used to divide humans into the three conventional races. These traits include skin color, hair color and texture, and facial features. Asians are usually identified primarily by the epicanthic eye fold, yet if this criterion were applied consistently, the San (Bushmen) of South Africa would be considered Asian. And while skin color certainly helps distinguish Swedes from the Masai of East Africa, it also distinguishes Swedes from Turks, both of whom are considered "white," and the Masai from the San, whose olive complexion more closely resembles the Turk's than the much darker Masai's.

Humans are visual creatures, so that in categorizing others, we fixate on differences of appearance. But these criteria are biologically arbitrary; other, less obvious traits associated with human subpopulations might just as easily be used. A common anatomic trait among Asians is front teeth that are "scooped out," or shovel shaped, in the back. Yet Swedes and Native Americans also share this trait, so we could divide the species into one race with shovel-shaped incisors, and one without. Considering biochemistry, some peoples produce lactase (an enzyme that aids milk digestion) into adulthood, while others do not. A "lactase-positive race" would include northern and central Europeans, Arabs, northern Indians, and many West Africans, while other Africans, Native Americans, southern Europeans, and Southeast Asians would be in the "lactase-negative race." Genetics multiplies the possibilities even further: antimalarial genes, including but not limited to the sickle cell gene, could be used to distinguish a "malaria-resistant race" (in which Greeks and Italians would be grouped with Southeast Asians, New Guineans, and tropical Africans) from the "malaria-susceptible race" (which would place Scandinavians with the Xhosa of South Africa). Because these various traits are nonconcordant, classifying the human species on the basis of one will produce a set of "races" entirely different from the set based on another trait.

Biologically speaking, then, all such classification schemes are both arbitrary and meaningless. The genetic variation contained *within* any identifiable human subpopulation, including the conventional "races," is vastly greater than the variation *between* populations. That is, any two Asian people are likely to have less in common than either has with a randomly chosen white person. To put it in slightly different terms, Harvard biologist Richard Lewontin once observed that if a holocaust wiped out everyone on earth except a small tribe deep in the New Guinea forest, almost all the genetic variation found in the four (now five) billion people currently on earth would be preserved (cited in Gould 1981). Grouping people into racial categories tells us nothing about how biologically related they are. It tells us only that we perceive them to share some trait that we humans have chosen to consider important.

If racial categories tell us nothing meaningful about biology, however, they tell us a great deal about history, as we can see from another argument against the traditional view of race: that individuals' racial identification can change as they move from one society to another. Americans are accustomed to thinking of black and white as two separate categories, and assigning people with any African ancestry to the former category. This is the "hypodescent rule," in which the offspring of a mixed union are assigned to the lower-ranked group. In Brazil, however, black and white are poles on a continuum, and individuals can be placed at any point on that continuum, depending on their facial features, skin color, and hair texture. Even siblings need not share the same identity, which also to some extent depends on social class: the expression "money bleaches" reflects the fact that upward mobility can move a person's racial assignment closer to the white end of the continuum (van den Berghe 1967). Thus, a black American who is light skinned and well to do may find that in Brazil he is not considered "black" at all, and may even be labeled "white." Should he go to South Africa instead, our light-skinned black American would be neither black nor white, but "coloured," the term that denotes a person of mixed ancestry in that society.

Finally, consider this consequence of the hypodescent rule: in America, a white woman can give birth to a black child, but a black woman cannot give birth to a white child. This convention is biologically nonsensical and arbitrary; it can only be understood historically. In the United States, hypodescent was carried to the extreme of the "one-drop rule," in which one drop of African blood was enough to designate a person as black. This practice evolved out of a desire to maximize the profitable slave population, and to maintain the "purity" of the white race. Clearly, the racial categories commonly used in America do not reflect an underlying biological reality, but rather the more grim chapters of our history. This point has important implications, as we can see by returning to the debate over the relationship between race and intelligence. If the precise nature and meaning of intelligence remains unclear, and if race itself has no biological significance at all, then how are we to interpret a statistical association between "race" and "intelligence"? It becomes little more than a mathematical exercise, yielding information of dubious value.

SOCIAL CONCEPTIONS OF RACE

While race may lack biological significance, it does have tremendous social significance. Sociologist W. I. Thomas's famous dictum is certainly true of race: "If men define situations as real, they are real in their consequences" (quoted in Coser 1977, p. 521). Racial distinctions are meaningful because we *attach* meaning to them, and the consequences vary from prejudice and discrimination to slavery and genocide. Since people believe that racial differences are real and important, and behave accordingly, those differences become real and important. Hitler, for example, believed that Jews

constituted a distinct and inferior race, and the consequences of his belief were very real for millions of Jews. Thus the major questions confronting sociologists who study race relations concern the social consequences of racial categorization. To what degree are different racial and ethnic groups incorporated into the larger society? How can we account for variations in the economic, political, legal, and social statuses of different groups?

American sociologists have found their own society to be a natural laboratory for the study of these issues. The United States has a wide variety of racial and ethnic groups, and some of these have been more successful in American society than others. Within any group there is substantial variation in economic achievement, and the success of "model minorities" is often exaggerated. Still, considered as groups, Jews and the Japanese have been more successful in America, in material terms, than have blacks and Mexicans. One explanation for these differences that has found some acceptance both within and outside scientific circles is that the cultures and values of these groups differ. Some groups' values are believed to be more conducive to success than others. Jews, for example, have traditionally been seen as valuing scholarship and business acumen; as a result they have worked hard in the face of discrimination, educated their children, and pulled themselves up from poverty. African Americans, by contrast, allegedly lacked these values; the result is their continued concentration in the poor and working classes.

Most sociologists reject this argument, which Stephen Steinberg (1981) refers to as the "ethnic myth." Steinberg argues that this line of reasoning is simply a new form of social Darwinism, in which the fittest *cultures* survive. A closer look at the experiences of immigrants in America (including African Americans) reveals that not all immigrant groups start at the bottom; some groups arrive with the skills necessary to compete in the American labor market while others do not. Furthermore, the skills possessed by some groups are in high demand in the United States, while other groups find fewer opportunities. Thus Steinberg argues that the success of an immigrant group depends on the occupational structure of its country of origin, the group's place in that structure, and the occupational structure of the new country.

Steinberg uses the case of American Jews to support his argument. In terms of education, occupation, and income, Jews have been highly successful. Thirty-six percent of the adult Jewish population had graduated from college in 1971, compared to 11 percent of non-Jews. Seventy percent of Jews were in business or the professions, compared with roughly a third of non-Jews. The median family income of Jews in 1971 was $14,000, approximately 30 percent more than the average American family. Again, it is possible to overstate Jewish success, since many Jews are still poor or working class; middle-class Jews are concentrated in small business and the professions, and are nearly absent from corporate hierarchies. Furthermore, Jews have experienced a great deal of economic and social discrimination. Nevertheless, when compared with other ethnic and racial groups in America, they have been quite successful.

This success, Steinberg argues, is attributable in part to the origins of Jewish immigrants, most of whom came from Russia and eastern Europe, and arrived in the United States in the late nineteenth and early twentieth centuries. Since Jews in eastern Europe could not own land, they tended to live in cities; even those who lived in rural areas were mostly merchants and traders, rather than farmers. The urban concentration and above-average literacy rates of Jews affected their occupational distribution: 70 percent of Russian Jews worked as artisans or in manufacturing or commerce in 1897; even unskilled Jews worked in industrial occupations. Sixty-seven percent of Jewish immigrants who arrived in America between 1899 and 1910 were skilled workers, compared to 49 percent of English immigrants, 15 percent of Italians, and 6 percent of Poles.

Furthermore, Jewish immigrants were disproportionately represented in the garment industry, which was growing at two to three times the rate of other American industries. Jobs in the garment industry were better paid than other industrial jobs, and Jews, with their higher skill level, tended to have the better-paid jobs within the industry.

The garment industry also offered unusual opportunities for individual entrepreneurship, since little capital was required to start a small clothing business.

In sum, Jewish immigrants did well in America because they brought industrial skills to an industrializing country. Although the majority of Jewish immigrants arrived with little money and encountered widespread discrimination, American industry could not afford to ignore them completely. Steinberg concludes that while a case can be made that Jews have traditionally valued educational and occupational achievement, and that this contributed to their success, Jews do not hold a monopoly on these values. Furthermore, if they had encountered an occupational structure that offered no hope for the fulfillment of these aspirations, Jews would have scaled their goals down accordingly.

The inability of other racial and ethnic groups to match the success achieved by Jewish Americans has also been attributed to the cultures and values of those groups. Glazer and Moynihan (1970), for example, blame the persistent poverty of blacks on "the home and family and community. . . . It is there that the heritage of two hundred years of slavery and a hundred years of discrimination is concentrated; and it is there that we find the serious obstacles to the ability to make use of a free educational system to advance into higher occupations and to eliminate the massive social problems that afflict colored Americans and the city" (pp. 49, 50). Yet, as Gutman (1976) has shown, the black family emerged from slavery relatively strong and began to exhibit signs of instability only when blacks became concentrated in urban ghettos. Furthermore, for generations after emancipation, blacks faced extreme educational and employment discrimination; the notion that a free educational system provided a smooth path to the higher occupations is simply inconsistent with blacks' experience in America.

Most sociologists tend, like Steinberg, to locate the cause of African Americans' poverty relative to white immigrant groups in the structure of opportunity that awaited them after slavery. The South was an economically backward region where blacks remained tied to the land and subject to conditions that were in many cases worse than those they had known under slavery. The vast majority of white immigrants settled in the North, where industry provided jobs and taxpaying workers provided schools. The more agricultural South had fewer educational opportunities to offer blacks or whites. Immediately after the Civil War, when they were provided access to education, blacks flocked to southern schools. This opportunity was short lived, however, since the scarcity of educational resources made it advantageous for whites to appropriate the blacks' share for themselves, a temptation they did not resist.

By the time large numbers of blacks migrated north, the industrial expansion that had provided so many jobs for immigrants was on the wane. Moreover, the newly freed slaves did not have industrial skills and were barred from industrial occupations. Given the generations of social, economic, political, and legal discrimination that followed, and the fact that blacks did take advantage of the opportunities that presented themselves, it is unnecessary to call on "inferior values" to explain the difference in achievement between African Americans and white immigrants. (For an interesting comparison of the struggle of blacks in the postbellum South and the North to that of black South Africans, see Frederickson 1981; for a comparison of the conditions faced by U.S. blacks and white immigrants, and the effects of these differences on each group's success, see Lieberson 1980.)

CONCLUSION

Ever since Darwin proposed that the evolutionary process of natural selection ensures that only the fittest species survive, social science has been bedeviled by the notion that some human groups, especially races, are more biologically or culturally fit than others. This extension of Darwin's principle to competition for survival *within* the human species, especially when applied to industrial or postindustrial societies, cannot withstand close scrutiny. While human subpopulations have evolved certain traits such as malaria resistance and the retention of lactase into adulthood as adaptations to environmental conditions, these physical traits do not sort our species into consistent categories, and they are hardly relevant to performance in today's school or workplace.

Furthermore, cultural differences between groups can be identified, and these differences may have economic consequences, but they are more likely to reflect a group's historical experiences than the value its members attach to economic success. Thus, the current trend in sociology is to explain differences in the success of racial and ethnic groups in terms of the economic and political resources possessed by those groups, and by the groups with whom they are in competition and conflict.

One reason for the longevity of the biological and cultural forms of social Darwinism may be that for many years most natural and social scientists have been white, and middle class to upper class. While the objective search for truth is the goal of the scientific enterprise, race is an emotionally and ideologically loaded concept, and even the most sincere humanitarians have been led to faulty conclusions by their own biases. An important prospect for the advancement of the scientific study of race, then, is the recruitment of new scholars with a wide diversity of ethnic, racial, and national backgrounds. This increasing diversity will help to broaden the exchange of ideas so necessary to scientific inquiry, and will yield an understanding of race that is more balanced and less subject to bias than it has been in the past.

REFERENCES

Begley, Sharon 1995 "Three Is Not Enough." *Newsweek* (February 13):67–69.

Cornell, Stephen, and Douglas Hartmann 1998 *Ethnicity and Race*. Thousand Oaks, Calif.: Pine Forge.

Coser, Lewis A. 1977 *Masters of Sociological Thought*, 2nd ed. New York: Harcourt Brace Jovanovich.

Fraser, Steven (ed.) 1995 *The Bell Curve Wars*. New York: Basic Books.

Frederickson, George M. 1981 *White Supremacy*. New York: Oxford University Press.

Glazer, Nathan, and Daniel Patrick Moynihan 1970 *Beyond the Melting Pot.* Cambridge: Massachusetts Institute of Technology Press.

Gould, Stephen Jay 1981 *The Mismeasure of Man.* New York: Norton.

Gutman, Herbert 1976 *The Black Family in Slavery and Freedom.* New York: Pantheon.

Herrnstein, Richard J., and Charles Murray 1994 *The Bell Curve.* New York: Free Press.

Lieberson, Stanley 1980 *A Piece of the Pie.* Berkeley: University of California Press.

Steinberg, Stephen 1981 *The Ethnic Myth.* New York: Atheneum.

van den Berghe, Pierre L. 1967 *Race and Racism.* New York: John Wiley.

—— 1981 *The Ethnic Phenomenon.* New York: Praeger.

SUSAN R. PITCHFORD

RACISM

See Discrimination; Prejudice; Race; Segregation and Desegregation.

RAPE

See Sexual Violence and Exploitation.

RATIONAL CHOICE THEORY

Rational Choice theory is typically seen as the use of economic reasoning in contexts that were traditionally the concern of disciplines other than economics, especially of political science, sociology, and anthropology. If we take a more nuanced historical view, however, we might as soon see mainstream economics as the stepchild of the kind of reasoning about larger social institutions, norms, behaviors, and so forth that was central to the Scottish Enlightenment in the works of David Hume, Adam Smith, and many others. The genius of these thinkers was to make sense of such institutions, norms, and so forth as the products of individuals acting from their own private incentives. Their concern was that of James Coleman (1990), to explain macrophenomena from microchoices. Through most of the past two centuries, economists increasingly focused such reasoning on explaining the nature and working of the market, for example on prices and conditions for an equilibrium of supply and demand, and the earlier concern with broader sociological issues faded. The great classical economists, such as Smith, Alfred Marshall, and Vilfredo Pareto, were interested not only in the market but also in broader social institutions and practices. Much of their work can readily be counted among the great contributions to sociology in their eras.

Contemporary rational choice theory represents a resurgence of such earlier efforts. The efflorescence of such theory in our time has followed on the development of game theory by John von Neumann and Oskar Morgenstern, Kenneth Arrow's demonstration that individual preferences do not aggregate into analogous collective preferences, and Anthony Downs's analysis of democratic participation. The largest bodies of contemporary work are those on the study of group behavior, under the rubric of Mancur Olson's logic of collective action, and on political participation, which in part can be seen as merely a special case of collective action. Perhaps the fastest-growing area of inquiry today is in the analysis of institutions, much of it focused on historical institutions, as in the work of Douglass North.

A cognate area is social exchange theory, which had its contemporary origins well before the works of von Neumann, Arrow, and Downs. Its origins were also distinctively sociological, as in the work of George Homans, and anthropological.

A seemingly cognate area is economic sociology, although much of economic sociology is like the bulk of voting studies in that it takes the form of simple correlations of behaviors with personal characteristics—gender, age, ethnicity, education, occupation, nationality, religion, and so on. Much of economic sociology might therefore be counted as behavioralist. Rational choice analysis at least implicitly assumes intentionality. Hence, in effect, rational choice theory is contrary to the behavioralism of much of sociology, especially political sociology, in the mid-twentieth century. The point of behavioralism is to avoid the use of mental or intentional explanations of behavior, to treat the mind as virtually a black box. Rational choice theory imputes preferences and intentions to actors. In part, of course, these might derive from or be explained by such sociological characteristics as race, gender, or religion. Although there is a large field of behavioral economics, economics in general was not centrally influenced by the behavioral movement just because it is largely about preferences and intentions. Indeed, much of the work on behavioral economics is directed primarily at establishing the nature and content of preferences and preference functions. It gives measures of the preferences that might go into intentionalist accounts of behavior.

Although much of rational choice theory explains behavior as a response to interests, such theory need not be so narrowly restricted. In its more general form, it explains behavior as the product of preferences, which can cover virtually anything from values to interests. For example, holding all else constant, you might prefer a higher to a lower income. But you might prefer a lower income with peace to a higher income in a state of war, even if your safety and livelihood are not at risk in the war. In many contexts, however, interests seem to be adequate to explain behavior, often because other values are not at stake in the behavior to be explained or because they are substantially less important than interests. Rational choice theory is commonly most compelling in contexts in which interests are predominant. In part, this is because interests can often be more systematically imputed to relevant actors than can other values, although this is not always true. For example, in a given population, particular religious values might regularly trump concern with interests to some substantial degree in some aspects of life. Even when we might suppose other values are very important, however, we might also suppose that analyzing the force of interests gives us a clear baseline for then coming to understand the import or weight of these other values in explaining behavior.

The value theory of rational choice theory is essentially the utility theory that has been developed over the past few centuries by economists and others. It is sometimes asserted that this is an empty value theory and that we can put almost anything we wish into utility functions. For example, I can put your pleasures or various normative commitments in my own utility function. While this is technically correct, most of the major results of rational choice analysis turn on the use of utility functions that are about as spare as we can imagine. They include nothing more than interests, which are conceived to be resources, such as money and time. The results surveyed here virtually all depend only on such simple utility functions. Or occasionally, in a somewhat fuller version, they require inclusion of some of the pleasure one gets from various consumptions, as in the account below of the norm of conformity to neighborhood tastes and manners.

Rational choice theory has been applied to so many diverse issues that a full survey of its characteristic results would be exhausting. I will therefore take up several applications, some of them especially important both in establishing rational choice theory and in recasting the nature of major problems that had already long been the focus of much research. I will first discuss the main methodological or fundamental theories behind rational choice theory. In applying such theory, I will begin with the grandest of sociological issues: the problem of social order. Then I will take up two major areas of research that got the contemporary field of rational choice theory under way: the study of group action and the corollary study of political participation. The first of these is historically a major focus of sociological research, while the second has naturally been the special domain of political science. Then I will take up three efforts that show the breadth of the approach. These are the analyses of institutions, norms, and functional explanation.

GAME THEORY

The methods of rational choice theory are essentially the methods of economics, including standard equilibrium analysis, price theory, econometrics, and game theory. Game theory is less a theory

Game Theory

GAME 1. PURE CONFLICT

	COLUMN	
Row	I	II
I	1,2	2,1
II	2,1	1,2

GAME 2. PURE COORDINATION

	COLUMN	
Row	I	II
I	1,1	2,2
II	3,3	1,1

GAME 3: PRISONER'S DILEMMA OR EXCHANGE

	COLUMN	
Row	Cooperate	Defect
Cooperate	2,2	4,1
Defect	1,4	3,3

Table 1

than a format for presenting the array of choices and outcomes that face two or more actors whose outcomes are determined by the joint choices or actions of all of them. Games can be represented in many forms. In the matrix form, each player has a set of choices or strategies, and outcomes are determined by the intersection of the strategy choices of all players. Games in which two players have two strategies each are called two-by-two games. Such games can be pure coordination, pure conflict, or a mixture of these two, as represented in Games 1–3, in Table 1. In each of these games, Row has two strategy choices available and Column also has two choices. When both have chosen their strategies, an outcome is determined. The payoffs in each outcome are given in ordinal terms. 1 is the best payoff, 2 next best, and so forth. The first payoff in each outcome is to Row and the second payoff is to Column.

In the pure conflict game, one player can be better off only if the other is worse off. In the pure coordination game, both players achieve their best payoff together. Mixed games are commonly called *mixed-motive games*. There are many different types. The one represented here is the prisoner's dilemma, which is surely the most studied of all simple games, probably because it represents ordinary exchange and is therefore ubiquitous and central in social interaction. In the prisoner's dilemma both players can be made better off together in the move from (3,3) to (2,2), so that the game has a strong element of coordination. But Row is made better off while Column is made worse off in the move to (1,4) from any other outcome, so that the game also has a strong element of conflict.

Unfortunately, the (3,3) outcome of a prisoner's dilemma is an equilibrium in the sense that we cannot move to the Pareto superior (2,2) outcome through individually beneficial or neutral moves, because my change of strategy from defecting to cooperating while you continue with your strategy of defecting makes me worse off. To move to the (2,2) outcome requires joint action. The prisoner's dilemma is the only one of the seventy-eight ordinally distinct two-by-two games that has a Pareto-dominated equilibrium. Its solution therefore commonly requires incentives from outside a single play of the game. The incentive can be from the benefits of cooperative play in an iterated series of plays of the game or from external enforcement by other parties, as under a legally binding contract.

SOCIAL ORDER

There are three grand schools on social order. One of these is the conflict school associated with Plato's Thrasymachus, Karl Marx's class theory, Ralf Dahrendorf, and many others. Another is the shared-values school of John Locke, Émile Durkheim, and Talcott Parsons. A third is the school of exchange theory associated with Adam Smith, George Homans, and others. These can be characterized by the three classes of games represented above. Because there can be all these—and many other—classes of interactions in society, all these theories are partially right about social order. There is a fourth plausible account of much of the order we see, an account that fits the coordination game. We do not coordinate only because we share values; we can coordinate merely to stay out of each other's way while we pursue our different values. (Indeed, in some sense we can share values—we both want the same thing—in such a way as to have severe conflict.)

One of the simplest of social coordinations is the coordination on driving that makes traffic flow much faster and with less mishap. In North America, we all drive to the right. That is merely one of two possible conventions that could work equally well. The other convention is that we all drive to the left; this convention is followed in the United Kingdom and many nations of the British Commonwealth. It is merely coordination that resolves the traffic problem. But when you and I coordinate on this convention, we do so not because we share any substantial values. We might each be utterly self-serving. The only value we share is to keep others out of our way as much as possible. This is characteristic of much of social order in contemporary liberal societies, in which rampant individualism and great diversity of values might seem to lead to great and disruptive conflict. Instead, it commonly gets channeled in ways that avoid conflict but that could hardly be called cooperative in the sense in which you and I might cooperate in building a house.

Coordination without confluence of values makes the problem of social order seem relatively simple, as it must be for many activities in which we spontaneously achieve order without either the imposition of power by authorities, as is required for the conflict school, or the relatively deliberate cooperation of the exchange school. While such coordination is not the original discovery of rational choice theory or game theory, it is made far more perspicuous by these because these give it a structure of motivation that makes sense of it in many contexts, just as they make the other major schools of social order clearer. Hume presented a clear account of coordination and convention in many social contexts in which stabilizing expectations is fundamentally important to social order. Game theory provides a framework for characterizing the interactions that we must govern if we are to achieve order. Most forcefully, perhaps, game theory suggests why we cannot ground an account of social order in merely one of the traditional

schools, because it displays the greater complexity of the forms of interaction that must be ordered.

GROUPS AND COLLECTIVE ACTION

There is a tradition, still alive today, in which it is supposed that if the members of a group share an interest in some result, they will act to provide themselves that result. For example, Karl Marx's theory of revolution requires this simplistic assumption coupled with his account of class consciousness. Against this tradition, Olson (1965) argued that, if our group interest requires for its achievement that each (or at least many) of us make a personally costly contribution to its achievement, then we commonly do not have individual incentive to act for the collective good. Each of us bears the full cost of our own contribution but receives only a minuscule part of the small piece of the larger collective good provided by that contribution. Typically, therefore, the collective benefit to me of my contribution to our collective provision will be less than the cost to me of that contribution. Hence, if I am narrowly self-interested, I will not make a contribution to the collective good but will hope merely to free ride on the provision that results from the contributions of others. If all other members of my group have my structure of interests, none of us will contribute and our collective good will not be provided. If we could vote to have ourselves compelled to contribute, we might all vote to do so. But if we must voluntarily contribute, none of us might do so. This is the logic of collective action.

Olson used standard micro-economic analysis to demonstrate this logic. He modeled the problem as an instance of Paul Samuelson's theory of public goods, in which the efficient price of access to the public good would be zero even though, at that price, there would be no voluntary supply of the good. Olson's logic can as well be demonstrated game theoretically as an instance of a large-number prisoner's dilemma (Hardin 1982). As in the discussion of game theory above, individually motivated action would not lead us out of the dismal equilibrium of no cooperation, even though the Pareto superior outcome in which all would contribute might be enormously superior to the status quo equilibrium in which all defect.

A very large literature has been directed at explaining the collective action and the achievement of collective benefits that we see despite this logic. For example, we apparently see a great deal of collective action in the form of social movements that sometimes entail great individual costs and even severe individual risks. Much of this literature supposes that people are motivated by commitments beyond self-interest, such as social and moral commitments, but much of it supposes that there are incentives apart from the direct logic of collective action. For example, there may be specific personal benefits corollary to the collective benefit. Alternatively, our group might be provided its collective good but not through spontaneous individual actions. Rather, an entrepreneur might see the possibility of making a career out of leadership in providing our group its collective benefit. Such an entrepreneur might especially arise if our group's good could be provided by government without requiring our voluntary cooperation.

POLITICAL PARTICIPATION AND DEMOCRACY

There are two main lines of theory on political participation in a democratic system. One of these began with Kenneth Arrow's ([1951] 1963) impossibility theorem. That theorem essentially says that collective preferences cannot be modeled simply on individual preferences. We might each individually have well-ordered preferences over all the choices we face, and yet we might collectively not have such well-ordered preferences. Indeed, we can generally expect not to have such collective preferences over any complex realm of choice, such as we often face in normal politics over the large array of policies at issue. This has far broader implications than merely that democratic choice may have problems. It is an important and broadly interesting instance of the fact that the imputation of various characteristics of individuals, such as their pattern of preferences, to groups composed of individuals is a fallacy of composition.

The typical implication of Arrow's theorem goes back to the Marquis de Condorcet and to Lewis Carroll. It is that our collective preferences may cycle through some set of possibilities. For example, in majority votes we may collectively prefer A to B, B to C, and C to A. If our collective preferences were as well behaved as our individual preferences, the fact that we prefer A to B and B to C would entail that we prefer A to C. In majority votes, the majority who prefer A to B can be different from that who prefers C to A. For example, my preferences may be A > B > C; yours may be B > C > A; and a third person's may be C > A > B. These preferences yield the cycle above if the three of us vote by manjority. Many institutional devices, such as legislative practices of opposing new laws against each other before opposing the winner of such a series against the status quo, tend to block any evidence of cyclic preferences; but such a device gives a strong conservative bias to collective choice.

The other main line of rational choice theory of democracy began with Joseph Schumpeter and was developed extensively by Downs (1957). There are two major classes of claims. First, Downs supposed that two parties or candidates in an election face an electorate that is divided along a left-right dimension. If the voters have a normal distribution about some central tendency on this dimension, the two candidates will want to place themselves at the peak of that normal distribution. Hence, the two candidates will tend to have quite similar positions. Second, he supposed each voter faces what is de facto a logic of collective action on whether to vote. Suppose there are some costs involved in casting a vote—waiting on line, traveling in foul weather, and paying a fee for registration. It follows that individual voters should see the election of candidate A over candidate B as essentially a collective good to be provided at individual cost to themselves. It is therefore subject to the perverse logic of collective action, and we should expect that many voters would not vote unless they have motivations that go beyond their own interests. Furthermore, if it is not in my interest even to vote, it is unlikely to be in my interest to learn enough about the issues to vote intelligently.

INSTITUTIONS

The rational choice analysis of institutions has roots in ancient accounts of the rise of civilization. Among many such accounts in the era of the Scottish Enlightenment is Smith's theory (1978) of the stages of development of society from very primitive, to pastoral, to more nearly modern society in his *Lectures on Jurisprudence* (these lectures were not published in Smith's time and have played little role in the development of such analyses since then). Smith's account turns very clearly on the incentives that individuals have to submit to various forms of social order and, eventually, government. His later analysis of the wealth of nations is itself a theory of one of the grandest of all institutions: the economy of a modern commercial society. Smith argued that the wealth of the nation is a function of the efforts of individuals to do well for themselves.

More recent work has gone in diverse directions. The two main directions are the microanalysis of institutions and the behavior of individuals within them and the more nearly macroanalysis of why certain institutional forms arise and prevail. The microanalysis is applied to a wide variety of institutions, most of them of relatively small scale, such as committee structures and formal organizations of many kinds. The macroanalysis is often broadly historical and is directed at accounting for the rise of economic and other institutions. For example, there is extensive work on the rise of devices for handling trade across a broad array of cultures in the absence of any centralized governmental authorities.

Much of the institutional analysis builds on accounts of transaction costs. According to the so-called Coase theorem, due to Ronald Coase, if there were no transaction costs, property rights assignments would have no effect on overall production. Introducing transaction costs can distort production substantially. Firms sometimes internalize functions for which transaction costs would be high if they had to deal with outside suppliers for those functions, and they externalize functions for which markets work well to reduce transaction costs so that competitive suppliers can drive down production costs. Attention to the structure of transaction costs therefore can explain much of an economic organization's structure. Attention to changes in markets over time can also explain the evolution of such organizations' structures. While most transaction cost analysis has so far been done by economists, including economic historians, it is also increasingly done by sociologists and others.

North (1990, p. 131) argues that the use of standard neoclassical economic methodologies exacts a heavy price in our effort to understand institutions. Because such understanding must of necessity be developmental, it must include stories of how the institutions came to be what they are. Neoclassical price theory is concerned with allocations at a specific moment in time under particular institutional arrangements. Game theory lends itself more readily to developmental stories, but to some extent we lack the methodology for putting such stories into order.

A clear implication of the transaction cost analysis of institutions is that, once in place, institutions influence incentives and interests, so that one cannot simply take institutions as dependent on rational choice. They are, additionally, shapers of rational choice. This is conspicuously true, of course, for such institutions as those of government and law, part of whose function is specifically to give people incentive to behave in some ways rather than others. It is true far more generally of essentially all institutions that have significant value to us, even institutions whose purpose might be seen as merely to produce certain goods or services. This means that the actual set of institutions we have and the set of individual behaviors we see are partly determined by the order and the era in which institutions have developed. Some part of what is commonly referred to as culture is merely the happenstance dependency of such historical developmental patterns.

NORMS

Much of the study of norms has been psychological or even psychoanalytic, and perhaps most of it has assumed that the motive for following norms is essentially normative or otherwise not self-interested. Efforts to explain the rise of norms, however, are often forced to take account of how the interests of at least some people are to act on and to enforce various norms. One way to characterize the problem of creating and maintaining a norm is as a problem of collective action. It would seemingly be in the interest of almost all of us if a certain norm prevailed, but it is in the interest of almost none of us actually to abide by the norm unless there is some sanctioning system to keep us in line. In some theories, norms are morally or psychologically internalized, so that the sanctioning system is internal to the actor. Such theories require a substantial account of just how the internalization works. No doubt, there is some internalization of norms, but many norms must still depend heavily on external sanctioning, either for them to work at all or for them to work very well. If that were not so, we could dispense with institutionalized law.

Against accounts that require external sanctions, it is sometimes supposed that sanctioning has costs, so that sanctioning a violator of a norm runs against the interests of those who would like to see the norm upheld. For many norms, this is apparently not true. For norms of exclusion, I may actually prefer to shun you if you violate our norm. Hence, I sanction you and benefit from doing so. For example, if you do not follow neighborhood norms of using a relevant slang or dressing in certain ways, I might actively prefer not to associate with you, because your behavior makes me uncomfortable. My reticence and that of others in our neighborhood affects you and damages the pleasures you might get from associating with us or even shuts you out of such association.

For universalistic norms the problem is more complex. Some of these, such as the norm of promise keeping or truth telling, are enforced between dyads or small numbers of participants. In these cases, it may commonly be my interest to sanction you by not cooperating with you on other matters if you break your promise to me on some current matter. Hence, these norms are like norms of exclusion in that they can also be backed by sanctions that serve the interest of the sanctioners.

For universalistic norms that govern large-number interactions that are essentially instances of collective action, there may be no sanctioning device that serves the sanctioner's interest, and such norms are, not surprisingly, relatively weak in comparison to dyadic universalistic norms and norms of exclusion (Hardin 1995).

FUNCTIONAL EXPLANATION

An example of the ways in which rational choice theory is applied to apparently contrary approaches is recent work on functional explanation. This work does not contribute to the older school of functionalism or structural functionalism, as represented in much of twentieth-century anthropology or in the sociology of Parsons and many others. Rather, it reconstructs functional accounts in terms of individual incentives, as did Robert Merton in his effort to be very clear about the logic of functional argument. Oddly, the most important contribution to this new work was intended as a dismissal of functional analysis. Jon Elster (1979) argued that, if the form of functional explanation is properly spelled out, then very few supposedly functional accounts fit that form.

Pared down to its essentials, Elster's account is as follows:

An institution or a behavioral pattern X is explained by its function F for group G if and only if:

1. F is an *effect* of X;

2. F is *beneficial* for G;

3. F maintains X by a causal *feedback* loop passing through G.

Many groups that benefit from some behavior on the part of their members induce that behavior through incentives that they give to their members.

As an example of a functional account of a major institution, return to the problem of social order, which is typically governed in substantial part by a legal system. A common view of much of law is that its function is to coordinate us or to facilitate our interactions. Hence in a functional explanation of law, F is coordination, X is law, and

G is our law-governed populace. The feedback loop passing through the populace is that our coordination by law enables us to coordinate to produce still further law to coordinate us still further. Hence, law is functional for us. But we would coordinate in such ways only because it is in our interest to coordinate. Hence, we can explain a major, pervasive, and seemingly all important social institution in functional terms as grounded in the rational choices of the actors.

CURRENT DIRECTIONS

Perhaps the easiest assessment of where the field of rational choice will go and where it should go is to extrapolate from current trends. Clearly, institutional work looms large for the near term and normative work seems likely to become more important. In both of these developments, one might hope and even urge that research in rational choice take the findings of other approaches seriously. Doing this would entail two quite different programs. The first and simpler program is merely to make extensive use of findings from other approaches. The second and intellectually more challenging program is to attempt to show the complementary relation of various other approaches to rational choice theory—or, alternatively, to demonstrate their incompatibility, which is often asserted but seldom shown. Sometimes, this might even entail showing that some other approach is, at least in some applications, equivalent to rational choice analysis. For example, work that has unpacked the logic of functional explanation often reveals the rationality of actors involved in replicating some supposedly irrational or extrarational behavioral pattern.

Perhaps the greatest challenge to rational choice theory is to fit it to vast bodies of behavioral research that does not focus on individual incentives and intentions. Part of the task here would be to impute incentives and intentions to relevant actors, perhaps by analogy from other studies and contexts. Another part of the task, as in the rational choice analysis of institutions, functional explanation, and norms, is to restructure the problems in ways that make their choice structures clear.

Unfortunately, rational choice theory is less well developed in sociology than in economics and even political science, in part because it is embattled. Despite the heyday of exchange theory in anthropology earlier in the twentieth century, rational choice theory is almost entirely absent from that discipline.

Finally, just because rational choice theory focuses on the incentives for microchoices that produce macroeffects, it is particularly suited to policy analysis. Empirical work on incentive systems and how they work can be put to use in designing policies to change behavior in productive ways. This is little more than common sense in many contexts, but a resolute focus on the relation of microincentives to macroresults is an especially natural part of rational choice analyses.

(SEE ALSO: *Social Exchange Theory*)

REFERENCES

Arrow, Kenneth J. (1951) 1963 *Social Choice and Individual Values*, 2nd ed. New Haven, Conn.: Yale University Press.

Coleman, James S. 1990 *Foundations of Social Theory*. Cambridge, Mass.: Harvard University Press.

Cook, Karen S., and Richard Emerson 1978 "Power, Equity, and Commitment in Exchange Networks." *American Sociological Review* 43:721–739.

Downs, Anthony 1957 *An Economic Theory of Democracy*. New York: Harper.

Elster, Jon 1979 *Ulysses and the Sirens*. Cambridge: Cambridge University Press.

Hardin, Russell 1982 *Collective Action*. Johns Hopkins University Press.

—— 1995 *One for All: The Logic of Group Conflict*. Princeton, N.J.: Princeton University Press.

Hirschman, Albert O. 1970 *Exit, Voice and Loyalty: Responses to Decline in Firms, Organizations, and States*. Cambridge, Mass.: Harvard University Press.

Homans, George Caspar (1961) 1974 *Social Behavior: Its Elementary Forms*. New York: Harcourt Brace Jovanovich.

Mueller, Dennis C. (ed.) 1997 *Perspectives on Public Choice: A Handbook*. New York: Cambridge University Press.

North, Douglass C. 1990 *Institutions, Institutional Change and Economic Performance*. Cambridge: Cambridge University Press.

Olson, Mancur, Jr. 1965 *The Logic of Collective Action*. Cambridge, Mass.: Harvard University Press.

Smith, Adam 1978 *Lectures on Jurisprudence* R. L. Meek, D. D. Raphael, and P. G. Stein, eds. Oxford: Oxford University Press. (From notes of Smith's lectures in 1762–1964.)

Ullmann-Margalit, Edna 1977 *The Emergence of Norms*. Oxford: Oxford University Press.

RUSSELL HARDIN

REFERENCE GROUP THEORY

See Role Theory; Role Theory: Foundations, Extensions and Applications; Self-concept.

REFUGEES

See Genocide; International Migration.

RELIABILITY

The reliability of a measured variable has two components, consistency and stability. *Consistency* is the degree to which two measures of the same concept provide the same assessment at the same time; consistency is based on "cross-sectional" research. *Stability* is the degree to which a measure of a concept remains unchanged across time; stability is based on "longitudinal" research. Let us illustrate consistency and stability on the measurement of height.

THE MEASUREMENT OF HEIGHT

As an example, we often measure how tall people are. Height, how tall someone is, is a measure of distance. In order to measure distance, we establish an arbitrary standard. A common arbitrary standard for measuring distance is the "yardstick."

The yardstick is 36 inches long, and is broken down into feet, inches, and fractions of inches. Another common measuring rod is the "meterstick." The meterstick is 100 centimeters long, and is broken down into decimeters, centimeters, and millimeters. If we know how tall someone is in inches, we can calculate how tall he or she is in centimeters, and vice versa. For example, rounding to two decimal places, a 70-inch-tall person is 177.80 centimeters tall (1 inch = 2.54 centimeters; $70 \times 2.54 = 177.80$). Conversely, rounding to two decimal places, if we know that someone is 160 centimeters tall, we also know that that person is 62.40 inches tall (1 centimeter = 0.39 inches; $160 \times 0.39 = 62.40$).

Indeed, the yardstick and the meterstick are highly consistent. With reasonable attention to proper measurement protocol, the correlation between height as measured by the yardstick and height as measured by the meterstick across a sample with sufficient variation in height would be very high. For all intents and purposes, the yardstick and the meterstick are interchangeable; the researcher need not establish their consistency. This leads to the *principle of consistency:*

> *If two measures of the same concept are perfectly consistent, they provide identical results. When this is so, the use of multiple measures is needlessly repetitive.*

In this situation, the researcher need only use either the yardstick or the meterstick; using both sticks provides no additional information.

When babies are born, they are usually 18–24 inches "tall." Parents (and developmental researchers) often measure how tall babies and children are as time passes. This over-time height measurement is a stability assessment. Ordinarily, children grow a rough average of 3 inches per year for 15 years, resulting in most 15-year-olds being between 63 and 69 inches tall. Then female height growth stops while male height growth continues. By the time females are 18 years old, they average about 66 inches tall, while males of the same age average about 72 inches. Their heights then remain roughly stable for the remainder of their adult lives. This leads to the *principle of stability:*

A measure of a concept is perfectly stable when it provides identical results at different points in time. When this is so, repeated measurement over time is needlessly repetitive.

Height measurement from year to year provides useful information for children but not for adults. This is because the children grow taller with the passage of time, but adults do not. Elderly people who suffer from osteoporosis (loss of bone density) will become shorter, but this decline in height is slight, compared to their growth when they were children.

Let us now turn to a discussion of how the principles of consistency and stability apply to the measurement of sociological concepts. We will first discuss the protocols of good sociological measurement. Then we will discuss the implications of these protocols for the assessment of the consistency of self-esteem and the stability of alienation.

PROTOCOLS OF GOOD MEASUREMENT

The Measurement of Self-Esteem. Researchers often attempt to measure how well people feel about themselves. Many decades ago, Charles Horton Cooley (1902) and George Herbert Mead (1934) theorized about the concept "self-esteem." In offering the "looking glass self," Cooley assumed that people develop a definition of themselves by evaluating what they believe others think of them. Mead differentiated between what a person actually is and what that person believes about himself or herself.

Rosenberg (1965) wished to measure self-esteem as conceptualized by Cooley and Mead. He did so by creating ten questionnaire items, each of which he believed would provide an empirical measure of the concept of self-esteem. His measurement attempt will be discussed in detail later in this paper. For now, let us assume that each of these items positively but imperfectly represents self-esteem. The positive representation implies that the concept "self-esteem" has a positive causal effect on each item. The imperfectness of the representation implies that there are other factors

that also cause each item. Under this condition, none of these ten different measures of self-esteem was nearly as consistent as the yardstick and the meterstick. That is, the correlations among these ten questionnaire items were far from perfect. When this is so, the use of multiple measures is more consistent than the use of any single measure alone. Thus, the *converse principle of consistency:*

> *If multiple measures of the same concept provide imperfect assessments of the same concept, then the use of multiple measures is more consistent than the use of any single measure alone.*

Commonly, items presumed to measure sociological concepts do so imperfectly. Therefore, sociological researchers often turn to the use of multiple items in social surveys as indexes to represent concepts. Combining their substantive knowledge of the literature with their clinical knowledge of people who exhibit various aspects of the concept, these researchers design items to represent each of these aspects. Then researchers are faced with the tasks of evaluating the consistency and stability of the items as measures of their respective concepts. In order to do this, good researchers employ a set of protocols of good measurement. We now turn to a discussion of these good measurement protocols.

Good measurement of sociological concepts satisfies the following criteria:

- Clear definitions of concepts.
- Multiple items.
- Clear definitions of items.
- Strong positive interitem correlation.
- Score construction.
- Known groups validity.
- Construct validity.
- Consistency.
- Stability.

These protocols represent the state of the art not only in sociology (Mueller 1997), but also in a wide variety of other scientific disciplines. A computer search of the literature revealed more than five hundred articles citing these protocols in the 1990s, including: political science (Jackman and Miller 1996); psychology (Hendrix and Schumm 1990); nursing research (Budd et al. 1997); the family (Grandin and Lupri 1997); sports and leisure (Riemer and Chelladurai 1998); computer information systems (McTavish 1997); management (Szulanski 1996); gerontology (Wright 1991); genetics (Tambs et al. 1995); social work (Moran et al. 1995); higher education (Aguirre et al. 1993); market research (Lam and Woo 1997); and preventive medicine (Saunders et al. 1997).

Let us briefly discuss each of these protocols in turn. Then we will focus the attention of the remainder of this paper on the two major focuses of reliability, consistency and stability.

Clear Definitions of Concepts. Good measurement protocol requires that each concept be clearly defined and clearly differentiated from every other concept. Good measurement protocol can document that an ambiguous concept is, indeed, ambiguous. Moreover, such protocol may suggest points of theoretical clarification. However, there is no substitute for clear theoretical thinking augmented by a thorough knowledge of the literature and a clinical immersion in the domain of content.

Multiple Items. Good measurement protocol requires that each aspect of a concept be assessed using multiple items. A single item, taken alone, suffers from measurement error. That is, the item is, in part, a representation of its respective concept. However, this same item may be a representation of other concepts, of systematic measurement error, and of random content. These other contents are called "error"; they reduce the degree to which the item accurately represents the concept it is designed to measure empirically. The rationale for the use of multiple items revolves around minimizing this measurement inaccuracy. That is, all items designed to measure a concept contain inaccuracies. If a single item is used to measure the concept, the researcher is, in essence, stuck with the specific inaccuracies of the single item. However, if multiple items designed to measure the same concept are used, the inaccuracies of one item may be offset by different inaccuracies of the other items.

Clear Definitions of Items. Good measurement protocol requires that each item be designed to measure one and only one concept. The response categories should be constructed so that the higher the code of the response category, the more positive the respondent's attitude on that concept.

Strong Positive Interitem Correlation. When multiple items are designed to measure a single variable, the standard of the research industry has long been that the items should be coded in such a way that the higher the score, the more positive the empirical representation on the concept. Good measurement protocol requires strong positive intercorrelations among items designed to measure a concept. Ordinarily, these intercorrelations are presented in a correlation matrix. A visual inspection of the correlation matrix will be revealing. An item that correlates strongly (e.g., $r > .4$) with other items will generally emerge as a strong contributor to the reliability of the resulting score; an item that has a zero correlation with other items will not add to the reliability of the score; and an item that inversely correlates with other items (assuming that it has been coded such that the higher the score on the item, the higher the measure of the concept) will detract from the reliability of the score.

To the author's knowledge, the sole exception to this principle was articulated by Curtis and Jackson (1962, p. 199) who argued that "two equally valid indicators of the same concept may. . . be strongly related to one another, or they may be totally unrelated (or negatively related)." The difficulty with the Curtis and Jackson position is that it effectively invalidates the most powerful empirical argument that can be made for multiple items representing a single dimension—that of the equivalence established using convergence. Instead, the author would argue that if two items are unrelated or negatively related to one another, either they represent different dimensions, or they are reflecting a method artifact or both. For a more detailed discussion of this matter, see Zeller and Carmines (1980, p. 77–136) or Carmines and Zeller (1979).

Factor analysis is the major statistical technique designed to describe a matrix of item intercorrelatedness. As such, factor analysis enables researchers to (1) describe a large number of items in terms of a small number of factors and (2) select those items which best represent each of the identified concepts (see Bohrnstedt 1970, p. 96; and Zeller and Carmines 1980, p. 19–46). Items that have high factor loadings on a factor that represents a concept are then retained. These items are then used to construct a score to represent the concept.

In evaluating the degree to which a large set of items represents a small number of theoretical concepts, the application of factor analytic techniques is as much an art as it is a science. This is because there are numerous ambiguities in the measurement setting. The researcher defines one or more concepts and explores the degree to which the factors coincide with the hypothesized concepts. For each item, the researcher wants to know the degree to which it is a function of the concept it was designed to measure, other concepts, method artifacts, and random error.

Score Construction. Once the number of factors and which items define which factors has been established, the researcher needs to create scores. One score should be created to represent each concept empirically for each respondent. If the items defining a concept have roughly equal variances, the simplest way to create a score is to sum the items defining the concept. In practice, researchers can tolerate moderate variation in the item variances. For example, if the item variances for a set of Likert items range from, say, .8 to 1.4, summing the items seems to make the most sense. However, if the variation in the items is severe (say from .5 to 2.5), then the researcher should first create standardized scores using the following formula: $z = (score - mean)/standard\ deviation$. The standardized scores have equal variances (i.e., 1); the sum of these standardized scores will create each desired score.

Known Groups Validity. Once scores have been constructed, comparisons of scores between groups known to be high and low on the dimensions of the concept should be made. Known groups validity is established if groups known to be high on the concept have substantially higher scores than groups known to be low on the concept.

Construct Validity. Construct validity is intimately related to theory testing. Construct validity involves (1) specifying theoretical relationships among concepts, (2) assessing empirical relationships among scores, and (3) interpreting how the evidence clarifies the validity of any particular measure. For more information on this concept, see Carmines and Zeller (1979, pp. 22–26).

Consistency. Good measurement protocol requires that the consistency among items designed to measure a concept should be strong. This means that the correlation between any two items designed to measure the same concept should positively and strongly correlate. We will apply the principle of consistency to Rosenberg's attempt to consistently measure the concept of self-esteem.

Stability. Good measurement protocol requires that, if a concept does not change over time, a score designed to measure that concept also does not change over time. The trick of consistency is that the researcher ordinarily does not know whether there is a change in the value of the concept over time. We will apply the principle of stability to the attempt by R. A. Zeller, A. G. Neal, and H. T. Groat (1980) to stably measure the concept of alienation.

When these protocols of good measurement are not followed, the researcher increases the risk of torpedoing the best of conceptual schemes and sentencing them to the intellectual trash heap, whether they belong there or not. High-tech statistical tools, such as structural equation modeling (SEM), make requirements that, by definition, are not present in the measurement development situation (Bollen 1989; Bollen and Long 1993; Hayduk 1987; and Hoyle 1995). That is, SEM requires both strong theory and strong measurement a priori. Indeed, SEM demands that the researcher know beforehand:

- How many factors there are.

- Which items represent which factors.

But these are precisely the major questions that the researcher wants to answer! The end result of the factor analysis should be that the researcher has inferred how many factors are represented by the items, and which items define which factors.

We now turn to a discussion of the consistency of self-esteem.

CONSISTENCY OF SELF-ESTEEM

Good measurement protocol requires that the consistency be strong among items designed to measure each dimension of a concept. This means that the correlation between any two items designed to measure the same concept should positively and strongly correlate. Often different measures of the same concept have relatively modest positive intercorrelations.

In constructing the self-esteem scale, Rosenberg created ten items using the response categories "Never true," "Seldom true," "Sometimes true," "Often true," and "Almost always true." Five of these were positive items; these items made a positive statement about self-esteem. The other five were negative items; these items made a negative statement about self-esteem. The response categories for the positive items were assigned the values 1 through 5, respectively, such that the higher the score, the higher that respondent's self-esteem was inferred to be. These positively stated items were:

- "I feel that I have a number of good qualities."

- "I feel that I'm a person of worth, at least on an equal place with others."

- "I take a positive attitude toward myself."

- "I am able to do things as well as most other people."

- "On the whole, I am satisfied with myself."

For the five negatively phrased items, a higher score indicated a lower self-esteem. These items had the same response categories as above, but the assignment of values was reversed. That is, the negatively stated items were assigned the values 5

through 1 respectively. That is, a "Never true" response to the item "I wish I could have more respect for myself" was assigned a 5 and an "Almost always true" response to that item was assigned a 1. These five negatively stated items were:

- "I wish I could have more respect for myself."

- "I feel I do not have much to be proud of."

- "I certainly feel useless at times."

- "All in all, I'm inclined to feel that I am a failure."

- "At times I think I am no good at all."

Given the reverse scoring for these items, a higher score indicated higher self-esteem. In order to create a self-esteem scale, the scores were summed into a value that ranged from 10 representing the lowest measured self-esteem possible to 50 for the highest possible measured self-esteem.

How consistent are these items? We suggest the following as a *consistency rule of thumb* for a variable to be used in sociological research:

- If r is above .8, the score is highly consistent.

- If r is between .6 and .8, the score is modestly consistent.

- If r is less than .6, the score may not be used in research.

In the author's research (Zeller and Carmines 1976), interitem correlations among the ten Rosenberg items designed to measure self-esteem ranged from a low of .05 to a high of .58 with a mean r of .32. These intercorrelations do not meet this rule of thumb. When properly analyzed, however, they will. We now turn to a discussion of the strategy for this analysis that will address this criterion of consistency.

Split-Half Consistency. The "split-half" approach to estimating the consistency of items designed to measure a concept is to divide the items into two subscores and calculate the correlation between those subscores. For example, the ten items can be divided into two subscores of five items each. The resulting split-half correlation between the two subscores provides an estimate of consistency. If the average interitem correlation equals .3, a score created by summing the responses to the ten items into two five-item subscores would have a split-half correlation of .68.

However, it is well known that, given items whose intercorrelations are equal (i.e., $r = .3$), the greater the number of items, the higher the consistency of a score resulting from those items. Thus, a ten-item score will have more consistency than a five-item score when both scores are made up of items that intercorrelate .3. The split-half reliability correlation, however, does not represent the ten-item score, it is two subscores made up of five items each. Therefore, this split-half correlation will be lower than the actual consistency of the ten-item score.

Two researchers, Spearman (1910) and Brown (1910), independently recognized and solved this statistical estimation problem. Specifically, they noted that the split-half reliability correlation can be adjusted to project what the consistency of a ten-item score would have been if it had been calculated on the basis of two ten-item subscores instead of two five-item subscores. They shared attribution for this solution and called the result the *Spearman-Brown Prophecy*. It is presented in formula (1):

$$r_{xx''} = 2r_{xx'} / (1 + r_{xx'})$$

where

$r_{xx''}$ is the Spearman-Brown Prophecy formula. (1)

$r_{xx'}$ is the split-half correlation coefficient.

Using the example from above, we can see that the Spearman-Brown Prophecy formula projects the consistency of the entire ten-item scale using formula (1) as follows:

$$r_{xx''} = 2r_{xx'} / (1 + r_{xx'}) = (2)(.68) /$$
$$(1 + .68) = 1.36 / 1.68 = .81$$

This .81 is an unbiased estimate of the consistency of the total score. Applying the above rule of thumb, such a scale is quite consistent and can be used in sociological research.

In actual research, intercorrelations among score items vary substantially. In the self-esteem example, item intercorrelations varied from .05 to .58. Moreover, the researcher must decide which items to assign to which subscales. One assignment of items to subscales will produce a different reliability estimate than another. When this occurs, the split-half reliability correlation between the two subscales is beset with the *problem of equivalence*: Which items are assigned to which subscales? We now turn to a way of handling variations in intercorrelations among items.

Equivalence Consistency The researcher could assign the even-numbered items to one subscore and the odd-numbered items to the other; or items 1, 2, 3, 4, and 5 to one subscore and 6, 7, 8, 9, and 10 to the other; or items 1, 4, 5, 8, and 10 to one score and 2, 3, 6, 7, and 9 to the other. There are many combinations of assignments that could be made. Which one should the researcher use?

Lee Cronbach (1951) solved this dilemma by creating *Cronbach's Alpha*. Cronbach's Alpha uses the average of all possible split-half reliability correlations that are Spearman-Brown projected to the number of items in the score. This is presented in formula (2):

$$\alpha_{xx} = N(\text{Mean } r_{xx}) / [1 + \text{Mean } r_{xx}(N - 1)]$$
where

α_{xx} is Cronbach's Alpha. (2)

N is the number of items.

Mean r_{xx} is the mean interitem correlation.

Applying formula (2) to the ten-item score designed to measure self-esteem where the mean interitem correlation is .3, we get:

$$\alpha_{xx} = N(\text{Mean } r_{xx}) / [1 + \text{Mean } r_{xx}(N - 1)]$$
$$= (10)(.3) / [1 + (.3)(9)] = 3 / 3.7 = .81$$

Thus, Cronbach's Alpha produces the same value that we obtained when we calculated a split-half correlation and applied formula (1), the Spearman-Brown Prophecy formula. This occurred because all the items were, we assumed, equally correlated with each other.

Both the number of items and the average interitem correlations influence the value of Cronbach's Alpha as follows:

- As the number of equally intercorrelated items increases, Cronbach's Alpha increases.

- As the average intecorrelation among the same number of items increases, Cronbach's Alpha increases.

We now turn to the implications of these two patterns:

Number of Items The researcher often faces the question "How many items should I use to measure a concept?" The oversimplified answer to this question is, "More!" The more equally intercorrelated items a researcher uses to measure a concept, the higher the reliability will be.

The trick, of course, is that the items must be equally intercorrelated. In most research situations, items designed to measure a concept are not equally correlated. Some items will intercorrelate more strongly with the set of items than others. When this occurs, the researcher's judgment must be employed to decide how much of a reduction in interitem correlation offsets the increase in the number of items in the score. At a minimum, the researcher does not want to add an item which decreases the Cronbach's Alpha consistency of a scale. Standard computer software provides an option which allows the researcher to examine the Cronbach's Alpha if any item is removed from the score. When the alpha with the item removed is higher than the alpha when that item is included, there is consistency justification for the removal of that item from the scale.

This question can be posed in terms of how many items the researcher needs to meet specific alpha reliability thresholds given the mean interitem correlations. Table 1 addresses this concern. In Table 1, three alpha reliability thresholds (.7, .8, and .9) and eight mean interitem correlations (1. through .8) are specified. We then solved formula

Sample Size Needed for Various Alphas with Various Mean Correlations

	CRONBACH'S ALPHA		
Mean *r*	.7	.8	.9
.1	21	36	81
.2	10	16	36
.3	6	10	21
.4	4	6	14
.5	3	4	9
.6	2	3	6
.7	1	2	4
.8	1	1	3

Table 1

(2) algebraically for the sample size needed to achieve each threshold, given each mean interitem correlation using formula (3):

$$N = [\alpha_{xx}(1 - \text{Mean } r_{xx})] / [(\text{Mean } r_{xx})(1 - \alpha_{xx})] \quad (3)$$

Using formula (3), the body of Table 1 presents the number of items needed for each Cronbach's Alpha threshold for each mean interitem correlation. For example, if the mean item intercorrelation is .2, sixteen items will be needed in order to achieve a Cronbach's Alpha of .8.

An examination of Table 1 reveals that when the mean interitem correlation is equal to .5, only three items are needed for an alpha of .7, four items for an Alpha of .8, and nine items for an alpha of .9. If the mean interitem correlation is .3, six, ten, and twenty-one items are needed for alphas of .7, .8, and .9, respectively. Moreover, if the mean interitem correlation is .1, twenty-one, thirty-six, and eighty-one items are needed for Alphas of .7, .8, and .9, respectively.

Thus, weak interitem correlations can be used to achieve consistency thresholds when many items are used. This is what ordinarily occurs in academic achievement tests. An exam of eighty-one items with a mean interitem correlation of .1 reaches the highly consistent .9 alpha; and an exam of only thirty-six items with a mean interitem correlation of .1 is a reasonably consistent .8 alpha. At the same time, strong interitem correlations reach these thresholds with a small number of items. This harkens back to the observation that if two measures correlate strongly, the researcher merely picks the most convenient measure and uses it with little concern for consistency reliability.

However, the law of diminishing returns suggests that at some point, additional items with the same average intercorrelation with other items will not provide sufficient value in exchange for the effort to be expended to include those additional items. When the number of items is small, an additional equally correlated item adds substantial enough value to the reliability of the score to warrant the effort needed to include it.

Table 2 presents Cronbach's Alphas for various numbers of items with various mean interitem correlations. An examination of Table 2 illustrates the law of diminishing returns. When the mean interitem correlation is .9, the alpha is .98 with five items; adding additional items does not, indeed cannot, increase the consistency much. This is so because the maximum consistency is a perfect 1.0. When the mean interitem correlation is .3, the alpha of .68 with five items is only marginally consistent. However, the alpha increases to an acceptable .81 when ten items are used and to a highly consistent .9 when twenty items are used. Finally, the alpha for five items with a mean interitem correlation of .1 is .37. In order for a score made up of such items to be adequately consistent, the number of such items must be increased substantially.

Cronbach's Alpha can be calculated using formula (2) above. Standard statistical computer software packages can also be used for this purpose. However, care must be taken in using these packages to assure that all the items and only the items that define a specific score be included in the calculations. Indeed, the attentive researcher will want to produce the Cronbach's Alpha by hand, using formula (2), and by computer. When these two measures are identical, the researcher can take comfort that both are likely to have been done

Cronbach's Alpha for Various Numbers of Items with Various Mean Correlations

Mean r	NUMBER OF ITEMS				
	5	10	20	30	50
.1	.37	.53	.69	.77	.850
.2	.56	.71	.83	.88	.930
.3	.68	.81	.90	.93	.960
.4	.77	.87	.93	.95	.970
.5	.83	.91	.95	.97	.980
.6	.88	.94	.97	.98	.990
.7	.92	.96	.98	.99	.990
.8	.95	.98	.987	.992	.995
.9	.98	.99	.994	.996	.998

Table 2

properly. As a postscript on this discussion, we note that the Cronbach's Alpha consistency of Rosenberg's ten-item self-esteem score calculated on the data presented in Zeller and Carmines (1980, p. 92) was equal to a reasonably consistent .83. More advanced procedures which take into account which items are more highly correlated with the total score, such as theta and omega, have been omitted from this discussion. For a discussion of theta and omega, see Carmines and Zeller (1979, pp. 60–62) or Zeller and Carmines (1980, pp. 60–63). Rosenberg's self-esteem scale continues to attract academic attention (e.g., GrayLittle et al. 1997).

STABILITY OF ALIENATION

The Measurement of Alienation. The concept of alienation is one of the major "unit ideas" of sociology (Nisbet 1966). But the concept is so imbued with different meanings that some have come to question its usefulness as a sociological concept (Lee 1972). Seeman (1959) believed that the conceptual confusion surrounding the study of alienation can be addressed by construing it as multidimensional. Neil and Rettig (1967) have operationalized Seeman's original conceptualizations. Following the protocols of good measurement described above, Neal and Groat (1974) theoretically defined and empirically confirmed powerlessness, normlessness, meaninglessness, and social isolation as the four dimensions of alienation. Specifically, they constructed items designed to measure each of the four dimensions of alienation, gathered data, conducted factor analyses, noted that the observed factor structure coincided with the conceptual dimensions, created factor-based scores, and conducted substantive analyses.

R. A. Zeller, A. G. Neal, and H. T. Groat (1980) conducted a consistency and stability analysis. Data on the same sample in 1963 and 1971 revealed that reliabilities ranged from .64 to .83 in 1963 and from .65 to .88 in 1971. The authors needed accurate consistency estimates because they wished to minimize the correction for attenuation. Correction for attenuation will be discussed shortly. Zeller and colleagues wished to describe the amount of stability in the dimensions of alienation over the turbulent years between 1963 and 1971. Specifically, they wished to assess the degree to which those who had high levels of alienation in 1963 would also have high levels of alienation in 1971. In order to do so, they created scores for each of the four dimensions of alienation in both 1963 and 1971. For each score, the correlation between the 1963 and the 1971 value represented the "stability" of that dimension over that time period. High correlations would suggest substantial stability in which respondents were alienated over that time period; low correlations would suggest substantial change.

Correction for Attenuation Due to Measurement Inconsistency. In order to assess the stability of the dimensions of alienation over time, Zeller et al. (1980) calculated correlation coefficients between the scale scores for each dimension of alienation. They found stability coefficients ranging from .40 for normlessness to .53 for social isolation. It would appear that there was substantial stability over the eight years under investigation. Before we jump to any conclusions, however, we must consider that measurement inconsistency attenuates (i.e., reduces) the observed correlation from what it would have been if each concept had been perfectly measured at each time point. That

is, they needed to correct their stability correlations for measurement inconsistency. Formula (4) presents the correction for attenuation:

$$r_{xtyt} = r_{xy} / SQRT(r_{xx}r_{yy})$$

where

r_{xtyt} is the correlation over time corrected for attenuation.

r_{xy} is the observed correlation between X and Y. (4)

r_{xx} is the Cronbach's alpha for X.

r_{yy} is the Cronbach's alpha for Y.

$SQRT(r_{xx}r_{yy})$ is the square root of the product of the alphas at the two points in time.

Let us apply the correction for attenuation to Zeller and his colleagues' meaninglessness score. The meaninglessness stability correlation = .52; meaninglessness had an omega consistency of .64 in 1963 and of .65 in 1971. Substituting these estimates into formula (4), we get:

$$r_{xtyt} = r_{xy} / SQRT(r_{xx}r_{yy}) = .52 / SQRT(.64 * .65)$$
$$= .52 / .64 = .81$$

Similar analyses were conducted on the other dimensions of alienation.

This analysis led Zeller and colleagues (1980, pp. 1202–1203) to conclude that their data "indicate substantial stability in the dimensions of alienation over an eight-year period." They believe that their longitudinal data "have provided evidence to suggest that operationalizing dimensions of alienation is not only feasible, but may be accomplished with a high degree of confidence in the (consistency) reliability of the measuring instruments. The obtained stability of alienation scores over a long period of time lends credence to the search for the causal, antecedent conditions."

Method Artifacts in Longitudinal Research. There are several method artifacts that can artificially attenuate or inflate the estimation of stability. As noted above, score inconsistency attenuates the stability estimate. Memory tends to inflate the stability estimate. That is, if, at time 2, respondents remember what they answered at time 1 and wish to present themselves as being stable in their answers, they will make the same response to the item at time 2 that they made at time 1. We do not believe that this "memory effect" operated to any great degree in the analysis by Zeller and colleagues, because we doubt that respondents would remember their specific response to a specific questionnaire item for eight years. However, when the interval between time 1 and time 2 is relatively short, memory becomes a problem.

A conventional wisdom in stability research is that the interval of time that elapses between time 1 and time 2 should be long enough that respondents will not remember their specific answers to specific items, but short enough that very little change (i.e., instability) takes place in the interim. We believe, on the contrary, that part of what we wish to estimate in stability research is how much change actually takes place. Given our perspective, it does not matter how much time elapses between time 1 and time 2.

Still, the threat of artifactual deflations and inflations to the stability estimate is real. Consider the effect of item-specific variance. The respondent may answer an item in a "stable" fashion over time not because of the stability of the concept it measures, but because of some idiosyncratic nuance of the item. Idiosyncratic nuances of items unrelated to the concept the item is designed to measure are systematic, not random, error. As such, idiosyncratic nuances of items threaten to inflate the stability estimate. We now turn to a statistically advanced discussion of the identification and removal of item specific variance from stability estimation. This section requires a working knowledge of path analysis as described in Asher [(1976), 1983].

COMBINING CONSISTENCY AND STABILITY INTO A MEASUREMENT MODEL

The path model presented in Figure 1 combines consistency and stability into a measurement path model. In this measurement model, X_1 and X_2 represent the value of the concept at time 1 and time 2; P_{21} is the theoretical causal path from X_1 on X_2, it represents stability, the theoretical effect of X_1 on X_2. This and the other effects in this model

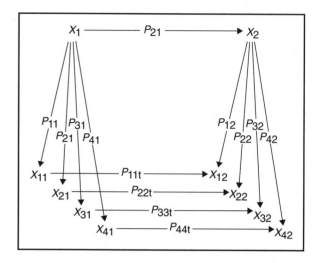

Figure 1. Consistency and Stability in a Measurement Model

can be thought of as path coefficients. The x_{ij} represent the observations; specifically, x_{21} is item 2 at time 1; x_{32} is item 3 at time 2. The p_{ij} are the epistemic correlations, the effect of the concept on each respective measure; specifically, p_{21} is effect of X_1 on item 2 at time 1; p_{32} is the effect of X_2 on item 3 at time 2. The p_{ijt} are the item specific effects over time, the effects of an item at time 1 on that same item at time 2; specifically, p_{11} is effect of x_{11} on x_{12} over and above the effect mediated through the concept. For a more complete discussion of epistemic correlations, see Blalock (1969).

Figure 2 presents this consistency and stability measurement model where the stability effect is $P_{21} = .8$, the epistemic correlation are $p_{ij} = .7$, and the item-specific effects are $p_{ijt} = .3$. These are approximately the effect parameters for the meaninglessness measurement over time in Zeller and colleagues (1980).

Table 3 presents the correlation matrix that results from applying the rules of path analysis [Asher (1976) 1983] to Figure 2. Specifically, within the measurement model, the correlation between x_{11} is x_{21} is equal to the product of the path from X_1 to x_{11} times the path from X_1 to x_{21}. That is, $r = (p_{11})(p_{21}) = (.7)(.7) = .49$. In the same way, all the time 1 measures intercorrelate .49; all the time 2 measures correlate .49.

The correlation between the time 1 and time 2 items must differentiate between the correlations

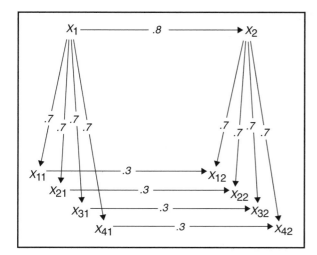

Figure 2. Hypothetical Consistency and Stability Data in a Measurement Model

between different items over time and the correlations between the same item over time. Let us first address correlations between different items over time.

The correlation between x_{11} (item 1 at time 1) and x_{22} (item 2 at time 2) is equal to the product of the path from X_1 to x_{11} times the path from X_1 to X_2 times the path from X_2 to x_{22}. That is, $r = (p_{11})(P_{21})(p_{22})$ = $(.7)(.8)(.7) = .39$. In the same way, all the time 1–time 2 correlations *among different items* are .39.

The correlation between x_{11} (item 1 at time 1) and x_{12} (item 1 at time 2) is equal to the product of the path from X_1 to x_{11} times the path from X_1 to X_2 times the path from X_2 to x_{12} plus p_{11t}. That is, $r = (p_{11})(P_{21})(p_{12}) + p_{11t} = (.7)(.8)(.7) + .3 = .69$. In the same way, all the time 1–time 2 correlations *for the same item* are .69.

Using formula 2, we can solve for the Cronbach's alpha, at both time 1 and time 2, as follows:

$$\alpha_{xx} = N(\text{Mean } r_{xx})/[1 + \text{Mean } r_{xx}(N-1)]$$
$$= (4)(.49)/[1 + (.49)(3)] = 1.96/2.47$$
$$= .79$$

Using the criteria described above, the score is modestly, and almost highly, consistent.

The correlation between two scores can be calculated using the correlation matrix with the following formula:

$$r = e/SQRT(a + 2b)SQRT(c = 2d)$$

where

r is the stability correlation between a score at time 1 and time 2.

a is the number of items in the time 1 score.

b is the sum of the correlations at time 1.

c is the number of items in the time 2 score.

d is the sum of the correlations at time 2.

e is the sum of the intercorrelations between the measures at times 1 and 2.

(5)

Applying formula 5 to the data in Table 3, we get:

$a = 4$

$b = (6)(.49) = 2.94$

$c = 4$

$d = (6)(.49) = 2.94$

$e = (12)(.392) + (4)(.692) = 7.472$

and

$$r = e / SQRT(a + 2b)SQRT(c = 2d) = 7.472 /$$
$$SQRT[4 + (2)(2.94)]^2$$
$$= 7.472/9.98 = .756$$

Correcting this correlation for attenuation using formula 4, we get:

$$r_{xtyt} = r_{xy} / SQRT(r_{xx}r_{yy}) = .76 /$$
$$SQRT(.79)^2 = .96$$

Thus, the stability coefficient is .96. But we specified this stability coefficient to be .8 in Figure 2! What is wrong with our procedures? Why did we overstate the stability of the model? We overstated the model's stability because we included the item specific effects as stability effects. That is, the observed correlations between the same item at time 1 and time 2 represented the effects of both stability and item-specific variance. We need to remove the item specific variance from our estimation of the stability coefficient.

We can estimate the item-specific effects by subtracting the mean of the correlations of different items at time 1 compared to time 2 (mean r = .39) from the mean of the correlations of the same item at time 1 compared to time 2 (mean r = .69). Then we use only the variance that is not item-specific in the same item correlations across time

Correlation Matrix among Four Measures at Two Points in Time

Item	x_{11}	x_{21}	x_{31}	x_{41}	x_{12}	x_{22}	x_{32}	x_{42}
x_{11}	—	.49	.49	.49	<u>.692</u>	.392	.392	.392
x_{21}		—	.49	.49	.392	<u>.692</u>	.392	.392
x_{31}			—	.49	.392	.392	<u>.692</u>	.392
x_{41}				—	.392	.392	.392	<u>.692</u>
x_{12}					—	.490	.490	.490
x_{22}						—	.490	.490
x_{32}							—	.490
x_{42}								—

Table 3

$(r = .69 - .30 = .39)$ as our estimate of what these correlations would have been if there had been no item-specific variance.

We now reapply formula 5 to the adjusted data in Table 3 to get:

$a = 4$

$b = (6)(.49) = 2.94$

$c = 4$

$d = (6)(.49) = 2.94$

$e = (12)(.39) + (4)(.39) = 6.24$

and

$$r = e / SQRT(a + 2b)SQRT(c = 2d) = 6.24 / SQRT[4 + (2)(2.94)]^2$$
$$= 6.24 / 9.98 = .63$$

Correcting this correlation for attenuation using formula 4, we get:

$$r_{xtyt} = r_{xy} / SQRT(r_{xx} r_{yy}) = .63 / SQRT(.79)^2 = .80$$

Thus, the stability coefficient corrected for the removal of item specific variance is .80; despite rounding, this is equal to the .8 which was the stability coefficient specified in Figure 2.

Estimating the stability of concepts measured by scores across time is complex. A simple correlation between a measure at time 1 and the same measure at time 2 is subject to a variety of influences. First, this stability coefficient is attenuated due to inconsistency of the item. We can address this by using multiple measures. The multiple measures allows us to estimate the consistency of the score and to correct the stability coefficient for the attenuation that occurs because the score is not perfectly consistent.

Second, the stability coefficient is artificially inflated because of item-specific variance. We can address this by estimating the size of the item-specific variance and removing it from the correlation matrix. Then we can correlate the score at time 1 and time 2 on the correlation matrix (with the item specific variance having been removed). This correlation, corrected for attenuation, is an unbiased estimate of the actual stability. For the past twenty years, the author has been searching in vain for someone who will solve for the model presented in Figure 2 from the correlation matrix presented in Table 3 using SEM techniques. Many have claimed to be able to do so, but so far, to my knowledge, no one has succeeded in doing so.

CONCLUSION

Thirty years ago, Hauser (1969, pp. 127–128) noted that "it is inadequate measurement, more than inadequate concept or hypothesis, that has plagued social researchers and prevented fuller explanations of the variances with which they are confounded." We have come a long way since then.

The scientific community has given greater attention to the measurement properties of the variables we use. Our capacity to conduct numerous alternative data analyses on large and well-documented data sets has been substantially enhanced. At the same time, nature is jealous of her secrets and there are many land mines buried along the paths we need to follow (or blaze) in order to make sense of our social scene. Moreover, there are many who seek shortcuts to sociological knowledge. Hence, we continue to address the challenges of establishing the consistency and stability of our measures.

REFERENCES

Aguirre, A., R. Martinez, and A. Hernandez 1993 "Majority and Minority Faculty Perceptions in Academe." *Research in Higher Education* 34(3):371–385.

Asher, H. B. (1976) 1983 *Causal Modeling*. Beverly Hills, Calif.: Sage.

Blalock, H. M. 1969 "Multiple Indicators and the Causal Approach to Measurement Error." *American Journal of Sociology* 75:264–272.

Bohrnstedt, G. W. 1970 "Reliability and Validity Assessment in Attitude Measurement." In G. F. Summers, ed., *Attitude Measurement*. Chicago: Rand McNally.

Bollen, K. 1989 *Structural Equations with Latent Variables*. New York: John Wiley.

——, and S. Long 1993 *Testing Structural Models*. Newbary Park, Calif.: Sage.

Brown, W. 1910 "Some Experimental Results in the Correlation of Mental Abilities." *British Journal of Psychology* 3:269–322.

Budd, K. W., D. RossAlaolmolki, and R. A. Zeller 1997 "Psychometric Analysis of the Self-Coherence Survey." *Archives Psychiatric Nursing* 11(5):276–281.

Carmines, E. G., and R. A. Zeller 1979 *Reliability and Validity Assessment*. Beverly Hills, Calif.: Sage.

Cooley, C. H. 1902 *Human Nature and the Social Order*. New York: Scribner's.

Cronbach, L. J. 1951 "Coefficient Alpha and the Internal Structure of Tests." *Psychometrika* 16:297–334.

Curtis, R. F., and E. F. Jackson 1962 "Multiple Indicators in Survey Research." *American Journal of Sociology* 68:195–204.

Fredman, L., M. P. Daly, and A. M. Lazur 1995 "Burden among White and Black Caregivers to Elderly Adults." *Journals of Gerontology Series-B-Psychological Sciences and Social Sciences* 50(2):S110–S118.

Grandin, E., and E. Lupri 1997 "Intimate Violence in Canada and the United States." *Journal of Family Violence* 12(4):417–443.

GrayLittle, B. V. S. Williams, and T. D. Hancock 1997 "An Item Response Theory Analysis of the Rosenberg Self-Esteem Scale." *Personality and Social Psychology Bulletin* May 23(5):443–451.

Hauser, P. 1969 "Comments on Coleman's Paper." Pp. 122–128 in R. Bierstedt, ed., *A Design for Sociology: Scope, Objectives, and Methods*. Philadelphia: American Academy of Political and Social Science.

Hayduk, L. 1987 *Structural Equation Modeling with LISREL*. Baltimore, Md.: Johns Hopkins University Press.

Hendrix, C., and W. Schumm 1990 "Reliability and Validity of Abusive Violence Scale." *Psychological Reports* 66(3):1251–1258.

Hoyle, R. 1995 *Structural Equation Modeling: Concepts, Issues, and Applications*. Newbury Park, Calif.: Sage.

Jackman, R. W., and R. A. Miller 1996 "A Renaissance of Political Culture?" *American Journal of Political Science* 40(3):632–659.

Lam, S. S., and K. S. Woo 1997 "Measuring Service Quality." *Journal of Marketing Research* 39(2):381–396.

Lee, A. M. 1972 "An Obituary for Alienation." *Social Problems* 20(1): 121–127.

McTavish, D. G. 1997 "Scale Validity–A Computer Content Analysis Approach." *Social Science Computer Review* 15(4):379–393.

Mead, G. H. 1934 *Mind, Self, and Society*. Chicago: University of Chicago Press.

Moran, J. R., D. Frans, and P. A. Gibson 1995 "A Comparison of Beginning MSW and MBA Students on Their Aptitudes for Human-Service Management." *Journal of Social Work Education* 31(1):95–105.

Mueller, C. 1997 "International Press Coverage of East German Protest Events, 1989." *American Sociological Review* 62(5):820–832.

Neal, A. G., and H. T. Groat 1974 "Social Class Correlates of Stability and Change in Levels of Alienation: A Longitudinal Study." *Sociological Quarterly* 15(4):548–558.

——, and S. Rettig 1967 "On the Multidimensionality of Alienation." *American Sociological Review* 32(1):54–64.

Nisbet, R. A. 1966 *The Sociological Tradition*. New York: Basic Books.

Riemer, H. A., and P. Chelladurai 1998 "Development of the Athlete Satisfaction Questionnaire." *Journal of Sport and Exercise Psychology* 20(2):127–156.

Rosenberg, M. 1965 *Society and the Adolescent Self Image.* Princeton, N.J.: Princeton University Press.

Seeman, M. 1959 "On the Meaning of Alienation." *American Sociological Review* 24:772–782.

Spearman, C. 1910 "Correlation Calculated from Faulty Data." *British Journal of Psychology* 3:271–295.

Szulanski, G. 1996 "Exploring Internal Stickiness." *Strategic Management Journal* 17:27–43.

Tambs, D., J. R. Harris, and P. Magnus 1995 "Sex-Specific Causal Factors and Effects of Common Environment for Symptoms of Anxiety and Depression in Twins." *Behavorial Genetics* 25(1):33–44.

Wright, L. K. 1991 "The Impact of Alzheimers Disease on the Marital Relationship." *Gerontologist* 31(2):224–237.

Zeller, R. A., and E. G. Carmines 1980 *Measurement in the Social Sciences: The Link between Theory and Data.* New York: Cambridge University Press.

—— 1976 "Factor Scaling, External Consistency, and the Measurement of Theoretical Constructs." *Political Methodology* 3:215–252.

Zeller, R. A., A. G. Neal, and H. T. Groat 1980 "On the Reliability and Stability of Alienation Measures: A Longitudinal Analysis." *Social Forces* 58:1195–1204.

RICHARD A. ZELLER

RELIGION, POLITICS, AND WAR

The Peace of Westphalia (1648) marked the end of the Thirty Years' War and the beginning of the modern European state system. The development and evolution of the principles laid out in the Westphalian treaties made the territorially defined independent sovereign state the dominant political unit for managing and governing populations. Those principles also led to recognition of the state as the primary unit for interaction (including the "interaction" of war) between territorially bounded populations. By the end of the twentieth century, the state system had encompassed the entire globe.

An understanding of the relationship between religion, politics, and war begins with an analysis of regimes (Swanson 1967). A state governs a population by means of a regime. A regime is responsible for maintaining peace and securing justice within the territorial bounds of a state. A regime acts by exercising its own autonomous powers and by implementing and enforcing laws.

Regimes take many forms, including (but not limited to) absolute monarchy (France under Louis XVI), personality-centered dictatorship (Hitler's Germany), government by cabinet embedded in a constitutional monarchy (the United Kingdom), an executive presidential system linked through a division of powers to legislative bodies (United States of America), and rule by a single party (People's Republic of China).

The autonomous powers of a regime are, in principle, unlimited, and they include the legitimate use of force. The powers of a regime and a regime's performance can be (and usually are) constrained and directed by laws and limitations such as traditional rights, even where the regime is a monarchy or dictatorship. In that regard, a major question in the analysis of the state pertains to the relationship between a regime and a society's political system or body politic. Can interests (including religious interests) be legitimately organized and expressed within a political system in ways that effectively influence a regime's actions? Answers to this question can be framed within answers to another fundamental question. What is the direct relation between a regime and the religious institutions of a society, the relation that is not mediated through an aggregation of interests in civil society and their expression in a political system? This question defines the church-state problematic.

CHURCH AND STATE

Although the categories "church" and "state" are products of the history and experience of the West, they can be applied to the analysis of religion, regimes, and politics across the contemporary world (see Martin 1978). Two ideal-type models and their variants specify the range of relations between religion and the state. The *interpenetration model* assumes a high degree of church-state (or religion-regime) congruence and the effective unity of religious and political action. Important variants of this model include theocracy and caesaro-papism. Where theocracy exists, the authority of religion is decisive for the state. In the case of caesaro-papism the tables are turned and the state dominates religion.

The *separation model* posits institutional autonomy for both religion and the state. Variants include the two-powers and the strict separation subtypes. The two-powers subtype recognizes the distinct jurisdictional domains of the state and religion within a framework of church-religion–state-regime accommodation that may include church establishment (the official recognition and support of a church by a state) but also may encompass mutual suspicion, struggle, and cross-institutional interference. Strict separation eliminates all traditional, legal, and organizational bonds and most forms of accommodation between the state and religion. Each institution is not only autonomous but also "out of bounds" with respect to the other.

Contemporary examples of the interpentration and separation models include the Islamic Republic of Iran (theocratic), Russia (caesaro-papist), Poland (two powers), and the United States of America (strict separation). The 1979 revolution in Iran led by Ayatollah Ruhollah Khomeini imposed Twelver Shi'a Islamic law and tradition on the Iranian state. This move invigorated the Iranian masses and was hailed as progressive in many parts of the Muslim world. It also led to tension between the development of Iran as a modern state and the application of Islamic rules, principles, and laws as the authentic seal of the revolution (Arjomand 1993). The lawmaking power of the state dominates the law finding power of the traditional Shi'a jurists in Iran. Nevertheless the country can be classified as a theocracy because the resolution of disputes is constitutionally in the hands of those who have been trained in Islamic religious jurisprudence. As well, lay citizens may serve in lower offices including the Majlis (parliament), but only clerics (religious jurists) can occupy high political, administrative, or judiciary positions in Iran.

The reforms of Peter the Great, czar of Russia from 1682 to 1725, transformed the administration of the Russian Orthodox Church into an office of the state and, thereby, instituted a caesaro-papist regime. All religious activities were governed by regulations promulgated by the czar. The church was the state's instrument for controlling and educating the population. It remained so until the Bolshevik Revolution in 1917 and the foundation of the Soviet state. Under Communist Party rule, with Marxism as the official ideology of the regime, Russian caesaro-papism became a negative, eradicating, secularizing force. Church property was confiscated. The church was sheared of all nonreligious functions. Religious practice was strictly controlled.

After the collapse of the Soviet state (1989–1991), a liberal constitution guaranteed freedom of expression and practice for all religions. No provision was made for an established church. Subsequently, however, the Russian Orthodox Church was recognized by the state as the preeminent church in Russia, thus formally linking the Russian state to the Russian church once again. In the former Soviet Union, the autocracy of the Communist Party replaced the autocracy of the Russian czar. In both cases there was a caesaro-papist relation between a regime and religion, a relation that persists in the recognition of the preeminence of the Russian Orthodox Church by the liberalized, post-Soviet Russian state.

Unlike the Russian Orthodox Church, the Roman Catholic Church in Poland has never acceded to nor successfully been forced into a caesaro-papist relation with the state. The two-powers variant of the separation model has always prevailed, even during the period of Communist rule (1948–1989).

In the early modern period, Poland did not develop a state controlled by an absolute prince. A protodemocratic republic of nobles resisted state autocracy and, thereby, prevented control of the church by a powerful, centralized regime. In the nineteenth century, Polish national identity was fused with Polish Roman Catholicism. Thus, the stage was set for the church to serve as the defender of the interests of the nation when those interests were at risk during the period of Communist rule.

Identified with the Polish nation, the Polish church stood against the Polish state in a two-powers relationship during most of the Cold War. The opposition of the church in Poland to the Communist regime made an important contribution to the downfall of communism in the Eastern bloc of European states. As one of the most powerful actors in the civil society of post-Communist Poland (having long organized itself as a hierarchic weapon in defense of its own interests), the Polish Roman Catholic Church now faces the challenge of dealing with the tendency "in victory" to become a quasitheocratic actor, a role that is inconsistent with the Vatican's position that national churches should be institutions with interests and not would-be hegemons in contemporary liberal democratic societies (Casanova 1994).

Where Poland exemplifies the two-powers variant of the separation model, the United States is the primary example of strict separation. Constitutionally guaranteed free religious practice and a constitutional provision forbidding the establishment or state sponsorship of any religion underwrite the autonomy and differentiation of religion and the state in a historically exceptional pattern. Unlike the case of Russia, for example, where the post-Communist state recognized the Russian Orthodox Church as the preeminent national religious body, no part (legislative, executive, or judicial) of any American government (local, state, or federal) can grant legal privileges to a religious organization. By the same token, American governments can neither limit nor curtail religious practice, as happened in the former Soviet Union, nor can they pass and enforce laws that impose religious norms and rules on a population, as is the case in Iran.

Unlike Poland, where the post-Communist liberal constitution has not prevented the government from granting funds to the Roman Catholic Church in support of church-sponsored education, no church or religious body could successfully petition any government in America for material support. On the other hand, American churches and religious organizations are not taxed by governments unless they are, in effect, business organizations within the meaning and application of the law. Thus, although the state neither interferes with religious institutions nor provides recognition and material support for them, there is a pattern of passive accommodation in America whereby the state allows religious organizations to operate as untaxed nonprofit corporate bodies. Where strict separation holds, the state is not anticlerical, nor is it a direct, overt benefactor of religion.

The examples adduced above do not exhaust the range of historical detail and local variance that will be discovered where the fit of the interpenetration or separation models to a particular state is assessed. The models, themselves, however, do exhaust the range of possibilities for the regime-religion relation and, thus, can be used to classify any state and organize the history of its intercourse with religion.

RELIGION, REGIMES, AND POLITICAL SYSTEMS

The analysis of the church-state relation focuses on links between the governing center of a society (a regime) and religious groups and institutions in a society. The analysis of religion and political systems, on the other hand, addresses questions pertaining to the organization and expression of interests in a society. Variation in the form of political systems and the relations between political systems and regimes affects the organization of interests in a society and the impact that interests including religious interests can have on regimes.

Do most of the members of a society have a role in determining who controls the society's regime? Do most of the members of a society have a role in selecting those who make the society's laws? For most of human history, the answer to both questions has been no. Kings, queens, emperors, military despots, dictators, patriarchs, oligarchs, leaders of single-party states, religious autocrats, petty tyrants, and the like—those who attain office without the broad-based consent of the people whom they dominate—were the rule, not the exception, until well into the twentieth century. Today, the democratic election of state leaders and lawmakers is a global norm, although there are many departures from it in practice (see Meyer et al. 1997).

The extent to which religious interests in a democratic society are organized and expressed in the society's political system is conditioned on the regime-religion (church-state) relation. As well, the organization of democratic political systems varies in ways that are independent of the regime-religion relation and that can affect the political expression of religious interests. Also, the properties of a society's population can have an impact on the political expression of religious interests. Finally, a state and its society may face external conditions that influence the internal relation between religion and politics.

Canada, the United States, and Israel, for example, are all modern democratic societies, but there are significant differences between them regarding religion and politics—differences that reflect variations in the regime-religion (church-state) relation, the organization of political systems, the populations, and external conditions. An examination of these variations illustrates the range of linkages between religion and politics in contemporary democracies.

A substantial majority of the population of Israel is Jewish. Where religious matters are politically salient in Israel, controversies and conflicts often reflect sharp differences between secular and observant as well as Zionist and non-Zionist Israeli Jews. Most Israelis do not identify themselves as religiously observant in a strict sense, although only about 20 percent of the population eschew all religious observance. The state was founded (in 1948) and continuously governed for many years by a social-democratic party (Labour) whose members were for the most part secularized Jews of eastern European origin. Immigration added a significant component of observant oriental Jews to the Israeli population. Notwithstanding the secular origins of the state and the persistent secular orientation of many Israelis, religion is highly salient in Israeli politics today (Liebman 1993).

The State of Israel does not have a written constitution. Thus, the relation between religion and the state is not formally defined in a constitutional sense. No legislative or administrative acts either separate religion and the state or establish a particular variant of Judaism as the religion of the state. This means, among other things, that the resources of the state can be allocated on an ad hoc basis to religious organizations, including schools and welfare organizations that are controlled by religious groups. In this circumstance, religious groups have formed political parties to obtain state support for their organizations and to secure political goals linked to religious ideologies.

Representation in the Israeli parliament (Knesset) is based on proportional voting for parties. Proportional voting enables small parties to win seats. This feature of the Israeli electoral system plus the absence of legal or constitutional provisions either specifying or restricting the use of state resources in support of religion have encouraged the development of religious political parties in Israel. In recent years both large secular parties (socialist Labour and Likud) and smaller religious parties have received enough votes to claim seats in the parliament, but no single party has secured enough seats (a majority) to form a government. In that circumstance a government is formed by bargaining between parties. The leader of the party with the most seats negotiates with other parties to form a majority coalition. Cabinet positions are the important bargaining chips in the process.

By entering into agreements with large secular parties when they need votes to form a government, some religious parties in Israel have secured cabinet portfolios. The electoral successes of some religious parties have enabled them to pursue interests and goals that in some cases are at considerable variance with the sensibilities and inclinations of secular Israelis, especially with regard to territorial settlements and peace, but also in matters pertaining to religious observance and the public presence of religion in Israeli life.

Israel, then, is a qualified variant of the theocratic model of religion-regime relations in the sense that there are no constitutional restrictions on the implementation of politically salient derivations that could flow from the ideology of a governing party. No religious party in Israel has succeeded, so far, in becoming a governing party, but were that to happen, there is no constitutional limitation that would, in principle, prevent a religious governing party from imposing its prescriptions and practices on the population of Israel.

Both Israel and Canada are parliamentary democracies, but the presence of religion in the contemporary political life of Canada is subdued in comparison with its visibility in the Israeli public arena. Reasons for this difference include the form of the constitutionalization of the church-state relationship in Canada, the organization of the Canadian political system, the secularization of cleavages or political fault lines in Canada, and the religious composition of the Canadian population.

The constitution of Canada underwrites a "soft" version of the caesaro-papist subtype of the interpentration model of church-state relations. There is both a guarantee of free religious practice and the recognition of a form of religious establishment whereby public funds flow in support of primary and secondary schools affiliated with some churches. As well, hospitals and other health care organizations owned by religious groups are publicly funded.

Where education and health care are constitutionalized provincial responsibilities, there are variations between provinces regarding patterns and levels of funding for church-related schools. Also, provinces are free to expand support beyond constitutionally required levels or to withdraw support in some circumstances. Thus, until 1999 Roman Catholic secondary schools in Ontario were not funded at the same level as public high schools. Following a provincial referendum in Newfoundland, church-related school boards were abolished in 1999, although public funds continue to support religious instruction in all schools in the province.

Constitutional and legal provisions pertaining to the church-state relation in Canada circumscribe the possibilities for political action by religious actors. The state will not provide material support to any religion for the asking, although it does provide funds in support of the educational and health care activities of designated churches, of which the Roman Catholic Church is the most notable example. This pattern has roots in the accommodation of Roman Catholic francophone Canada and Protestant anglophone Canada and the political balancing act that has kept Canada together since the founding of the Canadian state in 1867. Essentially, federal governments act in ways that are designed to ensure continuing accommodation between divisive political actors. The form that the constitutionalization of the church-state relation has taken in Canada enables governments to control the fissiparous tendencies of religiously oriented political actors through quasi-establishment (the funding of religiously affiliated schools and health care facilities) and caesaro-papist policies that, in effect, limit the public, political expression of divisive religious views (Simpson 1985).

The organization of the Canadian political system also encourages the containment of religious expression as a form of political action. The electoral rule of "first past the post" (a plurality of votes) makes it unlikely that the candidates of small parties will win seats in the federal House of Commons. This is unlike, say, the case in Israel, where the proportion of votes obtained by a party provides small parties with an opportunity for representation in the Knesset. Views on issues including religious views that lack a broad base in the Canadian population are not likely to be represented in government.

A Canadian government is formed by the appointment of a cabinet of ministers (who are the government) by the leader of the party with a majority of seats in the House of Commons. (Not every member of parliament is a member of a government.) Once formed, a government (as is the case in any parliamentary system) can work its will without bargaining with other parliamentary parties—assuming that it is a majority government, meaning that it has a majority of seats in the House of Commons. Typically, matters related to the country's economy and the unity of Canadian confederation dominate federal elections in Canada and, thus, rise to the level of government policy making, where they obscure other issues, including those that have a base in sectarian religious sensibilities.

The pattern of church-state articulation and the mechanics of the electoral system work against a simple, direct relation between religion and politics in contemporary Canada. As well, there has been shift in the last forty years in the nature of the cleavage that divides Canada into the nation of Quebec and the rest of Canada, a shift that has had implications for the tie between religion and politics. The rapid institutional secularization of Quebec in the 1960s and parallel movements in Anglophone Canada transformed the religion-language duality of Canada into a culture-language duality. Culture burst the bounds of religion and church control (see Borduas 1948). By the 1970s, Canada was officially defined as a bilingual and bicultural society, an understanding that was constitutionalized in 1982 along with provisions that, in effect, recognized rights pertaining to cultural maintenance and expression for all groups in Canada.

By moving the "game" of Canada to the politics of language, culture, and national expression and away from the politics of the religion-language link that was associated with Anglo dominance and the power of the Roman Catholic clergy in Quebec (a pattern that had been in place since British ascendance in the 1760s), the secularization of Canada in the post–World War II period gradually pushed religion out of the central place it had once occupied in the Canadian political system (Simpson 1988). While religion is no longer in a commanding position, its voice is not dead in the contemporary Canadian public arena. The Roman Catholic Church, mainline Protestant denominations, and Jewish organizations provide a public conscience in matters related to economic and social justice, and they engage the political system with pursuant representations that are underwritten by the pattern of elite accommodation that typifies the Canadian political system (Simpson and Macleod 1985).

In recent years, a number of highly charged issues pertaining to abortion, homosexuality, pornography, prayer in the schools, and extramarital sex have been thrust into the American political arena. While some of these matters have public visibility in Canada, they have not generated the same level of public attention and scrutiny that they have in the United States, nor have they been a source of sustained conflict and serious divisiveness within the political arenas of Canada. Why?

The sociomoral issues that have been politicized in America have a base in the moral practices of conservative, sectarian Protestants as well as those of Roman Catholics to some extent. The reincorporation of sectarian Protestants into the American presidential electoral party system in the late 1970s brought sociomoral issues into the American public domain with force (Simpson 1983). A comparison of the religious demography of the Canadian and American populations suggests why these issues, once they were defined as public concerns, have had more prominence in America than in Canada.

About 45 percent of Americans are conservative Protestant Christians, whereas less than 10 percent of the Canadian population falls into the same category. Mainline Christian churches (including Roman Catholic) account for about 65 percent of the Canadian population and 40 percent of the U.S. population (Simpson 1988; Kosmin and Lachman 1993). There are far fewer sectarian Protestants in Canada than in the United States. Canada, then, lacks the population base for generating, supporting, and sustaining a politics of sociomoral issues. In the United States, on the other hand, a substantial portion of the population resonates with sociomoral issues that provide a public presence for everyday moral sensibilities anchored in conservative Protestant beliefs and practices.

More than religious demography underwrites the presence and tenacity of sociomoral issues in the American political system. Once thematized as politically relevant, issues have staying power that can be traced to the organization of the American system of government and, for religiously anchored

sociomoral issues, to the constitutionalization of free religious practice and no establishment of religion. Regarding the latter, practices in civil society that are approved by many but have been legally undone because they are not constitutionally valid (for example, prayer in public schools) may be a source of political agitation. A sense of unresolvable grievance arises where unfettered religious practice in the circumstance of no establishment leads to voluntaristic integrity, strength, and, even, militance in pursuit of outcomes that can only be achieved by violating the rule (no establishment) that underwrites and sustains the integrity and strength of religious practice in the first place. Unresolvable grievances are the stuff of primordial political mobilization. A politician signals that she or he is "onside" and wishes that something could be done but that it cannot because it is unconstitutional. Where the principle of no establishment is constitutionally moot, as in Israel or Canada, for example, a sense of unresolved grievance pertaining to issues linked to religion is less likely to persist, since a problem can be solved, at least in principle, by political action that entangles religion and the state.

Issues including politically relevant sociomoral issues also persist because there are three centers of political authority in the American form of government: the president, the Senate, and the House of Representatives. Each center is elected separately, and law can be made only where there is agreement among them. In this circumstance, politicized issues have lives in multiple electoral jurisdictions that encompass local, state, and national publics.

Although the majority party organizes the business of the American House of Representatives and the Senate, it does not form a government as a majority party does in a parliamentary system (for example, Canada or Israel). A government in a parliamentary system does not need the agreement of other centers of political authority to make law since a parliamentary majority guarantees that the political will of the majority party leader and her or his cabinet can become law without external advice or consent. In parliamentary systems a politicized issue tends to have a "half-life" that is as long as the attention span of the leader of the government and her or his cabinet of ministers. Where the electorate, itself, is not attuned to issues by virtue of its demographic characteristics—as is the case in Canada regarding religiously linked sociomoral issues—it is unlikely that issues will rise to the level of serious consideration by a government, and even if they do, a government may not pay much attention to them. In the U.S. system, on the other hand, there is a tighter fit between what is on the public mind and the exercise of political authority. As long as an issue persists in the media, it has a guaranteed hearing in multiple centers of political power at the federal level.

Variations in the links between religion and politics in modern democratic systems have been illustrated above with an analysis of Israel, Canada, and the United States of America. The analysis could be extended to other democratic states and, as well, to political systems that are not democratic—for example, to the People's Republic of China where single party, top-down government has imposed a strict caesaro-papist pattern of control on religion. In any case, an analysis will examine the social forms and properties that inscribe the details of the relationship between religion and politics: the religion-regime linkage, the organization of a state's political system, and the religious demography of a state's population.

RELIGION AND WAR

The state system that emerged from the treaties ending the Thirty Years' War in 1648 led to the contemporary global international system. In this system, a state and its regime are the elementary units of interaction. Diplomacy, trade, and war are the fundamental forms of international behavior.

By the time of World War I (1914–1918), the international system was a mix of nation-states and imperial powers with nation-state cores. Western nation-states and imperial powers controlled nearly all the inhabited world. World War I dissolved the Ottoman Empire and the Austro-Hungarian Empire. World War II (1939–1945) led to the rapid decline and breakup of the British Empire. It also led to the bipolar Cold War that pitted the West against the Soviet Union and its client states. The bipolar system came to an end in 1989.

The outcome of each of the major wars in the twentieth century, including the Cold War, led to the decline or collapse of imperial and international structures. Each such decline or collapse, in turn, led to the formation of nation-states. Typically (but not always), states were constructed from the pieces of an imperial or a neo-imperial structure (the bipolar system of the Cold War). Thus, Turkey emerged from the Ottoman Empire and Hungary from the Austro-Hungarian Empire in the wake of World War I. India, Pakistan, Burma, and Indonesia were devolutions from the British Empire and the Dutch Empire, which were broken up following World War II. The end of the Cold War led to the formation or revival of nation-states that had been parts of the Russian empire constituted as the Soviet Union and the client states of the Warsaw Pact. They include (but are not limited to) the Baltic states (Estonia, Latvia, Lithuania), Ukraine, Georgia, Kazakhstan, and Azerbaijan.

The history of state formation in the twentieth century demonstrates a clear tendency for a nation—that is, a people who share territory, language, and religion—to form or seek to form a state in which the leash of imperial control or regional control with imperial-like features slackens or disappears. When the Cold War global structure collapsed, for example, so did the forces that were the basis for the integration of the former Yugoslavia, a regional, quasi-imperial power from the immediate post–World War II period to the end of the 1980s.

War and state formation in the former Yugoslavia followed the path of ethnoreligious differences. Slovenia (Roman Catholic) and Macedonia (Orthodox) were more or less peaceful devolutions. Serbs (Orthodox) and Croats (Roman Catholic) fought before the state of Croatia was secured. Serbs, Croatians, and Bosnians (Muslim) fought in Bosnia-Herzegovina prior to a Western-imposed settlement. Having receded to the Orthodox provinces of Serbia and Montenegro, Serb-dominated Yugoslavia attempted to drive out the ethnic Albanian (Muslim) population from the region of Kosovo (a part of Serbia) before the North Atlantic Treaty Organization (NATO) intervened in 1999.

Beyond the former Yugoslavia there are other contemporary armed conflicts that are also rooted in ethnoreligious differences. These include sporadic border fighting between India and Pakistan, and armed civil conflicts of one variety or another—guerrilla war, terrorism, state military suppression—in the Philippines, Northern Ireland, Indonesia, and Sri Lanka. In the Middle East, religiously oriented militant factions of Muslims and Jews have complicated the pursuit of peace. The successful testing of nuclear weapons by both India and Pakistan has fortified the division of the world along ethnoreligious lines.

Huntington (1996) argues that contemporary patterns of conflict in the world provide evidence that the ideologically based political divisions of the Cold War have been replaced by a set of differences that are grounded in the congruence of religion, language, and territory. These differences support, encourage, and sustain action that is rooted in collective and individual identities. At the global level, identities are embedded in civilizations, and civilizations, according to Huntington, are the key to understanding international order and disorder in the twenty-first century.

Analysis of the conflicts in the former Yugoslavia provides a sense of the developing pattern of global tension as envisioned by Huntington. Ethnoreligious divisions within collapsing Yugoslavia were replicated in the religious identities of the sources of support for the divisions in the outside world. Orthodox Serbia received economic, military, political, and diplomatic support from Orthodox Russia Germany and, in particular, the heavily Roman Catholic state of Bavaria supported Roman Catholic Croatia. Bosnians and ethnic Albanians received sympathy and aid from sources in the Muslim world.

Jumping to the global level, Huntington argues that divisions in the world will increasingly congeal along civilizational lines. The central civilizational players (and their core states) in the intercivilizatonal global system of the twenty-first century, according to Huntington, include Orthodox civilization (Russia), Confucian civilization (China), Hindu civilization (India), Japanese civilization (Japan), Islamic civilization (no core state), and Western civilization (a consortium of core states consisting of the United Kingdom, France, Germany, and the United States). International conflicts and wars will tend to occur along civilizational fault lines with core states leading and/or abating intercivilizational hostilities.

If Huntington is right, conflict and war at the intercivilizational level in the twenty-first century will resemble the European wars of religion (Roman Catholics versus Protestants)—the so-called Thirty Years War—that ended with the Peace of Westphalia in 1648. In each case, ethnoreligious or cultural identities have been the basis for the cross-state attribution of lethal patterns of "us versus them." Whereas the modern state emerged from the seventeenth-century European wars of religion as the dominant political unit for governing and managing populations, it remains to be seen whether new forms of political organization will arise from the intercivilizational tumults of the twenty-first century.

REFERENCES

Arjomand, Said Amir 1993 "Shi'ite Jurisprudence and Constitution Making in the Islamic Republic of Iran." In M. E. Marty and R. S. Appleby, eds., *Fundamentalisms and the State: Remaking Politics, Economics, and Militance.* Chicago: University of Chicago Press.

Borduas, Paul-Emile 1948 *Refus Global.* Montreal: Mithra-Mythe Editeur.

Casanova, José 1994 *Public Religions in the Modern World.* Chicago: University of Chicago Press.

Huntington, Samuel P. 1996 *The Clash of Civilizations and the Remaking of World Order.* New York: Simon and Schuster.

Kosmin, Barry A., and Seymour P. Lachman 1993 *One Nation under God: Religion in Contemporary American Society.* New York: Crown.

Liebman, Charles S. 1993 "Jewish Fundamentalism and the Israeli Polity." In M. E. Marty and R. S. Appleby, eds., *Fundamentalisms and the State: Remaking Politics, Economics, and Militance.* Chicago: University of Chicago Press.

Martin, David 1978 *A General Theory of Secularization.* New York: Harper and Row.

Meyer, John W., John Boli, George M. Thomas, and Francisco O. Ramirez 1997 "World Society and the Nation-State." *American Journal of Sociology* 103:144–181.

Simpson, John H. 1983 "Moral Issues and Status Politics." In R. C. Liebman and R. Wuthnow, eds., *The New Christian Right.* New York: Aldine.

—— 1985 "Federal Regulation and Religious Broadcasting in Canada and the United States: A Comparative Sociological Analysis." In William Westfall, Louis Rousseau, Fernand Harvey, and John Simpson, eds., *Religion/Culture: Comparative Canadian Studies.* Ottawa: Association for Canadian Studies.

—— 1988 "Religion and the Churches." In J. Curtis and L. Tepperman, eds., *Understanding Canadian Society.* Toronto: McGraw-Hill Ryerson.

———and Henry G. MacLeod 1985 "The Politics of Morality in Canada." In R. Stark, ed., *Religious Movements: Genesis, Exodus, and Numbers.* New York: Paragon House.

Swanson, Guy E. 1967 *Religion and Regime.* Ann Arbor: University of Michigan Press.

JOHN H. SIMPSON

RELIGIOUS FUNDAMENTALISM

*See*Religious Movements; Sociology of Religion.

RELIGIOUS MOVEMENTS

Most people do not perceive religious beliefs as changing very much over time. Religions, after all, are engaged in the propagation of eternal truths. While it is understandable that religious organizations may change, that process is perceived to occur only very slowly. Indeed, changes in beliefs are perceived to occur so slowly that adherents and leaders alike hardly notice.

Contrary to popular perceptions, both religious beliefs and religious organizations are dynamic, ever-changing phenomena. Changes in the beliefs and organizational structure of religions reflect adaptations, accommodations, and innovations to continuously changing cultural, political, and economic environments. Without more or less constant change, religions would become irrelevant to their environments, and would simply become defunct. Indeed, this has been the fate of many religions in the history of humankind.

Changes in both beliefs and organizational structure may occur as the result of actions taken by leaders empowered to make such changes, but even greater change occurs as the result of *religious movements.* How religious movements effect change, both within and outside religious organizations, is the subject of this essay. The essay unfolds in three parts. First, the classic scholarly literature about religious movements is examined within the framework of a simple typology that pivots on the origins and target of change sought by movements. Second, the phenomenon of religious fundamentalism is examined as an exemplar of religious

movements. Selection of fundamentalism is appropriate because it is one of the most important religious movements of the twentieth century. In the final part of the essay, the emerging theoretical work on religious movements is linked to some practical implications of religious movements and the future of religion in human cultures.

UNDERSTANDING RELIGIOUS MOVEMENTS

Religious movements may be understood as a subcategory of *social movements*—that is, *organized efforts to cause or prevent change.* There are three discrete types or categories of religious movements. First, *endogenous religious movements* constitute efforts to change the internal character of the religion. Second, *exogenous religious movements* attempt to alter the environment in which the religion resides. Third, *generative religious movements* seek to introduce new religions into the culture or environment.

Religions consist of beliefs, symbols, practices, and organizations. *Endogenous movements* seek to change one or more of these aspects of a religion. Some endogenous movements have had monumental impact on both history and culture—for example, the great schism that split Christianity into Western Catholicism and Eastern Orthodoxy in the eleventh century; and the Reformation, which developed in the sixteenth century and split Protestantism from Roman Catholicism. Other movements, while important to the participants, have been of little cultural significance.

Endogenous movements frequently result in a schism—the division of the religious organization into two or more independent parts. Protestantism has been particularly schism-prone. Melton (1996) has identified more than 750 Protestant groups in North America alone. New religious groups formed through the process of schism are known as *sects. Sectarian movements* tend to be led by laity, or lower-echelon clergy. Many religious movements result in reform rather than schism. *Reform* is a more likely outcome when movements are initiated by the religious leaders, or when the religious hierarchy responds to and coopts grass roots demands for change. Through the centuries, the Roman Catholic Church has been particularly effective in coopting and reincorporating movements into the church. We see them today as religious orders.

Pope John XXIII called the Second Vatican Council (1962–1965) in response to strong internal pressures to modernize the Roman Catholic Church and improve relations with other faiths. The Council produced many wide-sweeping changes in the Catholic Church. In addition, it spawned many other religious movements within the Catholic Church (e.g., liberation theology, the movement for women's ordination, and movements for greater lay participation).

A second important hierarchically initiated movement of the twentieth century was the Protestant *ecumenical movement*. After several centuries of denominational proliferation, mostly occurring as the result of schism, the second half of the twentieth century has witnessed a powerful ecumenical movement that has resulted in the union of diverse Protestant traditions.

Exogenous movements constitute a second general type of religious movement. They are concerned with changing some aspect of the environment in which a religious organization exists. All religious organizations bring four imperatives to the environments in which they exist: (1) survival, (2) economic viability, (3) status, and (4) ideology (Hadden 1980). As long as these interests are secure, the religious organization exists in equilibrium or harmony with its environment. This is the normal relationship between religions and the culture. In sociological literature, these groups are identified as *churches*, or *denominations*.

When a religious group's interests are threatened, or the leadership seeks to enhance or expand interests, religious movements may ensue. Often, exogenous religious movements are indistinguishable from social movements. Indeed, they are frequently pursued in coalition with secular social movement organizations.

In addition to legitimating religious movements with transcendental principles, religious leaders are often enlisted by secular social movement leaders to legitimate their movements. As a general proposition, religious leaders are specialists in the legitimization of social movement causes.

In the second half of the twentieth century, liberal Protestantism has forged coalitions with virtually every liberal cause on the scene. Evangelical (conservative) Protestantism, on the other hand, has coalesced with economically and socially conservative causes. In both instances, religious organizations engage in movement activity to promote some element of their ideology. At the same time, in doing so, they hope to enhance their status. Much of the exogenous social activism of evangelical Christian groups during the past quarter-century has been grounded in the presupposition that a morally corrupt society threatens the survival of culture itself.

The very essence of religious organizations is that they carry cultural values, ideals, customs, and laws that claim transcendental character. When religious leaders engage in exogenous religious movements, they almost always draw on these transcendental principles to legitimate their cause. The claim that movement objectives are part of a divine plan, or that God is on the side of the movement, may serve as a powerful motivation for adherents of the faith to participate. Witness, for example, the many occasions during the 1980s when Islamic leaders exhorted their followers to engage in *jihad* (holy war).

The civil rights movement in the United States was substantially a religious movement. It was led by black ministers, activities were organized in black churches, funds were raised in liberal white churches, white clergy bolstered the troops who marched and picketed, and idealistic black and white youth—motivated by their religious traditions—participated in civil rights campaigns and projects.

The strength of the movement came not only from the broad base of religious participation but also from the ability of the leaders to legitimate the movement constantly in terms of sacred religious principles. For example, civil rights leaders repeatedly quoted the passage in the Declaration of Independence that acknowledges the role of the Creator in human rights: "We hold these Truths to be self-evident, that all Men are created equal, that they are endowed by their Creator with certain unalienable Rights, that among these are Life, Liberty, and the Pursuit of Happiness. . . ."

The Solidarity labor movement in Poland, which was the first major social movement that led to the collapse of communism in eastern Europe, sought and received legitimacy from the Catholic

Church. Not only in Poland but also throughout eastern Europe, religious traditions were deeply involved in the movement for liberation from communism.

Not all exogenous religious movements are movements of liberation. Around the globe religious groups call on divine providence to help them in struggles against other religions, ethnic rivals, and unsympathetic governments.

There are literally hundreds of these movements around the world in various stages of ascendancy or abatement. In predominantly Hindu India, Muslims in the northern province of Kashmir seek independence or union with Pakistan, while Sikhs in the nearby province of Punjab have for many years waged a bloody confrontation with the government for independence. In Sri Lanka, just off India's southern shores, Tamils, members of a Hindu sect, seek an independent state in a nation that is predominantly Buddhist. In Northern Ireland, Protestants and Catholics have experienced periodic conflict since Protestant settlers arrived in the middle of the seventeenth century, but since 1968 the two rivals have been locked in a high level of tension punctuated with intermittent outbursts of violence.

The third type of religious movement is *generative*—a deliberate effort to produce a new religious movement. Either new religions are introduced to a culture externally by missionaries, or they are products of innovation (invention) by members of the culture. Whereas schismatic movements produce variations on an existing religion within a culture, new religions are novel to the host culture. Sociological scholars refer to these new religions as *cults*.

New religions are not necessarily newly created. Hare Krishnas, adorned in saffron robes and chanting on street corners, first appeared in the United States during the mid-1960s. The Krishnas brought with them Hindu beliefs and practices that were clearly novel to North America, but that had been first practiced in India in the sixteenth century. In contrast, the Reverend Sun Myung Moon, a Korean and founder of the Unification Church, created a religion that involved a blending of significantly reconstructed Christian beliefs with important elements of Eastern religions. In still another example, L. Ron Hubbard, a science fiction writer, published a book in 1950 titled *Dianetics*, which outlined psychotherapeutic or mental health techniques. The book became a bestseller, and in 1954 Hubbard founded the Church of Scientology.

In these three groups we have examples of, first, the importation of an old religion based on sacred texts of Hinduism (Hare Krishna); second, a newly created religion based on reported revelation from the God of the monotheistic traditions of Judaism and Christianity (Unificationism); and third, an indigenous religion based on techniques of modern psychotherapy (Scientology). All are new and novel to North American culture.

The late 1960s and early 1970s produced a flurry of new religious movements in the United States. The youth counterculture of the 1960s provided a receptive environment for new religions. Equally important, the repeal of the Oriental Exclusion Acts in 1965 paved the way for many Eastern gurus to come to the United States as missionaries of their faiths. While not nearly as extensive, this activity can be compared to that of the Christian missionaries, who flocked to Africa and Asia, during the late nineteenth and early twentieth centuries, to seek converts to their faith.

This period of rapid cult formation was not particularly unique. The nineteenth century, for example, produced a large number of cult and sectarian movements in the United States. Christian Science, Mormonism, Seventh-Day Adventism, Jehovah's Witnesses, and Theosophy are but a few examples of groups that emerged in that time frame and that remain viable in the late twentieth century.

Significant social science literature exists on all three types of religious movements: endogenous, exogenous, and generative. The focus of inquiry has shifted significantly over time, and the discipline of the investigators has influenced the selection of questions addressed.

During the formative years of sociology much attention was devoted to discerning how new religions arise and evolve. This interest was motivated by the legacy of early sociological writing on the *church-sect* typology by Max Weber and Ernst Troeltsch. Sects develop as a result of dissent within churches, when the dissenters break away and form sects. Over time, they institutionalize and gradually become more like the churches they earlier broke from, even as new sects are being formed. Sects tend to recruit disproportionately from the "disinherited," or the economically deprived classes. Further, sectarian groups tend to socialize their members to the dominant middle-class values of society.

Until the mid-1960s, much of the sociological literature focused on movements that have here been identified as endogenous. Much of this literature concerned questions relating to the formation of religious movements and could be classified as consisting of theories of: (1) deprivation (socioeconomic and other), (2) social dislocation, and (3) socioeconomic change.

Historical work has focused on exogenous and generative movements. Norman Cohn's monumental work *The Pursuit of the Millennium* concludes that revolutionary millenarian movements during the eleventh and sixteenth centuries drew their strength from groups on the margin of society. Cohn uses the term *marginal* to describe persons who are not just poor but who also have no "recognized place in society [or] regular institutionalized methods of voicing their grievances or pressing their claims" (1970, p. 282). Historical literature supports much sociological work that finds religious groups emerging on the fringe of society.

Anthropological literature tends to focus on generative movements. The question that dominates their inquiry was inherited from the evolutionary agenda of Social Darwinism in the late nineteenth century: What are the origins of religion? New religions, they conclude, emerge during periods of rapid social change, disorganization, and dislocation. In anthropological literature, this cultural strain is most often identified as the result of the invasion of an indigenous culture by a militarily advanced culture—the typical pattern of conquest and colonization by European cultures from the late fifteenth century forward.

The new religions are variously identified as "cargo cults," "messianic movements," "nativistic movements," and "revitalization movements." Anthropological literature postulates that new religions emerge as a means of dealing with cultural stress. La Barre (1972) generalizes from the scores of ethnographic studies of anthropologists to locate the origins of all religions in cultural crisis.

Lanternari, surveying anthropological and historical literature on new religions that emerged as a result of intercultural conflict, concludes that these religions "tend to seek salvation by immediate action through militant struggle or through direct and determined opposition to the foreign forces" (1965, p. 247).

Psychological literature has been much less concerned with religious movements. Following the logic of Sigmund Freud's cultural bias against religion, many psychologists have identified the leaders of religious movements as psychopathological and their followers as psychologically defective. This literature has not been particularly productive of insights about religious movements.

The ferment of generative religious movements in the wake of the youth counterculture of the late 1960s stimulated a tremendous volume of sociological inquiry. In terms of sheer volume, research and theorizing about "new religious movements" eclipsed all other subtopics of inquiry in the social scientific study of religion during the 1970s and 1980s (Bromley and Hadden 1993). These studies examined (1) the organizational development of new religions, (2) the structural and social-psychological dynamics of affiliation and disaffiliation, and (3) the persistence of intragroup conflict between new and established religious traditions.

In addition, the 1980s saw significant theoretical developments in the conceptualization of the role of religious movements in sustaining religion in human cultures. By the early 1990s, this literature was beginning to be recognized as a distinct departure from, and a challenge to, the prevailing model of religion that dominated the social sciences for most of the twentieth century. Indeed, from the inception of the social sciences, scholars worked within an intellectual framework that viewed religion as incompatible with the modern world that is dominated by science and reason.

In 1993 Stephen Warner published an article that proclaimed a "new paradigm" in the sociology of religion. The key theoretical ideas in Warner's argument were most closely identified with the work of Rodney Stark and his colleagues. Warner showed how support for the new paradigm has been mounting in much social research, but especially in the work of young social historians. We will return to the "new paradigm" in the final section of this essay and examine how it has altered our understanding of the role of religious movements in human culture. Further, we will see how the new paradigm restructures the central task of the sociology of religion as the study of religious movements.

We turn next to an examination of *fundamentalism*, a religious movement that spans most of the twentieth century. Several reasons are offered for exploring fundamentalism in some depth. First, fundamentalism is one of the most important movements of the twentieth century and, thus, deserves to be examined in its own right. Second, the widespread cultural prejudice against this conservative manifestation of religion has spilled over into scholarly literature, with the result that little empirical understanding of fundamentalism developed until near the end of the century. Third, the foundation for a much better understanding of fundamentalism is now in place. We shall briefly discuss the literature that constitutes this foundational work, and point to some research tasks that are required before a mature scholarly understanding of fundamentalism can be achieved.

RELIGIOUS FUNDAMENTALISM AS EXEMPLAR

Fundamentalism is an important religious movement that dates from the early twentieth century. Fundamentalism may be understood as protest against the quest of liberal Protestant scholars to resolve the apparent contradictions between religious knowledge and scientific discoveries. Such an effort, it was believed, could lead only to Christianity's capitulation to the ontological superiority of science as a path to truth.

From the early years of fundamentalism, most persons who have stood outside the movement have seen it through stereotypical lenses—provided substantially by the mass media—and have failed to grasp the complexity, nuances, and implications of the movement. Thus, almost from the beginning of the movement, fundamentalism has been a concept associated with religions that are perceived to be backward and potentially dangerous.

Fundamentalism has four distinct meanings. The first three meanings were in place by the end of the first quarter of the twentieth century; the

fourth does not appear until the last quarter of the century. The different meanings are often intermingled in both mass media and scholarly usage, with the result of considerable confusion and misunderstanding of the phenomenon. Significant theological and historical literatures are available on fundamentalism, but neither a theoretical nor an empirical sociological literature is well developed. This section of the essay of religious movements first identifies the four distinct meanings of fundamentalism and locates each in historical context. It then turns to a discussion of how a seriously flawed construct might be employed to better understand the phenomenon, and especially its utility for comparative sociological research.

First, fundamentalism refers to a Christian *theological movement* that experienced its greatest strength in the first quarter of the twentieth century. This movement was concerned with defending the faith against an internal movement seeking to make changes to accommodate Protestant Christianity to the modern world. As a theological movement, fundamentalism sought to purge the teachings of "modernism" from churches and theological schools. Modernist teachings had emerged during the late nineteenth century as a means of accommodating Christian doctrine to the evidence and teachings of science.

The most basic teaching of fundamentalism is that the scriptures are *inerrant*—that is, literally true. Closely related is the doctrine of *millenarianism*, which prophesies the imminent return of Christ. In the early days of the fundamentalist movement, these theological battles were waged in the leading theological seminaries of the nation (e.g., Princeton Theological Seminary).

An important development in this struggle was the publication, between 1910 and 1915, of a series of twelve books that sought to defend and reaffirm "fundamental" Christian principles in the face of the teachings of liberal scholars that did not believe the Bible should be understood as literal truth. Leading scholars from the United States and England contributed articles to the books, titled *The Fundamentals*, which were published by two wealthy Christian brothers, Lyman and Milton Steward. Copies of *The Fundamentals* were distributed gratis to over a quarter-million clergy members, seminary students, and teachers throughout the United States. These tracts provided the inspiration for the name of the movement. The term "fundamentalism," however, was not coined until 1920 by Curtis Lee Laws, a Baptist newspaper editor.

Defense of the faith against the encroachment of modernist theological teachings was at the core of the movement. But the *holiness movement* profoundly influenced fundamentalism, which was just as concerned with *correct behavior* as fundamentalism was with *correct belief*. The personal piety and renunciation of "worldly" vices of the holiness movement was combined with the combative spirit of theological fundamentalism to produce a *political fundamentalism*, the second distinct meaning of fundamentalism.

Fundamentalism as a political movement has had several phases. The first wave of political fundamentalism was a short-lived but vigorous conservative movement with several agendas, including temperance and anticommunism. The critical and ultimately fatal crusade of the fundamentalist movement occurred in the arena of public education policy. Charles Darwin's theory of evolution, which had gained popularity among scientists and teachers, was clearly incompatible with a literal reading of the Bible. Among other incompatible passages in the Bible, the Genesis story of creation states that the earth and all that dwells therein were created in six days. The fundamentalists launched a campaign to prohibit the teaching of Darwinism in public schools, a campaign that initially met with considerable success in several states.

The struggle came to a climax in 1925 in one of the most celebrated trials of the twentieth century. John Scopes, a substitute biology teacher, was charged with violating a Tennessee state law that prohibited the teaching of evolution. Dubbed the "Monkey Trial," this epochal event drew two of America's greatest trial lawyers to the tiny town of Dayton, Tennessee. Speaking for the prosecution was William Jennings Bryan, brilliant orator and presidential nominee of the Democratic Party on three occasions. Bryan was the unchallenged leader of the fundamentalist political movement. Clarence Darrow, a bitter foe of organized religion, defended Scopes. Darrow gained prominence as a defender of labor unions and in litigation against monopolistic corporations. He was believed by many to be the outstanding trial lawyer in the nation.

The highlight of the trial came when, in a surprise move, Darrow called Bryan as a witness. While Bryan claimed to have been a scholar of the Bible for fifty years, his ability to defend some of the finer points and implications of fundamentalist theology proved wanting. In the end, his testimony was a debacle for the prosecution. George Marsden described the scene thus:

Bryan did not know how Eve could be created from Adam's rib, where Cain got his wife, or where the great fish came from that swallowed Jonah. He said that he had never contemplated what would happen if the earth stopped its rotation so that the sun would "stand still." (Marsden 1980, p. 186)

The trial was quintessentially a confrontation between the emerging modern world and the forces of tradition. The drama was played out on the turf of traditionalism—a sleepy, small town in Tennessee—but journalists who were sages of the new modern order communicated the trial to the world. The fundamentalists were portrayed as fossilized relics from an era long past. Darrow himself portrayed the trial as a struggle of modern liberal culture against "bigots and ignoramuses" (Marsden 1980, p. 187).

John Scopes was convicted, but that fact seemed inconsequential. The forces of modernity and tradition had met face to face, and modernity triumphed. William Jennings Bryan collapsed and died a few days after the trial without ever leaving Dayton, Tennessee. In popular myth, Bryan died of a broken heart. Bryan had planned a national campaign to compel schools across the nation to teach evolution as a theory, not a scientific fact. There was no one else of Bryan's stature to pick up the cause. The first wave of political fundamentalism died when Bryan was unable to defend its theological underpinnings.

The third distinct meaning of fundamentalism emerges from a melding of the theological and political movements to create a *popular caricature* of small-town Americans as culturally unenlightened religious fanatics. Journalists H. L. Mencken and Sinclair Lewis, writing in the second and third decades of this century, set the tone and style of a genre of lambasting literature that subsequent generations of writers have admired and sought to emulate. Fundamentalists were portrayed as backwater fools preyed on by hypocritical evangelists, and as a withering species destined to disappear from the modern world. They could be meddlesome and annoying, but they were not viewed as politically dangerous. In time they would most certainly die off, even in the rural hinterlands of America.

The Scopes trial clearly marked the demise of the first wave of political fundamentalism. Fundamentalists in the major Protestant denominations lost ground to the modernists on the theological front. But biblical fundamentalism did not so much wane as pass from high public visibility. A number of leaders bolted from mainline Protestant churches and formed new denominations and seminaries. But out of the limelight of the press and mainstream culture, fundamentalism did not wither as had been forecast. Rather, it continued to grow, particularly in the Midwest and the South (Carpenter 1997).

Fundamentalists also were schism-prone, so that none of the scores of groups developed into large new denominations, such as occurred with the Baptists and Methodists in the nineteenth century (Finke and Stark 1992). This, too, served to diminish the fundamentalists' visibility. An important development occurred during the 1940s when fundamentalism effectively divided into two camps. The first, which was more insular and combative toward the larger culture, joined with Carl McIntire to create the American Council of Christian Churches (ACCC). McIntire was militantly antimodernist, and he viewed the ACCC as an instrument for doing battle with the liberal Federal Council of Churches (FCC), which in 1950 became the National Council of Churches.

A second and larger contingent of fundamentalists, who were neither with the militant McIntire contingent nor the modernist tradition aligned with the FCC, came together in 1942 to found the National Association of Evangelicals (NAE). Theologically the NAE might have considered themselves neofundamentalists, but they recognized the negative cultural stereotype associated with fundamentalism. The use of the term "evangelical" was a reappropriation of a term that most Protestant groups used to describe themselves before the modernist-fundamentalist schism. Some of the leaders of the NAE later admitted that the name "evangelical" was a strategy to escape the negative cultural stereotypes against fundamentalism. The concept of evangelicalism was simply more respectable.

Publicly NAE leaders stressed their desire to emphasize the positive aspects of their beliefs in contrast to the highly negative and combative posture of the ACCC toward both theological modernism and political liberalism. The label "evangelical" has served well those millions of Christians whose theological beliefs are hardly discernible from those identified as fundamentalists. Billy Graham, perhaps the most respected religious leader of the second half of the twentieth century, is considered an evangelical. Theologically speaking, his basic beliefs are virtually indistinguishable from those of fundamentalist Jerry Falwell, or from those of the leadership of the Southern Baptist Convention, which staged a takeover of the Southern Baptist denomination during the 1980s.

While fundamentalism continues to be defined in terms of assent to biblical literalism, fundamentalism in the United States is highly varied in terms of the social organization, nuances of belief, and social class background of adherents. To the general public, however, fundamentalists are known in terms of the caricature that is the legacy of the Scopes trial debacle—people who are narrow-minded, bigoted toward persons different from their own kind, obscurantist, sectarian, and hostile to the modern world. The mass media dredge up enough examples of people exhibiting these traits to keep the stereotype alive.

From the 1930s forward there have been periodic flurries of right-wing political activity led by preachers and laypersons who have been labeled fundamentalists. During the Depression, William Dudley Pelley, Gerald B. Winrod, and Gerald L. K. Smith led movements that blended religion with anti-Semitism. For many decades from the 1940s forward, Carl McIntire was a strident anti-Catholic propagandist; Frederick C. Schwarz, Billy James Hargis, and Edgar Bundy were among the most visible anticommunist crusaders of the post–World War II era.

Liberal political pundits and scholars have always viewed fundamentalist groups with mixed feelings. Some have unequivocally looked on them with great alarm, and that sense of alarm has always been greatest during periods when fundamentalist movements were highly visible. Outside periods of high visibility, the general consensus of scholars is that the fundamentalist right embodies doctrines and attracts an element that is on the fringe of the mainstream of American politics. While perhaps repugnant to the liberal ethos, they have not been widely perceived as a serious threat to democratic institutions.

This perception vacillated yet once more in 1979 when Jerry Falwell, a fundamentalist television preacher, founded a political organization named the Moral Majority. Initially the media paid little attention, but when Falwell and his fellow right-wing fundamentalists organized to help elect presidential candidate Ronald Reagan, interest picked up. When Reagan reached out and embraced the fundamentalists, attention escalated. Following the Reagan victory, along with the defeat of several ranking senators and congressmen, Falwell claimed responsibility. Pollster Lou Harris agreed that the fundamentalist vote was the margin of victory for Reagan. Postelection analysis did not support this claim (Hadden and Swann 1981), but the high media profile of Falwell and his fellow televangelists gave fundamentalism its highest public profile since the 1920s.

This wave of concern about the political power of fundamentalists might have blown over quickly were it not for the timing of the development with the rise of the Islamic imam Ayatollah Khomeini. Khomeini led a revolution that deposed the shah of Iran. Shortly thereafter, his followers held sixty-two Americans hostage for fourteen months. Political analysts concerned with the power of the fundamentalists in America were soon comparing the religious right in America with the followers of Ayatollah Khomeini and other radical Muslim factions in the Middle East. From these comparisons was born the concept of *Islamic fundamentalism*. This linkage was quickly followed by the labeling of selected politically active religious groups around the world as "fundamentalist."

Thus was born the concept of *global fundamentalism*, the fourth distinct meaning of fundamentalism. During the 1980s the idea of global fundamentalism became widely accepted by the mass media and scholars alike. But like previous uses of the term, global fundamentalism has suffered from lack of systematic conceptualization and consistent application. The global application of the concept thus has many of the same underlying presuppositions of the popular caricature of fundamentalism in U.S. Protestantism.

"Global fundamentalism," thus, is an uncomplimentary epithet for religious groups that are viewed as out of sync with the modern world. Fundamentalism, whether the American variety or of some other culture and faith, is characterized by blind adherence to a religious dogma or leader, and by zealous rejection of the modern world. It is also widely assumed that fundamentalists are contemptuous of democratic institutions. The concept is not applied to religious movements that are perceived to be on the side of human betterment. Thus, *liberation theology*, which is global in character, is not considered to be fundamentalist in spite of the fact that it bears some considerable resemblance to movements that have been characterized as fundamentalist.

Inconsistencies in the application of the concept fundamentalism are readily apparent. This was nowhere so evident as the failure to apply the concept to Afghan Muslim guerrillas who fought the Soviet army to a standstill during the 1980s. Both theologically and politically the Afghan rebels were unmistakably Islamic fundamentalists, but they were almost never so identified in the Western press. Rather, these Afghans are almost always referred to as the *mujaheddin*, usually with positive references such as "courageous," "brave," and "freedom fighting." But seldom did anyone mention that *mujaheddin* means, literally, one who fights a *jihad* or holy war. This and other instances of inconsistent application suggest that the concept of fundamentalism is reserved for religious zealots who are disapproved.

In sum, popular use of the concept of global fundamentalism has tended to connote the same stereotypical content that the term conveys when it is applied to Protestant fundamentalists in the United States. Given this history, it might be argued that fundamentalism has not been a concept of great utility for sociological analysis and, thus, its use should be discouraged. In support of this argument, it can be said that the social scientists have done little work to define, conceptualize, or measure fundamentalism.

To propose that fundamentalism should be abandoned as a social science concept may be premature. The introduction of the idea of global fundamentalism has served to focus rather considerable attention on the phenomenon—whatever it may be. The suggestion that the phenomenon might exist across cultures and world religions invites comparative analysis that was lacking when the concept was restricted to American Protestantism.

By the late 1980s serious comparative analysis of fundamentalism had begun. One of the first things learned from comparative inquiry is that fundamentalism cannot be explained away as part of a broader conservative cultural resistance to innovation. Bruce Lawrence's research on Islam led him to the conclusion that fundamentalism is a product of modernity and, thus, is a phenomenon that did not exist prior to modernity.

To view fundamentalism as merely an unenlightened backwater resistance to innovation is to give it a misplaced emphasis. Lawrence argues that fundamentalism is a product of modernity, and "because modernity is global, so is fundamentalism" (Lawrence 1989, p. 3).

Shupe and Hadden (1989) similarly argue that "fundamentalism is a truly modern phenomenon—modern in the sense that the movement is always seeking original solutions to new, pressing problems" (p. 112). Further, the solutions the propose are new. Secularization, the cognitive counterpart to modernization, has progressively sought to compartmentalize religion from, and defined it as irrelevant to, other institutional spheres. Fundamentalism acknowledges that religion has lost authority in the secular world. Further, it perceives secular values to be seriously at variance with the sacred tradition it proclaims.

Fundamentalism may be seen as a movement that seeks to reintegrate religion into the mainstream of culture. Thus conceived, *fundamentalism* may be defined as *a proclamation of reclaimed authority of a sacred tradition that is to be reinstated as an antidote for a society that has strayed from its cultural moorings.* Sociologically speaking, fundamentalism involves (1) a refutation of the radical differentiation of the sacred and the secular that has evolved with modernization and (2) a plan to dedifferentiate this institutional bifurcation and thus bring religion back to center stage as an important factor of interest in public policy decisions.

Fundamentalism is clearly an assault on the cognitive components of modernization. Insofar as the process of modernization is not globally uniform, the development of fundamentalism may be expected to manifest a different character in different cultures. Thus conceived, the varieties of fundamentalism can be examined without the baggage of presuppositions that assume it is necessarily a regressive force in culture.

So conceived, fundamentalism is not antimodern. Fundamentalists, for example, are typically not against the use of modern technology, but rather certain applications of technology viewed to be at variance with the faith. Fundamentalists have proved themselves to be particularly adept at utilizing technology, particular communications technology, to their own ends. From the invention of radio to the development of syndicated television broadcasting, fundamentalists have dominated the use of the airwaves for religious broadcasting in the United States. They have also succeeded in developing a significant global presence. In terms of sheer volume, the four major international religious broadcasting organizations transmit more hours per week in more languages than the BBC, Radio Moscow, and the Voice of America together (Hadden 1990, p. 162).

The American Academy of Arts and Sciences launched the most ambitious comparative study of fundamentalism to date in 1987 with a substantial grant from the John D. and Catherine T. MacArthur Foundation. Over a period of five years, the Fundamentalism Project, led by historian Martin E. Marty, brought together scholars of religion from around the world to prepare studies of groups that have been identified as fundamentalist.

This project was important for several reasons. First, it both encouraged a large number of scholars to study the phenomenon seriously, and provided resources for them to do so. Second, by bringing these scholars together to critique one another's work, the project significantly leavened the individual and collective intellectual products. Third, the monumental five-volume work published by the University of Chicago Press, with over one hundred research papers, constitutes an enormous repository of information about fundamentalist and fundamentalist-like groups in every major faith tradition around the world. (See Marty and Appleby 1991, 1993a, 1993b, 1994, 1995.)

The one major fault of this otherwise marvelous inquiry into the nature and scope of fundamentalism is that the leadership early made a strategic decision not to define the subject matter. From the onset, project leaders spoke of *family resemblances*. If a group shared some family resemblances, it was an appropriate group for investigation. This strategy served to avoid long debates that would most certainly have ensued among scholars from many disciplines, cultures, and faith traditions. But in the end, the family resemblances became a proxy for a definition. The proxy, in turn, became a typology that suffers the same conceptual flaw as the *church-sect* typology—the indiscriminate mixing of correlates with attributes in a definition (Stark and Bainbridge 1979).

A serious result of this study design flaw is an inability to differentiate between fundamentalism and that which is not fundamentalism. The implications of the flaw become evident when, for example, one seeks to differentiate between fundamentalist and nationalist movements. This criticism notwithstanding, the Fundamentalism Project has given an enormous boost to an understanding of the nature, origins, and scope of a phenomenon that has been substantially shrouded in misunderstanding for almost a century. Clearly, this is a fine example of scholarly inquiry into the study of religious movements moving in the right direction. Further, the raw data in the form of five volumes of published papers is a valuable resource for others to use in advancing understanding of fundamentalism.

EMERGING THEORETICAL UNDERSTANDING OF RELIGIOUS MOVEMENTS

During the last two decades of the twentieth century, the study of religious movement became the cutting edge in the development of sociological theory about religion. To understand how and why this occurred, it necessary to back track just a bit to explore the development of the sociology of religion during the century.

For the better part of the twentieth century, the sociology of religion was presaged by the classic writings by the founding generation of social science: Emile Durkheim, Sigmund Freud, William James, Bronislaw Malinowski, Karl Marx,

Max Weber, and a few other notables. By midcentury, the advent of survey research added a new dimension of interest in studying religion. Much of this work could be characterized as applied, not very theoretical, and conducted by nonacademic scholars. In the academy, scholars of religions studied the classics with an eye toward fine-tuning the founding fathers' brilliance, or aligning their own work with classic writings.

In 1973 Charles Y. Glock and Phillip Hammond, working under the imprimatur of the Society for the Scientific Study of Religion, published a volume of essays entitled *Beyond the Classics?* The question mark in the title of this stock-taking volume reveals the negative conclusion—social scientists had not moved much beyond the classic statements about religion.

Insofar as their perceptions of religion were concerned, the classic scholars held highly variable views, but they tended toward a common assessment of the future of religion. The prospects of religion against the rising tide of rational thought, science, and modernity were highly precarious. *Secularization theory* was a template laid over the work of the classicists to explain the fate of religion. In a phrase, secularization is the process whereby human cultures and institutions are loosed from ecclesiastical dominance.

From the perspective of secularization theory, the concept *religious movement* almost has the quality of an oxymoron. Many scholars who studied modernization during the second third of the century viewed religious movements as a kind of "residual noise" that had no relevance to the main currents of social change. Anthropologists frequently viewed religion as a prime mover in the formation of "revitalization movements," but the evidence of their case studies pointed to less than felicitous conclusions for aborigines; that is, in the end, modern cultures triumph over "primitive cultures." And modern culture is secular. If religion is moving toward extinction, the study of this phenomenon is less interesting than if it were perceived to have a buoyant quality in the face of dynamic new ways of understanding the world and the human condition.

Beginning in the 1960s, several factors would serve to point intellectual thought in the sociology of religion away from the presuppositions of secularization theory. First, those who studied the civil rights movement, and the human rights movements that quickly followed, could hardly ignore the role of religion both in leadership roles and as a force that legitimated movement activity. Second, the youth counterculture of the late 1960s began with young people's "freaking out" on drugs and then came to a conclusion with many of those same youths' "freaking out" on Jesus, or some guru from Asia. Third, the power of religion to energize large communities of people became increasingly evident in the late 1970s and early 1980s with the coincidence of a renewed fundamentalist political movement in the United States, and the politicized Muslim youth in Iran. Once scholars began to focus their attention beyond the United States, the presence of religious movements on every continent and in every faith tradition became increasingly clear.

Each of these developments drew the attention of scholars who found resources to investigate the phenomenon. In differing ways, each of these developments called attention to the incongruity of religion as a dynamic and vital force in culture and the inherited legacy of secularization theory that had long ago sentenced religion to extinction. If religion is dead, or about to slip into a comatose condition, why are religious movements thriving everywhere scholars turn?

In the discipline of sociology, more persons gravitated to the study of new religious (generative) movements then any of the other movements. Many scholars began their inquiries much as anthropologists might pursue ethnography, but soon they were engaged in comparative work, and looking at the history of new religions in the United States during the nineteenth century. Eventually the scholars of new religious movements would see the discordant implications of their work for secularization theory.

As noted in the conclusion to the first part of this essay, Warner has argued that the sociology of religion is in the midst of a process of ferment that he characterizes as a "paradigm shift." His argument is framed in Thomas Kuhn's classic statement, *The Structure of Scientific Revolutions* (1962). The accumulation of anomalous findings to the prevailing theory has mounted to the point of producing an intellectual crisis. Defenders of the old paradigm rally to shore up their position, while new evidence accumulates that simply cannot be incorporated.

The tone of Warner's unrelenting presentation of evidence in support of a new paradigm appears early in his forty-page essay:

The emerging paradigm begins with the theoretical reflection on a fact of U.S. history highly inconvenient to secularization theory: the proportion of the population enrolled in churches grew hugely throughout the 19th century and the first half of the 20th century, which, by any measures, were times of rapid modernization. (1993, pp. 1048–1049)

Warner draws heavily on historians who collectively have accumulated enormous evidence that demonstrates American religious history simply does not fit the secularization model. Warner finds an explanation for this in the historical fact of *disestablishment*, that is, the separation of church and state in the American Constitution. By protecting the institutionalization of religion, but protecting no religion in particular, the Constitution creates an environment in which religions can compete and, thus, thrive and grow, or atrophy and die. Sociologically speaking, the Constitution legitimated a social structure in which *pluralism* is not only permitted but also encouraged. Whereas religious monopolies discourage the expansion of religion, pluralism promotes the growth of religion.

Warner is cautious in not making his claim for a paradigm shift beyond the U.S. boundaries, but his limiting of the argument to the United States seems clearly to be overly cautious (Hadden, 1995). The role of disestablishment in promoting the growth of religion is important in the case of the United States, and Warner's argument can be fully incorporated into a larger framework of a global paradigm.

Over the past two decades, the seminal work of Rodney Stark and his colleagues has galvanized the study of religious movements and contributed almost immeasurably to the development of the new paradigm that Warner invisions. As the senior scholar in the enterprise, Stark has surrounded himself with a group of exceptionally able collaborators. Together they have developed a theory, identified a research agenda, pursued that research agenda vigorously, and inspired others who have joined the task of building a new model for understanding religion.

For almost a decade, Stark's principal collaborator was William Sims Bainbridge. Stark and Bainbridge's work together began in 1979 with an article that bore a modest subtitle, "Preliminary Concepts for a Theory of Religious Movements." In this paper they identified and defined key concepts for the study of religious movements. They then proceeded to fill in details with more than twenty published papers over the next five years. These papers were published together in 1985 under the title *The Future of Religion*. Two years later Stark and Bainbridge published *A Theory of Religion* (1987), a work of monumental importance. *A Theory of Religion* goes beyond religious movements to provide a comprehensive theory that accounts for the origins, dynamics, and persistence of religions in human cultures. Beginning with six axioms, these authors deductively create more than a hundred definitions and nearly three hundred and fifty propositions.

The theory has sweeping implications for an understanding of religion in the modern world. First, the theory deduces why religion must necessarily be ubiquitous in human cultures. Second, religious institutions are human constructions and, thus, subject to constant change. Third, religious movements are the principal mechanism through which religious change occurs. Hence, *if religious are constantly in flux, and religious movements constitute the principal mechanism for change, it follows that the core focus of inquiry for social science is the study of religious movements.*

The theory is clearly inspired by *rational choice theory*. Stark's collaborations with Roger Finke, a sociologist, and Lawrence Iannaccone, an economist, are especially rich with concepts and imagery from economics. They speak of a *religious economy* as embracing all the religious activity of a given culture, and they work comfortably with concepts like *markets, niches, supply-side religion, monopoly,* and *competition*. Still, both Stark and Bainbridge vigorously object to the criticism that the paradigm is "nothing more" than a wholesale borrowing from economics and rational choice theory. (See Bainbridge 1997, pp. 350–356; Stark and Finke 2000).

As of the writing of this essay, the new paradigm lacked a name and, hence, the reference to the "new paradigm." Rational choice theory has emerged as a significant development within American sociology. The American Sociological Association now has a rational choice section, and there is a journal entitled *Rationality and Society*. This perspective has also been referred to as the "theory of religious economy," but this too implies a narrower perspective than either Stark or Bainbridge wishes to communicate. In 1994 Lawrence Young, of Brigham Young University, convened a conference on "Rational Choice Theory and Religion," at which the principal contributors to the "new paradigm" were participants. Stark's own reservations to the name "rational choice theory" are communicated in his opening essay to the proceedings, entitled "Bringing Theory Back In." His concluding remark captures his commitment to follow theory wherever it may lead to fruitful insights: "My goal is to bring real theories into sociology, not to found a new theoretical sect."

Rejecting the names "rational choice theory" and "theory of religious economy" would appear to be a wise strategy, at least for the present time. Many scholars who are presently studying religious movements would also reject the identification of their work with either of these names. Still, a very large proportion of the emerging scholarship about religious movements is informed by and also adds credence to the emerging new paradigm. For a more detailed examination of this literature, and an annotated bibliography of religious movements studies that are informed by the new paradigm, see Hadden's Religious Movements Homepage on the Internet, http://www.religiousmovements.org (1999). To locate these materials, go to the front page and search on "new paradigm bibliography."

REFERENCES

Bainbridge, William S. 1997 *The Sociology of Religious Movements*. New York: Routledge.

Bromley, David G., and Jeffrey K. Hadden, eds. 1993 *Handbook of Cults and Sects in America*, 2 vols. Greenwich, Conn.: JAI.

Carpenter, Joel A. 1997 *Revive Us Again: The Reawakening of American Fundamentalism*. New York: Oxford University Press.

Cohn, Norman 1970 *The Pursuit of the Millennium*. New York: Oxford University Press.

Finke, Roger, and Rodney Stark 1992 *The Churching of America: 1776–1990.* New Brunswick, N.J.: Rutgers University Press.

Glock, Charles Y., and Phillip E. Hammond, eds. 1973 *Beyond the Classics?* New York: Harper and Row.

Hadden, Jeffrey K. 1980 "Religion and the Construction of Social Problems." *Sociological Analysis* 41:99–108.

—— 1990 "Precursors to the Globalization of American Televangelism." *Social Compass* 37:161–167.

—— 1995 "Religion and the Quest for Meaning and Order: Old Paradigms, New Realities." *Sociological Focus* 28:1(February):83–100.

—— 1999 "Annotated Bibliography of 'New Paradigm' Research in the Sociology of Religion." Religious Movements Homepage. University of Virginia. http://www.religiousmovements.org. Search on "new paradigm bibliography" to access.

——, and Charles E. Swann 1981 *Prime Time Preachers.* Reading, Mass.: Addison-Wesley.

Kuhn, Thomas S. 1962 *The Structures of Scientific Revolutions.* Chicago: University of Chicago Press.

La Barre, Weston 1972 *The Ghost Dance.* New York: Delta.

Lanternari, Vittorio 1965 *The Religions of the Oppressed.* New York: Mentor Books.

Lawrence, Bruce B. 1989 *Defenders of God.* San Francisco: Harper and Row.

Marsden, George M. 1980 *Fundamentalism and American Culture.* New York: Oxford University Press.

Marty, Martin E., and R. Scott Appleby, eds. 1991 *Fundamentalism Observed. The Fundamentalism Project*, vol. 1. Chicago: University of Chicago Press.

——, eds. 1993a *Fundamentalisms and Society. The Fundamentalism Project*, vol. 2. Chicago: University of Chicago Press.

——, eds. 1993b *Fundamentalisms and the State. The Fundamentalism Project*, vol. 3. Chicago: University of Chicago Press.

——, eds. 1994 *Accounting for Fundamentalisms. The Fundamentalism Project*, vol. 4. Chicago: University of Chicago Press.

——, eds. 1995 *Fundamentalism Comprehended. The Fundamentalism Project*, vol. 5. Chicago: University of Chicago Press.

Melton, J. Gordon 1996 *The Encyclopedia of American Religions*, 5th ed. Detroit, Mich.: Gale Research.

Robbins, Thomas 1988 *Cults, Converts and Charisma.* Newbury Park, Calif.: Sage.

Shupe, Anson, and Jeffrey K. Hadden 1989 "Is There Such a Thing as Global Fundamentalism?" In Jeffrey

K. Hadden and Anson Shupe, eds., *Secularization and Fundamentalism Reconsidered. Religion and the Political Order*, vol. 3. New York: Paragon House.

Smith, Christian 1998 *American Evangelicalism: Embattled and Thriving.* Chicago: University of Chicago Press.

Stark, Rodney 1987 "How New Religions Succeed: A Theoretical Model." In David G. Bromley and Phillip E. Hammond, eds., *The Future of New Religious Movements.* Macon, Ga.: Mercer University Press.

——, and William Sims Bainbridge 1979 "Of Churches, Sects, and Cults: Preliminary Concepts for a Theory of Religious Movements," *Journal for the Scientific Study of Religion* 18:2(June):117–131.

——, 1985 *The Future of Religion.* Berkeley: University of California Press.

——, (1987) 1996 *A Theory of Religion.* New Brunswick, N.J.: Rutgers University Press.

——, and Roger Finke 2000 *The Human Side of Religion.* Berkeley: University of California Press.

Wallace, Anthony F. C. 1966 *Religion: An Anthropological View.* New York: Random House.

Warner, Stephen 1993 "Work in Progress Toward a New Paradigm for the Sociological Study of Religion in the United States." *American Journal of Sociology* 98(March):1044–1093.

Young, Lawrence A. (ed.) 1997 *Rational Choice Theory and Religion.* New York: Routledge.

JEFFREY K. HADDEN

RELIGIOUS ORGANIZATIONS

The social organization of religion in the United States is diverse and complex. Most religious organizations are local churches (congregations, parishes, synagogues) tied to national religious bodies (usually referred to as denominations). The *Yearbook of American and Canadian Churches* lists 189 denominations in the United States with a total of almost 360,000 churches. The membership reported by these churches equals almost 58 percent of the U.S. population (Lindner 1999). The largest denominations are the Roman Catholic Church (61,207,914 members in 1996), the Southern Baptist Convention (15,891,514 members in 1997), and The United Methodist Church (8,496,047 members in 1996). Most denominations are quite small. In all, the twenty-one denominations with membership in excess of one million members account for more than 140,000,000 members—about 91 percent of all church members in the United States. In contrast, the seventy-seven denominations with fewer than 25,000 members account for about 586,000 members, fewer than one-half of 1 percent of church members (figures calculated from information in Lindner 1999).

Typically, local churches hold worship services at least once a week and also have educational activities, especially for children and youths. Most churches organize various groups within the church to accomplish particular tasks (for example, missions, evangelism, or community action), or for the association of persons with common interests (such as women, youths, or senior citizens). Women's groups are especially active. Many churches serve as community centers providing space for meetings of all sorts of neighborhood and community organizations. Ammerman's recent work (1997) shows the crucial role churches play in their communities. "Not only are they linked to other parts of the community through the multiple memberships and loyalties of their members, but they are also linked *as organizations* to larger organizational networks" (p. 360) that pursue community-based goals.

Local churches usually have a pastor (or a priest or rabbi) and a lay governing board. There is great variation from denomination to denomination on the authority of lay boards, and, within denominations, there is variation from church to church in informal power. Research has shown that control by inner circles of informal leaders is likely to emerge when formal mechanisms of control and official leaders are not performing effectively (Hougland and Wood 1979).

The degree of control of the denomination over the local church depends in large part upon the polity, or political structure, of the denomination. Students of religious organizations place denominations in three categories according to polity. *Congregational* polity is the weakest. In this polity the local church owns its own property and hires and fires its own pastor. In contrast, in a *hierarchical* (often *episcopal*) polity the national (or regional) body holds title to the property and controls the placement of pastors. An in-between category is often called *presbyterial*. There are a number of correlates of polity. For example, denominations with strong polities were more active

supporters of the civil rights movement and more aggressively pressed for the integration of their churches (Wood 1981).

Denominational polities continue to evolve as they adapt to changing social environments (Dykstra and Hudnut-Beumler 1992). Recent years have seen a growth in the influence of local congregations—with a concomitant gain in local control—even within the most hierarchical polities. Given the communications revolution, which allows the almost instant dissemination of information throughout the church, this trend toward local control is congruent with Michels' argument (1962) that leaders' control of information is a principal basis of hierarchical control. A major study being conducted by researchers at Hartford Seminary, "Organizing Religious Work for the 21st Century," will provide massive data for the understanding of how denominational polities are adapting to their changing environments.

Though the organization of Jewish synagogues is similar to that of many Protestant churches in the United States, the Jewish perspective on religious organization is somewhat different. In 1987 the officials of the congregational organizations of the Orthodox, Conservative, and Reform branches of Judaism reported 3,750,000 persons associated with their synagogues and temples. However, there are approximately six million Jews, who are seen as an ethnic, social, and religious community (Jacquet 1989, pp. 243–244). Daniel Elazar stresses that Jews see no meaningful line of separation between "churchly" purposes and other communal need, and hence Jewish organizations are not neatly divided into religious and nonreligious ones. "It is *not simply* association with a *synagogue* that enables a Jew to become part of the organized Jewish community. Affiliation with *any of a whole range of organizations*, ranging from clearly philanthropic groups to 'secularist' cultural societies, offers the same option" (Elazar 1980, p. 133). Elazar argues that local Jewish federations for welfare, educational, and cultural activities should be seen as religious organizations (p. 133).

RELIGIOUS ORGANIZATIONS IN SOCIOLOGICAL CONTEXT

Religious organizations provide patterns for the interaction of religious individuals. Social forces change these patterns, but in turn, the collective action of religious people influences society. Sociologists looking at religious organizations have been interested especially in their importance as plausibility structures that foster specific beliefs and values (Berger 1967) and as structures of action that mobilize people to seek social change.

Until the 1970s the sociological approach to religious organizations was guided primarily by the church-sect typology. This theoretical framework helped to explain the number and variety of religious bodies and differences in their behaviors by reference to the social class of their adherents. Max Weber distinguished between a church, a continuously operating rational, compulsory association that claims a monopolistic authority, and a sect, "a voluntary association [that] admits only persons with specific religious qualifications" (Weber 1978, p. 56). "One becomes a member of the church by birth . . . [but a] sect . . . makes membership conditional upon a contractual entry into some particular congregation" (p. 456). Weber's student, Ernst Troeltsch (1961), developed a typology from these concepts and some variation of the church-sect typology has been used repeatedly in studying U.S. religious organizations.

In the Weberian tradition, H. Richard Niebuhr stressed the sociological sources of sect formation and the way in which social forces tended to turn sects into churches. He argued that sects originate "in the religious revolts of the poor, of those who were without effective representation in church or state" (1954, p. 19) and who employed a democratic, associational pattern in pursuing their dissent because it was the only way open to them. Niebuhr observed that the pure sectarian character of organization seldom lasts more than one generation. As children are born to the voluntary members of the first generation,

> *the sect must take on the character of an educational and disciplinary institution, with the purpose of bringing the new generation into conformity with ideals and customs which have become traditional. Rarely does a second generation hold the convictions it has inherited with a fervor equal to that of its fathers, who fashioned these convictions in the heat of conflict and at the risk of martyrdom. As generation succeeds generation, the isolation of*

> *the community from the world becomes more difficult. Furthermore, wealth frequently increases when the sect subjects itself to the discipline of asceticism in work and expenditure; with the increase of wealth the possibilities for culture also become more numerous and involvement in the economic life of the nation as a whole can less easily be limited.* (Niebuhr 1954, pp. 19–20).

Nancy Ammerman's work continues the research tradition that relates the evolution of churches to social class backgrounds. Ammerman traces the rise of fundamentalism in the Southern Baptist Convention to the erosion of cultural support for traditional beliefs. She finds that fundamentalism decreases with increased levels of education and with increased levels of income. But "many at the edges of this transition are likely to respond by embracing fundamentalist beliefs more vigorously than ever (Ammerman 1986, p. 487).

According to James Beckford, "The question of the degree to which any particular organisation was church-like or sect-like was taken seriously for what it implied about that organisation's capacity to survive in the modern world" (1984, p. 85). The church-sect theorizing was dominated by considerations of rationalization and compromise. Beckford detected a shift in the focus of sociologists studying religious organizations in the 1970s toward "the capacity of religious organisations to foster a sense of personal authenticity, conviction and self-identity" (p. 85). The 1970s saw a great many studies about recruitment and mobilization by religious organizations. Many of these studies focused on the growth and decline of traditional organizations, but many others dealt with religious movements that were new, or at least new upon the U.S. scene. Beckford refers to a number of authors who have found that cultlike formations are appropriate to an age marked by rationalization, bureaucratization, and privatization. That is, small groups of people cultivating esoteric religion in private are flexible and adaptable to the conditions of highly mobile and rapidly changing societies. Some of these scholars have linked cults' ability to inspire and mobilize their members to their distinctive forms of organization.

In recent years more emphasis is placed on applying general organization theory to religious organizations. Many recent studies of religious organizations are characterized by an open-systems approach, which views organizations as adaptive organisms in a threatening environment (Scherer 1980). The questions of adaptability to the modern world and of inspiration and mobilization of followers come together in studies of the Roman Catholic Church. John Seidler and Katherine Meyer (1989) examine that denomination's accommodations to the modern world, many of which involve important structural changes, such as priest's councils, and other changes that allowed both priests and lay people to have more say in the operation of the church.

A relatively new theoretical perspective within the sociology of organizations and social movements—resource mobilization—has illuminated much of the current scene of new religious movements. Bromley and Shupe did a detailed resource mobilization analysis of the Unification Church. They argue that one key element in the church's establishment in the United States was the development of mobile fund-raising teams (1979).

CURRENT ISSUES

A more varied theoretical approach to religious organizations has allowed scholars to focus on different kinds of issues. A major concern has been the decline of the liberal mainline denominations and the significance of that decline (Roof and McKinney 1987; Hoge and Roozen 1979). The liberal mainline churches in the United States share with other churches in a vast mobilization of voluntary time and money in activities caring for individuals such as the poor, the sick, and the elderly. Churches are particularly effective at such mobilization because they instill philanthropic values and present information and opportunities for philanthropic activities in face-to-face settings such as worship services and Sunday School classes. The liberal churches have played the additional role of implementing socially liberal policies, that is, policies designed to change the structure of society so that, for example, income as well as opportunities for individual achievement are more widely distributed throughout society. The liberal social agenda also includes sharp criticism of the U.S. government's role as promoter of U.S. business interests abroad. Mobilizing individuals and

groups to press for the acceptance and implementation of a liberal social agenda may be these churches' most significant contribution to U.S. society (Wood 1990).

Social and cultural changes in the United States in the last three decades have led to important changes in most traditional denominations and to the decline of membership and resources in many of them. At the same time, a new form of religious organization—the megachurch—has spread rapidly. These large (usually having at least 2,000 members), multiservice congregations are rarely affiliated with any denomination. However, megachurches are often associated with one another in networks that provide some of the services that denominations provide their member churches. In the twenty-first century, megachuches and their networks continue to provide significant competition for denominations. Yet these churches are themselves not immune to social and cultural change. Already there are reports that some of the leading megachurches are finding it necessary to make major changes in their programs to attract post–baby boomers (Jorstad 1999).

Another issue related to denominational polity is the role of women in the ministry. Chaves (1997) argues convincingly that the great variability in denominations' approval of women's ordination can be explained as responses to the denominations' significant social environments.

In an era of rapid social and cultural change, religious organizations play a crucial role in the process of consensus formation in our society. Amitai Etzioni (1968) argues that a healthy society is one in which the relationship between citizens and national leaders is mediated by a large network of groups and organizations where multiple perspectives are reduced toward consensus. The effect of any direct appeal by national leaders or by mass media campaigns to individual citizens is determined largely by the multiple membership of the citizens in groups and organizations. This mediation protects against mass emotional manipulation. At the national level the many "legislatures" within the major religious bodies in this country are of enormous importance in shaping the working consensus that enables both the formulation and the implementation of national policies. The representative selection procedures for national meetings and the deliberative consensus formation processes typical of the major denominations are an important contribution to informed public opinion in U.S. society.

At the local level, congregations provide forums in which differing opinions can be expressed in a context of mutual respect. David Knoke and James Wood (1981) show that a wide variety of nonreligious social influence associations did not attract people with views as diverse as those in the church. They suggest that "in most of these organizations, policy-dissatisfied members probably do not feel the social pressure to remain in the organization comparable to that felt by dissatisfied church members" (p. 103). Churches' multiple goals and their emotional and value ties provide holding power that keeps members with different views together in the same church. Voluntary associations in which individuals can debate the critical issues face to face encourage individuals to act out their selfless values rather than their selfish interests, and provide a bulwark against the manipulation of the public by computer-generated direct mailing and mass media campaigns for a particular group's vested interest in ideology, money, or power.

Wood (2000) argues that the consensus formation process described above is contributing to the resolution of the issue of homosexuality, one of the most controversial social issues in church and society today.

OTHER RELIGIOUS ORGANIZATIONS

Robert Wuthnow (1988) has described the rise of numerous special-purpose organizations that are rooted in religion, drawing legitimation and resources from the more traditional religious organizations but with the objective of achieving a quite specific purpose.

These organizations provide new options for religious people in addition to participation in local churches. A wide variety of purposes are pursued, including the advancement of nuclear disarmament and meeting the spiritual needs of senior citizens. Wuthnow suggests that "as far as the society as a whole is concerned, these organizations may be the ones that increasingly define the public role of American religion. Rather than

religion's weight being felt through the pressure of denominations, it may be exercised through the more focused efforts of the hundreds of special-purpose groups now in operation" (1988, p. 121). Though these special-purpose groups are in many ways a revitalizing influence on traditional religious organizations (denominations and local churches), they may also have important sociological implications. For example, while the traditional organizations have often held together people of diverse social backgrounds, special-purpose groups may have a tendency toward homogeneity.

There are also a number of important umbrella organizations, such as the National Council of Churches and the National Association of Evangelicals, that facilitate the cooperation of sets of denominations. The National Council of Churches was particularly important in mobilizing a segment of the church population into the civil rights movement (Wood 1972). There has also been a growth of community councils of churches.

NEW RELIGIOUS ORGANIZATIONS

In recent years a number of the religious organizations have been in the news are unrelated either to the Judaeo-Christian heritage or to immigrant groups. They draw their adherents largely from the broad center of the U.S. middle class. Robert Ellwood and Harry Partin (1988) discuss more than forty of these groups. None of them are very large and in most of them most of their members remain affiliated for less than a year. Perhaps their greatest importance from the sociological perspective is that they introduce new organizational models into the U.S. scene.

THE FUTURE

New immigrant people are bringing their religions with them to the United States. Islam in particular is growing rapidly. People in the United States may have to start thinking of themselves as a Protestant, Catholic, Jewish, *Islamic* nation. According to one source, in 1973 there were fifteen or twenty local centers of Muslim worship in the United States; by 1980 these centers were reported in all of the three hundred largest cities in the United States. Two million adherents were reported in 1980; at the end of the century most authorities estimate that there are between three and four million Muslims in the United states (some estimates go as high as six million). Most Islamic organizations in the United States are local centers (variously called Islamic Societies, Islamic Centers, or Muslim Mosques). Each of these organizations provides a place of worship and a place for other religious, social, and educational activities. Islam does not have an organized hierarchy, but several regional and national groups help to coordinate the work of local groups and promote unity among them (Jacquet 1989). If, as Elazar contends, many Jewish organizations in addition to the synagogue play a religious role, in Islam it appears that the religious centers play many roles in addition to the religious one. Perhaps this is always the case with the churches of recent immigrants.

Stark and Bainbridge (1985) say that traditionally organized religion may decline drastically as more and more people pursue individualistic "careers" of going from one self-enhancement group to another. If they are correct, any societal influence of religious organizations would be felt more through influence on individuals than through collective action of large religious bodies. However, there is much evidence that the traditional structure of religious organization in the United States will persist in the twenty-first century.

REFERENCES

Ammerman, Nancy T. 1986 "The New South and the New Baptists." *The Christian Century* (May 14):486–488.

—— 1997 *Congregation and Community*. New Brunswick, N.J.: Rutgers University Press.

Beckford, James A. 1984 "Religious Organisation: A Survey of Some Recent Publications." *Archives de Sciences Sociales Des Religions* 57:83–102.

Berger, Peter L. Sector 1967. *The Sacred Canopy* Garden City, N.Y.: Doubleday.

Bromley, David G., and Anson D. Shupe, Jr. 1979 *"Moonies" in America: Cult, Church, and Crusade*. Beverly Hills, Calif.: Sage.

Chaves, Mark 1997 *Ordaining Women: Culture and Conflict in Religious Organizations*. Cambridge, Mass.: Harvard University Press.

Dykstra, Craig, and James Hudnut-Beumler 1992 "The National Organizational Structures of Protestant Denominations: An Invitation to a Conversation." In Milton J. Coalter, John M. Mulder, and Louis B.

Weeks, eds., *The Organizational Revolution: Presbyterians and American Denominationalism*. Louisville, Ky.: Westminster/John Knox.

Elazar, Daniel J. 1980 "Patterns of Jewish Organization in the United States." In Ross P. Scherer, ed., *American Denominational Organization*. Pasadena, Calif.: William Carey Library.

Ellwood, Robert S., and Harry B. Partin 1988 *Religious and Spiritual Groups in Modern America*. Englewood Cliffs, N.J.: Prentice Hall.

Etzioni, Amitai 1968 *The Active Society*. New York: Free Press.

Hoge, Dean R., and David A. Roozen 1979 *Understanding Church Growth and Decline: 1950–1978*. New York: Pilgrim.

Hougland, James G., Jr., and James R. Wood 1979 "'Inner Circles' in Local Churches: An Application of Thompson's Theory." *Sociological Analysis* 40:226–239.

Jacquet, Constant H., Jr. (ed.) 1973, 1980, 1989 *Yearbook of American and Canadian Churches*. Nashville, Tenn.: Abingdon.

Jorstad, Erling 1999 "Megachurch Regrouping after Growth Lull." *Religion Watch* 14:1.

Knoke, David, and James R. Wood 1981 *Organized for Action: Commitment in Voluntary Associations*. New Brunswick, N.J.: Rutgers University Press.

Lindner, Eileen W., ed. 1999 *Yearbook of American and Canadian Churches*. Nashville, Tenn.: Abingdon.

Michels, Robert 1962 *Political Parties*. New York: Free Press.

Niebuhr, Gustav 1998 "American Religion at the Millennium's End." *Word and World* 18(Winter):5–13.

Niebuhr, H. Richard 1954 *The Social Sources of Denominationalism*. Hamden, Conn.: Shoe String.

Roof, Wade Clark, and William McKinney 1987 *American Mainline Religion: Its Changing Shape and Future*. New Brunswick, N.J.: Rutgers University Press.

Scherer, Ross P. 1980 *American Denominational Organization*. Pasadena, Calif.: William Carey Library.

Seidler, John, and Katherine Meyer 1989 *Conflict and Change in the Catholic Church*. New Brunswick, N.J.: Rutgers University Press.

Stark, Rodney, and William S. Bainbridge 1985 *The Future of Religion: Secularization, Revival, and Cult Formation*. Berkeley, Calif.: University of California Press.

Thumma, Scott 1996 "The Kingdom, the Power, and the Glory: Megachurches in Modern American Society." Ph.D. diss., Emory University.

Troeltsch, Ernst 1961 *The Social Teachings of the Christian Churches*. New York: Harper and Row.

Weber, Max 1978 *Economy and Society*, vol. 1. Berkeley: University of California Press.

Wood, James R. 1972 "Unanticipated Consequences of Organizational Coalitions: Ecumenical Cooperation and Civil Rights Policy." *Social Forces* 50:512–521.

—— 1981 *Leadership in Voluntary Organizations: The Controversy over Social Action in Protestant Churches*. New Brunswick, N.J.: Rutgers University Press.

—— 1990 "Liberal Protestant Social Action in a Period of Decline." In Robert Wuthnow and Virginia A. Hodgkinson, eds., *Faith and Philanthropy in America: Exploring the Role of Religion in America's Voluntary Sector*. San Francisco: Jossey-Bass.

—— 2000 *Where the Spirit Leads: The Evolving Views of United Methodists on Homosexuality*. Nashville, Tenn.: Abingdon.

Wuthnow, Robert 1988 *The Restructuring of American Religion: Society and Faith since World War II*. Princeton, N.J.: Princeton University Press.

JAMES R. WOOD

RELIGIOUS ORIENTATIONS

Sociologists generally conceive of religion as a system of symbols that evokes a sense of holistic or transcendent meaning (Bellah 1970, p. 16; Geertz 1973, pp. 90–125). This definition reflects sociology's claim that symbols are essential to the human capacity to experience and interpret reality (Berger and Luckmann 1966). Symbols are acts, objects, utterances, or events that stand for something—that is, that give meaning to something by connecting it to something else. Symbols give order and meaning to life. Without them, life would be experienced as senseless and chaotic. Indeed, research suggests that individuals are able to experience and understand only those aspects of their worlds for which they have symbols (Farb 1973).

Sociologists' emphasis on holistic or transcendent meaning as the defining feature of religion arises from their view that meaning is always contextual (Langer 1951). The meaning of a particular word depends on the other words that form its immediate context. For example, the word "courts" means one thing if it appears with the word "tennis," but something different when the word "justice" or, the word "dating" is present. Similarly, in their daily lives people give meaning to their activities by associating them with various frames of reference. Hitting a tennis ball has meaning, for example, because it is associated with the rules of the game of tennis. Each frame of reference, moreover, has meaning because it can be placed within a more encompassing symbolic context (tennis, say, within the context of physical exercise and health). But if each symbolic framework requires a broader framework to have meaning, then, some form of holistic or transcendent symbol system that embraces all of life must be present. These are what sociologists call religious orientations or religious systems (Berger 1967; Roberts 1984).

The questions that typically invoke religious symbols involve the quest to make life itself meaningful. Such questions arise at the extremities of human existence: Where did I come from? Why am I here? What happens when I die? These questions, framed at the individual level, may also be asked about the collectivity to which one belongs or about humanity in general: How did our tribe originate? Where is humanity headed? Other questions focus on the absolutes or landmarks that make life recognizable in its most basic sense: What is beauty? What is truth? How can we know truth? What is essential about the human condition? There are also questions that arise because the events they deal with make no sense to us on the surface: Why must I die? Why is there suffering in the world? What is the reason for evil?

Transcendent symbol systems address these questions at a variety of levels. Elaborate philosophical and theological doctrines sometimes supply rational answers that satisfy canons of logic and empirical evidence. In daily life these questions are more likely to be addressed through narratives, proverbs, maxims, and ikonic representations rich with experiential connotations. Religious orientations are likely to be structured less by abstract deductive reasoning than by parables that raise questions but leave open precise answers, by personal stories that link experience with wider realities, and by creeds and images that have acquired meaning through long histories of interpretation in human communities (Greeley 1982, pp. 53–70).

Like other symbol systems, religious orientations are thought to be the products of social interaction. Although the role of such factors as divine revelation cannot be ruled out, sociologists focus on the ways in which symbols come to have meaning through the interaction of individuals and groups in human communities. Sometimes these communities invent collective symbols to articulate powerful experiences they may have undergone. More commonly, communities borrow symbols available within their cultural traditions, but then adapt these symbols to their own use, giving them new meanings and interpretations. Communities also underwrite the plausibility of religions belief systems (Berger 1967, p. 45). They do so by providing evidence that such beliefs are not the product of individual imaginations alone, by encouraging the public expression of beliefs, and by creating occasions on which beliefs may be enacted and predictions fulfilled. Without the ongoing interaction of people in communities, it is doubtful whether belief systems could long be sustained. Research has also demonstrated that personal religious orientations are more likely to have behavioral consequences if these orientations are supported by communities of like-minded individuals (Roof 1978).

In defining religion as a symbol system that deals with ultimate questions, sociologists assume that humans have the capacity to question their experience and a desire to make sense of their worlds. Whether all people pursue this desire with equal intensity is more doubtful. It is possible, for example, to explain a plane crash by observing that a rivet came loose. It is also possible to let the incident raise questions about the meaning of pain, the frailty of human existence, or the meaning and purpose of one's own life. How much the quest for holistic meaning and transcendence enters into people's lives is, therefore, a matter of variation. Studies indicate that most people say they have thought about the meaning and purpose of life, but individuals vary in the extent to which they have been troubled by this issue. They also vary in the amount of explicit attention they have devoted to it and in their views about the possibility of arriving at definite answers (Stark and Glock 1968, p. 77). Agnosticism, for example, is a religious orientation that grants the importance of ultimate questions about meaning and purpose but denies the possibility of finding answers to these questions.

The kinds of symbols that come into play in relation to such questions are also matters of variation. While all such symbol systems may perform functionally similar roles, it is useful to distinguish them substantively. These substantive distinctions are usually the basis on which religious orientations are delineated in popular discourse. At the broadest level, sociologists distinguish theistic meaning systems, which recognize the existence of a God or divine being, from atheistic systems, which do not acknowledge a divine being (Glock and Stark 1965, pp. 3–17). Christianity is an example of the former; Marxism, of the latter. Insofar as it addresses the same higher-order questions about the meaning of life, Marxism would be considered functionally similar to Christianity. But this does not mean that Marxism necessarily functions this way. Just as one might study Marxism to derive economic principles, so one might study Christianity simply as an example of literature. In neither case would it be appropriate to say that a religious orientation is at work. Only as they function to evoke holistic meaning and transcendence do symbol systems become religious orientations.

The distinction between theistic and atheistic meaning systems is useful when the relevant concept is the presence or absence of a divine entity. But this distinction may be less useful in other contexts. For example, contemporary discussions in theology and in science sometimes distinguish religious orientations on the basis of whether they posit a reality that is humanly knowable or ultimately mysterious, whether reality is empirical or includes a supraempirical dimension, or whether being implies something that is not being itself but the ground of being. In these debates the boundary between varieties of ultimate meaning systems is often ambiguous.

In contemporary societies religious orientations are often distinguished in popular belief according to the dominant force or power that people perceive as governing their lives (Wuthnow 1976). Some people may conceive of this force as God; others, as luck or fate. Natural or human causes may also be considered dominant; for example, the force of heredity, of scientific law, society, or individual willpower. Whether a part of elaborate philosophical systems or simple pieces of folk wisdom, such understandings help people to make sense of their lives by identifying the causal agents that control human events.

Sociologists have insisted that religious orientations become important to the study of human behavior insofar as these orientations are internalized as part of the individual's worldview. A worldview can be defined as a person's guiding outlook on life. The essential aspects of a religious orientation are the person's beliefs and assumptions about the meaning of life and such matters as the existence and nature of God, goodness and evil, life beyond death, truth, and the human condition. These beliefs and assumptions help the individual make sense of life cognitively. They also have an emotional dimension, perhaps including a feeling of awe, reverence, fear, or peace, comfort, and security. In addition, they are regarded as behavioral predispositions that lead to various actions, each as participation in worship, prayer, or ethical decisions (Spilka et al. 1985).

The importance of religious orientations for ethical decisions has been of longstanding interest to sociologists. In the classical work of Max Weber (1963), religious orientations were conceived of as symbolic frameworks that made sense of the world, in part, by providing explanations for the existence of evil (also known as theodicies). Some religious orientations, for example, explained evil as a struggle between God and the devil, others saw evil as part of a cycle of regeneration and renewal, while still others attributed evil to the workings of an all-powerful but inscrutable deity. The implications for ethical action derived from the prescriptions for salvation implied by these different conceptions of evil. In one tradition, for example, people might be expected to pray and meditate in order to escape from the cycle of evil and regeneration; in another tradition, they might be expected to do good deeds as a way of siding with the forces of good against those of evil.

Much of the research by sociologists on religious orientations has dealt with their subjective aspects (Blasi and Cuneo 1986). Assuming that the important feature of symbolism is its meaning, researchers have tried to discover what religious symbols mean to individuals. Efforts have been made to tap the deeper predispositions presumed to underlie such religious expressions as prayer and worship, to say how deeply implanted the religious impulse is, and to classify varieties of religious outlooks and experiences.

Recent developments in sociological theory have resulted in some rethinking of this emphasis on subjective religiosity. Current research is beginning to focus more on the observable manifestations of religious symbolism itself, rather than claiming to know what lies beneath the surface in the subjective consciousness of the individual (Wuthnow 1987). Discourse, language, gesture, and ritual have become more important in their own right (Tipton 1982). The contrast between this and the earlier approach can be illustrated by comparing two statements: "I believe God exists" and "God speaks to us through the Word." A subjective approach would treat both statements as manifestations of some inner conviction of the individual. The more recent approach would pay closer attention to the language itself, noting, for example, the more personalized style of the first statement and the collective reference contained in the second.

The value of the more recent approach is that it recognizes the public or social dimension of religious orientations. Observers may not know what goes on in the dark recesses of the believer's soul. But if that person tells a story, or participates in worship, the researcher can then study the observable manifestations of that person's faith.

To account for variations in religious orientations, sociologists usually look at the social conditions to which people are exposed. They assume that most people do not make up their own religions from scratch. Rather, they borrow from the various symbol systems that are available in their environment. The most significant borrowing occurs in early childhood. Family is thus an important factor, and it, in turn, is influenced by broader conditions such as social class, levels of education, race and ethnicity, and exposure to regional subcultures.

A generation ago, sociologists often held the view that scientific generalizations could be made about the relationships between social factors and religious orientations. For example, much work was inspired by the hypothesis that theistic religious orientations were more common among persons with lower levels of education than among persons in better-educated social strata. Another common hypothesis suggested that religious orientations were likely to be associated with various kinds of social deprivation, since the deprived would presumably seek solace in otherworldly beliefs. Empirical studies have found some support for such hypotheses, but the ability to make generalizations has remained limited. Different relationships seem to be present in different communities and in different time periods.

More attention has turned in recent years, therefore, toward describing the rich and complex processes by which religious orientations and social environments intermingle. In one setting people without college educations may turn to religious views that shield them from the uncertainties of science and other modern ideas. In another setting people with high levels of education may also turn to religion, but do so in a way that combines ideas from science and Scripture or that focuses on the therapeutic needs of people working in the professions. In both settings, religious orientations provide answers to ultimate questions. But the composition of these orientations reflects ideas present in the different social settings.

An earlier generation of social theorists also sought to explain the variations in religious orientations in ways that often reduced them to little more than the by-products of social or psychological needs. Sociologists following in the tradition of Karl Marx, for example, regarded religion merely as a reflection of class struggles, while some following Émile Durkheim viewed it as a reflection of the corporate authority of society (Swanson 1960, 1967). The reductionism in these approaches consisted not only of regarding social structure as more basic than religion but also of implying that religion would gradually disappear as people became more aware of its origins (Fenton 1970). Recent work is decidedly less reductionistic in its assumptions about religion. It still assumes that religion fulfills human needs and that it is influenced by social conditions, but regards religion as a more active contributor to human experience and considers its future more viable.

In addition to the more general social conditions that may influence the religious orientations of individuals, sociologists have also been particularly interested in the institutions that devote specific energies to the promulgation of religious orientations. These institutions supply the resources needed for religious orientations to be perpetuated. Leadership, producers of religious knowledge, specialists in the dissemination of such knowledge, organizational skills, physical facilities, and financial resources are all required for religious orientations to be maintained over time. Religious institutions must compete with other institutions, such as governments, businesses, and families, for these resources.

In most modern societies competition is also present among the adherents of various religious orientations (Wuthnow 1988a). When such competition has been recognized either governmentally or culturally, we say that a condition of religious pluralism exists (Silk 1988). Pluralism often becomes a kind of religious orientation itself, imposing norms of civility and tolerance on particularistic religious traditions. When multiple religious orientations are forced to compete with one another, the plausibility of any one such tradition may be diminished as a result of believers' seeing others who hold views different from their own. At the same time, pluralism appears to contribute to the overall vitality of religious orientations in a society by encouraging competition among them for adherents and by giving believers more options from which to choose (Christiano 1987).

It has been common in the past for individuals to choose one particular religious orientation with which to identify. Often these orientations have been defined by religious institutions, such as the Roman Catholic church, or by denominational organizations, such as the Presbyterian or Methodist churches (Greeley 1972). Increasingly, however, it appears that individuals in modern societies are exposed to a variety of religious institutions and orientations. As a result, they may pick and choose particular elements from several different faiths and traditions. Their religious orientation therefore takes on a more personalized character (Bellah et al. 1985, pp. 219–249; Roof and McKinney 1987, pp. 40–71).

Although some individuals work out highly coherent religious orientations that have internal consistency and integrity, it appears that the more common result of living in religiously pluralistic settings is a form of personalized eclecticism. People become heteroglossic—that is, they gain the capacity to speak with many religious voices. Their religious orientations may not provide a guiding philosophy of life that maintains an orderly view of the world. Rather, religious orientations become tool kits (Swidler 1987) assembled from a variety of personal experiences, social contacts, books, sermons, and other cultural repertoires, and from which the individual is able to draw as he or she is confronted with the challenges of life.

At present, research studies indicate that large proportions of the population in societies like the United States hold theistic religious orientations (Wuthnow 1988a). In other societies where religious institutions have had fewer resources in the past, such orientations are less common. In all societies, though, theistic orientations are confronted by the humanistic orientations promulgated by secular institutions. The outcome appears to involve a balance between pressures to adapt, on the one hand, and tendencies by religious adherents to resist these pressures, on the other hand (Hammond 1985; Beckford 1989). Much of the struggle depends on the ability of religious leaders to articulate visions that grow out of particular confessional traditions in ways that appeal to the universalistic norms governing wider social audiences.

Although religious orientations have become more diverse and eclectic as a result of cultural contact and mass communication, evidence also suggests that in some societies a basic polarization has emerged between those whose orientation involves traditionalistic, fundamentalistic, or conservative norms, on one side, and those whose orientation involves progressive, modernistic, or liberal norms, on the other side (Wuthnow 1988a). Conservatives are characterized by adherence to the authority of traditional scriptural texts, while liberals emphasize more the relativity of these texts and the need for reason and experience in interpreting them. Liberal religious orientations have been nurtured by relativistic views in higher education, in the professions, and in the mass media in market-oriented societies, but conservative orientations have grown as well, not only in reaction to liberalism, but also as a result of conservatives gaining educational or political advantages and seizing on opportunities created by the ill effects of rapid societal change (Ammerman 1987; Hunter 1987). Whereas earlier discussions predicted the demise of fundamentalist religious orientations, current studies are more concerned with the ongoing tensions between fundamentalist and more liberal or more humanistic religious orientations.

Research on religious orientations continues to be produced. Fundamentalism and evangelicalism have been examined comparatively and through quantitative studies (Marty and Appleby 1994; Shibley 1996; Smith 1998), and conflicts between fundamentalist or orthodox views and those of liberals or progressives have been examined (Hunter 1991; Wolfe 1997). Other important currents in recent research include studies emphasizing eclecticism, individualism, and instability in contemporary spiritual orientations (Roof 1993), the apparent shift in popular thinking from beliefs rooted in organized religion toward orientations emphasizing personal spirituality (Roof 1999), and the rising importance of spiritual practices in response to uncertainties about formal religious beliefs (Hall 1997; Wuthnow 1998).

(SEE ALSO: *Social Philosophy; Sociology of Religion*)

REFERENCES

Ammerman, Nancy Tatom 1987 *Bible Believers: Fundamentalists in the Modern World*. New Brunswick, N.J.: Rutgers University Press.

Beckford, James A. 1989 *Religion and Advanced Industrial Society*. London: Unwin Hyman.

Bellah, Robert N. 1970 *Beyond Belief: Essays on Religion in a Post-Traditional World*. New York: Harper and Row.

——, Richard Madsen, William M. Sullivan, Ann Swidler, and Steven M. Tipton 1985 *Habits of the Heart: Individualism and Commitment in American Life*. Berkeley: University of California Press.

Berger, Peter L. 1967 *The Sacred Canopy: Elements of a Sociological Theory of Religion*. Garden City, N.Y.: Doubleday.

——, and Thomas Luckmann 1966 *The Social Construction of Reality; A Treatise in the Sociology of Knowledge*. Garden City, N.Y.: Doubleday.

Blasi, Anthony J., and Michael W. Cuneo 1986 *Issues in the Sociology of Religion: A Bibliography*. New York: Garland.

Christiano, Kevin J. 1987 *Religious Diversity and Social Change: American Cities, 1890–1906*. Cambridge, England: Cambridge University Press.

Farb, Peter 1973 *Word Play*. New York: Bantam.

Fenton, John Y. 1970. "Reductionism in the Study of Religion." *Soundings* 53:61–76.

Geertz, Clifford 1973 *The Interpretation of Cultures.* New York: Harper and Row.

Glock, Charles Y., and Rodney Stark 1965 *Religion and Society in Tension.* Chicago: Rand McNally.

Greeley, Andrew M. 1972 *The Denominational Society: A Sociological Approach to Religion in America.* Glenview, Ill.: Scott Foresman.

—— 1982 *Religion: A Secular Theory.* New York: Free Press.

Hall, David D., ed. 1997 *Lived Religion in America: Towards a History of Practice.* Princeton, N.J.: Princeton University Press.

Hammond, Phillip E., ed. 1985 *The Sacred in a Secular Age.* Berkeley: University of California Press.

Hunter, James Davison 1987 *Evangelicalism: The Coming Generation.* Chicago: University of Chicago Press.

—— 1991 *Culture Wars: The Struggle to Define America.* New York: Basic.

Langer, Susanne K. 1951 *Philosophy in a New Key.* New York: Mentor.

Marty, Martin E., and R. Scott Appleby, eds. 1994 *Accounting for Fundamentalisms: The Dynamic Character of Movements.* Chicago: University of Chicago Press.

Roberts, Keith A. 1984 *Religion in Sociological Perspective.* Belmont, Calif.: Wadsworth.

Roof, Wade Clark 1978 *Community and Commitment: Religious Plausibility in a Liberal Protestant Church.* New York: Elsevier.

—— 1993 *A Generation of Seekers: The Spiritual Journeys of the Baby Boom Generation.* San Francisco: Harper San Francisco.

—— 1999 *Spiritual Marketplace: Baby Boomers and the Remaking of American Religion.* Princeton, N.J.: Princeton University Press.

——, and William McKinney 1987 *American Mainline Religion: Its Changing Shape and Future.* New Brunswick, N.J.: Rutgers University Press.

Shibley, Mark A. 1996 *Resurgent Evangelicalism in the United States: Mapping Cultural Change since 1970.* Columbia: University of South Carolina Press.

Silk, Mark 1988 *Spiritual Politics: Religion and America since World War II.* New York: Simon and Schuster.

Smith, Christian 1998 *American Evangelicalism: Embattled and Thriving.* Chicago: University of Chicago Press.

Spilka, Bernard, Ralph W. Hood, Jr., and Richard L. Gorsuch 1985 *The Psychology of Religion: An Empirical Approach.* Englewood Cliffs, N.J.: Prentice-Hall.

Stark, Rodney, and Charles Y. Glock 1968 *American Piety: The Nature of Religious Commitment.* Berkeley: University of California Press.

Swanson, Guy E. 1960 *The Birth of the Gods: The Origin of Primitive Beliefs.* Ann Arbor: University of Michigan Press.

—— 1967 *Religion and Regime: A Sociological Account of the Reformation.* Ann Arbor: University of Michigan Press.

Swidler, Ann 1987 "Culture in Action: Symbols and Strategies." *American Sociological Review* 51:273–286.

Tipton, Steven M. 1982 *Getting Saved from the Sixties: Moral Meaning in Conversion and Cultural Change.* Berkeley: University of California Press.

Weber, Max 1963 *The Sociology of Religion.* Boston: Beacon.

Wolfe, Alan 1997 *One Nation After All: What Americans Really Think about God, Country, Family, Racism, Welfare, Immigration, Homosexuality, Work, the Right, the Left and Each Other.* Boston: Viking.

Wuthnow, Robert 1976 *The Consciousness Reformation.* Berkeley: University of California Press.

—— 1987 *Meaning and Moral Order: Explorations in Cultural Analysis.* Berkeley: University of California Press.

—— 1988b "Sociology of Religion." In Neil J. Smelser, ed., *Handbook of Sociology.* Beverly Hills, Calif.: Sage.

—— 1988a *The Restructuring of American Religion: Society and Faith since World War II.* Princeton, N.J.: Princeton University Press.

—— 1998 *After Heaven: Spirituality in America since the 1950s.* Berkeley: University of California Press

ROBERT WUTHNOW

REMARRIAGE

Remarriages have become almost as common as first marriages in contemporary America. In fact, in recent years, almost half of all marriages involved at least one spouse who had been married previously (U.S. Bureau of the Census 1998). Remarriage rates in the United States (the number of people remarrying each year per 1,000 persons divorced or widowed) increased during the 1960s, declined precipitously across the 1970s, and have continued to decline throughout the 1980s and 1990s, although at a much slower rate (Sweet and Bumpass 1988; U.S. Bureau of the Census 1998).

Contemporary remarriages are more likely to follow divorce, in contrast to earlier centuries, in which remarriage typically followed the death of a spouse. For example, Demos (1970) reported that in the Plymouth Colony, approximately 40 percent of men and 26 percent of women over the age of 50 had been married more than once, due primarily to the death of the first spouse. In contrast, throughout the twentieth century, remarriages following the death of a spouse have been increasingly outnumbered by remarriages following divorce, owing to the combination of the dramatic decrease in the mortality rate in the first few decades of the century and the increase in the divorce rate. In fact, by 1990, remarriages in which both parties had been divorced occurred twenty times more often than remarriages in which both parties had been widowed (Clarke 1995).

While remarriage rates are related to divorce rates, they do not always follow the same trend. For example, the rise in remarriage rates in the 1960s accompanied the rise in divorce rates, but the decline in remarriage rates in the 1970s occurred at a time when the divorce rates were still growing. This apparent incongruence in the 1970s and early 1980s can be explained to a great extent by an increase in cohabitation among formerly marrieds across the same period (Bumpass et al. 1991).

WHO REMARRIES?

Rates of remarriage vary substantially by age, gender, race and ethnicity, and marital status (i.e., divorced or widowed).

Age at the time of termination of the first marriage is clearly the best predictor of remarriage—particularly for women—with younger people remarrying at much higher rates. For example, almost 90 percent of women under the age of 25 when their first marriage ends remarry, while fewer than one-third of women over the age of 40 at the time of termination remarry (Bumpass et al. 1990).

Remarriage rates also differ by *race and ethnicity*. White non-Hispanic women are substantially more likely to remarry than are black women, and somewhat more likely than Hispanic women (U.S. Bureau of the Census 1998). White non-Hispanic

women also remarry much more quickly than do either black or Hispanic women. Based on 1988 data, 35 percent of white women had remarried within two years, compared to only 16 percent of black women and 17 per cent of Hispanic women (U.S. Bureau of the Census 1998). Further, black and Hispanic women are less likely to cohabitate following divorce than are white women (U.S. Bureau of the Census 1998). Thus, the variations in remarriage appear to reflect a general tendency for white non-Hispanic women to be more likely than black or Hispanic women to establish new households following divorce.

Gender is a particularly important factor to consider when discussing remarriage, not only because remarriage rates vary by gender, but because gender interacts with several other factors that predict remarriage. Overall, three-quarters of divorced men and two-thirds of divorced women in the United Sates remarry (Cherlin and Furstenberg 1994). However, gender differences in likelihood of remarriage increase substantially across the life course. For formerly marrieds under 30 years of age, there is little difference in men's and women's likelihood of remarriage; however, by age 35, men are much more likely to remarry, and they are increasingly more likely in each successive age group. For example, among those aged 30–34, the rate of remarriage per 1,000 in the formerly married population is 138 for women, and 178 for men. In the age group 50–54, the gender discrepancy increases to a rate of 25 per 1,000 for women, and 75 per 1000 for men. By age 65 and over, the rate of remarriage rate for women is only 2 per 1,000 formerly marrieds in the population, compared to 15 per 1,000 for men (Clarke 1995). Thus, women's likelihood of remarriage not only decreases considerably across the life course, but decreases particularly markedly compared to that of men.

Various explanations for the overall lower remarriage rates for women than men have been developed. The most commonly cited explanation focuses on the limited "marriage market," or field of eligibles, for women who experience the termination of their marriage through divorce or death. First, there are fewer men than women, and this discrepancy increases with age (U.S. Bureau of the Census 1998). Also, women tend to marry men who are older than themselves, further limiting the pool of eligibles for women who are themselves older.

The effect of the *presence of children* on likelihood of remarriage also varies considerably by gender. In particular, the presence of children has much greater effects on the likelihood of remarriage for women than for men. For example, a recent study in New York State found that only 45 percent of divorced women with children remarried, compared to 67 percent of divorced men with children. Further, the likelihood of remarriage for women, but not men, declined as the number of children from the previous marriage increased (Buckle et al. 1996). About half of the women with one child remarried, but only about a quarter of the women with four children remarried. In contrast, about two-thirds of men with either one or four children remarried. It is possible to speculate that the lower rate of remarriage for women with children, particular those with multiple children, might be a function of the fact that women with several children are likely to be older than their childless counterparts; however, even when controlling on age (i.e., comparing women within the same age groups), the rate of remarriage is about one-quarter lower among mothers than among childless women (Bumpass et al. 1990).

Buckle and colleagues (1996) found that the presence of children also affected men's, but not women's, choice of a new partner. Divorced men who were childless were four times more likely to marry women who had not been married previously; in contrast, divorced men with children were almost twice as likely to marry a woman who had been married before. While divorced women were almost twice as likely to marry men who had previously been married than those who had not, this choice was not affected by whether the women had children.

Recent work by Sweeney (1997) suggests that the *age of children* must also be considered when examining the effect of children on their mothers' likelihood of remarriage. She found that preschoolers reduced women's likelihood of remarriage, while school-age children and teenagers had no effect, and children 18 years or older were associated with an *increased* likelihood of remarriage; these findings are similar to those reported by Koo and Suchindran almost twenty years earlier (1980),

suggesting little change across time in the effects of this factor on remarriage.

MATE SELECTION AMONG THOSE WHO REMARRY

One of the most striking patterns in first marriages is the tendency for individuals to marry others with similar social characteristics, such as age, educational attainment, religion, and socioeconomic background—a pattern known as homogamy. Although there is also a tendency toward homogamy in remarriage, the degree of similarity has been less than in first marriages, although this trend appears to be changing.

The differences in status similarity between first marrieds and remarrieds can be seen by examining partners' age discrepancies. Individuals who remarry tend to select mates from a wider field of eligibles compared to first marrieds, resulting in greater age difference between spouses in remarriage; however, the discrepancy appears to have decreased over the past two decades. Throughout the past thirty-five years, the groom in a first marriage has been, on average, two years older than the bride. Between the early 1960s and the mid-1970s, remarried grooms were, on average, four years older than their brides; however, since 1980, the discrepancy has declined to about three years (Clarke 1995). Thus, while there continues to be less age homogamy in remarriages than first marriages, the difference has become muted.

Individuals who are formerly married also appear to be increasingly likely to select a partner who shares the same marital status. For example, by 1990, divorced women were almost twice as likely to marry men who were also divorced as to marry men who had never been married (Clarke 1995). However, as in the case of age, homogamy of marital status was greater than in earlier years; in fact, the rate of divorced women marrying divorced men almost doubled from 1970 to 1990.

Socioeconomic factors appear to have somewhat different effects on patterns of first marriages and subsequent marriages—particularly for women. The women most likely to enter first marriages are those with greater socioeconomic prospects (cf. Goldscheider and Waite 1986; Lichter et al. 1992). However, the patterns are more complicated for remarriage. Haskey (1987) reported that women with higher occupational prestige were *less* likely to remarry; however, more recent research by Sweeney (1997) suggests that the effect of women's occupational prestige on remarriage may be more complex. She found that, among women under the age of 25 at the time of separation, those with higher occupational prestige were less likely to remarry; however, among women separating at age 45, higher occupational prestige was associated with an increased likelihood of remarriage. Thus, it appears that the middle-aged women who are the least able to support themselves are also the women least likely to be able to achieve economic stability through remarriage, further increasing the risk of poverty for women in this age group.

For men, it is less clear whether socioeconomic prospects have differential effects on entry into first marriages and remarriages. As in the case of women, greater economic prospects increase men's likelihood of entering into first marriages (cf. Goldscheider and Waite 1986; Lichter et al. 1992); however, evidence on economic factors and remarriage are less consistent. While Haskey (1987) found that men with higher occupational prestige were more likely to marry, Sweeney (1997) found no effects for any dimension of men's socioeconomic prospects, including educational attainment, job status, occupational aspirations, and work commitment.

Taken together, these findings suggest that patterns of remarriage may be becoming more similar to patterns of first marriages in terms of some demographic characteristics, such as age and previous marital status, but not necessarily in terms of socioeconomic prospects.

DIFFERENCES BETWEEN FIRST MARRIAGES AND REMARRIAGES

Marital Quality. While the popular press has debated the relative happiness of first marriages and remarriages, scholarly research on this issue has failed to find important differences. The most comprehensive review of this research to date (Vemer et al. 1989) found that first marrieds report only slightly greater marital satisfaction than do remarrieds. Elizabeth Vemer and her colleagues suggest that even this small difference may be accounted for by the fact that most studies combine data from individuals who had married twice with those who had married more than twice, and there is evidence that individuals in the latter group are less happy in general. Vemer and her colleagues also found that remarried men were more satisfied with their relationships than were remarried women; however, the differences were very small and paralleled the differences found between women's and men's satisfaction with first marriages. The absence of notable differences in marital quality between first marriages and remarriages has also been found in more recent investigations of this issue (cf. McDonald and DeMaris 1995). Thus, taken together, the findings indicate little difference in satisfaction between first marriages and remarriages for either men or women.

Division of Household Labor. The literature suggests that the division of household labor also differs for couples in first and subsequent marriages. Ishii-Kuntz and Coltrane (1992) found that husbands in remarriages contributed more to household tasks such as cooking, meal cleanup, shopping, laundry, and housecleaning than did men in first marriages, particularly when couples had only their own biological children. In families in which there were stepchildren, women performed a greater actual number of hours of household labor, but the *proportion* that they contributed relative to their spouses was still smaller than that of women in first marriages. Ishii-Kuntz and Coltrane suggest that this is because the "incomplete institutionalization" of remarriage leads to a reduction in gender traditionalism.

However, other studies suggest that whether the woman has been married previously may have more effect on the division of household labor than whether her husband has been married before. Funder (1986) found that women in second marriages perceived that household labor was shared more equally than in their first marriages; however, there was no such trend in men's perceptions. Further, Sullivan (1997) reported that women who had been previously married contributed a smaller proportion of household labor, but that men who were formerly married contributed no differently than did men in first marriages.

Children in Remarriages. The large majority of remarriages involve children. Not only do more than half of formerly married individuals bring children to their new marriages (Buckle et al. 1996), but the rate of childbearing in remarriages is relatively high. Approximately half of all women who enter remarriage under 35 years of age bear at least one child during that marriage, generally within the first two years (Wineberg 1990).

One question that is often raised in both the popular and the scholarly literature is the effect of the presence of children on marital quality. The presence of children has generally been found to have a negative effect on parents' marital quality; however, the effects of children specifically on *remarried* couples is less clear. While White and Booth (1985) found that the presence of stepchildren was associated with somewhat lower marital quality, Martin and Bumpass (1989) found no effect, and both Albrecht and colleagues (1983) and Kurdek (1989) reported that the presence of stepchildren was weakly but *positively* associated with marital quality. The findings regarding mutual children are also inconsistent. Ganong and Coleman (1988) found that mutual children had no effect on marital quality, but Albrecht and colleagues (1983) found a weak but positive effect. Thus, it is unclear how the presence of either mutual children or stepchildren affects marital quality among remarrieds.

Another question that is often the focus of research on stepfamilies (or blended families as they are increasingly labeled) concerns the effect of the remarriage on children. These effects are of considerable importance, given that about 15 percent of all children live in blended families, and it is estimated that between one-third and one-half of today's young people will become stepsons or stepdaughters at some point (Glick 1989; U.S. Bureau of the Census 1997). In the majority of these cases, the children in stepfamilies live with a biological mother and a stepfather.

Remarriage presents several challenges to the family. Members must make numerous decisions and adjustments to living arrangements and family relationships. In addition, parenting approaches and activities may change following the remarriage. Further, remarriage creates a complex set of relationships between former spouses, between stepparents and stepchildren, between step- and half-siblings and extended kin. These relationships are

often ill defined and lack the support of social expectations and norms. The ambiguous nature of these relationships can be seen when members of blended families are asked whom they consider to be family. While only 10 percent of children fail to mention a biological parent when asked to define their family, over 30 percent do not mention a stepparent (Furstenberg and Cherlin 1991).

Some studies have found that the bonds between stepparents and stepchildren are somewhat less warm, more conflictual, and less enduring than those between biological parents and children, while others have found substantial levels of closeness between stepparents and stepchildren (Kurdek and Fine 1993; White 1994). Such variation is not surprising, considering the wide variety of roles that stepparents adopt within the family. Some stepparents adopt a parental role, including the formation and maintenance of close emotional bonds with their stepchildren. Others take on the activities and roles of more distant relatives such as aunts or uncles, and still others act like adult boarders in the home, having little involvement with or showing little affection for the children (Arendell 1997).

Several factors appear to influence the nature of the stepparent-stepchild relationship. In a 1994 review, Cherlin and Furstenberg concluded that the primary factor influencing the character of the stepparent-stepchild relationship is the effort made by the stepparent to forge kinlike relations. Further, it appears easier to be a stepfather than a stepmother, in part because children seem more willing to accept substitute fathers than substitute mothers.

Other factors also affect the quality of the stepparent-stepchild relationship. For example, the younger the child at the time of the remarriage, the more likely he or she is to come to view the stepparent as a "real" parent. The more frequent the contact between the nonresidential parent and the child, the less likely the child is to develop a parentlike relationship with the stepparent (Arendell 1997).

Following remarriage, children often must adapt to the presence of step-siblings and half-siblings, as well as to stepparents. Such siblings may present additional challenges for the child's adjustment. For example, children may be asked to share space and material resources, as well as the attention of their biological parent. Children may also find that their positions in the household hierarchy have changed with the addition of step-siblings; for example, a child may suddenly find that he or she has lost the status of being the "oldest" or the "baby" of the family. Despite these changes, most step-siblings eventually adjust and form close relationships. In fact, even as adults, step-siblings often maintain contact, albeit on a less frequent basis than full siblings (White and Reidman 1992).

Research on blended families provides a mixed picture with regard to the degree to which stepfamilies differ from intact families in terms of children's adjustment (for reviews, see Amato and Booth 1997; Amato and Keith 1991a, 1991b; Hethering-ton et al. 1998). Children in stepfamilies appear to be at greater risk than children in intact families. For example, children in divorced and remarried families are more likely than children in intact families to have academic problems; to be less socially responsible; to have lower levels of self-esteem; to be withdrawn; to be less happy; to have trouble concentrating; and to have troubled relationships with parents, siblings, and peers. Adolescents may experience the same negative outcomes; they may also be more likely to drop out of school, to become sexually active at an earlier age, to have children out of wedlock, to be involved in delinquent activities, to abuse drugs and/or alcohol, and to be unemployed. Further, adult offspring of divorced and remarried families have been shown to be less satisfied with their lives, to have higher levels of marital instability, and to have lower levels of socioeconomic attainment.

Fortunately, despite their increased risk, the majority of children from divorced and stepfamilies do not experience these problems, and some studies suggest that many of the detrimental consequences of divorce of remarriage on children are temporary (c.f., Chase-Lansdale and Hethering-ton 1990; Emery and Forehand 1994; Hethering-ton 1993).

It is also important to note that the magnitude of differences in well-being and behavioral outcomes linked to family structure is reduced when the well-being and adjustment of the child prior to divorce and remarriage are taken into consideration. Further, there is a tendency for studies of children's adjustment following divorce and remarriage to combine different categories of stepfamilies together. This is particularly problematic due to the set of children that experience multiple transitions in family status. Approximately 10 percent of children experience at least two divorces by their custodial parent before they reach the age of 16 (Furstenberg 1988). The inclusion of children of multiple divorces with those of parents who have divorced and remarried a single time may artificially inflate the risks for children associated with remarriage, since these children are at greatest risk for negative outcomes. In fact, Kurdek (1994) argues that it is the children of the multiple-divorce group—not the stepfamily group—that are most at risk for negatives outcomes when compared to children of intact families.

Last, it is essential to point out that remarriage may help to compensate for some of the negative consequences of divorce. For example, remarriage improves the financial well-being of children and their divorced mothers. Only 8 percent of children in mother-stepfather households live below the poverty line, compared to 49 percent of children in single-mother households (Cherlin and Furstenberg 1994). Remarriage also provides an additional adult in the household, thus adding more opportunities for interaction between children and adults, taking some of the burden off the custodial parent, and providing another role model for the child. These factors may help to explain why some studies have found that children in blended families are at less risk for negative outcomes than are children in single-parent homes (Amato and Keith 1991b).

In sum, although there are special concerns and greater complexity in family relationships, many blended families manage to form relationships that are close, loving, and lasting, and to function as effective family units, with the same variation in relationship quality found in more traditional family forms.

Stability of Remarriages. Clearly, remarriages and first marriages differ in complexity. The remarried couple must develop ways of interacting with the former spouse; with children from the former marriage (regardless of whether the children are minors or adults); and, in some cases, with both the extended kin and the new partner of the former spouse. In addition, the emotional history of the relationship with the first spouse, positive and negative, may carry over to influence the new relationship, regardless of whether the first marriage was terminated by death or divorce. Further, material possessions and financial considerations emanating from the first marriage often have a significant impact on second marriages.

This complexity, and perhaps the attendant problems, might help to explain the slightly higher rate of divorce among remarried couples. Whereas about half of first remarriages end in divorce, approximately 60 percent of remarriages do so (Ihinger-Tallman and Pasley 1987).

There are several explanations for the higher rate of divorce among the remarried. Cherlin (1978) has suggested that there is an "incomplete institutionalization" of remarriage. Remarriages, according to Cherlin, are more difficult than first marriages due to the absence of guidelines in language, law, and custom for remarried couples.

Another interpretation of the higher rate of divorce among the remarried is offered by Furstenberg and Spanier (1984), who identify the predisposition to divorce of the remarried as the key explanatory factor. According to this perspective, since remarried individuals have already demonstrated their willingness to leave an unsatisfactory marriage, they will be willing to do so again if dissatisfied with the current relationship. Therefore, it may not be the quality of the marital relationship that precipitates divorce but the propensity to leave an unsatisfactory relationship.

Last, Martin and Bumpass (1989) have suggested that another explanation for the higher rate of divorce among the remarried is that these individuals have sociodemographic characteristics that increased the likelihood that their first marriage would end in divorce. These characteristics, such as low educational level, income instability, and parental divorce, are then carried into the remarriage, also increasing its instability. Further, Martin and Bumpass suggest that individuals who remarry are disproportionately likely to have married as teenagers, which may indicate differences in personality or experiences that might make it more difficult to maintain a successful marriage. Consistently with Martin and Bumpass's argument, there is evidence that men who are socially disadvantaged

remarry more quickly than their counterparts who are more advantaged (Monk-Turner and White 1995).

In sum, while the literature on remarriage emphasizes differences between first marriages and remarriages, it is important to reiterate that, overall, there is substantially more similarity than difference between the two. The patterns of mate selection, marital quality, and marital stability of individuals who remarry do not differ markedly from the patterns of individuals marrying for the first time.

CONCLUSION

In conclusion, married life in America today often involves a sequence of marriage, divorce, and remarriage, sometimes followed by a subsequent divorce. Many sociologists suggest that the high rate or remarriage followed by a subsequent divorce in America society indicates a strong commitment to married life, albeit of a slightly different form. These scholars argue that contemporary Americans are not rejecting marriage, they are only rejecting specific relationships that became unsatisfying. Taken together, the literature on remarriage and stepfamilies suggests that the individuals who choose to follow this pattern have approximately as great a likelihood of finding a satisfying and stable relationship as do those who marry for the first time.

For further discussions and reviews of work regarding remarriage, see Bumpass and colleagues (1990), Ganong and Coleman (1994), and Vemer and colleagues (1989). For a further discussion of literature on the effects of divorce and remarriage on children, see Amato and Booth (1997), Amato and Keith (1991a, 1991b), Cherlin and Furstenberg (1994), and Hetherington and colleagues (1998).

REFERENCES

Albrecht, Stan L., Howard M. Bahr, and Kristen L. Goodman 1983 *Divorce and Remarriage: Problems, Adaptations and Adjustments*. Westport, Conn.: Greenwood.

Amato, Paul R., and Alan Booth 1997 *A Generation at Risk: Growing Up in an Era of Family Upheaval*. Cambridge: Harvard University Press.

Amato, Paul R., and Bruce Keith 1991a "Parental Divorce and Adult Well-Being: A Meta-Analysis." *Journal of Marriage and the Family* 53:43–58.

—— 1991b "Parental Divorce and the Well-Being of Children: A Meta-Analysis." *Psychological Bulletin* 11:26–p46.

Arendell, Terry (ed.) 1997 *Contemporary Parenting Challenge, and Issues*. Thousand Oaks, Calif.: Sage.

—— 1983 "Divorce and Remarriage." *Contemporary Parenting: Challenges and Issues*. Thousand Oaks, Calif.: Sage.

Bolgar, R., H. Sweig-Frank, and J. Paris 1995 "Childhood Antecedents of Interpersonal Problems in Young Adult Children of Divorce." *Journal of the Academy of Child and Adolescent Psychiatry* 34:143–150.

Buckle, Leslie, Gordon G. Gallup, Jr., and Zachary A. Rodd 1996 "Marriage as a Reproductive Contract: Patterns of Marriage, Divorce, and Remarriage." *Ethology and Sociobiology* 17:363–377.

Bumpass, Larry, James Sweet, and Teresa Castro Martin 1990 "Changing Patterns of Remarriage." *Journal of Marriage and the Family* 52:747–756.

Bumpass, Larry, James Sweet, and Andrew Cherlin 1991 "The Role of Cohabitation in Declining Rates of Marriage." *Journal of Marriage and the Family* 53:913–927.

Chase-Lansdale, P. Lindsay, and E. Mavis Hetherington 1990 "The Impact of Divorce on Life-Span Developmental: Short and Long Term Effects." In D. Featherman and R. Lerner, eds., *Life Span Development and Behavior*, vol. 10. Hillsdale, N.J.: Lawrence Erlbaum.

Cherlin, Andrew J. 1978 "Remarriage as an Incomplete Institution." *American Journal of Sociology* 84:634–650.

——, and Frank F. Furstenberg 1994 "Stepfamilies in the United States: A Reconsideration." *Annual Review of Sociology* 20:359–381.

Clarke, Sally C. 1995 "Advance Report of Final Marriage Statistics 1989 and 1990." *Monthly Vital Statistics Report* 43 (July 14). Washington, D.C.: U.S. Department of Health and Human Services.

Demos, John 1970 *A Little Commonwealth: Family Life in Plymouth Colony*. London: Oxford University Press.

Emery, Robert E., and R. Forehand 1994 "Parental Divorce and Children's Well-Being: A Focus on Resilience." In R. J. Haggerty, L. R. Sherrod, N. Garmezy, and M. Rutter, eds., *Stress, Risk, and Resilience in Children and Adolescents*. Cambridge, England: Cambridge University Press.

Funder, K. 1986 "His and Her Divorce." In Peter McDonald, ed., *Setting Up: Property and Income Distribution on Divorce in Australia*. Sidney: Australian Institute of Family Studies, Prentice Hall.

Furstenberg, Frank F. 1988 "Child Care after Divorce and Remarriage." In E. Mavis Hetherington and J. D. Arasteh, eds., *Impact of Divorce, Single Parenting, and Stepparenting on Children*. Hillsdale, N.J.: Elrbaum.

——, and Andrew J. Cherlin 1991 *Divided Families*. Cambridge, Mass.: Harvard University Press.

Furstenberg, Frank F., and Graham B. Spanier 1984 "The Risk of Dissolution in Remarriage: An Examination of Cherlin's Hypothesis of Incomplete Insitutionalization." *Family Relations* 33:433–441.

Ganong, Lawrence H., and Marilyn Coleman 1988 "Do Mutual Children Cement Bonds in Stepfamilies?" *Journal of Marriage and the Family* 50:687–698.

—— 1994 *Remarried Family Relationships*. Thousand Oaks, Calif.: Sage.

Glick, Paul C. 1989 "Remarried Families, Stepfamilies, and Stepchildren: A Brief Demographic Analysis." *Family Relations* 38:7–26.

Goldscheider, Frances Kobrin, and Linda J. Waite 1986 "Sex Differences in the Entry into Marriage." *American Journal of Sociology* 92:91–109.

Haskey, J. 1987 "Social Class Differentials in Remarriage after Divorce: Results from a Forward Linkage Study." *Population Trends* 47:34–42.

Hetherington, E. Mavis 1993 "An Overview of the Virginia Longitudinal Study of Divorce and Remarriage with a Focus on Early Adolescence." *Journal of Family Psychology* 7:39–56.

——, Margaret Bridges, and Glendessa M. Insabela 1998 "What Matters? What Does Not? Five Perspectives on the Association between Marital Transitions and Children's Adjustment." *American Psychologist* 53:167–184.

Ihinger-Tallman, Marilyn, and Kay Pasley 1987 *Remarriage*. Thousand Oaks, Calif.: Sage.

Ishii-Kuntz, Masako, and Scott Coltrane 1992 "Remarriage, Stepparenting, and Household Labor." *Journal of Family Issues* 13:215–233.

Koo, Helen P., and C. M. Suchindran 1980 "Effects of Children on Women's Remarriage Prospects." *Journal of Family Issues* 1:497–515.

Kurdek, Lawrence A. 1989 "Relationship Quality for Newly Married Husbands and Wives: Marital History, Stepchildren, and Individual-Difference Predictors." *Journal of Marriage and the Family* 51:1053–1064.

—— 1994 "Remarriages and Stepfamilies Are Not Inherently Problematic." In Alan Booth and Judy Dunn, eds., *Stepfamilies: Who Benefits? Who Does Not?* Hillsdale, N.J.: Lawrence Erlbaum.

——, and Mark A. Fine 1993 "The Relation between Family Structure and Young Adolescents' Appraisals of Family Climate and Parenting Behavior." *Journal of Family Issues* 14:279–290.

Lichter, Daniel T., Diane K. McLaughlin, George Kephart, and David J. Landry 1992 "Race and the Retreat from Marriage: A Shortage of Marriageable Men?" *American Sociological Review* 57:781–799.

MacDonald, William L., and Alfred DeMaris 1995 "Remarriage, Stepchildren, and Marital Conflict: Challenges to the Incomplete Institutionalization Hypothesis." *Journal of Marriage and the Family* 57:387–398.

Martin, Teresa Castro, and Larry Bumpass 1989 "Recent Trends in Marital Disruption." *Demography* 26:37–51.

Monk-Turner, Elizabeth, and Garland White 1995 "Factors Shaping the Probability of Divorce and Early Remarriage among Young Men." *International Journal of Contemporary Sociology* 32:97–105.

Sullivan, Oriel 1997 "The Division of Housework among 'Remarried' Couples." *Journal of Family Issues* 18:205–223.

Sweeney, Megan M. 1997 "Remarriage of Women and Men after Divorce." *Journal of Family Issues* 18:479–502.

Sweet, James A., and Larry L. Bumpass 1988 *American Families and Households*. New York: Russell Sage Foundation.

U.S. Bureau of the Census 1997 *Statistical Abstract of the United States, 1997*. Washington, D.C.: Government Printing Office.

—— 1998 *Statistical Abstract of the United States, 1998*. Washington, D.C.: Government Printing Office.

Vemer, Elizabeth, Marilyn Coleman, Lawrence H. Ganong, and Harris Cooper 1989 "Marital Satisfaction in Remarriage: A Meta-Analysis." *Journal of Marriage and the Family* 51:713–725.

White, Lynn K. 1994 "Coresidence and Leaving Home: Young Adults and Their Parents." *Annual Review of Sociology* 20:81–102.

——, and Alan Booth 1985 "The Quality and Stability of Remarriages: The Role of Stepchildren." *American Sociological Review* 50:689–698.

White, Lynn K., and Agnes Riedman 1992 "When the Brady Bunch Grows Up: Step/Half- and Full-Sibling Relationships in Adulthood." *Journal of Marriage and the Family* 54:197–208.

Wilson, Barbara Foley 1989 "Remarriages and Subsequent Divorces" *National Vital Statistics*, series 21, no. 45. Hyattsville, Md.: National Center for Health Statistics.

Wineberg, Howard 1990 "Childbearing after Remarriage." *Journal of Marriage and the Family* 52:31–38.

J. Jill Suitor
Shirley A. Keeton

REPLICATION

Philosophers have long identified replication as an important facilitator of scientific progress. Several terms have been used to denote the ability to assess past work through replication, including "intersubjective testability," "reliability," and "verifiability by repetition." Authors of scientific papers typically describe the methods and materials they used in their research so that, at least hypothetically, others can repeat the work and reproduce the reported results. Successful replication of their own and others' work gives researchers confidence in its validity and reassures them about the fruitfulness of the general line of inquiry they are following. In contrast, inability to replicate one's own or others' results casts doubt upon the validity of the previous work. Critics argue that because sociologists infrequently attempt to replicate findings, they are both less able to identify valid lines of inquiry and more likely to follow spurious ones.

One can identify a continuum ranging from exact to weakly approximate replication. The former, also called repetition, consists of attempts to use the same materials and procedures as previous research to determine whether the same results can be obtained. Approximate replication, on the other hand, consists of using some but not all of the conditions of a previous study. By systematically varying research conditions in a series of approximate replications, it may be possible to determine the precise nature of a previous study's results and the extent to which they also hold for different populations and situations (Aronson et al. 1998). Researchers usually value successful approximate replication more than successful exact replication because the latter contributes less to existing knowledge.

In the natural sciences, experimentalists are usually expected to carry out successful exact replications of their own work before submitting it for publication. This reduces the likelihood of reporting spurious results and of misleading one's colleagues. Exact replications of others' research are often difficult and costly to execute, however, and natural scientists rarely attempt them except in cases where the original work is theoretically important or has high potential practical value, or where there is suspicion of fraud. Another disincentive for carrying out exact replications of already published work is that such work is usually difficult to publish. This is true not only because little new knowledge results from an exact replication, but also because the meaning of a failure to replicate exactly is often ambiguous. Failures can indicate that the original work was flawed, but they may also be due to inadequate specification of research procedures, the existence of a stochastic element in the production of results, or errors in the replication itself (Harry M. Collins 1985). By contrast, approximate replications, especially those involving the modification of research instruments and their application to new areas of inquiry, are common in the natural sciences, and this has led some to identify them as constituting a central element of "rapid-discovery, high-consensus science" (Randall Collins 1994).

Many hold that social scientists' opportunities to carry out replications, especially exact replications, are severely limited. This is partly because social scientists often use nonexperimental research techniques that are difficult to repeat exactly. In addition, changing social and historical contexts can influence studies' results. As a result, failures to obtain the same results as reported by previous studies are even more ambiguous in the social sciences than in the natural sciences (Schuman and Presser 1981). This ambiguity may account for social scientists' continued interest in concepts and theories stemming from studies whose results have repeatedly failed to be replicated (e.g., sex differences in fear of success and patterns of moral development).

Nevertheless, critics have long argued that behavioral scientists need to attempt more replications of previous research because their dependence on statistical inference produces many spurious reports of "statistically significant" results. Statistical inference allows researchers only to reject or fail to reject a null hypothesis. Each of these two outcomes is subject to error due to the probabilistic nature of statistical hypothesis testing; sometimes researchers reject null hypotheses that are actually true (type one error), and sometimes they fail to reject null hypotheses that are actually false (type two error). However, failure to reject a null hypothesis does not justify accepting it, and studies that do not yield rejections therefore are often judged as contributing little. As a result, scholarly journals tend to publish only papers that report the rejection of null hypotheses, some of which are the result of type one errors (Sterling 1959). Furthermore, to ensure that they will be able to reject null hypotheses, researchers sometimes use inappropriate analytic procedures that maximize their chances of obtaining statistically significant results (Selvin and Stuart 1966), increasing the likelihood that published findings are due to type one errors. To counteract these patterns, some have argued that behavioral science editors should set aside space in their journals for the publication of replication attempts, and to publish studies that fail to replicate earlier results even when the replications themselves fail to reject null hypotheses.

Despite the calls for increased replication, behavioral science journals publish few papers reporting replication attempts. In an early examination of this issue, Sterling (1959) reported that among 362 articles in psychology journals, 97 percent of those reporting a test of significance rejected the null hypothesis, but that none was an explicit replication. Ironically, many have replicated Sterling's results (cf. Dickersin 1990; Gaston 1979; Reid et al. 1981). These studies probably underestimate the prevalence of replication, because they do not count papers reporting a set of experiments that comprise both an original result and one or more approximate replications of it. By not encouraging more replication, however, behavioral science journals may foster elaborate and vacuous theorizing at the expense of identifying factual puzzles that deserve theoretical analysis (Cook and Campbell 1979, p. 25).

Although the traditional view of replication entails the collection of new data—including data on additional cases or additional measures—statisticians and social scientists have suggested alternative replication strategies. One is to build replication into a study from the start. For example, a researcher can draw a sample large enough to allow its random partition into two subsamples.

Data from one subsample can then be used to check conclusions drawn on the basis of analyses of data from the other. Another approach, requiring the intensive use of computing resources, is to draw multiple random subsamples from already collected data and then use these subsamples to crossvalidate results (Finifter 1972). This general strategy, which includes such techniques as "jack-knifing" and "bootstrapping," is also used to assess sampling variances for complex sampling designs (see *Sampling Procedures*). Still another elaboration of the basic idea of replication is the general approach called *meta-analysis*. Here the analyst treats previous studies on a topic or relationship as a sample of approximate replications. By statistically analyzing whether and how studies' results vary, one can determine how generalizable a finding is and the extent to which differences in study design account for variation in results (Hunter and Schmidt 1990). Finally, replication may also be fostered by the increased availability of already-collected data sets stemming from the establishment of data depositories, and funding agency requirements that data from supported projects be made accessible to other researchers. Access to previously collected data makes it possible to carry out both exact replications of previous analyses and approximate replications that alter the analytic procedures used by the original researcher.

(SEE ALSO: *Sampling Procedures*)

REFERENCES

Aronson, Elliot, Timothy D. Wilson, and Marilynn B. Brewer 1998 "Experimentation in Social Psychology." In Daniel T. Gilbert, Susan T. Fiske, and Gardner Lindzey, eds., *Handbook of Social Psychology*, 4th ed. Boston: McGraw-Hill.

Collins, Harry M. 1985 *Changing Order: Replication and Induction in Scientific Practice*. London: Sage.

Collins, Randall 1994 "Why the Social Sciences Won't Become High-Consensus, Rapid-Discovery Science." *Sociological Forum* 9:155–177.

Cook, Thomas D., and Donald T. Campbell 1979 *Quasi-Experimentation: Design and Analysis Issues for Field Studies*. Chicago: Rand-McNally.

Dickersin, Kay 1990 "The Existence of Publication Bias and Risk Factors for Its Occurence." *Journal of the American Medical Association* 263:1385–1389.

Finifter, Bernard M. 1972 "The Generation of Confidence: Evaluating Research Findings by Random Subsample Replication." In Herbert L. Costner, ed., *Sociological Methodology 1972*. San Francisco: Jossey-Bass.

Gaston, Jerry 1979 "The Big Three and the Status of Sociology." *Contemporary Sociology* 8:789–793.

Hunter, John E., and Frank L. Schmidt 1990 *Methods of Meta-Analysis*. Newbury Park, Calif.: Sage.

Reid, L. H., L. C. Soley, and R. D. Rimmer 1981 "Replications in Advertising Research: 1977, 1978, 1979." *Journal of Advertising* 10:3–13.

Schuman, Howard, and Stanley Presser 1981 "Mysteries of Replication and Non-Replication." In Howard Schuman and Stanley Presser, eds. *Questions and Answers in Attitude Surveys*. New York: Academic Press.

Selvin, Hannan C., and Alan Stuart 1966 "Data-Dredging Procedures in Survey Analysis." *American Statistician* 20:20–23.

Sterling, Theodore D. 1959 "Publication Decisions and Their Possible Effects on Inferences Drawn from Tests of Significance—Or Visa Versa." *Journal of the American Statistical Association* 54:30–34.

LOWELL L. HARGENS

RESEARCH FUNDING IN SOCIOLOGY

IMPORTANCE OF EXTERNAL FUNDING

Jesse Unruh, a well-known twentieth-century politician in California, is alleged to have said, "Money is the mother's milk of politics." Observers at the century's close may have made similarly accurate comments about the importance of money in the conduct of research. Natural scientists (including those in fields ranging from basic biomedical science to space exploration) have traditionally depended on funds beyond the internal resources of the organizations at which they are employed. Major discoveries in the natural sciences would be unthinkable without funding for particle accelerators, field expeditions, and clinical research staffs. Social scientists and particularly sociologists may be moving toward similar dependence on funding from beyond the boundaries of their universities and institutes. Such resources appear crucial for truly significant investigations, at least those which require original empirical data.

Sponsorship citation in the leading sociology journals in 1997 and 1998 provides an indication of the importance of external research support to sociologists. Volume 62 (1997) of the *American Sociological Review (ASR)* contains 55 articles. In 31 of these articles (56 percent), the authors cite sources of funding outside their home organizations. An additional 3 authors, all university based, cite internal sources of support (such as university research committees), which presumably grant awards through a competitive proposal process. *American Journal of Sociology (AJS)*, volume 103 (1997 and 1998), contains 27 articles; 9 of these cite funding sources, 6 (22 percent) of which are clearly outside agencies or internal units distributing funds obtained from outside. At century's end, external research funding appeared to be a frequent if not ubiquitous part of the research process in sociology.

Review of research published a generation ago presents a similar picture. Volume 42 of *ASR* (1977) contains 59 articles, 23 (39 percent) of which cite outside funding sources. An additional 4 authors cite funding sources internal to their institutions. Volume 83 of the *AJS* (1977 and 1978) includes 38 articles, of which 24 (63 percent) cite funding from sources outside the authors' universities, institutes, or agencies. An additional 3 *AJS* articles cite internal sources.

SOURCES OF FUNDING

Sources named in the above-cited *AJS* and *ASR* volumes provide an indication of where sociologists obtain research funds. Among the articles published in 1997 and 1998 that cite external funding, a plurality (17 citations) named the National Science Foundation (NSF) as the sole or primary source of support. The second most frequently cited source was the National Institute of Child and Human Development (NICHD), with three citations, followed by the National Institute on Aging (NIA), with two citations. One article cited the National Institute of Mental Health (NIMH) and the remainder acknowledged a variety of private funders, such as the Ford, Rockefeller, and Guggenheim foundations.

Among 1977 and 1978 journal articles that cited external funding, the National Science Foundation (NSF) received the most frequent acknowledgement (16 citations), followed by NIMH (eight citations), the Office of Economic Opportunity (four citations), the Ford Foundation (four citations), the National Institute of Education (two

citations), and the Russell Sage Foundation (two citations). An assortment of federal agencies and private foundation received one citation each, including the Social Security Administration (SSA), the Department of Labor (DOL), the National Endowment for the Humanities (NEH), the National Institute for Drug Abuse (NIDA), and the Grant and Guggenheim foundations.

Comparison of funding patterns in *ASR* and *AJS* across the decades carries some risk. These journals do not necessarily represent the most important work of general sociology and may not reflect patterns of support (or its absence) in subdisciplines, such as medical sociology and sociology of religion. Conventions and habits prevailing among authors regarding citation of funding sources may have changed between the 1970s and the 1990s, but inspection of acknowledgements in the articles cited above suggests that external funding of major sociological research remained as common a phenomenon in the late 1990s, when 43 percent of *ASR* and *AJS* articles cited external funding, as it was in the late 1970s, when 47 percent of *ASR* and *AJS* articles acknowledged such support. Funding of the research leading to these articles depended somewhat more on public agency support in the late 1970s than in the late 1990s. About 80 percent of the above-referenced 1977 and 1978 *ASR* and *AJS* articles which acknowledged external funding cited public sources and 20 percent cited private sources. About 71 percent of comparable *ASR* and *AJS* articles in 1997 and 1998 acknowledged public funding, 29 percent citing private sources.

STRUCTURE AND OPERATION OF FUNDING ORGANIZATIONS

Public and private sources of research funding comprise different social worlds. Representatives of each evaluate research proposals according to different rules and criteria. These differences derive from the distinct institutional surroundings of public agencies and private organizations.

Public Funding Organizations. Procedures followed by the U.S. Public Health Service (PHS) illustrate the processes by which public research funding takes place and the organizational components which facilitate these processes. The PHS, a subunit of the Department of Health and Human

Services (DHHS), houses a large number of agencies making research grants. These include several of the sources cited in the above-mentioned *AJS* and *ASR* volumes, such as the National Institute of Mental Health (NIMH), the National Institute of Aging (NIA) and the National Institute of Child Health and Disease (NICHD). Other PHS subunits such the National Cancer Institute (NCI) and the Agency for Health Care Policy and Research (AHCPR) have funded significant sociological work, principally in the fields of organizational and medical sociology. It appears likely that other governmental funding organizations, such as NSF, operate in a manner similar to these PHS units.

The institutional background and functioning of AHCPR provide a paradigm applicable to all federal funding organizations. Federal legislation established AHCPR through the Omnibus Budget Reconciliation Act of 1989 (AHCPR 1992). The legislation authorizes the secretary of DHHS to undertake "research, demonstration, and evaluation activities" regarding delivery of health services in the United States. The AHCPR administrator acts as operational head of the agency and derives his or her authority via delegation from the secretary of DHHS. By statute, the administrator is advised by the National Advisory Council for Health Care Policy, Research, and Evaluation. The council recommends priority areas for research funding. In addition, it provides "secondary review" of grant proposals. All PHS awarding organizations have a similar administrative structure and advisory council.

The council's composition is mandated to include seventeen public (nonfederal) members who have voting power. These are primarily scientifically qualified individuals. The council also includes health practitioners; individuals drawn from business, ethics, law, and policy; and consumer representatives. In addition, the council includes seven federal officials with voting power, appointed to serve *ex officio*.

Of key importance in the process of research funding by AHCPR and analogous groups is the Initial Review Group (IRG), sometimes referenced as the "scientific review group" or "study section." As mandated by statute, the IRG advises the secretary of DHHS on the scientific and technical merit of research grant applications within AHCPR's areas of responsibility. The AHCPR administrator

officially invites individuals selected for IRG membership to join. Selection is made with assistance from the Office of Scientific Review (OSR), the administrative body within the agency with responsibility for organizing the review of applications for grant support and reporting IRG findings to the AHCPR administrator. Normally, IRG members are appointed to overlapping four-year terms.

Official criteria for IRG membership include scientific expertise in areas of concern to the agency, often indicated by a history of receiving funds under the agency's jurisdiction. IRG members cannot be employees of the federal government. In 1992, AHCPR operated four IRGs, each covering a different specialty area or agency concern. Agencies such as AHCPR occasionally appoint special panels to evaluate proposals obtained in response to Requests for Applications (RFAs) issued to solicit interest in new or unusual areas of scientific concern.

The IRG meets three times each year, a few months after regularly scheduled deadlines for submission of grant applications. An official of the Office of Scientific Review, known as the Scientific Review administrator, in consultation with the IRG chair, assigns committee members the task of reviewing each application received by the agency. For each application, the Scientific Review administrator appoints a primary reviewer and at least two secondary reviewers.

At IRG meetings, primary and secondary reviewers present evaluations of the scientific merit of the proposals which they have been assigned. Discussion then takes place among all members of the IRG. The chair then requests a recommendation from the primary reviewer to assign a "priority score" to the proposal, defer discussion, or remove the proposal from further consideration. Priority scores are assigned ranging from 1.0 (most meritorious) to 5.0 (least meritorious). Following the reviewers' reports and ensuing discussion, all voting members of the IRG formulate priority scores according to their own judgment and submit them to the chair. Composite priority scores and summaries of the IRG's findings regarding scientific merit are reported to the council and the grant applicant.

The agency establishes a "pay line" indicating the priority score below which proposals are likely to receive funding. In the late 1990s, pay lines varied between priority scores of 1.80 and 2.20, criteria stringent in comparison with the early 1970s, when pay lines were often in the 300s. Strictly speaking, the findings of the IRG are advisory to the council and ultimately to the secretary. Rarely, the council or a high official may elect to fund a proposal "out of priority" due to extraordinary merit or urgent public need.

Government research organizations such as AHCPR review all grant applications that are complete and received on time. In a mid-1992 funding cycle, IRGs (including all those of AHCPR, the National Institute of Health [NIH], and related agencies) reviewed 8,017 applications (NIH Division of Research Grants 1993). Three such cycles occur annually. IRGs usually award priority scores resulting in funding of between 10 and 20 percent of the applications they review. Structure and procedures at the National Science Foundation appear somewhat simpler but similar in form to those of the PHS. Proposals are reviewed by technical staff (an NSF program officer) with the aid of outside reviewers. Final award decisions are made at the senior management level.

Private Funding Organizations. If review of funding sources cited in *ASR* and *AJS* provides a valid indication, most nongovernment funding for sociological research comes from private foundations. None of the journal articles acknowledge funding from corporations, which are major sources of research support in some fields, such as engineering and pharmacy.

A private foundation is a nongovernmental, nonprofit organization with funds from a permanent portfolio of investments known as an endowment. Typically, an endowment originates from a single source, such as an individual, a family, or a corporation. Legally, foundations are chartered to maintain or aid social, educational, religious, or other charitable activities serving the common good. They are owned by trustees who hold the foundation's assets "in trust" for the people of the jurisdiction in which they are chartered. Governance is carried out by a board of directors. Trustees usually sit on boards of directors, but directors are not always trustees. Foundations of significant size employ staff to recommend policy, evaluate applications for funding, and perform day-to-day administrative tasks.

Like federal agencies, private foundations identify areas of interest and disseminate this information to the grant-seeking community. New interests and areas of emphasis emerge periodically through initiation by staff or discussion among directors and trustees. Large foundations such as Robert Wood Johnson and W. K. Kellogg seem to change their areas of emphasis approximately every decade or upon accession of a new president. Foundations often develop initiatives articulating interests focused on specific concerns and issue program announcements and RFAs in these areas.

The process of evaluating grant requests appears considerably less formal in private foundations than it is in government. Typically, foundations advise potential grant applicants to submit short letters of interest as a first step. Typically, lower-level staff read these letters, screening them for conformity with the foundation's interests, credibility of the prospective applicant, and such nonstandard criteria for consideration as the foundation might maintain. Letters that pass this screening process are transmitted to higher-level staff, which may ask the applicant for a detailed proposal. Some foundations assemble review panels and hire outside consultants to evaluate proposals of a technical nature. More typically, though, foundation officials discuss full-scale proposals among themselves and formulate recommendations to the governing board, which makes final award decisions.

The percentage of letters of interest which result in eventual funding is quite low. Most letters of inquiry generate a notice of rejection via form letter. Likelihood of funding appears roughly comparable with federal sources. In 1999, the Robert Wood Johnson Foundation's Web site advised potential applicants that their chances of success were 1 in 20. In the 1990s, this foundation operated an investigator program in health policy. Each year, this program received over 400 letters of inquiry and awarded no more than 10 grants.

Some features of the private foundation's informality appear advantageous to applicants. Federal grant application forms are extremely long and detailed, requiring significant effort for completion. Foundation forms tend to be simpler. Many foundations require no standard form. Generally, though, federal agencies provide larger amounts of money to grantees than private foundations. In the late 1900s, for example, few Ford Foundation grants exceeded $100,000. Several AHCPR awards approached $1 million. Generous overhead recovery rates provided by federal grants are attractive to university officials. Many private foundations severely restrict overhead payments or allow no such funds in grantee budgets.

THE POLITICS OF RESEARCH FUNDING

The bureaucratic structure of public funding organizations clearly aims at promoting accountability and fairness. Legally, much of the grant award process is visible to the public. All successful grant applications may be obtained through the Freedom of Information Act. IRG deliberations, the venue in which key funding decisions take place, tend to be conscientiously conducted discussions in the manner of serious graduate-level seminars.

Key features of the operation of agencies such as AHCPR, though, raise questions about the degree to which awards are made strictly according to scientific merit. Deliberations of the Scientific Review Administrator and the agency administrator which result in IRG membership selection are subject to the same uncertainty as all dyadic interactions. Disciplinary bias, partiality to particular questions and approaches, and personal ties may affect IRG membership appointments. IRG membership, of course, strongly affects the agency's funding pattern.

Assignment of primary review responsibilities by the Scientific Review administrator and the IRG chair can also have a profound effect on funding decisions. Positively or negatively biased assignment of the primary reviewer responsibility can determine favorable versus unfavorable outcome. Although all IRG members are expected to read all applications, only the primary and secondary reviewers are expected to do so in detail. IRG members look to these individuals for guidance in their determination of priority scores. Given the competitiveness of funding, most applications have no chance of receiving priority scores below the pay line without strong support by their primary reviewers. In a sense, the primary reviewer must function as an advocate for the applicant. Officials

prejudiced against a particular investigator or approach could ensure selection of a primary reviewer who shared their negative inclination.

Advocacy plays a role of similar importance in private foundation funding. Communication with a foundation official is a virtual necessity prior to submission of a letter of interest. Established relations with these officials is necessary to avoid the screening process that eliminates most grant-seekers and to promote favorable action at each step in the decision-making process.

REFERENCES

National Institute of Health, Division of Research Grants 1993 *Grant Application Statistics.* NIH Peer Review Notes, (February), p. 8.

Agency for Health Care Policy and Research 1992 *Orientation Handbook for Members of AHCPR Review Groups.* Rockville, Md.: Agency for Health Care Policy and Research.

HOWARD P. GREENWALD

RESEARCH METHODS

See Case Studies; Comparative-Historical Sociology; Ethnomethodology; Ethnography; Evaluation Research; Qualitative Methods; Survey Research; Statistical Methods.

RETIREMENT

Retirement is primarily a twentieth-century phenomenon that developed through a convergence of public and private employment policies, a restructuring of the life span relative to work activity, and a redefinition of the terms of monetary compensation for work performed. It may be tempting to view retirement as the "natural" development of a social institution matched to the needs of older people experiencing declines in capacity; but the invention of a distinctive nonemployment status called *retirement* was not simply a response to human aging. Rather, in reconciling a transformed economy to an aging population with an increasing amount of surplus labor, an explicit policy of job distribution was produced. Retirement policies incorporated age as a characteristic that served as both a qualifying and an exclusionary principle for work and income. The fact that these policies were age-based can be linked to the social production of age as a predictor of individual capacity and potential, a production that had ideological roots in the science and larger culture of the time.

HISTORICAL DEVELOPMENTS

Whereas *retirement contracts* existed in both Europe and colonial America, Plakans (1989) argues that preindustrial retirement was a gradual transition. The head of a household transferred legal title to an heir in exchange for some combination of monetary payments, material provisions, and services as stipulated by the aged person or couple. These contracts were typical of agrarian economies in which land was the main factor in production; they represented the final step in a long and sometimes elaborate process of property transfer. These "stepping-down" practices were therefore most immediately linked to inheritance patterns; they could be used to ensure that family control of the land was maintained (Sorensen 1989).

Between 1790 and 1820, American legislatures introduced policies of mandatory retirement for certain categories of pubic officials. By the late 1800s, the majority of businesses still had no formal policies of fixed-age retirement. Instead, informal policies eliminated older workers from the labor force (Fischer 1977). This decline in the demand for older workers can be linked to changes in the structure of American capitalism. During the late 1800s the structure of American capitalism began to change from small-producer, competitive capitalism to large-scale corporate capitalism (Sklar 1988). Part of this reconstruction involved attempts to rationalize age relations in the workplace, a process that was embedded in a more general disenchantment with older workers and a devaluation of their skills. Indeed, the employment rates for men aged 65 and older showed a steady decline during this period, from 80.6 percent in 1870 to 60.2 percent in 1920 (Graebner 1980). According to Graebner's analysis, retirement became the impersonal and egalitarian method adopted by both public and private employers for dealing with superannuated workers. It allowed employers to routinize the dismissal of older workers, thereby restructuring the age composition of their workforces in a way they believed would enhance efficiency, a belief supported by the principles of scientific management. Pension plans legitimized this process and, at the same time, served as an effective labor control device.

The first pension plan (1875) is credited to the American Express Company, but benefits were restricted to permanently incapacitated workers who were at least 65 years old with a minimum of 20 years of service (Schulz 1976). In 1920, the first general piece of retirement legislation, the Civil Service Retirement Act, provided pension coverage for federal civilian employees. One year later, the Revenue Act of 1921 encouraged businesses to implement private plans by exempting both the income of pension and profit-sharing trusts and the employer contributions to these trusts from income tax liability. Nevertheless, coverage remained concentrated in a few industries, and 85 percent of the workforce continued to be without pension coverage.

By the 1930s, the problem of superannuated workers was coupled with the more general problem of managing surplus labor. The changing technology of the workplace helped transform the labor process. A subsequent increase in worker productivity and the growing recognition of the cyclical crises inherent in industrial capitalism broadened the concern beyond that of simple superannuation to that of job distribution and consumption capacity.

The Depression of the 1930s greatly exacerbated the growing problem of old-age poverty and unemployment. By 1935 unemployment rates among those 65 and older were well over 50 percent. Even those with pension benefits did not escape poverty; trade union plans were collapsing, and state and local governments were reducing or discontinuing pension payments (Olsen 1982). Legislative proposals for alleviating some of these problems included the Townsend Plan and the Lundeen Bill. The Townsend Plan proposed a flat $200 monthly pension for older Americans; recipients had to spend the pension within thirty days. The Lundeen Bill proposed benefits at the level of prevailing local wages for all unemployed workers aged 18 and older (including the elderly) until suitable employment was located. Neither of these plans was directly related to a retirement transition. The Townsend Plan granted equal benefits to all nonemployed persons over age 60. The Lundeen

Bill focused more on job creation for workers of all ages than on limiting labor supply through age exclusions.

In 1934, President Franklin Roosevelt appointed the Committee on Economic Security (CES) to develop legislation to address the problems of old-age poverty and unemployment. The Social Security Act of 1935 offered a solution that based benefits on the level of workers' contributions to a general trust fund. Upon their retirement, covered workers (primarily those in manufacturing) could draw retirement benefits, assuming they met the age and work eligibility requirements.

For the CES, retirement referred to complete withdrawal from the labor force. As stated by Barbara Armstrong, an original member of the CES, "[r]etirement means that you've stopped working for pay." According to Armstrong, the option facing the Roosevelt administration pitted older workers against younger workers (Graebner 1980, p. 186). Retirement would reduce unemployment by moving older workers out of the labor force, allowing industries characterized by surplus labor to transfer jobs from older to younger workers. The federal government could facilitate this process by shifting the focus of older workers' financial dependency from the wage contract to a federal income maintenance program. In that sense, the Social Security Act of 1935 established what was primarily a program of old-age relief; its limited coverage and low benefit levels precluded its serving as an effective instrument of retirement. However, in establishing a measure of income support for retired older workers, the act reinforced the view that in the competition for jobs, age was a legitimate criterion, and youth had the "higher claim" (Graebner 1980). Ironically, the mobilization for World War II created job opportunities for older workers, as it did for women. Even though these opportunities proved temporary, they challenged the connection between retirement and superannuation, a connection that was asserted more emphatically when the supply of labor exceeded the demand.

During the next several decades, considerable growth in private pension plans occurred; coverage increased from 4 million workers in the late 1930s to 10 million workers in 1950 and 20 million workers in 1960. The expansion was spurred by a number of factors including the desire of firms to encourage loyalty and reduce turnover, favorable tax treatment, and the 1949 Supreme Court decision to uphold a National Labor Relations Board (NLRB) ruling that pensions were appropriate issues of negotiation through collective bargaining (Schulz 1976). During this same period, Social Security coverage was extended to more workers, and Congress continued to raise benefits in response to changes in the cost of living, although real benefit levels remained relatively low (Derthick 1979).

DECLINING RATES OF LABOR-FORCE PARTICIPATION

Early research on retirement was centrally concerned with the question of voluntarism in the retirement transition, as well as with the financial, social, and psychological consequences of leaving the labor force. Even though the expansion of both government and employer-based pensions had improved the economic situation of older people in retirement, poverty rates among the elderly were still high. By 1960, 35.2 percent of persons aged 65 and older were below the poverty line, compared with 22.4 percent of the general population. Poverty was the norm for older white women and older African Americans (U.S. Bureau of the Census 1987).

During the 1950s, the Social Security Administration began studying the characteristics of newly entitled beneficiaries. Initial reports stated that early retirement occurred primarily because of poor health and difficulties finding and keeping jobs; the availability of Social Security retirement benefits played a secondary role (Wentworth 1945; Stecker 1955). Although these studies relied on beneficiary-reported reasons for retirement, a measurement strategy that was criticized because of its susceptibility to social desirability bias, the findings cannot be totally discounted. Retirement in the 1950s was not a financially attractive status for many older workers. Given that retirement income programs offered "fixed" benefits (benefits that remained nominally the same but, with inflation, declined in real terms), the financial security of middle- and working-class retirees was in jeopardy.

During the 1950s, retirement became more common. Insurance companies led the way in developing "retirement preparation" programs, as researchers attempted to define strategies for "successful aging." In an era of postwar prosperity, retirement came to be viewed as a "period of potential enjoyment and creative experience which accrues as a social reward for a life-time of labor" (Donahue et al. 1960, p. 361). Researchers investigating the effect of retirement on life satisfaction found that "retirement does not cause a sudden deterioration in psychological health as [had] been asserted by other writers" (Streib and Schneider 1971, p. 161). Rather than rejecting retirement, advocacy groups for the elderly lobbied for improved conditions of retirement, including more generous pension benefits. Mandatory retirement had not yet become an issue. Instead, the trend was in the direction of earlier retirement, that is, before the age of 65. In 1956 women and in 1962 men were allowed to retire at age 62 by accepting actuarially reduced Social Security benefits.

During the mid-1960s, in the context of Lyndon Johnson's War on Poverty, the issue of old-age poverty was again addressed. In the Older Americans Act of 1965, Congress established a "new social contract for the aged" (Achenbaum 1983, p. 85) by specifying a series of objectives that, if met, would significantly improve the quality of life enjoyed by older people. Among these objectives was an "equal opportunity to the full and free enjoyment of . . . an adequate income in retirement in accordance with the American standard of living . . . [and] retirement in health, honor, and dignity" (U.S. Department of Health, Education, and Welfare 1976, p. 2).

Richard Nixon's presidency inaugurated the era of modern retirement. Whereas previous amendments to the Social Security Act had brought more and more workers into the system, they had not significantly improved the level of retirement benefits (Munnell 1977). The presumption that Social Security benefits should serve as retirement income supplements rather than as the primary source of income had not been challenged. But the persistently high rates of old-age poverty lent credence to the charge that benefits were inadequate. During the decade following passage of the Older Americans Act, benefits were increased five times and indexed to changes in the consumer price index. Both the "real" level of benefits and

the replacement rate of benefits to previous earnings were improved. Enhanced retirement benefits allowed workers to maintain their standard of living across the retirement transition and helped redefine retirement as a legitimate nonwork status that average-income workers could afford to enter voluntarily. During the 1970s, employer-sponsored pensions were also being reorganized. The 1974 passage of the Employee Retirement Income Security Act (ERISA) regularized vesting plans and provided workers with some protection against benefit loss. Private sector initiatives aimed at inducing early retirement were also increasingly common (Barfield and Morgan 1969). Until the 1970s, workers choosing early retirement virtually always accepted reduced benefits. During the 1970s, however, employers began to offer early retirement incentive plans. Not only did these plans pay benefits at younger ages, but the present value of the benefits often exceeded that of normal retirement benefits.

The parallel changes in labor-force participation rates and in poverty rates among the elderly are noteworthy. In the latter part of this century, labor-force participation rates at older ages declined significantly. During the 1970s, rates for men aged 55–64 dropped from 83 percent (1970) to 75.6 percent (1975) to 72.1 percent (1980) (U.S. Department of Labor 1983). In addition, at the beginning of the decade, 24.6 percent of those aged 65 and older were living below the poverty line, twice the 12.1 percent that characterized the general population. By the end of the decade, the poverty rate among the elderly had dropped to 15.2 percent, compared to an overall poverty rate of 11.7.

As Figure 1 illustrates, the changes in labor-force participation rates (derived from the Current Population Survey) differ by both age and gender. Rates for men and women aged 65 and older appear to have stabilized and perhaps marginally increased from their lowest point. Rates for men aged 55–59 and 60–64 show overall declines with recent hints of a slight upturn. In contrast, rates for women in these age ranges have steadily increased during the last quarter-century, with rates for women in their late fifties surpassing rates for men in their early sixties during the last decade.

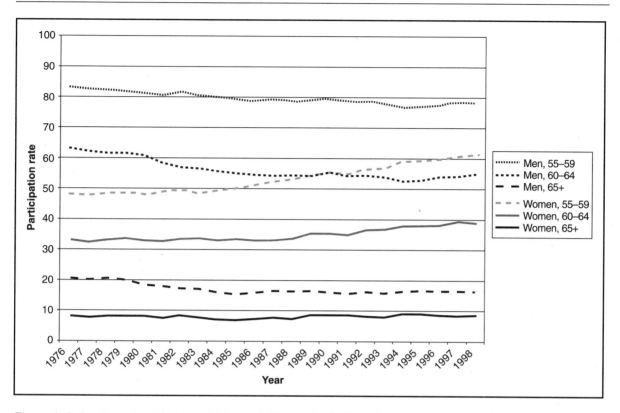

Figure 1. Labor-Force Participation of Men and Women in the United States, 1976–1998

DETERMINANTS OF RETIREMENT

Most current research examining retirement is of one of two types: national longitudinal studies that address the behavior of workers across a wide variety of occupations and industries (e.g., Quinn and Burkhauser, 1994; Hayward et al. 1989) and studies of specific firms that assess the retirement behavior of workers who share substantial commonality in workplace features (e.g, Hardy et al. 1996; Stock and Wise 1990). The former design maximizes variation in both work context and individual characteristics, using statistical controls to assess the relative impact of individual and job characteristics on retirement transitions. Because of the sampling strategy, results from these studies can be generalized to the national population of older workers. The second design—the case study—limits observations to workers who share a particular work context and attempts to explain variation in workers' responses to a common decisional matrix.

In both these designs, individualized models of retirement have been dominant, although the relative emphasis of "sociological" versus "economic" models may differ. Retirement models proposed by economists have emphasized the financial considerations involved in exchanging one income flow (e.g., wages and salary) for alternative sources of income (e.g., pensions and income from savings and investments). They have proposed measurement strategies based on the calculation of the present discounted values of the various income streams to attempt to disentangle relative effects. Sociological studies of retirement frequently focus either on the social psychological consequences of retirement or on the importance of occupational structure in shaping behavioral contingencies. Both opportunities and constraints are unequally distributed across workers. Whereas unionized manufacturing jobs may protect older workers through seniority systems, they also provide early retirement incentives through employer-based pension plans. Older workers are also vulnerable to plant closings and job dislocations that accompany mergers, downsizing, and cutbacks. This theoretical framework views retirement transitions as a career characteristic, with late-career behaviors being at least partially contingent on earlier career opportunities. In addition, retirement behavior is embedded in more general macroeconomic conditions. Rates of unemployment, changes in both government and employer pension programs, and the age structure of both the population and the labor force are implicated. Combining insights from both disciplines leads to models in which the financial trade-off is captured by the relative effects of current earnings and the present value of pension benefits; human capital (and, indirectly, the probability of alternative employment) through education, health status, skill level, and age; characteristics of career through years of seniority, history of recent layoffs, and overtime work; and family situation through marital status and the presence of children in the home.

MEASURING RETIREMENT

As the nature of retirement transitions changed, the question of measurement became more difficult. Armstrong's definition of "no longer working for pay" was being replaced by a variety of definitions oriented toward transitions out of career employment or full-time work, changes in major income sources (the receipt of Social Security or employer pension benefits), or changes in identity structures (e.g., through self-identification as a retiree). As definitions of retirement shifted toward receipt of pensions and the inclusion of part-time workers, the concerns of government turned toward the escalating cost of retirement and the advisability of delaying it. It became important to distinguish among exiting the labor force through "early" retirement, "regular" retirement, or disability, since these distinctions have implications for income replacement as well as labor-force reentry. Professionals, managers, and salespeople tend to delay retirement, whereas skilled and semiskilled blue-collar workers move more rapidly into retirement; clerical workers move more quickly into both retirement and disability statuses; and service workers experience relatively high rates of disability and death out of employment (Hayward et al. 1989). In addition, reentry into the labor force has become more common, with estimates of as many as one-third of retirees becoming reemployed, often within one to two years of their retirements. In short, the heterogeneity of what it means to be retired has increased considerably: it encompasses a broader age range;

it involves diversity of income sources; and it allows for some level of postretirement employment.

ISSUES OF GENDER AND RACE

The development of retirement policy has been primarily oriented around the work careers of men, predominantly white men. The original Social Security program excluded industries in which women and blacks were concentrated. Although later amendments eventually covered these categories of workers, the benefit structure continued to reward long and continuous attachment to the labor force and to penalize workers for extended or frequent work interruptions. The temporal organization of women's lives relative to work and family, paid and unpaid labor, put women "off schedule" in accumulating claims to retirement income.

Spousal and survivors' benefits were designed to support couples and (primarily) widows during their later years. Research on women's retirement often focused on unmarried women and found that the determinants of retirement for women were similar to the determinants that had been identified for men. Although unmarried women and men differed in occupational locations, wages, health, and access to employer-sponsored pensions, these determinants appeared to sort unmarried women into retirees and workers in much the same way as they sorted men.

The pattern of women's labor-force participation has changed in recent decades, and more women—particularly more married women—are in the labor market. In fact, the trends in rates of labor-force participation for older women reflect both the increasing employment rates for successive cohorts of women and the tendency for more recent cohorts of older working women to retire at younger ages. The increase in dual-earner couples suggests that retirement decisions may be interdependent, with age differences, relative earnings, and the relative health of spouses figuring into joint decisions about careers, retirement, and postretirement employment.

Work and income disadvantages that are experienced at earlier stages of the life course cast a shadow on retirement transitions among minority group members. Lower earnings, lower job status, and discontinuity in labor-force attachment all undermine the financial platform for retirement. Work histories characterized by frequent spells of unemployment, illness, or temporary disability are linked to lower average retirement benefits and lower rates of savings and asset accumulation. In addition, African Americans are less likely to be married than whites and therefore more likely to be limited to their individual earnings and retirement resources. African Americans are more likely to exit work through disability and also more likely to continue to work intermittently after retirement. Gibson (1987) argues that disability can be used as another pathway to retirement for older African Americans, one that offers financial advantages. Because work histories can appear sporadic in old age as well as youth, establishing the timing of retirement as an event also can be difficult (Gibson 1987).

INTERNATIONAL COMPARISONS

Industrialization, economic development, demographic shifts, and politics are implicated in international comparisons of both the prevalence and the financing of retirement. Pampel (1985) reports that, among advanced industrial nations, a pattern of low labor-force participation among aged males is related to the level of industrialization and population aging. Cross-national comparisons of employment-to-population ratios demonstrate a continued decline in labor-force participation between 1970 and 1990 for men aged 55 and older. This decline is not, however, consistent across all age groups. Employment rates for men aged 55–59 have not shown the same proportional decrease as rates for men aged 60–64, or for those aged 65 and older. Compared to other Organization for Economic Cooperation and Development (OECD) countries (see Figure 2), Canada, Finland, Japan, Sweden, and the United States have relatively high rates of labor-force participation for men and women aged 65 and older.

Despite an overall downward trend in average age of retirement, nations continue to differ in the patterns of labor-force exits. Early retirement in European countries such as France, the Netherlands, and Germany remains the norm, with one-half to three-quarters of 60–64-year-old men out of the labor market (Guillemard and Rein 1993). Whereas early retirement in the United States was

primarily financed through early retirement incentive programs (ERIPs) offered by private firms, more severe problems of unemployment in Europe fueled early retirement through expanded eligibility for state programs. Among some countries of western Europe and North America, disability programs also can operate as pseudo-retirement programs that allow workers to exit prior to normal retirement age. In contrast to the pattern of western Europe, Canada, and the United States, labor-force participation rates in Japan for men in all three age groups have been more resilient. Rates in 1990 remained relatively high, with more than one-third of men aged 65 and older participating in the labor force (Quinn and Burkhauser 1994). Cross-national comparisons of women's retirement patterns are more complicated. Whereas some countries show little change since 1970 (e.g., Canada, Australia, Italy, Japan, and the United States), others show patterns of labor-force withdrawal that parallel the trends for older men (e.g., Finland, France, West Germany, Spain, and the United Kingdom).

When comparing rates of labor-force participation, it is important to take into account national differences in census procedures, the definition of the labor force, and the kinds of activities that constitute "work." Because countries differ in the pathways workers take to retirement, using pension receipt as an indicator is also flawed. In Germany, for example, disability benefits and intermediate unemployment benefits also provide access to early retirement. Comparisons based on rates of labor-force participation confound country differences in full-time versus part-time employment, complete versus partial retirement, and unemployment and employment. In addition, cross-sectional figures do not allow a comparison of rates of withdrawal or reentry that would allow us to distinguish relatively stable from volatile labor markets.

Within each nation, policy development and social dynamics exert an important influence on retirement behavior. Recent debate in the United States and other countries has centered on the financial burdens of supporting a growing population of retirees and the desirability of reversing the trend toward early retirement. In 1983 the United States amended the Social Security Act to legislate a gradual increase in the age of full entitlement from 65 to 66 by 2009 and to 67 by 2027. Germany

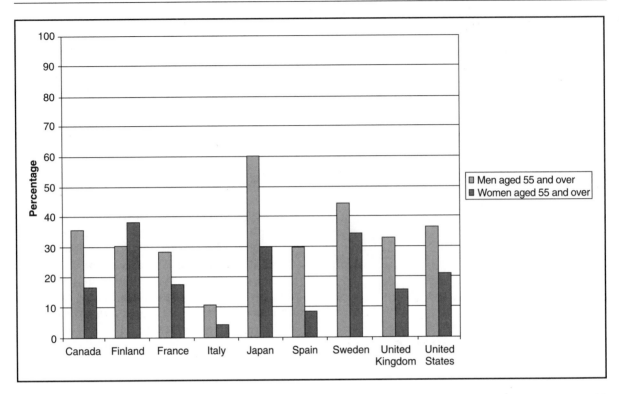

Figure 2. The Employment-to-Population Ratio for Men and Women Aged 55 and Over in OECD Countries, 1990

(1992 Pension Reform Act) and Italy have made similar policy changes. Japan tried to raise the retirement age from 60 to 65 but failed in their initial attempt. In 1990 Sweden succeeded in blocking the early retirement pathway through the disability fund, but in 1992 failed to abolish the partial retirement pension system. Even in France, where "old age is seen as a time of life when work is illegitimate (Guillemard 1983, p. 88) and where the legal retirement age was lowered to 60 in 1982, it is likely that the retirement age will be raised. This type of political reaction to demographic aging is one way of trying to shift the cost of early retirement from government programs to firms and individuals.

Other workplace policies linked to demographic aging, such as flexible retirement systems, are also being considered in countries like Germany, France, and Great Britain. Countries with lower rates of early exit, such as Japan and Sweden, provide an alternative approach to labor-market withdrawal which may alleviate the pressures of demographic aging. These countries structure retirement as a gradual process involving lowering

wages, reducing hours, and reassigning workers. To some extent this model is already in place in the United States through "bridge jobs," in Sweden through partial retirement pensions, and in Japan through wage reduction arrangements.

DIRECTIONS FOR RESEARCH

Sociologists are also interested in the social context in which retirement decisions are made and retirement policies are developed. Family contexts, work contexts, economic contexts, and historical contexts all provide important frames of reference in which these behaviors are negotiated. To date, retirement research has refined both the measurement of concepts and the complexity of the behavioral models. Many of these refinements have involved the economic dimensions of retirement. The financial trade-off between pensions and wages, the changes in accumulated pension wealth, and the age-earnings profiles of different occupations have been captured in current models. What models of retirement continue to lack, however, is sensitivity to the social frames of reference (e.g., the shop floor, the office, the firm, the family, and the community). Studies that have addressed some of these issues (e.g., Hardy and Hazelrigg 1999) suggest, for example, that firm level features may be implicated in both the rate and the determinants of early retirement.

Retirement behavior may be primarily motivated by financial considerations. But given a threshold of financial security, perhaps the unfolding of the retirement process also involves the culture of the workplace, family dynamics, and societal values. Our first task is to theorize the social aspects of these decisions so that we can develop hypotheses. To test these hypotheses, a different data collection strategy is required—one that samples a sufficient number of observations of individual workers within sufficient numbers of organizational or, more generally, cultural contexts that can themselves be measured in terms of their salient characteristics. What has become clear is that retirement decisions are shaped by individual preferences, but that these preferences are shaped by the opportunities and constraints that workers encounter.

REFERENCES

Achenbaum, W. Andrew 1983 *Shades of Gray: Old Age, American Values, and Federal Policies since 1920*. Boston: Little, Brown.

Atchley, Robert 1982 "Retirement: Leaving the World of Work." *Annals of the Academy of Political and Social Science* 464:120–131.

Barfield, Richard E., and James N. Morgan 1969 *Early Retirement: The Decision and the Experience*. Ann Arbor: University of Michigan Press.

Derthick, Martha 1979 *Policymaking for Social Security*. Washington, D.C.: Brookings Institution.

Donahue, Wilma, Harold Orbach, and Otto Pollak 1960 "Retirement: The Emerging Social Pattern." In Clark Tibbitts, ed., *Handbook of Social Gerontology*. Chicago: University of Chicago Press.

Fischer, David Hackett 1977 *Growing Old in America*. New York: Oxford University Press.

Gibson, Rose 1987 "Reconceptualizing Retirement for Black Americans." *Gerontologist* 27(6):691–698.

Graebner, William 1980 *A History of Retirement: The Meaning and Function of an American Institution 1885–1978*. New Haven, Conn.: Yale University Press.

Guillemard, Anne-Marie 1983 "The Making of Old Age Policy in France: Points of Debate, Issues at Stake, Underlying Social Relations." In Anne-Marie Guillemard, ed., *Old Age and the Welfare State*. Beverly Hills, Calif.: Sage.

——, and Martin Rein 1993 "Comparative Patterns of Retirement: Retirement Trends in Developed Societies." *Annual Review of Sociology* 19:469–503.

Hardy, Melissa A., and Lawrence Hazelrigg 1999 "A Multilevel Analysis of Early Retirement Decisions among Auto Workers in Plants with Different Futures." *Research on Aging* 21(2):275–303.

——, and Jill Quadagno 1996 *Ending a Career in the Auto Industry*. New York: Plenum.

Hayward, Mark D., Melissa A. Hardy, and William Grady 1989 "Labor Force Withdrawal Patterns among Older Men in the United States." *Social Science Quarterly* 70(2):425–448.

Munnell, Alicia H. 1977 *The Future of Social Security*. Washington, D.C.: Brookings Institution.

Olsen, Laura Katz 1982 *The Political Economy of Aging: The State, Private Power, and Social Welfare*. New York: Columbia University Press.

Pampel, Fred 1985 "Determinants of Labor Force Participation Rates of Aged Males in Developed and Developing Nations, 1965–1975." In Zena Blau, ed., *Current Perspectives on Aging and the Life Cycle*. Greenwich, Conn.: JAI Press.

Plakans, Andrejs 1989 "Stepping Down in Former Times: A Comparative Assessment of Retirement in Traditional Europe." In David Kertzer and K. Warner Schaie, eds., *Age Structuring in Comparative Perspective*. Hillsdale, N.J.: Erlbaum.

Quinn, Joseph F., and Richard V. Burkhauser 1994 "Retirement and Labor Force Behavior of the Elderly." In Linda Martin and Samuel H. Preston, eds., *Demography of Aging*. Washington, D.C.: National Academy Press.

Schulz, James H. 1976 *The Economics of Aging*. Belmont, Calif.: Wadsworth.

Sklar, Martin J. 1988 *The Corporate Reconstruction of American Capitalism, 1890–1916*. New York: Cambridge University Press.

Sorensen, Aage B. 1989 "Old Age, Retirement, and Inheritance." In David Kertzer and K. Warner Schaie, eds., *Age Structuring in Comparative Perspective*. Hillsdale, N.J.: Erlbaum.

Stecker, Margaret 1955 "Why Do Beneficiaries Retire? Who among Them Return to Work?" *Social Security Bulletin* 18:3.

Stock, James H., and David A. Wise. 1990. "The Pension Inducement to Retire." In David A. Wise, ed., *Issues in the Economics of Aging.* Chicago: University of Chicago Press.

Streib, Gordon F., and Clement Schneider 1971 *Retirement in American Society.* Ithaca, N.Y.: Cornell University Press.

U.S. Bureau of the Census 1987 *Statistical Abstract of the United States 1986.* Washington, D.C.: U.S. Government Printing Office.

U.S. Department of Health, Education, and Welfare 1976 *Older Americans' Act of 1965, as Amended and Related Acts, Bicentennial Compilation, March 1976.* Washington, D.C.: Office of Human Development, Administration on Aging.

U.S. Department of Labor, Bureau of Labor Statistics 1983 *Current Population Reports,* ser. P-60, no. 148. Washington, D.C.: U.S. Government Printing Office.

Wentworth, Edna C. 1945 "Why Beneficiaries Retire." *Social Security Bulletin* 8:16–20.

MELISSA A. HARDY
KIM SHUEY

REVOLUTIONS

Revolutions are rapid, fundamental transformations of a society's socioeconomic and political structures (Huntington 1968). Social revolutions differ from other forms of social transformation, such as rebellions, coups d'état, and political revolutions. *Rebellions* involve the revolt of society's subordinate classes—peasants, artisans, workers—but do not produce enduring structural changes. *Coups d'état* forcibly replace the leadership of states but do not fundamentally alter state structures. *Political revolutions* transform state structures but leave social structures largely intact. What is distinctive to social revolutions is that basic changes in social structures and political structures occur in a mutually reinforcing fashion (Skocpol 1979). A social revolution is more than a change in the state. It is a change in the state of an entire society.

Recent sociological work on revolutions recognizes their importance in the making of the modern world order and the opportunities revolutions offer for building theories of social and political change. These opportunities were most emphatically embraced by Marx, who placed the study and the making of revolution at the center of his lifework. Virtually all theories of revolution since Marx share his concern with three separate yet interrelated phenomena: (1) the social conditions that lead to revolution or its absence, (2) the character of participation in revolutions, and (3) the outcomes of revolutions (see Tucker 1978). This review examines Marx's theories in light of significant contemporary analyses of revolution, in order to evaluate how well his theories have stood the test of time and to consider how much of his legacy may endure in future sociological work.

First, Marx understood modern revolutions to be by-products of economic advance. Revolutionary situations emerged when contradictions between the forces of production (how the means of existence are produced) and the relations of production (how labor's product is distributed) within an existing mode of production reached their limits. For Marx, the coming of the 1789 French revolution lay in the irresolvable contradiction between feudal restrictions on land, labor, and credit and emerging capitalist arrangements advanced by an ascending bourgeoise. Revolutions brought the resolution of these contradictions by serving as bridges between successive modes of production, enabling the ascent of capitalism over feudalism and later the replacement of capitalism by socialism.

Second, Marx held that revolutions were accomplished through class struggle. In revolutionary situations, conflict intensified between the existing dominant class and the economically ascendant class. Under feudalism, class conflict pitted the aristocracy against the ascendant bourgeoisie. Under capitalism, the differing situations of segments of society determined their revolutionary tendencies. Some classes, such as the petite bourgeoisie, would become stakeholders in capitalism and allies of the dominant bourgeoisie. Others, such as the peasantry, that did not fully participate in wage labor and lacked solidarity, would stay on the sidelines. The industrial proletariat would be the midwife of socialist revolution, for wage labor's concentration in cities would generate solidarity and collective consciousness of the proletariat's exploitation by the bourgeoisie. Class consciousness was a necessary (though not a sufficient) condition for revolution.

Third, Marx believed that revolutions so thoroughly transformed class relations that they put in place new conditions enabling further economic advance. Revolutions were locomotives of history that brought in train new structures of state administration, property holding, and political ideology. Reinforcing the fundamental changes in class relations, these transformations culminated the transition from one mode of production to another.

In sum, Marx's theory identified the conditions that spawn revolutionary situations, the classes that would make revolutions, and the outcomes of revolutions. How well has Marx's analysis served later generations of scholars and revolutionaries? Many of the sociopolitical transformations since his death were unanticipated by Marx. In light of these events, contemporary sociologists have reconsidered his thinking.

Consider first the social conditions making for revolution or its absence. Social revolutions are rare. Modern capitalist societies have experienced severe economic crises that intensified class conflict and gave the appearance of revolutionary situations, but they have skirted actual revolution. Modern capitalist economies have great staying power, and reform rather than revolution is the rule in advanced nations. Indeed, the great revolutions of France, Russia, and China, and those in Third World societies such as Cuba, Vietnam, and Nicaragua, have occurred in predominantly agrarian economies where capitalist relations of production were only moderately developed. The 1917 Russian Revolution stands as proof of Lenin's claim that revolution was possible in Russia despite its failure to develop a fully capitalist economy in the manner of the western European states Marx saw as the likely candidates for socialist revolution.

Rather than growing from contradictions between the forces and the relations of production, revolutionary situations arise in political crises occasioned by international competitive pressures. States with relatively backward economies are vulnerable to military defeats, as occurred in Russia in 1917, and to financial crises like that of 1789 France after a century of costly struggle with Britain and Continental Powers. Nation-states that are disadvantaged within the international states system are most at risk to externally induced crises and to the possibility of social revolution.

A state's vulnerability to crisis, however, depends fundamentally on its autonomy, that is, the extent of its dependence on elites, whether nobles, landlords, or religious authorities. State managers are forever caught in a vice between their obligation to increase revenues to meet international competitive challenges and the resistance of angry elites to resource extraction. States that are weakly bureaucratized, where elites control high offices and key military posts, cannot act autonomously. When powerful elites paralyze the state's resource accumulation, severe crises occur, as in the English, French, and Chinese revolutions (Goldstone 1986).

However, externally induced crises may initiate an "elite revolution," as occurred in Japan's 1868 Meiji restoration and Ataturk's 1919 revolution in Turkey. In such regimes, a bureaucratic elite of civil and military officials emerged that lacked large landholdings or ties to merchants and landlords. In the face of Western military threats to national sovereignty and, consequently, to their own power and status, these elites seized control of the state apparatus. With the aim of resolving economic and military difficulties, they transformed existing sociopolitical structures through land reform, leveling of status distinctions, and rapid industrialization (Trimberger 1978). These transformative episodes, sometimes called "revolutions from above," are distinguished by the absence of popular revolts "from below."

Neopatrimonial regimes are highly vulnerable to revolutionary overthrow (Eisenstadt 1978). Examples include pre-1911 Mexico, pre-1959 Cuba, and pre-1979 Nicaragua. Centered on the personal decisions of a dictator, each of these regimes operated through extensive patronage networks rather than through a bureaucratized civil service and a professionalized military. Their exclusionary politics made reform nearly impossible and, in the event of withdrawal of support by stronger states, invited challenges that might overwhelm corrupt armed forces.

In contrast, revolution is unlikely in open, participatory regimes typical of modern capitalist democracies. By enfranchising new groups, these systems incorporate potential challengers. By redistributing wealth and opportunity—or appearing to do so through open markets and meritocracy—they are able to mute class antagonisms.

In sum, contradictions between the state apparatus and a society's dominant classes have been crucial to the onset of revolutionary situations. State bureaucrats are caught in the cross pressures between meeting the challenges of the international states system and yielding to the competing claims of elites. Consequently, state structures differ in their vulnerability to political crises.

Consider next the character of participation in revolutions. Critics of Marx's voluntarist theory assert that no successful social revolution has been made by a self-consciously revolutionary movement. They allow that revolutionaries do guide the course of revolutions, but assert that they do not create revolutionary situations which emerge from externally induced political crises. These critics also offer a different reading of the roles of social classes in revolution. Urban workers, favored by Marx's theory, played important parts in revolutions. However, their numbers were small and their protests lacked the impact of uprisings by peasants who composed the vast bulk of producers in agrarian societies. Indeed, peasant revolts provided the "dynamite" to bring down old regimes when political crises immobilized armies and upset food supplies and distribution (Moore 1966). Peasant revolts against the landed upper classes made it impossible to continue existing agrarian class relations and thereby reduced the prospects for liberal reforms or counterrevolution. It was the conjunction of political crisis and peasant insurrection that brought about the fundamental transformations identified with social revolutions in France, Russia, and China (Skocpol 1979).

But peasants do not act alone. A key difference between Old Regime revolutions and revolutions in the Third World is the importance of coalitions in the latter (Tilly 1978). Peasants in France and Russia lived in solitary and relatively autonomous village communities that afforded them the solidarity and tactical space for revolt (Wolf 1969). In the twentieth century, professional revolutionaries provided leadership and ideologies that cemented dispersed local groups with disparate interests into potent national movements. The success of their efforts depended in part on the breadth of the coalition they were able to realize among peasants, landless and migrant laborers, rural artisans, and sometimes landlords (Goodwin and Skocpol 1989).

Add to that the importance of urban groups which played crucial parts in making Third World revolutions. In Cuba and Nicaragua, students, professionals, clerics, and merchants joined workers and peasants in coalitions that toppled dictatorial regimes. Similarly, the 1979 overthrow of the Shah of Iran resulted from the mobilization of a broad coalition of merchants and workers, students and professionals, that met little resistance from powerful military forces (Farhi 1990).

Finally, revolutionary leaderships have not come from the ranks of an ascendant bourgeoisie or a risen proletariat. Rather, marginal political elites were most likely to consolidate power, for they were both skilled in the running of state organizations and tied by identity and livelihood to the aggrandizement of national welfare and prestige. Their role is clearest in revolutions from above but is no less prominent in social revolutions.

Consider, last, the outcomes of revolutions. For Marx, revolutions were bridges between successive modes of production. Bourgeois revolutions marked the transition from feudalism to capitalism; socialist revolutions opened the way for the transition from capitalism to communism, history's final stage. Through the dictatorship of the proletariat and the abolition of private property, socialist revolution would bring the end of class struggle and the disappearance of state power.

Revolutions did transform class structures, economic arrangements, and political institutions, however, in all successful social revolutions, the transformations were accomplished by new state structures. The state did *not* wither away. Moreover, the new states were more centralized and bureaucratized than their predecessors. For example, liberal parliamentary regimes appeared in the early phases of the 1789 French and 1917 Russian revolutions. In the face of threats to sovereignty from abroad and counterrevolutionary threats at home, these regimes gave way to centralized governments which rationalized the machinery of state for national defense and internal control. Liberal parliamentary regimes were similarly short-lived during revolutionary episodes in post–World War II Europe, Asia, Africa, and Latin America.

Indeed, what changed most in revolutions was the mode of social control of the lower strata as regimes centralized political power. All social revolutions ended with the consolidation of new mass-mobilizing state organizations through which peasants and urban workers were for the first time directly incorporated into national economies and polities. While they aimed for independence from colonial powers, national liberation movements in Asia and Africa shared with these newly formed revolutionary states the project of state-centered mass mobilization.

Last, and vastly more important than the ways that individual revolutions changed sociopolitical institutions where they occurred, is the collective legacy of four centuries of revolution for the modern world. The legacy is clear in ways that revolutions transformed the workings of the world order and altered our sense of human prospects and limits. Through new political institutions, revolutions created our vocabulary of citizenship and its opposite, the machinery of tyranny. Through new structures of labor and investment, revolutions boosted agricultural and industrial output. By breaking old alliances and creating new ones, they altered the international states system and the shape of world markets. With wars and depressions, revolutions rightfully became the major markers of world history. Past revolutions are a benchmark from which we reckon humankind's advance or descent. In all these ways, revolutions helped shape the structures and consciousness we know as modernity.

For a century, sociologists who study revolutions have pursued a project of revision. Informed by the study of recent sociopolitical transformations and by new interpretations of past revolutions, their work questions and qualifies much of Marx's analysis. It considers national revolutions in the context of the world economy and the international states system. It places the relations between states and social classes in a new light, and it examines how social transformations in the recent or distant past weigh on the course of revolutionary events. On balance, it largely affirms and continues the main thrust of Marx's perspective, notably his focus on actors embedded in concrete organizational settings within historically specific circumstances. This perspective—rather than a focus on personality, collective mentality, or system dysfunction—distinguishes the sociology of revolution. It owes much to Marx's legacy.

What future sociologists will take from Marx's legacy is an open question. Are revolutions in the coming century likely to differ in their causes, dynamics, or outcomes from the revolutions of centuries past? Will revolutions become unlikely as global prosperity shrinks the now yawning gap between rich and poor? Is it possible that new state structures, either more responsive or more repressive than those we now know, will bring revolutions to an end? These are questions for the next generation of theorists.

Their search for answers will surely cover old ground. There is no "Y2K problem" for revolutionary theory. Changing the calendar does not change the world. The familiar masterplots that made modern world history—notably, the globalization of markets, communications, and culture, the international states system, and persistent inequalities in power and resources—suggest the shape of revolutions to come.

Indeed, for many sociologists, the past is prologue. For example, in an analysis of revolution and rebellion in Europe, China, and the Middle East from 1500 to 1850, Goldstone (1991) links population growth and state breakdown. He identifies a process in which population growth overwhelms the administrative capacities of agrarian states, bringing inflation and fiscal crisis, intra-elite conflicts, popular unrest, and delegitimation of traditional regimes and their policies. Starting in roughly 1850, the underlying conditions changed when new forms of investment and infrastructure that accompanied urbanization and industrialization enabled modern states to manage population growth and prices. In much of the contemporary Third World, however, urbanization and industrialization did not strengthen the hand of state managers, but had the opposite effect. There, population growth and price pressures—often the unintended consequences of failed development schemes—continued to court state crises.

Nevertheless, Goldstone and other analysts assert revolutions will be rare. This is so because revolutions are not the result of a single cause, such as population pressure, but arise only when several causal elements, such as state crisis, elite withdrawal, and mass mobilization, converge in a rare revolutionary conjuncture. The worker masses of Sergei Eisenstein's films and massed peasants of Hollywood spectacles give a misleading impression of revolutionary causation. There have been many popular uprisings—some of them large and quite violent—which did not bring revolutionary transformations.

Lachmann (1997) calls attention to the pivotal role of elites. He develops an explanation for revolutionary outbreak and success in terms of varying combinations of elite unity or conflict and mass participation or quiescence. Lachmann finds that single, unified elites are immune to mass revolutionary challenges (as happened in Hungary in 1956 and Czechoslovakia in 1968). Conversely, mass mobilization succeeds at moments of heightened elite conflict (as in 1789 France). These conditions are self-reinforcing. By creating opportunities and potential alliances, elite conflict encourages nonelite mobilization (sometimes accidentally, sometimes intentionally), which, in turn, can alter the system of political domination and economic exploitation through which elites rule and live.

The study of mass-elite relations signals a turn toward understanding the importance of agency and ideology in making revolutions. The turn follows a generation of structural theories which spotlighted the crises through which revolutionary situations come, but left us unenlightened as to how revolutionary outcomes are realized in the actions of millions of men and women. For example, Markoff (1996) shows how in 1789 France, the abolition of feudalism was not foreordained by the state's fiscal crisis, but a contingent outcome of the interplay of waves of rural insurrection, Parisian mobs, and legislative concessions. Through their dialogue with the "people," revolutionary legislators created a form of discourse that defined the revolution as a watershed moment between the old order and the new. Markoff shows that words, as well as deeds make revolutions. While the French revolution was more than talk, talk became the frame in which action was interpreted and given form.

Revolutionary outcomes, though, depend on more than the unfolding of actions and the shaping of ideologies by the makers of revolution. History shows that revolutionary outcomes are constrained by global circumstances. Contrasting the outcomes of the Mexican (1910–1917) and Bolivian (1952) revolutions, Eckstein (1976) shows the impact of U.S. foreign investment and military assistance on class structure, party formation, and national well-being. While both modernized their economies, Mexico had greater economic diversification, productivity growth, and political stability than Bolivia. Their revolutions did not alter their standing relative to stronger states, leaving Bolivia with its weaker postrevolutionary state (and important tin mines) open to U.S. foreign aid and military assistance. Subsidized and schooled by the United States, the armed forces played the decisive role in the 1964 overthrow of the Bolivian regime that the United States had supported in 1952.

Revolutions will not disappear as long as nation-states remain the dominant form of world political organization. While the globalization of markets, communications, and culture seems to augur a new world, we live with the legacy of the capitalist world order. Ours is still a world of states, albeit one increasingly structured by regional alliances, multinational corporations, and international bodies like the United Nations. What Marx recognized in the late nineteenth century will likely hold in the century ahead: that persistent inequalities in power and resources between masses and elites and among the world's nation-states will shape revolutionary prospects and processes.

(SEE ALSO: *Marxist Sociology*)

REFERENCES

Eckstein, Susan 1976 *The Impact of Revolution: A Comparative Analysis of Mexico and Bolivia*. London: Sage.

Eisenstadt, S. N. 1978 *Revolution and the Transformation of Societies*. New York: Free Press.

Farhi, Farideh 1990 *States and Urban-Based Revolutions: Iran and Nicaragua*. Urbana: University of Illinois Press.

Goldstone, Jack A. 1986 "The Comparative and Historical Study of Revolutions." In J. A. Goldstone, ed., *Revolutions*. San Diego; Calif.: Harcourt Brace Jovanovich.

—— 1991 *Revolution and Rebellion in the Early Modern World*. Berkeley: University of California Press.

Goodwin, Jeff, and Theda Skocpol 1989 "Explaining Revolutions in the Contemporary Third World." *Politics and Society* 17:489–509.

Huntington, Samuel P. 1968 *Political Order in Changing Societies*. New Haven, Conn.: Yale University Press.

Lachmann, Richard 1997 "Agents of Revolution: Elite Conflicts and Mass Mobilization from the Medici to Yeltsin." In John Foran, ed., *Theorizing Revolutions*. New York: Routledge.

Markoff, John 1996 *The Abolition of Feudalism*. University Park: The Pennsylvania State University Press.

Moore, Barrington, Jr. 1966 *Social Origins of Dictatorship and Democracy*. Boston: Beacon.

Skocpol, Theda 1979 *States and Social Revolutions*. New York: Cambridge University Press.

Tilly, Charles 1978 *From Mobilization to Revolution*. Reading, Mass.: Addison-Wesley.

Trimberger, Ellen Kay 1978 *Revolution from Above: Military Bureaucrats and Development in Japan, Turkey, Egypt, and Peru*. New Brunswick; N.J.: Transaction.

Tucker, Robert (ed.) 1978 *The Marx-Engels Reader*. New York: Norton.

Wolf, Eric R. 1969 *Peasant Wars of the Twentieth Century*. New York: Harper and Row.

ROBERT C. LIEBMAN

ROLE CONFLICT

See Role Theory; Role Theory: Foundations, Extensions and Applications; Stress.

ROLE MODELS

See Gender; Role Theory; Role Theory: Foundations, Extensions and Applications; Socialization; Symbolic Interaction Theory.

ROLE THEORY

Role theory concerns the tendency for human behaviors to form characteristic patterns that may be predicted if one knows the social context in which those behaviors appear. It explains those behavior patterns, (or *roles*) by assuming that persons within a context appear as members of recognized social identities (or *positions*) and that they and others hold ideas (*expectations*) about behaviors in that setting. Its vocabulary and concerns are popular among both social scientists and practitioners, and role concepts have generated both theory and a good deal of research. Nevertheless, conflicts have arisen about the use of role terms and the focus of role theory, and different versions of the theory have appeared among groups of authors who seem to be unaware of alternative versions. Role theory has been weakened by association with controversial theories in sociology, as well.

HISTORY, DIFFERENTIATION, AND CONFUSION

Role theory arose when social scientists took seriously the insight that social life could be compared with the theater, in which actors played predictable "rôles." This insight was pursued independently by three major contributors in the early 1930s with somewhat different agendas. For Ralph Linton (an anthropologist), role theory was a means for analyzing social systems, and roles were conceived as "the dynamic aspects" of societally recognized social positions (or "statuses"). In contrast, George Herbert Mead (a social philosopher) viewed roles as the coping strategies that individuals evolve as they interact with other persons, and spoke of the need for understanding others' perspectives ("role taking") as a requisite for effective social interaction. And Jacob Moreno (a psychologist) saw roles as the habitual, sometimes harmful, tactics that are adopted by persons within primary relationships, and argued that imitative behavior ("role playing") was a useful strategy for learning new roles.

Additional insights for role theory were generated by other early authors, particularly Muzafer Sherif's studies of the effects of social norms; Talcott Parsons's functionalist theory, which stressed the importance of norms, consensus, sanctioning, and socialization; Robert Merton's analyses of role structures and processes; the works of Neal Gross, Robert Kahn, and their colleagues, which discussed role conflict and applied role concepts to organizations; Everett Hughes's papers on occupational roles; Theodore Newcomb's text for social psychology, which made extensive use of role concepts; and (in Europe) the seminal monographs of Michael Banton, Anne-Marie Rocheblave, and Ragnar Rommetveit, as well as Ralf Dahrendorf's essay "Homo Sociologicus."

The contrasting insights of these early contributors affected many subsequent writers, and various traditions of role theory have since appeared. Unfortunately, advocates for (or critics of) these differing traditions often write as if they are unaware of other versions. In addition, advocates may propose inconsistent uses for terms, or contrasting definitions for concepts, that are basic in role theory. To illustrate, for some authors the term "role" refers only to the concept of social position, for others it designates the behaviors characteristic of social position members, and for still others it denotes shared expectations held for the behaviors of position members. Such inconsistent uses pose problems for the unwary reader.

Also, role theorists may disagree about substantive issues. For example, some authors use role concepts to describe the social system, whereas others apply it to the conduct of the individual. Again, some writers assume that roles are always tied to functions, whereas others conceive roles as behaviors: that conform to expectations, that are directed towards other in the system, that are volitional, that validate the actor's status, or that project a self-image. Such differences in stance have reflected both accidents of intellectual history and the fact that role theorists have wrestled with differing social system forms.

Despite these differences, role theorists tend to share a basic vocabulary, an interest in the fact that human behavior is contextually differentiated and is associated with the social position of the actor, and the assumption that behavior is generated (in part) by expectations that are held by the actor and others. This means that much of role theory presumes a thoughtful, phenomenally aware participant, and role researchers tend to adopt methods that call for the observing of roles and for asking respondents to report about their own or others' expectations. Moreover, it also means that role theory may be contrasted with alternative theoretical positions that give stronger emphasis to unconscious motives or behavior-inducing forces of which the actor may be unaware (such as mechanisms that are not obvious but that serve to maintain structured inequalities of power, wealth, or status).

FUNCTIONALIST ROLE THEORY

One early perspective in role theory reflected functionalism. Functionalist thought arose from the contributions of Talcott Parsons and was, at one time, the dominant orientation in American sociology. This theory made use of role concepts, and some authors continue, today, to write as if role theory was or is largely an attempt to formalize functionalism.

Functionalist theory was concerned with the problem of explaining social order. Stable but differentiated behaviors were thought to persist within social systems because they accomplished functions and because actors in those systems shared expectations for behaviors. Such consensual expectations (or "roles") constituted norms for conduct, and actor conformity to norms was induced either because others in the system imposed sanctions on the actor or because the actor internalized them. In addition, those in the system were thought to be aware of the norms they held and could be counted on to teach them to (i.e., to socialize) neophytes as the latter entered the system.

Functionalist thought has been under attack since the 1950s, and many of its basic assumptions have been challenged. Critics have pointed out that persisting behaviors may or may not be functional for social systems, that norms for conduct are often in conflict, that actor conformity need not be generated by norms alone but can also reflect other modes of thought (such as beliefs or preferences), that norms might or might not be supported by explicit sanctions, that norms internalized by the actor may be at odds with those supported by external forces, and that processes of socialization are problematic. Above all, critics have noted that social systems are not the static entities that functionalist thought portrayed, and that human conduct often responds to power and conflicts of interest in ways that were ignored by functionalists. As a result of these attacks, interest in functionalist role theory has declined, although it is still possible to find writers who advocate (e.g., Bates and Harvey 1975) or denounce (Connell 1979) role theory as if it were merely a gloss for functionalism.

ROLE CONFLICT AND ORGANIZATIONAL ANALYSIS

Interest in organizational role theory began with the works of Neal Gross, Robert Kahn, and their associates, which questioned the assumption that consensual norms were required for social stability. Instead, these writers suggested that formal organizations were often characterized by *role conflict* (i.e., opposing norms that were held for actors by powerful others), that such conflicts posed problems for both the actors and the organizations in which they appeared, and that strategies for coping with or "resolving" role conflict could be studied. These insights stimulated both texts that applied role concepts to organizational analysis and many studies of role conflict and role conflict resolution in organizational contexts (see, for example, van de Vliert 1979; Van Sell et al. 1981; Fisher and Gitelson 1983).

In addition, the concept of role conflict has proven attractive to scholars who wanted to conceptualize or study problems that are faced by disempowered persons, particularly married women who must cope with the opposing demands of the workplace, home maintenance, and support for their husbands (Stryker and Macke 1978; Lopata 1980; Skinner 1980). Unfortunately (for the argument), evidence suggests that role conflicts are not always shunned by disempowered persons (see Sales et al. 1980) and that "resolving" those conflicts does not necessarily lead to empowerment.

Despite these problems, research on role conflict within the organization continues actively, and some proponents of the organizational perspective have recently turned their attention to the events of role transition—that is, to phenomena associated with entry into or departure from a role (see Allen and van de Vliert 1984; Ebaugh 1988).

THE STRUCTURAL PERSPECTIVE

Another use of role concepts has appeared among structuralists and network theorists. This third perspective reflects the early contributions of anthropologists such as S. F. Nadel and Michael Banton, sociologists such as Marion Levy, and social psychologists ranging from Dorwin Cartwright and Frank Harary to Oscar Oeser. As a rule, structuralists concern themselves with the logical implications of ways for organizing social systems (conceived as social positions and roles) and eschew any discussion of norms or other expectation concepts.

To date, much of the work in structural role theory has been expressed in formal, mathematical terms (see Burt 1982; Winship and Mandel 1983). This means that it has had greater appeal for scholars who are mathematically trained. It also constitutes one form of network analysis (although other network perspectives have appeared that do not use role concepts).

ROLE THEORY AMONG SYMBOLIC INTERACTIONISTS

Interest in role theory has also appeared among symbolic interactionists who were influenced not only by George Herbert Mead but also by Everett Hughes, Irving Goffman, and other influential figures. In general, symbolic interactionists think of a role as a line of action that is pursued by the individual within a given context. Roles are affected by various forces, including preexisting norms applying to the social position of the actor, beliefs and attitudes that the actor holds, the actor's conception and portrayal of self, and the "definition of the situation" that evolves as the actor and others interact. Roles need not have common elements, but they are likely to become quite similar among actors who face common problems in similar circumstances.

These concepts have been applied by symbolic interactionists to a host of interesting concerns (see, for example, Scheibe 1979; Gordon and Gordon 1982; Ickes and Knowles 1982; Stryker and Serpe 1982; Zurcher 1983; Hare 1985), and a continuing and useful contribution has flowed from Ralph Turner's interest in the internal dynamics of roles and the fact that roles tend to evolve over time (1979, 1990).

Unfortunately, some persons within this perspective have also been guilty of tunnel vision and have produced reviews in which role theory is portrayed largely as an extension of symbolic interactionist thought (see Heiss 1981; Stryker and Statham 1985). In addition, symbolic interactionism has attracted its share of criticism—among other things, for its tendencies to use fuzzy definitions, recite cant, and ignore structural constraints that affect behaviors—and some of these criticisms have tended to rub off on role theory.

COGNITIVE PERSPECTIVES IN ROLE THEORY

Empirical research in role theory has been carried out by cognitive social psychologists representing several traditions (see Biddle 1986, for a general review). Some of this work has focused on role playing, some of it has concerned the impact of group norms, some of it has studied the effects of anticipatory role expectations, and some of it has examined role taking.

In addition, cognitive social psychologists have studied conformity to many forms of expectations, including instrumental norms, moral norms, norms attributed to others, self-fulfilling prophesies, beliefs about the self (such as those induced by identity projection or labeling), beliefs about others, and preferences or "attitudes." These studies suggest that roles are often generated by two or more modes of expectational thought, and several models have also appeared from cognitive theorists reflecting this insight (see, for example, Bank et al. 1985).

Unfortunately, much of this effort ignores expectations for social positions and concentrates, instead, on expectations for individual actors. Cognitive role theory also tends to ignore the implications of its findings for structural analysis, and thus appears to be atheoretical from a sociological perspective. However, Bruce Biddle (1979) has authored a broad vision for role theory that uses information from cognitive research to build models for social system analysis.

RECENT TRENDS IN ROLE THEORY

Four recent trends in the development of role theory should be noted. First, although the term "role" continues to appear in most textbooks for basic courses in sociology and social psychology, it normally does not appear by itself as a major concept but rather is likely to surface in chapters on such topics as "the self," "groups," "institutions," and "role taking." In contrast, extensive discussions of roles and related concepts may be found in texts for various types of advanced courses for these fields. To illustrate, consider recent texts for courses on group dynamics. In the latest edition of his highly successful work, Donelson Forsyth (1999) devotes an entire chapter to "norms," "roles," and related issues, and in her new text, Joann Keyton (1999) focuses a major chapter on "group member roles," "group norms," and associated materials. As a rule, portrayals of role theory in such sources is straightforward: "roles" are deemed to refer to specific patterns of behavior that are associated with individuals or recognized identities; "norms" are shared expectations for conduct that may apply to all persons in the group or only to certain identities (such as "leaders"); and related concepts such as "socialization" and "role conflict" appear frequently.

Second, many authors continue to employ role concepts for discussing social relations within a specific institution or for portraying the lives of those who share an occupational identity. For example, a substantial literature has now appeared concerned with "the role of the school principal," and a useful summary of this work may be found in a recent review by Ronald Heck and Philip Hallinger (1999). In another example, Biddle (1997) provides an extensive overview of recent research on "the role of the school teacher." Again, much of this applied work makes clear use of concepts from role theory, with the "role" term normally used to refer to differentiated behaviors, whereas notions about behaviors that are thought to be appropriate for roles are normally termed "norms" or "role expectations."

Third, for at least a generation, authors who have written about differences between the conduct, problems, or outlooks of men and women have used role theory as a vehicle for interpreting their findings, and this interest continues. To illustrate, for years a key journal that publishes studies concerned with gender and its problems has borne the title *Sex Roles*, but recently a particularly strong advocate for using role theory to interpret evidence about gender differences in behavior has appeared in the person of Alice Eagly (1987, 1995). Eagly asserts that such differences appear as a result of structural forces in societies—hence may differ among countries—but are sustained and reproduced because men and women develop role-appropriate expectations for those behaviors. Given the earlier, pioneering studies of Margaret Mead, such assertions would seem unexceptionable, and yet they have touched off a storm of criticism from evolutionary psychologists who prefer to believe that gender differences in conduct are hard wired and culturally universal, and have arisen from the mechanisms of Darwinian selection. (See, for example, Archer [1996].) Unfortunately, in her 1987 book on the subject, Eagly did not make clear that her argument involved only one version of role theory, and it has seemingly not occurred to her evolutionary critics that there might be other versions of the role story that would also bear on their concerns. So, in criticizing her, they have made foolish assertions about "the scope of social role theory," and have condemned it for assumed stances that most role theorists would not advocate.

Fourth and last, every few years interesting works are published by authors who have apparently just discovered some version of role theory and are intrigued with its potential for generating insights or resolving problems in cognate fields. A good example of this type of work appears in a recent article by James Montgomery (1998). Montgomery begins by noting that, in a widely cited work, Granovetter (1985) had argued that economic action is embedded in social relationships and that rational choice theorists have subsequently explored this insight through research on prisoner's dilemma games in which long-term interaction is thought to be governed by general assumptions about "calculative trust." Empirical support for this thesis has been weak, and—drawing on work by James March (1994)—Montgomery argues that a stronger case can be made for assuming that, when engaged in long-term interaction, persons make assumptions about the social identities which they and others have assumed, and that these identities are associated with shared expectations about behaviors that are appropriate in the relationship. To illustrate, Montgomery suggests that expectations are far different when one assumes the other to be a "profit-maximizing 'businessperson'" than when the other is assumed to be a "nonstrategic 'friend.'"

Montgomery's arguments are well wrought, and their implications are spelled out through techniques of formal logic. Moreover, Montgomery points out how his arguments relate to recent work on various cognate concerns such as identity processes, artificial intelligence, situation theory, and cognitive psycholgy. So far so good, but (like too many recent converts) Montgomery seems not to be familiar with the bulk of work in the role field, and this leads him to make foolish errors. To illustrate, he refers to social identities as "roles" and shared expectations about behaviors as "rules"—idiosyncratic uses that will surely confuse readers. Worse, he seems not to be familiar with prior work by role theorists on his topic, including major works within the structural role theory tradition; with Ralph Linton's writings on the evolution of roles; and with the fact that much of his argument was actually made *forty* years ago by John Thibaut and Harold Kelley (1959). It does not help work in any field if scholars are unwilling to familiarize themselves with prior work on their subject, and one wonders how role theory is to make progress in the future if even its advocates are unwilling to do their homework.

ROLE THEORY AND THE FUTURE

As the foregoing examples suggest, role theory is currently weakened by terminological and conceptual confusion, diffuse effort, and the narrow visions of some of its proponents and critics. Nevertheless, role theory concerns central issues for sociology and social psychology, and assumptions about social positions, role behaviors, and expectations for human conduct appear widely in current social thought. Role theory will prosper as ways are found to discuss these issues with clarity, consistency, and breadth of vision.

REFERENCES

Allen, Vernon L., and Evert van de Vliert, eds. 1984 *Role Transitions: Explorations and Explanations*. New York: Plenum.

Archer, John 1996 "Sex Differences in Social Behavior: Are the Social Role and Evolutionary Explanations Compatible?" *American Psychologist* 51:909–917.

Bank, Barbara J., Bruce J. Biddle, Don S. Anderson, Ragnar Hauge, Daphne M. Keats, John A. Keats, Marjorie M. Marlin, and Simone Valantin 1985 "Comparative Research on the Social Determinants of Adolescent Drinking." *Social Psychology Quarterly* 48(2):164–177.

Bates, Frederick L., and Clyde C. Harvey 1975 *The Structure of Social Systems*. New York: John Wiley.

Biddle, Bruce J. 1979 *Role Theory: Expectations, Identities, and Behaviors*. New York: Academic Press.

—— 1986 "Recent Developments in Role Theory." In R. H. Turner, ed., *Annual Review of Sociology*, vol. 12. Palo Alto, Calif.: Annual Reviews.

—— 1997 "Recent Research on the Role of the Teacher." In B. J. Biddle, T. L. Good, and I. F. Goodson, eds., *International Handbook of Teachers and Teaching*. Dordrecht, The Netherlands: Kluwer.

Burt, Ronald S. 1982 *Toward a Structural Theory of Action: Network Models of Social Structure, Perception, and Action*. New York: Academic.

Connell, Robert W. 1979 "The Concept of 'Role' and What to Do with It." *Australian and New Zealand Journal of Sociology* 15:7–17. Reprinted in R. W. Connell, ed., *Which Way Is Up? Essays on Sex, Class and Culture*, chap. 10. Sydney: Allen and Unwin, 1983.

Eagly, Alice H. 1987 *Sex Differences in Social Behavior: A Social-Role Interpretation.* Hillsdale, N.J.: Lawrence Erlbaum.

—— 1995 "The Science and Politics of Comparing Women and Men." *American Psychologist* 50:145–158.

Ebaugh, Helen Rose Fuchs 1988 *Becoming an EX: The Process of Role Exit.* Chicago: University of Chicago Press.

Fisher, Cynthia D., and Richard Gitelson 1983 "A Meta-Analysis of the Correlates of Role Conflict and Ambiguity." *Journal of Applied Psychology* 68:320–333.

Forsyth, Donelson R. 1999 *Group Dynamics*, 3rd ed. Belmont, Calif.: Wadsworth.

Gordon, Chad, and Paddy Gordon 1982 "Changing Roles, Goals, and Self-Conceptions: Process and Results in a Program for Women's Employment." In W. Ickes and E. S. Knowles, eds., *Personality, Roles, and Social Behavior.* New York: Springer-Verlag.

Granovetter, Mark 1985 "Economic Action and Social Structure: The Problem of Embeddedness." *American Journal of Sociology* 91:481–510.

Hare, A. Paul 1985 *Social Interaction as Drama: Applications from Conflict Resolution.* Beverly Hills, Calif.: Sage.

Heck, Ronald H., and Philip Hallinger 1999 "Next Generation Methods for the Study of Leadership and School Improvement." In J. Murphy and K. S. Louis, eds., *Handbook of Research on Educational Administration*, 2nd ed. San Francisco: Jossey-Bass.

Heiss, Jerrold 1981 "Social Roles." In M. Rosenberg and R. H. Turner, eds., *Social Psychology: Sociological Perspectives.* New York: Basic Books.

Ickes, William, and Eric S. Knowles, eds. 1982 *Personality, Roles, and Social Behavior.* New York: Springer-Verlag.

Keyton, Joann 1999 *Group Communication: Process and Analysis.* Mountain View, Calif. Mayfield.

Lopata, Helena, ed. 1980 *Research in the Interweave of Social Roles: Women and Men–A Research Annual*, vol. 3. Greenwich, Conn.: JAI.

March, James G. 1994 *A Primer on Decision Making.* New York: Free Press.

Montgomery, James D. 1998 "Toward a Role-Theoretic Conception of Embeddedness." *American Journal of Sociology* 104(1):92–125.

Sales, Esther, Barbara K. Shore, and Floyd Bolitho 1980 "When Mothers Return to School: A Study of Women Completing an MSW Program." *Journal of Education for Social Work* 16(1):57–65.

Scheibe, Karl E. 1979 *Mirrors, Masks, Lies, and Secrets: The Limits of Human Predictability.* New York: Praeger.

Skinner, Denise A. 1980 "Dual-Career Family Stress and Coping: A Literature Review." *Family Relations* 29:473–481.

Stryker, Sheldon, and Anne Statham Macke 1978 "Status Inconsistency and Role Conflict." In R. Turner, J. Coleman, and R. Fox, eds., *Annual Review of Sociology*, vol. 4. Palo Alto, Calif.: Annual Reviews.

——, and Richard T. Serpe 1982 "Commitment, Identity Salience, and Role Behavior: Theory and Research Example." In W. Ickes and E. S. Knorales, eds., *Personality, Roles, and Social Behavior.* New York: Springer-Verlag.

——, and Anne Statham 1985 "Symbolic Interaction and Role Theory." In G. Lindzey and E. Aronson, eds., *Handbook of Social Psychology*, 3rd ed. New York: Random House.

Thibaut, John W., and Harold H. Kelley 1959 *The Social Psychology of Groups.* New York: John Wiley.

Turner, Ralph 1979 "Strategy for Developing an Integrated Role Theory." *Humboldt Journal of Social Relations* 7:123–139.

—— 1990 "Role Change." In W. R. Scott, ed., *Annual Review of Sociology*, vol. 16. Palo Alto, Calif.: Annual Reviews.

van de Vliert, Evert 1979 "Gedrag in Rolkonfliktsituaties: 20 Jaar Onderzoek Rond Een Theorie" (Behavior in Role Conflict Situations: 10 Years of Research About a Theory). *Nederlands Tijdschrift voor de Psychologie* 34:125–146.

Van Sell, Mary, Arthur P. Brief, and Randall S. Schuler 1981 "Role Conflict and Role Ambiguity: Integration of the Literature and Directions for Future Research." *Human Relations* 34:43–71.

Winship, Christopher, and M. Mandel 1983 "Roles and Positions: A Critique and Extension of the Blockmodeling Approach." Pp. 314–344 in S. Leinhardt, ed., *Sociological Methodology 1983–1984.* San Francisco: Jossey-Bass.

Zurcher, Louis A., Jr. 1983 *Social Roles: Conformity, Conflict, and Creativity.* Beverly Hills, Calif.: Sage.

BRUCE J. BIDDLE

ROLE THEORY: FOUNDATIONS, EXTENSIONS, AND APPLICATIONS

Role theory provides conceptual elements and dynamic relations across the social sciences. Indeed, the notion of *role* has become something of a "meta-construct" that has been adapted to the scholarly focus and methodological predilections of fields such as sociology, psychology, anthropology, and management, to name just a few. Such broad application, while suiting testimony to the importance of role constructs in social theory, has led to some conceptual confusion, formulamatic imprecision, and sharply diverging interpretations. Nevertheless, there remains a great deal of consensus about the integral nature of roles in the operation of social systems and the behavior of individuals.

Fundamentally, roles are organized behavioral patterns and expectations that attend a given position (hierarchical, functional, or social) or that accompany a specific situation. That is, roles encapsulate and invoke the accepted repertoire of individual conduct associated with a specific position or extant circumstance. In this way, roles provide behavioral guidelines, prescriptions, or boundaries in the form of *expectations*. These expectations can be formally assigned and explicitly stated—as in the case of occupational job descriptions—or informally assumed and tacit—as in the case of one who plays the "facilitator" role in a friendship clique. Additionally, by evoking behavioral expectations, roles affect how individuals cognitively frame, interpret, and process physical or social stimuli, and thus they further condition emotional responses. There is some controversy as to whether individuals are fully cognizant of the roles they play, but that is incidental to the underlying assumption that roles influence behavior, and thus are powerful predictors of individual action and key to understanding social systems.

This essay is not intended to provide a comprehensive review of role theory nor to propose new theoretical formulations. Rather, this essay will offer a framework for organizing role theory that hinges on *levels of analysis* and the particular *phenomenon of focus*.

There are two primary levels of analysis relevant to role theory. The first emphasizes how roles operate within and through *social systems*, such as societies or groups. The second level is concerned with how roles influence, or are influenced by, the *individuals* who inhabit them. This is essentially a classic *macro versus micro* distinction, the former being characteristic of sociological and anthropological inquiry, the latter of management and psychological inquiry (though there is, of course, some crossover). The phenomenon of focus refers

to the particular object of inquiry within each level of analysis. For instance, a researcher in the social systems tradition may focus on nations, ethnic heritage, or group cohesion, whereas a researcher in the individual tradition may focus on self-conceptions, cognitions, or conflict. The phenomena of focus vary widely within each level of analysis, and are discussed under subheadings.

SOCIAL SYSTEMS

The underlying assumption of role theory at the broadest level is that social systems—particularly societies, cultures, organizations, groups and families—are organized and operate through roles. Hence, roles function dynamically to structure the interaction of participants so as to maintain, defend, alter, innovate, or advance the purpose of social systems. In this way, roles become the primary linkage between the social system and the individual, and are designed to communicate the expectations of the larger concern to the particular actor. Roles, then, can be viewed as indispensable mechanisms that embody the values of the social system.

Societies and Stasis. One of the earliest uses of role theory in social science involved the proposal that societies, like organisms, have differentiated parts that function interdependently to allow the whole to operate. In any given society, those parts would include institutions like the state or the church, each of which carry out defined obligations that reflect the priorities of that society. However, institutions in and of themselves do not execute the role. To accomplish their purposes, institutions convey that responsibility to individuals through socialization and inculcation, who in turn are responsible for enacting them. Hence, roles become the primary theoretical construct for explaining *social stability*. That is, roles *function* in a manner conducive to social order and stasis. The term "function" is important here, as *functionalism* was the name given to the major school of thought at the time (Parsons 1951).

The chief concern of functionalism was how societies decided upon, designed, communicated, and enforced roles. This concern opened up a series of issues that have occupied sociological role theory, such as: which parties designate a role, the rationale for the privilege or status assigned given roles, the mechanisms by which the social system inculcates roles, and how to ensure a role is faithfully enacted (see Biddle 1986).

Culture and Change. Role theory has found its way into the study of cultures primarily through anthropology. Here, the dramatic, theatrical flavor of roles is clearly evidenced. The basic thrust is that all cultures have forms of ritual, ceremony, and pageantry that encompass symbolic societal roles which in turn play crucial social functions. Unlike sociologists, who see such institutions and their prescribed roles as maintaining stasis and order, anthropologists, notably Victor Turner (1986), argue that the purpose of such social drama is *change*. Specifically, Turner contends that, whenever individuals act in accordance with social scripts (i.e., roles), the possibility exists for "liminality": a lodgment in time and circumstance where individuals depart from proscribed patterns and initiate new ones. The very idea of roles is to trigger or generate novelty and creativity by stepping out from that which is expected, and thus bring new meaning to the dynamic represented in the social drama. It is the tension between norms and expectations and the stability they imply, versus the necessity for change for survival's sake, that animates the alteration of roles, which is viewed as the engine of cultural development.

Organizations and Performance. Whereas the emphasis is respectively on stability or change when societies or cultures are the phenomenon of focus, when organizations are the focus, the emphasis is squarely on *performance* (typically operationalized as productivity, or the difference between inputs and outputs, or costs and profits). Role theory finds its way into management at the macro level with research concerned with organizational design. The major concern is the proper way to arrange an organization for optimal performance, which constitutes a structure through which the organization is managed. Principles involved in organization design include differentiation, integration, centralization, complexity, and formalization. But a key element in the erection of an structure is the formal designation of roles that organizational actors are assigned to play (see Hall 1991).

The roles that individuals assume in organizations are typically assigned based on expertise and previous experience. That is, an individual is specifically trained or has the background to execute the relevant duties; he or she is prepared to fill a role. But beyond possessing the requisite skills, organizational roles are designed to place individuals into the particular structure of the organization. This is accomplished primarily through two formal mechanisms and one informal mechanism. The first is the job description, which is a detailed documentation of all duties and responsibilities. The job description, then, effectively posits expectations and sets strict behavioral boundaries. The second is the reporting relationship, which describes the hierarchical order of the organization, and thus dictates channels for approval and communication. The third, and informal, mechanism by which individual conduct is guided is the organizational culture. In this case, culture refers to the organizations climate as well as its tacit mores and traditions.

From the perspective of research in organizational design, the question is the relationship between structure and performance. For instance, in industries where there is a high rate of change, research suggests that looser structures, with fewer specifications for job descriptions and more open channels of communication, tend to perform better. Suffice it to say, nowhere are roles more formally communicated, monitored, and controlled than in the management of firm performance.

Groups and Functionality. Another area of inquiry where role concepts play a major part is groups. Defined as two or more interdependent individuals who have come together to achieve an objective, groups can include formal work teams, friendship cliques, and even families (though family relations is often treated as an independent, free-standing field of inquiry). The conceptual elements in group research are not fundamentally different from those involved in the study of societies, cultures, or organizations. That is, to accomplish its purpose—whether that purpose be completing an organizationally assigned task or comraderie—group members must function in a complimentary manner. That *functioning*, then, is typically arranged around roles that members are assigned or assume.

The role concepts most frequently employed in group research are role identity (the attitudes and behaviors consistent with a role), role perception (an individual's view of how to behavior in a given situation), role expectations (other's beliefs of how one should act in a given situation), and role conflict (the contradiction of two role's expectations). These concepts are then used to predict various group dynamics—such as conformity, status relations, and cohesiveness—and outcomes—such as performance, satisfaction, creativity, and efficiency (for a review, see Goodman et al. 1987).

INDIVIDUALS

Whether examining societies, cultures, organizations, or groups, roles are enacted by individuals. The term "enacted" is important here, since it belies the theatrical, dramaturgical roots of role theory (Simmel 1920). Moreno (1934) for instance, stressed the importance of *role playing* as a natural act of children in learning about themselves and their world, and an important aid for education as well as therapy. Perhaps the most memorable proposition is Goffman's powerful theatrical analysis (1959). Goffman's basic premise, not unlike that of Shakespeare's "all the world's a stage," is that *all* human behavior is acted, with some allowance for the nature or type of audience. Although varying in the degree of their theoretical commitments, these thinkers underscore the central place that the metaphor of *stage acting* commands in role theory, especially as an explanatory and illustrative aid in understanding individual behavior.

Identity and Interaction. There is no question that individual identity—the self-conception and personality of the individual—is impacted by the society in which individuals live, the family into which they are born, the community in which they were raised, and the people with whom they associate. Identity is surely a complex, interwoven interaction of the person and his or her situation. And that roles exert a strong influence on individual identity is equally obvious in individuals' descriptions of themselves, which invariably involve roles (e.g., daughter, husband, student, lawyer). Individuals, then, show a marked propensity to understand themselves through the roles they have assumed.

The study of roles in identity formation was largely sparked by a school of thought known as *symbolic interactionism*. According to this perspective, identity evolves through the dynamic process of a communicating society. Here, society is not a static structure that dictates roles and thus identity. Rather, it is built through interaction heavy in symbolic communication. Therefore, society is continually formed and reformed through the *reciprocal* influence of individuals taking into account one another's characteristics, and the symbolic meanings that emerge as they interact. Accordingly, neither society nor the individual ontologically precedes the other.

Traditional role theory (especially that which employees social systems as the level of analysis) and symbolic interactionism diverge on the precedence of the relationship between society, individuals, and roles. Traditional role theory assumes that roles are defined by society, which in turn logically determines identity. Symbolic interactionism, on the other hand, views roles as emerging from symbolic communication in a reciprocal relationship between the society and the individual. Here, individuals are credited with being active, creative, mindful, and volitional in their identity.

Symbolic interactionism is grounded in the philosophy of the American pragmatists (e.g., W. James, J. Dewey, and C. S. Pierce) and subsequent social scientists like G. H. Mead, C. H. Cooley, and E. Goffman. The basic premise is that the self emerges through symbolic interactions with socially recognized categories and the roles that correspond with those categories. Because roles *emerge* in relationship to others and society, the self does as well. The self is the way in which individuals understand themselves in relation to others (see Stryker and Statham 1985).

A practical implication of this is that how individuals think of themselves depends, to a great extent, on the social roles that they play. This is nicely captured by W. James: "Many a youth who is demure enough before his parents and teachers, swears and swaggers like a pirate among his tough young friends" (1890, p. 294). Also implicit is James's assertion that individuals have many selves and many social identities: "a man has as many social selves as there are individuals who recognize him and carry an image of him in their mind" (1890, p. 294). Thus, individuals can be said to have many linked selves as opposed to one united self.

The active and emergent nature of the self and identity is indicative of the work of those in the symbolic interactionism tradition. Individuals choose selves upon which to stake a claim and abandon others which did not prove adaptive or failed to garner positive feedback. Thus, self-esteem is directly tied to the choice of selves to maintain or dismiss. In addition, roles and selves are not merely foisted upon individuals, but rather the options available open the opportunity for the exploration of *possible* selves. Recent papers, derived from James's formulations, contemporary theories of evolution, and performative dynamics, have proposed a model of the exploration and construction of possible selves (Bailey and Ford 1994; Yost et al. 1992).

Cognition and Schematic Processing. Roles affect individual perceptions, determinations and judgments of people, events, and causal relations through *schematic processing*. A schema is a highly ordered cognitive structure composed of knowledge, beliefs, and feelings about persons, objects, and events. Schemas, then, are mental frameworks that coherently organize memory and associations that in turn facilitate the efficient processing of information. Although there are many types of schemas—such as event schemas (e.g., the script individuals follow when dining at a restaurant) or person schemas (e.g., the knowledge, feelings, and expectations an individual has about another)—role schemas are those that organize proper behavioral patterns according to position or situation.

The notion of role schema is central to the role construct inasmuch as roles are behavioral guidelines. From a cognitive perspective, the question is how role schemas influence individual information processing. This influence occurs in both directions; that is, as *observer* and as *actor*. Research demonstrates that, when observing another, the activation of a role schema influences attention, memory, and attribution. For instance, when observing an elderly person, individuals tend to notice, recall, and render causal explanations that are consistent with an age-based role schema (e.g., the older gentleman crinkled his nose because he disapproved of the loud music). In this way, role schemas provide observers with a richly interconnected network of information by which they can categorize and thus interpret the behavior of others. Of course, as a means for comprehending others, role schemas sacrifice accuracy for the sake of efficiency, as is the case with stereotypes. As an actor, role schemas refer to the mental representations of the expectations that attend a role. Similarly, individuals access and process information

more quickly when it is related to the role they are occupying at the moment (see Fiske and Taylor 1991).

Transition and Alteration. Research on role transition acknowledges that individuals develop and move from one role to another in the course of their lives. Hence, role transition refers to the movement from one role to another, and specifically how individuals adapt to the transition. For instance, a promotion from staff programmer to project supervisor requires learning new duties and expectations, but also altering attitudes toward others. The same holds true for transitions from son or daughter to parent, from student to employee, and from child to adult. Such role transitions, then, challenge individuals to reconceptualize their notion of themselves, their relations to others, and their opinions and attitudes toward domain-relevant objects and events. Role transition has been examined in the management arena, with emphasis on how to facilitate the transition in order to improve performance, and in the psychological counseling arena, with attention to assuaging the emotional distress that often accompanies such periods of adjustment.

Role change can be defined as an *alteration* in the consensual understanding of the behavioral patterns of an established role. This is not a transition from one role to another, but rather a change in the expectations and boundaries of an established role. The assumption here is that roles are not static entities, but must *evolve* in order to adequately address the demands of the cultural milieu, economic conditions, or social situation (see Turner 1990).

There are three fundamental ways in which roles can change. First, roles can change according to shifting societal priorities or cultural patterns. For instance, gender roles have gone through considerable alteration as attitudes toward equal rights, access to career opportunities, and traditional obligations have been reconsidered and reconfigured in society. Second, roles can change because of formal dictates from authority. For instance, one's job responsibilities could be expanded quantitatively (e.g., supervising more people) or quantitatively (e.g., involving an entirely different skill set). Third, and perhaps the most interesting, roles can be changed by the individual who inhabits the role. For instance, individuals may, because of either personal preferences or attitudes, redefine a "director" role to be less about planning and monitoring and more about mentoring and directing.

CONCLUSION

Role theory has come full circle. Early formulations, especially those of Parsons (1951), Moreno (1934), and Goffman (1959), have recently gained considerable currency. For instance, functionalism has proved useful as an analytic framework for describing alterations in emerging democracies. Moreno's emphasis on role playing has found its way into pedagogy in the form of classroom exercises to illustrate concepts and executive workshops for skill development, as well as a fruitful method for therapeutic intervention. And Goffman's reliance on stage acting has influenced current thinking on identity and even research methodology. What this suggests is that role theorists are acutely aware of their theoretical heritage and progenitors, and are willing to mine the past in order to better understand the present.

Roles change as broad conditions shift. Political, economic, and technological factors are especially volatile, each in its own way altering the social system in which individuals reside and the manner in which they understand themselves. Although role theory has not been as intensely researched in last decade—a victim of academic fashion—it continues to provide an intellectual and structural foundation for fields across the social sciences. Moreover, because the late twentieth century is marked as much by change as anything else, social conditions are changing at a dizzying pace. No theoretical construct is more suited to examine the impact of such changes on the social system and the individual than role theory.

REFERENCES

Bailey, J. R., and C. M. Ford 1994 "Of Methods and Metaphors: Theater and Self-Exploration in the Laboratory." *Journal of Applied Behavioral Science* 30:381–396.

Biddle, B. J. 1986 "Recent Developments in Role Theory." In R. H. Turner and J. F. Short, eds., *Annual Review of Sociology*, vol. 12. Palo Alto, Calif.: Annual Reviews.

Fiske, S. T., and S. E. Taylor 1991 *Social Cognition*. New York: Random House.

Goffman, E. 1959 *The Presentation of Self in Everyday Life*. New York: Doubleday.

Goodman, P. S., E. Ravlin, and M. Schminke 1987 "Understanding Groups in Organizations." In L. L. Cummings and B. M. Staw, eds., *Research in Organizational Behavior*. Greenwich, Conn.: JAI.

Hall, R. H. 1991 *Organizations: Structures, Processes, and Outcomes*. Englewood Cliffs, N.J.: Prentice Hall.

James, W. 1890 *Principles of Psychology*, vol. 1. New York: Dover.

Moreno, J. L. 1934 *Who Shall Survive?* Washington, D.C.: Nervous and Mental Disorders Publishers.

Parsons, T. 1951 *The Social System*. Glencoe, Ill.: Free Press.

Simmel, G. 1920 "Sur philosopie des schauspielers." *Logos* 1:339–362.

Stryker, S., and A. Statham 1985 "Symbolic Interaction and Role Theory." In G. Lindzey and E. Aronson, eds., *Handbook of Social Psychology*. New York: Random House.

Turner, R. H. 1990 *Role Change*. In W. R. Scott and J. Blake, eds., *Annual Review of Sociology*, vol. 16. Palo Alto, Calif.: Annual Reviews.

Turner, V. 1986 *The Anthropology of Performance*. New York: PAJ.

Yost, J. H., M. J. Strube, and J. R. Bailey 1992 "The Construction of the Self: An Evolutionary View." *Current Psychology: Research and Review* 11:110–121.

JAMES R. BAILEY
JOHN H. YOST

RURAL SOCIOLOGY

Rural sociology is the study of social organization and social processes that are characteristic of geographical localities where population size is relatively small and density is low (Warner 1974). Thus, rural sociology can be defined as the sociology of rural society. Since rural societies do not exist in isolation, rural sociology also addresses the relation of rural society to the larger society. Therefore, it deals also with spatial organization and the processes that produce spatial allocations of population and human activities (Newby 1980; Newby and Buttel 1980).

There is a temptation to equate rural sociology with American rural sociology because the latter is most thoroughly institutionalized and there are more practitioners in the United States than anywhere else in the world. While rural sociology, in its institutionalized form, originated in America, it has flourished in other regions of the world, especially since the end of World War II. No doubt this is due in large part to the "modernization" efforts in the many nations that gained independence since 1950. Outside North America, sociological investigations of rural society often are referred to as peasant studies, development studies, or village studies rather than rural sociology (Newby 1980). Moreover, some aspects of rural sociological analysis are closely related to other social science disciplines, such as settlement patterns with human geography, family and kinship systems with social anthropology, and land tenure and farming systems with agricultural and land economics.

ROOTS IN SOCIAL THOUGHT

Although the subject matter of rural sociology has been of keen interest to social thinkers for centuries, its treatment by the major nineteenth-century classical theorists led to a polarization that continues today (Duncan 1954; Hofstee 1963; LeFebvre 1953; Mendras 1969). Two points of view, both deeply embedded in the social thought and literature of Western culture, and both quite limiting if not erroneous, have predominated. The first tradition, an image drawn from the Arcadia of Greek mythology, has been the glorification of village life for the supposed pastoral virtue of its people. The second tradition has been that of the Enlightenment and modern Western rationalism, which viewed the technological and organizational character of urban industrial forces as being superior to the alleged backwardness of rural areas.

These two traditions were ultimately embraced in major nineteenth-century social theories (Nisbet 1966). Some theorists, typified by Emile Durkheim and by Karl Marx to a lesser extent, viewed the urban industrial complex as the center of a new civilization emerging from the social transformations of the industrial revolution. Rural society, in this perspective, was regarded as a residual of preindustrial society and increasingly to be relegated to a secondary status. Other theorists, such as Toennies [1887] (1957) and early-twentieth-century interpreters of Toennies (e.g., Sorokin

and Zimmerman 1929), viewed the emergent cities of industrial capitalism as monuments to the degradation of civilization. Both points of view are deeply imbedded in the social thought of Western culture and continue to shape the perspectives of rural sociology as a scientific enterprise.

RURAL SOCIOLOGY IN AMERICA

The roots of rural sociology in America lie in the social and political turmoil associated with America's version of the Industrial Revolution, which followed the Civil War. As industrial capitalism made its great surge, urban America was on the move, quickly surpassing earlier achievements of European nations—yet in the midst of obviously rising affluence there existed a paradoxical injustice of poverty and inequality, especially in rural areas (Goodwyn 1978). William Jennings Bryan was defeated in 1896 as the Populist Party candidate for president, but the political unrest in the countryside continued to be a source of concern to urban industrialists, who depended on farmers to provide a stable supply of cheap food for the growing army of industrial workers.

The Country Life Movement emerged at the turn of the century as an urban-sponsored alternative to the radical economic proposals of the rural Populists (Bowers 1974; Danbom 1979; Swanson 1972). It was a social, cultural, and moral reform movement that adopted the view that rural society was backward, lagging behind the evolution of an advanced urban society. The problems of rural people were viewed as stemming from a lack of organization, failures of rural social institutions, inadequate infrastructures, and technological backwardness, rather than from the failures of the industrial capitalist system, as the Populists claimed.

In 1908 President Theodore Roosevelt gave legitimacy to the reform movement by appointing the Commission on Country Life. Spurred by the President's Commission and the Country Life Movement, Congress in 1914 passed the Smith-Lever Act, which created the Cooperative Extension Service to modernize rural America (Hooks and Flinn 1981). In 1925 Congress passed the Purnell Act, which provided colleges of agriculture and agricultural experiment stations with funds to support rural sociological research. Shortly thereafter, departments of rural sociology began to emerge within universities, often separated from departments of sociology (Sewell 1965). The institutionalization of rural sociology was given further impetus in 1936, when rural sociologists established their own journal, *Rural Sociology*, and during the following year, when they divorced themselves from the American Sociological Society (now the American Sociological Association) by forming the Rural Sociological Society. During the Depression, rural sociology received substantial support for research regarding the socioeconomic status of farm families and the effectiveness of various New Deal federal programs (Larson et al. 1992).

Because of its historical roots, rural sociology has been an active participant in two conflicting social policies derived from the opposing views of rural society in social thought. The institutional separation of rural sociology from sociology, its organizational location in colleges of agriculture, and its functional integration with cooperative extension have given American rural sociology a strong attachment to technologically driven modernization. For many of its institutional sponsors, whose primary goal has been the technological advancement of agriculture, the predominant justification for supporting rural sociology research has been its presumed ability to enhance the process of modernization of rural society.

Two important consequences have followed from this sponsorship. First, the research agenda of rural sociology has been significantly influenced by politicians and administrators of colleges of agriculture and agricultural experiment stations. Thus, American rural sociological research has tended to be driven primarily by the need to be "useful" in solving practical problems involved in transforming rural society. Second, theoretical development within rural sociology has atrophied. Theoretical work that may contradict the prevailing social policy dogma and thereby threaten its financial and institutional support has been particularly uncommon. Thus, the practice of American rural sociology has been part of an explicit social policy of transforming rural society (Newby 1980).

The opposing cultural theme portrays rural society as a way of life that is superior to existence in the cities and threatened by urban industrial capitalism (Sorokin and Zimmerman 1929). It has protagonists within rural sociology and in society for whom the problem is how to preserve the wholesome qualities of rural society against the encroachments of urban industrial capitalism (e.g., how to avoid community disintegration, loss of local autonomy, the collapse of the family farm, the decline of the traditional rural way of life, degradation of the rural landscape, and depletion of nonrenewable natural resources). These Jeffersonian values of community, individualism, family entrepreneurship, and grass-roots democracy inspire private and public sponsorship of many rural sociological endeavors (Gilbert 1982). Thus, American rural sociology has been significantly involved in two explicit and conflicting social policies. First, it has contributed to positivistic social science by providing the basic descriptive information about rural populations, institutions, and social processes that have guided the development of programs to transform rural society. Second, it has served those committed to preserving selected elements of rural society, a practice that often is perceived by agricultural administrators and proponents of technological innovations as creating barriers to progress.

MAJOR RESEARCH TOPICS

Within the context of these conflicting and vacillating social policy orientations, rural sociology in America has generated a substantial body of research. Some research topics have emerged principally in response to the social policy of transforming rural society and have followed the paradigm of positivism. Other topics are associated more clearly with the preservationist policy orientation and the paradigm of critical sociology. While the alignment of social policy and scientific paradigms is not perfect, there is a clear pattern of association. Both sets of orientations have existed within rural sociology since its inception, with the modernization-positivism orientation clearly dominating the research enterprise until recently.

Modernization-Positivism—Oriented Research. One of the primary concerns of the Commission on Country Life was the lack of complete and accurate information about the conditions of life in rural America. Thus, study of the rural population was one of the first research topics to emerge (Brunner 1957). Initially research was devoted primarily to description of the rural population, not only in an effort to provide more accurate counts of people but also to report on their characteristics in greater detail and to describe demographic processes more accurately. Population studies continue to be extremely important in providing the basic descriptive information about the rural population that is needed to guide the development of programs to transform rural society (Fuguitt et al. 1989; Garkovich 1989).

To the extent that rural population studies depart from purely demographic analyses and venture into sociological investigations, they are usually guided by the systemic perspective of human ecology (Hawley 1950, 1986). In this more sophisticated systems model, population size and density are treated as interdependent with the environment, the level of technology, and the social organization of a locality. It is presumed that population size and density will expand to the maximum possible within the constraints imposed by the other components of the system, especially the technology of transportation and communication. While the perspective offers promise of merging social and spatial analysis, the results have been only partially successful. Rural population studies cum human ecology have yet to integrate the social and spatial levels of reality.

As more information about rural populations became available, comparisons with urban populations became possible, and there followed a prolific production of research to examine the belief that population size and density set the conditions of social action and social organization. This was a fundamental premise of the romanticists among the classical sociological writers noted earlier, and it was translated sociologically into the "rural-urban continuum" of Sorokin and Zimmerman (1929) and later the "folk-urban continuum" of Redfield (1947). The evidence that there are universal differences in the cultural and social characteristics that may be derived from differences in population size and density has not been convincing (Pahl [1966] 1970). Thus, while comparisons are drawn between rural and urban populations, the causality argument associated with the rural-urban continuum has been discarded by most rural sociologists.

Rural sociologists have conducted hundreds of community studies that serve as a major source of information for the design of community development programs (Bell and Newby 1972; Summers 1986, Luloff and Swanson 1990; Wilkinson 1991). From Galpin's pioneering study in 1915 until the mid-1960s, the study of community was almost synonymous with rural sociology in the United States. By that time the rural-urban continuum, which was the chief frame of reference for many investigators, was falling into disrepute (Pahl [1966] 1970). Their studies were being criticized for their impressionistic methodologies and their excessively descriptive nature (Colin Bell and Newby 1972). Moreover, proponents of the mass-society thesis argued that communities had been eclipsed by the forces of urbanization, bureaucratization, and centralization (Stein 1964; Vidich and Bensman 1958; Warren 1963). Community was alleged to be no longer a meaningful locus of social decision making. It was presumed that the increased presence of extralocal forces in the community (vertical integration) had destroyed the horizontal integration of communities and rendered small rural communities powerless in the face of broad and powerful forces of mass society. Although the tradition of holistic community studies has not returned to its former status, evidence clearly supports the argument that increased vertical integration does not necessarily destroy horizontal integration (Richards 1978; Summers 1986). Rather, it is more consistent with the empirical data to view local autonomy as a variable, and the impact of changes in vertical integration as varying according to a complex matrix of variables characterizing the external agent and the community.

In 1897, W. E. B. DuBois began a series of analyses of economic conditions among rural black groups and their relation to agriculture (DuBois 1898, 1901, 1904). Indeed, as we will stress later, since the turn of the century rural sociologists have been studying the "sociology of agriculture," although that expression did not come into use until the 1970s (Buttel et al. 1990). Land tenure and types of farming enterprises were studied to understand the relations of farming and agriculture-based businesses to the conditions of rural living. The methodology of these studies was often that of the community survey, and consequently there was much overlap with population and community studies. Most of these studies were descriptive in nature, and they generated taxonomies of farming enterprises, which provided further refinements of farm family and farming community characteristics. The resulting social maps of farming communities provided detailed information to guide modernization programs, especially those of the Cooperative Extension Service, with its offices in virtually every rural county in the United States.

Although technological innovations have been occurring in agriculture for centuries, technological change was revolutionized with the introduction of hybrid corn (Ryan and Gross 1943). With this innovation, adoption and diffusion research became a new research field led by rural sociology. The first research focused on identifying which farmers had the highest rates of adoption of hybrid corn and how the adoption process was diffused to other farmers. Soon the research encompassed other innovations and spread to other countries with the modernization era at the end of World War II (Rogers 1995; Fliegel 1993). The basic processes of adoption and diffusion are now reasonably well understood, and training programs based on this knowledge are being implemented worldwide in areas of human behavior that reach well beyond farming practices to include health and nutrition, resource conservation, business management, and many other areas.

Preservationist–Critically Oriented Research.
By the 1960s there was a strong and growing disillusionment with the societal consequences of positivistic social science and the absence of a structuralist perspective (Newby and Buttel 1980). It was claimed that theory and research had become uncoupled, with theory being excessively abstract and research exhibiting a mindless empiricism. Several rural sociologists involved in international development research offered challenges to the Western development orthodoxy by claiming that modernization was serving the interests of the powerful and wealthy rather than improving the social and economic well-being of peasants and poor people (Havens 1972; Havens and Flinn 1975; Thiesenhusen 1978). In North America and Europe similar claims were being expressed in the environmental, civil rights, and other social justice movements of the late 1960s. The emerging research topics in rural sociology manifest the intellectual ferment of a more critical perspective on existing public policies, especially

in relation to established institutions of agricultural and rural research and programs claiming to improve rural communities and institutions. The emergent critical perspective incorporates a diversity of theoretical views that recognize the active role of the state in public policy and argue that it is subject to the influences within society of powerful interest groups that often are formed along the lines of class, race, ethnicity, or gender. Thus, the contemporary theoretical debates within rural sociology draw heavily on neo-Marxist and neo-Weberian orientations, with the result that rural sociology and sociology are closer intellectual partners today than at any time in the past fifty years. Although virtually all facets of rural social organization and processes are subjected to the emergent critical perspective, some areas have received more attention than others.

As we note below, the most distinctive feature of this "new rural sociology" (Newby and Buttel 1980) was the prominence of Marxist and neo-Marxist interpretations of the social differentiation of agriculture. This critical new rural sociology was applied most extensively to understanding the paradox of the growth of large-scale capitalist agriculture accompanied by the persistence of the small-scale family or subfamily farm. Efforts to understand this duality of agricultural structure has led to sharp debates about the barriers to capitalist transformation of agriculture, the role of small-scale and part-time farms in a functionally integrated capitalist industrial and agricultural system, and the role of the state in promoting capitalist agriculture. These critical perspectives have also been directed to understanding the social significance of the research apparatus of the land grant university system itself, particularly as to whether land-grant agricultural science has essentially served as a state policy that has helped to underwrite the growth of large-scale capitalist agriculture (Busch et al. 1991; Goodman and Redclift 1991; Kloppenburg 1988).

Until the late 1960s and early 1970s, rural sociology's contribution to the sociology of development was confined largely to adoption-diffusion research related to new agricultural technologies in Third World countries (Hoogvelt 1997; Toye 1987; Webster 1990). Shortly thereafter, following on the growing disillusion with adoption-diffusion research, development-related inquiry in rural sociology shifted dramatically. Much of the impetus behind criticism of the adoption-diffusion approach came from rural social scientists who did Third World research and who became acutely aware of its shortcomings as a vehicle for understanding agricultural change in the developing countries (Havens and Flinn 1975; George 1976; Lipton 1977; Flora 1990). The theoretical ferment in rural sociology in the 1970s and 1980s was to a large extent derived from new concepts in the sociology of development, such as the "development of underdevelopment," "dependent development," "core-periphery relations," and "capitalist world-system," which were developed as critiques of modernizationism as applied to the developing world.

The "post-diffusion" phase of the sociology of development has led to a far more diversified program of rural sociological research on development processes in the Third World. Although rural sociologists who do sociology of development research tend, not surprisingly, to give particular stress to agricultural development and its environmental implications, increasingly rural sociologists in the United States and other advanced countries do research on development processes that is often indistinguishable from that conducted by scholars who are not identified as rural sociologists. Also, as noted earlier, in many developing countries rural sociology is virtually synonymous with sociology of development, development studies, peasant studies, village studies, and so on.

To a certain extent this emerging research area overlaps the political economy of agriculture with its emphasis on technological change and its effects of distribution of ownership and control of resources, as well as equity in the distribution of benefits of new technologies (Field and Burch 1988). There is the additional concern with the depletion and pollution of nonrenewable resources (Schnaiberg and Gould 1994; Bell 1998). Social and economic impact assessment has emerged as a research activity that often is characterized by its critical perspective (Freudenburg 1986). A comprehensive theory has not yet emerged that links technological change in natural resource industries to the full range of its ramifications for the environment, its socioeconomic impacts, and its associations with industrial structures. However, the magnitude of its potential impacts and the associated public concern suggests that this area of research has a viable future (Freudenburg 1992).

Since the 1920s, agriculture and natural-resource-based industries have been declining as sources of employment; the rate of decline accelerated dramatically after World War II. For a brief period during the 1970s manufacturing was a major source of employment growth in rural areas as industries sought cheaper land, lower taxes, and a nonunion labor force willing to work for lower wages and fewer benefits. Although this process continues, service industries have emerged as the major source of employment growth (Brown et al. 1988). These shifting labor demands have been accompanied by high unemployment in rural areas and a growth of temporary and part-time work, with resulting loss of wages and increasing levels of poverty. Rural labor market analysis has emerged as a new research area in rural sociology as a consequence (Summers et al. 1990). Much of the research is devoted to describing more precisely the nature and extent of rural unemployment and underemployment. However, the theoretical interpretations generally are sensitive to the linkages of rural labor markets to broader issues of economic restructuring. While labor demand–oriented and human capital explanations persist, there are attempts to understand the functioning of rural labor markets within the context of capitalist market institutions in a manner that is reminiscent of institutional labor economics.

Gender studies are not new to rural sociology; the role of women in farming has been a subject of research for at least a quarter-century (Haney and Knowles 1988). However, the past decade has witnessed the emergency of theoretical and empirical studies that attempt to explain how the institutions of capitalism, patriarchy, and the domestic ideology influence the work roles of men and women. A major focus of these recent studies has been the nature and extent of farm women's involvement in farm, household, and off-farm work. The rich descriptive detail of gender-based allocations of labor is being integrated into more comprehensive theoretical interpretations of structural changes in both agricultural and nonagricultural industries (Beneria 1985; Leon and Deere 1987; Sachs 1996).

For the past twenty-five years the United States has pursued a variety of programs and policies intended to alleviate poverty (Sanderfur and Tienda 1988; Snipp 1989; Wilson 1987). In spite of these efforts, poverty persists at rates that are higher in rural areas than in urban areas, and the difference is increasing. Moreover, rural poverty is disproportionately concentrated in minority populations. Within the critical perspective it is argued that past and present institutional barriers limit the access of minority populations to the means of economic well-being. Persons of working age are disproportionately handicapped by deficiencies of human capital and discriminatory practices in the labor market. Moreover, these failures have produced a generation of elderly persons who are denied access to important public insurance programs such as Social Security because they were excluded from the labor market in years past or were employed in industries that were not covered by such programs. Thus, the state is called into question for its poor performance in developing and implementing adequate public policies, a failure that is alleged to benefit the interests of the wealthy and powerful classes of society (Summers 1991).

AGRICULTURAL CHANGE AND THE SOCIOLOGY OF AGRICULTURE

As social scientists and historians have begun to reflect on the momentous and often convulsive changes that have occurred during the twentieth century, many have noted that the most far-reaching social change of the century has arguably been the rapid decline of peasantries and of farm life, particularly since World War II (Hobsbawm 1994). The "depeasantization" of the advanced industrial countries has proceeded the farthest, but the very rapid decline of the peasant societies along with massive streams of rural-to-urban migrants that is now occurring in the developing world is, if anything, more stark (Araghi 1995).

The manner in which rural sociologists have conceptualized the processes and the significance of social-structural changes in agriculture has involved not only debate between the two overarching theoretical positions that have long characterized rural sociology, but also political and ideological positions on agriculture in society at large. Thus, on one hand, theories in the sociology of agriculture tend to fall within either the modernizationist

tradition (e.g., adoption-diffusion) or the critically oriented tradition (e.g., Lenin's and Kautsky's theories of capitalism and rural differentiation; see Goodman and Redclift 1982) discussed earlier. Over and above the differences and debates across theoretical traditions are changing sociopolitical views about agriculture and food.

We noted earlier that, from the beginnings of rural sociology around the turn of the twentieth century, agriculture was one of its most central subject matters. But what was considered interesting or important about agriculture has changed dramatically over time. Early rural sociology was largely focused on the sociology of agricultural communities. Rural sociology was later dominated by the adoption and diffusion of agricultural innovations. While these two traditions differed in their views of what it was about agriculture that was most worthy of study, both were modernizationist perspectives that tended to see the decline of family farming and restructuring of agriculture as being natural components of rural (and overall social) development.

The term "sociology of agriculture" can be best understood as a movement among rural sociologists in the mid- to late 1970s in reaction to two related but distinct components of modernizationism. The sociology of agriculture was, in the first instance, a reaction against rural sociological theories which, at least implicitly, accepted the inevitability and desirability of the demise and destruction of peasantries in the developing world and family farming in the industrial world. What Newby and Buttel (1980) meant by the notion of the "new rural sociology" was that a more adequate rural sociology required a more critical theoretical view about how and why farmers and other rural people were witnessing disintegration of their ways of life. The second defining feature of the new rural sociology was that it sought to take seriously the growing public and social movement concerns about the loss of family farms, the problems faced by agricultural communities, and the role of land-grant universities and public research.

The pattern of farm structural change that has occurred in the United States is not entirely typical of that of the rest of the industrial world, but the past century of changes in the American structure of agriculture typify the theoretical and broader social issues at stake in the sociology of agriculture. In 1940, there were about 7 million American farms, home to about 30 million people (or about 25 percent of the U.S. population). By the end of the century there were only about 1.8 million farms, and the farm population (which numbered a little less than 7 million people) was less than 2 percent of the U.S. total. Even more striking is that fact that the last Census of Agriculture in the twentieth century (the 1997 Census) showed that a mere 26,000 farms with gross annual sales of $1,000,000 or more (representing only 1.4 percent of the total number) accounted for about 42 percent of gross farm sales; by contrast, less than twenty years earlier, farms with gross annual farm sales of $200,000 or more represented 3.3 percent of farms and about 44 percent of total sales (according to the 1978 Census of Agriculture). Thus, American farming has become increasingly concentrated. U.S. farm structure has also become highly dualistic; a handful of very large farms account for the bulk of output, while roughly 1.2 million small, "subfamily" (mostly part-time) farms account for the bulk of the farm population but very little of the output. In between, the middle stratum of farms—the prototypical medium-sized full-time family farm—has declined in numbers and percent of farm sales as the dualism of agriculture has been continued apace. Despite the rapid restructuring of agriculture from 1940 to the end of the century, nearly 95 percent of American farms continue to be family-proprietor or partnership farms. Thus, family farming—even if many of the largest and smallest family operations bear little resemblance to the traditional notion of a family farm—has persisted in the midst of otherwise convulsive change in agriculture and rural America.

The new rural sociology of agriculture in the late 1970s and early 1980s therefore ironically had two very different problematics—the decline/differentiation and the persistence of family farming—on which to focus its research. The new rural sociology drew on three major early-twentieth-century classical theories in focusing on these two problematics. V. I. Lenin tended to be the principal classical antecedent of theories of rural class differentiation (e.g., de Janvry 1980; Friedland et al. 1981; Havens et al. 1986), which tended to foresee agriculture undergoing differentiation into capital and labor, in much the same way that had occurred in nonfarm industry. A. V. Chayanov and K. Kautsky were most influential in the work of scholars who sought to explain the persistence of family farming. Theories of the persistence of family farming generally explain the phenomenon in terms of the obstacles or the forms of resistance that exist to the development of capitalist agriculture (e.g., how the seasonal-biological nature of agriculture makes farming unattractive for large-scale investments [Mann 1990] or how independent commodity producers exhibit different rationalities [Mooney 1988] or enjoy certain advantages over capitalist producers [Friedmann 1978]).

While the agrarian differentiation/persistence debate dominated the sociology of agriculture through the early 1990s, the sociology of agriculture has made two significant shifts—toward studies of farming styles, on one hand, and the globalization of agriculture, on the other—over the last decade. The most recent versions of the sociology of agriculture have been partly a response to the current era of "globalization," trade liberalization, hypermobility of financial capital, World Bank–International Monetary Fund (IMF) imposition of structural adjustment reforms on the developing world, the rapid industrialization of certain sectors of farming (especially livestock and fresh fruits and vegetables), and the remarkable pace of concentration in the agricultural inputs and agro-food industries. It also became apparent to many scholars that most of the theories that dominated the sociology of agriculture in the 1970s through the early 1990s had two possible weaknesses: First, "new rural sociology" theories tended to be somewhat economistic and deterministic. Second, these "new rural sociology" theories tended to locate the dynamics of agricultural change largely, if not entirely, within agriculture itself. These theories tended to give short shrift to the off-farm components of agro-food systems and to the global political-economic environment of agriculture.

The second generation of the sociology of agriculture can be understood as being a response to these two shortcomings of new rural sociology theories as well as to the intellectual and policy challenges posed by globalization. The first response has been the "farming styles" research tradition, and is often referred to as the "Wageningen School" approach because two of its most prominent researchers (van der Ploeg 1992; Long 1992) are located at Wageningen University in the Netherlands. The Wageningen School perspective is a neo-Weberian or "actor-oriented" approach which stresses how diverse rural cultures interacting within diverse national economies and natural environments tend to give rise to diverse "farming styles." Thus, it is argued that there are multiple sources of diversity in farming structures, technologies, rationalities, and practices that serve to obviate the otherwise powerful political-economic processes of globalization and homogenization.

The second, and most influential, new approach in the sociology of agriculture—the agro-industrial globalization tradition—reflects a conviction that chief among the factors propelling agricultural change are matters such as national political-economic processes, the world economy, and geopolitics which lie outside of the realm of agriculture per se (see Friedmann 1982; Friedmann and McMichael 1989). Many scholars working within this new agro-industrial globalization tradition have emphasized the growing ascendancy on the part of agribusiness multinationals as post–World War II protectionist institutions and regulations have been dismantled. Studies in this genre emphasize how private firms are increasingly assuming the standard-setting and regulatory functions formerly undertaken primarily by governments, and how large corporations are playing a growing role in shaping the structure and performance of agro-commodity chains (e.g., Bonanno et al. 1994). Other scholars stress how the emerging structure of the new world food order reflects the growing role of monetary instability and Third World debt. Monetary disorder and debt have created the political-economic conditions for the liberalization of agricultural trade through international regimes such as the World Trade Organization (WTO) and the North American Free Trade Agreement (NAFTA). For example, by serving to justify structural adjustment policies which require that development countries adopt agro-food export policies and reduce food subsidies in order to repay their loans, monetary disorder and debt have been crucial factors in the late twentieth century restructuring of food systems (Friedmann and McMichael 1989; McMichael 1994). These new global food systems contrast sharply with the postwar national-type food order in which world nations tended to control their own agricultural systems and food supplies through national food regulations and domestic agricultural policies.

CONCLUSION

These emergent research topics have not displaced those of an earlier period of rural sociology; they coexist. In doing so, rural sociology continues to serve two conflicting social policy agendas that reflect divergent views of rural society. The field has not escaped its origins in the social thought of nineteenth-century Europe. It does appear to be renewing its intellectual kinship with sociological theory.

The future of rural sociology as a research domain and as an intellectual endeavor appears to be very promising. Only a decade ago some observers were predicting its demise on the grounds that agriculture was declining as a source of employment and urbanization was continuing on a worldwide scale. However, predictions of the death of rural sociology seem to have been premature. The majority of the world population still lives in rural areas, and agriculture still plays a major role in the economies of most nations of the world. The globalization of food systems remains one of the most critical determinants of human well-being (Goodman and Watts 1997). The ending of the Cold War and the opening of the Eastern Bloc to greater scientific and intellectual exchanges create a vast new market for rural sociology, since all of these nations are predominately rural in composition. Finally, rural sociologists are expanding the scope of their work to include a much broader array of social phenomena and accepting the challenge of building the theoretical and empirical bridges between rural and urban aspects of society.

The growth of rural sociology professional associations is further evidence of its good health. In addition to the Rural Sociological Society, which was created in 1937, there are now the International Rural Sociological Association and independent associations in all the world's regions. Membership in all these associations is increasing; the Rural Sociological Society remains over 1,000, and annual meeting attendance has been in excess of 500 for most years in the 1990s.

(SEE ALSO: *Agricultural Innovation; Community; Human Ecology and the Environment; Population*)

REFERENCES

Araghi, Farshad 1995 "Global Depeasantization, 1945–1995." *Sociological Quarterly* 36 (Spring):337–368.

Bell, Colin, and Howard Newby 1972 *Community Studies: An Introduction to the Sociology of the Local Community*. New York: Praeger.

Bell, Michael 1998 *An Invitation to Environmental Sociology*. Thousand Oaks, Calif.: Pine Forge.

Beneria, Lourdes 1985 *Women and Development: Sexual Division of Labor in Rural Societies*. New York: Praeger.

Bonanno, Alessandro, Lawrence Busch, William H. Friedland, Lourdes Gouveia, and Enzo Mingione (eds.) 1994 *From Columbus to ConAgra*. Lawrence: University Press of Kansas.

Bowers, W. L. 1974 *The Country Life Movement in America, 1900–1920*. Port Washington, N.Y.: Kennikat.

Brown, David L., and Kenneth Deavers, eds. 1988 *Rural Economic Development in the 1980s*. Rural Development Research Report No. 69. Washington: U.S. Department of Agriculture, Economic Research Service.

Brunner, Edmund des. 1957 *The Growth of a Science: A Half-Century of Rural Sociological Research in the United States*. New York: Harper and Row.

Busch, Lawrence, William B. Lacy, Jeffrey Burkhardt, and Laura R. Lacy 1991 *Plants, Power and Profit*. Oxford: Basil Blackwell.

Buttel, Frederick H., Olaf F. Larson, and Gilbert W. Gillespie, Jr. 1990 *The Sociology of Agriculture*. Westport, Conn.: Greenwood.

Danbom, D. B. 1979 *The Resisted Revolution: Urban America and the Industrialization of Agriculture, 1900–1930*. Ames: Iowa State University Press.

de Janvry, Alain 1980 "Social Differentiation in Agriculture and the Ideology of Neopopulism." In F. H. Buttel and H. Newby, eds., *The Rural Sociology of the Advanced Societies*. Montclair, N.J.: Allanheld, Osmun.

DuBois, W. E. B. 1898 "The Negroes of Farmville, Virginia: A Social Study." *Bulletin of the Department of Labor* 3(14):1–38.

—— 1901 "The Negro Landholders of Georgia." *Bulletin of the Department of Labor* 6(35):647–777.

—— 1904 "The Negro Farmer." In U.S. Bureau of the Census, *Negroes in the United States*. Washington: U.S. Government Printing Office.

Duncan, Otis Durant 1954 "Rural Sociology Coming of Age." *Rural Sociology* 19(1):1–12.

Field, Donald R., and William R. Burch, Jr. 1988 *Rural Sociology and the Environment*. Westport, Conn.: Greenwood.

Fliegel, Frederick C. 1993 *Diffusion Research in Rural Sociology*. Westport, Conn.: Greenwood.

Flora, Cornelia Butler 1990 "Rural Peoples in a Global Economy." *Rural Sociology* 55(Summer):157–177.

Freudenburg, William R. 1986 "Social Impact Assessment." *Annual Review of Sociology* 12:451–478.

—— 1992 "Addictive Economies: Extractive Industries and Vulnerable Localities in a Changing World Economy." *Rural Sociology* 57(Fall):305–332.

Friedland, William H., Amy Barton, and Robert J. Thomas 1981 *Manufacturing Green Gold*. New York: Cambridge University Press.

Friedmann, Harriet 1978 "World Market, State, and Family Farm: The Social Basis of Household Production in an Era of Wage Labour." *Comparative Studies in Society and History* 20(4):545–586.

—— 1982 "The Political Economy of Food: The Rise and Fall of the Postwar International Food Order." *American Journal of Sociology* 88(Supplement):S248–S286.

——, and Philip McMichael 1989 "Agriculture and the State System: The Rise and Decline of National Agricultures, 1870 to the Present." *Sociologia Ruralis* 29(2):93–117.

Fuguitt, Glenn V., David L. Brown, and Calvin L. Beale 1989 *Rural and Small-Town America*. New York: Russell Sage Foundation.

Galpin, Charles J. 1915 *The Social Anatomy of an Agricultural Community*. Madison: Wisconsin Agricultural Experiment Station.

Garkovich, Lorraine 1989 *Population and Community in Rural America*. New York: Praeger.

George, Susan 1976 *How the Other Half Dies*. New York: Penguin.

Gilbert, Jess 1982 "Rural Theory: The Grounding of Rural Sociology." *Rural Sociology* 47(Winter):609–633.

Goodman, David, and Michael Redclift 1982 *From Peasant to Proletarian*. Oxford: Basil Blackwell.

—— 1991 *Refashioning Nature*. London: Routledge.

——, and Michael Watts (eds.) 1997 *Globalising Food*. New York: Routledge.

Goodwyn, Lawrence 1978 *The Populist Movement: A Short History of the Agrarian Revolt in America*. New York: Oxford University Press.

Haney, Wava G., and Jane B. Knowles (eds.) 1988 *Women and Farming: Changing Roles, Changing Structures*. Boulder, Colo.: Westview.

Havens, A. Eugene 1972 "Methodological Issues in the Study of Development." *Sociologia Ruralis* 12(3–4):252–273.

——, and William L. Flinn 1975 "Green Revolution Technology and Community Development: The Limits of Action Programs." *Economic Development and Cultural Change* 23(April):469–481.

——, Gregory Hooks, Patrick H. Mooney, and Max J. Pfeffer, eds. 1986 *Studies in the Transformation of U.S. Agriculture*. Boulder, Colo.: Westview.

Hawley, Amos H. 1950 *Human Ecology*. New York: Ronald.

—— 1986 *Human Ecology: A Theoretical Essay*. Chicago: University of Chicago Press.

Hobsbawm, Eric 1994 *The Age of Extremes*. New York: Pantheon.

Hofstee, E. W. 1963 "Rural Sociology in Europe." *Rural Sociology* 28(3):329–341.

Hoogvelt, Ankie M. M. 1997 *Globalization and the Postcolonial World*. Baltimore, Md.: Johns Hopkins University Press.

Hooks, Gregory M., and William L. Flinn 1981 "The Country Life Commission and Early Rural Sociology." *Rural Sociologist* 1(March):95–100.

Kloppenburg, Jack, Jr. 1988 *First the Seed*. New York: Cambridge University Press.

Larson, Olaf F., Edward O. Moe, and Julie Zimmerman (eds.) 1992 *Sociology in Government*. Boulder, Colo.: Westview.

LeFebvre, Henry 1953 "Perspectives de la Sociologie Rurale." *Cahiers Internationaux de Sociologie* (*International Journal of Sociology*) 14:122–140.

Leon, Magdalena, and Carmen Diana Deere (eds.) 1987 *Women and Rural Policy: Feminist Perspectives*. Boulder, Colo.: Westview.

Lipton, Michael 1977 *Why Poor People Stay Poor*. London: Temple Smith.

Long, Norman 1992 "From Paradigm Lost to Paradigm Regained: The Case for an Actor-Oriented Sociology of Development." In N. Long and A. Long, eds., *Battlefields of Knowledge*. London: Routledge.

Luloff, A. E., and Louis E. Swanson, eds. 1990 *American Rural Communities*. Boulder, Colo.: Westview.

McMichael, Philip (ed.) 1994 *The Global Restructuring of Agro-Food Systems*. Ithaca, N.Y.: Cornell University Press.

Mann, Susan Archer 1990 *Agrarian Capitalism in Theory and Practice*. Chapel Hill: University of North Carolina Press.

Mendras, Henri 1969 *Rural Sociology in France*. Paris: Mouton.

Mooney, Patrick H. 1988 *My Own Boss*. Boulder, Colo.: Westview.

Newby, Howard 1980 "Rural Sociology—A Trend Report." *Current Sociology* 28(1):1–141.

——, and Frederick H. Buttel 1980 "Toward a Critical Rural Sociology." In F. H. Buttel and H. Newby, eds., *The Rural Sociology of the Advanced Societies*. Montclair, N.J.: Allanheld, Osmun.

Nisbet, Robert 1966 *The Sociological Tradition*. New York: Basic.

Pahl, Ray E. (1966) 1970 "The Rural-Urban Continuum." *Sociologia Ruralis* 6(3–4):299–327. Reprinted in R. E. Pahl, ed., *Readings in Urban Sociology*. Oxford: Pergamon.

Redfield, Robert 1947 "The Folk Society." *American Journal of Sociology* 52(3):293–308.

Richards, R. O. 1978 "Urbanization of Rural Areas." In David Street and Associates, eds., *Handbook of Contemporary Urban Life*. San Francisco: Jossey-Bass.

Rogers, Everett M. 1995 *Diffusion of Innovations*, 4th ed. New York: Free Press.

Ryan, Bryce, and Neal C. Gross 1943 "The Diffusion of Hybrid Seed Corn in Two Iowa Communities." *Rural Sociology* 8:15–24.

Sachs, Carolyn 1996 *Gendered Fields*. Boulder, Colo.: Westview.

Sandefur, Gary D., and Marta Tienda (eds.) 1988 *Divided Opportunities: Minorities, Poverty, and Social Policy*. New York: Plenum.

Schnaiberg, Allan, and Kenneth Gould 1994 *Environment and Society*. New York: St. Martin's.

Sewell, William H. 1965 "Rural Sociological Research, 1936–1965." *Rural Sociology* 30(December):428–451.

Snipp, C. Matthew 1989 *American Indians: The First of This Land*. New York: Russell Sage Foundation.

Sorokin, P. A., and Carl C. Zimmerman 1929 *Principles of Rural-Urban Sociology*. New York: Henry Holt.

Stein, Maurice 1964 *The Eclipse of Community*. New York: Harper and Row.

Summers, Gene F. 1986 "Rural Community Development." *Annual Review of Sociology* 12:347–371.

—— 1991 "Minorities in Rural Society." *Rural Sociology* 56:177–188.

——, Francine Horton, and Christina Gringeri 1990 "Rural Labour-Market Changes in the United States." In Terry Marsden, Philip Lowe, and Sarah Whatmore, eds., *Rural Restructuring: Global Processes and Their Responses*. London: David Fulton.

Swanson, R. M. 1972 The country life movement, 1900–1940. Ph.D. diss. University of Minnesota.

Thiesenhusen, William C. 1978 "Reaching the Rural Poor and Poorest: A Goal Unmet." In H. Newby, ed., *International Perspectives in Rural Sociology*. New York: John Wiley.

Toennies, Ferdinand (1887) 1957 *Community and Society: Gemeinschaft und Gesellschaft*. New York: Harper and Row.

Toye, John 1987 *Dilemmas of Development*. New York: Basil Blackwell.

van der Ploeg, Jan Douwe 1992 "The Reconstitution of Locality: Technology and Labour in Modern Agriculture." In T. Marsden, P. Lowe, and S. Whatmore, eds., *Labour and Locality*. London: David Fulton.

Vidich, Arthur J., and Joseph Bensman 1958 *Small Town in Mass Society: Class, Power and Religion in a Rural Community*. Princeton, N.J.: Princeton University Press.

Warner, W. Keith 1974 "Rural Society in a Post-Industrial Age." *Rural Sociology* 39(3):306–317.

Warren, Roland 1963 *The Community America*. Chicago: Rand McNally.

Webster, Andrew 1990 *Introduction to the Sociology of Development*, 2nd ed. Atlantic Highlands, N.J.: Humanities Press International.

Wilkinson, Kenneth 1991 *The Community in Rural Society*. Westport, Conn.: Greenwood.

Wilson, William Julius 1987 *The Truly Disadvantaged: The Inner City, the Underclass, and Public Policy*. Chicago: University of Chicago Press.

GENE F. SUMMERS
FREDERICK H. BUTTEL

S

SAMPLE SELECTION BIAS

In a linear regression model, sample selection bias occurs when data on the dependent variable are missing nonrandomly, conditional on the independent variables. For example, if a researcher uses ordinary least squares (OLS) to estimate a regression model in which large values of the dependent variable are underrepresented in a sample, estimates of slope coefficients typically will be biased.

Hausman and Wise (1977) studied the problem of estimating the effect of education on income in a sample of persons with incomes below $15,000. This is known as a *truncated sample* and is an example of explicit selection on the dependent variable. This is shown in Figure 1, where individuals are sampled at three education levels: low (L), middle (M), and high (H). In the figure, sample truncation leads to an estimate of the effect of schooling that is biased downward from the true regression line as a result of the $15,000 ceiling on the dependent variable. In a variety of special conditions (Winship and Mare 1992), selection biases coefficients downward. In general, however, selection may bias estimated effects in either direction.

A sample that is restricted on the dependent variable is effectively selected on the error of the regression equation; at any value of X, observations with sufficiently large positive errors are eliminated from the sample. As is shown in Figure 1, as the independent variable increases, the ex-

pected value of the error becomes increasingly negative, making these two elements negatively correlated. Because this contradicts the standard assumption of OLS that the error and the independent variables are not correlated, OLS estimates become biased.

A different type of explicit selection occurs when the sample includes persons with incomes of $15,000 or more but all that is known about those persons is their educational attainment and that their incomes are $15,000 or more. When the dependent variable is outside a known bound but the exact value of the variable is unknown, the sample is *censored*. If these persons' incomes are coded as $15,000, OLS estimates are biased and inconsistent for the same reasons that obtain in the truncated sample.

A third type of selection that leads to bias occurs when censoring or truncation is a stochastic function of the dependent variable. This is termed *implicit selection*. In the income example, individuals with high incomes may be less likely to provide information on their incomes than are individuals with low incomes. As is shown below, OLS estimates also are biased when there is implicit selection.

Yet another type of selection occurs when there is *selection on the measured independent variable(s)*. For example, the sample may be selected on educational attainment alone. If persons with high levels of schooling are omitted from the model, an OLS estimate of the effect for persons with lower levels of education on income is unbi-

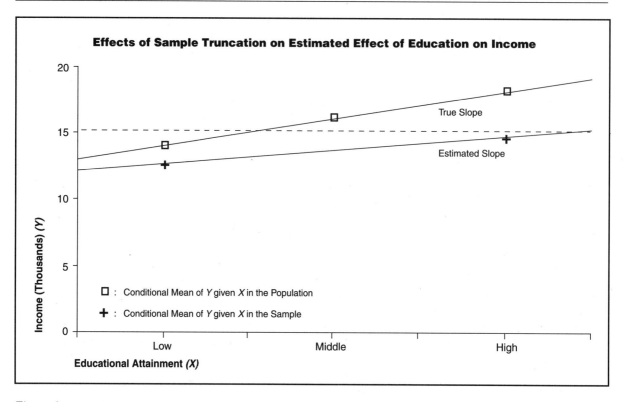

Figure 1

ased if schooling has a constant linear effect throughout its range. Because the conditional expectation of the dependent variable (or, equivalently, the error term) at each level of the independent variable is not affected by a sample restriction on the independent variable, when a model is specified properly OLS estimates are unbiased and consistent (DuMouchel and Duncan 1983).

EXAMPLES

Sample selection can occur because of the way data have been collected or, as the examples below illustrate, may be a fundamental aspect of particular social processes. In econometrics, where most of the basic research on selection bias has been done, many of the applications have been to labor economics. Many studies by sociologists that deal with selection problems have been done in the cognate area of social stratification. Problems of selection bias, however, pervade sociology, and attempts to grapple with them appear in the sociology of education, family sociology, criminology, the sociology of law, social networks, and other areas.

Trends in Employment of Out-of-School Youths. Mare and Winship (1984) investigate employment trends from the 1960s to the 1980s for young black and white men who are out of school. Many factors affect these trends, but a key problem in interpreting the trends is that they are influenced by the selectivity of the out-of-school population. Over time, that selectivity changes because the proportion of the population that is out of school decreases, especially among blacks. Because persons who stay in school longer have better average employment prospects than do persons who drop out, the employment rates of nonstudents are lower than they would be if employment and school enrollment were independent. Observed employment patterns are biased because the probabilities of employment and leaving school are dependent. Other things being equal, as enrollment increases, employment rates for out-of-school young persons decrease as a result of the compositional change in this pool of individuals. To understand the employment trends of out-of-school persons, therefore, one must analyze jointly the trends in employment and school enrollment. The increasing propensity of young blacks to remain in school explains some of the growing gap in the employment rates between blacks and whites.

Selection Bias and the Disposition of Criminal Cases. A central focus in the analysis of crime and punishment involves the determinants of differences in the treatment of persons in contact with the criminal justice system, for example, the differential severity of punishment of blacks and whites (Peterson and Hagan 1984). There is a high degree of selectivity in regard to persons who are convicted of crimes. Among those who commit crimes, only a portion are arrested; of those arrested, only a portion are prosecuted; of those prosecuted, only a portion are convicted; and among those convicted, only a portion are sent to prison. Common unobserved factors may affect the continuation from one stage of this process to the next. Indeed, the stages may be jointly determined inasmuch as legal officials may be mindful of the likely outcomes later in the process when they dispose cases. The chances that a person will be punished if arrested, for example, may affect the eagerness of police to arrest suspects. Analyses of the severity of sentencing that focus on persons already convicted of crimes may be subject to selection bias and should take account of the process through which persons are convicted (Hagan and Parker 1985; Peterson and Hagan 1984; Zatz and Hagan 1985).

Scholastic Aptitude Tests and Success in College. Manski and Wise (1983) investigate the determinants of graduation from college, including the capacity of the Scholastic Aptitude Test (SAT) to predict individuals' probabilities of graduation. Studies based on samples of students in colleges find that the SAT has little predictive power, yet those studies may be biased because of the selective stages between taking the SAT and attending college. Some students who take the SAT do not apply to college, some apply but are not admitted, some are admitted but do not attend, and those who attend are sorted among the colleges to which they have been admitted. Each stage of selection is nonrandom and is affected by characteristics of students and schools that are unknown to the analyst. When one jointly considers the stages of selection in the college attendance decision, along with the probability that a student will graduate from college, one finds that the SAT is a strong predictor of college graduation.

Women's Socioeconomic Achievement. Analyses of the earnings and other socioeconomic achievements of women are potentially affected by nonrandom selection of women into the labor market. The rewards that women expect from working affect their propensity to enter the labor force. Outcomes such as earnings and occupational status therefore are jointly determined with labor force participation, and analyses that ignore the process of labor force participation are potentially subject to selection bias. Many studies in economics (Gronau 1974; Heckman 1974) and sociology (Fligstein and Wolf 1978; Hagan 1990; England et al. 1988) use models that simultaneously represent women's labor force participation and the market rewards that women receive.

Analysis of Occupational Mobility from Nineteenth-Century Censuses. Nineteenth-century decennial census data for cities provide a means of comparing nineteenth- and twentieth-century regimes of occupational mobility in the United States. Although one can analyze mobility by linking the records of successive censuses, such linkage is possible only for persons who remain in the same city and keep the same name over the decade. Persons who die, emigrate, or change their names are excluded. Because mortality and migration covary with socioeconomic success, the process of mobility and the way in which observations are selected for the analysis are jointly determined. Analyses that model mobility and sample selection jointly offer the possibility of avoiding selection bias (Hardy 1989).

MODELS OF SELECTION

Berk (1983) provides an introduction to selection models; Winship and Mare (1992) provide a review of the literature before 1992. We start by discussing the censored regression, or tobit, model. We forgo discussion of the very closely related truncated regression model (Hausman and Wise 1977).

Tobit Model. The censored regression, or tobit, model is appropriate when the dependent variable is censored at an upper or lower bound as an artifact of how the data are collected (Tobin

1958; Maddala 1983). For censoring at a lower bound, the model is

$$Y_{1i}^* = X_i\beta + \varepsilon_i \tag{1}$$

$$Y_{1i} = Y_{1i}^* \quad \text{if } Y_{1i}^* > 0 \tag{2}$$

$$Y_{1i} = 0 \quad \text{if } Y_{1i}^* \leq 0 \tag{3}$$

where for the *i*th observation, Y_{1i}^* is an unobserved continuous latent variable, Y_{1i} is the observed variable, X_i is a vector of values on the independent variables, ε_i is the error, and ß is a vector of coefficients. We assume that ε_i is not correlated with X_i and is independently and identically distributed. The model can be generalized by replacing the threshold zero in equations (2) and (3) with a known nonzero constant. The censoring point also may vary across observations, leading to a model that is formally equivalent to models for survival analysis (Kalbfleisch and Prentice 1980).

Standard Sample Selection Model. A generalization of the tobit model involves specifying that a second variable Y_{2i}^* affects whether Y_{1i} is observed. That is, retain the basic model in equation (1) but replace equations (2) and (3) with

$$Y_{1i} = Y_{1i}^* \quad \text{if } Y_{2i}^* > 0 \tag{4}$$

$$Y_{1i} = 0 \quad \text{if } Y_{2i}^* \leq 0 \tag{5}$$

Variants of this model depend on how Y_{2i} is specified. Commonly, Y_{2i}^* is determined by a binary regression model:

$$Y_{2i}^* = Z_i\alpha + U_i \tag{6}$$

$$Y_{2i} = 1 \quad \text{if } Y_{2i}^* > 0 \tag{7}$$

$$Y_{2i} = 0 \quad \text{if } Y_{2i}^* \leq 0 \tag{8}$$

where Y_{2i}^* is a latent continuous variable. The classic example is a model for the wages and employment of women where Y_{1i} is the observed wage, Y_{2i} is a dummy variable indicating whether a woman works, and Y_{2i}^* indexes a woman's propensity to work (Gronau 1974). In a variant of this model, Y_{2i} is hours of work and equations (6) through (8) are a tobit model (Heckman 1974). In both variants, Y_{1i}^* is observed only for women with positive hours of work. One can modify the model by assuming,

for example, that Y_{1i} is dichotomous. If ε_i and υ_i follow a bivariate normal distribution, this leads to a bivariate probit selection model.

Estimation of equation (1) using OLS will lead to biased estimates. When $Y_{2i}^* > 0$,

$$\begin{aligned} Y_{1i} &= X_i\beta + E\left[\varepsilon_i | Y_{2i}^* > 0\right] + \eta_i \\ &= X_i\beta + E\left[\varepsilon_i | U_i - Z_i\alpha > 0\right] + \eta_i \end{aligned} \tag{9}$$

The OLS regression of Y_{1i} on X_i is biased and inconsistent if ε_i is correlated with $\upsilon_i - Z_i\alpha$, which occurs if ε_i is correlated with υ_i or Z_i or both. If the variables in Z_i are included in X_i, ε_i and Z_i are not correlated by assumption. If, however, Z_i contains additional variables, ε_i and Z_i may be correlated. When $\sigma_{\varepsilon\upsilon} = 0$, selection depends only on the observed variables in Z_i, not those in X_i. In this case, selection can be dealt with either by conditioning on the additional Z's or by using propensity score methods (Rosenbaum and Rubin 1983).

Equation (9) shows how selectivity bias may be interpreted as an omitted variable bias (Heckman 1979). The term $E[\varepsilon_i | Y_{2i}^* > 0]$ can be thought of as an omitted variable that is correlated with X_i and affects Y_1. Its omission leads to biased and inconsistent OLS estimates of ß.

Nonrandom Treatment Assignment. A model intimately related to the standard selection model that is not formally presented here is used when individuals are assigned nonrandomly to some treatment in an experiment. In this case, there are essentially two selection problems. For individuals not receiving the treatment, information on what their outcomes would have been if they had received treatment is "missing." Similarly, for individuals receiving the treatment, we do not know what their outcomes would have been if they had not received the treatment. Heckman (1978) explicitly analyzes the relationship between the nonrandom assignment problem and selection. Winship and Morgan (1999) review the vast literature that has appeared on this question in the last two decades.

ESTIMATORS

A large number of estimators have been proposed for selection models. Until recently, all these estimators made strong assumptions about the distribution of errors. Two general classes of methods—maximum likelihood and nonlinear least squares—typically assume bivariate normality of ε_i and υ_i. The most popular method is that of Heckman (1979), known as the lambda method, which assumes only that υ_i in equation (6) is normally distributed and $E[\varepsilon_i | \upsilon_i]$ is linear.

For a number of years, there has been concern about the sensitivity of the Heckman estimator to these normality and linearity assumptions. Because maximum likelihood and nonlinear least squares make even stronger assumptions, they are typically more efficient but even less robust to violations of distributional assumptions. The main concern of the literature since the early 1980s has been the search for alternatives to the Heckman estimator that do not depend on normality and linearity assumptions.

Heckman's Estimator. The Heckman estimator involves (1) estimating the selection model (equations [6] through [8]), (2) calculating the expected error, $\upsilon_i = E[\upsilon_i | \upsilon_i > -Z_i\alpha]$, for each observation using the estimated α, and (3) using the estimated error as a regressor in equation (1). We can rewrite equation (9) as

$$Y_{1i} = X_i\beta + E\left(\varepsilon_i | U_i > -Z_i\alpha\right) + \eta_i \qquad (10)$$

If ε_i and υ_i are bivariate normal and Var $(\upsilon_i) = 1$, then $E(\varepsilon_i | \upsilon_i) = \sigma_{\varepsilon\upsilon}\upsilon_i$ and

$$E\left(\varepsilon_i | U_i > -Z_i\alpha\right) = \sigma_{\varepsilon u}\phi\left(-Z_i\alpha\right) / [1 - \Phi\left(-Z_i\alpha\right)] = \sigma_{\varepsilon u}\lambda\left(-Z_i\alpha\right) \qquad (11)$$

where ϕ and Φ are the standardized normal density and distribution functions, respectively. The ratio $\lambda(-Z_i\alpha)$ is the inverse Mills's ratio. Substituting equation (11) into equation (10), we get

$$Y_{1i} = X_i\beta + \sigma_{\varepsilon u}\lambda\left(-Z_i\alpha\right) + \eta_i \qquad (12)$$

where η_i is not correlated with both X_i and $\lambda(-Z_i\alpha)$. Equation (12) can be estimated by OLS but is preferably estimated by weighted least squares since its error term is heteroskedastic (Heckman 1979).

The precision of the estimates in equation (12) is sensitive to the variance of λ and collinearity between X and λ. The variance of λ is determined by how effectively the probit equation at the first stage predicts who is selected into the sample. The better the equation predicts, the greater the vari-

ance of λ is and the more precise the estimates will be. Collinearity will be determined in part by the overlap in variables between X and Z. If X and Z are identical, the model is identified only because λ is nonlinear. Since it is seldom possible to justify the form of λ on substantive grounds, successful use of the method usually requires that at least one variable in Z not be included in X. Even in this case, X and $\lambda(-Z_i\alpha)$ may be highly collinear, leading to imprecise estimates.

Robustness of Heckman's Estimator. Because of the sensitivity of Heckman's estimator to model specification, researchers have focused on the robustness of the estimator to violations of its several assumptions. Estimation of equations (6) through (8) as a probit model assumes that the errors υ_i are homoskedastic. When this assumption is violated, the Heckman procedure yields inconsistent estimates, though procedures are available to correct for heteroskedasticity (Hurd 1979). The assumed bivariate normality of υ_i and ε_i in the selection model is needed in two places. First, normality of υ_i is needed for consistent estimation of α in the probit model. Second, the normality assumption implies a particular nonlinear relationship for the effect of $Z_{i\alpha}$ on Y_{2i} through λ. If the expectation of ε_i conditional on υ_i is not linear and/or υ_i is not normal, λ misspecifies the relationship between $Z_{i\alpha}$ and Y_{2i} and the model may yield biased results.

Several studies have analytically investigated the bias in the single-equation (tobit) model when the error is not normally distributed. In a model with only an intercept—that is, a model for the mean of a censored distribution—when errors are not normally distributed, the normality assumption leads to substantial bias. This result holds even when the true distribution is close to normal (for example, the logistic) (Goldberger 1983). When the normality assumption is wrong, moreover, maximum likelihood estimates may be worse than estimates that simply use the observed sample mean. For samples that are 75 percent complete, bias from the normality assumption is minimal; in samples that are 50 percent complete, bias is substantial in the truncated case but not in the censored case; and in samples that are less than 50 percent complete, bias is substantial in almost all cases (Arabmazar and Schmidt 1982).

The fact that estimation of the mean is sensitive to distributional misspecification suggests that the Heckman estimator may not be robust and raises the question of how often such problems arise in practice. In addition, even when normality holds, the Heckman estimator may not improve the mean square error of OLS estimates of slope coefficients in small samples (50 or less) (Stolzenberg and Relles 1990). This appears to parallel the standard result that when the effect of a variable is measured imprecisely, inclusion of the variable may enlarge the mean square error of the other parameters in the model (Leamer 1983).

No empirical work that the authors know of directly examines the sensitivity of Heckman's method for a standard selection model. Work by LaLonde (1986) using the nonrandom assignment treatment model suggests that in specific circumstances the Heckman method can inadequately adjust for unobserved differences between the treatment and control groups.

Extensions of the Heckman Estimator. There are two main issues in estimating equation (12). The first is correctly estimating the probability for each individual that he or she will be selected. As it has been formulated above, this means first correctly specifying both the linear function $Z\alpha$ and second specifying the correct, typically nonlinear relationship between the probability of selection and $Z\alpha$. The second issue is the problem of what nonlinear function should be chosen for λ. When bivariate normality of errors holds, λ is the inverse Mills's ratio. When this assumption does not hold, inconsistent estimates may result. Moreover, since X_i and Z_i are often highly collinear, estimates of ß in equation 12 may quite be sensitive to misspecification of λ.

The first problem is handled rather easily. In the situation where one has a very large sample and there are multiple individuals with the same Z, the simplest approach is to estimate the probability of selection nonparameterically by directly estimating the probability of being selected for individuals with each vector of Z's from the observed frequencies. With smaller samples, kernel estimation methods are available. These methods also consist of estimating probabilities directly by grouping individuals with "similar" Z's and directly calculating the probability of selection from weighted frequencies. Variants of this approach involve different definitions of similarity and/or weight (Hardle 1990). In both methods, the problem of

estimating how the probability of selection depends on Z is bypassed.

Semiparametric methods are also available. These methods are useful if their underlying assumptions are correct, since they generally produce more efficient estimates than does a fully nonparametric approach. These methods include Manski's maximum score method (1975), nonparametric maximum likelihood estimation (Cosslett 1983), weighted average derivatives (Stoker 1986; Powell et al. 1989), spline methods, and series approximations (Hardle 1990).

The problem in the second stage is to deal with the fact that one generally has no a priori knowledge of the correct functional form for λ. Since λ is simply a monotonic function of the probability of being selected, this is equivalent to asking what nonlinear transformation of the selection probability should be entered into equation (12). A variety of approaches are available here. One approach is to approximate λ through a series expansion (Newey 1990; Lee 1982) or by means of step functions (Cosslett 1991). An alternative is to control for λ by using differencing or fixed effect methods (Heckman et al. 1998). The essential idea is to control for the probability of selection by implicitly including a series of dummy variables in equation (1), with each dummy variable being used to indicate a set of individuals with the same probability of selection or, equivalently, the same λ. Generally, this will produce significantly larger standard errors of the slope estimates. This is appropriate, however, since selection increases uncertainty. With small samples, these methods can be generalized through kernel estimation (Powell 1987; Ahn and Powell 1990). Newey et al. (1990) apply a variety of methods to an empirical problem.

CONCLUSION

Selection problems bedevil much social science research. First and foremost, it is important for investigators to recognize that there is a selection problem and that it is likely to affect their estimates. Unfortunately, there is no panacea for selection bias. Various estimators have been proposed, and it is important for researchers to investigate the range of estimates produced by different methods. In most cases this range will be considerably broader than the confidence intervals for the

OLS estimates. Selection bias introduces greater uncertainty into estimates. New methods for correcting for selection bias have been proposed that may provide a more powerful means for adjusting for selection. This needs to be determined by future research.

REFERENCES

Ahn, H., and J. J. Powell 1990 *Semiparametric Estimation of Censored Selection Models with a Nonparametric Selection Mechanism*. Madison: Department of Economics, University of Wisconsin.

Arabmazar, A., and P. Schmidt 1982 "An Investigation of the Robustness of the Tobit Estimator to Non-Normality." *Econometrica* 50:1055–1063.

Berk, R. A. 1983 "An Introduction to Sample Selection Bias in Sociological Data." *American Sociological Review* 48:386–398.

Cosslett, S. R. 1983 "Distribution-Free Maximum Likelihood Estimator of the Binary Choice Model." *Econometrica* 51:765–781.

—— 1991 "Semiparametric Estimation of a Regression Model with Sampling Selectivity." In W. A. Barnett, J. Powell, and G. Tauchen, eds., *Nonparametric and Semiparametric Methods in Econometrics and Statistics*. Cambridge: Cambridge University Press.

DuMouchel, W. H., and G. J. Duncan 1983. "Using Sample Survey Weights in Multiple Regression Analyses of Stratified Samples." *Journal of the American Statistical Association* 78:535–543.

England, P., G. Farkas, B. Kilbourne, and T. Dou 1988 "Explaining Occupational Sex Segregation and Wages: Findings from a Model with Fixed Effects." *American Sociological Review* 53:544–558.

Fligstein, N. D., and W. Wolf 1978 "Sex Similarities in Occupational Status Attainment: Are the Results Due to the Restriction of the Sample to Employed Women?" *Social Science Research* 7:197–212.

Goldberger, A. S. 1983 "Abnormal Selection Bias." In S. Karlin, T. Amemiya, and L. A. Goodman, eds., *Studies in Econometrics, Time Series, and Multivariate Statistics*. New York: Academic Press.

Gronau, R. 1974 "Wage Comparisons—Selectivity Bias." *Journal of Political Economy* 82:1119–1143.

Hagan, J. 1990 "The Gender Stratification of Income Inequality among Lawyers." *Social Forces* 68:835–855.

——, and P. Parker, 1985. "White-Collar Crime and Punishment." *American Sociological Review* 50:302–316.

Hardle, W. 1990 *Applied Nonparametric Regression*. New York: Cambridge University Press.

Hardy, M. A. 1989 "Estimating Selection Effects in Occupational Mobility in a 19th-Century City." *American Sociological Review* 54:834–843.

Hausman, J. A., and D. A. Wise, 1977 "Social Experimentation, Truncated Distributions, and Efficient Estimation." *Econometrica* 45:919–938.

Heckman, J. J. 1974 "Shadow Prices, Market Wages and Labor Supply." *Econometrica* 42:679–694.

—— 1978 "Dummy Endogenous Variables in a Simultaneous Equation System." *Econometrica* 46:931–959.

—— 1979. "Sample Selection Bias as a Specification Error." *Econometrica* 47:153–161.

——, H. Ichimura, S. Smith, and P. Todd 1998 "Characterizing Selection Bias Using Experimental Data." *Econometrica* 6:1017–1099.

Hurd, M. 1979 "Estimation in Truncated Samples." *Journal of Econometrics* 11:247–58.

Kalbfleisch, J. D., and R. L. Prentice 1980 *The Statistical Analysis of Failure Time Data*. New York: Wiley.

Lalonde, R. J. 1986 "Evaluating the Econometric Evaluations of Training Programs with Experimental Data." *American Economic Review* 76:604–620.

Leamer, E. E. 1983 "Model Choice and Specification Analysis." In Z. Griliches and M. D. Intriligator, eds., *Handbook of Econometrics, vol. 1*. Amsterdam: North-Holland.

Lee, L. F. 1982 "Some Approaches to the Correction of Selectivity Bias." *Review of Economic Studies* 49:355–372.

Maddala, G. S. 1983 *Limited-Dependent and Qualitative Variables in Econometrics*. Cambridge: Cambridge University Press.

Manski, C. F., and D. A. Wise 1983 *College Choice in America*. Cambridge, Mass.: Harvard University Press.

Mare, R. D., and C. Winship 1984 "The Paradox of Lessening Racial Inequality and Joblessness among Black Youth: Enrollment, Enlistment, and Employment, 1964–1981." *American Sociological Review* 49:39–55.

Newey, W. K. 1990 "Two-Step Series Estimation of Sample Selection Models." Paper presented at the 1988 European meeting of the Econometric Society.

——, J. L. Powell, and J. R. Walker 1990 "Semiparametric Estimation of Selection Models: Some Empirical Results." *American Economic Review* 80:324–328.

Peterson, R. and J. Hagan 1984 "Changing Conceptions of Race: Towards an Account of Anomalous Findings of Sentencing Research." *American Sociological Review* 49:56–70.

Powell, J. L. 1987 *Semiparametric Estimation of Bivariate Latent Variable Models*. Working Paper No. 8704.

Madison: Social Systems Research Institute, University of Wisconsin.

——, J. H. Stock, and T. M. Stoker 1989 "Semiparametric Estimation of Index Coefficients." *Econometrica* 57:1403–1430.

Rosenbaum, P., and D. B. Rubin 1983 "The Central Role of the Propensity Score in Observational Studies for Causal Effects." *Biometrika* 70:41–55.

Stoker, T. M. 1986 "Consistent Estimates of Scaled Coefficients." *Econometrica* 54:1461–1481.

Stolzenberg, R. M., and D. A. Relles 1990 "Theory Testing in a World of Constrained Research Design: The Significance of Heckman's Censored Sampling Bias Correction for Nonexperimental Research." *Sociological Methods Research* 18:395–415.

Tobin, J. 1958 "Estimation of Relationships for Limited Dependent Variables." *Econometrica* 26:24–36.

Winship, C., and R. D. Mare 1992 "Models for Sample Selection Bias." *Annual Review of Sociology* 18:327–350.

——, and S. Morgan 1999 "The Estimation of Causal Effects from Observational Data." *Annual Review of Sociology.* 25:657–704.

Zatz, M. S., and J. Hagan 1985 "Crime, Time, and Punishment: An Exploration of Selection Bias in Sentencing Research." *Journal of Quantitative Criminology* 1:103–126.

CHRISTOPHER WINSHIP
ROBERT D. MARE

SAMPLING PROCEDURES

The analysis of data from samples constitutes a major proportion of contemporary research in the social sciences. For example, researchers use sample data from the U.S. population to estimate, with specified levels of confidence and precision, quantities such as average household size, the proportion of Americans who are unemployed during a given month, and the correlation between educational attainment and annual earnings among members of the labor force. Sample-based estimates are called *sample statistics*, while the corresponding population values are called *population parameters*. The most common reason for sampling is to obtain information about population parameters more cheaply and quickly than would be possible by using a complete census of a population. Sampling also is used sometimes when it is not feasible to carry out a complete census. For example,

except perhaps in a few nations with population registers, attempts to carry out a census in large countries invariably fail to enumerate everyone, and those who are missed tend to differ systematically from those who are enumerated (Choldin 1994). In these cases sampling may be the only way to obtain accurate information about population characteristics.

Researchers can use sample statistics to make inferences about population parameters because the laws of probability show that under specified conditions, sample statistics are unbiased estimators of population parameters. For example, if one used the same procedure to draw repeated samples from a population and determine the proportion of females in each sample, the average value of the observed sample proportions would equal the actual proportion of females in the population. The laws of probability also show that one can use data from a single sample to estimate how much a sample statistic will vary across many samples drawn from the population. Knowing the variability of a sample statistic (in statistical parlance, its *sampling variance*) in turn makes it possible to draw conclusions about the corresponding population parameter even though one has data for only a single sample. The key condition that must be met for these conditions to hold is that the data must come from a *probability sample*, a sample in which each case in the population (cases may be individuals, households, cities, days, etc.) has a known and nonzero probability of being selected into the sample. To produce this type of sample, a sampling technique must employ a random selection mechanism, one in which only the laws of chance determine which cases are included in the sample.

Researchers sometimes use *nonprobability samples*, such as convenience samples, quota samples, and snowball samples, to avoid the costs in time and money of probability sampling. *Convenience samples*, which consist of cases chosen simply because they are readily available (such as pedestrians passing by a street corner and volunteers from a classroom), sometimes are used in exploratory research and in the development of questionnaires or interview protocols. Opinion polls sometimes use *quota samples*, in which interviewers are assigned certain types of people to interview (e.g., a white female over age 50 living on a farm or a black male aged 20 to 30 living in a central city) but are free to select specific individuals fitting these criteria to interview, to gauge political opinions cheaply. *Snowball samples* are generated when investigators ask known members of a group to identify other members and subsequently ask those who are so identified to identify still other members. This procedure takes advantage of the fact that the members of certain small and hard to locate groups (for example, biochemists studying a particular enzyme) often know one another. None of these nonprobability sampling procedures ensures that all the cases in the target population have a known and nonzero probability of being included in a sample, however (Kalton 1983, pp. 90–93). As a result, one cannot be confident that these procedures will provide unbiased estimates of population parameters or make statistical inferences from the samples they yield. Unless cost and time constraints are severe, researchers seeking to estimate population parameters therefore nearly always use procedures that yield probability samples.

One should distinguish between the representativeness of a sample and whether it was drawn by using probability sampling procedures. Although probability samples have a decidedly better track record in regard to representativeness, not all probability samples are representative and not all nonprobability samples are unrepresentative. Political polls based on quota samples, for example, often produce results that come very close to the subsequent vote. However, there is usually no reason to believe that a nonprobability sampling procedure that has been successful in the past will continue to yield representative results. In contrast, probability sampling procedures are likely to produce representative samples in the future because they are based on a random selection procedure.

Sampling theory, a branch of statistical theory, covers a variety of techniques for drawing probability samples. Many considerations can influence the choice of a sampling procedure for a given project, including feasibility, time constraints, characteristics of the population to be studied, desired accuracy, and cost. Simple sampling procedures are often sufficient for studying small, accessible, and relatively homogeneous populations, but researchers typically must use more complicated procedures to study large and heterogeneous populations. Using complicated procedures requires

consultation with a sampling specialist at a survey organization (the University of Illinois Survey Research Laboratory provides a list of these organizations on its Web site: www.srl.uic.edu).

Any study in which a probability sample will be drawn must begin by defining the population of interest: the target population. The purpose of the study restricts the definition of the target population but rarely specifies it completely. For example, a study of characteristics of U.S. families obviously will define the population as consisting of families, but it will be necessary to define precisely what counts as a family as well as decide how to treat various cases from which it may be difficult to collect data (such as the families of U.S. citizens who live overseas). Sudman (1976, pp. 11–14) discusses general issues involved in defining target populations.

The next step in probability sampling is to construct a *sampling frame* that identifies and locates the cases in the target population so that they can be sampled. The most basic type of sampling frame is a list of the cases in the target population. Such lists are often unavailable, however, and so researchers usually must construct an alternative. For example, to draw a sample of U.S. public high schools, a researcher might begin with a list of U.S. census tracts, select a sample of those tracts, and then consult maps that indicate the locations of public high schools in the selected tracts. Here the sampling frame would consist of the list of census tracts and their corresponding maps.

A perfect sampling frame includes all the cases in the target population, no inappropriate cases, and no duplications. Most sampling frames are imperfect, however, with failure to include all the cases in the target population being the most serious type of *coverage error*. For example, telephone-number sampling frames, such as those employed in random-digit dialing procedures, do not cover people without a telephone, and sampling frames that are based on dwelling units do not cover homeless people. Undercoverage errors bias sample statistics, with the extent of the bias being positively related to (1) the proportion of the target population not covered by the sampling frame and (2) the magnitude of the difference between those covered and those not covered. Sampling experts have developed many methods to reduce coverage errors, including the use of multiple frames, multiplicity techniques, and postsurvey adjustments. Kish (1995, pp. 53–59, 384–439) and Groves (1989, pp. 81–132) provide helpful discussions of sampling-frame problems and possible solutions.

BASIC PROBABILITY SAMPLING PROCEDURES

Characteristics of one's sampling frame influence the specific sampling procedure appropriate for producing a probability sample. For example, some sampling procedures require that the sampling frame list all the cases in the population, while others do not. In addition, sampling procedures often are combined in situations where the sampling frame is complex. In all situations, however, the key element required for producing a probability sample is the use of a formally random procedure for selecting cases into the sample.

Simple Random Sampling. Simple random sampling (SRS) is the most elementary probability sampling procedure and serves as a benchmark for the evaluation of other procedures. To use SRS, one's sampling frame must list all the cases in the population. Usually the researcher assigns a unique identification number to each entry in the list and then generates random numbers by using a random number table or a computer program that produces random numbers. If a random number matches one of the identification numbers in the list, the researcher adds the indicated case to the sample (unless it has already been selected). This procedure is followed until it produces the desired sample size. It is important that only the randomly generated numbers determine the sample's composition; this condition ensures that the sampling procedure will be unbiased and that the chosen cases will constitute a probability sample.

With SRS, all cases in the sampling frame have an equal chance of being selected into the sample. In addition, for a sample of size n, all possible combinations of n different cases in the sampling frame have an equal chance of constituting the sample. The formulas for standard errors found in nearly all statistics textbooks and those used in statistical programs for computers assume that SRS generated the sample data. Most studies of human populations use sampling procedures that are less efficient than SRS, however, and using SRS

formulas in these instances underestimates the sampling variances of the statistics. As a consequence, researchers frequently conclude that differences or effects are statistically significant when they should not do so, or they may report misleadingly small confidence intervals.

Systematic-Simple Random Sampling. When a sampling frame contains many cases or the size of the prospective sample is large, researchers often decide to economize by setting a sampling interval and, after a random start, using that interval to choose the cases for the sample. For example, suppose a researcher wanted to select a sample of n cases from a population of size N and $n/N = 1/25$. To use systematic simple random sampling (SSRS), the researcher would draw a random number, r, between 1 and 25 and, starting with the rth case, select every twenty-fifth case in the sampling frame (for more complicated examples, see Kalton 1983, p. 17). This procedure gives all the cases in the frame an equal probability of being chosen for the sample but, unlike SRS, does not give all combinations of cases equal probabilities of selection. In the above example there are only 25 possible combinations of cases that could constitute the resulting sample (for example, cases 105 and 106 could never be in the same sample).

When the order of the cases in the sampling frame is random with respect to the variables of interest in a study, this property of SSRS is inconsequential, but when the frame is cyclically ordered, the results of SSRS can differ significantly from those of SRS. For example, suppose one wished to sample starting players on college basketball teams to determine their average height and had a sampling frame ordered by team and, within each team, by position. Since there are five starting players on each team, a sampling interval of any multiple of 5 would yield a sample composed of players who all play the same position. There would be a 1 in 5 chance that these players would all be centers (usually the tallest players) and a 2 in 5 chance that they would all be guards (usually the shortest). Thus, in this instance the sampling variation of the players' mean height would be substantially greater than the variation that SRS would produce. However, there are also situations in which stratified random sampling SSRS is equivalent to (StRS) (see below) and yields samples that have smaller sampling variances than those from SRS (Kish 1995, pp. 113–23). In practice, most lists of entire populations have orderings, often alphabetical, that are essentially random with respect to the purposes of a study, and lists with potential problems usually are obvious or are quickly recognized. Thus, in most applications SSRS is essentially equivalent to SRS (Sudman 1976, pp. 56–57).

Stratified Random Sampling. When a sampling frame consists of a list of all the cases in a population and also contains additional information about each case, researchers may use StRS. For example, a list of people also might indicate the sex of each person. A researcher can take advantage of this additional information by grouping individuals of each sex into a sublist (called a *stratum*) and then sampling, using SRS or SSRS, from each stratum. One can use either the same sampling fraction for each stratum, in which case the procedure is called *proportionate* StRS, or different fractions for different strata (*disproportionate* StRS). In either case one usually attempts to use the additional information contained in the sampling frame to produce a sample that will be more efficient than one derived from other sampling procedures (i.e., it will need fewer cases to produce a sample with a given precision for estimating a population parameter).

Efficiency is commonly measured by a sampling procedure's *design effect*, the ratio of the sampling variance of a statistic based on that procedure to the sampling variance of the same statistic derived from an SRS with the same number of cases (Kalton 1983, pp. 21–24). The efficiency of proportionate StRS is directly related to the correlation between the variable used to stratify the sampling frame and the variable or variables being studied. Thus, if one wished to determine the mean individual income of a population of Americans, proportionate StRS based on sex would produce a more efficient sample than would SRS and would have a design effect smaller than unity, because sex is correlated with income. In the limiting case in which the stratifying variable is perfectly correlated with the variable or variables being studied—for example, if each woman earned $15,000 per year and each man earned $25,000—proportionate SrRS would always yield a sample mean exactly equal to the population mean. By contrast, if sex were completely uncorrelated with income, proportionate StRS would be no more efficient than SRS, and the design effect of StRS would equal unity. In practice it is usually difficult to obtain sampling frames that contain information about potential stratifying variables that are substantially correlated with the variables being studied, especially when the cases are individuals. As a result, the gains in efficiency produced by proportionate StRS are often modest.

Proportionate StRS often yields small sample sizes for strata that consist of small proportions of a population. Thus, when researchers want to estimate parameters for the individual strata in a population, they sometimes employ disproportionate StRS to ensure that there will be enough cases from each stratum in the overall sample. A second reason for using disproportionate StRS is to design an optimal sample, one that produces the most precise estimates for a given cost, when there are differences between the strata in terms of (1) the cost of sampling and obtaining data, (2) the variability of the variables under study, or (3) prior knowledge about the variables under study. Sudman (1976, pp. 107–130) discusses and gives examples of each of these situations. The benefits of disproportionate StRS may be hard to attain when one wants to draw a multipurpose sample with observations on many variables, however, because the optimal procedures for the different variables may conflict. In addition, although proportionate StRS cannot have a design effect greater than unity, the design effects for disproportionate StRS can be larger than unity, meaning that disproportionate StRS can produce samples that are less efficient than those derived from SRS (Kalton 1983, pp. 20–26).

Cluster Sampling. All the sampling procedures discussed above require that the researcher have a sampling frame that lists the cases in the target population. Unfortunately, such sampling frames rarely exist, especially for human populations defined by area of residence. One can still draw a probability sample, however, if the population can be organized in terms of a grouping principle and each case can be assigned to one of the groups (called *clusters*). For example, dwellings in cities are located in blocks defined by streets. Even if a list of dwellings does not exist, it is possible to draw a probability sample by constructing a sampling frame that consists of a listing of the blocks, drawing a random sample of the blocks, and then collecting data on the dwellings in the chosen blocks.

This procedure, which is called cluster sampling (CS), is also advantageous when one wishes to use face-to-face interviewing to survey geographically dispersed populations of individuals. In this case CS is less costly because it allows the survey to concentrate interviewers in a small number of locations, thus lowering traveling costs. However, CS usually produces samples that have larger sampling variances than those drawn from SRS. The efficiency of CS is inversely related to (1) the extent to which clusters are internally homogeneous and differ from each other and (2) the number of cases sampled from each cluster. CS is maximally efficient when a population can be divided into clusters that are identical, because each cluster will then be a microcosm of the population as a whole. When clusters are internally homogeneous and differ sharply from each other, as tends to be true for human populations clustered by area of residence, CS is considerably less efficient than SRS (Kalton 1983, pp. 30–33). In this situation, researchers usually attempt to select only a few cases from each of many clusters, but that strategy eliminates the cost savings of CS.

Multistage Sampling. Researchers who want to collect data through face-to-face interviews with a probability sample of people living in a certain area, such as the United States, a state, or even a city, usually combine elements of the procedures discussed above in a multistage sampling procedure. For example, to draw a probability sample of U.S. adults, one might begin by obtaining a list of counties and parishes in the United States and collecting data on several characteristics of those units (region, average household income, etc.). These variables can be used to group the units, called *primary sampling units*, into strata so that one can use StRS. In addition, one would obtain estimates of the number of residents in each unit so that they could be sampled with probabilities proportional to their estimated population sizes (Sudman 1976, pp. 134–50). After selecting a sample of counties in this fashion, the researcher might proceed to draw a series of nested cluster samples. For example, one could divide each selected county into subareas (perhaps townships or other area-based governmental divisions) and then select a cluster sample from these units, with probabilities once again proportional to estimated population size. Next the researcher might divide each of the selected units into subareas (perhaps on the order

of the U.S. Bureau of the Census's "blocks") and draw a cluster sample of them. For each chosen block, the researcher might obtain a list of dwelling units and draw another cluster sample. Finally, from each chosen dwelling unit the researcher would choose, according to a specified procedure (Kish 1995, pp. 396–404), an individual to be interviewed. It is crucial that the selection procedure at each stage of the sampling process be based on a formally random selection procedure. For more detailed discussions and examples of the selection of multistage sampling procedures, see Kish (1995, pp. 301–383), Moser and Kalton (1972, pp. 188–210), and Sudman (1976, pp. 131–170). Multistage sampling usually requires considerable resources and expertise, and those who wish to draw such samples should contact a survey organization. Studies of the *design effects* of multistage samples, such as those carried out by the University of Michigan's Survey Research Center, show that they usually vary from 1.0 to 2.0, with values around 1.5 being common (Kish 1995, p. 581). A design effect of 1.5 means that the standard error of a statistic is twenty-two percent larger than estimated by standard statistics programs, which assume simple random sampling. There is also variation across kinds of statistics, with univariate statistics, such as the mean, often having larger design effects than do bivariate statistics, such as regression coefficients (Groves 1989, pp. 291–292). Unfortunately, estimating standard errors for a multistage sample is usually a complicated task, and this complexity, combined with the fact that popular statistics programs for computers use only SRS formulas, has led most researchers to ignore the problem, producing many spurious "statistically significant" findings.

RECENT ADVANCES

Sampling practitioners have made considerable progress in developing techniques for drawing probability samples of rare or elusive populations for which there are no lists and for which conventional multistage sampling procedures would produce sufficient cases only at an exorbitant cost. Sudman et al. (1988) review procedures for screening clusters to determine those that contain concentrations of a rare population's members and also discuss how multiplicity sampling procedures and capture-recapture methods can be applied to this problem. Researchers also have begun to use multiplicity sampling of individuals to draw probability samples of businesses and other social organizations to which individuals belong; Sudman et al. (1988) outline the general strategy involved, and Parcel et al. (1991) provide an informative discussion and an example. This approach also can produce "linked micro-macro samples" that facilitate contextual analyses.

Recent developments in statistical theory and computer software promise to make the calculation of standard errors for statistics based on multistage samples much easier. One approach to overcoming these difficulties is to use a computer program to draw many subsamples from an existing sample and then derive an overall estimate of a standard error from the many estimates given by the subsamples. There are several versions of this general approach, including "bootstrapping," "jackknife replication," and "cross-validation" (Hinkley 1983). A second approach is to develop computer statistical packages that incorporate information about the sampling design of a study (Wolter 1985, pp. 393–412, contains a list of such programs). The increased availability of such programs should produce greater recognition of the need to take a study's sampling procedure into account in analyzing the data the study yields.

There is now greater recognition that sampling error is just one of many types of error to which studies of human populations are subject. Nonsampling errors, including nonresponse error, interviewer error, and measurement error, also affect the accuracy of surveys. Groves (1989) comprehensively discusses both sampling and nonsampling errors and argues that minimizing one type can increase the other. Thus, decisions about sampling procedures need to take into account likely sources and magnitudes of nonsampling errors.

REFERENCES

Choldin, Harvey M. 1994 *Looking for the Last Percent: The Controversy over Census Undercounts*. New Brunswick, N.J.: Rutgers University Press.

Groves, Robert M. 1989 *Survey Errors and Survey Costs*. New York: Wiley.

Hinkley, David 1983 "Jackknife Methods." In Samuel Kotz and Norman L. Johnson, eds., *Encyclopedia of Statistical Sciences*, vol. 4. New York: Wiley.

Kalton, Graham 1983 *Introduction to Survey Sampling*. Newbury Park, Calif.: Sage.

Kish, Leslie 1995 *Survey Sampling*. New York: Wiley.

Moser, Claus A., and Graham Kalton 1972 *Survey Methods in Social Investigation*, 2nd ed. New York: Basic.

Parcel, Toby L., Robert L. Kaufman, and Leanne Jolly 1991 "Going Up the Ladder: Multiplicity Sampling to Create Linked Macro-to-Micro Organizational Samples." In Peter V. Marsden, ed., *Sociological Methodology*, vol. 21. Oxford, UK: Basil Blackwell.

Sudman, Seymour 1976 *Applied Sampling*. New York: Academic Press.

——, Monroe G. Sirken, and Charles D. Cowan 1988 "Sampling Rare and Elusive Populations." *Science* 240:991–996.

Wolter, Kirk M 1985 *Introduction to Variance Estimation*. New York: Springer-Verlag.

LOWELL L. HARGENS

SCALES AND SCORES

See Factor Analysis; Measurement.

SCANDINAVIAN SOCIOLOGY

Scandinavian sociology emerged in its modern form as an academic discipline just after World War II, although its roots go back considerably further. In Helsinki, the sociologist, ethnologist, and philosopher Edvard A Westermarck (1862–1939) lectured on sociology in 1890; in Göteborg, Gustaf Fredrik Steffen (1864–1929) became a professor of economics and sociology in 1903.

In 1850, the Norwegian clergyman Eilert Sundt (1817–1875) published a study of Norwegian tramps and the lowest stratum of the rural population. Between 1850 and 1869, when he became a vicar, Sundt received state support for his demographic and sociological studies of Norwegian manners and customs, poverty, and living conditions. In demography he is remembered for "Sundt's law," which states that irregularities in the age distribution at a given time generate similar irregularities in the next generation (Ramsøy 1998).

Westermarck held chairs in applied philosophy until 1930, and between 1907 and 1930 he also had a chair in sociology in London. He belonged to the small group of leading European sociologists and philosophers in the early part of the century. His best-known works are studies of the history of marriage (first volume published in 1891) and of the origin and development of moral ideas (1906–1908, 1932).

Between 1907 and 1913 the statistician A Gustav Sundbärg (1857–1914) directed "Emigrationsutredningen," an official investigation of Swedish emigration, which was considered one of the most serious problems in Sweden at that time (Sundbärg 1913). The final report was presented in 1913, and between 1908 and 1912 twenty appendices by Sundbärg himself; Nils R Wohlin (1881–1948), secretary of the investigation; and others were published. The investigation contains a wealth of statistical information of great interest.

EARLY SOCIOLOGY

In Scandinavia in the 1940s, sociology was confronted with an established discipline of demography, a reliable and accessible population registration system, a positivistic philosophy, and a reformist policy in need of empirical studies of societal problems. Until the late 1960s, Scandinavian sociologists engaged in empirical studies, mostly quantitative, of social inequality, social mobility and the educational system, work conditions, problems of physical planning and social epidemiology, alcohol problems, and delinquency. The works of Allardt in Helsinki (1965), Carlsson in Lund (1958), Rokkan (1921–1979) in Bergen (Rokkan and Lipset 1967), and Segerstedt (1908–1999) in Uppsala (1955) are representative of early mainstream sociology, and those of Aubert (1922–1988) in Oslo (1965) had a qualitative approach. There was a strong American influence from Scandinavians who had studied at American universities, from journals and textbooks, and from visiting Americans; Norway in particular received a series of Fulbright scholars. Scandinavian sociology became strongly empirical, technical, sociopsychological, and survey-oriented. There was less interest in functionalism, Talcott Parsons, and the classics than in survey analysis and social exchange theory.

In the late 1960s and throughout the 1970s, new sociological voices were heard in Scandinavia, perhaps more in Denmark and Sweden than in Finland and Norway. They can be characterized as aggressively political and Marxist, antipositivistic, antifunctionalistic, and antiquantitative. In general, the "new" sociology was more theoretical and sociophilosophical and less empirical than the main-

stream versions. Conflict theories, critical theory, symbolic interactionism, and the labeling perspective came to the fore, as did socioanthropological and hermeneutic methods.

INSTITUTIONAL STRUCTURE

In Denmark, the German refugee Theodor Geiger (1891–1952) was appointed a professor of sociology at Aarhus University in 1938. In 1955, Kaare Svalastoga (1914–1997), a Norwegian historian with a sociological education from the University of Washington in Seattle, became professor of sociology at Copenhagen, where a graduate program in sociology was started in 1958. In the 1960s and 1970s, additional chairs were created at Copenhagen and Aalborg and in sociological subdisciplines at unversities in Copenhagen, Aarhus, Aalborg, and Roskilde as well as at the Handelshøjskolen (School of Economics and Business Administration) in Copenhagen. Mostly as a result of problems at the two institutes at the University of Copenhagen, Danish sociology was in a state of crisis after the late 1960s. In 1986–1987 the government closed down the Copenhagen institutes, and by 1994 they had been reorganized into a new institute with two chairs. The institute offers (as did Aalborg after 1997) a three-year undergraduate program leading to a B.A., followed by a two-year master's program. At present there are only eight chairs in sociology in Copenhagen, Aalborg, Roskilde, and Handelshøjskolen. Outside the universities, the most important institute in sociology is the Socialforskningsinstituttet (Institute for Social Research). With Henning Friis as director from its start in 1958 until 1979, the institute has carried out many social investigations using its own field organization, for instance, the 1976 and 1986 Danish Welfare Surveys and the report on the 1992 follow-up of the 1968 youth study (Hansen 1995).

In Finland, two of Westermarck's ethnosociological students held chairs in sociology in Helsinki and Turku in the 1920s. In the mid-1940s, modern-type sociologists got chairs, such as the criminologist Veli Verkko (1893–1955) in Helsinki in 1946. Heikki Waris (1901–1989), professor of social policy from 1948 in Helsinki, also should be mentioned here. Sociology chairs were first established at Helsinki, Turku, Åbo Academy, and Tampere. At present, there are more than twenty professors of sociology and its subdisciplines at eleven universities and colleges: eight chairs at Helsinki University, four at Tampere, and two each at Jyväskylä and Turku, plus one at Åbo Akademi, also in Turku. Undergraduate studies lead to a master's degree after five years. There also are important research institutes outside the universities. The National Research and Development Centre for Welfare and Health (STAKES), under the Ministry of Social and Health Care, was established in 1992. Within STAKES there is a Social Research Unit for Alcohol Studies that conducts research on four principal areas, including narcotics. The research directors are Hannu Uusitalo and Jussi Simpura. There also is the Finnish Foundation for Alcohol Studies, which was established in 1950, with Klaus Mäkelä as its leading researcher.

In Norway, Sverre Holm filled the first sociology chair in 1949 in Oslo, and chairs were added in Bergen, Trondheim, and Tromsø in the 1960s. At present there are some twenty-five professorships. A basic undergraduate program takes four years, after which a two-year program leads to a "cand.polit." degree. Several institutes are important in sociological research and education: Institutt for Samfunnsforskning (Institute for Social Research [ISF]) since 1950, the newly established NOVA (Norwegian Institute for Research on Childhood and Adolescence, Welfare, and Aging), FAFO (Trade Union Movement's Research Foundation), and Statistisk Sentralbyrå (Statistical Central Bureau [SSB]). Institutt for Anvendt Sosialforskning (Institute for Applied Social Research [INAS]), which was established in 1968, is now included in NOVA. Natalie R Ramsøy was its research director until 1981.

In Sweden, the educator and sociologist E. H. Thörnberg (1873–1961) never held a university position. Gunnar Myrdal (1898–1987) could claim to be the first modern sociologist, but Torgny T. Segerstedt (1908–1999) became the first professor of sociology by converting his chair in applied philosophy to sociology at Uppsala in 1947. Sociology is now taught at Uppsala, Stockholm, Lund, Göteborg, Umeå, and Linköping as well as in several colleges, of which those at Karlstad, Växjö, and Örebro have become universities. There are about thirty sociology professors at the universities. A bachelor's program in sociology is scheduled for three years, a master degree for a fourth year, and a "licentiat" degree for a fifth

year. Outside the universities, Arbetslivsinstitutet (the National Institute for Working Life); Folkhälsoinstitutet (the National Institute of Public Health), established in 1992; the National Council for Crime Prevention (BRÅ), starting in 1974; and Statistics Sweden are important in Swedish sociology. The Institute for Social Research ([SOFI] 1972, beginning in with five sociology chairs) and the National Center for Social Research on Alcohol and Drugs (since 1999), with Robin Room as research director, are parts of Stockholm University. Since 1992 BRÅ has published *Studies on Crime and Crime Prevention*, an international biannual journal.

There is considerable interaction among the Scandinavian sociological communities: Professors hold chairs in neighboring countries, such as the leading Finnish alcohol researcher Kettil Bruun (1924–1985) who had a chair in Stockholm in 1982–1984 and Swedish sociologists from Lund who crossed the sound to Copenhagen; comparative studies of the Scandinavian countries are conducted; and there have been joint comparative projects with one editor from each of four countries.

The Scandinavian Sociological Association has some 2,500 members. Approximate memberships are 550 in Denmark, 50 in Iceland, 600 in Finland (in 1995), 700 in Norway, and 500 in Sweden. Since 1955 the association has published *Acta Sociologica*, a refereed quarterly journal. For the first twelve years Torben Agersnap of Handelshøjskolen in Copenhagen was the editor, and since then editorship has rotated among the countries, with three-year periods since 1985. Each Scandinavian country has a national sociological association. The Finnish Westermarck Society, founded in 1940, is the oldest and includes social anthropologists. There are also national journals: *Sociologia* (since 1990) in Denmark, *Sosiologia* in Finland, *Tidskrift for Samfunnsforskning* (since 1960) and *Sosiologisk Tidskrift* in Norway, and *Sociologisk forskning* (since 1964) in Sweden.

Most foreign contacts are still with the United States, although interaction with European, especially British, French, and German, sociologists tends to be more frequent now. Polish, Hungarian, and Estonian contacts are important to Finnish sociology. Comparative studies including non-Scandinavian European or OECD countries (Erikson and Goldthorpe 1992; Korpi and Palme 1998) are conducted frequently as a heritage from Stein Rokkan in political sociology. Comparisons often have been made with the United States and Canada, as occurred when Norway and Sweden were included in Tim Smeeding's and Lee Rainwater's so-called "Luxembourg Income Study" around 1980. Furthermore, several Scandinavian sociologists have been visiting researchers at the European Sociological Institute in Florence, Italy. The Danish welfare researcher Esping-Andersen (1990) has a chair at the University of Trent in Italy. Several Scandinavian sociologists have spent most or parts of their careers abroad, especially in the United States, for example, Aage Bøttger Sørensen from Denmark; the Norwegians Stein Rokkan, Jon Elster, and Trond Pedersen; and the Swedes Bo Andersson and Hans L. Zetterberg.

PRESENT SOCIOLOGY

Essays on Scandinavian sociology can be found in Bertilsson and Therborn (1997). New conceptions in Finnish sociology in the early 1990s and their relation to earlier structural-cultural traditions are discussed by Alapuro (1995), while Martinussen (1993) deals with present-day Norwegian sociology. Allardt et al. (1988) offer an official evaluation of Swedish sociology. Gunnlaugsson and Bjarnason (1994) describe Icelandic sociology.

Even after the wave of New Left sociology subsided toward the end of the 1970s, Scandinavian sociology remained diversified, with a continued interest in Marxism and the classics as well as in social exchange theory and a broad spectrum of data analysis. On balance, the focus now is somewhat more on theory and on macrosociology. Interest in theories of organizations (Ahrne 1994), economic sociology (Swedberg 1990), and, especially after Coleman's book (1990), rational-choice approaches (Hedströem and Swedberg 1998) has been increasing. The statistical analytic orientation has held its own, at least partly because of the rapid development of personal computers and their programs, which permit more adequate analyses. At the same time, the old interest in qualitative methods has remained, especially in connection with the growing field of gender studies.

In Norway, Østerberg (1986, 1988) writes in the hermeneutic and humanistic essay tradition, Yngvar Løchen (1931–1998) carried out action research in medical sociology with relevance to the lives of sociologists, and Elster is a well-known philosopher and social scientist (1989), favorably disposed to Marxism (1985) but closer to the rational-choice approach. In Sweden, Göran Therborn is an internationally respected Marxist and the social psychologist and essayist Johan Asplund has a prestigious position in the discipline; Antti Eskola is Finland's best known social psychologist.

A cluster of overlapping core areas concerning forms of inequality has remained central to Scandinavian sociology. Studies concern gender inequality as well as inequality among social classes and other groupings in regard to political, economic, educational, and social resources, which can be seen as constituting inequality of welfare in a broad sense; these studies present indicators of various welfare dimensions. Research institutes such as the Institute for Social Research in Copenhagen, INAS (now in NOVA) and ISF in Oslo, and SOFI in Stockholm have been important, as STAKES in Helsinki will be. One of the tasks of SOFI has been to follow up an officially commissioned 1968 study of low-income categories. The study was carried out by Sten Johansson, then at Uppsala, and his team, which published several reports in 1970–1971, creating considerable political commotion. SOFI has continued this study as a panel, Levnadsnivåundersökningen (Level of Living Study [LNU]), with new surveys in 1974, 1981, and 1991. A volume edited by Erikson and Åberg (1987) provided a partial summary. Comprehensive welfare studies (level-of-living studies) have been carried out in all Scandinavian countries since the 1970s (Erikson et al. 1987; Hansen et al. 1993). Statistics Sweden has conducted annual level-of-living surveys since 1974 (Vogel 1988). Studies by Gudmund Hernes in Norway have been influential both politically and sociologically. Hernes was the leading researcher in the first Norwegian level-of-living survey and in an official Norwegian 1972–1982 project on power in society (Hernes 1975, 1978, also involving exchange theory). The task force gave its final report in 1982 (Hernes 1982). The official Swedish study of societal power, ordered after the success of the Norwegian study, was run mainly by political scientists, historians, and economists, although Åberg (1990) was asked to repeat in modern form a community study from the 1950s (Segerstedt and Lundquist 1952, 1955). Here the different roles of Norwegian and Swedish sociology may reflect differences in public opinion: Norwegian sociologists have easy access to the mass media and the political elite. The criminologist Nils Christie has become a well-known participant in public discussion of social policy issues, and Hernes was the Labor Party's minister of education and research.

Social stratification and social mobility have long been an area of strong interest in Scandinavian sociology (Carlsson 1958; Svalastoga 1959, 1965). Later works in the field include those of Alestalo (1986), Erikson (1987), Knudsen (1988), and Erikson and Goldthorpe (1992). More recently Erikson and Jonsson reported an officially commissioned investigation of social selection to higher education (Erikson and Jonsson 1993, 1996).

In political sociology Stein Rokkan's (1921–1979) far-reaching project (Rokkan and Lipset 1967; Rokkan et al. 1970; Rokkan 1987) was left unfinished. Other important works in this field include Korpi (1989), Therborn (1986, 1995), Martinussen (1988), Alapuro (1988), and Mjøset (1992).

Gender studies are an exceptionally strong field in Norway and fairly strong in Scandinavia generally. In the late 1960s, Holter (1970) analyzed gender roles and their impact on work life, political behavior, and education. Several Norwegian gender studies, among others those by Helga Hernes and Kari Waerness, were published in the series "Kvinners levekår og livsløp" (Women's Level of Living and Life Course). In Sweden Edmund Dahlström and Rita Liljeström and in Finland Elina Haavio-Mannila pioneered the field.

Outside the sociological core area of inequality there are neighboring fields and sociological specialties. The Finnish demographer Tapani Valkonen is known for skillful context analyses and epidemiological studies. To revitalize Swedish demography, which had stagnated in the 1970s, the Norwegian demometrician Jan M. Hoem was called in from Copenhagen in 1983.

In the lively sociological subfield of literature and mass media, Karl-Erik Rosengren is the leading Swedish researcher. To some extent through east European contacts, the life-course narrative as a research instrument has been developed into a Finnish specialty, mostly by J.P. Roos.

Deviance is another subfield. Usually it is not considered a sociological core area, although it has long-term credentials as a central field both from the classics and from early Scandinavian sociology. The study of deviance has remained an important part of Scandinavian sociology in terms of both applied and basic research. Since the Finnish State Alcohol Monopoly established its research institute in 1950, alcohol studies have been a strong Finnish field. Bruun (Bruun and Frånberg 1985) was its longtime director, and Mäkelä (1996) was his successor. Also Skog (1985) in Oslo and Kühlhorn (Kühlhorn and Björ 1998) and Norström (1988) in Stockholm are well known in the field of alcohol and drug studies. Mathiesen's penology (1987) is a part of Norwegian sociology, just as studies of crime and crime prevention have been a part of Swedish sociology since the official 1956 juvenile delinquency project (Carlsson 1972) and early BRÅ projects.

Gunnlaugsson and Bjarnason (1994) claim that the four fields of welfare research, stratification research, women's studies, and cultural studies do not capture the structure of Icelandic sociology, which centers on two broad themes: social conditions and social and cultural problems associated with the development of Icelandic society. These problems essentially concern crime, in particular incidental violence by strangers, alcohol abuse, and the perceived threat of drug abuse, that is, deviance.

Finally, access to an extensive and reliable population registration system has made good sampling frames available to surveys, and governmental microdata have been helpful in longitudinal data sets in Scandinavian behavioral projects. However, since the mid-1970s, statistically oriented behavioral researchers, especially in Sweden, have had problems with privacy-protecting data legislation. According to the pioneering Swedish Data Act of 1973, running data on identified persons by computer requires a permit from a Data Inspection Board (DI). The DI expanded the informed-consent condition for the permit to include the computer use of identified governmental microdata accessed according to the century-old right-of-access principle. Although this condition has been waived in some cases, it has led to frequent and well-publicized controversies between the DI and social researchers, with the media usually supporting the DI. In Sweden, the media debated privacy issues mostly in connection with statistical data sets, whereas administrative files largely went unnoticed. Since the conflict came to a head in 1986 over the deidentification of the data set of Project Metropolitan, a longitudinal study of a cohort of Stockholmers, the tensions have smoothed out and access to register data has been made easier. The rich governmental microfiles, including the censuses, remain assets to Scandinavian sociology. In 1998, a new Swedish Personal Data Protection Act in line with EU regulations and modern Internet use was substituted for the 1973 Data Act.

REFERENCES

Ahrne, Göran 1994 *Social Organizations*. Newbury Park CA: Sage.

Alapuro, Risto 1995 "Structure and Culture: Finnish Sociology, 1990–94" *Acta Sociologica* 38(2):167–180.

Alestalo, Matti 1986 *Structural Change, Classes, and the State*. Helsinki: Research Group for Comparative Sociology.

Åberg, Rune, ed. 1990 *Industrisamhälle i omvandling* (Industrial Communities in Transition). Stockholm: Carlssons.

Allardt, Erik 1965 *Samhällsstruktur och sociala spänningar* (Societal Structure and Social Tension). Tampere: Söderströms. Also in Finnish.

——, Sverre Lysgaard, and Aage Bøttger Sørensen (1988) *Sociologin i Sverige* (Sociology in Sweden). Stockholm: HSFR.

Aubert, Vilhelm 1965 *The Hidden Society*. Totowa, N.J.: Bedminster.

Bertilsson, Margareta, and Göran Therborn, eds. 1997 *From a Doll's House to the Welfare State*. Copenhagen: ISA.

Bruun, Kettil, and Per Frånberg, eds. 1985 *Den svenska supen* (The Swedish Snaps). Stockholm: Prisma.

Carlsson, N. Gösta 1958 *Social Mobility and Class Structure*. Lund: Gleerup.

—— 1972 *Unga lagöverträdare II* (Young Law Violators II). Stockholm: SOU 1972:76

Coleman, James S. 1990 *Foundations of Social Theory*. Cambridge, Mass.: Belknap.

Elster, Jon 1985 *Making Sense of Marx*. Cambridge, UK: Cambridge University Press.

—— 1989 *Nuts and Bolts for the Social Sciences*. Cambridge, UK: Cambridge University Press.

Erikson, Robert 1987 "The Long Arm of the Origin." In Ulla Bergryd and Carl-Gunnar Janson, eds., *Sociological Miscellany*. Stockholm: Department of Sociology, University of Stockholm.

——, and Rune Åberg, (eds.) 1987 *Welfare in Transition*. Oxford, UK: Clarendon Press.

——, and John Goldthorpe 1992 *The Constant Flux: A Study of Class Mobility in Industrial Society*. Oxford, UK: Clarendon.

——, Erik Jørgen Hansen, Stein Ringen, and Hannu Uusitalo, eds. 1987 *The Scandinavian Model: Welfare State and Welfare Research*. Armonk, N.Y.: Sharpe.

——, and Jan O. Jonsson 1993 *Ursprung och utbildning* (Social Origin and Education). Stockholm: SOU 1993:85.

——, and —— (eds.) 1996 *Can Education Be Equalized?* Oxford, UK: Westview Press.

Esping-Andersen, Gøsta 1990 *The Tree Worlds of Welfare Capitalism*. Cambridge, UK: Cambridge University Press.

Gunnlaugsson, Helgi, and Thoroddur Bjarnason 1994 "Establishing a Discipline: The Impact of Society on the Development of Icelandic Sociology." *Acta Sociologica* 1994(3):303–312.

Hansen, Erik Jørgen 1995 *En generation blev voksen* (A Generation Grew Up) Copenhagen: Socialforskningsinstituttet, Report 95:8.

——, Stein Ringen, Hannu Uusitalo, and Robert Erikson, eds. 1993 *Welfare Trends in the Scandinavian Countries*. Armonk, N.Y.: Sharpe.

Hedström, Peter and Richard Swedberg 1998 *Social Mechanisms*. Cambridge: Cambridge University Press.

Hernes, Germund 1975 *Makt og avmakt* (Power and Powerlessness). Bergen, Norway: Universitetsforlaget.

—— 1978 *Forhandlingsøkonomi og blandingsadministration* (Transaction Economy and Mixed Administration). Bergen, Norway: Universitetsforlaget.

—— 1982 *Maktutredningen: slutrapport* (The Power Study: Final Report). Oslo: NOU 1982:3.

——, and Willy Martinussen 1980 *Demokrati og politiske resurser* (Democracy and Political Resources). Oslo: NOU 1980:7.

Holter, Harriet 1970 *Sex Roles and Social Structure*. Oslo: Norwegian University Press.

Knudsen, Knud 1988 "Class Identification in Norway." *Acta Sociologica* 31:69–79.

Korpi, Walter 1989 "Power, Politics, and State Autonomy in the Development of Social Citizenship." *American Sociological Review* 54:309–328.

——, and Joakim Palme 1998 "The Paradox of Redistribution and Strategies of Equality." *American Sociological Review* 63:661–687.

Kühlhorn, Eckart, and Jill Björ, eds. 1998 *Svenska alkoholvanor i förändring* (Changing Swedish Drinking Habits). Stockholm: Sober.

Martinussen, Willy 1988 *Solidaritetens grenser* (Limits of Solidarity). Oslo: Universitetsforlaget.

—— 1993 "A Snapshot of Present-Day Norwegian Sociology," *Acta Sociology*, 36, 305–392.

Mathiesen, Thomas 1987 *Kan fengsel forsvares?* (Can Prisons Be Justified?) Oslo: PAX; sec. ed. 1995.

Mjøset, Lars ed. 1992 *Contributions to the Comparative Study of Development*. Oslo: ISF, Report 92:2.

Norström, Thor 1988 "Alcohol and Suicide in Scandinavia." *British Journal of Addiction* 83:553–559.

Østerberg, Dag 1986 *Fortolkende sosiologi* (Interpretive Sociology). Oslo: Universitetsforlaget.

—— 1988 *Metasociology*. Oslo: Norwegian University Press.

Ramsøy, Natalie R. 1998 "Eilert Sundt."

Rokkan, Stein 1987 *Stat, nasjon, klasse* (State, Nation, Class). In B. Hagtvet, ed., Oslo: Universietsforlaget.

——, Angus Campbell, Per Torsvik, and Henry Valen 1970 *Citizens, Elections, Parties*. Oslo: Norwegian University Press.

——, and Seymour M. Lipset, eds. 1967 *Party System and Voter Alignments*. New York: Free Press.

Segerstedt, Torgny 1955 "Kriminalsociologi" (Sociology of Crime). In Ivar Agge, ed., *Kriminologi* (Criminology). Stockholm: Wahlström and Widstrand.

——, and Agne Lundqvist 1952 and 1955 *Människan i industrisamhället. del I och II* (Man in Industrial Society. Parts I and II). Stockholm: SNS.

Skog, Ole-Jørgen 1985 "The Collectivity of Drinking Cultures." *British Journal of Addiction* 81:365–379.

Sundbärg, Gustav 1913 *Emigrationsutredningen* (Investigation on Emigration). Stockholm: Offentligt betänkande. Twenty appendices 1908–1912.

Svalastoga, Kaare 1959 *Prestige, Class, and Mobility*. Copenhagen: Gyldendal.

—— 1965 *Social Differentiation*. New York: McKay.

Swedberg, Richard 1990 *Economics and Sociology*. Princeton: Princeton University Press.

Therborn, Göran 1986 *Why Are Some People More Unemployed Than Others?* London: Verso.

—— 1995 *European Modernity and Beyond*. Newbury Park, Calif.: Sage.

Vogel, Joachim 1988 *Inequality in Sweden*. Stockholm: SCB.

Westermarck, Edvard A. 1891 *History of Human Marriage*, 3 vols. London: Macmillan.

—— 1906–1908 *The Origin and Development of Moral Ideas*. London: Macmillan.

—— 1932 *Ethical Relativity*. New York: Harcourt; paperback ed. 1960 by Littlefield.

CARL-GUNNAR JANSON

SCIENCE

Sociologists of science study the social organization of science, the relationships between science and other social institutions, social influences on the content of scientific knowledge, and public policy regarding science. The definition of the term "science" is problematic. Science can refer to a changing body of shared knowledge about nature or to the methods used to obtain that knowledge; in that form, science has existed for millennia. Research on "indigenous scientific knowledge" is reviewed in Watson-Verran and Turnbull (1995). Sociologists of science are more likely to define science in institutional terms, and most research in that area studies those who work in differentiated social institutions. The "demarcation" problem of distinguishing between science and nonscience persists. Gieryn (1995, 1998) argues that scientists and their advocates continually engage in contested "boundary work" to demarcate science. He discusses the rhetorical and organizational devices used in those contests; thus, scientists are likely to emphasize the disinterested search for knowledge in their attempts to distinguish science from technology and stress the utility of scientific knowledge in their attempts to distinguish it from religion. Gieryn argues against the notion that there are "essential" features of science that determine the outcome of those contests; these "essential features" are instead "provisional and contextual results of successful boundary-work" (1995, p. 406).

Unless the production of knowledge about the empirical world is delegated to relatively autonomous specialists, knowledge accumulates at a slow pace. When beliefs about nature are closely linked to major social institutions, institutional rigidity tends to produce cognitive rigidity (Znaniecki 1940; Parsons 1951, pp. 326–348). There were communities of relatively autonomous specialists in several great civilizations in the past, but most failed to produce stable institutions. Modern science dates from seventeenth-century Europe. Europeans at that time believed in a deity that gave laws to nature as well as to people and expected to discover those laws. Seventeenth-century Europeans could build on the basis of a science produced by the medieval schoolmen. With the rise of capitalism, intellectual elites developed a strong interest in using new knowledge to improve material conditions and enrich themselves. Merton, the leading founder of the sociology of science, argued in 1938 (1970) that in addition to these conditions, Puritanism contributed to the scientific ethos through its emphasis on work in the everyday world, rationalism and empiricism, openness to free inquiry, and desire to glorify God by describing His creation. (This still-controversial thesis is reviewed in a symposium in *Isis* 1988. For a general review of theories about the scientific revolution, see Cohen 1994.)

A distinctive normative ethos was institutionalized in modern science. Merton (1973, chap. 13) identified four salient norms: (1) "Universalism" requires that scientific contributions be evaluated according to general impersonal criteria without regard to "irrelevant" characteristics of the contributors such as their race, religion, and nationality. It also requires that scientists be rewarded according to their scientific contributions without regard for those irrelevant criteria. (2) "Communism" requires that knowledge be shared, not kept secret. Thus, the only way a scientist can claim a discovery as "his" or "hers" is to make it known to others. In this regard, modern scientists differ from Renaissance mathematicians and magicians, who were often quite secretive. (3) "Disinterestedness" refers to the injunction that the procedures and products of science not be appropriated for private gain. This need not imply altruism, although scientists often are driven to discover as an end in itself, but in addition, situations usually are structured so that it is in a scientist's career interest to act in a disinterested manner. (4) "Organized skepticism" permits and encourages challenges to knowledge claims. Science tends to be unlike many other areas of social life, in which conformity in matters of belief is demanded as a sign of loyalty.

Merton's essay on the normative ethos of science, first published in 1942, has drawn fruitful criticism. While Merton argued that the scientific ethos was functional for the advancement of knowledge, Mitroff (1974) argued that scientists could invoke "counter-norms," for example, could fail to be skeptical about their own theories, and this could be equally functional in some situations. Mulkay (1980) invoked ethnomethodological ideas to make an argument of general significance: "We should not assume that *any* norm can have a single literal meaning independent of the contexts in which it is applied. . . . Scientists *must* engage in inferential and interpretive work on norms. They are likely to do this *after* their actions, in order to construct acceptable accounts of their behavior. The norms don't determine behavior."

Ambiguity involving the norm of universalism was present at the birth of modern science: Which characteristics of those who advance knowledge claims are relevant or irrelevant? Shapin (1994) argues that in England only the testimony of "gentlemen" was accepted as valid, and not all gentlemen; those who rejected the empiricism of men such as Francis Bacon and Robert Boyle and accepted the arguments from first principles of men such as Thomas Hobbes were excluded from the scientific community (Shapin and Shaffer 1985).

Scientists in the seventeenth and eighteenth centuries were usually amateurs, such as Robert Boyle and Benjamin Franklin, or the intellectual servants of amateurs. In the later eighteenth and nineteenth centuries, science was professionalized. Scientists received formal education in universities; found full-time employment, often in the universities; formed self-governing associations; and developed the modern scientific journal and other means of communication. A case study of the process for the newly emerging discipline of geology in the 1830s is presented in Rudwick (1985), where it is linked with the conduct of intense disputes about geological history; the "professionals" in those disputes got no special respect. The more general process of professionalization is described by Ben-David (1984, 1991), who notes the importance of national differences in the organization of science. Ben-David shows that there was more competition among universities in Germany and the United States in the late nineteenth and twentieth centuries than there was in those in Britain and France and claims that this partly accounted for the greater productivity of science in the first two countries. Other organizational characteristics of American science also help account for its superior productivity in the past half century: Science is not highly centralized, the competitive units are large enough and heterogeneous enough to provide a critical mass of closely interacting scientists, and senior scientists tend to have less authority over younger scientists than they have elsewhere. (For statistics on national science productivity, see U.S. National Science Board 1996.)

SOCIAL STRATIFICATION IN SCIENCE

Competition remains intense among organizations that engage in basic research in the United States, particularly universities. Organizational prestige is central; as is usually true when it is difficult to measure organizational outputs directly, social comparisons become more important. Periodic surveys of faculty members have been used to rate the prestige of research departments. While outputs are difficult to measure, departments with high prestige are more successful in obtaining research resources and have higher rates of research productivity.

Competition is also intense among individual scientists, who compete for recognition from their peers for being the first to make valued discoveries (Merton 1973, chaps. 14 and 15; Hagstrom 1965, 1974). Competition may lead to secretive behavior and premature publication; it also may encourage scientists to move into new areas where there is less competition. A common consequence of competition is simultaneous or multiply independent discovery (see Zuckerman 1988 and the references cited there). The frequency of such events shows the extent to which science is a social product. When apparently simultaneous discoveries occur, those involved often engage in priority disputes; they are often ambivalent in those disputes, torn between a desire for the recognition due to originality and the demand for humility, the recognition of their dependence on the work of others.

There is a great degree of inequality in the research productivity of scientists. The chances that a scientist will publish as many as n papers is $1/n^2$; in other words, about 6 percent of all scientists produce 50 percent of all published papers (Price 1986). This inequality is even greater if one looks at the distribution of citations of the work of scientists. With some reservations, the number of citations can be taken as a measure of the quality of scientific work; frequently cited papers are usually those which other scientists have found useful in their own research. If c is the number of citations, the chances that the work of a scientist will have c citations is proportional to $1/c^3$; that is, about 3 percent of all scientists receive 50 percent of all the citations of scientific papers.

Most of the variation in scientific productivity can be explained in terms of individual characteristics of scientists, such as years required to earn a doctorate, and characteristics of their employers, especially departmental prestige. While men have been more productive than women (the difference has been declining), that difference is almost entirely the result of differences in background and employer characteristics (Xie and Shauman 1998). In the United States (more than in most countries), there is considerable mobility of scientists among organizations. High research productivity predicts mobility to institutions of higher prestige and to a higher rank, but employment in a high-prestige organization in turn causes higher productivity (Allison and Long 1990). In general, American universities tend to conform to universalistic norms in making appointments and promotions (Cole and Cole 1973). There is an apparent exception to this in the early phases of careers, when productivity is difficult to assess; the prestige of a scientist's doctoral department is strongly correlated with the prestige of the initial employer.

Inequality of productivity increases over the careers of scientists (Allison et al. 1982) as a manifestation of Merton's (1973) "Matthew effect": "For unto every one that hath shall be given, and he shall have abundance: but from him that hath not shall be taken away even that which he hath." Initially productive scientists obtain more and better resources for research, their work is more visible to others, and they are more likely to interact with other highly productive scientists.

WORK GROUPS, SPECIALTIES, AND DISCIPLINES

Scientific research is a nonroutine activity; outcomes and problems cannot be predicted, and it is difficult to plan research. As organization theories lead one to expect in such situations, scientific work tends to be done in small groups with few hierarchical levels and a small degree of control by supervisors (Hagstrom 1976). Most basic research in universities is done by groups of four to nine graduate students and technicians led by one to a few professors. Over the course of time, faculty members have found it increasingly desirable to collaborate with their peers, and most publications are multiply authored. Some aspects of research can be routinized, and the extent to which this can be done varies among disciplines; for example, work is more readily routinized in chemistry than it is in mathematics (Hargens 1975). Thus, work groups are smaller in mathematics than in chemistry. Chemists can delegate tasks to assistants, whereas mathematicians cannot; while the number of assistants does not explain much of the variation in the productivity of mathematicians, it does so in regard to the productivity of chemists. In other areas of science, major changes in research methods have led to what is called big science, which is epitomized by high-energy physics. Despite the use of labor-saving devices, the work groups at high-energy particle laboratories can be very large, with well over 150 scientists. Such groups have a greater division of labor, a broader span of supervisory control, and greater centralization of decision making.

These work groups ordinarily are embedded in larger organizations such as universities and governmental or industrial establishments. They also are likely to be linked informally with other groups working on the same or related research problems in other establishments. These loosely linked and loosely bounded sets of work groups can be called "specialties" or, more evocatively, "invisible colleges" (Price 1986). Groups in a specialty simultaneously compete with one another and make contributions to one another's research. The number of groups in a specialty worldwide (there is a great deal of international collaboration) is ordinarily small, perhaps 50 on the average and seldom over 100, although specialties with over 500 groups exist. Scientists spend much of their time communicating with one another: writing papers, reviewing papers by others, attending meetings of scientific societies, and informally (Nelson and Pollock 1970).

The public nature of science tends to inhibit deviant behavior, but some deviance is to be expected. The extent of research fraud, such as forging and trimming data, is difficult to ascertain, as is the case in white-collar crime generally. Evidence and theories about such deviance are summarized in Zuckerman (1988). Fraud is most likely to occur when researchers are under pressure to get results (such as postdoctoral fellows and nontenured faculty members) and when it is less likely to be detected (as in collaborative research with workers from different disciplines, where one is unable to evaluate the work of another); both conditions are especially likely to exist in experimental research in the biomedical sciences. Of courses, scientists with a high reputation also have engaged in research fraud; the case of the psychologist Cyril Burt is discussed in Gieryn (1998).

Scientific specialties usually exist within disciplines represented by their own university departments and scientific societies, but interdisciplinary research is common. The growth of an interdisciplinary area can lead to the differentiation of disciplines, and so the number of scientific disciplines has grown (Hagstrom 1965). The different scientific disciplines differ greatly in the degree of consensus about theories and methods; one indicator of this is variation in the rejection rates of manuscripts submitted to scientific journals, which is high in fields such as sociology and low in fields such as physics (Hargens 1975, 1988). Variations in consensus can affect the careers of scientists by affecting judgments of the merits of the work of individuals; it is easier to achieve early success in disciplines with a high degree of consensus. Disciplines also vary in the degree to which the work of scientists depends on and contributes to the work of others in their disciplines. This interdependence is related to Durkheim's concept of "organic solidarity." It is lower in mathematics than it is in the empirical sciences, as is indicated by fewer references in and citations of papers written by mathematicians, and it can be experienced as a problem by mathematicians (Hagstrom 1965).

THE SOCIOLOGY OF SCIENTIFIC KNOWLEDGE

The Structure of Scientific Revolutions by the historian Kuhn (1970), first published in 1962, strongly influenced the sociology of science. Kuhn made a distinction between normal and revolutionary science. Normal science is a puzzle-solving activity governed by paradigms. A paradigm consists of shared commitments by a group of scientists to a set of values, presuppositions about nature, methods of research, symbolic generalizations such as Newton's laws, and exemplars such as particular experiments. In normal science, researchers force nature into agreement with the paradigm; apparently disconfirming evidence does not weaken commitment to the paradigm. Normally scientists are successful in explaining away apparently disconfirming evidence, but persistent critical anomalies can trigger a scientific revolution. In a successful revolution, one paradigm is succeeded by another paradigm with quite different presuppositions and exemplars. Kuhn (1970) argued that the contending paradigms in revolutionary situations are "incommensurable"; the choice between them is not and cannot be determined by evidence and formal decision rules alone. Kuhn illustrated his argument with evidence from major revolutions ranging from the Copernican Revolution of the sixteenth century to the revolutions that overthrew Newtonian physics in the twentieth century as well as smaller revolutions that affected the work of smaller sets of scientists.

The sociologists who developed the sociology of scientific knowledge, initially largely British, advanced radical arguments far beyond those of Kuhn. Not only are paradigms, or theories, "underdetermined" by data, theories are largely or entirely socially constructed. In Harry Collins's words, "the natural world has a small or nonexistent role in the construction of scientific knowledge. . . . [N]othing outside the courses of linguistics, conceptual and social behaviour can affect the outcome of these arguments" (quoted in Gieryn 1982). The constructivists have done a number of detailed case studies of changes in the content of science to support their claims. Their early work is summarized in Collins (1983), who shows how "data" were insufficient for resolving conflicts about an allegedly new type of laser. Others have studied cases such as disputes about gravity waves, the construction of quarks, and the history of statistics and genetics in the early twentieth century. In an ethnographic study of a laboratory that investigated neurohormones, Latour and Woolgar (1979) describe how facts were socially constructed. For example, initial claims constitute conjectures, and lower-order factual statements are qualified by the names of those making the claims. However, when they are successfully constructed, these qualifications are dropped and the facts are taken for granted, perhaps embedded in laboratory equipment or algorithms. Related work by other sociologists has involved detailed analyses of scientific discourse. Gilbert and Mulkay (1984) studied biochemists who did research on the process of oxidative phosphorylation. Those authors showed that the sober prose of the scientific papers, where evidence and argument lead to conclusions, was contradicted by the informal discourse of the same scientists, who were partly aware that evidence and argument would be insufficient to persuade their opponents.

The constructivist position naturally leads to a relativistic position: If theories are social constructs, they could equally well be different. From his detailed study of the ways in which physicists constructed quarks in the period 1964–1974, Andrew Pickering (1984) concluded that "there is no obligation upon anyone framing a view of the world to take account of what twentieth century physics has to say. The particle physicists of the late nineteen-seventies were themselves quite happy to abandon most of the phenomenal world and much of the explanatory framework which they had constructed in the previous decade. There is no reason for outsiders to show the *present* HEP worldview any more respect." This relativism leads constructivists to challenge the conventional demarcation between science and nonscience or pseudoscience. Thus, an article reporting a study of parapsychologists was titled "The Construction of the Paranormal: Nothing Unscientific Is Happening."

These extreme claims have elicited much controversy. Representative criticisms by sociologists can be found in Gieryn (1982) and Amsterdamska (1990). Some natural scientists have argued that constructivism, along with several other "postmodern" schools of thought in the social sciences and humanities, represents a dangerous form of antiscientism; see Gieryn (1998) for a discussion of these "science wars." Nevertheless, persuasive evidence has been produced about the importance of social factors in changing scientific knowledge. Stewart (1990) studied the recent revolution most widely known to the general public: plate tectonics in the 1950s and 1960s. He found strong resistance to the revolution. Earth scientists who had invested heavily in earlier perspectives were most likely to resist plate tectonics. Usually conversion to the new paradigm was gradual, sealed when scientists saw the relevance of the paradigm for their own research, but Stewart found some whose acceptance of plate tectonics came as the kind of "gestalt switch" described by Kuhn (1970).

In the conflicts accompanying the revolution, scientists on both sides deviated from conventional norms and used coercive methods to advance their positions and resist their opponents. Such intense conflict does not always accompany revolutions; in the one in physics that produced quarks, there was little acrimony or duress (Pickering 1984). In the earth sciences and physics, interests internal to the scientific disciplines affected the reception of theories. External interests also can have significant effects. Desmond (1989) shows how the interests of social classes interacted with religion in affecting the reception of Lamarckian ideas about evolution in England in the 1840s; the participants in the disputes were aware of the ideological implications of biological theories. Feminist sociologists of science have shown how gender interests have influenced perceptions of nature and the formulation of biological theories. See Keller (1995) for a review of some examples.

APPLIED RESEARCH AND DEVELOPMENT

The preceding discussion has concerned mostly basic research oriented primarily toward the advancement of knowledge. However, most research is done to advance other goals: corporate profits, weaponry, health, and human welfare. Of the 2 to 4 percent of their gross national products that advanced industrial countries devote to research and development (R&D), less than 10 percent is devoted to basic research (U.S. National Science Board 1996). Of the remainder, much is devoted to defense, particularly in the United States, where a substantial majority of federal R&D expenditures are devoted to that use.

Independent inventors are still an important source of innovations, but most applied scientists and engineers are salaried employees of corporations and mission-oriented government agencies. Such employees lack most of the autonomy of basic scientists. University-trained scientists are likely to chafe under this loss of autonomy, but successful applied research organizations have developed procedures for harmonizing their scientists' desires for autonomy with an organization's desire for useful knowledge (Kornhauser 1962). Engineers are important in translating knowledge into products and processes. Engineers are more pragmatic than scientists and are committed less

to paradigms and more to physical objects (when a scientist moves, he or she is likely to pack his or her journals first; when an engineer moves, she or he packs her or his catalogues). While scientists tend to seek autonomy in organizations, engineers tend to seek power; it is usually necessary to control organizational resources to do successful engineering work.

One of the conflicts that can occur between scientists and their industrial employers concerns communications. Scientists want to communicate their discoveries to their colleagues to gain recognition; their employers want to profit from the discoveries, and that may require keeping them secret. The patent system can provide an accommodative mechanism: Discoveries are made public, but those who wish to use the discoveries for practical purposes must pay royalties to the patent holder. The patent system represents one aspect of the commodification of knowledge. Marxist theories imply that in capitalist social formations, goods and services are produced for sale as commodities, not for use, and this is increasingly the case for scientific knowledge. Kloppenburg (1988) has applied Marxist thought effectively in his history of plant breeding. There were and are inherent problems in making seeds into a commodity, since seeds tend to reproduce themselves; they can be both objects of consumption and part of the means of production. Until recently, seeds seldom were produced as commodities; new varieties were exchanged among farmers or distributed to them by government agencies at little cost, and the farmers would then grow their own seeds. This changed first with the development of hybrid corn, where farmers could not use the corn they produced as seed and instead bought new seed from the seed companies each season. This process has since been extended to other crops. In addition, consistent with Marxist thought, the seed industry has become increasingly centralized and concentrated, with fewer and larger firms dominating it. Those firms also expand into world markets, acquiring germ plasm in third world countries and selling seeds as commodities in those countries. The development of biotechnology has increasingly taken this form. Rapid developments in this area blur the distinction between basic and applied research. The emerging pattern seems to be one in which research that cannot be used to generate a profit is done in universities and governmental agencies, usually at public expense, while research that can be used for profit is done in corporations.

Modern science has led to massive changes in the lives of people in all countries, and it has the potential for further changes. For example, it has made major contributions to economic growth (Mansfield 1991). However, not all these changes have been beneficial, and not all beneficial changes are allocated equitably. While polls show high support for science in general, there are intense public controversies in many areas, from the use of animals in biomedical research, to global warming, to military technologies (Nelkin 1995). Sometimes research and development efforts can achieve considerable autonomy. MacKenzie (1993) shows how those who developed the inertial navigation system for submarine-launched missiles successfully "black-boxed" their efforts so that political officials would not interfere. The navigation technology could have had seriously destabilizing effects in the cold war, without any deliberation by elected officials. The autonomy of engineers sometimes achieve does not imply autonomy for scientists. Thus, while oceanographers have made major discoveries in the past forty years, their expensive research has been driven largely by the interests of the U.S. Navy and their autonomy has been constrained by its interests (Mukerji 1990). Attempts have been made to develop more democratic means for developing science policy. Collingridge (1980) argues for an approach of "disjointed incrementalism": Since problems are rarely foreseen, policy making should be fragmented rather than centralized and will often be remedial; since it is not feasible to investigate all solutions, analysis and evaluation should be serial and incremental. Democratic governments have developed organizations to mediate between science and governmental institutions. These organizations can be nongovernmental, such as the National Academy of Sciences–National Research Council; part of the legislative branch, such as the Office of Technology Assessment of the U.S. Congress; or part of the executive branch, such as the Environmental Protection Agency. (For a description of these efforts in the United States and the difficulties they face, see Bimber and Guston 1995; Cozzens and Woodhouse 1995.) The growth and rapid change of science-based technologies present difficult problems in regard to support and control. Knowledge about the organization of science and its relationships with other institutions can help in dealing with those problems.

REFERENCES

Allison, Paul D., and J. Scott Long 1990 "Departmental Effects on Scientific Productivity." *American Sociological Review* 55:469–78.

———, J. Scott Long, and Tad K. Krauze 1982 "Cumulative Advantage and Inequality in Science." *American Sociological Review* 47:615–625.

Amsterdamska, Olga 1990 "Review of *Science in Action* by Bruno Latour." *Science, Technology, and Human Values* 15:495–504.

Ben-David, Joseph 1984 *The Scientist's Role in Society.* Chicago: University of Chicago Press.

——— 1991 *Scientific Growth: Essays on the Social Organization and Ethos of Science.* Berkeley: University of California Press.

Bimber, Bruce, and David H. Guston 1995 "Politics by the Same Means: Government and Science in the United States." In Sheila Jasanoff, G. Markle, J. C. Petersen, and T. Pinch eds., *Handbook of Science and Technology Studies.* Thousand Oaks, Calif. Sage.

Cohen, H. Floris 1994 *The Scientific Revolution: A Historiographical Inquiry.* Chicago: University of Chicago Press.

Cole, Jonathan R., and Stephen Cole 1973 *Social Stratification in Science.* Chicago: University of Chicago Press.

Collingridge, David 1980 *The Social Control of Technology.* London: Frances Pinter.

Collins, Harry M. 1983 "The Sociology of Scientific Knowledge: Studies of Contemporary Science." In *Annual Review of Sociology,* vol. 9. R. H. Turner and J. F. Short, Jr., eds. Palo Alto, Calif. Annual Review.

Cozzens, Susan E., and Edward J. Woodhouse 1995 "Science, Government, and the Politics of Knowledge." In Sheila Jasanoff, G. Markle, J. C. Petersen, and T. Pinch, eds., *Handbook of Science and Technology Studies.* Thousand Oaks, Calif.: Sage.

Desmond, Adrian 1989 *The Politics of Evolution.* Chicago: University of Chicago Press.

Gieryn, Thomas F. 1982 "Relativist/Constructivist Programmes in the Sociology of Science: Redundance and Retreat." *Social Studies of Science* 12:279–297.

——— 1995 "Boundaries of Science." In Sheila Jasanoff, G. Markle, J. C. Petersen, and T. Pinch eds., *Handbook of Science and Technology Studies.* Thousand Oaks, Calif.: Sage.

—— 1998 *Cultural Boundaries of Science*. Chicago: University of Chicago Press.

Gilbert, G. Nigel, and Michael Mulkay 1984 *Opening Pandora's Box: A Sociological Analysis of Scientists' Discourse*. Cambridge, UK: Cambridge University Press.

Hagstrom, Warren O. 1965 *The Scientific Community*. New York: Basic Books.

—— 1974 "Competition in Science." *American Sociological Review*. 39:1–18.

—— 1976 "The Production of Culture in Science." *American Behavioral Scientist* 19:753–768.

Hargens, Lowell L. 1975 *Patterns of Scientific Research: A Comparative Analysis of Research in Three Scientific Fields*. Washington, D.C.: American Sociological Association.

—— 1988 "Scholarly Consensus and Journal Rejection Rates." *American Sociological Review* 53:139–151.

Isis 1988 Symposium on the Fiftieth Anniversary of *Science, Technology and Society*, vol. 79, pp. 571–605.

Keller, Evelyn Fox 1995 "The Origin, History, and Politics of the Subject Called 'Gender and Science.'" In Sheila Jasanoff, G. Markle, J. C. Petersen, and T. Pinch eds., *Handbook of Science and Technology Studies*. Thousand Oaks, Calif.: Sage.

Kloppenburg, Jack R., Jr. 1988 *First the Seed: The Political Economy of Plant Biotechnology 1492–2000*. New York: Cambridge University Press.

Kornhauser, William 1962 *Scientists in Industry: Conflict and Accommodation*. Berkeley: University of California Press.

Kuhn, Thomas S. (1962) 1970 *The Structure of Scientific Revolutions*. Chicago: University of Chicago Press.

Latour, Bruno, and Steve Woolgar 1979. *Laboratory Life: The Social Construction of Scientific Facts*. Beverly Hills, Calif.: Sage.

MacKenzie, Donald A. 1993 *Inventing Accuracy: A Historical Sociology of Nuclear Missile Guidance*. Cambridge, Mass.: MIT Press.

Mansfield, Edwin 1991 "Academic Research and Industrial Innovation." *Research Policy* 20:1–12.

Merton, Robert K. (1938) 1970. *Science, Technology and Society in Seventeenth Century England*. New York: Howard Fertig.

—— 1973 *The Sociology of Science*. Chicago: University of Chicago Press.

Mitroff, Ian 1974 "Norms and Counternorms in a Select Group of Scientists: A Case Study in the Ambivalence of Scientists." *American Sociological Review* 39:579–595.

Mukerji, Chandra 1990 *A Fragile Power: Scientists and the State*. Princeton N.J.: Princeton University Press.

Mulkay, Michael J. 1980 "Interpretation and the Use of Rules: The Case of the Norms of Science." In T. F. Gieryn, ed., *Science and Social Structure: A Festschrift for Robert K. Merton*. New York: New York Academy of Sciences.

Nelkin, Dorothy 1995 "Scientific Controversies: The Dynamics of Public Disputes in the United States." In Sheila Jasanoff G. Markle, J. C. Petersen, and T. Pinch eds., *Handbook of Science and Technology Studies*. Thousand Oaks, Calif.: Sage.

Nelson, Carnot E., and Donald K. Pollock, eds. 1970 *Communication among Scientists and Engineers*. Lexington, Mass.: Heath.

Parsons, Talcott 1951 *The Social System*. Glencoe, Ill.: Free Press.

Pickering, Andrew 1984 *Constructing Quarks: A Sociological History of Particle Physics*. Chicago: University of Chicago Press.

Price, Derek J. de S. (1963) 1986 *Little Science, Big Science . . . and Beyond*. New York: Columbia University Press.

Rudwick, Martin J. S. 1985 *The Great Devonian Controversy: The Shaping of Scientific Knowledge among Gentlemanly Specialists*. Chicago: University of Chicago Press.

Shapin, Steven 1994 *A Social History of Truth: Civility and Science in Seventeenth-Century England*. Chicago: University of Chicago Press.

——, and Simon Shaffer 1985 *Leviathan and the Air-Pump: Hobbes, Boyle, and the Experimental Life*. Princeton N.J.: Princeton University Press.

Stewart, John A. 1990 *Drifting Continents and Colliding Paradigms: Perspectives on the Geoscience Revolution*. Bloomington: Indiana University Press.

U.S. National Science Board 1985 *Science and Engineering Indicators*. Washington, D.C.: National Science Foundation.

——, 1996 *Science and Engineering Indicators*. Washington, D.C.: National Science Foundation.

Watson-Verran, Helen, and David Turnbull 1995 "Science and Other Indigenous Knowledge Systems." In Sheila Jasanoff, G. Markle, J. C. Peterson, and T. Pinch eds., *Handbook of Science and Technology Studies*. Thousand Oaks, Calif.: Sage.

Xie, Yu, and Kimberlee A. Shauman 1998 "Sex Differences in Research Productivity." *American Sociological Review* 63:847–870.

Znaniecki, Florian 1940 *The Social Role of the Man of Knowledge*. New York: Columbia University Press.

Zuckerman, Harriet 1988. "The Sociology of Science." In Neil J. Smelser, ed., *Handbook of Sociology*. Newbury Park, Calif.: Sage.

Warren Hagstrom

SCIENTIFIC EXPLANATION

Science and scientific knowledge achieved high status in twentieth-century Western societies, yet there continues to be disagreement among scientists and those who study science (historians, philosophers, and sociologists of science) about the meaning of scientific explanation. Indeed, the use of the word "explanation" has been the subject of heated debate (Keat and Urry 1982).

One way to make sense of science is to "reconstruct" the logic scientists use to produce scientific knowledge. The reconstructed logic of science differs from what scientists actually do when they engage in research. The research process is seldom as clear, logical, and straightforward as the reconstructed logic presented in this article makes it appear. For a long time, the most popular reconstruction of the logic of the scientific process was the "hypothetico-deductive" model. In this model, "the scientist, by a combination of careful observation, shrewd guesses, and scientific intuition arrives at a set of postulates governing the phenomena in which he is interested; from these he deduces observable consequences; he then tests these consequences by experiment, and so confirms or disconfirms the postulates, replacing them, where necessary, by others, and so continuing" (Kaplan 1964, pp. 9–10; see also Braithwaite 1968; Nagel 1961). The description of scientific explanation presented here is broadly consistent with this model as it is used in the social sciences.

Scientific explanations can be contrasted to other, nonscientific types of explanation (Babbie 1989; Kerlinger 1973; Cohen and Nagel 1934). Some explanations obtain their validity because they are offered by someone in authority, for example, a police officer, the president, or parents. Validity also may rest on tradition. For instance, the correct way to do a folk dance is the way it has always been danced, handed down over the generations. This knowledge is not obtained by going through textbooks or conducting experiments but is stored in the memories and beliefs of individuals. Another way of knowing is a priori, or intuitive, knowledge. This knowledge is based on things that "stand to reason," or seem to be obvious, but are not necessarily based on experience. People tend to cling strongly to intuitive knowledge even if the "facts" do not match their experience. Situations that contrast with strongly held beliefs are explained away as unique occurrences that will not happen again. For example, it "stands to reason" that if you are nice to other people, they will be nice to you.

The scientific method is a way of obtaining information, or knowledge, about the world. Theoretically, the same knowledge will be obtained by everybody who asks the same questions and uses the same investigative method. Scientific explanation uses theories, deductive and inductive logic, and empirical observation to determine what is true and what is false. Unlike authoritarian, traditional, or intuitive explanations, scientific knowledge is always supposed to be open to challenge and continual correction.

A theory is a hypothetical explanation for an observation or a question such as Why is the sky blue? or Why do victims of child abuse often grow up to be perpetrators? Scientists develop and test theories by using deductive logic, trying to show that empirical observations are instances of more general laws. Scientific theories are hypothetical explanations that state the possible relationships among scientific concepts. Theories consist of "a set of interrelated constructs (concepts), definitions, and propositions that present a systematic view of phenomena by specifying relations among variables, with the purpose of explaining and predicting the phenomena" (Kerlinger 1973, p. 9). Theories also are used by scientists to interpret, criticize, and bring together established laws, often modifying them to fit unanticipated data. They also guide the enterprise of making new and more powerful generalizations (Kaplan 1964, p. 295).

Scientific theories generally take the form of "If X happens, then Y will happen." For instance, Karl Marx's theory of surplus value suggests that as the level of surplus value in a capitalist society increases, so will inequality. This is an attempt to determine causal relations, so that theories not only predict what will happen in the world but also explain why it happens.

In general, scientific explanations are derived using nomothetic methods, which have the goal of making generalizations or of establishing universal laws. The experiment is perhaps the best known nomothetic method. Scientific theories try to generalize, or predict, beyond the specific data that support them to other similar situations. In contrast, some forms of the social sciences and humanities use idiographic methods, which are designed to provide knowledge of one particular event which may be unique. The best known idiographic method may be the case study. For example, both social scientists and historians investigate wars. A social scientist tries to explain what is common to all wars, possibly so that she or he can develop a general theory of intersocietal conflict. In contrast, a historian studies individual wars and tries to chronicle and explain the events and conditions that cause a specific war, and is generally not interested in a scientific theory of what may be common to all wars.

It seems that there is a paradox here: Scientific explanations are the best explanations that can be offered for an event, yet scientific theories are always open to correction by a better explanation or theory. What counts as a "better" explanation or theory has been the subject of debate in the philosophy of science. Some people believe that the better theories are those which can explain anomalies that previous theories could not. In other words, the new, "better" theory can explain everything the old theory could but also can explain some things that it left unexplained. There are many debates among philosophers of science about how to judge the "goodness" of a theory. They all admit that theories can never be confirmed definitively by any amount of observational material. The possibility always exists of finding an event that does not fit the theory, thus falsifying it. However, some theories have so much observational evidence on their side that they are said to be well confirmed, and the possibility of finding observations that falsify them is considered negligible.

However, the philosopher of science Popper said that while one can never absolutely *confirm* theories, one can definitively *falsify* them (1959). In other words, it is possible to find definite events that disconfirm, or falsify, a theory. However, other philosophers argue that this is not necessarily true, because it is always an open question whether it is the theory that is wrong or one of the assumptions that is not tested when the theory is tested.

A famous example of this problem of falsification is provided by the philosopher of science Carl Hempel in his historical examination of the work of the Hungarian physician Semmelweiss (1966). Semmelweiss was concerned with the high rates of maternal mortality during childbirth. He theorized that those deaths resulted from blood poisoning, which was caused by infectious matter carried on the physician's hands. Physicians were examining women right after performing dissections in the autopsy room. Semmelweiss's hypothesis led him to believe that if the infectious matter was removed before the women were examined, the death rates would drop. To test this, he had doctors wash their hands in a solution of chlorinated lime *after* performing dissections and then examine women who had just given birth. As he predicted, the mortality rates fell as this procedure was practiced, providing evidence *confirming* his theory.

However, if the mortality rates had *not* fallen, that would not necessarily have meant that the theory was wrong. It could have meant that one of the unexamined assumptions, such as that chlorinated lime destroys infectious matter, was wrong. Thus, the theory would have been true but the experiment would not have provided evidence to confirm it because one of its untested assumptions was incorrect. Thus, falsification is a double-edged sword: When a theory is not confirmed, it is necessary to determine whether it is the thing that is being manipulated experimentally (the hand washing in chlorinated lime) that is the causal factor or whether one of the assumptions underlying the experiment is faulty (if it turned out that chlorinated lime did not kill infectious matter) (Hempel 1966, pp. 3–6). Scientists have to be careful not to give up on a theory too soon, even if early results appear to falsify it, because many major scientific achievements would not have occurred if they had been quickly abandoned (Swinburne 1964).

Whether philosophers of science hold to the confirmationist view or the falsificationist view of testing scientific theories, they agree on two things. The first is that scientific theories are universal statements about regular, contingent relationships in nature; the second is that the observations used to evaluate scientific theories provide an objective foundation for science (Keat and Urry, 1982, p. 16). One of the goals of science is to develop and test theories, although some scientists believe that science proceeds inductively, purely by amassing facts and building theories from the amassed data.

Scientific laws fall broadly into two types: deterministic laws and stochastic (probabilistic) laws. For deterministic laws, if the scientist knows the initial conditions and the forces acting on a system and those factors do not change, the state of the system can be determined for all times and places. Deterministic laws are the ideal of the Newtonian, or mechanistic, model of science. In this model, it is assumed that causes precede effects and that changes come only from the immediately preceding or present state, never from future states. It is assumed that if two systems are identical and are subject to the same initial conditions and forces, they will reach the same end point in the same way. Deterministic laws assume that it is possible to make a complete separation between the system and the environment and that the properties of the system arise from its smallest parts. The smallest parts of a system are those about which nothing can be determined except their location and direction. There is nothing in the parts themselves that influences the system, and all changes in the state of the system come from the forces acting on it. Deterministic laws are based on the assumption that the universe is regular and that connections between events are independent of time and space. The idea with a scientific explanation is that all other things being equal (ceteris paribus), identical circumstances lead to identical results.

Stochastic laws are expressed in terms of probability. For large or complex systems, it is not possible to identify precisely what state the system will be in at any given time but only to assess the probability of its being in a certain state. Quantum physics, chemistry, card games, and lotteries utilize stochastic laws. Those laws are stated in terms of probability over time and apply to classes of events rather than to specific instances. Most relationships in the social sciences are stated in stochastic terms because individual behavior is very difficult to predict. The use of probability does not mean that events are viewed as random, or uncaused, simply that the behavior of the individual elements of a system cannot be predicted with perfect accuracy.

Scientific theories are systematically linked to existing knowledge that is derived from other generally accepted theories. Each scientist builds on the work of other scientists, using tested theories to develop new theories. The scientific method is dedicated to changing theories, and scientific knowledge progresses through the challenge and revision of theories.

Often a new theory is preferred not because it is based on facts (data) that are different from those on which the old theory was based but because it provides a more comprehensive explanation of existing data. For example, Newton's theory of the solar system superseded Kepler's explanation of planetary motion because Newton's theory included the theory of gravity (which predicted a gravitational attraction between all physical bodies in the universe) as well as the laws of motion. The two theories together provided many circumstances that could "test" the theory because they *predicted* not only where planets should be in relation to each other at given times but also phenomena such as falling apples and swinging pendulums. Newton's theory was more comprehensive and more economical, and although it provided more opportunities for falsification than did Kepler's (which made it more vulnerable), it also resisted falsification better and became the accepted scientific explanation (Chalmers 1982).

The premises, or propositions, in a scientific theory must lead logically to the conclusions. Scientific explanations show that the facts, or data, can be deduced from the general theory. Theories are tested by comparing what deduction says "should" hold if the theory is true with the state of affairs in the world (observations). The purpose of a theory is to describe, explain, and predict observations.

The classic example of deductive logic is the familiar syllogism "All men are mortal; Socrates is a man; therefore, Socrates is mortal." Deductive conclusions include only the information included in the propositions. Thus, deductive reasoning can be logically correct but empirically incorrect. If a theory is based on empirically false premises, it probably will result in empirically false conclusions. A scientific test of the truth of the conclusions requires a comparison of the statements in the conclusion with actual states of affairs in the "real" world.

Scientific explanations and theories are usually quite complex and thus often require more information than can be included in a deductively valid argument. Sometimes it is necessary to know that a conclusion is probably true, or at least justified, even if it does not follow logically from a set of premises and arguments (Giere 1984). Thus, there is a need for inductive logic, which is based on particular instances (facts or observations) and moves to general theories (laws).

Many sociologists and other scientists believe that scientific knowledge is produced mainly by induction (Glaser and Strauss 1967). For example, after one has observed many politicians, a theory might postulate that most politicians are crooked. Although this theory is based on many observations, its proof, or verification, would require observing every politician past, present, and future. Falsifying the theory would require finding a substantial number of politicians who were not crooked. The absolute and final verification of scientific theories is not possible. However, it should be possible to "falsify" any scientific theory by finding events or classes of events that do not support it (Stinchcombe 1987; Popper 1959).

Because inductive arguments are always subject to falsification, they are stated in terms of probabilities. Good inductive arguments have a high probability associated with their being true. This high probability comes from a large number of similar observations over time and in different circumstances. For example, although it is not absolutely certain that if someone in North America becomes a medical doctor, he or she will earn a high income, the evidence provided by observing doctors in many places and many times shows that a high probability can be assigned to the assertion that medical doctors earn high incomes.

Inductive arguments are not truth-preserving. Even with true premises, an inductive argument can have a false conclusion because the conclusions of inductive arguments generally contain more information or make wider generalizations than do the premises (Giere 1984). Science requires both deductive and inductive methods to progress. This progress is circular: Theories are developed and tested, and new data give rise to new theories, which then are tested (Wallace 1971).

Several steps are involved in testing scientific theories. Theories first must be expressed in both abstract, verbal terms and concrete, operationalized terms. Concepts and constructs are rich, complex, abstract descriptions of the entity to be measured or studied. Concepts have nominal definitions (they are defined by using other words) and are specifically developed for scientific purposes. A variable is operationally defined to allow the measurement of one specific aspect of a concept. Operationalization is a set of instructions for how a researcher is going to measure the concepts and test the theory. These instructions should allow events and individuals to be classified unambiguously and should be precise enough that the same results will be achieved by anyone who uses them (Blalock 1979).

For example, one theory posits that the relationship between "anxiety" and test performance is curvilinear. This theory predicts that very little anxiety leads to poor performance on tests (as measured by grades), a medium amount of anxiety improves test performance, and very high anxiety causes poor test performance. If it were drawn on a graph, this curve would be an upside-down U. To test the theory, both anxiety and test performance must be measured as variables expressed in empirical terms. For an observation to be empirical means that it is, or hypothetically could be, experienced or observed in a way that can be measured in the same manner by others in the same circumstances.

As a concept, anxiety encompasses many different things. The measurement theory must specify whether anxiety will be measured as feelings, such as being tense, worried, or "uptight," or as physical reactions, such as shortness of breath, heart palpitations, or sweaty palms. The researcher may decide to measure anxiety by asking subjects how worried or tense they felt before an examination. Racing hearts, sweating palms, and upset stomachs are part of the concept, but they are excluded from the operationalization. The researcher must decide whether this is or is not a valid (measures what it purports to measure) and reliable (obtains the same results on repeated tests) measure of anxiety, in part by comparing the results of the research to other research on anxiety and test performance. It is also necessary to strike a balance between the scope of the concept (the different things it refers to) and precision. The wider the scope of a concept, the more it can be generalized to other conditions and the fewer conditions are required to construct a theory, making it more parsimonious. However, if the scope of a concept is too wide, the concept loses precision and becomes meaningless.

Scientific explanation involves the accurate and precise measurement of phenomena. Measurement is the assignment of symbols, usually numbers, to the properties of objects or events (Stevens 1951). The need for precise measurement has led to an emphasis on quantification. Some sociologists feel that some qualities and events that people experience defy quantification, arguing that numbers can never express the meaning that people's behavior holds for them. However, mathematics is only a language, based on deductive logic, that expresses relationships symbolically. Assigning numbers to human experiences forces a researcher to be precise even when the concepts, such as "anxiety" and "job satisfaction," are fuzzy.

Another important aspect of scientific explanations is that they attempt to be "objective." In science this term has two broad meanings. First, it means that observers agree about what they have observed. For example, a group of scientists observing the behavior of objects when they are dropped would agree that they saw the objects "fall" to the ground. For this observation to be objective, (1) there must be an agreed-on method for producing it (dropping an object), (2) it must be replicable (more than one object is released, and they all "fall"), and (3) the same results must occur regardless of who performs the operation and where it is performed (objects must behave the same way for all observers anywhere in the world). Scientific operations must be expressed clearly enough that other people can repeat the procedures. Only when all these conditions are met is it possible to say that an observation is objective. This form of objectivity is called "intersubjectivity" and it is crucial to scientific explanations.

The second use of the word "objective" in science means that scientific explanations are not based on the values, opinions, attitudes, or beliefs of the researcher. In other words, scientific explanations are "value-free." A researcher's values and interests may influence what kinds of things she or he chooses to study (i.e., why one person becomes a nuclear physicist and another becomes a sociologist), but once the problem for study is chosen the scientist's personal values and opinions do not influence the type of knowledge produced. The value-free nature of science is the goal of freeing scientific explanations from the influence of any individual or group's biases and opinions.

The relationships in a theory state how abstract constructs are to be linked so that antecedent properties or conditions can be used to explain consequent ones. An antecedent condition may be seen as either necessary or sufficient to cause or produce a consequent condition. For example, higher social status may be seen as *sufficient* to increase the probability that farmers will adopt new farming techniques (innovation). It also could be argued that awareness and resources are necessary conditions for innovation. Without both, innovation is unlikely (Gartrell and Gartrell 1979).

Relationships may be asymmetrical (the antecedent produces the effect) or symmetrical (both cause each other): Frustration may cause aggression, and aggression may cause frustration. Relationships may be direct, or positive (an increase in knowledge causes an increase in innovation), or negative (an increase in stress leads to a decrease in psychological well-being). They may be described as monotonic, linear, or curvilinear. Sociologists often assume that relationships are linear, partly because this is the simplest form of a relationship.

Relationships between variables are expressed by using a wide variety of mathematical theories, each of which has its own "language." Algebra and calculus use the concepts of "greater than," "less than," and "equal to." Set theory talks about things being "included in," and graph theory uses "connectedness" or "adjacency between." Markov chains attempt to identify a connectedness in time or a transition between states, and symbolic logic uses the terms "union" and "intersection" to talk about relationships.

Scientific explanation is also very explicit about the units to which relationships between propositions refer. Sociologists refer to a host of collectivities (cultures, social systems, organizations, communities), relationships (world systems, families), and parts of collectivities (social positions, roles). There is strength in this diversity of subject matter but also potential weakness in failing explicitly to define the unit of analysis. Some properties cannot be attributed to all units of analysis. For example, "income" is a concept that can apply to an individual or a group (e.g., "average" income), but "inequality" is always a property of an aggregate. The "ecological fallacy" (Hannan 1970) involves the incorrect attribution of properties of aggregates to individuals. Aggregation is not a matter of simple addition, and some relationships between subunits (homogeneity, complexity, inequality) have complicated aggregation algorithms. Care must be taken in switching units of reference from social collectivities to individuals. For example, communities with high divorce rates also may have high homicide rates, but this does not necessarily imply that divorced people kill one another or are more likely to be homicide victims or perpetrators.

To test theories, the relationships among concepts are stated as hypotheses, linking variables in an operationalized form. Since the existence of a relationship cannot be proved conclusively, a scientist instead tries to show that there is no relationship between the variables by testing hypotheses that are stated in the "null" form. In the test performance and anxiety example, a null hypothesis would state, "There is no curvilinear relationship between the number of correct responses on tests and the reported level of worry and tension." If this hypothesis was rejected, that is, found to be highly unlikely, the researcher would have evidence to support the alternative hypothesis suggested by the theory: There is a curvilinear relationship between the variables.

Social scientists use a variety of methods to study human behavior, including experiments, surveys, participant observation, and unobtrusive measures. In essence, experiments try to identify causal sequences by determining the effect of an independent variable (the stimulus) on a dependent variable. Experiments require stringent conditions that often are difficult to fulfill with human beings, sometimes for ethical reasons but more often because there is a wide variation in individual responses to the same stimulus (Babbie 1989; Kerlinger 1973; Cook and Campbell 1979).

Social scientists have developed other research methods, such as surveys and field research, which allow them to produce scientific knowledge without resorting to experimental manipulation. Statistical analysis of survey data allows social scientists to examine complex problems in large populations by statistically controlling several variables that represent competing explanations (Blalock 1964). The distinctive characteristic of survey research is that the subjects of the study tell the scientist about themselves.

Social scientists also use qualitative methods such as participant observation to conduct research in the "field" where phenomena actually occur. Field research focuses on the empirical richness and complexity of the whole subject in order to understand what is subjectively meaningful. Participant observation proceeds inductively rather than deductively. The researcher observes and participates in order to understand (subjectively) and then attempts to externalize the observations by constructing categories of responses, or theory. In contrast to other research designs, participant observation deliberately does not attempt to control conditions; the researcher strives to obtain an unbiased picture of how the subjects see things in their natural setting (Whyte 1961). The emphasis is on the richness of subjects' understanding of events and on subjectivity rather than on objectivity. Theory developed from this type of research is called grounded theory (Glaser and Strauss 1967). Unobtrusive methods such as content analysis focus on the study of artifacts (newspapers, homes), partly to overcome reactivity by subjects and biases on the part of the researcher.

CRITIQUES OF THE HYPOTHETICO-DEDUCTIVE MODEL OF SCIENCE

In the 1930s and 1940s, the dominant view of science was "radical positivism," which viewed science as a process based only on inductive generalizations and empirical verification. Abstract theoretical concepts that could not be observed were considered literally meaningless. The revision of positivism in the 1950s (logical empiricism) recognized the importance of abstract concepts and theories but continued to insist that all scientific statements be subject to empirical falsification. In short, the empiricists persisted in their belief that "facts" were purely objective entities and that what was viewed as a fact did not depend on theory or theoretical concepts. However, theories play as large a role in scientific change and knowledge production as do empirical observations. In part, this internal confusion laid the groundwork for a wide range of critiques of both positivism and empiricism (Alexander 1982; Bernstein 1976).

Reconstructed logic suggests that scientific knowledge can be accounted for by following formal rules of logic. The progress of knowledge is such that unscientific or prescientific explanations for phenomena are replaced successively by scientific explanations, which are ever closer approximations to the "truth." It stresses that the knowledge produced by the scientific method is objective and value-free, corresponding to states of the world as it really is, not as it is seen by a particular group of people in a particular social and historical location.

However, the "facts" on which scientific explanations are based are not independent of "point of view" (Polanyi 1958; Hanson 1972). All scientific data are theoretically informed. What is "fact" and what is "theory" are what is convenient to the focus of scientific attention at a particular time. Because science is a social and cultural activity, it is grounded in an everyday, taken-for-granted reality. Scientists can perceive "facts" only in a particular social and cultural context. Observations take place in a cultural milieu that literally affects what the observer perceives, not just how it is interpreted. The totally objective, theory-free observation aspired to in science is not possible; to "see" something is always to see it "as" something. For example, to observe the medical "facts" in an x-ray, a physician must first learn what parts of the picture to ignore. The "fact" that objects "fall" to the ground is a fact only in a social context in which gravity is an accepted explanation for the behavior of falling objects. Scientific facts are constructed and developed through situated human labor; they do not have an independent, objective existence of their own (Fleck 1979).

Most twentieth-century philosophers of science have assumed that there is something called the scientific method that applies equally to all sciences and that sciences can be judged by their ability to adhere to that method. This is called the "unity of the sciences" model. However, the philosophy of science has ignored the actual behavior of scientists, concentrating instead an reconstructing the logic of science. The result has been an idealized and unrealistic picture of how scientific knowledge is produced. When the actual practice of scientists is observed, it is apparent that in different sciences, scientists reason in a wide variety of modes.

These different modes of reasoning were hidden by the philosophical approach of viewing scientific knowledge as resulting from the simple application of scientific logic to problems. Scientific knowledge is better seen as the outcome of an active, work-oriented process than as an uninvolved description of a "passive" natural world. This means that scientific knowledge production consists largely in activities in which scientists make decisions about how to proceed in different circumstances. This does *not* imply that scientific knowledge is "made up" and thus completely relative but instead, by looking at scientific practice rather than only scientific logic, that the view of science has shifted from science as a "representation" of nature to science as "action" or "work" (Knorr Cetina 1981).

The most definitive research into how the various sciences produce knowledge differently is represented by the work of the sociologist of science Knorr Cetina (1999). Knorr Cetina has examined the practical activity and "cultures of knowing" of two very different sciences: molecular biology and high-energy physics. She has focused on the "concrete, mundane, everyday practices of inquiring and concluding through which participants establish, for themselves and for others, knowledge claims" (1991, p. 108). Her research shows that what counts as "scientific method" differs radically between these two sciences. In other words, the cultural structure of scientific methodology varies from science to science (1991, p. 107).

Knorr Cetina demonstrates that the epistemic culture in a molecular biology laboratory is such that molecular biologists have to become "repositories of unconscious experience" and individual scientists have to develop an embodied sense of a reasonable response to different situations (1992, p. 119). A practicing molecular biologist literally *becomes* a measurement instrument. These scientists become highly skilled at seeing things others cannot see, and their bodies learn to perform delicate operations in loading gels and manipulating DNA that cannot be taught, only learned through experience. In their scientific work, individual molecular biologists often have to *guess* what procedure is best in a given situation. For this reason, the sense of what counts as a successful procedure depends heavily on an individual's experience and the predictive ability "which individuals must somehow synthesize from features of their previous experience, and which remains implicit, embodied, and encapsulated within the person" (1992, p. 121). What counts as a successful procedure or as proper scientific method is implicit: It is a blend of the individual's experience and the culture in the laboratory. Knorr Cetina calls this kind of reasoning "biographical" because "it is sustained by a scientist's biographical archive and the store of his or her professional experience" (1991, p. 115).

In contrast to the highly individual and personalized culture of knowing in a molecular biology laboratory, high-energy physics laboratories are very different kinds of epistemic spaces. Their organization is best compared to that of a superorganism, such as highly organized colonies of bees, ants, or termites. High-energy physics involves more circularities and contingencies than does molecular biology; its experiments are long term and "supra-individual."

In high-energy physics (HEP) experiments, the work of producing knowledge is detached from the individual scientist and shifted to the group. These experiments can involve from 200 to 2,000 individuals from 200 different institutions around the world, all focused on a common goal, for up to twenty years (Knorr Cetina 1999, p. 160). Authorship belongs to the experiment as a whole; individual scientists feel that they are representatives of the whole, and there is a sense of collective responsibility among them. (Knorr Cetina 1995). Unlike the highly trained body and eyes of a molecular biologist, data interpretation in HEP is done not by individual scientists but by computers. In fact, individual scientists literally cannot run experiments. HEP experiments are huge, they take many years to run, and each experiment seeds new generations of experiments. High-energy physicists do not think in terms of individual achievements in months but of group successes over years and decades.

In HEP, forming a consensus about what counts as adequate scientific knowledge and the proper application of scientific method is very much a group process. In molecular biology, the group is involved in terms of the culture of the laboratory but each individual scientist is a highly skilled measuring instrument that makes most procedural decisions on his or her own. Thus, by examining the organization of the laboratories and the working practices of the scientists in these two domains, Knorr Cetina has challenged the philosophical assumption of a unitary scientific method.

Science is now widely regarded as a social activity rather than an application of logic to nature. It is seen as an interplay between practical activity, empirical observations, and broad theoretical "paradigms" (Kuhn 1970; Fleck 1979). Paradigms dictate the valid questions for research as well as the range of possible answers and can be so powerful that contradictory data (anomalies) are explained away under the assumption that they can be brought into the theory at a later time. Confronted by contradictory empirical evidence that cannot be ignored, the adherents of a theory often develop ad hoc hypotheses and residual categories to account for anomalies. Thus, they encompass or explain observations that contradict their theories and often cling to those theories in dogmatic fashion. The reconstructed logic of science leads one to believe that theories would be rejected under those conditions.

However, sociological research has shown that "the data" do not and cannot speak for themselves and decide between competing scientific theories. Sometimes a theory wins out over its competitors because its survival is in the best interests of a group or researcher (Woolgar 1981; Shapin 1979). For example, when high-energy particle physicists were searching for the subatomic particles now known as quarks, two competing explanations were advanced: the "charm" and "color" theories. Both models were consistent with the data. The ultimate success of the charm model occurred because more people had an interest in seeing it succeed. Charm theorists were more successful in relating their theory to an existing body of practice and interests. The color theory was never empirically refuted but eventually "died" because its proponents were reduced to talking to themselves (Pickering 1982).

Part of the problem is that the decision about whether certain experiments or observations are critical to the proof or falsification of a theory is possible only after the fact, not before, and the possibility always exists that an experiment failed because it was not performed competently. It is difficult to establish the criteria for determining whether an experiment has been successful. To know whether the experimental apparatus, the theory, and the competence of the researcher have combined to produce a successful experiment, it is necessary to know beforehand what the correct outcome is. However, the definition of a competently performed experiment is having a successful outcome, leading to the "experimenter's regress" (Collins 1985).

The replication of results is an essential criterion for the stability of scientific knowledge, but scientific inquiry requires a high degree of tacit or personal knowledge (Polanyi 1958). This knowledge is by nature invisible, but its importance is strongly denied by a scientific community that bases its claims to validity on the potential for replication. Scientific developments often cannot be replicated unless there is direct, personal contact between the original researcher and the people attempting to do the replication. Few replications are possible using published results and procedures, and successful replication often rests on the original researcher's tacit knowledge, which is not easily transferable (Collins 1985). To complicate matters, science reserves its highest rewards for original research rather than replication. As a consequence, there is little glory and less funding for replication, and the "replicability" requirement is reduced to demonstrating the possibility of replication.

Feminists have added their voice to critiques of science and the scientific method. The most successful feminist critiques of science are those identified as "feminist empiricist," which attempt to restructure "bad science" and provide a more objective, gender-free knowledge (Harding 1986). Feminists have pointed out some androcentric (male-centered) categories in science and have identified the patriarchal social organization of "science as an institution." Haraway has argued that there is no purely "objective" stance that can be taken; knowledge is always a "view" from somewhere (Haraway 1988). The concept of power based on gender has become a permanent category of analysis in feminist approaches (Smith 1987; Connel 1983).

By differentiating between "good science" and "bad science," feminist empiricists strive to separate the wheat from the chaff by eradicating gender biases in the scientific process. The ultimate goal is to provide more objective, value-free knowledge (Harding 1987). At the very least, feminist approaches often attempt to show the hidden biases in many scientific theories. The argument is that some types of knowledge are true only for certain social groups and do not reflect the experience of women, homosexuals, and many ethnic and racial groups, or other groups on the margins of society (Haraway 1988).

This perspective has had some success in the social sciences, perhaps because its revisions provide results that are intuitively appealing. By including categories that often are ignored, oppressed, and invisible to traditional sociology, feminist research gives a voice to what were previously "non-questions" under the mainstream, or as feminists call it, the male-stream model of science (Vickers 1982). For example, feminist research suggests that many women do not make a yes-or-no decision about having children but instead leave it to luck or time to decide. This type of decision-making behavior has implications for fertility and deserves the same theoretical status as the yes and no categories. However, a male-stream model of science that assumed that fertility decisions were the outcome of a series of rational cost-benefit analyses was blind to this conceptualization (Currie 1988).

It is ironic that while feminist empiricist criticisms of "bad" science aspire to strengthen science, they ultimately subvert the understandings of science they attempt to reinforce: "If the concepts of nature, of dispassionate, value free, objective inquiry, and of transcendental knowledge are androcentric, white, bourgeois, and Western, then no amount of more rigorous adherence to scientific method will eliminate such bias, for the methods themselves reproduce the perspectives generated by these hierarchies and thus distort our understandings" (Harding 1987, p. 291).

Another critique of science comes from the hermeneutic, or interpretive, perspective, which takes issue with the positivist assumption that the concepts, categories, and methods used to describe the physical world are applicable to human behavior. Human studies proponents insist that the universal categories and objective arguments required for prediction and explanation in the natural sciences cannot be achieved in the social sciences. The proper subject matter of the social sciences is the internal, or subjective, meanings of human behavior that guide human action. Because these meanings are nonempirical and subjective rather than objective, they cannot meet the requirements for scientific explanation. Therefore, the goal of the social sciences is to understand rather than predict and explain human behavior (Hughes 1961; Habermas 1971; Gadamer 1976). Validation of interpretations is one of the biggest problems with the hermeneutic position because no firm ground exists from which to judge the validity of different interpretations of meaning and behavior. Hermeneutic explanations are ultimately subjective and in their extreme form focus solely on the explanation of individual, unique events (Alexander 1982).

The value-free nature of scientific knowledge also has been challenged by critical theory, which suggests that scientific knowledge is knowledge that is one-sided and specifically oriented to the domination and control of nature. This "interest" in domination and control does not lie in the application of scientific knowledge but is intrinsic to the knowledge itself. In contrast, communicative knowledge is knowledge that is oriented to reaching understanding and achieving human emancipation (Habermas 1984).

CONCLUSION

Although scientific explanation has been the subject of many critiques, it is still the most methodical, reliable form of knowledge. It is ironic that while the natural sciences are becoming less positivistic and are beginning to recognize nonempirical, subjective, and cultural influences on scientific knowledge, the social sciences continue to emphasize the refinement of methodology and measurement in an attempt to become more positivistic (Alexander 1982). The result is that in sociology, theoretical inquiry is increasingly divorced from empirical research. Paradoxically, this schism may be a source of strength if the two sides can learn to communicate. Sociology may be in a unique position to integrate critiques of the scientific model with ongoing empirical research, perhaps producing a hybrid that is neither relativistic nor positivistic.

(SEE ALSO: *Causal Inference Models; Epistemology; Experiments; Measurement; Metatheory; Positivism; Quasi-Experimental Research Design; Reliability; Validity; Statistical Inference*)

REFERENCES

Alexander, Jeffrey C. 1982 *Positivism, Presuppositions and Current Controversies.* Berkeley: University of California Press.

Babbie, Earl 1989 *The Practice of Social Research,* 5th ed. Belmont, Calif: Wadsworth.

Bernstein, Richard J. 1976 *The Restructuring of Political and Social Theory.* Philadelphia: University of Pennsylvania Press.

Blalock, Hubert M. 1964 *Causal Inferences in Non-Experimental Research.* Chapel Hill: University of North Carolina Press.

——1979 *Social Statistics,* rev. 2nd ed. New York: McGraw-Hill.

Braithwaite, Richard Bevan 1968 *Scientific Explanation.* London: Cambridge University Press.

Chalmers, A. F. 1982 *What Is This Thing Called Science?* Milton Keynes, UK: Open University Press.

Cohen, M., and E. Nagel 1934 *An Introduction to Logic and Scientific Method.* New York: Harcourt.

Collins, H. M. 1985 *Changing Order. Replication and Induction in Scientific Practice.* Beverly Hills, Calif: Sage.

*Collins, H. M., and Pinch, T. 1998 *The Golem: What You Should Know about Science.* New York: Cambridge University Press.

Connell, R. W. 1983 *Which Way Is Up?* Boston: Allen and Unwin.

Cook, Thomas D., and Donald T. Campbell 1979 *Quasi-Experimentation: Design and Analysis Issues for Field Settings.* Chicago: Rand McNally.

Currie, Dawn 1988 "Re-Thinking What We Do and How We Do It: A Study of Reproductive Decisions." *Canadian Review of Sociology and Anthropology* 25:231–253.

Fleck, Ludwik 1979 *Genesis and Development of a Scientific Fact.* Chicago: University of Chicago Press (originally published in German in 1935).

Gadamer, Hans-Georg 1976 *Philosophical Hermeneutics.* Berkeley: University of California Press.

Gartrell, John W., and C. David Gartrell 1979 "Status, Knowledge, and Innovation: Risk and Uncertainty in Agrarian India." *Rural Sociology* 44:73–94.

Giere, Ronald N. 1984 *Understanding Scientific Reasoning,* 2nd ed. New York: Holt, Rinehart and Winston.

Glaser, Barney G., and Anselm L. Strauss 1967 *The Discovery of Grounded Theory.* Chicago: Aldine.

Habermas, Jurgen 1971 *Knowledge and Human Interests.* Boston: Beacon Press.

—— 1984 *The Theory of Communicative Action.* Boston: Beacon Press.

Hannan, Michael T. 1970 *Problems of Aggregation and Disaggregation in Sociological Research.* Chapel Hill: University of North Carolina Press.

Hanson, Norbert R. 1972 *Patterns of Discovery.* Cambridge, UK: Cambridge University Press.

Haraway, Donna 1988 "Situated Knowledges: The Science Question in Feminism and the Privilege of Partial Perspective." *Feminist Studies* 14:575–609.

Harding, Sandra 1986 *The Science Question in Feminism.* Ithaca, N.Y.: Cornell University Press.

—— 1987 "The Instability of the Analytical Categories of Feminist Theory." In Sandra Harding and Jean F. O'Barr, eds., *Sex and Scientific Inquiry.* Chicago: University of Chicago Press.

Hempel, Carl 1966 *Philosophy of Natural Science.* Englewood Cliffs, N.J.: Prentice-Hall.

Hughes, Stuart 1961 *Consciousness and Society.* New York: Vintage.

Kaplan, Abraham 1964 *The Conduct of Inquiry: Methodology for Behavioral Science.* San Francisco: Chandler.

Keat, R., and J. Urry 1982 *Social Theory as Science.* London: Routledge and Kegan Paul.

Kerlinger, Fred N. 1973 *Foundations of Behavioral Research*, 2nd ed. New York: Holt, Rinehart and Winston.

Knorr Cetina, Karin 1981 *The Manufacture of Knowledge. An Essay on the Constructivist and Contextual Nature of Science.* Oxford, UK: Pergamon Press.

—— 1991 "Epistemic Cultures: Forms of Reason in Science" *History of Political Economy*, 23(1):105–122.

—— 1992 "The Couch, the Cathedral, and the Laboratory: On the Relationship between Experiment and Laboratory in Science." In Andrew Pickering, ed., *Science as Practice and Culture.* Chicago: University of Chicago Press.

—— 1995 "How Superorganisms Change: Consensus Formation and the Social Ontology of High-Energy Physics Experiments." *Social Studies of Science* 25:119–47.

—— 1999 *Epistemic Cultures. How the Sciences Make Knowledge.* Cambridge and London: Harvard University Press.

Kuhn, Thomas 1970 *The Structure of Scientific Revolutions*, 2nd ed. Chicago: University of Chicago Press.

*Latour, Bruno 1987 *Science in Action: How to Follow Scientists and Engineers through Society.* Cambridge, Mass.: Harvard University Press.

——, and Steve Woolgar 1986 *Laboratory Life.* Princeton, N.J.: Princeton University Press.

Nagel, Ernest 1961 *The Structure of Science: Problems in the Logic of Scientific Explanation.* New York: Harcourt, Brace and World.

Pickering, Andrew 1982 "Interests and Analogies." In B. Barnes and D. Edge, eds., *Science in Context.* Milton Keynes, UK: Open University Press.

Polanyi, Michael 1958 *Personal Knowledge.* Chicago: University of Chicago Press.

Popper, Karl R. 1959 *The Logic of Scientific Discovery.* London: Hutchinson.

Shapin, Steven 1979 "The Politics of Observation: Cerebral Anatomy and Social Interests in the Edinburgh Phrenology Disputes." In Roy Wallis, ed., *On the Margins of Science: The Social Construction of Rejected Knowledge.* Monograph 27, *1979 Sociological Review.*

Smith, Dorothy 1987 *The Everyday World as Problematic.* Boston: Northeastern University Press.

Stevens, S. S. 1951 "Mathematics, Measurement, and Psychophysics." In S. S. Stevens, ed., *Handbook of Experimental Psychology.* New York: Wiley.

Stinchcombe, Arthur L. 1987 *Constructing Social Theories.* Chicago: University of Chicago Press.

Swinburne, R. G. 1964 "Falsifiability of Scientific Theories." *Mind*, 73:434–436.

Vickers, Jill 1982 "Memoirs of an Ontological Exile: The Methodological Rebellions of Feminist Research." In Angela Miles and Geraldine Finn, eds., *Feminism in Canada: From Pressure to Politics.* Montreal: Black Rose.

Wallace, Walter L. 1971 *The Logic of Science in Sociology.* Chicago: Aldine.

Whyte, William Foote 1961 *Street Corner Society: The Social Structure of an Italian Slum*, 2nd ed. Chicago: University of Chicago Press.

*Woolgar, Steve 1988 *Science, the Very Idea.* London, New York: Tavistock.

Woolgar, Steve 1981 "Interests and Explanation in the Social Study of Science." *Social Studies of Science* 11:365–394.

LINDA DERKSEN
JOHN GARTRELL

SCIENTIFIC METHOD

See Epistemology; Positivism; Scientific Explanation.

SECONDARY DATA ANALYSIS AND DATA ARCHIVES

The creation and growth of publicly accessible data archives (or data banks) have revolutionized the way sociologists conduct research. These resources have made possible a variety of secondary analyses, often utilizing the data in ways never anticipated by their creators. Traditionally, secondary data analysis involves the use of an available data resource by researchers to study a problem different from the one treated in the original analysis. For example, a researcher might have conducted a survey of workers' reactions to technological change and analyzed those data to evaluate whether the workers welcomed or resisted such change in the workplace. As a matter of secondary interest, the researcher collects data on workers' perceptions of the internal labor-market structures of their firms. She then lends those data to a colleague who studies the determinants of (workers' perceptions of) job-ladder length and complexity in order to understand workers' views on prospects for upward mobility in their places of employment. The latter investigation is a secondary analysis.

More recently, however, the definition of a secondary analysis has expanded as more data sets have been explicitly constructed with multiple purposes and multiple users in mind. The creators, or principal investigators, exercise control over the content of a data set but are responsive to a variety of constituencies that are likely to use that resource. The creators may undertake analyses of the data, addressing questions of intellectual interest to themselves while simultaneously releasing the data to the public or depositing the data resource in an archive. Data archives are depositories where data produced by a number of investigators are available for secondary analyses. The data bank generally takes responsibility for providing documentation on the data sets and other information needed for their use. The term also refers more generally to any source of data already produced that an investigator may uncover in the course of an investigation, such as government or business records housed in libraries. For example, the U.S. government archives thousands of government documents yearly in libraries around the world. The data in those documents cover a wide variety of topics and are often useful in sociological investigations. It remains the responsibility of the analyst to configure the data in a way that is useful to his or her investigation. This entry illustrates these expanded opportunities by describing one key data archive and indicating the extent and breadth of data resources that this and other archives include. It then describes the process of conducting secondary analyses from resources such as these.

DATA ARCHIVES AND DATA SOURCES

One of the most important data archives for social scientists is the Interuniversity Consortium for Political and Social Research (ICPSR) at the University of Michigan, Ann Arbor. The ICPSR publishes an annual *Guide to Resources and Services* (much of this description was taken from the 1996–1997 volume). Additional information is available at the ICPSR Web site (www.icpsr.umich.edu). The consortium was founded in 1962 as a partnership between the Survey Research Center at the University of Michigan and twenty-one U.S. universities. In 1997 the holdings included over 3,500 titles, some of them capturing several panels of data on the same respondents or several waves of data involving comparable information. These titles are available to researchers at member institutions. The consortium charges fees on a sliding scale to academic institutions for membership privileges; researchers whose institutions are not members can obtain data for a fee. In 1997, over four hundred institutions in the United States, Canada, and countries throughout the world were members. While ICPSR originated as a service to political analysts, it currently serves a broad spectrum of the social sciences, including economics, sociology, geography, psychology, and history as well, and its data resources have been used by researchers in education, social work, foreign policy, criminal justice, and urban affairs.

Although ICPSR provides training in research and statistical methods and helps members in the effective use of computing resources, its central function is the archiving, processing, and distribution of machine-readable data of interest to social scientists. Although data capturing elements of the U.S. political process are well represented in its holdings, data are available on consumer attitudes, educational processes and attainment, health care utilization, social indicators of the quality of American life, employment conditions, workers' views on technology, and criminal behavior. The data come from over 130 countries, include both contemporary and historical censuses, and are not confined to the individual level but also provide information on the characteristics of nations and organizational attributes. ICPSR actively seeks out high-quality data sets, and the user fees finance additional data acquisition as well as other operations. It also encourages investigators to deposit their data holdings in the archives to make them available to researchers for secondary analyses. Researchers whose data production efforts are funded by federal agencies such as the National Science Foundation are required to make their data publicly available after their grants have expired, and ICPSR is a logical depository for many data sets produced in the social sciences.

ICPSR maintains over ninety serial data holdings, including the earlier waves of the National Longitudinal Surveys of Labor Market Experience (NLS) (discussed below), the Survey of Income and Program Participation, the General Social Surveys, National Crime Surveys, the Panel Study of Income Dynamics, the Detroit Area Studies, the U.S. Census of Population and Housing, and the American National Elections Studies. These serial holdings include longitudinal surveys (in which the same respondents are interviewed repeatedly over time) such as the NLS and the Panel Study of Income Dynamics. These resources are particularly useful in determining the impact of earlier life events on later life outcomes, since the causal orders of all events measured on the data sets are clearly indicated. The holdings also include sets of cross-sectional studies conducted at regular intervals, such as the Detroit Area Studies and the General Social Surveys (GSS). These studies contain different cross sections from the same populations over time and are useful in charting trends in the attitudes of the respective populations over time, assuming that the same questions are repeated. Sources, such as the GSS, that ask the same questions over several years allow the researcher to pool samples across those years and obtain larger numbers of cases that are useful in multivariate analyses.

To illustrate one data set, consider the National Longitudinal Surveys of Labor Market Experience. These surveys are produced by the Center for Human Resource Research (CHRR) at Ohio State University. The CHRR produces a yearly *NLS Handbook*, and much of the following information regarding the NLS was taken from the 1998 *NLS Handbook*. These surveys began in 1966 with a study of older men aged 45–59 and a survey of young men aged 14–24, continued in 1967 with a survey of mature women aged 30–44, and were followed up with a survey of young women aged 14–24 in 1968. In 1979, CHRR began a survey of over 12,000 youths aged 14–22, known as the NLSY79. In 1997, CHRR surveyed a new cohort of over 9,000 youths aged 12–16, called the NLSY97, and is continuing with yearly surveys of this cohort. The six major surveys contain a wealth of data on labor-force experience (e.g., labor-force and employment status, work history, and earnings) as well as investment in education and training, marital status, household composition and fertility, background material on respondents' parents, work-related attitudes, health, alcohol and drug use, and region of residence.

Each of these cohorts has been followed at varying intervals since the surveys' inceptions. For example, the Young Women were surveyed nineteen times between 1968 and 1997. The NLSY79 respondents were surveyed every year until 1994, when surveys in even-numbered years began. The Older Men were surveyed every year until 1983, and they or their widows were resurveyed in 1990. Data production for the Older Men and Young Men is complete; data production for the Mature Women and Young Women is ongoing biennially. In 1986 the NLS added a survey of the children of the NLSY79 cohort's women; that described the social, cognitive, and physiological development of those children and, given the longitudinal nature of the data on the mothers, allows an explanation of these child outcomes in terms of maternal background and current maternal characteristics. Surveys of the children occur in even-numbered years; this accumulated longitudinal database on child outcomes allows important inferences regarding the process of child development, with the numbers of children surveyed far exceeding those in most other sources. This additional resource has expanded NLSY79's usefulness to other disciplines, including psychology, and to other researchers interested in child development.

The NLS data sets are produced with the cooperation of CHRR, NORC (formerly the National Opinion Research Center) at the University of Chicago, and the U.S. Bureau of the Census. For example, for NLSY79, the CHRR takes responsibility for questionnaire construction, documentation, and data dissemination, while NORC has handled sample design, fieldwork, and data reduction. The Census Bureau has handled sample design, fieldwork, and data reduction for the four original cohorts. All data are available on CD-ROM from CHRR. Waves of data prior to 1993 are also available from ICPSR, as was noted above.

Social scientists from several disciplines, including sociology, economics, and industrial relations, have found the NLS to be a critical resource for the study of earnings and income attainment, human capital investment, job searches, fertility, racial and sex discrimination, and the determinants of labor supply. Inferences from these studies have been useful in regard to theory as well as policy formation. Other topics the data resource can usefully inform include family structure and processes, child outcomes, and aging processes. The CHRR estimates that by 1998 over 3,000 articles, books, working papers, and dissertations were produced using the NLS data. The 1998 *NLS Handbook* provides a wealth of detail regarding the designs of the surveys, survey procedures, variables, and CD availability. It also describes the extensive documentation available on the NLS data sets and lists references to key Web sites, including one that contains NLS publications. This handbook is indispensable for any researcher considering a secondary analysis using NLS data. The CHRR at Ohio State University disseminates the data and provides documentation and assistance to users with questions about the data sets. This summary gives a glimpse of the tremendous potential for secondary analyses of NLS data; this potential is multiplied many times over when one considers the number of other data sets available to researchers.

Because of the increase in resources devoted to survey research in sociology and related social sciences, the ICPSR holdings containing surveys of individuals have grown rapidly. However, ICPSR also archives data produced at varying levels of aggregation, thus facilitating secondary analyses in which the theoretically appropriate units of analysis are countries or organizations. For example, ICPSR archives the World Tables of Economic and Social Indicators, 1950–1992, provided by the World Bank. These data contain economic and social indicators from 183 countries, with the indicators including measures such as gross national product, value of imports and exports, gross national savings, value added across major industrial categories, net direct foreign investment, public

long-term debt, international reserves excluding gold, and gold holdings at the London market price. Demographic and social variables include population, total fertility rate, crude birthrate, percentage of the labor force in agriculture, percentage of the labor force that is female, and primary and secondary school enrollment rates. An older data set, also from the World Bank, contains similar measures from 1950 to 1981 as well as additional indicators not included in the data set covering the 1950–1992 period. Because these are also longitudinal data sets, there is the potential for pooling across time variation in these measures across the countries so that cross-sectional and longitudinal variations can be studied simultaneously.

ICPSR also maintains a small number of holdings useful for studying organizational processes. For example, a 1972 study of industrial location decisions obtained from the Economic Behavior Program of the Survey Research Center at the University of Michigan surveyed 173 industrial plants in Detroit, Chicago, and Atlanta. The interviewees were organizational informants such as president, vice president, general manager, and public relations director. The items included reasons for the location of the plant and the advantages and disadvantages of a location; other constructs measured included duration of plant operations, levels of sales and production, production problems, and plans for future expansion.

More recent arguments, however, have suggested that although sociology has invested considerably in surveys of individuals, it has invested insufficiently in surveys of organizations (Freeman 1986; see also Parcel et al. 1991). Kalleberg et al. (1996) present results from the National Study of Organizations, a National Science Foundation–sponsored study of a representative cross section of organizations that addresses their structures, contexts, and personnel practices. Although they demonstrate the utility of this design for addressing some questions regarding organizational functioning, these data cannot address issues of organizational change. A possible solution would be to produce a longitudinal database of organizations. The characteristics of a representative sample of organizations would be produced across time, analogous to the panel data sets of individual characteristics described above. Such a resource would enable researchers to study processes of organizational change with models that allow a clear causal ordering of variables. This type of resource also would permit analyses of pooled cross sections. Most important, the resource would allow organizational theories to be subjected to tests based on a representative sample of organizations, in contrast to the purposive samples that are used more frequently. To date, the resources have not been sufficient to approach the panel design suggested above. Clearly, the capacity to conduct secondary analyses at the organizational level is in its infancy relative to studies of individual-level processes and phenomena.

Finally, ICPSR also archives a variety of data sets that make possible historical analyses of social, economic, and political processes. For example, it archives the Annual Time Series Statistics for the United States, 1929–1968, which includes 280 variables for most of that period, although only 127 variables are available for the period 1947-1968. Available data include population characteristics, measures of political characteristics of the U.S. Congress, business and consumer expenditures, and expenditures by various federal government departments. ICPSR also archives Political Systems Performance Data for France, Sweden, and the United States, 1950–1965, in which the central constructs measured include size of public debt, gross national product (GNP), energy consumption, income tax rates, birthrates and death rates, labor force and unemployment, voting behavior, urbanization, and agricultural growth. Each of these historical data sources makes possible time series analyses of the macro-level phenomena they measure.

Additional major archives include the Roper Center for Public Opinion Research at the University of Connecticut and the Lewis Harris Data Center at the University of North Carolina at Chapel Hill. Kiecolt and Nathan (1985) provide additional information on the major archives, and Stewart (1984) outlines the extensive holdings in U.S. Government Document Depositories, especially the products of the U.S. Bureau of the Census. Other important archives include several in Europe with which ICPSR maintains a relationship, such as the Norwegian Social Science Data Services, the Australian Social Science Data Archives, and the Zentralarchiv far empirische Sozialforschung (ZA) at the University of Cologne. There is the potential for member institutions to obtain from ICPSR data contained in those local archives as well. The International Social Survey Program (ISSP) has worked toward coordinating survey research internationally by asking common questions cross-nationally in given years, facilitating cross cultural analyses of social phenomena. For example, in 1990 social surveys in Austria, West Germany, Great Britain, Hungary, Ireland, Israel, Italy, the Netherlands, and Norway all included questions on work, including the consequences of unemployment, union activities, working conditions, and preferred job characteristics. A comparable module in 1987 focused on social inequality in Australia, Austria, West Germany, Great Britain, Hungary, Italy, and the United States. The 1993 module focused on nature, the environment, recycling, and the role of science in solving environmental problems. Data from the ISSP are available from ICPSR.

THE NATURE OF SECONDARY DATA ANALYSIS

The key advantage of secondary data analysis is also the key disadvantage: The researcher gains access to a wealth of information, usually far in excess of what he or she could have produced with individual resources, but in exchange must accept the myriad operational decisions that the investigators who produced the data have made. On the positive side, the researcher frequently is able to take advantage of a national sample of respondents or data produced on national populations when individual resources would have supported only local primary data production. The numbers of cases available in secondary resources often far outstrip the sample sizes individual investigators could have afforded to produce; these large sample sizes enhance the precision of parameter estimates and allow forms of multivariate analyses that smaller sample sizes preclude. A secondary analyst also can take advantage of the significant expertise concentrated in the large survey organizations that produce data sets for secondary analysis. This collective expertise usually exceeds that of any single investigator. Despite these advantages, the researcher must carefully match the requirements of the research project to the characteristics of the data set. When the match is close, the use of secondary data will enhance the research effort by making use of existing resources and taking advantage of the time, money, and expertise of others devoted to data production. If the match is poor, the research project will fail because the data will not address the questions posed.

Because many secondary analyses are conducted on survey data, effective use of secondary survey sources frequently depends on knowledge of sample design, question wording, questionnaire construction, and measurement. Ideally, the researcher conceptualizes precisely what he or she wishes to do with the data in the analysis, since analytic requirements must be met by existing data. If the research questions posed are longitudinal in nature, the researcher must be sure that the survey questions are measured at time points that mirror the researcher's assumptions of causal order.

The researcher also must be certain that the survey samples all the respondents relevant to the problem. For example, analyses of racial differences in socioeconomic outcomes must use data sets in which racial minorities are oversampled to ensure adequate numbers of cases for analysis. The researcher also must be certain that a data set contains sufficient cases for the analysis she or he intends to perform. Kiecolt and Nathan (1985) stress the challenges for trend and cross-cultural studies that result from changes in sampling procedures over time. For example, suppose a researcher wants to ascertain whether more people support a voucher system for public education in 2000 compared with 1990. Changes in the sampling frame over the decade may introduce variations into survey responses that would not otherwise exist. These variations can be in either direction, and hypotheses regarding their direction are a function of the nature of sampling changes. Gallup surveys have increased their coverage of noninstitutionalized civilian adult populations over time, with the result that there has been an artifactual decrease in the levels of education they report (Kiecolt and Nathan 1985, pp. 62–63), since the later surveys have progressively included groups with lower levels of schooling. Sampling changes also can occur over time because of changes in geographic boundaries. Cities change boundaries owing to annexation of areas, and Metropolitan Statistical Areas (MSAs, formerly Standard Metropolitan Statistical Areas [SMSAs]) are created over time as increased numbers of counties meet the population and economic criteria for defining MSAs.

The most common problem in conducting secondary analyses, however, occurs in the questionnaire coverage of items needed to construct appropriate measures. It is likely that the original survey was constructed with one purpose and asked adequate numbers and forms of questions regarding the constructs central to that problem but gave only cursory attention to other items. A secondary researcher must evaluate carefully whether the questions that involve his or her area of central interest are adequate for measurement and for analytic tasks. The biggest fear of a secondary researcher is that some variables needed for proper model specification have been omitted. Omitted variables pose potentially severe problems of misspecification in estimating the parameters of the variables that are included in the models. In these cases the researcher must decide whether an adequate proxy (or substitute) variable exists on the data set, whether the research problem can be reformulated so that omission of that construct is less critical, or whether the initially chosen data set is unsuitable and another must be sought. Researchers can also purchase time on major social surveys such as the GSS administered by NORC. This strategy enables researchers with adequate financial resources to be certain that the questions needed to investigate the issues of interest to them will be included in a national survey. This strategy mixes primary data production with secondary analysis of a multipurpose data set. The entire data resource then becomes available to other secondary analysts.

Other challenges for secondary analysts occur as a function of the particular form of secondary analysis used. For example, Kiecolt and Nathan (1985) note that survey researchers who produce series of cross sections of data that are useful in studying trends may "improve" the wording of questions over time. In regard to the problem of voucher systems in public education, the researcher may observe increased percentages of survey respondents favoring this option over the period covered by the surveys but still may have difficulty eliminating the possibility that question wording in the later survey or surveys may have encouraged a more positive response. Such changes also can occur if the wording of the question remains the same over time but the nature of the response categories changes. Secondary analysts who conduct cross-cultural comparisons must be sensitive to the fact that the same question can mean different things in different cultures, thus interfering with their ability to compare the same social phenomenon cross-culturally.

Dale, et al. (1988) note that in-depth studies of specific populations may be most realistic with national samples that provide sufficient cases for analyses of the subgroups while allowing the researcher to place those data within a broader empirical context. It is also possible that surveys produced by different survey organizations will produce different results even when question wording, response categories, and sampling procedures remain the same (Kiecolt and Nathan 1985, p. 67). A secondary analyst must be certain that the survey organization or individual responsible for producing the data set exercised appropriate care in constructing the data resource. As was noted above, detailed familiarity with the documentation describing the data set production procedures is essential, as is a codebook indicating frequencies on categorical variables, appropriate ranges for continuous variables, and codes for missing data.

There is often an interactive nature to the process of conducting a secondary data analysis. While the researcher's theoretical interests may be reasonably well formulated when he or she identifies a useful data set, the variables present in the data resource may suggest additional empirical opportunities of theoretical interest that the researcher had not previously considered. Also, familiarity with data resources can facilitate the formulation of empirical investigations that otherwise might not be initiated. Once a researcher is familiar with the features of a particular secondary source, accessing additional variables for the analysis of a related problem may require less investment than would accessing a new data resource. However, there is general agreement that data availability should never dictate the nature of a research question. Although it is legitimate for a researcher to use his or her awareness of data resources to recognize that analyses of problems of long-standing interest are now empirically possible, "data dredging" has a deservedly negative connotation and does not result in the advancement of social science. Hyman's (1972) classic treatment of secondary analyses of survey data richly chronicles the experiences of a number of sociologists as they interactively considered the matching of theoretical interests and data availability in formulating and conducting secondary analyses. He also describes a number of ways in which secondary analysts can configure existing data to test hypotheses.

Recent developments in technology have streamlined several steps in secondary analyses that formerly were time-consuming and labor-intensive. Many secondary data sets are now available on CD-ROM (compact disk-read only memory); the NLS data discussed above are only one example. With many computers having attached CD readers, analysts can read the disks and extract from them the variables and cases they wish to study. Often the disks also contain searching devices that enable researchers to locate variables of interest easily. These "search engines" simultaneously enable analysts to select a sample and obtain the variables needed on each case. These capabilities totally bypass older technologies involving nine-track tapes containing data. In tape-based technologies, analysts had to write original computer programs to extract the needed variables and cases. A typical analyst no longer depends on a centralized computing facility for storing, mounting, and reading magnetic tapes.

The next steps in secondary analysis differ only slightly from the steps that investigators who produce primary data undertake. In both cases, data must be cleaned to remove coding errors that might result in erroneous findings. Similarly, both investigators need to address problems with missing data. The primary data producer is close enough to the actual data production not only to identify such problems but also to resolve many of them appropriately. For example, if the researcher is studying a single organization and notes that a respondent has failed to report his or her earnings, the researcher, knowing the respondent's occupation, may be able to obtain data from the organization that approximates that respondent's earnings closely. The secondary analyst would not have access to the original organization but might approximate the missing data by searching for other respondents who reported the same occupation but who also reported earnings. Variations on this theme involve the imputation of missing data by using mathematical functions of observed data to derive reasonable inferences about values that are missing (Little and Rubin 1987, 1990; Jinn and Sedransk 1989).

Both types of investigator have to be familiar with the descriptive properties of their data. For a primary investigator, observing distributions of respective variables as well as their central tendencies should be an outgrowth of data production itself. A secondary analyst has less familiarity with the data someone else produces but is under the same obligation to become familiar with the descriptive properties of the data in a detailed way. For both researchers, good decisions involving measurement of variables and model specification for multivariate analyses depend on knowledge of the descriptive properties of the data.

Within the respective multipurpose data sets, research traditions often arise from the sometimes unique suitability of certain resources for addressing given problems. These traditions derive from the fact that several investigators have access to the data simultaneously, a feature that distinguishes secondary data analysis from analyses undertaken by different primary investigators, each of whom has a unique data set. For example, in the late 1980s and into the 1990s, the NLSY79 with Mother and Child Supplements was virtually unique in combining a large sample size, longitudinal data on maternal familial and work histories, observed child outcomes, and oversamplings of racial minorities. Problems tracing the impact of maternal events on child outcomes are addressable with this data resource in a way that they were not with other resources. Investigators with an interest in these issues use the data and exchange information regarding strategies for measuring constructs and data analysis and then exchange their findings. Over time, bodies of findings emerge from common data sources where the findings are contributed by a number of secondary investigators, although the particular problems, theoretical frameworks, and empirical strategies represented in each one may differ markedly. As was suggested above, multipurpose data sets frequently allow secondary analyses by researchers from several disciplines. The products of these investigations bear the stamps of their respective disciplines. In addition, the NLSY79 with Mother and Child Supplements has served as a model for the Michigan Panel Study of Income Dynamics (PSID) in its 1997 Child Development Supplement on the PSID respondents. This new data resource, which combines longitudinal data on parents and developmental assessments of children from birth to age 12, will enable replication of key findings produced with the NLSY79 child data set as well as the production of new findings. For example, both data sets contain age-appropriate cognitive assessments for children, permitting findings produced with the NLSY79 child data set to be replicated with the PSID Child Development Supplement. The PSID, however, contains data on how children spend their time. These variables should allow researchers to understand the effects of children's time use on several developmental outcomes, something that the NLSY79 child data do not permit.

The wealth of secondary data sources also permits investigators to use more than one data source to pursue a particular line of inquiry. No single data set is perfect. Researchers can analyze several data sets, all with key measures but each with unique strengths, to check interpretations of findings and evaluate alternative explanations. McLanahan and Sandefur (1994) use this approach in their study of the effects of single parenthood on the offspring's academic success and social adjustment. Their data sources include the NLSY79, the PSID, and the High School and Beyond Study. The result is a stronger set of findings than those which could have been produced with any one of those sources.

Another model for conducting secondary research is suggested by researchers who use census data produced by the U.S. Department of Commerce. Census holdings cover not only information on the general U.S. population but also data on businesses, housing units, governments, and agricultural enterprises. Researchers who use these sources singly or in combination must be familiar with the questionnaires used to produce the data and with the relevant features of sample coverage. While some census data are available on machine-readable tape, other data exist only in printed form. In these cases, the researcher must configure the needed data into a form suitable for analyses, in many cases a rectangular file in which cases form row entries and variables form column entries. Data produced on cities from the County and City Data Books, for example, allow a variety of analyses that involve the relationships among urban social and economic characteristics. In these analyses, the unit of analysis is probably an aggregate unit such as a county or city, illustrating the applicability of secondary analysis to problems conceptualized at a level of aggregation higher than that of the individual.

Another advantage of secondary analyses is the potential for those most interested in a particular set of findings to replicate them by using the same data and to introduce additional variables or alternative operationalizations as a method for evaluating the robustness of the first secondary investigator's findings. A classic example is Beck et al.'s 1978 investigation of differences in earnings attainment processes by economic sector. Hauser's (1980) reanalysis of those data suggested that most of the differences in sectoral earnings reported in the original study were a function of coding decisions for low-earnings respondents, since the differences disappeared when the code for low earnings was changed. Despite this criticism, the impact of the original investigation has been enormous, with many additional investigators exploring the structure and implications of economic sectors. The point, of course, is that such debate is more likely to occur when researchers have access to common data sets, although gracious investigators often lend their data resources to interested critics. Hauser (1980) acknowledges that Beck et al. shared their original data, although he could have obtained the original data set from ICPSR.

Secondary data sets can be augmented with additional data to enrich the data resource and allow the derivation of additional theoretical and empirical insights. Contextual analysis, or the investigation of whether social context influences social outcomes, is a key example. Parcel and Mueller (1983) used the 1975 and 1976 panels from the PSID to study racial and sex differences in earnings attainment. To evaluate the impact of occupational, industrial, and local labor-market conditions on workers' earnings, they augmented the PSID data with archival data from U.S. Census and Dictionary of Occupational Titles sources that were based on the occupations, industries, and local markets of respective PSID respondents. Illustrative contextual indicators included occupational complexity, industrial profitability, and local-market manufacturing-sector productivity. Analyses then suggested how these contextual, as well as individual-level, indicators affected workers' earnings differently depending on ascriptive statuses. Computer software is now available to correct for problems in estimating models that use contextual data.

The potential for many sociologists to use secondary analysis to conduct studies of theoretical and practical importance probably has contributed to a change in productivity standards in sociology, particularly in certain subfields. The fact that certain issues can be addressed by using existing data can result in enormous savings in time relative to the time that would be required if primary data had to be produced. Research-oriented departments either implicitly or explicitly take this into account in assigning rewards such as salaries, tenure, and promotion. The potential for secondary analyses thus may create pressures toward increased scientific productivity; whether these pressures work generally for the good of social science or against it may be a matter of debate.

It is undeniable that progress in addressing some of the most important problems in social science has been facilitated greatly by the existence of multipurpose data sets and secondary resources. It is also true that the resources needed to produce and disseminate these data are considerable and that the existence and continuation of these resources are vulnerable to changes in political climate and priorities when those priorities influence resource allocation. It is critical that such decisions on resource allocation, particularly those made at the level of the federal government, recognize the important role that secondary resources have played in furthering both basic social science and applications informing social policy.

(SEE ALSO: *Census, Social Indicators, Survey Research*)

REFERENCES

Beck, E. M., Patrick Horan, and Charles W. Tolbert II 1978 "Stratification in a Dual Economy: A Sectoral Model of Earnings Determination." *American Sociological Review* 43:704–720.

Dale, Angela, Sara Arber, and Michael Proctor 1988 *Doing Secondary Analysis*. London: Unwin Hyman.

Freeman, John 1986 "Data Quality and the Development of Organizational Social Science: An Editorial Essay." *Administrative Science Quarterly* 31:298–303.

Guide to Resources and Services, 1996–1997. Ann Arbor, Mich.: Interuniversity Consortium for Political and Social Research, University of Michigan.

Hauser, Robert 1980 "Comment on 'Stratification in a Dual Economy.'" *American Sociological Review* 45:702–712.

Hyman, Herbert H. 1972 *Secondary Analysis of Sample Surveys: Principles, Procedures, and Potentialities.* New York: Wiley.

Jinn, J. H. and J. Sedransk 1989 "Effect on Secondary Data Analysis of Common Imputation Methods." *Sociological Methodology* 19:213–241.

Kalleberg, Arne L., David Knoke, Peter V. Marsden, and Joe L. Spaeth 1996 *Organizations in America: Analyzing Their Structures and Human Resource Practices.* Thousand Oaks, Calif.: Sage.

Kiecolt, K. Jill, and Laura E. Nathan 1985 "Secondary Analysis of Survey Data." Sage University Paper Series on Quantitative Applications in the Social Sciences, series no. 07-053. Beverly Hills, Calif.: Sage.

Little, Roderick J. A. and Donald B. Rubin 1987 *Statistical Analysis with Missing Data.* New York: John Wiley and Sons.

—— 1990 "The Analysis of Social Science Data with Missing Values." Pp. 375–409 in John Fox and J. Scott Long, eds., *Modern Methods of Data Analysis.* Newbury Park, Calif.: Sage Publications.

McLanahan, Sara, and Gary Sandefur 1994 *Growing Up with a Single Parent: What Hurts, What Helps.* Cambridge, Mass.: Harvard University Press.

NLS Handbook 1998. Columbus, Ohio: Center for Human Resource Research, Ohio State University.

Parcel, Toby L., and Charles W. Mueller 1983 *Ascription and Labor Markets: Race and Sex Differences in Earnings.* New York: Academic Press.

——, Robert L. Kaufman, and Leeann Jolly 1991 "Going Up the Ladder: Multiplicity Sampling to Create Linked Macro-Micro Organizational Samples." *Sociological Methodology, 1991.* 21:43–80.

Stewart, David W. 1984 *Secondary Research: Information Sources and Methods.* Beverly Hills, Calif.: Sage.

U.S. Department of Commerce [various years] *County and City Data Book.* Washington, D.C.: U.S. Government Printing Office.

TOBY L. PARCEL

SECULARIZATION

Secularization is the process by which the sacred gives way to the secular, whether in matters of personal faith, institutional practice, and political power. It involves a transition in which things once revered become ordinary, the sanctified becomes mundane, and the otherworldly loses its prefix. Whereas the term "secularity" refers to a state of sacredlessness and "secularism" is the ideology devoted to that state, secularization is a historical dynamic that may occur gradually or suddenly and may be replaceable (if not reversible).

The concept of secularization has been both an organizing theme and a source of contention among scholars of religion since the beginning of the European "Enlightenment" in the seventeenth century. One might expect an increasing consensus on a matter so long on the scholarly agenda, but discord has crescendoed in recent years. Secularization has taken on different meanings in different camps. It matters whether the reference is to religion's displacement, decline, or change; to the sacred at the level of the individual, the institution, the community, or the culture; or to a pattern that is long term, linear, and inevitable or short term, cyclical, and contingent.

The object of this essay is to disentangle both the issues and the combatants. After describing the early protagonists and more recent sociological proponents of secularization, this article considers recent arguments against their theses. In the face of a seemingly intractable conflict, it is important to describe the issues in dispute. This will lead to a consideration of secularization and sacralization as opposite phenomena that actually are more mutually linked than mutually exclusive.

EARLY AND RECENT CONCEPTIONS OF SECULARIZATION

Any conception of the sacred is likely to engender skeptical—if often marginal—detractors. While both the process and the thesis of secularization have precursors early in Western history, it was the Enlightenment that provided their first codification.

The term "secularization" dates back to France in the mid-seventeenth century. The first high priest of this antichurch was the French bourgeois intellectual Voltaire (1694–1778). A professed "deist" whose belief in impersonal forces stood in sharp contrast to "theistic" conceptions of a personal God, Voltaire railed against the Catholicism's superstitions and ecclesiastical trappings (Voltaire 1756). However, Voltaire was not the most materialist figure of his day and he was distinguished more by the expression of his views than by their substance, including his sense that the end of religion was near, possibly in his lifetime. The main thrust of his views was shared by many Europeans and Americans, including Benjamin Franklin and Thomas Jefferson.

The prophets of secularization soon multiplied. By the second half of the nineteenth century, they included the father or at least namer of "sociology," the French positivist Comte (1852). Comte's conception of a future that belonged more to the social sciences than to religion was shared by Britain's Spencer (1874), whose sales rivaled those of Dickens. Marx ([1844] 1963) envisioned a denarcotized future once the masses learned the real secret of their misery, substituted class consciousness for false consciousness, and exchanged otherworldly sighs for this-worldly action.

Weber and Durkheim continued the tradition in the first two decades of the twentieth century. Both provided key statements about the importance of religion: Weber's "Protestant ethic" as a precondition of capitalism and Durkheim's conception of religion as the latent worship of society. However, neither was personally religious, and both envisioned a secularized future without predicting it directly.

For Weber ([1905] 1993), secularization was an implication of the "rationalization" that was uniquely characteristic of the West. He was ambivalent about the results. On the one hand, he appreciated its cultural underpinnings of everything from capitalism and bureaucracy to architecture and music. On the other hand, he wrote in the tradition of German historiography and a concern for the spirit of every age. Weber lamented a dark side of rationality that would lead to secularized disenchantment. Toward the end of *The Protestant Ethic and the Spirit of Capitalism*, he commends the cynical sentiment:

Specialists without spirit, sensualists without heart; this nullity imagines that it has attained a level of civilization never before achieved.
([1905] 1993, p. 182)

Durkheim worked selectively within the tradition of Comte and French positivism and therefore was more positive about secularization. Durkheim (1961) was optimistic about a secular morality and an autonomous ethic for society. Although religious beliefs would be displaced by science, the sense of society as a sacred collectivity would remain. On the eve of World War I, he described France as undergoing a period of "moral mediocrity," but he was certain that it would soon be revitalized through a sense of "collective effervescence" and sacred renewal, possibly independently of conventional religion (Durkheim 1912).

By the middle of the twentieth century, secularization had become one of the master motifs of the social sciences. It was at least implicit in major transitional distinctions such as Durkheim's "mechanical versus organic solidarity" Toennies's ([1887] 1957) "Gemeinschaft" versus "Gesellschaft" societies, and Redfield's (1953) "folk" versus "urban" cultures. At the same time, prophecies had given way to theories as sociology began to develop more nuanced versions of secularization. The 1960s produced a bumper crop of new works, among the most influential of which were Berger's *The Sacred Canopy* (1967) and Wilson's *Religion in Secular Society* (1966).

Berger dealt with both the rise and the decline of religion. Having described religion's importance as a source of meaning for a cosmos that is often inchoate, he then noted factors involved in religion's erosion. These included privatization, pluralism, and a new religious marketplace, all of which contributed to a secularization he defined as "the process by which sectors of society and culture are removed from the domination of religious institutions and symbols" (1967, p. 107). Berger did not place all the blame for the decline of religion on external factors. Liberal clergy and theologians were often ahead of the process in diluting religion to avoid conflicts with a secular society.

If Berger's conception of secularization suggests society pulling away from a still-religious core, Wilson conveys a scenario in which religion recedes to the margins and suffers a diminution of influence. For Wilson, secularization is "the process whereby religious institutions, actions, and consciousness lose their social significance" (1966, p. xiv). However, Wilson was aware of a profound difference between the declining influence of the established churches and the surging growth of sectarian movements (Wilson 1998): As society becomes more complex, all its institutions become more differentiated from each other and have more autonomy but less influence. However, the process does not occur equally, and traditional institutions such as religion are more affected by these changes. Often seen as part of a larger process of "modernization," differentiation has been a prominent theme among functionalists such as Parsons (1977) and Luhmann (1982) and neofunctionalists such as Bell (1976) and Habermas (1988).

Differentiation takes different forms and exacts different tolls. The Belgian scholar Dobbelaere (1981) draws a parallel between secularization and the French term "laicization," which Durkheim and others used to denote a loss of priestly control, with a consequent decanonization of religion. While developing the concept for European settings, Dobbelaere draws two sets of distinctions: between the processes of differentiation, decline, and change (1981) and between the levels of the individual, the organization, and the society (Dobbelaere 1985).

By this time, secularization had become a major priority for social scientists examining religion. In analyzing the United States, Fenn (1979) stresses that secularization involves a blurring rather than a sharpening of the boundaries between the sacred and the secular; more recently, Fenn refers to secularization as the "domestication of charisma" (1993). Meanwhile, the concept is at least a subtheme of Bellah et al. (1985) in a work that depicts the community's losing struggle with individualism, perhaps the ultimate form of differentiation at the personal level.

Roof and McKinney (1987) describe a similar pattern as a "new voluntarism" that has displaced old denominational loyalties. Similarly, Wuthnow (1988) notes how other forces of differentiation have shifted religious action away from the denominations and congregations and in the direction of "special-purpose groups" whose single-issue agendas are often more a reflection of political morality than of religious doctrine or theology. Wuthnow also describes a differentiation between America's liberal and conservative "civil religions" and the rise of a third national faith in the form of secular technology.

Finally, Chaves (1993) documents the emergence of differentiated "dual structures" within denominations. This duality represents a split between declining "religious" authority and increasing secular "agency" authority. This formulation is consistent with other traditions of organizational analysis in religion, including the classic distinction between "sects" and "churches" and the process by which the purity of sects is compromised by their transformation into accommodating churches.

SECULARIZATION MYTHOLOGIZED

Originally, the detractors of secularization were defenders of the faith. More recently, they have portrayed themselves as critics of a very different faith, which they have played a large role in constructing. Recent years have seen the attribution of a full-blown "secularization thesis" that is not so much a series of questions for investigation as a definitive answer with all the qualities of an epochal narrative. Here the older eighteenth-century prophetic vision of secularization has been substituted for more recent and less sweeping versions. Secularization is presented as a tenuous article of faith that is suspended between two mythical points. The first point involves the fiction of a deeply and universally religious past; the second involves the conceit of a religionless present and future (Stark 1992). Thus, secularization has been recast as a sweeping saga that serves as a sort of antisacred doctrine, in its own right—though it is important to bear in mind that it is the critics of secularization who have both popularized this version and savaged it.

The British anthropologist Douglas (1982) was among the first to chastise proponents of secularization for imagining a mythical past against which the present inevitably comes up short. In her case, the past involved those simple, undifferentiated societies studied by anthropologists but used by others as convenient foils. Thus, even here religious piety and participation are not always deep or universal. If these societies are the beginnings of the neoevolutionary process of modernization, their religion has inconvenient similarities with the religion of complex societies toward the end of the process.

Stark (1998) elaborates this point for early Western societies. To the extent that a secularizing trend depends on a contrast with a pious ancient and medieval Europe, Stark cites evidence suggesting that this past is also mythical. Once one looks beyond the public displays of ecclesiastical officialdom, the masses appear to be antichurch, if not antireligious. Attitudes toward organized faith were conspicuous for their alienation, corruption, and raucousness. Many "Christian" nations founded in the late middle ages were only inches deep as surface monopolies atop an impious base.

What of the myth of religious demise? Martin (1969) was among the first to find religion in the midst of putative nonreligion, in this case in "highly secularized" Great Britain. In fact, Martin called for dropping the term "secularization" because of the confusion it had elicited, though ten years later he adopted the semantic fashion by publishing *A General Theory of Secularization* (1978).

Stark has also been a relentless critic of the second myth, and he has had company. His book with Finke, *The Churching of America* (Finke and Stark 1992), uses actual and reconstructed church membership data to argue that the real "winners" over the past two centuries have been conservative churches while liberal (and more secular) churches have been the "losers." Critics note that the work is not without problems; for example, its thesis refers to rates of growth and decline rather than absolute size, and it assumes that membership is a reliable measure of general religiosity over time (Demerath 1992).

Many other scholars have noted the continued vitality of religion in America. Warner's "new paradigm" (1993) provides a systematic description of how the American case may differ from the European scene that spawned secularization theory. Meanwhile, Stark has taken his methods and "market" model of religion abroad. He and the economist Iannaccone (1994) developed a nonmonopolistic, "supply-side" interpretation of European religion, arguing that its death and secularization have been greatly exaggerated. This argument has had both supporters (Davie 1994; Swatos 1997) and detractors (Bruce 1995; Dobbelaere 1993; Wilson 1998).

Meanwhile, the dispute over secularization is not restricted to the West. In fact, the Western version of the debate is comparatively innocuous because it is confined largely to scholars removed from political conflicts and because the politics of religion has generally been laid to rest except in a few cases, such as the tragic violence in Northern Ireland and the anticlimactic decision of Sweden to sever state ties with the Lutheran Church as of 2000. Once one leaves the West, however (Demerath 2000), assessments of secularization and secularity have become volatile public issues exacerbated by the ideological conflict between forthright pro- and antisecularists.

Moving from Poland and eastern Europe through the remains of the Soviet Union to Afghanistan, from the Balkans through Turkey and into Iran, from Algeria through Egypt to Israel, from Pakistan through India to Sri Lanka, and from Indonesia through China to Japan, one sees countries whose national identities are being defined by a prolonged conflict over secularization (Juergensmeyer 1993). In each case, the struggle involves less one religious group versus another than religion generally versus secular alternatives.

In addition to what might be termed a "bottom-up" process of seeping secularization, there are instances of a "top-down" coercive scenario, and the two are not mutually exclusive. The former Soviet Union, Turkey, and China illustrate the latter process through political systems headed by Lenin, Ataturk, and Mao Tse-Tung and their followers, respectively. This structurally imposed secularization had cultural effects as specifically defined state rituals became common alternatives to traditional religious ceremonies. However, in all these countries, traditional religion remains in evidence in the private sphere and occasionally bursts into the public arena.

Although there are examples of externally coerced secularization (e.g., the U.S. insistence on Japan's abolishing "State Shinto" after World War II), secularization generally takes a far less direct form. Consider India as a case in point. Over the centuries, the south Asian subcontinent has given the world Hinduism, Buddhism, Jainism, and Sikhism, but from the early sixteenth century until the mid-twentieth century, it was dominated by outside rulers representing first Islam in the Moghul period and then Christianity under the British "raj." When independence was won in 1947, the partitioning of Pakistan and India created two states, one Muslim and the other dominantly Hindu. The religious resorting involved a massive cross-migration as long-time residents of each area moved to the other so that they could live among their coreligionists. The violence that ensued is estimated to have left from 250,000 to 500,000 people dead.

Religious conflict has continued in both areas, but in each case, it is not simply one religion against another but also religion versus secularity.

After independence, India instituted a national government that followed the Western model of a secular and thus religiously neutral state. However, after a half century, a series of violent conflicts between Hindus, Muslims, and Sikhs have left a cloud over India's state secularity. In the 1990s, the dominant and secularist Congress Party lost its voting plurality to the Hindu nationalist Bharatiya Janata Party (BJP). Momentum is gathering on behalf of a Hindu state that would reflect the country's Hindu majority. Nor is the movement confined to right-wing religious zealots. A number of India's most prominent intellectuals have entered the fray and produced a series of strident exchanges (Nandy 1990; Madan 1998 Beteille 1994). For many people, the commitment to state secularity has ebbed; paradoxically, secularism has been secularized.

FINDING A MUDDLED GROUND

Today it is common to hear that secularization has been categorically "disproved" and that anyone who still uses the term is more of an ideological antediluvian than an *au currant* scholar. Yet one must be wary of throwing out the baby with a bathwater both drawn and drained by the critics themselves. And certainly one must always be suspicious of prophets who predict the vindication of their own ideology. Most of the early visionaries of secularization and a disproportionate number of the theorists who have followed have been personally nonreligious, if not necessarily antireligious. At the same time, the ranks of the antisecularizationists have included a number of theorists with personal religious loyalties. Although a scholarly discipline should provide methods to avoid or transcend these biases, history indicates otherwise.

A full review of the empirical literature on the secularization debate is beyond the scope of this article, and it is not feasible to conduct an investigation that would constitute a critical test. However, this is not an issue that can be settled empirically. Statistical arguments will be irrelevant until a series of pressing ideological and conceptual issues are confronted.

One must decide what to test before deciding how to test it. Because the two great myths attributed to the secularizationists by their critics are

by their nature overblown, they are not hard to puncture. Debating the matter at such mythical levels lends an all-or-nothing quality to the dispute: Insofar as the thesis fails to document a shift from all to nothing, it is suspect. However, no recent secularization theorists stake their claim in those terms.

It is not difficult to refute the first myth of secular dynamics concerning a seamless and universal religiosity in tribal settings and in the historical past. However, for the past to be more religious, it is not necessary for it to be either consistently or totally so. For a society to have been dominated by religion as political power, it need not have been more religious at the level of the individual and *vice versa*. Even at that level, of the individual, the past may be more religious in terms of personal piety and belief without necessarily being more religious in terms of formal institutional participation. Also, to say that one group or society's past was more religious than its present is not necessarily to say that another's must be the same. Finally, there are multiple pasts, none of which need be linear in their linkages.

Meanwhile, the second myth of secular dynamics is even easier for critics of secularization to deflate. The notion of religion's actual death and disappearance has shifted from the sublime to the ridiculous, especially in the formulations of eighteenth- and nineteenth-century figures, some of whom foresaw the end in their own lifetimes (Stark 1998). Somehow religion survived the eighteenth and nineteenth centuries, not to mention the twentieth. Again, however, it is not clear that this is either necessary or sufficient to disprove a more nuanced conception of secularization. Today it is common to reject the concept of secularization simply because religion persists, but mere persistence masks a host of questions concerning religion's changing terms and circumstances.

The "secularization thesis" with a mythical beginning and a mythical end is erroneous, but it is a largely noninstructive error akin to "denying all climatology and the particular hypothesis of global warming because we have not yet been burned to a crisp and the nights do, after all, still get cooler" (Demerath 1998b, p. 9).

Clearly secularization as a textured social process remains a fruitful concept. In fact, once the focus shifts to a less extreme version, the consensus widens considerably. Consider two recent remarks from arch critic Stark:

> *This refers to a decline in the social power of once-dominant religious institutions whereby other social institutions, especially political and educational institutions, have escaped from prior religious domination. If this were all that secularization means, there would be nothing to argue about. Everyone must agree that, in contemporary Europe, for example, Catholic bishops have less political power than they once possessed, and the same is true of Lutheran and Anglican bishops. . . . Nor are primary aspects of public life any longer suffused with religious symbols, rhetoric, or ritual. (1998, pp. 4–5)*
>
> *Of course, religion changes. Of course, there is more religious participation and even greater belief in the supernatural at some times and places than in others, just as religious organizations have more secular power in some times and places than in others. Of course, doctrines change–Aquinas was not Augustine, and both would find heresy in the work of Avery Dulles. But change does not equate with decline. (1998, p. 29)*

These statements greatly narrow the gap between secularization's advocates and one key antagonist. For many of the former, Stark's first passage suggests a battlefield conversion, though it is not a new position for him (Stark and Bainbridge 1985). While the second remark is correct in that change and declension are not identical, the implied invitation to deconstruct the two should be welcomed.

There is little question that secularization has come to connote decline. Whether in its long-range mythical or short-term process form, secularization posits some variant of religious erosion, if not extinction. However, all these versions represent a myopic and one-sided perspective compared to the alternative that follows.

PARADOXES OF SECULARIZATION AND SACRALIZATION

At a time when work on secularization might be expected to yield a consensually validated paradigm (Tschannen 1991), it is far closer to producing a new set of divisive paradoxes. Much of this conflict results from the terms at issue. Both "secular" and "sacred" are mutually referential in that each makes a statement about the other. To be secular is to be nonsacred; to be sacred is to transcend and transform the secular. The same is true when one shifts from semantics to social processes. Just as an object must have been sacred for it be subsequently secularized, it must have been secular for it to be subsequently "sacralized." Just as secularization marks a decline of the sacred, sacralization denotes an increase in the sacred in one form or another and at one level or another.

However, linking the processes of secularization and sacralization can have paradoxical results. The following eight propositions can serve as examples:

1. Religious revivals and "great awakenings" require previous eras of religious decline and secular "naps." American religious history has been charted in terms of its eighteenth-, nineteenth-, and possibly twentieth-century awakenings (McLoughlin 1978), but an opposite focus has equal merit (May 1949; Erikson 1966; Turner 1985). It is the combination of the two that establishes the basic rhythm of a country's religious history.

2. Modernization may lead to both secularization and sacralization. The grand narrative of the secularization thesis is that religion beats a steady and linear retreat in the face of mounting modernization. There is considerable truth to this but also some half-truth. This is what Berger referred to in recanting some of his earlier writing on secularization (Berger 1997). Modernization often leads to forms of secularization, but those often spark a sacralizing response—one that uses the means of modernity to protest the ends of modernity. This characterizes "fundamentalisms" everywhere, whether in the original Christian version in the United States or in the Islamic and Hindu variants around the global girdle of religious extremism. As was noted earlier, many countries demonstrate religion's continuing presence, but these countries also bear witness to the incursions of secularity as a perceived threat to religious interests. If either religion or secularity

3. The rise of a vital "religious market-place" is evidence of both secularization and sacralization. An increase in religious competition often reflects the decline of religion's structural monopolies and/or cultural hegemonies. Religious dominations once taken for granted are now subject to doubt and dismissal, yet the new consumer's mentality may involve more stained-glass window shopping than long-term buying (actually joining a church). The debate over changing patterns of religiosity turns on this point, as does a current dispute over the significance of religious "switching" in the United States (Demerath and Yang 1998a).

4. Because movements that go against the societal grain often create more friction than do trends that go with it, one must be careful not to mistake the sacred exceptions for the secular rule. It is tempting to interpret the flames of a small religious movement as being more important than the smoking embers of its larger and more secularized context. In the same spirit, one must be wary of confusing growth rates with size. Both have their place, but even small, conservative religious movements with high growth rates may be marginal to the larger population and culture. As an example, see the "winners" and "losers" cited by Finke and Stark (1992).

5. Sacred manifestations may reflect secular forces, and vice versa. The relationship between any form of behavior and the motivations behind it is problematic. Standard indicators of religiosity such as civil religious loyalty, church membership, church attendance, and religious belief are all subject to myriad interpretations, not all of which are unambiguously sacred (Demerath 1998a; Haddaway et al. 1993). It may be more the case that the civil is religious than that the religious is civil: Church membership and attendance reflect a variety of sacred and secular meanings that vary across a population and across time, and affirming a religious belief may be less a matter of cognitive conviction than of cultural affiliation and continuity. Even the various "fundamentalist" movements may not be as uniformly or fanatically "religious" as they are often portrayed. Many of their members have a predominantly secular agenda that religion legitimizes (Demerath 2000). Similarly, a withdrawal from conventional religious frameworks may coexist with a more privatized faith (see the "little voice" of the pseudonymous Sheila Larson in Bellah et al. 1985, p. 221). Finally, there are any number of conventionally secular commitments that take on sacred valences for their devotees (see below).

6. Moderate secularization can be a prophylactic against ultimate secularization. Changing social conditions require changing forms of the sacred. Hence, some degree of secularization may serve as a form of sacred adaptation. This has been a tactical assumption in the trajectory of liberal Protestantism over the last century as pastors and theologians have made concessions to their secularizing adherents (Berger 1967; Demerath 1992). This tactic has been challenged by advocates of strict doctrine and strict churches (Kelley 1972; Iannaccone 1994), but cleaving to strictness may have cost the churches far more defections than has the alternative.

7. Secularization and sacralization are engaged in a dialectical oscillation in which each is contingent on and responsive to the other. The presence of one does not necessarily involve the absence of the other. As was noted above, a secularization that goes too far is likely to elicit a sacralizing reaction. Similarly, sacralizing may exceed the bounds of pertinence, propriety, credibility, or convenience in a complex social context. Thus, lapsing and laicization of various sorts result in a secularizing adjustment. Without suggesting that secularization is always balanced by a corresponding sacralization to create a religious equilibrium, one can say that this mutual responsiveness is an important

reason why secularization, like a sense of the sacred itself, will always be with us.

8. Focusing on the fate of old forms of religion may deflect attention from new forms of the sacred. An obsession with secularization in the past may preclude an analysis of sacralization in the present and future. Just as conventional religion may not necessarily be sacred, new sources of the sacred are not necessarily religious. Today one hears a good deal of talk about a growing distinction between religion and spirituality and about profound sacred commitments in everything from socialism to sex. Just because they have attained cliché status does not mean that these concepts should be jettisoned as possibilities for deeper investigation.

These eight propositions lead to a series of issues beyond the scope of this article: Does every individual need a sense of a sacred commitment and a regimen that is self-consciously maintained and ritually reinforced? Does every collectivity and society require something similar that is shared among its members? If the answers to these questions are affirmative, what is the relation between the sacredness required and conventional religion on the one hand and more secular sources on the other? To what extent can the sacred reside in high and low culture, moral and ethical convictions, and movements on behalf of political causes, personal identities, and nationalist ambitions? Is it possible to investigate these matters without falling into tautology and teleology? Precisely because these questions are so old, it is time for freshly conceptualized and newly researched answers.

The alternation of secularization and sacralization is a crucial historical dynamic not just for religion but for culture as a whole. Secularization without sacralization is a nearly defining characteristic of putative *postmodernity*, with its loss of grand narratives and collective bearings. At the other extreme, sacralization without secularization is a similarly defining characteristic of stereotypic *premodernity*, where the sacred is static and unchallenged. However, it is in historical *modernity* that secularization and sacralization play off each other in both producing and responding to change. Whether causes or effects, these are critical processes in the world of time as opposed to timelessness.

SUMMARY

The importance of any scholarly issue is revealed in the debates it engenders. By this standard, secularization qualifies as very important indeed. As a matter that seems to defy either empirical or ideological consensus, it has become a kind of Gordian knot for social scientific scholarship on religion.

Clearly, it is possible to construct versions of secularization that are either outrageous or reasonable. It matters greatly how the concept is deployed. For some, it is a prophecy of religious demise, whether a tragic jeremiad or a triumphant anticipation. For others, it is a set of historically and sociologically specified processes that move less linearly and with less certainty through time. For still others, secularization converges with sacralization to form a stream of constantly shifting conceptions and locations of the sacred. Whichever option is at issue, the stakes are high, and the sight of scholars impaled upon them is not uncommon.

REFERENCES

Bell, Daniel 1976 *The Cultural Contradictions of Capitalism.* New York: Basic Books.

Bellah, Robert N., Richard Madsen, William M. Sullivan, Ann Swidler, and Steven M. Tipton 1985 *Habits of the Heart.* Berkeley: University of California Press.

Berger, Peter L. 1967 *The Sacred Canopy.* Garden City, N.Y.: Doubleday.

—— 1997 "Epistemological Modesty: An Interview with Peter Berger." *Christian Century* 114:972–978.

Beteille, Andre 1994 "Secularism and the Intellectuals." *Economic and Political Weekly* 29(10):559–566.

Bruce, Steve 1995 "The Truth about Religion in Britain," *Journal of the Scientific Study of Religion* 34:417–430.

Chaves, Mark 1993 "Denominations as Dual Structures: An Organizational Analysis." *Sociology of Religion* 54:147–169.

Comte, August 1852 (1891) *The Catechism of Positive Religion*, 3rd ed. London: Routledge.

Davie, Grace 1994 *Religion in Britain since 1945: Believing without Behaving.* Oxford, UK: Blackwell.

—— 1998a "Excepting Exceptionalism: American Religion in Comparative Relief." *The Annals* 558:28–39.

—— 1998b "Secularization Disproved or Displaced." In Rudy Laermans, Bryan Wilson, and Jaak Billiet, eds., *Secularization and Social Integration*. Leuven: Belgium: Leuven University Press.

Demerath, N. J. III 1992 "Snatching Defeat from Victory in the Decline of Liberal Protestantism: Culture versus Structure in Instituional Analysis." in P. D. Demerath, T. Schmitt, and R. H. Williams, eds., *Sacred Companies*. New York: Oxford University Press.

—— 2000 *Crossing the Gods: Religion, Violence, Politics and the State across the World*. New York: Rutgers University Press.

Dobbelaere, Karel 1981 "Secularization: A Multi-Dimensional Concept." *Current Sociology* 20:1–216.

—— 1985 "Secularization Theories and Sociological Paradigms." *Sociological Analysis* 46(4):377–387.

—— 1993 "Church Involvement and Secularization: Making Sense of the European Case." In Eileen Barker, James A. Beckford, and Karel Dobbelaere, eds., *Secularization, Rationalism, and Sectarianism*. Oxford, UK: Clarendon.

Douglas, Mary 1982 "The Effects of Modernization on Religious Change." In Douglas and Tipton and Steven M. Tipton, eds., *Religion in America: Spirituality in a Secular Age*. Boston: Beacon.

Durkheim, Emile 1912 (1995) *The Elementary Forms of the Religious Life*, trans. Karen Fields. New York: Free Press.

—— 1961 *Moral Education*. New York: Free Press.

Erikson, Kai 1966 *Wayward Puritans*. New York: Wiley.

Fenn, Richard 1979 *Toward a Theory of Secularization*. Provo, Utah: Society for the Scientific Study of Religion.

—— 1993 "Crowds, Time, and the Essence of Society." In Eileen Barker, James A. Beckford, and Karel Dobbelaere, eds., *Secularization, Rationalism and Sectarianism*, Oxford, UK: Clarendon.

Finke Roger, and Rodney Stark 1992 *The Churching of America, 1776–1990: Winners and Losers in Our Religious Economy*. New Brunswick, N.J.: Rutgers University Press.

Habermas, Jurgen 1988 *The Theory of Communicative Action*, 2 vols. Cambridge, UK: Polity Press.

Haddaway, C. Kirk, Penny Long Marler, and Mark Chaves 1993 "What the Polls Don't Show: A Closer Look at U.S. Church Attendance." *American Sociological Review* 58:741–752.

Iannaccone, Laurence R. 1994 "Why Strict Churches Are Strong." *American Journal of Sociology* 99:1180–1211.

Juergensmeyer, Mark 1993 *The New Cold War: Religious Nationalism Confronts the Secular State*. Berkeley: University of California Press.

Kelley, Dean 1972 *Why Conservative Churches Are Growing*. Macon, Ga.: Mercer University Press.

Luhmann, Niklas 1982 *The Differentiation of Society*. New York: Columbia University Press.

Madan, T. N. 1998 *Modern Myths, Locked Minds*. Delhi: Oxford University Press.

Martin, David 1969 *The Religious and the Secular*. New York: Schocken.

—— 1978 *A General Theory of Secularization*. New York: Harper & Row.

Marx, Karl (1844) 1963 "Contribution to the Critique of Hegel's Philosophy of the Right." In Thomas B. Bottomore, ed., *Early Writings*. New York: McGraw-Hill.

May, Henry F. 1949 *Protestant Churches in Industrial America*. New York: Harper.

McLoughlin, W. G. 1978 *Revivals, Awakenings, and Religious Change*. Chicago: University of Chicago Press.

Nandy, Ashish 1990 "The Politics of Secularism and the Recovery of Religious Tolerance." In Veena Das, ed., *Mirrors of Violence*. Delhi, India: Oxford University Press.

Parsons, Talcott 1977 *The Evolution of Societies*. Englewood Cliffs, N.J.: Prentice-Hall.

Redfield, Robert 1953 *The Primitive World and Its Transformations*. Ithaca, N.Y: Cornell University Press.

Roof, Wade Clark, and William McKinney 1987 *American Mainline Religion*. New Brunswick, N.J.: Rutgers University Press.

Spencer, Herbert 1874 1915 *Essays Scientific, Political, Speculative*, 3 vols. New York: Appleton.

Stark, Rodney 1992 "Sociology of Religion." In *Encyclopedia of Sociology*. New York: MacMillan.

—— 1998 "Secularization R.I.P." Paper presented at Meetings of the Society for the Scientific Study of Religion. *Sociology of Religion*.

——, and William H. Bainbridge, Jr. 1985 *The Future of Religion*. Berkeley: University of California Press.

——, and Laurence R. Iannaccone 1994 "A Supply-Side Interpretation of the 'Secularization' of Europe." *Journal for the Scientific Study of Religion* 33:230–252.

Toennies, Ferdinand (1887) 1957 *Community and Society*, trans. and ed. Charles Loomis. East Lansing: Michigan State University Press.

Tschannen, Oliver 1991 "The Secularization Paradigm: A Systematization." *Journal of the Scientific Study of Religion* 30:395–415.

Turner, James 1985 *Without God, Without Creed*. Baltimore: Johns Hopkins University Press.

Voltaire, Francois-Marie Arouet 1756 (1963) *Essai sur les Moers et l'Esprit des Nations*, 2 vols. Paris: Garnier.

Warner, Steven 1993 "Work in Progress toward a New Paradigm for the Sociological Study of Religion in the U.S." *American Journal of Sociology* 98:1044–1093.

Weber, Max (1905) 1993 *The Protestant Ethic and the Spirit of Capitalism*, trans T. Parsons, intro. Randall Collins. Los Angeles: Roxbury.

Wilson, Bryan 1966 *Religion in Secular Society*. London: Penguin.

—— 1998 "The Secularization Thesis: Criticisms and Rebuttals." In Rudy Laermans, Bryan Wilson, and Jaak Billiet, eds., *Secularization and Social Integration*. Leuven, Belgium: Leuven University Press.

Wuthnow, Robert 1988 *The Restructuring of American Religion*. Princeton, N.J.: Princeton University Press.

N. J. DEMERATH III

SEGREGATION AND DESEGREGATION

In the early years of the American colonies and the new republic of the United States, segregation was not only impractical but undesirable. To benefit from slavery, slave masters had to manage and control slaves; therefore, they had to work with them. Not all slaves were field hands or agricultural workers; some were domestic servants, and so the slave master and mistress had to share their private quarters with slaves. Thus, many white Americans, especially Southerners in the pre-Civil War South, accepted daily, intimate, personal, primary face-to-face contact with slaves as a necessity. They insisted, however, that all such contacts reflect proper social distance: slaves were always to be subservient, behavioral assimilation was allowed only to a point, and slaves were supposed to know the dominant-group culture, use it appropriately, and always recognize that they were not the equals of their masters. Although structural assimilation occurred at a primary level, it was not among equals.

With the Emancipation Proclamation of 1863 and the ratification of the Thirteenth Amendment in 1865, some Americans seriously considered the idea of separating blacks and whites. As some blacks emigrated to poor urban areas in the South and as their numbers increased, some whites recognized that blacks were becoming a threat to the hard-won victories of higher-priced white labor

(Bonacich 1972). They recognized that the former mechanisms of deference and social distance would no longer allow whites to maintain the subordination of black men and women, and so they insisted on a system of separation. It was not enough to separate residentially; it was necessary to establish a caste system that would deny blacks equal access to most jobs, social and governmental services, schools and colleges, public accommodations, and the right to vote.

In both the South and the North, segregation was practiced long before it became embodied in law. It was a Supreme Court decision, however, that in 1896 established segregation as the law of the land. It was through the medium of statutes, therefore, that domination was ultimately exercised. In other words, it was the polity, not the economy, that suppressed the competition of black urban laborers and that established the shift from paternalistic to competitive race relations (Scott 1977; van den Berghe 1967).

Segregationist laws were passed as early as 1875 in Tennessee; they rapidly advanced throughout the South, and by the 1880s blacks were not only separated on all modes of transportation (Franklin 1947). However, the Civil Rights Act of 1875, which guaranteed black Americans all the privileges and rights of citizenship, was an impediment to the policy of segregation. Consequently, the impediment was removed in 1883, when the Supreme Court declared the Civil Rights Act of 1875 unconstitutional. Soon after that decision, black Americans were banned from most Southern venues, from hotels and other places of public accommodation—restaurants, theaters, and places of public amusement. The process of limiting opportunities for blacks continued, and by 1885 most Southern states had enacted laws requiring separate schools for blacks and whites. Finally, on May 18, 1896, the Supreme Court in the infamous *Plessy v. Ferguson* decision made segregation the law of the land (Kromkowski 1991). Although the North and the South were elated, the implication of the decision and the way it was to be implemented would be considerably different in the two regions. As a result, the consequences and effects of segregation in the South would be different from those in the North.

If segregation had not legitimated the rights of Southern whites to degrade and control blacks,

blacks might have seen opportunities for independent growth in segregation. Segregation in the South meant biracialism, and biracialism meant the creation of black institutions that were to some extent administered and controlled by blacks. Although most blacks in the South worked for whites, they did not have to depend on them for all their basic services: They had separate schools, hospitals, and churches. Most blacks in the South became sharecroppers, working rented land. The land meant debt for the sharecropper, but it also meant a certain amount of daily independence. It is conceivable, therefore, that under a more positive set of circumstances blacks could have focused on the "equal requirement" of the *Plessy* "separate but equal" decision. However, because segregation became the detested symbol of injustice, Southern blacks insisted on destroying it.

As blacks struggled against segregation, they were beaten and murdered. Law enforcement participated in those affronts either by refusing to protect black people or by becoming the perpetrators of violence. Such actions reinforced the view of Southern blacks that segregation was the symbol of black inferiority. As blacks struggled to defend themselves, they learned that sheriffs and law enforcement officials, mayors, governors, the FBI, the federal government, the attorney general of the United States, and even the president participated in one way or another in the maintenance of a system of segregation that declared black people inferior and denied them equal access to the labor market and to educational opportunity.

Although Southern blacks were eventually successful in destroying the system of segregation in the South, blacks in the North, where the *Plessy* decision had been implemented differently, often failed. Because the major problem in the North was not segregation, the strategies of Southern blacks were inappropriate for the problems of Northern blacks and those who moved north. Desegregationist strategies were designed for problems such as residential segregation but not for problems such as poverty and differential access to occupational opportunities. This is why the Southern Christian Leadership Conference left the urban slums of Chicago in 1965, where the the real problems were, and attacked the issue of segregated housing in Cicero, Illinois, which for blacks at that time was insignificant.

Although Southern whites insisted on black inferiority, one should not assume that they therefore wanted to dispose of blacks. They needed blacks for at least two reasons: to establish their alleged superiority and to exploit black labor. Blacks had been their slaves, had worked their fields, had stablized and maintained their households, and had been a source of wealth and sometimes pleasure. Many Southern whites had even developed a degree of affection for blacks.

Northern whites were quite different in this regard. Some knew the value of black Americans, but their major goal was to make certain that blacks and whites remained apart. A biracial system was not required because occupational and economic discrimination kept blacks and whites apart. When and where necessary, whites would use restrictive real estate practices to keep the races separate. Whites in the North wanted blacks to stay completely to themselves unless there was some need for their labor. With the exception of hiring black women, whites did not really want to make competitive use of black labor. It seems that Northern whites wanted blacks to disappear, and so they pretended that they did not exist.

In the South, segregationist policies eventually led to a biracial system that produced unanticipated consequences. It actually laid the groundwork for the development of a black middle class composed of clergy, college administrators and professors, medical doctors, journalists, schoolteachers, artisans, and skilled craftspeople, all of whom had learned to be independent in their respective institutional settings. They were the decision makers and leaders of their people. They would train the new teachers, the new professionals, and even a new business elite. Their protégés would become the new entrepreneurs and open businesses of various kinds—barbershops, beauty shops, grocery stores, restaurants, and nightclubs. They would establish black banks, publish black newspapers, and establish professional societies. Many of the college graduates would become ministers and establish their own churches. In time, all these professionals would combine their resources and expertise and, using their two institutional bases, the school and the church, lead a struggle against the very system that made their existence possible: the system of segregation. In the South segregation did not mean separation only. It meant the right of whites to degrade blacks and treat blacks unjustly, but mostly it meant the right to keep blacks in an inferior position by denying them equal access and equal opportunity.

Eventually the black church, a product of segregation and discrimination, would become the institutional base for the fight against segregation and discrimination. Not only did the black church provide the leadership, it also provided the following. However, since black churches had existed for decades and their congregations had been ready for change for decades, why did the "movement" take until 1955 to start? A critical component is the size of the black middle and skilled-working classes. In the middle to late 1950s, those two classes constituted approximately 39 percent of the black community, a larger percentage than ever before. World War II had been a major period of opportunity for African Americans, and as a result, they garnered more resources and consequently expected more from the system. In short, they experienced a revolution of rising expectations. They had become intolerant of abuse, the various forms of discrimination they had experienced, and insults to their dignity. They were in need of a social movement.

DESEGREGATION: THE CIVIL-RIGHTS MOVEMENT

The impetus for the civil-rights movement, the movement to desegregate the South, actually began before Mrs. Rosa Parks's heroic refusal in 1955 to give up her bus seat to a white person. The initial stimulus was the May 17, 1954, decision of the Supreme Court in *Brown* v. *Board of Education* (1954) that the 1896 *Plessy* decision was unconstitutional. Black soldiers returning from World War II and the burgeoning black middle class praised the decision and proclaimed that the *Brown* decision must usher in a new social order.

No sooner had the decision been made, however, than the nation was shocked by the grisly murder of a young teenager, Emmett Till, in Sumner, Mississippi. That murder dramatized the fact that no change in the law would change the customs of Southern whites, and the case demonstrated how the circumstances of blacks in the South were radically different from those of blacks in the North. According to Emmett Till's uncle, Emmett had been bragging to some black youngsters outside a rural store. He claimed to have

white friends, even white girlfriends, in Chicago and showed photographs of his friends. Emmett had just arrived in Sumner and was trying to impress those young boys to gain their friendship. One of the boys apparently said to Emmett, "I bet you won't go into that store and say something to that white lady." Till accepted the challenge, went in, purchased some candy, and in leaving said, "'Bye, baby." Late the same night, two or more white men knocked at the door of Emmett's grandfather, Mose Wright, and took the boy away in a car. When Emmett Till was found, he had been mutilated and beaten beyond recognition, with a bullet hole through his temple. The picture of Emmett Till's disfigured body was published in *Jet* magazine by Johnson Publications, a black publishing firm, and black people throughout the nation saw the picture. Till's mother insisted on an open casket. Two men were charged with the murder, but both were found not guilty. Black people recognized that a change in the law was not enough. More had to be done.

Emmett Till was a Northern urban kid who had grown up and apparently gone to school with some liberal whites, and although the commingling of whites and blacks in the North could lead to violence, in some circles it was tolerated. Because the issue in the North was residential separation, it was easy for a black person to find himself in a predominantly black school, though generally there were at least a few white students. More important, however, was the fact that the overwhelming majority of the teachers were white (Jones 1985, p. 180). Those teachers and other professionals usually lived outside the school districts in which they taught. Although they insisted that black schoolchildren obey them, they did not insist that blacks be subservient and inferior. As teachers, they were proud of their successful black students. Northern blacks thus developed self-esteem, a sense of "somebodyness," a belief that they were the equals of others. That attitude was reinforced in black urban enclaves. In the South, however, every contact a black person had with a white person required a demonstration of black inferiority and even fear. The idea of being equal to whites was generally unthinkable, that is, if the idea was to be put into action. Northern blacks were always warned by their relatives when they went to the South that the rules were different there, that not obeying them could place everybody in jeopardy and could even lead to the loss of life.

Emmett Till was a tough urban kid, not unlike many of the gang members of the 1990s, and the fact that he was not afraid of his captors and refused to stop fighting back made them angrier. He obviously did not know that what he did in the North could get him killed in the South. He had not been warned, or he did not heed the warning.

Emmett Till's murder and the injustice of the final verdict produced mounting frustration. Thus, on December 1, 1955, Mrs. Rosa Parks told a bus driver who asked her to give her seat to a white person, which was the law, that she would not. This galvanized the entire black population of Montgomery, Alabama. The black community organized a bus boycott, and soon the buses were empty. The leadership was surprised (Raines 1977). Black people were fed up. They had always been angered by such demands and customs, but as Christians they had been taught to accept them and hope for change. Now, however, former soldiers and their families who had been patriotic and had sacrificed during World War II had become intolerant. Segregation did not mean biracialism to them. Instead it meant abuse and insult. A social movement had started.

Soon a brilliant young black Baptist minister would join the movement, and even though he was only twenty-six years of age, he would become the leader. That leader, Martin Luther King, Jr., defined the enemy as segregation. Segregation, King insisted, "scars the soul of the segregated. . . . It not only harms one physically, but injures one spiritually." It is a system, asserted King, that "forever stares the segregated in the face saying you are less than, you are not equal to." Segregation denies a human being the right to express his or her true essence; therefore, it must be destroyed. King declared that nonviolence would be the movement's strategy and philosophy. Nevertheless, violence erupted immediately. Whites were resisting, but the Montgomery Improvement Association won its victory when the Supreme Court declared segregated busing unconstitutional. King and his leadership cadre immediately set about the task of desegregating other public facilities in Montgomery. The movement had begun, and from that point on other struggles would erupt sponta-

neously across the South, all of them devoted to desegragation.

As African-American college students observed the activities of Dr. King and his organization, the Southern Christian Leadership Conference (SCLC), they agreed to continue the process of desegregation. Dr. King was desegregating downtown department stores in Montgomery; they would desegregate lunch counters. It was the custom in the South not to serve blacks at lunch counters in the various dime stores, especially the Woolworth's chain. On November 1, 1960, four students from the local black college took seats at the lunch counter in Greensboro, North Carolina. They asked to be served, and when the management refused, they resolved to stay. After a day or two, violence broke out. A group of young white toughs and some older adults began to pull them out of their seats and beat them. The police were called in, but they refused to arrest the perpetrators of the violence. Instead they arrested the victims, those who were involved peacefully in what became known as sit-ins. As a result of the police actions, Southern blacks noted again that not only were the citizens of the South opposed to their rights, so were public officials. Segregation had to be destroyed "lock, stock, and barrel, top to bottom, left to right" (Carmichael 1971) because it also corrupted public officials and officers of the law whose sworn duty it was to protect the citizenry. From this point on segregation was the enemy, and going to jail to end it became a badge of honor.

The issue of segregation on buses involving interstate travel remained a problem even after the Montgomery victory. Therefore, it was not long before groups of Freedom Riders were mobilized to test the Supreme Court decision's relevance to interstate travel. The Freedom Riders included blacks and whites, a fact that should not be forgotten. The Freedom Rides began in May 1961 and were immediately confronted with violence. Buses were bombed. Freedom Riders were beaten unmercifully at several destinations, and some were permanently disabled. The perpetrators were indiscriminate: they beat blacks and whites. Their hatred seemed greater for whites— "nigger lovers," they were called then. The Freedom Riders expected to be protected by the FBI, but J. Edgar Hoover, the director, made it clear that his agency had no intention of protecting those agitators. The failure of the federal government to uphold the law in this instance finally communicated to black people and some whites that the existence of segregation had corrupted not just local public officials but even officials of the federal government. The fight had to begin at the top.

The next major chapter in the effort to desegregate the South took place in Albany, Georgia, in 1961. Failing in their desegregation efforts there, King and the SCLC launched a new project to protest segregated lunch counters in downtown Birmingham, Alabama. King was jailed. While in jail, he wrote his philosophically brilliant "Letter from a Birmingham Jail." Although Birmingham's white business leaders agreed on a desegregation plan, King's motel was still bombed. Medgar Evers was shot to death in neighboring Jackson, Mississippi, and four young children were murdered in the bombing of the Sixteenth Street Baptist Church in Birmingham. Blacks learned that even if they could get local public officials and businessmen to change segregationist policies, some Southern whites, perhaps even the majority, would not accept change. They also learned that among the majority there were those who were willing to use violence. Blacks had to have protection from another source.

In 1964, the Student Nonviolent Coordinating Committee (SNCC) began its Freedom Summers Project in Mississippi. Mississippi was considered by blacks the most dangerous state in the South, and it lived up to its reputation. On Sunday, August 4, 1964, Mississippi claimed the lives of James Chaney, Michael Swerner, and Andrew Goodman—the latter two were white. All three were members of SNCC's Freedom Summer Project. Their only offense was that they had volunteered to teach black youth, work with the rural poor, and register blacks to vote. If it was not apparent during the Freedom Rides, it was now apparent that Southern whites would kill anybody, whites included, who opposed their way of life.

Blacks now had a growing collection of concerned Northern whites. Swerner's wife commented that it was unfortunate, but apparently whites had to die before other, complacent whites would listen. The parents of the two young white students, Swerner and Goodman, talked about the martyrdom of their children. They were proud but grief-stricken. They insisted that the monstrous evil of segregation must be destroyed. Black members of the Congress of Racial Equality (CORE) and SNCC were furious. Some of them had been personal friends of James Chaney, who was black. They blamed the governor of the state and the federal government for what happened in Philadelphia, Mississippi, during the summer of 1964.

As a result of those murders, SNCC and SCLC mobilized a march to Montgomery. Near the end of their march, however, they were attacked by mounted sheriff's officers wielding clubs. Men and women, as well as young adults and children, were beaten.

In summary, the central focus of black struggle in the South from 1955 to 1965 was desegregation. Blacks insisted on desegregating public transportation facilities, public eating establishments, public water fountains, public bathrooms, and public institutions of higher education. As a result of the violence they experienced, black Southerners learned that desegregation required more than protests, it required changes in the law at the national level. A civil-rights bill was required. Certainly a change in the law was required, but even that was not enough. In order for changes to be implemented, government officials had to demonstrate a willingness to protect and defend the rights of African Americans.

It was not long after Selma that Watts, an urban ethnic enclave near Los Angeles, exploded, beginning a series of race riots that developed spontaneously throughout the latter half of the 1960s. Stores were torched and looted. Surveying the destruction in Watts, Dr, King and SCLC decided that it was time to take their movement north. What they were not aware of was that their desegregation strategies would not solve the problems of Northern blacks, because the central problem for that group was *not* segregation. To understand this, it is necessary to contrast the evolution of the black middle class in the South with that in the North.

DESEGREGATION VERSUS INTEGRATION

A biracial system similar to that in the South never surfaced in the American North. As a result, blacks there depended almost completely on whites for employment. Northern whites, furthermore, had not come to depend on black labor, with the possible exception of domestic labor. Domestic labor, however, did not produce wealth; it was a symbol of surplus wealth. In addition, Northern whites who wanted to remain physically (residentially) separated from blacks did not feel any need to employ them, with the exception of menial labor jobs. With the influx of European immigrants, Northern whites preferred to hire the sons and daughters of Europe rather than the emancipated slaves of the South (Blauner 1972; Jones 1985). Indeed, from the turn of the century to the beginning of World War II. Northern blacks never established a foothold in the manufacturing industries of the North (Jones 1985). According to Blauner, even in ancillary industries such as meatpacking where blacks initially gained a foothold because of the unhealthy working conditions they were actually displaced by European immigrants during the 1930s.

Given their background, the problem for the black middle class in the North was different from that for the black middle class in the South, and the leadership of the civil-rights movement knew it. At one point, Dr. King said that "the struggles of the past decade were not national in scope; they were Southern; they were specifically designed to change life in the South" (1968, p. 70). Northern blacks had only been segregated (de facto) residentially. Otherwise they could ride public transportation and eat at many of the major restaurants, although it was understood that some owners would discourage blacks from coming by being discourteous. The major concern of Northern middle-class blacks, therefore, was not formal desegregation but discrimination and unequal access. They insisted that they should get the same quality of goods or service for their money. Their major concern was reflected in their insistence on greater job opportunities. They rejected the idea of caste barriers in employment, and they insisted that promotions be tied fairly to evaluation, irrespective of race. They rejected job ceilings and the idea of determining job status on the basis of race. These kinds of problems could not be solved by civil rights marches. They could not be solved simply by desegration or changing the law. Such changes would help, perhaps, but what was required was to get the federal government to establish civil-rights policies that would declare such acts as violations of the law and then, even more important, connect those policies to some kind of enforcement device so that private corporations and governmental agencies would comply with the law. This is exactly what the Civil Rights Act of 1964 in combination with affirmative action, did.

THE FAILURE OF INTEGRATION: THE URBAN POOR

Soon after the Civil Rights Act was passed by Congress and signed by President Lyndon B. Johnson, Executive Orders 11246 and 11375 were issued. Those orders led to the policy of affirmative action (Black 1981). Affirmative action policies essentially required that all city, state, and federal agencies, as well as any private corporation that contracted with the federal government, make every reasonable attempt to increase the proportion of minority workers in their workforces. Affirmative action was to be a device to address the effects of past discrimination. It did not take long to realize, however, that mostly middle-class blacks were benefiting from affirmative-action policies (Wilson 1987). The reason for this was twofold. First, middle-class blacks were the only ones who had competitive resources (such as skills they had acquired from higher education), owned businesses, or had parents who as a result of their professional status (doctors, dentists, ministers, etc.) were able to provide a competitive advantage for their children. Second, the American economy underwent structural changes that created more opportunities for professional, technical, human service, and clerical staff. As these opportunities increased, affirmative-action policies increased the likelihood that some of those jobs would go to black Americans. It was not long, however, before it also became apparent that neither affirmative-action policies nor the structural shift in the economy would aid black Americans who were poor and unskilled. In fact, as the economy shifted from a majority of manufacturing industries to a majority of service industries, a segmented labor market developed. A segmented labor market generated differential rates of mobility for differing class segments of the same group (Wilson 1978; 1981; 1987).

It is not surprising that when Mayor Richard Daly of Chicago and Martin Luther King, Jr., met early in 1966 and King complained about the slum housing of poor blacks in that city, Daly responded, "How do you expect me to solve the problems of poverty and joblessness overnight?'' King had no answer. He would quickly leave Chicago and the North after unsuccessful attempts both to help the impoverished and to desegregate Cicero, Illinois. It is to Dr. King's credit, however, that he recognized that the problems of the poor had not been solved and that a Poor People's Campaign was required.

Oblivious to the needs of the poor in the black community, Northern blacks who had turned a desegregationist movement into an integrationist movement (those Sowell [1984] incorrectly labels as people with a civil-rights vision) pursued integration with a vengeance. When the Civil Rights Act of 1964 became the law of the land, affirmative action was to be its guiding policy and equal opportunity and equal access the measure of fairness. It was not long, however, before civil-rights advocates recognized that something was amiss not only for the Northern black poor but also for the middle class. For example, although data from the 1970 census showed that black male college graduates in 1969 received a slightly higher average income than did comparable whites, other data demonstrated that the majority of black college students did not graduate from college. In fact, when Fleming (1985) researched this issue and compared the performance of black colleges with limited resources to that of predominantly white urban universities with considerably more resources that attracted black students with higher SAT scores, she found that the black colleges produced more intellectual and psychosocial development among black students than did the white colleges. Further, she found that typically white colleges produced "academic deterioration" among black students and concluded that better facilities and more institutional resources do not necessarily translate into a higher-quality college or university education (Fleming 1985. p. 186). She added that similar findings were reported in desegregated or so-called integrated public schools (Knowles 1962).

The fact is that whether or not schools are integrated, the situation confronting black children in most Northern and Southern public schools is catastrophic. Indeed, for the most part integration has failed black children. Once they enter school, they fall quickly behind their white counterparts on most measures of intelligence and scholastic achievement (Coleman 1966; Denton

1981). In fact, the longer black children remain in school, the further they fall behind. Denton (1981) reports that compared to white children, black children are three times as likely to be labeled mentally retarded, twice as likely to be suspended for discipline and attendance problems, and twice as likely to drop out of high school (White 1984, pp. 102–103). Black students who remain in school on average are two to three years below grade level in the basics—reading, writing, and arithmetic.

Educational integration consequently has often led to less growth and, even worse, the actual deterioration of the academic potential of black students in institutions of higher education. In those situations where deterioration does not actually occur, stagnation does (Black 1981).

These kinds of problems compound in later life such that black students have only "half as much . . . chance as a white child of finishing college and becoming a professional person," twice as much chance of being unemployed, and a one in ten chance of getting in trouble with the law (and, if these students are young males, a one in four chance of involvement with the criminal justice system); finally, as they age, black students have a life expectancy that is five years shorter than that of white adults (White 1984, p. 103).

Without an adequate education, black males become less employable, less marriageable, and more criminal.

Wilson (1981, 1987) examined the combined indicators of unemployment rates, labor-force participation rates, employment-population ratios, and work experience and concluded that not only do these indicators reveal a disturbing picture of joblessness, they also indicate that a growing percentage of young black males are not marriageable, that is, cannot contribute to the support of a family. Examining rates of teenage pregnancy; crime and violence, especially homicide; and increases in substance abuse, Wilson argues that many of these young men are more likely to become predators than responsible workers.

Further, according to Wilson, poverty has compounded in black urban ethnic enclaves. He demonstrates that there has been a significant increase in what he refers to as extreme poverty areas (i.e., areas with a poverty rate of at least 40 percent) in the black urban ethnic enclave. Wilson contrasts the growth of these areas with low-poverty areas (census tracts with a poverty rate of at least 20 percent) and high-poverty areas (with a poverty rate of at least 30 percent). The number of extreme poverty areas, he emphasizes, increased by a staggering 161 percent.

Wilson also demonstrates that the black community is losing its vertical class integration. Black middle-class and stable working-class families are choosing to live in the suburbs, and as they do, the institutions they used to staff, support, and nourish decline in number and importance.

The eventual demise of ethnic enclaves in urban areas has been experienced by all ethnic groups in America; for Europeans the process has taken from four to six generations. For blacks the process began in the late 1960s and early 1970s. Of course there was resistance to residential integration, as mirrored in the hostility that exploded in Cicero, Illinois, in the 1960s, and it continued in the 1990s. Although blacks residing in white suburbs are often racially harassed, residential integration is gaining momentum even as some whites move out of suburbia to exurbia or back to the city.

It should be noted, however, that the process of ethnic enclave decline for blacks is fundamentally different from that for European ethnics. Europeans settled in urban areas at a time when urban job opportunities were increasingly plentiful. Most of the jobs were in manufacturing and did not require skilled labor. And since Europeans were preferred over blacks, the sheer numbers of jobs allowed them to lift a whole mass of people out of squalor. As economic stability increased, European ethnics began the process of preparing themselves for increased mobility within the American occupational structure. To do this, education was critical—educational institutions are essentially preparatory institutions. In sum, the occupational and economic success of European ethnics required a stable economic base first, education second, and occupational success third (Greeley 1976). The circumstances of black Americans (a sizable segment of whom were denied stable employment opportunities in the North) were totally different, particularly in urban areas and especially in the North.

European ethnics were preferred over black laborers. Consequently, while European ethnics were reaping the benefits of full employment, blacks were denied equal access to the labor market, undermining their ability to establish a stable economic base. And for those who would come later, after manufacturing jobs actually began to diminish because of the restructuring of the economy, there world be nothing but long-term unemployment. These groups would eventually form the black underclass as one generation of unemployed workers would quickly give rise to another. European ethnics were described by the sociologists of the 1920s and 1930s as socially disorganized (Thomas and Zananiecki 1927). Their communities were plagued by crime, delinquency, gangs, prostitution, and filth, but the availability of employment opportunities in the 1940s and 1950s allowed many to "lift themselves up by their own bootstraps."

The jobs that are available to blacks now because of the growth in the service sector of the American economy are either jobs that do not pay enough for a person to support a family or require considerable education and training, and so black urban ethnic enclaves are likely to undergo a different kind of transformation than did the European ethnic enclaves of the early 1900s. The middle class will be increasingly siphoned off from such enclaves, leaving behind a large residue of the most despondent and dependent, the most impoverished, the most violent, and the most criminal elements. Without new institutions to play the role of surrogate parents, without some kind of mandatory civilian social service corps, blacks in those communities may become a permanent underclass. A residue was also left behind by European ethnics, but it was much smaller and therefore much less problematic. As the black middle class leaves, it leaves its ethnic community devoid of the leadership or resources needed to regain its health. And as the numbers of female-headed families increase, the middle class will eventually have left the majority of black people behind. Integration, then, has undermined the health and the integrity of the black community.

The counterposition is now being proffered by many people, organizations, and school systems throughout the United States. This can be seen in the proliferation of segregated black programs where black youngsters are being taught only by black teachers. In this context, race clearly is the critical issue. Gender however, has also become an issue. In many of these schools, black males insist that only they can do the job. Since black women have had to bear the burden of rearing children alone for so long, there is no doubt that they can use some help. One critical problem remains for people of this persuasion, however, and that is the continuing trend of black middle-class and stable working-class flight. Can the black community stem the tide? It is not suggested here that the black middle class can solve the problem alone but rather that it must provide the leadership, as it did in the segregated black institutions of the South, and that government must pay for it. Can the exodus be diminished?

Possibly, the passage of anti-affirmative action legislation and the increased reliance on standardized testing in higher education may alert the black middle class that the opportunities for their children are diminishing. Already they are starting to send their children to historically black colleges and universities in record numbers. This is a major shift in black higher education, and the number of available admissions is limited. As their children's opportunities decrease, maybe they will come to see that in America the opportunities of black Americans will always be dependent upon the amount of pressure that blacks as a people can bring to bear on the system.

In the last few months of 1998, several anti-affirmative action programs were passed—Proposition 209 in California and Initiative 200 in Washington, for example. These initiatives were passed despite the demonstrated benefits of affirmative action for the broader society.

(SEE ALSO: *Apartheid; Discrimination; Equality of Opportunity; Ethnicity; Prejudice; Race; Segregation and Desegregation; Slavery and Involuntary Servitude*)

REFERENCES

Black, Albert N., Jr. 1977 "Racism Has Not Declined, It Has Just Changed Form." *Umojo* 1, no. 3 (fall).

—— 1981 "Affirmative Action and the Black Academic Situation." *Western Journal of Black Studies* 5:87–94.

Bowen, William, G., and Derek Bok 1998 *The Shape of the River: Long-Term Consequences of Considering Race in College and University Admissions.* Princeton N.J.: Princeton University Press.

Blauner, Robert 1972 *Racial Oppression in America.* New York: Harper and Row.

Bonacich, Edna 1972 "A Theory of Ethnic Antagonism: The Split Labor Market." *American Sociological Review* 37 (October): 547–559.

Coleman, James S. 1966 *Equality of Educational Opportunity.* Washington, D.C.: U.S. Government Printing Office.

Denton, Herbert 1981 "Future Still Bleak for Black Children, Lobbying Group's Statistics Show." *Los Angeles Times*, January 14(1A):4.

Fleming, Jacqueline 1985 *Blacks in College.* San Francisco: Jossey-Bass.

Franklin, John Hope 1947 *From Slavery to Freedom: A History of Negro Americans*, 4th ed. New York: Knopf.

Greeley, Andrew M. 1976 "The Ethnic Miracle." *The Public Interest* 45: 20–36.

Jones, Jacqueline 1985 *Labor of Love, Labor of Sorrow: Black Women, Work and the Family, From Slavery to the Present.* New York: Vintage.

—— 1998 *American Work: Four Centuries of Black and White Labor.* New York: Norton.

King, Martin Luther, Jr. 1968 *Where Do We Go From Here: Chaos or Community?* Boston: Beacon Press.

Knowles, L. W. 1962 "Part 1, Kentucky." In United States Commission on Civil Rights, *Civil Rights USA: Public Schools, Southern States.* Washington, D.C.: U.S. Government Printing Office.

Krombowski, John A., ed. 1991 *Annual Edition: Race and Ethnic Relations, 91 to 92.* Guilford, Conn.: Dushkin.

Massey, Donald, and Nancy Denton 1993 *American Apartheid: Segregation and the Making of the Under-class.* Cambridge, Mass.: Harvard University Press.

Raines, Howell 1977 *My Soul Is Rested.* New York: Penguin.

Scott, Joseph W. 1977 "Afro-Americans as a Political Class: Towards Conceptual Clarity." *Sociological Focus* 10 (4):383–395.

Sowell, Thomas 1984 *Civil Rights: Rhetoric or Reality?* New York: Morrow.

Thomas, William I., and Florian Zananiecki 1927 *The Polish Peasant in Europe and America.* New York: Alfred A. Knopf.

Van den Berghe, Pierre L. 1967 *Race and Racism: A Comparative Perspective.* New York: Wiley.

White, Joseph 1984 *The Psychology of Blacks: An Afro-American Perspective.* Englewood Cliffs, N.J.: Prentice-Hall.

Wilson, William J. 1978 "The Declining Significance of Race: Revisited but Not Revised." *Society*, vol. 15.

—— 1981 "The Black Community in the 1980s: Questions of Race, Class, and Public Policy." *Annals of the American Academy of Political and Social Science*, vol. 454.

—— 1987 *The Truly Disadvantaged: The Inner City, Underclass, and Public Policy.* Chicago: University of Chicago Press.

—— 1996 *When Work Disappears: The World of the New Urban Poor.* New York: Vintage.

ALBERT WESLEY BLACK, JR.

SEGREGATION INDICES

Residential segregation has been a prominent topic in sociology since Burgess (1928) published his landmark study more than seventy years ago, and for almost as long, sociologists have argued about how to measure it. The debate has ebbed and flowed, and for a time the issue seemed to have been settled. In 1955, Duncan and Duncan published a landmark article (Duncan and Duncan 1955) demonstrating that there was little information in any of the prevailing indices that had not been captured already by the index of dissimilarity. For twenty years afterward, that measure was employed as the standard index of residential segregation.

This *Pax Duncanae* came to an abrupt end in 1976 with the publication of a critique of the dissimilarity index by Cortese and colleagues, ushering in a period of debate that has not ended (Cortese et al. 1976). Over the ensuing decade, a variety of old indices were reintroduced and new ones were invented, yielding a multiplicity of candidates. In an effort to bring some order to the field, Massey and Denton (1988) undertook a systematic analysis of twenty segregation indices they had identified from a review of the literature. They argued that segregation is not a unidimensional construct but encompasses five distinct dimensions of spatial variation. No single dimension is intrinsically more "correct" than any other; each reflects a different facet of the spatial distribution of social groups.

The five dimensions they identified are evenness, exposure, clustering, concentration, and centralization. To verify that conceptualization, Massey and Denton (1988) carried out a factor analysis of indices computed from 1980 census data for U.S. metropolitan areas. Their results showed that each index correlated with one of five factors corresponding to the dimensions they postulated. On theoretical, empirical, and practical grounds, they selected a single "best" indicator for each dimension of segregation. The dimensional structure of segregation and Massey and Denton's (1988) selection of indices have been reaffirmed using 1990 census data (Massey et al. 1996).

The first dimension of segregation is evenness, which refers to the unequal distribution of social groups across areal units of an urban area. A minority group is segregated if it is unevenly spread across neighborhoods. Evenness is not measured in an absolute sense but is scaled relative to another group. It is maximized when all areal units have the same relative number of minority and majority members as the city as a whole and is minimized when minority and majority members have no areas in common.

The index of dissimilarity quantifies the degree of departure from an even residential distribution. It computes the number of minority group members who would have to change neighborhoods to achieve an even distribution and expresses that quantity as a proportion of the number that would have to change areas under conditions of maximum unevenness. The index varies between zero and one, and for any two groups X and Y it is computed as:

$$D = .5 \sum_{i=1}^{n} \left| \frac{x_i}{X} - \frac{y_i}{Y} \right| \qquad (1)$$

where x_i and y_i are the number of group X and group Y members in areal unit i and X and Y are the number of group X and group Y members in the city as a whole, which is subdivided into n areal units.

Among its properties, the index is inflated by random factors when the number of minority group members is small relative to the number of areal units (Cortese et al. 1976). It is also insensitive to the redistribution of minority group members among areal units with minority proportions above or below the city's minority proportion

(James and Taeuber 1985; White 1986). Only transfers of minority members from areas where they are overrepresented (above the city's minority proportion) to areas where they are underrepresented (below the minority proportion) affect the value of the index.

The property means that the dissimilarity index fails the "transfers principle," which requires that segregation be lowered whenever minority members move to areas where they constitute a smaller proportion of the population. This and other problems led James and Taeuber (1985) to recommend using another measure of evenness, the Atkinson index (Atkinson 1970). Massey and Denton (1988), however, pointed out that the Atkinson index and dissimilarity indices are highly correlated and generally yield the same substantive conclusions. Moreover, the Atkinson index is actually a family of indices, each of which gives a slightly different result, creating problems of comparability. Given that D has been the standard index for more than thirty years, that its use has led to a large body of findings, and that that index is easy to compute and interpret, Massey and Denton (1988) recommended using it to measure evenness in most cases.

White (1986) points out, however, that another index may be preferred in measuring segregation between multiple groups, since the dissimilarity index is cumbersome to compute and interpret when the number of groups exceeds two. Thus, if one wants to generate an overall measure of segregation between ten ethnic groups, separate dissimilarity indices will have to be computed between all possible pairs of groups and averaged to get a single measure. An alternative index is Theil's (1972) entropy index, which yields a single comprehensive measure of ethnic segregation. The entropy index also can be expanded to measure segregation across two or more variables simultaneously (e.g. ethnicity and income) and can be decomposed into portions attributable to each of the variables and their interaction (see White 1986).

The second dimension of segregation is exposure, which refers to the degree of potential contact between groups within the neighborhoods of a city. Exposure indices measure the extent to which groups must physically confront one another because they share a residential area. For any city, the degree of minority exposure to the majority is defined as the likelihood of having a neighborhood in common. Rather than measuring segregation as a departure from an abstract ideal of "evenness," however, exposure indices get at the *experience* of segregation from the viewpoint of the average person.

Although indices of exposure and evenness are correlated empirically, they are conceptually distinct because the former depend on the relative size of the groups that are being compared, while the latter do not. Minority group members can be evenly distributed among the residential areas of a city but at the same time experience little exposure to majority group members if they constitute a relatively large share of the population of the city. Conversely, if they constitute a small proportion of the city's population, minority group members tend to experience high levels of exposure to the majority regardless of the level of evenness. Exposure indices take explicit account of such compositional effects in determining the degree of segregation between groups.

The importance of exposure was noted early by Bell (1954), who introduced several indices. However, with the establishment of the *Pax Duncanae* in 1955, sentiment coalesced around the dissimilarity index and exposure was largely forgotten until Lieberson reintroduced the P^* index in the early 1980s (Lieberson 1980, 1981). This index has two basic variants. The interaction index ($_xP^*_y$) measures the probability that members of group X share a neighborhood with members of group Y, and the isolation index ($_xP^*_x$) measures the probability that group X members share an area with each other.

The interaction index is computed as the minority-weighted average of each neighborhood's majority proportion:

$$_xP^*_y = \sum_{i=1}^{n} \left[\frac{x_i}{X} \right] \left[\frac{y_i}{t_i} \right] \qquad (2)$$

where x_i, y_i, and t_i are the numbers of group X members, group Y members, and the total population of unit i, respectively, and X represents the number of group X members citywide. The isolation index is computed as the minority-weighted average of each neighborhood's minority proportion:

$$_xP^*_x = \sum_{i=1}^{n} \left[\frac{x_i}{X} \right] \left[\frac{x_i}{t_i} \right] \qquad (3)$$

Both indices vary between zero and one and give the probability that a randomly drawn group X member shares a neighborhood with a member of group Y (in the case of $_xP^*_y$) or with another group X member (in the case of $_xP^*_x$). Values of $_yP^*_x$ and $_yP^*_y$ can be computed analogously from equations (2) and (3) by switching the x and y subscripts. When there are only two groups, the isolation and interaction indices sum to one, so that $_xP^*_y + _xP^*_x = 1.0$ and $_yP^*_x + _yP^*_y = 1.0$. The interaction indices are also asymmetrical; only when group X and group Y constitute the same proportion of the population does $_xP^*_y$ equal $_yP^*_x$.

P^* indices can be standardized to control for population composition and eliminate the asymmetry (Bell 1954; White 1986). Standardizing the isolation index yields the well-known correlation ratio, or eta^2 (White 1986). Stearns and Logan (1986) argue that eta^2 constitutes an independent dimension of segregation, but Massey and Denton (1988) hold that it straddles two dimensions. Since it is derived from P^*, eta^2 displays some properties associated with an exposure measure, but standardization also gives it the qualities of an evenness index. Massey and Denton (1988) demonstrate this duality empirically and argue that it is better to use D and P^* as separate measures of evenness and exposure. Nonetheless, Jargowsky (1996) has shown that one version of eta^2 yields a better and more concise measure of segregation when one wishes to measure segregation between multiple groups simultaneously (e.g., between income categories).

The third dimension of segregation is clustering, or the extent to which areas inhabited by minority group members adjoin one another in space. A high degree of clustering implies a residential structure in which minority areas are arranged contiguously, creating one large enclave, whereas a low level of clustering means that minority areas are widely scattered around the urban environment, like a checkerboard.

The index of clustering recommended by Massey and Denton (1988) is White's (1983) index of spatial proximity, SP. It is constructed by calculating the average distance between members of

the same group and the average distance between members of different groups and then computing a weighted average of those quantities. The average distance, or proximity, between group X members is

$$P_{xx} = \sum_{i=1}^{n} \sum_{j=1}^{n} \frac{x_i x_j c_{ij}}{X^2} \qquad (4)$$

and the average proximity between members of group X and group Y is

$$P_{xy} = \sum_{i=1}^{n} \sum_{j=1}^{n} \frac{x_i y_j c_{ij}}{XY} \qquad (5)$$

where Y is the number of group Y members citywide, x_i and y_j are the numbers of group X and group Y members in units i and j, and c_{ij} is a distance function between these two areas, defined here as a negative exponential: $c_{ij} = \exp(-d_{ij})$. The term d_{ij} represents the linear distance between the centroids of units i and j, and d_{ij} is estimated as $(.6a_i)\cdot5$, where a_i is the area of the spatial unit. Use of the negative exponential implicitly assumes that the likelihood of interaction declines rapidly as the distance between people increases.

Average proximities also may be calculated among group Y members (P_{yy}) and among all members of the population (P_u) by analogy with equation (4). White's SP index (1983) represents the average of intragroup proximities, P_{xx}/P_u and P_{yy}/P_u, weighted by the fraction of each group in the population:

$$\text{SP} = \frac{XP_{xx} + YP_{yy}}{TP_{tt}} \qquad (6)$$

SP equals one when there is no differential clustering between group X and group Y and is greater than one when group X members live nearer to each other than they do to group Y members. In practice, SP can be converted to a zero-to-one scale by taking the quantity SP−1 (Massey and Denton 1988). White (1984) also has proposed a more complex standardization by taking $f(d_{ij}) = d_{ij}^2$, which yields a statistic equivalent to the proportion of spatial variance explained.

Jakubs (1981) and Morgan (1983a, 1983b) have proposed that D and P^* be adjusted to incorporate the effects of clustering. Massey and Denton

(1988) argue against this procedure because it confounds two different dimensions of segregation. They maintain that it is better to measure clustering directly as a separate dimension than to try to adjust other measures to reflect it.

The fourth dimension of segregation is centralization, or the degree to which a group is located near the center of an urban area. In the postwar period, African-Americans became increasingly isolated in older central cities as whites gravitated to the suburbs. Centralization is measured by an index that reflects the degree to which a group is spatially distributed close to or far away from the central business district (CBD). It compares a group's distribution around the CBD to the distribution of land area around the CBD by using a formula adapted from Duncan (1957):

$$CE = \left(\sum_{i=1}^{n} X_{i-1} A_i \right) - \left(\sum_{i=1}^{n} X_i A_{i-1} \right) \qquad (7)$$

where the n areal units are ordered by increasing distance from the CBD and X_i and A_i are the respective cumulative proportions of group X members and land area in unit i.

In most circumstances, the centralization index varies between plus one and minus one, with positive values indicating a tendency for group X members to reside close to the city center and negative values indicating a tendency for them to live in outlying areas. A score of zero means that the group has a uniform distribution throughout the metropolitan area. The index states the proportion of group X members who would have to change their area of residence to achieve a uniform distribution around the CBD.

The last dimension of segregation is concentration, or the relative amount of physical space occupied by a minority group in the urban environment. Concentration is a relevant dimension of segregation because discrimination restricts minorities to a small set of neighborhoods that together account for a small share of the urban environment. The index of concentration takes the average amount of physical space occupied by group X relative to group Y and compares that quantity to the ratio that would obtain if group X were maximally concentrated and group Y were maximally dispersed:

$$CO = \frac{\displaystyle\sum_{i=1}^{n} \frac{x_i a_i}{X} \sum_{i=1}^{n} \frac{y_i a_i}{Y} - 1}{\displaystyle\sum_{i=1}^{n_1} \frac{t_i a_i}{T_1} \sum_{i=n_2}^{n} \frac{t_i a_i}{T_2} - 1} \qquad (8)$$

where areal units are ordered by geographic size from smallest to largest, a_i is the land area of unit i, and the two numbers n_1 and n_2 refer to different points in the rank ordering of areal units from smallest to largest: n_1 is the rank of the unit where the cumulative total population of units equals the total minority population of the city, summing from the smallest unit up, and n_2 is the rank of the areal unit where the cumulative total population of units equals the majority population, totaling from the largest unit down. T_1 equals the total population of areal units from 1 to n_1, and T_2 equals the total population of areal units from n_2 to n. As before, t_i refers to the total population of unit i and X is the number of group X members in the city.

In most circumstances, the resulting index varies from minus one to plus one; a score of zero means that the two groups are equally concentrated in urban space, and a score of minus one means that group Y's concentration exceeds group X's to the maximum extent possible; a score of positive one means the converse. In certain circumstances, however, Egan et al. (1998) demonstrate that whenever the number of group X members is very small and the areas in which they live are very large, the index becomes unbounded in the negative direction. Thus, caution should be used in measuring the concentration of groups with very few members.

Which of these five indices of segregation is chosen for a particular application depends on the purpose of the study. All are valid measures, and arguments about which one is "correct" or "best" are meaningless, since they measure different facets of segregation. D provides an overall measure of evenness that is highly comparable with prior work, widely understood, readily interpretable, and independent of population composition. P^* captures the degree of inter- and intragroup contact likely to be experienced by members of different groups and directly incorporates the effect of population composition. Most recent work has relied most heavily on these two segregation measures (Massey and Denton 1993; Frey and Farley 1994, 1996; Massey and Hajnal 1995; Peach 1998).

Neither D nor P^* is inherently spatial, however, and each may be applied to study nongeographic forms of segregation, such as segregation between men and women across occupations (see Jacobs 1989). The remaining three dimensions are relevant whenever it is important to know about the physical location of a group in space. If the extent to which group members cluster is important, SP should be computed; if it is important to know how close to the city center a group has settled, CE may be calculated; and if the amount of physical space occupied by a group is relevant, CO is the appropriate index.

The most comprehensive understanding of residential segregation is achieved, however, when all five indices are examined simultaneously. That multidimensional approach yields a fuller picture of segregation than can be achieved by using any single index alone. Thus, Massey and Denton (1989) found that blacks in certain U.S. cities were highly segregated on all five dimensions simultaneously, a pattern they called "hypersegregation." Denton (1994) has shown that this pattern not only persisted to 1990 but extended to other metropolitan areas. By relying primarily on the index of dissimilarity, prior work overlooked this unique aspect of black urban life and understated the severity of black segregation in U.S. cities.

REFERENCES

Atkinson, A. B. 1970 "On the Measurement of Inequality." *Journal of Economic Theory* 2:244–263.

Bell, Wendell 1954 "A Probability Model for the Measurement of Ecological Segregation." *Social Forces* 32:357–364.

Burgess, Ernest W. 1928 "Residential Segregation in American Cities." *Annals of the American Academy of Political and Social Science* 14:105–115.

Cortese, Charles F., R. Frank Falk, and Jack C. Cohen 1976 "Further Considerations on the Methodological Analysis of Segregation Indices." *American Sociological Review* 41:630–637.

Denton, Nancy A. 1994 "Are African Americans Still Hypersegregated?" In Robert D. Bullard, J. Eugene Grigsby III, and Charles Lee, eds., *Residential Apartheid: The American Legacy.* Los Angeles: CAAS Publications, University of California.

Duncan, Otis D. 1957 "The Measurement of Population Distribution." *Population Studies* 11:27–45.

——, and Beverly Duncan 1955 "A Methodological Analysis of Segregation Indices." *American Sociological Review* 20:210–217.

Eagan, Karla L., Douglas L. Anderton, and Eleanor Weber 1998 "Relative Spatial Concentration among Minorities: Addressing Errors in Measurement." *Social Forces* 76:1115–1121.

Frey, William H., and Reynolds Farley 1994 "Changes in the Segregation of Whites from Blacks during the 1980s: Small Steps toward a More Integrated Society." *American Sociological Review* 59:23–45.

—— 1996 "Latino, Asian, and Black Segregation in U.S. Metropolitan Areas: Are Multiethnic Metros Different?" *Demography* 33:35–50.

Jacobs, Jerry A. 1989 *Revolving Doors: Sex Segregation and Women's Careers.* Stanford, Calif.: Stanford University Press.

Jakubs, John F. 1981 "A Distance-Based Segregation Index." *Journal of Socio-Economic Planning Sciences* 15:129–136.

James, David R., and Karl E. Taeuber 1985 "Measures of Segregation." In Nancy B. Tuma, ed., *Sociological Methodology 1985.* San Francisco: Jossey-Bass.

Jargowsky, Paul A. 1996 "Take the Money and Run: Economic Segregation in U.S. Metropolitan Areas." *American Sociological Review* 61:984–998.

Lieberson, Stanley 1980 *A Piece of the Pie: Blacks and White Immigrants since 1880.* Berkeley and Los Angeles: University of California Press.

—— 1981 "An Asymmetrical Approach to Segregation." In Ceri Peach, Vaughn Robinson, and Susan Smith, eds., *Ethnic Segregation in Cities.* London: Croom Helm.

Massey, Douglas S., and Nancy A. Denton 1988 "The Dimensions of Residential Segregation." *Social Forces* 67:281–315.

—— 1989 "Hypersegregation in U.S. Metropolitan Areas: Black and Hispanic Segregation along Five Dimensions." *Demography* 26:373–393.

—— 1993 *American Apartheid: Segregation and the Making of the Underclass.* Cambridge, Mass.: Harvard University Press.

Massey, Douglas S., and Zoltan Hajnal 1995 "The Changing Geographic Structure of Black-White Segregation in the United States." *Social Science Quarterly* 76:527–542.

Massey, Douglas S., Michael J. White, and Voon-Chin Phua 1996 "The Dimensions of Segregation Revisited." *Sociological Methods and Research* 25:172–206.

Morgan, Barrie S. 1983a "An Alternate Approach to the Development of a Distance-Based Measure of Racial Segregation." *American Journal of Sociology* 88:1237–1249.

—— 1983b "A Distance-Decay Interaction Index to Measure Residential Segregation." *Area* 15:211–216.

Peach, Ceri 1998 "South Asian and Caribbean Ethnic Minority Housing Choice in Britain." *Urban Studies* 35:1657–1680.

Stearns, Linda B., and John R. Logan 1986 "Measuring Segregation: Three Dimensions, Three Measures." *Urban Affairs Quarterly* 22:124–150.

Theil, Henri 1972 *Statistical Decomposition Analysis*. Amsterdam: North Holland.

White, Michael J. 1983 "The Measurement of Spatial Segregation." *American Journal of Sociology* 88:1008–1019.

—— 1984 "Reply to Mitra." *American Journal of Sociology* 90:189–191.

—— 1986 "Segregation and Diversity: Measures in Population Distribution." *Population Index* 52:198–221.

DOUGLAS S. MASSEY

SELF-CONCEPT

The self is the central concept used to represent the individual in sociological social psychology. The importance of the self reflects the influence of symbolic interactionism in sociology. In the last twenty years social psychologists trained in psychology also have developed a strong interest in the self as their emphasis has shifted from behaviorism to cognitive theories (Baumeister, 1998).

STABLE SELF-CONCEPTS

The social psychological conception of the self is based on the idea that people are reflexive, responding to themselves just as they respond to other "objects." Since reflexive thinking requires language, it is assumed that infants and nonhuman animals lack a self-concept. However, there is some evidence that chimpanzees are aware of what they look like, since they notice markings on their faces (Gallup 1977). This self-recognition suggests that some animals and prelinguistic humans have a rudimentary sense of self but that it lacks meaning or content.

Some sociologists, particularly those with a philosophical and qualitative orientation, view the self as a process involving people's internal conversations. Those with a more positivistic and quantitative orientation emphasize more stable aspects of the self. From their point of view, the self-concept refers to all the ways in which people describe themselves. These linguistic descriptions refer to the way people think they are, no to their actual personal characteristics.

People describe themselves in many different ways. One way to find out about the content of the self-concept is to ask respondents to answer the question "Who am I?" Studies of responses to this question reveal that people often think of themselves in terms of their roles (or role identities). For example, people often describe themselves on the basis of their sex, age, race, and occupation. Stryker (1968) suggests that these and other roles are organized in a hierarchy according to their salience for a person. The salience of a role is based in part on the extent to which adequate performance of that role affects relationships with "significant others." Salience is also a function of how distinctive a role is (McGuire and Padawer-Singer 1976). For example, a female is more likely to mention her gender in describing herself if she is in a group of males.

People also describe themselves in terms of personal attributes, such as "lazy," "smart," and "attractive." In contrast to roles—which usually are described with nouns—these self-concepts are more likely to be defined by adjectives. They often reflect individuals' conceptions of their abilities or performance in different roles. For example, on a questionnaire children can be asked, "How smart in school do you think you are, among the smartest, above average, average, or below average?" Respondents sometimes try to be objective in answering this type of question and to place themselves according to the criteria they think the researcher is using. Sometimes they report more subjective feelings about where they stand in accordance with their own standards. For example, professional athletes may be dissatisfied with their level of play even if they think they are better than most people. Other personal attributes involve self-attributed traits such as "aggressive" or "nice." Also included here are the ways in which people characterize their beliefs and attitudes. For example, people may conceive of themselves as prejudiced or not independently of whether they are prejudiced by an objective standard.

While individuals think of themselves in terms of specific roles and specific evaluations of their personal attributes, they also have a more general opinion of themselves (Gecas and Burke, 1995). This global evaluation Brown, 1993 called *self-esteem* and is measured by statements such as "I feel I do not have much to be proud of" and "At times I think I am no good at all" (Rosenberg 1965). The global nature of self-esteem is indicated by the tendency of individuals to describe themselves as consistently positive or negative on different personal attributes. However, self-esteem also has different dimensions, such as self-efficacy and self-worth (Gecas 1982). Self-esteem, like depression and anxiety, usually is considered an aspect of mental health. Research using longitudinal data has shown that self-esteem affects and is affected by depression among adolescents (Rosenberg et al. 1989).

There is considerable evidence that people are motivated to enhance their self-esteem. For example, respondents tend to give inflated evaluations of themselves on anonymous questionnaires. In addition, subjects in experiments are more likely to explain their successes in terms of internal attributes, such as effort and ability, while attributing their failures to external factors, such as task difficulty (Bradley 1978).

SITUATIONAL SELF-IMAGES

Some self-statements are more temporary than those described above, involving the roles or personal attributes people use to describe themselves in particular situations. For example, a woman may think of herself as a "teacher" when she is talking to her students and as "foolish" when she has made a mistake. If repeated, these situational images may become stable as people come to believe them. Emotions also can be considered temporary self-concepts if one thinks of them as statements about how people say they feel rather than as a physiological process. Thinking about emotions in this way leads to the examination of how emotions are affected by social processes.

Some scholars focus on the presentation of situational self-images to others (Goffman 1959). Borrowing language from the theater, they view behavior as a performance displayed in front of an audience, a form of self-presentation or impression management. This approach presents a challenge to those who attempt to measure self-concepts, since it suggests that responses on questionnaires reflect self-presentation rather than privately held beliefs. Researchers try to minimize this problem by using carefully worded questions and guaranteeing anonymity.

Situational self-images often are studied in laboratory experiments. For example, subjects may be asked to respond after receiving false feedback about themselves. To determine whether a self-description involves impression management, the privacy of subjects' responses may be manipulated. When behavior in front of an audience is different from behavior performed in private, this suggests that the behavior reflects impression management rather than privately held beliefs. This type of research also can tell researchers something about how behavior is affected by subjects' awareness that they are being studied. Some behaviors in experimental settings have been shown to result from subjects doing what they think is expected of them (Orne 1962).

Self-presentation behavior is particularly likely to occur when people have done something that is apt to gain disapproval from an audience. When people find themselves in these "predicaments," they are embarrassed and engage in various forms of "facework" to avoid a negative image. Frequently, people give excuses and justifications in an attempt to explain their behavior and avoid condemnation from others. Research shows that subjects are more likely to use self-presentation tactics when they are dependent on the audience for rewards. An important role of self-presentation in conformity, altruism, aggression, and other behaviors has been demonstrated. For example, self-presentation processes are important in explaining the behavior of bullies and the tendency for people to retaliate when attacked (Tedeschi and Felson 1994).

DEVELOPMENT OF SELF-APPRAISALS

Three processes have been used to explain why people have favorable or unfavorable opinions about themselves: (1) attribution, (2) comparison, and (3) reflected appraisal. The first two processes have been emphasized by psychological social psychologists, while the third has been the focus of sociological social psychologists, particularly those sympathetic toward symbolic interactionism.

According to attribution theory, people learn about themselves and others in similar ways. Individuals base judgments about themselves on observations of their own behavior just as they base judgments about others on their observations of those people's behavior (Bem 1972). These judgments are socially influenced, since beliefs about the association of behaviors and personal attributes are learned from others. In judging their abilities, for example, people rely in part on observations of their performances on tasks they believe reflect those abilities. Thus, children who get high grades tend to attribute more ability to themselves. Individuals are likely to attribute a high level of ability to themselves when there is a consistent pattern of success (Kelley 1967).

When people view their behavior as being caused by external forces, they treat it as uninformative about themselves. However, when they view their behavior as being internally caused, there is likely to be some change in their self-appraisals. For example, research shows that external rewards sometimes can reduce the motivation of children to do things they have enjoyed in the past, such as playing with magic markers (Deci and Ryan 1980). If they are rewarded for playing with magic markers, they tend to lose interest when they are no longer rewarded because they attribute their behavior to the reward rather than to their intrinsic motivation. The external reward can decrease their interest in the behavior because it affects their judgments about why they did it. More generally, there is evidence that people's behaviors can affect their attitudes, just as their attitudes can affect their behaviors (Liska et al. 1984). For example, a person may decide that she likes an activity because she observes herself voluntarily engaging in that activity.

Comparison processes are also important factors in the development of self-appraisals. They affect the standards people use in evaluating their behavior. For example, students may think a B is a good grade or a poor grade depending on the standard they use. Standards are a function of two types of comparisons. A *temporal comparison* is a comparison of present performance and past performance. People are likely to judge their recent performances more harshly if they have been suc-

cessful in the past. A *social comparison* is a comparison of one's own behavior to the behavior of others. The more successful the others are, the higher the standard is and the more negative the self-appraisal is. Thus, subjects are more negative in describing themselves when there is another person with very positive qualities present than they are when that person has negative qualities (Morse and Gergen 1970). This implies that self-appraisals tend to be more favorable if one is a "big fish in a small pond." For example, research shows that high school students tend to have more negative self-appraisals of their academic ability if their schoolmates are bright (Felson and Reed 1986). However, sometimes the performance of others has a positive effect on self-appraisal. This occurs when people "borrow status" from successful others with whom they are associated and "bask in reflected glory" (Cialdini et al. 1976).

Festinger (1954) suggested that social comparison processes result from the desire to gain accurate appraisals of one's abilities and to find out whether one's opinions are correct. When objective information is not available, people compare themselves to others. Further, Festinger suggested that people usually choose similar others for comparison because the behavior of those persons provides the most information. Some research has examined the hypothesis that people evaluate their abilities by comparing themselves to others who are similar to themselves on attributes (other than ability) that are related to performance. For example, comparisons with people who have engaged in a similar effort will be the most informative. Similarly, if a boy believes that gender is related to athletic performance, he will compare himself to other boys in order to decide how much athletic ability he has.

According to the reflected appraisal process, people come to see themselves as others see them, or at least as they think others see them. This notion of the "looking-glass self" focuses on how individuals think they appear to others (Cooley 1902). According to Mead (1934), this helps explain the initial formation of self in young children. Mead suggested that when children role-play, they respond to themselves when they play the role of others. This role-taking process leads them to see themselves as objects. Later, the appraisals of significant others shape the specific content of people's self-concepts. The appraisals of others are accurately perceived and then are incorporated into the self-concept. Significant others may have special expertise or may be parents or close friends, but those who influence one aspect of the self-concept do not necessarily influence other aspects.

Experimental research suggests that subjects' self-appraisals are affected by the false feedback they receive from others. Survey research—which examines correlations between self-appraisals, the appraisals of significant others, and a person's perception of those appraisals—suggests that the appraisals of significant others are not perceived very accurately (Schrauger and Schoeneman 1979). Apparently, rules of politeness limit the amount of open communication—particularly criticism—making it difficult for people to find out what others think of them (Felson 1980). When feedback is given, it tends to involve specific comments about behavior rather than global evaluations. When praise is given, it often is not believed. As a result, people usually have only vague, general impressions of what others think of them and self-appraisals tend to be idiosyncratic and idealized (Felson 1989). While others are in some agreement about a person, that person does not share in the consensus. In addition, ambiguous feedback allows people to think more favorably about themselves and thus protect their self-esteem.

This discussion also applies to global self-esteem. Educators and parents may overemphasize the importance of praise in the development of self-esteem in children. While there is evidence that parents' praise and other supportive behavior affects the self-esteem of children (Felson and Zielinski 1989), successful performance in activities that children value may be more important.

There are other processes that increase the correspondence between people's appraisals of themselves and the appraisals of others. First, in some instances, people have access to the same information others have. For example, children's self-appraisals of their ability and their friends' appraisals of them correspond, because both are affected by the children's grades. Second, some other people can influence self-concepts if they have control over formal evaluations. For example, evidence shows that teachers influence self-concepts because they assign grades, but that is usually the extent of their influence in this area.

The discussion above has focused on the interpersonal environment. Social-demographic characteristics also affect self-appraisal. Social class, for example, has been shown to affect the self-esteem of adults but not that of children (Rosenberg and Pearlin 1978). Blacks and whites, by contrast, have similar levels of self-esteem (Porter and Washington, 1993; Wylie, 1979). A key element here appears to be whether people associate with others who are like themselves. The self-esteem of minority group members is likely to be lower in more heterogeneous settings where invidious comparisons are made and where members of higher-status groups may act in prejudicial ways.

CONSEQUENCES OF SELF-CONCEPTS

The way individuals think of themselves has an important impact on how they behave. Thus, people who think of themselves in terms of particular role identities tend to act in ways that are consistent with those identities. For example, a man who identifies himself as a father will engage in the behaviors he associates with being a father. These roles provide links between the individual and society. Individuals are plugged into the social structure through the roles that are mapped onto selves. In other words, role performance reflects the way people think about themselves. Of course, people vary in terms of the importance they attach to different roles. When people must decide between roles, they tend to choose the role more salient to them (Stryker 1968). For example, the choice between doing work and playing with children on a Sunday afternoon may reflect the relative salience of family and occupational roles.

Success and failure frequently are attributed to variations in self-confidence. Self-appraisals and performance are certainly correlated, but this does not necessarily mean that the former causes the latter. Longitudinal studies, which attempt to disentangle these causal relationships, suggest that students' global self-esteem does not affect their academic performance. However, there is evidence that specific self-appraisals of ability affect performance. Longitudinal analyses of high school students suggest that self-appraisals of academic ability have an effect on grades (Felson 1984). Self-appraisals of ability affect performance through two processes: effort and test anxiety. Those who are self-confident about their ability are likely to work harder because they think effort will bring success. In addition, they are less anxious when they are tested, and so nervousness does not interfere with their performance. However, the effect of self-appraisal on performance probably is not as strong as people think. The effect of grades on self-appraisal is much stronger, suggesting that success is more likely to lead to self-confidence than self-confidence is to lead to success.

Causal interpretation has been problematic in the study of the effects of self-concept on other behaviors as well. While self-esteem and various self-appraisals have been shown to correlate with behavior, it is difficult to show that the self-concepts cause the behaviors. Relatively few studies have attempted to sort out these relationships. Exceptions include longitudinal studies that suggest that low self-esteem increases delinquency among adolescents (e.g., Kaplan 1980; Rosenberg et al. 1989). In general, criminologists today are more likely to attribute criminal behavior to low self-control than to low self-esteem.

An interesting experimental method for examining the effects of self-concept on behavior has been suggested by Duval and Wicklund (1972). They suggest that since much human behavior is automatic or habitual, people do not always think about themselves before they engage in a behavior. These authors argue that self-concepts affect behavior when attention is directed toward the self rather than toward the environment, a condition they call "objective self-awareness." Objective self-awareness is likely to occur when people are in unfamiliar surroundings, when there are disruptions in social interaction, and when people find themselves in a minority. Mirrors are commonly used in experiments to create objective self-awareness. These studies show that subjects are more likely to engage in behavior that is consistent with their self-standards when they are facing a mirror (e.g., Beaman et al. 1979). In addition, there are individual differences: Some people are more chronically focused on themselves as objects. The behavior of such people is more likely to be consistent with their self-appraisals and internalized standards.

A number of researchers have examined the role of self-concepts in resisting change. For example, research suggests that people are motivated to reaffirm self-concepts when they are challenged (Swann 1984). Markus (1977) considers the generalizations people make about themselves as "self-schemas" that affect the way they process information. Self-schemas usually refer to personality traits (e.g., "independent" and "generous") that people attribute to themselves on the basis of past actions. Once formed, they affect the information people attend to and remember and how quickly they process it. For example, people are more likely to learn and recall information that is associated with their self-schemas. In other words, self-schemas act like filters, guiding the processing of incoming information. Thus, self-schemas have a conservative function because they lead people to focus on information that is consistent with their views of themselves.

SUMMARY

The determinants and consequences of the self have become central concerns for both sociologically and psychologically trained social psychologists. Self-concepts depend on the way individuals think they are viewed by others, on individuals' observations of their behavior, and on the standards individuals use to judge that behavior. These judgments in turn depend on the performance (for comparison) and appraisals of others. Self-concepts have consequences in that they affect which roles are performed and how successfully they are performed. They also affect conformity and deviance and the management of impressions. Finally, they are important in their own right as indicators of mental health.

REFERENCES

Baumeister, Roy 1998 "The Self." In D. T. Gilbert, S. T. Fiske & G. Lindzey, eds., *Handbook of Social Psychology*, 4th ed. New York: McGraw-Hill.

Beaman, A. L., B. Klentz, E. Diener, and S. Svanum 1979 "Objective Self-Awareness and Transgression in Children: A Field Study." *Journal of Personality and Social Psychology* 37:1835–1846.

Bem, Daryl 1972 "Self-Perception Theory." In L. Berkowitz, ed., *Advances in Experimental Social Psychology*, vol. 6. New York: Academic Press.

Bradley, G. W. 1978 "Self-Serving Biases in the Attribution Process: A Reexamination of the Fact or Fiction

Question." *Journal of Personality and Social Psychology* 36:56–71.

Brown, J. D. 1993 "Self-esteem and Self-evaluation: Feeling is Believing." In J. Suls, ed., *Psychological Perspectives on the Self.* Hillsdale, NJ: Erlbaum.

Cialdini, R. B., R. J. Borden, A. Thorne, M. R. Walker, S. Freeman, and L. R. Sloan 1976 "Basking in Reflected Glory: Three (Football) Field Studies." *Journal of Personality and Social Psychology* 34:366–374.

Cooley, Charles H. 1902 *Human Nature and the Social Order.* New York: Scribner's.

Deci, E. L., and R. M. Ryan 1980 "The Empirical Exploration of Intrinsic Motivational Processes." In L. Berkowitz, ed., *Advances in Experimental Social psychology*, vol. 13. New York: Academic Press.

Duval, S., and R. A. Wicklund 1972 *A Theory of Objective Self-Awareness.* New York: Academic Press.

Felson, Richard B. 1980 "Communication Barriers and the Reflected Appraisal Process." *Social Psychology Quarterly*, 43:223–233.

Felson, Richard B. 1984 "The Effects of Self-appraisals of Ability on Academic Performance." *Journal of Peronality and Social Psychology* 47:944–952.

—— 1989 "Parents and the Reflected Appraisal Process: A Longitudinal Analysis." *Journal of Personality and Social Psychology* 56:965–971.

——, and Mark Reed 1986 "The Effect of Parents on the Self-Appraisals of Children." *Social Psychology Quarterly*, 49:302–308.

——, and Mary Zielinski. 1989 "Children's Self-Esteem and Parental Support." *Journal of Marriage and the Family* 51:727–735.

Festinger, Leon 1954 "A Theory of Social Comparison Processes." *Human Relations* 7:117–140.

Gallup, G. G., Jr. 1977 "Self-Recognition in Primates: A Comparative Approach to the Bidirectional Properties of Consciousness." *American Psychologist* 32:329–338.

Gecas, Viktor 1982 "The Self-Concept." *Annual Review of Sociology* 8:1–33.

Gecas, Viktor, and Peter J. Burke 1995 "Self and Identity." In K. S. Cook, G. A. Fine and J. S. House, eds., *Sociological Perspectives on Social Psychology* Needham Heights, Mass.: Allyn & Bacon.

Goffman, Erving 1959 *The Presentation of Self in Everyday Life.* New York: Doubleday.

Kaplan, Howard B. 1980 *Deviant Behavior in Defense of Self.* New York: Academic Press.

Kelley, H. H. 1967 "Attribution Theory in Social Psychology." In D. Levine, ed., *Nebraska Symposium on Motivation.* Lincoln: University of Nebraska Press.

Liska, A., R. Felson, M. Chamlin, and W. Baccaglini 1984 "Estimating Attitude-Behavior Relations within a Theoretical Specification." *Social Psychology Quarterly* 47:15–23.

Markus, H. 1977 "Self-Schemata and Processing Information about the Self." *Journal of Personality and Social Psychology* 35:63–78.

McGuire, William J., and A. Padawer-Singer 1976 "Trait Salience in the Spontaneous Self-Concept." *Journal of Personality and Social Psychology* 33:743–754.

Mead, G. H. 1934 *Mind, Self and Society.* Chicago: University of Chicago Press.

Morse, S., and K. J. Gergen 1970 "Social Comparison, Self-Consistency, and the Concept of Self." *Journal of Personality and Social Psychology* 16:148–156.

Orne, Martin T. 1962 "On the Social Psychology of the Psychological Experiment: With Particular Reference to Demand Characteristics and Their Implications." *American Psychologist* 17:776–783.

Porter, J. R., and R. E. Washington 1993 "Minority Identity and Self-esteem." Annual Review of Sociology 19:139–161.

Rosenberg, M. 1965 *Society and the Adolescent Self-Image.* Princeton, N.J.: Princeton University Press.

——, and Leonard Pearlin 1979 "Social Class and Self-Esteem among Children and Adults." *American Journal of Sociology* 84:53–87.

——, Carmi Schooler, and Carrie Schoenback 1989 "Self-Esteem and Adolescent Problems." *American Sociological Review* 54:1004–1018.

Schrauger, J. S., and T. J. Schoeneman 1979 Symbolic Interactionist View of Self: Through the Looking Glass Darkly. *Psychological Bulletin*, 86:549–573.

Stryker, Sheldon 1968 "Identity Salience and Role Performance: The Relevance of Symbolic Interaction Theory for Family Research." *Journal of Marriage and the Family* 30:558–564.

Swann, W. B. 1984 "Self-Verification: Bringing Social Reality into Harmony with the Self." In J. Suls and A. G. Greenwald, eds., *Psychological Perspective on the Self*, vol. 2. Hillsdale, N.J.: Erlbaum.

Tedeschi, James T. and Richard B. Felson 1994 *Violence, Aggression, & Coercive Actions.* Washington, D.C.: APA Books.

Wylie, Ruth 1979 *The Self-Concept: Revised Edition*, vol. 2: *Theory and Research on Selected Topics.* Lincoln: University of Nebraska Press.

RICHARD B. FELSON

SELF-ESTEEM

Self-esteem is a concept that has been used to explain a vast array of emotional, motivational, and behavioral phenomena. Most Americans believe intuitively that low self-esteem is undesirable; indeed, the link between low self-esteem and depression, shyness, loneliness, and alienation supports the general idea that low self-esteem is an aversive state. The view that self-esteem is a vital component of mental health is also evident in the popular media and in educational policy. Low self-esteem has been viewed as the root cause of societal problems ranging from drug abuse to teenage pregnancy to poor school performance. A number of educational and therapeutic programs have been developed to solve these problems by increasing self-esteem. Self-esteem is one of the most frequently examined constructs in sociology and psychology, with more than 15,000 research articles referring to it over the past thirty years. This entry reviews the research that has focused on the conceptual and functional basis of self-esteem.

Self-esteem is defined as the evaluative component of the self-concept, the extent to which people view themselves as likable and worthy as opposed to unlikable and unworthy. As a self-reflexive attitude, self-esteem is composed of cognitive and affective components. Self-esteem is related to personal beliefs about skills, abilities, and future outcomes as well as the strategies people use to gain self-knowledge. However, the personal experience of self-esteem is more emotional than rational. Some people dislike themselves in spite of objective evidence suggesting that they should feel very good about themselves. Many successful doctors, lawyers, professors, and entrepreneurs are filled with self-loathing despite their objective career success.

The term "self-esteem" sometimes is used interchangeably with terms such as "self-confidence," "self-efficacy," and even "self-concept," but such usage is inaccurate and should be discouraged. Self-confidence and self-efficacy refer to the belief that one can attain specific outcomes. Although people with high self-esteem often are self-confident, evaluative reactions to personal outcomes vary greatly, and it is possible for people to be confident about attaining a goal without feeling good about themselves in the process. The term "self-concept" refers to the components of self-knowledge and includes things such as name, race, ethnicity, gender, occupation, likes and dislikes, and personality traits. As such, self-concept refers to cognitive beliefs and other forms of self-relevant knowledge (Felson 1992). Although self-esteem clearly is influenced by the contents of the self-concept, they are not the same thing.

STRUCTURE AND MEASUREMENT OF SELF-ESTEEM

An important issue in the literature on self-esteem is whether self-esteem is best conceptualized as a unitary global trait or a multidimensional trait with independent subcomponents. An example of a multidimensional trait model is Tafarodi and Swann's (1995) differentiation between self-liking and self-competence. From this perspective, it is possible for people to like themselves generally but view themselves as not particularly efficacious at various tasks. Conversely, it is possible for people to view themselves as generally competent but not really like themselves. Mismatches between self-liking and self-competence lead to biases in the interpretation of social and performance feedback that confirm the level of self-liking. For instance, those who are high in self-liking but low in self-competence perceive negative feedback more positively than do those who are low in self-liking but high in self-competence.

Global self-esteem is best conceptualized as a hierarchical construct with three major components: *performance* self-esteem, *social* self-esteem, and *physical* self-esteem. Each component can be broken down into progressively smaller subcomponents. Performance self-esteem refers to one's sense of general competence and includes intellectual ability, school performance, self-regulatory capacities, self-confidence, efficacy, and agency. People who are high in performance self-esteem believe that they are smart and capable. As will be discussed below, personal beliefs about performance are poorly related to objective outcomes. Social self-esteem refers to how people believe they are perceived by others. It is perception rather than reality that is critical here. If people believe that others, especially significant others, value and respect them, they experience high social self-esteem even if others truly dislike them or hold them in contempt. The influence of these reflected appraisals on self-esteem is an integral part of Cooley's (1902) "looking-glass self" and has been implicated in the development of self-esteem by sociological theorists such as George Herbert Mead and Stanley Rosenberg. People who are low in social self-esteem often experience social anxiety and are high in public self-consciousness. They are highly attentive to their public images and worry about how others view them. Physical self-esteem refers to how people view their physical bodies and includes things such as athletic skills, physical attractiveness, and body image as well as physical stigmas and feelings about race and ethnicity.

How are these subcomponents of self-esteem related to global self-esteem? James (1892) proposed that global self-esteem is the summation of specific components of self-esteem, each of which is weighted by its importance to the self-concept. In other words, people have high self-esteem to the extent that they feel good about the things that matter to them. Not being good at tennis is irrelevant to the self-concept of a nonathlete, and doing poorly in school may have little impact on inner-city youth who do not identify with mainstream values (Steele 1997). Pelham (1995) and Marsh (1995) debated the value of global versus specific component models. Pelham's research generally supports the Jamesian view that the centrality of self-views is an important predictor of the emotional response to the self (i.e., one's feelings of self-esteem), whereas Marsh claims that domain importance does not have a strong impact on self-esteem. Although the jury is still out on this issue, the concept of domain importance is a central feature of most theories of self-esteem.

In terms of measurement, most research uses global measures of self-esteem, since this is viewed as having the greatest theoretical importance (Baumeister 1998). The most widely used measure of global self-esteem is the Rosenberg (1965) scale, which consists of ten general statements such as "On the whole, I am satisfied with myself," "I certainly feel useless at times," and "I take a positive attitude toward myself." Unfortunately, scores on this scale tend to be tightly clustered around its mean, limiting its predictive value. A review of self-esteem measures conducted by Blascovich and Tomaka (1991) recommended the Revised Feelings of Inadequacy Scale (Fleming and Courtney 1984), which is a modified version of the Janis and Field (1959) scale. This scale has five factors: social

confidence, school abilities, self-regard, physical appearance, and physical ability. The total score on this scale is widely used as a measure of global self-esteem.

Another issue in the measurement and definition of self-esteem is whether it is best conceptualized as a stable personality *trait* or a context-specific *state*. Most theories of self-esteem view it as a relatively stable trait: If one has high self-esteem today, one probably will have high self-esteem tomorrow. Around this stable baseline, however, there are fluctuations; although people generally may feel good about themselves, there are times when they may experience self-doubt and even dislike themselves. In terms of research, the selection of trait or state measures of self-esteem depends on whether one is interested in predicting long-term outcomes or in the immediate effects associated with feelings about the self. Obviously, measures of state self-esteem are more useful for the latter group. The State Self-Esteem Scale (Heatherton and Polivy 1991) is a commonly used measure that has been shown to be sensitive to laboratory manipulations of self-esteem. This scale measures context-specific feelings related to performance, social, and physical self-esteem. Measures of trait and state self-esteem are highly correlated. However, frequent fluctuations in state self-esteem have been found to be associated with increased sensitivity to and reliance on social evaluations, increased concern about how one views the self, and even anger and hostility (Kernis 1993). In general, those with a fragile sense of self-esteem respond extremely favorably to positive feedback and extremely defensively to negative feedback.

SOURCES AND FUNCTIONS OF SELF-ESTEEM

A central issue in self-esteem pertains to its source. Research in psychology and sociology has focused on the role of early childhood experiences, especially in terms of parental treatment. Harter has incorporated the Jamesian and Cooley views of the development of self-esteem into a general model of self-esteem development (Harter 1993). Harter proposes that reflected appraisals about important dimensions affect the development of self-esteem but that specific domains are closely linked to potential audiences. According to her theory, parents are particularly concerned about behavioral conduct and school performance, and therefore, children's beliefs about how their parents view them on these dimensions influence self-esteem. Children who do well scholastically and behave in accordance with parental expectations believe that their parents support and love them. However, parents have less impact than do peers on self-perceptions related to physical appearance, athletic ability, and peer likability. To obtain the support of one's peers, children believe they have to be attractive, athletic, and likable. Failure to obtain support from either parents or peers can lead to feelings of hopelessness, depression, and poor global self-esteem. Harter's model offers a significant advance over earlier developmental theories by integrating importance and social support from a domain-specific perspective.

Further evidence for socialization processes can be found when one considers the influence of gender differences. A number of studies suggest that boys and girls diverge in their primary sources of self-esteem, with girls being more influenced by relationships and boys being more influenced by objective success. Stein et al. (1992) examined participants in an eight-year longitudinal study of adolescent growth and development. During adolescence, an agentic orientation predicted heightened self-esteem for males but not for females, whereas a communal orientation predicted heightened self-esteem for females but not for males. The possibility that males and females differ in terms of what constitutes the self-concept was also addressed by Josephs et al. (1992). In a series of studies, men and women were given false feedback indicating that they had deficits either on a performance dimension (e.g., competition, individual thinking) or on a social dimension (e.g., nurturance, interpersonal integration). Consistent with predictions, men high in self-esteem enhanced their estimates of being able to engage successfully in future performance behaviors, whereas women high in self-esteem enhanced their estimates of being able to engage successfully in future social behaviors. The authors of this entry recently compared the experiences of boys and girls in a summer tennis camp designed to increase self-esteem (Hebl et al. 1999). Scores on a children's version of the state self-esteem scale showed that both boys and girls had increases in overall self-esteem during the tennis camp, but whereas boys gained self-esteem primarily in the performance self-esteem

domain, girls gainedself-esteem primarily in the social self-esteem domain. In each case it can be seen that boys gain self-esteem from getting ahead whereas girls gain self-esteem from getting along.

From a completely different perspective, some researchers have begun to explore the possibility that self-esteem is determined more by biology than by socialization. Although direct evidence is minimal, there is circumstantial evidence that some components of self-esteem are based in biology. Twin studies have suggested that self-esteem is moderately heritable, with estimates ranging from 30 to 50 percent (Kendler et al. 1998). In addition, traits known to be associated with self-esteem, such as extraversion and neuroticism, have long been known to have a genetic component. Kramer (1993) argues that self-esteem is rooted in activity of the serotoninergic neurotransmitter system. He notes that pharmacological treatments that increase the activity of serotonin are associated with an increased sense of self-confidence and self-esteem. However, there have not been any systematic or rigorous tests of this hypothesis. The possibility that self-esteem has a biological component remains an important empirical issue.

Some theorists have portrayed self-esteem as a mechanism that has evolved through adaptation to promote survival of the species. Accordingly, self-esteem is viewed as a force that promotes feelings of confidence and competence that may lead to superior performance across a broad range of activities. Interestingly, this perspective can be used to explain gender differences in the major sources of self-esteem. Throughout human evolutionary history, males were of value to the group primarily through their role as hunters and protectors whereas women gathered food and nurtured offspring. Hence, being good at tasks closely associated with ancestral sex roles may be associated with increased feelings of self-esteem. However, because theories of evolution and socialization predict the same gender pattern for self-esteem, it is impossible to clarify which perspective is correct or whether they are equally correct or incorrect. Baumeister (1998) has noted that simple evolutionary accounts of self-esteem are difficult to accept because of the rather negligible benefits associated with self-esteem and the possibility that high self-esteem may promote overconfidence and excessive risk taking.

A novel and important functional account of self-esteem has been proposed by Leary and his colleagues. Leary begins with the assumption that humans have a fundamental need to belong that is rooted in evolutionary history (Baumeister and Leary 1995). For most of human evolution, survival and reproduction depended on affiliation with a group. Those who belonged to social groups were more likely to survive and reproduce than were those who were excluded from groups and left to survive on their own. According to Leary, self-esteem functions as a monitor of the likelihood of social exclusion. When people behave in ways that increase the likelihood that they will be rejected, they experience a reduction in state self-esteem. Thus, self-esteem serves as a monitor, or sociometer, of social acceptance and/or rejection. At the trait level, those with high self-esteem have sociometers that indicate a low probability of rejection and therefore do not worry about how they are perceived by others. By contrast, those with low self-esteem have sociometers that indicate the imminent possibility of rejection and therefore are highly motivated to manage their public impressions.

CONSEQUENCES OF HAVING HIGH OR LOW SELF-ESTEEM

Self-esteem has both cognitive and affective components. Accordingly, a number of researchers have examined the cognitive and affective reactions of those with high and low self-esteem. The overall view suggests that people process information in a way that confirms and supports their chronic self-views. People with high self-esteem actively defend their positive self-views, whereas those with low self-esteem appear to be less able to do so. This section reviews research that has examined differences between individuals with high and low self-esteem.

Self-esteem differences have been reported for a wide range of intrapsychic phenomena, including emotional reactions, cognitive processes, and motivational states. There are obvious differences in how individuals with high and low self-esteem feel about themselves; the positivity and negativity of self-feelings are of course central to self-esteem. For instance, people with low self-esteem are more likely to report being depressed and anxious than are those with high self-esteem. These differences appear to be more subjective

than objective. Researchers have used diary studies to examine whether high and low self-esteem people differ in their daily moods and emotions (Campbell et al. 1991). Compared with individuals with high self-esteem, individuals with low self-esteem judged the events in their lives more negatively and as having a greater impact on their moods. However, when outside judges read participants' diaries, they could not distinguish between the events experienced by participants with high and low self-esteem. Thus, similar circumstances are perceived and experienced differently as a function of a person's self-esteem level. In terms of specific emotional states, there are no differences in how high and low self-esteem individuals experience impersonal emotions (e.g., happiness), but there are differences in how they experience self-relevant emotions (e.g., pride and shame). People with high self-esteem are more likely to report pride, whereas those with low self-esteem are more likely to report shame. Once again, this pattern is independent of actual events in the lives of people with high and low self-esteem.

A robust finding in social psychological research is that everyone feels good after receiving positive feedback regardless of one's self-esteem level. People with low self-esteem like to hear good things about themselves just as much as do people with high self-esteem, and both groups hope to be successful in life. However, people with high self-esteem are much more likely to believe positive feedback. People with low self-esteem are distrustful of overly positive feedback because it contradicts what they believe to be true about themselves. Swann (Swann et al. 1987) argues that people with low self-esteem are attracted to negative information because it validates and confirms their negative self-views. Swann likens the conflict between an emotional preference for positivity and a cognitive preference for negativity to being caught in the cross fire between two warring factions.

A consistent theme in the literature on self-esteem is that self-esteem involves a cognitive bias in processing evaluative and social information. In a world filled with ambiguities and uncertainties, people selectively construct their own reality through biased encoding, retrieval, and interpretation of life events. Research on information-processing styles shows that high self-esteem is associated with cognitive strategies aimed at enhancing self-appraisals and thinking of oneself in the most positive way. These objectives are accomplished by means of deeper encoding and more frequent retrieval of positive self-knowledge coupled with an avoidance of negative self-relevant information. That is, people with high self-esteem pay attention to information that says good things about them but ignore information that challenges a positive self-view. By contrast, the processing style associated with low self-esteem is one of self-consciousness and rumination. Individuals with low self-esteem focus on their own thoughts and feelings, often dwelling on negative life events. They are vigilant for information that confirms a negative self-view and ruminate on past failures, embarrassments, and setbacks in a nonproductive fashion.

Biased information processing helps people maintain their existing self-views. For example, an individual with high self-esteem may create a personal definition of what it means to be a "good student" that includes areas in which he or she excels while downplaying the importance of areas of personal deficiency. People with high self-esteem also believe that their talents are unique and special but that their weaknesses are common and trivial. As a result of their selective processing of evaluative information, people with high self-esteem are more adept at defending their self-esteem from external threats. Thus, people with high self-esteem discredit sources of negative feedback while readily accepting positive feedback. These people are also more likely to show a self-serving bias, which refers to the tendency of individuals to take personal credit for success but to blame failure on external circumstances. Some studies in fact find a reversal of the self-serving bias in individuals with low self-esteem such that they credit success to the environment (e.g., an easy task or luck) and blame themselves for failure. People with low self-esteem appear to be generally less able to put a positive spin on negative personal information. For instance, after receiving a negative evaluation, individuals with low self-esteem are more likely to dwell on their weaknesses while individuals with high self-esteem recruit thoughts about their strengths. Differential responses to feedback appear to be an automatic consequence of self-esteem that does not require effort or conscious initiation (Dodgson and Wood 1998).

Baumeister and Tice (Baumeister et al. 1989) have proposed that the basic distinction between high self-esteem and low self-esteem is motivational. People with high self-esteem are concerned primarily with self-enhancement, whereas people with low self-esteem are concerned primarily with self-protection. The self-enhancement motive emphasizes feeling good about oneself with the aim of increasing one's self-esteem. Thus, people with high self-esteem look for areas in which they can excel and stand out. When they fail at a task, they set higher goals so that they can prove they possess exceptional skills. By contrast, people with low self-esteem are concerned with avoiding humiliation, embarrassment, and rejection. Low self-esteem individuals' self-protective orientation guards against feeling even worse about themselves. Thus, when they fail at a task, they set more modest goals so that they do not lose further esteem through failure.

Self-esteem is known to be relevant to interpersonal behavior. For instance, high and low self-esteem people differ in their perceptions of interpersonal acceptance or rejection. A study in which participants were told that they had been rejected or accepted by their peers (Nezlek et al. 1997) showed that individuals with low self-esteem perceived peer inclusion and exclusion accurately, corresponding to experimental feedback. High self-esteem individuals, however, always perceived inclusion, even when they had been told they had been personally rejected. In general, people with high self-esteem believe that others admire, like, and respect them, whereas people with low self-esteem do not feel that others provide them with adequate support. This pattern fits in well with the reflected appraisal model of self-esteem that was discussed earlier. Because they are concerned with how others view them and are uncertain about their own beliefs, people with low self-esteem are especially yielding; they change their minds and behaviors to conform to the beliefs and opinions of others. Conversely, people with high self-esteem are confident about their opinions and tend not to be influenced by others. Indeed, they often view their own ideas and beliefs as being superior to those of others.

The currently available evidence paints the cognitive, affective, and social worlds of those with high and low self-esteem to be quite different. But do people truly differ as a function of self-esteem? When people are interviewed, there appear to be great differences between those with high and low self-esteem. When describing themselves, high self-esteem people say they are physically attractive, intelligent, socially skilled, outgoing, upbeat, optimistic, and satisfied with the state of their lives. Low self-esteem people depict themselves in a much less positive light and describe themselves by using more neutral and negative self-aspects than do those with high self-esteem. Unfortunately, the use of self-reports is problematic because they are confounded by one's level of self-esteem. High self-esteem people generally like and believe favorable things about themselves, and it is not surprising that they rate themselves highly on positive personality traits. However, the extent to which high self-esteem individuals actually possess and exhibit these positive traits—and the extent to which they do not possess or exhibit negative traits—is not well known.

The few studies that have compared claims by high and low self-esteem people to objective standards have not found differences between self-esteem groups. For instance, although people with high self-esteem think of themselves as more attractive than do people with low self-esteem, both groups are seen as equally attractive by others (Diener et al. 1995). Ratings of intelligence show the same pattern: High self-esteem people claim to be more intelligent, but intelligence tests show no differences as a function of self-esteem (Gabriel et al. 1994). Similarly, self-report data indicate that high self-esteem individuals are more likable than are low self-esteem individuals. However, likability ratings of high and low self-esteem people by interaction partners show no relation to self-esteem (Brockner and Lloyd 1986). Overall, most researchers have concluded that there are few differences in objective outcomes between those high and low in self-esteem (Baumeister 1998). A review of the literature by the California Task Force to Promote Self-Esteem and Personal and Social Responsibility (1990) conceded that "the associations between self-esteem and its expected consequences are mixed, insignificant, or absent" (Mecca et al. 1989, p. 15). Self-esteem appears to be related to *subjective* rather than *objective* life outcomes.

It is even possible that high self-esteem is associated with negative outcomes in some contexts. For instance, although high self-esteem typically is associated with superior self-regulation, some evidence suggests that high self-esteem may interfere with self-regulation when self-esteem is threatened. Relative to when they succeed, failure elicits higher goals and increased persistence—even on unsolvable tasks—in those with high self-esteem (McFarlin et al. 1984). Baumeister et al. (1993) demonstrated that ego threats sabotage self-regulation among those with high self-esteem. In this research, high and low self-esteem participants chose performance contingencies in which greater payoffs were associated with loftier and riskier personal goals. In the control condition, those with high self-esteem set appropriate goals and showed superior self-regulation. However, after ego threat (being told to play it safe if they "didn't have what it takes"), high self-esteem participants set inappropriate, risky goals and ended up with smaller monetary rewards than did participants with low self-esteem. Under threat, participants with high self-esteem also were significantly more likely to choke under pressure (i.e., to show performance decrements under conditions where superior performance is important) than were participants with low self-esteem. These findings suggest that people with high self-esteem are prone to self-regulatory failure in certain situations.

Similarly, extremely positive self-appraisals have been linked to poor interpersonal outcomes, especially when such self-appraisals are challenged or discredited. Baumeister et al. (1996) examined the literature linking self-esteem to interpersonal violence. In contrast to widely held assumptions that low self-esteem is associated with violent actions, they found a consistent pattern in which those who thought highly of themselves but encountered a threat or challenge to their positive self-views were more likely to act in hostile and violent ways. Similarly, Kernis and colleagues (Kernis 1993) have demonstrated that when it is unstable, high self-esteem is associated with increased hostility and aggression. They found that those with unstable high self-esteem are likely to respond to ego threats with self-aggrandizement and defensiveness (Kernis et al. 1997).

Other evidence suggests that those with highly positive self-views may exhibit poor interpersonal skills. Colvin et al. (1995) examined individuals with apparently inflated self-views, as indicated by the difference between self and other ratings. They found that those individuals were viewed by others as hostile and unlikable. In addition, during a structured and highly charged debate, such individuals engaged in a variety of negatively evaluated interpersonal behaviors, such as bragging, interrupting their partners, and showing an overall lack of genuine concern for their partners. Once again, these patterns are most likely to occur when high self-esteem individuals feel personally challenged. Schlenker et al. (1990) exposed high and low self-esteem subjects to contexts in which they were motivated to make a positive impression on a critical or a supportive audience. They found that high self-esteem subjects became egotistical when the evaluative pressures were greatest. They concluded that "people with high self-esteem become more boastful as the social stakes increase" (p. 891). Similar findings have been reported by Schneider and Turkat (1975), who found that high self-esteem subjects who also expressed high needs for social approval presented themselves much more positively after negative feedback than they did after positive feedback. Perhaps ironically, high self-esteem subjects who receive negative feedback about their intellectual abilities claim to have especially good social skills. However, the available evidence does not support their claims.

SUMMARY

Having high self-esteem confers a number of benefits to those who possess it: Such people feel good about themselves, are able to cope effectively with challenges and negative feedback, and live in a social world in which they believe that people value and respect them. Although there may be some negative consequences associated with having extremely high self-esteem, most people with high self-esteem lead happy and productive lives. People with low self-esteem see the world through a more negative filter, and their general dislike for themselves influences their perceptions of everything around them. It is striking that the objective record does not validate the subjective experiences of those with high and low self-esteem. The interesting unanswered questions about self-esteem are related to what allows people to hold such positive or negative views of themselves in spite of objective evidence. For instance, it is possible that self-esteem is rooted in neurochemistry and therefore is not sensitive to contextual influence, but this has not been established. It is equally plausible that self-esteem is a cognitive style that develops through early socialization experiences, but this perspective also requires more conclusive evidence. In any case, the subjective experience of having high or low self-esteem plays an important role in how people interpret the world around them.

REFERENCES

Baumeister, R. F. 1998 "The Self." In D. T. Gilbert, S. T. Fiske, and G. Lindzey, eds., *Handbook of Social Psychology* 4th ed. Boston: McGraw-Hill.

——, T. F. Heatherton, and D. M. Tice 1993 "When Ego Threats Lead to Self-Regulation Failure: Negative Consequences of High Self-esteem." *Journal of Personality and Social Psychology* 64:141–156.

——, and M. R. Leary 1995 "The Need to Belong: Desire for Interpersonal Attachments as a Fundamental Human Motivation." *Psychological Bulletin* 117:497–529.

——, L. Smart, and J. M. Boden 1996 "Relation of Threatened Egotism to Violence and Aggression: The Dark Side of High Self-Esteem." *Psychological Review* 103:5–33.

——, D. M. Tice, and D. G. Hutton 1989 Self-Presentational Motivations and Personality Differences in Self-Esteem." *Journal of Personality* 57:547–579.

Blascovich, J., and J. Tomaka 1991 "Measures of Self-Esteem." In J. P. Robinson, P. R. Shaver, and L. S. Wrightsman, eds., *Measures of Personality and Social Psychological Attitudes*, vol. 1. San Diego, Calif.: Academic Press.

Brockner, J., and K. Lloyd 1986 "Self-Esteem and Likability: Separating Fact from Fantasy." *Journal of Research in Personality* 20:496–508.

Campbell, J. D., B. Chew, and L. S. Scratchley 1991 "Cognitive and Emotional Reactions to Daily Events: The Effects of Self-Esteem and Self-Complexity." *Journal of Personality* 59:473–505.

Colvin, C. R., J. Block, and D. C. Funder 1995 "Overly Positive Self-Evaluations and Personality: Negative Implications for Mental Health." *Journal of Personality and Social Psychology* 68:1152–1162.

Cooley, C. H. 1902 *Human Nature and the Social Order.* New York: Scribner's.

Diener, E., B. Wolsic, and F. Fujita 1995 "Physical Attractiveness and Subjective Well-Being." *Journal of Personality and Social Psychology* 69:120–129.

Dodgson, P. G., and J. V. Wood 1998 "Self-Esteem and the Cognitive Accessibility of Strengths and Weaknesses after Failure." *Journal of Personality and Social Psychology* 75:178–197.

Felson, R. B. 1992 "Self-Concept." In E. Borgatta, ed., *Encyclopedia of Sociology*, New York: Macmillan.

Fleming, J. S., and B. E. Courtney 1984 "The Dimensionality of Self-Esteem: Hierarchical Facet Model for Revised Measurement Scales." *Journal of Personality and Social Psychology* 46:404–421.

Gabriel, M. T., J. W. Critelli, and J. S. Ee 1994 "Narcissistic Illusions in Self-Evaluations of Intelligence and Attractiveness." *Journal of Personality* 62:143–155.

Harter, S. 1993 "Causes and Consequences of Low Self-Esteem in Children and Adolescents." In R. Baumeister, ed., *Self-Esteem: The Puzzle of Low Self-Regard*. New York: Plenum.

Heatherton, T. F., and J. Polivy 1991 "Development and Validation of a Scale for Measuring State Self-Esteem." *Journal of Personality and Social Psychology* 60:895–910.

Hebl, M., T. F. Heatherton, and C. Lloyd 1999 "Differential Bases of Boys' and Girls' State Self-Esteem." Unpublished manuscript. Dartmouth College.

James, W. 1892 *Psychology: The Briefer Course*. New York: Henry Holt.

Janis, I. L., and P. Field 1959 "Sex Differences and Personality Factors Related to Persuasibility." In C. Hovland and I. Janis, eds., *Personality and Persuasibility*. New Haven, Conn.: Yale University Press.

Josephs, R. A., H. R. Markus, and R. W. Tafarodi 1992 "Gender and Self-Esteem." *Journal of Personality and Social Psychology* 63:391–402.

Kendler, K. S., C. O. Gardner, and C. A. Prescott 1998 "A Population-Based Twin Study of Self-Esteem and Gender." *Psychological Medicine* 28:1403–1409.

Kernis, M. H. 1993 "The Roles of Stability and Level of Self-Esteem in Psychological Functioning." In R. Baumeister, ed., *Self-Esteem: The Puzzle of Low Self-Regard*. New York: Plenum.

——, K. D. Greenier, C. E. Herlocker, C. R. Whisenhunt, and T. A. Abend, 1997 "Self-Perceptions of Reactions to Doing Well or Poorly: The Roles of Stability and Level of Self-Esteem." *Personality and Individual Differences* 22:845–854.

Kramer, P. D. 1993 *Listening to Prozac*. New York: Viking.

Marsh, H. W. 1995 "A Jamesian Model of Self-Investment and Self-Esteem: Comment on Pelham." *Journal of Personality and Social Psychology* 69:1151–1160.

McFarlin, D. B., R. F. Baumeister, and J. Blascovich 1984. "On Knowing When to Quit: Task Failure, Self-Esteem, Advice, and Nonproductive Persistence." *Journal of Personality* 52:138–155.

Mecca, A. M., N. J. Smeiser, and J. Vasconcellos, eds. 1989 *The Social Importance of Self-Esteem*. Berkeley: University of California Press.

Nezlek, J. B., R. M. Kowalski, M. R. Leary, T. Belvins, and S. Holgate 1997 "Personality Moderators of Reactions to Interpersonal Reactions: Depression and Trait Self-Esteem. *Personality and Social Psychology Bulletin* 23:1235–1244.

Pelham, B. W. 1995 "Self-Investment and Self-Esteem: Evidence for a Jamesian Model of Self-Worth." *Journal of Personality and Social Psychology* 69:1141–1150.

Rosenberg, M. 1965 *Society and the Adolescent Self-Image*. Princeton, N. J.: Princeton University Press.

Schlenker, B. R., M. F. Weigold, and J. R. Hallam 1990 "Self-Serving Attributions in Social Context: Effects of Self-Esteem and Social Pressure." *Journal of Personality and Social Psychology* 58:855–863.

Schneider, D. J., and D. Turkat 1975 "Self-Presentation Following Success or Failure: Defensive Self-Esteem Models. *Journal of Personality* 43:127–135.

Steele, C. 1997 "A Threat in the Air: How Stereotypes Shape Intellectual Identity and Performance." *American Psychologist* 52:613–629.

Stein, J. A., M. D. Newcomb, and P. M. Bentler 1992 "The Effect of Agency and Communality on Self-Esteem: Gender Differences in Longitudinal Data." *Sex Roles* 26:465–483.

Swann, W. B., Jr. 1996 *Self-Traps: The Elusive Quest for Higher Self-Esteem*. New York: W. H. Freeman.

——, J. J. Griffin, Jr., S. C. Predmore, and B. Gaines 1987 "The Cognitive-Affective Crossfire: When Self-Consistency Confronts Self-Enhancement. *Journal of Personality and Social Psychology* 52:881–889.

Tafarodi, R., and W. B. Swann, Jr. 1995 "Self-Liking and Self-Competence as Dimensions of Global Self-Esteem: Initial Validation of a Measure." *Journal of Personality Assessment* 65:322–342.

SENTIMENTS

To define the affective state, four terms can be used: passion, state of mind, emotion, and sentiments. The term "passion" is linked with the philosophical and literary tradition and designates a violent tension that the individual sustains for a certain duration. States of mind or moods are affective states of low intensity that are durable and pervasive, lack an immediately perceptible cause, and can influence initially neutral events. The term "emotion" indicates an intense affective state of short duration with a precise external or inner cause, a clear cognitive content, and the ability to reorient attention. Most scholars agree that emotion is a psychological construct with several components: (1) cognitive: finalized by the stimulus caused by emotion, (2) physiological: from the participation of the neurovegetative system, (3) expressive: linked with movement, (4) motivational: linked with intentions and the tendency to act or react, and (5) subjective: consisting of the sentiment felt by the individual.

Sentiments are more enduring than are emotions (e.g., hatred compared with a momentary explosion of anger) and are more cognitively structured. Sentiments may last seconds (embarrassment) or months (mourning) and may be more or less intense, conscious or unconscious, and controllable or outside one's control. When an individual names a sentiment by using a certain terms he or she refers to different elements: affection, cognitive contents or structures of evaluation, awareness of the level of readiness for action, and awareness of the body. Sentiments pervade daily life and are found in several artistic forms: music, poetry, literature, and painting.

In the philosophical tradition, the affective dimension appeared as a perturbation of human behavior that was considered the result of reasoning. Plato was the first to define passions as "diseases of the spirit." For the Stoics, passion was a disease that gets hold of the entire spirit at the expense of reason: Crisippo considered it an unbridled agitation, an unstoppable force that makes the ego leave the self. For Aristotle, passions act as a destabilizer of the rational powers of the individual. An ambivalent attitude toward passions developed at the beginning of the modern age. They were execrated during the age of illuminism, exalted during the romantic era, condemned during the period of critical rationalism and rehabilitated in the postmodern age.

THE INATTENTION OF THE FOUNDERS

For a long time sociology, evidently influenced by the hegemonic philosophical paradigm, excluded the study of the affective dimension from its theoretical concerns. Affects thus were relegated to anthropology and psychology. The founders of sociology saw the role of sentiments in social life as rather marginal. An interest in sentiments can be found in Durkheim, who saw them as agents and factors of cohesion in the formation of solidarity and morality. In his view, sentiments are learned and internalized during rituals and collective ceremonies through the sharing of emotions.

In Pareto's terminology, *residui* are sentiments or the expressions of sentiments inscribed in human nature and *derivazioni* are the conceptual systems of justification with which individuals disguise their passions or give an appearance of rationality to propositions or behaviors that are not rational. People rarely behave in a logical way but always want to make their fellow people believe that their conduct is logical. The main characteristic of human nature is that it lets itself be guided by sentiments and puts forward pseudological justifications for sentimental attitudes. According to Pareto, nonlogical is not necessarily equivalent to illogical: Emotions follow some principles. The logic of sentiments Pareto identified can be summarized in five points. First, while reason is analytic, sentiment is synthetic. Second, sentiment follows justificational and persuasive principles. Third, sentiments are inaccurate, indefinite, and indeterminate. Fourth, sentiments may be ambivalent and conflicting. Fifth, sentiments can take on extreme, absolute characteristics that prevent learning from reality.

Weber begins by distinguishing four types of action: rational action in relation to an aim, rational action in relation to a value, affective or emotional action, and traditional action. The action Weber calls affective results from the state of mind or mood of an individual: the slap a mother gives to her unbearable child or the fist of a soccer player who loses his temper. Action, that is, is defined with reference not to an aim or system of values but to the emotional reaction of an agent who finds himself or herself in certain circumstances. The distinctive characteristic of the world in which people live is rationalization: a firm is rational, as is the bureaucratic management of a state, while scientific action is a combination of a rational action in relation to an aim and a rational action in relation to a value, which is truth.

The importance of the emotional factor in the formation of charisma and the religious spirit is mentioned explicitly by Weber. Perhaps the spirit of capitalism is seen by Weber as deriving from the pressure of strong and pervasive emotions such as anxiety, desperation, and fear on which Calvinist doctrine was founded. Weber does not ignore affection, but he considers it a parasite of reason, a noise producer, a disturber in the ascent to rationality.

SOME PRECURSORS

Sentiments are central in the work of Simmel, who thoroughly analyzed their role and formation, especially in his essay on love and his reflections on sociability. For Simmel, emotional reality is the foundation of an individual's experience and social interactions. Individuals, he maintains, enter into relationships with one another through the sentiments. Social relations produce other sentiments that therefore are always connected to interactions. The Italian protosociologist Ferrero studied fear and tried to read the historical existence of civilizations in the light of such sentiments. For Ferrero, fear is the spirit of the universe. People, like all creatures, are molded by fear: To overcome fear, people arm themselves, but because they are armed, they cannot help fearing each other. Consequently, people become the most frightening and the most frightened beings because they are the only ones able to manufacture deadly and thus frightful instruments of offense. Moreover, fantasy creates imaginary dangers of all kinds. The human condition therefore is characterized by a permanent dialogue with fear. Even sacrificial rituals are interpreted as expedients to exorcise the fear that every person has of her or his fellow creatures, who are seen as potential bearers of death. Thus, the salute is a technique of mutual reassurance, a ceremony through which one manifests the absence of aggressive intentions toward others. The main instrument for defeating the original fear is power: the institutionalization of the monopoly of violence. This solution transforms people into subject by taking away their freedom. As a result of the monopoly of violence among those who exercise command, peace is guaranteed, but its price is very high. The fear of war of all against all is eliminated, but it is replaced by fear of power.

However, Ferrero emphasizes that those in power fear the subjects over whom they exercise command. No government is certain of the total obedience of its citizens, and a revolt can break out among the most compliant subjects. In this way, feedback develops between the use of force and fear: The more those in power fear their subjects, the more they resort to instruments of repression, the more they are repressive, and the more they feel fear. For the usurper of power there is not only an external threat, as Plato, Senofonte, Machiavelli, and Montesquieu showed, but also an internal torment: fear of one's own illegitimacy. In *Community and Society*, Toennies, in theorizing about the fundamental category of "community," emphasized the sentiment of belonging. He recognized in sentiments a relative autonomy when he assumed that they were a guide for action and that the fundamental directions of human action depend largely on inner conditions (dispositions) and to a lesser extent on external conditions (circumstances). Veblen based his concept of the wealthy class on a complex mix of sentiments (superiority and inferiority, emulation and imitation) and showed their influence on collective behavior.

Scheler showed, through a phenomenology of resentment, the tight link between the sphere of individual sentiments and that of collective behavior. For Scheler, the forming of resentment and its mode of expression have an individual component tied to temperament and a social component: "The way and the measure in which resentment takes shape in entire groups and in individuals is linked in the first place to the disposition of the human material at issue, in the second place to the structure of society in which this lives." Therefore, there is constant interaction between individual attitudes and collective mentality. The manifestation of resentment is linked to social inequalities and the inability to heal an offense, true or presumed, through vengeance or rebellion. The spreading of resentment creates the psychological premises that become linked with the structural premises, leading to the explosion of mass movements.

For Scheler, "the formal structure of the expression of resentment is always the same: A is approved of, supported and praised not for his intrinsic qualities, but with the intention—that remains unsaid in words—to deny, devaluate and reprove B." The refusal of wealth is nothing but a repressed desire for wealth among the poor, who despise what they want but cannot have. Like

Tocqueville, Scheler sees in democracy the fuel of resentment. He maintains: "It will possess a maximum charge of resentment a society in which political rights and others of almost equal kind, jointly with a formal social parity publicly recognized, go together with great differences of power, of effective possession of assets and effective cultural formation."

In the 1960s, MacIver explored the sentiment of attachment to a community, referring to the complex of memories, traditions, customs, and institutions shared by the members of a community. This sentiment of community, which is acquired through the socialization process, has three main elements: (1) the sentiment of we, (2) the sentiment of role, and (3) the sentiment of dependence. The first leads to the identification of a person with the others; the second is associated with the functions individual members perform in the community and expresses the way in which the individual normally realizes his or her belonging to the entire community. The sentiment of dependence expresses the dependence of a person on the community, which is considered a necessary condition for his or her existence, lessening his or her isolation. In modern society, an individual belongs not only to a single community but also to specific associations, as social life is subject to the process of differentiation and specialization. Moreover, the sentiment of belonging to the community seems to persist only in rural areas; in urban areas, it is replaced by attachment to other, less inclusive and more sectorial groups. In rural areas, the sentiment of attachment to the community remains strong because of people's longer periods of residence. An enlarged sentiment of community is the sentiment of nationality, which is produced by historical circumstances and supported by common psychological factors.

Helen Lynd was the first to recognize the importance of shame in the complex dynamics of identity growth. According to Lynd, the values of a culture do not stimulate the experience and communication of emotions such as shame, joy, wonder, and love. However, once trust has been created—allowing one to reveal oneself and thus look for the ways in which to communicate shame—the risk of being exposed may become an experience of abandonment, self-revelation, and intimacy with others. Once accepted, shame leads a person to a greater awareness and to an enrichment of his or her personality.

CONTEMPORARY APPROACHES

Sociologists' interest in emotions and sentiments can be traced to the mid-1970s. In that period, one of the foundations of sociology—the idea of a rational social actor guided in his or her conduct, motivation, and choices by a utilitarian and instrumental logic while sentiments play a residual and socially insignificant role—was questioned. This model started showing its abstractness and rigid partiality and its inadequacy in explaining the complexity of individual and collective action, which depends on how people feel and manage their emotions. Thus, emotions started losing their residual and even disturbing function and were recognized as integral parts of social action.

This crack in the rational actor construction went together with a new cultural climate characterized by attention to the self and to the world of private and interpersonal relations, a desire for authenticity, and the revaluation of sentiments. Emotions and sentiments became objects of knowledge, attention, and communication both in daily life and in sociological reflection. In women and youth subcultures especially, the expression of one's sentiments was encouraged. Advertising saw the positive value of the affective dimension and used it in its campaigns by linking it to products potentially able to stimulate emotions, such as sports, film, television, cars, and even food. The revaluation of the affective dimension also was stimulated by the increase in the number of magazines dealing with psychoanalytic issues and the growth of university courses on psychological subjects: In many textbooks, at least one chapter is devoted to the dynamics of sentiments and emotions. A widespread representation of emotions has resulted from cinematic and television fiction.

In the growing social sciences literature on sentiments and emotions, five approaches can be singled out: (1) sociohistorical, (2) positivist, (3) functionalist, (4) conflict, (5) interactionist, and (6) socialconstructivist.

The Sociohistorical Approach. According to Elias, the phenomenon of civilization is a matter of controlling emotions and natural impulses. From the documents he collected, it can be inferred that anger, which now seems psychopathic, was in medieval times considered normal, and that the desire to destroy was openly confessed, while it now is admitted with shame or used to attract attention.

For Elias, emotions and their expressive forms are strongly correlated with the social contexts in which they manifest themselves. Every social structure, he maintains, corresponds to a structure of emotions and sentiments, and their inhibition, repression, or free expression depends on their being functional to different social systems.

According to Elias's theory of the process of civilization, daily life in the Middle Ages was characterized by abuse and violence. People, lived in a permanent state of insecurity and fear. The situation began to change when a stronger territorial power prevailed on the weaker ones and the monopoly of the state's legal violence gradually was established. Violence, reserved to specialized bodies, began to be excluded from other areas of life, and some calm, protected zones started to form. Within those areas, "good manners" developed and eventually replaced violence and abuse in interpersonal relations. Starting in the higher ranks, individuals began to abandon spontaneity and impetuousness and learned to dominate themselves, control their impulses and passions, and regulate aggressiveness.

For Elias, institutionalized sports channel and often divert people's natural emotions. Hunting, for example, often has been recognized as a substitute for war. In their free time, people can carry out activities that incite emotions closely tied to those of normal life.

The Positivist Approach. According to Kemper's positivist approach, people have philogenetically inherited a set of primary emotions—fear, anger, joy, and depression—that serve evolutionary and adaptive needs and are sensitive to certain contingent environmental situations. For human beings, the main contingent environmental situations are of a social nature; therefore, social vicissitudes determine emotions unless society intervenes normatively with different demands.

Kemper states that emotions are universally elicited by two fundamental dimensions of social relationships: power and status. Possessing adequate power produces feelings of security, possessing excessive power produces feelings of guilt, and possessing inadequate power produces anxiety. Fear develops when the power of two interacting individuals is uneven.

Anger emerges from interactions in which an expected, habitual status is denied or withdrawn by an actor considered responsible for the status reduction. Depression is tied to a loss of status, and the person considers himself or herself responsible for the loss. Individuals feel shame if they perceive that their status is too high; in the opposite case, they feel depression. Satisfaction results from interactions in which power is not felt as threatening and the status is expected and desired.

The positivist approach to the study of emotions attempts to (1) treat emotion as a variable, (2) undertake studies that embrace various cultures, (3) develop the history of particular emotions, and (4) examine the link between emotions and sociological variables such as social class, gender, and ethnicity.

The Functionalist Approach. In the functionalist perspective, innate emotional behavior may have developed in the course of evolution because of its value in being functional to adaptation. The purpose of emotions is to face emergency situations by estimating the importance of the events in order to organize appropriate action. First, emotions prepare the body to react to hostile or dangerous situations, predisposing the organism for the emergency and thus leading to rebalance and adaptation. As Darwin noted, fear is an emotion common to various species, as it is conducive to survival, aids in adaptation, and is linked to a safeguarding mechanism that is evident in the first phases of life.

Emotions also have the function of interpersonal signaling. That is, they produce the effect of communicating the state of the organism to the outside world. The variety and specificity of emotions reflect the flexibility of the forms of adaptation to the environment. Therefore, for example, fear helps avert danger, sadness is a call for help, and happiness is a phase of recovery after the attainment of a goal.

The Conflict Approach. The conflict theory of emotion can be found in the works of Coser and

Collins, according to whom the crucial determinant of emotion is membership in competing groups and classes. Emotion, Coser says, is a resource that can be mobilized, directed, and exploited in conflicts over power. Moreover, it can be used to create emotional loyalty and solidarity. Human biological nature supplies emotional energy, but the differentiation and management of emotion are achieved by competing groups that fight for control over the means of emotional reproduction, that is, the resources for assembling the ritualistic arousal of emotions in support of one's group. According to conflict theory, persons not only manage their own emotions but also to stimulate, suppress, or transform emotions in other people. This also happens at the collective level. For example, hostility perceived as coming from external groups increases in-group solidarity, and emotion is intensified by the presence of a large number of people in an expressive ritual.

For Collins, emotional energy is an essential part of the model of chain ritual interaction, and he maintains that the basis of every interaction is a minimum feeling of positivity toward others. Thus, a person accepted in a conversation receives from that experience not only an increase of positive emotional energy but also additional emotional resources (trust, warmth, enthusiasm) with which to negotiate in the next interaction.

The Interactionist Approach. In the interactionist approach, emotions essentially result from social interaction. They differ according to the social and cultural worlds one belongs to and thus continuously change.

Symbolic interactionists draw a distinction between biological emotions and social sentiments. An emotion is fixed in the human organism, is experienced concurrently with bodily change, and consists of a fixed configuration of bodily sensations and gestures in response to simple, standard stimuli. In contrast, a sentiment originates through cultural definition and social interaction and continues over time in enduring social relationships. The expressive gestures and internal sensations of a sentiment are culturally defined and can be altered according to the situation and on a broader cultural scale, since sentiments are not fixed in human biological nature. In the course of interaction, differences among sentiments are developed,

and sentiments are redefined continuously through encounters and relationships.

Goffman has examined the system of rules that dominate interaction and the efforts made by individuals to be in tune with the emotional states of a situation. This control of impressions essentially is a strategy for avoiding embarrassment or shame and is inspired by pride and the desire to make a positive impression.

According to Goffman, embarrassment is linked to the impression of people transmitted to others and is a phenomenon that blocks interactions among individuals and makes them unable to interact. The attitudes deriving from this process violate behavioral standards shared with others and cause inappropriate behaviors. Embarrassment, however, is a normal part of everyday life, since it is a manifestation of adaptation to social organization. One structures in several ways other people's perception of oneself according to the various roles one takes on. What creates embarrassment and uneasiness for an individual is the diversity of multiple interactive situations, which imply different and often discordant rules of behavior. Goffman also describes the process of emotion management: By managing the impressions others have of them, people facilitate their goals and attract the responses they need. Often, however, expression management involves inauthentic sentiments to avoid situationally inappropriate emotional gestures, such as laughter at a funeral or a forced smile on meeting an enemy. Emotion management is guided by implicit and shared social rules about appropriate or inappropriate displays of sentiment and emotion. These emotional rules constitute a normative framework of expectations that people take into account.

The Social Constructivist Approach. For costructionist theorists, emotions are not natural answers but experiential and expressive models determined by the sociocultural context; they are learned answers that have neither natural contents nor functions and are tied to the conservation of the individual and the species. From the costructionist point of view, emotions are complex syndromes whose meaning and function can be understood only by referring to the social system of which they are part.

According to costructionists, emotions are functional, as they are socially constructed and prescribed to maintain and support a certain system of values. Therefore, a community will try to promote emotional manifestations that are functional to the maintenance of a socially founded moral order and will try to penalize and remove emotions that are in opposition to the moral order. Examples of how an emotion with a negative connotation, such as hatred, can be promoted and prescribed by a community include Nazi Germany and the Ku Klux Klan. In both cases, hatred became the accepted emotional behavior, as its negative side was socially nationalized. Does the ethics of success on which contemporary Western culture is founded not use in a functional way the emotion of envy as a motivational force for the individual?

SOCIAL IMPACT OF SENTIMENTS

Imagining a passionate individual in total isolation is impossible: Passions require sharing, participation, and a common horizon of values and rules. A person perceives his or her passions through those he or she is able to stimulate in other people and decodes them on the basis of their reactions. There is no passion without a mental or a real relational context.

"Others" are necessary interlocutors for the expression of sentiments that involve a mutual exchange: Often children wait to be in the presence of an obliging listener before venting their emotions. Moreover, some places are considered socially more suitable than others for expressing certain emotions. For example, aggressiveness is more often shown in a stadium than in a church.

Research on large social groups shows that the distribution of specific emotions (pain, jealousy, love) varies from one social group to another, while studies conducted at the micro level indicate that the experience and expression of an emotion, as well as attempts to control it, are influenced by socialization and the prevailing situational factors.

A society is certainly founded on some sociostructural presuppositions, but it cannot function if it does not also rest on sentiments, beliefs, and obligations. These factors act as a social glue, as an "a priori" that, without being the object of codification or knowledge from individuals is nonetheless necessary for society to function.

One of these psychosocial elements is trust, which represents a precontractual requirement of the fulfillment of social exchanges. As Simmel maintained, society would disintegrate in the absence of trust among men.

It is not trust alone that supports social order, but trust is one of the psychosocial elements that play a fundamental role in maintaining the social system, even if structural theories neglect it. Trust is a powerful cultural resource, a precondition for a full use of other resources, such as entrepreneurship, citizenship, and legality. It is an intangible resource, like the spirit of belonging or consent.

Different social objects can be invested with trust, and so there can be various types of trust:

1. Generalized trust gives people an ontological security about the system.

2. Segmental trust involves entire institutional segments of society, such as the economy and justice.

3. Technological trust involves the expert systems such as transportation and computer science networks.

4. Organizational trust refers to real organizations such as the army and the university.

5. Commercial trust refers to goods with a specific trademark or produced in certain countries.

6. Positional trust is invested in particular social roles, such as priests and doctors.

7. Personal trust can refer to virtues revealed by public or private persons.

The social objects in which trust is placed can be found in one's own society or in foreign societies. From this fact arises the distinction between inner trust and outer trust. One speaks of focused trust when trust is placed in a particular category of objects; one speaks of diffuse trust when one metaphorically refers to the trustful or distrustful atmosphere that pervades the society. This climate can be incorporated in a culture as well as in a normative perspective. For example, a large part of Italian fiscal legislation appears to be based on distrust of the honesty of the contributors. Trust in a specific object can be justified in an indirect way, when its reliability depends on the trust that is placed in bodies of supervision and control. In contrast, distrust feeds conflict and social atomization, therefore becoming a powerful destructive force.

Once distrust has been initiated, it soon becomes impossible to know if it was justified, since it has the ability to fulfill itself, to generate a reality that is coherent with it. Observing events that refute past fiduciary relations, for example, finding out that certain scientific data have been counterfeited so that one can publish spectacular results, can cause an unexpected loss of trust. The absence of trust involves an excessive increase in vigilance and the creation of more complex systems of control.

The slump in institutional trust is reflected in a generalized loss of trust in monetary means of exchange, the authorities' legitimacy, the credibility of the political system, and the effectiveness of specialized spheres such as scholastic and religious institutions. A similar collapse of institutional trust can lead to a loss of trust in individuals.

In the postcommunist societies of eastern Europe, there is a widespread lack of trust that leads to a spreading syndrome of diffidence. The Polish sociologist Sztompka has cited some indicators. The strongest behavioral indicator of generalized distrust in the society to which one belongs is choosing to emigrate. This is the obvious form of escape people choose when living conditions become unbearable and signs of improvement cannot be seen. Another form of escape is withdrawing from public life and taking refuge in primary groups. Here there is a horizontal trust that compensates for the lack of vertical trust in institutions. Another indicator of public distrust is the number of protest demonstrations. Yet another is reluctance to think about the long-term future. In the economic field, an indicator of distrust is neglecting investment forms and spending a lot on consumer goods, especially foreign-made goods. The opening and dissemination of casino chains are also important indicators of distrust. Finally, in the postcommunist societies of eastern Europe, trust is undermined because of normative disorganization and the high level of expectations after the "glorious" revolution of 1989.

Some sentiments may derive from the social order, such as loneliness and historical contingencies that generate fear. Some demographic transformations, such as the lengthening of life, and other social changes, such as breaking the bond of marriage or choosing to remain single, amplify the sentiment of loneliness. Feeling lonely has two sides: It is a sad sentiment connected with loss, refusal, and isolation, but it is also a source of serenity, as it means staying with oneself. This develops the inner world and fosters creativity and the birth of the new.

A large amount of the research on loneliness has established only simple correlations between loneliness and other variables. On the whole, it seems that loneliness is more common among women than men, poor people than rich, and adolescents than elderly people. Data on attitudes and sentiments generally indicate that a person who feels lonely also feels distrust and hostility, is rarely attracted by other people, and expects to be rejected. A large number of studies have found positive correlations between loneliness and feelings of impotence and inadequacy, a tendency to self-devaluation, and self-deprecation. A gap can be found in research on loneliness concerning the etiology of the phenomenon. Sociologists are not in a position to establish which factors cause loneliness and which are facilitating conditions. Sociologists do not know, for example, the relationship between objective causes (mournings, transfers, separations) and subjective causes (introversion, shyness, low self-esteem).

In regard to fear, it is necessary to assume that in the past, some events connected to the adversities of nature generated emotional reactions that were stronger than those of today. The historian Delumeau showed how in past centuries, primary concrete fears (of war, scarcity, plague, tyranny, and earthquake) were grafted onto secondary fears that resulted from cultural processes and movements that singled out dangers and adversaries (the heretic, the Hebrew, the witch, the demon, the vampire, the plague spreader) on which it was easier to unload the anguish caused by real but frightening and unmanageable phenomena.

In modern society, fear of machines has sometimes developed. In England at the beginning of the nineteenth century, the Luddites were organized bands of laborers who destroyed textile machines, which caused layoffs of many craftsmen.

Fear of the dominion of the machine is found in many science fiction, utopian, and dystopian novels in this century. In *Erehwon* by Samuel Butler, there are no machines; in Spengler, the machine is devilish and is seen as the dissolver of Western civilization. In the *Brave New World* by Aldous Huxley and *1984* by George Orwell, pervasive technology supplantes people's individuality. Similarly dark scenes are accompanying the current computer science phase that features the presence of apocalyptic Cassandras afraid of the effect of computers on the human brain.

In the second half of the 1980s, after the Chernobyl accident, a strong fear of nuclear energy developed, while the 1990s were characterized by the fear of ecological catastrophes tied to the greenhouse effect or the perforation of the ozone layer. The modern age has brought new threats in the form of drugs and the acquired immune deficiency syndrome (AIDS). Sometimes a social fear may be born, the perception, that is, of a "barbarization" of social life, of a progressive loss of freedom, the feeling of being a pawn in the mosaic of daily life, impotent before the great bureaucratic and occult powers. Another source of fear is food, which in Europe was manifested after the Chernobyl accident and during the mad cow crisis. Today a great fear is that of being killed by someone whom one does not know and who has no reason to direct his anger against an individual. Bodyguards represent a new defense against this fear, while the fear of burglars, especially in cities and urban areas, is causing a rush to purchase electronic systems for defense for the home. In Europe, the fear of a demographic decline accompanies the fear of immigration and of being submerged by other ethnic groups.

EMOTIONS AND CULTURE

A common question among those who study sentiments and emotions is whether these affective states are culturally universal or vary from culture to culture. There are two schools of thought. According to the universalistic school, emotions are always the same in all cultures, while for the relativistic school, they vary in time and among different cultures. Cross-cultural studies have shown differences among cultures concerning the language, the meaning, the objects, and the appraisal of emotions: One therefore would have to speak of ethnotheories of emotions.

One of the distinctions made by anthropologists is based on the prevalence of sentiments of shame versus guilt. In regard to the fact that a certain culture attributes a preponderant importance to the former or the latter emotion, one speaks of "cultures of shame" and "cultures of guilt": cultures of shame regulate individual behavior through external sanctions, while cultures of guilt are based on interiorized sanctions; that is, guilt is caused by the knowledge of having transgressed important moral or social norms. The cultures of guilt would therefore be those of Western societies, characterized by the Judeo-Christian tradition or the Protestant ethic.

In cultures that systematically resort to humiliation as an educational method, the sentiment of shame is present in massive doses. This happens, for example, in the Japanese culture, which is defined by anthropologists as "the culture of shame." Anthropological data on some cultures of New Guinea show that shame may have a paralyzing effect. In New Guinea, people who have not made a good impression shelter under the porch of the house, cover their faces in chalk powder and wait for the others members to come and playfully reproach them. After a few days, such a person washes his or her face and reenters the group.

The geography of jealousy also shows some variation. In fact, anthropological research shows that jealousy is more widespread and accepted in cultures that are based on private property, authorize sex only within marriage, and grant the status of a responsible adult only to married persons.

In some cultures there are social classes in which a quarrel is unthinkable and an accusation of another person makes clear one's own victimized state. Examples are ritual sounds among the Australian aboriginals, accusing the object of one's anger of witchcraft, and the icy silence of the English bourgeois. In some cultures, such as the Korean, a person who offends is treated with intensified respectful manners, that is, with an increased formality of words and intonation. It is said that the Tasaday did not have in their language a word to express anger. Among the Ibo in Nigeria, anger also seems to be completely absent. A culture, such as the Tahitian, in which social life is little differentiated, produces few emotions; in this case, one speaks of hypocognition or underidentification.

EMOTION NORMS

Emotion norms indicate the expected range, intensity, duration, and target of a specific emotion in specific situations. The principles that govern emotion are of four types:

1. Rules of appraisal that define how a situation is perceived and evaluated

2. Rules of behavior that establish how an emotion has to be expressed

3. Prognostic rules that indicate the correct duration of an emotion

4. Rules of attribution that legitimate an emotion in regard to the social system

The rules of expression defined by a given culture and subgroup influence how much the emotional state is expressed in self-description, behavior and bodily expression. Emotion rules prescribe the depth and duration of feelings and provide a measure of how much a certain feeling is unusual, crazy, unsuitable, or normal in a certain social context.

Feeling and expression rules are an integral part of what has been called "emotion culture." Moreover, emotion culture includes beliefs concerning sentiments as well as concepts regarding the way in which one should lend attention, codify, evaluate, control, and express feelings. Emotion culture is reflected in films, religion, psychiatric theories, and the law. Many systems of law mention, for example, two sentiments, widespread among the population, that are worth of being safeguarded: decency and honor.

Decency. The sentiment of decency concerns the intimate sphere of one's personality, the area a person thinks should be private and confidential. Analyses carried out in the social sciences reveal extreme variability in the sphere of decency: In different epochs and cultures, different actions and behaviors are considered as damaging this feeling, whereas in other contexts they appear totally legitimate. However, the sentiment of decency is present in all ages and cultures, and

through it, a peculiar relationship occurs between subjective perceptions and objective images of confidentiality, especially in the sexual sphere. Reflecting on the characteristics of the sentiment of decency in a society makes it possible to individuate the prevailing values of a social group concerning the protection of confidentiality but also to explore in depth the reasons for behaviors that do not fall within the sphere of the individual. For example, the meticulous and detailed Starr report on President Clinton disseminated by electronic mail all over the world is an example of the absence of decency in the American judicial system.

Honor. Honor is the pretension and the right to be proud, but it also means that society acknowledges this individual pretension. The sentiment of honor spurs honored behavior. Honor is the social acknowledgment of those who fulfill the duties of their status.

In contemporary society, there are a great number of ritual situations in which specific persons are given, while alive, special honors or special offices, degrees, or prizes. After death, these persons are honored with symbolic actions: A recent example was the garlands of flowers that were laid on Mother Teresa's coffin.

A call to honor is made when a citizen sees his or her name and respect wounded by his or her fellow citizens. Civil and penal laws protect honor legally. There are professional groups that supervise the observance of specific norms by means of a code of honor. In this epoch, honor brings to mind retrograde and fragmented elements. In past societies, honor was not only a particular type of sentiment linked to occasional events and one that operated as a cultural superstructure: The conceptions of honor were more than simple accessories of life; they went beyond abstract values one referred to only occasionally. For centuries, they determined the style of life of wide layers of people in premodern societies, orienting their social and private conduct.

Through honor, the individual identifies as member of a group, which in turn confers a status, that is, a dignity and a value in the social relations occurring within and outside the group to which one belongs. The functional cost an individual has to face consists of control of morals through endorsement mechanisms whose most qualifying phase is the formation and application of honor codes. Acts of violence in defense of the honor of one's family were widely tolerated by the law until relatively recent times.

The Mediterranean culture of honor has been characterized as a phenomenon of archaic societies that have not reached a high level of civilization. With modernization, it was maintained, this dark phase would disappear. Instead, the culture of honor has succeeded in preserving its importance among immigrants in the industrialized metropolis.

The fact that the code of honor has not lost its valence, at least in the Mediterranean area, makes one question whether the linear concept of modernization is truly valid or whether a concept based on a permanent dialectic between persistence and change is more valid.

The regulation of emotion comes largely from social sources that consist partly in the interests that others have and in the norms of social interaction and partly in the expression and feelings rules of society: Boys should not cry, and mourning should not be shown too much, at least in the Nordic countries. Expression rules are specific to a given culture or social role: English people, for example, are little inclined to express how they feel, and the clergy behave with dignity. In some cultures, jealousy cannot be felt, while in others, it must be; in some cultures, an offense to honor is strongly felt, while in others, the honor concept is almost nonexistent. The rules are often explicit to the point of being codified in books of ethics and good manners. In the Western culture, the ethic of control of emotional impulses prevails.

Anger also is subject to social rules. For every class, there are prescriptive rules that indicate the choices that have to be made and proscriptive rules that indicate those to avoid. For example, one can show anger for a behavior that attacks one's honor, freedom, or property (prescriptive rule), but anger cannot exceed the limits of what is necessary to correct the situation (proscriptive rule).

SENTIMENTS IN THE POSTMODERN AGE

In the contemporary world, several indications seem to point to a situation in which the consumer society is increasingly inviting people to be passionate but people are distanced from passion. The threshold of emotional involvement has become high to protect people from a useless daily mobilitation: In post-modern culture, emotions and social action seem more and more separated.

The process of "blaseization" that Simmel saw at the beginning of the century thus has accelerated. However, certain episodes occur, like Princess Diana's death, that are experienced with a sentiment of pain that is almost cosmic, so that Pareto's *residuo* of "displaying sentiments with exterior acts" seems still present, although only latently.

The relevance of the affective dimension also is evidenced within the religious and family domain. In religion, several scholars maintain that once people get rid of ritualistic and pretentious display and once reciprocal aggressiveness has disappeared, the prevalent function of religion is to provide affective support of people against the uncertainties of the world. The family which has lost some of its fundamental functions, such as economic and socialization, has maintained and perhaps strengthened its function of affective support both horizontal and vertical.

Within the job world concerns about feelings of alienation during the assembly line period, have been replaced by concerns about the burnout phenomenon, which is a feeling of powerlessness and indifference, which affects especially the health, helping, and education professions.

According to some management scholars, in the next decades a resource to contrast these negative phenomena could be the development of emotional intelligence, which is the ability to effectively perceive, realize, and apply the strength and perspicacity that emotions—meant as sources of energy, information, relations and influence—provide human beings with.

In the 1990s, different authors tried to individuate the prevalence of some sentiments in society or in parts of it. At the beginning of the twenty-first century a sentiment that seems widespread is narcissism, understood as self-complacency and desire to be admired. Some indicators of this feeling are the cult of the body, abandoning every emotional involvement, the proliferation of interpersonal relationships governed by appearance, and a flight from the social. Post-modern society thus seems to be pervaded with a dominant passion: love for the self, which is translated into vanity and desire for power, wish to control anxiety over self-approval, self-interest, and egoism. Such syndrome, however, seems to co-exist with an altruistic dimension, normally rather latent but that grows in emergencies. The prevailing sentiments seem however to be linked to the spreading of post-materialistic values, such as love and friendship. Along the continuum localism—cosmopolitan, following Huntington, it seems that we are moving towards an attachment for intermediate cultural areas, essentially configurated according to the religious tradition.

Contrary to the expectations raised by the fall of the Berlin wall, in various parts of the world (Burundi, Algeria, Bosnia, Kosovo) during the 90s there were carnages caused also by feelings of interethnic hatred.

Another sentiment, felt especially by younger generations, is a worry about the future that generates anxiety and is capable of determining behaviors that are aggressive and antisocial.

Lately mass media scholars complain about the spreading, especially in television and movies, of a certain provocative impudence, together with the weakening of feelings of shame. Moreover, some psychologists have noticed an increase in interpersonal aggressiveness that parallels the increase in the time devoted to city mobility.

In a time of increasing globalization of markets the McDonaldization of tastes, the process of conforming seems to proceed also in the affective sphere, with the consequent weakening of passions and the misting over of the ability to suffer but also to feel joy, indignation, and pity. All these worries had been expressed by the antiutopians, by Riesman, and by the supporters of the critical theory of society. Leading to the valorization of sentiments as bulwark against any attempt of hegemonic oppression. In postmodernity, it thus seems appropriate to place *Homo sentiens* near *Homo faber* and *Homo sapiens*.

REFERENCES

Alberoni, Francesco 1991 *Gli Invidiosi*. Milan: Garzanti.

Cooper, Robert K., and Ayman Sawaf 1999 *Il Fattore Emozione*. Milano: Sperling and Kupfer.

D'Urso, Valentina, and Rosanna Trentin 1998 *Introduzione alla Psicologia delle Emozioni*. Bari: Laterza.

Elias, Norbert 1978 *The Civilizing Process: The History of Manners*. Oxford, UK: Basil Blackwell.

Gambetta, Diego 1988 *Trust: Making and Breaking Cooperative Relations*. Oxford, UK: Basil Blackwell.

Goffman, Erving 1967 *Interaction Ritual*. Garden City, N.Y.: Doubleday.

Hancock, Barry W. 1986 *Loneliness: Symtoms and Social Causes*. Lanhah: University Press of America.

Hochschild, Arlie Russel 1985 *The Managed Hearth*. Berkeley: University of California Press.

Lewis, Michael 1992 *Shame: The Exposed Self*. New York: Free Press.

Misztal, Barbara 1996 *Trust in Modern Societies*. Cambridge, UK: Polity Press.

Turnaturi, Gabriella 1995 *La Sociologia delle Emozioni*. Milan: Anabasi.

Van Sommers, Peter 1988 *Jealousy*. London: Penguin Books.

Zingerle, Arnold ed. 1991 "Sociologia dell'Onore." *Annali di Sociologia* 7.

BERNARDO CATTARINUSSI

SEX DIFFERENCES

"Sex differences" is the label used in describing variations between women and men. The term "sex" reflects the division of women and men into two groups on the basis of their unique biological features; the term "differences" derives from the tradition of differential psychology, in which distinct groups of people (defined by natural categories such as sex or constructed categories such as socioeconomic class) are compared in terms of an outcome.

Both terms have been criticized. To many people, references to sex differences imply a biological determinism that ignores the role of socialization and context. The more contemporary term "gender" directs attention to the social meanings assigned to the categories of male and female. With either term, however, it is not necessary to assume a particular causal factor for an observed pattern of variation. A problem with the term "differences" is that it suggests that *dis*similarities are the norm and similarities are the exception. More appropriately, one makes comparisons between groups to see whether there are similarities or differences.

Regardless of the rubric used to characterize the investigation, comparisons between women and men pervade social science literature. Thousands of studies have analyzed sex-related patterns in physical performance, cognitive abilities, personality traits, moral reasoning, social interaction, occupational choice, sexual behavior, attitudes, aggression, depression, self-esteem, leadership, nonverbal behavior, self-disclosure, intelligence, life satisfaction, workplace achievement, and almost every other domain of human activity. To learn how these behaviors emerge, developmental psychologists explore the ways in which specific socialization practices contribute to observed differences between girls and boys and, by extension, women and men. Sociologists study structural features that shape the roles of women and men in organizational settings, family units, and labor markets. All these analyses contribute to the understanding of gender.

Not all of these topics can be discussed in this entry, and this review will not deal with sexual behavior or the biological basis of sex-related differences. Instead, this article will examine some of the main theoretical accounts of sex differences and then turn to 1) sex differences in four domains that were highlighted in early reviews (verbal, quantitative, and spatial ability and aggression), 2) differences in mathematics and science achievement, 3) other analyses of sex differences, and 4) contextual influences on sex-related patterns of behavior.

THEORETICAL ACCOUNTS OF SEX DIFFERENCES

Two predominant and contrasting theoretical accounts of sex differences are evolutionary approaches and a variety of social roles, expectations, and/or status perspectives (Eagly and Wood 1999). Evolutionary theory predicts that "the sexes will differ in precisely those domains in which women and men have faced different sorts of adaptive problems" in evolutionary history (Buss 1995, p. 164). These domains primarily are those relevant to reproduction, such as mate selection and sexual behavior (Feingold 1992), but also may include physical skills, the commission of violent crimes (Daly and Wilson 1988), and thresholds for physical risk taking (Wilson and Daly 1985). The evolutionary perspective suggests that in domains irrelevant to sexual selection, the sexes should and do tend to be psychologically similar.

The social roles and/or expectations perspective focuses on the relationship between male gender and high status in American and other societies. Sex differences in behavior may emerge because men are expected to be more competent and authoritative than women, and many social situations are structured to support this outcome (Foschi 1998; Geis 1993; Ridgeway and Diekema 1992). Eagly's (1987) social role theory further suggests that the unequal distribution of men and women in social roles (e.g., homemaker versus paid employee) contributes to both biased perceptions of the sexes and the development of skills and behavior that fit those roles.

The literature on self-fulfilling prophecy (Geis 1993; Rosenthal and Jacobson 1968) is consistent with this perspective. Expectations lead people to behave in ways that make the expected outcome more likely to occur. Gender-stereotyped beliefs of parents, for example, predict students' performance in mathematics courses: Parents who believe that girls are inferior in mathematical ability are more likely to have daughters who do poorly in mathematics (Eccles 1985). Deaux and Major's (1987) interactionist perspective further details how contextual factors determine whether and how gender-related expectations are translated into gendered behavior.

Other accounts of sex differences exist, including biological approaches (emphasizing hormones, brain structure, and genetics), developmental and/or learning approaches (e.g., social learning theory and gender schema theory) (Jacklin and Reynolds 1993), and constructionist perspectives (which describe "doing gender" rather than "having gender") (West and Zimmerman 1987). The basic theme of "biology or environment" pervades these perspectives. As is discussed below, any theoretical account faces the challenge of accounting for the size and pattern of sex differences across domains and the susceptibility of those differences to contextual moderation.

WELL-ESTABLISHED SEX DIFFERENCES?

In discussing sex differences, one can begin with Maccoby and Jacklin's (1974) landmark book *The Psychology of Sex Differences*. In this volume, the authors review the literature on sex differences and highlight several that are "fairly well established" (p. 351): Females tend to have greater verbal ability than males, and males tend to surpass females in quantitative ability, spatial ability, and aggression.

After the appearance of this narrative review, the statistical technique of "meta-analysis" was developed, enabling researchers to quantitatively combine results across many studies. Rather than rely on subjective impressions of the literature or a "count" of significant and nonsignificant effects, meta-analysis is based on calculation of an effect size (d) that reflects the mean sex difference in pooled standard deviation units in a given study. D's are combined across studies to compute an average effect size. As a rough guide, Cohen (1977) suggests that d's of .20 are small, those of .50 are medium, and those of .80 are large in magnitude. (To take a familiar example of a physical sex difference, the effect size for U.S. male–female differences in height is very large at $d = 1.93$.)

Meta-analyses of the four "established" sex differences have reached somewhat different conclusions than did Maccoby and Jacklin's (1974) narrative review. For example, females and males appear to be comparable in verbal ability in general and in most specific types of verbal ability, such as vocabulary, verbal analogies, and reading comprehension (overall $d = .11$) (Hyde and Linn 1988); positive d's indicate a relative female advantage. This effect was fairly stable across age despite Maccoby and Jacklin's (1974) conclusion that the onset of sex differences in verbal ability occurs at around age 11. A possible exception to the smallness of sex differences is verbal fluency (e.g., speed and accuracy of speech production and the production of sentences meeting meaning requirements), where females more clearly outperform males ($d = .33$) (Hyde and Linn 1988). It is also the case that males are more prevalent at the low end of the verbal abilities distribution. For example, there are three to four times as many male stutterers as female stutterers (Skinner and Shelton 1985), and severe dyslexia is about 10 times more common in males than in females (Sutaria 1985; see also Halpern 1992).

In regard to quantitative ability, some meta-analyses have reported modest differences between males and females in performance on tests of mathematical skill ($d = -.36$ and $-.43$) (Feingold 1988; Hyde 1981). A more recent study, however, found a very small overall effect in the direction of female superiority ($d = .05$), although differences favoring men emerged in high school ($d = -.29$) and college samples ($d = -.32$) (Hyde et al. 1990). Sex differences also tend to be greater among selected samples of mathematically talented youth tested on the mathematics section of the Scholastic Aptitude Test (Benbow 1988). Overall, the average scores of 12- and 13-year-old boys are higher than those of girls of the same age in these samples; the variability in the boys' scores is also greater. As a result, in the upper 3 percent of the distribution defined as mathematically precocious, boys outnumber girls in ratios that sometimes are dramatic (Benbow and Lubinski 1993).

Spatial ability has a possible (though still unclear) link to mathematical aptitude and scientific and engineering achievement. Meta-analyses of sex differences in visual-spatial ability have shown a variety of effect sizes, depending on the specific type of task or skill assessed. For example, on tasks of mental rotation, in which one is asked to visualize the rotation of a three-dimensional object, large sex differences favoring males have been found on one specific type of test (the Shepard-Metzler test; $d = -.94$) but not on others ($d = -.26$) (Linn and Peterson 1986). Tasks involving spatial perception (e.g., determining the true vertical plane when one is seated in a tilted chair) also indicate relatively smaller sex effects ($d = -.44$), and those involving spatial visualization (e.g., finding a simple shape in a complex pattern of shapes) show virtually no sex difference ($d = -.13$) (Linn and Peterson 1986; see also Masters and Sanders 1993; Voyer et al. 1995). Thus, sex differences in this domain are quite task-specific.

The only social behavior highlighted in Maccoby and Jacklin (1974) was aggression. Two meta-analyses of sex differences in aggression that were published a decade apart produced comparable, small effect sizes that indicated less evidence of aggression among females than among males ($d = -.24$ and $d = -.29$ in Eagly and Steffen 1986 and Bettencourt and Miller 1996, respectively). Bettencourt and Miller (1996) also identified an important moderating condition of this sex effect: Unprovoked men tend to be more aggressive than are unprovoked women ($d = -.33$), but under conditions of provocation, this sex effect is much smaller ($d = -.17$). A sense of the relatively small size of these effects can be gleaned by comparing them to the effect of provocation on aggression ($d = .76$). Although sex differences in aggression emerge, they do not seem to be as strong or straightforward as previously was thought.

MATHEMATICS AND SCIENCE ACHIEVEMENT

Although meta-analyses indicate relatively small sex differences in quantitative ability, an important related question is whether females and males differ in real-world achievements in quantitative domains such as mathematics, science, and engineering.

A report on women's representation in science and engineering by the National Science Foundation (1999) describes several significant findings. First, with regard to secondary education, male and female students are similar in their completion of high school mathematics and science courses (about 17 percent of both sexes have taken trigonometry, and about 25 percent have taken physics). Furthermore, average mathematics scores for females and males in the eighth and twelveth grades are not significantly different, although science scores among twelfth-graders are slightly higher for males than for females (based on the 1996 National Assessment of Educational Progress mathematics and science assessment).

On the mathematics portion of the Scholastic Assessment Test (SAT), men tend to score about 35 points higher than do women, a gap that remains even for students who reported having taken calculus and physics courses in high school. However, this difference appears to be due in part to the fact that a larger number of women than men who take the SAT are from lower-income families. Because parental income is related to SAT scores, the greater proportion of low-income women may reduce the overall female average (National Science Foundation 1999). It is unclear whether this income factor also accounts for findings regarding men's and women's performance on the 1996 College Board Advanced Placement (AP) tests. These data indicated a male advantage over females on AP tests in physics, computer science, chemistry, and calculus (d from $-.26$ to $-.52$) as well as an overrepresentation of males in the upper tail and an underrepresentation in the lower

tail of the distribution of test scores (Stumpf and Stanley 1998). Interestingly, across twenty-nine different AP tests, the size of the effect favoring males was highly correlated with the percentage of males taking a given test ($r = .71$). That is, the greater proportion of male to female high school students who choose to take a given AP test, the greater the male advantage in performance. Students taking AP tests are college-bound and self-select test subjects on the basis of their levels of preparation and expertise. Thus, this finding demonstrates that males feel more competent than females in the domains where they outperform females and that sex differences are apparent even among this highly self-selected group of "prepared" male and female students.

The National Science Foundation report (1999) details larger differences in female versus male achievement in regard to the attainment of advanced degrees and employment. Although women received 46 percent of science and engineering bachelor's degrees in 1995, they earned only 31 percent of the total science and engineering doctoral degrees in that year (up from 26 percent in 1985). The only science field in which women received the majority of doctoral degrees (64 percent) was psychology.

With regard to employment, women represent 46 percent of the total U.S. labor force but only 22 percent of scientists and engineers. Representation differs dramatically across fields: More than half of psychologists and 47 percent of sociologists are women, but women account for only 12 percent of physicists and 9 percent of engineers (National Science Foundation 1999). Among those with academic employment, women with science training are more likely than are men to work in elementary or secondary schools and two-year colleges. In four-year colleges, women are less likely than men to be tenured (35 percent versus 59 percent) or full professors (24 percent versus 49 percent). Men also are more likely than women to be managers, and across fields, full-time male scientists and engineers earn more than do females (overall median salary of $52,000 versus $42,000). Some, but not all, of these differences in employment placement may be due to differences in age, and women in science and engineering tend to be younger than men. Similarly, salary differences are due in part to age and field differences, since men are more likely than women to enter the high-paying fields of computer science and engineering. Nonetheless, differences in academic rank remain after one controls for age, and with increasing age, the gap in salaries between female and male scientists and engineers widens (National Science Foundation 1999)

OTHER SEX DIFFERENCES AND SIMILARITIES

It is impossible to provide a thorough overview of other research on sex differences in this brief article. In addition to the thousands of original empirical studies, over 180 meta-analyses have been published since Hall's (1978) initial meta-analytic study of sex differences in the decoding of nonverbal cues (where $d = .40$).

In a review of the "science and politics of comparing women and men," Eagly (1995) summarizes meta-analytic research by suggesting that the sizes of sex differences vary considerably across domains. The largest differences ($d > .80$) tend to be found for (1) some physical abilities (e.g., throwing distance, speed, and accuracy), (2) the Shepard-Metzler mental rotation task described above, (3) social behaviors such as facial expressiveness, (4) sexual behaviors such as the frequency of masturbation and attitudes toward casual sex, and (5) nurturant personality traits (tender-mindedness) (Feingold 1994). Most other examined attributes, however, tend to support sex differences that are small to moderate (or negligible) in size. For example, the mean effect size is $-.14$ for studies of sex differences in self-esteem (Major et al. 1999), .21 for fine eye-motor coordination (Thomas and French 1985), .02 for perceived leadership effectiveness (Eagly et al. 1995), .26 for negative attitudes toward homosexuality (Whitley and Kite 1995), and .07 for competitiveness in negotiation (Walters et al. 1998). Ashmore (1990) summarizes his review of the meta-analytic sex differences literature by noting that "relatively large sex differences are demonstrated for physical abilities and for body use and positioning; more modest differences are shown in abilities and social behaviors; and many negligible sex differences are sprinkled across all domains" (p. 500).

Whether one views observed sex differences as "meaningful" depends on one's opinion and perspective. On the one hand, as Eagly (1995) points out, even a large effect size translates into substantial overlap between the sexes: A d of around .80 indicates about a 53 percent overlap in female–male distributions. In this manner, findings of difference may mask substantial similarity between the sexes. Furthermore, many sex differences are quite small in magnitude compared with other important psychological phenomena (e.g., the provocation–aggression link of .76 described above and the effect of group pressure on conformity of $d = 1.06$) (Bond and Smith 1996).

On the other hand, a number of other sex differences are comparable in magnitude to psychological effects that typically are interpreted as both theoretically and socially meaningful. For example, the effect of exposure to media violence on aggression is $d = .27$ (Wood et al. 1991), and the effect of having a type A personality style on systolic blood pressure is $d = .33$ (Lyness 1993). It is also the case that sex differences based on general population samples may be smaller than the differences that appear when one looks at selected populations or those in the "tails" of frequency distributions. The greater representation of males among the mathematically precocious, the verbally challenged, and the most violently criminal, for example, suggests that for some highly salient important outcomes, sex differences may be more striking than one might assume based on observations of "average" people encountered in everyday experience.

Some have questioned the wisdom of overreliance on meta-analysis, as this quantitative approach cannot overcome the shortcomings or biases in the original set of studies on which the data summary is based. For example, in Eagly and Crowley's (1986) meta-analysis of sex differences in helping behavior, the authors note that their findings are based primarily on studies that involve short-term helping of strangers ("heroic helping"), a type of helping that is more consistent with the male role than the female role. Any finding of sex differences must be taken in light of this fact and not generalized across all helping situations.

Others have illustrated the limitations of meta-analysis for making causal inferences (Knight et al. 1996). For example, a number of meta-analyses of sex differences have indicated a "year of publication" effect: Studies published relatively recently suggest smaller sex differences in domains such as aggression; verbal, cognitive, and mathematical abilities; helping behavior; influenceability; leadership; and sexuality. Although some have interpreted these findings to mean that sex differences are disappearing (an interpretation more supportive of an environmental than a biological account), changes in research methodology over time may provide an alternative explanation. Indeed, in revisiting a meta-analysis of sex differences in aggression, Knight et al. (1996) found that statistically controlling for method characteristics (e.g., experimental or not, observational or self-report measures, physical or verbal aggression) removed the year of publication effect; small sex differences in aggression appear to have remained stable over time.

The entire enterprise of studying sex differences has its critics, and a number of relevant issues have been questioned and debated in several recent venues (*American Psychologist* 1995; *Feminism and Psychology* 1994; *Journal of Social Issues* 1997). Criticisms center on the tendency in this work to treat females and males as belonging to polar, global categories that ignore the other social characteristics of individuals (race, class, age, sexual orientation), invoke unsophisticated nature versus nurture explanations, ignore social context, and imply that a difference means a deficit. Despite these criticisms, the research literature continues to grow, and there appears to be a trend "toward a more contextualized version of gender-related behavior" (Deaux and LaFrance 1998, p. 816).

CONTEXTUAL INFLUENCES ON SEX-RELATED PATTERNS

As is indicated in many of the patterns of sex difference described above, researchers often find important moderators of the sex differences that emerge. For example, experimental work has demonstrated that the way in which a task is framed can affect performance outcomes. Thus, when the "spatial nature" of a spatial reasoning task was emphasized, men outperformed women, but when this aspect of the task was ignored, no sex difference emerged (Sharps et al. 1993). Similar findings have appeared with regard to mathematics performance, as predicted by Steele's (1997) theory of "stereotype threat." This perspective suggests that women's (and minorities) weaker mathe-

matics performance may be based in part on the threat of being judged consistently with negative group stereotypes. When that threat is lifted, performance differences should disappear. In one study, when a mathematics test was described as producing sex differences, women performed worse than did similarly qualified men; when the test was described as not producing sex differences, women and men did not differ in performance (Spencer et al. 1999). Other testing characteristics also may affect the size of sex differences. For example, structured tests that use a free-response format tend to produce smaller sex differences than do those which use a multiple-choice format (Kimball 1989).

The contextual setting also can play a role in the size of sex differences. A case in point is the analysis of leadership effectiveness, where military settings promote sex differences of moderate size ($d = -.42$) but other organizational contexts produce effect sizes of a much smaller magnitude or reversed direction, ranging from $-.07$ to $.15$ (Eagly et al. 1995). An analysis of gender and self-esteem indicated the importance of considering age and ethnicity in discussions of sex differences (Major et al. 1999). No sex difference in self-esteem was apparent before adolescence ($d = -.01$), but very modest differences began to emerge around ages 11 through 13 ($d = -.12$). Similarly, sex differences in self-esteem are apparent among whites ($d = -.20$) but virtually nonexistent among North American minority groups, especially African-Americans ($d = .03$). Finally, many abilities addressed in studies of sex differences are easily modified by experience. For example, spatial skills improve with exposure, and specific training programs designed to improve spatial skills are equally effective for women and men (Baenninger and Newcombe 1989).

Thus, task characteristics, familiarity, and social context can create sex differences or make them disappear. As Deaux and Major (1987) suggest, the basic behavioral repertoires of women and men are quite similar (e.g., both women and men know how to be aggressive, how to be helpful, how to smile). What men and women actually do is determined less by differential abilities than by the context in which they act. Norms, expectations, the actions of others, and the actor's goals and objectives may all combine to produce sex differences in behavior in some circumstances.

No doubt people will continue to ask how or why women and men differ, but the answers will never be simple and the explanations will not fall squarely on the side of biology or that of environment. Evolutionary and social role models ultimately may complement each other in their relative emphases on distal (distant) versus proximal (immediate) causal factors. The causal direction of some reasoning may need to be examined further. For example, observed differences between the sexes cannot be used as a simple explanation for broader gender roles. Instead, accepted roles may channel men and women into different patterns of behavior. Whatever the patterns observed, most sex differences will continue to reflect a gendered environment and be subject to change as social factors shift over place and time.

REFERENCES

American Psychologist 1995 Current Issues. 50:145–171.

Ashmore, R. D. 1990 "Sex, Gender, and the Individual." In L. A. Pervin, ed., *Handbook of Personality: Theory and Research*. New York: Guilford Press.

Baenninger, M., and N. Newcombe 1989 "The Role of Experience in Spatial Test Performance: A Meta-Analysis." *Sex Roles* 20:327–344.

Benbow, C. P. 1988 "Sex Differences in Mathematical Reasoning Ability in Intellectually Talented Preadolescents: Their Nature, Effects, and Possible Causes." *Behavioral and Brain Sciences* 11:169–232.

——, and D. Lubinski 1993 "Consequences of Gender Differences in Mathematical Reasoning Ability and Some Biological Linkages." In M. Haug, R. E. Whalen, C. Aron, and K. L. Olsen, eds., *The Development of Sex Differences and Similarities in Behaviour*. London: Kluwer Academic.

Bettencourt, B. A., and N. Miller 1996 "Gender Differences in Aggression as a Function of Provocation: A Meta-Analysis." *Psychological Bulletin* 119:422–447.

Bond, R., and P. B. Smith 1996 "Culture and Conformity: A Meta-Analysis of Studies Using Asch's (1952b, 1956) Line Judgment Task." *Psychological Bulletin* 119:111–137.

Buss, D. M. 1995 "Psychological Sex Differences: Origins through Sexual Selection." *American Psychologist* 50:164–168.

Cohen, J. 1977 *Statistical Power Analysis for the Behavioral Sciences*. San Diego, Calif.: Academic Press.

Daly, M., and M. Wilson 1988 *Homicide*. New York: Aldine de Gruyter.

Deaux, K., and M. LaFrance 1998 "Gender." In D. T. Gilbert, S. T. Fiske, and G. Lindzey, eds., *The Handbook of Social Psychology*, 4th ed. Boston: McGraw-Hill.

——, and B. Major 1987 "Putting Gender into Context: An Interactive Model of Gender Related-Behavior." *Psychological Review* 94:369–389.

Eagly, A. E. 1987 *Sex Differences in Social Behavior: A Social Role Interpretation*. Hillsdale, N.J.: Erlbaum.

—— 1995 "The Science and Politics of Comparing Women and Men." *American Psychologist* 50:145–158.

——, and M. Crowley 1986 "Gender and Helping Behavior: A Meta-Analytic Review of the Social Psychological Literature." *Psychological Bulletin* 100:283–308.

——, S. J. Karau, and M. Makhijani 1995 "Gender and the Effectiveness of Leaders: A Meta-Analysis." *Psychological Bulletin* 117:125–145.

——, and V. J. Steffen 1986 "Gender and Aggressive Behavior: A Meta-Analytic Review of the Social Psychological Literature." *Psychological Bulletin* 100:309–330.

——, and W. Wood 1999 "The Origins of Sex Differences in Human Behavior: Evolved Dispositions versus Social Roles." *American Psychologist* 54:408–423.

Eccles, J. E. 1985 "Sex Differences in Achievement Patterns." In T. B. Sonderegger, ed., *Psychology and Gender*. Nebraska Symposium on Motivation, 1984. Lincoln: University of Nebraska Press.

Feingold, A. 1988 "Cognitive Gender Differences Are Disappearing" *American Psychologist* 43:95–103.

—— 1992 "Gender Differences in Mate Selection Preferences: A Test of the Parental Investment Model." *Psychological Bulletin* 112:125–139.

—— 1994 "Gender Differences in Personality: A Meta-Analysis." *Psychological Bulletin* 116:429–456.

Feminism and Psychology 1994 "Special Feature: Should Psychologists Study Sex Differences?" 4:507–546.

Foschi, M. 1998 "Double Standards: Types, Conditions, and Consequences." *Advances in Group Processes* 15:59–80.

Geis, F. L. 1993 "Self-Fulfilling Prophecies: A Social Psychological View of Gender." In A. E. Beall and R. J. Sternberg, eds., *The Psychology of Gender*. New York: Guilford Press.

Hall, J. A. 1978 "Gender Effects in Decoding Nonverbal Cues." *Psychological Bulletin* 85:845–857.

Halpern, D. F. 1992 *Sex Differences in Cognitive Abilities*, 2nd ed. Hillsdale, N.J.: Erlbaum.

Hyde, J. S. 1981 "How Large Are Cognitive Gender Differences? A Meta-Analysis Using w^2 and d." *American Psychologist* 36:892–901.

——, E. Fennema, and S. J. Lamon 1990 "Gender Differences in Mathematics Performance: A Meta-Analysis." *Psychological Bulletin* 107:139–155.

——, and M. C. Linn 1988 "Gender Differences in Verbal Ability: A Meta-Analysis." *Psychological Bulletin* 10:53–69.

Jacklin, C. N., and C. Reynolds 1993 "Gender and Childhood Socialization." In A. E. Beall and R. J. Sternberg, eds., *The Psychology of Gender*. New York: Guilford Press.

Journal of Social Issues 1997 "The Significance of Gender: Theory and Research about Difference." 53:213–408.

Kimball, M. M. 1989 "A New Perspective on Women's Math Achievement." *Psychological Bulletin* 105:198–214.

Knight, G. P., R. A. Fabes, and D. A. Higgins 1996 "Concerns about Drawing Causal Inferences from Meta-Analyses: An Example in the Study of Gender Differences in Aggression." *Psychological Bulletin* 119:410–421.

Linn, M. C., and A. C. Peterson 1986 "A Meta-Analysis of Gender Differences in Spatial Ability: Implications for Mathematics and Science Achievement." In J. S. Hyde and M. C. Linn, eds., *The Psychology of Gender: Advances through Meta-Analysis*. Baltimore: Johns Hopkins University Press.

Lyness, S. A. 1993 "Predictors of Differences between Type A and Type B Individuals in Heart Rate and Blood Pressure Reactivity." *Psychological Bulletin* 114:266–295.

Maccoby, E. E., and C. N. Jacklin 1974 *The Psychology of Sex Differences*. Stanford, Calif.: Stanford University Press.

Major, B., L. Barr, J. Zubek, and S. H. Babey 1999 "Gender and Self-Esteem: A Meta-Analysis." In W. B. Swann, J. H. Langlois, and L. A. Gilbert, eds., *Sexism and Stereotypes in Modern Society*. Washington, D.C.: American Psychological Association.

Masters, M. S., and B. Sanders 1993 "Is the Gender Difference in Mental Rotation Disappearing?" *Behavior Genetics* 23:337–341.

National Science Foundation 1999 *Women, Minorities, and Persons with Physical Disabilities in Science and Engineering: 1998*. NSF Publication No. 99-87, February 1999.

Ridgeway, C. L., and D. Diekema 1992 "Are Gender Differences Status Differences?" In C. L. Ridgeway, ed., *Gender, Interaction, and Inequality*. New York: Springer-Verlag.

Rosenthal, R., and L. Jacobson 1968 *Pygmalion in the Classroom: Teacher Expectation and Pupils' Intellectual Development*. New York: Holt, Rinehart, & Winston.

Sharps, M. J., A. L. Walton, and J. L. Price 1993 "Gender and Task in the Determination of Spatial Cognitive Performance." *Psychology of Women Quarterly* 17:71–83.

Skinner, P. H., and R. L. Shelton 1985 *Speech, Language, and Hearing: Normal Processes and Disorders*, 2nd ed. New York: Wiley.

Spencer, S. J., C. M. Steele, and D. M. Quinn 1999 "Stereotype Threat and Women's Math Performance." *Journal of Experimental Social Psychology* 35:4–28.

Steele, C. M. 1997 "A Threat in the Air: How Stereotypes Shape Intellectual Identity and Performance" *American Psychologist* 52:613–629.

Stumpf, H., and J. C. Stanley 1998 "Stability and Change in Gender-Related Differences on the College Board Advanced Placement and Achievement Tests." *Current Directions in Psychological Science* 7:192–196.

Sutaria, S. D. 1985 *Specific Learning Disabilities: Nature and Needs*. Springfield, Ill.: Charles C Thomas.

Thomas, J. R., and K. E. French 1985 "Gender Differences across Age in Motor Performance: A Meta-Analysis." *Psychological Bulletin* 98:260–282.

Voyer, D., S. Voyer, and M. P. Bryden 1995 "Magnitude of Sex Differences in Spatial Abilities: A Meta-Analysis and Consideration of Critical Variables." *Psychological Bulletin* 117:250–270.

Walters, A. E., A. F. Stuhlmacher, and L. L. Meyer 1998 "Gender and Negotiator Competitiveness: A Meta-Analysis." *Organizational Behavior and Human Decision Processes* 76:1–29.

West, C., and D. H. Zimmerman 1987 "Doing Gender." *Gender and Society* 1:125–151.

Whitley, B. E., and M. E. Kite 1995 "Sex Differences in Attitudes toward Homosexuality: A Comment on Oliver and Hyde (1993)." *Psychological Bulletin* 117:146–154.

Wilson, M., and M. Daly 1985 "Competitiveness, Risk Taking, and Violence: The Young Male Syndrome." *Ethology and Sociobiology* 6:59–73.

Wood, W., F. Y. Wong, and J. G. Chachere 1991 "Effects of Media Violence on Viewers' Aggression in Unconstrained Social Interaction." *Psychological Bulletin* 109:371–383.

MONICA BIERNAT
KAY DEAUX

SEX-ROLE MODELS

See Gender; Femininity/Masculinity; Role Theory; Socialization.

SEXISM

See Feminist Theory; Gender.

SEXUAL BEHAVIOR IN MARRIAGE AND CLOSE RELATIONSHIPS

The scientific study of sexuality is not limited to a single discipline but involves scholars from a variety of fields, including sociology, psychology, and biology. The multidisciplinary nature of sexuality research lends itself to various and often contradictory theoretical interpretations of sexual phenomena. Furthermore, individuals have various perspectives on the purpose of sexual behavior and engage in a variety of sexual behaviors. For example, Reiss (1960) asserts that individuals take one of three general approaches to sexuality. Some individuals have a "procreational orientation," believing that the purpose of sexual intercourse is reproduction; others have what Reiss (1960) refers to as a "relational orientation," believing that sexual intercourse is for the purpose of expressing emotional attachment to a partner; and still others have a "recreational orientation," viewing the purpose of sexual behavior as enjoyment. Other researchers (e.g., Peplau et al. 1977) have constructed similar typologies. These perspectives or standards are likely to overlap; for example, couples who engage in sexual intercourse in order to reproduce also express their love and affection for each other and may enjoy themselves in the process. However, Reiss (1960) argues that individuals have one of these orientations as a primary explanation for engaging in sexual behavior. This article focuses on sexuality within close relationships. It begins by presenting some of the theoretical perspectives on sexuality and then discusses recent research findings on sexuality in close relationships.

THEORETICAL FRAMEWORKS

As was stated above, numerous theories have been developed to explain why certain individuals engage in sexual activities with certain other individuals and the context in which sexual behaviors occur. These theories generally fall on either side of an essentialist versus social constructionist dichotomy (DeLamater and Hyde 1998).

Essentialism. According to the essentialist perspective, certain behaviors are biologically driven and thus are natural and ubiquitous. An example of essentialist theories would be evolutionary theories such as sociobiology and sexual strategies theory (Buss 1998; DeLamater and Hyde 1998). According to those theories, which often are applied to gain an understanding of mate selection, certain contemporary sexual behaviors have emerged over time in response to environmental conditions. For example, both men and women are thought to strive to maximize their reproductive success (Oliver and Hyde 1993). Men are theorized to want to pass their genes to successive generations; therefore, they wish to impregnate as many women as possible to increase the likelihood that they will have offspring. Women also want to maximize their reproductive success, but they do so by striving to secure a long-term partner who will provide for their children financially (Chodorow 1978). Because men would not be passing along their genetic heritage by caring for another man's child, a woman's sexual exclusivity to one man has been socially desirable. These theories correspond to Freudian theories in psychology ("anatomy is destiny") and structural functionalist theories in sociology, which argue that traditional heterosexual marriage is the only appropriate forum in which sexual behaviors should occur, as the integrity of families and societies can be maintained only by that institution (see Parsons and Bales 1955).

Social Constructionism. Social constructionist theories minimize the influence of biological drives in explaining sexuality, instead focusing on how sexuality, like other phenomena, is socially constructed (DeLamater and Hyde 1998). For example, instead of arguing that men are biologically driven to be sexually promiscuous while women are biologically driven to be sexually exclusive, social constructionists argue that men and women engage in specific sexual behaviors as a result of the cultural messages they receive through socialization. Examples of theories within this framework are symbolic interactionism, social learning, social exchange, and conflict theories (Longmore 1998; Oliver and Hyde 1993; Sprecher 1998).

According to symbolic interactionism, individuals create meaning through their interactions with others; that is, they learn their sexual identities by communicating with others. Indeed, individuals learn and follow sexual scripts (Laumann et al. 1994; Longmore 1998; Oliver and Hyde 1993) that are specific to their culture, gender, race, social class, and so forth. These scripts are fluid; individuals frequently modify them to adapt to their environments. According to network theory (Laumann et al. 1994), sexual relationships are embedded in larger social networks that influence intimate dyads (Sprecher et al. in press). More specifically, network members influence who pairs up with whom, what behaviors (sexual and otherwise) should be encouraged and/or tolerated in an intimate relationship, and whether dissolution should occur.

To explain sexual behavior, social exchange theories postulate that the members of a dyad exchange resources with each other in an attempt to maximize their rewards and minimize their costs (Sprecher 1998). Examples of social exchange theories are equity theory (individuals reward their partners or withhold rewards in an attempt to influence the balance of equity in the relationship; Sprecher 1998) and choice theory (individuals pursue goals on the basis of the resources available to them, such as energy, physical attractiveness, and money; Laumann et al. 1994).

In explaining sexuality, conflict theories emphasize the power struggle inherent in intimate relationships. According to this perspective, men sexually dominate and exploit women in order to achieve their own goals, while women, lacking power, service men's sexual needs (Weis 1998b). While men may be better positioned to dominate and exploit because of their greater average physical strength, the power struggle is social and is based on the system of patriarchy (see Richardson 1996 for a discussion of this issue).

Summary. Despite these theoretical perspectives, sexuality research has been accused of being atheoretical (Weis 1998a, 1998b). Weis argues that theories of sexuality are still in an early stage compared to the theoretical development of other scholarly fields because of a lack of sexuality research that tests hypotheses (below, it will be seen that much sexuality research is descriptive) and because few strong connections have been established between theory and research. Christopher and Sprecher (in press) concur; in their decadelong review of sexuality in close relationships, they note the limited progress made in theories of sexuality despite the considerable increase in research in-

terest in this topic. They call for more theoretical advancements in future research on sexuality.

The following sections present some of the research findings concerning sexuality in close relationships. Several large-scale studies have been conducted within the last decade (most notably the National Health and Social Life Survey in addition to the second wave of the National Survey of Families and Households and several waves of the General Social Survey, which include measures tapping sexual behavior) despite the politicized nature of conducting studies on sexual behavior. These studies have greatly increased sociological understanding of sexuality in committed relationships. The discussion here focuses on three main concerns: (1) descriptive information on sexual behavior in close relationships (e.g., frequency of intercourse, number of partners), (2) the character of extramarital/extradyadic sex, and (3) qualities of homosexual close relationships.

DESCRIPTIVE CHARACTERISTICS OF SEXUAL BEHAVIOR

As was stated above, much sexuality research is descriptive. Thus, there is considerable knowledge of how frequently individuals engage in sexual behaviors, the types of behaviors in which they engage, how many sexual partners individuals have had over the course of their lives, the prevalence and character of extramarital or extradyadic sex, and the extent of sexual and overall life satisfaction, in addition to numerous other behavioral and attitudinal characteristics. This section focuses on the frequency of sex, the number of partners, and sexual and overall life satisfaction.

The state of descriptive knowledge of sexual behavior has increased considerably over the last several years as a result of the implementation of large-scale national surveys that use rigorous sampling methods. In particular, the National Health and Social Life Survey, which is based on a national sample of the noninstitutionalized population between ages 18 and 59, has provided extensive information on the sex lives of U.S. citizens (Laumann et al. 1994). The design of this survey is much more rigorous than that of the famous Kinsey studies (Kinsey et al. 1948, 1953), which relied largely on volunteers, calling into question the extent to which their data represented the general population.

Frequency of Sex. Contrary to the popular opinion that married couples engage in sex less than anyone else does, Laumann et al. (1994) found that only 1.3 percent of married men and 3.0 percent of married women did not engage in sex in the past year (respondents defined the meaning of engaging in sex, which may or may not have included vaginal intercourse). Twenty-two percent of the never-married/noncohabiting men and 30.2 percent of the never-married/noncohabiting women did not engage in sex in the past year. These figures are similar to those for divorced, separated, or widowed individuals who were not cohabiting (23.8 percent of the men and 34.3 percent of the women, respectively). However, all the cohabiting men and all the divorced/separated/widowed cohabiting women had engaged in sex at least a few times in the past year (1.4 percent of the never-married cohabiting women reported not engaging in sexual activity in the past year). According to Laumann et al. (1994), then, while cohabitors on average are more likely to engage in sex than are respondents in any other heterosexual category, sexual activity occurs in nearly all marriages.

According to Laumann et al. (1994), cohabitors are also more likely than are other heterosexuals to engage in frequent sex. More specifically, 18.6 percent of never-married cohabiting men (11.1 percent of divorced/separated/widowed cohabiting men) and 16.7 percent of never-married cohabiting women (11.3% of divorced/separated/widowed cohabiting women) engaged in sex at least four times a week, compared with 7.3 percent of married men and 6.6 percent of married women. Blumstein and Schwartz (1983), who conducted face-to-face interviews and collected questionnaire data from a convenience sample of heterosexual married couples, heterosexual cohabiting couples, and gay and lesbian cohabiting couples, found more substantial differences. They report that while 45 percent of couples in short marriages (two years or less) engage in sex at least three times a week or more, the corresponding figure for short-term cohabitors is 61 percent. This pattern persists when one compares marital and cohabiting unions of two to ten years (27 percent of the marrieds and 38 percent of the cohabitors engage in sex at least three times a week) (Blumstein and Schwartz 1983). Similarly, Rao and DeMaris (1995), using National Survey of Families and Households

data, found that the mean monthly frequency of sexual intercourse among cohabitors was approximately 1.3 times the mean frequency of the legally married.

As was noted above, those who are not currently married and are not cohabiting are more likely than anyone else not to have engaged in sex in the last year (Laumann et al. 1994). However, never-married/noncohabiting men and women who do engage in sex are slightly more likely than are married men and women, respectively, to have sex four or more times a week (7.6 percent of the noncohabiting men versus 7.3 percent of the married men and 7.0 percent of the noncohabiting women versus 6.6 percent of the married women). The divorced/separated/widowed respondents who are not cohabiting are less likely than are married couples to engage in sex at least four times a week (4.6 percent of the noncohabiting men and 3.7 percent of the noncohabiting women engage in sex this frequently).

Blumstein and Schwartz (1983) also found that gay men engaged in sexual behaviors more frequently than did anyone else in their sample (67 percent of gay men in short-term relationships of less than two years reported engaging in sex three or more times a week, compared with 32 percent of gay men in unions of two to ten years). Lesbians engaged in sex less frequently than did anyone else in the sample (33 percent of lesbians in relationships of less than two years engaged in sex at least three times a week; only 7 percent of lesbians in unions of two to ten years engaged in sex that frequently). However, Laumann et al. (1994) found no statistically significant difference in the frequency of sex among gay men versus all men. Statistically significant differences also did not appear among the women (however, the sample size of lesbians was very small).

In summary, cohabitors engage in more sex than do other heterosexuals, but marital sex is not the anomaly that popular opinion asserts (in other words, that sex rarely occurs in marriage; see Blumstein and Schwartz [1983] for a discussion of this issue). However, sexual frequency does decline with increasing age and duration of marriage (see Donnelly 1993; Marsiglio and Donnelly 1991; Call et al. 1995). Findings concerning the frequency of sex among homosexual men and women compared with their heterosexual counterparts are mixed.

Number of Sexual Partners. Individuals vary in terms of their number of lifetime (since age 18) sexual partners as a function of gender and relationship status. First, women are much more likely than men to have had only one sex partner since age 18 (31.5 percent of women report one partner compared with 19.5 percent of men) (Laumann et al. 1994). Men are more likely to report having had at least eleven sexual partners since age 18 (32.9 percent of men and 9.2 percent of women reporting having had at least eleven sexual partners).

Married individuals are less likely than are individuals in any other relationship status to have had numerous sex partners since age 18 (Laumann et al. 1994). More specifically, 37.1 percent of married respondents have had only one sex partner since age 18, compared with 24.6 percent of the never-married cohabitors and none of the divorced/widowed/separated cohabitors (who have all had more than one sexual partner). Nearly 15 percent of the never-married/noncohabitors have had only one sex partner (12.3 percent have had no sex partners), and 11.1 percent of the divorced/widowed/separated noncohabitors have had only one sex partner (0.2 percent have had no sex partners). The percentage of respondents who have had two to four sex partners since age 18 is quite similar across all relationship statuses. However, married respondents are consistently less likely than are respondents in all other relationship statuses (with the exception of never-married cohabitors) to have at least five or more sex partners since age 18. Those in other relationship statuses are quite similar in terms of the percentages who have had at least twenty-one sex partners. Thus, while cohabitors are more likely to engage in sexual behaviors and do so more frequently than other heterosexuals do, they do not differ appreciably from heterosexuals in all other nonmarital relationship statuses in the likelihood of having a high number of sexual partners.

Sexual Satisfaction. Sexual frequency is associated with overall perceptions of the quality of one's sex life (Blumstein and Schwartz 1983). Among those who engage in sex at least three times a week, the vast majority are satisfied with the quality of their sex lives (89 percent of both husbands and wives, 87 percent of male cohabitors,

88 percent of female cohabitors, 85 percent of gay men, and 95 percent of lesbians report satisfaction). The percentages of respondents who are satisfied with the quality of their sex lives decreases linearly with decreasing sexual frequency in all types of unions. For example, among those engaging in sex once a month or less, only 32 percent of husbands and wives are satisfied with the quality of their sex lives, compared with 4 percent of male cohabitors, 30 percent of female cohabitors, 26 percent of gay men, and 37 percent of lesbians. Other research has confirmed these findings (e.g., Call et al. 1995; Donnelly 1993).

The number of sexual partners a respondent has within the last year also influences physical pleasure and emotional satisfaction (Laumann et al. 1994). Married and cohabiting respondents who have had only one sexual partner in the last year are identical in terms of the the percentage reporting that they are extremely or very physically pleased with their relationships (87.4 percent and 84.4 percent, respectively). However, married and cohabiting respondents with more than one partner in the last year are less physically pleased by their primary partners (61.2 percent and 74.5 percent, respectively). The majority of those who are neither spouses nor cohabitors are also extremely or very physically pleased with their primary relationships regardless of whether they have one or more partners (78.2 percent with one partner are extremely or very physically pleased, compared with 77.9 percent of those with more than one partner).

Spouses with only one sexual partner in the last year are more likely than are respondents in the other union types to report that they are extremely or very emotionally satisfied with their relationships (84.8 percent; 75.6 percent of the cohabitors and 71.0 percent of those who are neither married nor cohabiting report that they are extremely or very emotionally satisfied). However, only 56.7 percent of marrieds with more than one partner report being extremely or very emotionally satisfied with their primary partners (the corresponding figures for cohabitors and those who are neither married nor cohabiting are 57.9 percent and 61.7 percent, respectively). In short, these numbers indicate that most individuals with one partner are quite physically pleased and emotionally satisfied with their relationships. Unfortunately, statistics are not provided comparing homosexual relationships to heterosexual relationships.

Overall Satisfaction with Life. As previous researchers have argued (e.g., Cupach and Comstock 1990; Edwards and Booth 1994; Greeley 1991; Lawrance and Byers 1995), sexual satisfaction is associated with overall relationship satisfaction, which is associated with overall satisfaction with life. Men and women are very similar in terms of their self-reports of overall life satisfaction (Laumann et al. 1994). There are, however, differences by marital status, sexual frequency, and number of partners. First, married respondents are more likely than are the never married, the divorced, the widowed, and the separated to state that they are extremely or very happy overall (67.5 percent, compared with 51.9 percent of never-marrieds, the next highest percentage) (Laumann et al. 1994). Similarly, they are less likely than are those in other statuses to report that they are fairly unhappy or unhappy with life most times (8.7 percent versus 15.2 percent of the never-married, the next lowest percentage in the sample). Unfortunately, Laumann et al. (1994) did not compare cohabitors, nonmarried/noncohabitors, or gays and lesbians to the legally married on this measure. However, they report that 62.5 percent of heterosexual men and 59.2 percent of heterosexual women are extremely or very happy, compared with only 47.1 percent of homosexual men and 45.6 percent of lesbians.

Respondents with only one sexual partner in the last year are happier overall (63.4 percent report being extremely or very happy) than are those with no sexual partners in the last year (40.7 percent) and those with more than one sexual partner (44.9 percent of those with two to four sexual partners and 47.2 percent of those with five or more sexual partners) (Laumann et al. 1994). Furthermore, the frequency of sex is associated with overall happiness in a generally linear fashion: The proportion of respondents stating that they are extremely or very happy increases with increasing frequency of sex in the past year unless the respondents engage in sex at least four times a week; the proportion reporting that they are extremely or very happy decreases slightly at this point. Again, Laumann et al. (1994) do not report distinctions among the respondents based on union status (married, cohabiting, homosexual, etc.).

Summary. These results clearly indicate that sex in marriage is not boring or non-existent for most couples and that unattached (not married and not cohabiting) individuals are not having all the fun. Indeed, because frequency of sex is associated with satisfaction with one's sex life and with overall feelings of happiness, one would expect married individuals to exhibit high levels of well-being in this regard, since most have steady access to a sexual partner. Also, variety of sexual experience as a function of having numerous partners is not associated with increasing feelings of happiness; instead, exclusive attachment to one sexual partner is associated with high levels of well-being for most respondents. These results raise the question: Why do some individuals engage in extramarital/extradyadic sex?

EXTRAMARITAL/EXTRADYADIC SEX

Behavioral Incidence. Kinsey et al. (1948, 1953) estimated that approximately half of married men have engaged in extramarital intercourse; the corresponding proportion for married women is approximately one-fourth. More recent figures that are based on more rigorous sampling methods indicate that on average, approximately 25 percent of men and 15 percent of women have experienced extramarital sex (Laumann et al. 1994). In additional analyses conducted by Laumann et al. using 1991 General Social Survey data, 21.7 percent of men and 13.4 percent of women (both between the ages of 18 to 59, consistent with their own sample) reported having extramarital sexual experience. These figures are consistent with those of Wiederman (1997), who, using data from the General Social Survey, found that 22.7 percent of men and 11.6 percent of women have engaged in extramarital sex. In their analysis of the National AIDS Behavioral Survey, Choi et al. (1994) found that 2.9 percent of men in the national sample (4.1 percent of men in the urban sample) and 1.5 percent of women in the national sample (1.0 percent of women in the urban sample) had engaged in extramarital sexual activity within the last twelve months (these percentages would increase with longer periods of exposure to opportunities for extramarital sex). Laumann et al. (1994) found that 3.8 percent of the married respondents had engaged in extramarital sex within the last twelve months (they did not differentiate between men and women among marrieds).

Blumstein and Schwartz (1983) found that 26 percent of husbands and 21 percent of wives had been nonmonogamous in their current relationships. According to those authors, 29 percent of nonmonogamous husbands had only one extramarital partner, while 42 percent reported having two to five extramarital partners. The corresponding figures for wives are 43 percent and 40 percent, respectively. Blumstein and Schwartz (1983) also found that 33 percent of male cohabitors and 30 percent of female cohabitors had engaged in extradyadic sex. Thirty-six percent of nonmonogamous male cohabitors had only one extradyadic partner (49 percent reported having had two to five partners). Forty-four percent of nonmonogamous female cohabitors reported having had only one extradyadic partner (41 percent reported having had two to five partners). Furthermore, 82 percent of gay men have engaged in extradyadic sex; among them, only 7 percent reported having had only one extradyadic partner (43 percent reported having had at least twenty). Blumstein and Schwartz (1983) report that 28 percent of lesbians were nonmonogamous; 53 percent had only one extradyadic partner, while 42 percent had two to five.

Unfortunately, Laumann et al. (1994) did not present the percentages of those in nonmarital/noncohabiting relationships who are sexually nonexclusive. However, Forste and Tanfer (1996) found that 18 percent of dating women between ages 20 and 37 had engaged in a least one instance of extradyadic sex.

As these results indicate, when respondents are asked if they have engaged in extramarital/extradyadic sex, the majority (with the exception of gay men) report sexual exclusivity with their spouses/partners. Also, at young ages (those under age 40), there does not appear to be a gender difference in sexual nonexclusivity among married respondents (Wiederman 1997). Over the age of 40, however, men are more likely to have engaged in extramarital sex. For example, 29.3 percent of men in their forties have engaged in extramarital sex, compared with 19.3 percent of women in their forties (Wiederman 1997). The greatest gender difference was found among respondents in their sixties, among whom 34 percent of men but only 7.6 percent of women reported having engaged in extramarital sex. It appears that the extramarital sexual behavior of women is becoming more similar to that of men as younger cohorts age.

Attitudes. According to Sprecher and McKinney (1993), much research has been conducted on attitudes toward extramarital sex. Generally, the measures employed in these studies assess either normative attitudes (those concerning the acceptability of extramarital sex in general) or personal standards (those assessing the acceptability of extramarital sex for oneself). Most research on normative standards has found that the majority of Americans disapprove of sexual relations with someone other than a person's spouse (Davis 1980; Greeley 1991). For example, Laumann et al. (1994) found that 77.2 percent of their (unweighted) sample believe that extramarital sex is "always wrong." Similarly, using General Social Survey data and restricting the sample to those between the ages of 18 and 59, they found that 74.3 percent believe that extramarital sex is "always wrong." However, other studies measuring personal standards have found that among younger men (under age 40), 70 percent envision themselves as having extramarital affairs at some point (Pietropinto and Simenaur 1977). Furthermore, Atwater (1982) reports that current predictions assert that as young married women age, approximately 50 percent will engage in extramarital sex. Of course, there is considerable difference between actual behavior, attitudes toward behavior for oneself versus others, and predictions concerning the future, as these numbers indicate. It may be expected that statistics on actual behavior are the most accurate in determining the prevalence of extramarital sex.

Explanations for Extramarital/Extradyadic Sex. Why do individuals engage in extramarital/extradyadic sex? It appears that the answer to this question depends in part on one's gender and relationship status. Extradyadic sex appears to be part of the culture of male homosexuality (Blumstein and Schwartz 1983). Indeed, it may be part of the socialization experience of most young men, who may enjoy high status among their peers for being sexually nonexclusive, while women are encouraged to be sexually exclusive (Peplau et al. 1977; Rubin 1990). Also, cohabitors in general (both men and women) tend to be much more liberal than are married couples on a variety of measures, such as premarital sex, abortion, and divorce (Blair 1994; Denmark et al. 1985; Macklin 1983a, 1983b). These liberal attitudes may correspond with more liberal attitudes and behaviors regarding sexuality, including extradyadic sexual behaviors.

Atwater (1982) conducted an in-depth study of married women who engaged in extramarital affairs with single men. She argues that married men and women engage in extramarital affairs for different reasons. Married women who have such affairs report that their self-esteem and confidence increase as a result of an affair; they report feeling more powerful, independent, and resourceful. Married men, in contrast, typically become involved in extramarital affairs in response to unsatisfying marital sex or the belief that their wives (or any one woman, for that matter) could not possibly satisfy all their sexual needs (Meyers and Leggitt 1975; Yablonsky 1979).

In a study of justifications for extramarital sex, Glass and Wright (1992), found that men and women differ in their approval of specific justifications. They found that men are more likely to support sexual justifications for extramarital sex, including engaging in extramarital sex for the purposes of enjoyment, curiosity, excitement, and novelty. Women, in comparison, are more likely to support love justifications (getting love and affection and falling in love) and emotional justifications (intellectual sharing, understanding, companionship, enhanced self-esteem, and respect for extramarital sex). The data collection methods employed in this study were not rigorous (questionnaires were handed out on the street to be completed and mailed back, with a response rate of 36 percent), and only respondents' attitudes were assessed, not actual justifications for their own extramarital sexual experience. However, this research suggests that men and women think differently about extramarital/extradyadic sex (as they do about other forms of sexuality, as evidenced by the sexual double standard; see Sprecher and McKinney 1993). Future research should continue to explore the use of justifications by men and women for engaging in extramarital/extradyadic sex.

The Character of Extramarital/Extradyadic Relationships. What are extramarital/extradyadic relationships like? The perspectives of those involved probably differ. Such relationships have been explored in depth only among legally married spouses involved with single individuals. Thus, the discussion here applies only to married cou-

ples, although the findings presented may apply to cohabitors as well.

In an extensive analysis of the relationships between married men and single women, Richardson (1985, 1988) discusses the power play inherent in an extramarital (and, by extension, an extradyadic) relationship. Popular opinion would suggest that the unmarried partner is the one with the power because at any moment she could reveal the affair to her married lover's wife. However, the partner who is married typically holds most of the power. Being married typically requires that the extramarital relationship be maintained in secret and thus in privacy. Often the home of the unmarried partner becomes "their" home because it provides the only safe setting in which the partners can come together. Furthermore, the married partner decides when and how much time the couple will spend together. The man is more likely to have competing obligations (notably a spouse and children), and so the unmarried partner often makes herself constantly available to her married lover whenever he can find time to spend with her. As a result, the single woman often constructs her entire life around her married lover, as she cannot obtain social support for her relationship from other family members and friends (because the relationship is maintained in secret). By being so dependent on her married lover, the single woman empowers him while giving up any control she formerly had.

Also, the unmarried partner has much to lose by revealing the affair to her married lover's wife (Richardson 1985). She may lose the relationship altogether, since the married partner's spouse would in most situations call for an immediate end to the relationship. Also, the betrayed spouse could destroy the reputation of the other woman by accusing her of being a home wrecker, causing emotional distress to the betrayed spouse and her children, causing financial problems, and so on. Furthermore, if the other woman works with her married lover, she may be labeled as "sleeping her way to the top," which could mean career and financial problems. This does not mean, however, that the single woman never reveals to the wife that her husband is having an extramarital affair. Block (1978) reports that some of these women (and men, in addition to the married lovers) intentionally plant evidence of an affair in an attempt to force a marital separation. However, it is not the case that the single woman could only benefit from such a revelation.

Popular opinion also states that the "wife is always the last to know" about her husband's extramarital liaisons, but it is more accurate to say that the wife is always the last to acknowledge an affair. Indeed, numerous researchers (e.g., Atwater 1982; Block 1978; Framo et al., 1975; Richardson 1985; Yablonsky 1979) have discussed the lengths to which a monogamous spouse will go to pretend that the affair does not exist, some bordering on the absurd. Atwater (1982) refers to such feigned ignorance of an affair as a "'pretense' context" (p. 86). Most wives pretend not to know about the affair because admitting knowledge of it would force them to feel compelled to respond to such a transgression (Framo et al. 1975). These women appear to have been lulled into a sense of complacency. They do not want to believe that their comfortable (although possibly dull) marriages may be in danger. Therefore, feigning ignorance may be a strategy to maintain the marriage (Richardson 1985). This may be especially important to wives who feel they have few alternatives to the marriage. Women in midlife, who have minimal chances of successfully competing with other women to find a long-term heterosexual relationship, and women who have been financially dependent on their husbands for many years may feel they have no choice but to stay with their husbands.

Similarly, a single woman interested in a permanent relationship with a married man (not all of these women are interested in permanent relationships, as that typically would entail performing housework and other services for the man, something their wives do instead; Richardson 1985) often denies the existence of the wife in order to more easily engage in her fantasies of permanence (Richardson 1985; Yablonsky 1979). Thus, feigned ignorance allows both women to indulge in their preferred fictions. The result, of course, is that the married man has the implicit permission of his wife to engage in the extramarital affair, while the single woman does not place undue pressure on him to divorce his wife.

Sometimes the evidence of an extramarital affair cannot be ignored. In these cases, there are several possible outcomes. One may be the immediate end of the extramarital affair (Framo et al. 1975). Another may be the eventual end of the marriage. Even if the marriage ends, however, it is unlikely that the newly divorced husband will marry the other woman even if he leaves his wife for her (Richardson 1985). A third possible outcome is that the married couple will arrive at an understanding of the husband's infidelity. For example, upon the discovery of the husband's extramarital liaison, the couple may engage in a tremendous and ugly conflict, followed by the husband promising to never stray again and the couple maintaining their relationship. However, few wives place much faith in a husband's new claims to fidelity (Ziskin and Ziskin 1973). Other couples construct an arrangement in which husbands are permitted to engage in extramarital sex, presumably because of their greater sexual need (Yablonsky 1979), but wives are expected to remain monogamous (Ziskin and Ziskin 1973). The wives typically accept this arrangement with resignation: They believe that they will not be able to stop their husbands from engaging in extramarital sex, and as long as the husband continues to remain married to the wife, does not allow himself to develop a deep emotional attachment to any of the other women with whom he is involved, and does not bring home a sexually transmitted disease, the stability of the marriage is not threatened (Block 1978; Yablonsky 1979; Ziskin and Ziskin 1973). A few wives may believe that they benefit from this situation, as they are granted the ability to pursue their own interests (rather than responding to the husband's needs), while the husband has some of his needs met by other women (Moultrup 1990). Finally, some spouses construct a new agreement in which both spouses are permitted to engage in extramarital sex (Myers and Leggitt 1975; Yablonsky 1979).

Summary. These results indicate that extramarital/extradyadic sex is not a majority experience. Indeed, with the exception of gay men, most individuals in committed relationships are sexually monogamous. These results also indicate that single women involved in extramarital affairs are not necessarily home wreckers or are looking to "steal away" another woman's husband. Furthermore, the married men involved in these affairs are not the hapless victims of single women's feminine wiles, powerless to reject any and all sexual advances. Finally, the monogamous husbands and wives left at home while their spouses rendezvous with single lovers are not necessarily the fools that others make them out to be but are often making a conscious choice to ignore a spouse's infidelity because of a lack of attractive alternatives to the current relationship.

As this discussion illustrates, little research has been conducted on extradyadic affairs among cohabitors, gay men, and lesbians, with the exception being the collection of statistics on the incidence of such experiences, as was discussed above. While heterosexual cohabitors may experience the same conditions and responses to their own or their partners' infidelity as do the legally married, future research should specifically address the experience of extradyadic sex among them in addition to infidelity among homosexual couples.

As has been suggested throughout this article, the relationships of homosexuals may be both similar to and different from those of heterosexuals in important respects (as an example, recall the very high relative rates of nonmonogamy among gay men, while the rates of nonmonogamy are similar among lesbians and heterosexual wives). Indeed, the relationships of gay men and lesbians are similar to and different from each other in important ways as well. The following section presents the results of research indicating the incidence and prevalence of homosexuality for both men and women as well as how those relationships may be similar to and different from the relationships of heterosexuals.

HOMOSEXUALITY

Behavioral Incidence. In discussing statistics on the prevalence of homosexual experience among men and women, one must be extremely cautious. Even at the end of the twentieth century, homosexuality was still a decidedly stigmatized status. This can be seen in attitudes toward homosexuality: In their analysis of General Social Survey data, Davis and Smith (1987) found that 75 percent of adults in the United States believe that sexual relations between two adults of the same sex are "always wrong." Only 12 percent of adults believe that sexual relations between two same-sex partners are "not wrong at all." This stigma probably results in some individuals claiming no homosexual experience when such experience has occurred or continues to occur for those individuals. Thus, one may suspect that reported statistics on the incidence and prevalence of homosexuality are inaccurately low.

Furthermore, homosexuality may be measured in a number of ways. For example, homosexuality may be defined as having same-gender sex partners, as expressing homosexual desires, or defining oneself as homosexual, bisexual, heterosexual, and so on (Laumann et al. 1994). Such variability leads Laumann et al. to conclude that there is "unambiguous evidence that no single number can be used to provide an accurate and valid characterization of the incidence and prevalence of homosexuality in the population at large" (1994, p. 301).

Laumann et al. (1994) report different percentages of the incidence and prevalence of homosexuality depending on how homosexual experience is defined. For example, they found that 0.6 percent of men and 0.2 percent of women have exclusive homosexual experience; that is, these men and women have never engaged in sexual activity with a person of the opposite sex. However, when respondents were asked if they had had any same-gender sex partners since the age of 18, 4.9 percent of the men and 4.1 percent of the women reported having had same-gender sex partners. Furthermore, 9.1 percent of men and 4.3 percent of women reported having engaged in at least one sexual practice with a same-gender partner since puberty (these practices include oral and anal sex). Also, 2.0 percent of men and 0.9 percent of women define themselves as homosexual (0.8 percent of men and 0.5 percent of women define themselves as bisexual; the remainder define themselves as heterosexual). In short, as these statistics illustrate, accurately determining the incidence and prevalence of homosexuality is both a political issue and a methodological issue.

The Character of Homosexual Relationships. Today most individuals maintain their intimate relationships in ways that differ from the traditional model (i.e., a breadwinning father and a stay-at-home mother). These various methods of maintaining relationships typically are referred to by social scientists and the larger public as "alternatives" rather than as legitimate family relationships (Boswell 1994; Scanzoni et al. 1989). Defining these relationships as alternatives to the standard (the traditional nuclear family) implies that such relationships are somehow not as legitimate or valid as the standard (Scanzoni et al. 1989).

A closer examination of these relationships, however, indicates that dyads that do not conform to the traditional standard are similar in certain important respects to traditional heterosexual relationships, particularly in the dyads' search for emotional intimacy and permanence (Scanzoni et al. 1989). More specifically, both heterosexual and homosexual individuals often seek potential partners who are similar to themselves in important ways (Murray 1996). For example, in her analysis of the relationships of homosexual dyads, Sherman (1992) interviewed numerous couples who specifically stated that they chose their current partners on the basis of shared behaviors or interests. For example, John and Reid, a couple that had been together for seventeen years, discussed how

> when we first got together, we talked a great deal about life goals and how we felt about relationships. . . . We decided early on that we wouldn't allow anything to come between us. We've really worked at that. We've made sacrifices about where we wanted to live and what we did professionally to help the other out at different points (p. 60).

However, both men agreed that while their relationship comes before the pursuit of individual interests, "we both sense the importance of being individuals and helping the other toward self-actualization" (p. 60). Thus, this couple struck a balance between pursuing their individual autonomy and maintaining their relationship on the basis of their similar values.

Similarly, in a study of eighty-four lesbian couples, Weber (1998) interviewed numerous couples who emphasized the importance of shared interests in forming and maintaining their relationships. A 46-year-old educator and a 43-year-old registered nurse who had been cohabiting for two years reminisced about how they came together: "We met at a Democratic fund-raiser, so through our work there we gained respect for each other overall and realized that we are intellectual and political equals. We also noted that we are peers on an educational and vocational level" (p. 57).

It appears that similarity in relevant characteristics attracts potential long-term partners to each other regardless of whether the couple consists of heterosexual partners, gay men, or lesbians. These long-term couples share a strong sense of commitment and the expectation of permanence based on similar values, making their relationships similar.

However, the relationships of both gay men and lesbians differ in some important respects from those of heterosexual couples, mainly because of the lack of social support homosexual couples experience as a result of their stigmatized status. More specifically, legal and religious institutions for the most part do not acknowledge the legitimacy of homosexual relationships. While in some cities homosexual couples may obtain domestic partnership certificates that publicly acknowledge their relationships, they still may not legally marry in the United States (Wisensale and Heckart 1993; Worsnop 1992). Also, while some representatives of mainstream religious organizations are willing to perform commitment ceremonies (see Sherman 1992 for a discussion of couples who engaged in these ceremonies), the official position of Catholicism, Judaism, and mainstream Protestantism is not to acknowledge such relationships in a religious sense.

Homosexuals confront numerous issues that do not affect heterosexuals. For example, homosexuals often must come to terms with a sexual identity that is stigmatized by the society in which they live. They also must decide whether they will "come out" to family members, friends, and co-workers, recognizing that doing so may jeopardize their relationships and employment. Heterosexuals do not "come out" with their sexual identity, as it is assumed that they are straight, and such an identity is encouraged and valued. Also, heterosexuals are rarely concerned that their sexual identity may result in social ostracism. One may expect that such concerns have an impact on the relationships of homosexual couples, something that is not experienced by heterosexual couples.

Homosexual couples often are shunned by family members and heterosexual friends when they reveal their sexual identity and introduce their partners to others. As a result, friends who do support the couple become defined by that couple as family (Nardi 1992). Those friends may be more important to the support of homosexual relationships than are the friends and family members of heterosexual couples, who also enjoy societywide support for their relationships, as was noted above.

Homosexuals are clearly aware of their second-class status in U.S. society. As a 35-year-old Department of Defense worker explained (Weber 1998, p. 50): "I am a valid and vital human being. I am a taxpayer, a property owner, a veteran, a professional, and also happen to be a lesbian. It is one aspect of who I am, yet it is the only aspect by which I am judged." A 36-year-old school counselor shared her experiences with the pressure associated with her socially ascribed second-class status (Weber 1998, pp. 51–52):

I love my child. I work. I pay taxes. I follow the Ten Commandments. I have friends and relatives that love me and I love them. I would help anyone in their time of need. I live next door to you in a clean house with a manicured yard. I live with my spouse, my child, and two dogs. I'm so normal that I'm boring. Yet, while I call her my spouse, I cannot legally marry the love of my life. While I love and support and care for my child, she could be taken away from me at the drop of a hat. While I have a responsible job at which I am very good, I could get fired without recourse. While I pay taxes, I cannot claim "head of household" or file jointly with my partner. While I follow the Ten Commandments, many churches will not allow me to attend their services.

My family and friends are the most important things in my life, yet if many of my friends knew what my family included, they would cease to be my friends. How can this be? Because I am a lesbian, and according to the laws of this country and the moral judgments of most of you, I am a pervert that should not be allowed to exist.

In discussing both lesbian and gay male relationships together and comparing them to heterosexual relationships, it should not be assumed that homosexual relationships are similar regardless of the gender of the partners (indeed, it should not be assumed that all heterosexual relationships, all lesbian relationships, or all gay male relationships are similar). As was noted above, gay men and lesbians differ significantly with regard to sexual frequency, number of partners, and other characteristics. However, lesbians and gay men suffer from the same stigmatized status as homosexuals. Future research should continue to explore the various coping mechanisms employed by homosexual couples in dealing with this stigma as well as

the ways in which their relationships are affected by it.

Summary. As this discussion illustrates, homosexual relationships are similar in a variety of ways to heterosexual relationships, particularly with regard to the degree of commitment in long-term relationships and the expectation for permanence. Although, as was noted earlier, the majority of gay men are sexually nonexclusive, one should not interpret this to mean that among gay men involved in long-term unions, few are committed to their partners as evidenced by sexual nonexclusivity. Indeed, there are heterosexual couples who engage in nonmonogamy yet remain committed to their primary unions (see the above discussion of extramarital sex). Monogamy should not be confused with commitment to one's relationship, and nonmonogamy should not be considered an indication of a lack of commitment.

Homosexual relationships do, however, differ in important respects from heterosexual relationships as a result of the second-class status of their unions. One may suspect that this stigma has an impact on the relationship dynamics of homosexual unions. Future research is needed to understand more fully how societal conditions affect these intimate relationships.

CONCLUSIONS

This article has demonstrated that even in examining only close, committed relationships, knowledge of sexual behavior is largely descriptive. Researchers need to explore in much greater depth the sexual dynamics of these relationships. More specifically, there is a need for a better understanding of how couples negotiate their sexual behaviors. Who decides how frequently a couple will engage in sexual activity and in what behaviors they will engage in and when? What is the negotiation process? Also, there is virtually no understanding of how the larger society affects the sex lives of individuals and couples, with the exception of theories of gender socialization in explaining differences between men and women. Of course, asking these questions is a political as well as a methodological endeavor that requires a strong financial and philosophical commitment on a societal basis. While the knowledge of sexual behavior in close relationships has progressed considerably the last few years, a greater understanding is needed of how individuals negotiate and manage their sex lives in the context of committed relationships rather than simply understanding what individuals *do* sexually. (Note: The authors wish to thank Susan Sprecher for her assistance on this article.)

(SEE ALSO: *Courtship; Sexual Behavior Patterns; Sexual Orientation*)

REFERENCES

Atwater, L. 1982 *The Extramarital Connection: Sex, Intimacy, and Identity*. New York: Irvington.

Blair, S. L. 1994 "Marriage and Cohabitation: Distinctions and Similarities across the Division of Household Labor." *Family Perspective* 28:31–52.

Block, J. D. 1978 *The Other Man, the Other Woman: Understanding and Coping with Extramarital Affairs*. New York: Grosset & Dunlap.

Boswell, J. 1994 *Same Sex Unions in Premodern Europe*. New York: Morrow.

Blumstein, P., and P. Schwartz 1983 *American Couples*. New York: Morrow.

Buss, D. M. 1998 "Sexual Strategies Theory: Historical Origins and Current Status." *Journal of Sex Research* 35:19–31.

Call, V., S. Sprecher, and P. Schwartz 1995 "The Incidence and Frequency of Marital Sex in a National Sample." *Journal of Marriage and the Family* 57:639–652.

Chodorow, N. 1978 *The Reproduction of Mothering*. Berkeley: University of California Press.

Choi, K., J. A. Catania, and M. M. Dolcini 1994 "Extramarital Sex and HIV Risk Behavior among U.S. Adults: Results from the National AIDS Behavioral Survey." *American Journal of Public Health* 84:2003–2007.

Christopher, F. S., and S. Sprecher In press "Sexuality in Marriage, Dating, and Other Relationships: A Decade Review." *Journal of Marriage and the Family*.

Cupach, W. R., and J. Comstock 1990 "Satisfaction with Sexual Communication in Marriage: Links to Sexual Satisfaction and Dyadic Adjustment." *Journal of Social and Personal Relationships* 7:179–186.

Davis, J. A. 1980 *General Social Surveys, 1972–1988. Cumulative Data*. Chicago: National Opinion Research Center.

——, and T. W. Smith 1987 *General Social Surveys, 1972–1988*. Chicago: National Opinion Research Center.

DeLamater, J. D., and J. S. Hyde 1998 "Essentialism vs. Social Constructionism in the Study of Human Sexuality." *Journal of Sex Research* 35:10–18.

Denmark, F. L., J. S. Shaw, and S. D. Ciali 1985 "The Relationship among Sex Roles, Living Arrangements, and the Division of Household Responsibilities." *Sex Roles* 12:617–625.

Donnelly, D. A. 1993 "Sexually Inactive Marriages." *Journal of Sex Research* 30:171–179.

Edwards, J. N. and A. Booth, 1994 "Sexuality, Marriage, and Well-Being: the Middle Years." In A. S. Rossi, ed., *Sexuality Across the Life Course*. Chicago: University of Chicago Press.

Forste, R., and K. Tanfer 1996 "Sexual Exclusivity among Dating, Cohabiting and Married Women." *Journal of Marriage and the Family* 58:33–47.

Framo, J. L., Y. A. Cohen, H. A. Otto, C. Symonds, A. Ellis, L. G. Smith, J. R. Smith, and L. Salzman 1975 "How Does an Affair Affect a Marriage? 7 Views." In L. Gross, ed., *Sexual Issues in Marriage: A Contemporary Perspective*. New York: Spectrum.

Glass, S. P., and T. L. Wright 1992 "Justifications for Extramarital Relationships: The Association between Attitudes, Behaviors, and Gender." *Journal of Sex Research* 29:361–387.

Greeley, A. M. 1991 *Faithful Attraction: Discovering Intimacy, Love, and Fidelity in American Marriage*. New York: Doherty.

Kinsey, A. C., W. B. Pomeroy, and C. E. Martin 1948 *Sexual Behavior in the Human Male*. Philadelphia: Saunders.

——, and P. H. Gebhard 1953 *Sexual Behavior in the Human Female*. Philadelphia: Saunders.

Laumann, E. O., J. H. Gagnon, R. T. Michael, and S. Michaels 1994 *The Social Organization of Sexuality: Sexual Practices in the United States*. Chicago: University of Chicago Press.

Lawrance, K., and E. S. Byers 1995 "Sexual Satisfaction in Long-Term Heterosexual Relationships: The Interpersonal Exchange Model of Sexual Satisfaction." *Personal Relationships* 2:267–285.

Longmore, M. A. 1998 "Symbolic Interactionism and the Study of Sexuality." *Journal of Sex Research* 35:44–57.

Macklin, E. D. 1983a. "Nonmarital Heterosexual Cohabitation." In A. S. Skolnick and J. H. Skolnick, eds., *Family in Transition*, 4th ed. Boston: Little, Brown.

—— 1983b "Nonmarital Heterosexual Cohabitation: An Overview." In E. D. Macklin and R. H. Rubin, eds., *Contemporary Families and Alternative Lifestyles*. Beverly Hills, Calif.: Sage.

Marsiglio, W., and D. Donnelly 1991 "Sexual Relations in Later Life: A National Study of Married Persons." *Journal of Gerontology: Social Sciences* 46:S338–344.

Meyers, L., and H. Leggitt 1975 "A Positive View of Adultery." In L. Gross, ed., *Sexual Issues in Marriage: A Contemporary Perspective*. New York: Spectrum.

Moultrup, D. J. 1990 *Husbands, Wives, and Lovers: The Emotional System of the Extramarital Affair*. New York: Guilford Press.

Murray, S. O. 1996 *American Gay*. Chicago: University of Chicago Press.

Nardi, P. M. 1992 "That's What Friends Are for: Friends as Family in the Gay and Lesbian Community." In K. Plummer, ed., *Modern Homosexualities: Fragments of Lesbian and Gay Experience*. London: Routledge.

Oliver, M. B., and J. S. Hyde 1993. "Gender Differences in Sexuality: A Meta-analysis." *Psychological Bulletin* 114:29–51.

Parsons. T., and R. F. Bales 1955 *Family, Socialization, and Interaction Process*. Glencoe, Ill.: Free Press.

Peplau, L. A., Z. Rubin, and C. T. Hill 1977 "Sexual Intimacy in Dating Relationships." *Journal of Social Issues* 33:86–109.

Pietropinto, A., and J. Simenaur 1977 *Beyond the Male Myth*. New York: New American Library.

Rao, K. V., and A. DeMaris 1995 "Coital Frequency among Married and Cohabiting Couples in the United States." *Journal of Biosocial Science* 27:135–150.

Reiss, I. L. 1960 *Premarital Sexual Standards in America*. New York: Free Press.

Richardson, D. 1996 *Theorising Heterosexuality: Telling It Straight*. Buckingham, UK: Open University Press.

Richardson, L. 1985 *The New Other Woman: Contemporary Single Women in Affairs with Married Men*. New York: Free Press.

—— 1988 "Secrecy and Status: The Social Construction of Forbidden Relationships." *American Sociological Review* 53:209–219.

Rubin, L. B. 1990 *Erotic Wars: What Happened to the Sexual Revolution?* New York: HarperCollins.

Scanzoni, J., K. Polonko, J. Teachman, and L. Thompson 1989 *The Sexual Bond: Rethinking Families and Close Relationships*. Newbury Park, Calif.: Sage.

Sherman, S. 1992 *Lesbian and Gay Marriage*. Philadelphia: Temple University Press.

Sprecher, S. 1998 "Social Exchange Theories and Sexuality." *Journal of Sex Research* 35:32–43.

——, and K. McKinney 1993 *Sexuality*. Newbury Park, Calif.: Sage.

Sprecher, S., D. Felmlee, T. L. Orbuch, and M. C. Willetts In press "Social Networks and Change in Personal Relationships." In A. Vangelisti, H. Reis, and M. A. Fitzpatrick, eds., *Advances in Personal Relationships*, vol. 2: *Stability and Change in Relationship Behavior*. Cambridge.

Weber, J. C. 1998 *Lesbian Dyads as Families*, Ph.D. dissertation. University of Florida.

Weis, D. L. 1998a "Conclusion: The State of Sexual Theory." *Journal of Sex Research* 35:100–114.

—— 1998b "The Use of Theory in Sexuality Research." *Journal of Sex Research* 35:1–9.

Wiederman, M. W. 1997 "Extramarital Sex: Prevalence and Correlates in a National Survey." *Journal of Sex Research* 34:167–174.

Wisensale, S. K., and K. E. Heckart 1993 "Domestic Partnerships: A Concept Paper and Policy Discussion." *Family Relations* 42:199–204.

Worsnop, R. L. 1992 "Domestic Partners." *CQ Researcher* 2:762–783.

Yablonsky, L. 1979 *The Extra-Sex Factor: Why over Half of America's Men Play Around*. New York: Times Books.

Ziskin, J., and M. Ziskin 1973 *The Extra-Marital Sex Contract*. Los Angeles: Nash.

MARION C. WILLETTS
JANIS C. WEBER

SEXUAL BEHAVIOR PATTERNS

In the face of significant political and methodological obstacles, social science researchers have continued to advance the understanding of human sexuality. Clearly, the political climate surrounding sex research has improved since Kinsey and his colleagues conducted their pioneering studies on male and female sexuality in the late 1940s and early 1950s (Kinsey et al. 1948, 1953), but the politics of sex research continue to impede progress in this area. One prominent research team, for example, was forced to abandon its efforts to secure federal funding and turn to private foundations to support a landmark study on human sexuality in the general population (Laumann et al. 1994b).

Despite the efforts of some conservative politicians, policymakers have become more willing to fund research on sexuality and related issues. This funding pattern is documented by the numerous large-scale national surveys that were supported by federal monies during the late 1980s and 1990s. These studies dealt extensively with sex and related issues (e.g., National AIDS Behavioral Survey, National Surveys of Adolescent Males, National Surveys of Men) or included a small battery of sex-related questions in surveys dealing primarily with other topics (e.g., ADD Health Surveys, National Household Survey of Drug Use, National Surveys of Families and Households, National Survey of Labor Market Experience–Youth, Youth Risk Behavior Survey). Funding agencies such as the Social Science Research Council Sexuality Research Fellowship Program are expanding studies of sexuality by offering crucial support for both quantitative and qualitative research projects about sexuality (Di Mauro 1997). Efforts also are being made to expand international studies of sexual behavior (Parker 1997). Most observers agree that the human immunodeficiency virus/ acquired immune deficiency syndrome (HIV/ AIDS) epidemic has provided the major impetus for this turnaround.

While a great deal has been learned about sexual behavior in recent years, especially among adolescent and young adult men, much of this research has focused on sexuality within a "social problems" context. This research typically has dealt with issues associated with teenage sexuality and pregnancy, HIV/AIDS, coercive sexuality, or another form of sexuality that has attracted a "deviant" label. As a result, relatively little attention has been devoted to studying the expression of sexuality in noncontroversial, everyday life circumstances.

Sex research took an impressive step forward with the publication of *The Social Organization of Sexuality: Sexual Practices in the United States* (Laumann et al. 1994a) and *Sex in America* (Michael et al. 1994), the less technical version of this study prepared for the general public. These publications were based on data drawn from the National Health and Social Life Survey (NHSLS) that included face-to-face interviews and supplemental self-administered questionnaires given to 3,432 respondents aged 18–59 who were selected randomly from the noninstitutionalized population. The NHSLS represents the most comprehensive sex survey to date that uses a probability sample of the general noninstitutionalized U.S. population.

Conducting sex surveys or other types of research in this area continues to be difficult because sex researchers, compared with researchers in most other areas, deal with particularly sensitive and personal topics and therefore face serious difficulties with issues related to response bias, sample representativeness, measurement, and ethics. With these methodological issues in mind (Bancroft 1997; Bentler and Abramson 1980; Jayne 1986; Kelley 1986) and given this article's space limitations, this review assesses the available research on sexual *behavior* in the United States. The brevity of this article precludes a review of all the literature on individuals' subjective perceptions of sexuality. Notably, much of the research on gay, lesbian, and bisexual experiences has revolved around identity, etiology, community, and AIDS (Risman and Schwartz 1988). While this entry discusses same-sex sexual behavior patterns, the reader should consult "Sexual Orientation" in this encyclopedia for a summary of literature about gay, lesbian, bisexual, and transsexual/transvestite identities and experiences. Since much of the literature on sexuality subsumes behavior under identity, this discussion uses the terms "heterosexual," "homosexual," and "bisexual" as adjectives rather than nouns and uses the terms "gay," "lesbian," and "bisexual" to refer to self-identity as reported in research studies (Risman and Schwartz 1988).

This discussion takes into account five basic and interrelated features of sexuality: (1) patterns of behavior, emphasizing gender, race, and sexual orientation, (2) the varied meaning of sexuality at distinctive periods throughout the life course, (3) social control aspects, particularly as they relate to prostitution, (4) the consensual and coercive contexts within which sex occurs, and (5) the relationship between the HIV epidemic and sexual behavior. While this entry reviews primarily social science literature, a number of studies have been published in the popular press, some of which have received considerable attention from the lay population, that are based on self-selected samples of persons who returned magazine surveys (Kelley 1986 provides a review of these works) or volunteered for qualitative interview studies (Rubin 1990).

SEXUALITY IN THE LIFE COURSE

Childhood Sexual Behavior. Given the Western view of children as asexual beings, little social science research has been conducted on childhood sexuality in the United States; most of the limited research has occurred within northern Europe. Data that are available typically rely on adults' recollections of their childhood experiences or the reports of parents about their children. While this research is methodologically limited, it does offer a glimpse of children's sexual behavior and play.

Anthropological research has shown clearly that while individuals in Western cultures tend to view children as asexual, children are seen as being capable of sexual activity in many nonindustrialized, non-Western countries (Ford and Beach 1951). Parents in non-Western countries sometimes tolerate and even encourage their children to pursue heterosexual behaviors (including intercourse), homosexual behaviors (e.g., fellatio), or both. In some societies mothers masturbate their children to soothe them.

The available research indicates that prepubertal boys are much more likely to experience intense sexual interest and masturbate and to do so at younger ages than their female counterparts. Boys also appear to participate more frequently throughout childhood in both heterosexual and homosexual play activities that have sexual overtones (e.g, "doctor and nurse"). These activities typically include an element of exhibition, exploration, and experimentation. In a unique longitudinal study of children in California, researchers found that about 48 percent of mothers reported that their children had engaged in interactive sex play (77 percent when masturbation was included) before age 6 and that exposure to such sex play was not related to children's long-term adjustment at ages 17 to 18 (Okami et al. 1997).

Other researchers focusing on heterosexual and lesbian women in Brazil, Peru, the Philippines, and the United States found similarities across cultures in regard to memories of childhood sexual behavior. Self-identified lesbians were found to be more sexually active as children and reported earlier contact than did heterosexual women. Lesbians also were more interested in girls than heterosexual women were in boys, even though lesbians reported more early attractions to men than did heterosexual women (Whitam et al. 1998). Another study of gay and bisexual male youth ranging in age from 17 to 23 also depends on memories of childhood to understand early childhood same-sex attractions. The results of this study show that in most cases, same-sex attractions began in childhood and were given sexual meaning at the onset of puberty (Savin-Williams et al. 1996). Both studies suggest that same-sex attractions are felt in childhood and are acted on in adolescence.

Adolescent and Young Adult Sexual Behavior. In contrast to childhood sexuality, an expansive body of literature on adolescent heterosexual behavior has emerged during the past two decades, and much more extensive data are now available on young males (Moore et al. 1995, 1998; Sonenstein et al. 1997). Much of this research has used one of several national data sets to document and examine rates and trends for age at first intercourse and sexual activity patterns, with particular attention given to racial patterns.

The bulk of the evidence suggests that there was a sizable increase in the rate of sexual activity among teenage females in the 1970s and 1980s, although that increase appears to have leveled off in the 1990s. In fact, among 15- to 19-year-old females, while the proportion that had ever had intercourse increased from 29 percent in 1970 to 55 percent in 1990, it declined slightly to 50 percent in 1995. About 77 percent of 19-year-old females have had sex at least once. The main reason teenage females remain virgins is that having sex would violate their religious or moral values. While rates among African-American and white females have converged over the past two decades, black females are still more likely to report being sexually active than are their white counterparts. Whereas 90 percent of black females have had intercourse by age 19, about 75 percent of whites and Hispanics have had coitus.

Sexual activity rates among comparably aged males have increased since the 1970s and have always been higher than those of females. A 1998 study compared three separate national samples of males aged 17–19 living in metropolitan areas in 1979, 1988, and 1995 and found that the percentage of respondents who had ever had heterosexual intercourse shifted from 66 percent, to 76 percent, to 68 percent (Ku et al. 1998). However, these changes were restricted to nonblack males because the rates for blacks increased from 1979 to 1988 and then remained basically constant between 1988 and 1995. A similar curvilinear pattern for the overall sample (but not for blacks) was observed when researchers examined the proportion of teenage males who had had intercourse in the four-week period before the interview. Meanwhile, the average number of times young males engaged in sexual intercourse during the previous twelve-month period increased from fourteen in 1979 to seventeen in 1988 to twenty-one in 1995. While black males did not experience a change in frequency between 1979 and 1988, they reported a significant increase from 1988 to 1995 (thirteen versus twenty-four acts per year).

Attempts to explain why youth initiate sex have focused primarily on the direct and indirect influence of sociodemographic, social psychological, and biological factors. Most of the research designs, especially those used in studying females, are not ideal for concluding a causal relationship between beliefs, attitudes, or values and sexual behavior because these variables tend to be measured simultaneously. Despite this methodological shortcoming, a number of factors appear to be related positively (when controlling for numerous variables) to the probability of individuals engaging in heterosexual intercourse at a young age: being black, living in a poverty area, having weak religious beliefs, attending a segregated school (for blacks), attending an integrated school (for whites), lower parental education, having a mother who was sexually active at a young age, living in a single-parent household, having more siblings, and having a low level of academic achievement.

In addition to these social variables, a small number of researchers have used cross-sectional and longitudinal designs to study the relationship between adolescent hormones and heterosexual behavior (Udry 1988). While this research has produced mixed results, hormones and biological markers associated with puberty appear to be related to adolescents' sexuality (both attitudes and behavior). Consequently, a growing number of social scientists are advocating the development of biosocial models that take into account the complex interrelationship among the pubertal process, sexual identity development, sexual behavior, and societal norms. Collecting saliva and blood samples has become an acceptable, and increasingly expected, component of national data collection efforts that target adolescent sexuality and fertility.

The discussion of social and biological factors leading toward the initiation of sexual behavior is also present in studies of same-sex attractions, desires, and behaviors. Similar to heterosexual onset of active sexuality, gay, lesbian, and bisexual youth report the development of sexual interest during puberty. Gagnon (1977) explains that young men typically self-identify as gay and have homosexual experiences at an earlier age than do young women. Jay and Young (1979) report awareness of same-sex attraction for young men developing at the median age of 13 or 14 and for young women at age 18. Cohen and Savin-Williams (1996, pp. 120–121) summarize the results of ten different studies of the initiation of sexual behavior (mostly among young men) and find that the average age of reported first experience of homosexual sex is 15 for young men, with young women reporting an average age of 16. Importantly, same-sex sexual behavior is not always correlated with the development of a gay, lesbian, or bisexual identity. Studies show that youth will participate in homosexual activities without later "coming out" as gay, lesbian, or bisexual. In particular, as a result of cultural understandings of gender and sexuality, Chicano men who participate in same-sex anal intercourse do not consider it "gay sex" unless one is in the subordinant (receptor) role (Almaguer 1993; Alonso and Koreck 1993; Carrier 1989). Research in this area supports the supposition that social and cultural factors are important in the initiation of same-sex sexual behavior and its attendant meaning.

Research on adolescent homosexual and bisexual behavior is complicated by the stigma associated with a gay, lesbian, or bisexual identity, and so many youths do not self-report same-sex activities (Savin-Williams et al. 1996). While many self-identified gay, lesbian, and bisexual adolescents report desiring steady, loving same-sex relationships, many maintain heterosexual relationships and fear revealing close same-sex friendship because of the stigma associated with being "gay" (Hetrick and Martin 1987). Thus, studies of sexual behavior among gay, lesbian, and bisexual adolescents have documented heterosexual behavior, although with a lesser frequency than is the case with heterosexual counterparts. Interestingly, lesbian and bisexual female adolescents tend to report more heterosexual experiences than do gay and bisexual male adolescents (Herdt and Boxer

1993). Research on the frequency of sexual activity among gay, lesbian, and bisexual young adults indicates that for some populations, entry into college allows an increase in the frequency of sexual experiences (Evans and D'Augelli 1996).

While most research has focused on heterosexual intercourse, a number of studies of adolescent and young adult populations have examined issues related to the number of sexual partners, frequency of sexual intercourse, other types of sex acts, and the sequencing of petting behaviors (Laumann et al. 1994a; Moore et al. 1995 ; Warren et al. 1998). The majority of teenagers and those in their twenties tend to have one sexual partner at a time, a form of serial monogamy. One study found that 72 percent of women aged 18–29 reported having only one partner in the previous year, and another found that only about 10 percent of females have two or more partners in a three-month period. Among the sexually experienced, about 77 percent of 15- to 19-year-old females and 85 percent of those aged 20–24 report having sex more than once a month. Among sexually experienced teenage males aged 15–19, 54 percent report having had no more than one partner in the previous year, 80 percent report having had two partners, and 6 percent report having had five or more.

Researchers also have shown that the prevalence of oral sex has grown tremendously in this century. Kinsey's data revealed that very few college women born between 1910 and 1935 performed fellatio (11 percent) or received cunnilingus (12 percent). More recent studies in California and North Carolina suggest that between one-third and one-half of adolescents aged 15–18 have engaged in oral sex (Hass 1979; Newcomer and Udry 1985), while nonrepresentative studies of college students in the United States and Canada indicate that between 32 and 86 percent of females have administered oral sex and between 44 and 68 percent say they have received it (Herold and Way 1983; Young 1980). Furthermore, Kinsey's data suggested that oral sex was primarily experienced only among those who also had experienced coitus (only 5 percent of male and female virgins reported performing it), but more recent research indicates that a sizable minority of youth are experiencing oral sex while they are technically virgins.

Single-Adult Sexual Behavior. Because researchers have not clearly and consistently distinguished between young adult (18- to 24-year-olds) and adult sexual behavior in presenting their findings, it is difficult to present a clear-cut review of "adult" sexual behavior among single persons. Research has shown that rising divorce rates and postponement of marriage for heterosexual men and women have increased the population of single adults (Blumstein and Schwartz 1983). The inability of gay and lesbian partners to marry legally also contributes to the growing population of "single adults" because some persons in committed relationships are categorized as single. This growing population of single adults and the typical transition from experimentation and dating to long-term, committed relationships bring into focus a significant type of adult sexual behavior. While these demographic patterns are noteworthy, a large proportion of individuals still experience a significant proportion of their adult sexual histories within committed relationships or marriage.

For single adults, it is known that individuals today move through the sequence from first kiss to first intercourse much more quickly than did older cohorts of a similar age. Many of these first sexual experiences with a new partner occur within an arrangement that is perceived in some ways to be a relationship. Although men are more likely to find recreational sex outside a relationship acceptable, both men and women prefer to have sex within an ongoing romantic relationship. Thus, contrary to stereotypical images, most adults have sex infrequently when they are not in a relationship. Indeed, national data based on a sample of 18- to 59-year-olds who report being sexually active in the past year indicate that without controlling for age, 48 percent of men and 54 percent of women who have never been married and are not currently cohabiting have had sex only a few times or not at all in the past year. These figures varied only slightly for men (46 percent) and women (58 percent) who were divorced, separated, or widowed but were not married or cohabiting. The mean monthly frequency of sex (vaginal, oral, or anal) was 5.6 and 5.3 for men and women who never married and were not currently cohabiting and 5.4 and 5.1 for men and women who were divorced, separated, or widowed. Only 8 to 9 percent of men and women who had never married but were currently cohabiting—persons who could be perceived technically as being single—reported similarly low levels of sexual activity: a few times a year or not at all. Meanwhile, among never married, noncohabiting persons, 29 percent of men and 21 percent of women reported giving oral sex to their partners during the most recent sexual experience. Among the entire sample, regardless of whether the respondents had sex in the past year, 67 percent of men and 70 percent of women reported that they had engaged in active oral sex at some point during their lives.

One of the revelations of Kinsey's early research was the extent to which people had same-sex sexual experiences without identifying themselves as gay, lesbian or bisexual. Since Kinsey's research, this finding has been reproduced in a variety of different contexts. Laumann et al.'s comprehensive sex study (1994a) illustrates how the interaction of behavior, attraction, and sexual identity complicates the measurement of the number of people who could be understood to be gay, lesbian, or bisexual. Ultimately, Laumann et al. (1994a) conclude that there is a core group of people who define themselves as "homosexual or bisexual," have same-gender partners, *and* express homosexual desires. Yet there are also a number of men and women who have adult same-sex sexual experiences or desires but do not identify themselves as "homosexual or bisexual." Additionally, variables (e.g., place of residence and level of education) are found to influence the number of homosexual experiences. Because of the complexity of measurement, Laumann et al. (1994a) conclude that there is no single answer to the prevalence of homosexuality. Studies of adult sexual experiences among men of color in the United States and men of color in other cultures also have illustrated the extent to which heterosexual adults engage in same-sex sexual behavior: Research has identified a large population of men who have sex with men (MSM) yet do not self-identify as gay or bisexual (Manalansan 1996). Research since Kinsey's original attempt to develop a comprehensive (although nonrepresentative) understanding of sexual behavior in the United States has shown that some adults participate in homosexual behavior without self-identifying as such.

Despite the complexity of sexual identity and behavior, a great deal of research on same-sex adult behavior patterns has been comparative, creating a binary heterosexual-homosexual comparison. This dualistic approach is so prevalent that many sexual activities are understood as being in the domain of only heterosexual behavior or only homosexual behavior. For example, tranvestitism (cross-dressing) has been defined in the psychological literature as primarily the domain of heterosexual men, yet more recent research suggests that men with cross-dressing habits behave as homosexual, bisexual, and asexual as well as heterosexual, suggesting a complexity to adult sexual behavior patterns that is not fully understood (Bullough and Bullough 1997). In a significant study comparing same-sex sexual behavior patterns with opposite-sex behavior patterns, Masters and Johnson (1979) found some general trends of similarity for adult "heterosexuals" and "homosexuals" (both men and women). Overall, their research shows that "heterosexuals" and "homosexuals" have similar fantasy patterns and physiological responses to sexual stimuli. In other words, response to sexual stimuli is not conditioned by a particular sexual identity. Some differences between heterosexuals and nonheterosexuals emerge when women's experiences are highlighted. A study of 70 self-categorized heterosexual, bisexual, or homosexual women showed that bisexual and lesbian women were significantly more likely than were heterosexual women to describe their orgasms as "strong." In addition, bisexual and lesbian women put more emphasis on oral and manual sexuality, while heterosexual women put more emphasis on intercourse as a source of sexual response (Bressler and Lavender 1986). Overall, comparative studies suggest a similarity of sexual response and fantasy for both heterosexual and homosexual behaviors but some distinctions in terms of actual sexual activities participated in by self-identified gay, lesbian, or bisexual individuals.

Another arena of research that compares heterosexual behavior to gay and lesbian behavior is the study of committed relationships. A great deal of research illustrates the prevalence of stereotypes about gay, lesbian, and bisexual people being promiscuous and not involved in long-term, committed relationships. However, in one of the few large-scale studies of relationships (including heterosexual, gay, and lesbian couples), Blumstein and Schwartz (1983) found that many lesbians and gay men establish lifelong partnerships. Research also shows that in established couples, gay men and lesbians report as much satisfaction (measured in numerous ways) as heterosexuals do (Peplau 1982). Specific research about sexual behavior among gay and lesbian couples has shown some interesting trends. A notable finding in Blumstein and Schwartz's (1983) research is that the frequency of sex in lesbian couples is low compared to that in other couples. Among lesbian couples who had been together two to ten years, more than 25 percent reported having sex once a month or less. This finding has been explained in terms of women's sexual socialization, different definitions of sexuality, and age of couples (Blumstein and Schwartz 1983; Johnson 1990). By contrast, Blumstein and Schwarz (1983) report that gay male couples report higher sexual frequency than do married couples (of one to ten years). This often is explained in terms of men's socialization to value sexuality. Research on sexual frequency in committed couples illustrates the significance of gender and thus the diversity of relationships and attendant sexual behavior among self-identified gay men and lesbians.

Research about the diversity of sexual behaviors among gay, lesbian, and bisexual adults expanded in the 1990s. In general, gender is understood to account for variation of sexual behavior in the gay, lesbian, and bisexual population: Men having sex with men are understood to do so differently (in terms of frequency and activities) than women having sex with women. Variation also has been found within sexual identity categories. For example, it has been found that individuals involved in bisexual behavior have a variety of relationship types (Blumstein and Schwartz 1976). Meanwhile, distinctions in regard to adult same-sex sexual behavior in terms of race are not well understood. In a national-level study of more than 700 coupled, homosexually active African-American men and women, most of the respondents reported satisfying sex lives with their current partners and variation of sexual frequency among couples but no systematic difference between women and men (Peplau et al. 1997). The varieties of sexual behavior within gay, lesbian, and bisexual categories and couples are just being discovered.

The politics of sexuality research in the era of HIV/AIDS has expanded the understanding of sexual behavior among adults, but only in particular arenas. For example, national-level research on sexual behaviors among bisexual men and women and lesbians remains limited (Doll 1997). In addition, the way in which studies of male homosexuality have been conducted differentially operationalizes

"homosexual" as an identity, so that populations of men who have sex with men (MSM) sometimes are included and at other times are excluded (Carballo-Dieguez 1997; Sandfort 1997). Clearly, studies of sexuality expanded dramatically in the 1990s, yet this growth pattern has been shaped by concerns associated with an era of HIV/AIDS.

Sexual Behavior among Elderly Persons. Although the proportion of the U.S. population over age 50 continues to grow, research addressing the relationship between aging and sexuality, in particular the sexual behavior of the elderly population (65 and older) is quite limited because of its frequent use of small nonrepresentative samples, its cross-sectional research designs, and its narrow, youth-oriented definition of sexuality as coitus. Consequently, generalizations are difficult to make, and most research on elderly persons' sexual behavior deals with the physiological and psychological aspects of this phenomenon. The Viagra revolution undoubtedly will prompt researchers to devote more attention to older persons' sexuality (Butler 1998).

Two of the more frequently cited, though perhaps dated, studies of aging and sexuality issues are the Starr-Weiner Report (1981) and the second Duke Longitudinal Study (George and Weiler 1981), neither of which was based on random sampling techniques. The former study included 800 sociodemographically diverse participants in senior centers, while the latter included a panel design of men and women health insurance program participants who were 46 to 71 years of age at the first observation period in 1969 and were followed for six years ($n = 348$ for those enrolled in all four data collection points). Seventy-five percent of the respondents in the first study reported that sex felt as good as or better than it did when they were younger. The results from an analysis restricted to the 278 married respondents who had been retained throughout the Duke study revealed that pattens of sexual interest and activity remained fairly stable over time, men reported higher levels of sexual interest and activity than did their female age peers, and younger cohorts of respondents reported higher levels of sexual interest and activity.

Compared to earlier studies (e.g., the Kinsey reports), the Starr-Weider and Duke studies as well as more recent ones have found higher levels of sexual activity among older persons. Accordingly, Riporetelia-Muller (1989, p. 214) concluded that "for those elderly who remain sexually active and have a regular partner, the rate of decline is not as great as formerly believed." However, many older persons do not remain sexually active. Using data from the second Duke study, George and Weiler (1981) found that among those who were at least 56 years of age at the first observation date, 21 percent of men and 39 percent of women reported six years later that they had abstained from sexual relations throughout the study or were currently inactive.

In a study using data from a nationally representative household sample (Marsiglio and Donnelly 1991), about 53 percent of all married persons 60 years of age and older reported having sex in the past month, with 65 percent of those 60 to 65 years old being sexually active compared to 44 percent of those 66 or older. Among those who had been sexually active during the past month, the overall mean frequency for sexual relations was 4.3 times. In a multivariate context, persons were most likely to have had sex during the past month if they were younger, had a higher sense of self-worth and competency, and were married to a spouse who self-reported his or her health status as favorable. Surprisingly, when an interaction term was used to compare husbands and wives, no significant differences were observed in the way the partner's health status was related to sexual behavior, although other research has found that both husbands and wives report that males' attitude or physical condition tends to be the principal reason why they have curtailed or ceased to have sexual relations. Meanwhile, other research indicates that being widowed is the most frequently cited reason for not being sexually active among older women overall. While data on persons who are institutionalized are scarce, it appears that their sexual activity levels are low.

Being without a spouse does not necessarily mean that older persons are sexually inactive. Brecher (1984) reported, for example, that among unmarried persons 60 years of age and older, about 75 percent of men and 50 percent of women were sexually active. This is reinforced by Starr and Weiner's (1981) finding that 70 percent of their respondents over 60 were sexually active, although only 47 percent were married. Finally, masturbation is an option used by some elderly

persons to express their sexuality, presumably in a nonsocial setting. In a few studies, about one-third of women and slightly less than one-half of men over 70 report masturbating.

Just as stereotypes about elderly people and sexuality abound, so do stereotypes about the sexuality of gay, lesbian, and bisexual elders. However, research suggests that gays and lesbians offer a model of successful aging (Berger 1996). In terms of actual sexual behaviors, many of the gay men interviewed for this study reported that their frequency of sex had changed as they aged, supporting the idea that age is associated with a lower frequency of sexual relations (Berger 1996). Similarly, another study based on self-report data obtained from men between 40 and 77 years old found that the majority of these self-identified gay men were currently sexually active, although sexual interest declined somewhat with age. The majority reported no change in their enjoyment of sex from their younger years to the present (Pope and Schulz 1990). The myth of sexual and emotional isolation for lesbians is also challenged by a series of in-depth interviews with 20 women over age 50 who self-identified as lesbian. This research found that lesbians continue to be sexually active and tend to seek out other older women as partners (Raphael and Robinson 1992). Like other research on aging and sexuality, research on self-identified gay and lesbian elders shows that they have continued interest in expressing themselves sexually.

CONSENT AND COERCION

In recent decades, researchers have increasingly focused on "rape and other forms of sexual coercion" (Muehlenhard 1994, p. 143). A few observers have reacted by asserting that the data assessing sexual coerciveness among adults who are known to one another are seriously flawed and thus exaggerate their substantive and policy significance (Roiphe 1993; Muehlenhard et al. 1994). However, most social scientists and clinicians consider sexual coerciveness to be both serious and significant and have begun to scrutinize the conceptual and measurement problems that underlie its use.

Perhaps the most significant historical distinction in this realm was between stranger versus nonstranger, or unknown versus known. Rape occurred most convincingly—to the minds of jurors, for example—when a man who was totally unknown to a woman executed penile penetration. If the man had been known to the woman in any way, her charge of forcible sex could be undermined, depending on how well she knew the man. If, for example, the man was her husband, she could not claim rape at all because consenting to be married carried the obligation to give her body to him unreservedly.

Koss and her colleagues were among the first to expand the discourse on sexual coercion beyond its conventional historical understanding. Using a national survey of college students, they reported that 38 percent of female college students reported sexual victimization that met the legal criterion for rape or attempted rape and almost 8 percent of males admitted to behaviors that could be classified as raped or attempted rape with at least one woman since the fourteenth birthday (Koss et al. 1985, 1988). Their conclusions were supported by other studies (Mosher and Anderson 1986; Rapaport and Burkhart 1984). Using data from the 1987 wave of the National Survey of Children, Moore et al. (1989) found that about 7 percent of U.S. adults aged 18–22 (females being more likely than males) confirmed that they had sex against their will or had been raped on at least one occasion. Other researchers have reported that between 10 and 12 percent of women report having been raped by dates and between 8 and 14 percent of wives report that their husbands have sexually assaulted or raped them (Finkelhor and Yilo 1985; Russell and Howell 1982).

Estimating the prevalence of the various forms of coercive sexuality is exceedingly difficult because the Uniform Crime Reports are widely believed to underreport the true rate of sex crimes and anonymous, self-report surveys vary widely in sampling techniques and findings. Nevertheless, Grauerholz and Solomon's (1989) review of research in this area suggests that a large proportion of the U.S. population has experienced or will experience coercive sexual relations as a victim, a perpetrator, or both. A comparison of sexual coercion among university students in the United States and Sweden found higher rates in the United States (Lottes and Weinberg 1996). Researchers' estimates of the pervasiveness of incest in the United States may vary the most. Whereas some researchers have observed that about 1 percent of

U.S. females have been incest victims (Kempe and Kempe 1984), others have reported much higher figures. For example, Russell (1984) found that 16 percent of her large household sample of women 18 years of age and older in San Francisco had experienced incest before age 18, and 20 percent of Finkelhor's (1979) predominantly white, middle-class New England college student sample who were raised primarily in nonmetropolitan areas reported having been an incest victim. The 1998 National Violence Against Women survey of 8,000 women estimated that some 17.7 million women in the United States, nearly 18 percent, have been raped or have been the victim of attempted rape. Nearly half the victims were assaulted before their seventeenth birthday. Some three-quarters of those saying they had been raped or assaulted as adults reported that the perpetrator was a current or former husband, a cohabiting partner, or a date.

Not only is sexual coercion an issue for many women, there is evidence to suggest that it is pertinent for some boys and men as well (Finkelhor 1979; Moore et al. 1989). A study of 115 sexually assaulted men found that the majority were assaulted at age 15 or younger, about half were assaulted more than once, and a majority knew their assailants. Among the 115 surveyed, 100 were assaulted by at least one man, 7 by a man and a woman, and 8 by women (King and Wollett 1997). Further, much of the research about sexual assault on men assumes that it is primarily heterosexual men who are the perpetrators of sexual assault on other men, doing so to express power and control. However, in a study of 930 "homosexually-active males" in England and Wales, about 28 percent reported having been sexually assaulted or having had sex against their will at some point in their lives. Moreover, 33 percent of the respondents reported being forced into sexual activity by men with whom they had previously had or were currently having consensual sexual activity. This research suggests that sexual assault in the gay, lesbian, and bisexual community needs to be researched further (Hickson et al. 1994). Some studies (Struckman-Johnson and Struckman-Johnson 1994) indicate that some men report that they were pressured or coerced by women into a sexual experience. Other studies focus on men both in and outside of prison who coerce and/or physically force other men into having sex (King and Wollett 1997; Struckman-Johnson et al. 1996).

In an effort to clarify matters of coercion and consent in the case of both sexes, O'Sullivan and Allgeier (1998) proposed a series of points along a continuum. First, there is sexual activity among persons known to each other that is the result of actual or threatened restraint, aggression, or force. It can be done by men against women and by men against men. Logically, it could involve women against women, but empirically that appears to be quite rare even in a prison situation (Struckman-Johnson et al. 1996), although Renzetti's (1992) research on partner abuse among lesbian couples suggests that lesbian couples experience a cycle of violence that can include sexual assault. Nevertheless, the general lack of empirical evidence about coercive sex between women could indicate either lower rates of occurrence or gaps in the research. Coercive sex also could be initiated by women against men, but again, this seems to be rare and is associated with the male having become intoxicated (Struckman-Johnson and Struckman-Johnson 1994). O'Sullivan and Allgeier (1998, p. 234) summarize the first category as "coercive interactions in which a person [submits] to . . . sexual activity but does so under duress."

Their second category of sexual activity occurs as the result of "seduction interactions in which one partner is clearly resistant," [and a third is] "'token resistance' interactions in which a person expresses nonconsent but is willing and intends to engage in the sexual activity." Their final category is "willing participation in an unwanted sexual activity." This refers to "situations in which a person freely consents to sexual activity . . . without experiencing a concomitant desire for the initiated sexual activity." They review literature suggesting the validity of these four categories and present their own research in support of the last one. Future research, they imply, should utilize these and/or other constructs to sort out differences along the consent-coercion continuum.

With evidence that coercive sexuality is prevalent, the question remains: Why do many men and some women coerce others to have sex with them? Some theorists argue that males are more likely to engage in various forms of coercive sexuality if they have strong ties to a peer group that supports sexually aggressive behavior. Compared to their less stereotypically masculine counterparts, men studied in the research noted above who possess traditionally masculine personality characteristics and hold rigid views of gender stereotypes are more likely to report that they have used physical force and threats to have sex and probably would use physical force to obtain sex if they could be assured that they would not be prosecuted. Other theorists have argued that a small percentage of women may facilitate different forms of coercive sexuality by playing sexually receptive or seductive roles. Not surprisingly, it is common for sexual assailants to believe, or at least report, that their victims were willing participants who enjoyed themselves while being sexually assaulted, even though these perceptions are clearly inconsistent with the victims' accounts (Scully and Marolla 1984).

While the several forms of coercive sexuality share a number of themes, such as the objectification of women, individual factors and circumstances may be significant in accounting for why particular types of coercive sexuality occur. One of the important factors that seem to distinguish the typical stranger or acquaintance rapist from the "average" date rapist is the former's greater tendency to have been sexually or physically abused by his parents or others. Date rapes tend to involve partners who knew one another and had established at least a modicum of interpersonal trust by making a commitment to spend time together. The dynamic nature of the interaction episodes that typify date rapes and the fact that at least one of the persons often has been influenced by drugs, alcohol, or both can obscure the participants' intentions and behavior. Furthermore, the more individuals' sexual scripting is influenced by traditional gender socialization, the more likely it is that coercive sexuality will occur because of sexual miscommunication and males' reliance on coping strategies that emphasize dominance and aggression. Many men assume that women will offer token resistance to their sexual advances to create an impression that they are not sexually "promiscuous" (Check and Malamuth 1985). One study of 610 female undergraduates revealed that almost 40 percent had engaged in this type of token resistance at least once (Muehlenhard and Hollabaugh 1988). While these patterns should not be used to justify date rape, it is not surprising that some men distort the consensual petting that generally precedes date rape as a woman's way of acknowledging her willingness to engage in more intimate forms of sexual interaction, even if this means that in some cases men will be required to pursue it forcefully. Finally, while there are many factors related to fathers' incestuous behavior, one of the more frequently noted arguments underscores the common pattern in which a father pursues sexual and emotional intimacy with his female children (usually a series of episodes over time with the oldest female child) to compensate for his unfulfilling relationship with the adult female, who generally has withdrawn from her roles as mother and wife (partner).

SEXUAL RISK-TAKING BEHAVIOR

Despite the well-documented overall increase in condom use in the 1990s, most research on risk-taking behavior indicates that a high percentage of people still regularly place themselves at risk of getting pregnant and/or contracting a sexually transmitted disease (STD) and/or HIV/AIDS. These patterns persist despite increased efforts at safe-sex education programs and services. Some trends are becoming increasingly evident. Data from face-to-face interviews with adult men and women aged 18–59 in the 1996 National Household Survey on Drug Abuse showed that 19 percent of the respondents used a condom during their last sexual experience (vaginal, oral, or anal sex, with no distinction being made in terms of the gender of the partner) when the event occurred within a relationship, while 62 percent did so when sex occurred outside an ongoing relationship (Anderson et al. 1999). Ninety-five percent of the respondents indicated that their last sexual experience occurred within a relationship. These data also showed that once relationship status was statistically controlled, individuals with high-risk sex and drug use profiles did not use condoms at a higher rate than did their counterparts who were not classified as being at an increased risk for HIV infection. Only about 22 percent of high-risk individuals used a condom at last intercourse within an ongoing relationship. Thus, both the casual and steady partners of high-risk individuals continue to place themselves at risk.

Meanwhile, a study of college students highlights gender differences in which men are found to be engaged in more risk-taking behaviors relevant to partner choice and sexual practices (Poppen 1995). Another study indicates that college women tend to put themselves at risk for sexually transmitted diseases by rarely using condoms and only

minimally discussing sexual history with a partner (Sheahan et al. 1994). Further, differences in behavior based on sexual identity are empirically supported. Interview data from gay and bisexual men suggest different behavior patterns in regard to "safe sex." These data suggest that gay men were more likely to have had a steady male partner and to have engaged in unprotected anal sex than were bisexual men (Stokes et al. 1997). Other studies indicate that young gay men's reports of having unprotected anal intercourse were more common when they knew their partners. Also, increased involvement in the gay community was related to higher levels of risk-taking behavior (Meyer and Dean 1995). Bisexual men use condoms inconsistently with male and female partners, seldom disclose their bisexuality to female partners, and are more likely than men who participate exclusively in same-sex sexual relations to report risk behaviors associated with HIV. The four factors found to raise HIV risk for bisexual men were (1) male prostitution, (2) injection drug use, (3) sexual identity exploration, and (4) culturally specific gender roles and norms such as those characterizing some African-American and Hispanic communities (Doll and Beeker 1996).

PROSTITUTION

Sociological research on prostitution emerged from studies of crime and delinquency, with an emphasis on theories of innate criminal drives. Contemporary sociological research on prostitution more often focuses on actual behaviors. In fact, the commercial sex industry has become a renewed area of research interest and funding as it has been identified as a site of potentially high transmission of HIV. Most research on prostitution still typically relies on self-report data with small-scale, situationally specific convenience samples. Thus, Kinsey's nonrepresentative data, which are more than forty-five years old, remain the best available comprehensive data on commercial sexual behavior. The available data on commercial sexual behavior identifies a variety of types: heterosexual prostitution of women (street prostitutes, brothels, etc.), heterosexual prostitution of men (e.g., escort services), homosexual prostitution of men (hustlers), homosexual prostitution of women, transvestite/transsexual prostitution, and the global/tourist sex industry (Brock and Thistlethwaite 1996; Perkins and Bennett 1985). Among these types of prostitution, some trends are increasingly visible.

The most historically well known form of prostitution is the heterosexual prostitution of women. Feminists offer a variety of interpretations for why women enter into prostitution, ranging from exploitation to legitimate work (Jenness 1990). Gagnon (1977) suggests that the six most common reasons men visit prostitutes are (1) sex without negotiation, (2) sexual involvement without commitment, (3) sex for eroticism and variety, (4) a form of socializing, (5) sex away from home, and (6) sex without rejection. Some sociologists believe that prostitution serves a useful societal function by providing men with a convenient sexual outlet, which in turn minimizes the numbers of sexual transgressions against "respectable" women. Other sociologists view female prostitution as an extreme form of sexism.

Rather than addressing this debate, let us note some empirical trends. Kinsey reported that before World War II, between 60 and 70 percent of adult men had visited a prostitute and about 15 to 20 percent used them regularly. However, many commentators have indicated that rates of prostitution, a form of commercialized sex that in the past provided men with sexual opportunities in a less sexually open society, have decreased drastically since World War II. Notably, current research on sexual behavior in the context of prostitution shows the preponderance of incidents of sexual violence and the increased use of condoms. For example, Miller's (1993) study of 16 women incarcerated for prostitution found that almost all had experienced some form of sexual assault and other violent crimes. Benson and Mathews (1995) surveyed vice squads, women working as prostitutes on the streets and in brothels, and clients and resident groups in England, finding that most street prostitutes began working in their teens and have been victims of repeated sexual and physical attacks, while the majority of clients have regular partners or are married and tend to be middle-class and middle-aged. A study in the Netherlands of 559 male clients of female prostitutes found that 14 percent of the clients do not use condoms (De Graaf et al. 1997). Typically, men who are less educated, have more commercial sex contacts, and have more contacts with prostitutes are the least likely to use condoms. It is not known if similar trends are characteristic of the heterosex-

ual prostitution of men or the homosexual prostitution of women because there is little empirical research. Thus, it is difficult to determine whether similar patterns of sexual violence and safe sex are present across gender and sexuality lines.

The concern about the transmission of HIV/AIDS has, however, stimulated new and more comprehensive research about the homosexual prostitution of men and transvestite/transsexual prostitution. For example, Browne and Minichiello (1996) illustrate that many early studies of homosexual prostitution of men (from the 1960s to the 1980s) focused on biopsychological concerns, creating the need for future studies to focus on the behaviors and attendant risk for HIV infection of both the prostitute and the client. A study of 211 male street prostitutes and 15 male customers further makes this point (Morse et al. 1992). Morse et al. (1992) found that despite knowledge of HIV infection and its transmission, customers engage in high-risk sexual and drug use behaviors with prostitutes. However, another study contradicts these findings. Waldorf and Lauderback (1992) interviewed 552 men who solicit clients in public places (hustlers) and men who solicit by telephone and advertisements (call men) and found that 90 percent of the respondents used condoms in the past year and 75 percent used them in the past week. Similar studies of risk behavior are emerging for the transvestite/transsexual prostitution population. For example, Boles and Elifson (1994) interviewed 52 transvestite prostitutes and found that those who are socially isolated tend to be at more risk of HIV infection and those networked with nontransvestite male prostitutes tend to have a lower risk of HIV infection. Sociological research on men involved in homosexual prostitution and transvestites involved in prostitution suggests that sexual behaviors have been altered in an era of HIV/AIDS. However, little research about sexual behavior patterns outside the context of risk behaviors has been reported.

Another area of research in prostitution concerns the growing global sex industry. Sex tourism has long existed, but increasing globalization of travel and Internet advertising have sparked research in this area. Sociologists often explain the global sex industry as an outgrowth of "third world" poverty and the inequity of a global economy. Sex tourism does not involve only heterosexual prostitution of women; homosexual prostitution of men is also prevalent. Empirical studies of sexual behavior in the global sex industry remain minimal as it is illegal in many countries and most research is still done on European or American prostitution (Brock and Thistlewaite 1996).

Sociological studies of the varieties of prostitution in the United States and around the world point to a more general trend of contemporary empirical research focusing on sexual risk behaviors. Many of these studies indicate that the study of sexuality is complicated by both politics and the complexities of research methodology. However, the emergence of HIV/AIDS also reminds the sociological community of the importance of studies of sexual behavior and patterns.

CONCLUSION

This review has documented the extensive efforts of social scientists in recent decades to enhance the understanding of human sexual behavior. Indeed knowledge of sexual behavior has increased dramatically since the days of Kinsey's early studies. This review also serves as a reminder, however, that knowledge about human sexual behavior, in some areas more than in others, remains limited because sex research is a function of both political and ethical decisions. For example, knowledge about homosexual experiences will continue to be less reliable and complete than it is for heterosexual behavior because the political commitment and considerable resources needed to secure nationally representative samples of gays, lesbians, and bisexuals are missing. Thus, just as social scientists can be held accountable for any shortcomings associated with the prevailing theoretical approaches to sexuality issues, the larger society and its institutionalized, politicized mechanisms for providing research support are responsible for impeding the research community's efforts to understand sexual behavior. Because sexual activity tends to be a highly private social experience, social scientists' incremental advances in documenting and explaining it are linked to the lay population's commitment to this type of research endeavor.

(SEE ALSO: *Courtship, Sexual Behavior, and Marriage; Sexual Orientation; Sexual Violence and Abuse*)

REFERENCES

Almaguer, Tomas 1993 "Chicano Men: A Cartography of Homosexual Identity and Behavior." In Henry Abelove, Michele Aina Barale, and David M. Halperin, eds., *The Lesbian and Gay Studies Reader*. New York: Routledge.

Alonso, Ana Maria, and Maria Teresa Koreck 1993 "Silences: 'Hispanics,' AIDS, and Sexual Practices." In Henry Abelove, Michele Aina Barale, and David M. Halperin, eds., *The Lesbian and Gay Studies Reader*. New York: Routledge.

Anderson, John E., Ronald Wilson, Lynda Doll, Stephen Jones, and Peggy Barker 1999 "Condom Use and HIV Risk Behaviors among U.S. Adults: Data from a National Survey." *Family Planning Perspectives* 31:24–28.

Bancroft, John 1997 *Researching Sexual Behavior: Methodological Issues*. Bloomington: Indiana University Press.

Benson, Catherine, and Roger Matthews 1995 "Street Prostitution: Ten Facts in Search of a Policy." *International Journal of the Sociology of Law* 23(4):385–415.

Bentler, P. M., and P. R. Abramson 1980 "Methodological Issues in Sex Research: An Overview." In R. Green and J. Weiner, eds., *Methodological Issues in Sex Research*. Rockville, Md.: National Institute of Mental Health. U.S. Department of Health and Human Services.

Berger, Raymond M. 1996 *Gay and Grey: The Older Homosexual Man*. New York: Haworth Press.

Blumstein, Philip W., and Pepper Schwartz 1976 "Bisexuality in Women." *Archives of Sexual Behavior* 5(2):171–181.

—— 1983 *American Couples: Money, Work, Sex*. New York: Morrow.

Boles, Jacqueline, and Kirk W. Elifson 1994 "The Social Organization of Transvestite Prostitution and AIDS." *Social Science and Medicine* 39(1):85–93.

Brecher, Edward 1984 *Love, Sex, and Aging: A Consumer Union Report*. Mount Vernon, N.Y.: Consumers Union.

Bressler, Lauren C., and Abraham D. Lavender 1986 "Sexual Fulfillment of Heterosexual, Bisexual, and Homosexual Women." *Journal of Homosexuality* 12(3–4):109–122.

Brock, Rita Nakashima, and Susan Brooks Thistlewaite 1996 *Casting Stones: Prostitution and Liberation in Asia and the United States*. Minneapolis: Fortress Press.

Browne, Jan, and Victor Minichiello 1996 "Research Directions in Male Sex Work." *Journal of Homosexuality* 31(4):29–56.

Bullough, Bonnie, and Vern Bullough 1997 "Are Transvestites Necessarily Heterosexual?" *Archives of Sexual Behavior* 26(1):1–12.

Butler, Robert N. 1998 "The Viagra Revolution." *Geriatrics* 53(10):8–9.

Caraballo-Dieguez, Alex 1997 "Sexual Research with Latino Men Who Have Sex with Men." In John Bancroft, ed., *Researching Sexual Behavior: Methodological Issues*. Bloomington: Indiana University Press.

Carrier, Joseph M. 1989 "Gay Liberation and Coming Out in Mexico." *Journal of Homosexuality* 17:225–252.

Check, J. V. P., and N. M. Malamuth 1983 "Sex Role Stereotyping and Reactions to Depictions of Stranger vs. Acquaintance Rape." *Journal of Personality and Social Psychology* 45:344–356.

Cohen, Kenneth M., and Ritch C. Savin-Williams 1996 "Developmental Perspectives on Coming Out to Self and Others." In Ritch C. Savin-Williams and Kenneth M. Cohen, eds., *The Lives of Lesbians, Gays, and Bisexuals: Children to Adults*. New York: Harcourt Brace.

De Graaf, Ron, and Gertjan Van Zessen, Ine Vanwesenbeeck, Cees J. Straver, and Jan H. Visser 1997 "Condom Use by Dutch Men with Commercial Heterosexual Contacts: Determinants and Considerations." *AIDS Education and Prevention* 9(5):411–423.

Di Mauro, Diane 1997 "Sexuality Research in the United States." In John Bancroft, ed., *Researching Sexual Behavior: Methodological Issues*. Bloomington: Indiana University Press.

Doll, Lynda S. 1997 "Sexual Behavior Research: Studying Bisexual Men and Women and Lesbians." In John Bancroft, ed., *Researching Sexual Behavior: Methodological Issues*. Bloomington: Indiana University Press.

——, and Carolyn Beeker 1996 "Male Bisexual Behavior and HIV Risk in the United States: Synthesis of Research with Implications for Behavioral Interventions." *AIDS Education and Prevention* 8(3):205–225.

Evans, Nancy J., and Anthony R. D'Augelli 1996 "Lesbians, Gay Men and Bisexual People in College." In Ritch C. Savin-Williams and Kenneth M. Cohen, eds., *The Lives of Lesbians, Gays and Bisexuals*. New York: Harcourt Brace.

Finkelhor, D. 1979 *Sexually Victimized Children*. New York: Free Press.

——, and K. Yllo 1985 *License to Rape*. New York: Holt, Rinehart and Winston.

Ford, Clellan, and F. Beach 1951 *Patterns of Sexual Behavior*. New York: Harper.

Gagnon, John 1977 *Human Sexualities*. Glenview, Ill.: Scott, Foresman.

George, L. K., and S. J. Weiler 1981 "Sexuality in Middle and Late Life." *Archives of General Psychiatry* 38:919–923.

Grauerholz, Elizabeth, and Jennifer Crew Solomon 1989 "Sexual Coercion: Power and Violence." In Kathleen McKinney and Susan Sprecher, eds., *Human Sexuality: The Societal and Interpersonal Context*. Norwood, N.J.: Ablex.

Hass, W. 1979 *Teenage Sexuality*. New York: Macmillan.

Herdt, Gilbert, and Andrew Boxer 1993 *Children of Horizons: How Gay and Lesbian Teens Are Leading a New Way Out of the Closet*. Boston: Beacon.

Herold, W., and L. Way 1983 "Oral-Genital Sexual Behavior in a Sample of University Females." *The Journal of Sex Research* 19:327–338.

Hetrick, Eric, and A. D. Martin 1987 "Developmental Issues and Their Resolution for Gay and Lesbian Adolescents." *Journal of Homosexuality* 14:25–44.

Hickson, Ford C. I., Peter M. Davies, Andrew J. Hunt, Peter Weatherburn, Thomas J. McManus, and P. M. Anthony 1994 "Gay Men as Victims of Nonconsensual Sex." *Archives of Sexual Behavior* 23(3):281–294.

Jay, Karla, and Allen Young, eds., 1979 *The Gay Report: Lesbians and Gay Men Speak Out about Sexual Experiences and Lifestyles*. New York: Simon and Schuster.

Jayne, C. E. 1986 "Methodology on Sex Research in 1986: An Editor's Commentary." *The Journal of Sex Research* 22:1–5.

Jenness, Valerie 1990 "From Sex as Sin to Sex as Work: COYOTE and the Reorganization of Prostitution as a Social Problem." *Social Problems* 37(3):403–420.

Johnson, Susan E. 1990 *Staying Power: Long Term Lesbian Couples*. Tallahassee, Fla.: Naiad Press.

Kelley, K. 1986 "Integrating Sex Research." In D. Byrne and K. Kelly, eds., *Alternative Approaches to the Study of Sexual Behavior*. Hillsdale, N.J.: Erlbaum.

Kempe, R. S., and H. Kempe 1984 *The Common Secret: Sexual Abuse of Children and Adolescents*. New York: Freeman.

King, Michael, and Earnest Woollett 1997 "Sexually Assaulted Males: 115 Men Consulting a Counseling Service." *Archives of Sexual Behavior* 26(6):579–588.

Kinsey, Alfred C., Wardell Pomeroy, and Clyde Martin 1948 *Sexual Behavior in the Human Male*. Philadelphia: Saunders.

——, ——, Clyde Martin, and Paul Gebhard 1953 *Sexual Behavior in the Human Male*. Philadelphia: Saunders.

Koss, Mary, Kenneth E. Leonard, Dana A. Beezley, and Cheryl J. Oros 1985 "Nonstranger Sexual Aggression: A Discriminant Analysis of the Psychological Characteristics of Undetected Offenders." *Sex Roles* 12:981–992.

——, Thomas E. Dinero, Cynthia A. Seibel, and Susan L. Cox 1988 "Stranger and Acquaintance Rape: Are

There Differences in the Victim's Experience?" *Psychology of Women Quarterly* 12:1–23.

Ku, Leighton, Freya Sonenstein, Laura D. Lindberg, Carolyn H. Bradnere, Scott Boggess, and Joseph H. Pleck 1998 "Understanding Changes in Sexual Activity among Young Metropolitan Men: 1979–1995." *Family Planning Perspectives* 30:256–262.

Laumann, Edward O., John Gagnon, Robert T. Michael, and Stuart Michaels 1994a *The Social Organization of Sexuality: Sexual Practices in the United States*. Chicago: University of Chicago Press.

Laumann, Edward O., Robert T. Michael, and John Gagnon 1994b "A Political History of the National Sex Survey of Adults." *Family Planning Perspectives* 26:34–38.

Lottes, Ilsa L., and Martin S. Weinberg 1996 "Sexual Coercion among University Students: A Comparison of the United States and Sweden." *The Journal of Sex Research* 34:67–76.

Manalansan, Martin F. 1996 "Double Minorities: Latino, Black and Asian Men Who Have Sex With Men." In Ritch C. Savin-Williams and Kenneth M. Cohen, eds., *The Lives of Lesbians, Gays and Bisexuals*. New York: Harcourt Brace.

Marsiglio, William, and Denise Donnelly 1991 "Sexual Intercourse in Later Life: A National Study of Married Persons." *Journal of Gerontology* 46:S338–344.

Masters, William H., and Virginia E. Johnson 1979 *Homosexuality in Perspective*. Boston: Little, Brown.

Meyer, Ilan H., and Laura Dean 1995 "Patterns of Sexual Behavior and Risk Taking among Young New York City Gay Men." *AIDS Education and Prevention* 7:13–23.

Michael, Robert T., John H. Gagnon, Edward O. Laumann, and Gina Kolata 1994 *Sex in America*. Boston: Little, Brown.

Miller, Jody 1993 "'Your Life is on the Line Every Night You're on the Streets': Victimization and the Resistance among Street Prostitutes." *Humanity and Society* 17(4):422–446.

Moore, Kristin Anderson, Anee K. Dirscoll, and Laura Duberstein Lindberg 1998 *A Statistical Portrait of Adolescent Sex, Contraception, and Childbearing*. Washington, D.C.: National Campaign to Prevent Teen Pregnancy.

——, Brent C. Miller, Dana Glei, and Donna Ruane Morrison 1995 *Adolescent Sex, Contraception, and Childbearing: A Review of Recent Research*. Washington, D.C.: Child Trends.

——, Christine Winquist Nord, and James L. Peterson 1989 "Nonvoluntary Sexual Activity among Adolescents." *Family Planning Perspectives* 21:110–114.

Morse, Edward V., Patricia M. Simon, Paul M. Balson, and Howard J. Osofsky 1992 "Sexual Behavior Patterns of Customers of Male Street Prostitutes." *Archives of Sexual Behavior* 21(4):347–357.

Mosher, D. L., and R. D. Anderson 1986 "Macho Personality, Sexual Aggression, and Reactions to Guided Imagery of Realistic Rape." *Journal of Research in Personality* 20:77–94.

Muehlenhard, Charlene L. 1994 "Controversy about Rape Research and Activities." *Journal of Sex Research* 31:143.

——, and L. C. Hollabaugh 1988 "Do Women Sometimes Say No When They Mean Yes?: Prevalence and Correlates of Women's Token Resistance to Sex." *Journal of Research in Personality and Social Psychology* 54:872–879.

——, Susie C. Sympson, Joi L. Phelps, and Barrie J. Highby 1994 "Are Rape Statistics Exaggerated? A Response to Criticism of Contemporary Rape Research." *Journal of Sex Research* 31:144–146.

Newcomer, S., and J. Udry 1985 "Oral Sex in an Adolescent Population." *Archives of Sexual Behavior* 14:41–46.

Okami, P., R. Olmstead, and P. R. Abramson 1997 "Sexual Experiences in Early Childhood: 18-Year Longitudinal Data from the UCLA Family Lifestyles Project." *The Journal of Sex Research* 34:339–347.

O'Sullivan, Lucia, and Elizabeth Rice Allgeier 1998 "Feigning Sexual Desire: Consenting to Unwanted Sexual Activity in Heterosexual Dating Relationships." *The Journal of Sex Research*, 35:234–243.

Parker, Richard G. 1997. "International Perspectives on Sexuality Research." In John Bancroft, ed., *Researching Sexual Behavior: Methodological Issues*. Bloomington: Indiana University Press.

Peplau, Latitia Anne 1982 "Research on Homosexual Couples: An Overview." *Journal of Homosexuality* 8(2):3–7.

——, Susan D. Cochran, and Vicki M. Mays 1997 "A National Survey of the Intimate Relationships of African-American Lesbians and Gay Men." In Beverly Green, ed., *Ethnic and Cultural Diversity among Lesbians and Gay Men*. Thousand Oaks, Calif.: Sage.

Perkins, Roberta, and Gary Bennett 1985 *Being a Prostitute: Prostitute Women and Prostitute Men*. London: George Allen & Unwin.

Pope, Mark, and Richard Schulz 1990 "Sexual Attitudes and Behavior in Midlife and Aging Homosexual Males." *Journal of Homosexuality* 20(3–4):169–177.

Poppen, Paul J., 1995 "Gender and Patterns of Sexual Risk Taking in College Students." *Sex Roles* 32(7–8):545–555.

Rapaport, K., and B. R. Burkhart 1984 "Personality and Attitudinal Correlates of Sexual Coercive College Males." *Journal of Abnormal Personality* 93:216–221.

Raphael, Sharon M., and Mina K. Robinson 1992 "The Older Lesbian: Love Relationships and Friendship Patterns." In Wayne R. Dynes and Stephen Donaldson, eds., *Sociology of Homosexuality*. New York: Garland.

Renzetti, Claire M. 1992 *Violent Betrayal: Partner Abuse in Lesbian Relationships*. Newbury Park, Calif.: Sage.

Riportella-Muller, Roberta 1989 "Sexuality in the Elderly: A Review." In Kathleen McKinney and Susan Sprecher, eds., *Human Sexuality: The Sexual and Interpersonal Context*. Norwood, N.J.: Ablex.

Risman, Barbara J., and Pepper Schwartz 1988. "Sociological Research on Male and Female Homosexuality." *Annual Review of Sociology* 14:125–147.

Roiphe, Katie 1993 *The Morning After: Sex, Fear, and Feminism*. Boston: Little, Brown.

Rubin, Lillian 1990 *Erotic Wars: What Happened to the Sexual Revolution*. New York: HarperPerennial.

Russell, D. E. H. 1984 *Sexual Exploitation*. Beverly Hills, Calif.: Sage.

——, and N. Howell 1982 *Rape in Marriage*. New York: Macmillian.

Sandfort, Theo G. M. 1997 "Sampling Male Homosexuality." In John Bancroft, ed., *Researching Sexual Behavior: Methodological Issues*. Bloomington: Indiana University Press.

Savin-Williams, Ritch C., and Kenneth M. Cohen 1996 "Memories of Childhood and Early Adolescent Sexual Feelings among Gay and Bisexual Boys: A Narrative Approach." In Ritch C. Savin-Williams and Kenneth M. Cohen, eds., *The Lives of Lesbians, Gays, and Bisexuals: Children to Adults*. New York: Harcourt Brace.

Scully, D., and J. Marolla 1984 "Convicted Rapists' Vocabulary of Motive: Excuses and Justification." *Social Problems* 31:530–544.

Sheahan, Sharon L., Stephen Joel Coons, John P. Seabolt, Lance Churchill, and Dale Thomas 1994 "Sexual Behavior, Communication, and Chlamydial Infections among College Women." *Health Care for Women International* 15(4):275–286.

Sonenstein, Freya, Kellie Stewart, Laura Duberstein Lindberg, Marta Pernas, and Sean Williams 1997 *Involving Males in Preventing Teen Pregnancy: A Guide for Program Planners*. Washington, D.C.: Urban Institute.

Starr, Bernard D., and Marcella B. Weiner 1981 *The Starr-Weiner Report on Sex and Sexuality in the Mature Years*. Briarcliff Manor, N.Y.: Stein & Day.

Stokes, Joseph P., Peter Vanable, and David J. McKirnan 1997 "Comparing Gay and Bisexual Men on Sexual Behavior, Condom Use and Psychosocial Variables Related to HIV/AIDS." *Archives of Sexual Behavior* 26(4):383–397.

Struckman-Johnson, Cindy, and David Struckman-Johnson 1994 "Men Pressured and Forced into Sexual Experience" *Archives of Sexual Behavior* 23:93–114.

——, David Struckman-Johnson, Lila Rucker, Kurt Bumby, and Stephan Donaldson 1996 "Sexual Coercion Reported by Men and Women in Prison." *Journal of Sex Research* 33:67–76.

Udry, J. Richard 1988 "Biological Predispositions and Social Control in Adolescent Sexual Behavior." *American Sociological Review* 53:709–722.

Waldorf, Dan, and David Lauderback 1992 "The Condom Use of Male Sex Workers in San Francisco." *AIDS & Public Policy Journal* 7(2):108–119.

Warren, Charles W., John S. Santelli, Sherry A. Everett, Laura Kann, Janet L. Collins, Carol Cassell, Leo Morris, and Lloyd J. Kolbe 1998 "Sexual Behavior among U.S. High School Students, 1990–1995." *Family Planning Perspectives* 30(4):170–172, 200.

Whitam, Frederick L., Christopher Daskalos, Curt Sobolewski, and Peter Padilla 1998 "The Emergence of Lesbian Sexuality and Identity Cross-Culturally: Brazil, Peru, the Phillipines, and the United States." *Archives of Sexual Behavior* 27(1): 31–56.

Young, M. 1980 "Attitudes and Behaviors of College Students Relative to Oral-Genital Sexuality." *Archives of Sexual Behavior* 9:61–67.

WILLIAM MARSIGLIO
JOHN H. SCANZONI
KENDAL L. BROAD

SEXUAL INEQUALITY

See Discrimination; Sex Differences; Social Stratification.

SEXUAL ORIENTATION

As Nietzsche noted, "[O]nly that which has no history is definable" ([1887] 1968, p. 516). This observation is clearly supported by the dramatic changes in the ways in which sexual orientation has been conceptualized over the last quarter century and, in particular, the last decade. As a result, the concept of sexual orientation may be difficult to define with any assurance of general agreement. It is currently mired, and surely will continue to be mired, in conflicting interpretations of the history of the behaviors that are assumed to be the expression of specific sexual orientations. The question of sexual orientation remains a conceptual battleground where many of the most critical issues regarding the nature of human sexuality, if not the human condition itself, are debated.

Sexual orientation generally can be described as the integration of the ways in which individuals experience the intersection of sexual desires and available sexual social roles. For some people, this intersection is experienced happily as an unproblematic confluence of personal and social expectations. For others, it is experienced as a persistent conflict. For still others, issues of sexual orientation are experienced as an occasion for experimentation, compromise, and sometimes change in how they see themselves, how they present themselves to others, and how different segments of social life respond to such outcomes.

Sexual orientation is also part of the conceptual apparatus of contemporary scientific and popular discourse; it has become a way in which people recognize and "explain" sexual behavior. It is as if establishing an individual's sexual orientation, however inaccurately, were enough to explain most of what has to be known about that individual's sexuality. As a result, the discourses of sexual orientation often become a point of contact with the discourses of age, gender, morality, and law.

SEXUAL ORIENTATION AND GENDER

Following Freud's distinction between the "object" (the "who") and the "aim" (the "what") of sexual desire ([1905] 1953), current conceptions of sexual orientation can be said to focus primarily on the nature of the object defined in narrow terms of gender. This almost exclusive distinction derives from the dimorphic nature of the human species, that is, two genders giving rise to three possible categories—homosexual, heterosexual, and bisexual—although within each of these categories there is a wide range of variations in both sexual and nonsexual attributes of individuals and there are many aspects of sexual preference that are shared across these categories. Among such aspects of desire would be the other's age, race, social class, and ethnic status; the nature of the emotional bond; and the conventions of physical

beauty. Important differences regarding sexual aims, such as sadomasochism, pedophilia, hebophilia (sexual attraction to postpubescent minors), and transvestism, are most often subsumed within each of these gender-based categories. Most often, they become adjectives modifying the label "homosexual" or "heterosexual."

The continuing significance of gender may reflect the fact that within modern Western societies, gender is possibly the last fully pervasive aspect of identity that provides cohesion among the increasingly complex components of multiple social roles. Gender serves this role in a social context of continuing change because of its seeming permanence and seemingly *ascriptive* character. As a result, the gender of the object of one's desires continues to dominate the meaning of sexual orientation almost to the exclusion of all the other attributes of potential partners that contribute to or preclude sexual interest or excitement.

This emphasis on the gender of the object of desire may be a culturally specific development. Some, for example, have argued that in other cultural or historical contexts, gender may be less significant in defining categories of legitimate sexual access than are other social distinctions. Thus, the acceptability of same-gender sexual contacts among males in ancient Greece was contingent on differences in age (mature adult versus youth) and social status (free citizen versus slave). Respect for those distinctions in social status required that there be no direct reciprocity, that the "active" role (the seeking of sexual pleasure) and the "passive" role (the providing of sexual pleasure) remain respectful of social status (Halperin 1989). Men engaging in such behavior were viewed as conventional so long as those rules were maintained. Such examples indicate that not all persons engaging in sexual acts experience their participation as erotic or experience those activities in the context of what might be termed sexual excitement. By the same token, they also indicate that not all motives for engaging in specific sexual acts derive from intrinsically sexual motives.

Through much of the twentieth century, the question of sexual orientation would not have appeared problematic. In a range of theoretical positions, from Freud's assumption of an inherent bisexuality ([1905] 1953) to those postulating an exclusive heterosexuality, sexual orientation was taken as being so firmly rooted in the "natural" process of human psychosexual development that it was treated as a transcultural phenomenon (Simon 1996). This was true for heterosexuality, which often was, and for many people still is, viewed as being phylogenetically programmed as a requirement of species survival (Symons 1979; Wilson 1978). Homosexuality and bisexuality were viewed as a disturbance of "normal" development (Freud [1905] 1953), an inherited decadence (Ellis 1937), a gender-discordant development (Krafft-Ebing [1896] 1965), later as a normal but minor genetic variant (Kinsey et al. 1948), and more recently as a sociocultural construction (see below). This social constructionist position has been extended to the treatment of heterosexuality as well (Katz 1995; Richardson 1996).

Explanations of sexual orientation currently might be described as a continuum anchored at one polar position by the assumption of an entirely biological or phylogenetic source (essentialism) and at the other polar position by sources reflecting the adaptation of specific individuals within given sociocultural settings (constructionism) and still more recently as the reflection of the sociocultural construction of gender as a binary phenomenon (queer theory).

Essentialist Perspectives. The extreme essentialist position leads to a view of sexual orientation (as gender preference) that is potentially present in all human populations, varying only in its manifest expression as a result of differing qualities of encouragement or repression (Gladue 1987; Boswell 1983; Whitam 1983; LaVay 1996). Other biologically oriented explanations link biological developments with experiential adaptations. Typically, those approaches link variations in phenomena such as prenatal hormonal chemistry with critical but often unpredictable postnatal experiences in the shaping of sexual orientation (Money 1988).

The essentialist end of the conceptual continuum assumes that at some basic level of character or personality, there are objective, constitutional sources of sexual orientation (Green 1988). It is almost as if such approaches viewed different categories of sexual orientation as different species or subspecies, as if all those included within a specific category of sexual interactions shared a common origin. A commitment to such permanent distinctions is often evident in the use of a concept such

as *latent homosexuality*, which implies that even when such differences fail to be manifested or are manifested late in life, this orientation is viewed as the "real" one.

Constructionist Perspectives. At the other end of this continuum are constructionists, who view sexual orientation as the product of specific historical contingencies, as something to be acquired or perhaps even "an accomplishment" (Stoller 1985a). Most of those holding this position reject the idea of a sexual drive or at best see such a drive as an unformed potential that is largely dependent on experience to give it power and directionality. "Every culture has a distinctive cultural configuration with its own 'anthropological' assumptions in the sexual area. The empirical relativity of these configurations, their immense varity, and luxurious inventiveness, indicate that they are products of man's own socio-cultural formations rather than a biologically fixed human nature" (Berger and Luckman 1966, p. 49).

For most constructionists, sexual orientation is a reflection of the more general practices of a time and place and is expressive of social power (Foucault 1978; Weeks 1985; Padgug 1979; Greenberg 1988; Halperin 1989). Others would add concern for the specific contexts of interaction and the management of identities and social roles (Simon and Gagnon 1967; McIntosh 1976; Plummer 1975; Ponse 1968; Weinberg 1983), and still others would add concern for the experiences that constitute primary socialization (Gagnon and Simon 1973; Stoller 1985b; Simon and Gagnon 1986; Mitchell 1988).

From a constructionist perspective, the concept of sexual orientation itself is viewed as an aspect of the very cultural practices that sustain the differential evaluations of the sexual behaviors the concept purports to explain. The focusing of attention on something that can be called sexual orientation is seen as signifying an importance to be assigned to the sexual that may not be intrinsic to it but may derive from the evolved meanings and uses that constitute the sexual in specific sociohistorical contexts.

Whereas essentialists tend to view the sexual as a biological constant that presses on evolving social conventions, constructionists view the sexual as the product of the individual's contingent response to the experiencing of social conventions. For essentialists, the sexual might be said to develop from the inside out, whereas for constructionists, the sexual, like most other social practices, is learned from the outside in. A middle ground is taken by many who view sexual behavior as the outcome of a dialectical relationship between biology and culture (Erikson 1950).

CURRENT CONCEPTS

If only in recognition of the enormous diversity of sexual practices in different cultural and historical settings despite the relative stability of human physiology, almost everyone who has approached the study of human sexuality admits the need for some degree of sociological explanation of specific patterns of sexual interaction and the significance accorded to them (Gregersen 1983). The question of homosexuality was the dominant issue in most discussions of sexual orientation until relatively recently. Heterosexuality, insofar as it was viewed as doing what came naturally, seemingly required no "explanation" unless it was expressed in unconventional ways. Instead, it was homosexuality that was viewed as problematic, if not pathological, and whose explanation was more urgent. The medicalization of same-gender sexual preference, which preceded the initial public use of terms such as "homosexuality" and "heterosexuality" in 1880 (Herzer 1985), involved the "disease" model of seeking a specific cause as well as a mode of prevention and possible cure. This implicitly homophobic commitment persists in some of the scientific community's considerations of homosexuality (Irving 1990).

The acceptance of homosexuality as an alternative life-style, however, did not necessarily require the abandonment of a concern for explaining its appearance; it merely made it more obvious that heterosexuality cannot be taken for granted but requires explanation (Katz 1990). One characteristic of the modern Western condition is that it has made sexual orientation and the closely related issue of sexual identity problematic. The question, What will I be when I grow up? is asked of an ever-growing number of dimensions of life, including the sexual, and is asked with increasing uncertainty regarding the possible answers.

Heterosexuality. Heterosexuality, defined as *cross-gender sexual intercourse*, has been a preference in all societies, though not necessarily an exclusive

preference in all societies. Nor does the universality of this preference establish the full range of definitions of with whom, when, where, or in what manner it should occur. Thus, outside of incest taboos involving immediate family members and a variable list of other close relatives, different cultures and periods of history have defined legitimate and illegitimate sexual contacts in dramatically contrasting ways (Bullough [1978] 1980). These differences involve not only what might be called the mechanics of sexual acts, that is, matters of relationship, time, place, costume, sequence of gestures, and positions, but also the determinants of their relative significance.

The potential reproductive consequences of heterosexual genital intercourse inevitably led to a linking of the desire for sex with a conscious or unconscious desire for reproduction. This view has been criticized as resting on the questionable assumption of a biologically rooted commitment to species survival (Beach 1956). Valid or not, such views constitute a cultural legacy that gives credence to many current norms regarding sexual acts, norms that enhance the social regulation of reproduction in the name of an assumed natural mandate.

More specifically, expectations regarding gender and family, influenced by many aspects of social life, generally have shaped the social meaning of sexual acts. Current language for describing cross-gender sexual contacts explicitly assumes a relationship to the family—marital, premarital, postmarital, and extramarital sex—and implicitly evaluates behaviors in terms of their "distance" from location within the family.

Similarly, genital intercourse still is viewed commonly as the ultimate or purest form of sexual exchange, as the "fulfillment of nature's intent." As a result, it continues to serve as the measure of the "normality" of alternative forms of sexual contact. This was reflected in the historical, but declining, practice of criminalizing not only sexual acts occurring outside of marriage but also those involving oral or anal contact or in viewing masturbation as pathogenic when practiced by the young and symptomatic when practiced by adults, although recent research (Lauman et al. 1994) indicates that masturbation occurs in North America among significant segments of postpubertal individuals at all stages of the life course.

Many of the conventions surrounding gender expectations also directly reinforced the "scripting," or construction, of heterosexuality. This involves presenting images of the sexual that both naturalize and normalize evolved Western heterosexual practices, making them appear unquestionably proper. The labels "active" and "passive," terms that had applications in many domains of social life, virtually became synonymous with "masculine" and "feminine," respectively. Even physical positions in sexual intercourse—"Who is on top?"—have often had to pay homage to prevailing patterns of social domination.

The nineteenth century witnessed the elaboration of images of the female as fragile, domestic, nurturant, receptive, and either only minimally sexual or capable of insatiable lusts. These images of femininity were complemented by images of the male as strong, given to exploratory curiosity, possessively protective, and aggressively lustful. Although applied diffusely, these implicit norms were not always applied equally. The restraint and fragility of the female found a common application in the parlors and bedrooms of the urban middle class and rural gentry but was applied far less in the fields, factories, servants' quarters, and brothels of the day.

While the images of heterosexuality reinforced patterns of family life and gender differentiation, it is equally appropriate to speak of the ways in which patterns of family life and gender differentiation reinforced prevailing concepts of the "naturalness" of heterosexuality. This same gender-based division of labor within the family was taken for granted by mid-twentieth century sociological theorists (Parsons and Bales 1955), as it was inscribed in the most widely held views regarding "normal" human development (Erikson 1950).

From the late nineteenth century on, concepts of the family became substantially more voluntary and egalitarian. However, those modifications further empowered the heterosexual scenario, which now plays an even more important role in the creation of marital bonding and the preservation of the nuclear family. Heterosexuality, given the assumption of its powers as a basic drive, simultaneously became a nearly constant threat to and vital aspect of family life. This in turn gave rise to various methods, both formal and informal, of restricting nonmarital expressions of sexual activity.

The emphasis placed on the heterosexual scenario led in turn to a greater emphasis on the subjective aspects of one's sexual orientation. Faith in the mute logic of "nature's" intent gave way to concern for the fashioning and maintenance of individual desire. Women increasingly were expected not only to be receptive but to desire as well as to be desirable. Men increasingly were expected to use the sexual to affirm their masculinity not only by their ability to find sexual pleasure but also by their ability to provide pleasure to their partners. Heterosexual preference continued to be taken for granted while heterosexual competence was being placed on the agenda in new and unanticipated ways.

In recent years, evident trends have called into question many of these practices, challenging many earlier basic expectations regarding family and gender. The conjugal family is no longer the exclusive social address for heterosexuality. Premarital sex has become *statistically* normal at all social levels, and it approaches becoming *attitudinally* normative. Moreover, the age at which sexual intercourse first occurs has declined, particularly for females. By age 18, over half are no longer virgins, which is more than double the proportion of nonvirgins reported two generations ago. This suggests that most of what occurs by way of sexual activity among adolescents and young adults can be described as pre-premarital, as much of this early sexual behavior occurs outside the context of family-forming courtship, where much of the premarital experience of older generations took place.

Similarly, at the premarital and postmarital stages, there has been increasing acceptance of nonmarital cohabitation in the sense that it tends to be more openly acknowledged with little anticipation of social rejection or stigmatization. While the number of middle- to upper-middle-class females who have deliberately borne children without marriage or an acknowledged male partner is not great, the fact that this practice has achieved considerable visibility and implicit legitimacy is significant.

Reflecting the diffusion of feminist values, support for women with regard to sexual interest, sexual activity, and especially sexual competence, with the latter measured by the capacity to achieve orgasm, has visibly increased (Ehrenreich et al. 1986). As a result, gender stereotypes with regard to sexual behavior have experienced changes that for the most part have served to blur many of the gender distinctions that previously appeared to give heterosexuality its distinctive complementarity.

Specific behaviors, such as oral sex, that once were associated with devalued sexual actors, homosexuals, and prostitutes in recent years have become a conventional part of the heterosexual script. This is particularly true at higher social class levels, where oral sex tends to occur regularly, often substituting for genital intercourse (Gagnon and Simon 1987; Blumstein and Schwartz 1983; Simon et al. 1990).

Heterosexuality remains the dominant erotic imagery of Western societies. However, changing concerns for reproduction, continuing changes in the organization of family life, and the constraints describing gender presentations indicate that present trends toward a pluralization of the ways in which heterosexuality is experienced and the contexts within which it is expressed will continue into the imaginable future.

Homosexuality. Same-gender sexual interactions have been reported in a sufficient number of social settings to suggest that they fall within the normal range of human behaviors (Ford and Beach 1951; Gregersen 1983). As Kinsey and associates (1948) observed, "The homosexual has been a significant part of human sexual activity ever since the dawn of history, primarily because it is an expression of capacities that are basic in the human animal" (p. 666). This essentialist view implies that a predisposition to same-gender sexual acts is an immutable fact of nature like gender and race and as such is totally independent of personal preference and societal values (Green 1988).

The fact that same-gender sexual involvements fail to be reported or occur as atypical behaviors in sufficient numbers suggests that there is little about them on which to predicate a universal or singular explanation. Where homosexual behavior occurs, the specific forms it takes, and the kinds of sexual acts and the relations within which they occur, as with most aspects of heterosexuality, vary so much that a full understanding must be sought in terms of the contingent features of specific social contexts. In other words, apparent uniformity of acts, such as members of the same gender engaging in sexual acts, allows one to assume very little, if any, uniformity of actors, their development, their mo-

tives, or the social and personal meanings of their behavior. When constructionists assert that the homosexual is an invention of the modern world, they are not suggesting that same-gender contacts were unknown in earlier periods of Western history or in other cultural settings. What they do suggest is that the processes that constitute the behavior, that give it meaning, and that transform otherwise identical forms of "behavior" into different forms of evaluated "conduct" may be of a fundamentally different character.

The variety of meanings given to same-gender "sexual" contacts is as wide as that given to cross-gender contacts. "Sexual" is placed in quotation marks as a reminder that while genital contact and orgasm may be present, in many instances the behavior is not necessarily experienced as sexual in the contemporary Western sense of that word. Such same-gender contacts range from those which are incidental to religious rites or rites of puberty, to those specific to certain statuses that may be temporary and that are not in themselves significant aspects of the individual's social identity, to those in which same-gender contacts are defined as permanent features of the individual's character.

An example of age-specific sexual contact can be found among the Sambians of New Guinea. Male children at about age 6 are removed to the men's hut, where they ingest semen, a practice that is viewed as necessary for full masculine development, by engaging in fellation with older, unmarried fellow villagers. At puberty, such males enter the role of semen donor by making their penises available to their younger fellow villagers. During early adulthood, they enter arranged marriages and are expected to practice heterosexual sex exclusively for the remainder of their lives. Observers report a nearly universal absence of fixation with regard to the activities of earlier stages or a reversal of age roles (Herdt 1981; Stoller 1985a).

This of course stands in dramatic contrast with the modern Western experience, in which the imagery of the behavior is associated with powerful meanings whose very invocation is often capable of exciting intense emotional responses of all kinds. Thus, negative images promote strong feelings of homophobia and at times cause "homosexual panic" in which the fear of being or becoming homosexual generates highly charged nonrational responses. At the same time, the possibility of same-gender sexual contacts often generates responses sufficiently strong to allow many individuals to experience and accept themselves as being homosexual despite the homophobic character of their immediate social settings (Bell and Weinberg 1978; Weinberg 1983).

In the examples of both the Sambians and the contemporary Western experience, the biological processes associated with arousal and orgasm are undoubtedly the same. What vary are the meanings and the representations that occasion arousal. As Beach noted, "Human sexual arousal is subject to extensive modification as a result of experience. Sexual values may become attached to a wide variety of biologically inappropriate stimulus objects or partners" (1956, p. 27).

Patterns of homosexual behavior, like those of heterosexual behavior, have manifested persistent change. While same-gender sexual contact was known in premodern Europe and was severely sanctioned, often treated as a capital offense, it was not viewed as being the behavior of a different kind of person but as a moral failing, a sin, to which all might be vulnerable (Bray 1982). Some have argued that a conception of homosexuality as a sexual orientation involving a distinct kind of person was a correlate of many of the changing patterns and values associated with the emergence of urban, industrial capitalism (Adam 1978; Hocquenghem 1978; Foucault 1978).

Within the category of male homosexuality, different styles of homosexual activity predominated in different periods of history and different social settings. If the concept of homosexuality is to have any meaning, such variations suggest that modern forms of homosexuality reflect an eroticization of gender, not a fixation on a specific form of sexual activity. In other words, it is the gender of the participants that generates and sustains sexual interest and only secondarily the specific form of sexual activity (Gagnon 1990; Simon et al. 1990).

The significance of gender in considerations of homosexuality has marked much of its recent history. Initial nineteenth-century views defined and implicitly explained homosexuality as an inversion of gender. Lesbians often were viewed as "men trapped in women's bodies," and gay men the reverse. Consistent with this, a common designation was "invert." Despite this early view, more recent research indicates that in many respects lesbians and gay men tend in their sexual development and subsequent behavior to approximate their genders. This suggests that sexual development tends to follow gender socialization: Gender roles and gender role expectations influence sexuality more often than sexuality prompts changes in gender identity (Gagnon and Simon 1973; Blumstein and Schwartz 1983).

Change in sexual patterns has been a critical aspect of recent social history. Whereas heterosexual practice might be described as being increasingly privatized and dissociated from the major institutions of society, homosexual practice has moved from the margins of society to sharing the central stage. Whereas the family becomes less and less the exclusive legitimate context for heterosexual activities, the appearance and survival of bonded relationships among homosexuals, particularly gay men, has visibly increased. Whereas the larger community appears increasingly anomic, gay communities (which once were limited to bars, discreet networks of friends, and, for gay men, locations for anonymous sexual contacts) now rival even the most solidary of ethnic groups. There is a flowering of recreational, religious, welfare, political, and other affinity groups and organizations as well as of areas of residential dominance (Epstein 1987; Escoffier 1998; Levine 1998).

Homosexuality remains negatively valued, remains stigmatized. Discrimination in employment and housing, instances of "gay bashing," and criminalization of same-gender sexual activity in some jurisdictions speak directly to continued homophobic practices and fears. However, on the whole, the 1960s, 1970s, and 1980s witnessed increasing acceptance of both homosexuality and the homosexual. Even the identification of gay men with transmission of the HIV virus, which initially was associated with an incipient moral panic and occasioned expressions of antihomosexual attitudes, became an occasion for sympathetic representation in the major public media and broadened understanding of gay men, their life-styles, and the many roles they play in and contributions they make to the larger society.

Currently, possibly owing to the heightened visibility of lesbians and gay men, the homogenizing of identities has been called into question. What once was viewed as a singular phenomenon is now more generally seen as pluralized. It now encompasses different developmental histories, affording different ways of incorporating a homoerotic commitment within a specific life history. The same is true for the development of a heterosexual orientation (Murray 1984; Stoller 1985a). As a consequence, the major questions that previously dominated issues of homosexuality (What is *the* cause? How many are there?) have become incurably cloudy as claims for a "biology of identity" conflict with what has been called the "politics of identity." Same-gender sexual interactions remain a characteristic of a minority of persons (Lauman et al. 1994), but the actual number cannot be established without resolving the question of what a homosexual is. Reflecting the complexity of these questions, Lauman et al. (1994) distinguish between three critical dimensions: same-gender sexual *behavior*, same-gender sexual *attraction* or *desire*, and *identity* as a homosexual. They found that among the 10.1 percent of the men in their survey who reported *any* adult same-gender sexuality, only 24 percent reported positive responses on all three dimensions and among the 8.6 percent of the women reporting *any* adult same-gender sexuality, only 15 percent were positive on all three dimensions. (p. 298)

What is clear is that there may be many more reasons for developing a homosexual orientation than there are ways of giving it expression. Aspects of development such as variations in the development of a gender identity may be significant in the development of homosexual orientations for some individuals (Harry 1982; Green 1987), but these aspects may have to be reconsidered as society modifies its more general beliefs and practices regarding gender identity. For example, the question must be asked, On what basis should "effeminacy" in male children be treated as symptomatic of some pathology any more than comparable displays of "effeminacy" in female children? Or the reverse, regarding what is commonly referred to as "tomboyishness" among young females?

Individuals with a marked homosexual preference appear in virtually all social contexts: different types of community settings; at different class levels; in all racial, ethnic, and religious categories; and from all manner of family backgrounds (Gebhard and Johnson 1979; Bell et al. 1981). There are differences between such categories, but in the absence of unbiased and comprehensive data, it is difficult to determine with any confidence whether significant effects are associated with possible differentials. There is reason to suspect that such statistics can provide only an approximation of current populations and a poor guide to future developments, developments that depend more on society's conceptions and uses of sex and gender, which appear to be in continuing transition.

Whether rooted in biology, social experience, or some combination of these elements, homosexuality as a concept, as a class of persons, and as social groups will persist into the twenty-first century. However, factors such as the greater visibility of representations in the media that challenge prior negative stereotypes and folk psychologies, the depathologizing of homosexuality by medical and social science communities, and its greater acceptance by conventional major institutions may be in the process of transforming what was once a closeted, isolated group into one that that is different but is seen as neither abnormal nor threatening. Indeed, one may be observing a process of the *normalization* of homosexuality. Some, in effect, have raised the question of the disappearance of homosexuality through its assimilation into mainstream social life as minor variant. (Bech 1997; Seidman et al. 1999). Alternative arguments suggest that this ultimate assimilation is an unrealistic and undesirable possibility based on conceptions of gender (queer theory) that are ethnocentrically biased in their narrow emphasis on the North American and Western European experiences (Murray 1996).

Bisexuality. Bisexuality is a complex concept and, like homosexuality and heterosexuality, has become more complex in recent years as the framing concepts of gender have become less arbitrarily complementary and distinct (Butler 1993; Weinberg et al. 1994). Bisexuality can refer to behavior (those who have had both homosexual and heterosexual experience), psychic response (those capable of being erotically aroused by both homosexual and heterosexual imagery), and either social labeling or self-labeling. Substantial numbers of people have had, if only incidentally, both homosexual and heterosexual experiences while retaining a firm self-identity as being one or the other (Lauman et al. 1994). Even larger numbers have or can be assumed to have experienced sexual arousal in association with both heteroerotic and homoerotic imagery (Kinsey et al. 1948, 1953;

Bell and Weinberg 1978; Bell et al. 1981). The mere experience of having sex with members of both genders may not be sufficient to justify the application of the term "bisexual." What can be called "situational same-gender, sexual contacts," such as those which occur in single-gender penal institutions, may represent little more than conventionally styled heterosexual orientations expressed in restrictive circumstances (Gagnon and Simon 1973).

Relatively few people conceive of themselves as bisexual or can be labeled as such, particularly if the concept is defined as an attraction to both genders and an attraction for the sexual behaviors commonly attributed to both genders. However, bisexual identification probably has increased as an expression of an increase among younger cohorts of "open gender schemas" (Weinberg et al. 1994).

Many people whose sexual histories involve interaction with both genders still see themselves as being either homosexual or heterosexual in orientation. This may be a reflection of the fact that outside of relatively few "bisexual support groups," until recently neither heterosexual nor homosexual social worlds appeared to accept or validate such an identity. The very concept of bisexuality, when used to refer to a specific type of person, was viewed with skepticism (Tripp 1987). Having bisexual interests often was viewed as a mask or apology for an underlying orientation. Undoubtedly, for some people the bisexual label served as a transitional phase in the complicated task of identity transformation. Although a large number of the psychotherapeutic communities accept bisexuality as a distinct type of psychosexual development (Hill 1989), even among those who identify themselves as bisexual there are some who tend to have patterns of sexual behavior that are "amazingly diverse and that [their] day to day life roles are greatly different from one another . . . [and] it is clear that people come to bisexuality in an incredibly diverse number of ways" (Blumstein and Schwartz 1976, p. 180).

Bisexuality as denoting a special orientation tends to be a recent conceptualization, that reflects the increased recognition of gender as a crystallization of erotic responses that are not necessarily coded by the logic of an excluding complementarity. Prior images of bisexuality re-flected the assumed differences of masculinity and femininity such as the persistently masculinized dominant sexual actor and the individual who could switch between stereotypical presentations of gender. Increased recognition of a bisexual possibility follows the recognition of the possible absence of complementarily, that is, with each participant providing what is absent in and desired by the other, within many heterosexual and homosexual relationships and the calling into question an implicit complementarity within existing conceptions of gender (Garber 1995).

Transvestism and Transsexuality. These two concepts do not represent discrete categories so much as a continuum describing the degree to which an individual biologically of one gender desires and enacts the identities or aspects of the identities of the other (Feinbloom 1976). For an unknown number of people this is limited to using the clothing of the other gender to elicit sexual excitement, with little more being directly involved. For most, however, more is involved; for most it involves adopting and enacting, if only for an audience of oneself, aspects of the identity and selected roles of the other gender, not merely cross-dressing but cross-gendering. However, for transvestites, cross-dressing is temporary, and they do not abandon their primary gender identity; they play at being the other (Newton 1979).

At the other end of the continuum is the transsexual who ideally seeks to adopt permanently the gender, costumes, and roles of the other gender (Green 1974). While an absolute realization of this aspiration is impossible, combined modern surgical and pharmacological techniques and permissive bureaucracies (the former cosmetically "redesigning" the body, while the latter allow for a redesigning of one's identifying credentials) have brought about the possibility of coming close to allowing some people to more fully realize their aspiration to live their lives, as fully as possible, in the costumes and roles of the other gender (Bolin 1988; Lothstein 1983).

The desirability of supporting transsexuality remains a matter of continuing contention that involves issues of mental health and gender. Several medical centers that once maintained programs of "surgical gender reassignment" have suspended those programs after reporting results that were too mixed to justify their continuation. Additionally, feminists have criticized such programs as catering to the desire to enact some of the most extreme forms of gender stereotypes (Irving 1990).

Midway between these extremes, between the erotic fetishizing of the clothing of the opposite gender and the desire to become the opposite gender, are those who prefer the costumes and behavior roles of the opposite gender without wanting to or needing to abandon their own initial gender or genitalia. This ranges from those who deliberately blur costumes and the coding or semiotics of gestures to obscure distinctions—women who have masculinized or men who have feminized their presentation of self—to those who experience a continuing conflict between a "masculine self" and a "feminine self," feeling that each of these components of a divided self requires its own costumes, vocabulary of gestures, and social space. (Bullough et al. 1997)

Again, as is true for most forms of stigmatized behavior, estimates of how many individuals are involved in such practices are virtually impossible to determine with any accuracy. Across this continuum of cross-gendering, both males and females can be observed. Most researchers speculate that more males than females are involved, generalizing the apparent tendency for significantly more males than females to be involved in various kinds of sexual deviance.

This speculation is made additionally plausible by the manifest tendency for violations of gender by men to generate more nervousness and be more heavily sanctioned than are comparable violations by females. It is possible for many females to mask their transvestic desires through the broader range of fashion available to women. For example, female cross-dressing in film and literature often involves the beginnings of romantic investment, while male cross-dressing is almost entirely restricted to the comic mode.

These two concepts, transvestism and transsexuality, perhaps more than any other, speak to the powers of gender and its multiple correlates They speak as well to the complex relationship between gender and sexuality. For relatively few people are gender presentations altered to facilitate a specific sexual aim; more often the sexual is organized to facilitate desired gender effects. Little that is manifestly sexual appears in the cross-gendering of some people, as in the case of many male heterosexual transvestites. In the case of the transsexual, surgical procedures often diminish orgasmic capacity. However, confirmation is often one of the major motives for engaging in sexual behavior and a major source of its capacity to gratify, a capacity that may go well beyond the narrow physicalist emphasis on orgasm.

However, conflict between the sexual as genital involvement and the sexual as gender confirmation has been seen by some as an expression of the application of a socially constructed arbitrary binary system that coercively mutes existing heterogeneities of desires and identity themes. This recently articulated perspective views *transgendering* as a moment of potential liberation from an arbitrary binary gender system, allowing individuals to give fuller expression to the totality of their eroticized and noneroticized desires (Stone 1991).

CONCLUSIONS

Sexual orientation is a complex construct rather than a simple thing. While it tends to identify individuals in terms of commitment to similar sexual preferences, it also has the capacity to mask differences among those who appear to otherwise share identical orientations. This is not surprising. Sexual behaviors, like many other aspects of human experience that are linked in critical ways to biology, are also historical and subject to change and as such reflect the very connections of the sexual ultimately to the total fabric of social life.

At the same time, concepts of sexual orientation are aspects of the cultural apparatus of a time and place and are used to explain the behaviors of others as well as one's own behavior. As such, they have the capacity to influence the very behaviors they appear merely to describe. Thus, to view the sexual in isolation from the continuing dynamic of social life, which until recently has largely been its fate, is to run the risk of unself-consciously transforming the science of social life into an oppressive disciplinary instrument of social life.

(SEE ALSO: *Alternative Life-Styles*; *Heterosexual Behavior Patterns*; *Sexual Behavior and Marriage*)

REFERENCES

Adam, Barry 1978 "Capitalism, the Family, and Gay People." *Sociologists Gay Caucus Working Papers I.*

Beach, Frank 1956 "Characteristics of Masculine Sex Drive.'" In Marshall R. Jones, ed., *Nebraska Symposium on Motivation.* Lincoln: University of Nebraska Press.

Bech, Henning 1997 *When Men Meet: Homosexuality and Modernity.* Chicago: University of Chicago Press.

Bell, Allen C., and Martin S. Weinberg 1978 *Homosexualities: A Study of Diversity among Men and Women.* New York: Simon & Schuster.

——, ——, and Susan Hammersmith 1981 *Sexual Preference.* Bloomington: Indiana University Press.

Berger, Peter, and Thomas Luckman 1966 *The Social Construction of Reality.* Garden City, N.Y.: Doubleday.

Blumstein, Phillip W., and Pepper Schwartz 1976 "Bisexuality in Women." *Archives of Sexual Behavior* 5(2):171–181.

—— 1983 *The American Couple.* New York: Morrow.

Bolin, Anne 1988 *In Search of Eve: Transsexual Rites of Passage* Parsagr. South Hadley, Mass: Bergin and Garvey.

Boswell, John 1983 "Revolutions, Universals, and Sexual Categories." *Salamgundi* 58–59:89–113.

Bray, Alan 1982 *Homosexuality in Renaissance England.* London: Gay Men's Press.

Bullough, Bonnie, Vern Bullough, and James Elias 1997 *Gender Blending.* Amherst, N.Y.: Prometheus.

Bullough, Vern L. (1978) 1980 *Sexual Variance in Society and History.* Chicago: University of Chicago Press.

Butler, Judith 1993 *Bodies That Matter: On the Discursive Limits of "Sex."* London: Routledge.

Ehrenreich, Barbara, Elizabeth Hess, and Gloria Jacobs 1986 *The Feminization of Sex.* New York: Doubleday, Anchor.

Ellis, Havelock 1937 *Studies in the Psychology of Sex,* vol. 2. New York: Random House.

Epstein, Steven 1987 "Gay Politics, Gay Identities: The Limits of Social Construction." *Socialist Review* 93/94:9–53.

Erikson, Erik 1950 *Childhood and Society.* New York: Norton.

Escoffier, Jeffrey 1998 *American Homo: Community and Perversity.* Berkeley: University of California Press.

Feinbloom, Deborah 1976 *Transvestites and Transsexuals: Mixed Reviews.* New York: Delacorte.

Ford, Clellan, and Frank A. Beach 1951 *Patterns of Sexual Behavior.* New York: Harper.

Foucault, Michel 1978 *The History of Sexuality,* vol. I: *An Introduction.* New York: Pantheon.

Freud, Sigmund (1905) 1953 "Three Essays on the Theory of Sexuality." *Standard Edition,* vol. 7. London: Hogarth.

Gagnon, John H. 1990 "Gender Preferences in Erotic Relations, the Kinsey Scale and Sexual Scripts." In David McWhorter, Stefanie Sanders, and June Reinisch, eds., *Heterosexuality, Homosexuality, and the Kinsey Scale.* New York: Oxford University Press.

——, and William Simon 1973 *Sexual Conduct: The Social Sources of Human Sexuality.* Chicago: Aldine.

—— 1987 "The Scripting of Oral Genital Contacts." *Archives of Sexual Behavior* 16(1):1–25.

Garber, Marjorie 1995 *Vice Versa: Bisexuality and the Eroticism of Everyday Life.* New York: Simon and Schuster.

Gebhard, Paul H., and Alan B. Johnson 1979 *The Kinsey Data: Marginal Tabulation of the 1938–1963 Interviews Conducted by the Institute for Sex Research.* Philadelphia: Saunders.

Gladue, Brian A. 1987 "Psychobiological Contributions." In Louis Diamant, ed., *Male and Female Homosexuality: Psychological Approaches.* New York: Hemisphere.

Green, Richard 1974 *Sexual Identity Conflict in Children and Adults.* New York: Basic Books.

—— 1987 *The "Sissy Boy Syndrome" and the Development of Homosexuality.* New Haven, Conn.: Yale University Press.

—— 1988 "The Immutability of (Homo)Sexual Orientation: Behavioral Science Implications for a Constitutional (Legal) Analysis." *Journal of Psychiatry and Law* Winter, pp. 537–557.

Greenberg, David F. 1988 *The Construction of Homosexuality.* Chicago: University of Chicago Press.

Gregersen, Edgar 1983 *Sexual Practices: The Story of Human Sexuality.* New York: Franklin Watts.

Halperin, David M. 1989 *One Hundred Years of Homosexuality and Other Essays on Greek Love.* New York: Routledge, Chapman, and Hall.

Harry, Joseph 1982 *Gay Children Grow Up.* New York: Preager.

Herdt, Gilbert H. 1981 *Guardians of the Flute.* New York: McGraw-Hill.

Herzer, Manfred 1985 "Kertbeny and the Nameless Love." *Journal of Homosexuality* 12(1):1–23.

Hill, Ivan, ed. 1989 *The Bisexual Spouse: Different Dimensions in Human Sexuality.* New York: Harper Prennial.

Hocquenghem, Guy 1978 *Homosexual Desire,* Danniella Dangoor, trans. London: Allison and Busby.

Irvine, Janice M. 1990 *Disorders of Desire: Sex and Gender in Modern American Sexology*. Philadelphia: Temple University Press.

Katz, Jonathan M. 1990 "The Invention of Heterosexuality." *Socialist Review* 90/91:7–34.

—— 1995 *The Invention of Heterosexuality*. New York: Dutton.

Kinsey, Alfred C., Wardell B. Pomeroy, Cyde E. Martin, and Paul H. Gebhard 1948 *Sexual Behavior in the Human Male*. Philadelphia: Saunders.

—— 1953 *Sexual Behavior in the Human Female*. Philadelphia: Saunders.

Krafft-Ebing, Richard von (1886) 1965 *Psychopathia Sexualis*, trans. by Harry E. Wedeck. New York: Putnam's.

Lauman, Edward O., John H. Gagnon, Robert T. Michael, and Stuart Michaels 1994 *The Social Organization of Sexuality: Sexual Practices in the United States*. Chicago: University of Chicago Press.

LaVay, Simon 1996 *Queer Science*. Cambridge, Mass.: MIT Press.

Levine, Martin P. 1998 *Gay Macho: The Life and Death of the Gay Clone*. Michael S. Kimmel (ed.). New York: New York University Press.

Lothstein, Leslie 1983 *Female to Male Transsexualism: Historical, Clinical, and Theoretical Issues*. Boston: Routledge and Kegan Paul.

McIntosh, Mary 1976 "The Homosexual Role." *Social Problems* 16(2):182–192.

Mitchell, Stephan A. 1988 *Relational Concepts in Psychoanalysis*. Cambridge, Mass.: Harvard University Press.

Money, John 1988 *Gay, Straight, and In-Between: The Sexology of Erotic Orientations*. New York: Oxford University Press.

Murray, Stephen O. 1984 *Social Theory, Homosexual Reality*. New York: Gay Academic Union.

—— 1996 *American Gay*. Chicago: University of Chicago Press.

Newton, Esther 1979 *Mother Camp: Female Impersonators in America*. Chicago: University of Chicago Press.

Nietzsche, Frederic (1887) 1968 *On the Genealogy of Morals*. In Walter Kaufmann trans., *The Basic Writings of Nietzsche*. New York: Modern Library.

Padgug, Robert A. 1979 "Sexual Matters: On Conceptualizing Sexuality in History." *Radical History Review* 20:3–33.

Parsons, Talcott, and Robert F. Bales 1955 *Family Socialization and Interaction Process*. New York: Free Press.

Plummer, Kenneth 1975 *Sexual Stigma: An Interactionist Approach*. London: Routledge and Kegan Paul.

Ponse, Barbara 1978 *Identity in the Lesbian World*. Westport, Conn.: Greenwood.

Richardson, Diane, ed. 1996 *Theorizing Heterosexuality*. Buckingham, U.K.: Open University Press.

Seidman, Steven, C. Meeks, and F. Traschen 1999 "Beyond the Closet: The Changing Meaning of Homosexuality in the United States." *Sexualities* 2(1):11–34.

Simon, William 1996 *Postmodern Sexualities*. London: Routledge.

——, and John H. Gagnon 1967 "Homosexuality: The Formulation of a Sociological Perspective." *Journal of Health and Human Behavior* 2(1):9–37.

—— 1986 "Sexual Scripts: Permanence and Change." *Archives of Sexual Behavior* 15(2):97–120.

——, D. Kraft, and H. Kaplan 1990 "Oral Sex: A Critical Overview." In June Reinisch, Bruce Vollmer, and Michael Goldstein, eds., *AIDS and Sex: A Biomedicial and Behavioral Approach*. New York: Oxford University Press.

Stoller, Robert J. 1985a *Observing the Erotic Imagination*. New Haven, Conn.: Yale University Press.

—— 1985b *Presentations of Gender*. New Haven, Conn.: Yale University Press.

Stone, Sandy 1991 "The Empire Strikes Back: A Posttranssexual Manifesto." In Julia Epstein and Kristina Straub, eds., *Body Guards: The Cultural Politics of Gender Ambiguity*. New York: Routledge.

Symons, Donald 1979 *The Evolution of Human Sexuality*. New York: Oxford University Press.

Tripp, Clarence 1987 *The Homosexual Matrix*, 2nd ed. New York: New American Library.

Weeks, Jeffrey 1985 *Sexuality and Its Discontents: Meanings, Myths, and Modern Sexualities*. London: Routledge and Kegan Paul.

Weinberg, Martin S., Colin J. Williams, and Douglas W. Pryor 1994 *Dual Attractions: Understanding Bisexuality*. New York: Oxford University Press.

Weinberg, Thomas S. 1983 *Gay Men, Gay Identities*. New York: Irvington.

Whitam Frederic L. 1983 "Culturally Invariable Properties of Male Homosexuals." *Archives of Sexual Behavior* 12:207–222.

Wilson, Edward O. 1978 *On Human Nature*. Cambridge, Mass.: Harvard University Press.

WILLIAM SIMON

SEXUAL VIOLENCE AND EXPLOITATION

Sexual violence and exploitation are social problems that were relatively neglected as research topics until the late 1960s. This article focuses primarily on the different categories of rape, sexual harassment, child sexual abuse, and related issues.

RAPE AS A FORM OF SEXUAL VIOLENCE

Rape was not conceptualized as a major problem in the United States until the late 1960s; this awareness accompanied the resurrected women's movement and the establishment of the National Center for the Prevention and Control of Rape. After this awakening of interest, enough information was generated to document the fact that there were explanations for rape that went beyond the biological and psychological. Society and its institutions, laws, and attitudes were seen as contributing greatly to the problem. In the 1970s, rape was clearly defined as a social problem.

The works of three feminists contributed to advancing awareness of rape or sexual violence against women: Millet's *Sexual Politics* (1972), Griffin's "Rape: The All American Crime" (1971), and Brownmiller's *Against Our Will: Men, Women, and Rape* (1975). Millet argued that rape is linked to the concept of patriarchy, in which men use power and coercion to control women's sexuality. Nowhere is this better articulated than in the "crimes of honor" concept or social norm still evident in many Middle Eastern countries. Griffin's article focused on the nature of rape. She argued that rape is not a sexual act but a violent political act and that the threat of being raped controls women socially. This social control is present even among very young females. In response to the survey questions, "Would you rather be a man or woman?" and "Why?" a 10-year old girl replied that she would rather be a man, because women get killed and raped (Renzetti and Curran 1995, p. 338). Research indicates that rape is the crime women fear most, and this fear is compounded by the possibility of getting pregnant and contracting AIDS. Brownmiller's book is a historical account of rape that expands on the ideas of Millet and Griffin. The writings of these women clearly demonstrated that rape is more a sociological than a psychological phenomenon.

The definition of rape that served as the basis for most rape laws is grounded in English common law: "the unlawful carnal knowledge of a woman by force and against her will." Implicit in this idea is the assumption that the assailant is a man. In the 1970s, many states redefined rape laws to more comprehensively describe the behaviors that constituted rape and define the age of consent. By the end of the decade, forty-one states had passed some form of rape shield laws that limited the use in court of victims' prior sexual conduct with persons other than the offender (Green 1988, pp. 16–40). Many states have abandoned the concept of rape in favor of the more gender-neutral concept of sexual assault.

The Federal Bureau of Investigation (FBI) indicates that a rape happens every five minutes in the United States. American women are eight times more likely to be raped than are European women and twenty-six times more likely than Japanese women. In the 1980s, the rate of rape in the United States rose four times faster than did the total crime rate. While the number of rapes appears to have fallen over the last few years, rape is still the most frequently committed and least reported violent crime. A total of 97,464 forcible rapes were reported to law enforcement bodies in 1995, the lowest number since 1989. Based on this statistic, it is estimated that in 1995, 72 of every 100,000 females were reported rape victims (U.S. Department of Justice 1995). However, a study funded by the U.S. Department of Health and Human Services found that 683,000 women had been raped in 1990, a figure more than five times as high as the 130,260 reported to the police in that year (Johnston 1992).

Victimization studies such as the National Crime Survey (NCS) and other research projects were initiated to get better estimates of the prevalence of rape. These studies show that the amount of rape is greatly underestimated, although prevalence rates vary from study to study and are hard to reconcile because of variations in research design, sampling, and geographic location.

Rape is described in a number of ways. Sometimes it is discussed in terms of the number of offenders per victim: the single-offender, two-offender, or multiple, group, or gang rape. Victimization statistics for these forms of rape are, respectively, 81 percent, 10 percent, and 8 percent (Koss and Harvey 1987, p. 10). Rape also is classified as stranger rape, in which the victim and offender have no relationship to one another, or acquaintance rape, which includes date rape and rape between individuals who knew each other before the assault. According to the U.S. Department of Justice, about 55 percent of rapes are acquaintance rapes; the younger the victim is, the more likely it is that she knew the rapist. Acquaintance rapes are especially common on college campuses. Warshaw (1988, chap. 1), citing statistics from the *Ms.* magazine Project on Campus Assault, reports fewer stranger (16 percent) and group rapes (15 percent), with the vast majority of incidents (95 percent) being individual assaults that involve acquaintances or dates (84 percent). The NCS's rape statistics indicate that 27 percent of rapes involve multiple offenders. While acquaintance rapes are more common, women raped by strangers are ten times more likely to report the incident (Renzetti and Curran 1995, p. 341).

Many researchers have attempted to classify rapists into types. Some typologies suggest as few as two or three types (e.g., Groth 1979), while others describe five (e.g., Rada 1978). A review of this literature leads to the conclusion that the typologies are tied closely to the developer's theoretical orientation and educational background.

Rape legally occurs when a person uses force or the threat of force to engage in sexual intercourse (vaginal, oral, or anal) with another person. This seems like a straightforward definition that may lead to the conclusion that rape cases are easy to prosecute. However, one of the most common defenses in rape cases involves the issue of consent. For example, if the victim was drinking, how can she be sure she did not consent? Many rapists have learned that the "alcohol excuse" can help them escape rape charges. A more insidious drug, rohypnol, is being used on college campuses and in bars and nightclubs to facilitate raping and getting away with it. It is dropped into a potential victim's drink. The symptoms are dizziness,

disorientation, lack of coordination, and passing out. The victim is then raped but has no memory of the sexual assault. The question again is posed, If she cannot remember, how does she know she did not consent?

According to the Center for Women Policy Studies (1991, pp. 3–4), fewer than 40 percent of reported rapes result in charges against the offenders and only 3 percent result in convictions. Many researchers have commented on the comparatively light sentences associated with rape convictions. There appear to be several reasons for this, including the tendency to blame the victim rather than the perpetrator: "She should have been more cautious or more sensible or not been walking alone at night." Closely associated with blaming the victim is the notion of "victim precipitation," or the idea that the victim did something to provoke the rape. This can be tied to how the victim was dressed, her profession (e.g., a prostitute), or where she was when the rape happened (e.g., in a fraternity member's room or a male's hotel room, as in the Mike Tyson rape case). Many researchers who have studied rape and the criminal justice system argue that women who are rape victims are "double victims." They are victimized by both the rapist and the criminal justice system.

OTHER TYPES OF RAPE AS SEXUAL VIOLENCE

Marital Rape. Most discussions of rape focus on date rape or acquaintance rape and stranger rape. A third type of rape among intimates that has received increased attention since the 1980s is marital rape. This type of rape occurs when the victim and offender are spouses or are living in a spouselike arrangement. Although this was thought to be rare, Russell (1984, p. 59) found that 8 percent of ever-married women reported being raped by their husbands. Some researchers believe that marital rape is more common than all other types combined. The 1980s brought about many changes, as spousal immunity laws, which historically prevented husbands from being charged with raping their wives because a wife was viewed as a husband's property, were challenged.

In 1977, Oregon repealed the marital exemption to its rape statute, and in 1979, James K. Chretien became the first person in the United States to be convicted of marital rape. Currently all states prohibit forced sex between a husband and a wife, although most include numerous spousal exemptions. As of 1990, seventeen states and the District of Columbia allowed the prosecution of husbands for raping their wives without exemptions. In twenty-six states, husbands are exempt from prosecution in certain circumstances, such as if only force is employed (Wallace 1999, p. 509) but there is no additional violence such as the threat of using a weapon. In eight states (Kentucky, Missouri, New Mexico, North Carolina, Oklahoma, South Carolina, South Dakota, and Utah), a husband cannot be prosecuted for raping his wife unless they are living apart, are legally separated, or have filed for divorce. In five states, exemptions are extended to unmarried cohabiting couples, and there is an exemption for dating relationships in Delaware.

Males as Victims of Sexual Violence. Males appear to be victimized both in and out of prison by heterosexual and homosexual males and by females. Currently, men are thought to make up less than 10 percent of all rape victims (Renzetti and Curran 1995, p. 39.) In *Rape in Prison* (1975), Scacco emphasized that rape in prisons is not an act of homosexuality. Rather, it is an extension of the traditional male sex role and the patriarchal culture in which a single male or group of males seeks to dominate another person through a violent act. In the absence of females, those who are powerful, dominant conquerors are viewed as the "real" or "masculine" men and those who are raped are relegated to a lower status. As Scacco puts it, the victims of rape become "a punk, a queen, or a female." They have, in the words of the rapists, "had their manhood taken" (1975, p. 52). Scacco's interpretation of male rape in prison fits into most feminist theories of rape: Rape is an act of power and control rather than a sexual act. While the prevalence rates for the rape of males in prisons appear to vary from one institution to another, it seems safe to conclude that these rates are higher in prisons than outside prisons, where women are available targets.

Rape Outside Prisons. Outside the prison environment, most people think rape happens only to women. Scacco (1975) argues, however, that rape would not exist in prison if it did not exist first on the streets. A survey of literature on males raping males indicates that the overwhelming majority of rapists are heterosexual both in and out of prison. However, as more is learned about sexual assaults of males, rape is found to be part of gay men's relationships as well as involving gay men raping women and other men. If, as most rape theorists agree, rape is a crime of power and not sex, there is no reason to believe that some homosexual males do not commit rape. Russell (1984, p. 74) argues that the insignificant number of females raping males (less then 1 percent) has received more attention than has rape by homosexual men. She notes that this politically controversial issue has resulted an avoidance of even discussing the issue (1984, p. 74).

While there is no agreement about the prevalence of males being raped, there is a consensus that men get raped by other men and women, that homosexual and heterosexual males are rape victims and offenders, that rape happens in all parts of society and not just in prisons, and that men are less likely than women to report rape. It is known that male victims share some of the traumas of female victims as well as having special concerns. Those added concerns include issues of masculinity and/or sexuality, medical procedures, reporting to the police, telling others, and finding resources and support.

Rape and War. Brownmiller's (1975, chap. 3) historical account of rape provides evidence that rape has always been a part of war. This applies whether one analyzes biblical accounts or the raping of women by American soldiers during the Vietnam War.

There is much documentation that the rape of women and even children is not, as some military and government officials argue, an unfortunate but inevitable part of war. Instead, Brownmiller argues, it is a planned part of war strategy that has included not only rape during the conquest of a village, town, or city but women being captured and used as sexual slaves. She contends that it is the winning side or the conquerors in battle who do the raping. Rape is not only a way of measuring victory but also the way males assert their masculinity. Consistent with the idea that women are property, women are seen as tangible rewards of war.

Rape during war is considered a criminal act under international law, punishable by imprisonment or death, but wartime rape continues. This violence against women generated public attention as a human rights issue when, in 1993, the U.S. and European media reported the systematic rape, sexual enslavement, torture, and murder of Bosnian Muslim women and children by Serbian military forces in the former Yugoslavia. The estimate of the number of rapes in 1993 was 20,000 (Riding 1993). In 1999, the rape of women and children by the Serb military continued. Investigations of these atrocities conclude, as did Brownmiller, that rape is used as a weapon of war. They argue that it is a central part of the Serbian ethnic cleansing campaign. Bosnian and Kosovar men are murdered, while the women are raped with the objective of impregnating them to produce offspring with Serbian genetic characteristics. It is also psychological warfare, with the intent to demoralize and terrorize Muslims and drive them from their homes. European investigators reported that many women and children died during sadistic and brutal rapes. Brownmiller's historical account of rape and war indicates that an additional consequence of rape and impregnation is suicide and infanticide.

Rape during war often takes the form of group or gang rape. There are documented cases of gang rape by police and military personnel in numerous countries, including Haiti, Honduras, El Salvador, and Iran (Sontag 1993). There are also recent accounts of Algerian women being raped by Islamic radicals. Muslim women in Bosnia, Kosovo, and Algeria who survive rape face psychological problems associated not only with rape but with living in a culture that values sexual purity, by which the male's honor as well as the family's honor is defined.

The motivations for rape and violence against women in war are similar to those for rape between strangers, acquaintances, and intimates in everyday society and prisons. It is an attempt to socially control and harm individuals who are viewed as having lower or undesirable statuses or are viewed as the enemy. In war, the rapes occur on a larger scale.

In the 1990s, the United Nations attempted to develop policies to eliminate all forms of discrimination against women. However, as long as rape of women and children remains an open or hidden part of war strategy, this violent act will continue.

EXPLANATIONS FOR RAPE

Explanations for rape come from a variety of disciplines, although many explanations have been dominated by the psychiatric perspective and the medical model (Koss and Leonard 1984, pp. 213–232). The basic assumption underlying this thinking is that rapists are psychologically sick and that rape is sexually motivated. Hence, many explanations focus on developing profiles of rapists (e.g., Groth 1975), leading to a body of research whose validity is questioned because it is based primarily on nonrepresentative clinical or prison populations.

Sociological explanations of rape focus on the social dynamics of society that promote, treat, or proscribe such behaviors and include sociocultural, sociohistorical, and sociopsychological analyses. While these types of explanations lagged behind those of psychology and biology, they offer an alternative to individual-based theories.

Sociocultural explanations of rape are supported by large cross-cultural studies of tribal societies (Sanday 1981) and large studies in nonindustrialized nations. All these studies draw similar conclusions. Rape-prone societies endorse the macho personality and a fundamental belief in the inferiority of females, a belief system that incorporates an acceptance of physical aggression, a high amount of risk taking, and a casual attitude toward sex. Rape also is related to a culture's socioeconomic structure.

Among industrialized societies, the United States has high rape rates. Baron and Straus's

(1989, p. 180) state-level analyses show that rape rates vary by region and state within the United States and that those rates are positively related to the amount of social disorganization, sex magazine circulation (pornography), and gender inequality in a state or region. This adds weight to earlier research that ties rape-specific myths and attitudes to a larger attitudinal construct supportive of sex role stereotyping, violence against women, and adversarial sexual beliefs.

Sociocultural and sociopsychological explanations of rape support the sociohistorical analysis of Brownmiller (1975). While Brownmiller has been criticized for exaggerating the notion of male intimidation, sociological and anthropological research indicates that rape is a socially created phenomenon that is much more likely to occur in cultures that support patriarchy and violence. Sociocultural explanations also may explain why the majority of offenders are male irrespective of whether the victims are male or female, adult or child.

Regardless of the varied theoretical perspectives, most researchers agree that multifactorial (psychological and sociological factors), compared with single-factor, explanations are better predictors of rape. Russell (1984, p. 111) notes that most rape theories could fit into Finkelhor's (1984) four-factor explanation of child sexual abuse, which is discussed in a later section.

SEXUAL HARASSMENT

Sexual harassment is a form of violence against both males and females, but the overwhelming majority of victims are women and most of the perpetrators are men. While the exact prevalence seems to vary from one study to another, it is safe to conclude that sexual harassment in the workplace is widespread. While sexual harassment can occur in other social institutions, such as colleges and schools where professors and teachers use their positions of power to obtain sexual favors from students, most sexual harassment research has focused on the workplace.

Sexual harassment policies, laws, and rulings generally have relied on Title VII of the Civil Rights Act of 1964, which prohibits employment discrimination on the basis of race, color, religion, sex, pregnancy, or national origin. In 1980, the Equal Employment Opportunity Commission (EEOC) adopted guidelines that specifically address discrimination on the basis of sex. While these guidelines were not binding, they were used by courts in making decisions in sexual harassment cases. In 1993, the Supreme Court further articulated the meaning of sexual harassment in *Harris v. Forklift Systems, Inc.* Basically, the case focused on the "nature" of sexual harassment and ruled that there was no requirement that the severity of the harassing conduct cause the victim psychological or physical harm. The Court held that victims alleging sexual harassment met their burden of proof if they proved that the environment was *perceived* as hostile or abusive. The circumstances for making such a judgment could include the frequency of the alleged harassment, whether it was physically threatening or humiliating, and the extent to which it interfered with an employee's work performance.

Sexual harassment may take two forms that are not mutually exclusive: quid pro quo harassment and hostile environment harassment. The former type occurs when the victim is placed in a situation where an employer or supervisor uses his or her position to request sexual favors as a basis for continued employment or job benefits. The victim is put in the position of choosing between providing sex and losing employment or benefits. Hostile environment harassment happens when victims are exposed to a series of unwelcome sexual acts that result in psychological harm or humiliation. The difference between the two types of harassment is that the quid pro quo form focuses on harassment that is tied to economic disadvantage, while the hostile environment type focuses on psychological harm.

Tangri et al. (1982) offer several models to explain sexual harassment: the biological, organizational, and sociocultural models. The biological model assumes that sexual behavior in the workplace is an extension of human sexuality or strong sex drives. The organizational model focuses on the situation in which the workplace offers opportunities for sexual aggression. This model focuses on power that derives from formal roles in an organization. The sociocultural model is derived from theories of patriarchy in which men are viewed as dominant in Western culture and are the gatekeepers of political and economic power. This explanation is the most congruent with a feminist view of sexual harassment.

Two prominent sexual harassment cases have captured the public's attention. The first involved Anita Hill and Clarence Thomas. Hill, a law professor, testified to the U.S. Congress that Thomas, who had been nominated to the Supreme Court, had sexually harassed her. The second was the case of *Paula Jones v. William J. Clinton.* Jones brought charges against President Clinton, alleging that when he was governor of Arkansas and she was an employee of that state, he asked her to engage in sexual activities. Her reluctance, she argued, led to the loss of job benefits. Both cases demonstrated the difficulties of proving sexual harassment cases. They also sent messages that bringing charges against very powerful males can lead to additional reputational, economic, and psychological victimization.

Simply having agencies and courts establish procedures and policies to process sexual harassment will not terminate this behavior. The public must send a clear message that it stands behind sexual harassment laws and that everyone, regardless of social status, must be held accountable. Accounts of sexual harassment, rape, or sexual exploitation by President Clinton of Gennifer Flowers, Paula Jones, Monica Lewinsky, Kathleen Willey, Juanita Broaddrick, and others raise questions about the public's concern about these issues as well as the issue of a double standard. The public seems willing to support or excuse some offenders, such as President Clinton, while punishing others.

CHILD SEXUAL ABUSE

Since the mid-1970s, there has been increased interest in understanding child sexual abuse. This concern led to the founding of the National Cen-

ter on Child Abuse and Neglect and the passage of the 1977 Protection of Children against Sexual Exploitation Act. A review of the child sex abuse research (Finkelhor et al. 1986) demonstrates many similarities with what is known about rape. Paralleling Brownmiller's (1975) historical analysis of rape, for example, is Rush's (1980) analysis of child sexual abuse. Like Brownmiller, Rush elevates child sexual abuse to the level of a social problem by tracing its roots to patriarchal societies and their social institutions, belief systems, and myths. However, there are groups that do not view child–adult sex as a problem, such as the North American Man Boy Love Association; in fact, they advocate it.

In general, child sexual abuse can be defined as sexual exploitation of or sexual activities with a child by an adult, in which the child's health or welfare may be harmed or threatened. While all states consider child sexual abuse a crime, definitions vary from state to state and some states leave the interpretation to the courts. There is no real agreement among social scientists about the true extent of child sexual abuse, but all concede that the number of reported cases is increasing and that the actual numbers are underestimated, particularly for males. A comparison of national findings with less comprehensive research studies reveals conflicting estimates of the incidence of child sexual abuse. Commonly cited estimates suggest that one in four girls and one in six to seven boys will be sexually abused by the time they reach age 18.

Studies do not support a general social characteristics profile of the victims or offenders, although females tend to be at somewhat greater risk of victimization than males and males are overwhelmingly the offenders. The ages of greatest risk for victimization appear to be between 4 and 9. Most offenders are either known by or related to their victims and are not old. Only about 10 percent of child sexual abusers are strangers, although the Internet could change this statistic.

The impact of being a victim of child sexual abuse has been widely studied. It generally is agreed that the amount of trauma experienced varies with the type of abuse, how the offender is related to the child, how long the abuse lasted, how sexually intrusive the abuse was, the age when the abuse began, the reactions of others to the disclosure of the abuse, and the child's personality.

As an ever-increasing number of child sexual abuse cases have moved into the courts, particularly in cases involving divorce and custody, concern for balancing the needs of the legal system against those of children has arisen. Placing children in the courtroom subjects them to many of the same problems faced by rape victims: victim blaming and other courtroom-produced traumas. Although still in the early stages, reforms are being implemented and suggested, with one area of legislative reform focusing on increasing convictions and community notification once sex offenders are released. The latter was largely an outgrowth of Megan's Law, which was named after Megan Kanka, a 7-year-old who was molested and killed in 1994 by a released sex offender who was living in her neighborhood without residents' knowledge of his history of sexually abusing children. By 1995, forty-three states had adopted laws requiring offenders to register with a law enforcement agency when they were released.

The late 1980s and early 1990s ushered in a new area of child sexual abuse. Children 12 years of age and younger have sexually abused other children. These young offenders have predatory patterns that are very similar to those of adult and adolescent molesters. Some, but not all, are reacting to their own victimization. An interesting finding from this research is that females tend to be about as likely to be perpetrators as are males and are equally aggressive in their sexual acts. Questions have been raised about why females are not found in larger numbers among the adolescent and adult sex offender populations. The family system appears to be the learning and training ground for these youthful (some as young as 2 years old) perpetrators (Araji 1997).

Studies of child sexual abuse do not offer a consistent link between social class, race, and ethnic group, although the lower socioeconomic classes tend to be overrepresented, as are, in the case of young perpetrators, single-parent families. It is too early to make accurate cross-national comparisons of the extent of child sexual abuse. Some research has been conducted in other countries and Finkelhor (1994) suggests that, as in the United States, the problem is widespread. There have been no cross-cultural studies of children who sexually abuse other children.

EXPLANATIONS OF CHILD SEXUAL ABUSE

The development of child sexual abuse explanations has been similar to that of explanations for rape, as most early studies focused on offenders' psychopathological or biological motivations or attempted to develop profiles of child molesters, victims, and families. As with rape, most explanations offered only single-factor explanations, an approach criticized by Araji Finkelhor (1986, chap. 34). As an alternative, those authors proposed a four-factor explanation of child sexual abuse that includes the categories of emotional congruence, sexual arousal, blockage, and disinhibition. Respectively, these factors incorporate explanations of why an adult would have an emotional need to relate to a child, could be sexually aroused by a child, would not have alternative sources of gratification, and would not be deterred from such an interest by normal prohibitions (Araji and Finkelhor 1986, p. 117). The model includes both individual (e.g., arrested emotional development) and sociocultural (pornography) factors. As was noted above, Russell (1984) believes that this model could be adapted to explain rape.

With respect to explaining youthful perpetrators' sexual aggression, Araji (1997) found much of the same theoretical history noted above. She proposes systems theory as a necessary explanatory and remedial guide.

INCEST

Most researchers and practitioners consider incest different from child sexual abuse, with incest viewed as intrafamilial and child sexual abuse viewed as extrafamilial sexual relations. While some argue that the two types of abuse have much in common, one of the most significant differences is that the victims of incest are always betrayed by someone who has been charged with loving and protecting them. Much of the sexual abuse committed by children 12 years of age and younger is intrafamilial. Such experiences can have extremely destructive results, but this varies with the factors discussed above.

The most common type of incest researched and written about is between father and daughter (Herman and Hirschman 1981), although the most common type may be brother–sister. As stepfamilies are formed, the probability for incestuous relationships involving stepfathers increases. Estimates of incest range from a high of 38 percent of females in Russell's (1984) study to about 25 percent in several other survey studies (e.g., Finkelhor 1979). However, the same research problems surrounding rape and child sexual abuse apply to incest literature: underestimating the extent of the crime, not accurately defining it, and theory and sampling problems.

TREATMENT AND PREVENTION

A considerable body of literature on the prevention and treatment of sexual violence and abuse has emerged from applied disciplines such as social work and clinical psychology as well as from community and feminist organizations. An extensive discussion is beyond the scope of this article, and so only a few generalizations are noted. First, as treatment programs are informed by a variety of theories of rape and sexual abuse, it is not surprising that there is an array of treatment programs. With respect to offenders, most programs focus on punishment and/or rehabilitation (Groth 1979; Conte and Berliner 1981), and many are based on the psychiatric or medical model. In cases of child sexual abuse and incest, programs typically focus on helping the victims and their families get through the crisis. In the area of rape, programs have been aimed primarily at treating victims and families for the rape trauma syndrome and have been directed at females. Treatment programs have also been developed to deal with the short- and long-term effects of abuse (Brown and Finkelhor 1986) and can be either clinical or community-based. Some

are beginning to focus on sexual and ethnic differences. At present, however, there remain debates among professionals and practitioners about what the appropriate treatments are, which ones work, and how well.

Stemming from myths and callous societal attitudes toward sexual aggression and the extensive involvement of feminists, prevention programs have followed a victim advocacy model (Araji 1989, chap. 17). Under this concept, potential victims are taught in various ways how to protect themselves from becoming victims. Some newer programs are aimed at men and promote the development of a nurturant rather than a macho male image.

SUMMARY AND CONCLUSIONS

Extensive public and professional attention to sexual violence and exploitation has come about only since 1960 and has been primarily a grassroots movement. As a result, a large body of cross-disciplinary literature has developed and various reforms have taken place. While no consensus exists about the scope of these problems, the rates at which they are increasing or decreasing, definitions, explanations, social policies, and solutions, sociologists, particularly feminists, have concluded that sexual violence and exploitation will not be reduced or eliminated until societies stop supporting and/or promoting aggression, violence, exploitation, and inequality.

However, the prognosis that sexual violence and exploitation involving women and children will soon end is not convincing. As long as societal members, many of them women, are willing to turn a blind eye to predatory behaviors toward women on the part of the president of the United States and surveys of college, high school, and elementary students report large percentages (31 to 87 percent) of students believing that it is acceptable for males to engage in forced sex or rape of females under certain circumstances (White and Humphrey 1991) or if they do not get caught (Malamuth 1981), one must conclude that the fight against sexual violence and exploitation of women and children is still in the beginning stages.

REFERENCES

Araji, S. 1989 "The Effects of Advocates on Prevention." In N. C. Barker, ed., *Child Abuse and Neglect: An Interdisciplinary Method of Treatment*. Dubuque, Iowa: Kendall/Hunt.

—— 1997 *Sexually Aggressive Children: Coming to Understand Them*. Thousand Oaks, Calif.: Sage.

——, and D. Finkelhor 1986 "Abusers: A Review of the Research." In D. Finkelhor, S. Araji, L. Baron, A. Brown, S. Doyle Peters, and G. E. Wyatt, eds., *A Sourcebook on Child Sexual Abuse*. Beverly Hills, Calif.: Sage.

Baron, L., and M. Straus 1989 *Four Theories of Rape in American Society*. New Haven, Conn.: Yale University Press.

Brown, A., and D. Finkelhor 1986 "Impact of Child Sexual Abuse: A Review of the Research." *Psychological Bulletin* 99:16–77.

Brownmiller, S. 1975 *Against Our Will: Men, Women, and Rape*. New York: Simon & Schuster.

Center for Women Policy Studies 1991 *More Harm Than Help: The Ramifications of Mandatory HIV Testing of Rapists*. Washington, D.C.: Center for Women Policy Studies.

Conte, J. R., and L. Berliner 1981 "Prosecution of the Offender in Cases of Sexual Assault against Children." *Victimology* 6:102–109.

Finkelhor, D. 1994 "The international epidemiology of child sexual abuse." *Child Abuse & Neglect, 18,* 409–417.

—— 1979 *Sexually Victimized Children*. New York: Free Press.

—— 1984 *Child Sexual Abuse: New Theory and Research*. New York: Free Press.

——, S. Araji, L. Baron, A. Brown, S. Doyle Peters, and G. E. Wyatt 1986 *A Sourcebook on Child Sexual Abuse*. Beverly Hills, Calif.: Sage.

Green, W. M. 1988 *Rape*. Lexington, Mass.: Lexington Books.

Griffin, S. 1971 "Rape: The All-American Crime." *Ramparts*, September.

Groth, N. 1979 *Men Who Rape*. New York: Plenum.

Herman, J. L., and L. Hirschman 1981 *Father-Daughter Incest*. Cambridge, Mass.: Harvard University Press.

Johnston, D. 1992 "Survey Shows Number of Rapes Far Higher Than Official Figures." *New York Times* April 24, p. A14.

Koss, M., and M. Harvey 1987 *The Rape Victim: Clinical and Community Approaches to Treatment*. Lexington, Mass.: Stephan Green Press.

Koss, M. P., and K. E. Leonard 1984 "Sexually Aggressive Men: A Review of Empirical Findings." In N. Malamuth and E. Donnerstein, eds., *Pornography and Sexual Aggression*. New York: Academic Press.

Malamuth, N. M. 1981 "Rape Proclivity among Males." *Journal of Social Issues* 37:138–157.

Millett, K. (1970). *Sexual Politics*. New York: Doubleday.

Rada, R. T., Ed. 1978 *Clinical Aspects of the Rapist*. New York: Grune & Stratton.

Renzetti, C. M., and D. J. Curran 1995 *Women, Men and Society*. Boston: Allyn and Bacon.

Riding, A. 1993 "European Inquiry Says Serbs' Forces Have Raped 20,000," *New York Times*, January 1, p. 4.

Rush, F. 1980 *The Best Kept Secret: Sexual Abuse of Children*. New York: McGraw-Hill.

Russell, D. 1984 *Sexual Exploitation, Rape, Child Sexual Abuse, and Workplace Harassment*. Beverly Hills, Calif.: Sage.

Sanday, P. R. 1981 "The Socio-cultural Context of Rape: A Cross-cultural Study." *Journal of Social Issues* 37:5–27.

Scacco, A. M., Jr. 1975 Rape in Prison. Springfield, Ill.: Charles C Thomas

Sontag, D. 1993 "Women Asking U.S. Asylum Expand Definition of Abuse." *New York Times* September, 27 pp. A1, A13.

Tangri, S., M. Burt, and L. Johnson 1982 "Sexual Harassment at Work: Three Explanatory Models." "*Journal of Social Issues* 38: 33–54.

U.S. Department of Justice, Federal Bureau of Investigation 1995 *Crime in the United States: Uniform Crime Reports, 1995*. Washington, D.C.: U.S. Government Printing Office.

Wallace, H. 1999 *Family Violence: Legal, Medical and Social Perspectives*. Boston: Allyn and Bacon.

Warshaw, R. 1988 *I Never Called It Rape*. New York: Harper & Row.

White, J. W., and J. A. Humphrey 1991 "Young People's Attitudes toward Acquaintance Rape." In A. Parrot, ed., *Acquaintance Rape: The Hidden Crime*. New York: Wiley.

SHARON K. ARAJI

SEXUALITY

See Sexual Behavior Patterns; Sex Differences; Sexual Orientation.

SEXUALLY TRANSMITTED DISEASES

Until the 1980s, social science research on sexually transmitted diseases (STDs) focused primarily on the history of various pestilences, the epidemiology of those diseases, and the description of mass disasters (Brandt 1985; Aral and Holmes 1999). The disease that was most commonly researched was syphillis, long the best identified and most feared STD. Historians and anthropologists wrote numerous treatises on its origin and the social consequences of its introduction into isolated, tribal, or third world societies (Wood 1978; Hart 1978). In the early 1980s, the consequences of other STDs were studied, especially as sequelae of prostitution (Kalm 1985; Poherat et al. 1981).

When awareness of the "sexual revolution" finally induced social scientists and epidemiologists to think about the effects of STDs on less sexually active populations than prostitutes and their clients, the literature turned to the newly sexually active: vulnerable teenagers (Washington et al. 1985) and other young people who engaged in premarital sex (O'Reilly and Aral 1985). The exponential intensification of the discussion of and social science research on STDs, however, came only after the medical commmunity's horrified acknowledgment that the newest STD to become epidemiologically important, the acquired immune deficiency syndrome (AIDS), was also the deadliest and that social, not just biological, information was essential in order to combat it.

When AIDS first began to be discussed in 1981, the medical community was already alarmed at its mystery and virulence (Aral and Holmes 1999). Unhappily, it took years before more focused measures, such as those taken by fundraising organizations and institutes devoted to AIDS research, were initiated. Journalists, most notably Randy Shilts (1987), have persuasively ar-

gued that the lack of a strong reaction from the start was due to the fact that the early victims were gay men, not American Legionnaires or Girl Scouts. Today the basic facts of AIDS have been well disseminated. Almost everyone knows, for example, that in the United States gay men are disproportionately affected, as are people who mix blood while exchanging hypodermic needles. However, in the early 1980s, information was abysmally inadequate and myth and rumor educated more people than did social or medical research.

With the accuracy of hindsight, it is evident that sociologists should have looked at sociocultural histories of recent sexual behavior and used that information to help study disease transmission. But no one was proactive, and it took years for a pertinent literature to emerge. The exceptions were a small group of social researchers at the Centers for Disease Control (CDC), whose work was restricted to STD-related topics, and a few epidemiologists studying the social location of this disease among gay American men (Aral and Holmes 1999) and among heterosexuals in Africa. Otherwise, the analysis of AIDS remained mostly ghettoized in the medical literature until the mid-1980s. Until the publication in 1994 of the results from a large national survey of adult sexuality in the United States (Laumann et al. 1994), the best available data on sexual behavior were the Kinsey studies from the 1940s and early 1950s.

Finally, the combination of organized gay activism and public alarm created the kind of political pressure that made more money available and launched a flood of AIDS research. Indeed, interest in sex research in general, previously an area treated like a poor relation, received more credibility, though not enough to allow the funding of a nationally representative study of sexual behaviors. A large national study slated to be funded by the National Institutes of Health was stopped in 1990 after Senator Jesse Helms helped persuade the U.S. Senate that Americans should not be exposed to such questions. Nonetheless, research on sexuality, especially on STDs, found funds and larger and more diverse professional audiences. Even before the prevalence of AIDS among gay men was understood or publicized, some research described how great numbers of anonymous sexual contacts in gay bars, baths, and parks happened and how such activity set the stage for infection (Darrow 1979; Ross 1984; Klovdahl 1985). By the 1990s research attention had become focused on how sexual cultures, such as a "gay lifestyle," increased exposure to the human immunodeficiency virus (HIV). Later, the issue was reframed to focus on behaviors that place people at risk (rather than on the groups to which they belong) and the social and psychological factors that influence sexual decision making. This avenue of research affirms that sex is a social behavior that must be studied in its social context.

Current AIDS literature centers on two main issues: (1) who is at risk and why and (2) risk-reduction factors, including education.

WHO IN THE UNITED STATES IS AT RISK AND WHY

Most researchers include in their lists of risk factors number of partners, sex of partners, intravenous (IV) drug use or an IV-drug-using partner (Ehrhardt et al. 1995), frequency of intercourse (Aral and Cates 1989), use of condoms (Morrison et al. 1995), contact with commercial sex workers (Plummer et al. 1999), and sex with bisexual men (Doll and Ostrow 1999). The last factor has been of increasing interest, since there seems to be more bisexuality than mainstream research acknowledged previously and because this is an obvious bridge between high- and low-HIV-rate populations. Information about bisexuality has become important in efforts to understand AIDS transmission. For example, a study of lesbian women, a group usually thought of as low-risk, showed that not only had 81 percent of these women had sex with men, at least one-third of their male partners had had sex with other men. Women with bisexual male partners were also more likely to have had anal sex, an activity thought to be an especially efficient mode of HIV transmission (Padian et al. 1987). Bisexuality among men constitutes a greater risk factor than was previously recognized because these men may make regular forays into the gay male world unknown to their female partners.

This may be more likely to occur among married couples or in some minority communities, where the behavior itself may necessitate the utmost secrecy and may even be defined by the participants as "not homosexual" and therefore not risky (Carrier 1985; Blumstein and Schwartz 1977; Humphreys, 1975).

Other, less obvious risks include the possibility of deviousness or outright lies from a partner. In a poll conducted by Cochran and Mays (1990), 196 men and 226 women aged 18–25 completed an anonymous questionnaire on sexual strategies. The findings indicated that a significant number of both men and women had told a lie in order to have sex. Men lied more frequently than did women, but both sexes were actively and passively willing to deceive a date.

Sociodemographic characteristics also have been studied as risk factors. Age is one such factor. Among U.S. teenagers the rate of AIDS is low overall (less than 1 percent of AIDS cases); however, such data underestimate the risk because of the long incubation period from HIV infection to the development of AIDS (ten or more years). Moreover, AIDS rates are higher among more vulnerable subpopulations of adolescents, such as runaway and homeless youth, STD clinic populations, and young people in the juvenile justice system. Such youths are more likely to engage in activities, such as drug use and "survival sex," that put them at high risk of HIV infection. Particularly worrisome is the high rate of other STDs among teenagers, especially young women, because having an STD is thought to enhance the probability of becoming infected with HIV after exposure. Unfortunately, although condom use has increased among teenagers, adolescents still do not use condoms consistently (Sonenstein et al. 1998.). Teenagers in the United States have higher rates of nonmarital pregnancies than do their counterparts in any other industrialized nation despite the fact that they are no more sexually active than are teens in other countries. These facts suggest that teenagers in the United States are not adequately protecting themselves against the outcomes of their sexuality. This may be the result of a lack of comfort with the idea of teenage sexuality in a nation that sends mixed messages to its youth.

In general, better-educated persons are more likely to use condoms. College students, however, are surprisingly casual about condom use. In a study by Reinish et al. (1990), less than two-thirds of the students studied had used a condom in the previous year, less than one-third had used a condom the last time they had had vaginal or anal intercourse, and only half had ever used contraceptive methods that also prevent STD transmission. Those in exclusive sexual relationships reported the highest levels of intercourse. This finding prompted concern among the researchers that while it seems that being in a committed sexual relationship lowers the overall risk of HIV infection by reducing the number of partners, risk may be increased because of frequency of relations unless partners use condoms or have accurate information about each other's sexual and drug use histories. Even well-educated college students tend to use criteria irrelevant to AIDS transmission, such as "just knowing" a partner is safe, as a means of determining when condom use is necessary (Civic, in press). A set of qualitative research notes indicates that condom use may decrease, even among populations that most need to use them, for socioemotional reasons. Kane's (1990) population of women with HIV-probable partners in the drug culture refused, as an act of solidarity, to use condoms. These women felt that using a condom would indicate their awareness and condemnation of the partner's addiction, alienating him and harming the relationship.

In the United States, not all racial and ethnic groups have been equally affected by the AIDS epidemic. Although European-Americans initially were the group with the highest rate of AIDs, this is no longer true: AIDS rates among racial and ethnic minority groups have increased substantially since the beginning of the epidemic. Data from the CDC show that in 1990 whites accounted for over half the AIDS cases (56 percent in January 1990), but they now account for fewer than half the cases (46 percent in January 1998). African-Americans in impoverished inner cities have been especially hard hit. In January 1990, 27 percent of AIDS cases occurred among African-Americans, but by January 1998, this figure had increased to 35 percent.

The infection rate also has been increasing among Americans of Hispanic origin (18 percent of cases in January 1998).

One of the newest groups in the United States to receive research attention is women. Since AIDS surfaced in this country among gay men, the lack of attention to women might seem reasonable until one remembers that as partners of bisexual men or drug users, as drug users themselves, or as inhabitants of countries where AIDS is not a "gay disease," women always were at risk. AIDS has been increasing steadily among women in the United States. CDC figures show that in January 1989 women represented only 9 percent of AIDS cases, but by January of 1998 this figure rose to 16 percent, a 44 percent increase in less than a decade. Women also have substantially higher rates of chlamydia—the most prevalent bacterial STD—as well as genital herpes. Unfortunately, STDs are more likely to be asymptomatic in women, thus causing delayed treatment, increased complications such as infertility, and increased vulnerability to HIV infection.

Initially, IV drug use was the primary mode of AIDS transmission among U.S. women, but today, heterosexual intercourse is the primary mode. In late 1989, 52 percent of AIDS cases among women were attributable to IV drug use, whereas in June 1998, only 23 percent of cases were thought to be IV drug use–related. Most women with AIDS are of childbearing age. This increases the chances of transmission from an infected pregnant woman to her unborn baby as well as increasing the number of children, often in single-parent families, who are forced to cope with the prolonged illness and then loss of a mother. The effects of AIDS on children have only recently begun to be studied. Studies show that between 13 and 35 percent of babies born to HIV-positive women are HIV-infected, a figure that has been rapidly declining since the beginning of the AIDS epidemic, largely as a result of the advent of newer antiviral drugs. Many pregnant HIV-infected women, even with knowledge of the risk, choose not to abort (*Proceedings NIMH/NIDA Conference on Women and AIDS* 1989). AIDS concerns attend other reproductive issues as well, such as the safety of artificial insemination. While the American Fertility Association has guidelines that exclude high-risk men from donating sperm, methods for testing for HIV seem to be inconsistent, and private physicians may not test at all (Campbell 1990).

The use of alcohol and drugs has been shown to be related to unsafe sex practices, although there have been contradictory findings (Leigh and Stall 1993 provide for a review). Fullilove and Fullilove (1989), for example, found that 62 percent of the 222 black inner-city teenagers they studied used crack, and 51 percent of the users said they combined crack use with sex. Forty-one percent of the teenagers surveyed had had at least one STD; those who used crack with sex had a significantly higher rate of STD infection. The correlation between crack use, sex, and STD transmission has been found by many other investigators (Aral and Holmes 1999). Although crack use has declined substantially since the late 1980s, the use of other drugs (e.g., methamphetamines) that also appear to be related to unsafe sex has risen. Leigh (1990) found that patterns of drug use and the effects of drugs on behavior differ among groups: Gay men were less affected by drinking and engaged in more risk taking when using cocaine, whereas heterosexual risk taking was predicted largely by total frequency of sex, with only a small amount of the variance explained by having partners who used drugs or alcohol. A note of caution is warranted in interpreting the findings of studies of the relationship between sexual practices and substance use. Most of this research that shows a relationship between substance use and risky sex has not demonstrated that substance use *causes* risky sex, because researchers rarely have information on which came first. Moreover, it is conceivable that a third factor, such as a propensity to take risks, is responsible for both substance use and sexual risk taking (Leigh and Stall 1993). Clearly, more research is needed.

Research has increasingly concentrated on infection resulting from exchange of blood caused by mutual use of needles during intravenous drug use. In a paper by Freeman et al. (1987), a comparison of gay males and IV drug users showed that peer support helped create safer sexual practices

for gays while lack of social organization reduced IV drug users' chance of self-protection. Among the drug users, 95 percent were well aware of their exposure and 68 percent knew that needle sharing could transmit AIDS. Some individual attempts at decreasing the use of potentially contaminated needles had been made, but the authors felt that the only way to reduce risk in this population was to create organizations for needle dispensation that eventually could create a culture of mutual protection. Opinion has changed from considering IV drug users uneducable to recognizing substantial successes in changing their drug-taking practices to include more self-protective habits. Still, ethnography shows that needle sharing between addicted partners is seen as an intimate and bonding behavior, and this makes change more difficult. Moreover, despite their demonstrated effectiveness, needle-exchange programs are under attack by conservatives who claim that they encourage drug use, even though there is no evidence to support that contention.

Although sexual behavior certainly has biological underpinning, it is clear from the research that sexual behavior and the spread of STDs are socially driven. Sociocultural factors, not biology, determine not only with whom one has sex, whether and when one is likely to have sex, and the specific forms of sexual expression in which one engages but even which persons, activities, and things are experienced as erotic. This fact is eminently evident in the early studies of the Kinsey group, Ford and Beach's (1951) cross-cultural studies, and more recent research (e.g., Laumann et al. 1994).

RISK REDUCTION AND EDUCATION IN THE UNITED STATES

It is difficult to discuss risk without touching on risk reduction. Indeed, a growing body of research literature reports the results of studies investigating specific risk-reduction strategies, curricula, and behavior modification that targets specific populations—such as gay men, minority group members, teenagers, mothers, and drug users—with what is hoped to be a useful approach.

The most encouraging findings indicate that it is possible to change risky sexual behavior. This is a significant discovery, since many personal habits, such as drinking and overeating, are notoriously resistant to sustained modification. In the 1980s, researchers in San Francisco found that gay men there had reduced their numbers of partners and frequency of sex and increased their use of safer sex practices (McKusick et al. 1985). However, since much of this change was attributed to the extraordinary social power of organized gay groups in that city, the question arose whether such dramatic changes could occur among gay men who are less embedded in gay communities (Fisher 1988). However, change has occurred across the United States, indicating both the strength of educational and social control efforts among gay activists and, perhaps, the great motivation for change that exists when suffering and death are not only possible but probable (Martin 1987; Siegal and Glassman 1989; Roffman et al. 1998).

This conclusion is not self-evident because change in gay male circles has not been complete. Changes in behavior are associated with proximity to populations with high incidences of the disease: The more distance, the less change in behavior (Fox et al. 1987). Furthermore, even in densely infected areas, a significant minority of HIV-infected persons seem to continue engaging in risky sexual practices (Kelly et al. 1998). There is even evidence that for some men, fear wears off and unprotected sex practices increase (Martin 1987), whereas for others, initial changes toward safer sex are difficult to maintain in the long run (Kelly et al. 1998).

Naturally, there is a great deal of pressure on researchers to find out what helps all kinds of people protect themselves from AIDS. Depressingly but predictably, is has been found education alone is inadequate to induce behavior change. For example, Calabrese et al. (1987) reported that for gay men outside big cities, attendance at a safe-sex lecture, reading a safe-sex brochure, HIV antibody testing, advice from a physician, and counseling were all inadequate. Other sex education efforts have had a limited effect, often for a limited period. For example, researchers assessed the impact of a ten-week university course on human sexuality and AIDS-related behavior. While stu-

dents who had taken the course possessed more information about actual risk, worried about AIDS more, and asked sexual partners more questions relating to AIDS than did a control group, they did not increase their use of condoms or other contraceptives, decrease the number of sexual partners, or spend a longer time getting to know a prospective partner (Baldwin et al. 1990). Studies have consistently shown that sex education for adolescents is necessary but not sufficient to produce behavioral changes (Kirby and Coyle 1997).

The disappointing results of sex education have led researchers to search for more viable strategies. Because self-esteem, confidence, and ego strength have been hypothesized to help individuals protect themselves from others' as well as their own desires, a number of researchers have looked for ways to bolster these characteristics (Becher 1988). To date, the most promising programs appear to be ones that are conceptually based and provide information and skill building, enhance motivation and normative support for change, and are ethnically and culturally sensitive (Fisher and Fisher 1992 provide a review).

No one believes that any single approach is appropriate for all audiences. Increasingly, this literature has been investigating separate strategies for different groups. Students of race, ethnicity, and gender understand not only that various groups use language differently but also that reality is filtered through culture. This sociological truism has benefited research and education among at-risk populations. An example is understanding how gender differences affect health behavior. Campbell (1990) noted the limitations of educational programs aimed at women, especially non–IV drug users, who resist feeling at risk. She found that the partners of IV drug users are unlikely to be assertive and to insist on safer sex. Most of these women are already in subordinate, if not abusive, situations, and their vulnerability and passivity have to be addressed before progress can be made. This fact is underscored by findings from a study in which Beadnell et al. (in press) report that a strong predictor of the extent of at-risk women's attendance at a multi session AIDS prevention intervention is whether they are in an abusive relationship. Campbell (1990) warns that there are special considerations about condom use among minority group women, since minority group men may reject condoms more resolutely than do white men. Campbell also reminds the reader that in educating commercial sex workers both for their own safety and for that of others, one needs to take into account the dual issues of their gender and their profession. She argues against overreliance on women as the safety net in sexual relations. To date, little AIDS research has focused on heterosexual men.

Among working and lower-income African-Americana women, gender issues often make safe-sex guidelines seem impossibly theoretical. Unemployment has put African-American men in transient relations with African-American women, and partners are unlikely to engage in the kind of cooperative communication many safe-sex guidelines assume (Fullilove, et al. 1994). Fullilove et al. also highlight black women's and teenagers' increased vulnerability to disease because of relatively high rates of nonmonogamy among potential partners. Those authors feel that individual strategies are unlikely to be as powerful as a "reknitting of community connections" for the evolution of protective norms. Social disorganization further complicates the problem by giving less and less accurate information to African-American and Hispanic populations.

Even designing messages for minorities or finding community outlets for their dissemination does not begin to handle the difficulty of reaching and influencing at-risk persons. Target audiences for prevention are not necessarily self-identified. For example, almost no AIDS-prevention research has been conducted with lesbian women who may have occasional intercourse with bisexual partners and do not consider themselves at risk. Latino men who occasionally visit gay bars and have anal intercourse often do not use condoms with their wives in part because, as the "activo," they do not see themselves as homosexual or as having participated in a homosexual act and therefore do not perceive themselves as being at risk (Magana 1990). Similarly, because virginity before marriage is highly valued in Latino culture, young unmarried Latinas may engage in higher-risk anal sex in order to remain "technical virgins." Given the high value placed on motherhood among Latinas, using condoms during vaginal sex can imply that a man's intentions are less than honorable by eliminating the possibility of motherhood. Almost nothing is known about the sexual practices of Asian-Americans, perhaps because they have been depicted as the "model" minority. However, some data suggest that Asian-American youths are less knowledgeable about AIDS than are other groups (Wells et al. 1995), and a substantial minority of Asian-American adolescents have been shown to engage in unprotected sex (Schuster et al. 1998). Issues of identification, culture, and gender relations bedevil both researchers and health workers.

Despite the optimism of biomedical researchers, there is still no cure for AIDS or an effective vaccine against contracting HIV. Therefore, behavioral change remains the best hope for controlling the epidemic. Sociological and psychological theories have generated a number of programs that appear to be effective in reducing an individual's risk of contracting HIV. Most of these programs have focused on changing individuals' skills, knowledge, attitudes, and behaviors. However, sexual intercourse is inherently dyadic, and partner issues will need greater attention for such programs to achieve maximum effect, especially for women, who often do not have control over their sexuality. Moreover, the advent of new antiviral drugs and protease inhibitors has transformed the character of the AIDS epidemic to the public at large and the researchers as well as to those with HIV infection. Many people in the United States now view AIDS as a manageable chronic illness rather than a death sentence. Persons with AIDS are living longer, mortality rates have decreased, and those infected with HIV do not appear to be developing AIDS at the same rate as was the case before the use of these new drugs. In response to this change, the focus of AIDS research has changed: Researchers are increasingly studying how to prevent or reduce adverse outcomes, such as depression and relapse to unsafe behaviors, and enhance the quality of life among those living with HIV and AIDS (Kelly et al. 1998 provide a cogent discussion). However, the new drugs are not a panacea. For some, they do not work at all; for others, they appear to work initially but then gradually become ineffective; and for far too many, the enormous cost of the drugs is beyond their means. The latter fact is even more tragic when one considers that in the United States most new cases of HIV infection are occurring among society's most vulnerable populations.

THE INTERNATIONAL SCENE

Data on STDs, including AIDS, from other countries are inadequate because many countries, especially third world nations, do not have sophisticated systems to monitor these diseases. The World Health Organization (WHO) estimates that the current annual prevalence of STDs is about 333 million cases worldwide, with about 5.8 million persons being newly infected with HIV in 1997. In 1999 there were nearly 31 million persons living with HIV or AIDS worldwide. If the current trend continues, WHO estimates that more than 40 million persons will be infected with HIV by the year 2000. To date, over eleven million people worldwide have died of AIDS, and in 1998 alone, about 2.3 million deaths were attributable to AIDS, 46 percent of which occurred among women. The vast majority of cases of STDs worldwide, including AIDS, have occurred in developing countries, and the growth of the AIDS epidemic has been fastest in sub-Saharan Africa, which is thought to have two-thirds of the world's population of persons infected with HIV. Although rates of infection are lower in Asia, where the epidemic started later, the number infected there is estimated to be quite large. In North America, western Europe, Australia and New Zealand, and a few third world countries that have sound economies (e.g., Costa Rica, Thailand), rates of several STDs (e.g., syphilis and gonorrhea) have been declining steadily over the past decade, but they have been skyrocketing (or being reported better) in regions such as China and Russia and remain high in Africa and Asia.

Why is the AIDS epidemic so heavily concentrated in the developing world? Decosas (1996) argues that differences in sexual behaviors alone cannot explain this fact. He argues that the high incidence of untreated STDs that increase vulnerability to HIV infection, cultural factors such as age differences between male and female sexual partners (older persons typically have more sexual partners and therefore an increased likelihood of exposure to HIV), and demographic factors such as large-scale labor migration and refugee movements have all contributed to the difference. All these factors are related directly or indirectly to poverty and gender inequality. Young women in third world countries, for example, often have limited access to education or vocational training and may have few alternatives for economic survival other than having sex with men. Studies in Africa suggest that women in traditional relationships typically do not engage in risky sexual practices, yet they are increasingly being infected with HIV (Way et al. 1999). Even women who report having only one sexual partner in their lives and who believe that they are in monogamous relationships are found to be infected with HIV. In many regions of Africa, however, men not infrequently engage in extramarital sexual relations, often with higher-risk partners such as commercial sex workers (Way et al. 1999).

Today, the AIDS epidemic worldwide is spread primarily through heterosexual contact. As more women of childbearing age become infected, perinatal transmission from mother to infant is increasing. In urban areas of Uganda, Zambia, Malawi, and parts of Southern Africa, for example, HIV infection among pregnant women has been increasing rapidly; more than one-fifth, and in some areas up to 40 percent, of these women have been found to be HIV-positive (Way et al. 1999). There are important differences across the globe in the main mode of AIDS transmission and who has been infected as well as substantial differences in these factors within regions. In China, for example, there appears to be two epidemics: one among IV drug users in the mountainous regions and the southwestern areas and the other in the more prosperous eastern coastal areas, where commercial sex is reemerging in response to the growing gap between rich and poor. Ironically, AIDS was virtually unknown in China before that country it opened its borders. In Africa, the highest HIV prevalence rates occur in urban as opposed to rural areas. In Mexico and Latin America, the epidemic is concentrated among the poorest and most marginalized members of society, as is becoming increasingly true of the United States. In eastern Europe, IV drug use accounts for the majority of new infections. Not only are there important differences in the major modes of AIDS transmission worldwide, the modes of transmission within regions have changed over time (Way et al. 1999). This is evident in the United States, where the AIDS epidemic first appeared among gay men, then among IV drug users, and now among racial and ethnic minorities and women. In Latin America, AIDS was first concentrated among IV drug users and gay men, but heterosexual sex is playing an increasing role in its transmission. The epidemic in Asia is moving rapidly from high-risk populations to the general population, largely as a result of heterosexual transmission. In developing nations particularly, new AIDS cases are occurring among younger persons.

The rate of STDs worldwide is alarming because although the most common nonviral STDs (syphilis, gonorrhea, chlamydia, and trichomoniasis) are curable, they are often initially asymptomatic. This is especially so for women, who also are more likely than men to become infected if exposed. Moreover, the increased mobility of populations, accompanied by urbanization, poverty, sexual exploitation of women, and changes in sexual behaviors, places an increasing proportion of the world's population at risk. Because younger people make up a much larger proportion of the population in developing nations than they do in industrialized ones and because younger persons today have more sexual partners than was previously the case, one can expect to see a steeper rise in the rate of AIDS in these countries.

Uganda was among the first nations to respond to the AIDS epidemic, making a strong effort to prevent the spread of the disease that appears to be having an effect, as is evident in the declining proportion of persons infected with HIV (Asiimwe-Okiror et al. 1997). This decline is consistent with behavioral studies that show increased condom use, delay in sexual initiation, and a decline in the number of sex partners. Similarly, in Zaire, condom use among commercial sex workers dramatically increased from zero to 68 percent after a three-year condom promotion program (Adler 1998). The result was a marked decline in STDs. In Thailand, which is believed to have the best documented AIDS epidemic among developing countries, an aggressive and sustained national campaign to reduce HIV infection rates was instigated once authorities recognized that there was an epidemic. The campaign focused on increasing condom use, promoting respect for women, discouraging men from having sex with commercial sex workers, and increasing opportunities for education and employment to keep younger women from becoming commercial sex workers. The effects of this campaign have demonstrated the success of a concerted national effort. The use of condoms among commercial sex workers rose from 14 percent in 1989 to over 90% by 1994, rates of STDs declined, and the rate of new HIV infections has been declining, especially among commercial sex workers and their clients (Rojanapithayakorn and Hanenberg 1996). The success of this campaign has been attributed to several factors, including use of the existing infrastructure, a focus on a limited goal (improving condom use among commercial sex workers rather than trying to eliminate prostitution), widespread advertising, and a systematic means of monitoring the epidemic. Although less dramatic, local programs in other third world countries appear to be having some impact, as they have had in the United States. In Uganda, for example, a longitudinal study in an urban area showed a substantial increase in condom use, delay of sexual initiation, and a decrease in casual sex among adolescents over a period of two years. These changes were accompanied by a 40 percent decline in HIV seroprevalence among pregnant women who attended antenatal clinics (Asiimwe-Okiror et al. 1997). Similarly, a study of urban factory workers in Tanzania showed a decline over a two-year period in the number of sexual partners and casual sex, although condom use did not increase substantially (Ng'weshemi et al. 1996). A behavioral risk reduction program targeting truckers in Kenya has shown significant declines in extramarital sex and sex with commercial sex workers, although condom has not changed. These behavioral changes were accompanied by significant declines in STDs such as gonorrhea. In Bolivia, an HIV prevention intervention aimed at commercial sex workers appears to have increased condom use and resulted in lower STD rates in this high-risk group (Levine et al. 1998). In Jamaica, researchers have concluded that a comprehensive HIV/STD control program has resulted in reduced rates of STDs and increased condom use, although a significant minority continue to have unprotected sex in high-risk situations (Figueroa et al. 1998). Officials in some countries, such as India, deny that AIDS is a problem in their regions, and few efforts have been launched to stem the possibility of a widespread AIDS epidemic in those areas.

CONCLUSIONS

Studies have demonstrated that the psychosocial and economic impact of AIDS extends far beyond the persons infected (Carael et al. 1998). Families have been shown to suffer from stress, economic hardship, stigma, and discrimination when one of their members has AIDS. Women, especially in third world countries, are in structurally less powerful positions than men and often have little or no control over their own sexual safety. These socioeconomic effects of AIDS, along with increasing mortality from AIDS among those in the most productive years of their lives, are expected to increase the gap between rich and poor and contribute to the feminization of poverty (Decosas 1996). Moreover, an infrequently mentioned consequence of AIDS in developing nations is its effect on children, who are being orphaned at alarming rates; WHO estimates that over eight million children in the world have been orphaned because of AIDS. In some areas of the world, AIDS may be changing the demography. It has been estimated that in areas hardest hit by the epidemic, life expectancy has declined by as much as seventeen years and mortality rates for children under age 5 have increased by 74 percent (Stover and Way 1998). Demographers project that by the year

2005, there will be 13 to 59 million fewer people and a 27 percent reduction in life expectancy in countries with the most severe epidemic compared with what have been the case if AIDS had not hit those regions (Stover and Way 1998). Mortality rates from AIDS are expected to continue to increase, and the gap in the death rates from AIDS in developing and developed countries is expected to grow wider. Finally, most people in third world countries cannot afford or do not have access to the new drugs that have prolonged lives of persons living with HIV or AIDS in the United States; thus, mortality rates there are not likely to drop. This may mean, as Way et al. (1999, p. 90) predict, that "the worst is yet to come."

The emergence of AIDS as a social issue not only has revitalized interest in the social context and consequences of STDs, it has caused medical research to understand more fully how disease can never be studied effectively apart from social conditions or without adequate information about relevant social actors. Still in its infancy is a fuller consideration of institutional and public responses to STDs, for example, how public policy gets made and by whom (Volinn 1989) or why some communities respond with compassion, others with fear, and others not at all. The social construction of disease, and that of STDs in particular, is an important and understudied area of social science research.

REFERENCES

Adler, M. 1998 "Strategies for the Prevention and Treatment of Sexually Transmitted Diseases." *International Journal of STD & AIDS* 9:8–10.

Aral, S., and W. Cates 1989 "The Multiple Dimensions of Sexual Behavior as Risk Factors for Sexually Transmitted Disease: The Sexually Experienced Are Not Necessarily Sexually Active." *Sexually Transmitted Diseases* 16:173–177.

——, and K. Holmes 1999 "Social and Behavioral Determinants of the Epidemiology of STDs: Industrialized and Developing Countries." In K. Holmes, P. F. Starling, P. A. Mardh, S. Lemon, W. Stamm, P. Piot, and J. Wasserheit, eds., *Sexually Transmitted Diseases*, 3rd ed. New York: McGraw-Hill.

Asiimwe-Okiror, G., A. A. Opio, J. Musinguzi, E. Madraa, G. Tembo, and M. Carael. 1997 "Change in Sexual Behaviour and Decline in HIV Infection among Young Pregnant Women in Urban Uganda. *AIDS* 11:1757–1763.

Baldwin, J. I., S. Whitely, and J. D. Baldwin 1990 "Changing AIDS and Fertility Related Behavior: The Effectiveness of Sexual Education." *Journal of Sex Research* 27:245–262.

Beadnell, B., S. A. Baker, D. M. Morrison, and K. Knox (in press) "HIV/STD Risk Factors for Women with Violent Male Partners. *Sex Roles*.

Becher, M. H. 1988 "AIDS and Behavior Change." *Public Health Review* 16:1–11.

Blumstein, P., and P. Schwarz 1976 "Male Bisexuality." *Urban Life.*5:339–358.

Brandt, A. M. 1985 *No Magic Bullet*. New York: Oxford University Press.

Calabrese, L. H., B. Harris, and K. Easly 1987 "Analysis of Variables Impacting on Safe Sexual Behavior among Homosexual Men in an Area of Low Incidence for AIDS." Paper presented at the Third International Conference on AIDS, Washington, D.C.

Campbell, C. A. 1990 "Women and AIDS." *Social Science and Medicine* 30:407–415.

Carael, M., B. Schwartlander, and D. Zewdie 1998 Preface to *AIDS* 12(suppl 1):S1–S2.

Carrier, J. M. 1985 "Mexican Male Bisexuality." *Journal of Homosexuality* 1:75–85.

Civic, D. in press "College Students' Reasons for Non-Use of Condoms within Dating Relationships." *Journal of Sex and Marital Therapy.*

Cochran, S. D., and V. M. Mays 1990 "Sex, Lies and HIV." *New England Journal of Medicine* 322:774–775.

Darrow, William 1979 "Sexually Transmitted Diseases in Gay Men. An Insider's View." *Sexually Transmitted Diseases* 6:278–280.

Decosas, J. 1996 "HIV and Development." *AIDS* 10(suppl 3):S69–S74.

Doll, L. S., and D. G. Ostrow 1999 "Homosexual and Bisexual Behavior." In K. Holmes, P. F. Starling, P. A. Mardh, S. Lemon, W. Stamm, P. Piot, and J. Wasserheit, eds., *Sexually Transmitted Diseases*, 3rd ed. New York: McGraw-Hill.

Ehrhardt, A. A., C. Nosetlinger, H. F. L. Meyer-Bahlburg, T. M. Exner, R. S. Gruen, S. L. Yingling, J. M. Gorman, W. El-Sadr, and S J. Sorrell 1995 "Sexual Risk Behavior among Women with Injected Drug use

Histories." *Journal of Psychology and Human Sexuality* 7:99–19.

Figueroa, J. P., A. R. Brathwaite, M. Wedderburn, E. Ward, K. Lewis-Bell, J. A. Amon, Y. Williams, and E. Williams 1998. "Is HIV/STD Control in Jamaica Making a Difference?" *AIDS* 12(suppl 2):S89–S98.

Fisher, J. D. 1988 "Possible Effects of Reference Group Based Social Influence on AIDS-Risk Behavior and AIDS Prevention." *American Psychologist* 49:914–920.

——, and W. A. Fisher 1992 "Changing AIDS-Risk Behavior." *Psychological Bulletin* 111:455–474.

Ford, C. S., and F. A. Beach 1951 *Patterns of Sexual Behavior.* New York: Harper.

Fox, R., D. Ostrow, R. Valdiserri, B. Van Rader, and B. F. Pall 1987 "Changes in Sexual Activities among Participants in the Multi Center AIDS Cohort Study." Paper presented at the Third International Conference on AIDS, Washington, D.C.

Freeman, S. R., D. C. Des Jarlais, J. L. Sotheran, J. Garber, H. Cohen, and D. Smith 1987 "AIDS and Self-Organization among Intravenous Drug Users." *International Journal of Addictions* 23:201–219.

Fullilove, M. T., and R. E. Fullilove 1989 "Intersecting Epidemics: Black Teen Crack Use and Sexually Transmitted Disease." *Journal of American Women's Association* 44:146–153.

——, R. E. Fullilove, K. Hayes, and S. Gross 1994 "Black Women and AIDS Prevention: A View toward Understanding the Gender Rules." *Journal of Sex Research* 27(1):47–64.

Hart, G. 1978 "Social and Psychological Aspects of Venereal Disease in Papua New Guinea." *British Journal of Venereal Disease* 54:215–217.

Humphreys, L. 1975. *Tearoom Trade: Impersonal Sex in Public Places*. Chicago: Aldine.

Kalm, F. 1985 "The Two Faces of Antillean Prostitution." *Archives of Sexual Behavior* 14:203–217.

Kane, S. 1990 "AIDS, Addiction and Condom Use: Sources of Sexual Risk for Heterosexual Women." *Journal of Sex Research* 27:427–444.

Kelly, J. A., L. L. Otto-Salaj, K. J. Sikkema, S. D. Pinkerton, and F. R. Bloom 1998 "Implications of HIV Treatment Advances for Behavioral Research on AIDS: Protease Inhibitors and New Challenges in HIV Secondary Prevention." *Health Psychology* 17:310–319.

Kirby, D., and K. Coyle 1997 "School-Based Programs to Reduce Sexual Risk-Taking Behavior." *Children and Youth Services Review* 19:415–436.

Klovdahl, Alden S. 1985 "Social Networks and the Spread of Infectious Diseases: The AIDS Example." *Social Science Medicine* 21:1203–1216.

Laumann, E. O., J. H. Gagnon, R. T. Michael, and S. Michaels 1994 *The Social Organization of Sexuality.* Chicago: University of Chicago Press.

Leigh, B. C. 1990 "Sex and Drugs." *Journal of Sex Research* 27:199–213.

——, and R. D. Stall 1993 "Substance Use and Risky Sexual Behavior for Exposure to HIV: Issues in Methodology, Interpretation, and Prevention." *American Psychologist* 48:1035–1045.

Levine, W. C., R. Revollo, V. Kaune, J. Vega, F. Tinajeros, M. Garnica, M. Estenssoro, J. S. Lewis, G. Higueras, R. Zurita, L. Wright-DeAguero, R. Pareja, P. Miranda, R. L. Ransom, A. A. Zaidi, M. L. Melgar, and J. N. Kuritsky 1998. "Decline in Sexually Transmitted Disease Prevalence in Female Bolivian Sex Workers: Impact of an HIV Prevention Project." *AIDS* 12:1899–1906.

Magana, Raul 1990 "Bisexuality among Hispanics." Paper Presented at *CDC Workshop on Bisexuality and AIDS, American Institutes for Research.*

Martin, J. L. 1987 "The Impact of AIDS on Gay Male Sexual Behavioral Patterns in New York City." *American Journal of Public Health* 77:578–584.

McKusick, L., J. A. Wiley, T. J. Coates, R. Stall, G. Saika, S. Morin, K. Charles, W. Horstman, and M. A. Conant 1985 "Reported Changes in the Sexual Behavior of Men at Risk for AIDS in San Francisco 1982–84: The AIDS Behavioral Research Project." *Public Health Report* 100:622–629.

Morrison, D. M., M. R. Gillmore, and S. A. Baker 1995 "Determinants of Condom Use among High-Risk Heterosexual Adults: A Test of the Theory of Reasoned Action." *Journal of Applied Social Psychology* 25:651–676.

Ng'weshemi, J. Z. L., J. T. Boerma, R. Pool, L. Barongo, K. Senkoro, M. Maswe, R. Isingo, D. Schapink, S. Nnko, and M. W. Borgdorff 1996 "Changes in Males' Sexual Behaviour in Response to the AIDS Epidemic: Evidence from a Cohort Study in Urban Tanzania." *AIDS* 10:1415–1420.

O'Reilly, K. R., and S. O. Aral 1985 "Adolescence and Sexual Behavior: Trends and Implications for STDs." *Journal of Adolescent Health Care* 6:262–270.

Padian, N., L. Marquis, D. P. Francis, R. E. Anderson, G. W. Rutherford, P. M. O'Malley, and W. Winkelstein 1987 "Male to Female Transmission of Human Immunodeficiency Virus." *Journal of the American Medical Association* 258:788–790.

Plummer, F. A., R. A. Coutinho, E. N. Ngugi, and S. Moses 1999 "Sex Workers and Their Clients in the Epidemiology and Control of Sexually Transmitted Diseases." In K. Holmes, P. F. Starling, P. A. Mardh, S. Lemon, W. Stamm, P. Piot, and J. Wasserheit, eds., *Sexually Transmitted Diseases*, 3rd ed. New York: McGraw-Hill.

Poherat, J. J., R. Rothenberg, and D. C. Bross 1981 "Gonorrhea in Street Prostitutes: Epidemiology and Legal Implications." *Sexually Transmitted Diseases* 8:241–244.

Proceedings NIMH/NIDA Conference on Women and AIDS: Promoting Health Behavior 1989 Washington, D.C.: American Psychiatric Press.

Reinish, J. M., C. A. Hill, S. A. Sanders, and M. Ziemba-Davis 1990 "Sexual Behavior among Heterosexual College Students" *Focus* 5:3.

Roffman, R. A., R. S. Stephens, L. Curtin, J. R. Gordon, J. N. Craver, M. Stern, B. Beadnell, and L. Downey 1998 "Relapse Prevention as an Interventive Model for HIV Risk Reduction in Gay and Bisexual Men." *AIDS Education and Prevention* 10:1–18.

Rojanapithayakorn, W., and R. Hanenberg 1996 "The 100% Condom Program in Thailand." *AIDS* 10:1–7.

Ross, M. W. 1984 "Sexually Transmitted Diseases in Homosexual Men: A Study of Four Societies." *British Journal of Venereal Disease* 60:52–66.

Schuster, M. R. Bell, G. Nakajima, and D. Kanouse 1998. "The Sexual Practices of Asian and Pacific Islander High School Students." *Journal of Adolescent Health* 23:221–231.

Shilts, R. 1987 *And the Band Played On.* New York: St. Martin's.

Siegal, K., and M. Glassman 1989 "Individual and Aggregate Level Change in Sexual Behavior among Gay Men at Risk for AIDS." *Archives of Sexual Behavior* 18:335–348.

Sonenstein, F. L., L. Ku, L. D. Lindberg, C. F. Turner, and J. H. Pleck 1998. "Changes in Sexual Behavior and Condom Use among Teenaged Males: 1988 to 1995." *American Journal of Public Health* 88:956–959.

Stover, J., and P. Way 1998. "Projecting the Impact of AIDS on Mortality." 1998 *AIDS* 12(suppl 1):S29–S39.

Volinn, I. 1989 "Issues of Definitions and Their Implication: AIDS and Leprosy." *Social Science and Medicine* 20:1157–1162.

Washington, A. E., R. L. Sweet, and M. A. B. Shafer 1985 "Pelvic Inflammatory Disease and Its Sequelae in Adolescents." *Journal of Adolescent Health Care* 6:298–310.

Way, P. O., B. Schwartlander, and P. Piot 1999. "The Global Epidemiology of HIV and AIDS." In K. Holmes, P. F. Starling, P. A. Mardh, S. Lemon, W. Stamm, P. Piot, and J. Wasserheit, eds., *Sexually Transmitted Diseases*, 3rd ed. New York: McGraw-Hill.

Wells, E. A., M. J. Hoppe, E. E. Simpson, M. R. Gillmore, D. M. Morrison, and A. Wilsdon 1995. "Misconceptions about AIDS among Children Who Can Identify the Major Routes of HIV Transmission." *Journal of Pediatric Psychology* 20:671–686.

Wood, C. S. 1978 "Syphillis in Anthropological Perspective." *Social Science and Medicine* 12:47–55.

PEPPER SCHWARTZ
MARY ROGERS GILLMORE

SLAVERY AND INVOLUNTARY SERVITUDE

Many observers view slavery and freedom as polar opposites, but both slave and free wage labor systems rely on compulsion. Slave systems depend ultimately on physical coercion to force slaves to work for masters, although cultural, ideological, and economic pressures typically augment physical force. Wage labor systems, by contrast, depend on workers being free "in the double sense" (Marx [1867] 1967, pp. 168–169): Not only must workers be free to seek employment and choose among potential employers, they also must be free of all other means of subsistence that would allow voluntary withdrawal from the labor market. In the absence of subsistence alternatives, economic necessity compels "free" workers to exchange labor services for wages. Although wage labor systems depend primarily on labor-market processes to supply employers with workers, physical coercion often supplements those processes, especially during periods of economic decline. Cultural expectations and ideological appeals also reinforce market mechanisms. Nevertheless, large-scale labor systems are maintained primarily by a mixture of physical and economic coercion that varies with the availability of subsistence alternatives.

The way in which the constellation of physical and economic coercion and subsistence alternatives is determined by the power of contending groups as well as historically specific cultural and ideological factors has been of great interest to social scientists. Perhaps the simplest and most durable statement of the causes of slavery is a conjecture known as the Nieboer–Domar hypothesis (Nieboer 1900; Domar 1970; Engerman 1986a; see Patterson 1977b for a critique), which links slavery to an abundance of arable land combined with a shortage of labor. The way in which slavery differs from other forms of involuntary servitude is explained in the next section. The Nieboer–Domar hypothesis is then amended to provide a provisional explanation for the worldwide trend away from slavery and toward freedom in large-scale labor systems over the last several hundred years. Finally, the Nieboer–Domar hypothesis is reevaluated in light of current patterns of slavery and involuntary servitude around the world.

SLAVERY AND OTHER FORMS OF INVOLUNTARY SERVITUDE

Patterson (1982, p. 13) argues that slavery is defined by three conditions. First, slaves suffer perpetual domination that ultimately is enforced by violence. The permanent subjugation of slaves is predicated on the capacity of masters to coerce them physically. Second, slaves suffer natal alienation, or the severance of all family ties and the nullification of all claims of birth. They inherit no protection or privilege from their ancestors, and they cannot convey protection or privilege to their descendants. Third, slaves are denied honor, whereas masters are socially exalted. This condition appears to be derivative rather than definitive of slavery because all hierarchical social systems develop legitimating ideologies that elevate elites and denigrate those at lower levels. The first two conditions, which distinguish slavery from other forms of involuntary servitude, constitute the working definition used in this article.

In chattel slave systems, slaves are movable property owned by masters and exchanged through market processes. Because some societies constructed elaborate slave systems without well-developed notions of property and property rights, property relationships cannot be an essential defining element of slavery (Patterson 1982; 1977a). Nevertheless, property relations and economic processes had important effects on slavery and other forms of unfree labor in the Americas, Europe, and Africa in the period after the fifteenth century, which is the major focus of this analysis.

An unfree laborer cannot voluntarily terminate service to a master once the servile relationship has been established. Slavery maximizes the subordination of servant to master. Other servile workers, such as indentured and contract laborers, debt servants, peons, and pawns, are less dominated than slaves are and do not suffer natal alienation. Pawns, for example, were offered by their families in return for loans. Pawns maintained kinship ties to their original families, a situation which gave them some protection, and were freed once the loans were repaid. Indentured servants agreed to be bound to a master for a specific term, such as seven years, in exchange for a benefit such as passage to America or release from prison (Morris 1946; Smith 1947; Morgan 1975). Contract laborers also were bound for specified terms but could not be sold against their will to other masters, as was the case with indentured servants. Debt servitude consists of labor service obligations that are not reduced by the amount of work performed (Morris 1946; Sawyer 1986). Peons are tied to land as debt servants and owe labor services to a landlord. Serfs are not debt servants, but they are tied to land and perform labor services on their lords' estates. The right to labor services enjoyed by European feudal lords was vested in their political authority rather than in land ownership, although serfs were reduced to slaves in all but name in some instances (e.g., Russia in the nineteenth century) (Kolchin 1987).

Indentured servants and contract laborers may agree to the initial terms of their servitude, but they cannot willingly end it during its term once it begins. Usually some form of coercion, such as poverty, debt, or impending imprisonment, was necessary to force people to agree to terms of contractual servitude or pawnship. By contrast, the status of the slave, serf, peon, and debt servant typically was inherited or imposed on workers against their will.

SLAVERY, THE LAND–LABOR RATIO, AND THE STATE

In its simplest form, the Nieboer–Domar hypothesis states that abundant free land makes it impossible for free workers and nonworking landowners to coexist. If free land is available and laborers can desert landowners whenever they choose, landowners will be unable to keep enough workers to maintain their status as nonworkers. If landlords can compel workers to perform labor services despite the availability of free land, landlords become labor lords and workers are not free. By contrast, scarce land combined with an abundant labor supply drives wages down, making wage laborers less expensive than slaves and other servile workers. When they are denied access to land, hunger forces workers to labor for wages and wage labor systems displace slave labor systems.

This model appears to be deficient in at least four ways. First, as Domar recognized, political factors determine the degree of freedom enjoyed by workers. Chief among those factors is the extent to which the state protects the interests of landowners when they conflict with those of laborers. Large-scale slave labor systems cannot exist without states that defend the power of slave masters to control and utilize the labor of slaves. A powerful state is essential for protecting slave masters against slave rebellions, capturing runaways, and enforcing slave discipline. State power is required for the enslavement of new supplies of slaves. If the state is responsive to the demands of workers or if workers can voluntarily withdraw their labor services, unfree labor systems cannot be maintained.

Second, the model presumes that slave masters exploit slaves in response to economic incentives, but slaves and other unfree laborers often provided military, administrative, domestic, and sexual services largely unrelated to economic activities (Roberts and Miers 1988; Patterson 1982).

The Nieboer–Domar hypothesis therefore does not apply to societies that employ slaves and other servile workers in noncommercial or minor economic roles (Lovejoy 1983; Finley 1968). It also does not apply to states that use race, religion, gender, or other status criteria to restrict the freedom of workers for noneconomic reasons (James 1988).

Third, the key issue from an employer's perspective is not simply the ratio of land to labor but the relative costs and benefits of different forms of labor that can be profitably employed using existing capital (including land). A more general version of the Nieboer–Domar model compares the stock of available capital to the availability of different forms of labor at prevailing prices. Thus, labor scarcity means the scarcity of labor at prices that allow it to be employed profitably.

Fourth, the simple version of the Nieboer–Domar hypothesis ignores the organizational capacities of workers and capitalists' ability to adopt labor-saving innovations. If workers demand concessions that threaten profits or engage in strikes and other production disruptions, capitalists experience "labor shortages" that stem not from insufficient numbers but from the organized resistance of the workers who are present (Miles 1987). Faced with such disruptions, capitalists with sufficient capital may adopt labor-saving innovations if they are available. When capitalists are unable to adopt those innovations, they may resort to coercive strategies to curb workers' market-based demands (Paige 1975). This case contradicts the Nieboer–Domar hypothesis, which assumes that high ratios of labor to capital (or land) make coercive labor control strategies unnecessary.

UNFREE LABOR IN THE AMERICAS

From the fifteenth through the nineteenth centuries, Europe, Africa, and the Americas were closely linked by flows of people and commodities (Lovejoy 1983; Eltis 1987). The colonization of the Americas by strong European states provided vast, lightly populated lands for commercial exploitation. Expanding markets in Europe for sugar, cotton, tobacco, coffee, and other commodities stimulated the demand for greater supplies of servile labor to work the plantations and mines of the Americas. Weak states in large areas of sub-Saharan Africa left large populations vulnerable to armed predation by stronger states that supplied the expanding markets for slaves.

Estimates of the numbers of bondsmen and slaves transported to the Americas are subject to sizable errors because of the paucity and unreliability of existing records, but relative magnitudes are thought to be reasonable (see Table 1). Differences in the sources of servile labor produced different racial compositions across American regions. Slaves from Africa outnumbered arrivals from Europe nearly four to one before 1820, and most were bound for sugarcane plantations in Brazil and the West Indies. British North America was atypical because its early immigrants were predominantly white indentured servants from Britain, Ireland, and Germany; perhaps two-thirds of the white immigrants who arrived before the American Revolution were bonded servants (Smith 1947, p. 336). Before being displaced by African slaves, white bondsmen were the principal source of labor in the plantation regions of all British colonies, including those in the Caribbean (Engerman 1986a; Galenson 1981).

Indentured servitude was the principal method of defraying the costs of supplying the colonies with workers. British laws and customs regulating master–servant relationships were modified significantly to fit American circumstances (Galenson 1981). Because of the high costs of transatlantic passage, longer periods of service were required, typically four to seven years rather than one year or less in England. English servants could not be sold against their will to another master, but that practice was sanctioned in colonial laws and customs because European servants could not negotiate terms with perspective masters before immigrating to America. Finally, opportunities for escape were much greater in America. Consequently, elaborate state enforcement mechanisms were implemented to discourage runaways and to catch, punish, and return those who did. Most indentured servants were transported to plantation re-

Immigration to and Populations of Regions in the Americas (in thousands)

TOTAL IMMIGRATION TO THE AMERICAS UP TO AROUND 1820

	African	European	Total	% African
United States	550	651	1,201	46
Continental Spanish America	1,072	750	1,822	59
Brazil and the West Indies	6,777	964	7,741	88
Total	8,399	2,365	10,764	78

TOTAL POPULATION AROUND 1650

	Native Americans and Mestizos	Europeans	Blacks and Mulattos	Total
North America	860 (86%)	120 (12%)	22 (2%)	1,002 (100%)
Continental Spanish America (excluding Peru)	8,773 (90%)	575 (6%)	437 (4%)	9,785 (100%)
Brazil, the West Indies, and the Guyanas	843 (51%)	154 (9%)	667 (40%)	1,664 (100%)
Total	10,476 (84%)	849 (7%)	1,126 (9%)	12,451 (100%)

TOTAL POPULATION AROUND 1825

	Native Americans and Mestizos	Europeans	Blacks and Mulattos	Total
North America	423 (4%)	9,126 (80%)	1,920 (17%)	11,469 (100%)
Continental Spanish America (excluding Peru)	12,660 (79%)	2,937 (18%)	387 (2%)	15,984 (100%)
Brazil, the West Indies, and the Guyanas	381 (5%)	1,412 (20%)	5,247 (75%)	7,040 (100%)
Total	13,464 (39%)	13,475 (39%)	7,554 (22%)	34,493 (100%)

Table 1

SOURCES: Immigration rates are adapted from Eltis (1983, p. 278). Population figures are adapted from Slicher Van Bath (1986, p. 21), in which the West Indies include the Spanish islands but exclude the Bahamas.

gions because plantation labor produced greater returns than did any other economic activity in the Americas (Galenson 1981). Employers in areas such as New England could afford few or no servants because they specialized in trades with lower labor productivity and lower profit margins.

White servile labor was replaced by black slavery throughout the Americas between 1600 and 1800. Racial prejudice encouraged the shift but probably was not decisive (Morgan 1975). First, the limited supply of indentured servants could not satisfy the demand for servile labor, whereas the supply of African slaves was almost completely elastic. Improving economic conditions in Britain and state restrictions on the emigration of British servants reduced the numbers seeking passage to America, causing the price of servants to increase. As the price of servants exceeded the price of slaves, first for unskilled and later for skilled workers, slaves came to be preferred to bonded servants (Galenson 1981). Second, Africans were more resistant to the diseases of the tropics, where the most important export crops were grown (Eltis 1983).

Third, slaves could be compelled to comply with the labor-intensive plantation work regime that developed (Fogel 1989). Slaves were more efficient and profitable than free or indentured workers in sugar, cotton, coffee, rice, and tobacco agriculture because the work required by those crops could be performed efficiently by slave work gangs. Work gangs were organized according to specialized tasks, and slaves were assigned to particular gangs according to their skills and capacities. The work was performed under close supervision to maintain work intensity and quality. Slave masters often used brutal violence to enforce discipline, but naked force might have been used less than once was thought. Slave masters experimented with different mixtures of positive and negative incentives, to encourage slaves to maximize their output (Fogel 1989). Thus, slave plantations anticipated the discipline of workers in the great factories of industrial capitalism, where assembly lines regulate the rhythms and intensity of work.

Forced migration from Africa greatly exceeded all migration from Europe as sugar production became the greatest consumer of servile labor in the Americas. High death rates and a preference for male slaves in the sugar-producing regions led to net population declines among blacks and mulattoes (compare immigration numbers to population sizes in Table 1), but the proportion of blacks in the British West Indies increased from 25 to 91 percent between 1650 and 1770 (Fogel 1989, p. 30). By the 1820s, the proportion of blacks and mulattoes in Brazil, the Guyanas, and the West Indies reached 75 percent (Table 1).

British North America was an exception to this pattern as both black and white populations had high rates of natural increase. Almost all major slave societies were unable to maintain the size of slave populations without continuous replenishment from outside sources. By contrast, the slave population in the United States multiplied because of unusually high fertility rates and low mortality rates (see Table 1 and Fogel 1989).

Political factors also encouraged the transition from white servitude to black slavery (Engerman 1986b; Galenson 1981). As British citizens, indentured servants retained state-protected natal rights that their masters were obliged to respect. For example, masters could beat servants and slaves to enforce work discipline, but colonial courts protected servants against unfair punishment (Smith 1947). Importantly, Europeans could choose the place of their servitude, and most refused transportation to the plantation regions from the eighteenth century on. African slaves could not avoid the plantation regions and were citizens of no state in Africa or America that could or would defend their interests.

Because Spain conquered the continental regions with the largest Native American populations (Table 1), it had less need of African slaves. Instead, Spanish colonists installed a coercive labor system patterned on Spanish feudalism that forced natives to work part-time on colonial estates although slavery was still preferred in the mines (Slicher Van Bath 1986; Kloosterboer 1960). Unfree labor markets and compulsory labor endured for 400 years, eventually evolving into debt servitude in the nineteenth century. Native Americans and mestizos accounted for nearly 80 percent of the population of continental Spanish America by 1825 but were almost annihilated in the West Indies (Table 1).

Nowhere in the Americas was slavery in danger of withering away economically at the time when it was abolished (Eltis 1987). Furthermore, with the principal exception of Haiti in 1804, slave rebellions were not successful in conquering slave masters and transforming a slave system into a wage labor system. Paradoxically, Britain played the dominant role in abolishing slavery and the transatlantic slave trade even though it controlled half the transatlantic commerce in slaves and half of the world's exports in sugar and coffee, which were produced primarily on slave plantations (Eltis 1987). Britain outlawed the slave trade in 1808 and freed the slaves in its West Indian colonies in 1833 over the strenuous objections of slave owners. The United States prohibited the importation of slaves after 1808, and civil war led to abolition in 1865. By the 1870s, all the major European and American maritime and commercial powers had acquiesced to British pressure and outlawed the slave trade. Brazil, the last state in the Americas to abolish slavery, did so in 1888.

The land–labor ratio strongly affected planters' responses to abolition. In places where ex-slaves could find no alternative to plantation work, such as Barbados and Antigua, the transition to free labor was rapid, and plantation production did not decline appreciably (Boogaart and Emmer 1986). In places where land or alternative employment was available, such as Jamaica and Trinidad, the ex-slaves abandoned the plantations, and plantation productivity declined (Engerman 1985). In response, planters implemented a variety of servile labor systems with mixed results. A second wave of indentured servants was imported chiefly from Asia, especially China and India, which more than compensated for the labor shortages induced by abolition in some cases, such as Mauritius and British Guiana (Engerman 1985, 1986b). China and colonial India eventually banned the recruitment of servants because of objections to employers' poor treatment of servants, and Brazil was never able to gain access to Asian indentured laborers (Boogaart and Emmer 1986).

In areas where planters retained a degree of political power, such as the West Indies and Brazil, vagrancy statutes and other compulsory labor schemes forced workers to accept wages below free market levels (Kloosterboer 1960; Huggins 1985). Indentured labor and other forms of involuntary servitude were banned in the United States in 1865 by the Thirteenth Amendment to the U.S. Constitution, but planters regained substantial influence over black workers through their control of racially discriminatory state and local governmental institutions (James 1988). Blacks were disfranchised by 1900, making them vulnerable to racial segregation, physical coercion, and economic discrimination. The extent to which racial discrimination interfered with free labor markets in the South is controversial (Wright 1986). Nevertheless, the most determined resistance to the civil rights movement of the 1960s occurred in the plantation regions (James 1988). The success of that movement led to increased protection of the citizenship rights of blacks and doomed widespread coercive labor control practices. The transition to capital-intensive agricultural practices was rapid during that period.

UNFREE LABOR IN AFRICA AND ASIA

Slavery was an indigenous institution in Africa and Arabia for centuries before Europeans entered

the African slave trade (Thornton 1998). While approximately 9.9 million Africans were transported to the Americas before the Atlantic slave trade was suppressed (Fogel 1989), an additional 5.2 million African slaves were transported across the Sahara, the Red Sea, and the Indian Ocean into the Islamic world between 1500 and 1900. Moreover, perhaps 6.4 million more were exported to Islamic societies between A.D. 650 and 1500 ("a rough approximation," Lovejoy 1983, p. 24). Many thousands more were enslaved in African societies in that period (Thornton 1998).

Whereas chattel slavery in the Americas was predicated on profit making, African slavery typically did not have a narrowly economic basis. African slaves were menial servants and field workers, but they also were concubines, surrogate kin, soldiers, commercial agents, and candidates for human sacrifice (Roberts and Miers 1988, p. 5). Female slaves were especially valued because women performed most agricultural and domestic work. African societies were based on kinship relations in which all individuals were linked in a complex network of dependency. Because power in kinship systems depends on the size of social groups, slave masters could increase their power by obtaining more slaves. Furthermore, slaves were immune to the appeals of their masters' rivals within kin groups because they had no kinship ties that mediated their subordination to their masters. Large numbers of persons were enslaved as a result of military victories in wars between African kingdoms and societies.

African slave masters also responded to economic incentives. An increasing number of slaves were provided to the Atlantic slave trade as the demand for slaves in the Americas increased. Thornton (1998, p. 125) concludes that African participation in the slave trade was voluntary because European slavers did not have the economic or political power to force African leaders to sell slaves. The established African practices of holding and trading slaves made it possible for African states to respond to the increasing European demand so long as the prices paid were attractive.

Islamic slavery also differed from chattel slavery in important ways. Islamic law prohibited the enslavement of Muslims but permitted the enslavement of people born to slave parents or captured for the purpose of conversion to Islam (Gordon 1989). Concubines could not be sold if they bore a child to a master, and the child could not be enslaved. Allowing slaves to purchase their freedom brought honor to former masters. Manumitting slaves was also meritorious and could atone for certain sins and offenses.

Islamic slaves typically were employed as household servants, domestic workers, concubines, and to a lesser extent soldiers. Female slaves typically brought higher prices than did males because the heads of patriarchal Muslim families prized female slaves for assignment to sexual and domestic roles in their households. Slave eunuchs performed special tasks in large households and usually brought higher prices than did female slaves. Consequently, pre-twentieth-century slave traders castrated large numbers of African slave boys in crude operations that killed up to 90 percent of them (Gordon 1989, pp. 91–97). However, Islamic slave masters also responded to economic incentives as did their American counterparts when market opportunities arose. During the nineteenth century, over 750,000 slaves were transported to the clove plantations on Zanzibar and other locations on the east coast of Africa, for example (Cooper 1977; Lovejoy 1983, p. 151).

British diplomatic and military pressure finally led to the suppression of the Islamic and African slave trades as it did with the transatlantic traffic. In 1890, all the European powers agreed to suppress slave trading and slave raiding and to assist ex-slaves, a commitment that legitimated the conquest of Africa in the eyes of European citizens. However, European colonial administrators were reluctant abolitionists (Roberts and Miers 1988). Inadequate military and administrative power, fear of economic and political disruptions, and unfamiliarity with African customs delayed the process.

Colonial governments outlawed slavery almost everywhere in sub-Saharan Africa by the 1930s, but involuntary servitude persisted. Roberts and Miers (1989, pp. 42–47) identify three factors that retarded the emergence of free labor markets in Africa. The first two were responses to abundant land and scarce labor. First, colonial states conscripted natives, imposed labor levies that local chiefs had to fill, and implemented other compulsory labor mechanisms to maintain a supply of cheap labor for European employers and administrators. Second, many Africans had access to land or livestock and were unwilling to work for wages. Colonial states tried to reduce the attractiveness of nonwage occupations by, for example, raising taxes above what peasant agriculturalists and pastoralists could pay and prohibiting Africans from growing lucrative cash crops. In settler colonies such as South Africa, native Africans were pushed off the land and confined to strictly regulated labor markets by pass laws. Third, Africans resorted widely to pawnship after abolition.

The reluctance of colonial administrators and the power of postcolonial states allowed slavery to survive in some nations in north Africa and the Arabian peninsula well into the twentieth century. In 1926, the League of Nations codified its opposition to slavery by adopting the Convention to Suppress the Slave Trade and Slavery, which defined slavery as the ownership of another person. Gradually, the remaining slave states abolished slavery officially: Ethiopia in 1942, Saudi Arabia in 1962, Muscat and Oman in 1970, and Mauritania for the third time in 1980. Nevertheless, reports of slavery persisted. Saudi Arabia allegedly failed to free some 250,000 slaves in the late 1960s; an estimated 100,000 chattel slaves existed in Saharan regions of Mauritania in 1980, although many were freed by 1984; and nomadic tribesmen allegedly held 250,000 slaves in the Sahelian districts of Mali in 1984 (Gordon 1989, pp. 232–234; United Nations 1984, pp. 18–19; United Nations 1988, p. 197; Sawyer 1986, p. 14).

In 1956, the United Nations increased the international attack on slavery and involuntary servitude by adopting the Supplementary Convention on the Abolition of Slavery, the Slave Trade, and Institutions and Practices Similar to Slavery. In addition to outlawing slavery, the Supplementary Convention pledged signatory nations to suppress debt bondage, serfdom, the pawning of children, and servile marriage (forcing women to marry in exchange for payments to their family members or assigning wives, after the death of their husbands, to others as an inheritance). Progress has been slow. For example, India outlawed bondage in 1976, but a survey found more than 2.5 million bonded workers in 1978; only 163,000 had been freed by 1985 (Sawyer 1986, pp. 124–134). Debt servitude has been reported since 1970 among landless peasants in India and Nepal and among Native American rubber collectors in the Peruvian Amazon. As late as 1986, the Dominican Republic used its army to round up Haitian immigrants for forced work on sugar plantations during the harvest season (Plant 1987).

PATTERNS OF SLAVERY AND UNFREE LABOR SINCE 1990

Large-scale systems of slavery and involuntary servitude can be maintained only if slave owners and labor lords can use physical coercion to maintain labor discipline. Hence, large-scale systems of unfree labor depend on state institutions that deny citizenship rights to unfree workers and augment the power of dominant classes to coerce their workers physically. Today no nation officially protects the rights of employers to reduce their workers to slavery or involuntary servitude. Virtually all members of the United Nations have ratified the Supplementary Convention on the Abolition of Slavery, the Slave Trade, and Institutions and Practices Similar to Slavery (see United Nations [1957] 1999 for the current list of ratifying nations). Ratification of the Supplementary Convention officially commits a nation to the elimination of slavery and involuntary servitude within its borders and obligates it to cooperate with other nations in suppressing those practices. Although it took 200 years, the international antislavery campaigns led by politically powerful nations with wage labor markets were successful. Large-scale systems of slavery and involuntary servitude supported and protected by complementary state institutions no longer exist.

The expansion of capitalism and increasing world population displaced large numbers of people from subsistence agriculture and other means of support in many regions. Great disparities between rich and poor nations drive people across state boundaries in search of jobs and improved living conditions. State power plays a crucial role in shaping migration and molding the relationship between capital and labor, but states with expanding economies now prevent the entrance of many willing workers rather than compelling the entrance of the unwilling. The whip of unemployment and poverty replaces the slave master's lash as free labor replaces slave labor.

However, slavery and forced labor persist and are widespread in some areas. Anti-Slavery International, the world's oldest human rights organization, estimates that over 200 million people, about 3 percent of the world's population, labor in some form of bondage. Table 2 provides examples of some existing systems of unfree labor. Because reliable information is difficult or impossible to obtain in some cases, the examples in Table 2 should not be considered exhaustive or the most egregious. The best available information suggests that slavery and involuntary servitude occur with the greatest frequency in nations that are ravaged by civil war or have weak states that are unwilling or unable to suppress coercive labor practices.

Somalia, Sudan, and Uganda provide examples of how civil war places defenseless people at the mercy of powerful military groups. A United Nations special rapporteur confirmed that armed militia groups abducted people in southern Sudan for use as forced laborers or for sale as slaves. Prisoners were subjected to beatings, electric shock, exposure to the sun for long periods, pouring of cold water on the naked body, rape and the threat of rape, sleep deprivation, and the refusal of food and medical treatment. Sudanese government security forces and allied militias as well as insurgent groups were guilty of conscripting children and forcing them to fight as soldiers (United Nations 1997). The civil war in Sudan has disrupted agricultural production to the extent that some impoverished parents give or sell their children to others to prevent their starvation (Finnigan 1999).

A large and active chattel slavery market is in operation in Sudan. Its magnitude is not known,

Examples of Slavery and Involuntary Servitude in 1998

COUNTRY	Servitude Type	Sector of Employment	Legal Status of the Servitude	Estimates of the Scope of Involuntary Servitude
Bangladesh	Bonded labor; forced labor; forced child labor; forced prostitution	Garment industry; forced prostitution	Prohibited by constitution	10,000 to 29,000 child prostitutes; bonded labor is not widespread; trafficking in women and children is widespread
Benin	Bonded labor; forced child labor	Agriculture; domestic service	Prohibited by labor codes	Some poor parents indenture their children
Brazil	Forced labor; bonded labor; forced child labor	Agriculture; sugar industry; mining industries	Prohibited by constitution	The government conducted more than 400 raids between 1995 and 1997 that freed more than 130,000 forced laborers; forced workers numbered 1.3 million in 1992 (Sutton 1994)
Burma	Forced labor; forced child labor;	Irrigation, transportation, and tourism services, and military service	No law prohibits forced or bonded labor by children	Government use of forced labor is widespread; bonded labor is not practiced
Cambodia	Forced and bonded labor; child prostitution	Military; wood-processing, rubber, and brick industries; prostitution	Labor law prohibits forced or bonded labor, including children	Prostitution and trafficking in children is widespread; bonded labor occurs but is not widespread
Cameroon	Slavery; forced and bonded child labor; contracting prison labor to private employers	Agriculture	Labor code does not protect children	The slavery still practiced in northern Cameroon is primarily enslavement of Kirdi by Fulani, a Muslim group that conquered the Kirdi 200 years ago
China	Contracting prison labor to private employers; forced prostitution	Manufacturing; agriculture; mines	Government prohibits export of goods made by prisoners and prohibits forced labor by children	Kidnapping and sale of women and children for prostitution is a problem recognized by the government; prohibitions against private use of prison labor have not been enforced effectively
Ethiopia	Sexual bondage	Children, especially girls, used as prostitutes	Prohibited by constitution and criminal code	Large-scale use of children as prostitutes; children are kidnapped and sold for about $36; some poor parents sell their children

Table 2

SOURCE: United States Department of State (1999) unless otherwise noted.

but international human rights groups estimate that chattel slaves number in the tens of thousands and that the market may extend as far as Saudi Arabia and the Gulf states (Finnigan 1999, p. 71). Anti-Slavery International (1999a) reports that more than 2,700 slaves were freed during the first four months of 1999 in return for over $100,000 in payments. Finnigan (1999) photographed a Sudanese Arab slaver who hoped to sell over 130 individuals to a Christian antislavery organization for $50 each. If that plan failed, he decided that he might return the former slaves to their families for a much lower price. Many others were not so fortunate. Slaves in Sudan are subject to severe punishment; are stripped of their cultural, religious, and personal identities; and can become the property of another person for life, traded and inherited, branded and bred.

Continued

COUNTRY	Servitude Type	Sector of Employment	Legal Status of the Servitude	Estimates of the Scope of Involuntary Servitude
India	Bonded labor; forced labor; indentured and bonded child labor; forced prostitution; contracting prison labor to private employers and brothels	Carpet industry; prostitution; domestic servants; gemstone, glass, footwear, textiles, silk, and fireworks industries	Prohibited by constitution and criminal code	5 million bonded laborers; 300,000 forced child laborers in the carpet industry alone; frequent reports of sale of children and women for forced domestic service and prostitution; some poor parents sell their children
Indonesia	Bonded labor; bonded child labor; forced prostitution	Fishing industry; prostitution	Law prohibits forced labor	Several thousand bonded child laborers; hundreds of bonded adults; widespread forced prostitution; 1,500 child prostitutes in one province
Mauritania	Slavery and vestiges of slavery; unpaid labor; forced child labor	Agriculture; shepherds and herdsmen	Slavery officially abolished several times, most recently in 1980	Slavery in the form of forced and involuntary servitude reportedly persists in some isolated areas; psychological, tribal, and religious bonds continue to tie former slaves to their prior masters; forced child labor is now rare
Morocco	Adoptive servitude of children	Domestic servants	Forced and compulsory labor prohibited by statute in 1957	The adoption of young girls for domestic service is socially accepted, and the government does little to discourage the practice
Nepal	Bonded labor; child labor; trafficking in women and children for sex work	Agriculture; forced prostitution; carpet industry	Prohibited by constitution	100,000 bonded labors in one region; 40,000 bonded child laborers; 5,000 to 7,000 girls forcibly transported to India as prostitutes annually; forced prostitution is widespread; forced child labor in carpet industry has been greatly reduced to international pressure
Nigeria	Child sexual slavery; forced labor	Domestic servants; prostitution	Prohibited by constitution but children are not protected	Child slavery rings operated between Nigeria and neighboring countries; also see Effah (1996); forced labor is now rare

Table 2, continued

Some slavery and slavery-like practices in India, Benin, Mauritania, Morocco, and Pakistan are supported by local customs and traditions that have long histories (Table 2). Mauritania and India have attempted to eliminate these practices, whereas other states are more reluctant or unable to act decisively. Debt bondage is widespread in the rural areas of India, but involuntary servitude has been adapted to the economic opportunities provided by the operation of global markets. Just as European demand for sugar and coffee drove the Atlantic slave trade in the seventeenth and eighteenth centuries, employers of servile labor in poor countries find opportunities to supply consumer demands for cheap goods in economically advanced countries. For example, India, Pakistan, and Nepal employed as many as one million servile child workers in the hand-knotted carpet industry

Continued

COUNTRY	Servitude Type	Sector of Employment	Legal Status of the Servitude	Estimates of the Scope of Involuntary Servitude
Pakistan	Bonded labor; bonded child labor; forced prostitution of children	Carpet, fish, glass and brick industries; agriculture; construction industry; prostitution	Forced labor is specifically prohibited by law	Bonded labor is widespread; landlords held 4,500 bonded laborers in one region; poor parents traditionally sell children to rich landlords as permanent bond servants in exchange for money or land; significant numbers of women and children are forced to work as prostitutes.
Somalia	Forced labor; child labor	Agriculture; military service	Civil war has eliminated any effective governmental system for the protection of human rights	Widespread vulnerability to forced labor in the service of warlords; in contrast to previous years, there were no reports of the use of forced labor by multinational fruit export firms
Sudan	Slavery including enslavement of prisoners of war, forced labor, and child labor	Agriculture; domestic service; concubines; trafficking in slaves; military service	Law prohibits forced or compulsory labor, but civil war has eliminated effective protection of human rights in many areas	Widespread use of slavery and forced labor by government troops and their allies; government forces and insurgents forcibly conscript children; international religious organizations paid $50 each to purchase the freedom of slaves captured by raiding parties (Finnigan 1999)
Thailand	Trafficking of women and children for sex work; bonded child laborers	Prostitution, especially in response to tourists' demand; agriculture	Constitution prohibits forced labor but does not protect children	Forced prostitution is often protected by government officials who profit from it; child prostitutes number 20,000 to 40,000.
Togo	Forced labor; indentured servitude	Domestic servants	No law addresses forced or compulsory labor by adults or children	International trafficking in children, especially girls, for use as indentured servants or slaves; the government attempts to suppress the practice.
Uganda	Bonded labor; forced child labor; contracting prison labor to private employers	Agriculture; domestic service; concubines; soldiers	Prohibited by law	Government forces were too weak to defend rights of citizens; an insurgent militia group abducted 3000 Ugandan children and forced them to become soldiers or sexual slaves

Table 2, continued

in 1994 (United States Department of Labor 1995). The United States imported $329 million worth of hand-knotted carpets in 1996, a large proportion of which were produced in those countries (United States Department of Labor 1997). Children in India have been kidnapped and transported from their villages to face years of forced labor in the carpet industry. Forced child labor is characterized by long hours, threats of violence, dangerous conditions, little or no pay, and poor or nonexistent health care (United States Department of Labor 1994, 1998; Anti-Slavery International 1999b). Other commercial products produced by bonded and forced child workers for export are brassware, silk cloth and silk garments, and stone and glass products (United States Department of Labor 1997).

Thailand, Nepal, Indonesia, and Cambodia are examples of weak states or states crippled by corruption that facilitate the persistence of forced labor and forced sexual prostitution. The flourishing Asian sex trade involves the transport of women and children across borders to work in brothels for foreign and domestic customers. Victims are lured by false promises of decent employment, kidnapped or sold by family members, or reduced to debt bondage by poverty. In Thailand, debt bondage sometimes continues from generation to generation as a result of very low wages, high interest charges, and fraudulent debts that cannot be repaid (U.S. Department of Labor 1994, 1996, 1998). Because of the spread of AIDS, brothel customers increasingly prefer very young girls who are supposedly disease-free. Consequently, brothel owners purchase or kidnap young girls from the surrounding countries to supply the demand. Girls from Burma, Cambodia, China, Laos, and Vietnam can be found in the brothels of Thailand (United States Department of Labor 1995).

The Asian sex trade is huge. UNICEF estimates that 100,000 child prostitutes are employed in Thailand alone, but the number could be more than 200,000 (U.S. Department of Labor 1995). Patterns vary from country to country, but the brothels typically are patronized by local customers and to a lesser extent by foreigners, including tourists, businessmen, and military personnel from the United States and Europe. Travel agencies arrange sex tours that include accommodations and a choice of escorts (United States Department of Labor 1995, 1996). As is the case with many handmade and manufactured products, the Asian sex trade and the exploitation of servile workers are intimately connected to the global economy.

In contrast to Britain's use of the navy to suppress the Atlantic slave trade in the nineteenth century, current international efforts to suppress slavery and involuntary servitude are weak. One enforcement tactic is to expose governments that do not suppress servile labor practices to the condemnation of world opinion. For example, the United Nations Commission on Human Rights investigates patterns of human rights violations within countries, including slavery and servitude, and disseminates its reports widely. The Interna-

tional Labor Organization, a special agency of the United Nations, formulates international labor standards and monitors the compliance efforts of governments (United Nations 1991). A wide variety of nongovernmental organizations are involved in the publicity campaigns against human bondage. Perhaps the most famous is Anti-Slavery International, which promotes the eradication of slavery and slavery-like practices by supporting the victims of those practices and through the collection and dissemination of information on specific cases. The negative publicity created by the public exposure of servile labor practices can diminish servile labor practices, but governments often do not cooperate because negative publicity alone is a feeble enforcement tool.

Economic pressure may be more effective than the investigative reporting and publicity efforts of the United Nations and other governmental and nongovernmental organizations. For example, the annual reports of the U.S. Department of State on Human Rights Practices are provided to the U.S. Congress to assist it in formulating foreign aid policies (Table 2 is based on the 1999 report). Countries are encouraged to suppress slavery and unfree labor practices to continue receiving aid from the United States and international organizations. Pressure from consumer organizations is effective in some cases. For example, a number of product-labeling programs were created to reassure buyers that products imported into affluent countries were not made by children. A nongovernmental organization in India initiated the RUGMARK program in 1994, which encourages carpet manufactures to stop using child labor by providing a labeling service that certifies that products are not made by children (United States Department of Labor 1997). By mid-1997, RUGMARK inspections had found over 1,000 illegal child workers in the carpet industry. Other labeling programs cover leather footwear, soccer balls, and the tea industry (United States Department of Labor 1997).

The historical decline in the land–labor ratio did not produce the abolition of slavery and involuntary servitude. The simple version of the Nieboer–Domar hypothesis is inadequate. From the middle of the nineteenth century until the present, political factors have played a decisive role in breaking the link between the availability of land and unfree labor. Rather than defending slavery when land was plentiful, Britain used its political power to abolish slavery and suppress the slave trade even though it was not in its economic interest to do so.

By the late twentieth century, most nations had officially prohibited slavery and slavery-like practices, but both persist. As the modified Niebor–Domar hypothesis predicts, some employers will use physical coercion to drive down the cost of labor when opportunities arise. Weak or corrupt state institutions cannot or will not defend the rights of those who are most vulnerable to coercion. Civil wars destroy the ability of states to maintain order and subject citizens to the depredations of warring militias. In some areas of the world, cultural support for servile labor and grinding poverty combine to make it difficult to eliminate some forms of slavery and forced labor. In all cases, the typical victims of these practices are the weakest and most vulnerable groups: women, children, migrant workers, low-status class or caste groups, and racial, ethnic, and religious minorities (Table 2).

All nations regulate the passage of individuals across their borders and assign superior rights and privileges to citizens compared to noncitizens. In advanced capitalist democracies with ostensibly free labor markets, the state-enforced distinction between citizen and noncitizen is a key mechanism in maintaining dual labor markets that disproportionately relegate noncitizens to the lowest-paying jobs (e.g., Thomas 1985; Miles 1987; Cohen 1987). Typically, noncitizen "guest workers" are less likely to enjoy state protection and more vulnerable to discrimination. Because the demand for cheap labor often can be satisfied by choosing among citizens and noncitizens who have no other labor market alternatives, democratic states can regulate noncitizens' access to domestic labor markets rather than forcibly import unfree workers from foreign lands.

However, many states are not liberal democracies. Thousands were confined for political reasons in forced labor camps during the Stalin era in the Soviet Union. Nazi Germany forced Jews and other minorities into slavery where they were to be "worked to death" (Sawyer 1986). Blacks were disfranchised and rigidly segregated in the southern United States for much of the twentieth century, making them vulnerable to coercive labor practices. The Republic of South Africa's now abolished policy of apartheid denied citizenship status to indigenous blacks and exposed them to forced labor practices. Since 1988, the military government of Burma has engaged in systematic human rights abuses, including the imposition of forced labor on large segments of the population for military purposes and for the construction and development of infrastructure (Bureau of International Labor Affairs 1998).

The international condemnation of slavery and involuntary servitude represents a great victory for those who support and defend human rights. The use of forced and other forms of servile labor has not been eliminated, but it has been widely branded as criminal activity. As a consequence, those who would employ servile labor must risk prosecution or search for opportunities in countries with weak or corrupt political institutions that cannot or will not suppress slavery and involuntary servitude. Although the struggle to eradicate servile labor practices has not been won, nations and international human rights organizations appear to be more concerned about the loss of life and other human rights violations that accompany civil wars and international conflicts. For example, NATO recently intervened to stop the murder and forced displacement of thousands of ethnic Albanians in Kosovo. A similar intervention into the affairs of anther nation to eliminate slavery or involuntary servitude is unlikely.

REFERENCES

Anti-Slavery International 1999a "Slavery in Sudan—Appeal for Releases." News Release available from the Anti-Slavery International website (www.charitynet.org/~asi/).

—— 1999b. "What Is Modern Slavery?" Available from the Anti-Slavery International website (www.charitynet.org/~asi/)

Boogaart, Ernst Van Den, and P. C. Emmer 1986 "Colonialism and Migration: An Overview." In P. C. Emmer, ed., *Colonialism and Migration*. Dordrecht, Netherlands: Martinus Nijhoff.

Bureau of International Labor Affairs 1998 "Report on Labor Practices in Burma." Washington, D.C.: U.S. Department of Labor.

Cohen, Robin. 1987. *The New Helots*. Brookfield, Vt.: Gower.

Cooper, Frederick 1977 *Plantation Slavery on the East Coast of Africa*. New Haven, Conn.: Yale University Press.

Domar, Evesy D. 1970 "The Causes of Slavery or Serfdom: A Hypothesis." *Journal of Economic History* 30:18–31.

Effah, Josephine 1996 *Modernised Slavery: Child Trade in Nigeria.* Lagos, Nigeria: Constitutional Rights Project.

Eltis, David 1983 "Free and Coerced Transatlantic Migrations: Some Comparisons." *American Historical Review* 88:251–280.

—— 1987 *Economic Growth and the Ending of the Transatlantic Slave Trade.* New York: Oxford University Press.

Engerman, Stanley L. 1985 "Economic Change and Contract Labour in the British Caribbean." In D. Richardson, ed., *Abolition and Its Aftermath.* London: Frank Cass.

—— 1986a "Slavery and Emancipation in Comparative Perspective: A Look at Some Recent Debates." *Journal of Economic History* 46:317–339.

—— 1986b "Servants to Slaves to Servants: Contract Labour and European Expansion." In P. C. Emmer, ed., *Colonialism and Migration.* Dordrecht, Netherlands: Martinus Nijhoff.

Finley, M. I. 1968 "Slavery." In David Sills, ed., *International Encyclopedia of the Social Sciences*, vol. 14, pp. 307–313. New York: Macmillan.

Finnigan, William 1999 "The Invisible War." *The New Yorker*, January 25, pp. 50–73.

Fogel, Robert W. 1989 *Without Consent or Contract.* New York: Norton.

Galenson, David W. 1981 *White Servitude in Colonial America.* New York: Cambridge University Press.

—— and Stanley L. Engerman 1974 *Time on the Cross: The Economics of Negro Slavery*, 2 vols. Boston: Little, Brown.

Gordon, Murray 1989 *Slavery in the Arab World.* New York: New Amsterdam Books.

Huggins, Martha K. 1985 *From Slavery to Vagrancy in Brazil.* New Brunswick, N.J.: Rutgers University Press.

James, David R. 1988 "The Transformation of the Southern Racial State: Class and Race Determinants of Local-State Structures." *American Sociological Review* 53:191–208.

Kloosterboer, W. 1960. *Involuntary Labour since the Abolition of Slavery.* Leiden, Netherlands: E. J. Brill.

Kolchin, Peter 1987 *Unfree Labor: American Slavery and Russian Serfdom.* Cambridge, Mass.: Harvard University Press.

Lovejoy, Paul E. 1983 *Transformations in Slavery.* Cambridge, UK: Cambridge University Press.

Marx, Karl. (1867) 1967 *Capital*, vol. 1. New York: International Publishers.

Miles, Robert 1987 *Capitalism and Unfree Labour.* London: Tavistock.

Morgan, Edmund S. 1975 *American Slavery, American Freedom.* New York: Norton.

Morris, Richard B. 1946 *Government and Labor in Early America.* New York: Columbia University Press.

Nieboer, Herman J. 1900 *Slavery as an Industrial System.* The Hague, Netherlands: Martinus Nijhoff.

Paige, Jeffery 1975 *Agrarian Revolution.* New York: Free Press.

Patterson, Orlando. 1977a "Slavery." *Annual Review of Sociology* 3:407–449.

—— 1977b "The Structural Origins of Slavery: A Critique of the Nieboer Domar Hypothesis." *Annuals of the New York Academy of Sciences* 292:12–34.

—— 1982 *Slavery and Social Death.* Cambridge, Mass.: Harvard University Press.

Plant, Roger 1987 *Sugar and Modern Slavery.* London: Zed.

Roberts, Richard, and Suzanne Miers 1988 "The End of Slavery in Africa." In S. Miers and R. Roberts, eds., *The End of Slavery in Africa.* Madison: University of Wisconsin Press.

Sawyer, Roger 1986 *Slavery in the Twentieth Century.* London: Routledge and Kegan Paul.

Slicher Van Bath, B. H. 1986 "The Absence of White Contract Labour in Spanish America during the Colonial Period." In P. C. Emmer, ed., *Colonialism and Migration.* Dordrecht, Netherlands: Martinus Nijhoff.

Smith, Abbot Emerson 1947 *Colonists in Bondage.* Chapel Hill: University of North Carolina Press.

Sutton, Alison 1994 *Slavery in Brazil.* London: Anti-Slavery International.

Thomas, Robert J. 1985 *Citizenship, Gender, and Work.* Berkeley: University of California Press.

Thornton, John 1998 *Africa and Africans in the Making of the Atlantic World, 1400–1800*, 2nd ed. Cambridge, UK: Cambridge University Press.

United Nations 1984 "Slavery: Report Prepared by B. Whitaker, Special Rapporteur of the Sub-Commission on Prevention of Discrimination and Protection of Minorities." New York.

—— 1988 "United Nations Action in the Field of Human Rights." New York.

—— 1991 "Contemporary Forms of Slavery." New York: Center for Human Rights.

—— 1997 "Situation of Human Rights in the Sudan." New York: Commission on Human Rights.

—— (1957) 1999 "The Supplementary Convention on the Abolition of Slavery, the Slave Trade, and Institutions and Practices Similar to Slavery," including a current list of ratifying nations as well as all the major documents and treaties concerning human rights. Available on the United Nations website, www.unhchr.ch/html/intlinst.htm.

United States Department of Labor 1994 *By the Sweat and Toil of Children vol. 1: The Use of Child Labor in American Imports.* Washington, D.C.: Bureau of International Labor Affairs.

—— 1995 *By the Sweat and Toil of Children, vol. II: The Use of Child Labor in U.S. Agricultural Imports & Forced and Bonded Labor.* Washington, D.C.: Bureau of International Labor Affairs.

—— 1996 *Forced Labor: The Prostitution of Children.* Washington, D.C.: Bureau of International Labor Affairs.

—— 1997 *By the Sweat and Toil of Children, vol. IV: Consumer Labels and Child Labor.* Washington, D.C.: Bureau of International Labor Affairs.

—— 1998 *By the Sweat and Toil of Children, vol. V: Efforts to Eliminate Child Labor.* Washington, D.C.: Bureau of International Labor Affairs.

United States Department of State 1999 *Country Reports on Human Rights Practices for 1998.* Washington, D.C.: U.S. Government Printing Office. Available on the State Department website, www.state.gov/www/global/human_rights/1998_hrp_report.

Wright, Gavin 1986 *Old South, New South.* New York: Basic Books.

DAVID R. JAMES
SARA HEILIGER

SMALL GROUPS

In sociology, the concept "group" implies more than simply an aggregate of individuals. Additional elements involved are (1) structure—interaction patterned in terms of statuses and roles, (2) history—some frequency and regularity of interaction over time, (3) interdependence—some degree of members' mutual reliance on each other for needed or valued material and nonmaterial resources, and (4) common identity—grounded in shared meanings, values, experiences, and goals. Frequently there is a group product, not necessarily of a material nature, which is the outcome or consequence of collective effort and interaction.

These elements are dimensional in that groups possess and manifest them to a greater or lesser degree. At one extreme, family groups typically have well-established and enduring structures, share extensive histories, encompass a wide range of activities, exert a broad scope of influence, and provide the basis of individual identity. At the other extreme, ad hoc work groups (and groups studied in laboratory experiments) may be assembled to perform specific tasks of very limited duration with little or no relevance for or influence on the members outside a clearly defined situation and range of activity. McGrath (1984) developed a comprehensive typology of groups in terms of origin, scope of activity, task, duration, and interaction.

Groups are regarded as small if meaningful and direct face-to-face interaction can take place among all members. The number of members usually is thought of as ranging from two to twenty, with three to seven common in many laboratory studies of groups.

PRIMARY AND SECONDARY GROUPS

Cooley (1909) identified a fundamental type of small group that is characterized by intimate association and cooperation, which he regarded as the basic building block of society. Cooley called groups of this sort "primary groups" and held them to be forms of association found everywhere. Primary groups work on the individual to form and develop the social nature of the person. "This nature consists of certain primary social sentiments and attitudes, such as consciousness of one's self in relation to others, love of approbation, resentment of censure, emulation, and a sense of social right and wrong formed by the standards of a group" (1909, p. 32).

Membership and participation in primary groups are valued and rewarding for their own sake. The groups typically are long-lasting. Members interact as "whole persons" rather than merely in terms of specialized, partial roles. Primary groups are basic sources of socioemotional support and gratification, and participation in them is considered essential for a person's psychological and emotional well-being. Some (the family, the neighborhood peer group) are also primary in the sense that they are settings for early childhood socialization and personality development.

In contrast are groups formed and maintained to accomplish a task, to which people belong for extrinsic purposes (because they are paid or to achieve an external goal). These "secondary groups" are characterized by limited, instrumental relationships. They may be relatively short-term, and their range of activity is restricted. Affective ties and other "irrational" personal influences are intended to be minimized or eliminated.

It has been widely observed, however, that primary relationships develop pervasively within secondary groups and organizations. In a synthesis of observations and research findings, Homans (1950) attempted to identify universal variables of group behavior. He sought to develop a general theoretical scheme that would permit an understanding of groups as diverse as an industrial work unit, a street-corner gang, and a Polynesian family. Homans approached the small group as a system in which activity, interaction, and sentiment are interrelated. He concluded that interaction among group members increases their liking for one another and that they tend to express their friendship in an increasing range of activities and to interact more frequently. Affective elements emerge in virtually all ongoing groups and may enhance or interfere with the purposes for which a group was established. Soldiers are motivated to fight and workers are motivated to increase or restrict work output by loyalty to their friends and the norms of the immediate group.

BASES AND DEVELOPMENT OF SMALL GROUP RESEARCH

Sociological interest in small groups has several bases, including (1) the perception of small groups as fundemental, universal social units on which all larger organizational structures depend, (2) a concern with the description and understanding of particular small groups both for their own importance and as a source of observations from which hypotheses and general theories can be developed, and (3) the usefulness of the laboratory group as a research context in which to study the characteristics of the group as the unit of interest and as a setting for the investigation of social influence on individual cognition and behavior.

Foundations for small group research may be seen in nineteenth-century sociological thought, such as Emile Durkheim's analyses of the development of social structures, specialization and task differentiation, and the bases of social cohesion and Georg Simmel's work on the importance of group size and coalition formation. Early in the twentieth century Charles H. Cooley and George Herbert Mead stressed the social construction of the self through interaction within immediate group settings.

In the 1930s and 1940s, Jacob L. Moreno developed a systematic approach to the understanding and charting of group structure and Muzafer Sherif conducted key studies of group influence and conformity. William Foote Whyte's field study of a street-corner gang demonstrated the existence and importance of group norms and structure in an urban milieu generally thought to lack social organization. Of major importance was Kurt Lewin's work, which provided direction and inspiration for the postwar generation of social psychologists. Lewin combined principles of Gestalt psychology and concepts from the physical sciences to develop field theory in social psychology as a basis for the study of group dynamics. Interested in both theoretical and applied aspects of group interaction, in 1945 he established the first organization devoted to research on group dynamics. The widely utilized sensitivity-training group method originated serendipitously in sessions Lewin organized in 1946.

The period from the end of World War II to the early 1960s produced burgeoning activity in small group research (Hare et al. 1965). The pervasiveness of Lewin's ideas was evident in the growth of group dynamics as an area of research and theoretical development. Cartwright and Zander's important compilation, *Group Dynamics* (1968), first published in 1953, presented a theoretical overview and numerous influential studies of cohesiveness, group pressures and standards, individual motives and group goals, leadership and group performance, and the structural properties of groups.

Substantial work with a different orientation reflected concerns with functional needs that groups must meet in order to survive and with the relationship of those functions to dimensions of interpersonal behavior and personality traits. At the same time, influences from anthropology, economics, and behavioral psychology were being melded in a view of social interaction as an exchange of resources, a perspective applied to the analysis of interdependence, cooperation and competition, and interpersonal relationship (Homans 1950, 1974; Thibaut and Kelley 1959). During those years small group research shared the methodological advances that were occurring throughout the social sciences, developing an increasing sophistication in research design, measurement, and analysis. The excitement, optimism, and productivity of the field led some to define social psychology as the study of small groups.

Small group research since the 1960s has not been as prominent, prolific, or influential as it was during the immediate postwar years, when social psychology was virtually dominated by the small groups "movement" (Borgatta 1981). The production of studies is steady, if moderate compared to the enthusiasm of the peak period, and some significant attempts have been made to organize and integrate the diverse body of work and theory that has accumulated (Hare 1982; McGrath 1984; Foschi and Lawler 1994). There is renewed interest in conceptualizing groups as entities with distinctive properties that cannot be understood in terms of reductionist individual psychology (Turner 1987). Many aspects and procedures of group process and dynamics are commonly utilized in applied settings, while practical concerns with group productivity, efficiency, and success are widespread (Hare et al. 1992; Forsyth 1999).

APPROACHES TO SMALL GROUP RESEARCH

Small group studies are characterized by a wide variety of research techniques and theoretical and practical concerns. Research methods vary in regard to the types of groups and circumstances studied—whether "natural" or contrived for research purposes—and in the intrusiveness of research procedures. Some investigators are concerned with properties of the group itself as the unit of interest, while others use the small group setting as context for exploring individual behavior. Although laboratory studies have predominated, the research techniques employed include direct observation of groups in natural as well as controlled settings; the use of structured observa-

tional systems to code communication or other aspects of behavior; the use of checklists, questionnaires, or interviews to elicit ratings, choices, opinions, or attitudes from group members; and field experimentation.

Laboratory studies have marked advantages in terms of the control and manipulation of variables in the precision of observation and measurement. The procedures employed normally permit replication of observation under controlled conditions. The experimental method is regarded as superior to others for rigorously testing causal hypotheses. Fundamental technical issues are whether relevant variables can be brought into laboratory situations and whether a meaningful range of variation can be achieved.

Criticisms of laboratory research center on the artificiality of the setting and the short-term nature of most studies. Representativeness of subject groups and thus the generalization of the findings also are questioned. Concerns for protecting the rights and well-being of human subjects have led to procedural safeguards that now inhibit or prevent practices that were typical of some well-known earlier studies.

The technical advantages of laboratory procedures, the desire to emulate the natural sciences in developing theory based on experimental evidence, and the compatibility of laboratory methods with the academic environment within which most researchers work all have contributed to the proliferation of laboratory studies that constitute much of small group research.

Direct observation of group behavior under basically uncontrolled ("natural") conditions may be coupled with the investigator's more or less active participation in the affairs of the group. Such research can employ structured systems for coding behavior and interaction patterns that are used by uninvolved "objective" observers, as when a children's play group is studied by adults. A more informal ethnographic approach was employed by Goffman (1964) in collecting the information that illustrated his characterization of human interaction as an elaborate sequence of symbolic presentations of self and groups as collaborating teams of performers.

Participant observation is a procedure in which the researcher acts as part of a (usually natural) group to understand a situation from within, as members of the group define and experience it. Group members may know that the observer is an outsider who is there for his or her own purposes or may be led or allowed to believe that the observer is simply another "genuine" group member. In either case the observer's status influences and constrains both the kinds and amount of information available and the opportunities for recording information. The observer also has some influence on the situations and processes being studied, thus producing outcomes different from those which would have occurred in his or her absence. The use of multiple observers increases opportunities for observation while also increasing the effect of the research on the group's behavior (Festinger et al. 1964). For these reasons, reliability and validity are particularly problematic issues in using this technique.

Participant observation is regarded as useful primarily for descriptive and exploratory research and for generating or illustrating, as opposed to testing, theory. It is favored by those who want to understand the meanings of situations and actions generated and maintained by groups in their natural, everyday environments.

An important naturalistic study was conducted in the late 1930s by Whyte (1955), who studied a street-corner gang as a participant observer over a period of three and a half years. (The appendix to his monograph provides an informative discussion of practical and ethical issues in participant observation.) Whyte gained access to the gang through his association with its leader, and his view is from the top of the social structure. He described the recurrent patterns of relationships among members, group values and codes of behavior, the existence of implicit exchange relationships, territorial behavior, and the nature and functions of gang leadership. His observations of the ways in which members' social rankings in the group affected their performance in athletic competition suggested a program of experimental studies of diffuse status characteristics: an exploration of the manner in which "logically" irrelevant social rank affects the amount of influence an individual has on others in activities ranging from pedestrian behavior to the making of perceptual judgments.

Sociometry, a seminal form of network analysis developed by Moreno (1953), is a technique for eliciting and representing the patterns and structure of choices and liking among group members. While the most common procedure is for researchers to ask group members who they like, dislike, would prefer to work with, or would like to "be like," ratings also can be based on direct observations of members' behavior. The information can be represented as a sociogram showing individuals as circles and choices as arrows between the circles: The diagram depicts group structure in terms of affective relations. Indices of liking or disliking can be computed for each member, and ratings can be organized in a matrix format. The density and patterning of choices may be taken as indicators of group cohesiveness. In practical applications, sociometric data are used to restructure groups on the basis of members' mutual choices.

Interaction Process Research. A prominent research concern has been the description and analysis of group interaction processes, focusing primarily on communication. The approaches employed have ranged from purely formal examination of the amount of communication sent and received by each member of the group to extremely detailed analyses of linguistic and paralinguisitic material, including posture, gestures, and inflection.

The widely used system for Interaction Process Analysis (IPA) developed by Bales (1950, 1970) involves a set of twelve categories for coding units (acts) of communication. The categories reflect Bales's conclusion that all groups confront two domains of concerns: instrumental concerns related to the task the group must accomplish and expressive concerns associated with the socioemotional needs and interrelationships of the group members. Both sets of concerns operate continuously and must be dealt with if a group is to succeed and survive, and there is a virtually constant conflict between them. The set of categories is used by observers to code types of active and passive task-related acts and positive and negative socioemotional acts, as they are generated by group members in the course of interaction.

Numerous studies using the IPA system have sought to document the patterns or "phase movements" of instrumental and expressive communication as groups try to establish the equilibrium necessary to operate. Interaction process scores have been related to personality characteristics and to peer assessments and self-assessments (Borgatta 1962). Attention also has been paid to the roles of particular group members in exercising task leadership or socioemotional leadership.

The division of group leadership into instrumental and expressive functions proved compatible with accepted notions of "typical" male and female personal attributes and with a conceptualization of the family (at least in the Western world) as a small group with the father as task leader and the mother as socioemotional specialist. However, recent research comparing "natural" families with ad hoc laboratory groups indicates that the instrumental versus expressive specialization found in the laboratory seldom holds for groups in natural settings. There is greater diversity of behavior and less gender-linked stereotypical conduct in longer-lasting groups that cover a greater scope of activities (McGrath 1984).

The IPA system has been criticized on both theoretical and operational grounds, and numerous revisions and alternatives have been proposed. Bales and his colleagues developed an elaborated observational system, SYMLOG (Bales and Cohen 1979), that models personal space in three dimensions: dominant-submissive, friendly-unfriendly, and instrumentally controlled–emotionally expressive. Group interaction is observed and members' behaviors are coded on each dimension by outside observers or by the group members themselves. On the basis of combinations of multiple observations, each individual is located within the three-dimensional space and the positions of all group members are charted. The resulting diagram and indices based on the scores indicate the degree to which members are perceived as acting in a similar fashion. Interest in the SYMLOG technique is substantial, and it is utilized in many studies of group structure and performance.

GROUP COHESIVENESS

The understanding of what holds a social unit together, a central issue in sociology, also has been central in small group analysis. Cohesion—the sum of the forces that bind members to the group—was viewed by Lewin and other Gestaltists as a property or characteristic of the group itself, a sort of force field analogous to a magnetic or gravitational field. However, the assessment of cohesion usually depends on observations of the attitudes and behaviors of the individual group members: their self-reported attraction to the group, their feeling of being accepted by the group, similarity in expressions of sentiment, how regularly they attend group meetings, how prompt or tardy they are, or how responsible they are in performing actions that benefit the group. Members also may asked to describe the unity of the group (Evans and Jarvis 1986; Bollen and Hoyle 1990). Although Steiner (1972) suggested that "A true test of a group's cohesion would entail observation of its members' reaction to disruptive influences," he rejected this procedure on technical and ethical grounds (1972, p. 161).

The bases of cohesion include (1) rewards available within and through the group, (2) the congruence between individual goals and group goals, (3) the attraction and/or liking of members for each other, (4) the importance of the group as a source or ground of the individual's identity and self-perception and his or her internalization of group culture and values, and (5) in psychoanalytic group theory, the members' identification with and attraction to the group leader and "the alignment between particular individual superego formation and its corresponding punitive group structure" (Kellerman 1981, p. 11).

Although high cohesiveness often is taken as indicating a "healthy" group, its effect is to heighten members' susceptibility to influences in the group. Thus, group productivity, for example, may be increased or decreased depending on the nature of the predominant influences. A positive association between group cohesion and performance was found by Evans and Dion (1991) in a review of previous studies, but the relationship was modest.

Major importance in the study of cohesiveness has been placed on interpersonal attraction and interdependence, emphasizing the exchange of emotional and affective resources. Work by Tajfel (1981) and Turner (1987) supports, alternatively, an emphasis on social identity and self-categorization. A concept of cohesion based on interpersonal liking that is not mediated by shared group membership and depersonalized attraction to the group is held to be inadequate. Group membership and the resultant self-categorization occur prior to interaction and the emergence of interdependence, cooperation, influence, and cohesion.

Hogg (1987, 1992) advocates research that will produce answers about group solidarity and social identity rather than about interpersonal relationships.

Self-categorization in a most elemental form has been demonstrated in "minimal group" experiments (Tajfel 1981). Subjects are divided into two groups, sometimes presumably on the basis of an arbitrary and unimportant criterion and sometimes in an obviously random manner. The participants do not interact within or between groups during the experiment. Given the task of dividing a sum of money between two persons about whom they know nothing except their group membership, subjects show a marked bias in favor of members of their own group.

Interdependence in a most elemental form has been realized in experiments with the "minimal social situation" (Sidowski 1957). Two subjects, each of whom controls resources that may reward or punish the other and each of whom depends primarily on the other's behavior as a source of reward or punishment, learn to exchange rewards despite being completely unaware of the nature of the situation.

Thibaut and Kelley (1959) identified two criteria individuals use in evaluating the rewards available within a particular situation: a usual, expected level of reward to which the person feels entitled, called the "comparison level," and the person's perceived best level of reward available outside the situation, called the "comparison level for alternatives." An individual's satisfaction with his or her group membership and participation depends on the relationship of rewards available within the group to his or her comparison level, while the likelihood that one will stay in or leave a group depends on the comparison level for alternatives.

Although the value and availability of rewards are usually emphasized in assessing the attractiveness of a group, Leon Festinger has pointed out the persistence of loyalty to "lost causes" and the effect that insufficient reward, or even aversive experiences, can have in strengthening members' positive attitudes. In one experiment (Aronson and Mills 1959), potential group members who were subjected to a severe initiation expressed greater liking for the group than did those who had a mild initiation. And while an equitable and balanced exchange of rewarding outcomes is considered important in sustaining interpersonal relationships and participants' satisfaction with them, Kelley and Thibaut (1978) noted that problematic situations provide particular opportunities. Attributions about a partner's personality and motivations and self-presentations that encode messages of commitment and concern for the other person are facilitated when behavior cannot be explained simply in terms of "rational" self-interest. Such attributions and encodings strengthen affective ties and promote interdependence of the characteristics and attitudes displayed in the relationship.

GROUP INFLUENCE

Social Facilitation and Inhibition. In a study credited as the first social psychological experiment (1897), Triplett measured the average time his subjects took to wind 150 turns on a fishing reel, working both alone and in competition with one another. Subjects working in competition wound the reels faster than did those working alone. Numerous subsequent experiments (including some with nonhuman subjects) have supported and modified these results. It was found that the mere presence of other persons (as observers or coactors, whether or not they were competitors) facilitated well-learned responses but that the presence of others interfered with the acquisition of new responses. This "audience effect" thus facilitates performance but inhibits learning. Various explanations of social facilitation and inhibition have been proposed, generally incorporating the idea that the presence of others increases motivational arousal. Such arousal is a basic feature of the group environment (Zajonc 1966).

Conformity. Similarities of values, attitudes, beliefs, perceptions, and behavior are a ubiquitous and virtually defining feature of group existence. These similarities can facilitate coordination of goal-directed activity, motivate the members, provide sources of psychological security and emotional reward, reinforce members' identification with the group, and increase cohesiveness. They also may prevent reasoned consideration of alternatives to group decisions and the potential consequences of group actions, reduce flexibility in adapting to new circumstances, and inhibit change in general. Closed circles of conformity in cohesive groups that are isolated from dissenting viewpoints, producing "groupthink" (Janis 1982), have been implicated in producing military blunders, fascist atrocities, government scandals, and space shuttle disasters. Conformity (to modeled indifference or uncertainty) is a factor in the failure of bystanders to help others in emergencies.

The amount of conformity in a group may be seen as a characteristic of the collectivity. Experimental studies, however, usually have been concerned with effects on the individual. Considered from this viewpoint, conformity is defined as a change in an individual's attitudes, beliefs, or behavior in the direction of a group norm. It is an example of social control resulting from peer influence (as distinct from, for example, obedience to a constituted authority) (Milgram 1974). Two types of conformity have been identified: belief (or informational) conformity and behavioral (or normative) conformity. Both types are increased by strong group cohesiveness.

Belief conformity involves an internalized and lasting change grounded in an individual's dependence on social sources of information and guidance. Once they are internalized, the group's standards and perceptions are constantly carried with the individual and constitute an ongoing element of social control.

Sherif (1935) asked individual subjects to judge the apparent movement of a pinpoint of light in an otherwise totally dark room. Under these conditions the light, which in fact was stationary, appeared to most people to move. Different individuals perceived different amounts of movement. Assembled in small groups viewing the light together, the subjects began to agree on the amount of movement they perceived: A group norm emerged in an ambiguous situation. After the group interaction, subjects were asked to view the light, again in isolation. They continued to see the amount of movement agreed on by the group rather than the amount they originally perceived individually. The group's perceptions apparently had been internalized.

The strength of belief conformity varies with the ambiguity and unfamiliarity of the situation, the individual's trust in the credibility of the group, the individual's attraction to and identification with the group, and the individual's prior experience and confidence.

Behavioral conformity is grounded in the potential rewards and punishments dispensed by the group and in the individual's previous experience with the consequences of conformity and nonconformity. The consequences of agreeing with others' judgments and opinions, emulating others' behaviors, and following the customs of a group are usually pleasant, while disagreement and deviancy generally lead to unpleasant effects. Group members who hold deviant opinions typically receive, at first, greater than normal amounts of communication in an attempt to influence them to conform. If these efforts fail, they are likely to be isolated or rejected, depending on the severity of the deviance. Monitoring of behavior is necessary if reward or punishment is to depend on its occurrence; thus this type of influence is effective only if and when an individual's actions are known to the group.

Experiments conducted by Asch (1951) demonstrated behavioral conformity. The subjects engaged in a perceptual estimation task that required them to pick out lines of the same length printed on boards that were presented side by side. The boards were presented in pairs, and the judgment of each pair constituted one experimental trial. In a typical experiment there was only one genuine subject; the other participants were employed by Asch, and their judgments were prearranged. After a number of trials in which correct judgments were given, the confederate "subjects" began stating unanimous wrong judgments. The genuine subjects conformed to a substantial extent by expressing judgments that agreed with those of the group. When removed from the group or allowed to state judgments in private, the real subjects did not persist in making these errors. Their conformity occurred only when it was witnessed by the other group members.

The strength of behavioral conformity varies with the size and unanimity of the group, the importance of the group to the individual, and the disclosure of relevant judgments or behaviors to the group.

Belief and behavioral conformity can be distinguished analytically (and empirically under some laboratory conditions), but in natural situations they operate in conjunction. The group member not only is rewarded for conforming but also depends on others as models for behavior and guides for judgments and opinions. While it is common to think of beliefs and attitudes as existing before the behaviors that reflect them, a large body of research indicates that people come to believe the opinions they express. "Mere" behavioral conformity can lead to internalization.

Conformity effects usually are thought to reflect the majority influence in a group, but evidence shows that a determined minority can prevail. Minority influence seems especially relevant in regard to internalization (Moscovici 1980).

Group Polarization. Early theories of "group contagion" and the madness of crowds notwithstanding, a general assumption has been that conformity processes within a group operate to bring extreme opinions and judgments in toward the center of the range of opinions and judgments. However, a body of research has contradicted the notion that group actions are more moderate than those of individuals.

The experimental procedure called for individual subjects to evaluate each of twelve "choice dilemmas," situations in which a person was asked to choose between a highly desirable risky alternative and a less desirable but certain alternative. The subjects were instructed to indicate for each dilemma, the lowest probability of success they would accept in recommending that the desirable risky alternative be chosen. Probabilities were averaged for each subject over all dilemmas to generate a "riskiness" score for that person. Small groups of subjects were then formed and instructed to discuss each situation, reach a group decision, and indicate the group riskiness score for the dilemma. A group's scores were averaged over the twelve situations, and that value was compared to the mean of the individual scores of the group members.

Initial research that employed the choice dilemmas procedure found a significant "risky shift" in the group decisions compared to the mean of the individual scores. Numerous experiments and further analyses followed that extended and qualified those findings (Cartwright 1973). Certain kinds of choice dilemma scenarios produced risky shifts, while others produced conservative shifts or showed no significant difference. Shifts tended to move in the direction of the initial inclinations of the group: The interaction resulted in a collective outcome more extreme than might have been predicted on the basis of the individual positions, but the individual positions forecast the nature of the shift.

Group polarization, as the effect is now called, has been theoretically interpreted in terms of risk as a cultural value, the persuasive influence of "risky" individuals, and the diffusion of responsibility in group action. However, the effect can be explained as being due to the normative and informational influences involved in conformity processes (McGrath 1984).

GROUP INTERACTION AND PERFORMANCE

Group performance in terms of problem solving, productivity, or effectiveness is a subject of both practical and theoretical concern that has generated numerous studies and a large body of theory. Productivity may refer to the quality of a group product, the efficiency of output per unit time or progress toward a group goal, or the realization of group potential. The establishment of an appropriate basis of evaluation is often problematic, and expected outcomes depend heavily on the type of task undertaken. When groups fall short of what (from some standpoint) it is felt they should accomplish, the failure often is attributed to "process losses" resulting from problems in interaction.

Steiner (1972) distinguished between tasks that require a coordinated division of effort, which he labeled "divisible," and those with a single outcome or product, which he called "unitary." Disjunctive unitary tasks are those which can be accomplished successfully by one individual alone. In such cases the group should be as "good" as the best member. Conjunctive unitary tasks require all the members to contribute successfully; in these tasks, the group can be only as good as the worst member. Tasks in which members' contributions are simply summed to produce the group outcome are called additive, and group performance should depend on the "average" member. Numerous laboratory studies of ad hoc groups performing a wide range of judgment tasks have been conducted. Overall, the results indicate that groups seldom do as well as the best member but usually do better than the average member.

Field studies of industrial workers in natural settings illustrate how influence processes in the group can regulate behavior. Work groups develop norms with respect to what they, not the company, regard as an appropriate day's output. While pay, potential promotion, and retention or termination may be controlled by the employer, the immediate group controls powerful social rewards and sanctions that are brought to bear on a day-to-day basis. Those who exceed the group's production norm ("rate busters") and those who fail to produce an acceptable amount or attain an acceptable standard of quality are subjected to group pressure ranging from "kidding" and mild criticism to serious harassment. Since group cohesiveness increases conformity, some companies find it desirable to move workers frequently and attempt in other ways to inhibit the formation of interpersonal ties and identification with the group. Other organizations attempt to mobilize small group processes to support their goals.

Successful performance requires that a group have the necessary resources (material resources and members' skills, knowledge, and competencies) and time needed to accomplish its tasks. In addition, issues of coordination and motivation arise. When it confronts a disjunctive unitary task, the group simply must assure that the "best" member has the opportunity, recognition, and authorization to function and is motivated to do so. The only coordination needed may be to prevent interference from other members. For other types of tasks the quality, sequence, and articulation of many or all members' contributions are important (Miller and Hamblin 1963).

Allocation of opportunity to participate and evaluation of members' actions constitute elements of the status structures of groups. The explanation of how interaction inequalities in task groups are developed and maintained is the concern of expectation states theory (Foschi 1997; Foschi and Lawler 1994).

Group members hold expectations about the nature, quality, and value of each other's performances. Their expectations influence the quality of those performances and affect the evaluation of performances after they occur; they are in this sense self-fulfilling prophecies.

Though expectations may derive from first-hand task experience within the group, they also are based on "external" status characteristics of the members. Diffuse status characteristics such as age, race, gender, or perceived social rank may influence expectations whether or not they are objectively relevant to the group's task and goals. Inequalities in participation, evaluation of performance outputs, and influence over the group's decisions reflect inequalities in status characteristics that members bring to the group. These inequalities tend to be maintained within the group regardless of their pertinence. Evaluations of performance output depend on previous evaluations, and expectations that arise out of group interaction influence subsequent interaction to produce their own confirmation (Berger et al. 1972, 1980). Thus the degree of influence exerted by group members and the impact of their contributions to the group's effort may not be highly correlated with their task-related competence and abilities.

Processes of influence and conformity may degrade performance quality. Majorities generate social pressure whether or not they are competent. Techniques have been devised to control these effects by regulating the kind of interaction that can take place. Some procedures, such as Multi-Attribute Utility Analysis, require the clear identification of task elements and their accomplishment in specified sequences. Group members can interact freely but must adhere to the task stages. Other approaches impose rules for communication in decision-making processes.

Many studies have been concerned with evaluating the effects of different patterns of interaction, primarily communication, on performance. "Brainstorming," a group interaction technique in which members generate as many ideas as possible within a given time period without evaluation or criticism, is intended to overcome inhibiting social influence processes while taking advantage of those which stimulate creativity. However, research indicates that a brainstorming group is generally less effective in producing ideas than are the same number of individuals working alone. The Delphi Method and the Nominal Group Technique are two approaches to regulating the combination of individual effort with group feedback or interaction to reduce the deleterious effects of social relations within the group, conformity, and personalized conflict. In the Delphi Method individuals, without communicating with each other, make judgments that are combined into a group "product." The results are made known to the participants, who then make another round of judgments. This procedure is repeated until a final group judgment is attained. The Nominal Group Technique, which is used for developing plans or ideas or for choosing a correct or best solution, begins by having individuals work separately to generate plans, ideas, or judgments. The group then collectively lists and evaluates the material that was produced individually. These methods have advocates, but the desirability of some of their results is questionable and the time and cost involved in their utilization may be significant (McGrath 1984).

A substantial body of research has compared the relative effectiveness of structured networks of communication available to members of problem-solving groups. Typically, groups of three to five persons were required to combine information distributed across the individual members, communicating only through channels provided by the experimenters. Various networks of communication channels have been investigated to see how they affect a group's efficiency and the members' satisfaction. The networks differ in terms of how centralized or open they are. The most centralized network compels all messages to flow through one position, while the most open permits direct communication among all the members.

The conclusions from this research are that centralized networks are most efficient in dealing with simple tasks but that group members tend to be dissatisfied, except for the person occupying the central position. In more complex tasks the advantages of centralization are lost. Burgess (1969) suggested that the network experiments were basically flawed in failing to provide meaningful consequences for group performance and in studying groups only for brief periods, while they were learning to use the networks. His research demonstrated that when subjects had enough time to learn to use the channels provided, and received rewards based on performance, the type of network made no difference. Given time and motivation, groups adapted efficiently to overcome the structural constraints.

A type of process loss observed in both physical and cognitive tasks is the reduction in effort people put into group performance compared with the effort they make when working individually. This effect, called social loafing, has been observed in numerous cultures and is related to group size: As groups get larger, individual effort tends to diminish. Social impact theory explains social loafing in terms of a conflict between a person's sense of responsibility and his or her feeling that inaction is the safest or least costly course of behavior. Diffusion of personal responsibility occurs in group situations and reduces the blame for inaction. Also, a lack of individual identification and the absence of evaluation by others become more likely as group size increases. Thus both rewards for effort and punishment for lack of effort become less certain and less consistent. While laziness and "goldbricking" often occur in individual situations, those behaviors can be concealed more easily in a crowd. Nonetheless, members who identify with and value a group and hold strongly to its norms will exert effort on behalf of the group (Hogg 1992). As was noted above, there is a positive association between group cohesion and productivity in groups with norms that support good performance. This relationship is reciprocal: Group success tends to increase cohesion.

The social loafing effect is confounded with problems of coordination, since both increase as the number of persons involved in a task gets larger. In addition, members' impatience and/or frustration with coordination problems can undermine their motivation and sense of responsibility, exacerbating social loafing.

Although researchers have paid much attention to process loss, there also are many significant process gains in group interaction. Social facilitation, stimulation, learning, socioemotional support, development and reinforcement of identity, and even conformity processes can enhance creativity, productivity, and effectiveness. While questions of individual versus group superiority may be provocative, most human endeavor occurs in group contexts and requires group effort.

The recognition that productivity can be affected substantially by the functions and quality of leadership in a group has stimulated much research and theorizing about leadership styles and effectiveness. An early experimental program conducted by Lewin et al. (1939) systematically varied the behavior of adult leaders of clubs of 11-year-old boys engaged in craft work and recreational activity. The leaders were trained to enact democratic, authoritarian (autocratic), and laissez-faire styles of leadership, and those styles were experienced by each club for several weeks. The resulting changes in the boys' task performance, social relationships and interaction, and motivation as well as some aspects of group "climate" were intensively documented and analyzed. The results of the study, while complex, generally favored the democratic leadership style both for producing increased motivation and originality and for fostering more mutual friendliness and group-mindedness among the boys. Group members preferred the democratic leader to either the autocratic or the laissez-faire leader.

A contingency model of leadership effectiveness has been developed by Fiedler (1981), whose concepts of task-motivated versus relationship-motivated style recall Bales's identification of instrumental and socioemotional leadership functions. A leader's effectiveness results from the combination of style and situation: Task leaders are most effective in situations that are either highly favorable or unfavorable, while relationship leaders are most effective in middle-range situations. The contingency model, though supported by a large body of research, is questioned by some who feel that effective leaders are those who deal with both task and relationship elements of group situations.

COOPERATION AND COMPETITION IN GROUPS

Two different orientations are evident in research on competition and cooperation within groups. In one approach cooperation and competition are treated as imposed external conditions that influence the quality of group interaction and task performance. Alternatively, cooperation and competition have been studied as dependent behaviors that are affected by reward and risk contingencies, the availability of communication, and other situational factors.

Numerous studies have compared the productivity and efficiency of groups working under cooperative conditions (defined as working for group goals) and competitive conditions (defined as working for individual goals). The concept of cooperation in early research usually specified only mutual dependency of outcomes, with little attention paid to the interdependency of the members' task activities. The findings indicated that the efficiency of work under competition was greater than that under cooperation for tasks that did not require coordination of effort. Some research indicated that cooperative groups worked together more frequently and were more highly coordinated.

Analysis of research focusing on the nature of tasks used as criteria in comparing cooperative and competitive reward structures points to the importance of "means interdependence," the degree to which group members are reliant on one another (Schmitt 1981, 1998). When tasks are simple, requiring no division of labor or sharing of information or resources, the advantage of cooperative contingencies seems to hold. However, cooperative contingencies are typically superior for tasks high in means interdependence involving distribution of effort, coordination of responses, or information sharing. Also, the long-term consequences of different reward structures may be substantial in natural groups, involving issues of morale and sustained member motivation that seldom arise in relatively brief laboratory studies. Such consequences can depend on the way in which competitive payoffs are determined; the possibility that some group members may become perpetual "losers" while others are constant winners will affect the efforts of all the members.

In a number of cases an additional element of competition between groups has been found to increase the productivity of internally cooperative groups. Turner (1987) observed that competition (for mutual distinctiveness) can develop between groups even in the absence of conflicts of interest. This striving to enhance positive social identity increases group cohesiveness and solidarity, making cooperation more likely.

Laboratory research treating cooperation as a dependent effect has focused on the participants' choice of cooperative rather than competitive behaviors and the distribution and coordination of responses. The effects of threat and communication were investigated in a well-known "trucking game" study (Deutsch and Krauss 1962). Two subjects could cooperate by taking turns using a "short route" to reach a destination and thus make money. Cooperation was reduced when one subject could block the route with a gate ("unilateral threat") and was extremely rare when both subjects had gates ("bilateral threat"). Communication between subjects did not increase cooperation under the threat conditions.

Communication sometimes has been found to increase cooperation in some of the many studies using the "Prisoner's Dilemma." In this situation, two participants benefit moderately if both choose to cooperate and lose substantially if both "defect." If either one chooses to cooperate while the other defects, the cooperator suffers a very large loss and the defector's outcome is highly favorable. Thus, cooperation involves risk while defection implies motives of self-protection, exploitation, or both. The structure of outcomes is paradoxical: The rational choices of each individual lead to poor collective consequences.

The rates of cooperation observed in these studies are low. The Prisoner's Dilemma epitomizes the class of situations called social traps, in which individual (usually short-term) "rational" self-interest conflicts with the (usually longer-term) well-being of the group, leading to collective irrationality (Kollock 1998).

Inequity of outcomes and the presence of risk have been found to reduce cooperation across a wide range of experimental research (Marwell and Schmitt 1975). Beneficial effects of communication were dependent on the timing of its availability and the pattern of behavior that had occurred before communication took place.

Studies of cooperation and competition have addressed problems of motivation and coordination, issues of equity, the effects of short-term and long-term consequences, and the relationship of individual outcomes to collective outcomes. The analysis of these topics is a notable feature of recent small group research, particularly as concern with social traps and dilemmas resonates with the environmental and social issues facing contemporary society.

REFERENCES

Aronson, Elliot, and Judson Mills 1959 "The Effect of Severity of Initiation on Liking for a Group." *Journal of Abnormal and Social Psychology* 59:177–181.

Asch, Solomon E. 1951 "Effects of Group Pressure upon the Modification and Distortion of Judgments." In H. Guetzkow, ed., *Groups, Leadership, and Men.* Pittsburgh: Carnegie.

Bales, Robert F. 1950 *Interaction Process Analysis: A Method for the Study of Small Groups.* Cambridge, Mass.: Addison-Wesley.

—— 1970 *Personality and Interpersonal Behavior.* New York: Holt, Rinehart and Winston.

——, and Stephen P. Cohen 1979 *SYMLOG: A System for the Multiple Level Observation of Groups.* New York: Free Press.

Berger, Joseph, Bernard P. Cohen, and Morris Zelditch, Jr. 1972 "Status Characteristics and Social Interaction." *American Sociological Review* 37:241–255.

——, Susan J. Rosenholtz, and Morris Zelditch, Jr. 1980 "Status Organizing Processes." *Annual Review of Sociology* 6:479–508.

Bollen, Kenneth A., and Rick H. Hoyle 1990 "Perceived Cohesiveness: A Conceptual and Empirical Examination." *Social Forces* 69:479–504.

Borgatta, Edgar F. 1962 "A Systematic Study of Interaction Process Scores, Peer and Self-Assessments, Personality and Other Variables." *Genetic Psychology Monographs* 65:269–290.

—— 1981 "The Small Groups Movement: Historical Notes." *American Behavioral Scientist* 24:607–618.

Burgess, Robert L. 1969 "Communication Networks: An Experimental Evaluation." In R. L. Burgess and D. Bushell, Jr., eds., *Behavioral Sociology: The Experimental Analysis of Social Process.* New York: Columbia University Press.

Cartwright, Dorwin 1973 "Determinants of Scientific Progress: The Case of Research on the Risky Shift." *American Psychologist* 28:222–231.

——, and Alvin Zander, eds., 1968 *Group Dynamics: Research and Theory,* 3rd ed. New York: Harper & Row.

Cooley, Charles H. 1909 *Social Organization.* New York: Charles Scribner's Sons.

Deutsch, Morton, and Robert M. Krauss 1962 "Studies of Interpersonal Bargaining." *Journal of Conflict Resolution* 6:52–76.

Evans, Charles R., and Kenneth L. Dion 1991 "Group Cohesion and Performance: A Meta-Analysis." *Small Group Research* 22(2):175–186.

Evans, Nancy J., and Paul A. Jarvis 1986 "The Group Attitude Scale: A Measure of Attraction to Group." *Small Group Behavior* 17:203–216.

Festinger, Leon, Henry W. Riecken, and Stanley Schachter 1964 *When Prophecy Fails.* New York: Harper & Row.

Fiedler, Fred E. 1981 "Leadership Effectiveness." *American Behavioral Scientist* 24:619–632.

Forsyth, Donelson R. 1999 *Group Dynamics,* 3rd ed. Belmont, Calif.: Brooks/Cole-Wadsworth.

Foschi, Martha 1997 "On Scope Conditions." *Small Group Research* 28(4):535–555.

——, and Edward J. Lawler, eds. 1994 *Group Processes: Sociological Analyses.* Chicago: Nelson-Hall.

Goffman, Erving 1959 *The Presentation of Self in Everyday Life*. Garden City, N.Y.: Doubleday.

Hare, A. Paul 1982 *Creativity in Small Groups*. Beverly Hills, Calif.: Sage.

——, Herbert H. Blumberg, Martin F. Davies, and M. Valerie Kent 1992 *Small Group Research: A Handbook*. Norwood, N.J.: Ablex.

——, Edgar F. Borgatta, and Robert F. Bales, eds. 1965 *Small Groups: Studies in Social Interaction*, rev. ed. New York: Knopf.

Hogg, Michael A. 1987 "Social Identity and Group Cohesiveness." In J. C. Turner, ed., *Rediscovering the Social Group*. Oxford, UK: Basil Blackwell.

——, 1992 *The Social Psychology of Group Cohesiveness: From Attraction to Social Identity*. New York: New York University Press.

Homans, George C. 1950 *The Human Group*. New York: Harcourt, Brace.

—— 1974 *Social Behavior: Its Elementary Forms*, rev. ed. New York: Harcourt Brace Jovanovich.

Janis, Irving L. 1982 *Groupthink: Psychological Studies of Policy Decisions and Fiascos*, 2nd ed. Boston: Houghton-Mifflin.

Kellerman, Henry 1981 "The Deep Structures of Group Cohesion." In H. Kellerman, ed., *Group Cohesion: Theoretical and Clinical Perspectives*. New York: Grune & Stratton.

Kelley, Harold H., and John W. Thibaut 1978 *Interpersonal Relations: A Theory of Interdependence*. New York: Wiley.

Kollock, Peter 1998 "Social Dilemmas: The Anatomy of Cooperation." *Annual Review of Sociology* 24:183–214.

Lewin, Kurt, Ronald Lippit, and Ralph K. White 1939 "Patterns of Aggressive Behavior in Experimentally Created 'Social Environments.'" *Journal of Social Psychology* 10:271–299.

Marwell, Gerald, and David R. Schmitt 1975 *Cooperation: An Experimental Analysis*. New York: Academic Press.

McGrath, Joseph E. 1984 *Groups: Interaction and Performance*. Englewood Cliffs, N.J.: Prentice-Hall.

Milgram, Stanley 1974 *Obedience to Authority*. New York: Harper & Row.

Miller, L. Keith, and Robert L. Hamblin 1963 "Interdependence, Differential Rewarding, and Productivity." *American Sociological Review* 28:768–778.

Moreno, Jacob L. 1953 *Who Shall Survive?* rev. ed. Beacon, N.Y.: Beacon House.

Moscovici, Serge 1980 "Toward a Theory of Conversion Behavior." In L. Berkowitz, ed., *Advances In Experimental Social Psychology*, vol. 13. New York: Academic Press.

Ofshe, Richard A., ed. 1973 *Interpersonal Behavior in Small Groups*. Englewood Cliffs, N.J.: Prentice-Hall.

Olmstead, Michael, and A. Paul Hare 1978 *The Small Group*, 2nd ed. New York: Random House.

Schmitt, David R. 1981 "Performance under Cooperation or Competition." *American Behavioral Scientist* 24:649–679.

——, 1998 "Effects of Reward Distribution and Performance Feedback on Competitive Responding." *Journal of the Experimental Analysis of Behavior* 69:263–273.

Sherif, Muzafer 1935 "A Study of Some Social Factors in Perception." *Archives of Psychology* 27, no. 187.

Sidowski, Joseph B. 1957 "Reward and Punishment in a Minimal Social Situation." *Journal of Experimental Psychology* 54:318–326.

Steiner, Ivan D. 1972 *Group Process and Productivity*. New York: Academic Press.

Tajfel, Henri 1981 *Human Groups and Social Categories*. Cambridge; UK: Cambridge University Press.

Thibaut, John W., and Harold H. Kelley 1959 *The Social Psychology of Groups*. New York: Wiley.

Triplett, N. 1897 "The Dynamogenic Factors in Pacemaking and Competition." *American Journal of Psychology* 9:507–533.

Turner, John C. 1987 *Rediscovering the Social Group: A Self-Categorization Theory*. Oxford, UK: Basil Blackwell.

Whyte, William F. 1955 *Street Corner Society: The Social Structure of an Italian Slum*, 2nd ed. Chicago: University of Chicago Press.

Zajonc, Robert B. 1966 *Social Psychology: An Experimental Approach*. Belmont, Calif.: Brooks/Cole.

Robert W. Shotola

SOCIAL AND POLITICAL ELITES

At one level, elites can be defined simply as persons who hold dominant positions in major institutions or are recognized leaders in art, education, business, and other fields of achievement. Such individuals exist in all societies, but beyond this mundane observation, social scientists are interested in why particular individuals attain positions of status and power. Does achievement reflect superior talent, or is it a product of social or cultural advantage? Why are some achievements valued over others? How does the distribution of elite positions in society reflect the particular social structures in which they exist? These questions are the focus of much research on stratification and social inequality.

In the social sciences, the concept of elites refers to a more specific issue as well: the concentration of societal power—especially political power—in the hands of a few. At the heart of theoretical debates and empirical research on elites is the famous assertion of Mosca (1939, p. 50): "In all societies . . . two classes of people appear—a class that rules and a class that is ruled." One can distinguish the conception of "functional elites" in a variety of institutional contexts from that of a "ruling" or "political" elite that in some sense wields societal-level power. Then the key questions concern the existence and nature of this dominant group. Is power over the major institutions of society highly concentrated, or is it broadly dispersed as "pluralists" claim? If a cohesive ruling elite exists, then who is in it and what is the basis of its power? What is the extent of its power in relation to the nonelite "masses"? Does this societal elite exercise power responsibly in the interests of society as a whole, or do elites maximize their own interests against those of subordinate groups?

CLASSICAL ELITE THEORY

Social thought on elites goes back at least to Plato and Aristotle, but contemporary debates usually begin with the "neo-Machiavellians" Pareto (1935), Mosca (1939), and Michels ([1915] 1959). Reacting to the turmoil of European society in the early twentieth century, each developed arguments supporting the inevitability of elite rule in opposition to classical democratic theory, Marxian class analysis, and socialist political movements. For Pareto, elites in general were those holding leadership positions in business, politics, education, and other areas of accomplishment. Those individuals could be distinguished from the rest of "nonelite" society. He further distinguished between the "governing elite"—the segment of the elite with broad political power—and the nongoverning elite. His best known statements concerned the former group. Though famous for his work in mathematical economics, Pareto believed that most human behavior was nonrational, the expression of

deep-seated "sentiments" and their observable manifestations, or "residues." These motivational orientations led to behaviors that were then "explained" through our post hoc rationalizations, or "derivations" (1935, chap. IX). For Pareto, the governing elites were those with dominant talents or leadership skills derived primarily from superior individual attributes. Borrowing from Machiavelli, he distinguished two ideal types of political leaders on the basis of their dominant personal qualities and motivations ("residues"). "Lions" appealed to the conservative instincts that were most common in the masses, relying on tradition, strength, and coercion to rule. "Foxes" were more innovative leaders who relied on cunning, new ideas, and manipulation. Both types were necessary, but Pareto tended to see a cyclical pattern of rule in societies in which "foxes" dominated in periods of upheaval and transition, only to be displaced by "lions" after the restoration of social order (1935, chap. XII).

Pareto also noted that individuals in positions of power often attempt to maintain their privileged positions by closing off access for others. This risks social disruption by shutting off avenues of achievement and power to other talented individuals, who then mobilize to affect change. The "circulation of elites" refers to the process by which the ruling class is renewed periodically by superior individuals from other ranks. For Pareto, obstacles to elite circulation often resulted in the stagnation of the ruling class. Closed aristocracies and caste-like systems fostered tension, conflict, and eventually social change.

Like Pareto, Mosca began with the assertion that elite rule is an empirical fact in all societies. Although he also noted the superior individual attributes of the "ruling class," his analysis was considerably more sociological than that of Pareto. Mosca emphasized the organizational advantages of the ruling elite in that they represented a relatively cohesive and easily organized minority against the disorganized masses (Mosca 1939, p. 53). He also discussed the role of the "subelite," a technocratic stratum of managers, intellectuals, and bureaucrats that was increasingly important for elite rule in modern societies (1939, pp. 404–409; see also Marger 1987, p. 54). Mosca's conception of social change and the circulation of elites was also more sociological. Social, economic, and technological changes often generated new opportunities and called forth new talents, bringing new elites into prominence. Mosca agreed with Pareto that closed systems of rule threatened social stability, since a stagnant elite impeded adaptation to change.

In *Political Parties* ([1915] 1959), Michels traced the necessity of elite rule in modern societies to the imperatives of complex organization. His classic study analyzed the German Social Democratic Party, but his arguments have been applied to a variety of organizational contexts. Influenced by Weber's ([1921] 1968) work on politics and bureaucracy, Michels's most famous conclusion is summarized in his "Iron Law of Oligarchy," the argument that large-scale organizations necessarily concentrate power in the hands of a few at the top. Once in power, leaders in organizations such as labor unions and political parties act to preserve their positions. Those who rise from lower levels in the organization are co-opted in a process that preserves the structure of power. The resources available to institutional leaders and their relative unity of interest and perspective give them numerous advantages in maintaining their power over the unorganized rank and file. Over time, leaders develop similar interests and intraelite attachments that reflect their elevated position and separate them from the masses. For their part, Michels saw the masses contributing to elite rule through their general apathy and acquiescence. With his focus on organizational factors, Michels has been very influential in the development of contemporary elite approaches to power (see Marger 1987, pp. 56–58; Burton and Higley 1987).

C. WRIGHT MILLS AND THE ELITE-PLURALIST DEBATE

Among elite theorists there is an important distinction between those who see the concentration of power as inevitable or desirable and those who do not. The former group includes the classical elite theorists and those who have extended their ideas (see Field and Higley 1980; Burton and Higley 1987). In contrast, "critical" or "radical" elite theorists recognize the concentration of power in society but argue that this condition is neither inevitable nor desirable. Unlike the classical theorists who emphasized mass apathy or incompetence, critical elite theorists argue that elite domination

is maintained through the manipulation and exploitation of nonelites.

The most influential representative of the critical elite perspective is Mills (1956). Mills, Hunter (1953), and other critical elite theorists developed their work in response to the dominance of "pluralist" studies of political power in the United States. Pluralism, as represented in the work of Dahl (1956), Truman (1951), Riesman (1950), and others, held that power in modern democratic societies was widely dispersed and that those in decision-making positions were subject to significant mass pressures (through electoral or other processes) or the countervailing power of other institutional elites or organized interest groups. For Mills, the notion of a pluralist balance of power between competing interest groups was a romantic ideal rather than a description of political reality in the United States. He acknowledged the activities of labor unions, farm groups, professional associations, and other organized interest groups but argued that those groups operated mainly at the secondary, local, and "middle levels" of power. The power to make decisions of national and international scope rested with a "power elite" of individuals in top positions of authority in major corporations, the executive branch of government, and the military. Congress was consigned to the middle levels of power, along with most of the interest groups studied by pluralist social scientists. Mills traced the historical consolidation of the power elite to the growth of the federal government in the 1930s and especially during World War II, as industrial production was coordinated with military needs through the government. That institutional alignment was strengthened in the Cold War years as the state expanded its commitment to national security, social welfare, and the direction of economic policy. By the 1950s there was a significant shift in power from Congress to the executive branch, reflecting an expansion of government that required a complex information-gathering and administrative capacity. Congress lacked the resources and coherence required for modern state administration.

Mills argued that most of the members of the power elite had similar values and interests, which reflected their similar backgrounds, common schools, shared membership in elite social clubs, and informal social interaction. He also emphasized the continuous professional interaction between these institutional leaders and the frequent exchange of top personnel between major corporations, the military, and the executive branch of government. Another factor contributing to the relative homogeneity of the power elite was their common experience at the apex of bureaucratic institutions. The skills, status, and even personality type required for success were similar in each sphere, reflecting their similarity of organizational structure (Mills 1956, p. 15).

The other side of Mills's conception of the power elite was that of mass society. The same social processes that had concentrated political power had created a society of increasingly fragmented individuals whose lives and interests were shaped for them from above. Information filtered selectively through bureaucratized institutions of mass education and the mass media, which became more susceptible to elite manipulation as they became more centralized. The media emphasized entertainment and consumption over information and critique. Educational institutions had developed into sites of large-scale vocational training rather than havens for the development of critical thought and an informed citizenry necessary for democratic politics (Mills 1956, chap. 13).

Mills's work became the touchstone for debates about the structure of power in the United States that have continued to this day. Pluralists argue that he exaggerated the unity of functional elites and neglected the influence of the electoral process and interest group competition. From the other direction, neo-Marxist and other class-theoretical analysts have been critical of the Millsian model for not acknowledging the extent to which political power is shaped by dominant economic interests (see the debates collected in Domhoff and Ballard 1968). A key question in these disputes concerns the degree of elite cohesion. How much consensus (or competition) between elites is required to support an elite (or pluralist) model? What is the extent of elite competition? Is there a hierarchy of elites, with a ruling class or "power elite" on top, or a "polyarchy" (Dahl 1971) of diverse institutional powers? Elite theorists acknowledge that individuals with different skills and constituencies hold leadership positions in a variety of institutions such as prestigious universities, private foundations, major civic organizations,

and the media (see Dye 1995). Pluralists view these institutions as relatively autonomous sources of societal influence. Although one may identify "strategic elites," or influential leaders, in a variety of fields (Keller 1963), they see no overall cohesion or uniform coordination of policy within a single ruling group. However, those defending an elite perspective argue that disagreements over particular interests occur within a general elite consensus on basic ideology and acceptable policy. Developing Mills's arguments, elite theorists have studied a variety of coordinating mechanisms that foster elite cohesion, such as private school ties, social networks, shared membership in policy planning organizations, and the general recruitment process in which future leaders are instilled with attitudes conducive to maintaining the existing structure of power (see Prewitt and Stone 1973; Marger 1987; Bottomore 1993; Dye 1995; Domhoff 1998). Some who work in this tradition go further than Mills in emphasizing the prominence of *class* interests and corporate power over the political process and other institutions in capitalist societies (Miliband 1969; Useem 1983; Domhoff 1990, 1998). Indeed, the distinction between "elite" and "class "analysis disappears in many such works (on the similarities and differences, see Marger 1987). From this perspective, prestigious Ivy League universities may harbor intellectuals critical of the existing power structure, that but only those academics with "acceptable" views are selected as advisers to political elites in turn must maintain acceptable levels of business confidence and campaign finance to remain in power.

In a similar vein, all parties agree that in a modern democratic system, the "elite," however defined, must pay some attention to the "masses." The question is, How much attention must be paid, and how do public preferences impose themselves on elites? Pluralists hold that the public has a significant influence on elite decision making through voting, public opinion, and the threat of social protest. From a different starting point, some class-based analysts note the role of working class mobilization or the effects of other nonelite social movements, such as the civil rights movement, that force changes in the polity and society (Piven and Cloward 1977). By contrast, those who emphasize elite power tend to leave little room for the influence of nonelites in promoting major social change. Change is viewed as the result of elite mobilization, intraelite conflict, or the circulation of elites. Mills, for example, viewed the major societal decisions in the United States as the product of elite decision making, while more specific, localized issues were more likely to be negotiated at the "middle levels" of power. Domhoff (1998) considers major policy formation processes by looking at the "agenda-setting" power of elites, noting that while pluralistic interest group competition does occur on specific issues, the general parameters of public discourse and public policy are set in advance and behind the scenes through organizations such as policy planning groups and presidential task forces that bring elites together to build a consensus on major policy issues before specific proposals enter the formal legislative process. Other elite theorists point out that even in periods of mass mobilization over policy issues, the power of elites over the public agenda allows public sentiment to be deflected or diffused by temporary measures or by redirecting public attention to peripheral issues (Prewitt and Stone 1973, pp. 107–108).

MODERNIZATION, MERITOCRACY, AND ELITE RECRUITMENT

The dominant view of elites in the 1950s developed out of the structural functionalism of Parsons (1940; 1951) and the "end-of-ideology" arguments that appeared around that time (see Waxman 1968). This perspective, which is popular again today, holds that with the emergence of modern industrial societies and liberal democracy, elites increasingly represent a stratum of talented individuals filling important positions of leadership in dominant institutions (see especially Keller 1963; see also Mannheim 1940; Aron 1950). Variations on this theme point to a "New Class" of "knowledge" workers in "postindustrial" managerial and information-based professions and a proliferation of new institutional elites that transcend the old hierarchies of caste and class (Keller 1963; Bell 1974). From this perspective, modern elites are functionally necessary in a society of complex organizations and increasingly specialized occupations. Echoing Davis and Moore's (1945) functionalist theory of stratification, status and material rewards are seen to reflect the high skill and social responsibility required for those positions. The legitimacy of functional elites is supported to the

extent that relatively equal opportunities to attain those positions are available to all talented and motivated individuals.

The validity of this "meritocracy" model of power is directly related to the issue of elite recruitment and the extent to which positions of power are open to nonelites. Once again, at one level there is general agreement among all parties on the relative openness of modern societies in comparison to traditional systems in which elite "recruitment" often was based on birth. In contemporary societies, differentiation fostered a proliferation of institutional elites requiring specific talents and skills in a variety of fields (see Keller 1963). However, beyond this empirical fact, the questions of contention are: (1) How much openness is there? and (2) Does it matter?

The first question has been the subject of much research in stratification and will be dealt with only briefly here. The meritocracy model assumes equal opportunity for individuals, but considerable research has challenged this assumption. For example, if elite positions are based on merit, educational institutions must provide avenues for mobility and equal opportunity for talented individuals from nonelite backgrounds, but a basic criticism of functionalist theories of stratification is that existing structures of inequality create barriers to nonelite achievement (see Tumin 1953). Beyond the obvious inequality of economic resources and formal educational institutions, the work of Bourdieu and others (Bourdieu 1984; Bourdieu and Passeron 1977; DiMaggio and Mohr 1985) has shown how the unequal distribution of "cultural capital" among groups in different locations in the class structure contributes to the reproduction of inequality in a variety of subtle ways. This research also points to the difficulty in assessing differences in "talent" among individuals or groups, since indicators such as "intelligence," cultural appreciation, and political knowledge may reflect a preexisting distribution of cultural resources.

A more fundamental question regarding the openness of elite recruitment is: Does it matter? First, if the concern is the overall structure of power, as it was for Mills and most elite theorists, the success of a few upwardly mobile individuals from the lower strata does not affect the analysis: Power still may be concentrated in a few in key positions. Second, elite recruitment from the lower ranks does not necessarily affect the *content* of elite decision making, given the selection process involved in the rise of "talented" individuals into elite positions. Most analysts agree that in modern societies, attainment of elite positions often requires a degree of talent, effort, and achievement, but elite theorists argue that those who make it to the top are selected for specific orientations that are compatible with existing structures of power. Those from privileged backgrounds, with access to economic, social, or cultural capital, have a definite advantage, but it is possible for nonelites people who possess the right attitudes and skills to rise into positions of power. This maintains the existing structure of power while providing legitimating examples of individual success. Limited avenues for mobility also provide a mechanism for the co-optation of promising leaders from below, as Pareto and Mosca would recognize (see the discussions of elite recruitment in Prewitt and Stone 1973; Marger 1987; Bottomore 1993; Dye 1995; Domhoff 1998).

ELITES AND DEMOCRACY

There have been a number of modifications of both "elite" and "pluralist" theory that have brought the two closer together. The work of Weber, Michels, and others influenced later theorists who viewed the concentration of power in modern institutions as necessary. From this vantage point, the issue was not whether broad "democratic" participation in political, economic, and other institutions was possible (it was not) but whether the interests of nonelites could be preserved in the face of modern bureaucratic organization. *Democratic elitism* represented a refinement of pluralist assumptions that redefined democracy in a manner congruent with elite rule. Given the inevitable concentration of power in modern societies, the central problem became: What legitimates elite rule or preserves elite "accountability"? The traditional answer of conservative elitists had been the "virtue," "character," or inward convictions of elite leaders in comparison to the selfish and undisciplined masses. In this tradition, with adherents from Plato to Pareto, elites have a stronger commitment to the "public interest" than do the "people" (Prewitt and Stone 1973, pp. 188–196). The meritocracy model represents a contempo-

rary variation of this viewpoint: Modern institutions require skilled leadership, and this means that institutional elites are increasingly likely to be selected on the basis of superior talent.

Another source of public accountability important for "democratic elitists" is elite competition for electoral support. Political elites must compete for votes in formal democracies, and this acts as a broad restraint on their actions. However, once in office, elite decision makers are relatively free to act as they see fit as long as their actions remain within acceptable limits. In a well-known formulation by Schumpeter (1942), elite rule is preserved both by superior talent and by the general mass apathy that he saw as functional for political rule. For Schumpeter (1942, pp. 269–296) and other conservative advocates of democratic elitism, the efficiency of modern representative governments depends on the "people" selecting their leaders and then leaving them alone. Note that the definition of "democracy" has been transformed from an emphasis on maximum public participation in political life to an assertion of the functional necessity of *non*participation. Far from government "by the people," democracy is now defined as a procedure for the selection of political elites. This underscores the difficulty in weighing empirical claims concerning "democratic" representation made by competing theories, given the radically divergent definitions of the key concept. Classical theories of democracy emphasized the importance of political participation as an end in itself, one that was necessary for the *creation* of political citizens capable of democratic self-rule (Pateman 1970). Critics of conservative elitism such as Bottomore (1993, p. 95) wonder if "a person can live in a condition of complete and unalterable subordination for much of the time, and yet acquire the habits of responsible choice and self government which political democracy calls for." This issue is muddier for the fact that many *critical* elite theorists are ambivalent about the possibilities for participatory democracy in modern society. If elite rule is undesirable, it would seem necessary to provide an alternative. Mills held up participatory democracy as an ideal from which to judge the contemporary United States in his concept of "publics" (1956, pp. 302–304), but he was not very clear about how that ideal could be implemented in modern "mass society." Other critical elite theorists seem to have accepted the classical argument for the inevitability of elite rule in modern, bureaucratically organized socities (see Prewitt and Stone 1973; Marger 1987; Burton and Higley 1987). For these critics, the only option to a "democracy" of mass apathy is one in which political institutions and decision-making elites are as open as possible to public scrutiny by a truly informed electorate.

LIMITATIONS OF THE ELITE PARADIGM

The elite paradigm–and by extension the "elitism-pluralism" debate as it usually is formulated–focuses on the leaders of large-scale organizations and organized institutions. Power is based on command over organizational resources; the elites are those in positions of organized power. While there are other ways to conceptualize elites, this is the dominant model in the social sciences today (see Marger 1987; Burton and Higley 1987; Dye 1995). Most scholars agree that power is concentrated in such organizations. The disagreements occur over whether there is a unified "ruling elite" above and beyond these multiple institutional elites that characterize all modern societies.

This controversy has led to much fruitful research and theoretical debate, but the "elitist-pluralist" framework is less adequate for dealing with other dimensions of societal power. For example, many of the social and cultural processes involved in the reproduction of class, gender, and racial inequality cannot be encompassed within an organizational paradigm. This includes socialization processes and everyday practices within the family, school, and workplace that reproduce the hegemony of a dominant culture. Further, it is possible to map the formal leadership structure of educational institutions, research foundations, and media organizations without explaining the *content* of their decisions. One might ask: Elite power, yes, but power for what? With its emphasis on the power of individuals within organizations, the elite paradigm neglects many structural and cultural forces that constrain those organizations and the elites within them. For example, how do global economic conditions and the imperative of "business confidence" constrain the decisions of political and economic elites? How are the ideologies and cultural practices that govern gender relations reproduced in the boardroom or the executive

mansion? These questions are significant, because without them it is difficult to explain why elites make the decisions they do or why some societal interests are better represented than others are in the decision-making process. It is necessary to consider elites and the organizations they command in their larger social and cultural context.

This issue was highlighted many years ago in debates over the "managerial revolution thesis." This was an argument that modern corporations are different from traditional capitalist enterprises because of their separation of ownership from management. Managers were seen to have aims different from those of capitalists, reflecting their organizational position. They were more interested in long-term growth, stability, labor peace, and good community relations–good management–and less concerned with profit maximization (Berle and Means 1932; Burnham 1941) The simple but fundamental weakness in such an argument was that managers–the "elites" who wield organizational power in modern corporations–were still constrained by the imperatives of the market and capital accumulation. Time has shown that their ability to act "managerially" reflected a brief postwar period of U.S. dominance in the world economy. Global competition has since required that corporate elites act more like representatives of capital.

The same might be said about political elites as well, which brings one back to the issue of the relationship between political power and class interest. Recent debates in political sociology over the degree to which state institutions, governing officials, and policy intellectuals are "relatively autonomous" from the constraints of class interest or other societal pressures have again brought into focus the relationship between political power and economic interest (see Skocpol 1985; Jessop 1990). Class theorists have argued that the decisions of political elites are shaped not only by the superior resources of a dominant class but also by the structural constraints on the state in a market economy (see Block 1977; Lindbloom 1977). Others have traced a clear class bias and pro-capital selectivity inherent in the very institutions of modern states and the dominant political discourse (Jessop 1990). Parallel arguments have been made by feminists who hold that patriarchal domination is embedded in the very structure of the state (e.g.,

MacKinnon 1989). These lines of inquiry do not negate the importance of research on elites, but they lead one to ask questions about the larger social forces that shape their decisions.

REFERENCES

Aron, Raymond 1950 "Social Structrure and the Ruling Class." *British Journal of Sociology* 1:126–144.

Bell, Daniel 1974 *The Coming of Post-Industrial Society*. New York: Basic Books.

Berle, A. A., and G. C. Means 1932 *The Modern Corporation and Private Property*. New York: Macmillan.

Block, Fred 1977 "The Ruling Class Does Not Rule." *Socialist Revolution* 7(3):6–28.

Bottomore Tom 1993. *Elites and Society*. London: Routledge.

Bourdieu, Pierre 1984 *Distinction: A Social Critique of the Judgment of Taste*. Cambridge, Mass.: Harvard University Press.

——, and J. C. Passeron 1977 *Reproduction in Education, Society, and Culture*. Beverley Hills, Calif.: Sage.

Burnham, James 1941 *The Managerial Revolution*. New York: Day.

Burton, Michael G., and John Higley 1987 "Invitation to Elite Theory." In G. William Domhoff and Thomas Dye, eds., *Power Elites and Organizations*. Newbury Park, Calif: Sage Publications pp. 219–238.

Dahl, Robert A. 1956 *A Preface to Democratic Theory*. Chicago: University of Chicago Press.

—— 1971 *Polyarchy*. New Haven, Conn.: Yale University Press.

Davis, Kingsley, and Wilbert Moore, 1945 "Some Principles of Stratification." *American Sociological Review* 10(2): 242–249.

DiMaggio, Paul, and John Mohr 1985 "Cultural Capital, Educational Attainment, and Marital Selection." *American Journal of Sociology* 90: 1231–1261.

Domhoff, G. William 1990 *The Power Elite and the State*. New York: Aldine de Gruyter.

—— 1998 *Who Rules America? Power and Politics in the Year 2000*. Mountain View, Calif.: Mayfield.

—— and Hoyt B. Ballard, eds. 1968 *C. Wright Mills and the Power Elite*. Boston: Beacon Press.

Dye, Thomas 1995 *Who's Running America? The Clinton Years*. Englewood Cliffs, N.J.: Prentice Hall.

Field, G. Lowell, and John Higley 1980 *Elitism*. London: Routledge and Kegan Paul.

Hunter, Floyd 1953 *Community Power Structure*. Chapel Hill: University of North Carolina Press.

Jessop, Bob 1990 *State Theory: Putting Capitalist States in their Place*. University Park: Penn State University Press.

Keller, Suzanne 1963 *Beyond the Ruling Class: Strategic Elites in Modern Society*. New York: Random House.

Lindbloom, Charles 1977 *Politics and Markets*. New York: Basic Books.

MacKinnon, Catherine 1989 *Toward a Feminist Theory of the State*. Cambridge, Mass.: Harvard University Press.

Mannheim, Karl 1940 *Man and Society in an Age of Reconstruction*. London: Kegan Paul.

Marger, Martin N. 1987 *Elites and Masses: An Introduction to Political Sociology*. Belmont, Calif.: Wadsworth.

Michels, Robert (1915) 1959 *Political Parties*. New York: Dover.

Miliband, Ralph 1969 *The State in Capitalist Society*. New York: Basic Books.

Mills, C. Wright 1956 *The Power Elite*. New York: Oxford University Press.

Mosca, Gaetano 1939 *The Ruling Class*. New York: McGraw-Hill.

Pareto, Vilfredo 1935 *The Mind and Society*. New York: Harcourt Brace.

Parsons, Talcott 1940 "An Analytical Approach to the Theory of Social Stratification." *American Journal of Sociology* 45:841–862

1951 *The Social System*. Glencoe, Ill.: Free Press.

Pateman, Carole 1970 *Participation and Democratic Theory*. Cambridge, UK: Cambridge University Press.

Piven, Frances, and Richard Cloward 1977 *Poor People's Movements*. New York: Random House.

Prewitt, Kenneth, and Alan Stone 1973 *The Ruling Elites*. New York: Harper & Row.

Riesman, David 1950 *The Lonely Crowd*. New Haven, Conn.: Yale University Press.

Schumpeter, Joseph A. 1942 *Capitalism, Socialism, and Democracy*. New York: Harper Colophon.

Skocpol, Theda 1985 "Bringing the State Back In: Strategies of Analysis in Current Research." In Peter Evans, Dietrich Reuschemeyer, and Theda Skocpol, eds. *Bringing the State Back In*. Cambridge, UK: Cambridge University Press.

Truman, David B. 1951 *The Governmental Process*. New York: Random House.

Tumin, Melvin, 1953 "Some Principles of Stratification: A Critical Analysis." *American Sociological Review* 18: 387–393.

Useem, Michael 1983 *The Inner Circle: Large Corporations and the Rise of Business Political Activity in the U.S. and the U.K.* New York: Oxford University Press.

Waxman, Chaim I. ed. 1968 *The End of Ideology Debate*. New York: Clarion.

Weber, Max, (1921) 1968. *Economy and Society*, vols. Berkeley: University of California Press.

PATRICK AKARD

SOCIAL BELONGING

THE DIMENSIONS OF HUMAN INVOLVEMENT

It is necessary to distinguish four different dimensions or states in the involvement of individuals in the context of human relations: territorial location, ecological participation, social belonging, and cultural conformity (Pollini 1990) (Figure 1). *Territorial location*, as Weber showed in his famous sociological analysis of the medieval European city (Weber 1921) does not involve any form of social relation among the individuals of a population in a particular territorial area. This dimension was subsequently defined by Parsons as one of the three primary relational criteria, with the other two being biological position and temporal location (Parsons 1959, pp. 89–96).

Unlike territorial location, *ecological participation* involves some sort of reciprocal relationality among the individual members of a human population, whether settled in the same territorial area or not. To use the terminology of human and social ecology in reference to nonsymbolic social relations, recalling Mead's well-known distinction (Mead 1934), ecological participation involves a specific form of interdependence among individuals ("symbiosis") (Park 1936, 1939) that is distinctly different from social interaction (Quinn 1939). For Parsons, the ecological system is "a state of mutually oriented interdependence of a plurality of actors who are not integrated by bonds of solidarity to form a collectivity but who are objects to one another" (1959, p. 93). Thus, instrumentally, the customers of a commercial firm, the participants in a market, and the antagonists in a struggle, and expressively, a network of purely personal friendships and the inhabitants of a neighborhood or district in a modern metropolis are paradigmatic examples of the dimension of participation in networks of ecological interaction or in purely ecological systems. Parsons defined the state of ecological participation as a secondary relational criterion.

Social belonging refers to the state in which an individual, by assuming a role, is characterized by inclusion in the social collectivity, which is exclusively a *Gemeinschaft*, according to Weber (Weber 1922, 136), and which is a *Gemeinschaft* (an organization or association), according to Parsons (Parsons 1959, p. 100). In this frame of reference, the dimension of social belonging relates to any form of social collectivity, whether predominantly expressive (nonrational in Weber's terms) or predominantly instrumental. Strictly speaking, the status of belonging concerns only the *symbolic* dimension of human and social relations and interactions (Durkheim 1912; Pareto 1916; Weber 1921, 1922; Mead 1934; Park 1939; Parsons 1959; Merton 1963; Shils 1975). Parsons defines it as a secondary relational criterion.

Cultural conformity is symbolic in character. This dimension differs from social belonging in that it involves the sharing by individuals of value systems and therefore of attitudes of "*consensus*" as defined by Weber (Weber 1913) as well as, though not necessarily, conformism (Parsons 1959). The distinction between social belonging and cultural conformity demonstrates that belonging to a collectivity can be compatible with the exercise of internal opposition; thus, social membership does not exclude the possibility of disagreement, especially in regard to value orientations.

The distinction between social belonging and cultural conformity also has been drawn by Robert K. Merton, who expressly asserts the noncoincidence between membership groups and reference groups. The latter groups constitute a focus of reference toward which a certain degree of positive orientation is shown rather than being an already-established social bond that is manifest in the interactions among the individual members of a group (the membership group).

On the basis of the distinction between ecological participation and social belonging—both of which are secondary relational criteria, according to Parsons—it is possible to use the findings of human ecology and sociological analysis to differentiate between attachment to the community and belonging to the *Gemeinschaft*. Whereas attach-

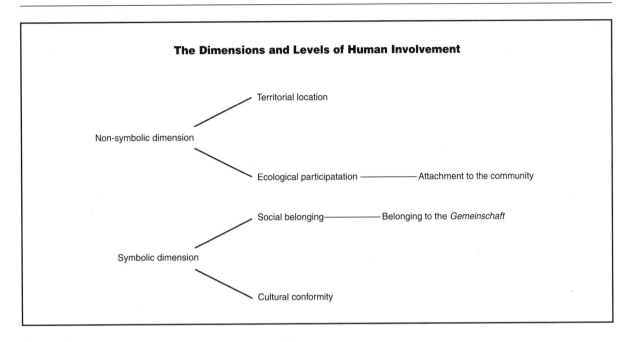

The Dimensions and Levels of Human Involvement

Non-symbolic dimension
- Territorial location
- Ecological participatation ———— Attachment to the community

Symbolic dimension
- Social belonging———— Belonging to the *Gemeinschaft*
- Cultural conformity

Figure 1

SOURCE: Pollini 1990, p. 188.

ment to the community involves the ecological concept of community defined as "a) a population, territorially organized; b) more or less completely rooted in the soil it occupies; c) its individual units living in a relationship of mutual interdependence that is symbiotic rather than societal" (Park 1936, p. 148), the belonging to the *Gemeinschaft* concerns that sociological concept of *Gemeinschaft* as defined by Toennies (1887), Weber (*Vergemeinschaftung*) (1922), and Parsons (1959), although for Parsons as well as for some others, social belonging concerns not *Gemeinschaft* alone but any social collectivity and the social collectivity *qua talis*.

THE STRUCTURE OF SOCIAL BELONGING

The distinction between attachment to the ecological community and belonging to the social collectivity (particularly the *Gemeinschaft*) introduces the fundamental question of the structure of social belonging and the relations among its main components, which from an analytic and multidimensional perspective include attachment. Using Parsons's scheme of reference, together with the contributions of other sociologists, the structure of social belonging can be described by

starting from the relations among the four chief components that define it as such: *attachment, loyalty, solidarity*, and the *sense of affinity* or *we-feeling* (Figure 2).

Attachment is a form of investment or "cathexis" (from the Freudian term *Besetzung*, denoting the relationship between emotional energy and an object) in a social object (the collectivity in this case), where "cathexis" refers to "the significance of ego's relation to the object or objects in question for the gratification-deprivation balance of his personality" (Parsons 1959, p. 17). Attachment involves an "orientation to alter in which the paramount focus of cathective-evaluative significance is in alter's attitudes" (Parsons 1959, p. 213), where "the relation to alter is the source, not merely of discrete, unorganized, ad hoc gratifications for ego, but of an organized *system* of gratifications which include expectations of the future continuance and development of alter's gratificatory significance" (Parsons 1959, p. 77).

When attachment is organized into a symbolic pattern, particularly a pattern of expressive symbols whose meaning's shared between ego and alter, become values—in other words, when they serve as a criterion or standard for selection (or an

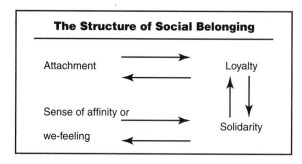

The Structure of Social Belonging

Attachment → ← Loyalty

Sense of affinity or → we-feeling ← Solidarity

Figure 2

appreciative criterion in this case, which concerns expressive symbolism) among the alternatives of orientation that are intrinsically available in the situation—*loyalty* arises (Parsons 1959, p. 77). In the case of social belonging, loyalty defines the relation between ego as a subject and the collectivity as social object of which the ego is a member. Besides being the social object of attachment, the social collectivity thus becomes the object of loyalty as well. This raises the question of the trust the collectivity requires and the individual grants.

Along with attachment and loyalty, social belonging involves the *solidarity* of the collectivity. Solidarity, which "involves going a step beyond 'loyalty,'" is defined by Parsons as "the institutionalized integration of collectivity," and it is distinguished from loyalty because it entails that "collectivity-orientation converts this 'propensity' into an institutionalized obbligation of the role-expectation. Then whether the actor 'feels like it' or not, he is obligated to act in certain ways and risks the application of negative sanctions if he does not" (Parsons 1959, p. 98).

The final component that defines the structure of social belonging is what has been called the "sense of affinity" (Shils 1975) or the "we-feeling" (MacIver and page 1949, p. 5ff). (Weber treated belonging in terms of *Zusammengehoerigkeit*, or "subjective feeling of the parties, whether affectual or traditional, that they belong together") (Weber 1922, p. 136). Although this component can be considered the final outcome of attachment, loyalty and solidarity, it also can be viewed as the component that controls and legitimates the others and therefore performs the function of pattern maintenance in the system of social belonging. It may include, at least in part, two of the factors that

Merton states constitute a collectivity as a social group: people's definition of themselves as "members" of the group and definition by others as "belonging to the group," with the others, including fellow members and nonmembers (Merton 1963).

In short, social belonging is constituted by the relations of interdependence among the dimensions of attachment, loyalty, solidarity, and sense of affinity, according to paths that extend from attachment to a sense of affinity or we-feeling and back, passing through the intermediate components of loyalty and solidarity.

From the point of view of the collectivity as a social system, belonging is the dimension that can be called a "residue," to use Pareto's term. A residue is the relatively constant symbolic-social element that can be deduced from the symbolic-linguistic expressions (or nonlogicoexperimental theories) associated with the nonlogical actions of associated individuals and that performs a function of "persistence of aggregates" maintain the equilibrium of the system. This equilibrium is characterized by the interdependence relations among the residues of various classes, genera, and specie, and between these and the system's other "internal' elements," such as derivations, interests and social heterogeneity, and which is the circulation among the parts (Pareto 1916; Pollini 1987).

In regards to attachment, Shils, adopting a concrete rather than an analytic perspective, has drawn up a typology of four kinds of attachment that can be compared with the notions presented here. Shils's first type of attachment is the *primordial attachment* that arises among individuals by virtue of "particularist existential connections" (such as the biological bond of kinship) and stable sexual relations or the sharing of a territorial area. It can be compared with the community attachment of human ecology and, more generally, the cathexis in a broad sense involved in ecological participation.

Personal attachment and *civil attachment* operate at different levels of the process of social structuring. They are distinctive of the social belonging defined by the "emerging" components of loyalty, solidarity, and the we-feeling.

Sacred attachment is grounded in beliefs and therefore also in notions of truth, justice, goodness, and beauty. It mainly but not exclusively includes cultural conformity and a consensus on beliefs, although it gives rise to a social community that Shils views as a community of *believers* (Shils 1961).

SOCIAL BELONGING AND ITS RELATIONS WITH OTHER COMPONENTS OF HUMAN ACTION

This discussion of the structure of social belonging and its main components has identified a number of elements by which it is constituted and conditioned. By adding further elements of fundamental importance, we may outline a complete frame of reference which social belonging involves interrelations among the following subsystems or "complexes": the ecological complex of *territorial location* and *ecological interaction*, the mental complex of the *identity* of the personality, the social complex of the *solidarity* of the collectivity, and the cultural complex of *expressive and evaluative symbolism* (Figure 3).

Starting from territorial location and ecological interaction, central importance is assumed by the relationship between the *identity* of the personality and the *solidarity* of the collectivity, both of which stand in relation to the complex of *expressive and evaluative symbolism*. It is the latter factor in particular that, through internalization and institutionalization, characterizes personal identity and collective solidarity (Durkheim 1912), of which the personal identity involves the process by which the symbolic complex is acknowledged and the collective solidarity later involves the process by which it is represented.

The process by which the social collectivity relates to the individual person can be called the process of *inclusion*, while the mental process by which a person comes to be inducted in a collectivity may be called the mechanism of *identification*, or the mechanism by which a person learns "to play a role complementary to those of other members in accord with the pattern of values governing the collectivity" (Parsons 1958, p. 91). In other words, identification is "motivational 'acceptance'—at levels of 'deep' motivational 'commitment'—of membership in collective systems" (Parsons 1970, p. 356).

From the point of view of the personality, the multiple social belongings or even belonging to multiple collectivities or social circles so distinctive of the individual condition today are inevitable components of an identity (Parsons 1968, p. 21), to the point where the perception of personal individuality is determined by membership in a collectivity or social circle (first sociological *a priori*) (Simmel 1890, 1908). However, just as the individual as a member of society (a social person) is determined not wholly by the fact that she/he is a member of society but also by the fact that she or he is "not socialized" (second sociological *a priori*) (Simmel 1890, 1908), identity marks out "the individual autonomy relative to *any* role and collectivity membership" (Parsons 1968, p. 20).

Simmel defined the relations between individual identity and belonging to social circles on the basis of the following principles:

1. A positive correlation exists between the development of personal identity and the widening of the social circle of belonging.

2. There is a positive correlation between the increased extension of the social circle and the centrifugal tendency of the individual toward other circles.

3. The individual belongs to an intermediate social circle that fosters the individualization of identity even in very large communities.

4. The determinacy of personal identity increases in direct proportion to belonging to other social circles.

5. The determinacy of individual identity is positively correlated with the dispersion and diffusion of the multiple social circles of belonging rather than with their overlapping, concentration and coincidence.

6. The shared belonging of several individuals to the same social circle may not be incompatible with their single and distinct belonging to other competing and conflicting circles.

7. The modern form of belonging displays voluntary and autonomous, rather than coercive and heteronomous, belonging to a social circle or circles.

8. In the modern age, the totalizing and globalizing nature of belonging to a single and all-encompassing social circle tends

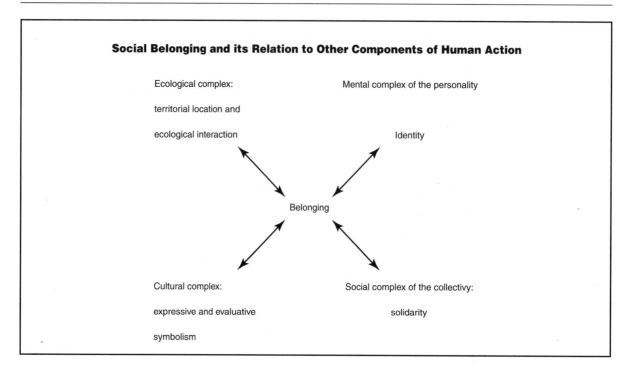

Social Belonging and its Relation to Other Components of Human Action

Ecological complex:

territorial location and

ecological interaction

Mental complex of the personality

Identity

Belonging

Cultural complex:

expressive and evaluative

symbolism

Social complex of the collectivy:

solidarity

Figure 3

to give way to the functional feature of belonging to multiple social circles (Simmel 1890, 1908).

A person's role as member of the collectivity, which is acquired by means of the mechanism of identification by which social belongings come to constitute inevitable components of personal identity, entails acknowledgment and internalization by the individual personality of the symbolic complex. This is both the foundation of the social collectivity and its representation. According to Durkheim, for whom the social group is defined by the symbolic complex and especially by the totemic symbol (Durkheim 1912), and according to Parsons, for whom expressive symbolism involves not only individual members or units (in that it is shared by each of them) but the entire collectivity constituted as a social object by symbolic social interaction, membership in the social collectivity is not expressed and represented only by the symbolic complex and by distinct symbols and emblems. More important, it is reinforced, developed, and augmented by them, in particular by participation in specific symbolic actions and rituals such as ceremonies, celebrations, gatherings, and meetings and by the projection of shared

value sentiments into individual members, especially those who assume the role of chief or leader and thus symbolically embody shared value patterns (Parsons 1959, pp. 395–399). Thus, ritual participation does not only express and manifest belonging to the collectivity and group; it also strengthens and develops this belonging, in particular the component of it denominated we-feeling or sense of affinity.

MEMBERSHIP AND NONMEMBERSHIP GROUPS

On the basis of the theory of the reference group, Merton has examined the limiting condition of nonmembership, which he defines as a positive orientation toward groups that, although not belonged to, are nevertheless reference groups. It is thus possible to identify a diversified set of nonmembership features that depend on the one hand on the nonmember's attitudes toward membership and on the other hand on possession of the qualities necessary for membership established by the group. Merton uses these two distinct dimensions to draw up a typology of a nonmembership group that includes a variety of forms and conditions of nonmembership that may or may not eventually give rise to membership. These forms range from the "antagonistic nonmember" (outgroup) to the "candidate for membership" through the intermediate types "potential member," "autonomous nonmember," "marginal man," and "detached nonmember." Merton thus overcomes the membership-nonmembership dichotomy by proposing gradations of nonmembership and investigating the various types of membership that cannot be defined by lack of membership.

A brief discussion is required of the type of nonmembership Merton calls "marginal man," following Stonequist (1937) and Park (1928). This is the individual who, although he or she aspires to join a particular group, does not fulfil the requirements established by the group to do so. In other words, the marginal man is a person who, by simultaneously participating in two cultures, tends to occupy not the center but the margins of both. As a consequence, he is not fully accepted by either culture. More precisely, the "marginal man" is the individual who seeks to abandon his membership group, leaving its institutionalized value patterns and norms behind, but is unable to belong to the new group to which he aspires even though he has already absorbed its values and norms to some extent. This process by which the "marginal man" absorbs the values and groups of the group to which he aspires but does not yet belong is called "anticipatory socialization" by Merton (1963).

The "marginal man" also may be likened to the "stranger" described by Simmel (1908, 1964) and Schutz (1944).

BELONGING: INCLUSION AND PARTICIPATION

Belonging to a collectivity or social group characterized by solidarity through the assumption of some sort of role within it by an individual is brought about by two concomitant processes: *inclusion* and *participation*. By means of the process of inclusion, the social collectivity constantly retains or acquires individuals within its relational ambit, thus responding to the problem of integration by eliminating possible exclusion. The intensity of the inclusion process by which individuals become full-fledged members of the collectivity may vary greatly with the features of the collectivity, primarily according to the criteria that must be fulfilled to join it. These criteria are defined by the collectivity itself and can be characterized as universalism or particularism (Levy 1952).

At the micro level it is possible to identify a number of ways in which the inclusion process comes about: physical and mental coercion, monetary and symbolic remuneration, persuasion, and co-option. At the macro-sociological level, the ways in which individuals are included in collectivities have been variously defined, mainly in the context of membership in the national community (i.e., citizenship) (Turner 1993; van Steenbergen 1994) and in relation to immigration (Alexander 1980; Bauböck 1994; Miles and Thränhardt 1995). With no claim to exhaustiveness, one can point out some of these forms of inclusion: adjustment (Eisenstadt 1954), incorporation (Smith 1974; Horowitz 1975; Portes and Boeroecz 1989; Schmitter Heisler 1992), absorption (Eisenstadt 1954), and assimilation (Park 1913; Gordon 1964; Horowitz 1975; Geazer 1993).

While inclusion is the process that moves from the collectivity to the individual as object, participation is the process that moves from the individual as subject to the collectivity.

The etymology of the term "participation" has a twofold meaning by which it can denote either "taking part in" something or "being part of" something. It is therefore advisable to distinguish the concept of participation from that of belonging by defining "participation" only in the former sense, in other words, on the basis of the action of "taking part in," and defining "belonging" as "being part of." However, it is possible to identify a relationship between belonging and participation, since participation denotes the action of "taking part in" the collectivity, of which one "becomes part" by virtue of the process of inclusion activated by the collectivity.

Besides operating "transitively"—through the relationship a person establishes with the collectivity as a symbolic-social object of attachment and loyalty—participation operates "intransitively" through the relationship the person establishes with himself or herself while participating. By undertaking the action of "taking part in" the collectivity, a person exerts effects on himself or herself, generally in the direction of change in the elements, aspects, and traits of the psychic structure of his or her personality. Participation thus not only helps reinforce belonging but changes and develops the various components of the individual unit.

From the transitive point of view or from that of the individual vis-à-vis the collectivity, Smelser's theory of collective behaviour (Smelser 1963) and Merton's modes of individual adaptation (Merton 1963) provide the basis for the identification of at least four dimensions of participation: *diffuse* participation, *technical decision-making* participation, *reformatory* participation, and *revolutionary* participation.

Diffuse participation is the dimension of participation, of adaptive character, that accepts the institutionalized means and ends established by the collectivity and attempts to ensure its continued functioning. Technical decision-making participation is the dimension of participation that, while accepting the ends of the collectivity of membership, attempts to change its institutionalized means, which are deemed unable to achieve the goals established. Innovative-reformatory participation accepts the collectivity's means or at any rate is unconcerned by them and attempts instead to change its ends and goals. Revolutionary participation endeavours to change the institutionalized means and ends of the collectivity with a view to creating a "collectivity of the future" that differs from the "collectivity of the present."

REFERENCES

Alexander, Jeffrey C. 1980 "Core Solidarity, Ethnic Outgroups and Structural Differentiation: Toward a Multidimensional Model of Inclusion in Modern Societies." In Jacques Dofny and Akinsola Akiwowo, eds., *National and Ethnic Movements*. Los Angeles and London: Sage.

Bauböck, Rainer 1994 *From aliens to citizens: redefining the status of immigrants in Europe*. Alolershot: Avebury

Durkheim, Emile 1912 *The Elementary Forms of Religious Life*. London: Allen & Unwin, reissued 1976.

Eisenstadt, Shmuel N. 1954 *The Absorption of Immigrants*. London: Routledge & Kegan Paul.

Glazer, Nathan 1993 "Is Assimilation Dead?" *Annals of the American Academy of Political and Social Science*, vol. 530, nov., pp. 122–136

Gordon, Milton M. 1964 *Assimilation in American Life. The Role of Race, Religion and National Origins*. New York: Oxford University Press.

Horowitz, Donald L. 1975 "Ethnic Identity." In Nathan Glazer, and Daniel P. Moynihan, eds., *Beyond the Melting Pot*. Cambridge, Mass: Harvard University Press and MIT Press, originally published 1963.

Levy, Marion J., Jr. 1952 *The Structure of Society*. Princeton, N.J.: Princeton University Press.

MacIver, Robert M., and Charles H. Page 1949 *Society: An Introductory Analysis*. New York: Holt, Rinehart & Winston, reissued 1961.

Mead, George H. 1934 *Mind, Self and Society: From the Standpoint of a Social Behaviorist*. Chicago: University of Chicago Press, reissued 1959.

Merton, Robert K. 1963 *Social Theory and Social Structure*. Glencoe, Ill.: Free Press.

Miles, Robert, and Dietrich Thränhardt 1995 *Migration and european integration: the dynamics of inclusion and exclusion* London: Pinter

Pareto, Vilfredo 1916 *Trattato di sociologia generale*. Florence: G. Barbèra.

Park, Robert E. 1913 "Racial Assimilation in Secondary Groups." *American Sociological Review* VIII:66–83.

—— 1928 "Human Migration and Marginal Man." *American Journal of Sociology* XXXIII(6):881–893.

—— (1936) "Human Ecology." In *Human Communities: The City and Human Ecology*. New York: Free Press, reissued 1952.

—— 1939 "Symbiosis and Socialization: A Frame of Reference for the Study of Society." *American Journal of Sociology* XLV(1):1–25.

Parsons, Talcott 1958 "Social Structure and the Development of Personality: Freud's Contribution to the Integration of Psychology and Sociology." In *Social Structure and Personality*. New York: Free Press, reissued 1964.

—— 1959 *The Social System*. Glencoe, Ill.: Free Press, first edition 1951.

—— 1968 "The Position of Identity in the General Theory of Action." In Chad Gordon and Kenneth J. Gergen, eds., *The Self in Social Interaction*, vol. 1. New York: Wiley.

—— 1970 "Equality and Inequality in Modern Societies, or Social Stratification Revisited." In Talcott Parsons, Social Systems and the Evolution of Action Theory, New York: Free Press, pp. 321–380

Pollini, Gabriele 1987 *Appartenenza e identità: Analisi sociologica dei modelli di appartenenza sociale* (Belonging and Identity: Sociological Analysis of Models of Social Belonging). Milan: Franco Angeli.

—— 1990 "Appartenenza socio-territoriale e mutamento culturale" (Socioterritorial Belonging and Cultural Change). In Vincenzo Cesareo, ed. (a cura di), *La cultura dell'Italia contemporanea*. Turin: Fondazione G. Agnelli.

——, 1999 "The socio-territorial belonging." In Renzo Gubert, ed., *The Territorial Belonging between Ecology and Culture*. Trento, Italy: University of Trento Press.

Portes, Alejandro, and Jòzsef Boeroecz 1989 "Contemporary Immigration: Theoretical Perspectives on Its Determinants and Modes of Incorporation." *International Migration Review* 23(3): 606–630.

Quinn, James A. 1939 "Ecological versus Social Interaction." *Sociology and Social Research*. 28:565–570.

Schmitter Heisler, Barbara 1992 "The Future of Immigrant Incorporation: Which Models? Which Concepts?" International Migration Review XXVI(2): 623–645

Schutz, Alfred 1944 "The Stranger." *American Journal of Sociology* XLIX(6):499–507.

Shils, Edward A. 1961 "Society: The Idea and Its Sources." *Revue Internationale de Philosophie* 15:93–114.

—— 1975 *Center and Periphery: Essays in Macrosociology*. Chicago: University of Chicago Press.

Simmel, Georg 1890 *Ueber soziale Differenzierung: Sociologische und psychologische Untersuchungen*. Leipzig: Dunker & Humblot.

—— 1908 *Soziologie: Untersuchungen ueber die Formen der Vergesellschaftung*. Berlin: Duncker & Humblot, reissued 1983.

—— 1964 "The Stranger." In Kurt H. Wolff, ed., *The Sociology of Georg Simmel*. New York: Free Press.

Smelser, Neil J. 1963 *Theory of Collective Behavior*. New York: Macmillan.

Smith, M. G. 1974 *Corporations and Society*. London: Duckworth.

Stonequist, Everett V. 1937 *The Marginal Man*. New York: Scribner's.

Toennies, Ferdinand 1887 *Community and Society*. New Brunswick, N.J.: Transaction, reissued 1988.

Turner, Bryan S. 1993 ed., *Citizenship and Social Theory*, London: Sage.

van Steenbergen, Bart 1994 ed., *The Condition of Citizenship* London: Sage.

Weber, Max 1913 "Ueber einige Kategorien der verstehenden Soziologie." In *Gesammelte Aufsaetze zur Wissenschaftslehre*. Tuebingen: Mohr, 2d ed. 1951.

—— 1921 *The City*. New York: Free Press, reissued 1958.

—— 1922 *The Theory of Social and Economic Organization*. New York: Free Press, reissued 1966.

GABRIELE POLLINI

SOCIAL CAPITAL

Social capital is a form of capital that exists within relationships among individuals. According to Bourdieu (1986), capital is accumulated labor that can be appropriated by individuals or groups for their exclusive use to further their interests and increase their capital holdings. By drawing on the social capital resources in their relationships, individuals can further their own goals. For example, the larger the social network an individual has while looking for a job, the more resources—through company contacts, information, and higher-status references—that individual can draw on. Greater availability of resources increases the likelihood that the individual will find a job better than will an individual with fewer social network resources. It is also likely that a well-connected individual will find employment sooner. Simply put, social capital is "an elegant term to call attention to the possible individual and family benefits of sociability" (Portes and Landolt 1996, p. 94).

Some scholars have remarked on the "plethora of capitals" recently appearing in social and economic theories that refer to virtually all aspects of social life as a form of capital (Baron and Hannan 1994). The notion of physical capital, as embodied in machines, tools, and equipment, has been extended by economists to include human capital. Just as investments can be made to improve physical capital—newer and better tools—human capital can be increased by enlarging an individual's skills or knowledge base. Social capital, then, is created when relationships are used to enable actions by individuals to further their own interests. According to Coleman (1988), each actor has control over and interests in certain resources and events. Social capital constitutes a specific kind of resource that is available to an actor. Unlike other resources, social capital is based on reciprocity and thus comes with the expectation that obligations will be repaid as requested by other individuals in the network. Social capital does not have a set rate of exchange, and payments often are made according to need rather than in standard purchase terms as is done with equipment and education.

The theoretical foundation of the concept of social capital is still in a nascent phase, and there is much debate about its definition, creation, and utility as well as its role in public policy and modernization strategies. Advanced most notably in the work of the French sociologist Bourdieu and further developed by Coleman, the notion of social capital has been put forth as a conceptual tool to bridge two divergent theories of social action: economism and semiologism (Bourdieu 1986). Economism reduces all social exchanges to economic transactions in which independent social actors pursue their own self-interest with little attention to social context. In this view, social action is based on the principle of maximizing utility. In contrast, semiologism reduces social exchanges to communicative acts by socialized actors and downplays the impact of economic factors. In this theoretical orientation, social action is governed by social norms, rules, and obligations. The notion of social capital mediates these divergent orientations by acknowledging both the self-interest of actors and the influence of the social and economic context.

As social capital refers to the aspects of the social structure that are of value to social actors as resources that can be mobilized in pursuit of their interests, it is defined by its function. Social capital is not located in the actors themselves (as with human capital) or in any physical implements of production (as with physical capital). Instead, it is located in the relationships and personal networks between and among social actors. Social capital, then, appears in a variety of forms that have two common elements: (1) Social capital appears as an aspect of social structures, and (2) actors are able to use social capital as a resource to achieve their goals within the social structure.

Coleman (1988, 1990) conceives of social capital as a social structural resource that is a capital asset for the individual. It is productive, making it possible to achieve certain goals that cannot be achieved in its absence, and it is constituted within social organizations often as a by-product of activities undertaken for other purposes. For Coleman,

the value of the concept lies primarily in accounting for different outcomes of individual efforts and illuminating how resources can be combined with other resources to create system-level differences. The concept of social capital is most useful in qualitative analyses of social systems and studies relying on qualitative indicators.

FORMS OF SOCIAL CAPITAL

Coleman (1990) identifies six forms of social capital: obligations and expectations, information potential, norms and effective sanctions, authority relations, appropriable social organizations, and intentional organizations.

Obligations and Expectations. A social system that relies heavily on reciprocal actions creates obligations and expectations on the part of its participants. Each "favor" is expected to be repaid, and those who can provide "favors" are expected to do so when requested. This form of exchange engenders social capital for a group member who has done many favors without collecting reciprocal favors in return. These unreciprocated favors create obligations that allow the favor-granting member to request aid from those who are obligated to her or him. These unpaid obligations accrue in the form of social capital that the member can use.

This form of social capital has two critical elements: the mutual trust within the social system and the extent of outstanding obligations. Without trust that obligations will be reciprocated, there is no incentive to accrue social capital. For social capital to have value, there must be trust that the resources will be there to be drawn on when needed. Furthermore, it is the extent of outstanding obligations that denotes the amount of social capital an individual can draw on. Indeed, the overall number of outstanding obligations within a system can be a measure of its interconnectedness as members are obligated to one another. This connectedness also increases the resources available to each member.

Information Potential. By interacting with informed members, individuals can increase their knowledge without having to obtain the information directly, whether by reading the newspaper or by interpreting research findings. A member also may become privy to specialized information—

such as unadvertised business opportunities—through informal information exchange. Useful information can be the impetus for action that furthers the individual's on goals and can be a beneficial commodity.

Norms and Effective Sanctions. Within a social system, norms can support and provide rewards for specific behaviors. Norms that encourage the subjugation of self-interest to the needs of the community are an especially powerful form of social capital. By promoting certain activities, norms by nature constrain other activities. Criminal pursuits are an obvious example of activities that communities want to constrain. Less obvious examples would be that the promotion of athletic activities constrains the time available for other interests and that norms that promote conformity constrain innovation. Effective "norms can constitute a powerful form of social capital" (Coleman 1990, p. 311).

Authority Relations. Within groups organized to address a specific issue, a leader often is chosen and given the right to make decisions and speak for the group. Thus, the members of the group transfer the "rights of control" to one individual, who then has access to an extensive network of social capital that can be directed toward a specific goal. When the rights of control are located in one individual, the social capital of all the members is amplified. Examples of this form of social capital can be found in political action groups, business cartels, and grassroots organizations.

Appropriable Social Organizations. Social organizations usually are created to address a specific issue, and after that issue is resolved, the organization often continues to exist through a redefinition of its goals. Thus, an organization that was developed for one purpose can be appropriated for another purpose. This constitutes a form of social capital available for use.

Intentional Organizations. This form of social capital occurs when individuals join together to create an organization that will benefit them directly. An example of this can be a joint business venture or a voluntary association that produces a public good, such as a Parents and Teachers Association (PTA) chapter. This form of social capital advances the interests of those who invest in it. Additionally, it can create two by-products as social capital: a public good that benefits others who did not invest directly and a social organization that can be appropriated for other purposes.

These six forms of social capital have certain properties that distinguish them from other assets. Social capital's value lies in its use and cannot be exchanged easily. Additionally, it is not the private property of those who benefit from it. Rather, it is most often a by-product of other intentioned actions. Individuals who invest in the creation of the necessary social structures (norms, reciprocal obligations, etc.) are not the primary beneficiaries of the social capital that is generated. Instead, the social capital profits all those who are part of the social structure. Thus, it is not necessarily in an individual's self-interest to bring social capital into being. If another form of assistance that does not incur an obligation, such as a government program, is available or if individuals can meet their needs through self-sufficiency, they may choose to utilize these resources rather than those which accrue social capital through reciprocity. Using such forms of assistance or sufficiency does not increase the general pool of social capital in the community.

Coleman (1990) identifies factors that can increase or diminish social capital. A high degree of *closure* in a social network strengthens its ability to engender norms and effective sanctions. Closure is also important in achieving mutual trust among members. Conversely, lower closure reduces the effective norms and trust that would lessen the social capital engendered. The *stability* of a social structure affects the development or destruction of social capital. Individual mobility can threaten the stability of an organization, which in turn threatens its social capital. Organizations and social relations that are dependent on specific individuals are less stable than are those which rely on positions that can be filled by various individuals. Those organized around positions have more stability and thus a more steady supply of social capital on which the members may draw. *Ideology* can create social capital by influencing individuals to act in the interest of the whole rather than in their own interests. Religious ideologies are an example of this factor. Alternatively, ideologies of self-sufficiency or individualism can hinder the generation of social capital. Other factors Coleman mentions include affluence, availability of official aid such as governmental support, and other factors that may make individuals less dependent on each other. Additionally, social capital must be maintained, as it depreciates over time and must be renewed.

REFINING SOCIAL CAPITAL THEORY

Portes and Sensenbrenner (1993) have extended Coleman's basic theory of social capital, claiming that it contains two specific shortcomings. First, they call for a more defined discussion of the forms of social capital and how they are developed. Second, they question Coleman's optimistic instrumentalist orientation which focuses on the positive side of social capital. Furthermore, Portes and Sensenbrenner reidentify the sociological origins of notions of social capital by grounding their contribution in the works of classical social theorists. They begin by redefining social capital as "those expectations for action within a collectivity that affect the economic goals and goal-seeking behavior of its members" (1993, p.1323). This definition differs from Coleman's emphasis on social structures that can facilitate individual actions.

Portes and Sensenbrenner (1993) outline four different types of social capital, with each one corresponding to a classical tradition. From Parsons and Durkheim, they define *value introjection* as the first source of social capital because it promotes behaviors based on morals and values rather than on self-interest. From Durkheim's work, they conceive of economic transactions as reflections of an underlying moral order and contracts as reframing existing norms or values rather than creating new rules. Their second source of social capital—*reciprocity transactions*—comes from the work of Simmel and focuses on the dynamics of group membership. Reciprocity transactions are the obligations and expectations, backed by norms of reciprocity, that emerge through social networks of exchange. The third form of social capital is *bounded solidarity*, developed from Marx and Engels's writings on situational circumstances that lead to principled group action. This type of social capital is created when individuals join together in response for an adverse situation. The fourth form of social capital is drawn from Weber's distinction between formal and substantive rationality in market transactions; *enforceable trust*. Enforceable trust refers to the different mechanisms that formal institutions and particularistic group settings use to engender members' disciplined compliance with group norms

and expectations. Formal institutions use legal, rational mechanisms, whereas particularistic groups utilize substantive, social means.

Acknowledging the Negative Effects. Portes and Sensenbrenner also point out the negative effects of social capital in direct contrast to Coleman's more positive position. The same social structures "that give rise to appropriable resources for individual use can also constrain action or even derail it from its original goals" (1993, p. 1338). The costs of solidarity can be obligations and interconnections within the community. The costs of community conformity can constrain individual freedom. Obligations to the community can inhibit attempts to succeed in a broader network with a richer array of rewards. Individuals may come to see these costs of developing and maintaining social capital as being too high and not in their best interest.

In spite of its inchoate state and the ongoing debates, Coleman's optimistic discussion of social capital has become popular with policymakers who see it as the key to solving a variety of social problems. These policy proponents identify social capital as the features of social organizations (networks, norms, and social trust) that enable cooperative efforts for mutual benefit. Social capital is favored for its ability to promote and maintain voluntary associations that allow individuals to work together to resolve collective difficulties. In direct response, Portes and Landolt (1996) warn of the "downside" of social capital by making three specific criticisms of this use of social capital. First, social capital is discussed as the property of groups (communities), not individuals. Second, no distinction is made between the ability to access resources and the quality of those resources: Having networks is not enough; the networks need to have sufficient resources of value to make a difference. Third, policy proponents focus exclusively on the positive benefits of high levels of social capital and ignore the possibility of negative consequences.

Portes and Landolt (1996) specifically identify the less desirable possibilities of developing social capital. Social networks can promote "public bads" just as easily as public goods. Social capital can contribute to discrimination, restriction of individual freedom and creativity, lack of economic opportunity, and overwhelming obligations. Strong voluntary associations, communities, and social networks that maintain high levels of solidarity often do so by excluding outsiders. Thus, noninsiders are disadvantaged within those groups. Additionally, high social capital is contingent on a high degree of conformity within the group, and nonconformists can be ostracized. This greatly impinges on personal freedom and expression. It also can result in a great deal of power for those in leadership positions in the group. Mafia-type power structures are an example of this.

Tight social networks also can undermine entrepreneurial activity. Successful business owners often are expected to help others, and this can affect their ability to maintain their businesses. Portes and Landolt (1996) identify further "downward leveling pressures" that can be consequences of social capital. The pressure to conform to group norms in order to access group resources (which may be perceived as the only resources available) can keep an individual from attempting to enter the mainstream and find a way up from poverty. Portes and Landolt use the examples of prostitution rings and youth gangs. The network norms function to keep individuals within the familiar group culture. Any attempt by a member to achieve something outside the network may be seen as a threat to group solidarity and is discouraged.

SOCIAL CAPITAL AND SOCIOLOGY

Within the discipline, sociologists recognize the need to conduct empirical investigations as an important component of theory building. The concept of social capital has been advanced in many diverse subfields of sociology. Sociologists have applied it to the macro issues of modernization, economic development or lack of it, networks, and organizations. Others have studied the empirical implications of social capital for families and youth behavior problems, schooling and education, community life, work and organizations, democracy and governance, and collective action (see Woolcock 1998 for an overview).

As a theoretical concept, social capital holds great promise for furthering the sociological understanding of social action. There is still much to learn; the perspective needs to be grounded in established bodies of empirical research before it can be translated into optimistic public policies. Its greatest promise, Woolcock (1998, p.188) points

out, "is that it provides a credible point of entry for sociopolitical issues into a comprehensive multi- and interdisciplinary approach to some of the most pressing issues of our time." Social capital may be seen as a common theoretical language that can allow historians, political scientists, anthropologists, economists, sociologists, and policymakers to work together in an open and constructive manner.

REFERENCES

Baron, James, and Michael Hannan 1994 "The Impact of Economics on Contemporary Sociology." *Journal of Economic Literature*, 32:1111–1146.

Bourdieu, Pierre 1986 "The Forms of Capital." In John G. Richardson, ed., *Handbook of Theory and Research for the Sociology of Education*. New York: Greenwood Press.

Coleman, James 1988 "Social Capital in the Creation of Human Capital." *American Journal of Sociology*, 94: S95–S120.

—— 1990 *Foundations of Social Theory*, Cambridge, Mass. Belknap Press of Harvard University Press.

Portes, Alejandro, and Patricia Landolt 1996 "The Downside of Social Capital" *American Prospect*, 26:18–21, 94.

——, and Julia Sensenbrenner 1993 "Embeddedness and Immigration: Notes on the Social Determinants of Economic Action." *American Journal of Sociology*, 98(6):1320–1350.

Woolcock, Michael 1998 "Social Capital and Economic Development: Toward a Theoretical Synthesis and Policy Framework" *Theory and Society*, 27(2):151–208.

TRACY X. KARNER

SOCIAL CHANGE

Social change is ubiquitous. Although earlier social scientists often treated stability as normal and significant social change as an exceptional process that required a special explanation, scholars now expect to see change at all times and in all social organizations. Much of this type of change is continuous; it occurs in small increments and reveals long-term patterns such as growth. Discontinuous changes, however, are more common than has been assumed. From the perspective of individual organizations, these changes are relatively common and often result in sharp departures from previous states such as when corporations are created, merged, or terminated. From the perspective of larger populations of such organizations, relatively few discontinuous changes result in comparably sharp departures from long-term patterns and trends. Even revolutions that result in dramatic changes of political and legal institutions generally do not transform all of society equally. Some previous patterns continue; others are restored.

Cumulative social change must be distinguished from recurrent fluctuations and the processual aspect of all social life. Both sociologists and historians study the latter by focusing on those dynamic processes through which the social lives of particular individuals and groups may change even though overall patterns remain relatively constant. Marriages and divorces are major changes in social relationships, but a society may have a roughly constant marriage or divorce rate for long periods. Similarly, markets involve a continuous flow of changes in regard to who possess money or goods, who stands in the position of creditor or debtor, who is unemployed or unemployed, and so forth. These specific changes, however, generally do not alter the nature of the markets. Researchers both study the form of particular transactions and develop models to describe the dynamics of large-scale statistical aggregations of such processes (see "Social Dynamics.")

As Bourdieu (1977, 1990) and Giddens (1986) suggest, it is necessary to see human social life as always being structured, but incompletely so. "Structuration," to use their term, is as much a process of change as a reflection of stability. Indeed, the existence of stable social patterns over long periods requires at least as much explanation as does social change. This situation has led to renewed attention to social reproduction, or the ways in which social patterns are re-created in social action. This contrasts with earlier views of continuity as a matter of inertia or simple endurance. Some continuity in the social order is achieved intentionally by actors with enough power to resist changes desired by others; rulers thus maintain their rule by force. Much social reproduction, however, works at a less consciously intentional level and is based on the ways in which people learn to think and act rather than on overt, material force. Bourdieu and Passeron (1977), for example, follow Weber in studying the ways in which

ingrained, habitual ways of deciding what new action fits an individual's situation work without conscious intention to reproduce overall social patterns. A pattern of inequality in educational attainment that is understood officially as meritocratic and is genuinely intended by teachers to be so thus may be reproduced in part because students from nonelite backgrounds unconsciously lower their expectations for themselves, expecting elites to do better. Teachers may unconsciously do the same thing. When decisions are to be made, such as whether to go to university, or which university to choose, elite students and their families are more likely to have the confidence and knowledge to invest in options with a higher long-term payoff.

To understand social change, thus, it is necessary also to understand what produces social continuity. It would be a mistake to explain social change always in terms of a new factor that intervenes in an otherwise stable situation. Rather, social change commonly is produced by the same factors that produce continuity. These factors may change in quantity or quality or in relation to each other.

Sometimes, however, specific processes of social life undergo long-term transformations. These transformations in the nature, organization, or outcomes of the processes are what is usually studied under the label "social change." Social life always depends, for example, on the processes of birth and death that reproduce populations through generations. These rates (adjusted for the age of a population) may be in equilibrium for long periods, resulting in little change in the overall size of a population. Alternatively birthrates may exceed death rates most of the time, resulting in gradual population growth, but periodic disasters such as war, famine, and pestilence may cut the population back. In this case, the population may show little or no cumulative growth, but instead exhibit a dynamic equilibrium in which every period of gradual increase is offset by one of rapid decline. Approximations to these two patterns characterize most of world history. Population growth generally has been quite slow, although periodic declines have not offset all the increases. In the last three hundred years, however, a new phenomenon has been noted. As societies industrialize and generally grow richer and change the daily lives of their members, they undergo a "fertility transition." First, improvements in nutrition, sanitation, and health can allow people to live longer. This results in population growth that can be very rapid if the improvements are introduced together rather than gradually developing over a long period. After a time lag, this encourages people to have fewer children because more of the children they do have survive. As fertility rates (birthrates standardized by the number of women of child-bearing age) also drop, a new equilibrium may be reached; population growth will slow or stop. This is a cumulative transition, because after it, the typical rates of birth and death are much lower even though the population may be much larger. A variety of other changes may follow from or be influenced by this process. For example, family life may change with declining numbers of children, parents' (especially mothers') lives are likely to change as fewer of their years are devoted to bearing and raising children, and childhood deaths may become rarities rather than common experiences.

Social history is given its shape by such cumulative social changes. Many of these changes are quite basic, such as the creation of the modern state; others are more minor, such as the invention and spread of the handshake as a form of greeting. Most, such as the development of team sports, fast-food restaurants, and the international, academic conference, lie in the broad area in between. Thus, cumulative social changes may take place on a variety of different scales, from the patterns of small group life through institutions such as the business corporation or church to overall societal arrangements. Significant changes tend to have widespread repercussions, however, and so it is rare for one part of social life to change dramatically without changing other parts.

While certain important changes, such as an increasing population, are basically linear, others are discontinuous. There are two senses of discontinuity. The first is abruptness, such as the dramatic contraction of the European population in the wake of plague and other calamities of the fourteenth century and the occurrence of the Russian Revolution after centuries of tsarist rule and failed revolts. Second, some social changes alter not just the values of variables but the relationship of variables to each other. Thus, for much of history the military power and wealth of a ruler was based directly on the number of his or her subjects; growing populations meant an increasing total

product from which to extract tribute, taxes, and military service. With the transformation first of agriculture and then of industrial production in the early capitalist era or just before it, this relationship was in many cases upset. Increasingly, from the sixteenth through eighteenth centuries, for example, the heads of Scottish clans found that a small population raising sheep could produce more wealth than could a large one farming; their attempt to maximize this advantage contributed to the migration of Scots to Ireland and America. This process was of course linked also to growing demand for wool and the development of the industrial production of textiles. Those factors in turn involved new divisions of social labor and increased long-distance trade. At the same time, the development of industrial production and related weapons technologies reduced the military advantages of large population size by contrast to epochs when wars generally were won by the largest armies; indeed, population may be inversely related to power if it impedes industrialization.

This case provides an example of how shifts in the relationships of certain variables can alter not only overall social patterns but broad cultural orientations to social change. Along with industrialization (and other dimensions of modern social life) has come a continuous process of technological and social innovation. As Weber (1922) emphasized, this process is at odds with a traditional orientation to social life. Traditionalism implies an expectation of continuity and respect for the ways in which things have always been done. Constant innovation is linked to the pursuit of more efficient ways to do things and an expectation of continuous change. Leaders of China, long thought the absolute size of armies would be decisive in conflict. They were shocked when both Japan and Western powers were able to win victories in the nineteenth century mainly on the basis of superior technology rather than superior size. This helped produce not only the collapse of a specific imperial dynasty but a crisis in a whole pattern of traditionalism. Instead of assuming that the best lessons for military strategy lay in the teachings of the past, some leaders recognized that they needed to look for new ways in which to make the country strong. This produced a tension between trying to preserve cultural identity by continuing to do things the same way and trying to achieve technological and other gains by innovating. This tension is common in societies that have undergone broad patterns of social change in the modern era. In China, after the death of Mao Zedong leaders decided that strengthening the country and improving people's lives depended on technological advancement and economic development. Recognizing both that large armies would not win wars against enemies with technologically advanced weapons and that rapid population growth would make it difficult to educate the whole population and produce rapid economic growth, Deng Xiaoping and other leaders introduced policies to reduce population growth rates. They also decided that they needed to liberalize the economy and encourage private business because state-owned enterprises could not innovate rapidly enough. On the one hand, they encourage innovation in economy and technology, and on the other hand, they resist change in politics and culture. Although perhaps contradictory, these two responses have been typical of leaders in societies undergoing the process of modernization. Although it is impossible to prevent major changes in technology and the economy from having an impact on politics and culture, it is possible to shape what those impacts will be.

Sociologists generally have taken three approaches to studying cumulative social changes. The first is to look for generalizable patterns in how all sorts of changes occur, the second is to seek an explanation for the whole overall pattern of history, and the third is to analyze historically specific processes of change.

Following the first of these approaches, sociologists have looked for characteristic phases through which any social innovation must pass, such as skepticism, experimentation, early diffusion among leaders, and later general acceptance. Ogburn ([1922] 1950) was a pioneer in this sort of research, examining topics such as the characteristic "lag" between cultural innovations and widespread adjustments to them or exploitation of their potential. In regard to the fertility transition, when improved health care and nutrition make it possible for nearly all children to survive to adulthood, it takes a generation or two before parents stop having large families as "insurance policies" to provide for support in their old age. Earlier researchers often hoped to find general laws that would explain the duration of such lags and account for other features of all processes of social change. Contemporary sociologists tend to place much more emphasis on differences among various kinds of social change and their settings; accordingly, their generalizations are more specific. Researchers may limit their studies to the patterns of innovation among business organizations, for example, recognizing that those organizations may act quite differently from others. They also may ask questions such as, Why do innovations gain acceptance more rapidly in formal organizations (e.g., businesses) than in informal, primary groups (e.g., families), or what sorts of organizations are more likely to innovate? The changes may be very specific, such as the introduction of new technologies of production, or very general, such as the Industrial Revolution as a whole (Smelser 1958). The key distinguishing feature of these sorts of studies is that they regard changes as individual units of roughly similar sorts and aim to produce generalizations about them.

The second major sociological approach to cumulative change—seeking an explanation for the whole pattern of cumulation—was long the province of philosophies of history that culminated in the sweeping syntheses of the nineteenth century. Sociology was born partly out of the attempt to understand the rise of science, industry, and urban society. These and related transitions were conceptualized in frameworks that emphasized shifts from tradition to modernity, feudalism to capitalism, and monarchy to republicanism or democracy. As Sztompka (1993) points out, three basic visions were developed, each of which has left a mark on sociology and continues to be influential in research: cycles, evolutionary progress, and historical materialism. The roots of the cyclical vision stretch back to antiquity. The image of the human life cycle, from birth and infancy to old age and death, for example, was used to conceptualize the rise and fall of whole societies and of imperial dynasties that were thought to be vigorous in youth and feeble in old age. Few scientific sociologists have regarded such images as more than metaphors, but they have been influential among writers attempting to generalize about the course of history (e.g., Spengler [1918] 1939; Toynbee 1934–1961). A number of sociologists, however, have studied more specific cyclical patterns. Pareto ([1916] 1980) analyzed what he called the circulation of elites, a pattern in which specific groups rose into and then fell from social dominance. Sorokin (1937) analyzed cultural cycles, especially the oscillating dominance of ideational (spiritual, intellectual) and sensate (sensual, materialist) orientations. More recently, sociologists have identified cycles in social movements and collective action (Tilly 1989; Tarrow 1998; Traugott, 1995).

Both historical materialism and evolutionism are indebted to another ancient idea, that of progress. Here the idea is that social change tends to produce a pattern of improvements in human life as measured in relationship to a standard of evaluation. In this regard, sociological evolutionism has commonly differed from evolutionary theory in biology, which has been less focused on the overall direction of change and normative evaluation. The great nineteenth-century evolutionary thinkers Comte([1830–1842, 1851–1854] 1975) and Spencer (1893) conceptualized history as progress through a series of stages. Comte based his analysis on what he saw as improvements in social knowledge through theological, metaphysical, and positive stages. Spencer, who was also an originator of evolutionary theory in biology, had a much more complex and sophisticated theory, focusing on the way structures developed to meet functional imperatives and gaining direction from the idea that "incoherent homogeneity" progressively gives way to "coherent heterogeneity" through the process of structural differentiation. Spencer (1893) addressed particularly the transition from military to industrial societies, which he saw as basic to modernity. Durkheim (1893) developed a similar analysis in his description of the movement from mechanical to organic solidarity.

[[1] Schrecker (1991) has analyzed a pattern in which something similar to Spencer's two stages alternated cyclically in Chinese society rather than forming the basis for a single evolutionary trend. Periods of increasing industrialization and commercialization (*fengjian*) were followed by eras in which agriculture and military prowess figured more prominently (*junxian*). Schrecker (1991) suggests that this intriguing combination of evolutionary and cyclical theories initially was developed by classical Chinese scholars, although it was recast after the importation of Spencerian evolutionary theory.]

Historical materialists, starting with Marx (1863), also analyzed stages in historical development (such as feudalism and capitalism), but with three crucial differences from other evolutionary theories. First, Marx and his followers argued that material factors, especially the mode of production, shape the rest of society and that change is driven largely by improvements in the capacity for material production. Second, following a dialectical logic, Marxists emphasized the internal contradictions within each stage of development. Capitalism, for example, generated tremendous increases in productivity but distributed the resulting wealth so unequally that it was prone to economic crises and social revolutions. Rather than a simple, incremental progress, thus, Marxists saw evolution as taking place in discontinuous breaks marked by clashes and struggles. Third, most versions of Marxist theory gave greater emphasis to human agency or ability consciously to shape the direction of social change than was typical of evolutionary theory. The question of the extent to which evolution can be directed consciously has, however, recently come to the fore of non-Marxist evolutionary theory as well, as in in the work of the sociobiologist Wilson (Wilson and Wilson 1999).

The most important contemporary theories of social evolution attempt to generate not only overall descriptions of stages but causal explanations for social change. Lenski, for example, has argued that increases in technological capacity (including information processing as well as material production and distribution) account for most of the major changes in human social organization (Lenski et al. 1994). In his synthesis, Lenski arranges the major forms of human societies in a hierarchy based on their technological capacity and shows how other features, such as their typical patterns of religion, law, government, class inequality, and relations between the sexes, are rooted in those technological differences. In support of the idea that there is an overall evolutionary pattern, Lenski et al. (1994) point to the tendency of social change to move only in one direction. Thus, there are many cases of agricultural states being transformed into industrial societies but very few (if any) examples of the reverse. Of course, Lenski acknowledges that human evolution is not completely irreversible; he notes, however, not only that cases of reversal are relatively few but that they commonly result from an external cataclysm. Similarly, Lenski indicates that the direction of human social evolution is not strictly dictated from the start but only channeled in certain directions. There is room for human ingenuity to determine the shape of the future through a wide range of potential differences in invention and innovation. There are a number of other important versions of the evolutionary approach to cumulative social change. Some stress different material factors, such as humanadaptation to ecological constraints (Harris 1979; White 1949); others stress culture and other patterns of thought more than material conditions (Parsons 1968; Habermas 1978).

Adherents to the third major approach to cumulative social change argue that there can be no single evolutionary explanation for all the important transitions in human history. They also stress differences as well as analogies among particular instances of specific sorts of change (Stinchcombe 1978). These historians and historical sociologists emphasize the importance of dealing adequately with particular changes by locating them in their historical and cultural contexts and distinguishing them through comparison (Abrams 1982; Skocpol 1984; Calhoun 1995, 1998). Weber was an important pioneer of this approach. A prominent variety of Marxism has stressed the view that Marx's mature analysis of capitalism emphasizes historical specificity rather than the use of the same categories to explain all of history (Postone 1993). Historical sociologists have argued that a particular sort of transformation, such as the development of the capacity for industrial production, may result from different causes and have different implications on different occasions. The original Industrial Revolution in eighteenth- and nineteenth-century Britain thus developed with no advance model and without competition from established industrial powers. Countries that are industrializing today are influenced by both models and competition from existing industrial countries, along with influences from multinational corporations. The development of the modern world system thus fundamentally altered the conditions of future social changes, making it misleading to lump together cases of early and late industrialization for the purpose of generalization. Similarly, prerequisites for industrial production may be supplied by different institutional formations; one should compare not just institutions but different responses to similar problems.

Accident and disorder also have played crucial roles in the development of the modern world system. Wallerstein (1974–1988) shows the centrality of historical conjunctures and contingencies: the partially random relationships between different sorts of events (on historical accidents, see also Simmel 1977; Boudon 1986). For example, the outcome of military battles between Spain (an old-fashioned empire) and Britain (the key industrial-capitalist pioneer) were not foregone conclusions. There was room for bravery, weather, strategy, and a variety of other factors to play a role. However, certain key British victories, notably in the sixteenth century, helped make not only British history but world history different by creating the conditions for the modern world system to take the shape it did. Against evolutionary explanation, historical sociologists also argue that different factors explain different transformations. Thus, no amount of study of the factors that brought about the rise of capitalism and industrial production can provide the necessary insight into the decline of the Roman Empire and the eventual development of feudalism in Europe or the consolidation of China's very different regions into the world's most enduring empire and most populous state. These different kinds of events have their own different sorts of causes.

Predictably, some sociologists seek ways to combine some of the benefits of each type of approach to explaining cumulative social change. Historical sociologists who emphasize the singularity of specific transformations can learn from comparisons among such changes and achieve at least partial generalizations about them. Thus, different factors are involved in every social revolution, yet certain key elements seem to be present, such as crises (financial as well as political) in a government's capacity to rule (Skocpol 1979; Goldstone 1991). This recognition encourages one to focus on structural factors that may help create potentially revolutionary situations as well as the ideologies and actions of specific revolutionaries. Similarly, even though a variety of specific factors may determine the transition to capitalism or industrialization in every instance, some version of a fertility transition seems to play a role in nearly all cases. Although evolutionary theory is widely rejected by historical sociologists, some look to evolutionary arguments for suggestions about what factors might be important. Thus, Lenski's emphasis on technology and Marx's focus on the relationship of production and class struggle can provide foci for research, and that research can help determine whether those factors are equally important in all societal transformations and whether they work the same way in each one. More radically, evolutionary socioglogy might follow biology in focusing less on the selection of whole populations (societies) for success or failure and look instead at the selection of specific social practices (e.g., the bearing of large numbers of children) for reproduction or disappearance. Such an evolutionary theory might provide insight into how practices become more or less common, following biology in looking for mechanisms of reproduction and inheritance, the initiation of new practices (mutation), and the clustering of practices in interacting groups (speciation) as well as selection. It would, however, necessarily give up the capacity to offer a single explanation for all the major transitions in human social history, which is one of the attractions of evolutionary theory to its adherents.

Certain basic challenges are particularly important in the study of cumulative social change today. In addition to working out a satisfactory relationship among the three main approaches, perhaps the most important challenge is to distinguish social changes that are basic from those which are ephemeral or less momentous. Sociologists, like historians and other scholars, need to be able to characterize broad patterns of social arrangements. This is what sociologists do when they speak of "modernity" or "industrial society." Such characterizations involve at least implicit theoretical claims about the crucial factors that distinguish these eras or forms. In the case of complex, large-scale societal processes, these factors are hard to pin down. How much industrial capacity does a society need to have before one can call it industrial? How low must employment in its increasingly automated industries become before one can call it postindustrial? Is current social and economic globalization the continuation of a longstanding trend or part of a fundamental transformation? Although settling such questions is difficult, debating them is crucial, for sociologists cannot grasp the historical contexts of the phenomena they study if they limit themselves to studying particulars or seeking generalizations from them without attempting to understand the differences among historical epochs (however hard to define sharply) and cultures (however much they may shade into each other with contact). Particularly because of the many current contentions that

humanity stands on the edge of a new age—postmodern, postindustrial, or something else—researchers and theorists need togive strong answers to the question of what it means to claim that one epoch ends and another begins (Calhoun 1999).

Many prominent social theorists have treated all of modernity as a continuous era and stressed its distinction from previous (or anticipated future) forms of social organization. Durkheim (1893) argued that a new, more complex division of labor is central to a dichotomous distinction of modern (organically solidary) from premodern (mechanically solidary) society. Weber (1922) saw Western rationalization of action and relationships as basic and as continuing without rupture through the whole modern era. Marx (1863) saw the transition from feudalism to capitalism as basic but held that no change in modernity could be considered fundamental unless it overthrew the processes of private capital accumulation and the commodification of labor. Recent Marxists thus argue that the social and economic changes of the last several decades mark a new phase within capitalism but not a break with it (Mandel 1974; Wallerstein 1974–1988; Harvey 1989). Many sociologists would add a claim about the centrality of increasing state power as a basic, continuous process of modernity (e.g., Tilly 1990; Mann 1986–1993). More generally, Habermas (1984–1988) has stressed the split between a life world in which everyday interactions are organized on the basis of mutual agreement and an increasingly prominent systemic integration through the impersonal relationships of money and power outside the reach of linguistically mediated cooperative understanding. Common to all these positions is the notion that there is a general *process* (not just a static set of attributes) common to all forms of modernity. Some claim to discern a causal explanation; others only point to the trends, suggesting that those trends may have several causes but that there is no single "prime mover" that can explain an overall pattern of evolution. All would agree that no really basic social change can be said to have occurred until the fundamental processes they identify have ended, been reversed, or changed their relationship to other variables. Obviously, a great deal depends on what processes are considered fundamental.

Rather than stressing the common processes that organize all forms of modernity, some scholars have followed Marx (and recent structuralist theory) in pointing to the disjunctures between relatively stable periods. Foucault (1973), for example, emphasized basic transformations in the way knowledge is constituted and an order is ascribed to the world of things, people, and ideas. Renaissance culture was characterized by an emphasis on resemblances among the manifold different elements of God's single, unified creation. Knowledge of fields as diverse to modern eyes as biology, aesthetics, theology, and astronomy was thought to be unified by the matching of similar characteristics, with those in each field serving as visible signs of counterparts in the others. The "classical" modernity of the seventeenth and early eighteenth centuries marked a radical break by treating the sign as fundamentally distinct from the thing it signified, noting, for example, that words have only arbitrary relationships to the objects they name. The study of representation thus replaced that of resemblances. In the late eighteenth and early nineteenth centuries, another rupture came with the development of the modern ideas of classification according to hidden, underlying causes rather than superficial resemblances and an examination of human beings as the basic source of systems of representation. Only this last period could give rise to the "human sciences"—psychology, sociology, and so forth—as they are known today. Similarly, Foucault (1977) argued that the modern individual is a distinctive form of person or self, produced by an intensification of disciplining power and surveillance. Where most theories of social change emphasize processes, Foucault's "archaeology of knowledge" emphasizes the internal coherence of relatively stable cultural configurations and the ruptures between them.

Foucault's work has been taken as support for the claim (which was not his own) that the modern era has ended. Theories of "postmodernity" commonly argue that at some point the modern era gave way to a successor, though some scholars (e.g., Lyotard 1977) have indicated, against the implications of the label "postmodern," that they mean not a simple historical succession but a recurrent internal challenge to the dominant "modernist" patterns (see Lash 1990; Seidman 1995; Harvey 1989; Calhoun 1995). Generally, they hold that where modernity was rigid, linear, and focused on universality, postmodernity is flexible, fluidly multidirectional, and focused on differ-

ence. Some postmodernist theories emphasize the impact of new production technologies (especially computer-assisted flexible automation), while others are more exclusively cultural. The label "postmodernity" often is applied rather casually to point to interesting features of the present period without clearly indicating why they should be taken as revealing a basic discontinuous shift between eras.

At stake in debates over the periodization of social change is not just the labeling of eras but the analysis of what factors are most fundamentally constitutive of social organization. Should ecology and politics be seen as determinative over, equal to, or derivative of the economy? Is demography or technological capacity prior to the other? What gives capitalism, feudalism, a kinship system, or any other social order its temporary and relative stability? Such questions must be approached not just in terms of manifest influence at any single point in time or during specific events but also in terms of the way particular factors figure in long-term processes of cumulative social change.

REFERENCES

Abrams, Philip 1982 *Historical Sociology*. Ithaca, N.Y.: Cornell University Press.

Boudon, Raymond 1986 *Theories of Social Change*. Cambridge, UK: Cambridge University Press.

Bourdieu, Pierre 1977 *Outline of a Theory of Practice*. Cambridge, UK: Cambridge University Press.

——, 1990 *The Logic of Practice*. Stanford, Calif.: Stanford University Press.

——, and Jean-Claude Passeron 1977 *Reproduction in Education, Culture, and Society*. London: Sage

Calhoun, Craig 1995 *Critical Social Theory: Culture, History, and the Challenge of Difference*. Cambridge, Mass.: Blackwell.

—— 1998 "Explanation in Historical Sociology: Narrative, General Theory, and Historically Specific Theory." *American Journal of Sociology* 108:846–871.

—— 1999 "Nationalism, Social Change, and Historical Sociology," In F. Engelstad and R. Kalleberg, eds., *Social Change and Historical Sociology*. Oslo: Scandinavian University Press.

Comte, Auguste (1830–1842, 1851–1854) 1975 *Auguste Comte and Positivism: The Essential Writings*, edited by G. Lenzer. New York: Harper.

Durkheim, Emile 1893 *The Division of Labor in Society*. New York: Free Press.

Foucault, Michel 1973 *The Order of Things: An Archaeology of the Human Sciences*. New York: Random House.

—— 1977 *Discipline and Punish*. New York: Pantheon.

Giddens, Anthony 1986 *The Constitution of Society*. Berkeley: University of California Press.

Goldstone, Jack 1991 *Revolution and Rebellion in the Early Modern World*. Berkeley: University of California Press.

Habermas, Jurgen 1978 *Communication and the Evolution of Society*. Boston: Beacon.

—— 1984–1988 *The Theory of Communicative Action*, 2 vols. Boston: Beacon

Harris, Marvin 1979 *Cultural Materialism*. New York: Vintage.

Harvey, David 1989 *The Postmodern Condition*. Oxford, UK: Oxford University Press.

Lash, Scott 1990 *Postmodern Sociology*. London: Routledge.

Lenski, Gerhard, Jean Lenski, and Patrick Nolan 1994 *Human Societies*, 7th ed. New York: McGraw-Hill.

Lyotard, Jean-François 1977 *The Postmodern Condition*. Minneapolis: University of Minnesota Press

Mandel, Ernst 1974 *Late Capitalism*. London: Verso.

Mann, Michael 1986–1993 *The Sources of Social Power*. Cambridge, UK: Cambridge University Press.

Marx, Karl 1863 *Capital*, vol. 1. New York: Viking.

Ogburn, W. F. (1922) 1950 *Social Change with Respect to Culture and Original Nature*. New York: Viking.

Pareto, Wilfredo (1916) 1980 *Compendium of General Sociology*. Minneapolis: University of Minnesota Press.

Parsons, Talcott 1968 *The Evolution of Societies*. New York: Free Press.

Postone, Moishe 1993 *Time, Labor and Social Domination*. New York: Cambridge University Press.

Schrecker, John 1991 *The Chinese Revolution in Historical Perspective*. New York: Praeger.

Seidman, Steven 1995 *The Postmodern Turn: New Perspectives on Social Theory*. New York: Cambridge University Press.

Simmel, Georg 1977 *The Problem of the Philosophy of History*. New York: Free Press.

Skocpol, Theda 1979 *States and Social Revolutions*. New York: Cambridge University Press.

——, ed. 1984 *Vision and Method in Historical Sociology*. New York: Cambridge University Press.

Smelser, Neil J. 1958 *Social Change in the Industrial Revolution*. London, Routledge and Kegan Paul.

Sorokin, Pitirim 1937 *Social and Cultural Dynamics*, 4 vols. New York: American Book Company.

Spencer, Herbert 1893 *Principles of Sociology*, 3 vols. London: Williams and Norgate.

Spengler, Oswald (1918) 1939 *The Decline of the West*. New York: Knopf.

Stinchcombe, Arthur 1978 *Theoretical Methods in Social History*. New York: Academic Press.

Sztompka, Piotr 1993 *The Sociology of Social Change*. Oxford: Blackwell.

Tarrow, Sidney 1998 *Power in Movement: Social Movements and Contentious Politics*. Cambridge, UK: Cambridge University Press.

Tilly, Charles 1989 *The Contentious French*. Cambridge, Mass.: Harvard University Press.

—— 1990 *Coercion, Capital, and European States, AD 990–1990*. Oxford, UK: Blackwell.

Toynbee, Arnold 1934–1961 *A Study of History*, 12 vols. Oxford, UK: Oxford University Press.

Traugott, Mark, ed. 1995 *Repertoires and Cycles in Collective Action*. Durham, N.C.: Duke University Press.

Wallerstein, Immanuel 1974–1988 *The Modern World System*, 3 vols. San Diego: Academic Press.

Weber, Max 1922 *Economy and Society*. Berkley: University of California Press.

White, Leslie 1949 *The Science of Culture*. New York: Grove Press.

Wilson, Edward O., and Edmund O. Wilson 1999 *Consilience*. New York: Random House.

CRAIG CALHOUN

SOCIAL COMPARISON PROCESSES

How do people come to understand themselves? A response to this age-old question involves what has been labeled everyone's "second favorite theory" (Goethals 1986): social comparison. The original formulation of social comparison theory (Festinger 1954) demonstrated how, in the absence of objective standards, individuals use other people to fulfill their informational needs to evaluate their own opinions and abilities. The process of social comparison underlies social evaluation (Pettigrew 1967) and relates to reference group processes (e.g., Hyman and Singer 1968), which in turn are critical to understanding diverse sociological issues pertaining, for example, to identity development, justice, interpersonal and intergroup relationships, and group decision making. Thus, the "second favorite" status of social comparison theory reflects the preference of researchers for particular theories about each of these topics, which nonetheless promote the centrality and breadth of social comparison processes in sociological pursuits. To explain the multifaceted role of social comparisons, this article first describes the theory and its elaborations and then shifts to a sampling of the extensive applications of that theory.

SOCIAL COMPARISON THEORY

For nearly fifty years, social comparison theory has shifted between the categories of "lost and found" (Goethals 1986): The theory flourishes for a while and then lies dormant. Suls (1977) outlines the first twenty years of social comparison research, beginning with its inception in 1954 by the psychologist Festinger and then describing its theoretical decline while applications to affiliation (Schachter 1959), emotions (Schachter and Singer 1962), and justice (Adams 1965) emerged; its momentary revival in a 1966 issue of the *Journal of Experimental Social Psychology*; and its second, more enduring revival in 1977 in the form of a landmark volume of collected essays (Suls and Miller, 1977). During its fourth decade, the resurgence of social comparisons research (Wood 1989) anchored it firmly in the "found" category. Almost fifty years after its inception, its contribution to numerous substantive areas appears to be unrivaled (Suls and Wills 1991).

Festinger (1954) incorporates his observations regarding research on aspiration levels and social pressures into the premises of his formal theory of social comparison. First, individuals are driven to evaluate their abilities and opinions. That drive increases with the importance of the ability or opinion, its relevance to immediate behavior, the relevance of the group to the ability or opinion, and the individual's attraction to the group. These factors also increase the pressure toward uniformity with relevant others. Second, people first attempt to make these evaluations through objective, nonsocial means, but if those means are unavailable, they are likely to compare themselves with others. Third, individuals are likely to choose for comparison someone close to the opinion or ability in question (the "similarity hypothesis"). Festinger notes that social comparisons may be

based on the similarity of attributes related to the dimension under evaluation (the "related attributes hypothesis"). As a rationale for the preference for similar comparison others, he argues that comparisons with divergent others produce imprecise and unstable evaluations. Comparisons with moderately different others (those within tolerable limits of discrepancy), however, produce changes in individuals' evaluations of their own or the others' abilities or opinions. These changes ensure uniformity in the group and reinforce stable and precise evaluations.

Although Festinger (1954) treats abilities and opinions similarly in most respects, he notes a major distinction that may influence the consequences of comparisons. In the case of abilities, the cultural value of doing "better and better" encourages individuals to make upward comparisons. Typically, because of the pressure toward uniformity, the upward drive is limited to comparisons with those who are slightly better. This unidirectional drive upward, however, inspires competition among group members that may inhibit the emergence of social uniformity. In contrast, no upward drive characterizes comparisons of opinions. In light of the pressure toward uniformity, the absence of an upward drive and the greater flexibility of opinions (compared with the nonsocial constraints on changes in abilities) suggest that a state of social quiescence is more likely to emerge in terms of the evaluation of opinions.

Despite the greater likelihood of opinion uniformity, Festinger (1954) notes that if potential comparison others have highly discrepant opinions, the cessation of the comparison process may result in hostility toward or derogation of those others. These negative reactions stem from the belief that opinion discrepancy means that an individual's opinions are incorrect. In contrast, no negative implications characterize discrepancy in abilities, which are more independent of relative value orientations, indicating different forms of "correctness."

As is suggested by his emphasis on group uniformity, one of Festinger's (1954) major concerns was to describe the role of social comparison processes in group formation and maintenance as well as social structure. Presumably, people who have similar abilities and opinions group together; as a result of their distinguishing themselves from others, segments form in society. These two implications of social comparison processes are represented in research on group decision making and intergroup relations (see below). Although Festinger's perspective suggests a wide range of implications, his theory is not definitive; in fact, Arrowood (1986) has labeled the 1954 version a "masterpiece of ambiguity." Points of ambiguity involve theoretical issues regarding the nature of social comparison per se, the motivations that underlie comparison choices, and the choice of a comparison other (especially the meaning of similarity).

In Festinger's (1957) formulation, the nature of the social comparison is oblique, referring only to nonobjective information regarding abilities and opinions. Others have extended the domain of social comparisons to include emotions (Schachter and Singer 1962), outcomes (Adams 1965), health (Buunk and Gibbons 1997), relationships (VanYperen and Buunk 1994), and traits (Thorton and Arrowood 1966, but see Suls 1986). Nonobjective information may include personal comparisons (see Masters and Keil 1987). These comparisons involve information about the self and draw attention to time as an important factor in determining the nature of comparisons. Temporal comparisons (Albert 1977) involve a "now versus then" dimension, meaning that a person compares pieces of information about an ability or opinion at different points in time.

Arrowood (1986) describes several forms of nonobjective (ability) information used in social comparison studies, for example, the presentation of two ratings (the evaluator's and that of an unidentified other), the display of a distribution of ratings that includes the evaluator's, and the presentation of the evaluator's rating along with the identifying characteristics of potential comparison others and their ratings. The latter two factors allow the development of an estimate about others in general, with the last one also allowing an assessment of similarity. Compared with objective information, relative standing generally exerts greater influence except when the desirability of objective information is great (Klein 1997). Not all methods, however, truly capture social comparison. To address this problem, Wood (1996) stresses the need for consistency between definitions and measures and the need to be wary of alternative interpretations. Insofar as information presentation stimulates the comparison process, its effects may depend on the motivations that drive the comparison.

The most explicit but general, motivation included in Festinger's (1954) perspective is that people need information. Later work, however, demonstrates that the motivations underlying social comparisons are far more extensive. Twenty years ago, Fazio (1979) specified two types of information motivations that underlie self-evaluations: (1) the "construction" motivation, referring to a person's desire to obtain information he or she lacks, and (2) the "validation" motivation, representing the use of information to determine the valid source (e.g., the person or the entity) of a person's judgment about an entity. Fazio argues that individuals appear to be motivated by construction when they lack information and by validations when they have sufficient information. Validation, however, is distinct from a third motivation: self (or ego) enhancement. Festinger (1954) hinted at the possibility of self-enhancement when he posited that in evaluating abilities, individuals are likely to make upward comparisons; by noting "how close" an individual is to a superior performer, that individual enhances the evaluation of his or her own ability. In addition to self-evaluation and self-enhancement goals, one study (Hegeson and Mickelson 1995) lists four other motives for social comparison: common bond, self-improvement, altruism, and self-destruction.

A recent trend in distinguishing among motivations is to focus on the role of self-esteem in social comparisons. Generally, individuals low in self-esteem rely more on social comparison information to meet goals of accuracy, self-enhancement, and self-improvement than do those high in self-esteem (Wayment and Taylor 1995). However, insofar as people with low self-esteem are more oriented to self-protection, they are likely to seek social comparison information that is "safe" (i.e., that carries little risk of humiliation) after receiving success feedback (Wood et al. 1994). In effect, low-esteem individuals are seizing a safe form of self-enhancement. Threats to self-esteem, especially among those who have high self-esteem, seem to stimulate more egocentric contrasts in judgments of others (Beauregard and Dunning 1998), suggesting that individuals tailor their evaluations of others to affirm their own self-worth.

That tailoring of evaluations coincides with other evidence that challenges Festinger's assumption that individuals are rational and accurate in information processing. Wood (1989) demonstrates that people are not unbiased evaluators of information about themselves and potential comparison others, and Hoorens's (1995) study captures some of those biases. Subjects comparing themselves to another person show more unrealistic optimism and illusory superiority regarding future positive events and traits than do subjects who compare another person to themselves. In other words, people perceive themselves more favorably than they perceive others. Motivations, coupled with perceptual processes, are critical in determining the choice of comparison others.

In an extensive review of the choice of comparison others, Gruder (1977) examines the conflict between evaluation and enhancement motivations. He concludes that the evaluation motivation is important in new situations and that under such conditions, individuals are likely to choose others who are similar to themselves in terms of the ability or opinion at issue. Enhancement motivations arise when enhancement is feasible. For example, in the absence of threats to self-esteem, individuals are likely to make upward, self-enhancing comparisons that provide useful information for self-improvement (Collins 1996; Blanton et al. 1999). If an upward comparison is unavoidable, individuals may deflect a threat to their self-esteem by perceptually distorting through exaggeration the performance of the other person (Alicke et al. 1997). When self-esteem is unavoidably threatened, people are more likely to make downward (defensive) comparisons (e.g., Hakmiller 1966; Taylor and Lobel 1989). In effect, to protect their self-esteem, individuals choose dissimilar others (i.e., inferior performers) for their comparisons. Researchers are examining a number of additional factors that may affect responses to upward and downward comparisons (e.g., Aspinwall and Taylor 1993). Whether individuals choose similar or dissimilar others for comparison depends in part on the nature of the dimension under scrutiny, the context (including the characteristics of potential comparison others), and the importance of the enhancement goal (Wood 1989).

Questions about the choice of comparison others typically raise the issue of the meaning of similarity. Festinger (1984) offers different yet potentially complementary definitions of similarity: closeness of ratings on abilities or opinions and attributes related to the evaluation dimension. Goethals and Darley (1977) note that similarity in the first sense is paradoxical: "[P]resumably the comparison is made in order to find out what the other's opinion or score is, yet prior knowledge of the similarity of his score or opinion is assumed as the basis for comparison" (p. 265). Those authors advocate the interpretation of similarity on the basis of "related attributes." One is likely to choose others for comparison who *should be* close to one's own ability or opinion by virtue of their standing on characteristics related to the evaluative dimension. Wheeler et al. (1982) review the extensive support for the related attributes hypothesis. Two trends, however, qualify that support. Kulik and Gump (1997) show that related attribute information has an effect only in the absence of information on relative performances. And Wood (1989) indicates that people choose comparisons with those with similar characteristics regardless of whether the attribute relates to the dimension under scrutiny; for example, people of the same sex are more likely to compare themselves to each other even if sex is unrelated to the ability that is being compared.

Concern with related attributes similarity and its evaluative consequences provides the basis for one of the main elaborations of social comparison theory: Goethals and Darley's (1977) attributional approach. Their approach applies Kelley's (1973) attributional concepts of discounting and augmentation (see Howard in this volume) to assess the certainty of one's standing on an ability or opinion. With regard to abilities, attribution logic focuses on the configuration of possible comparison others and one's own ability level. For example, a person who compares himself or herself to an advantaged other expects his or her performance to be worse. The implications for an ability evaluation are ambiguous, however, because other plausible causes (the superior related attributes) allow the discounting of low ability. In contrast, if an individual performed as well as or better than the advantaged other, he or she overcame inhibitory causes (the inferior related attributes), and this augments a claim to higher ability. In general, conclusive ability evaluations are likely when a person compares herself or himself to others with similar attributes. The role of attributions in evaluating opinions is more complicated because the unexpected cases (disagreement with similar others and agreement with dissimilar others) result in more useful information for validating an opinion than do the expected cases (agreement with similar others and disagreement with dissimilar others). More recent research has concentrated less on attributions than on other cognitive processes (e.g., the use of heuristics and memory) (see Masters and Keil 1987) and perceived control (see Major et al. 1991) to better understand social comparisons.

Complementing the intra- and interpersonal level focus of psychologists are sociological extensions to the level of intergroup relations. Tajfel and Turner (1979) build on Festinger's (1934) assumption that a major consequence of social comparisons to similar others is the development of groups or, in their terminology, social categories. They argue that social comparisons between categories, complemented by individuals' needs for a positive group identity (i.e., the self-enhancement motive), are likely to stimulate in-group bias. People tend to emphasize the positive characteristics of their group while derogating those of other groups. Evidence of such bias is particularly strong in competitive situations. Intergroup discrimination and conflict are the potential consequences of these intergroup comparisons.

Intergroup comparison processes form the main thrust of current research and raise issues of motivations, identity, and choice of comparison. For example, results from Rothgerber and Worchel (1997) confirm Tajfel and Turner's (1979) expectations about perceptions of groups resulting from intergroup comparisons. Disadvantaged in-group members harmed and saw as more homogeneous a disadvantaged out-group whose performance was similar to or better than that of the in-group. The effects of group status and performance, however, may be conditioned by the extent to which actors identify with their groups. High identifiers are likely to demonstrate group solidarity when there are threats to group identity in the form of a superior-status out-group comparison (Spears, Doosje, and Ellemers 1997). And Major et al. (1993) show how upward and downward group comparisons influence self-evaluations: People who compared unfavorably with in-group members reported lower self-esteem and more depressed af-

fect than did those who compared unfavorably with out-group members.

Gartrell (1987) also emphasizes the connection between the individual and the group. Rather than relying on motives for a positive social identity, his analysis concentrates on networks—relations among concrete entities—to highlight an often overlooked aspect of comparison choice: the social context in which individuals make comparisons. The examination of a person's social network relations is a way to understand more clearly not only the selection of relevant comparisons but also whether people seek comparisons actively or passively accept those which are readily present in the network. In addition, network analyses may inform how comparison choices affect the network and influence the ties among a person's multiple networks.

SOCIAL COMPARISON AND SOCIAL BEHAVIOR: APPLICATIONS OF THE THEORY

This review of developments in social comparison theory raises issues at the individual, group, and intergroup levels. Similarly, the extensive applications of the theory cross levels of analysis.

Festinger's (1954) assumption that individuals are driven to evaluate themselves implies a concern with self-knowledge that underlies self-concept and identity formation as well as self esteem. A number of studies examine the role of social comparisons in shaping individual identity through the life course. For example, Chafel (1988) concludes that during childhood, achievement identities reflect first autonomous self-generated norms, then social comparison norms, and finally an integration of the two. Another study (Young and Ferguson 1979) demonstrates that across all grade levels (grades 5, 7, 9, and 12), parents are the comparison choice for the evaluation of moral issues whereas peers typically serve as a reference point for social issues, especially among older students. Moreover, it appears that social comparisons remain a major source of self-evaluation throughout a person's life (Robinson-Whelen and Kiecolt-Glaser 1997).

Just as the choice of a comparison other provides the basis for self-knowledge, comparisons of opinions within a group affect group dynamics. A large body of research examines choice shift or group polarization, in which the group voices a more extreme opinion than would be expected on the basis of initial individual opinions (see Myers and Lamm 1976). The social comparison explanation of polarization states that insofar as people want their own opinions to remain distinct from those of others, exposure to others' opinions stimulates shifts in stances to retain that uniqueness. Consequently, the subsequent group opinion is more extreme.

Concerns with justice potentially stimulate social comparisons at all levels. To assess justice, people evaluate how their rewards or outcomes stack up against what they have earned in the past (internal comparison), what another individual like them earns (local or egoistic comparison), what members of their group typically earn (referential comparison), and what their group earns compared to another group (intergroup or fraternalistic comparison). The type of comparison and the specific person or group chosen define whether an individual is likely to perceive himself or herself or the group as being unfairly treated. Justice obtains when outcomes (or the ratio of outcomes to inputs) are equal across the comparison. Equity theory (Adams 1965; "Equity" in this volume) focuses on local comparisons as the basis for individual reactions to an imbalance in outcome–input ratios, while relative deprivation theory (focusing on outcomes only) attempts to explain when an individual or group will feel deprived and opt for collective action to redress that deprivation (see Masters and Smith 1987; Olson et al. 1986).

Social comparisons underlying justice processes have been extended in two ways beyond the traditional concerns that were noted above. First, researchers have begun to explore the role of social comparisons in understanding procedural justice and its relationship to distributive justice. There is, however, contradictory evidence about whether internal self-referents (Van den Bos et al. 1998) or social referents exert greater influence on that relationship (Ambrose et al. 1991). A second emphasis is more applied: To what extent do comparisons contribute to an understanding of perceptions of fair levels of pay? For example, although women earn lower wages than men do, they do not necessarily perceive this inequality as unfair. It appears that women's perceptions stem from their comparisons with other women rather than with men in general or even with men in their same occupations, resulting in lower pay entitlements (e.g., Moore 1991; Demarais and Curtis 1997).

Although justice concerns have been applied to close relationships, the role of social comparisons in those relationships is a relatively new area of inquiry. VanYperen and Buunk (1994) review research on individuals' decisions to compare themselves to their partners or to their reference groups and the implications of those decisions. For example, people with egalitarian sex-role beliefs are likely to use their partners as a source of comparisons and in doing so enhance their relationship satisfaction; in contrast, individuals with a more traditional sex-role orientation use reference group comparisons to ensure satisfaction. Highlighting the role of motivations in the research reviewed above, Beach et al. (1998) find that reactions to comparisons between individuals in a close relationship support a self-evaluation maintenance model. Comparisons made by intimate couples also appear to parallel those which are evident in intergroup relationships: Subjects have more positive beliefs and fewer negative ones about their own relationships than they do about other relationships (Lange and Rusbult 1995)

A growing body of research examines applications of social comparison theory to health concerns (see Buunk and Gibbons 1997); as in research on close relationships, the application confirms and extends existing theoretical ideas. For example, Buunk and Ybema (1997) introduce an identification–contrast model to explain the choice of comparisons among individuals coping with stress. They suggest that individuals attempt to maintain their self-esteem by identifying upward and by finding ways, such as downward comparisons, to feel that they are doing better than others are. Affleck and Tennen (1991) also stress that downward comparisons are a means for victims of illness to find meaning in their plight and mitigate threats to their self-esteem. These authors also raise important issues involving the role of temporal comparisons in coping with illness and the need to recognize the distinctions between the comparison process and the comparison conclusion. Further extending the domain of social comparison theory, Croyle (1992) attempts to incorporate comparison concerns into standard models of stress and coping and the self-regulation of illness behavior.

CONCLUSIONS AND FUTURE DIRECTIONS

The applications attest to the pivotal role of social comparisons in explaining diverse phenomena. They also reiterate a number of theoretical and empirical issues. Future research should examine conditions affecting the motivations that underlie social comparison processes. Such work also would entail the conditions, such as uncertainty, that stimulate comparisons. The establishment of social contexts activating various motivations will allow a clearer assessment of the cognitive processes that influence social comparisons. In turn, this knowledge may enhance understanding of the choice among comparison others and allow an assessment of the extent to which choices vary with nonmotivational factors. Finally, as much of the applied work suggests, additional studies may reveal the range of consequences of social comparisons for individuals, relationships, and groups. Specific theories about identity formation, group decision making, justice, intimate relationships, and health may be "favorites," but their explanatory success depends on everyone's second favorite theory: social comparison.

REFERENCES

Adams, J. Stacy 1965 "Inequity in Social Exchange." *Advances in Experimental Social Psychology* 2:267–299.

Affleck, Glenn, and Howard Tennen 1991 "Social Comparison and Coping with Major Medical Problems." In Jerry Suls and Thomas Ashby Wills, eds., *Social Comparison: Contemporary Theory and Research*. Hillsdale, N.J.: Erlbaum.

Albert, S. 1977 "Temporal Comparison Theory." *Psychological Review* 84:485–503.

Alicke, Mark D., Frank M. LoSchiavo, and Jennifer Zerbst 1997 "The Person Who Outperforms Me Is a Genius: Maintaining Perceived Competence in Upward Social Comparison." *Journal of Personality and Social Psychology* 73:781–89.

Ambrose, Maureen L, Lynn K. Harland, and Carol T. Kulik 1991 "Influence of Social Comparisons on Perceptions of Organizational Fairness." *Journal of Applied Psychology* 76:239–246.

Arrowood, A. John 1986 "Comments on 'Social Comparison Theory: Psychology from the Lost and Found.'" *Personality and Social Psychology Bulletin* 12:279–281.

Aspinwall, Lisa G., and Shelley E. Taylor 1993 "Effects of Social Comparison Direction, Threat, and Self-Esteem on Affect, Self Evaluation, and Expected Success." *Journal of Personality and Social Psychology* 64:708–722.

Beach, Steven R. H., Abraham Tesser, and Frank D. Fincham 1998 "Pleasure and Pain in Doing Well, Together: An Investigation of Performance-Related Affect in Close Relationships." *Journal of Personality and Social Psychology* 74:923–938.

Beauregard, Keith S., and David Dunning 1998 "Turning Up the Contrast: Self-Enhancement Motives Prompt Egocentric Contrast Effects in Social Judgments." *Journal of Personality and Social Psychology* 74:606–621.

Blanton, Hart, Bram P. Buunk, Frederick X. Gibbons, and Hans Kuyper 1999 "When Better-Than-Others Compare Upward: Choice of Comparison and Comparative Evaluation as Independent Predictors of Academic Performance." *Journal of Personality and Social Psychology* 76:420–430.

Buunk, Bram P., and Frederick X. Gibbons 1997 *Health, Coping, and Well-Being: Perspectives from Social Comparison Theory*. Mahwah, N.J.: Erlbaum.

Buunk, Bram P., and Jan F. Ybema, 1997. "Social Comparisons and Occupational Stress: The Identification-Contrast Model." In Bram P. Buunk and Frederick X. Gibbons, eds., *Health, Coping and Well-Being: Perspective from Social Comparison Theory*, pp. 359–388. Mahwah, NJ: Erlbaum.

Chafel, Judith A. 1988 "Social Comparisons by Children: Analysis of Research on Sex Differences." *Sex Roles* 18:461–487.

Collins, Rebecca L. 1996 "For Better or Worse: The Impact of Upward Social Comparison on Self-Evaluations." *Psychological Bulletin* 119:51–69.

Croyle, Robert T. 1992 "Appraisals of Health Treats: Cognition, Motivation, and Social Comparison." *Cognitive Therapy and Research* 16:165–182.

Demarais, Serge, and James Curtis 1997 "Gender Differences in Pay Histories and Views on Pay Entitlement among University Students." *Sex Roles* 37:623–642.

Fazio, Russel H. 1979 "Motives for Social Comparison: The Construction–Validation Destination." *Journal of Personality and Social Psychology* 37:1683–1698.

Festinger, Leon 1954 "A Theory of Social Comparison." *Human Relations* 14:48–64.

Gartrell, C. David 1987 "Network Approaches to Social Evaluations." *Annual Review of Sociology* 13:49–66.

Goethals, George R. 1986 "Social Comparison Theory: Psychology from the Lost and Found." *Personality and Social Psychology Bulletin* 12:261–278.

——, and John M. Darley 1977 "Social Comparison Theory: An Attributional Approach." In J. Suls and R. L. Miller, eds., *Social Comparison Processes: Theoretical and Empirical Perspectives*. Washingtron, D.C.: Hemisphere.

Gruder, Charles L. 1977 "Choice of Comparison Persons in Evaluations of Oneself." In J. Suls and R. L. Miller, eds., *Social Comparison Processes: Theoretical and Empirical Perspectives*. Washingtron, D.C.: Hemisphere.

Hakmiller, K. 1966 "Threat as a Determinant of Downward Comparison." *Journal of Experimental Social Psychology* 1(suppl.):32–39.

Hegeson, Vicki S., and Kristin D. Mickelson 1995 "Motives for Social Comparison." *Personality and Social Psychology Bulletin* 21:1200–1209.

Hoorens, Vera 1995 "Self-Favoring Biases, Self-Presentation, and the Self-Other Asymmetry in Social Comparison." *Journal of Personality* 63:793–817.

Hyman, Herbert H., and Eleanor Singer 1968 *Readings in Reference Group Theory and Research*. New York: Free Press.

Kelley, Harold H. 1973. "The Process of Causal Attribution." *American Psychologist* 28:107–128.

Klein, William M. 1997 "Objective Standards Are Not Enough: Affective, Self-Evaluative, and Behavioral Responses to Social Comparison Information." *Journal of Personality and Social Psychology* 72:763–774.

Kulik, James A., and Brooks B. Gump 1997 "Affective Reactions to Social Comparison: The Effects of Relative Performance and Related Attributes Information about Another Person." *Personality and Social Psychology Bulletin* 23:452–468.

Lange, Paul A. M. van, and Caryl E. Rusbult 1995 "My Relationship Is Better Than—and Not as Bad as—Yours Is: The Perception of Superiority in Close Relationships." *Personality and Social Psychology Bulletin* 21:32–44.

Major, Brenda, Anne M. Sciacchitano, and Jennifer Crocker 1993 "In-Group Versus Out-Group Comparisons and Self-Esteem." *Personality and Social Psychology Bulletin* 19:711–721.

——, Maria Testa, and Wayne H. Bylsma 1991 Responses to Upward and Downward Social Comparisons: The Impact of Esteem-Relevance and Perceived Control." In Jerry Suls and Thomas Ashby Wills, eds., *Social Comparison: Contemporary Theory and Research*. Hillsdale, N.J.: Erlbaum.

Masters, John C., and Linda J. Keil 1987 "Generic Comparison Processes in Human Judgment and Behavior." In J. C. Masters and W. P. Smith, eds., *Social Comparison, Social Justice, and Relative Deprivation*. Hillsdale, N.J.: Erlbaum.

——, and William P. Smith, eds. 1987 *Social Comparison, Social Justice, and Relative Deprivation*. Hillsdale, N.J.: Erlbaum.

Moore, Dahlia 1991 "Entitlement and Justice Evaluations: Who Get More and Why." *Social Psychology Quarterly* 54:208–223.

Myers, D. G., and David Lamm 1976 "The Group Polarization Phenomena." *Psychological Bulletin* 83:602–627.

Olson, James M., C. Peter Herman, and Mark P. Zanna, eds. 1986 *Relative Deprivation and Social Comparison*. The Ontario Symposium, vol. 4. Hillsdale, N.J.: Erlbaum.

Pettigrew, Thomas F. 1967 "Social Evaluation Theory." In D. Levine, ed., *Nebraska Symposium on Motivation*. Lincoln: University of Nebraska Press.

Robinson-Whelen, Susan, and Janice Kiecolt-Glaser 1997 "The Importance of Social versus Temporal Appraisals among Older Adults." *Journal of Applied Social Psychology* 27:959–966.

Rothgerber, Hank, and Stephen Worchel 1997 "The View from Below: Intergroup Relations from the Perspective of the Disadvantaged Group." *Journal of Personality and Social Psychology* 73:1191–1205.

Schachter, Stanley 1959 *The Psychology of Affiliation*. Stanford, Calif.: Stanford University Press.

——, and Jerome E. Singer 1962 "Cognitive, Social, and Physiological Determinants of Emotional State." *Psychological Review* 69:379–399.

Spears, Russell, Bertjan Dooseje, and Naomi Ellemers 1997 "Self-Stereotyping in the Face of Threats to Group Status and Distinctiveness: The Role of Group Identification." *Personality and Social Psychology Bulletin* 23:538–553.

Suls, Jerry M. 1977 "Social Comparison Theory and Research: An Overview from 1954." In J. Suls and R. L. Miller, eds., *Social Comparison Processes: Theoretical and Empirical Perspectives*. Washington, D.C.: Hemisphere.

—— 1986. "Notes on the Occasion of Social Comparison Theory's Thirtieth Birthday." *Personality and Social Psychology Bulletin* 12:289–296.

——, and Richard L. Miller, eds. 1977 *Social Comparison Processes: Theoretical and Empirical Perspectives*. Washington, D.C.: Hemisphere.

——, and Thomas Ashby Wills 1991 *Social Comparison: Contemporary Theory and Research*. Hillsdale, N.J.: Erlbaum.

Tajfel, Henri, and John C. Turner 1979 "An Integrative Theory of Intergroup Conflict." In W. G. Austin and S. Worchel, eds., *The Social Psychology of Intergroup Relations*. Monterey, Calif.: Brooks/Cole.

Taylor, Shelley E., and Marci Lobel 1989 "Social Comparison Activity under Threat: Downward Evaluation and Upward Contacts." *Psychological Review* 96:569–575.

Thorton, D., and A. John Arrowood 1966 "Self-Evaluation, Self-Enhancement, and the Locus of Social Comparison." *Journal of Experimental Social Psychology*. 1(suppl.):40–48.

Van den Bos, Kees, Henk A. Wilke, Allan E. Lind, and Riel Vermunt 1998 "Evaluating Outcomes by Means of the Fair Process Effect: Evidence for Different Processes in Fairness and Satisfaction Judgments." *Journal of Personality and Social Psychology* 74:1493–1503.

VanYperen, Nico W., and Bram P. Buunk 1994 "Social Comparison and Social Exchange in Marital Relationships." In Melvin J. Lerner and Gerold Mikula, eds., *Entitlement and the Affectional Bond: Justice in Close Relationships*. New York: Plenum.

Wayment, Heidi A., and Shelley E. Taylor 1995 "Self-Evaluation Processes: Motives, Information Use, and Self-esteem." *Journal of Personality* 63:729–757.

Wheeler, L., R. Koestner, and R.E. Driver 1982 "Related Attributes in the Choice of Comparison Other: It's There, but It Isn't All There Is." *Journal of Experimental Social Psychology* 18:489–500.

Wood, Joanne 1989 "Theory and Research Concerning Social Comparisons of Personal Attributes." *Psychological Bulletin* 106:231–248.

—— 1996. "What Is Social Comparison and How Should We Study It?" *Personality and Social Psychology Bulletin* 22:520–537.

——, Maria Giordano-Beech, and Kathryn L. Taylor 1994 "Strategies of Social Comparison among People with Low Self-Esteem: Self-Protection and Self-Enhancement. *Journal of Personality and Social Psychology* 67:713–731.

Young, James W., and Lucy Rau Ferguson 1979 "Developmental Changes through Adolescence in the Spontaneous Nomination of Reference Groups as a Function of Decision Content." *Journal of Youth and Adolescence* 8:239–252.

KAREN A. HEGTVEDT

SOCIAL CONTROL

NOTE: *Although the following article has not been revised for this edition of the Encyclopedia, the substantive coverage is currently appropriate. The editors have provided a list of recent works at the end of the article to facilitate research and exploration of the topic.*

The study of social control has been an integral part of sociology since its inception. Originally, the concept was defined as any structure, process, relationship, or act that contributes to the social order. Indeed, to some extent, the study of social order and social control were indistinguishable. This conceptual problem was particularly evident in the early Chicago perspective in which the concepts *social disorganization, social control,* and *deviance* were not distinguished. Deviance was thought to be the consequence of lack of social control and was often used to measure the presence of social control. Within the structural functionalism of the late 1940s and 1960s, the study of social control was allocated to the sidelines. It dealt with residual problems of deviance in a social system assumed to be generally integrated and well functioning. By the early 1960s society was, again, assumed to be considerably less orderly and integrated and, again, the concept of social control rose to the forefront. Studies examined both the causes and the consequences of social control. Thus, by the mid-1960s the intellectual ground had been laid for renewed scholarly interest in the study of social control. This chapter reviews the study of social control from that time through the 1970s and 1980s.

A consensus is now emerging that distinguishes social control from the social order it is meant to explain and that distinguishes among social-control processes. One basic distinction is among processes of internal control and external control. The former refers to a process whereby people adhere to social norms because they believe in them, feeling good, self-righteous, and proud when they do and feeling bad, self-critical, and guilty when they do not. This process has recently been termed *socialization*. External control refers to a social process whereby people conform to norms or rules because they are rewarded with status, prestige, money, and freedom when they do and are punished with the loss of them when they do not. This process has sometimes been termed *coercive, external,* or just *social* control.

Reflecting contemporary usage, this chapter emphasizes social control as external or coercive control. Research is organized, first, and foremost by whether social control is studied as an independent or dependent variable and, second, by whether it is studied at the micro level (the study of individuals) or the macro level (the study of cities, states, regions, and countries).

SOCIAL CONTROL AS AN INDEPENDENT VARIABLE

Social-control theories assume that norm violations can frequently be so pleasurable and profitable that many, if not most, people are motivated to violate them. Thus, it is not necessary to study deviant motives; rather it is necessary to study what constrains or controls most people from acting on their deviance motives most of the time. Studies of social control as an independent variable focus on the relative effectiveness of social relationships and arrangements in constraining behavior to social norms and laws. Three general areas have developed. One examines the effectiveness of social ties (bonds, relationships, attachments) to conventional institutions in constraining people from acting on deviant motives. The second examines the effectiveness of macro structures and processes in providing the foundation for these ties. The third examines the effectiveness of the criminal justice system in constraining people from violating the law.

Drawing on a long tradition of work, Hirschi (1969) published an influential formulation of micro social-control theory. He states that the relationship between people and conventional society consists of four bonds: belief, attachment, commitment, and involvement. *Belief* refers to the extent to which conventional norms are internalized (another term for internal control). *Commitment* refers to the extent to which people's social rewards are tied to conformity; the more people have to lose upon being socially identified as norm violators, the lower their likelihood of violating the social norms. *Attachment* refers to people's sensitivity to the opinions of others; the more people are concerned with the respect and status afforded them by others, the more they are subject to social control. *Involvement* refers to the amount of time people spend on conventional activities; the more

people are involved in conventional activities, the less time they have left for deviant activities.

This theory has inspired considerable research on juvenile delinquency. Studies from the 1960s to the 1980s (e.g., Kornhauser 1978; and Matsueda 1982) show that, as attachment to parents and school increase, delinquency decreases. These studies, however, do not show the casual order underlying the relationship between social attachment and delinquency. The theory assumes that low attachment leads to high delinquency; yet high delinquency could very well lead to low attachment. Trying to unravel these causal processes, Liska and Reed (1985) show that low parent attachment leads to high delinquency and that high delinquency leads to low school attachment.

From the 1920s onward, sociologists at the University of Chicago have been interested in the ecological distribution of deviance. Their studies of delinquency, mental illness, and suicide, for example, show that deviance tends to center in cities, particularly in the area where residential and business activity intermesh. They argued that the ecological conditions that disrupt traditional social-control processes are accentuated in these areas, and, when social-control processes weaken, deviance occurs. Industrialization creates a need for the concentration of labor, thereby increasing population size and density through migration and immigration. Both industrialization and urbanization lead to value and norm conflicts, social mobility, cultural change, and weak primary ties. These social conditions, in turn, disrupt internal and external processes of social control. The internal process is weakened because people are unlikely to accept normative standards as right and proper when they experience value and norm conflicts and social change. The external process is weakened because people are unlikely to constrain their behavior to conventional norms when social support for unconventional behavior is readily visible and primary ties to family and conventional friends are weak. In small towns, for example, people may conform even though they may not accept the moral standard because their deviance is easily visible to family and conventional friends.

Perhaps the major problem with this line of research was the failure to measure the disruptive processes directly and the tendency to infer them from either remote causes such as industrialization and urbanization or more immediate causes such as the social, racial, and class composition of areas. Unable to solve this problem, the theory withered from the 1950s through the 1970s.

During the 1980s a group of young sociologists reexamined the theory to understand the renewed disorder of cities. Directly addressing the problem of measuring the processes that disrupt social control, Sampson and Groves (1989) show how community structural characteristics (such as racial, class, and ethnic composition; residential mobility; and divorce rate) affect crime by weakening ties to conventional institutions. Contrary to the early Chicagoans, Bursik (1986) shows that the ecological distribution of crime is no longer stable over time, that crime rates actually influence community characteristics, and that changes in these structures influence social deviance.

A third body of research examines the effectiveness of the criminal justice system in controlling crime. The underlying theory (deterrence) ignores inner controls and emphasizes punishment as the means of social control, particularly state-administered punishment. It assumes that people are rational and that crime is the result of calculating the costs and benefits of law violations; therefore, it assumes that, the higher the costs of crime, the lower the level of crime. As state-administered punishment is a significant cost of crime, it follows that the higher the level of such punishment, the lower the level of crime.

Two types of deterrence processes have been studied: general and specific. *General* refers to a process by which the punishment of some law violators provides information about the costs of crime to those unpunished (the general public), thereby reducing their law violations. *Specific* refers to a process by which punishment reduces the future law violations of those punished. Research focuses on three dimensions of punishment: severity, certainty, and celerity. *Severity* refers to the harshness of punishment, such as the length of incarceration; *certainty* refers to the probability of punishment, such as the likelihood of being arrested; and *celerity* refers to the swiftness of punishment. In sum, deterrence theory predicts that crime is lowest when punishment is severe, certain, and swift.

The political climate of the 1980s stimulated considerable interest in this theory, leading to hundreds of studies (Cook 1980). Yet, after all this research, it is still difficult to find any firm evidence for either specific or general deterrence. Regarding general deterrence, which has generated the bulk of the research, there is little consistent evidence of a severity effect. There is somewhat more evidence for a certainty effect, although its strength and duration remain unclear. For example, some studies suggest that, as certainty of punishment increases, crime rates decrease but that the decrease does not occur until certainty reaches about 30 percent, which is infrequently reached (Tittle and Rowe 1974). Some studies suggest that the certainty effect only occurs for crimes about which people have the opportunity to think and calculate, like property crimes, but not for violent crimes. And some studies of drunken driving suggest that the certainty effect occurs only if high certainty is well publicized, and even this effect is short lived (Ross 1984).

In sum, assuming that people are generally motivated to deviate, researchers have tried to understand how people are constrained from acting on their motives. Contemporary studies of social control focus on three areas: the interpersonal relationships that constrain people from acting on their motives, the macro structures and processes that provide the social foundation for these relationships, and the criminal justice system as a source of legal constraints.

SOCIAL CONTROL AS A DEPENDENT VARIABLE

During the 1960s sociologists began to question the assumption of normative consensus and stability and, thus, by implication the viability of the theories built on them. Without clear and stable references points from which to judge behavior, deviance is difficult to define. Many sociologists came to define it in terms of visible social efforts to control it. Deviance is thus defined as that behavior that society controls, and deviants are defined as those people whom society controls. Research shifts from studying social control as a cause of deviance to studying the causes of social control.

Micro-level studies examine the social processes by which acts and people are defined, labeled, and treated as deviants by family, friends, the public, and formal agencies of social control such as the criminal justice and mental health systems. Drawing on labeling and conflict theories, many sociologists argue that social control is directed against those who are least able to resist (the disadvantaged and the unfortunate) and that social-control agencies are used by the powerful to control the behavior of others.

During the 1960s, research reported that resources and power (as indicated by class, ethnicity, and race) significantly affect defining, treating, and controlling people as criminals (Black and Reiss 1970), such as arresting, prosecuting, and sentencing them. Unfortunately, these studies do not adjust for the effects of legal considerations, such as seriousness and frequency of offense, which are related to social resources. Without examining the effects of both legal and social resource variables in the same analysis it is difficult to isolate the effects of one from those of the other.

During the 1970s studies addressed this issue. The results are inconsistent, some studies showing race and class effects and some showing no such effects (Cohen and Kleugel 1978).

During the 1980s research tried to resolve these inconsistencies. One group of researchers tried to show that the effect of resources depends on the stage of the criminal justice process (e.g., arrest, prosecution) and the characteristics of the local community. Some stages may be more sensitive to social status and social power than are others, and some communities may be more sensitive to status and power than are others. Dannefer and Schutt (1982) report more racial discrimination at the arrest stage than at other stages, arguing that police have more discretion than do other decision makers, and they report more racial discrimination when the percentage of nonwhites is high, arguing that a high percentage of nonwhites is threatening to authorities.

Macro studies of social control examine the level and the form of social control across such units as cities, states, regions, and countries. They study why one form of control (physical pain) occurs at one time and place and another form (incarceration) occurs at another time and place.

Since the 1970s, conflict theory has provided the major stimulus for this research. It assumes that social control is more likely when the ruling class or the authorities perceive their interests to be threatened. Threat is thought to be associated with the presence of disruptive acts (crime, civil disorders, social movements) and problematic people (the unemployed, minorities, the urban lower class). The theory assumes that, as disruptive acts and problematic people increase, authorities expand the capacity for social-control bureaucracies and pressure existing bureaucracies to expand the level of control.

Research has focused on the expansion and contraction of three such bureaucracies: the criminal justice system, the mental health system, and the welfare system. It generally suggests that the expansion of the criminal justice system is not necessarily a response to crime, that the expansion of the mental health system is not necessarily a response to mental health, and that the expansion of the welfare system is not necessarily a response to economic need. Rather the expansion and contraction of all three are responses by authorities to the acts and people deemed threatening to their interests.

Studies of the criminal justice system have examined the expansion of the police force in the late 1960s and 1970s, as an indicator of the potential for social control, and the expansion of the prison population in the 1980s, as an indicator of the actual level of control. Liska, Lawrence, and Benson (1981) report that, while the size of the police force is sensitive to the crime rate, it may be even more sensitive to the level of civil disorders, the relative size and segregation of the minority population, and the level of economic inequality. Studies of the prison population and admission rates show that, while these rates, too, are sensitive to the crime rate, they are equally sensitive to the size of problematic or threatening populations such as the unemployed. Studies in England, Canada, and the United States show a substantial relationship between the prison admission rate and the unemployment rate, adjusting for the crime rate (Berk et al. 1981; Inverarity and McCarthy 1988).

Some historical studies (Foucault 1965) assert that mental asylums emerged in the seventeenth century as another social mechanism for controlling the poor urban masses. During the twentieth century the population of mental asylums in the United States continually increased, reaching about

550,000 by the mid-1950s, while the prison population, in comparison, was less than 200,000 at the time. The mental health system seemed to be taking over the role of the criminal justice system in controlling problematic populations. However, since that time the trends for both bureaucracies have reversed. The mental asylum population has decreased from 500,000 to 150,000 and the prison population has increased from 200,000 to 300,000. These trend reversals have stimulated research to examine the extent to which the two bureaucracies are functional alternatives for controlling threatening or problematic populations and acts. Some research (Steadman 1979) studies how various threatening populations that in the past might have been admitted directly into asylums are now first processed in the criminal justice system. Then some of them remain in local jails and others, through various mechanisms such as pleas of *Incompetent to Stand Trial* and *Not Guilty by Reason of Insanity* are channeled into asylums.

Welfare is frequently conceptualized as a form of social control. Piven and Cloward (1971) have stimulated considerable controversy by arguing that the welfare expansion in the United States during the mid- and late 1960s was a response to the urban riots of that period, an attempt to control an economically deprived and threatening population. Various studies provide some support for this thesis. Schram and Turbett (1983) report that the riots affected welfare in two stages. Riots during the mid-1960s prodded the federal government to liberalize welfare policies generally; these policies were then more likely to be implemented in the late 1960s by those states experiencing the most rioting.

In sum, the 1970s and 1980s evidenced a research effort to explain the expansion and contraction of bureaucracies of social control, not so much as responses to crime, mental illness, or economic need, but as responses by authorities to control acts and populations deemed threatening to their interests.

The study of social control has come a long way since its inception at the birth of sociology, at which time it was vaguely defined and not distinguishable from the concept *social order*. Contemporary usage distinguishes the sources of social order from the order itself. The concept *socialization* has come to refer to internal sources of control, and the concept *social control* has come to refer to external sources of control, the processes whereby people conform to social norms because they are rewarded when they do and punished when they do not. Studying social control as an independent variable, a body of research examines the relative effects of interpersonal relations, social institutions, and formal agencies in constraining social behavior. Studying social control as a dependent variable, another body of research examines how social resources influence social control and how the aggregate amount and form of control varies over time and place.

(SEE ALSO: *Crime Theories of; Criminal Sanctions; Criminology; Deviance Theories; Juvenile Delinquency, Theories of: Law and Society; Sociology of Law*)

REFERENCES

Ben-Yehuda, Nachman 1997 "Political Assassination Events as a Cross-Cultural Form of Alternative Justice." *International Journal of Comparative Sociology* 38:1–2.

Berk, Richard A., David Rauma, Sheldon L. Messinger, and Thomas F. Cooley 1981 "A Test of the Stability of the Punishment Hypothesis: The Case of California, 1851–1970." *American Sociological Review* 46:805–829.

Black, Donald J., and Albert J. Reiss 1970 "Police Control of Juveniles." *American Sociological Review* 35:63–77.

Blomberg, Thomas G. and Stanley Cohen (eds.) 1994 *Punishment and Social Control: Essays in Honor of Sheldon Messinger*. New York: Aldine de Gruyter.

Bridges, George S. and Martha A. Myers (eds.) 1994 *Inequality, Crime and Social Control*. Boulder, Colo.: Westview Press.

Bursik, Robert Jr., 1986 "Ecological Stability and the Dynamics of Delinquency." In Albert J. Reiss and Michael Tonry, eds., *Communities and Crime*, pp. 35–66. Chicago: University of Chicago Press.

Cohen, Lawrence E., and James R. Kluegel 1978 "Determinants of Juvenile Court Dispositions." *American Sociological Review* 43:162–177.

Cook, Philip J. 1980 "Research in Criminal Deterrence: Laying the Groundwork for the Second Decade." In Norval Morris and Michael Tonry, eds., *Crime and Justice: An Annual Review of Research*, pp. 211–268. Chicago: University of Chicago Press.

Dannefer, Dale, and Russell K. Schutt 1982 "Race and Juvenile Justice Processing in Court and Police Agencies." *American Journal of Sociology* 87:1113–1132.

Foucault, M. 1965 *Madness and Civilization*. New York: Vintage.

Guthrie, Douglas J. 1994 "From Cultures of Violence to Social Control: An Analysis of Violent Crime in U.S. Counties with Implications for Social Policy." *Berkeley Journal of Sociology* 39:67–99.

Hirschi, Travis 1969 *Causes of Delinquency*. Berkeley: University of California Press.

Horwitz, Allan V. 1990 *The Logic of Social Control*. New Brunswick N.J.: Rutgers University Press.

Inverarity, James, and Daniel McCarthy 1988 "Punishment and Social Structure Revisited: Unemployment and Imprisonment in the United States, 1948–1984." *Sociological Quarterly* 29:263–279.

Johnson, W. Wesley 1996 "Transcarceration and Social Control Policy: The 1980s and Beyond." *Crime and Delinquency* 42:114–126.

Katovich, Michael A. 1996 "Cooperative Bases of Control: Toward an Interactionist Conceptualization." *Social Science Journal* 33:257–271.

Kornhauser, Ruth 1978 *Social Sources of Delinquency*. Chicago: University of Chicago Press.

Lacombe, Dany 1996 "Reforming Foucault: A Critique of the Social Control Thesis." *British Journal of Sociology* 47:332–352.

Liska, Allen E., Joseph J. Lawrence, and Michael Benson 1981 "Perspectives on the Legal Order: The Capacity for Social Control." *American Journal of Sociology* 87:412–426.

Liska, Allen E., and Mark Reed 1985 "Ties to Conventional Institutions and Delinquency: Estimating Reciprocal Effects." *American Sociological Review* 50:547–560.

—— 1997 "Modeling the Relationships between Macro Forms of Social Control." *Annual Review of Sociology* 23:39–61.

Lyon, David and Elia Zureik (eds.) 1996 *Computers, Surveillance and Privacy*. Minneapolis: University of Minnesota.

Matsueda, Ross L. 1982 "Testing Control Theory and Differential Association: A Causal Modeling Approach." *American Sociological Review* 47:489–504.

McConville, Michael and Chester L. Mirsky 1990 "Understanding Defense of the Poor in State Courts: The Sociolegal Context of Nonadversarial Advocacy." *Studies in Law, Politics, and Society* 10:217–242.

Ross, H. Lawrence 1984 "Social Control through Deterrence: Drinking and Driving Laws." In Ralph H. Turner and James F. Short, Jr., eds., *Annual Review of Sociology*, Palo Alto, Calif.: Annual Reviews.

Piven, Frances Fox, and Richard A. Cloward 1971 *Regulating the Poor: The Functions of Public Welfare*. New York: Vintage.

Sampson, Robert J., and W. B. Groves 1989 "Community Structure and Crime: Testing Social Disorganization Theory." *American Journal of Sociology* 94:774–802.

Schram, Stanford F., and J. Patrick Turbett 1983 "Civil Disorder and the Welfare Expansion: A Two-Step Process." *American Sociological Review* 48:408–414.

Staples, William G. 1997 *The Culture of Surveillance: Discipline and Social Control in the United States*. New York: St. Martin's Press.

Steadman, Hank J. 1979 *Beating a Rap*. Chicago: University of Chicago Press.

Stenson, Kevin and David Cowell 1991 *The Politics of Crime Control*. Newbury Park, Calif.: Sage Publications.

Tittle, Charles R., and Allan R. Rowe 1974 "Certainty of Arrest and Crime Rates: A Further Test of the Deterrence Hypothesis." *Social Forces* 52:455–562.

ALLEN E. LISKA

SOCIAL DYNAMICS

The term "social dynamics" is used in a wide variety of contexts that vary in level from the societal to the individual and in approach from qualitative (verbal) to quantitative (mathematical). For example, on the societal level, one can point to Sorokin's ([1937–1941] 1957) qualitative approach in *Social and Cultural Dynamics*. At the other extreme, though also at the global level, there are works such as Forrester's (1971) mathematical, computer-oriented approach in *World Dynamics* and the statistical, empirical approaches found in Ramirez et al.'s (1997) study of the adoption of women's suffrage throughout the world and Frank et al.'s (1997) research on the spread and development of a world environmental regime. On the individual level, examples of qualitative approaches include Hareven's (1982) *Family Time and Industrial Time* and the relevant chapters in Bertaux and Thompson's *Pathways to Social Class* (1997). Also on the individual level, there are mathematical approaches such as White's *Chains of Opportunity* (1970) and statistical, empirical approaches such as Zhou et al.'s (1996, 1997) studies of stratification dynamics in China. Studies that combine qualitative and quantitative approaches are rare. A classic example is Elder's *Children of the Great*

Depression (1974). Because of the great diversity in substance and approach, one cannot identify a single line of cumulative research on social dynamics. Instead, there are distinct, loosely related developments that arise in several contexts.

This article has five main sections. The first describes the three main sociological contexts for studies of social dynamics and summarizes their contributions to cumulative sociological research. Since the term "social dynamics" invariably implies a focus on change over time in a social entity, it is closely related to the term "social change." Some of the key differences between the two terms are discussed in the second section. The third section summarizes reasons for studies of social dynamics in general and the formulation of dynamic models in particular. The fourth section explains the fundamental differences between dynamic models and other types of models. The fifth section reviews the main variations in the types of dynamic models that sociologists have used.

MAIN CONTEXTS

In one context, social scientists refer to the *dynamics of a phenomenon*, meaning that they focus on how it changes over time. In this traditional usage, the emphasis is primarily on a substantive social phenomenon, and research progress depends on acquiring a deeper theoretical understanding and expanding empirical knowledge about that phenomenon. Topics vary, for example, from "group dynamics" (social interactions among the members of a small group over time) to the "dynamics of development" (change from a traditional rural society to a modern urban industrial society and then to a postindustrial society that belongs to a global system). It is hard to identify substantive commonalities across disparate topic areas except ones of the most abstract sort, for example, that social change is universal but varies in speed. Despite the limited number of substantive generalizations about social dynamics, the study of social dynamics is theoretically and methodologically helpful for reasons that are summarized in the third section.

In a second context that is more typical in recent work, researchers refer to a *dynamic model of a phenomenon*, meaning that their goal is to formulate, test, or explore the consequences of a set of mathematical assumptions or a computer algorithm that is intended to mimic the behavior of the phenomenon of interest. For example, researchers may use a model of population growth and decline in a society; a model of foundings, reorganizations, divestments, mergers, and failures in businesses or other organizations; or a model of the diffusion of an innovation through a population (e.g., the adoption of a new social policy by governments or a new contraceptive by women). Despite the substantive diversity, the formal properties of dynamic models of different phenomena are often similar. This similarity has fostered cumulative progress in studies of social dynamics because a model developed for one topic may be transferable to another topic after only minor modifications of its formal properties. For example, the notion that growth rates are "density-dependent" (depend on population size) arose first in dynamic models of population growth, with the main rationale being that a growing population increases competition among members of the system and depletes environmental resources, eventually leading to a lower rate of population growth. Later this notion was applied to explorations of dynamic models of the formation and survival of unions, businesses, and other kinds of organizations and how those processes depend on the structure of competition (Hannan and Carroll 1992; Carroll and Hannan 2000).

In a third context, authors use a *dynamic analysis* of empirical data on a phenomenon, meaning some form of temporal (longitudinal) analysis of data pertaining to different points in time. Since dynamic analyses are based on dynamic models, work done in the second and third contexts has close parallels. Typically, however, a focus on dynamic models implies a greater emphasis on the model itself, whereas a focus on dynamic analyses indicates a greater stress on the problems of estimating and testing the model as well as the resulting substantive empirical findings. Advance made in methods for the dynamic analysis of one social phenomenon often can be used in dynamic analyses of other phenomena. This also has facilitated cumulative progress in research on social dynamics. For example, Tuma et al.'s (1979) proposal for *dynamic analysis of event histories*, which originally was applied to data on marriage formation and dissolution, subsequently has been applied to dynamic analysis of data on occupational and geographic mobility, organizational mergers and failures, changes in political regimes, the adoption of governmental policies, and many other social phenomena.

SOCIAL DYNAMICS VERSUS SOCIAL CHANGE

Although the terms "social dynamics" and "social change" both indicate a focus on change over time, they are used in different circumstances. Social dynamics has a more precise meaning.

First, social dynamics usually presumes change within a social *system*. That system may consist of similar entities (e.g., members of a family, families in a neighborhood, nations in the world) or disparate entities (e.g., different types of actors in a political or economic system) or various attributes of a single social entity (e.g., an individual's education, occupational prestige, and income or a business firm's age, size, and structure). The system usually is regarded as bounded, allowing the rest of the world to be ignored for purposes of explanation.

Whether the system consists of actors or variables, the term "system" presumes interdependence and typically involves feedback. Thus, action by one entity in the system leads to counteraction by another entity. For example, managers of a firm may counter a strike by workers by acquiescing to the workers' demands, outwaiting them, or hiring nonunion laborers. Alternatively, change in one variable in the system leads to an opposing or reinforcing change in one or more other variables. For example, an increase in educational level is followed by an increase in prestige and then an increase in income. Changes resulting from interdependent forces and feedback effects within the system are called *endogenous* changes.

There also may be *exogenous* changes, that is, unexplained (perhaps random) changes that influence change within the system under study but whose causes originate outside that system. For example, in analyses of interaction between a husband and wife, changes in the economy and society in which the couple lives usually are treated as exogenous changes that affect the couple's behavior, but the societal-level changes themselves are not explained.

Because of interdependent forces and feedback effects as well as possible exogenous changes,

social dynamics typically implies a concern with *complex changes*. Simple linear changes or straightforward extrapolations of previous trends are rarely of primary interest.

Second, social dynamics connotes social changes that have a *regular pattern*. That pattern may be one of growth (e.g., economic expansion, growth of a population), decline (e.g., rural depopulation, the extinction of a cultural trait), cyclical change (e.g., boom and bust in the business cycle), a distinctive but nonetheless recurring transition (e.g., ethnic succession in neighborhoods, societal modernization, the demographic transition from high mortality and fertility to low mortality and fertility), or simply a drift in a particular direction (e.g., the slow but accelerating spread of a social belief or practice through a population).

Third, social dynamics usually implies a degree of *predictability*: Social change not only can be comprehended in terms of post hoc reasons but also can be explicitly modeled. The model, whether it consists of verbal statements or mathematical equations or computer instructions, involves a set of assumptions or propositions that permit fundamental patterns of change to be deduced. In contrast, although a unique historical event may foster social change, its uniqueness makes successful prediction impossible. One challenge in studies of social dynamics is therefore to convert phenomena that are unique on one level to ones that are representative and therefore predictable on another level. Thus, what some regard as a unique historical event, others see as an example of a regular pattern of change. For example, to a historian, the Russian Revolution of 1917 is a unique event, whereas a sociologist may regard it as exemplifying a response to changes in underlying social conditions. Thus, while recognizing many distinctive factors, Skocpol (1979) argues that similar patterns of causes underlie the dramatic political and social transformations that historians call the French, Russian, and Chinese revolutions.

Fourth, the term "social dynamics" is used more commonly than is the term "social change" when regularity in patterns of change is associated with some kind of *equilibrium* (steady state or homeostasis), that is, when feedback effects are such that small deviations from equilibrium lead to compensating effects that cause equilibrium to be restored. For example, in the United States, the distribution of family income (the share of total income received by different families) was remarkably stable throughout the twentieth century despite tremendous growth in population and economic output and social upheavals such as the civil rights and women's liberation movements. This stability suggests that the process governing the allocation of family income was nearly in equilibrium. The term "social change," especially change seen as part of a unique historical process, usually is associated with change from one distinctive situation to another, very different situation. It implies the antithesis of social equilibrium. The way in which the social status of women and minorities has changed during the twentieth century exemplifies social disequilibrium.

Studies of social dynamics do not necessarily assume the existence of an equilibrium. This point is made clear by studies of the dynamics of economic growth, which often envision a process of never-ending expansion and improvement. Similarly, some dynamic processes imply not a steady-state condition but continual oscillation between conditions. A classic sociological example is Pareto's (1935) analysis of the circulation of elites.

Fifth, the term "social dynamics" is almost always used in situations in which there is an interest in the *process* of change: the step-by-step sequence of causes and effects and the way in which intermediary changes unfold. It is rarely used when only a simple before–after comparison of the condition of the system is the object of interest. Instead, when authors use the term "social dynamics," there is usually a sense that the details and sequencing of changes are important because changes are contingent: If the sequence had been interrupted or altered at an intermediary point, the final outcome might have been different. For example, models of social protest often recognize that the state's response to protests may range from peaceful conciliation to violent suppression. The nature of the state's response is an important contingency because it affects the likelihood, timing, and character of future protests.

Sometimes the sequence of changes occurs on the level of the system as a whole rather than on the level of individual members. For example, in a simple model of population growth, individual-level changes are very elementary: birth followed by death, with the timing of the two being the only

question. On the population level, the addition and loss of individuals over time represent a sequence of changes even though on the individual level there may be few, if any intermediary changes and thus little sense of a sequence of causes and effects.

REASONS FOR STUDYING SOCIAL DYNAMICS

What motivates sociological interest in social dynamics in general and dynamic models in particular? The most potent reason is the long-standing interest of sociologists in social change, coupled with an increasing recognition that a tremendous amount of scientific leverage can be gained from identifying regularities in patterns of change and then formulating sociological theories that explain them, that is, from studying social dynamics and not just unique historical events. Leverage comes not only from the increased richness of theories of social dynamics but also from greater methodological power in discriminating among competing explanations, as is indicated in more detail below.

As observers of the great social transformations of the nineteenth century, the founders of modern sociology (e.g., Marx, Spencer, and Weber) were keenly interested in social change. However, in the middle of the twentieth century, when structural functionalism and Parsonian thought were dominant, social change was regarded as a minor subfield of sociology. Interest in social change was renewed after a reawakened recognition of social conflict and the concomitant criticism of the assumption of social equilibrium in structural functional theories.

An accelerating pace of global change has added to this interest (Sassen 1988; Boli and Thomas 1997). Rapid growth of the world's population; high levels of mobility of people, goods, and capital between and within nations; the transformation of agricultural societies to industrial and postindustrial societies; social upheavals ranging from strikes, to social protests, to revolutions, to wars; the creation of new organizational forms (e.g., holding companies, multinational corporations, international organizations); fundamental transformations of political regimes, including the failure of communist governments; steady increases in the number and volume of new technological innovations; depletion of natural resources; extinction of plant and animal species; and changes in climate induced by human activities are only a few of the world-level changes that make it virtually impossible for sociologists who study large-scale social systems not to be interested in social change.

Although some scholars view many of these changes as historically unique, the concrete social and economic problems that result from them motivate attempts to find regular patterns and predict future changes, in short, to develop dynamic models of societal and global changes. Consider the massive changes in eastern European nations that began in the late 1980s. From the late 1940s to the late 1980s, those nations were governed by totalitarian polities and had command-type socialist economies. Now most of them appear to be headed in the direction of market-type capitalist economies and democratic polities. The intellectual challenge, as well as a major problem for policymakers, is to develop a theory of the transition from one to the other, that is, a theory of the dynamics of the social change that is expected to occur. The fact that no satisfactory theory existed when the transition began was apparent to the general public as well as to social scientists. It points to the practical as well as scholarly value of studying social dynamics.

Sociologists who study micro-level phenomena (individuals and families) also cannot ignore social change. The life course of individuals in modern societies has a typical sequence of activities associated with aging (e.g., birth, day care, school, work, marriage, child rearing, retirement, death) that commands considerable attention by sociologists. Historical changes in family patterns (e.g., increases in premarital cohabitation, delays in marriage, changes in husband–wife roles, increases in divorce, baby booms and baby busts, increasing institutionalization of the elderly) also put social change at the forefront of the attention of sociologists who study the family. These subjects are perhaps more easily viewed in terms of social dynamics than are ones pertaining to global and societal changes because similar patterns across individuals and families are more readily apparent.

Sociologists who study behavior in small groups were among the earliest to express an interest in social dynamics. This interest received a major boost from Bales's *Interaction Process Analysis* (1950).

Game theorists, who attempt to explain the moves and countermoves of actors in highly structured situations, also exemplify a concern with social dynamics in small groups, though they, much more than Bales and his intellectual descendants, concentrate on formal models and deemphasize hypothesis testing and empirical results (see Shubik 1982).

There are also metatheoretical and methodological reasons for studying social dynamics even when the primary intellectual concern is with statics, that is, with relationships among actors or variables at a single point in time.

First, studies of relationships at a single point in time implicitly assume a steady state or equilibrium. Otherwise relationships at a given time point must be transitory and in the process of changing, a situation that would degrade their potential contribution to enduring sociological knowledge. A steady state may or may not exist. If it does not exist, one needs to study social dynamics to understand relationships at a point in time. If a steady state does exist, much can be learned by studying social dynamics that cannot be learned easily by studying relationships at a single point in time. For one thing, two theories may imply the same relationship among variables at a given point in time but imply different time paths of change. In that case, a study of social dynamics can differentiate between them, whereas a study of the steady state cannot. For another thing, a theory of relationships at a point in time is invariably the special case of one or more theories of change over time, and the latter theories almost always have a richer set of implications than do the former. This means that in general there are more ways to test theories of social dynamics than to test theories of social statics.

THE NATURE OF DYNAMIC MODELS

As was noted earlier, developments in dynamic models (and derivative developments in methods of dynamic analysis) are the major commonality in sociological studies of social dynamics. To understand the main features of dynamic models, it is important to differentiate them from other types of models.

The most basic distinction is between *static* and *dynamic* models. Static models describe relationships among social actors in a system or among the attributes of a social entity at a given point in time. As was noted earlier, they implicitly assume a steady state or equilibrium, a phenomenon that is about as common in nature as a vacuum. In contrast, dynamic models describe the process or sequence of changes among actors in a social system or among the attributes of a social system.

Dynamic models also can be contrasted with *comparative static models*, which are especially common in economic analyses and analyses of social experiments. Although both deal with change over time, they differ in an important way. The process of change leading from conditions at the earlier time point to conditions at the later time point is fundamental to a dynamic model. In contrast, the change process is ignored in a comparative static model, which resembles a black box that relates conditions at one point in time to conditions at a later time.

To illustrate this distinction, consider alternative ways of explaining a son's occupational prestige. In a comparative static model, the son's prestige may be related to his father's socioeconomic status and his own education without any attention being paid to the mechanisms and processes that lead from those background conditions to the son's condition as an adult. In a dynamic model, the father's socioeconomic status and the son's education may be seen as giving access to certain entry-level jobs, which in turn provide opportunities for further career mobility, leading to jobs with varying levels of prestige. In a dynamic model, the timing and sequence of job shifts are of concern, not just the son's initial condition (i.e., his father's social status and his own education). In summary, dynamic models are used to explain not only why the later condition of a phenomenon differs from its earlier condition but also how a sequence of changes leads from one condition to the other.

TYPES OF DYNAMIC MODELS

Different types of dynamic models are distinguished on the basis of a variety of formal properties. One basic distinction seems to be whether the components of the system are social actors or the attributes of a social entity. In the former case, dynamic models of the behavior of social actors are developed: Actor A does X, in response actor B

does Y, then actor A does Z, and so on. Although much of game theory is not concerned with dynamic models, some of it formulates precisely these kinds of models. In the latter kind of dynamic model, values of variables describing the social entity are related to one another. Ecological theories of organizational survival utilize these models, for example, relating the degree of environmental variability and the degree of specialization of various types of social organizations in the environment to the survival of these types (Hannan and Freeman 1987). The distinction between systems of actors and systems of variables is not as important as it may seem at first because the behaviors of actors usually can be translated into variables.

A more basic and important distinction is whether time is discrete or continuous. Most empirical phenomena can change at any moment, and this leads one to expect that time should be treated as continuous in most dynamic models. In fact, time more often is treated as discrete for two main reasons. First, the empirical data used to test a dynamic model usually measure time at only a few discrete points. Some researchers then find it convenient to build a dynamic model of the data rather than model the underlying social process. Second, some researchers consider discrete-time models to be simpler and believe that little information is lost from approximating truly continuous-time processes with discrete-time models. If the discrete time points in the data are sufficiently numerous and close together, the approximation is almost always satisfactory. If they are not, important intermediary steps in the process are likely to be ignored, possibly resulting in misleading conclusions. Whether discrete-time models are simpler than continuous-time models is less clear. To some extent, it is a matter of a researcher's taste and training.

Another key distinction concerns whether the variables that describe the social system are discrete, metric, or a mixture of the two. Discrete variables have a finite set of values; for example, political regimes may be categorized into a small number of basic types. Metric variables have a continuum of values; for example, a person's income and occupational prestige usually are treated as continuous variables. In fact, in both instances, the number of values is finite but is so large that treating the values as continuous may be convenient and is often fairly realistic. Age is a continuous variable, but measurements of it are always discrete (e.g., to the nearest year, month, or day).

A distinction also may be made in the way in which variables in a system change over time. By their nature, discrete variables change only in jumps. For example, there may be a sudden change from a military political regime to a multiparty government. Metric variables often are regarded as changing gradually. For example, a firm's profits may be treated as shifting upward or downward by small increments. In fact, metric variables also may change in jumps. For example, income may fall from a high value to nearly zero when a family's main breadwinners lose their jobs.

Another important distinction is whether the change process is treated as deterministic or stochastic (having a random component). There is a broad consensus that stochastic models are almost always more realistic. Few social changes occur in a strictly determined fashion, and those which do change deterministically are rarely sociologically interesting. Nevertheless, deterministic models can be useful when the solution of realistic stochastic models presents severe technical problems. Those formidable problems tend to occur when there is a high degree of interdependence in the social system (e.g., in models of the diffusion of an innovation) and when both time and outcomes are treated as continuous.

Whether time is treated as discrete or continuous, models of changes in discrete variables are invariably stochastic because changes by jumps almost dictate reference to probabilities. By contrast, continuous-time models of changes in metric variables are typically deterministic.

Some progress has been made in developing empirically estimable stochastic models of heterogeneity in the spread of a social practice in the presence of interdependent influences in a social system (Strang and Tuma 1993). Davis and Greve (1997) provide an intriguing application of this modeling approach to the use of "poison pills" and "golden parachutes" among firms.

Formal dynamic models are of two main types. In one type, the model consists of a set of mathematical equations that relate some elements of the system to other elements. In the other type, the model consists of a set of computer instructions that relate inputs of various variables and/or actors at one time to outputs at a later time. The computer instructions in fact represent mathematical equations that are so complex that they cannot be solved in practice without the aid of a computer. Still, it is convenient to think of computer models as very complicated mathematical models.

A clear introduction to both discrete-time and continuous-time deterministic models of metric variables can be found in Baumol's *Economic Dynamics* (1951), which also introduces several economic theories of potential interest to sociologists, including theories of wages and profits in firms and economic growth. For a discussion of deterministic models of change in metric variables, see Doreian and Hummon (1976).

Two of the early classic discussions of stochastic models of change in discrete variables are Coleman's *Introduction to Mathematical Sociology* (1964) and Bartholomew's *Stochastic Models for Social Processes* (1973). Tuma and Hannan's *Social Dynamics: Models and Methods* (1984) discusses both deterministic and stochastic models of change in metric variables in continuous time as well as continuous-time stochastic models of change in discrete variables. This work also discusses metatheoretical and methodological reasons for studying social dynamics, applies dynamic models to a variety of different sociological problems, and provides an extensive bibliography pertaining to models and methods used in studying social dynamics. It also contains a comprehensive introduction to event history analysis.

CONCLUSION

Sociologists, whether studying whole societies or small groups, have had a long-standing and far-reaching interest in social change. Traditional approaches focused on specific substantive phenomena and, especially in macro-level studies, often stressed unique historical occurrences rather than common dimensions underlying patterns of change. Recent studies of social dynamics usually focus on what is regular and predictable about social change and the social mechanisms that generate a sequence of contingent changes. Often they embed ideas about change in dynamic models and test them in dynamic analyses of over-time data. This approach has been especially valuable in fostering cumulative research.

(SEE ALSO: *Cohort Perspectives; Diffusion Theories; Game Theory and Strategic Interaction; Life Course; Life Histories and Narrative; Longitudinal Research; Paradigms and Models; Social Change; Social Forecasting*)

REFERENCES

Bales, Robert F. 1950 *Interaction Process Analysis: A Method for the Study of Small Groups*. Cambridge, Mass.: Addison-Wesley.

Bartholomew, David J. 1973 *Stochastic Models for Social Processes*. New York: Wiley.

Baumol, William J. 1951 *Economic Dynamics: An Introduction*. New York: Macmillan.

Bertaux, Daniel, and Paul Thompson eds. 1997 *Pathways to Social Class: A Qualitative Approach to Social Mobility*. Oxford, UK: Clarendon Press.

Boli, John, and George M. Thomas 1997 "World Culture in the World Polity: A Century of International Non-Governmental Organization." *American Sociological Review* 62:171–190.

Carroll, Glen R., and Michael T. Hannan 2000 *The Demography of Corporations and Industries*. Princeton, N.J.: Princeton University Press.

Coleman, James S. 1964 *Introduction to Mathematical Sociology*. New York: Free Press.

Davis, Gerald F., and Henrich R. Greve 1997 "Corporate Elite Networks and Governance Changes in the 1980s." *American Journal of Sociology* 103:1–37.

Doreian, Patrick, and Norman P. Hummon 1976 *Modeling Social Processes*. Amsterdam: Elsevier.

Elder, Glen H. 1974 *Children of the Great Depression: Social Change in Life Experience*. Chicago: University of Chicago Press.

Forrester, Jay W. 1971 *World Dynamics*. Cambridge, Mass.: Wright-Allen.

Frank, David J., Ann Hironaka, John W. Meyer, Evan Schofer, and Nancy Brandon Tuma 1997 "The Structuring of a World Environmental Regime, 1870–1990." *International Organization* 51:623–651.

Hannan, Michael T., and Glenn R. Carroll 1992 *Dynamics of Organizational Populations*. New York: Oxford University Press.

——, and John Freeman 1989 *Organizational Ecology*. Cambridge, Mass.: Harvard University Press.

Hareven, Tamara 1982 *Family Time and Industrial Time: The Relationship between the Family and Work in a New England Industrial Community*. Cambridge, UK: Cambridge University Press.

Pareto, Vilfredo 1935 *The Mind and Society*, vol. III, Arthur Livingston, ed.; Andrew Bongiorno and Arthur Livingston, trans. New York: Harcourt, Brace.

Ramirez, Francisco O., Yasemin Soysal, and Suzanne Shanahan 1997 "The Changing Logic of Political Citizenship: Cross-National Acquisition of Women's Suffrage Rights, 1890 to 1990." *American Sociological Review* 62(5):735–745.

Sassen, Saskia 1988 *The Mobility of Labor and Capital: A Study in International Investment and Labor Flow*. Cambridge, UK: Cambridge University Press.

Shubik, Martin 1982 *Game Theory in the Social Sciences: Concepts and Solutions*. Cambridge, Mass.: MIT Press.

Skocpol, Theda 1979 *States and Social Revolutions in France, Russia, and China*. Cambridge, UK: Cambridge University Press.

Sorokin, Pitirim A. (1937–1941) 1957 *Social and Cultural Dynamics: A Study of Change in Major Systems of Art, Truth, Ethics, Law and Social Relationships*, revised and abridged version. Boston: Porter Sargent.

Strang, David G., and Nancy Brandon Tuma 1993 Spatial and Temporal Heterogeneity in Diffusion." *American Journal of Sociology* 99:614–639.

Tuma, Nancy Brandon, and Michael T. Hannan 1984 *Social Dynamics: Models and Methods*. Orlando, Fla.: Academic Press.

——, ——, and Lyle P. Groeneveld 1979 "Dynamic Analysis of Event Histories." *American Journal of Sociology* 84:820–854.

White, Harrison C. 1970 *Chains of Opportunity: Systems Models of Mobility in Organizations*. Cambridge, Mass.: Harvard University Press.

Zhou, Xueguang, Nancy Brandon Tuma, and Phyllis Moen 1996 "Stratification Dynamics under State Socialism: The Case of Urban China, 1949–1993." *Social Forces* 74:759–796.

—— 1997 "Institutional Change and Job Shift Patterns in Urban China, 1949–1994." *American Sociological Review* 62 339–365.

NANCY BRANDON TUMA

SOCIAL EXCHANGE THEORY

Social exchange theory is a major theoretical perspective in sociology. Within this framework, social behavior is viewed primarily in terms of the pursuit of rewards and the avoidance of punishment and other forms of cost. Individuals engage in interaction to meet their needs. The basic unit of analysis is the relationship between actors. Thus, exchange theorists view social relations and the social structures generated by the ties that bind people in different forms of association as the central object of sociological inquiry. Major topics of study within this tradition of research include the nature and effects of the interconnections among actors and the distribution of power within exchange structures. Power and status relations among actors in different types of social structures are considered key forces in determining the nature of structural change over time. The major exchange theorists all have treated power, structural sources of power, and the dynamics of power use as primary in their theoretical formulations.

Social exchange theory derives from several distinct lines of theoretical work in the social sciences, including social behaviorism, utilitarianism, and functionalism (Turner 1986). Major proponents of the social exchange perspective within sociology include Homans (1961, 1974), Blau (1964, 1987), and Emerson (1962, 1972a, 1972b). Within psychology, the work of Thibaut and Kelley (1959; Kelley and Thibaut 1978) bears a strong resemblance to social exchange theory in its emphasis on the interdependence of actors and the social implications of different forms of interdependence. Anthropologists such as Malinowski (1922), Mauss (1925), Schneider (1974), and Levi-Strauss (1949, 1969) have contributed in different ways to the emergence of this theoretical perspective (see Ekeh 1974). In addition, the foundation of microeconomics has much in common with some variants of social exchange theory (Heath 1976). This affinity is clearest in Blau's *Exchange and Power in Social Life* (1964) and in subsequent theoretical developments (e.g., Cook and Emerson 1978; Coleman 1972, 1990). The breadth of the intellectual heritage of social exchange theory accounts in part for its continued significance in the social sciences.

Homans's well-known essay "Social Behavior as Exchange" (1958) clarified the nature of this theoretical orientation and introduced it into mainstream sociology. An elaboration of Homans's perspective was published in *Social Behavior: Its Elementary Forms* (revised in 1974). An important distinguishing feature of Homans's work was its reliance on the language and propositions of behavioral psychology. The use of operant psychol-

ogy as the behavioral basis of exchange theory created much of the early controversy surrounding the utility of this perspective for sociologists. In particular, the corresponding claim made by Homans that laws of social behavior could be "reduced to" the basic underlying principles of psychological behaviorism generated much debate (e.g., Deutsch 1964). According to Homans, "The general propositions we shall use in explanation are psychological in two senses: they refer to the actions of individuals and they have . . . been formulated and tested by psychologists" (1974, p. 12). However, Homans explicitly took as the major theoretical task the explanation of social phenomena. This emphasis on social behavior and the social structures generated and altered by human social interaction has sustained the influence of social exchange theory in sociology. In this regard, Homans viewed the line drawn between psychology and sociology as fundamentally arbitrary.

The initial theoretical formulation developed by Homans (1961) and revised in 1974 included five main propositions, all of which have to do with the fact that behavior is a function of its payoffs: the consequent rewards and punishments. The first proposition is the "success proposition," which states that the more frequently an activity is rewarded, the greater is the likelihood of its performance. Behavior that generates positive consequences for the individual is likely to be repeated. The second proposition, the "stimulus proposition," stipulates that similar environmental or situational circumstances will stimulate behavior that has been rewarded on similar occasions in the past. This allows for the generalization of behavioral responses to "new" situations. The "value proposition" specifies that the more valuable the result of an action is to the actor, the more likely that action is to be performed. This proposition is qualified by the "deprivation-satiation" proposition, which introduces the general ideal of diminishing marginal utility. According to this proposition, the more often a person has recently received a particular reward for an action, the less valuable is an additional unit of that reward. Thus, some rewards become less effective over time in eliciting specific actions, though this is less true for generalized rewards such as money and affection and for anything for which satiation is less likely to occur except at extreme levels. The fifth theoretical proposition in Homans's basic framework specifies the conditions under which persons react emotionally to different reward situations. This proposition has two parts. People who do not receive what they anticipate are expected to become angry and behave aggressively, based on the original Miller and Dollard (1941) "frustration-aggression" hypothesis (see Homans 1974, p. 37). People who receive more than they expect or do not receive anticipated punishments will be happy and will behave approvingly. This system of propositions forms the original core set of ideas of what has come to be called social exchange theory.

Homans's (1961, 1974) uses this set of theoretical ideas to explain phenomena such as the exercise of power and authority, cooperation, conformity and competition, structures of sentiment and interaction, status and influence, satisfaction and productivity, leadership, distributive justice, and the emergence of stratification. He addressed these social phenomena primarily in terms of the nature of the interpersonal relations involved. Furthermore, he emphasized "elementary" forms of behavior, or what he referred to as the "subinstitutional" level of analysis. "We gain our fullest understanding of the elementary features of social behavior by observing the interactions between members of small, informal groups," Homans (1974, p. 356) argued. By studying such forms of behavior, he hoped to illuminate the elementary, informal subinstitutional bases of more complex forms of social behavior that often are more formal and institutionalized. What he bequeathed to modern-day sociology, besides his particular form of theorizing, was an emphasis on the microfoundations of social structures and social change.

Whereas Homans focused on elementary forms of behavior and the subinstitutional level of analysis, Blau (1964, 1987) moved beyond the micro level to the institutional level, dealing with authority and power, conflict, and change in the context of institutionalized systems of exchange. In disagreement with Homans's reductionistic strategy, Blau (1987, p. ix) claims that his "theory is rooted in the peculiarly social nature of exchange, which implies that it cannot be reduced to or derived from psychological principles that govern the motives of individuals, as Homans aims to do." In distinct contrast to Homans's reductionism, Blau assumed that social structures has "emergent" properties that cannot be explained by character-

istics or processes that involve only the subunits. Thus, Blau parted company from Homans in two major ways. First, Blau's framework was not based on principles of behavioral psychology; instead, he introduced microeconomic reasoning into the analysis of distinctly social exchange. Second, he explicitly introduced the notion of emergent processes into his theoretical treatise, not only rejecting reductionism but also expanding the theory to extend far beyond its original subinstitutional base.

Blau (1964) developed a general framework for analyzing macro structures and processes based on an extension of his micro-level theory of social exchange processes. Drawing on Simmel's understanding of social life, he explains the general structure of social associations rooted in psychological processes, such as attraction, approval, reciprocation, and rational conduct. Group formation, cohesion, and social integration as well as processes of opposition, conflict, and dissolution are explained in terms of social exchange processes. These forms of social association generated by exchange processes come to constitute very complex social structures (and substructures) over time. These more complex social structures are then examined by Blau as they are created and changed by power processes and the dynamics of legitimation and political opposition. Common values mediate and make possible indirect exchanges and thus the coordination of action in large collectivities. According to Blau, they also "legitimate the social order." Throughout this major work, Blau contrasts and compares social exchange processes in simple structures with those in more complex social structures and institutions. The major social forces he analyzes include differentiation, integration, organization, and opposition that sets up the dialectic necessary for the explanation of structural change.

The strategy of building a theory of macro structure and processes on an explicitly micro-level theory was a distinguishing feature of Blau's (1964) original work, which also became the focus of a major stream of theoretical work in sociology on the "micro–macro link" in the 1980s and 1990s. Ironically, Blau (1986) himself challenged the utility of his approach in his subsequent writings (Blau 1987), fueling the debate further. In his introduction to the second printing of his book on exchange and power (1986), he argues that microsociological and macrosociological theories "require different approaches and conceptual schemes though their distinct perspectives enrich each other" (1986, p. xv). This theoretical debate will not be over soon since it lies at the heart of the nature of sociological analysis and relates to broad issues of the primacy of particular units and levels of analysis as well as to complex metatheoretical and methodological issues.

Blau (1964) and subsequently Emerson (1962, 1972, 1972b) made power the central focus of analysis. Blau treated power, authority, opposition, and legitimation as key topics in his discussion of macro structures and the dynamics of structural change. Emerson's (1962) theory of power-dependence relations was partially encorporated into Blau's (1964) treatment of power imbalance and the conditions of social independence. For Emerson (1962), these strategies were power-balancing mechanisms. The central proposition in Emerson's (1962) article classic was that power, defined in relational terms, is a function of the dependence of one actor on another. In a two-party exchange relation, the power of one party (A) over another party (B) is a function of the dependence of B on A. Dependence is a function of the value one actor places on the resources (or valued behavior) mediated by the other actor and the availability of those resources from alternative sources. The greater the availability of these resources from other actors (or alternative sources), the lower one actor's dependence on another. Two features of this approach to power are important: (1) It treats power as relational (a feature of a social relation, not simply a property of an actor), and (2) it treats power as potential power; that is, it may or may not be exercised. This relational conception of power became the basis for most subsequent work on exchange and power.

Emerson (1972a, 1972b) expanded his treatment of power and dependence to form a more extensive exchange theory of social relations. In many ways, his work combined the approaches of Homans (1961) and Blau (1964). In the original formulation, Emerson (1972a) adopted the language and principles of behavioral psychology to form a theory of social relations. However, he quickly moved beyond behavioral principles.to the formation of more complex propositions regarding the emergence of various kinds of social structures. Here the theory picks up the Simmelian focus of Blau's work as well as the concern with emergent properties and complex social structures. Emerson (1972b), like Blau (1964, 1986), viewed the major task of exchange theory as the creation of a framework in which the primary dependent variable is social structure and structural change. The major task was eminently sociological, not psychological, even though all three theorists explicitly encorporated into their thinking notions about the psychology of actors. Emerson and Cook's subsequent work (e.g., Cook and Emerson 1978) adopted a more cognitive perspective on the actors involved in social exchange. Molm's (1981, 1987) earlier work extended the original behavioral underpinnings of the theory.

Exchange theory, though originally dyadic in focus, has been extended to apply to the analysis of exchange networks. Both Homans and Blau recognized the ubiquity of social networks and different forms of social association, but Emerson (1972b) made networks and corporate groups a central focus of his theoretical formulation. The definition of exchange relations as being "connected" in various ways to form network structures was the key to this development in the theory. Emerson defined two major types of connections between exchange relations: negative connections and positive connections. Two relations are negatively connected if the magnitude or frequency of exchange in one is negatively correlated with the magnitude or frequency of exchange in the other. In essence, the two relations are strictly alternatives. If a supplier gets parts in an exchange with one vendor, he or she does not need to get the same parts from another vendor. Negatively connected relations are thus competitive in nature. In contrast, when two relations are positively connected, exchange in one relation enhances exchange in the other. For example, the resources one party gets in exchange with one supplier can be used to obtain needed goods from another supplier. In this case, a positive connection exists and the two exchange relations are positively correlated. Such exchange relations are more cooperative than competitive in nature and form the basis for some types of division of labor and specialization within exchange networks. Subsequent theorists such as Willer (1987), Markovsky et al. (1988), Bonacich (1986), and Yamaguchi (1996) have developed other ways of classifying types of exchange connections. Some of this work is discussed below in the discussion of alternative perspectives.

A key concept in Emerson's exchange theory of power is the idea that exchange relations can be balanced or imbalanced. A power inequality results from an imbalance in power relations between two or more actors. An exchange relation is balanced if both parties are equally dependent on each other for exchange (or resources of value). If they are equally dependent, they have equal power. The central idea that power is based on dependence allows for the specification of ways in which dependencies are altered so that they affect the balance of power in the exchange relation and in networks of exchange relations.

Emerson postulated four power-balancing mechanisms to explain some of the ways in which exchange relations and the networks they form change either to maintain and preserve existing structural arrangements and distributions of power or to alter them. Coalition formation is one of the mechanisms by which power-disadvantaged actors in less powerful network positions can gain power through the collective advantage gained through cooperative action. Not all coalitions are power-balancing, however. In subsequent work, Emerson addressed the kinds of coalitions that form between powerful actors (sometimes referred to as collusion) or between powerful actors and a subset of the less powerful actors (a divide-and-conquer strategy).

Division of labor, or specialization within a network, may operate as a power-balancing mechanism, since it can result in changes in the distribution of power in a network through modifications in the distribution of resources and the nature of the structural arrangements. For example, two suppliers of the same resource who have been competitors may decide to specialize and offer different services in a way that makes them no longer competitive with each other in a particular network. Network extension also can alter the balance of power in a network as new exchange partners become available. In addition, when other strategies are not available, actors can devalue what they obtain from a more powerful actor as a way to reduce their dependence on the relationship. This strategy may be a precursor to an exit from the relation in many instances. Various theorists have continued this line of work, specifying the principles that predict the distribution of power in different exchange structures and the

processes that modify it (e.g., Cook et al. 1983, 1986; Bonacich 1986; Yamaguchi 1996).

Other extensions of the exchange theory originally developed by Emerson have focused on the links between structure and process and on other bases of power. In a major research program that extended over a ten-year period, Molm (1997) investigated the role of coercive power in social exchange. Emerson's work and that of most of the exchange theorists had focused almost exclusively on reward power, or the control over positively valued goods and services. Coercive power is the ability to control negative events (e.g., to withhold rewards) or to inflict punishment on another in an exchange relation. Unlike reward power, coercive power is used less often in exchange relations, especially by those in power-advantaged positions, who seem to understand that it may be viewed as unjustified in many circumstances. The fear of retaliation is also a deterrent to the use of coercive power. The use of coercive power is more costly since it imposes losses on the exchange partner in addition to the opportunity costs involved. Molm's (1989, 1997) major accomplishment was to expand the treatment of power in the classic power-dependence formulation to include forms of coercion. Since exchange relations often involve control over both things people value and things people wish to avoid, this is a significant extension of the theory.

Alternative theoretical formulations have been developed for investigating power processes in exchange networks. They include the "elementary theory" developed by Willer and his collaborators (e.g., Willer and Anderson 1981; Markovsky et al. 1988), Friedkin's (1992) "expected value model" of social exchange, and game theory, which has been applied to the analysis of exchange networks by Bienenstock and Bonacich (1992). While some of these formulations have an affinity with the original power-dependence framework developed by Emerson (1972a, 1972b), most have explored other bases of power. For example, Willer and his collaborators have developed a different terminology for specifying the nature of the relations in an exchange network. They define three types of relations: null (no connection), inclusion (when someone has to be involved in an exchange for it to take place) and exclusion (when someone may be involved in an exchange but is in competition with others and thus may be excluded from the exchange at any time). These theorists go on to develop different principles for the distribution of power in networks characterized by different types of relations. Exclusion is viewed as the main determinant of power. The ability to exclude others from exchange is thus the key source of power in this theory.

Bienenstock and Bonacich (1992, 1997) analyze exchange networks by using a game theory perspective. They attempt to understand the efforts of actors to maximize certain well-defined interests by adopting strategies that can be analyzed usefully with the tools of game theory. Based on different solution concepts (e.g., the core, the kernel), they make predictions concerning the outcomes of the exchanges in various types of network structures. In addition, this application of game theory provides predictions about the role of information in exchange processes. Building on the early contributions of Blau, Coleman, Emerson, and Cook, Yamaguchi (1996) works out a rational choice model for predicting the distribution of power and the effects of network centrality in what he terms substitutable and complementary exchange relations.

Further developments in the theory of exchange include the formulation of explicit propositions concerning the use of power in different types of exchange network structures and the specification of some of the determinants of power use. These factors include concern over the fairness of the distribution of outcomes, the commitments that emerge between actors (e.g., Lawler and Yoon 1996), the formation of coalitions, particular strategies of action, and whether the power is reward power or punishment power. More recent developments focus more on methodologies for specifying the distribution of power in complex network structures (see, for example, Markovsky's work). Interest in this topic is in part driven by the potential for synthesizing exchange theoretic conceptions of power with network models of social structure (see Cook 1987; Cook and Whitmeyer 1992). Another arena of current theoretical and empirical work is the specification of dynamic models of power use and structural change that include a more sophisticated model of the actors involved and the strategies they adopt in their attempts to obtain resources and services that are of value to them. These general theoretical and empirical efforts will be important if exchange theory is to fulfill its promise of providing an approach to linking micro-level theories of action and interaction with macro-level explanations of structure and processes of social change, an agenda that was originally set by Homans, Blau, and Emerson.

The application of exchange theory to understanding a variety of social phenomena has grown over the last two decades. Early applications focused on the explanation of the initiation and termination of social relations in work settings and families and then in the domain of romantic relationships and dating. Topics of interest to researchers included the conception of fairness in social exchange relations and its link to relational satisfaction and dissolution, the use of power in social relations based on control of both rewards and costs, and the abuse of power as well as the role of coalitions in altering the balance of power among actors in a network of individuals or organizations. Beyond the application to family and work settings, exchange theory has been applied in many different contexts to the study of organizations and interorganizational relations. Since organizations typically require resources from other entities much of their time is devoted to the strategic management of those dependencies. The resource dependence perspective (Pfeffer and Salancik 1978) in the field of organizations represents a straightforward application of exchange reasoning to the strategic actions of organizations and their subunits (e.g., at the divisional level). The developing field of economic sociology is now drawing to some extent on ideas derived from exchange theory to explain the emergence of network forms of organization and the nature of the power processes that emerge in those networks. Network effects on labor practices, informal influence among organizations, the organization of business groups, and the formation of international linkages that cross traditional national boundaries of economic and productive activity are central topics of inquiry in economic sociology. Some of these efforts involve understanding the effects of network location on outcomes and the various strategies actors use to enhance their bargaining power and influence. These efforts derive in part from the power-dependence reasoning first introduced by Emerson and Blau into exchange theorizing.

Other applications of exchange theory include broader efforts to investigate the balance of power in the health care industry, the strategic role of insurance companies in an era of managed care, and the response of physicians to the loss of power and autonomy. Several researchers have attempted to analyze the nature of physician referrals in network exchange terms and to characterize the nature of physician–patient interaction as an exchange relation in which power is asymmetrical (or imbalanced) and trust plays a key role in "balancing" that power differential. The patient must place his or her fate in the hands of a more competent, more informed actor and trust that the physician will do no harm. Future applications of the exchange model of interaction and of network exchange in other domains will help clarify and extend the underlying theoretical framework.

REFERENCES

Blau, P. M. 1964 *Exchange and Power in Social Life*. New York: Wiley, 2d printing, 1986. New Brunswick: N.J.: Transaction.

—— 1987 "Microprocess and Macrostructure." In K. S. Cook, ed., *Social Exchange Theory*. Newbury Park, Calif.: Sage

Bienenstock, Elisa I., and Phillip Bonacich 1992 "The Core as a Solution to Negatively Connected Exchange Networks." *Social Networks* 14:231–243.

—— 1997 "Network Exchange as a Cooperative Game." *Rationality and Society* 9:937–965.

Bonacich, P. 1986 "Power and Centrality: A Family of Measures." *American Journal of Sociology* 92:1170–1182.

Coleman, J. S. 1972 "Systems of Social Exchange." *Journal of Mathematical Sociology* 2:145–163.

—— 1990 *The Foundations of Social Theory*. Cambridge, Mass.: Harvard University Press

Cook, Gillmore and Yamaguchi 1986 "Point and line vulnerability as bases for predicting the distribution of power in exchange networks: Reply to Willer." *American Journal of Sociology* 92:445–448.

Cook, K. S., ed. 1987 *Social Exchange Theory*. Newbury Park, Calif.: Sage.

——, and R. M. Emerson 1978 "Power, Equity, and Commitment in Exchange Networks." *American Sociological Review* 43:721–739.

——, ——, M. R. Gillmore, and T. Yamagishi 1983 "The Distribution of Power in Exchange Networks: Theory and Experimental Results." *American Journal of Sociology* 89:275–305.

Cook and Whitmeyer 1992 "Two Approaches to Social Structure: Exchange Theory and Network Analysis." *Annual Review of Sociology*. 18:109–127

Deutsch, M. 1964 "Homans in the Skinner Box." *Sociological Inquiry* 34:156–165.

Ekeh, P. P. 1974 *Social Exchange Theory: The Two Traditions*. Cambridge, Mass.: Harvard University Press.

Emerson, R. M. 1962 "Power-Dependence Relations." *American Sociological Review* 27:31–40.

—— 1972a "Exchange Theory, Part I: A Psychological Basis for Social Exchange." In J. Berger, M. Zelditch, and B. Anderson, eds., *Sociological Theories in Progress*, vol. 2. Boston: Houghton Mifflin.

—— 1972b. "Exchange Theory, Part II: Exchange Relations and Networks." In J. Berger, M. Zelditch, and B. Anderson, eds., *Sociological Theories in Progress*, vol. 2. Boston: Houghton Mifflin.

Friedkin, Noah E. 1992 "An Expected Value Model of Social Power: Predictions for Selected Exchange Networks." *Social Networks* 14:213–229.

Heath, A. 1976. *Rational Choice and Social Exchange: A Critique of Exchange Theory*. Cambridge, Mass.: Cambridge University Press.

Homans, G. C. 1958 "Social Behavior as Exchange." *American Journal of Sociology* 62:597–606.

—— 1961 *Social Behavior: Its Elementary Forms*. New York: Harcourt, Brace, and World.

—— 1974 *Social Behavior: Its Elementary Forms*, 2nd ed. New York: Harcourt, Brace, and World.

Kelley, H. H., and J. Thibaut 1978 *Interpersonal Relations: A Theory of Interdependence*. New York: Wiley.

Lawler, Edward J., and Jeongkoo Yoon 1996 "Commitment in Exchange Relations: A Test of a Theory of Relational Cohesion." *American Sociological Review* 61:89–108.

Levi-Strauss, C. 1949 *Les Structures Elementaires de la Parents*. Paris: Presses Universitaires de France.

—— 1969 *The Elementary Structures of Kinship*. Boston: Beacon.

Malinowski, B. 1922 *Argonauts of the Western Pacific*. London: Routledge and Kegan Paul.

Markovsky, B., D. Willer, and T. Patton 1988 "Power Relations in Exchange Networks." *American Sociological Review* 53:220–236.

Mauss, M. 1925 *Essai sur le don in Sociologie et Anthropologie*. Paris: Presses Universitaires de France. Translated into English by Ian Cunnison as *The Gift*. New York: Free Press, 1954.

Miller, N. E. and J. Dollard 1941 *Social Learning and Imitation*. New Haven, Conn.: Yale University Press.

Molm, L. D. 1981. "The Conversion of Power Imbalance to Power Use." *Social Psychology Quarterly* 44:151–163.

—— 1987 "Power-Dependence Theory: Power Processes and Negative Outcomes." In E. J. Lawler and B. Markovsky, eds., *Advances in Group Processes*, vol. 4. Greenwich, Conn.: JAI Press.

—— 1989 "Punishment Power: A Balancing Process in Power-Dependence Relations." *American Journal of Sociology* 94 (6):1392–1418.

Molm, Linda D. 1997 *Coercive Power in Social Exchange.* Cambridge, UK: Cambridge University Press.

Pfeffer, Jeffrey, and Gerald R. Salancik 1978 *The External Control of Organizations: A Resource Dependence Perspective.* New York: Harper and Row.

Schneider, H. K. 1974 *Economic Man: The Anthropology of Economics.* New York: Free Press.

Thibaut, J., and H. H. Kelley 1959 *The Social Psychology of Groups.* New York: Wiley.

Turner, J. H. 1986 *The Structure of Sociological Theory*, 4th ed. Chicago: Dorsey Press.

Willer, David 1987 *Theory and Experimental Investigation of Social Structures.* New York: Bordon and Breach.

Willer and Anderson 1981 Willer, David and Bo Anderson, eds. 1981. *Networks, Exchange and Coercion.* New York: Elsevier/Greenwood

Yamaguchi, K. 1996 "Power in Networks of Substitutable and Complementary Exchange Relations: A Rational-Choice Model and an Analysis of Power Centralization." *American Sociological Review* 61:308–322.

KAREN S. COOK

SOCIAL FORECASTING

Forecasting has been important in sociological thought. Early European sociologists argued that societies progress through inevitable historical stages; those theories helped sociologists predict all societies' futures. Early American sociologists adopted the pragmatists' rule that a science proves it "works" by predicting future events (Schuessler 1971). Sociologists, however, have only recently adopted methods appropriate for those early goals. The review in this article of the delayed development of social forecasting includes (1) three sociologists' conceptual uses of forecasting and some reasons their suggestions were not followed, (2) qualitative and quantitative methods of forecasting, and (3) recent indications of increased interest in forecasting.

FORECASTING TRADITIONS

Sociologists have contributed several social forecasting concepts that were historically significant enough to become traditional orientations in the analysis of the future. William F. Ogburn "held that in the modern world technological inventions commonly come first and social effects later. By reason of this lag, it is possible, he argued, to anticipate the future and plan for its eventualities" (Schuessler 1971, p. 309). For example, new possibilities came into conflict with family values when the invention of effective birth control gave women new choices. Ogburn's contribution was to suggest that cultural lags are inevitable but that the period of disruption they cause can be shortened (Reiss 1986).

Merton (1949) challenged Ogburn's idea that the effects of inventions can be easily anticipated. Each invention has an apparent goal, or manifest function, that it is hoped it will perform in society. Each change, however, also contains the possibility of performing a number of *latent functions*. These are unanticipated side effects that often are not desired and sometimes are dangerous. The institutions of society are closely intertwined, and an invention in one area can cause shocks throughout the system. The automobile is an example. Its manifest function of changing transportation has been fulfilled, but at the cost of serious ecological and sociological changes.

Merton's (1949) second warning was that social forecasting is unique because it tries to predict the behavior of humans, who change their minds. The *self-fulfilling prophecy* is a forecast that makes people aware of real or imagined new opportunities or dangers to be avoided. Merton demonstrated that false forecasts can have powerful effects if they gain public acceptance. For example, a sound bank can be destroyed by a run on its funds caused by a prediction of failure. Henshel's more inclusive concept—the self-altering prediction—shows that forecasts can be self-defeating as well as self-fulfilling. W. I. Thomas's theorem, "If men define situations as real, they are real in their consequences," applies particularly to the definitions societies make of the future (Henshel 1978, p. 100).

Moore challenged sociologists to go beyond safe prophecy based on orderly trends and attack the difficult problem of "how to handle sharp changes in the magnitude of change, and sharp (or at least clear) changes in direction" (Moore 1964, p. 332). There are four types of *discontinuous societal change*: (1) Some societies are changed drastically by an *exogenous variable*, an idea or value from another society. Modern Japan is an example. (2) A society's rate of development can increase spontaneously, creating an abundance of new ideas. This is an exponential acceleration, a *change in the rate of change*. (3) Moore attributes *changes in the direction of change* to the existence of a dialectic of values in each society's apparent trend. For example, a society may appear to be profit-oriented and ecologically exploitative, but there also exists a counterset of values that stress harmony with each other and with nature. If a shift in such basic value emphases could be predicted, many other associated forecasts could be made. (4) Finally, Moore recognizes that there are pure *emergents*, inventions such as money and writing, that cannot be thought of as parts of trends.

Moore drew a methodological moral from these complexities: "One must somehow move from discrete necessary conditions to cumulative and sufficient ones" (Moore 1964, p. 334). That is, the search for the one trend or causal variable that drives societal change should be abandoned. The summation and particularly the interaction of many component developments create events.

In 1966 Moore asked sociologists to put aside value-free scientific rules and attempt to construct *preferable futures* that might help "mankind survive for the next twenty years" (Moore 1966, p. 270). Moore was confronting what he felt to be the main reason why forecasting was done so infrequently. It is professionally permissible for sociologists to examine social change both currently and retrospectively, but making a forecast leaves one liable to being labeled a utopian (Winthrop 1968, p. 136). Utopian thinking is in disrepute because past advocates allowed their values to cloud their constructions. However, images of the future provide goals and determine how people plan and therefore how they behave in the present. Moore sought utopias that would perform a necessary social planning function by constructing alternative directions for human purpose.

WHY SOCIAL FORECASTING HAS DEVELOPED SLOWLY

Sociologists' basic methodological orientations preclude an interest in forecasting. Sociologists analyze society's static interconnections and concentrate on the social structures that persist. They have not developed skill in isolating the sequences of dynamic social behavior (Moore 1966). They are better at categorizing and typing people than at predicting how individuals might change from one type to another.

Many sociologists feel that not enough is known to predict future events. They point to economists and demographers and ask, If they are failing with their more quantifiable data, how can complex social changes be anticipated? One school of thought sees sociology as a qualitative art form that will never be a statistically modeled science. Critical sociologists object on moral grounds. They feel that society requires essential restructuring before positive change can be effected. Since most forecasting is based on models of the current structure, they feel that it sanctions unjust social arrangements (Henshel 1982).

JUDGMENTAL AND QUALITATIVE FORECASTING METHODS

The futurists (Bell 1997; Kurian and Molitor 1996) see "the challenge being not just to forecast what the future will be, but to make it what it ought to be" (Enzer 1984, p. 202). The actual future is too complex to be predefined, but possible futures can be constructed that can be instructive. In addition, secondary forecasts can be made that estimate the effects of policy actions on the original course of development (Colquhoun 1996). The pace of change is considered too rapid to be captured by traditional methods reliance on a careful quantitative reconstruction of the past. This justifies the use of experts' opinions, and futurists' methods are ways of systematizing those judgments (Allen 1978, p. 79).

A discontinuous social change usually is preceded by a "substantial restructuring of basic tenets and beliefs" (Holroyd 1978, p. 37). Such paradigm shifts are revolutionary, such as the rejection of the earth as the center of the universe. They appear in fields of knowledge in which one system of thought seems to be in control but is unable to solve important problems. Holroyd, for example, predicts a paradigm shift in economics because its current theories are unable to deal with essential problems such as scarcity of natural resources. Futurists anticipate shifts by compiling lists of crucial issues in the institutions of society. When the gap between current and desired conditions is large, that area is monitored closely for discontinuous change (Holroyd 1978, p. 38).

Cross-impact matrices are constructed by listing all possible future events in the problem area under study (Allen 1978, pp. 132–145). Each event is recorded as a row and a column in a square matrix. This allows the explicit examination of every intersection of events when one asks: What is the probability that the first will occur if it has been preceded by the other? The probabilities of occurrence can be derived from available data but are often judgments. Cross-impact analysis is a systematic way of heeding Merton's warning about not overlooking possibly damaging latent consequences. It is a tool for spotting crucial turning points or originating novel viewpoints by examining the intersections of change at which experts' judgments conflict.

Delphi surveys constitute an ingenious method for allowing the interaction of expert judgments while avoiding the contamination of social status or damage to reputations because of radical or mistaken pronouncements (Henshel 1982). In a series of survey rounds, everyone sees the distribution of others' responses without knowing the proponents' identities. A composite forecast emerges as anonymous modifications are made at each round.

After a review of forecasting methods, Ascher (1978) chose *scenarios* as one of only two methods he could recommend. A scenario is "a hypothetical sequence of events constructed for the purpose of focusing attention on causal processes and decision points" (Herman Kahn, quoted in Wilson 1978, p. 225). It is a story, but a complex one based on all available data and usually constructed after a cross-impact analysis has isolated possible turning points. Usually, two or three related scenarios are constructed to illustrate alternative futures that could be determined by particular decisions.

It is not surprising that an expert's decision process can be made explicit. What is surprising is that in many studies the systematic model of an expert often forecasts better than the person does (Armstrong 1978). In *bootstrapping*, the forecaster's individualized decision procedures become the "bootstraps" by which a systematized procedure is "lifted" into an orderly routine. Such a model can be made deductively through interviews that isolate and formalize the decision rules or inductively by starting with a series of past forecasts and attempting to infer the rules that accounted for the differences between them.

Metaforecasting (Makridakis 1988) represents an essential summary of these considerations and a bridge to more quantitative methods. It combines judgmental and statistical estimates. It attempts to include historical and social information to overcome the tendency to ignore or overreact to changes in established patterns or relationships.

SOCIAL DEMOGRAPHY

Demography is the most established form of social forecasting, and its methods and record can be found elsewhere (Henshel 1982). This article will discuss only two elements from its continuing development: a method that has had wide influence and what can be learned from its frequent failures to predict future population sizes.

A cohort is an aggregate of individuals of similar age who therefore experience events during the same time period (Reiss 1986, p. 47). *Cohort analysis* was first used by Norman Ryder to study the changing fertility behaviors of women born during the same five-year periods. Since that time, cohorts have been used in the study of many areas of social change to differentiate the changes that are result from individuals maturing through the stages of life from those caused by powerful societal events or value shifts.

Demographers failed to anticipate the postwar baby boom and the onset of its decline. These errors were due to *assumption drag*, "the continued use of assumptions long after their validity has been contradicted by the data" (Ascher 1978, p. 53). Henshel (1982) says that demographers probably ignored these turning points because they simply talked to each other too much. They reassured each other that their assumptions and their extrapolations from past trends would soon reassert themselves in the data. Recognition of this error of developing an isolated club of forecasters has helped economists and will help sociologists avoid a similar regimentation of estimates.

The mix of assumptions and actual data varies widely in *simulation models*. The most useful models test a set of explicit assumptions so that no interactions between variables are overlooked. Models have contributed the idea of the feedback loop as an important caution against unidirectional thinking. This common system characteristic occurs when an effect reaches a sensitive level and begins a reaction that modifies its own cause (Simmons 1973, p. 195). Often, however, the mix of assumptions and facts in simulations leans too heavily toward judgments. So-called black-box modeling (McLean 1978), in which equations are hidden, can produce output that is plausible and provocative but also unrealistic. The creator of the *Limits to Growth* study admitted that "in *World Dynamics* . . . there is no attempt to incorporate formal data. . . . All relationships are intuitive" (Simmons 1973, p. 208). That study extrapolated what have come to be seen as extreme assumptions of geometric growth unchecked by social adaptation. Its dramatic predictions of imminent shortages had a wide but unwarranted impact (Cole et al. 1973). A comment on those failed predictions and their popularity at the time of their publication sets the context in which all "modeled" forecasts should be received: "The apparent detached neutrality of a computer model is as illusory as it is persuasive. Any model of a social system necessarily involves assumptions about the workings of that system, and these assumptions are necessarily colored by the attitudes and values of the individuals or groups concerned. . . . [C]omputer models should be regarded as an integral part of political debate. . . . The model is the message" (Freeman 1973, p. 7).

PRAGMATIC STATISTICAL ANALYSIS OF TIME SERIES

Attention has shifted to techniques that are less concerned with demonstrating the effects of assumed patterns. Time series are records of observations through time. Traditional *time series analysis* projects "future values of a variable based entirely on the past and present observations of that vari-

able" (Levine et al. 1999). It involves isolating the trend inside the many "noisy" or seasonal factors that may obscure it. The techniques have been well developed, are taught in undergraduate management statistics courses, and have been adapted for spreadsheet software available on most computers. The problem, however, is how much faith one can put in the idea that "people do what they usually do." Time series projections are essential first steps in discovering patterns of behavior of aggregates of people over time. Such patterns often persist, but some shock (invention, immigration, social redefinition such "the sixties," or adjustment of tradition such as decreasing sexism) may cause disruption. In recognition of these sociological disruptions, time series are being explored from the viewpoint that any variable may be uniquely complex and subject to sudden change.

Time series regressions uncover structural relationships involved in the history of two or more variables. Before the relationship can be assessed, sources of error must be isolated and controlled. The most important of these errors are (1) the overall trend of change that would obscure any specific interrelationship and (2) the autocorrelation effect of internal dependence of an observation on previous observations. If a relationship seems to explain the data series' movements, it is tested with ex-post forecasts that can be verified within the range of available data. If these succeed, "ex-ante-forecasts can be used to provide educated guesses about the path of the variables into the blind future" (Ostrom 1990, p. 77).

Autoregressive moving average (ARIMA) models predict a variable's current status by using a combination of its previous observations and mathematically approximated random shocks. The goal is to find a pattern that fits the immediate data, not to understand relationships. ARIMA models are useful in interrupted *time series analysis*, in which the impact of a policy or another intervention can be examined by seeing how different the variable's patterns are before and after the intervention (McDowall et al. 1980). Autoregressive models have a limitation important for social forecasting, in which historical data are relatively scarce. "Because ARIMA models must be identified from the data to be modeled, relatively long time series are required" (McCleary and Hay 1980, p. 20). Fifty observations are recommended.

Exponential smoothing is widely used and is as reliable as more complicated methods (Gardner 1985). In its simplest form, the next period's forecast is based on the current forecast plus a portion of the error it made. That is, the difference between the current time period's forecast and the actual value is weighted and used to adjust the next period's expected value. The higher the value of the weight used is, the more the error adjustment contributes and the more quickly the model will respond to changes. Exponential smoothing is used in early detection of curvilinear changes, when the rate of change speeds or slows (Gardner 1987).

FUTURE TRENDS

Forecasting is being done. It is central in business and government planning. Even though many of these forecasts' essential variables are social or are found in social contexts (such as family decisions to move, build, and purchase or the development of social problems), economists have become society's designated forecasters (Henshel 1982; Stimson and Stimson 1976). Sociologists will not change this imbalance easily, but there are some indications that forecasting may finally become part of everyday sociological work.

Assumptions that a particular cycle or curve is the natural or underlying process of all change have been abandoned, and pragmatic methods are now widespread. It is also accepted that a forecast is developed only to be monitored for possible discontinuities. Trend extrapolations rarely are done without accompanying methods for describing the expected deviations.

Two forecasting methods are particularly promising because they allow sociologists to build on traditional skills. Componential or segmentation forecasting (Armstrong 1978) recognizes that an aggregate forecast can be improved by combining forecasts made on the population's component social groups. Sociologists are best able to distinguish the groups that should be treated separately. Pooled time series analysis (Sayrs 1989) combines cross-sectional descriptions such as one-time surveys. Sociologists are expert at describing interconnections in the structures of organizations or societies, and now they have the opportunity to study these social arrangements over time.

Society has recognized the wisdom of the early concern about anticipating the latent effects of social and technological inventions. Progress no longer seems inevitable. The popular question now is, Can someone assure us that a new element will not be as destructive as past changes?

Sociologists seem to be uniquely suited to help forecasting become more plausible because their working assumptions counter the weaknesses of current methods. The idea that technological innovation or economic cycles drive social change has produced today's mechanistic, ultrarational, anti-individualistic models that assume that the population is homogeneous (Dublin 1992). All these weaknesses are naturally contradicted when sociologists expand their vision of a population to include the cultural diversity of the social contexts that produce, accept or reject, and always modify the effects of technological and economic circumstances.

The future acceptance of forecasting also depends on sociologists' ability to improve the preparation and presentation of forecasts by using their traditional strengths. Forecasts will be accepted by policymakers and the public only when the quasi-theories they hold about the future are specifically addressed and proved false. Sociologists know this better than other social scientists do; they often are called on to dispel labels and popular theories that are so entrenched that they make any new attempt at explanation seem a "fool's experiment" to the forecaster's audience They also are used to the idea of various and multiple causes acting in a situation and therefore are skilled at isolating "unanticipated consequences."

Forecasts will improve and become more plausible when they place less importance on traditional scientific formulations. A forecast is not a hypothesis. Hypotheses must be made in advance of the behavior they are meant to predict to assure a full and objective test of the theories that produced them. Forecasts demand monitoring of predictions and adaptation of forecasts to circumstances. A forecast is as good as its ability to anticipate and allow the inclusion of changing social forces. That is, its main function is not to make an accurate prediction of future events but to isolate and interrelate the many factors in the current situation that may be causally powerful. Understanding the current social situation's complexity is the most important factor.

REFERENCES

Allen, T. Harrell 1978 *New Methods in Social Science Research: Policy Sciences and Futures Research*. New York: Praeger.

Armstrong, J. Scott 1978 *Long-Range Forecasting: From Crystal Ball To Computer*. New York: Wiley.

Ascher, William 1978 *Forecasting: An Appraisal for Policymakers and Planners*. Baltimore: Johns Hopkins University Press.

Bell, Wendell 1997 *Foundations of Futures Studies*, vols. I and II. New Brunswick, N.J.: Transaction.

Cole, H. S. D., Christopher Freeman, Marie Jahoda, and K. L. R. Pavitt, eds. 1973 *Models of Doom: A Critique of the Limits to Growth*. New York: Universe.

Colquhoun, Robert 1996 "The Art of Social Conjecture: Remembering Bertrand de Jouvenel." *History of the Human Sciences* 9(1): 27–42

Dublin, Max 1992 *FutureHype: The Tyranny of Prophecy*. New York: Plume.

Enzer, Selwyn 1984 "Anticipating the Unpredictable." *Technological Forecasting and Social Change* 26:201–204.

Freeman, Christopher 1973 "Malthus with a Computer" In H. S. D. Cole, Christopher Freeman, Marie Jahoda, and K. L. R. Pavitt eds., *Models of Doom: A Critique of the Limits to Growth*. New York: Universe.

Gardner, Everette S., Jr. 1985 "Exponential Smoothing: The State of the Art." *Journal of Forecasting* 4:1–28.

—— 1987 "Short-Range Forecasting." *LOTUS* 3:54–58.

Henshel, Richard L. 1978 "Self-Altering Predictions." In Jib Fowles, ed., *Handbook of Futures Research*. Westport, Conn.: Greenwood Press.

—— 1982 "Sociology and Social Forecasting." In Ralph H. Turner and James F. Short, eds., *Annual Review of Sociology*, vol. 8. Palo Alto, Calif.: Annual Reviews.

Holroyd, P. 1978 "Change and Discontinuity: Forecasting for the 1980s." *Futures* 10:31–43.

Kurian, George T., and Graham Molitor 1996 *Encyclopedia of the Future, vols. I and II*. New York: Macmillan.

Levine, David M., Mark L. Berenson, and David Stephan 1999 *Statistics for Managers Using Microsoft Excel*. Upper Saddle River N.J.: Prentice-Hall

Makridakis, Spyros 1988 "Metaforecasting: Ways of Improving Accuracy and Usefulness." *International Journal of Forecasting* 4(3):467–91.

McCleary, Richard, and Richard A. Hay, Jr. 1980 *Applied Time Series Analysis for the Social Sciences*. Beverly Hills, Calif.: Sage.

McDowall, David, Richard McCleary, Errol E. Meidinger, and Richard A. Hay, Jr. 1980 *Interrupted Time*. Newbury Park, Calif.: Sage.

McLean, J. Michael 1978 "Simulation Modeling." In Jib Fowles, ed., *Handbook of Futures Research*. Westport, Conn.: Greenwood Press.

Merton, Robert K. 1949 *Social Theory and Social Structure*, rev. ed. Glencoe, Ill.: Free Press.

Moore, Wilbert E. 1964 "Predicting Discontinuities in Social Change." *American Sociological Review* 29:331–338.

—— 1966 "The Utility of Utopias." *American Sociological Review* 31:756–772.

Ostrom, Charles W., Jr. 1990 *Time Series Analysis. Regression Techniques*, 2nd ed. Newbury Park, Calif.: Sage.

Reiss, Albert J., Jr. 1986 "Measuring Social Change." In Neil J. Smelser and Dean R. Gerstein, eds., *Behavioral and Social Science: Fifty Years of Discovery*. Washington, D.C.: National Academy Press.

Sayrs, Lois W. 1989 *Pooled Time Series Analysis*. Beverly Hills, Calif.: Sage.

Schuessler, Karl 1971 "Continuities in Social Prediction. "In H. L. Costner, ed., *Sociological Methodology, 1971*. San Francisco: Jossey-Bass.

Simmons, Harvey 1973 "System Dynamics and Technocracy." In H. S. D. Cole, Christopher Freeman, Marie Jahoda, and K. L. R. Pavitt eds., *Models of Doom: A Critique of the Limits to Growth*. New York: Universe.

Stimson, John, and Ardyth Stimson 1976 "Sociologists Should Be Put to Work as Forecasters." *American Sociologist* 11:49–56.

Wilson, Ian H. 1978 "Scenarios." In B. Fowles, ed. *Handbook of Futures Research*. Westport, Conn.: Greenwood Press.

Winthrop, Henry 1968 "The Sociologist and the Study of the Future." *American Sociologist* 3:136–145.

JOHN STIMSON

SOCIAL GERONTOLOGY

See Aging and the Life Course; Cohort Perspectives; Filial Responsibility; Intergenerational Relations; Intergenerational Resource Transfers; Long-Term Care, Long Term Care Facilities; Retirement; Widowhood.

SOCIAL IMITATION

See Behaviorism; Socialization; Social Psychology.

SOCIAL INDICATORS

Social indicators are statistical time series that are "used to monitor the social system, helping to identify changes and to guide intervention to alter the course of social change" (Ferriss 1988, p. 601). Examples are unemployment rates, crime rates, estimates of life expectancy, health status indices such as the average number of "healthy" days (or days without activity limitations) in the past month for a specific population, school enrollment rates, average achievement scores on a standardized test, rates of voting in elections, and measures of subjective well-being such as satisfaction with life as a whole.

HISTORICAL DEVELOPMENTS

Social Indicators in the 1960s. The term "social indicators" was given its initial meaning in an attempt by the American Academy of Arts and Sciences for the National Aeronautics and Space Administration in the early 1960s to detect and anticipate the nature and magnitude of the second-order consequences of the space program for American society (Land 1983, p. 2; Noll and Zapf 1994, p. 1). Frustrated by the lack of sufficient data to detect such effects and the absence of a systematic conceptual framework and methodology for analysis, some in the project attempted to develop a system of social indicators—statistics, statistical series, and other forms of evidence—with which to detect and anticipate social change and to evaluate specific programs and determine their impact. The results of this part of the project were published in a volume (Bauer 1966) called *Social Indicators*.

The appearance of this volume was not an isolated event. Several other influential publications commented on the lack of a system for charting social change and advocated that the U.S. government establish a "system of social accounts" that would facilitate a cost-benefit analysis of more than the market-related aspects of society already indexed by the National Income and Product Accounts (National Commission on Technology, Automation and Economic Progress 1966; Sheldon and Moore 1968). The need for social indicators also was emphasized by the publication of *Toward a Social Report* on the last day of the Johnson administration in 1969. The report was conceived of as a prototypical counterpart to the annual economic reports of the president, and each of its chapters addressed major issues in an area of social concern (health and illness; social mobility; the physical environment; income and poverty; public order and safety; learning, science, and art; and participation and alienation) and provided an assessment of the current conditions. In addition, the document firmly linked social indicators to the idea of systematic reporting on social issues for the purpose of public enlightenment.

Generally speaking, the sharp interest in social indicators in the 1960s grew out of the movement toward the collection and organization of national social, economic, and demographic data that began in Western societies in the seventeenth and eighteenth centuries and accelerated in the twentieth century (Carley 1981, pp. 14–15). The work of the sociologist William F. Ogburn and his collaborators at the University of Chicago in the 1930s and 1940s on the theory and measurement of social change is more proximate and sociologically germane (Land 1975). As chairman of President Herbert Hoover's Research Committee on Social Trends, Ogburn supervised the production of the two-volume *Recent Social Trends* (1933), a pathbreaking contribution to social reporting. Ogburn's ideas about the measurement of social change influenced several of his students—notably Albert D. Biderman, Otis Dudley Duncan, Albert J. Reiss, Jr., and Eleanor Bernert Sheldon—who played major roles in the emergence and development of the field of social indicators in the 1960s and 1970s.

Social Indicators in the 1970s and 1980s. At the end of the 1960s, the enthusiasm for social indicators was sufficiently strong and broad-based for Duncan (1969, p. 1) to write of the existence of a social indicators movement. In the early 1970s, this led to, among other things, the establishment in 1972, with National Science Foundation support, of the Social Science Research Council Center for Coordination of Research on Social Indicators in Washington, D.C.; the publication of several major efforts to define and develop a methodology for the measurement of indicators of subjective well-being (Campbell and Converse 1972; Andrews and Withey 1976; Campbell et al. 1976); the commencement of a federal government series of comprehensive social indicators books of charts, tables, and limited analyses (U.S. Department of Commerce 1974, 1978, 1980); the initiation of several continuing data series based on periodic sample surveys of the national population (such as the annual National Opinion Research Center's [NORC] General Social Survey and the annual National Crime Survey of the Bureau of Justice Statistics); the publication in 1974 of the first volume of the international journal *Social Indicators Research*; and the spread of social indicators and/or social reporting to numerous other nations and international agencies, such as the United Nations and the Organization for Economic Cooperation and Development.

Social indicators activities slowed in the 1980s as funding cuts and nonrenewals led to the closing of the Center for Coordination of Research on Social Indicators; the discontinuation of related work at several international agencies; the termination of government-sponsored social indicators reports in some countries, including the United States; and the reduction of statistical efforts to monitor various aspects of society. Several explanations have been cited for this slowdown (Andrews 1989; Bulmer 1989; Innes 1989; Johnston 1989; Rockwell 1987). Certainly, politics and the state of national economies in the early 1980s are among the most salient proximate causes. Administrations that came to power in the United States and elsewhere based decisions more on a "conservative ideology" and less on current social data than had been the case earlier. Also, faltering economies that produced large government budget deficits provided an incentive to make funding cuts. In addition to these immediate factors, there was a perceived lack of demonstrated usefulness of social indicators in public policymaking that was due in part to an overly simplistic view of how and under what conditions knowledge influences policy; this topic is treated more fully below in the discussion of current uses of social indicators. Before that, a more detailed discussion of types of indicators and their measurement and organization into accounting systems is necessary.

THREE TYPES OF SOCIAL INDICATORS

Criterion Indicators. On the basis of the premise that social indicators should relate directly to social policymaking considerations, an early definition by the economist Mancur Olson, the principal author of *Toward a Social Report*, characterized a social indicator as a "statistic of direct normative interest which facilitates concise, comprehensive and balanced judgments about the condition of major aspects of a society" (U.S. Department of Health, Education, and Welfare 1969, p. 97). Olson stated that such an indicator is in all cases a direct measure of welfare and is subject to the interpretation that if it changes in the "right" direction while other things remain equal, things have gotten better or people are better off. Accordingly, by this definition, statistics on the number of doctors or police officers could not be social indicators, whereas figures on health or crime rates could be.

In the language of policy analysis (Fox 1974, pp. 120–123), social indicators are "target" or "output" or "outcome" or "end-value" variables toward changes in which a public policy (program or project) is directed. This use of social indicators requires (Land 1983, p. 4) that (1) society agree about what needs improving, (2) it be possible to decide unambiguously what "getting better" means, and (3) it be meaningful to aggregate the indicators to the level of aggregation at which the policy is defined.

In recognition of the fact that other meanings have been attached to the term "social indicators," the tendency among recent authors is to use a somewhat different terminology for the class of indicators identified by Olson. For instance, Land (1983, p. 4) termed this the class of "normative welfare indicators." Building on the Olson approach, MacRae (1985, p. 5) defined "policy indicators" as "measures of those variables that are to be included in a broadly policy-relevant system of public statistics." With a meaning similar to that of MacRae, Ferriss (1989, p. 416) used the felicitous term "criterion indicators."

Life Satisfaction and/or Happiness Indicators. Another class of social indicators has its roots in the work of Campbell and Converse in the early 1970s. In *The Human Meaning of Social Change* (1972), they argued that the direct monitoring of key social-psychological states (attitudes, expectations, feelings, aspirations, and values) in the population is necessary for an understanding of social change and the quality of life. In this approach, social indicators are used to measure psychological satisfaction, happiness, and life fulfillment by employing survey research instruments that ascertain the subjective reality in which people live. The result may be termed "life satisfaction," "subjective well-being," or "happiness indicators."

The Campbell-Converse approach led to two major methodological studies in the 1970s (Andrews and Withey 1976; Campbell et al. 1976) and a subsequent edited volume (Andrews 1986) exploring the utility of various survey and analytic techniques for mapping individuals' feelings of satisfaction with numerous aspects ("domains") of their experiences. These studies examine domains ranging from the highly specific (house, family, etc.) to the global (life as a whole). A large number of other studies and applications of these concepts and techniques have appeared over the past three decades (for reviews, see Diener 1994; Diener et al. Smith1999; and Veenhoven 1996) and continue to appear; one or more studies of subjective well-being indicators can be found in almost every issue of *Social Indicators Research*. Research on the related concept of happiness as an index of well-being was surveyed by Veenhoven (1984).

The principle that the link between objective conditions and subjective well-being (defined in terms of responses to sample survey or interview questions about happiness or satisfaction with life as a whole) is sometimes paradoxical; therefore, the idea that subjective as well objective states should be monitored is well established in the social indicators literature. However, numerous studies of the measurement and psychodynamics of subjective well-being over the last three decades have led to a better understanding of this construct (Cummins 1995, 1998). While research continues and the debates have not been settled, it appears that this construct may have both *traitlike* (i.e., a durable psychological condition that differs among individuals and contributes to stability over time and consistency across situations) and *statelike* (i.e., a condition that is reactive to situational differences) properties (Stones et al. 1995; Veenhoven 1994, 1998).

With respect to the statelike properties of subjective well-being, Davis (1984) used an accumulated sample from several years of NORC General Social Surveys to document the responsiveness of happiness with life as a whole to (1) "new money" (recent changes in the respondents' financial status compared with the current income level), (2) "an old man/lady" (being married or having an intimate living partner), and (3) "two's company" (a household size of two compared to living alone or in a family of three or more). Many other studies have found additional factors that are more or less strongly associated with variations in subjective well-being, but the relevance of intimate living conditions and/or family status almost always is replicated. The connection of subjective well-being to income levels has been an intriguing problem for social indicators researchers since Easterlin's (1973) finding that income differences between nations predict national differences in happiness but that the association of happiness with income within countries is much weaker (for a review of this research literature, see Ahuvia and Friedman 1998). However, Davis's finding of a positive relationship between "new money" or recent income changes and happiness has been replicated by Saris (1998), using data from a panel study conducted in Russia in the period 1993–1995.

Descriptive Social Indicators. Building on Ogburn's legacy of research on social trends, a third approach to social indicators focuses on social measurements and analyses designed to improve the understanding of what the main features of society are, how they interrelate, and how these features and their relationships change (Sheldon and Parke 1975, p. 696). This produces *descriptive social indictors*—indices of the state of society and the changes taking place within it. Although descriptive social indicators may be more or less directly (causally) related to the well-being goals of public policies or programs and thus include policy or criterion indicators, they are not limited to such uses. For instance, in the area of health, descriptive indicators may include preventive indicators such as the percentage of the population that does not smoke cigarettes as well as criterion indicators such as the number of days of activity limitations in the past month and an index of self-reported satisfaction with health. Ferriss (1990) published a compilation of descriptive indicators for the United States at the end of the 1980s; regularly published national social indicator compilations for other nations also contain numerous examples.

The various statistical forms descriptive social indicators can take are described by Land (1983, p. 6). These forms can be ordered by degree of abstraction from those which require only one or two data series and little processing (e.g., an age-specific death rate) to those which involve more complicated processing into a single summary index (e.g., years of life expectancy at a given age and years of active or disability-free life expectancy at a given age). Descriptive social indicators can be formulated at any of these levels of abstraction. Moreover, as described in Juster and Land (1981), these indicators can, at least in principle, be organized into demographic- or time-budget-based systems of social accounts.

THE ENLIGHTENMENT FUNCTION: MONITORING, SOCIAL REPORTING, AND FORECASTING

The social indicators movement was motivated by the principle that it is important to *monitor changes over time* in a broad range of social phenomena that extend beyond the traditional economic indicators and include *indicators of quality of life* (Andrews 1989, p. 401; Noll and Zapf 1994, p. 5). Many organized actors in contemporary society—including government agencies, organizations and activists interested in social change programs, scholars, and marketing researchers interested in market development and product innovations—monitor indicators in which they have a vested interest and want to see increase or decline (Ferriss 1988, p. 603).

A second principle that has been part of the social indicators movement from the outset (Biderman 1970; Land 1996) is that a critically important role of social indicators in contemporary democratic societies is *public enlightenment through social reporting*. In brief, modern democracies require social reporting to describe social trends, explain why an indicator series behaves as it does and how this knowledge affects interpretation, and highlight important relationships among series (Parke and Seidman 1978, p. 15).

It also is important to document the consequences that are reasonably attributable to changes in a series. This includes the systematic use of social indicators to *forecast trends in and/or turning points in social conditions* (Land 1983, p. 21). The area of projection or forecasting is filled with uncertainties. Techniques range from the naive extrapolation of recent trends to future scenario construction to complicated model building with regression, time series, or stochastic process techniques. Moreover, there appear to be intrinsic limits to the accuracy of forecasts in large-scale natural and social systems (Land and Schneider 1987). However, demands for the anticipation of the future (at a minimum, a description of "what will happen if present trends continue"), foresight and forward thinking in the public and private sectors, and the assessment of critical trends (Gore 1990) appear to be an intrinsic part of contemporary postindustrial societies. Thus, it is prudent to expect that "anticipation" will become an increasingly important part of the enlightenment function of social indicators.

Social Reporting at the Turn of the Century. As the decade of the 1990s unfolded, the model of a comprehensive national social report in the tradition pioneered by Ogburn and Olson clearly faltered in the United States, at least in the sense of federal government sponsorship and/or production. However, the key ideas of monitoring, reporting, and forecasting were evident to a greater or lesser extent in the production of continuing periodic subject-matter-specific publications by various federal agencies, including *Science Indicators* (published by the National Science Foundation), *The Condition of Education* (published by the Department of Education), the *Report to the Nation on Crime and Justice* (published by the Department of Justice), and numerous Census Bureau publications. Special topics involving groups of federal agencies also receive attention from time to time. For instance, in 1997 the Federal Interagency Forum on Child and Family Statistics began the annual publication *America's Children: Key National Indicators of Well-Being*. In addition, numerous private research organizations, policy institutes, and scholars continue to produce reports, monographs, and books interpreting social trends and developments in several areas of social concern.

In contrast to the situation in the United States, comprehensive social reports and social indicators compendiums continue to be published periodically in several other countries. Examples are the *Social Trends* series published annually since 1970 by the United Kingdom's Central Statistical Office, the *Datenreport* series published biennially since 1983 by the Federal Republic of Germany, the *Social and Cultural Report* published biennially by the Social and Cultural Planning Office of the Netherlands, and *Australian Social Trends* published annually by the Australian Bureau of Statistics. Citations and summary reviews of these and other social indicators and social reports publications can be found in the quarterly newsletter and review of social reports *SINET: Social Indicators Network News* (see the World Wide Web home page: http://www.soc.duke.edu/dept/sinet/index.html).

The difference between the organization of social indicators and reporting work in the United States and that in other countries is in part attributable to the lack of a central statistical office responsible for the coordination of all government statistical activities in the United States. More generally, it is indicative of the fact that despite the invention of the ideas of social indicators and comprehensive social reporting in the United States, this nation has lagged in their institutionalization (Johnston 1989). Whether a new round of legislative efforts (e.g., then-Senator Albert Gore, Jr.'s, proposed Critical Trends Assessment Act [Gore 1990]) will create the necessary institutional base remains to be seen. Perhaps marking a turning point and indicative of things to come is Public Law 100-297, enacted April 28, 1988, which requires an annual education indicators report to the president and Congress.

Quality of Life as a Unifying Concept. Another development became vividly apparent in the 1990s (Land 1996): the widespread political, popular, and theoretical appeal of the "quality-of-life" (QOL) concept. As was noted above, this concept emerged and became part of the social indicators movement in the late 1960s and early 1970s as doubts were raised in highly developed Western industrial societies about economic growth as the major goal of societal progress (Noll and Zapf 1994, pp. 1–2). The "social costs" of economic growth were cited, and there was increasing doubt about whether "more" should be equated with "better." The QOL concept that resulted from this discussion was posed as an alternative to the increasingly questionable concept of the affluent society and entered discussions of social policy and politics as a new but more complex multidimensional goal. As a goal of social and economic policy, QOL encompasses all (or at least many) domains of life and subsumes, in addition to individual material and immaterial well-being, collective values such as freedom, justice, and the guarantee of natural conditions of life for present and future generations. The political use of the idea of QOL is paralleled in the private sector by the widespread use and popularity of numerous rankings—based on weighted scales of multiple domains of well-being—of the "best" places to live, work, do business, play, and so on, whether they are cities, states, regions, or nations.

The theoretical appeal of the QOL concept as an integrating notion in the social sciences and related disciplines is due in part to the perceived importance of measuring individuals' subjective assessments of their satisfaction with various life domains and with life as a whole, as was reviewed above. For instance, QOL has become a concept that bridges the discipline of marketing research and strategic business policy with social indicators. Marketing is an importance social force—with far-reaching direct and indirect impacts on the prevailing QOL in a society—through consumer satisfaction (Samli 1987; Sirgy and Samli 1995) and its impact on satisfaction with life as a whole. The intersection of marketing research with social indicators through the QOL concept led to the organization in the mid-1990s of the International Society for Quality-of-Life Studies (for information about the society and its activities, see its Web homepage: http://www.cob.vt.edu/market/isqols/). Sociologists who want to become more involved in the field of social indicators should participate in this international and interdisciplinary society.

Summary Indices of the Quality of Life. As the twenty-first century approaches, it is evident that the field of social indicators is entering a new era of the construction of summary social indicators. Often these indices attempt to summarize indicators (objective and/or subjective) of a number of domains of life into a single index of the quality of life. They thus attempt to answer one of the original questions that motivated the social indicators movement: How are we doing overall in terms of the quality of life? With respect to our past? With respect to other comparable units (e.g., cities, states, regions, nations)? Many pioneers of the social indicators movement in the 1960s and 1970s backed away from the development of summary indices to concentrate on conducting basic research on social indicators and the measurement of the quality of life and the development of a richer social database. With the tremendous increase in the quality of social data available for many societies today compared to two or three decades in the past, a new generation of social indicators researchers has returned to the task of summary index construction. Some examples are (1) at the level of the broadest possible comparisons of nations with respect to the overall quality of life, the Human Development Index (United Nations Development Programme 1993), Diener's (1995) Value-Based Index of National Quality of Life, and Estes's (1988, 1998) Index of Social Progress and (2) at the level of comparisons at the national level over time in the United States, the *American Demographics Index of Well-Being* (Kacapyr 1996), *The Fordham Index of Social Health* (Miringoff 1996), and the *Genuine Progress Indicator* (Redefining Progress 1995). The field of social indicators probably will see several decades of such index construction and competition among various indices, with a corresponding need for careful assessments to determine which indices have substantive validity for which populations in the assessment of the quality of life and its changes over time and across social space.

THE POLICY ANALYSIS FUNCTION: POLICY GUIDANCE AND DIRECTED SOCIAL CHANGE

Policy analysts distinguish various ways of guiding or affecting public policy, including *problem definition, policy choice and evaluation of alternatives,* and *program monitoring* (MacRae 1985, pp. 20–29). The social reporting–public enlightenment approach to social indicators centers on the use of social indicators in problem definition and the framing of the terms of policy discourse. Indeed, studies of the actual use of social indicators suggest that this is precisely the manner in which they have affected public action (Innes 1989).

However, policy analysts from Olson to MacRae always have hoped for more from social indicators: the shaping of public policy and planing through the policy choice process. At a minimum, this requires the identification of key variables that determine criterion indicators and changes in them

(i.e., causal knowledge). More generally, it requires the construction of elaborate causal models and forecasting equations (often in the form of a "computer model") that can be used to simulate "what would happen if" under a variety of scenarios involving policies and actions. An example of this is the development of the National Cancer Institute model for the control and reduction of the incidence of cancer in the United States to the year 2000 (Greenwald and Sondik 1986). Various policy and action scenarios involving prevention, education, screening, and treatment and their implications for cancer mortality were simulated and estimated with this computer model. These simulations led to a decision to allocate funds to prevention, education, screening, and treatment, and their implications for cancer mortality were simulated and estimated with this computer model. These simulations led to a decision to allocate funds to a prevention program rather than to additional clinical treatment.

At a more discursive level, the following *model for directed social change* has emerged in policy uses of social indicators in areas such as health, education, and the welfare of children and youth in the United States (Ferriss 1998):

1. *Identify trends in criterion indicators*, the direction or rate of change of which should be changed.

2. *Gather intelligence* from experiments, field research, or theory that suggests what should be done to bring about the desired change.

3. *Launch a decentralized program to effect change in specific criterion indicators* by specific amounts, to be attained by a target date.

4. *Monitor progress* by periodically assessing trends on the specific indicators, modifying strategies as needed.

5. As initial goals are reached, *set new goals* for continued progress.

Many more applications of social indicators to policy choice and evaluation are likely to appear in the future. In particular, such applications probably will occur in three areas. The first is the additional development of well-grounded, theoretically informed, and policy-relevant indicators and models for national and/or regional-level analyses in fields such as health, education, crime, and science (Bulmer 1989). In such applications, the phenomena to be included are definable and delimited and the limitations of the data on which the indicators are based are known. The second is the use of social indicators in the field of social impact assessment (Finsterbusch 1980; Land 1982), which has arisen as part of environmental impact assessment legislation and attempts to anticipate the social effects of large-scale public projects (e.g., dams, highways, nuclear waste disposal facilities) as well as to assess damage from both natural and human-made disasters (e.g., earthquakes, oil spills, nuclear plant accidents). This application of social indicators in impact assessments brings the field back full circle to its point of origination in the American Academy's effort of the 1960s. Finally, the many times series of indicators now available will increasingly be used by sociologists to assess theories, hypotheses, and models of social change, thus bringing social indicators data to bear on core issues in sociology.

(SEE ALSO: *Attitudes; Longitudinal Research; Public Opinion; Quality of Life; Social Change; Social Forecasting*)

REFERENCES

Ahuvia, Aaron C., and Douglas C. Friedman 1998 "Income, Consumption, and Subjective Well-Being: Toward a Composite Macromarketing Model." *Journal of Macromarketing* 18:153–168.

Andrews, Frank M., ed. 1986 *Research on the Quality of Life*. Ann Arbor, Mich.: Institute for Social Research.

—— 1989 "The Evolution of a Movement." *Journal of Public Policy* 9:401–405.

——, and Stephen B. Withey 1976 *Social Indicators of Well-Being: Americans' Perceptions of Life Quality*. New York: Plenum.

Bauer, Raymond A., ed. 1966 *Social Indicators*. Cambridge, Mass.: MIT Press.

Biderman, Albert D. 1970 "Information, Intelligence, Enlightened Public Policy: Functions and Organization of Societal Feedback." *Policy Sciences* 1:217–230.

Bulmer, Martin 1989 "Problems of Theory and Measurement." *Journal of Public Policy* 9:407–412.

Campbell, Angus, and Philip E. Converse 1972 *The Human Meaning of Social Change*. New York: Russell Sage Foundation.

——, ——, and Willard L. Rodgers 1976 *The Quality of American Life: Perceptions, Evaluations, and Satisfactions*. New York: Russell Sage Foundation.

Carley, Michael 1981 *Social Measurement and Social Indicators: Issues of Policy and Theory*. London: Allen and Unwin.

Cummins, Robert A. 1995 "On the Trail of the Gold Standard for Subjective Well-Being." *Social Indicators Research* 35:170–200.

—— 1998 "The Second Approximation to an International Standard for Life Satisfaction." *Social Indicators Research* 43:307–334.

Davis, James A. 1984 "New Money, An Old Man/Lady and "Two's Company': Subjective Welfare in the NORC General Social Survey." *Social Indicators Research* 15:319–351.

Diener, Ed 1994 "Assessing Subjective Well-Being: Progress and Opportunities." *Social Indicators Research* 31:103–157.

—— 1995 "A Value-Based Index for Measuring National Quality of Life." *Social Indicators Research* 36:107–127.

——, Eunkook M. Suh, Richard E. Lucas, and Heidi L. Smith 1999 "Subjective Well-Being: Three Decades of Progress." *Psychological Bulletin* 110: forthcoming.

Duncan, Otis Dudley 1969 *Toward Social Reporting: Next Steps*. New York: Russell Sage Foundation.

Easterlin, Richard 1973 "Does Money Buy Happiness?" *The Public Interest* 30:3–10.

Estes, Richard J. 1988 *Trends in World Development*. New York: Praeger.

—— 1998 "Social Development Trends in Transition Economies. In K. R. Hope, Sr., ed., *Challenges of Transformation and Transition from Centrally Planned to Market Economies*. Nagoya, Japan: United Nations Centre for Regional Development.

Ferriss, Abbott L. 1988 "The Uses of Social Indicators." *Social Forces* 66:601–617.

—— 1989 "Whatever Happened, Indeed!" *Journal of Public Policy* 9:413–417.

—— 1990 "The Quality of Life in the United States." *SINET: Social Indicators Network News* 21:1–8.

—— 1998 "Slow Progress toward Education 2000 Goals." *SINET: Social Indicators Network News* 53:11–12.

Finsterbusch, Kurt 1980 *Understanding Social Impacts: Assessing the Effects of Public Projects*. Beverly Hills Calif.: Sage.

Fox, Karl A. 1974 *Social Indicators and Social Theory: Elements of an Operational System*. New York: Wiley-Interscience.

Gore, Albert, Jr., 1990 "The Critical Trends Assessment Act: Futurizing the United States Government." *The Futurist* 24:22–28.

Greenwald, Peter, and Edward J. Sondik, eds. 1986 *Cancer Control Objectives for the Nation: 1985–2000*, NCI Monographs 2. Washington, D.C.: U.S. Government Printing Office.

Innes, Judith Eleanor 1989 "Disappointment and Legacies of Social Indicators." *Journal of Public Policy* 9:429–432.

Johnston, Denis F. 1989 "Some Reflections on the United States." *Journal of Public Policy* 9:433–436.

Juster, F. Thomas, and Kenneth C. Land, eds. 1981 *Social Accounting Systems: Essays on the State of the Art.* New York: Academic Press.

Kacapyr, Elia 1996 "The Well-Being Index." *American Demographics* 18:32–43.

Land, Kenneth C. 1975 "Theories, Models and Indicators of Social Change." *International Social Science Journal* 27:7–37.

—— 1982 "Ex Ante and Ex Post Assessment of the Social Consequences of Public Projects and Policies." *Contemporary Sociology* 11:512–514.

—— 1983 "Social Indicators." *Annual Review of Sociology* 9:1–26.

—— 1996 "Social Indicators and the Quality-of-Life: Where Do We Stand in the Mid-1990s?" *SINET: Social Indicators Network News* 45:5–8.

——, and Stephen H. Schneider 1987 "Forecasting in the Social and Natural Sciences: An Overview and Statement of Isomorphisms." In K. C. Land and S. H. Schneider, eds., *Forecasting in the Social and Natural Sciences*. Boston: Reidel.

MacRae, Duncan, Jr., 1985 *Policy Indicators: Links between Social Science and Public Policy.* Chapel Hill: University of North Carolina Press.

Miringoff, Marc L. 1996 *1996 Index of Social Health.* Tarrytown, N.Y.: Fordham Institute for Innovation in Social Policy.

National Commission on Technology, Automation and Economic Progress 1966 *Technology and the American Economy*, vol. 1. Washington, D.C.: U.S. Government Printing Office.

Noll, Heinz-Herbert, and Wolfgang Zapf 1994 "Social Indicators Research: Societal Monitoring and Social Reporting." In I. Borg and P. P. Mohler, eds., *Trends and Perspectives in Empirical Social Research*. New York: Walter de Gruyter.

Parke, Robert, and David Seidman 1978 "Social Indicators and Social Reporting." *Annuals of the American Academy of Political and Social Science* 435:1–22.

President's Research Committee on Social Trends 1933 *Recent Trends in the United States*. New York: McGraw-Hill.

Redefining Progress 1995 *The Genuine Progress Indicator: Summary of Data and Methodology.* San Francisco: Redefining Progress.

Rockwell, Richard C. 1987 "Prospect for Social Reporting in the United States: A Receding Horizon." In Jesse R. Pitts and Henri Mendras, eds., *The Tocqueville Review*, vol. 8. Charlottesville: University Press of Virginia.

Samli, A. Coskun 1987 *Marketing and the Quality-of-Life Interface.* Westport, Conn.: Quorum.

Saris, Willem E. 1998 "The Strength of the Causal Relationship between Living Conditions and Satisfaction." Paper presented at the fourteenth World Congress of Sociology Meeting, Montreal, Canada, July 26–August 1, 1998.

Sheldon, Eleanor B., and Wilbert E. Moore, eds. 1968 *Indicators of Social Change: Concepts and Measurements.* New York: Russell Sage Foundation.

——, and Robert Parke 1975 "Social Indicator." *Science* 188:693–699.

Sirgy, M. Joseph, and A. Coskun Samli, eds. 1995 *New Dimensions in Marketing/Quality-of-Life Research.* Westport, Conn.: Quorum.

Stones, M. J., T. Hadjistavropoulos, J. Tuuko, and A. Kozma 1995 "Happiness Has Traitlike and Statelike Properties." *Social Indicators Research* 36:129–144.

United Nations Development Programme 1993 *Human Development Report 1993*. New York: Oxford University Press.

U.S. Department of Commerce 1974 *Social Indicators, 1973.* Washington, D.C.: U.S. Government Printing Office.

—— 1978 *Social Indicators, 1977.* Washington, D.C.: U.S. Government Printing Office.

—— 1980 *Social Indicators, III.* Washington, D.C.: U.S. Government Printing Office.

U.S. Department of Health, Education, and Welfare 1969 *Toward a Social Report.* Washington, D.C.: U.S. Government Printing Office.

Veerhoven, Ruut 1984 *Conditions of Happiness.* Boston: Reidel.

—— 1994 "Is Happiness a Trait? Tests of the Theory That a Better Society Does Not Make People Any Happier." *Social Indicators Research* 33:101–160.

—— 1996 "Developments in Satisfaction Research." *Social Indicators Research* 37:1–46.

—— 1998 "Two State-Trait Discussions on Happiness: A Reply to Stones et al." *Social Indicators Research* 43:211–225.

KENNETH C. LAND

SOCIAL INEQUALITY

Social inequality refers to the graduated dimensions (Blau 1977), vertical classifications (Ossowski 1963: Schwartz 1981) and bounded categories (Tilly 1998), or hierarchical relations (Burt 1982) by which human populations at varying levels of aggregation are differentiated. This concept is among the oldest and most diversely defined in sociology, extending back at least as far as Plato's conception of the republic and developed subsequently in the social theories of Marx [1859] 1976–1978, Mosca (1939), Weber [1947] 1978, Simmel (1896), Sorokin (1941), Eisenstadt (1971), Merton (1968), and others. The construct often is used interchangeably with related (though relatively more specific) concepts such as social class, social stratification, socioeconomic status, power, privilege, cumulative advantage, dependence, and dominance. It is relevant for the study of social systems that range in size from the dyad (Simmel 1896) to the modern world system (Wallerstein 1974).

SOCIAL INEQUALITY AS A GRADUATED DIMENSION

When social inequality is conceptualized as a graduated dimension, it is treated as a distributional phenomenon. Here the approach is to define inequality in terms of the distribution of socially valued attributes such as education, income, information, health, and influence in a population. However, distributional phenomena can be examined from one of two very different assumptions. The first assumption views inequality as being an outcome of or generated by the underlying distribution of valued traits among individuals. In this sense, it refers to "regular differences in power, goods, services, and privileges among defined sets" of actors (Granovetter and Tilly 1988). The second assumption views inequality strictly as a system-level property with individual-level differences that are defined as derivative rather than generative (Blau 1977). Distributions such as the size of the system and its total volume of resources are examined as higher levels of aggregation, with the goal of determining the overall level of inequality (oligarchy) across systems and without reference to individual differences (e.g., Lenski 1966; Mayhew 1973; Mayhew and Schollaert 1980).

Both approaches operationalize inequality along criteria that usually are measurable at the level of individual actors (persons, races, gender categories, organizations, nation-states) in a system. Early applications of the first assumption can be found in Pareto's ([1897] 1980) examinations of income distributions and the circulation of elites. Pareto proposed that economic and political inequality emerged from the distribution and redistribution of "congenital abilities" that were valued within social systems. Sorokin (1941) proposed similar arguments to explain social and cultural processes of mobility and inequality.

Among the most influential and controversial conceptualizations of inequality as a graduated dimension emerging from individual differences was Davis and Moore's (1945) functionalist statement of the principles of stratification. Those authors argued that social inequality results from the differential distribution of societal rewards to individuals on the basis of their relative achievement of ranked social positions. This achievement process, with its implications for social mobility, was formally specified by Blau and Duncan (1967), who established that educational attainment mediated the process of intergenerational social mobility among men. Those researchers defined social inequality as socioeconomic status based on the economic and prestige rewards accorded to achieved occupational positions in American society. The strong parallel between this model of inequality and the neoclassical model of human capital (see Becker 1964) is well established (Wright 1978).

The most prominent distributional theories of inequality, however, are founded on macrosocial views of the division of labor, the rationalization of authority, and the distribution of social and economic rewards in industrial societies. Weber's ([1947] 1978) theory of economic organization proposed that capitalist systems of property, power, and prestige developed out of the conjunction of changing systems of economic exchange (money economies) and accounting (double-entry bookkeeping) with rationalized systems of social control (rational-legal authority). Thus, social inequality in industrial society developed along economic and political dimensions to produce the multidimensional bases of inequality: class, status, and party. Lenski's (1966) comparative study of the evolution of inequality attempted to test Weber's rationalization thesis that inequality evolves necessarily (functionally) with increasing differentiation in the direction of systems of privilege based on rational authority and away from socially illegitimate systems of force or economic dominance.

Accordingly, distributional inequality can be concerned with more than the single dimension of individual socioeconomic outcomes. It also addresses macrosocial patterns of inequality (Eisenstadt 1971). According to Blau (1977), the parameters of social structure include inequality and heterogeneity—or graduated and nominal dimensions, respectively—which intersect to constrain and differentiate individuals' opportunities as well as their motivations and outcomes. The intersection of graduated and nominal parameters creates diverse systems or populations with differing distributional properties that cannot be reduced to an original individual source. Blau's distributional theory is "macrosocial in the sense that the 'cases' are populations or communities and the 'variables' measure some aspect (a rate or a distributional property) of these populations" (Skvoretz and Fararo 1986, p. 30). Following this approach, indicators of inequality can be defined in terms such as Lorenz curves (e.g., Gini indices, Theil coefficients), social welfare functions, or similar distributional properties (see Allison 1978; Wolfson 1997).

The emergence of the new global economy over the last two decades of the twentieth century has been associated with what has been characterized as a "surge" in wage and household income inequality (Gottschalk and Smeeding 1997) and a "winner-take-all income market" (Levy 1998) in advanced industrial countries. By and large, the growth of very high incomes in some sectors and the stagnation of wages in selected labor markets have produced a widening distribution of income. Distributional measures of economic inequality such as Gini and Theil coefficients reveal growing inequality among employed workers across advanced industrial societies with some of the highest inequality observed in the United States.

Economic inequality also may intersect with the nominal category of race, for example, and produce more diverse outcomes than traditional functional or neoclassical economic theories would predict. Examinations of patterns of interracial/interethnic marriage, for example, indicate that the association between occupational achievement and race is mediated by the extent of interracial/interethnic marriage in a community (see Blum 1984; Blau et al. 1982). This treatment of inequality, which is based on notions of dispersion and association, departs from the simple reduction of unequal outcomes to individual attributes and embeds the process in extended distributional contexts.

Other distributional approaches introduce constructs to explain inequality at levels above individual attributes, although individuals usually remain the units of analysis. Spatial and temporal contexts, for example, define and constrain distributions of individual outcomes. The examination of occupational mobility within organizational or labor-market contexts attempts to nest the process of inequality in the workplace within organizational and occupational boundaries. The availability of occupational positions within a system is seen as being independent of the motivations and other attributes of workers. White's (1970) influential notion of "vacancy chains" exemplifies this approach with its argument that job vacancies produce opportunity structures for individual mobility and define the mobility chances, and thus distributional outcomes, of individuals. Vacancy-chain models have been particularly useful for examining closed opportunity systems, such as internal labor markets (Sorensen 1977).

Distributions of individuals in systems of inequality also are influenced by temporal factors. Merton's (1968) provocative discussion of the "Matthew effect" in scientific career systems argues that over time, initial inequalities in a system bias distributional outcomes in favor of initial advantage. Formal extensions and applications of Merton's notion of accumulative advantage have been applied across contexts (Cole and Cole 1973; Allison and Stewart 1974) to establish patterns of temporal regulation of distributional outcomes over and above the attributes of individuals over time. The cumulative advantage hypothesis has received considerable attention in research on the relationship between age and inequality within cohorts (Dannefer

1987; O'Rand and Henretta 1999). Succeeding cohorts of U.S. populations display growing inequality across the age span, with higher coefficients of inequality at older ages within cohorts and (in recent decades) increased inequality among the aged in successive cohorts (Crystal 1995).

SOCIAL INEQUALITY AS A VERTICAL CLASSIFICATION OR BOUNDED CATEGORY

When social inequality is conceptualized as a vertical classification system, it is treated as an oppositional phenomenon. Here the approach is to define inequality in terms of "the relative position in a matrix of oppositions" (Schwartz 1981, p. 94) of social categories that determine relations of dominance, such as class, race, and gender. Vertical classifications grow out of antagonistic and contradictory interests in the relations of "objective" positions in the social division of labor, not out of the dispersed motivations and interests of individuals. Dominance and subordination emerge from the objective opposition of social categories. Dichotomous, binary, and polar conceptions of inequality (e.g., ruler–ruled, rich–poor, white–black, masculine–feminine) generally are informed by an oppositional framework. Some researchers have argued that this approach to inequality may be the most ancient in human social consciousness (Ossowski 1963; Schwartz 1981).

Class theories that follow Marxian frameworks dominate this approach (Braverman 1974; Wright 1985). Marx's theory of class proposes that class relations in capitalist systems are inevitably in conflict. Since all value is ultimately produced by labor, all (capitalist) profit must be at the expense of labor. The objective positions of the owning class (bourgeoisie) and the laboring class (proletariat) therefore are necessarily antagonistic. Advanced capitalist systems sustain the exploitation of labor through rationalized job-definition systems and the degradation of work (Braverman 1974). Wright (1978) has argued, furthermore, that in advanced capitalist societies, the elaborate differentiation of functions originally embodied in entrepreneurial capitalism into many different categories has not overcome the fundamental oppositional inequality of its origins; contradictory class positions continue to exist as a result of the underlying structure of capitalist relations.

Oppositional frameworks lend themselves to the examination of classlike relations such as those observable in race- and gender-centered systems of inequality. Oppositional approaches to the examination of race inequality can be traced to Myrdal's (1944) pioneering analysis of racial exploitation in the U.S. context. These approaches argue that race is an invariant principle of vertical classification that is masked by ideologies of economic progress and attainment (Pinkney 1984). Debates regarding the inevitability of racial opposition as the basis of inequality center on the substitutability of race and class as categories in the recent history of U.S. inequality. Wilson (1980) has proposed the controversial argument that class inequality has superseded race inequality as the basis of cross-race differences in economic and social outcomes.

Theories of gender inequality extend back to Mill's libertarian essay on the subjection of women (Mill 1859) and Engels's Marxian analysis two decades later (Engels [1884] 1942) of the relationship between private property and the stratification of family (gender) roles. However, contemporary feminist theories provide the strongest argument for gender inequality as an oppositional, vertical classification system. The sex/gender system, it is argued, subordinates women in patriarchal relations that exist over and above class relations (Jaggar 1984), since male dominance over women's productive and reproductive roles predates the emergence of capitalism (Harding 1983). This system of inequality leads inevitably to a conflict of interests and to the emergence of competing ideologies.

Since the notion of dominance is central to vertical-classification approaches to inequality, these approaches are readily applied to the analysis of large-scale systems of inequality, such as the state (Skocpol 1979) and the modern world system (Wallerstein 1974). Mechanisms of domination extend beyond class (or classlike) interests and are observable in the historical relations of nation-states (Reddy 1987) and multistate sectors of the modern world system (Wallerstein 1974). Asymmetrical relations of exchange and dependence between states and geopolitical state sectors create relations of dominance, which define global inequalities. Those inequalities can be formulated as distributional phenomena by following a functional framework; however, the historical analysis of dominance systems lends itself more readily to oppositional analysis. The classification of the world system into core and periphery sectors that resulted from historically contingent factors introduces notions of centrality and dominance that suggest more than an underlying distribution of resources (Wallerstein 1974).

Tilly's (1998) statement on "durable inequalities" argues that persistent inequalities based on exploitation, opportunity hoarding, adaptation, and emulation largely take the form of bounded (usually dichotomous) categories (male–female, slave–owner, citizen–foreigner, white–black, etc.) that are resilient and readily generalizable across time and social systems. Relationships of inequality persist because participants in paired categories adapt to and participate in the perpetuation of those arrangements.

SOCIAL INEQUALITY AS HIERARCHICAL RELATIONS

When social inequality is conceptualized as hierarchical relations, it is treated as a system of interactions or interdependencies characterized by relative symmetry (equality) and asymmetry (inequality) among relations. Here the approach usually is to define the form of social relations rather than the attributes of individuals in those relations and to account for patterns of unequal relations without referring to oppositions. Inequality or dominance stems from positions in hierarchical relations, not from the a priori possession or control of resources or power by individuals, groups, or categories (Marsden 1983). This relational approach to inequality can be traced to Simmel (1896), whose studies of the structures of superordination–subordination by persons, groups, and principles continue to inform research on hierarchical relations and social networks in modern life (Coleman 1982).

Because social relationships have formal properties such as connectedness, transitivity, reciprocity, and multiplexity, they are measurable units of analysis in the study of social inequality within populations at all levels, from siblings to communities to transnational trading systems (Lin and Marsden 1982). These social units make up complex configurations of social relations within which distinctive positions of relative equivalence or cen-

trality can be revealed (Burt 1982). Thus, in their study of coalitions and elite structures in the German community of Altneustadt, Laumann and Pappi (1976) determined the relational bases of influence between natives and newcomers by using network techniques that emphasized associational patterns rather than personal attributes. Patterns of social distance and connectedness among corporate actors, not the preexisting distribution of resources, defined the influence process in that community.

A study by Granovetter (1974) of the job-search process clearly demonstrates the relative utility of relational over distributional approaches to inequality. Granovetter demonstrates that weak ties, rather than strong ties, in a community prevail in a successful job search. The "strength of weak ties" hypothesis (related to Simmel's *tertius gaudens*, or the third who enjoys) provides the counterintuitive argument that weaker (secondary) social contacts increase individuals' access to jobs more than stronger (primary) ties do. These ties operate independently of the attributes of individual job seekers.

The "strength of weak ties" phenomenon can be extended beyond the job-search process to examine structures of relational inequality in different contexts. Studies of interlocking directorates and informational brokerage systems, for example, demonstrate that loosely coupled relational systems of different forms produce different systems of social inequality (Burt 1982). The network of ties constitutes a social-constraint context within which actors are "captured." Burt's (1983) study of corporate philanthropy as a cooptive relation is a specific example of the relational bases of inequality in a market context. Using Internal Revenue Service data on firm expenditures for advertising and philanthropy, Burt demonstrates that firm philanthropy co-opts the household sector by legitimizing the firm to the public as a protector and by improving the ability of specific classes to purchase the firm's products (Burt 1983, p. 424). The strength of this approach is that advertising, which is more blatantly co-optive, does not escape public suspicion, whereas philanthropy does so more easily. Firms in an economic sector perform unequally as a result of their relative co-optive relations with the public, and the public has a co-optive relationship as consumers in that context.

Finally, it should be mentioned that despite the rationale provided above for the bulk of sociological research on relational inequality, the relational approach has been used to examine the importance of individual resources for social inequality. Indeed, early experimental efforts to study small group processes of inequality demonstrated that both individual resources and social relations can create systems of inequality, whether measured as leadership processes or as communication networks (Thibaut and Kelley 1959). More recently, studies of what Burt (1982) has termed "ego-centered" networks examine network position itself as an individual resource with implications for social inequality.

APPROACHES TO SOCIAL INEQUALITY

The three major approaches to the study of social inequality outlined above have different implications for theory as well as for method. The distributional approach that examines social inequality as a graduated dimension depends primarily on sample data and can be directed toward individual as well as structural explanations of inequality. The oppositional approach to vertical classifications and bounded categories may use sample data but has tended to adopt historical and qualitative approaches to study the institutionalization of dominance in various forms, such as class, race, and gender, as well as other forms of domination/subordination. The relational approach, which provides a direct method for examining the social context of inequality, may use sample or case data to map the configurations of the relations of inequality with implications for explanation at both the individual and structural levels.

(SEE ALSO: *Equality of Opportunity; Social Stratification*)

REFERENCES

Allison, Paul D. 1978 "Measures of Inequality." *American Sociological Review* 43:865–880.

——, and John A. Stewart 1974 "Productivity Differences among Scientists: Evidence for Accumulative Advantage." *American Sociological Review* 99:596–606.

Becker, Gary S. 1964 *Human Capital*. Chicago: University of Chicago Press.

Blau, Peter M. 1977 *Inequality and Heterogeneity*. New York: Free Press.

——, Terry C. Blum, and Joseph E. Schwartz 1982 "Heterogeneity and Intermarriage." *American Sociological Review* 47:45–62.

——, and Otis Dudley Duncan 1967 *The American Occupational Structure*. New York: Wiley.

Blum, Terry C. 1984 "Racial Inequality and Salience: An Examination of Blau's Theory of Social Structure." *Social Forces* 62:607–617.

Braverman, Harry 1974 "Labor and Monopoly Capital: The Degradation of Work in the Twentieth Century." *Monthly Review* 26:1–134.

Burt, Ronald S. 1982 *Toward a Structural Theory of Action: Network Models of Social Structure, Perception, and Action*. New York: Academic Press.

——, 1983 "Corporate Philanthropy as a Cooptive Relation." *Social Forces* 62:419–449.

Cole, Jonathan R., and Stephen Cole 1973 *Social Stratification in Science*. Chicago: University of Chicago Press.

Coleman, James S. 1982 *The Asymmetric Society*. Syracuse, N.Y.: Syracuse University Press.

Crystal, Stephen 1995 "Economic Status of the Elderly." In Robert H. Binstock and Linda K. George, eds., *Handbook of Aging and the Social Sciences*, 4th ed. New York: Academic Press.

Dannefer, Dale 1987. "Aging As Intracohort Differentiation: Accentuation, The Matthew Effect, and the Life Course." Sociological Forum 2: 211–236.

Davis, Kingsley, and Wilbert E. Moore 1945 "Some Principles of Stratification." *American Sociological Review* 10:242–249.

Eisenstadt, S. M. 1971 *Social Differentiation and Stratification*. Glencoe, Ill.: Scott Foresman.

Engels, Frederick (1884) 1942 *The Origin of the Family, Private Property and the State*. New York: International Publishers.

Granovetter, Mark 1974 *Getting a Job*. Cambridge, Mass.: Harvard University Press.

——, and Charles Tilly 1988 "Inequality and Labor Processes." In Neil J. Smelser, ed., *Handbook of Sociology*. Beverly Hills, Calif.: Sage.

Gottschalk, Peter, and Timothy Smeeding 1997 "Cross-National Comparisons of Earnings and Income Inequality." *Journal of Economic Literature* 35:633–687.

Harding, Sandra C. 1983 *Discovering Reality: Feminist Perspectives on Epistemology, Metaphysics, Methodology, and Philosophy of Science*. Dordrecht, Holland: D. Reidel.

Jaggar, Allison M. 1984 *Feminist Frameworks: Alternative Theoretical Accounts of the Relations between Men and Women,* 2d ed. New York: Academic Press.

Laumann, Edward O., and Franz U. Poppi 1976 *Networks of Collective Action: A Perspective on Community Influence Systems.* New York: Academic Press.

Lenski, Gerhard E. 1966 *Power and Privilege.* New York: McGraw-Hill.

Levy, Frank 1998 *The New Dollars and Dreams: American Incomes and Economic Change.* New York: Russell Sage.

Lin, Nan, and Peter V. Marsden, eds. 1982 *Social Structure and Network Analysis.* Beverley Hills, Calif.: Sage

Marsden, Peter V. 1983 "Restricted Access in Networks and Models of Power." *American Journal of Sociology* 88:686–717.

Marx, Karl (1859) 1976–1978 *Capital: A Critique of Political Economy.* Harmondsworth, UK: Penguin.

Mayhew, Bruce H. 1973 "System Size and Ruling Elites." *American Sociological Review* 38:468–475.

——, and Paul T. Schollaert 1980 "The Concentration of Wealth: A Sociological Model." *Sociological Focus* 13:1–35.

Merton, Robert K. 1968. "The Matthew Effect in Science." *Science* 159:56–63.

Mill, John Stuart (1859) 1970 *The Subjection of Women.* New York: Source Book Press.

Mosca, G. 1939 *The Ruling Class.* New York: McGraw-Hill.

Myrdal, Gunnar 1944 *An American Dilemma: The Negro Problem and Modern Democracy.* New York: Harper and Brothers.

O'Rand, Angela M., and John C. Henretta 1999 *Age and Inequality: Diverse Pathways through Later Life.* Boulder, Colo.: Westview.

Ossowski, Stanislav 1963 *Class Structure in the Social Consciousness.* New York: Free Press.

Pareto, Vifredo (1897) 1980 *Compendium of General Sociology.* Minneapolis: University of Minnesota Press.

Pinkney, Alphonso 1984 *The Myth of Black Progress.* New York: Cambridge University Press.

Reddy, William 1987 *Money and Liberty in Modern Europe.* Cambridge, UK: Cambridge University Press.

Schwartz, Barry 1981 *Vertical Classification.* Chicago: University of Chicago Press.

Simmel, Georg 1896 "Superiority and Subordination as Subject Matters of Sociology," trans. A. Small. *American Journal of Sociology* 2:167–189, 392–415.

Skocpol, Theda 1979 *States of Social Revolutions.* New York: Cambridge University Press.

Skvoretz, John, and Thomas J. Fararo 1986 "Inequality and Association: A Biased Net Theory." *Current Perspectives in Social Theory* 7:29–50.

Sorensen, Aage 1977 "The Structure of Inequality and the Process of Attainment." *American Sociological Review* 42:965–978.

Sorokin, Pitirim A. 1941 *Social and Cultural Dynamics.* New York: Bedminster.

Thibaut, John W., and Harold H. Kelley 1959 *The Social Psychology of Groups.* New York: Wiley.

Tilly, Charles 1998 *Durable Inequality.* Berkeley: University of California Press.

Wallerstein, Immanuael Maurice 1974 *The Modern World System.* New York: Academic Press.

Weber, Max (1947) 1978 *Economy and Society,* vols. I and II. Berkeley: University of California Press.

White, Harrison C. 1970 *Chains of Opportunity.* Cambridge, Mass.: Harvard University Press.

Wilson, William J. 1980 *The Declining Significance of Race: Blacks and Changing American Institutions.* Chicago: University of Chicago Press.

Wolfson, Michael C. 1997 "Divergent Inequalities: Theory and Empirical Results." *Review of Income and Wealth* 43:401–421.

Wright, Erik Olin 1978 *Class, Crisis, and the State.* London: NLB.

——, 1985 *Classes.* London: Verso.

ANGELA M. O'RAND

SOCIAL JUSTICE

Justice is a basic element of social life. It is a central moral standard in human affairs that involves the necessity of "assuring that each person receives what she or he is due" (Cohen 1986, p. 1). Distributive justice is in the eye of the beholder, and debate usually surrounds the questions of what each person is due and what principles and procedures should be used to decide this. These differences not only occur among persons and social categories within a society but also vary across time and across cultures. A range of competing principles—rights or entitlements, equality of outcomes, equality of opportunity, equity or proportionality of rewards, and the satisfaction of basic needs—are prevalent standards of justice in most realms of social existence. These principles compete for recognition and application in human affairs, and there is considerable interest in this subject among philosophers, social and behavioral scientists, and others; substantial effort has been invested in the understanding of justice in human life.

Questions of justice, or fairness, arise in virtually all aspects of social life, and the topic of social justice covers a vast array of subjects. The social goods that are of concern in questions of distributive justice include a wide array of things that people want, usually referred to as *primary goods*, including basic freedoms, political enfranchisement, power, authority, status, income and wealth, education and employment opportunities, housing, and health care. In most discussions, it is assumed that those things are scarce, although in some cases that is clearly not always the case; for example, there should be an unlimited supply of basic freedoms in a well-ordered democracy. However, even if social goods are abundant, they have inherent satisfaction value—they are things that bring both extrinsic and intrinsic satisfaction to the individual—and their distribution is governed in part by principles of justice.

A major form of justice that concerns sociologists as well as legal scholars is *criminal or legal justice*, but justice issues pervade many other types of social relationships as well. Justice issues arise very often when inequalities of outcomes exist, but equalities of outcomes also raise questions in regard to justice. In *Nichomachean Ethics*, Aristotle (1953) stated: "For if the persons are not equal, they will not have equal shares; it is when equals possess or are allotted unequal shares, or persons not equal, equal shares that quarrels and complaints arise." Thus, in certain circumstances, equality of outcomes may be perceived as unjust while inequality of results may be seen as perfectly just.

The experimental literature in social psychology indicates that when persons perceive "inequitable" inequalities, they frequently experience cognitive tensions and a drive to reduce those tensions by changing their judgments about relative investments and contributions or changing their values in regard to the importance of reward-relevant criteria. Research also shows that when experimental subjects in task-oriented settings have well-defined expecatations linked to objective indica-

tors and contributions and investments, they find reward inequalities more acceptable (Brickman 1977; Cook 1975). Inequalities in the distribution of rewards also result from power differentials, and those in disadvantaged positions are more likely to view such inequalities as unfair (Cook and Hegtvedt 1986; Molm 1991).

There are several overlapping spheres of equality/inequality in which justice issues are especially important. These spheres concern the *legal, political, economic*, and *social* realms of existence and cover a broad range of human social behavior. They can be summarized as follows: (1) *legal justice*: the application of laws and procedures to individuals and organizations through a system of rules laid down or established, whether by custom or through the will of the state, for which penalties exist for disobedience, (2) *political justice*: other aspects of social life in which issues of dependence/independence arise from interdependence and from the extent of power and influence held by actors and other parties to the relationship, (3) *economic justice*: the distribution of the material outcomes of existence, where the economic well-being of parties to the relationship is at issue, including access to basic needs and shelter, and (4) *social justice*: the realm of status, respect, and the sense of worth given and received in social interaction or in relation to society.

Because questions of justice in society are so pervasive, most social sciences claim to understand the ways in which human societies deal with them. Thus, the literature on justice is massive and is perceived differently from a variety of perspectives. Extensive scholarship exists in philosophy (Buchanan and Mathieu 1986), anthropology (Nader and Sursock 1986), economics (Boulding 1981; Solo and Anderson 1981; Worland 1986), psychology (Deutsch 1975, 1986; Folger 1984; Furby 1986; Greenberg and Cohen 1982; Mukula 1980; Messick and Cook 1983), and political science (Barry 1981; DiQuattro 1986; Elster 1989; Hochschild 1981; Rae 1981). Justice is also a prominent theme in many traditions within sociology (Alwin 1987; Hamilton and Rauma 1995; Hegtvedt and Markovsky 1995; Kluegel et al. 1995; Markovsky 1985; Rytina 1986; Jasso 1980; Jasso and Wegener 1997), but the issues of justice have been studied primarily by those working in the tradition of social psychology; this article reflects that emphasis.

PERCEIVING JUSTICE

As was noted above, justice sentiments occur with respect to what each person receives relative to what he or she is expected to receive in regard to an important social good in which expectations may be governed by the application of a principle of justice. People's expectations and perceptions of justice focus on a wide range of phenomena, such as sentiments about the fairness of social exchange and contracts, fairness in interpersonal relationships, and the treatment of themselves and others by a social group or by society as a whole. Justice concerns thus represent a ubiquitous aspect of social life at many different levels and in many different spheres.

Expectations are formed not only by reward recipients but by others as well, including both people who are involved in the relationship and observers. Justice sentiments thus derive from comparisons of what is received with what one believes should be received, that is, a comparison of the real with the ideal in a particular context. Those evaluations of differences between these two entities or quantities engage human faculties of perception, cognition, and emotion. Even if one knows little else about justice evaluations, one knows that they are subjective, and justice almost always refers to "justice in the eyes of the observer" (Walster et al. 1973). Of course, these facts complicate the application of justice principles because, even setting aside the issue of which principle of justice to invoke in a particular situation, actors may not agree on what is real, that is, what the true outcomes are. However, to paraphrase a theme in interactionist sociology (from W. I. Thomas), *what is real in the perceptions of humans is real in its consequences.* Thus, if individuals perceive the social mechanisms for allocating scarce social resources and/or rewards as just, presumably the resulting distribution of outcomes also will be perceived as just.

From a social psychological viewpoint, then, a focus on justice is a focus on *beliefs* about inequality and *perceptions* of justice. Justice perceptions are pervasive in interpersonal interaction and exchange as well as in the nature of the relationship of the individual to the larger social collective in the macro-social realm. One way to simplify the vastness of this sociological terrain is to separate questions of justice and its evaluation posed at the micro-social level from those which occur at the macro level of society or the state (Brickman et al. 1981; Markovsky 1985; Hegtvedt and Markovsky 1995). Micro justice concerns justice evaluations at the individual level with regard to a person's immediate circumstances. Macro justice involves the evaluation of justice above the individual level, for groups or for society as a whole. Clearly, justice evaluations take place across several domains at different levels and focus on the abstract or the concrete. Within each level, one also may distinguish between beliefs about inequality and perceptions of justice at an abstract level, such as how things should be distributed in a fair world, and the evaluation of justice in the "real world," that is, assessments of how fair things are in reality (Kluegel and Smith 1981). In most cases, these various levels and degrees of abstraction cannot be easily separated, for example, in the evaluation of the fairness of child support payments (Schaeffer 1990), the fairness of child custody resolutions (Elster 1989), and the fairness of economic rewards (Sennett and Cobb 1972), but it is useful to draw many of these conceptual distinctions for research purposes.

PHILOSOPHICAL ROOTS

The historical roots of Western conceptions of justice lie in classical philosophy, the Judeo-Christian religious traditions, and the theoretical and ideological underpinnings of legal, economic, and political arrangements. Aristotle's *Nichomachean Ethics* (Book V) provides the classical formulation of the problem of justice. Aristotle's work sought to clarify principles of distributive and retributive justice and formulate the rules for the regulation of social exchange. The Aristotelian logic of justice in market relationships stressed the *proportionality* principle with regard to expected reward given considerations of merit and indicated that most contracts and purchases comply with the going rate of exchange (Cohen and Greenberg 1982, p. 4). Of course, it is not always easy for parties to agree on the "going rate." Worland suggests a crucial dilemma is revealed in Aristotle's work involving competition between justice principles:

It becomes clear that the reference to two different kinds of justice and two different rules of proportions poses a crucial dilemma. If commodities sell at their fair price—or at a price that reflects the "fair" rate of exchange—then how can society guarantee that exchange at such prices will also provide society's participants with an income proportionate to their relative "merit" or their standing in the community? How is the rule requiring distribution of common goods in proportion to "merit" to be reconciled with the rule requiring "reciprocal proportionate equality" in the contractual, private exchange of commodities? (1986, p. 48)

Eighteenth- and nineteenth-century philosophers and social theorists resolved this dilemma in a number of competing ways. Marx's labor theory of value (see Buchanan and Mathieu 1986, p. 12) suggested that the need for principles of justice provided evidence that social institutions would be restructured, abolishing the market system and private goods. Although the notion of communal ownership of the means of production can be traced back to early Greek philosophy and before, this has not been viewed as the most adequate solution to Aristotle's dilemma. Indeed, communism poses its own dilemmas, and the recent unpopularity of socialism as a political and economic system may provide some evidence of this (see Alwin et al. 1996, p. 124). Markets exist even under state socialism, and from the point of view of studying justice, the existence of a market for social exchange, as well as its comprehension and acceptance, seems to represent an important component in understanding the fairness of social interaction (Thiabaut and Kelley 1959; Lane 1986, p. 384).

Adam Smith, who is considered the philosophical father of modern capitalism, posed the Aristotelian dilemma differently. He observed that the modern economic system had become specialized in the sense that the production, distribution, and exchange of social goods had evolved to a stage in which economic activity was highly differentiated as an institution (Worland 1986, p. 50). Smith believed the "natural" rules by which markets developed and the moral issues of justice were resolved could be determined empirically. What is just, then, was clearly a question of what individual actors considered just not only at the subjective level but also at the macro-social level. The operation of principles of supply and demand to set a going rate was seen as providing the answer to the moral question of justice. Thus, Smith propounded an early example of a principle that later was articulated in the social psychology literature: the principle that "what is" determines "what ought to be" (see Homans [1961] 1974, p. 250; Heider 1958, p. 235). This, however, falls short of resolving the Aristotelian dilemma because it gives too great a role to existential factors in defining justice.

As Worland (1986, p. 57) suggests, Marx's theory of surplus value, in which Marx identified the real sources of profit and nonwage income as exploitation of working people by the capitalist class, did much to clarify what can now be seen as a condemnation of capitalist economies in Aristotelian terms. The twentieth-century response to Marx's critique of capitalism in economics is known as marginal utility theory, which explains the issue of injustice in terms of market imperfections and the existence of monopolistic forms of capitalism instead of real free enterprise. According to Worland (1986, p. 81), the neoclassical response is able only to isolate and clarify "the rules that a market society needs in order to comply with the Aristotelian moral imperative." It does not answer the deeper question of moral psychology concerning "whether such a society would be able to achieve the social consensus necessary for the practical implementation of the rules."

The perspective offered by neoclassical economics on moral issues of justice often is seen more as a justification for social inequalities than as a "natural law" of justice. It is reminiscent of Cohen and Greenberg's (1982) suggestion that each social and economic system evolves its own unique concept of justice. For neoclassical economics, the idea that there may be merit in nonproductive activities or considerations is foreign. By contrast, contemporary political philosophers have attempted to address the broader question of merit. Rawls (1971) evaluates the Aristotelian imperative from a nonmaterial, rational perspective. Rawls's principles of justice are as follows (quoted from Buchanan and Mathieu 1986, p. 27):

1. *The principle of greatest equal liberty: Each person is to have an equal right to the most extensive system of equal basic liberties compatible with a similar system of liberty for all.*

2. *The principle of equality of fair opportunity: Offices and positions are to be open to all under conditions of equality of fair opportunity–persons with similar abilities and skills are to have equal access to offices and positions.*

3. *The difference principle: Social and economic institutions are to be arranged so as to benefit maximally the worst off.*

According to Rawls (1971), these principles are ordered in terms of their primacy; that is, if principles conflict, the one listed first takes precedence. These principles obviously refer not only to social contracts and exchanges but also to the basic structure of society, including legal, political, economic, and social institutions. In most societies, that includes charters and constitutions, the means of production, competitive markets, the family, the legal system of laws and procedures, and so forth. The basic structure of society is said to specify how and by what principles society should distribute primary goods: basic liberties, powers, authority, opportunity, income, and wealth. The principle of greatest equal liberty specifies Rawls's theory of how basic liberties are distributed, the principle of equality of fair opportunities regulates the distribution of life chances or prospects in the domains of power and authority, and the difference principle governs the distribution of income and wealth (see Buchanan and Mathieu 1986, p. 28).

It is beyond the scope of this article to review Rawls's theory in full or summarize the critical comment that followed, except to note that his theory is utopian in the sense that it describes an ideal society run on the basis of just principles. Rawls does not spell out how one moves from states of injustice such as those found in contemporary society to the ideal situation. Still, no single book has generated more discussion and critique than his *A Theory of Justice*. A prominent contemporary critique is Nozick's (1974) entitlement theory, which departs radically from Rawls by stressing a libertarian view that a person is entitled to the ownership of a social good if it was acquired through just principles. Walzer (1983) argues that it is not possible to write a general theory of justice in the abstract without attempting to assay the "substantive ways of life" of different cultures. To Walzer, "justice" is a relative term, and no abstract

theory of the ideal society can really work because justice does not exist in an abstract theoretical sense but only in terms of social meanings ordained by a particular way of life.

DISTRIBUTIVE VERSUS PROCEDURAL JUSTICE

Distributive justice issues arise when one considers two sets of questions: Who gets what, and how? and Who should get what, and how? Some writers have suggested that the distinction between the concepts of *procedural justice* and *distributive justice* is critical to a complete understanding of the ways in which people evaluate justice (see Cohen 1986; Hegtvedt and Markovsky 1995; Thibaut et al. 1975; Tyler 1984, 1986). Procedural justice refers to the mechanisms or decision rules by which reward allocations of social goods are made, while distributive justice is concerned with the resulting allocation. These are two aspects of the same process and are clearly related, but conceptually they purport to refer to two distinct features of justice. Typically, distributive justice issues are thought of in terms of the comparison of the rewards received by a person or a group with a standard of fairness or deservedness, whereas procedural justice issues refer to the "mechanics" of the system that regulates the process of distribution.

It is useful to distinguish three components of the distributive justice process: (1) the principles for the allocation of goods, (2) the system that governs the application of those allocative principles, and (3) the resulting distribution. While separable in this sense, these are all components of what is best thought of in terms of distributive justice, which is the overriding concept. This view is in agreement with the work of Deutsch (1986, p. 35), who states that "procedural justice is a key aspect of distributive justice," not something that is necessarily separate or separable. Procedural justice matters come to the forefront, suggests Deutsch, and arouse complaints of injustice more often than do the principles of justice, primarily because justice principles are often taken for granted, whereas procedural matters are not.

From this formulation, one can see that these three components—principles, procedures, and distributive outcomes—are likely to be confounded and confused in social life. If there is consensus on evaluative principles and if a clear and just set of procedures can be said to exist to implement those values, distributive justice presumably will follow. Procedural justice thus is an important component in the evaluation of distributive justice, and in the pure case the evaluation of distributive justice is not problematic. If, however, there is no consensus on the principles for allocating rewards in a social group or society or if there is a consensus but procedures are seen as ineffective or corrupted, distributive justice will be called into question. In such situations, the evaluation of distributive justice focuses on the evaluative principles that should be used, the application of the principles, or both. Therefore, the principles of allocation and the procedural aspects of allocation may be intrinsically inseparable, and it may not be clear whether unjust outcomes result from the "wrong" principle being used or from misapplication of the "right" principle.

In summary, while it seems useful to distinguish procedural justice from other components of the distributive process, it is not at all clear that procedural and distributive justice are really different forms of justice. Instead, they are different aspects of a common process. Clearly, distributive justice issues arise when persons perceive the allocative mechanisms to be unjust or perceive imperfections in the application of just mechanisms to real life. It can be seen, then, that overall evaluations of justice at the micro-social level or the macro-social level may be influenced by perceptions of the fairness of procedural or distributive justice issues. However, this distinction ultimately becomes the empirical issue of whether and under what sets of conditions distributive versus procedural injustice is perceived by the actors involved.

EQUITY THEORY

Much current research on distributive justice traces its theoretical roots to Homans's (1976, p. 249) discussion of the rule of distributive justice, which hypothesizes that unless persons' perceived inputs (contributions, investments, resources, etc.) are equal, some inequality of outcomes or rewards can be expected, and that rewards generally are expected to be allocated in proportion to inputs (see also Heider 1958, p. 288). Responding to what they saw as the need for a general theory of social behavior, Walster and her colleagues (see Walster

et al. 1973, 1978; Berkowitz and Walster 1976) formulated equity theory to integrate the insights from a variety of social psychological theories, including reinforcement theory, cognitive consistency theory, psychoanalytic theory, and exchange theory (Walster et al. 1978, p. 2). Building on the work of Homans, Lerner, and others, equity theory as formulated by Walster et al. (1978, p. 6) contains four basic propositions:

Proposition I: Individuals will try to maximize their outcomes.

Proposition IIA: Groups can maximize their collective reward by evolving accepted systems for equitably apportioning resources among their members. Thus, groups will evolve such systems of equity and attempt to induce their members to accept and adhere to those systems.

Proposition IIB: Groups generally will reward members who treat others equitably and punish members who treat others inequitably.

Proposition III: When individuals find themselves particpating in inequitable relationships, they will become distressed. The more inequitable the relationship, the more distress individuals will feel.

Proposition IV: Individuals who discover they are in an inequitable relationship will attempt to eliminate their distress by restoring equity. The greater the inequity that exists, the more distress they will feel and the harder they will try to restore equity.

To define justice, equity theory distinguishes *inputs* and *outcomes*, both of which are expressed in the same units, say, dollars, points, or another unit. Assuming that inputs are positive (for simplicity), the equity principle states that under conditions of justice, there is an equality of relative gains. For two actors (persons, groups, nations, etc.) engaged in social exchange, equity is said to exist when the ratio of profits (outcomes minus inputs) to inputs is the same for both actors involved in the exchange.

While it is clear that rational self-interest is a strong motive for behavior in many types of situations and may be a safe assumption in competitive situations, there are other motivations for behavior (Becker 1996; Elster 1984, 1989). This can be seen as one of the unnecessarily restrictive assumptions of equity theory; the prevalence of altruism, cooperation, and other forms of prosocial behavior strongly questions this basic assumption. There is plenty of evidence that competitive behavior in mixed-motive games such as the Prisoner's Dilemma can evolve into stable cooperation under certain conditions, such as the anticipation of future interaction (Axelrod 1984). In relationships where intimacy and identification are present, the importance of self-interest as a motive for behavior is considerably lessened (Austin 1977). As was noted earlier, Rawls's (1971) theory of justice, for example, suggests that one principle that underlies the moral judgments made in human society is the principle that social and economic arrangements are established to maximally benefit those who are less advantaged with respect to desirable social goods. Thus, one can see that equity theory as stated by Walster et al. (1978) probably overstates the need to specify a type of utilitarian-based logic for defining justice.

Implicit in this theoretical statement and the experimental literature on which it is based are the assumptions of cognitive dissonance theory (Festinger 1959). Thus, an important way to resolve dissonance is to adjust one's beliefs to conform to reality. However, while the theory's allowance for changes in beliefs is an important feature, there are limits to what people will believe. Elster comments as follows on the concept of "belief adjustment":

> Dissonance reduction can also take the form of belief adjustment. Workers who take jobs in unsafe industries alter their estimated probabilities of accidents. As a result, when safety equipment becomes available, they may choose not to purchase it. Here, as in other cases, misformation of private beliefs (or preferences) creates a case for government intervention. . . . Belief-oriented dissonance reduction is a form of wishful thinking [but] . . . acting on beliefs formed in this way can be disastrous and is likely to force a change in beliefs. When action is not called for, the wishful beliefs can be more stable. The "just-world" theory, for instance, suggests that people adjust their beliefs about guilt and responsibility so as to preserve their belief that the world is fundamentally just. The best-known example is the "blame the victim" syndrome. . . . (Elster 1989, pp. 22–23)

Presumably, many beliefs, including beliefs about inequality and justice, achieve a high degree of stability relatively early in adulthood and may not be subject to alteration (Alwin 1994). Expectations may not be altered easily if they are rooted in firmly held beliefs about the legitimacy of inequality.

FROM EQUITY TO DISTRIBUTIVE JUSTICE

In the early 1970s, Deutsch (1975) began to question the proportionality, or equity, principle implicit in much theorizing about justice. He, among others, argued that equity is only one of several principles used to evaluate the justice of outcomes in social life. Principles of justice are used as a basis of "judging individual persons and in judging the basic structure of societies" (Cohen 1986, p. 1). At least five competing principles—equality, equality of opportunity, equity, rights or entitlement, and need—are applied routinely in most realms of social existence. Other principles, such as chance, are really devices for ensuring that a principle of justice—namely, equality of opportunity—is procedurally adhered to (see the discussion of lotteries in Elster 1989, pp. 62–122). While these principles may more or less exhaust the possible criteria for evaluating justice, perhaps the equity principle has been seen as most relevant in many cases. For example, in the work of Homans ([1961] 1974), the proportionality principle is given a prominent place in the discussion of distributive justice, and it is clearly present in many discussions of equity theory (see Adams 1965; Berkowitz and Walster 1976; Cook and Hegtvedt 1983).

However, with time, theoretical work and empirical research have cast the problem of equity into the broader framework of distributive justice, in which justice may be evaluated by one principle or a combination of many different principles. Contemporary interest in the study of distributive justice can be traced to the early articulation of relative deprivation theory, particularly in the work of Stouffer, Merton, and Homans (see Williams 1975). In the last several decades, issues of distributive justice have moved from a primary focus on the psychological and behavioral consequences of patterns of social reward distributions in small group settings (see reviews by Adams 1965; Berkowitz and Walster 1976; Crosby 1976; Cohen and Greenberg 1982; Hegtvedt and Markovsky 1995) to a more recent focus among sociologists on studying principles of justice evaluation (Alves and Rossi 1978; Jasso and Rossi 1977; Jasso 1978, 1980; Jasso and Wegener 1997).

Justice Evaluation and Social Comparison

Current theories of distributive justice implicitly or explicitly specify *social comparison* as the basis for justice evaluation and the reference standard persons use in evaluating the fairness of social rewards. The following discussion summarizes the author's theory of justice evaluation and social comparison (Alwin 1987). As in most contemporary theories, it is assumed that in evaluating the fairness of a particular reward allocation, persons compare themselves with others (see Berger et al. 1972; Pettigrew 1967; Williams 1975; Gartrell 1982). For example, Homans's rule of distributive justice often is stated as follows (see Walster et al. 1978):

$$Justice = [P\text{'s Reward} / P\text{'s Inputs}] - [O\text{'s Reward} / O\text{'s Inputs}] = 0 \tag{1}$$

Here P and O are two persons in a *local exchange* in which P is assumed to evaluate his or her comparison ratio or rewards to inputs against that of another individual, O. If P perceives that O's comparison ratio is equal to his or her own, then he or she will perceive a state of justice. If this is not the case, some degree of injustice is presumed to exist, and P will perceive that he or she is underrewarded or overrewarded relative to O.

The term "inputs" is used in equation (1) to represent the general reward-relevant characteristics of individuals that are involved in making assessments of the fairness or justice of rewards. These may be contributions, investments, resources, or global status characteristics (see Cook 1975; Cook and Yamagishi 1983). This formulation ignores the concept of costs and their effects on rewards and inputs. In other words, inputs and rewards are thought of as positive quantities. For a somewhat different formulation involving negative inputs and rewards, see Walster et al. (1978).

Several investigators (e.g., Blau 1971; Berger et al. 1972; Jasso 1978) have pointed out that in viewing this identity (equation [1]) objectively, it is impossible to determine which parties are over- or underrewarded when perfect justice does not prevail. Moreover, formulations of justice evaluation as local comparisons cannot cope with the possibility that from the perspective of a more general

referential standard, both P and O may be unjustly rewarded even though their comparison ratios may be equal. This view in no way denies that people make local comparisons of such ratios. The point is that when people make local comparisons, referential standards existing outside the local situation typically are invoked to evaluate fairness.

Berger et al. (1972, p. 122) criticize this formulation, arguing that distributive justice issues arise only in the presence of a stable frame of reference and that justice evaluations are inherently made on the basis of reference to generalized individuals rather than specific others. Using this observation as a basis for reconceptualizing the classical exchange-based conception of justice, Berger et al. (1972) formulate a "theory of status value" that formalizes the process by which persons evaluate the fairness of rewards. They formulate the process in terms of *referential standards*: frames of reference that contain existing information regarding the characteristics and rewards of generalized others. The referential structure formalized by Berger et al. (1972) consists of information about the relationship between levels of characteristics possessed by general classes of persons and the associated levels of social reward. According to this theory, through social exchange persons develop normative expectations about the reward levels typically associated with general classes of individuals, and when persons perceive their reward-relevant characteristics to be similar to those of a particular general class of individuals, they come to expect that their reward levels also are similar. As a consequence of these beliefs about "what is," normative expectations are formed about reward levels that persons can legitimately claim (Berger et al. 1972, p. 139). This conclusion is consistent with Homans's ([1961] 1974) and Heider's (1958) observations that the "ought" is determined in the long run by the "is" and with recent sociological theorizing that argues that social inequalities are often the major basis of their own legitimation (Sennett and Cobb 1972; Della Fave 1980; Stolte 1983).

The Berger et al. (1972) *status-value formulation*, however, is limited in its consideration of the process by which a person selects a referential comparison standard among the many possibilities. Referential comparisons may be based on relatively small groups of persons such as one's coworkers or large classes of persons such as occupational categories. This may appear to be a flaw in the status-value theory; however, it also may be viewed as an asset in that it allows flexibility in specifying the role of various types of referential standards in justice evaluation processes.

Referential Comparisons. While near consensus exists in the social psychological literature that persons use referential comparisons to evaluate how satisfactory their outcomes are, Gartrell (1982) observes that little is known about the origin and visibility of comparative frames of reference. In his own research, for example, Gartrell finds that information on wage rates is often invisible, and such information for persons in other jobs frequently originates from concrete, personal references rather than from knowledge of rates for broad social categories. Moreover, the awareness of wage comparisons frequently appears to relate to somewhat idiosyncratic factors, such as informal social contacts (see Walster et al. 1978). This is consistent with other studies of relative deprivation and status comparison, in which persons are found to rely heavily on information from their own social circles (see Runciman 1966; Rainwater 1974; Coleman and Rainwater 1978). Thus, it may be difficult to specify the origin or basis of a person's referential comparison with objective accuracy. Some experimental research (Major and Forcey 1985) suggests that subjects are most interested in same-sex and same-job wage comparisons.

Moreover, the individual's subjective judgment regarding the "fairness" of a given reward outcome may be a more relevant concept. Jasso's (1978, 1980) theory of distributive justice introduces the term "just reward" to refer to the reward level individuals expect on the basis of referential comparisons conceived in general terms. Jasso formulates the status-value model of Berger et al. (1972) for justice evaluation as follows (1978, p. 1402):

$$Justice = \text{P's Actual Reward} - \text{P's Just Reward} = 0 \tag{2}$$

That is, for a person to determine the justice or fairness of his or her reward, the actual level of reward is simply compared with the reward expected on the basis of existential (or other) criteria.

This formulation is more general than the one given by Berger et al. (1972) because it permits a wide range of reference group comparisons and because both existential and nonexistential criteria may be used in the calculus of the "just reward" (see Jasso 1978, 1980). As Blau (1971, pp. 58–59) points out in his criticism of Homans ([1961] 1974), "not all existing practices reflect justice; some are unjust by prevailing moral standards, and the fact that they are expected to continue to exist does not make them just." Thus, there are both existential and nonexistential standards of justice, and either or both may be combined to determine the "just reward."

This "comparison difference" formulation of distributive justice makes the nature of over- or underreward clear, unlike the formulation used by most equity theorists (e.g., Walster et al. 1978). Moreover, in contrast with the classical formulation given in equation (1), both quantities in the equation are expressed in the same units: units of reward. Further, this formulation (equation [2]) satisfies the notion that the individual's subjective judgment regarding the "expected" or "deserved" reward may be the most relevant concept. Finally, the distinction between kinds and degrees of injustice can be measured on a scale that starts at zero, where "perfect justice" occurs. Southwood (1978, p. 1157) has proposed a model very similar to Jasso's model involving what he calls "subtractive interaction" that is intended to estimate the effects of departures of actual reward from expected (or just) reward. This model simply involves estimating the effects of the quantity $x_1 - x_2$, where x_1 represents the actual reward and x_2 represents the expected reward.

Reformulating the Justice Evaluation Model. Using Jasso's concept of the just reward, it is possible to reformulate the classical exchange-based conception in a way that permits the measurement of the direction and magnitude of departures from justice. First, it is necessary to recast Homan's ([1961] 1974) "rule of distributive justice" given in equation (1) as an equivalence of the ratio of P's and O's rewards to the ratio of their inputs as follows (see Patchen 1961; Adams 1965; Homans [1961] 1974, 1976):

$$Justice = \text{P's Actual Reward} - \text{P's Just Reward} = 0 \tag{3}$$

Here the comparison ratios are different from those in the classical statement (Walster et al.

1978). They now involve terms in common units: reward units on the one hand and units of input on the other hand. The present formulation of the classical model has two desirable properties: It is intuitively simpler to have the numerator and denominator of such ratios in the same units, and this formulation fits with the psychological mechanism often assumed in justice evaluation: Persons expect their inputs (contributions, investments, resources, or general status characteristics) to be in constant proportion to the rewards they associate with a standard of comparison.

If the Berger et al. (1972) theory of status value is correct is stating that a person, P, uses referential structures that specify levels of reward-relevant characteristics that are similar, indeed equivalent, to his or her own (see also Pettigrew 1967; Williams 1975), it is possible to equate P's and O's inputs on the right-hand side of equation (3), setting the second term on the right at unity, as follows:

$$Justice = [P's\ Reward\ /\ O's\ Reward] - 1 = 0 \quad (4)$$

If one generalizes the concept of "O's reward" to be the same as Jasso's "just reward," the justice evaluation process devolves to a comparison of P's actual and expected/just rewards:

$$Justice = [P's\ Actual\ Reward\ /$$
$$P's\ Expected\ Reward]\ -1 = 0 \quad (5)$$

An examination of this expression indicates that the classical formulation restated in this way permits the distinction between kinds and degrees of injustice measured on a scale that starts at zero, where perfect justice occurs. These units may conveniently be thought of as justice units because when the comparison exeeds zero, overreward occurs, and when it is less than zero, P is said to be underrewarded.

Note the convergence of the reformulation of the classical model given here with that proposed by Jasso (1978), which was derived empirically from the analysis of vignette data. The natural logarithm of equation (5), which is derived from classical exchange and status value theories, equals the formulation for justice evaluaton proposed by Jasso. I have derived theoretically a principle of justice evaluation that is equivalent to Jasso's (1978, 1980) empirically derived "Universal Law of Jus-

tice Evaluation." This formulation can be used as a basis for defining departures from justice.

Jasso argues, however, that the simple ratio of actual to just rewards does not capture the justice evaluation phenomenon precisely: It does not account for the fact that positive departures from justice (overreward) are not equivalent to negative departures (underreward), and "this appears to violate the human experience that deficiency is felt to be more unjust than a comparable excess" (Jasso 1978, p. 1403). In other words, the injustice created by an actual reward above the just reward k is not equivalent to the injustice created by an underreward of the same magnitude. Jasso (1978, p. 1415) resolves the problem by proposing the natural logarithm of the comparison ratio (i.e., actual reward/just reward). Such a formulation assumes that an overreward of k times is equal in the magnitude of injustice to an underreward of $1/k$ times. Using satisfaction with material well-being, Alwin (1987) empirically examined Jasso's hypothesis that the effects of underreward are more potent than the effects of overreward. While support was found for the importance of the sense of injustice in the prediction of material satisfaction, the hypothesis that the extent of satisfaction depends on measured departures from justice was not supported.

BELIEFS ABOUT INEQUALITY

As was mentioned above, distributive justice issues arise in response to two sets of questions: (1) the realm of the ideal, that is, who should get what, and how, and (2) the real, or who gets what, and how. As was noted, these issues may be phrased with regard to the individual, the micro-justice level, or groups of individuals or the whole society (i.e., macro-justice). Regardless of the justice principles one espouses, behavior and sentiment are conditioned by how the system works or is perceived to work. One of the important aspirations of social science is the understanding of who gets what and how, and it was the major focus of several important works on social stratification and mobility in the 1960s and 1970s (e.g. Blau, and Duncan 1967; Hauser and Featherman 1977; Featherman and Hauser 1978; Jencks et al. 1972, 1979; Levy 1988; Moynihan 1968; Sewell and Hauser 1975; Wright and Perrone 1977). As a result of that work, a great deal more is known about the ways in which race, gender, and class affect inequalities and the manner in which families and educational institutions operate to promote or deny access to opportunities for socioeconomic advancement. However, the study of social stratification and mobility is an arcane field of inquiry, and there is not always agreement among social scientists about the main factors that create socioeconomic inequalities (see Herrnstein and Murray 1994 and the debate it provoked, e.g., Fischer et al. 1996).

Sociologists often assume that there is a causal linkage between the structural conditions of society (e.g., the standard of living and economic inequality) and public beliefs and sentiments regarding the acceptability of those conditions, but little is known about the nature of that linkage. There is a growing body of empirical data regarding trends in income distribution and income inequality, much of which indicates growing economic inequality and hardship for segments of the population (e.g., Duncan and Rodgers 1991; Levy 1988; Levy and Murnane 1992; Thurow 1987), but much less is known about subjective interpretations of economic conditions. Thus, while social scientists attempt to understand the inner workings of the stratification system, there is much that remains to be understood, and it is important to realize that a person's beliefs about sources of inequality affect evaluations of justice as much as if not more than objective conditions do (see Kluegel and Smith 1981, 1986; Robinson and Bell 1978; Kluegel et al. 1995).

SOCIAL JUSTICE RESEARCH

This article has argued that one can distinguish three components of the distributive justice process with regard to any primary good: (1) the principles for the allocation of goods, (2) the system that governs the application of those allocative principles, and (3) the resulting distribution. Justice sentiments derive from comparisons of what is received with what one believes should be received, that is, a comparison of the real with the ideal in a particular context.

According to Jasso and Wegener, empirical justice analysis has four major objectives:

(i) to obtain numerical approximations of the quantities and relations identified by jus-

tice theory; (ii) to gauge the extent of interindividual and intergroup variation in the quantities and relations; (iii) to explain their etiology, including the effects of social structure and of the observer's position in the stratification structure; and (iv) to assess their behavioral and social consequences (1997, p. 393).

Three fundamental quantities pertain to justice: the actual condition, the just condition, and the justice evaluation. While justice evaluations involve the comparison of the other two quantities, it is not clear that individuals actually quantify justice in the way theoretical formulations suggest, and it remains to be seen whether most people "calculate" more than a general "sense of justice" from this comparison.

To summarize current research on social justice, one would have to focus on a wide range of distributional issues with respect to the primary social goods of distributed in society, including basic freedoms, political rights, power, authority, status, income and wealth, education and employment opportunities, housing, health care, and the pursuit of happiness. Below, this article briefly mentions five areas in which a consideration of justice theory is relevant to sociological understanding: (1) income inequality and the welfare state, (2) discrimination and affirmative action, (3) gender, work, and comparable worth, (4) divorce, child custody, and child support, and (5) intergenerational relations.

Income Inequality and the Welfare State. One of the central preoccupations of sociologists who study distributive justice has been the economic realm, with an explicit focus on wages or earnings (e.g. Alves and Rossi 1978; Gartrell 1982; Gartrell and Paille 1997; Jasso 1978, 1999; Jasso and Rossi 1977; Patchen 1961; Randall and Mueller 1995; Robinson and Bell 1978). Research in the United States shows convincingly that individualistic attributions for poverty and wealth predominate (Kluegel and Smith 1986). Such attributions are found across the spectrum of socioeconomic positions, and among lower socioeconomic status (SES) groups these beliefs are held concurrently with structural explanations. At the same time, Americans show considerable antagonism toward any form of systemwide redistribution of income beyond current welfare assistance to children, the disabled, and the indigent and current forms of social security for senior members of the population.

Whereas Americans hold equality as the standard of justice in the political realm, inequality is the standard in the economic realm. A recent multinational comparison of a U.S. sample with comparable data from other Western nations showed that in assessing the deservingness of their own earnings, "what ought to be" is strongly linked to "what is" (Alwin et al. 1996). Thus, existential considerations play a strong role in the development of judgments about levels of deserved income, although there was considerable variation in the magnitude of those linkages. The weakest effects, as predicted on the basis of perceived system legitimacy, were in the postcommunist economies of eastern and central Europe and the former republics of the Soviet Union. The strongest effects were in the Western capitalist democracies. Indeed, the linkage between job desserts and job income was so strong in those countries (Germany, Great Britain, the Netherlands, the United States, and Japan) that it seemed hardly possible that any factors other than current income levels could contribute to variation in perceptions of justice. By contrast, the level of perceived family need played a much stronger role in evaluations of the justice of earnings in the eastern European countries than it did in the West (see Alwin et al. 1996, pp. 123–128).

Discrimination and Affirmative Action. Discrimination by dominant groups against ethnic minorities and women has been a significant concern of those interested in equality and justice. This set of issues can be addressed easily within the framework of social justice as an instance of the lack of congruence between justice principles such as equality of opportunity and the actual workings of society. Although considerable progress has been made in establishing constitutional prohibitions against discrimination on the grounds of race, ethnic origin, and sex in employment practices, education, and public accommodations, reality has lagged behind those ideals. Substantial inequalities among racial groups persist despite substantial opinion that racial discrimination is no longer a problem in American society (Blauner 1989). Considerable research has focused on the consequences of discrimination.

The concept of *affirmative action* has been used in the United States and other countries to refer to social policies that go beyond prohibitions against discriminatory practices that deprive minorities of their rights and aim social policy toward remedying the effects of past discrimination. Affirmative action represents an effort to restore equity to social groups, rather than to individuals, by targeting women and minorities for educational opportunities, jobs, promotion, government contracts, and other arenas where past discrimination has been documented. Affirmative action policies have been controversial because they appear to represent a form of *reverse discrimination* inasmuch as they violate the principle of of equal opportunity by giving preferential treatment on the basis of race and national origin. These policies have faced a number of legal challenges that are likely to continue as long as they are perceived to be unjust by some members of society. Regardless of how one views these policies, they have placed increased numbers of women and minorities in good jobs and selective educational institutions, but they may have increased tensions over these matters.

Gender, Work, and Comparable Worth. An important application of the social justice framework has been the examination of equity in the job rewards of men and women. In the United States, as in other countries, there are legislative guarantees to the right of equal pay for equal work, such as Title VII of the Civil Rights Act of 1964. The concept of *comparable worth* was designed to go beyond this mandate to describe a situation of equal pay for work of equal value, that is, work that requires comparable levels of effort, skills, and responsibility. Rather than being a remedy for past discrimination, as in the case of affirmative action, this approach is aimed at developing policies that will guarantee equal treatment for men and women. While this idea seems to be catching on, there are still substantial gaps in the workplace authority and earnings of men and women throughout the world (see Wright et al., 1995; Jasso and Wegener, 1999), and researchers face a "paradox of the contented female worker" (Crosby 1982). Generally speaking, women have jobs with lower pay, less autonomy, and less authority than jobs held by men, but their level of earnings satisfaction is no different from that of men. Mueller and Wallace (1996) suggest that when levels of perceived justice are taken into account, substantial amounts of the difference between men and women in their satisfaction with earnings can be explained. What remains to be understood are the factors that contribute to differences between men and women in perceptions of what is just.

Divorce, Child Custody, and Child Support. Marital disruption is a conspicuous feature of the contemporary family that raises issues of justice not only for the people involved but for the public as well. Apart from justice matters arising from the division of property and assets in a divorce, when children are involved, the settlement becomes more complicated. Child custody disputes and child support issues present unique problems for justice analysis because in the first case the primary goods are indivisible and in the second case costs (or negative rewards) are being allocated. Procedures for resolving both sets of issues are governed by state and federal statutes or guidelines as well as by local customs and have varied considerably across time and culture. Historically, courts have employed justice principles involving parental entitlements to various degrees, but in recent times, the principle has evolved that the best interests of the child ought to be the sole or major consideration in custody decisions. As Elster (1989, p. 126) puts it, "although the child may to some extent and for some purposes be considered a consumption good for the parents, he is also and predominantly a person in his own right" who has an interest in the allocation. Elster argues, however, against the principle of the best interests of the child and suggests that in contemporary society, when joint custody is not feasible, three options present themselves: a presumption in favor of the mother, a presumption in favor of the primary caretaker (usually the mother), and tossing a coin.

Child support payments are vastly more determinate, and those judgments are considerably less Solomonic. Indeed, courts generally have allowed the participants, on the advice of counsel, to negotiate the nature of the awards. In child support situations, decision making occurs in two steps. There is a preliminary determination of an amount to be divided based on the needs of the child and then a decision on how that amount should be divided based on the relative resources of the parents. As Schaeffer (1980, p. 158) puts it, "beliefs abut child support awards differ in important ways from other beliefs about justice . . . [because] allocating child support obligations involves allo-

cating not rewards, but responsibilities expressed as contributions." Schaeffer (1980) analyzed beliefs about the fairness of child support judgments by using a factorial survey involving vignettes. She found that child support awards are allocated according to a "proportional contribution-variable need" system in which parents' contributions are proportional to their resources. She concluded that preferences for child support awards embody a "modified version of 'from each according to their abilities, to each according to their needs'" (1980, p. 172).

Intergenerational Relations. Relationships among generations are one of the most important structural features in all societies. Some authors have argued that the prevailing social contract between generations in Western society regarding expectations, obligations, and well-being is changing (Bengtson and Achenbaum 1993). This is due to the changing demography of age but also to shifting cultural understandings of age differences and issues of equity. Bengtson (1993, p. 4) argues that "we have reached a cultural watershed concerning the implicit understanding of rights and obligations between age groups and generations in human societies. Never before have so many elders lived so long; never before have so relatively fewer members of younger age groups lined up behind them in the succession of generations." He argues further that as a consequence, "we are faced with new and historically unique dilemmas of family life and social policy agendas regarding the expectable life course and the succession of generations."

These observations raise a number of questions regarding the nature of intergenerational conflict and the linkage between age and economic expectations, economic performance, and evaluations of material well-being. The concept of justice has been applied to the study of intergenerational relations (see Norris 1987), but little work has explicitly linked social psychological theory regarding equity or justice evaluation to this range of issues. Moreover, researchers often have settled for conclusions based on conjecture or weak and inappropriate kinds of evidence. There is a wide range of intergenerational issues to which the justice framework can be applied, including not only the material well-being of older age groups but also the sense of obligation that adult children have about the support of their elderly parents as well as public concern about the future health care and social security systems that will support the elderly in the future.

(SEE ALSO: *Affirmative Action; Comparable Worth; Decision-Making Theory and Research; Gender; Interpersonal Power; Poverty; Social Psychology; Utopian Analysis and Design*)

REFERENCES

Adams, J. Stacy 1965 "Inequity in Social Exchange." In L. Berkowitz, ed., *Advances in Experimental Social Psychology*, vol. 9. New York: Academic Press.

Alves, Wayne M., and Peter H. Rossi 1978 "Who Should Get What? Fairness Judgments of the Distribution of Earnings." *American Journal of Sociology* 84:541–564.

Alwin, Duane F. 1987 "Distributive Justice and Satisfaction with Material Well-Being." *American Sociological Review* 52:83–95.

—— 1994 "Aging, Personality and Social Change: The Stability of Individual Differences Across the Life-Span." In D. L. Featherman, R. M. Lerner, and M. Permutter, eds., *Life-Span Development and Behavior*, vol. 12. Hillsdale N.J.: Erlbaum.

——, Galin Gornev, and Ludmilla Khakhulina 1996 "Comparative Referential Structures, System Legitimacy, and Justice Sentiments: An International Comparison." In *Social Justice and Political Change: Public Opinion in Capitalist and Post-Communist States*. New York: Aldine de Gruyter.

Aristotle 1953 *Nichomachean Ethics*, trans. J. A. K. Thompson. London: George Allen and Unwin.

Austin, William 1977 "Equity Theory and Social Comparison Processes." In J. M. Suls and R. L. Miller, eds., *Social Comparison Processes: Theoretical and Empirical Perspectives*. Washington D.C.: Hemisphere.

Axelrod, Robert 1984 *The Evolution of Cooperation*. New York: Basic Books.

Barry, Brian 1981 "Social Science and Distributive Justice." In Robert A. Solo and Charles W. Anderson, eds., *Value Judgment and Income Distribution*. New York: Praeger.

Becker, Gary S. 1996 *Accounting for Tastes*. Cambridge, Mass.: Harvard University Press.

Bengtson, Vern L. 1993 "Is the 'Contract across Generations' Changing? Effects of Population Aging on Obligations and Expectations across Age Groups." In V. L. Bengtson and W. A. Achenbaum, eds., *The Changing Contract across Generations*. New York: Aldine de Gruyter.

——, and W. Andrew Achenbaum 1993 *The Changing Contract across Generations*. New York: Aldine de Gruyter.

Berger, Joseph, Maurice Zelditch, Bo Anderson, and Bernard P. Cohen 1972 "Structural Aspects of Distributive Justice: A Status-Value Formulation." In J. Berger, M. Zelditch, and B. Anderson, eds., *Sociological Theories in Progress*, vol. 2. Boston: Houghton-Mifflin.

Berkowitz, Leonard, and Elaine Walster, eds. 1976 *Equity Theory: Toward a General Theory of Social Interaction. Advances in Experimental Social Psychology*, vol. 9. New York: Academic Press.

Blau, Peter M. 1971 "Justice in Social Exchange." In H. Turk and R. L. Simpson, eds., *Institutions and Social Exchange: The Sociologies of Talcott Parsons and George C. Homans*. New York: Bobbs-Merrill.

——, and Otis Dudley Duncan 1967 *The American Occupational Structure*. New York: Wiley.

Blauner, Robert 1989 *Black Lives, White Lives*. Berkeley: University of California Press.

Boulding, Kenneth E. 1981 "Allocation and Distribution: The Quarrelsome Twins." In R. A. Solo and C. W. Anderson, eds., *Value Judgment and Income Distribution*. New York: Praeger.

Brickman, Philip 1977 "Preferences of Inequality." *Sociometry* 40:303–310.

——, et al. 1981 "Micro-Justice and Macro-Justice." In M. J. Lerner and S. C. Lerner, eds., *The Justice Motive in Social Behavior*. New York: Plenum.

Buchanan, Allen, and Deborah Mathieu 1986 "Philosophy and Justice." In R. L. Cohen, ed., *Justice: Views from the Social Sciences*. New York: Plenum.

Cohen, Ronald L., ed. 1986. *Justice: Views from the Social Sciences*. New York: Plenum.

Cook, Karen S. 1975 "Expectations, Evaluations and Equity." *American Sociological Review* 40:372–388.

——, and Karen A. Hegtvedt 1983 "Distributive Justice, Equity, and Equality." *Annual Review of Sociology* 9:217–241.

——, and —— 1986 "Justice and Power: An Exchange Analysis." In H. W. Bierhoff, R. L. Cohen, and J. Greenberg, eds., *Justice in Social Relations*. New York: Plenum.

——, and Toshio Yamagishi 1983 "Social Determinants of Equity Judgments: The Problem of Multidimensional Input." In D. M. Messick and K. A. Cook, eds., *Equity Theory: Psychological and Sociological Perspectives*. New York: Praeger.

Crosby, Faye 1976 "A Model of Egoistical Relative Deprivation." *Psychological Review* 83:85–113.

—— 1982 *Relative Deprivation and Working Women*. New York: Oxford University Press.

Davis, James A. 1959 "A Formal Interpretation of the Theory of Relative Deprivation." *Sociometry* 22:280–296.

Della Fave, L. Richard 1980 "The Meek Shall Not Inherit the Earth: Self-Evaluation and the Legitimacy of Social Stratification." *American Sociological Review* 45:955–971.

Deutsch, Morton 1975 "Equity, Equality and Need: What Determines Which Value Will Be Used as the Basis of Distributive Justice." *Journal of Social Issues* 31:137–149.

—— 1986 *Distributive Justice: A Social Psychological Perspective*. New Haven Conn.: Yale University Press.

DiQuattro, Arthur 1986 "Political Studies and Justice." In R. L. Cohen, ed., *Justice: Views from the Social Sciences*. New York: Plenum.

Duncan, Greg, and Willard Rodgers 1991 "Has Children's Poverty Become More Persistent?" *American Sociological Review* 56:538–550.

Elster, Jon 1984 *Ulysses and the Sirens: Studies in Rationality and Irrationality*, rev. ed. Cambridge, UK: Cambridge University Press.

—— 1989 *Solomonic Judgements: Studies in the Limitations of Rationality*. New York: Cambridge University Press.

Farkas, Arthur J., and Norman H. Anderson 1979 "Multidimensional Input in Equity Theory." *Journal of Personality and Social Psychology* 37:879–896.

Featherman, David L., and Robert M. Hauser 1978 *Opportunity and Change*. New York: Academic Press.

Festinger, Leon 1959 *A Theory of Cognitive Dissonance*. Stanford, Calif.: Stanford University Press.

Fischer, Claude S., et al. 1996 *Inequality by Design: Cracking the Bell Curve Myth*. Princeton, N.J.: Princeton University Press.

Folger, Robert 1984 *The Sense of Injustice: Social Psychological Perspectives*. New York: Plenum.

Furby, Lita 1986 "Psychology and Justice." In R. L. Cohen, ed., *Justice: Views from the Social Sciences*. New York: Plenum.

Gartrell, C. David 1982 "On the Visibility of Wage Referents." *Canadian Journal of Sociology* 7:117–143.

——, and Bernard E. Paille 1997 "Wage Cuts and the Fairness of Pay in a Worker–Owned Plywood Cooperative." *Social Psychology Quarterly* 60:103–117.

Greenberg, Jerald, and Ronald L. Cohen 1982 *Equity and Justice in Social Behavior*. New York: Academic Press.

Hamilton, V. Lee, and David Rauma 1995 "Social Psychology of Deviance and the Law." In Karen Cook, Gary Fine, and James House, eds., *Sociological Perspectives on Social Psychology*. Boston: Allyn and Bacon.

Hauser, Robert M., and David L. Featherman 1977 *The Process of Stratification: Trends and Analyses*. New York: Academic Press.

Hegtvedt, Karen A., and Barry Markovsky 1995 "Justice and Injustice." In Karen Cook, Gary Fine, and James House, eds., *Sociological Perspectives on Social Psychology*. Boston: Allyn and Bacon.

Heider, Fritz 1958 *The Psychology of Interpersonal Relations*. New York: Wiley.

Herrnstein, Richard J., and Charles Murray 1994 *The Bell Curve: Intelligence and Class Structure in American Life*. New York: Free Press.

Hochschild, Jennifer L. 1981 *What's Fair? American Beliefs about Distributive Justice*. Cambridge, Mass.: Harvard University Press.

Homans, George C. (1961) 1974 *Social Behavior: Its Elementary Forms*. New York: Harcourt, Brace Jovanavich.

—— 1976 "Commentary." In L. Berkowitz and E. Walster, eds., *Equity Theory: Toward a General Theory of Social Interaction*. New York: Academic Press.

Jasso, Guillermina 1978 "On the Justice of Earnings: A New Specification of the Justice Evaluation Function." *American Journal of Sociology* 83:1398–1419.

—— 1980 "A New Theory of Distributive Justice." *American Sociological Review* 45:3–32

—— 1999 "How Much Injustice Is There in the World? Two New Justice Indexes." *American Sociological Review* 64:133–168.

——, and Peter H. Rossi 1977 "Distributive Justice and Earned Income." *American Sociological Review* 42:639–651

——, and Bernd Wegener 1997 "Methods for Empirical Justice Analysis: Part 1. Framework, Models, and Quantities." *Social Justice Research* 10:393–430.

—— 1999 "Gender and Country Differences in the Sense of Justice." *International Journal of Comparative Sociology* 40:94–116.

Jencks, Christopher S., et al. 1972 *Inequality: A Reassessment of the Effect of Family and Schooling in America*. New York: Basic Books.

—— 1979 *Who Gets Ahead? The Determinants of Economic Success in America*. New York: Basic Books.

Kluegel, James R., David S. Mason, and Bernd Wegener 1995 *Social Justice and Political Change: Public Opinion in Capitalist and Post-Communist States*. New York: Aldine de Gruyter.

——, and Eliot R. Smith 1981 "Beliefs about Stratification." *Annual Review of Sociology* 7:29–56.

—— 1986 *Beliefs about Inequality: Americans' Views of What Is and What Ought to Be*. New York: Aldine de Gruyter.

Lane, Robert 1986 "Market Justice, Poltical Justice." *American Political Science Review* 80:383–402.

Levy, Frank 1988 *Dollars and Dreams: The Changing American Income Distribution*. New York: Norton.

——, and Richard J. Murnane 1992 "U.S. Earnings Levels and Earnings Inequality: A Review of Recent Trends and Proposed Explanations." *Journal of the Economic Literature* 30:1333–1381.

Major, Brenda, and Blythe Forcey 1985 "Social Comparisons and Pay Evaluations: Preferences for Same-Sex and Same-Job Wage Comparisons." *Journal of Experimental Social Psychology* 21:393–405.

Markovsky, Barry 1985 "Toward a Multilevel Distributive Justice Theory." *American Sociological Review* 50:822–839.

Messick, David M., and Karen A. Cook 1983 *Equity Theory: Psychological and Sociological Perspectives*. New York: Praeger.

Mikula, Gerald 1980 *Justice and Social Interaction: Experimental and Theoretical Contributions from Psychological Research*. New York: Springer-Verlag.

Molm, Linda D. 1991 "Affect and Social Exchange: Satisfaction in Power-Dependence Relations." *American Sociological Review* 56:475–493.

Moynihan, Daniel Patrick 1968 *On Understanding Poverty*. New York: Basic Books.

Mueller, Charles W., and Jean E. Wallace 1996 "Justice and the Paradox of the Contented Female Worker." *Social Psychology Quarterly* 59:338–349.

Nader, Laura, and Andree Sursock 1986 "Anthropology and Justice." In R. L. Cohen, ed., *Justice: Views from the Social Sciences*. New York: Plenum.

Norris, Joan E. 1987 "Justice and Intergenerational Relations: An Introduction." *Social Justice Research* 1:393–403.

Nozick, Robert 1974 *Anarchy, State, and Utopia*. New York: Basic Books.

Patchen, Martin 1961 *The Choice of Wage Comparisons*. Englewood Cliffs, N.J.: Prentice-Hall.

Pettigrew, Thomas F. 1967 "Social Evaluation Theory: Convergences and Applications." In D. Levine, ed., *Nebraska Symposium on Motivation*. Lincoln: University of Nebraska Press.

Rae, Douglas 1981 *Equalities*. Cambridge, Mass.: Harvard University Press.

Rainwater, Lee 1974 *What Money Buys*. New York: Basic Books.

Randall, Christina S., and Charles W. Mueller 1995 "Extensions of Justice Theory: Justice Evaluations and Employee Reactions in a Natural Setting." *Social Psychology Quarterly* 58:178–194.

Rawls, John 1971 *A Theory of Justice*. Cambridge, Mass.: Harvard University Press.

Robinson, Robert V., and Wendell Bell 1978 "Equality, Success and Social Justice in England and the United States." *American Sociological Review* 43:125–143.

Runciman, W. 1966 *Relative Deprivation and Social Justice*. Berkeley: University of California Press.

Rytina, Steve 1986 "Sociology and Justice." In R. L. Cohen, ed., *Justice: Views from the Social Sciences*. New York: Plenum.

Schaeffer, Nora Cate 1990 "Principles of Justice in Judgments about Child Support." *Social Forces* 69:157–179.

Sennett, Richard, and Jonathan Cobb 1972 *The Hidden Injuries of Class*. New York: Vintage Books.

Sewell, William H., and Robert M. Hauser 1975 *Education, Occupation, and Earnings: Achievement in the Early Career*. New York: Academic Press.

Solo, Robert A., and Charles W. Anderson 1981 *Value Judgment and Income Distribution*. New York: Praeger.

Southwood, Kenneth E. 1978 "Substantive Theory and Statistical Interaction: Five Models." *American Journal of Sociology* 83:1154–1203.

Stolte, John F. 1983. "The Legitimation of Structural Inequality." *American Sociological Review* 48:331–342.

Thibaut, John W., and Harold H. Kelley 1959 *The Social Psychology of Groups*. New York: Wiley.

——, et al. 1975 *Procedural Justice: A Psychological Analysis*. Hillsdale, N.J.: Erlbaum.

—— 1987 "A Surge in Inequality." *Scientific American* 256:30–37.

Tyler, Tom R. 1984 "Justice in the Political Arena." In R. Folger, ed., *The Sense of Injustice: Social Psychological Perspectives*. New York: Plenum.

—— 1986 "The Psychology of Leadership Evaluation." In H. W. Bierhoff, R. L. Cohen, and J. Greenberg, eds., *Justice in Social Relations*. New York: Plenum.

Walster, Elaine, Ellen Berscheid, and G. William Walster 1973 "New Directions in Equity Research." *Journal of Personality and Social Psychology* 25:151–176.

Walster, Elaine G., William Walster, and Ellen Berscheid 1978 *Equity: Theory and Research*. Boston: Allyn and Bacon.

Walzer, Michael 1983 *Spheres of Justice: A Defense of Pluralism and Equality*. New York: Basic Books.

Williams, Robin M., Jr. 1975 "Relative Deprivation." In L. A. Coser, ed., *The Idea of Social Structure: Papers in Honor of Robert K. Merton.* New York: Harcourt Brace Jovanovich.

Worland, Stephen T. 1986 "Economics and Justice." In R. L. Cohen, ed., *Justice: Views from the Social Sciences.* New York: Plenum.

———, and Luca Perrone 1977 "Marxist Class Categories and Income Inequality." *American Sociological Review* 42:32–55.

Wright, Eric Olin, Janeen Baxter, and Gunn Elisabeth Birkelund 1995 "The Gender Gap in Workplace Authority: A Cross-National Study." *American Sociological Review* 60:407–435.

DUANE F. ALWIN

SOCIAL MOBILITY

The term "social mobility" describes the nature and amount of change in social position over time. In principle, this change can be defined for any social entity. Thus, one can study the "collective mobility" of classes, ethnic groups, or entire nations in terms of, for example, average health status, literacy, education, or gross domestic product per capita. More commonly, the term is used in connection with the movement of individuals or families. However, even though social mobility typically is defined with respect to micro units of society, the pattern of mobility across those units generally is considered a core characteristic of a society's social structure, and the study of this mobility generally is recognized as a fundamental area of macro-level sociology.

Social mobility typically is conceptualized in terms of the quantity of movement and the distribution of its direction and distance. The different rates that together constitute the mobility structure of a society is highly complex, however, for several reasons. First, societies have more than one dimension along which mobility can occur. Thus, one can speak of occupational mobility, social class mobility, educational mobility, job mobility, income mobility, wealth mobility, and so on. In principle, one also can use the term "social mobility" to describe movement among nonhierarchical social statuses, such as religious affiliation mobility and geographic mobility or mobility across categories that describe attitudes, belief systems, life styles, and the like. The dominant use of the term in the literature, however, concerns mobility along a social hierarchy that defines a dimension of social inequality in a society. Second, even with respect to a single hierarchy, the mobility structure is not easy to summarize. A different rate of mobility can be calculated with respect to each combination of origin and destination position along the social hierarchy in question. Empirically, it may be possible to summarize this collection of rates accurately in terms of a function of the social distance between origin and destination or in terms of specific relationships between the origin and destination categories. In general, however, an accurate summary cannot be expressed in terms of a single number. Thus, for each social hierarchy, there is not a single rate of social mobility but a core set of rates that, taken together, can be termed the structure of mobility with respect to the particular hierarchical dimension.

Social mobility is an important issue in sociology for several reasons. For one thing, it is relevant to social equity. Philosophical and moral evaluations of social inequality often depend not only on the level of inequality in a society but also on the extent to which individuals or families can leave disadvantaged states during their lifetimes or across generations. Social mobility is also an important explanatory factor in social theory. The basic stratification variables affect a wide variety of social outcomes and behaviors, but these effects accumulate over time; social mobility therefore affects outcomes by changing the states and durations of these key explanatory variables. The societal rate of mobility also may have macro-level consequences. An early conjecture in this area appears in the work of Werner Sombart, who argued that the failure of early twentieth century socialist parties in the United States stemmed in part from the high rate of American social mobility, which prevented the formation of strong class identification.

The longest-standing tradition in sociological mobility research concerns mobility in occupational groupings or social classes. Much of this work has used "mobility tables" (cross-classifications of origin by destination position) to study "intergenerational mobility," that is, the extent to which the social position of adults differs from that of their parents. Another large body of work has focused on "intragenerational mobility," or the mobility experienced by individuals or families over the course of their adult lives. Because male labor force participation generally has been higher and more persistent than female participation and because of the somewhat controversial presumption that the status of a family derives from the status of the male breadwinner, for many years these studies focused on intergenerational mobility between fathers and sons, although more recent literature has examined the structure of mobility for women as well.

An important question in intergenerational mobility research is whether overall rates of intergenerational social mobility differ by country. Earlier in the century, scholars hypothesized that the United States had especially high rates of mobility, and some argued that those rates were a consequence of the American meritocratic value system. More recently, it became clear that the primary factors in cross-national differences in mobility rates are structural, not cultural. Differences in so-called structural mobility across countries arise from the extent to which the distribution of positions for sons or daughters differs from the distribution of positions for their fathers. Changes in this distribution across generations (as well as more subtle factors such as class differences in fertility, death rates, and migration rates) necessarily produce intergenerational social mobility. Countries whose occupational distribution is changing rapidly (high rates of structural change) therefore have greater levels of mobility than do countries whose occupational distribution is changing slowly.

Not all social mobility occurs as a result of structural change. The component of social mobility that occurs beyond the amount produced by structural change is typically called circulation mobility, exchange mobility, or relative mobility. The Featherman, Jones, Hauser (FJH) hypothesis of the mid-1970s asserts that cross-national and historical differences in social mobility are accounted for almost completely by differences in levels of structural mobility. According to the strong form of this hypothesis, once structural mobility is taken into account, the pattern of relative mobility chances is invariant over time and across countries. This pattern has three principal features: (1) relatively high immobility at the top and bottom of the hierarchy, (2) higher levels of short-range mobility than long-range mobility (moves from the top to the bottom or from the bottom to the top of the hierarchy are especially rare), and (3) a relatively small impact of origins on destinations in the middle of the hierarchy.

More recent research has determined that even though the weak form of the FJH hypothesis (overall mobility differences are due largely to differences in structural mobility) is supported by the data, the strong form (invariance of relative mobility chances) appears to be false. However, further progress on this issue has been elusive. In particular, the question of whether cross-national differences in relative mobility chances are the subject of such complex national historical differences that they are idiosyncratic or whether they are the product of a more parsimonious set of structural forces (e.g., the extent to which the political system is democratic, the level of modernization, and the level of social inequality) remains to be answered.

Another continuing challenge in mobility research concerns conceptualization and measurement of the component of mobility that is due to structural change. The specification of this causal force in terms of differences in the distribution of positions of fathers and their adult children is problematic for subtle but important reasons. Such an identification assumes that the observed destination distribution is caused by forces (such as technological change) that are not affected by (and therefore are a legitimate cause of) the observed mobility process. This amounts to assuming that the observed destination distribution constitutes a rigid supply constraint, a set of preexisting empty vacancies that are filled by the movement of sample members with respect to their origin positions. This assumption is never perfectly true. If the "supply constraint" is not rigid (and it is unlikely to be so), the observed distribution of destination positions (which by definition represents a summing up of the mobility outcomes for a particular statistical sample) is a consequence of the mobility process as well as of the "structural forces" that constrain the character of this destination distribution. It therefore cannot be taken to be a pure cause of social mobility. The logic of structural mobility becomes especially problematic when subgroups of the population are studied in this fashion. For example, if the distribution of women's occupations shifts toward high-status occupations relative to the total occupational distribution, it is problematic to argue that the relative improvement of women's destinations is a "cause" of women's higher levels of social mobility as opposed to being a consequence of that mobility. This problem, which is sometimes referred to as the "reflection" problem, has not had a satisfactory solution.

Although structural change is a major part of the explanation for overall levels of intergenerational social mobility in a society, it cannot explain differences in the likelihood that particular individuals will be upwardly or downwardly mobile. The prevailing pattern of circulation mobility that was noted above (relatively high levels of immobility at the top and bottom, the predominance of short-range over long-range mobility, etc.) implies that class of origin is a significant predictor of the types of mobility that do occur. However, an explanation for destination positions that relied solely on the status of origin would be unsatisfactory in two respects: First, the predictive power of social origins by itself is relatively weak; second, the explanation does not indicate how and why social origins matter.

Efforts to redress these deficiencies stem largely from the publication of Blau and Duncan's *The American Occupational Structure* (1967). A major goal of that work was to understand whether the educational system operated primarily as a device that transmitted the status of parents to their children or as an engine of social mobility that freed children from the effects of the status of their parents. To accomplish that goal, Blau and Duncan developed what has come to be known as the status attainment model. Their approach to the study of mobility assumed a dominant metric to social hierarchy: the socioeconomic status of occupations. Their research showed that, at least for men (Blau and Duncan did not study the mobility of women), education was a more important determinant of a son's adult socioeconomic status than were his socioeconomic origins. Furthermore, while educational attainment was strongly influenced by socioeconomic origin, most of the individual-level variation in educational attainment was not explained by socioeconomic origin. Those authors also showed that most of the effect of socioeconomic origins on outcomes was indirect, derived from the effect of those origins on education. Finally, the effect of education on occupational attainment regardless of social background was much larger in the United States than was the direct effect of father's socioeconomic background

(regardless of the son's education). These findings led many to interpret Blau and Duncan's research to mean that the United States more closely approximated an "achievement" than an "ascription" society, although others pointed to the still large (even if not decisive) disadvantage arising from low socioeconomic origin along with the disadvantages associated with being a first-generation immigrant, an African-American, or a woman as constituting important qualifications to such a generalization.

The Blau and Duncan approach essentially divided the intergenerational mobility process into three segments. The first segment concerned the process of educational attainment, the second concerned the transition from school to work, and the third concerned the "intragenerational" mobility that occurs over the working life. Leaving aside the powerful but difficult to specify force of structural change, this division may offer the best possibility for understanding the mechanisms that lie behind intergenerational social mobility as well as identifying possible policy interventions and shedding light on three processes that have great importance in their own right. Each of these processes calls attention to specific institutions (in particular, the educational system and the labor market) that facilitate, limit, or channel social mobility. The focus on how institutional forces constrain the impact of individual resources on individual outcomes sometimes is referred to as the "fourth generation" of social mobility research (with early mobility studies being the first generation, the status attainment tradition being the second, and statistically sophisticated analyses of mobility tables being the third).

A large body of literature has grown around each of these components of the intergenerational mobility process. With respect to education, scholars have conceptualized the educational career as a set of transitions to successively higher grades and have asked whether family background has the same influence at each grade level of this transition process. Results for the United States and several other countries suggest that the effects of family background decline at higher-grade transitions, though these findings are controversial. Assuming that the decline is real, some scholars have argued that the historical raising of the minimum school-leaving age should have reduced the impact of family of origin on outcomes over time.

Again, however, while there is some evidence that the effects of family background have declined during the twentieth century and that these declines are caused by the expansion of education, empirical studies have failed to confirm this conjecture decisively.

A second major focus in the literature concerns the reasons why socioeconomic background is associated with educational performance. It has been appreciated since Sewell and associates developed the "Wisconsin model" in the early 1970s that there is a social psychological component to mobility in which family status is related to parental expectations for the child. In combination with grades in school, peer group influences, and teachers' expectations, this shapes a student's educational and occupational aspirations. More recent work has reconceptualized these family advantages or disadvantages in terms of cultural resources ("cultural capital"), which sometimes are specified as a family's participation in "high-cultural" activities (exposure to art museums, opera, theater, dance, etc.); in other studies, they are defined more broadly (and vaguely) as encompassing all the cultural advantages a family may possess that affect a child's ability to do well in school. Other recent literature focuses on "social capital," which sometimes is interpreted to mean the level and quality of interaction parents have with their children and at other times is interpreted to refer to the resources embedded in the parents' social networks that could in principle influence a child's outcomes. A third, rather controversial focus of attention in recent years concerns possible links between socioeconomic status and genes and the extent to which intergenerational correlations among status variables (particularly educational outcomes) indicate the presence of a genetic force. A fourth focus concerns the specific consequences of low income on children's development and later socioeconomicoutcomes. A fifth focus concerns the extent to which the characteristics of schools, neighborhoods, and communities can mute or exaggerate the impact of family characteristics on educational outcomes.

The second mobility component is the transition from school to work. A large body of literature focuses specifically on aspects of this transition, including variation in the extent to which the diplomas, degrees, and advanced degrees provided by schools are linked by law or custom to specific occupational careers; the extent to which credentials are standardized in a country; the extent to which the supply of those credentials is controlled by schools in light of estimated demand; and the extent to which students who graduate with these diplomas or degrees are provided with knowledge of the relevant job market. Many policy concerns in the United States focus on those who leave school before the tertiary level and the extent to which they are provided with a mix of academic and vocational skills and credentials that is valuable on the job market. Vocational education in particular is organized quite differently across industrialized societies, and in recent years comparative research on this transition has accelerated.

The third component concerns intragenerational mobility over the life course. This research has taken different forms. The Blau and Duncan approach largely emphasized the mean or typical pattern of life-course development as a function of education, first job, and father's occupation. In this form, the question of mobility is reduced to a question about the average status "return" to the resources an individual possesses on first entering the labor market. Although this approach is informative about the typical level of status advancement during the work career as a function of origin conditions, it suffers from two deficiencies: First, it does not explain how education and the first job lead to the current job; second, it does not provide an explanation of the frequency or consequences of deviations from the typical amount of status advancement during the work career.

An understanding of the full distribution of outcomes (i.e., both upward and downward career mobility) is made possible through the use of the "mobility table" approach that has been applied to the study of intergenerational mobility between the status of the father and the status of the son or daughter. The prevalent approach in recent sociology, however, has been more institutional. One line of work has focused on structural linkages between jobs in particular occupational or organizational labor markets. This work has addressed the implications of entering these "internal labor markets" for subsequent career advancement, with an important subset of it directed at questions about whether these institutional mechanisms reproduce, enhance, or mute racial or gender differences. Because these job linkages generally are not expressed in terms of abstract hierarchical measures such as class and socioeconomic status, studies of these organized labor markets frequently have turned away from the earlier focus on class or status and toward more concrete reward variables such as earnings and job level within an organizational hierarchy. Jobs outside of organized hierarchies that lacked other forms of institutional protection (such as professional licensing requirements) were characterized as "open" or (if low-quality) "secondary" labor market jobs. For several years, sociologists hoped that a parsimonious set of labor market "boundaries" could be operationalized and used to explain labor market outcomes in terms of labor market segment early in one's career. The promise of this "segmented labor market" approach to career mobility has faded, however. It is now recognized thatthe boundary between unstable, low-paying jobs in what once was commonly referred to as the "secondary labor market" and "internal labor market" jobs is by no means impermeable, especially in the early years of the adult life course. The segmented labor market approach has been undermined further by the appreciation of the numerically high levels of mobility (including involuntary mobility) out of corporate jobs, often as a result of plant closings and corporate restructuring. Literature on "displaced workers" that has developed largely in labor economics rather than sociology has attempted to quantify the short-term and medium-term career consequences of job displacement (the literature shows only transitory effects on employment but more durable effects on earnings). It can be assumed that job displacement is a principal mechanism by which structural change produces short-term and longer-term intragenerational (and ultimately intergenerational) occupational mobility. However, sociologists have only begun to explore the connection between job displacement and the structural mobility observed in mobility tables.

A separate body of literature has addressed the intragenerational mobility of people who at one time or another in their lives are poor. Aside from questions about the intergenerational transmission of poverty, much of this literature has focused on whether poverty is a permanent or transitory status. It has been recognized that most poverty in the United States is transient, although an important fraction of the poor remain poor for long periods, while many who escape poverty have a relatively high probability of returning to poverty in the future. Much of this literature addresses the factors that influence rates of entry into and exit from poverty.

Poverty studies use a measure of income, especially income in relation to needs, rather than class or status as the basic measure of position. They typically make the family the relevant unit of measurement because it is family income, not individual earnings or status, that most directly determines poverty status. They also direct attention to the facts that income mobility is a household, not an individual-level, concept; that income mobility can be generated by labor market events involving one's partner as well as oneself; that public transfers can be an important source of income and can play a significant role in determining levels of income mobility; and that changes in household composition (including marriage, cohabitation, and union dissolution) can strongly influence income mobility.

More recent mobility literature has focused as much attention on instability as on stability (or stable "career advancement") over time. This emphasis raises important questions about an important presupposition underlying the sociological framework for mobility studies: that it was meaningful to conceptualize the socioeconomic status of the family of origin as a stable point and the "current" status of the adult son or daughter as a "realized" socioeconomic status that could be compared with the point of origin. Early studies were forced by the limitations of data to use parental status at a single point in time (e.g., the point at which the respondent was 16 years old) as the measurement of family status over the duration of childhood. The growing availability of multigenerational panel data that provide information about the possibly changing status of the family of origin during childhood has made it possible for scholars to study how temporal variations in the status of parents affect the process of intergenerational transmission. These more extensive data on the lives of parents and their grown-up children are allowing scholars to study intergenerational and intragenerational mobility with respect to statuses such as income, wealth, and poverty, which are perhaps more volatile than are occupational status and class position.

Questions about racial and/or ethnic or gender differences in mobility have largely been subordinated to gender and racial and/or ethnic inequality and changes in levels in inequality over time. In other words, the focus has been more on the *collective* mobility of these groups with respect to white males than on whether the structure of individual-level mobility within groups defined by race or gender is different from the structure of mobility for white males. This literature has perhaps paid more attention to economic outcomes than to class or status outcomes. Research on gender inequality in particular has avoided the use of status metrics or broad occupational groups, which understate the gender inequality that is visible in earnings. The issue of mobility still plays an important role in this literature because of the possible role of mobility processes in explaining how gender or racial and/or ethnic inequality comes about. In the case of women, the literature has focused on why women take a different mix of academic subjects than men do and on how gender differences in the transition from school to work and in career mobility produce differences in the average earnings of women and men over the life course. In this literature, the pattern and quantity of work experience and the different distribution of men and women across jobs and occupations ("sex segregation") have been the issues of greatest interest. In contrast, the role of specifically intergenerational processes and their possible impact on gender inequality or on the well-documented declining level of gender inequality in earnings has received less attention.

The issue of race is in some respects parallel to that of gender but has its own unique features. Women and men grow up in the same families, while whites and nonwhites grow up in different families, and these differences involve socioeconomic factors as well as race or ethnicity per se. Furthermore, racial and/or ethnic segregation by educational major, job, or occupation has not been as extreme as gender segregation in recent years. However, just as research has shown that the effects of race on income declined over the postwar years (though the trend has stalled and perhaps reversed since about 1980), it also has shown that the direct effects of race on socioeconomic attainment have declined, at least through the late 1980s. African-Americans experience no disadvantage at all in educational attainment because of race per se (though they experience a disadvantage stemming from their lower average socioeconomic origins). Specifically race-based intergenerational factors still may affect the levels of black–white inequality in the next generation, but they probably operate through the quality (as opposed to quantity) of schooling, and these effects are not well understood.

Comparative analyses of mobility that go beyond the mobility table approach described above are complicated by substantive differences in institutional structures across nations and differences in the measurement of key variables. Nonetheless, progress is being made. In perhaps the most notable application of the original Blau and Duncan model to comparative analysis, Treiman and Yip used the ratio of the net effect of education on occupational attainment to the direct effect of the father's socioeconomic background (this might be conceptualized as a ratio of "achievement" to "ascription") to compare the process of attainment in different countries. This ratio varies from a relatively high level in industrialized societies (particularly in Scandinavia) to a low level in less industrialized societies (with India having the lowest value in their study). Scholars also are focusing on comparative studies of topics such as the transition from school to work, job mobility, earnings mobility, sex segregation, and family dynamics. Many of these studies are being carried out with newly available panel data on demographic and socioeconomic outcomes that are being collected in many industrialized societies. These new sources of data are complex, and it will take several years before a broad-based comparative literature that uses them becomes available. The direction and pace of research, however, are encouraging. Social mobility is likely to retain its vitality as well as its centrality in sociology for the foreseeable future.

REFERENCES

Blau, Peter, and Otis Dudley Duncan 1967 *The American Occupational Structure*. New York: Wiley.

Corcoran, Mary 1995 "Rags to Rags: Poverty and Mobility in the United States." *Annual Review of Sociology* 21:237–267.

Duncan, Greg J., and Jeanne Brooks-Gunn, eds. 1997 *Consequences of Growing Up Poor*. New York: Russell Sage Foundation.

Erikson, Robert, and John H. Goldthorpe 1992 *The Constant Flux: A Study of Class Mobility in Industrial Societies*. Oxford, UK: Clarendon Press.

Fischer, Claude S. 1996 *Inequality by Design: Cracking the Bell Curve Myth*. Princeton, N.J.: Princeton University Press.

Ganzeboom, Harry B. G., Donald J. Treiman, and Wout C. Ultee 1991 "Comparative Intergenerational Stratification Research: Three Generations and Beyond." *Annual Review of Sociology* 17:277–302.

Grusky, David B. 1994 *Social Stratification: Class, Race, and Gender in Sociological Perspective*. Boulder, Colo.: Westview.

Jacobs, Jerry A. 1996 "Gender Inequality and Higher Education." *Annual Review of Sociology* 22:153–185.

Kerckhoff, Alan 1995 "Institutional Arrangements and Stratification Processes in Industrial Societies." *Annual Review of Sociology*. 21:323–347.

Reskin, Barbara 1993 "Sex Segregation in the Workplace." *Annual Review of Sociology* 19:241–269.

Rosenbaum, James E., T. Kariya, R. Settersten, and T. Maier 1990 "Market and Network Theories of the Transition from High School to Work: Their Application to Industrialized Societies." *Annual Review of Sociology* 16:263–299.

Rosenfeld, Rachel 1992 "Job Mobility and Career Processes." *Annual Review of Sociology* 18:39–61.

Shavit, Yossi, and Hans-Peter Blossfeld 1993 *Persistent Inequality: Changing Educational Attainment in Thirteen Countries*. Boulder, Colo.: Westview.

——, and Walter Müller, eds. 1997 *From School to Work: A Comparative Study of Educational Qualifications and Occupational Destinations*. Oxford, UK: Oxford University Press.

Sørensen, Annemette 1994 "Women, Family, and Class." *Annual Review of Sociology* 20:27–47.

THOMAS A. DIPRETE

SOCIAL MOVEMENTS

Social movements can be described most simply as collective attempts to promote or resist change in a society or group. The degree of change advocated and the level at which changes are pursued vary across all types of social movements, whether religious, political, or student. Some movements clamor for sweeping, revolutionary transformations, whereas others pursue specific moderate reforms. The level at which changes are sought varies from global and national alterations of social structures to attitudinal, spiritual, and lifestyle changes.

TYPES OF MOVEMENTS

Revolutionary movements such as the Bolshevik, Palestinian, Islamic jihad, and Irish Republican movements seek fundamental structural changes. These movements pursue radical changes in a society's basic institutions or, in some cases, major changes in the world order. Because these groups challenge the legitimacy of extant authorities, powerful elites typically use every means, including violence, to repress revolutionary movements.

Reform movements, in contrast, attempt to modify structural relations without threatening existing institutions. Consequently, while some elites oppose any reforms, they are usually more tolerant of reform movements than they are of revolutionary ones. Some reform movements, such as the peace, women's, and environmental movements, are general in scope (Blumer 1946) and often blend a plethora of political and lifestyle objectives. Peace movements, for example, not only pursue a variety of political objectives (e.g., preventing and stopping wars, opposing specific weapons, promoting disarmament, changing foreign policy, establishing conflict resolution institutions) but also strive to persuade individuals to change their attitudes and live more peaceful everyday lives.

Other reform movements, such as the antiabortion, women's temperance, and anti-drunken-driving movements, focus on specific issues. Although specific reform movements are considerably narrower in scope than general reform movements are, they also may organize around both political and lifestyle objectives (Staggenborg 1987).

Still other reform movements, such as various self-help, human potential, and New Age movements, focus almost exclusively on lifestyle and identity issues. In contrast to other movements, these movements tend to disregard social structural issues. Instead, they concentrate on changing individuals.

Finally, social movements frequently generate organized opposition in the form of countermovements. Countermovements attempt to prevent revolutionary or reform movements from securing the changes they promote. As a result of their counterreformist tendencies, most countermovements (e.g., the antibusing, McCarthyist, stop-ERA, and Moral Majority movements) are conservative (Lo 1982); that is, they attempt to preserve extant institutions, cultural practices, and lifestyles.

Regardless of the particular type of social movement and the scope and level of change it advocates or opposes, all movements share certain common characteristics that are of interest to social scientists. First, all movements emerge under a specific, complex set of historical, cultural, and structural conditions. Second, as a movement emerges, a variety of participation issues arise, including recruiting new members, building commitment, and sustaining participation. Third, every movement is organized to some degree. The most visible manifestations of movements are their organizations and their strategies and tactics. Third, by virtue of its existence, every social movement has some consequences, however minimal. Although researchers frequently are concerned with the extent to which movements affect social change, definitive answers to this question have proved illusory.

MOVEMENT EMERGENCE

Social scientists have devoted considerable attention to the factors associated with the emergence of social movements. Early theory and research asserted that movements arise when societies undergo structural strain, such as during times of rapid social change (Smelser 1962). These "breakdown theories" posit that "large structural rearrangements in societies—such as urbanization and industrialization" lead to the dissolution of social controls and heighten "the impulse toward antisocial behavior" (Tilly et al. 1975, p. 4). Hence, these systemic "breakdowns" were said to cause an increase in strikes, violent collective action, and social movements.

Later social movement scholars criticized breakdown theories on empirical and theoretical grounds. Rather than viewing movement emergence and participation as aberrations, scholars now view them as "simply 'politics by other means,' often the *only* means open to relatively powerless challenging groups" (McAdam 1988, pp. 127–128).

However, if these groups are powerless, it is important to understand the conditions that affect the likelihood that they will mobilize. To do so researchers first turned to the structural factors that are conducive to the emergence of social movements.

One macro structural factor concerns the "structure of political opportunities" (Eisinger 1973). Movements emerge when there is a "receptivity or vulnerability of the political system to organized protest" (McAdam et al. 1988, p. 699). Researchers exploring the U.S. civil rights movement, for instance, conclude that that movement's emergence was facilitated by a series of interrelated changes in the structure of political opportunities. Those changes included the decline of cotton markets, African-American migration to the North, the expansion of the black vote, and the electoral shift to the Democratic party (McAdam 1982).

Additionally, researchers have identified the absence of repression as a related macro structural factor. Social movements sometimes are spared a violent or otherwise repressive response from the authorities not only during times of breakdown or regime crisis but also during periods of expanding political opportunities such as times of state building. For example, as the former Soviet Union took strides between 1985 and 1989 to open discourse and other political opportunities ("perestroika"), there was a dramatic increase in protest activities (Zdravomyslova 1996). The result is what researchers have termed a cycle of contention: "the phase of heightened conflict across the social system" (Tarrow 1998, p. 142).

During times of increased movement activity, the authorities can, and sometimes do, take an active stance toward challenging groups. However, while their initial attempts to repress movements often fan the flames of discontent and fuel further protest activities, research suggests that the relationship between collective action and repression is bell-shaped (Tilly 1978). If the authorities later respond by increasing the severity of the repression, as occurred when the Chinese authorities ordered tanks and troops into Tiananmen Square to fire on student demonstrators, the cost of collective action usually becomes too high for movements to continue their challenges.

A nation-state can vary in structural factors such as institutional strength, access of challengers to polity membership and/or decision making, and configurations of power (Kriesi 1996; Rucht 1996; Ferree and Gamson 1999). The political environment, or context structure, of a nation-state then can influence movements and movement emergence. For instance, France after 1981 had a strong, exclusive government and a political party system with large inter- and intraparty divisions. In this case, movement emergence and growth depended in part on the left's support of solidarity movements to gain political advantage. In contrast, Switzerland had a weak but inclusive government in the 1980s, allowing for the growth of diverse groups with multiple areas of focus (Kriesi 1996).

Many contemporary social movements are affected increasingly by globalization, or the creation and intensification of "worldwide social relations which link distinct localities in such a way that local happenings are shaped by events occurring miles away and vice versa" (Giddens 1990, p. 64). Technological revolutions in communications and transportation as well as economic, cultural, and political developments have increased global interdependence and consciousness of the global whole. Globalization thus spawns similarities in movement mobilizations and context structures across different nations (della Porta and Kriesi 1999). These similarities often lead to the cross-national diffusion of values and beliefs, facilitated in part by direct and indirect links between similar movements in various countries. German students studying in the United States in the early 1960s, for example, drew on the American student movement and later on access to networks they found during their stay in the United States in mobilizing their own student movement in Germany (McAdam and Rucht 1993).

Operating in much the same way as cross-national linkages, preexisting organizations in a nation-state serve as communication networks for the discontented members of a population (Freeman 1973). In fact, they can aid or inhibit the spread of information from cross-national linkages. More important, they provide a base for mobilizing the resources needed to sustain a movement. Churches, for example, were important indigenous organizations that contributed to the emergence of the contemporary peace, civil rights, and Moral Majority movements.

Several European scholars contend that state intervention into private domains of life has generated new social movements. According to this perspective, various structural changes in Western industrialized societies, especially changes in the system of production, led the state to seek control over previously private domains. Consequently, private domains such as sexual relations, biological identity, birth and death, illness and aging, and one's relationship to nature "have entered the realm of 'public' conflict" (Melucci 1980, p. 219). New social movements (e.g., the women's, gay rights, euthanasia, and environmental movements) emerged to reclaim those areas from the state.

The foregoing analysis indicates that numerous structural factors are crucial to providing an opportunity for the emergence of social movements, yet those factors alone cannot account for the rise of a particular movement. Why is it that when the structural conditions appear to be ripe for the emergence of a particular movement, frequently no movement appears? To address this question, some researchers have begun to investigate both the cultural and the micro interactional factors associated with the emergence of social movements. What is most important here are the reasons people take action in the first place: their grievances.

As a commonly shared stock of knowledge and activity, culture plays a role in movement emergence by giving individuals a sense of commonality with others. Specifically, culture can aid in the creation of a common identity that sets itself apart from that of other groups. Furthermore, when groups feel subservient in a society, they may create forms of activities and beliefs that express opposition to the dominant culture. This opposition can result in interests and needs that conflict with the dominant culture and in the development of grievances. In the 1980s, for example, the naming of the *Québécois* nationalist movement in Canada set that group apart from the rest of Canadian society by emphasizing the common culture shared by the group's members and symbolized a collective desire for political empowerment (Jenson 1995).

Culture is important in the emergence and cross-national diffusion of social movements, then, because it provides a common way in which to view the world and ways to express that worldview. Indeed, movements, such as the Japanese-based

Nichiren Shoshu/Sokagakkai Buddhist group may actively attempt to spread their worldviews and the cultural actions and artifacts to which they are attached to facilitate movement emergence in other countries (Snow and Benford 1999).

Worldviews are also important because they provide a yardstick by which to evaluate events. When an event fails to measure up against that yardstick, people experience a moral shock that can lead to movement emergence (Jasper 1997). However, although a single event may generate several movements with similar goals, culture can play a role in amplifying the moral shock that leads to collective action. Protests against the Gulf War emerged throughout the world more quickly than they had during previous wars, and there initially appeared to be similarity in the information received by those movements, along with the timing and stances taken by them. For example, the slogan "No Blood for Oil" was used by movements globally (Koopmans 1999). However, while they all were against the Gulf War, the peace movements in various countries mobilized differently on the basis of culturally filtered considerations. French peace movements, for instance, were against any coalition with the Americans. By contrast, the German peace movement was against any potential use of the German military on foreign soil.

The bulk of micro interactional research focuses on individuals' processes of interpreting grievances. These processes refer to the means by which people collectively arrive at similar definitions of a situation or "interpretive frames" regarding social changes they support or oppose (Snow et al. 1986). Aggrieved but previously unmobilized people must revise the manner in which they look at a problematic condition or aspect of life; social arrangements must come to be seen as "unjust and mutable" (Piven and Cloward 1977, p. 12). This process of cognitive liberation typically involves an attributional shift from blaming oneself to blaming the system for particular problems (McAdam 1982). The expression of these understandings—the definitions of problems, protagonists, antagonists, ideas for change, and reasons for action—constitutes a movement's collective action frame.

As a cycle of contention continues, movement emergence is influenced indirectly by the movements that emerged early in the cycle. In addition to the structural influences, cultural influences, and need for cognitive liberation mentioned above, latecomers in a cycle must align their collective action frame with a master frame (Snow and Benford 1992). Early collective action frames may gain in both attention and popularity; they may resonate with the audience for which they are intended. In the minds of individuals, these frames are translated into generic codes that indicate how both audiences and movements should understand and react to events. Later attempts to extend the frames by adding further diagnoses, prognoses, and rationales for action may be met with resistance, constraining the emergence of a new movement.

In sum, social movements are most likely to emerge when the structural conditions for mobilization are ripe, cultural contexts provide a common worldview and set of activities to be applied to the situation, the collective interpretation of grievances produces cognitive liberation, and, if necessary, collective action frames are aligned to at least a minimal degree with a master frame.

MOVEMENT PARTICIPATION

Closely related to the issue of movement emergence are questions regarding movement participation: Who joins and why? What conditions affect the likelihood of participating? How do movements build membership and sustain participation? Initial attempts to address questions about movement participation were influenced by breakdown theories. Movement participation was viewed as an irrational response to social structural strains. The factors regarded as key determinants of movement participation ranged from alienation and social isolation to status strains and relative deprivation. Each of these approaches suggested that some sort of psychological malaise or personality defect predispose some individuals to react to structural strains by participating in social movements.

The outburst of collective action and the proliferation of social movements in the 1960s led many social scientists to reconsider the assumptions of breakdown theory. Some theorists redefined movement participation as a rational choice. According to this perspective, people take part in social movement activities only when they perceive that the anticipated benefits outweigh the expected costs of participation (Klandermans 1984). Research on the conditions affecting cost-benefit participation decisions indicates that this is a complex process that involves numerous structural and social psychological factors (Snow and Oliver 1995).

Social networks also have a crucial effect on differential recruitment to social movements. Movements tend to recruit the majority of their new members from the networks of existing members (Snow et al. 1980). A person typically decides to attend her or his first movement function because a friend, coworker, or relative invited her or him. Those outside such networks are less likely to be aware of the existence of specific movement groups. They also are less likely to attend a movement function if they are not sure there will be others present whom they know.

Overlapping networks in a community increase the probability that an individual will participate in a social movement. For instance, during the 1871 Paris uprisings, persons who were in Parisian National Guard units drawn from their own neighborhoods were more likely to defect and join the communal revolution. Participation increased further when adjacent neighborhoods had similar overlapping networks. In short, the interaction and intricacy of multiple networks increased the likelihood of social movement participation (Gould 1991).

While having social ties to people who are movement participants increases the likelihood of movement participation, other social ties can diminish that probability. Social ties in the form of family and career attachments can constrain movement participation in a number of ways. For one thing, these competing commitments may result in role conflict. The demands of being a movement participant and the demands of being a parent or employee may be incompatible. Married persons who have parental responsibilities as well as full-time jobs may not have sufficient discretionary time to participate in social movements (McCarthy and Zald 1973). Furthermore, spouses and employers can be displeased by a person's participation in a social movement.

To justify their movement participation to themselves and others, participants develop vocabularies of motives. These are rationales that offer compelling reasons for their participation, particularly when their actions are called into question by employers, family members, or friends. Movement participants socially construct these vocabularies of motive as they interact with one another. Activists in turn employ these rationales to encourage sympathizers and adherents to take action on behalf of movement goals.

Vocabularies of motives not only facilitate recruitment to movements but also serve as commitment-building mechanisms. They help participants justify to themselves making sacrifices for a cause. The more sacrifices the participants make, the more costly leaving the movement seems to be. As they relinquish old attachments in favor of new ones, their commitment grows deeper (Kanter 1968). Research indicates that contrary to popular myths regarding participation in new religious movements and cults, these conversion and commitment-building processes are typically voluntary (Snow and Machalek 1984).

Closely related to social ties and vocabularies of motives is the concept of collective identity. Usually based on shared values, beliefs, and personal identities, a collective identity refers to the qualities and characteristics attributed to a group by the members of that group (Hunt 1991). Movement actors develop this sense of "weness" or "groupness" in the course of participating in social movement activities. Participants who have made an emotional commitment to a movement "communicate, influence each other, negotiate and make decisions" (Melucci 1995, p. 45). During these interactions with others, participants continually create and re-create consensus on a movement's goals, strategies, and sites of activity.

Movements generate their collective identity in part by articulating the ways in which movement goals and interests appear to be aligned with the beliefs and values of potential supporters. In the case of the 1989 Chinese Democracy Movement, students framed their goals in ways that were consistent with traditional Chinese cultural narrations. Drawing on Confucian principles, communist ideology, and the rhetoric of nationalism, the students fashioned collective action frames and protest tactics that were concerned with patriotism and the way in which it was defined and dramatized. Through their words and deeds, the student demonstrators conveyed their deep sense of responsibility to their country and willingness to offer themselves in sacrifice for the greater good. Those framings tended to resonate well among the general population. Consequently, the Chinese Democracy Movement spread rapidly from students to ordinary citizens (Zuo and Benford 1995).

The emotional component is also important, since it can be changed through persuasion and thus can become a powerful motivation for initial involvement in a movement. Animal rights groups, for example, use pictures of stabbed bulls, starved dogs, clubbed baby seals, and cats with electrodes implanted in their skulls to create anger and draw recruits. Emotions also can help sustain participation. For instance, the songs and dances of Diablo Canyon nuclear power plant protestors in California generated a degree of bonding that helped sustain activity at the protest site (Jasper 1997).

By presenting images of movement participation, the mass media play an important role in the recruitment of individuals. Mass media allow the public to form a response to a potential social problem quickly because events are covered instantaneously. The media provide movements with a larger audience and at times are the only resource people have in constructing the meaning of an event. Although media representations of reality are filtered through people's experiences, the media serve as gatekeepers of information and thus exercise considerable influence on the framing of social problems and thus social movement recruitment.

Social movements do not necessarily rely exclusively on traditional media, however; sometimes movement activists devise their own means of communicating with their target audiences. In the Chinese Democracy Movement, the "illegitimate" status of the student protests precluded student activists from accessing major state-controlled media outlets such as newspapers, television, and radio. During the "crisis," the state even cut off student telephone and telegram services in most Beijing universities. To cope with communication problems, student leaders devised a number of creative means of communication, including protest notices and posters reporting the latest movement decisions and suggestions on campus building walls and bulletin boards, bicycles to relay strategic and tactical information between campuses, pirate radio broadcasts, E-mail, fax machines, and on-campus speeches and press conferences, to mobilize additional support (Zuo and Benford 1995).

Taken together, research on social movements reveals that participation factors, motives, and experiences are diverse. No single explanation can account for movement participation. Instead, a confluence of factors affect the decision to participate. Similarly, there are a variety of ways in which individuals may participate, ranging from those which require little commitment of time, such as signing a petition and writing a letter to a political official, to those requiring extensive commitment, such as coordinating national campaigns and committing acts of civil disobedience.

MOVEMENT ORGANIZATIONS

The activities of movements and their participants are coordinated by social movement organizations (SMOs). These organizations vary in a number of ways. An important way in which they differ relates to their origins. Some SMOs are organized at the grassroots level by people directly affected by a particular social problem. For example, a woman whose child had been killed by a drunken driver founded Mothers Against Drunk Driving (MADD). Other SMOs are established and sustained by powerful elites from the top downward. Before the disintegration of the Soviet bloc, the state orchestrated official "peace movements" in several communist countries.

Social movement organizations also vary in terms of the level or levels at which a group operates. Some SMOs operate at only a local level, focusing their attention solely on community issues. Others operate primarily at a state, provincial, or regional level, mobilizing around issues that affect that jurisdiction. Still others mobilize at a national level, often attempting to affect national decision making, policies, and legislation. Finally, some SMOs operate in several countries simultaneously. Many of those transnational SMOs focus on issues of human rights (Smith 1995).

Finally, SMOs vary in terms of how they are structurally linked to one another. At one end of the continuum, SMOs are formally linked to a central authority, usually a national or international SMO. Local Amnesty International chapters, for example, must follow specific guidelines and rules dictated by headquarters. At the other end of the continuum, SMOs are relatively autonomous, not answering to any central authority beyond their own group. Between those two poles, the social movement sector yields a variety organizational arrangements, including loosely federated clusters of SMOs, ad hoc coalitions, and more permanent coalitions.

Most general reform movements spawn numerous SMOs. For instance, by 1984, the U.S. nuclear disarmament movement included some 3,000 independent SMOs as well as another 1,000 local chapters of national organizations. Specific reform movements, by contrast, tend to generate fewer SMOs. Regardless, SMOs are formal groups that can be thought of as the command posts of movements. They acquire and deploy resources, mobilize adherents, and plan movement strategy.

Resource mobilization theorists were among the first to emphasize the importance of SMOs in performing these functions. In particular, they point out that in the absence of an organization, it is difficult for movements to acquire the resources needed to sustain their challenges (Tilly 1978). Contemporary movements require money for advertising, printing, postage, lobbying, staff, and the like.

Other resource mobilization theorists have suggested that studying SMOs reveals how the macro and micro levels are reciprocally linked (McAdam et al. 1988). For example, the resource level of a society affects the resources available to SMOs, which in turn affect recruitment efforts (McCarthy and Zald 1977). In times of economic prosperity, such as the 1960s, the entire social movement sector expands because there are more discretionary resources available for movements in those periods. In this illustration, the macro level (a society's surplus resources), mediated by SMOs, affects the micro level (individual participation).

However, many movements also try to affect the macro level from below, with SMOs again playing a mediating role. Individuals with similar grievances get together in an informal, small group setting, what McAdam (1988) refers to as a "micro-mobilization context." Sometimes the participants in those ad hoc meetings decide to establish a more formal, enduring organization (i.e., an SMO) to act on their collective grievances. The SMO in turn devises a strategy aimed at changing the system in some way. Occasionally, SMOs succeed in bringing about macro-level changes.

The strategies and tactics a movement employs in pursuit of its objectives typically are selected or devised by SMOs. A movement strategy refers to the broad organizing plans for the acquisition and use of resources toward achieving movement goals. For instance, as was suggested above, movements may pursue social change by devising strategies aimed at changing structural arrangements, strategies aimed at changing people, or both. Similarly, movements may choose between legal and illegal strategies and between violent and nonviolent strategies.

Tactics refer to the specific techniques movements employ to carry out their strategies. Teach-ins, sit-ins, marches, rallies, strikes, and mass mailings are only a few of the tactics contemporary reform movements typically utilize. There appears to be considerable tactical borrowing across the political spectrum. Conservative movements of the 1980s and 1990s in the United States, such as the Moral Majority and the antiabortion movements, for example, employed many of the tactics originally developed by the civil rights and New Left movements of the 1960s.

Tilly made a similar observation regarding eighteenth-century American revolutionary movement tactics. He accounted for tactical similarities across movements and SMOs by noting that every place and time has limited "repertoires of collective action" that are well defined but limited compared with the various theoretically available tactical options. These "standard forms are learned, limited in scope, slowly changing, and peculiarly adapted to their settings" (Tilly 1979, p. 131).

While tactical diffusion across movements and SMOs occurs, a division of tactical labor also commonly arises within movements. Each SMO tends to develop its own specific tactical preferences and expertise. These specializations arise as a consequence of cooperation and competition among the various SMOs that constitute a movement. By refining and employing specialized tactics, an SMO is able to carve out a niche the movement that distinguishes it from other movement organizations.

Once an SMO establishes an organizational identity, it can build a stable resource base. Some SMOs have been so successful in that regard that they have survived the decline of a movement. Research on the women's movement indicates that such "abeyance organizations" provide continuity from one cycle of movement activity to the next (Taylor 1989) by sustaining activist interaction and commitment during periods when the opportunity structures are unfavorable to mass mobilization. In sum mary, SMOs contribute stability to what is otherwise a fluid, emergent phenomenon.

MOVEMENT OUTCOMES

What effects, if any, do social movements have on social change? This crucial question is not as easy to answer as might be assumed. Because of the difficulties associated with studying a large sample of movements, most researchers study movements one at a time. Although these case studies provide researchers with rich, detailed data on specific movements, they are not helpful in making generalizations. However, even in case studies, the question of the effects of a particular movement is difficult to answer. First, the logic employed is counterfactual (Moore 1978). That is, in evaluating the effects of a particular movement, researchers have to speculate about what the outcome would have been if that movement had *not* existed. Second, the effects of movements are not always immediate and apparent. Some movements, such as the civil rights and women's movements, produce rippling effects that gradually engulf societal institutions, sometimes generating effects several decades after a movement's most intense period of agitation has ended.

To evaluate the outcomes of a movement, researchers examine its explicit and implicit goals, the direction of those goals, and the intended and unintended outcomes of attempting to reach those goals. For example, while the women's movement has ostensibly been geared toward enacting and changing policy, there is also an underlying goal of raising the consciousness of society concerning women's issues (e.g., women's health, reproductive rights, violence against women, employment). Movement success may be evaluated with respect to a variety of dimensions, including a movement's ability to mobilize people to act, the diffusion of ideas across many cultures or countries, changes in a specific culture and individual sensibilities, and social policy changes. However, while a movement may succeed in some areas, it may fail in others. On the one hand, the women's movement could be considered successful in that it mobilized women both in the United States and elsewhere to take part in the struggle for rights and brought issues such as sexual harassment and unequal occupational status into the open. On the other hand, it has failed to persuade Congress to enact the Equal Rights Amendment, and despite popular myths to the contrary, women still suffer gross inequities in the workplace and at home.

In general, research suggests that movements seem to be more effective in producing cultural than structural change. The enduring legacy of the movements of the 1960s, for example, appears to be cultural. These cultural changes are reflected in attitudinal shifts regarding women and minorities, fashion trends (e.g., blue jeans), popular music, hedonistic lifestyles (e.g., the proliferation of illicit drugs), and the like. By contrast, these movements have had negligible success in terms of structural changes. While civil rights legislation helped dismantle caste restrictions and nearly equalized voting rights in the South, African-Americans continue to suffer "grinding poverty" and "persistent institutional discrimination in jobs, housing, and education" (McAdam 1982, p. 234). Women have realized even fewer structural gains. Finally, the sweeping changes in the economic, political, and educational institutions advocated by student activists never came to pass.

Social movements have been able to affect the sensibilities of both localized and broad publics. Researchers have argued that part of the function of social movements is to make use of and spread the knowledge created in various institutions (Eyerman and Jamison 1991). In the 1950s, a local grassroots environmental movement in Minamata, Japan, for instance, made use of rallies, disruptive protests, legal action, and increasingly favorable media attention during a cycle of contention to bring attention to what medical authorities called

"Minamata disease," a methyl mercury poisoning caused by local industrial waste that contaminated the fish the local residents ate. Knowledge of how industries affect the inhabitants of the areas in which they operate became a matter of national attention by the late 1960s. However, the goal of obtaining local control over pollution eventually failed in the face of the nation's need to sustain economic growth through increased national influence on industry after the mid-1970s (Almeida and Stearns 1998). Nevertheless, success may be judged on the basis of the movement's ability to open lines of communication with the public and its use of those lines to spread new knowledge as it attempts to affect social change.

It should not be inferred, however, that movements always fail to achieve their structural objectives. The mid-nineteenth-century abolitionist movement succeeded in abolishing slavery. Over a century later, the global movement against apartheid in South Africa yielded dramatic successes. In the late 1980s and early 1990s, grassroots movements radically transformed the totalitarian political structures of a number of eastern European countries into more democratic states. Similarly, the transnational social movement organization Greenpeace has aided in the creation, enforcement, and increasing support for international policies controlling the trade in toxic waste. In short, although movements occasionally achieve dramatic outcomes, social structures initially tend to be more resistant than cultures to the revolutionary or reform efforts of social movements.

Gamson (1990) is one of the few researchers who have attempted to identify systematically the conditions under which social movements are likely to achieve their objectives. He traced the activities of a representative sample of fifty-three "challenging groups," SMOs that emerged in the United Sates between 1800 and 1945. Gamson measured the relative success or failure of those SMOs in terms of whether they (1) gained new advantages and/or (2) gained acceptance from their antagonists. He found that thirty-one (58 percent) of them gained new advantages or acceptance while twenty (38 percent) gained both.

One of Gamson's strongest findings pertained to the degree of change advocated. Movement groups that sought to displace extant elites rarely succeeded. Gamson reported that the SMOs most likely to succeed exhibited the following characteristics: selective incentives for participants (some form of inducement, including rewards and punishments, to participate); unruly tactics (e.g., strikes, violence), especially when the target was relatively weak; bureaucratic, centralized organizational structures; and the absence of factional splits in a group. Although Gamson's research has been criticized as being too simplistic, it identifies several factors that affect the outcomes of social movements.

In examining the effectiveness of a social movement, it is important to see that success in changing worldviews can be linked to success in changing social structures. Movement activists devote considerable time to the task of transforming the ways in which people view or frame a social issue or domain of life: their interpretive frames (Snow et al. 1986). If a movement's framing efforts are successful either locally or on a global scale, a general shift in public opinion can occur, as has been the case for the movement against drunk driving (Gusfield 1981). Drivers who once were thought of as foolish or careless have been redefined as "killer drunks." Subsequently, the movement has found it relatively easy to secure legislation raising minimum drinking ages and increasing the penalties for driving under the influence of alcohol. Although favorable public opinion is not a sufficient condition for social change to occur, it can lead to advantageous changes in the opportunity structure as well as the availability of resources.

Social movements may not always succeed in achieving their goals. Movements have, however, played a significant role in changing the way their members understand their world, the way others understand their world, and most societal reforms, revolutions, and changes in the world order.

REFERENCES

Almeida, Paul, and Linda Brewster Stearns 1998 "Political Opportunities and Grassroots Environmental Movements: The Case of Minamata." *Social Problems* 45:37–60.

Blumer, Herbert 1946 "Collective Behavior." In A. M. Lee, ed., *A New Outline of the Principles of Sociology*. New York: Barnes and Noble.

della Porta, Donatella, and Hanspeter Kriesi 1999 "Social Movements in a Globalizing World: An Introduction." In D. McAdam, J. D. McCarthy, and M. N. Zald, eds., *Comparative Perspectives on Social Movements:*

Political Opportunities, Mobilizing Structures, and Cultural Framings. Cambridge, UK: Cambridge University Press.

Eisinger, Peter K. 1973 "The Conditions of Protest Behavior in American Cities." *American Political Science Review* 67:11–28.

Eyerman, Ron, and Andrew Jamison 1991 *Social Movements: A Cognitive Approach*. University Park: Pennsylvania State University Press.

Ferree, Myra Marx, and William A. Gamson 1999 "The Gendering of Abortion Discourse: Assessing Global Feminist Influence in the United States and Germany." In D. McAdam, J. D. McCarthy, and M. N. Zald, eds., *Comparative Perspectives on Social Movements: Political Opportunities, Mobilizing Structures, and Cultural Framings*. Cambridge, UK: Cambridge University Press.

Freeman, Jo 1973 "The Origin of the Women's Liberation Movement." *American Journal of Sociology* 78:792–811.

Gamson, William A. 1990 *The Strategy of Social Protest*, 2nd ed. Belmont, Calif.: Wadsworth.

Giddens, Anthony 1990 *The Consequences of Modernity*. Cambridge, UK: Polity Press.

Gould, Roger V. 1991 "Multiple Networks and Mobilization in Paris Commune, 1871." *American Sociological Review* 56:716–729.

Gusfield, Joseph R. 1981 *The Culture of Public Problems: Drinking-Driving and the Symbolic Order*. Chicago: University of Chicago Press.

Hunt, Scott A. 1991 "Constructing Collective Identity in a Peace Movement Organization." Ph.D. dissertation, Department of Sociology, University of Nebraska, Lincoln.

Jasper, James 1997 *The Art of Moral Protest: Culture, Biography, and Creativity in Social Movements*. Chicago: University of Chicago Press.

Jenson, Jane 1995 "What's in a Name? Nationalist Movements and Public Discourse." In H. Johnston and B. Klandermans, eds., *Social Movements and Culture*. Minneapolis: University of Minnesota Press.

Kanter, Rosabeth M. 1968 "Commitment and Social Organization: A Study of Commitment Mechanisms in Utopian Communities." *American Sociological Review* 33:499–517.

Klandermans, Bert 1984 "Mobilization and Participation: Social-Psychological Expansions of Resource Mobilization Theory." *American Sociological Review* 49:583–600.

Koopmans, Ruud 1999 "A Comparison of Protests against the Gulf War in Germany, France, and the Netherlands." In D. della Porta, H. Kriesi, and D. Rucht, eds., *Social Movements in a Globalizing World*. London: Macmillan.

Kriesi, Hanspeter 1996 "The Organizational Structure of New Social Movements in a Political Context." In D. McAdam, J. D. McCarthy, and M. N. Zald, eds., *Comparative Perspectives on Social Movements: Political Opportunities, Mobilizing Structures, and Cultural Framings*. Cambridge, UK: Cambridge University Press.

Lo, Clarence Y. 1982 "Countermovements and Conservative Movements in the Contemporary U.S." *Annual Review of Sociology* 8:107–134.

McAdam, Doug 1982. *Political Process and the Development of Black Insurgency, 1930–1970*. Chicago: University of Chicago Press.

—— 1988. "Micromobilization Contexts and Recruitment to Activism." *International Social Movement Research* 1:125–154.

——, John D. McCarthy, and Mayer N. Zald 1988 "Social Movements." In N. Smelser, ed., *Handbook of Sociology*. Newbury Park, Calif.: Sage.

——, and Dieter Rucht 1993 "Cross-National Diffusion of Social Movement Ideas." *Annals of the American Academy of Political and Social Science* 528:56–74.

McCarthy, John D., and Mayer N. Zald 1973 *The Trend of Social Movements in America: Professionalization and Resource Mobilization*. Morristown, N.J.: General Learning Press.

—— 1977 "Resource Mobilization and Social Movements: A Partial Theory." *American Journal of Sociology* 82:1212–1241.

Melucci, Alberto 1980 "The New Social Movements: A Theoretical Approach." *Social Science Information* 19:199–226.

—— 1995 "The Process of Collective Identity." In H. Johnston and B. Klandermans, eds., *Social Movements and Culture*. Minneapolis: University of Minnesota Press.

Moore, Barrington, Jr. 1978 *Injustice: The Social Bases of Obedience and Revolt*. White Plains, N.Y.: Sharpe.

Piven, Frances Fox, and Richard A. Cloward 1977 *Poor Peoples' Movements: Why They Succeed, How They Fail*. New York: Vintage.

Rucht, Dieter 1996 "The Impact of National Contexts on Social Movement Structures: A Cross-Movement and Cross-National Comparison." In D. McAdam, J. D. McCarthy, and M. N. Zald, eds., *Comparative Perspectives on Social Movements: Political Opportunities, Mobilizing Structures, and Cultural Framings*. Cambridge, UK: Cambridge University Press.

Smelser, Neil J. 1962 *Theory of Collective Behavior*. New York: Free Press.

Smith, Jackie 1995 "Transnational Political Processes and the Human Rights Movement." *Research in Social Movements, Conflict and Change* 18:187–221.

Snow, David A., and Robert D. Benford 1992 "Master Frames and Cycles of Protest." In A. D. Morris and C. M. Mueller, eds., *Frontiers in Social Movement Theory*. New Haven, Conn.: Yale University Press.

——, and —— 1999 "Alternative Types of Cross-National Diffusion in the Social Movement Arena." In D. della Porta, H. Kriesi, and D. Rucht, eds., *Social Movements in a Globalizing World*. London: Macmillan.

——, and Richard Machalek 1984 "The Sociology of Conversion." *Annual Review of Sociology* 10:167–180.

——, and Pamela E. Oliver 1995 "Social Movements and Collective Behavior: Social Psychological Dimensions and Considerations." In K. S. Cook, G. A. Fine, and J. S. House, eds., *Sociological Perspectives on Social Psychology*. Boston: Allyn and Bacon.

——, E. Burke Rochford, Jr., Steven K. Worden, and Robert D. Benford 1986 "Frame Alignment Processes, Micromobilization, and Movement Participation." *American Sociological Review* 51:464–481.

——, Louis A. Zurcher, Jr., and Sheldon Ekland-Olson 1980 "Social Networks and Social Movements: A Microstructural Approach to Differential Recruitment." *American Sociological Review* 45:787–801.

Staggenborg, Suzanne 1987 "Life-Style Preferences and Social Movement Recruitment: Illustrations from the Abortion Conflict." *Social Science Quarterly* 68:779–797.

Tarrow, Sidney 1998 *Power in Movement: Social Movements and Contentious Politics*, 2nd ed. Cambridge, UK: Cambridge University Press.

Taylor, Verta 1989 "Social Movement Continuity: The Women's Movement in Abeyance." *American Sociological Review* 54:761–775.

Tilly, Charles 1978 *From Mobilization to Revolution*. Reading, Mass. Addison-Wesley.

—— 1979 "Repertoires of Contention in America and Britain, 1750–1830." In M. N. Zald and J. D. McCarthy, eds., *The Dynamics of Social Movements*. Cambridge, Mass.: Winthrop.

——, Louise Tilly, and Richard Tilly 1975 *The Rebellious Century: 1830–1930*. Cambridge, Mass.: Harvard University Press.

Zdravomyslova, Elena 1996 "Opportunities and Framing in the Transition to Democracy: The Case of Russia." In D. McAdam, J. D. McCarthy, and M. N. Zald, eds., *Comparative Perspectives on Social Movements: Political Opportunities, Mobilizing Structures, and Cultural Framings*. Cambridge, UK: Cambridge University Press.

Zuo, Jiping, and Robert D. Benford 1995 "Mobilization Processes and the 1989 Chinese Democracy Movement." *The Sociological Quarterly* 36:131–156.

ROBERT D. BEAFORD
TIMOTHY B. GONGAWARE
DANNY L. VALADEZ

SOCIAL NETWORKS

Social networks—structures of relationships linking social actors—are omnipresent in contemporary society. People often obtain information about such things as job opportunities, housing, and medical care through interpersonal contacts rather than from formal sources such as the mass media. Networks provide emotional support in times of crisis as well as instrumental aid such as help with household tasks. Identities are constituted by locations in networks; opinions are formed and decisions are made in light of information and conformity pressures that flow through network linkages. Also, social networks are important channels through which both infectious diseases and innovations are diffused.

Ties among individuals in social networks give rise to important larger-scale social patterns. Levels of socioeconomic or ethnoreligious segregation in a society, for example, reflect the degree to which social ties such as marriage and friendship are confined to sets of persons with a common social status or heritage. Such characteristics become salient as markers of differentiation to the degree that they serve as bases for the formation of intimate social relationships. Networks that link individuals to supraindividual units such as work organizations and voluntary associations may serve as modes of integration or separation. Thus, the study of networks contributes to the linking of micro and macro levels of analysis in sociology.

Many macro-level social phenomena can be understood as networks. Increasingly, systems of production for goods (such as automobiles) and services (such as care for the severely mentally ill) are located in multiorganizational fields consisting of separate but interdependent units linked by contingent cooperation rather than in self-contained units administered through elaborate formalized sets of rules. Innovations in corporate strategy and governance diffuse through overlapping boards of directors and other interorganizational structures. Patterns of consensus and cleavage in community and national politics are shaped by alliances and conflicts in networks of governmental agencies, interest groups, and party organizations. In international relations, network ties among nation-states and international organizations define geopolitical alignments.

Emphasis on social networks grew as a result of substantive observations about contemporary society. Many early twentieth-century observers posited that large-scale transformations associated with industrialization—especially urbanization, bureaucratization, and the development of mass media—led to a "mass society" of atomized individuals in which formal, special-purpose ties supplanted diffuse interpersonal relations.

Several lines of research, however, pointed to the continuing vitality of social ties. Industrial sociologists found that informal structures were crucial to the day-to-day functioning of work organization. Indeed, workplace social networks came to be seen as a solution to the inflexibility and excess formalization of bureaucracies and as important incentives for (or impediments to) the performance of individual employees. Urban sociologists found that friendship, neighboring, and informal assistance remained prominent in large cities, although technological innovations in transportation and communication reduced the extent to which the formation and maintenance of those social ties were constrained by spatial considerations. Rural-to-urban and international migrants were not rootless citizens in a normless society but tended to settle in districts populated by persons from their places of origin. In contrast to the expectations of theories predicting protest and activism among those marginal and peripheral to society, researchers found that those active in social movements tended to be drawn from among the persons best integrated into communities, and social ties proved to be important channels through which new members were recruited to social movements.

A social network perspective highlights the interdependence among social actors. This extends beyond the competitive interdependence of actors competing for shares of a stock of scarce resources to encompass obligations and commitments that accumulate as a result of past social

interaction. Individual action is embedded in, and therefore continually affected by, preexisting ties between specific actors (Granovetter 1985). In some theories, individuals are viewed as largely passive recipients of environmental pressure; in this structural emphasis, social networks constitute constraints that limit an actor's discretion. An alternative view makes more room for individual agency, viewing networks as structures of opportunity or social resources. Assuming a context of constrained voluntarism, it treats individuals as proactive, self-interested agents who use networks to manipulate outcomes to their advantage (Haines 1988; Emirbayer and Goodwin 1994).

Social scientists have used the term "social network" metaphorically for some time. Beginning in the 1970s, however, scholarly attention to the analytic development of the social network approach increased. It is now seen as a distinct specialty within several social science disciplines, especially sociology and anthropology, and has many adherents in professional schools, particularly those of business administration and public health. Mathematicians and statisticians have participated in this work, especially the development of novel techniques for studying relations between interdependent social units. These methods are distinct from the conventional ones used to study relations between variables within presumably autonomous units. The theoretical assumptions of formal network models are often implicit (Granovetter 1979), and a distinct "network theory" has not developed. Contemporary studies of social networks instead draw on diverse sociological and social psychological theories.

PRECURSORS

Some foundations of a methodology for studying networks of social relations were laid in Moreno's *Who Shall Survive?* (1934). Moreno coined the term "sociometry" to refer to methods for describing group structures and individual positions within them. His work focused on the affinities and disaffinities of individuals for one another, and his "sociometric test" accordingly stressed affective choices and rejections. These network data were mapped in "sociograms" in which persons were located at different points, with lines indicating the connections between them. Such graphic representations are also common in contemporary network analysis (Figure 1). On the basis of their locations in sociometric networks of affect, individuals were classified as attractive, isolated, rejected, and so forth.

Jennings collaborated with Moreno in developing sociometric methods; her (1943) work reported studies of attractiveness and emotional expansiveness. Sociometry as practiced by Moreno and Jennings had an applied component: They attempted to use sociometric measurements as a basis for rearranging groups to enhance both group functioning and individual creativity.

Displays such as sociograms are extremely useful as visualization devices but do not facilitate formal analysis. Forsyth and Katz (1946) and Luce and Perry (1949) were among the first to attempt to surmount the limitations of sociograms by representing networks in the form of matrices. They argued that this would reduce the subjectivity of statements about sociometric structure and allow objective identification of chains, groups, and cliques in network data. In later studies, the application of graph theory (Harary et al. 1965) to the analysis of networks has extended those early efforts.

A second set of influences on the development of social network analyses has emanated from the fieldwork of social anthropologists in complex societies. Those analysts observed that the categorical concepts of a structural-functional approach were insufficient for the study of societies in which not all behavior was regulated by "corporate groups"—institutions of kinship, community, or work. Barnes (1954) is credited with the first use of the term "social network" to refer to a set of existing social relationships as distinct from cultural prescriptions about the construction of such ties. In its initial formulations, the concept was used to refer to informal or extrainstitutional links, but it was soon noted that formalized relations and groups also could be analyzed as networks of interactions.

Classic studies in the anthropological tradition display the same variability in theoretical orientations seen in present-day work: Bott (1957) treated social networks as sources of norms prescribing an appropriate allocation of tasks between spouses, while Boissevain (1974) stressed the potential use of networks by maneuvering, self-interested entrepreneurs.

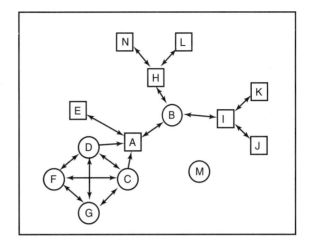

Figure 1. A Social Network Diagram

STRUCTURAL PROPERTIES OF NETWORKS

Social networks are studied from many standpoints, including the sociocentric and egocentric perspectives. Researchers with a sociocentric orientation examine complete networks of actors and relations, studying the global properties of a network and characterizing the position of any given actor by reference to all the others. Egocentric network analysis takes the perspective of individual actors and the "personal networks" surrounding them, focusing on the local structure of each actor's interpersonal environment.

Figure 1 depicts a complete network with fourteen actors, with each one represented as a circle or square. Lines connecting those points indicate relationships between pairs of actors, such as communication ties and expressions of affect. An actor's "first-order" egocentric network consists of the other actors to which it is linked and the relationships among them; actor G's egocentric network includes C, D, and F, while that of H consists of B, L, and N. The "second-order" zone of a focal actor's egocentric network includes those to which the actor is linked via one intermediary; the second-order zone of G's network consists of actor A, while that of H includes both A and I.

Arrows indicate directionality; for example, actors A and E are involved in a *reciprocal* relationship, while A and C are linked by an *asymmetric* tie in which the relationship flows in only one direction. *Indirect* relationships join actors to one another through intermediaries: for instance, H and I are indirectly linked through B.

The *density* of a network reflects the overall intensity of connectedness among actors. In Figure 1, sixteen of the ninety-one distinct pairs of actors have direct relationships, and so the network has a density of 18 percent. There are, however, wide variations in the density of the egocentric networks surrounding actors: G is in a very dense or closely knit locality, while H is in a sparse or loosely knit region.

Diagrams of more complicated networks might use lines of different thicknesses to represent relationships of varying intensity or different types of lines to show distinct relationships, such as providing emotional support versus giving instrumental aid. Different types of actors can be represented by different symbols; the actors in circles in Figure 1 might be men, while those in squares might be women. When a relationship typically joins actors that have the same attributes or statuses, as in Figure 1, it is said to display *homophily*.

Social ties, especially those involving positive sentiment, often create *transitive* configurations. In Figure 1, for example, transitivity implies that by virtue of the links between C and D and between C and F, there will also be a tie between D and F. Strong tendencies toward transitivity create closure and tend to fragment a group into distinct *cliques*: The mutually interconnected set of four actors (C, D, F, and G) provides an illustration. Relationships that do not conform to the transitivity principle are important sources of integration between otherwise separate parts of a social structure (Granovetter 1973): in Figure 1, the I–B and A–B ties exemplify *bridges* of this kind.

Actors may be *central* in a network because they are involved in many relationships, are in a controlling position between other pairs of actors, or are comparatively close to others (Freeman 1979). Sociometry referred to central actors as "sociometric stars." In Figure 1, actors A and B occupy relatively central locations. Those such as E, J, and L are *peripheral* within the network. Actor M is not involved in any relationships and is said to be an *isolate*.

Two actors are said to occupy the same *position* in a social network when they have profiles of relationships to other actors that are identical in a particular way (Borgatti and Everett 1992); these actors are therefore substitutable for each other from an observer's standpoint. Two actors having the same relationships to the same others are *structurally equivalent*. In Figure 1, actors J and K both have a reciprocal relationship with actor I but no direct relationship with each other or any of the other actors. J and K are thus structurally equivalent, as are three other pairs: C and D, F and G, and L and N. Actors are said to be *role-equivalent* when they have the same types of relationships to the same types of other actors. Actors L and K are role-equivalent, but not structurally equivalent; although they occupy similarly peripheral locations in the system of relations, L's direct link is to H, while K's is to I.

Additional patterns often appear in networks that involve more than one type of social relationship. *Exchange* patterns arise when a flow of one type in one direction is directly or indirectly reciprocated by a flow of a second type. A *multiplex* pattern occurs when the relationship between two actors consists of two or more distinct strands, such as kinship and emotional support; a *uniplex* relationship has only one strand.

Concepts and methods for identifying subgroups within networks have drawn much attention. The two dominant approaches focus on cohesion and equivalence as grouping principles. Techniques that emphasize cohesion locate subsets of densely interconnected actors; fully connected cliques are a limiting case. Blockmodel analysis (White et al. 1976) and related positional methods group equivalent actors together. This yields considerable flexibility. Social positions can be defined by the common ties of actors to outsiders rather than by actors' links to one another; for example, those in "broker" roles occupy mediating locations between other positions but are not necessarily linked to other brokers. Moreover, positional approaches are not confined to a single type of tie; they can identify subgroups on the basis of patterns in multistranded relations rather than focusing on a single type of tie extracted from its context, as approaches resting on cohesion generally must. Thus, positional analyses of international trade relations may examine flows of raw materials and flows of processed goods simultaneously.

THE STRUCTURING OF NETWORKS

Rational choice explanations of the formation of network ties are based on exchange theory: Social relations form when actors depend on one another for resources. Related behaviorist accounts stress a reinforcement history. An exemplar is Blau's (1955) description of the exchange of advice for expressions of deference among coworkers in a bureaucracy. The terms of exchange and thus the relative power of the actors involved depend on the number of alternative actors who control different resources, the extent of unity among those with a given resource, and the parties' relative interests in outcomes controlled by others (Cook 1982; Burt 1980).

Exchange-theoretic reasoning provides a basis for some commonly observed micro-level network patterns. To maintain autonomy and avoid power disadvantages, actors should avoid asymmetric relations in favor of reciprocal ones. Multiplex ties in which relations of solidarity overlie instrumental exchange links can protect people against exploitation by actors in positions of power. These ideas have played an important role in resource dependence theories of interorganizational relations. Such theories suggest, for example, that interdependent organizations tend to form network ties such as long-term contracts, joint ventures, interlocking directors, and mergers (Pfeffer 1987).

Some attempts to explain tendencies toward homophily are preference-driven accounts in which people actively seek out similar associates. From this viewpoint, communication is easier if people share implicit premises regarding interaction and trustworthiness in the face of uncertainty is enhanced if partners can assume that they have shared interests and predispositions.

Other lines of theorizing about the sources of homophily stress the structure of opportunities for association. Feld (1981) observes that most relationships arise within "foci" of association such as families, neighborhoods, workplaces, and voluntary associations. When segregating processes create foci composed of persons with similar attributes, they create systematic biases toward homophily. Blau's macrosociological theory (Blau and Schwartz 1984) postulates that networks vary with opportunities for association. Blau shows, without any assumptions about preferences, that intergroup relations—the converse of homophilous ones—

are more likely for small than for large groups, when there is great inequality or heterogeneity in a population instead of little, and when different characteristics (e.g., socioeconomic status, race, ethnicity) that structure the formation of social ties are intersecting (or uncorrelated) rather than consolidated. The implications of these factors for intergroup relations depend on the degree to which they penetrate into substructures such as Feld's foci: Distributional effects on intergroup association are strongest when heterogeneity, inequality, and intersection lie within rather than between substructures.

Transitivity has been most intensively studied for relations of positive sentiment; there the theoretical case for it rests on balance theories that posit pressures toward cognitive consistency (Davis and Leinhardt 1972). Tendencies toward closure also may result from increased opportunities for contact resulting from the copresence of actors in a triad, or an actor in contact with two others may facilitate or serve as a guarantor for a venture involving the other two. Principles of expectation states theory predict transitivity in dominance relations (Fararo and Skvoretz 1986).

CONSEQUENCES OF NETWORKS

A network perspective lends itself to the construction of theories at multiple levels. Contextual theories that examine the effects of an actor's position in a network on achievement, well-being, and other individual-level outcomes are common, and extensive research literatures have developed around some of them. Network entrepreneurship, diffusion and influence, social support, and power are among the most prominent themes in such works. Group-level theorizing about the properties of complete networks is less typical, although there have been important efforts in this direction. As Coleman (1990) stresses, group-level theorizing is a demanding enterprise.

Granovetter's (1973) discussion of "weak ties" has been a fruitful source of ideas for network analysts. Although Granovetter defines tie strength in terms of dyadic content (intimacy, intensity, exchange of services and time commitments), the "strength of weak ties" arises from their location within a network structure. Weak ties are less subject than strong ones to the transitivity pressures that induce closure and thus are more likely to be bridges that join distinct subgroups, thereby serving as channels for integration and diffusion. Different contextual theories positing network effects may stress the virtues of either strong or weak ties.

The purposive use of networks as individual-level "social capital" is a prominent theme in writing about network effects. Much research has been done on how networks facilitate or impede instrumental actions, particularly job seeking. Granovetter (1995) stressed the informational advantages of wide-ranging networks composed of many weak ties. He reasoned that such networks are likely to connect actors to diverse information sources that provide novel information and access to powerful others; by contrast, persons in a densely connected clique are apt to have similar social standing and know similar things. Other writing in this vein emphasizes the content rather than the form of networks. Lin (1990) contends that networks composed of highly ranked contacts are the most advantageous to an actor. Weak ties may facilitate access to social resources, but the aid such contacts can provide reflects their power and influence rather than the type of channel that links them to the actor.

Burt (1992), developed influential ideas about network entrepreneurship. Like Granovetter, Burt stressed the benefits of loosely knit networks for obtaining information quickly. Structural holes refer to the absence of connections between an actor's contacts in a sparse network; thus, in Figure 1 there are holes separating actor B's contacts (A, I, and H). Beyond providing actors with the ability to acquire information sooner than competitors can, Burt argues that networks rich in structural holes confer control benefits. Actors at the middle of networks that bridge many holes gain autonomy and leverage over others by virtue of their unique interstitial positions. They are able to place their contacts in competition with one another, avoid excessive dependence, and negotiate favorable bargains. Empirical applications in diverse settings lend support to these ideas: Structural holes have proved advantageous in studies of competition for promotions and bonuses in firms and studies of comparative profit margins in manufacturing industries.

Studies of the role of networks in diffusion and influence processes echo debates over cohesion and equivalence as bases for defining network subgroups (Marsden and Friedkin 1993). This work posits that networks provide actors with a basis for constructing reference groups and social comparisons (Erickson 1988). Approaches that stress the socializing potential of cohesive ties contend that people look to close associates for guidance toward appropriate attitudes or conduct in conditions of uncertainty. Network closure thus is viewed as a source of locally defined norms, as persons in dense networks respond to consistent conformity pressures from their strong ties.

Burt (1987) suggests an important alternative process of diffusion or influence, arguing that in seeking normative direction, actors look not to their close contacts but to their competitors. They engage in a process of role taking, examining the views held or the actions taken by structural peers who occupy similar positions within a system of relations. Conformity to norms here is less a matter of social pressure from the environment than the result of an actor's mimicry of others (DiMaggio and Powell 1983).

An extensive research literature on the sociology of health and illness draws a connection between social networks, exposure to stressors, the availability of social support, and well-being (House et al. 1988; Thoits 1995). Social networks are "structural" elements that may facilitate access to supportive contacts but also may expose someone to additional stressors, conflicts, and demands; hence, the quality as well as the structure of ties within networks must be considered. A "direct effect" view states that receiving social support enhances health and well-being in all conditions. The "buffering hypothesis" suggests a conditional effect in which those with supportive networks have less severe responses to stressful life events.

Several mechanisms have been suggested to account for the way in which aspects of social networks translate into social support and measures of physical and mental well-being. Some of these suggestions have a Durkheimian emphasis, reasoning that people integrated into dense networks—that is, strongly tied to a number of partners who are strongly tied to each other—have better-defined social identities, stronger senses of internal control, and more positive self-evaluations, which in turn may lead to the use of more effective coping strategies under stress. Collins

(1988) suggests that network density indicates that an individual is integrated into the "interaction rituals" of a solidary group, a situation that produces moral sentiments and energies that enhance well-being.

It is relatively well established that the availability of a strong tie or confidant has health-promoting effects (Thoits 1995). Theories stressing the availability of support resources imply that the size of a personal network is linked to physical and psychological health. Large, diverse networks are thought to facilitate adjustment to change. Contacts in one's network may offer companionship as well as both instrumental and emotional assistance; they can both provide health information and focus attention on it. Social contacts also may be sources of regulation and control, providing social feedback on one's behavior and performance, discouraging harmful behaviors such as substance abuse, and encouraging beneficial ones such as adherence to treatment protocols. It is increasingly recognized that providing social support can be burdensome and that stress as well as aid may emanate from relationships within social networks.

Network theorists have given substantial attention to the connection between an actor's location in a social network and social standing or prestige. Freeman's (1979) discussion of the conceptual foundations of centrality measures focused on processes in communication networks. He observed that distinct measures are sensitive to communication activity, the capacity to control the communications of others, and the capacity to avoid the controlling actions of others. Many empirical studies have documented an association between centrality and manifestations of power or influence.

Exchange-theoretic approaches observe that actors with predominantly favorable exchange ratios with others are central within networks of dependency relations and hence acquire power (Cook 1982). No universal principle leads to that connection, however; instead, it depends on a particular form of exchange. For Cook this is "positively connected" or "productive" exchange in which actors must combine diverse resources to be successful; hence, the use of one exchange relation tends to encourage the use of others, and advantages emerge for those in intermediary "bro-

ker" positions. Willer (1992) terms these "flow" networks. For Coleman (1990), the requisite conditions include resource transferability or fungibility: For systems of social exchange to develop fully, actors must be able to transfer not only control over resources but also the right to further transfer such control.

Under other conditions of exchange, network positions have different consequences for power. Among these are what Cook (1982) calls "negatively connected" exchange networks and Willer (1992) terms "restricted" exchange networks. In these networks, resources do not flow through positions and the use of one relation rules out or makes less likely the use of others. Matching systems such as marriage and dating markets exemplify negatively connected or restricted networks. In these conditions no special advantages accrue to an actor in a central position; instead, power is concentrated in actors who can exclude others from exchanges (Markovsky et al. 1988). The capacity to exclude others can depend both on the nuances of a network's structure and on the incentives or rules governing exchange in any given situation. Depending on such subtleties, there may be a nonlinear association between centrality and power; a network also may decompose into small substructures as some potential exchange relations fall into disuse.

Theorizing about network effects at the level of aggregates is less extensive than is that about networks as contexts for individual action. One line of work examines the implications of structural biases toward homophily or transitivity for the spread of diseases and innovations (Morris 1993). Another considers how the centralization or dispersion of networks shapes differences in system performance or effectiveness (Laumann and Knoke 1987). Still another deals with networks and collective action: Social density has been viewed as an infrastructure that allows latent "interest groups" to overcome social dilemmas (Marwell et al. 1988). Granovetter (1973) warns against excessive closure, however: Once formed, a coalition or "collective actor" may lack the social connections required for ultimate political success.

Some theorists have developed the notion of social capital as a collective rather than an individual property. Coleman (1990) suggests that closed social networks can create trust and enforce strong norms that facilitate collective action. Actors in densely interconnected systems can expect to encounter one another frequently in the future, and a reputation for trustworthiness therefore becomes valuable. Moreover, frequent communication among densely linked actors means that information about a failure to honor obligations diffuses quickly and that sanctions can be applied rapidly. Coleman asserts that strong norms of trust are essential to the creation of "social credit": aid or assistance contributed in exchange for future compensation. Preexisting social networks thus are valuable as sources of social capital to the extent that they are appropriable for new purposes.

Different varieties of network theory make contrasting observations about network density. Density can integrate an actor into a subculture, provide a well-defined social identity, create and enforce norms, and promote the production of collective goods it simultaneously may subject one to conformity pressures and limit the diversity of one's affiliations. Reconciling these seemingly conflicting effects of density represents a challenge in the contemporary study of networks. Understanding the manner in which networks channel and block transactions among the elements of society will remain a crucial and intriguing task for twenty-first-century sociology.

FURTHER LITERATURE

A number of review articles and collections treat aspects of network analysis in greater depth. Mitchell (1974) provides a useful review of the anthropological approach. Wellman (1983) reviews basic principles from a sociological perspective. Review articles on substantive applications appear in Wasserman and Galaskiewicz (1994). The journal *Social Networks* (1978–present), edited by Linton Freeman, presents methodological advances and substantive studies. Marsden (1990) surveys the literature on measurement, and Wasserman and Faust (1994) provide a comprehensive review of analytic methods.

REFERENCES

Barnes, J. A. 1954 "Class and Committees in a Norwegian Island Parish." *Human Relations* 7:39–58.

Blau, Peter M. 1955 *The Dynamics of Bureaucracy*. Chicago: University of Chicago Press.

——, and Joseph E. Schwartz 1984 *Crosscutting Social Circles*. New York: Academic Press.

Boissevain, Jeremy 1974 *Friends of Friends*. New York: St. Martin's.

Borgatti, Stephen P., and Martin G. Everett 1992 "Notions of Position in Social Network Analysis." In Peter V. Marsden, ed., *Sociological Methodology 1992*. Oxford, UK: Blackwell.

Bott, Elizabeth 1957 *Family and Social Network* London: Tavistock.

Burt, Ronald S. 1980 "Autonomy in a Social Topology." *American Journal of Sociology* 85:892–925.

—— 1987 "Social Contagion and Innovation: Cohesion versus Structural Equivalence." *American Journal of Sociology* 92:1287–1335.

—— 1992 *Structural Holes: The Social Structure of Competition*. Cambridge, Mass.: Harvard University Press.

Coleman, James S. 1990 *Foundations of Social Theory*. Cambridge, Mass.: Harvard University Press.

Collins, Randall 1988 *Theoretical Sociology*. New York: Harcourt Brace Jovanovich.

Cook, Karen S. 1982 "Network Structures from an Exchange Perspective." In Peter V. Marsden and Nan Lin, eds., *Social Structure and Network Analysis*. Beverly Hills, Calif.: Sage.

Davis, James A., and Samuel Leinhardt 1972 "The Structure of Positive Interpersonal Relations in Small Groups." In Joseph Berger, Morris Zelditch, Jr., and Bo Anderson, eds., *Sociological Theories in Progress*. Boston: Houghton Mifflin.

DiMaggio, Paul, and Walter W. Powell 1983 "The Iron Cage Revisited: Institutional Isomorphism and Collective Rationality in Organizational Fields." *American Sociological Review* 48:147–160.

Emirbayer, Mustafa, and Jeff Goodwin 1994 "Network Analysis, Culture, and the Problem of Agency." *American Journal of Sociology* 99:1411–1454.

Erickson, Bonnie H. 1988 "The Relational Basis of Attitudes." In Barry Wellman and S. D. Berkowitz, eds., *Social Structures*. New York: Cambridge University Press.

Fararo, Thomas J., and John Skvoretz 1986 "E-State Structuralism: A Theoretical Method." *American Sociological Review* 51:591–602.

Feld, Scott L. 1981 "The Focused Organization of Social Ties." *American Journal of Sociology* 86:1015–1035.

Forsyth, Elaine, and Leo Katz 1946 "A Matrix Approach to the Analysis of Sociometric Data: Preliminary Report." *Sociometry* 9:340–347.

Freeman, Linton C. 1979 "Centrality in Social Networks I: Conceptual Clarification." *Social Networks* 1:215–239.

Granovetter, Mark S. 1973 "The Strength of Weak Ties." *American Journal of Sociology* 78:1360–1380.

—— 1979 "The Theory-Gap in Social Network Analysis." In Paul W. Holland and Samuel Leinhardt, eds., *Perspectives on Social Network Research*. New York: Academic Press.

—— 1985 "Economic Action and Social Structure: The Problem of Embeddedness." *American Journal of Sociology* 91:481–510.

—— 1995 *Getting a Job: A Study of Contacts and Careers*, 2d ed. Chicago: University of Chicago Press.

Haines, Valerie A. 1988 "Social Network Analysis, Structuration Theory and the Holism-Individualism Debate." *Social Networks* 10:157–182.

Harary, Frank, Robert Z. Norman, and Dorwin C. Cartwright 1965 *Structural Models: An Introduction to the Theory of Directed Graphs*. New York: Wiley.

House, J. S., D. Umberson, and K. R. Landis 1988 "Structures and Processes of Social Support." *Annual Review of Sociology* 14:293–318.

Jennings, Helen Hall 1943 *Leadership and Isolation*. New York: Longmans, Green.

Laumann, Edward O., and David Knoke 1987 *The Organizational State*. Madison: University of Wisconsin Press.

Lin, Nan 1990 "Social Resources and Social Mobility." In Ronald L. Breiger, ed., *Social Mobility and Social Structure*. New York: Cambridge University Press.

Luce, R. Duncan, and Albert D. Perry 1949 "A Method of Matrix Analysis of Group Structure." *Psychometrika* 14:95–116.

Markovsky, Barry, David Willer, and Travis Patton 1988 "Power Relations in Exchange Networks." *American Sociological Review* 53:220–236.

Marsden, Peter V. 1990 "Network Data and Measurement." *Annual Review of Sociology* 16:435–463.

——, and Noah E. Friedkin 1993 "Network Studies of Social Influence." *Sociological Methods and Research* 22:127–151.

Marwell, Gerald, Pamela E. Oliver, and Ralph Prahl 1988 "Social Networks and Collective Action: A Theory of the Critical Mass III." *American Journal of Sociology* 94:502–534.

Mitchell, J. Clyde 1974 "Social Networks." *Annual Review of Anthropology* 3:279–299.

Moreno, J. L. 1934 *Who Shall Survive?* Washington, D.C.: Nervous and Mental Disease Publishing.

Morris, Martina 1993 "Epidemiology and Social Networks: Modeling Structured Diffusion." *Sociological Methods and Research* 22:99–126.

Pfeffer, Jeffrey 1987 "A Resource Dependence Perspective on Intercorporate Relations." In Mark S. Mizruchi and Michael Schwartz, eds., *Intercorporate Relations*. New York: Cambridge University Press.

Thoits, Peggy A. 1995 "Stress, Coping, and Social Support Processes: Where Are We? What Next?" *Journal of Health and Social Behavior*, extra issue, pp. 53–79.

Wasserman, Stanley, and Katherine Faust 1994 *Social Network Analysis: Methods and Applications*. New York: Cambridge University Press.

——, and Joseph Galaskiewicz, eds. 1994 *Advances in Social Network Analysis: Research in the Social and Behavioral Sciences*. Thousand Oaks, Calif.: Sage.

Wellman, Barry 1983 "Network Analysis: Some Basic Principles." *Sociological Theory* 1:155–199.

White, Harrison C., Scott A. Boorman, and Ronald L. Breiger 1976 "Social Structure from Multiple Networks I: Blockmodels of Roles and Positions." *American Journal of Sociology* 81:730–780.

Willer, David 1992 "Predicting Power in Exchange Networks." *Social Networks* 14:187–211.

PETER V. MARSDEN

SOCIAL NORMS

See Compliance and Conformity; Deviance Theories; Socialization; Social Control; Social Values and Norms.

SOCIAL ORGANIZATION

NOTE: *Although the following article has not been revised for this edition of the Encyclopedia, the substantive coverage is currently appropriate. The editors have provided a list of recent works at the end of the article to facilitate research and exploration of the topic.*

It is necessary to highlight this central area selectively, considering the breadth and variety in its specification, and to emphasize current concerns, relying on past overviews to detail their origins (e.g., by Znaniecki 1945; Gerth and Mills 1953; Faris 1964; Eisenstadt 1968; Parsons 1968; Udy 1968; Smelser 1988).

Social organization is nonrandom *pattern* within human populations that comprise society by sharing the main aspects of a common existence over time as well as nonrandom *patterning*, the human and interhuman activities through which patterns are formed, retained, altered, or replaced. These twin aspects of social organization had been considered *structure*, relatively stable patterns of interrelations among persons or other social units, and *process*, the manner in which the patterns are produced, reproduced, or transformed (see, e.g., Faris 1964). The distinction is blurred to the extent that interrelations vary in *degrees* of regularity, uniformity, and permanence in the rhythms of coexistence, contact, or avoidance of which they consist (Williams 1976). In short, structure can also be viewed as patterned process among human agents (e.g., Blumer 1969, pp. 78–89; Giddens 1979, pp. 49–95; Coleman 1990, esp. pp. 1–44).

At issue is not what is patterned or how, but simply the extent to which there is any pattern or patterning at all. The antithesis of social organization is not opposition or discord. Conflict and other aspects of tension or unrest can, for example, exhibit regularity and uniformity as readily as can union, harmony, and tranquillity. Rather it is randomness, consisting of chaos, formlessness, and idiosyncratic human behavior (Blau 1975) and is called social disorganization. Yet patterned *occurrence* of disorganization is no contradiction.

Social organization is characterized by *interdependence*—that is, what occurs among certain components has, to varying degree, consequences for some or all of the other components and their relations with one another. These consequences can range from loss, even annihilation, to survival and other types of gain. Subsumed are regulation and stability as well as replacement and transformation.

The socially organized units or sets of units are generally activities or actors, individual or plural, that affect one another more immediately—even if simply by coexisting or by their sheer numbers — than do other activities or actors. The former are therefore distinguished (to varying extents) from an environment that might include those other units.

The units considered vary in their distinguishability, modifiability, and permanence. For some purposes they have been defined as concrete entities, such as persons or countries, or as activities by these entities, such as acts of persuasion or conquest. For other purposes the units have been defined abstractly as only certain aspects of concrete entities or of their activities, called roles or functions (e.g., Hawley 1986, pp. 31–32), that signify position or participation in a particular aspect of collective living, or as complexes of these entities or activities. Examples are worker, labor, industry in production; official or bureau, directive, central administration in governance; judge or court, adjudication, court system in jurisprudence; supplicant or temple, prayer, denomination in religion; friend or friendship group, attachment, solidary web in emotional bonding; and lecturer or college, teaching, school system in social learning. It will be noted from these examples that units can be sets or combinations of other units. They are called substructures when they constitute broad components of social organization not detailed as to their composition. Examples of *societal* substructures are political state, economy, or moral community.

Structure subsumes both form and content: form generally in the senses of numbers, sizes, shapes, assemblage, connections among units, and directions of flow (say, of resources or persuasion); content in the sense of type of unit, substructure, relationship, or process. Clearly this distinction, though convenient for exposition, is not absolute. Units have been assigned to types on the basis of their forms. And there is form when the same everyday dramas can be "performed" in virtually any setting, whether work or nonwork (Goffman 1959).

FORM

In conventional usage, form implies arrangement in space (not necessarily physical space) and in time. It also implies relationships among elements, in this case the units, against a background—the environment—which is conceived as external to structure (Hawley 1986, pp. 10–44; Smelser 1988). The environment may contain units with which concrete portions of the structure have relationships. Thus environment's separation from structure is often abstract, especially where environment's nonphysical attributes are concerned.

Form can be classified by the processes that occur among the units. Among pure types that are widely investigated are markets, characterized by competition and exchange; arenas, characterized by interunit struggle and alliance; collectivities, characterized by cooperation in joint activity—that is, acting in concert (Parsons and Smelser [1956] 1965, p. 15), even if coerced; and aggregates, characterized by the absence of relations between the units.

These forms occur with a variety of contents. For example, markets not only process goods, services, and labor; they can also process social resources, such as information, intimacy, commitment, information, influence, and prestige. Arenas need not only be political; they can also exist within, say, the family. Collectivities may be found in any or all aspects of human living. And labor forces, electorates, viewerships, school enrollments, and populations of organizations (Aldrich and Marsden 1988) may all be conceived to constitute aggregates. Crosscutting the degrees to which these pure types are approximated are the variables of segmentation, stratification, specialization, scale, and endurance.

Segmentation. Segmentation is division into or banding together of like units (Parsons and Smelser [1956] 1965, p. 256; Parsons [1966] 1977, p. 25; Luhmann [1977] 1982, pp. 231–235, 242–245; Wallace 1988). Tribal societies, for example, can, in their inception, be considered markets constituted by exchange of spouses among relatively small family groups—the segments—that avoid internal marriages (Habermas [1981] 1987, pp. 161–162). In the case of collectivities, segmentation—called categoric organization (Hawley 1986, pp. 70–73)—enables each to accomplish more than could be accomplished separately, as, say, in the union of family groups in hunting and gathering societies (Duncan 1964; Lenski 1975; Hawley 1986, pp. 34–35), in a union of persons pursuing the same occupation, or in the replacement of one national corporation with several regional units. Categoric organization can also replace, at least in part, what would otherwise be mutually destructive competition or conflict or can otherwise create a more predictable environment for the participating unit. Examples are umbrella units that form among populations of special collectivities facing unpredictability in "turbulent environments" (cited by Scott 1987, pp. 122–123), even if they serve as no more than clearinghouses for information. All things being equal, ethnic pluralism—that is, subdivision into collectivities having different histories and life-styles—is another illustration of segmentation.

Stratification. For present purposes, stratification means the ranking of units or sets of units in their capacities to affect the existence and activity of other units or sets by controlling resources. This occurs through manipulation or struggle, as a result of competition or exchange, or voluntarily. Stratification and segmentation can co-occur. Where agriculture is the main economic activity, for example, it has been observed that rank tends to be associated primarily with size of landholding, if any; and where land ownership is also associated with other ranking criteria, as in earlier India, it is likely to serve as a basis either for strata (layers) or for collectivities of same-rank kinship units (Landecker 1981, pp. 33–34, 97). More complex social organization can consist of stratification among units that are themselves stratified. For example, it has been shown that the nations of the world are both internally stratified and stratified vis-à-vis one another (Wallerstein 1979), although effects of the one structure on the other are variable (see, e.g., Evans and Stephens 1988).

Specialization. In its pure sense, specialization refers to composition of unlike units that only taken together can accomplish all that is deemed significant. As a division of labor (Smith [1789] 1976; Durkheim [1902] 1964; Rueschemeyer 1986), specialization is characterized by greater interdependence—facilitative *or* inhibitory—than in the cases of simple segmentation or stratification. Segments can be added or lost with little effect; specialties cannot. Specialization ranges from little more than by age and sex in hunting and gathering societies, possibly with part-time political and religious leadership, to thousands of occupational specialties and nonoccupational roles in industrial and postindustrial societies (Lenski 1975, 1979; Hawley 1986, pp. 31–37, 64–67).

Generally also stratified, this form of social organization has been called corporate in distinction to categoric (Hawley 1986, pp. 68–69). The specialized units can be individuals or certain of their roles, as in a family, a small commune, or a small business enterprise; or they can themselves be segmented, stratified, or specialized internally.

Scale. Frequently associated with other aspects of social organization is its scale, variously specified as, for example, the number of units encompassed; the number of levels at which units are nested into progressively more comprehensive units; or lengths of chains in the modification and flow of materials and services, information, influence, or command.

Contrasted with today's enormous urban settlements and nation-states are the unspecialized and unnested bands of twenty-five to forty or so hunters and gatherers (Lenski 1979). Specific examples of nesting—often accompanying or accompanied by stratification and one type of chain—are world system, country, province, and locality; Catholic Church, archdiocese, diocese, parish, and priest or parishioner; corporation, division, department, and job. Nesting is bypassed when, for example, transnational corporations become disassociated from local, provincial, or national jurisdictions; when religious ties crosscut nation-states; or when staff activities or occupational associations occur irrespective of level (Turk 1977, pp. 923–224; Tilly 1984, p. 136; Hawley 1986, p. 104).

The more activities become organized into large, specialized, but unnested units at higher levels of social organization, according to one body of theory, the less likely are the constituent units to be interconnected (references cited by Turk 1977, p. 65; McAdam et al. 1988). Each of the aggregates that result, sometimes the set of all such aggregates, is called a mass. An example is loss of relationships based on common residence to the extent that the local community is penetrated by specialized large-scale nonlocal collectivities called organizations (e.g., Turk 1977, pp. 65–66, 208–209).

Endurance. An important basis of classifying structure—or, for that matter, any complex unit or relationship that comprises structure—is by the extent to which it predates and outlives, or is otherwise independent of, specific units. Factory workers and managers are relatively replaceable, but a marriage does not substitute a new spouse for one that has been lost without becoming a different marriage. A market can be independent of particular producers and consumers, but a partnership or international bloc is not. Moreover, general features of factory, family, market, partnership, or bloc—or the means of generating these—tend to predate and survive as prototypes any of their specific instances (see, e.g., Jackson 1990).

Combinations. Hybrid forms, some of them complex, occur when segmentation, stratification, specialization, and nesting are considered with respect to one another or with respect to markets, arenas, collectivities, and aggregates. Further, units can themselves be composed of other units in ways other than by nesting, or they can themselves be patterned. A few illustrations follow.

Organizations are specialized collectivities. Defined as complexes of more or less cooperative relations directed toward more or less specific objectives, these units have been said to occur in every known society as "the major vehicle through which concentrated goal-directed effort takes place" (Udy 1979). They, the aggregates they comprise, and relations among them—including organizations of organizations—are considered to be primary units of social organization, at least in industrial and postindustrial communities and nations (see, e.g., Turk 1077, 1985; Skocpol 1979; Perrow 1986; Evans and Stephens 1988; Perrucci and Potter 1080; Coleman 1990).

Markets and arenas generally affect and are affected by collectivities—including ones that they nest or in which they are nested, that they constrain or by which they are constrained—shaping units so they can compete, exchange, struggle, or ally themselves with one another (see, e.g., Stinchcombe 1986; Coleman 1990, esp. pp. 266–321, 371–396, 689). Indeed, organizations and other kinds of collectivities can affect the conditions under which other organizations are formed in substitution for markets (Williamson 1990). Clearly, positions within the organizational substitutes may be filled in turn by labor markets (Stinchcombe 1986; Granovetter and Tilly 1988).

Sizes of aggregates can affect social organization (see citations by Eisenstadt 1068). Sheer numbers make it impossible for each unit to have relations with each other one. This affects the probabilities of positions, networks, or organizations that channel and mediate social relationships (research stimulated by Simmel 1908, pp. 55–56). More recent work shows how specific interconnections, such as marriage or crowd behavior under conditions of threat, can be affected by aggregates, by their relative sizes and other properties, and by relations among these properties (e.g., Blau 1987, Coleman 1990).

Network analysis has added precision to the measurement of form—say, of stratification or of degrees of interconnectedness—by detailing the connections (links) among units and the patterns that these provide (see, e.g., Cook 1977; Leinhardt 1977; Burt 1982; Turner 1986, pp. 287–305). Its techniques are uniquely suited to the chains, clusters, and sequences of exchange, cooperation, alliance, or command over which goods, services, money, information, or influence flow. Associated with scale, for example, can be the number of points between origin of flow and its completion. Network formulations have also proven especially useful in identifying relations among organizations that affect concerted action locally (Turk 1977; Galaskiewicz 1989) and ones that affect it nationally (Laumann and Knoke 1989).

Complexity. The very complexity of social organization—the number and variety of units, levels, and interconnections—is itself an aspect of form. Though admittedly crude (Luhmann [1977] 1982, pp. 232–233; Tilly 1984, pp. 48–50; Rueschemeyer 1986, p. 168), this variable can be used to account for other aspects of social organization (e.g., Lenski 1075, 1979; Turk 1977; Habermas [1981] 1987, pp. 153–197; Luhmann [1977] 1982, pp. 229–254; Rueschemeyer 1986).

CONTENT

Classification of units—including complex units—is necessary for similarity, stratification, or specialization to signify more than simply differences in form. Among many, two bases of classification stand out. Sometimes applied jointly, the one emphasizes objective consequences—positive, negative, or neutral, and varying from 0 in degree—the other communicated, remembered, or recorded meanings and rules. Examples of the two bases follow.

Consequences. Substructure has been classified according to its consequences for stability and change in overall structure (e.g., Marx and Engels [1846] 1970; Marx [1859] 1971; Parsons [1966, 1971] 1977; Luhmann [1977] 1982; Habermas [1981] 1987; Hawley 1986). Among these, adaptation to the environment and of units to one another have been stressed (see, e.g., Duncan 1964; Lenski 1975, 1979; Parsons [1966, 1971] 1977; Habermas [1981] 1987; Luhmann [1974–1977] 1982; Hawley 1986), quite likely because socially organized life has been observed to be the major

adaptive means available to primates (e.g., by Lenski 1975).

Thus, the distinction is often made between (1) economic substructure affecting environmental adaptation for the generation and distribution of general resources (e.g., gross national product, homelessness) and (2) political substructure affecting the generation and distribution of general capacity to mobilize resources for concerted action, including action by opposing collectivities (e.g., national efforts, party campaigns, uprisings). Further distinction involves (3) substructure affecting the generation and distribution of general bonds or schisms that provide harmony or discord among units (e.g., community cohesion, solidary antagonism; see Parsons and Smelser [1956] 1965, pp. 48–49; Parsons [1966] 1977, pp. 135–140; Hawley 1986, p. 66; Coleman 1990, pp. 91–116, 175–196, 517–527) and (4) substructure affecting the generation, distribution, and maintenance of participation in structure: recruitment of units (including but not limited to procreation) and their training, allocation, motivation, and retention—in short, the populating and regulating of social structure.

Meanings and Rules. The classification of content can also rest on disputed or common meanings, understandings, purposes, or binding rules (including law) that are communicated about environment and structure. Communication can involve all kinds of participants or only certain ones and can be modified depending on the context (Goffman 1959). The products of communication vary in their permanence through repetition, recording, or recall; in their breadth of dissemination and acceptance; and in their association with sanction—that is, support by enforcement or other incentives to comply. They can, but often do not, coincide with the structure's objective consequences (Habermas [1981] 1987, esp. pp. 153–197) but can affect it.

Most theories of social organization allow for the effects on stability and change of sanctioned agreement, or of oppositions among sanctioned agreements, calling the product institutional or cultural. They differ in terms of the importance the institutional component is said to have for structure.

Near the one extreme, institutional rules are viewed as "higher level" determinants of social organization (Parsons [1971] 1977, pp. 234–236), not only of relations among units but also of the units themselves (Meyer et al. 1987; Coleman 1990, pp. 43–44, 325–70). Here the rules governing specific structure are considered to be products of more inclusive structure, such as political state or church (Znaniecki 1945; Turk 1977, pp. 210, 215–221), or to be elements of a world "culture pool" (Moore 1988; Meyer et al. 1987). Near the other extreme, meanings ("ideas") are viewed primarily as by-products of the material relations of production (Marx and Engels [1846] 1970, pp. 57–60) or in terms of their significance for organized adaptive processes vis-à-vis the environment (e.g., Duncan 1964; Lenski 1975). Meaning, if the concept is employed at all, is restricted to the acting unit's purposive rationality: its adoption, within the limits of error and imperfect knowledge or skill, of means that are appropriate to specified outcomes (see, e.g., Hawley 1986, pp. 6–7).

A second source of variability is the degree to which the institutional can be seen as analytically distinct from structure. Some consider the institutional to be an aspect of the environments of substructures and other units (Parsons 1968; Meyer and Rowan 1978; Hawley 1986, p. 79; Meyer et al. 1987; Coleman 1990, pp. 43–44). Others see it as relatively inextricable from structure (e.g., Giddens 1979, pp. 49–85), specifically where structure is viewed as formed and modified through interpretive interaction between persons or groups, in which interpretations are frequently but not always shared (Blumer 1969, pp. 86–88).

The third issue regards the degree to which structure is "spelled out" by the institutional. There can be precise rules that govern even the minutiae, as on an assembly line or in religious ritual. There are also general principles that reduce the number of structural alternatives without determining structure precisely (Parsons [1971] 1977, pp. 193–194), as in such ideals as freedom, rationality, retribution, obedience, protest, solidarity, revolution, contract, and property. Relatedly, there can be shared common-sense reasoning (Collins 1988, pp. 273–291 on Garfinkel) on the basis of which "sense" is made of structure. Or there can be broad myths that serve to provide accounts of social organization (Meyer and Rowan 1978, Goffman 1959) on the basis of which, rather than on the basis of performance, structure is justified.

Agency, as do most theories incorporating meaning, rests on the general idea of interest—variously called purpose, intention, motive, or goal and variably emerging during a course of action—and on the availability of action alternatives (e.g., Giddens 1979, pp. 55–56). Agency is the extent to which purposive action by and interaction among the units affect social organization. There is little need to consider what individual units contribute to organization or why (Hawley 1986, pp. 6–7). When structure, environment, or rule are viewed as an absolute constraint or as providing only limited choice (see, e.g., Blau 1987), or where social organization results from natural selection (Lenski 1975, 1979).

This is not the case where structure and culture simply set loose conditions for action and interaction. Important here for structural and cultural stability and change are the processes (1) by which interests are pursued under the influence and constraint of other actors (Homans 1975); (2) by which the conditions of action are interpreted through social interaction (Blumer 1969); (3) by which the acting unit monitors and adjusts the components of action, even intention, throughout (Giddens 1979, pp. 53–59); and (4) by which individual and collective actors choose means of implementing their interests (Coleman 1990). These processes are significant both to the reproduction and to the transformation of structure and institutional rule.

Classifications of meaning are numerous. Yet they frequently rest on one or more of the following variables (polar approximations in parentheses): (1) specificity: the scope of the relationship, from specific to diffuse content (e.g., organizations or special markets vs. unspecialized collectivities or conflict arenas); (2) universalism: the extent to which relationships hold for all units belonging to a category or only for particular ones from that category (e.g., upholding sovereignty of any nation or opposition toward all governments vs. a treaty or a declaration of war); (3) neutrality: the extent to which relationships are means to ends vs. ends in themselves (e.g., banking transactions or job competition vs. flag-raising or flag-burning ceremonies); and (4) performance: the extent to which relationships are based on what units do rather than on what they are (e.g., production relations or industrial conflict vs. aristocracy or racial conflict).

Concrete as well as abstract structures have been classified according to various combinations of values of these variables, leading to widely used typologies. More generally, any variables used to define content and form serve the analysis of overall structure by describing its various aspects or its different parts.

FORM AND CONTENT

Structure can vary in the extent to which substructures—such as the four whose consequences were noted—are abstractions, involving the same concrete units rather than different ones. At the low end of this continuum, the units comprise a single unstratified and unspecialized collectivity, approximated by a tribal society or a commune, in which each act affirms the totality (Durkheim [1902] 1964; Luhmann [1974] 1982, 1987, pp. 153–197), having every kind of consequence for it. In it myth tends to blur distinctions among the objective, social, and subjective worlds and between society and its natural surroundings (Habermas [1981] 1987, pp. 158–159), and there is comprehensive and detailed regulation of activity. The units not only resemble one another but also tend not to have separate identities. In short, relations tend to be particular to the given collectivity, not universal; affective, not neutral; ascriptive, not performance-based; and diffuse, not specific.

In examples of this noncomplex instance, economic and political organization tend to be extensions of family, extended family, religious group, and common territory, which overlap to considerable degrees. Commitment to any one aspect of social life tends to be supported and sanctioned within all of the others (Habermas [1981] 1987, pp. 156–157), and there are relatively few conflicting constraints, structural or cultural (Blumer 1969, pp. 87–88).

Compliance to one cluster of rules and understandings is approximated, with utility, sanction, attachment, and/or commitment as its basis or bases. Here change has been attributed, in the main, to changes in the environment or in ways of coping with it (e.g., Hawley 1986, pp. 15–18) or to ubiquitous "tension" between rules of action and the situation of the acting unit (e.g., Parsons and Smelser [1956] 1965, esp. pp. 50–51). There is little institutional provision for change.

With greater complexity, however, activities can be removed from these primordial units and assumed by large-scale economic, political, and other kinds of organizations (e.g., Lenski 1979; Coleman 1990, pp. 584–585). Varied organizational purpose as well as interaction among organizations can constitute bases of change that are themselves institutionalized.

Domination. Stratification implies domination—that is, setting the conditions of existence by certain units for other units through disposition over key resources; over the generation and selection of often self-serving meanings and rules (see, e.g., Landecker 1981); and over the means of securing compliance. Such disproportion is one of the most widely considered sources of strain, hence of change through conflict (see, e.g., the modifications of Marxian theory by Dahrendorf 1959 and Skocpol 1979).

Considered under various names (see, e.g., Marx and Engels [1846] 1970; Parsons and Smelser [1956] 1965; Dahrendorf 1959; Duncan 1964; Hawley 1986; Giddens 1985), domination includes disposition over means of coercion, material inducement, social support, or rules of command (adapted from Weber [1920] 1978, pp. 53–54; Hawley 1986, pp. 33–37). Domination reflects power, the capacity to affect action and its outcomes (Giddens 1979, pp. 88–94). Suggested by Weber ([1920] 1978, p. 53) as the probability that the acting unit can carry out its will despite resistance, power has also been defined as the structure's capacity to mobilize resources in effecting outcomes through concerted action, such as the production of sustenance (or other ways of supporting units) and environmental control (Parsons and Smelser [1956] 1965, p. 48; Hawley 1986, pp. 36–37). This capacity is conceived to be distributed in different ways, depending on the structure under consideration (Hawley 1986, pp. 74–77), serving political relations as money serves economic relations (Parsons 1975).

Domination can effect both form and content. For example, domination can cause segmentation to give way to stratification, frequently as a result of conquest, as when multicommunal societies become kingdoms or empires (Lenski 1979) or numerous petty sovereignties are gathered under nation-states (Tilly 1984, p. 48). By setting the conditions for competition and exchange or more directly by affecting concerted action that favors certain specialties or even by imposition, domination can also make specialization possible or influence its nature and degree (Habermas [1981] 1987, pp. 161–163; Hawley 1986, pp. 64–67, 91–95; Rueschemeyer 1986).

The resources on which domination is based need not only be material. They can be social—for example, active support, institutionalization by organizations and movements that generate and implement ideology or legality, and the absence of opposition. Generalized control over all manner of resources has been called hegemony, and political processes have been characterized as struggles for hegemony (Wallerstein 1979, 1984; Tuchman 1988). Domination has been conceived, in its extreme form, as rendering certain alternatives invisible (Giddens 1985, pp. 8–10) through taken-for-granted opposition by powerful units (Polsby 1980, pp. 189–218), lack of relevant language (Parsons 1975), absence of relevant substructures, agendas set by the mass media of communication (Tuchman 1988), and uncontested legitimacy—that is, common understandings as to what is valid or binding. The elementary stratified society is, by definition, hegemonic, since it is unspecialized in terms of the control of various types of resources.

Domination can be by one or more substructures over the others. History shows, for example, cases of kinship-based, religious, military, economic, and political domination (e.g., Tilly 1984; Evans and Stephens 1988). The hypothesis has been suggested that the greater the specialization, the less stable is domination through fusion of, say, political with economic activities (Parsons and Smelser [1956] 1965, p. 83). The expected trend is for substructures to become concretely separate. For example, underground markets arise as responses to shortages and bottlenecks in socialist societies, which are characterized by political domination of economic activity, or by the "informally" organized demands of their workers (Jones 1984).

Pluralism and Plasticity. The degree to which meanings are single or plural can be affected by segmentation or specialization. Different collectivities, constituted, say, on the basis of different fundamental beliefs, different descent, or different economic circumstances (Landecker 1981), coexist segmentally either by loose agreement or by coercive regulation, each with separate rules and un-

derstandings (Tenbruck 1989), or struggle with one another over which ones shall prevail (e.g., Landecker 1981, pp. 136–169; Wallace 1988).

The greater the specialization among units, all things being equal, the greater also is the plurality of interests, according to some models. A recurrent theme is that this form of pluralism affects the probabilities of different degrees of involvement by given units and of different alignments among units from one issue to the next. Such differential participation can have a negative effect on the probability of broad or intense conflict (Dahrendorf 1959, pp. 215–231; Polsby 1980, pp. 84–97, 122–138; Turk 1977, pp. 97–103, 1985; McAdam et al. 1988).

Specialized forms, including organizations, are by definition relatively indifferent to the activities or aspirations of supporting, component, or utilizing units in other social settings (Luhmann [1975] 1982, pp. 78–79; Labovitz and Hagedorn 1977, pp. 12–15). Entire areas of indifference are seen to result, for example, from "gaps" left between interests served by organizations (Luhmann [1975] 1982, pp. 79–80, 87, [1977] 1982, p. 237). The intrusion of, say, race and gender in contemporary labor markets suggests, however, that organizational indifference is a matter of degree (see, e.g., Stinchcombe 1986; Granovetter and Tilly 1988).

Accompanying segmentation or specialization, according to several theories, is plasticity: the probability of loose and variable connections among segments or among organizations subsumed by substructures like the four singled out. Here overall organization is limited to compatibility, falling short of the pursuit of unified or concerted outcomes across substructures (see, e.g., Luhmann [1975] 1982, pp. 78–79). Change is endemic in the absence of overall structure, save for markets and conflict arenas and rules that govern these (Luhmann [1977] 1982, pp. 238–242). It tends to occur as accommodation (1) through exchange, say, between segments or between political and economic substructures (Parsons and Smelser [1956] 1965), or (2) through new forms and modification of older ones in responses to changes elsewhere, as in the case of the family's loss of economic activity in the United States but its growing importance in providing incentive for such activity (Schumpeter, cited by Suttles and Janowitz 1979).

The greater the segmentation or specialization, the more general the accommodative meanings and rules that encompass social organization overall—for example, the idea of tolerance and its enforcement, or of universal civility (Parsons [1971] 1977, pp. 182–193; Hawley 1986, p. 66). Another example is the idea of freedom in classic liberal society, implemented as economic laissez faire, religious autonomy, voluntary rather than arranged marriage, political competition for electoral support, and stratum membership on the basis of achievement rather than family (Gerth and Mills 1964, pp. 354–357).

There is disagreement about the extent of hegemony under conditions of specialization, even where, say, political or economic organizations overshadow other organizations in control over resources. At the one extreme incumbents of dominant positions within the various specialized organizations have been conceived as constituting a single elite capable of joint domination (e.g., Mills 1956) or as being generally dominant to the extent that they hold positions in multiple organizations (Perrucci and Pilisuk 1970). Relatedly, large organizations have been observed to divorce themselves from the interests they were established to represent—as, say, those of capital and labor—and strike bargains with one another (Evans and Stephens 1988). These conceptions of unified domination have partly been verified and partly refuted (e.g., by Lieberson 1971; Mizruchi 1982; Johnsen and Mintz 1989).

Specialized as they are, according to another partly verified view, the same set of organizations can facilitate one another in certain respects and be in mutual struggle in others, therefore resisting direct domination by any one or a few of their number (citations in Turk 1985). Under these conditions policy that is the basis for binding domination is formed through action by those masses or by those nonpermanent coalitions of public agencies and private organizations that are concerned with any particular matter (Turk 1977, pp. 136–205; Galaskiewicz 1989; Laumann and Knoke 1989).

Crosscutting the issue is the question of whether, given specialization, either an organized elite or an interorganizational coalition has the capacity for concerted action that transcends the substructures. Specialization can mean that, at the most, even the most powerful organization is dominant only with respect to one or two issue areas (Luhmann [1975] 1982, pp. 76–89; Polsby 1980, pp. 122–128). However, even within organizations the normal decision process has been defined as organized anarchy by certain investigators (e.g., citations by Scott 1987, pp. 277–282; Meyer and Rowan 1978). Carried to an extreme, the question is one of the extent to which coordination by domination is haphazard, whether actual coordination might not result from the "invisible hand" of a market (Smith [1789] 1976, Vol. 1, pp. 477–478) or of an arena of conflict.

Standardization. Mitigating the diversifying possibilities of segmentation and specialization that have been noted are tendencies for units to become alike in certain aspects of form and content—that is, isomorphic (Hawley 1986, pp. 66–70; Udy 1979; Kerr 1983, pp. 85–89). This can be because units require similar internal arrangements for purposes of connection with one another (Hawley 1986, p. 70), or model themselves after other units in the preservation of competitive effectiveness (suggested by Aldrich and Marsden 1988, citing DiMaggio and Powell). It can also be through institutionalization by drawing upon a common "culture pool" available, say, to the countries of the world (Moore 1988) or through, say, political or religious imposition within a given society (Znaniecki 1945; Landecker 1981, p. 136) or by either (Hawley 1986, p. 66; Meyer et al. 1987).

Not only can there be standardization of form, there can also be standardization of process. For reasons of predictability and economy of effort, among others, the joint reproduction of habitual patterns has been considered to lie at the heart of social life (e.g., Berger and Luckmann 1966). This not only accounts in part for compliance with meanings and rules that standardize feeling, thinking, and acting in such relatively unspecialized settings as tribal societies, it also accounts for standardized, partly area-specific media and codes that symbolize and routinize all manner of activities and products where there is more specialization. Examples are language (Habermas [1981] 1987, pp. 56–57), money, property, prestige, influence, power, legality, administrative principles, criteria of truth (Parsons 1975, Habermas [1981] 1987, pp. 153–197, 367–373; Luhmann [1974] 1982, pp. 168–170), and credentialed expertise (Collins 1988, pp. 174–184; Luhmann [1976] 1982, pp. 303–331; Bauman 1989). These standardize and objecify aspects of markets, conflict arenas, collectivities, or aggregates. Unless it fails noticeably, it is believed, routine tends not to be questioned, especially where relevant knowledge is not widely pursued and alternatives are not at hand.

Collective Agency. Mainly based on exchange, conquest, or revolution, change is seldom institutionalized in segmental or stratified society. Pluralism generally includes provisions for categoric organization in the form of mass action, say through referenda, or in the form of movement and interest organizations, which not only participate in the coalitions that seek to dominate given matters but also define matters for action by the mass. These institutionalized means of structural and cultural change through collective agency are thought to occur where pluralism means lack of overall institutional detail (e.g., Gusfield 1979). Recent investigations have not only examined their causes and effects but also their forms and ways of acting (Zurcher and Snow 1981; McAdam et al. 1988). Their efforts can be toward increasing the material and social resources controlled by given categories of units, as in the case of gay rights, or they can be directed toward broad structural changes or changes in meaning that occur for their participants and for nonparticipants alike, as in the case of civil liberties (Gusfield 1979). Like revolutions, movements have been considered to be processes that can begin by effecting transitional social organization and end with new institutionalized structure (Alberoni [1981] 1984).

Commitment and Trust. Commitment of units to one another and to their common structure is a widely recognized influence. The "we" that characterizes collectivities (Cooley 1902, 1916) or the "consciousness" that causes support of existing social organization or generates struggle within it (Marx and Engels [1846] 1970; Durkheim [1902] 1964) is seen as having either of two effects. It can be direct, producing commitment to the given structure, or indirect by habitualizing the commitment and trust that serves participation in a variety of settings, even ones that are specific and neutral (also see Coleman 1990, p. 297).

Increasing specialization and other forms of organizational complexity and increasing scale have been viewed as negative influences on commitment, even on commitment to disputing factions or to revolutionary movements seeking structural change. Commitment to large-scale organizations comprising specialized substructure is generally considered less than to other kinds of collectivities because of anonymity among the constituent units, which are likely to have the characteristics of a mass, and because only part of the constituent is involved.

With complexity and scale, participation in one substructure is less contingent on participation in others, incurring separate, possibly conflicting obligations; indeed, everyday interactions that produce common meaning have been considered divorced from structure and rules (Luhmann [1974–1977] 1982, 1987; Habermas [1981] 1987, pp. 117, 153–197), and even everyday life is penetrated by the actions and generalized media controlled by organizations (e.g., legal and monetary), reducing its potential for social integration (Habermas [1981] 1987, pp. 267, 330–331, 367–373). Under these conditions the influence of trust on social organization is less likely (Coleman 1990, pp. 300–321), and benefits are more likely sought without corresponding contributions (Coleman 1990, pp. 650–655).

The greater the specialization and accompanying standardization, it has been observed, the more of the population can be included in whatever substructures comprise various areas of social life (Parsons [1966] 1977)—that is, the more universalistic, for example, are criteria for suffrage and military service, access to public facilities, mass education, and employment opportunity. One reason follows. The more social structure consists of aggregates of organizations whose concerted activities are narrowly focused on specialized consequences—meaning specific and neutral orientation toward performance—that tend to be unranked, the less relevant these aggregates are to one another as criteria of exclusion (Luhmann [1977] 1982, pp. 236–238). Examples can be found in references to "customer," "patient," "student," or "defendant," independently of the beneficiary's other social attributes. At its extreme it can even lead to "the gall bladder in bed 27." Aided by standardized media such as money, the result of inclusion can be the diminution of commitment and trust through the transformation of agents into commodities for exchange (e.g., Marx [1859] 1971, pp. 78–84), or their more general removal from meaningful communicative interaction (Habermas [1981] 1987, e.g., p. 343).

The other side of inclusion is regulation. The more central that large, specialized organizations are to social structure, it has also been claimed, the less social organization depends on commitment and the greater is the shift from mutual trust to trust in expertise. The state, for example, is said to require less legitimacy as its expert-driven political technology provides, say, surveillance, "correction," welfare supervision, "medicalization," or "psychiatrization" (Bauman 1989). Indeed, the electorate's growing cynicism about government (e.g., Institute for Social Research 1979) has had little apparent effect on political structure in the United States.

(SEE ALSO: *Organizational Structure; Social Dynamics; Social Network Theory; Social Structure*)

REFERENCES

Ahrne, Goran 1994 *Social Organizations: Interaction Inside, Outside and Between Organizations.* Beverly Hills, Calif.: Sage.

Alberoni, Francesco (1981) 1984 *Movement and Institution*, trans. P.C.A. Delmoro. New York: Columbia University Press.

Aldrich, Howard E., and Peter V. Marsden 1988 "Environments and Organizations." In N.J. Smelser, ed., *Handbook of Sociology.* Beverly Hills, Calif.: Sage.

Alvarado, Felix 1996 "Concerning Postmodernity and Organizations in the Third World: Opening a Debate and Suggestions for a Research Agenda." *Organization Science* 7:667–681.

Bauman, Zygmunt 1989 "Legislators and Interpretors: Culture as Ideology of Intellectuals." In H. Haferkamp, ed., *Social Structure and Culture.* New York: Walter de Gruyter.

Berger, Peter L., and Thomas Luckmann 1966 *The Social Construction of Reality: A Treatise in the Sociology of Knowledge.* Garden City, N.Y.: Doubleday.

Blau, Judith R. 1996 "Organizations as Overlapping Jurisdictions: Restoring Reason in Organizational Accounts." *Administrative Science Quarterly* 41:172–179.

Blau, Peter M. 1975 "Introduction: Parallels and Contrasts in Structural Inquiries." In P. M. Blau, ed., *Approaches to the Study of Social Structure.* New York: Free Press.

—— 1987 "Contrasting Theoretical Perspectives." In J. C. Alexander, B. Giesen, R. Mënch, and N. J. Smelser, eds., *The Micro-Macro Link.* Berkeley: University of California Press.

Blumer, Herbert 1969 *Symbolic Interactionism: Perspective and Method.* Englewood Cliffs, N.J.: Prentice-Hall.

Brass, Daniel J. 1992. "Power in Organizations: A Social Network Perspective." *Research in Politics and Society* 4:295–323.

Burt, Ronald S. 1982 *Toward a Structural Theory of Action: Network Models of Social Structure, Perception, and Action.* New York: Academic Press.

Coleman, James S. 1990 *Foundations of Social Theory.* Cambridge, Mass.: Harvard University Press.

Collins, Randall 1988 *Theoretical Sociology.* New York: Harcourt Brace Jovanovich.

Cook, Karen S. 1977 "Exchange and Power in Networks of Interorganizational Relations." *Sociological Quarterly* 18:62–82.

Cooley, Charles Horton 1902 *Human Nature and the Social Order.* New York: Scribners.

—— 1916 *Social Organization: A Study of the Larger Mind.* New York: Scribners.

Dahrendorf, Ralf 1959 *Class and Class Conflict in Industrial Society.* Stanford, Calif.: Stanford University Press.

Duncan, Otis Dudley 1964 "Social Organization and the Ecosystem." In R. E. L. Faris, ed., *Handbook of Sociology.* Chicago: Rand McNally.

Durkheim, Emile (1902) 1964 *The Division of Labor in Society*, trans. George Simpson. New York: Free Press.

Edelman, Lauren B. and Mark C. Suchman 1997 "The Legal Environments of Organizations." *Annual Review of Sociology* 23:479–515.

Eisenstadt, Shmuel N. 1968 "Social Institutions, I: The Concept." In D. L. Sills, ed., *International Encyclopedia of the Social Sciences.* New York: Macmillan.

Evans, Peter B., and John D. Stephens 1988 "Development and the World Economy." In N. J. Smelser, ed., *Handbook of Sociology.* Beverly Hills, Calif.: Sage.

Faris, Robert E. L. 1964 "Social Organization (Sociology)." In J. Gold and W. L. Kolb, eds., *A Dictionary of the Social Sciences.* New York: Free Press.

Galaskiewicz, Joseph 1989 "Interorganizational Networks Mobilizing Action at the Metropolitan Level." In R. Perrucci and H. R. Potter, eds., *Networks of Power: Organizational Actors at the National, Corporate, and Community Levels.* New York: Aldine de Gruyter.

Gerth, Hans, and C. Wright Mills (1953) 1964 *Character and Social Structure: The Psychology of Social Institutions.* New York: Harcourt, Brace and World.

Gherardi, Silvia 1995 *Gender, Symbolism and Organizational Cultures.* Beverly Hills, Calif.: Sage.

Giddens, Anthony 1979 *Central Problems in Social Theory: Action, Structure and Contradiction in Social Analysis.* Berkeley: University of California Press.

—— 1985 *The Nation-State and Violence.* Berkeley: University of California Press.

Goffman, Erving 1959 *The Presentation of Self in Everyday Life.* Garden City, N.Y.: Doubleday.

Granovetter, Mark, and Charles Tilly 1988 "Inequality and Labor Processes." In N. J. Smelser, ed., *Handbook of Sociology.* Beverly Hills, Calif.: Sage.

Gusfield, Joseph 1979 "The Modernity of Social Movements: Public Roles and Private Parts." In A. H. Hawley, ed., *Societal Growth: Processes and Implications.* New York: Free Press.

Habermas, Jurgen (1981) 1987 *The Theory of Communicative Action.* Vol. 2: *Lifeworld and System: A Critique of Functionalist Reason,* trans. Thomas McCarthy. Boston: Beacon Press.

Hawley, Amos H. 1986 *Human Ecology: A Theoretical Essay.* Chicago: University of Chicago Press.

Homans, George C. 1975 "What Do We Mean by Social 'Structure'?" In P. M. Blau, ed., *Approaches to the Study of Social Structure.* New York: Free Press.

Institute for Social Research 1979 "Deepening Distrust of Political Leaders Is Jarring Public's Faith in Institutions." *ISR Newsletter* 7:4–5.

Jackson, John E. 1990 "Institutions in American Society: An Overview." In J. E. Jackson, ed., *Institutions in American Society: Essays in Market, Political, and Social Organizations.* Ann Arbor: University of Michigan Press.

Johnsen, Eugene, and Beth Mintz 1989 "Organizational versus Class Components of Director Networks." In R. Perrucci and H. R. Potter, eds., *Networks of Power: Organizational Actors at the National, Corporate, and Community Levels.* New York: Aldine de Gruyter.

Jones, A. Anthony 1984 "Models of Socialist Development." In Lenski, Gerhard, ed., *Current Issues and Research in Macrosociology.* Leiden, Neth.: E. J. Brill.

Kerr, Clark 1983 *The Future of Industrial Societies: Convergence or Continuing Diversity?* Cambridge, Mass.: Harvard University Press.

Labovitz, Sanford, and Robert Hagedorn 1977 "Social Norms." In Sanford Labovitz, *An Introduction to Sociological Concepts.* New York: Wiley.

Landecker, Werner S. 1981 *Class Crystallization.* New Brunswick, N.J.: Rutgers University Press.

Laumann, Edward O., and David Knoke 1989 "Policy Networks of the Organizational State: Collective Action in the National Energy and Health Domains." In R. Perrucci and H. R. Potter, eds., *Networks of Power: Organizational Actors at the National, Corporate, and Community Levels.* New York: Aldine de Gruyter.

Leinhardt, Samuel (ed.) 1977 *Social Networks: A Developing Paradigm.* New York: Academic Press.

Lenski, Gerhard E. 1975 "Social Structure in Evolutionary Perspective." In P. M. Blau, ed., *Approaches to the Study of Social Structure.* New York: Free Press.

—— 1979 "Directions and Continuities in Societal Growth." In A. H. Hawley, ed., *Societal Growth: Processes and Implications.* New York: Free Press.

Levy, Marion J., Jr. 1996 *Modernization and the Structure of Societies.* Vol. 2: *The Organizational Contexts of Societies.* New Brunswick, N.J.: Transaction.

Lieberson, Stanley 1971 "An Empirical Study of Military-Industrial Linkages." *American Sociological Review* 76:562–585.

Luhmann, Niklas (1974–1977) 1982 *The Differentiation of Society,* parts trans. S. Holmes and C. Larmore. New York: Columbia University Press.

—— 1987 "The Evolutionary Differentiation Between Society and Interaction." In J. C. Alexander, B. Giesen, R. Münch, and N. J. Smelser, eds., *The Micro-Macro Link.* Berkeley: University of California Press.

Marx, Karl (1859) 1971 *The Grundrisse,* D. McLellan, ed. and trans. New York: Harper and Row.

Marx, Karl, and Frederick [sic] Engels (1846) 1970 *The German Ideology,* ed. C. J. Arthur, trans. W. Lough, C. Dutt, and C. P. Magill. New York: International Publishers.

McAdam, Doug, John D. McCarthy, and Mayer N. Zald 1988 "Social Movements." In N. J. Smelser, ed., *Handbook of Sociology.* Beverly Hills, Calif.: Sage.

McKinlay, Alan and Ken Starkey, eds., 1998 *Foucault, Management and Organization Theory.* Beverly Hills, Calif.: Sage.

Meyer, John W., John Boli, and George M. Thomas 1987 "Ontology and Rationalization in the Western Cultural Account." In G. M. Thomas, J. W. Meyer, F. O. Ramirez, and J. Bali, eds., *Institutional Structure: Constituting State, Society, and the Individual.* Beverly Hills, Calif.: Sage.

Meyer, John W., and Brian Rowan 1978 "The Structure of Educational Organizations." In M. Meyer and associates. *Environments and Organizations.* San Francisco: Jossey-Bass.

Mills, C. Wright 1956 *The Power Elite.* New York: Oxford University Press.

Mizruchi, Mark S. 1982 *The American Corporate Network, 1904–1974.* Beverly Hills, Calif.: Sage.

Monge, Peter R. 1995 "Theoretical and Analytical Issues in Studying Organizational Processes." In G. P.

Huber, and A. H. Van deVen, eds. *Longitudinal Field Research Methods: Studying Processes of Organizational Change*. Beverly Hills, Calif.: Sage.

Moore, Wilbert E. 1988 "Social Change." In E. F. Borgatta and K. S. Cook, eds., *The Future of Sociology*. Beverly Hills, Calif.: Sage.

Orlikowski, Wanda J. 1992 "The Duality of Technology: Rethinking the Concept of Technology in Organizations." *Organization Science* 3:398–427.

Parsons, Talcott 1968 "Social Systems." In D. L. Sills, ed., *International Encyclopedia of the Social Sciences*. New York: Macmillan.

—— 1975 "The Present Status of 'Structural-Functional' Theory in Sociology." In L. A. Coser, ed., *The Idea of Social Structure: Papers in Honor of Robert K. Merton*. New York: Harcourt Brace Jovanovich.

—— (1966, 1971) 1977 *The Evolution of Societies*, ed. Jackson Toby. Englewood Cliffs, N.J.: Prentice-Hall.

Parsons, Talcott, and Neil J. Smelser (1956) 1965 *Economy and Society: A Study in the Integration of Economic and Social Theory*. New York: Free Press.

Perrow, Charles 1991 "A Society of Organizations." *Theory and Society* 20:725–762.

Perrow, Charles 1992 "Organisational Theorists in a Society of Organisations." *International Sociology* 7:371–380.

—— 1986 *Complex Organizations: A Critical Essay*, 3rd ed. New York: Random House.

Perrucci, Robert, and Marc Pilisuk 1970 "Leaders and Ruling Elites: The Interorganizational Bases of Community Power." *American Sociological Review* 35:1040–1057.

Perrucci, Robert, and Harry R. Potter 1989 "The Collective Actor in Organizational Analysis." In R. Perrucci and H. R. Potter, eds., *Networks of Power: Organizational Actors at the National, Corporate, and Community Levels*. New York: Aldine de Gruyter.

Polsby, Nelson W. 1980 *Community Power and Political Theory: A Further Look at Problems of Evidence and Inference*, 2nd ed. New Haven, Conn.: Yale University Press.

Rueschemeyer, Dietrich 1986 *Power and the Division of Labor*. Stanford, Calif.: Stanford University Press.

Scott, W. Richard and Soren Christensen 1995 *The Institutional Construction of Organizations: International and Longitudinal Studies*. Beverly Hills, Calif.: Sage.

Scott, W. Richard 1987 *Organizations: Rational, Natural, and Open Systems*, 2nd ed. Englewood Cliffs, N.J.: Prentice-Hall.

Simmel, Georg 1908 *Soziologie: Untersuchungen über die Formen der Vergesellschaftung*. Leipzig: Duncker und Humblot.

Skocpol, Theda 1979 *States and Social Revolutions: A Comparative Analysis of France, Russia, and China*. New York: Cambridge University Press.

Slappendel, Carol 1996 "Perspectives on Innovation in Organizations." *Organization Studies* 17:107–129.

Smelser, Neil J. 1988 "Social Structure." In N. J. Smelser, ed., *Handbook of Sociology*. Beverly Hills, Calif.: Sage.

Smith, Adam [1789] 1976 *The Wealth of Nations*. Chicago: University of Chicago Press.

Stinchcombe, Arthur L. 1990 *Information and Organizations*. Berkeley: University of California Press.

—— 1986 "Economic Sociology: Rationality and Subjectivity." In U. Himmelstrand, ed., *Sociology: From Crisis to Science?*, vol. 1, *The Sociology of Structure and Action*. Beverly Hills, Calif.: Sage.

Strang, David and Sarah A. Soule 1998 "Diffusion in Organizations and Social Movements: From Hybrid Corn to Poison Pills." *Annual Review of Sociology* 24:265–290.

Suttles, Gerald, and Morris Janowitz 1979 "Metropolitan Growth and Democratic Participation." In A. H. Hawley, ed., *Societal Growth: Processes and Implications*. New York: Free Press.

Tenbruck, Friedrich H. 1989 "The Cultural Foundations of Society." In H. Haferkamp, ed., *Social Structure and Culture*. New York: Walter de Gruyter.

Tilly, Charles 1984 *Big Structures, Large Processes, Huge Comparisons*. New York: Russell Sage Foundation.

—— 1998 *Durable Inequality*. Berkeley: University of California Press.

Tuchman, Gaye 1988 "Mass Media Institutions." In N. J. Smelser, ed., *Handbook of Sociology*. Beverly Hills, Calif.: Sage.

Turk, Herman 1977 *Organizations in Modern Life: Cities and Other Large Networks*. San Francisco: Jossey-Bass.

—— 1985 "Macrosociology and Interorganizational Relations: Theory, Strategies, and Bibliography." *Sociology and Social Research* 69:487–500. (Reprint with corrected typography is available.)

Turner, Jonathan H. 1986 *The Structure of Sociological Theory*, 4th ed. Chicago: Dorsey Press.

—— 1990 "Emile Durkheim's Theory of Social Organization." *Social Forces* 68:1089–1103.

Udy, Stanley, H., Jr. 1968 "Social Structure: Social Structural Analysis." In D. L. Sills, ed., *International Encyclopedia of the Social Sciences*. New York: Macmillan.

——— 1979 "Societal Growth and Organizational Complexity." In A. H. Hawley, ed., *Societal Growth: Processes and Implications*. New York: Free Press.

Wallace, Walter L. 1988 "Toward a Disciplinary Matrix in Sociology." In N. J. Smelser, ed., *Handbook of Sociology*. Beverly Hills, Calif.: Sage.

Wallerstein, Immanuel 1979 "World Networks and the Politics of the World Economy." In A. H. Hawley, ed., *Societal Growth: Processes and Implications*. New York: Free Press.

——— 1984 "The Three Instances of Hegemony in the History of the Capitalist World Economy." In G. Lenski, ed., *Current Issues and Research in Macrosociology*. Leiden, Neth.: E. J. Brill.

Weber, Max (1920) 1978 *Economy and Society: An Outline of Interpretive Sociology*, G. Roth and C. Wittich, eds.; E. Fischoff, H. Gerth, A. M. Henderson, C. W. Mills, T. Parsons, M. Rheinstein, G. Roth, and C. Wittich, trans. Berkeley: University of California Press.

Wharton, Amy S. 1994 "Structure and Process: Theory and Research on Organizational Stratification." *Current Perspectives in Social Theory* supplement 1:119–148.

Williams, Raymond 1976 *Keywords: A Vocabulary of Culture and Society*. New York: Oxford University Press.

Williamson, Oliver E. 1990 "Chester Barnard and the Incipient Science of Organization." In O. E. Williamson, ed., *Organization Theory: From Chester Barnard to the Present and Beyond*. New York: Oxford University Press.

Znaniecki, Florian 1945 "Social Organization and Institutions." In G. Gurvitch and W. E. Moore, eds., *Twentieth Century Sociology*. New York: Philosophical Library.

Zurcher, Louis A., and David A. Snow 1981 "Collective Behavior: Social Movements." In M. Rosenberg and R. H. Turner, eds., *Social Psychology: Sociological Perspectives*. New York: Basic Books.

HERMAN TURK

SOCIAL PERCEPTION

Social perception theories and investigations deal with the nature, causes, and consequences of perceptions of social entities, including one's self, other individuals, social categories, and aggregates or groups to which one may or may not belong. The content of a perception can be virtually any property. Individual attributes may include personality traits, behavioral dispositions, physical characteristics, and ability evaluations. Group attributes can include properties such as size, cohesiveness, cultural traits, stratification patterns, network patterns, legitimacy, and historical elements. With some notable exceptions, however, the field of social perception traditionally has emphasized the micro side, focusing on individual inferences regarding one individual or a very small number of other individuals.

Social perception is best viewed as an umbrella label that covers a range of loosely related and usually loosely formulated theoretical conjectures and associated research. Today "social cognition" may be the more popular label, subsuming theory and research indexed under numerous other headings: person perception, social judgment, social representation, schema theory, reference group theory, impression formation, attribution theory, and more. Little of this work will be discussed here, although most of it is easy to access. Reference lists in books, chapters, and articles under the various headings tend to intersect rather than be isolated. Review articles have appeared with regularity, and so it is relatively easy to locate the seminal, general, or esoteric references one seeks.

This article provides an introduction and selective overview of the social perception area, with additional attention to some threads that have been or could be of particular interest within sociology. First there is a brief discussion of perception in general, followed by sections that divide the field into three major realms: self-perception, person perception, and group perception.

PERCEPTION

Social perception is only one manifestation of the general phenomenon of human perception. All perceptions begin with energy-producing events, either inside people or from the environment. Each of the senses operates as a "transducer," encoding a particular form of energy (e.g., radiant, kinetic, chemical) into neurological signals that are carried to the brain as complex, parallel streams of bioelectrical impulses. In the brain, these streams of information are filtered and transformed through several stages, producing dynamic neural representations almost instantaneously. Depending on anatomic factors, prior experiences, and the nature of the signals, these representations may or may not reach the level of conscious awareness.

When sensations survive this elaborate preprocessing and exceed sensory thresholds, however, they break through into a person's conscious awareness, appearing as coherent and meaningful perceptions: hunger pangs, one's reflection in the mirror, a smile from a friend. These perceptions seem to capture all the essential properties of the events that instigated them.

Roughly speaking, then, people acquire energetic impulses from internal and external environments that, in turn, impinge on the sensory apparatuses as sensations and are transformed by the brain into perceptions. This suggests a close relationship between the perceptions that are formed and the subsequent actions taken on their behalf. For instance, on the basis of perceptions of the personal qualities of others (and perceptions of others' perceptions of those qualities), people make judgments about those qualities (e.g., good or bad); on the basis of those judgments, people formulate intentions about how they will behave toward others (e.g., plan to engage with them or avoid them); on the basis of those intentions, the actions of others, the prevailing context, and so on, people enact their impressions and intentions in social interactions.

Three qualities of perceptions bear further elaboration: *Structure, stability,* and *meaning* are definitive subjective properties (Schneider et al. 1979). A fourth quality—*accuracy*—is best understood as an objective property of perceptions, at least in principle. Accuracy and bias in social perception are addressed later in this article.

Structure. Humans experience the world as structured. Rather than seeming chaotic and unpredictable, elements and events generally appear to correspond to one another in patterned ways. Things seem to happen for reasons. Much of this patterning is imposed, however, and one person's perceptions may be very different from those of others, even under identical conditions. This is especially relevant in regard to the interpretations people impose on complex phenomena. For instance, people tend not to be aware of how differences in the expectations they bring to a situation color their perceptions. People cannot take in information on everything around them and those expectations direct a person to attend selectively to the available stimuli in a situation. This biasing of attention can have a tremendous influence on interpretations of the situation. Moreover, each person may impose a unique subjective structure on the same objective reality. Every sports fan has experienced the perception that compared to the opponent, his or her favored team is consistently the victim of "bad calls" by the officials. Supporters of the opponent generally disagree, and rarely does one perceive the opposition to have been treated unfairly by officials. What fans actually "see" are slices of reality unconsciously chosen to conform with their beliefs and expectations.

Stability. Different sports fans may see different things, but if pressed, they probably could identify broad areas of the game they agree about and take for granted. They would agree that there were no sudden changes in the sport they were watching; they would profess not to have seen players on the field dematerializing in one place and rematerializing elsewhere; the ball appears to stay the same size and shape even as it moves nearer to and farther from the fans' points of view. In general, while observers may disagree on some points, most of what is observed has an underlying sense of continuity. Indeed, among the myriad sensations to which one might attend in a given situation, the bias is toward those which engender a sense of stability—a sense of the temporal endurance of these patterned sensations.

Meaning. If structure and stability were the only properties of experience, the world would appear merely as successions of discrete, insignificant objects and events, each with no particular import transcending the moment. In contrast, most perceptions seem meaningful. That is, perceptions are conceived of as threads in a larger fabric. Through their interconnections and the patterns they form, they seem to have significance, purpose, causes, and consequences beyond their own existence. With cognitive development comes the ability to recognize and select impressions and events that are significant in terms of the information they convey. As will be discussed below, meaningfulness and significance do not imply accuracy. Perceptions—especially social perceptions—are imperfect representations that can be highly misleading.

Among the variety of ways in which one could organize the social perception literature, one of the simplest and most useful proceeds from the individual perceiver, to perceptions of other individuals, and finally to group perceptions. These categories define the three sections below, which are followed by some remarks about future directions.

SELF-PERCEPTION

Self-perception is social perception with the self as the object. Through introspection and information from others, people develop beliefs about their many qualities: personality, physical appearance, behavioral tendencies, moral stature, athletic prowess, and the like. "Self-concept" is the general term for the system of beliefs about the self. Although introspection is a source of self-knowledge (Andersen and Williams 1985), mounting evidence suggests that it is not the predominant source that people used to believe it is and that it is generally biased and inaccurate (Nisbett and Wilson 1977; Wilson et al. 1981).

One major branch of self-perception research focuses on inaccuracies in self-knowledge, and a second on how information from others shapes the self-concept. An example of work in the first branch is a review by Greenwald (1980) of evidence of three types of self-conceptual biases: (1) *egocentricity*: the anchoring of judgments, recollections, thought experiments, and attributions about others with reference to the self, (2) *beneffectance*: the tendency to perceive the self as generally efficacious, and (3) *cognitive conservatism*: a resistance to cognitive change. Bem's influential self-perception theory (1972) asserts that in conditions of uncertainty, people use their own behavior as a guide to inferences about their inner selves. Later approaches to the self-concept focus on structures such as category systems, conceptual networks, and complex schemas that can represent explicit connections and nonconnections among elements of the self-concept (Greenwald and Pratkanis [1984] provide a review).

The early insights of Cooley (1964[1902]) and Mead (1934) still guide sociological theory and research on the social origins of the self-concept, the second branch mentioned above. Cooley described the "looking-glass self" as the use of others' appraisals as mirrors of the "true" self. Mead noted that the images people form of themselves are greatly affected by how they imagine significant others would respond to and evaluate them. Social comparison theory (Festinger 1954; Suls and Miller 1977) deals with, among other issues, the question of whom one refers to when seeking comparative self-knowledge and the effects of the various available social referents on one's self-concept and behavior.

Under the rubric of self-perception also are found topics such as self-efficacy, self-evaluation, self-esteem, and self-identity. Self-efficacy is the perception of one's competence with respect to specific tasks (Bandura 1986; Cervone and Peake 1986). Self-esteem is the extent to which one thinks positively about oneself (Rosenberg 1979). The concept of self-evaluation, when distinguished from efficacy and esteem, has been used in theory and research on how the characteristics of evaluators affect self-evaluations in specific, collective task situations (Webster and Sobieszek 1974). There are two major approaches to self-identity: identity theory (Stryker 1980; Burke 1991) and social identity theory (Hogg and Abrams 1988; Hogg et al. 1995). Although there are many shared concepts in these approaches, identity theory is distinguished by a greater emphasis on the performance of social roles as the source of self-definitions; in contrast, social identity theory emphasizes the ways in which self-categorizations hinge on salient properties of the groups with which individuals align themselves.

The more strongly a person's identity is tied to a particular social role or category, the greater is the extent to which that individual empathizes with other occupants of that role or category. It is as if the boundary between self and others became blurred, and the individual empathizes with similar others to whom good things and bad things happen. For instance, an experiment by Markovsky (1985) subtly emphasized self-identification versus group identification and created unjust reward allocations to both individuals and groups. The subjects responded more strongly to the type of injustice that corresponded to their identification.

PERSON PERCEPTION

The core of social perception theory and research addresses how people formulate impressions about the inner qualities and outward behaviors of other individuals. The focal points for this work include the properties of the people who are perceived and the characteristics of the situations in which a perception is developed, the logic by which basic sensations are integrated to form complex social perceptions, and the way in which perceptions, once formed, are affected by new information.

Attribution theories are concerned with how people form inferences about the causes of others' behaviors. The basic question in these approaches concerns the conditions under which another person's behavior is attributed to an internal disposition or to aspects of the situation in which it occurred (Jones et al. 1989). The so-called fundamental attribution error is the pervasive tendency for observers to underestimate the impact of situational factors on others' behavior (Ross 1977). In fact, people tend to make personal attributions for others' behavior and situational attributions for their own (Jones and Nisbett 1972). Gilbert (1989) has modified this question in a fruitful way by asserting that personal attributions occur automatically; situational attributions occur only as the possible result of an effortful search for additional information (Gilbert et al. 1988).

Although *schemas* could be discussed under the "self-perception" and "group perception" headings, most often they are invoked in theory and research on person perception. Schemas are organized structures of cognitions pertaining to social objects such as the self, other persons, groups, roles, and events (Taylor and Crocker 1981). Thus, one's schema for "college professor" may include beliefs such as "intelligent" and "scattered," negative attitudes such as "inaccessible" and "too political," and expectations for behaviors such as "lecturing" and "conducting research." Schemas have a variety of effects on social perception. For instance, they induce people to attend to certain social and situational features, influence people's judgments by inducing particular expectations for the consequences of their actions, and affect how people recollect social events by making some pieces of information more salient than others. Schemas also transcend individuals by becoming cultural elements that can be communicated among group members or from parent to child.

Other approaches to person perception focus on the integration of bits of information associated with particular others. Information integration theory (Anderson 1981) provides rigorous mathematical models of how an observer employs weighted combinations of another individual's traits to form an overall impression. Social applications of psychophysics (Stevens 1975; Lodge 1981) apply a magnitude scaling technology first developed for expressing judgments of physical properties (e.g., weight, brightness, numerosity, sound pres-

sure, saltiness) to the quantification and validation of judgments of personal or social properties (e.g., competence, fairness, attractiveness). Status characteristics theory (Berger et al. 1985) explains the emergence of status and influence hierarchies in collective, task-performing groups on the basis of individuals' relative standings on combinations of salient characteristics that can order interaction whether or not they are explicitly relevant to a task.

The accuracy of social perceptions was an early research focus but languished for years because of conceptual and methodological roadblocks (Cronbach 1955; Zebrowitz 1990; Fiske 1993). One problem is that determining accuracy requires the existence of a criterion against which a social perception is judged. Often, however, there is no assurance that the criterion is accurate because it may be arbitrary, subjective, or biased. Research in this area has seen a resurgence in recent years, however, partly as a result of approaches like Kenny and Albright's (1987) social relations model. That approach measures the accuracy of judgments of a given characteristic by using multiple observers and targets, permitting the researcher to control for observers' response sets, targets' attributes, and other aspects of the relationships between observers and targets. A mere recent trend is to attempt to disentangle the combined effects of observers' expectancies and targets' characteristics, specifying the conditions under which either set of factors predominates in determining social perceptions.

In a related vein, attributional and social perceptual biases constitute a vast field of inquiry. In recent years, a number of universal human perceptual inclinations have been cataloged that are capable of generating perceptual biases. Many perceptions depend on the ability to gauge one's relevant behaviors and characteristics, yet people often have difficulty assessing their own qualities and properties in an absolute way (Bem 1972). Preconceived notions powerfully influence subsequent perceptions by inducing selective perceptions. Once an idea is accepted, falsifying information is discounted and verifying information is accepted uncritically. People not only are subject to such errors of perception, they also underestimate the degree to which this is so. They are overconfident in their judgments; employ useless, distracting, and unrepresentative information contained in anecdotes; and infer illusory covariations among social characteristics. In recent years, cognitive and social psychologists have begun to identify and systematically examine these and other types of social perceptual biases. (For some examples, see Taylor and Fiske 1978; Taylor et al. 1978; Nisbett and Ross 1980; Kahneman et al. 1982; and Goldstein and Hogarth 1997.)

GROUP PERCEPTION

Two sets of approaches to group perception predominate: those concerned with reference group choices and effects, and those addressing social categorization processes. A reference group is a set of individuals whose standing or perspective is taken into account by an actor in selecting a course of action or making a judgment about a specific issue (Farmer 1992).

Research on reference group phenomena represents one of the first and longest-lived attempts in sociology and social psychology to understand how individuals orient themselves to groups, which groups they choose, and the consequences of their choices. (See the early work of Newcomb [1943] and Merton and Rossi [1968] and the more recent review by Singer [1981].) Among the functions of reference groups are providing sources for normative information and offering bases for social comparisons (Gecas 1982). Normative information dictates ostensibly correct and incorrect courses of action and positive and negative values. For example, people may adopt as their own the expressed values of respected members of the community or may assert a position opposite to that held by a disrespected group. In a similar way, social comparisons with reference groups provide bases for evaluating one's beliefs, actions, and accomplishments. For instance, without making reference to the set of people with incomes comparable to one's own, it is impossible to gauge one's level of generosity in donating money to charitable organizations. Three hundred dollars donated in a year may seem high until one discovers that the average donation of people in one's income bracket is ten times that amount.

Although virtually everyone makes use of reference groups, *which* reference groups one selects for one's comparisons and what consequences follow from those selections are more complex issues. Reference group choices have been shown in both natural and experimental settings to be influenced by numerous factors, including attitude similarity, structural inducements, and normative prescriptions. The consequences of referential comparisons that have been studied include the treatment of social deviants and the emergence of negative social evaluations, changes in self-esteem, and feelings of relative deprivation, gratification, or inequity. Although a good deal of interesting research and many theoretical conjectures have been associated with this area of inquiry, as Singer (1981) noted, there is no reference group theory per se, and the explanatory promise of this area remains unfulfilled. However, many of the research lines spawned by interest in reference groups remain active.

The reference group literature takes as given the existence of groups and the issue of which people are and are not members. Social categorization approaches (Tajfel 1981; Wilder 1986; Abrams and Hogg 1999) are closely related to the social identification literature noted earlier and view the perception of membership versus nonmembership as problematic. In general, people say that they detest being categorized and avoid categorizing others. However, social categorization is a manifestation of a perceptual process that is fundamental to survival. Everyone does it, consciously or not. By learning to recognize and categorize elements of their environments, humans are able to distinguish nutriment from poison and ally from adversary.

Despite its indispensability, the categorization process has side effects in the social realm. The most important and robust of these effects is the tendency for people to overestimate differences between groups and underestimate differences among group members. "They" appear uniform, but "we" are individuals (Quattrone 1986). This phenomenon lies at the heart of stereotyping: the overgeneralization of perceived group attributes (Stangor and Lange 1994). Once formed, stereotypes are maintained by virtue of the types of perceptual biases previously noted, such as forming illusory correlations and relying on anecdotes. A classic finding in research on social identity (Tajfel 1982; Turner 1987) demonstrated that arbitrary we-they distinctions created by random assignments to groups in a laboratory setting were sufficient to produce in-group favoritism and a variety of negative attributions regarding the out-group.

Discrimination—the differential treatment of others solely on the basis of their group memberships—and prejudice—negative attitudes toward certain groups and their members—are common behavioral manifestations of perceptual stereotyping. In American society and in the social and behavioral sciences, gender- and race-based forms of discrimination and prejudice have received the most attention (Eagly 1987; Dovidio and Gaertner 1986, respectively), although the list of bases for discrimination is probably as long as the list of conceivable social characteristics.

FUTURE DIRECTIONS

Social perception theory and research embrace multiple levels of analysis: cognitive processing, individual and interpersonal behavior, perceptions of groups, and group behavior. The social perception theories that may hold the greatest promise for the future are those amenable to integrating explicit formulations developed within these different levels of analysis. Undoubtedly, much social perception research in the near term will be business as usual, identifying new theoretical contingencies and empirical patterns. However, social and behavioral scientists are developing new approaches to modeling social and social psychological phenomena that may prove fruitful in social perception research.

Burt (1982) integrated a psychophysical model of human perception with explicit models of social network structure. The result is a conceptualization of social groupings at any scale in which network members (1) receive information about certain properties of others (e.g., resource holdings, attitudes), (2) take into account structural information about those others (e.g., the patterns of their social relations and of their relations' relations), (3) evaluate and combine the information received, and (4) make self-referential comparisons involving the information obtained from the network (e.g., relative resource holdings). The models show precisely how structural configurations of social relationships, in combination with individually based social perception and comparison processes, can theoretically account for a far broader class of phenomena than can either individual-level theories that do not consider structures or structural theories that do not consider individuals. Unfortunately, this formulation has not inspired a corresponding program of research, and the potential contributions of this innovative approach have not been tapped.

Significant progress has been made, however, using network models of a different sort. Within a broader class of approaches known as complexity theory (Eve et al. 1997), neural network models (Read and Miller 1998) and related alternatives (Carley and Svoboda 1996; Macy and Skvoretz 1998; Gilbert and Conte 1995) are beginning to account for social perception phenomena using parallel distributed processing models. This is a type of computer simulation in which numerous interconnected elements (e.g., neurons or agents) repeatedly receive, process, and respond to information from their environments, which may consist largely of similar elements. For example, using this approach, Smith and DeCoster (1998) devised a unified computational model that accomplishes several feats: It learns the social characteristics it "perceives" in individual cases and recognizes those characteristics from partial cues, learns stereotypes from exposure to multiple cases and recognizes those stereotypes from partial cues, and develops novel concepts from old ones. Although so-called connectionist approaches are relatively new, findings such as these bode well for further investigations.

There is no lack of good ideas in the social perception field, and this area may well play a central role in future attempts to integrate micro and macro sociology. Lacking, however, are concerted, programmatic efforts to develop and test explicit and rigorous social perception theories. Some exceptions were noted above. For the most part, however, the absence of explicitness and rigor has resulted in a minimal level of competition among different approaches, virtually no critical testing between formulations, and few time-tested conceptual and methodological refinements. However, this area remains attractive to a large number of psychologists and sociologists, in part because of its many unanswered questions and the ubiquity of its phenomena.

REFERENCES

Abrams, Dominic, and Michael A. Hogg, eds. 1999 *Social Identity and Social Cognition: An Introduction.* Oxford, UK: Blackwell.

Andersen, Susan M., and Marirosa, Williams 1985 "Cognitive/Affective Reactions in the Improvement of Self-Esteem: When Thoughts and Feelings Make a Difference." *Journal of Personality and Social Psychology* 49:1086–1097.

Anderson, Norman H. 1981 *Foundations of Information Integration Theory*. New York: Academic Press.

Bandura, Albert 1986 *Social Foundations of Thought and Action*. Englewood Cliffs, NJ: Prentice-Hall.

Bem, Daryl 1972 "Self-Perception Theory." In Leonard Berkowitz, ed., *Advances in Experimental Social Psychology*, vol. 6. New York: Academic Press.

Berger, Joseph, M. Hamit Fisek, Robert Z. Norman, and Morris Zelditch, Jr. 1985 "Expectation-States Theory." In Joseph Berger and Morris Zelditch, Jr., eds., *Status, Rewards, and Influence*. San Francisco: Jossey-Bass.

Burke, Peter J. 1991 "Identity Processes and Social Stress." *American Sociological Review* 56:836–849.

Burt, Ronald S. 1982 *Toward a Structural Theory of Action*. New York: Academic Press.

Carley, Kathleen, and David M. Svoboda 1996 "Modeling Organizational Adaptation as a Simulated Annealing Process." *Sociological Methods and Research* 25(1):138–168.

Cervone, Daniel, and Philip K. Peake 1986 "Anchoring, Efficacy, and Action: The Influence of Judgmental Heuristics on Self-Efficacy Judgments and Behavior." *Journal of Personality and Social Psychology* 50:492–501.

Cronbach, Lee. J. 1955 "Processes Affecting Scores on 'Understanding of Others' and 'Assumed Similarity.'" *Psychological Bulletin* 52:177–193.

Cooley, Charles Horton 1964 *Human Nature and the Social Order*. New York: Schocken [originally published 1902].

Dovidio, John F., and Samuel L. Gaertner, eds. 1986. *Prejudice, Discrimination, and Racism: Theory and Research*. Orlando, Fla.: Academic Press.

Eagly, Alice H. 1987 *Sex Differences in Social Behavior: A Social-Role Interpretation*. Hillsdale, N.J.: Erlbaum.

Eve, Raymond A., Sara Horsfall, and Mary E. Lee, eds. 1997 *Chaos, Complexity and Sociology: Myths, Models, and Theories*. Thousand Oaks, Calif.: Sage.

Farmer, Yvette 1992 "Reference Group Theory." In Edgar F. Borgatta and Marie L. Borgatta, Eds., *Encyclopedia of Sociology*. New York: Macmillan.

Festinger, Leon 1954 "A Theory of Social Comparison Processes." *Human Relations* 7:117–140.

Fiske, Susan T. 1993 "Social Cognition and Social Perception." *Annual Review of Psychology* 44:155–194.

Gecas, Viktor 1982 "The Self-Concept." *Annual Review of Sociology* 8:1–33.

Gilbert, Daniel T. 1989 "Thinking Lightly about Others: Automatic Components of the Social Inference Process." In James S. Uleman and John A. Bargh, eds., *Unintended Thought: Limits of Awareness, Intention, and Control*. New York: Guilford.

——, Brett W. Pelham, and Douglas S. Krull 1988 "On Cognitive Busyness: When Person Perceivers Meet Persons Perceived." *Journal of Personality and Social Psychology* 54:733–740.

Gilbert, Nigel, and Rosaria Conte, eds. 1995 *Artificial Societies: The Computer Simulation of Social Life*. London: UCL Press.

Goldstein, William M., and Robin M. Hogarth, eds. 1997 *Research on Judgment and Decision Making*. New York: Cambridge University Press.

Greenwald, Anthony G. 1980 "The Totalitarian Ego: Fabrication and Revision of Personal History." *American Psychologist* 35:603–618.

——, and Anthony R. Pratkanis 1984 "The Self." In Robert S. Wyer, Jr., and Thomas K. Srull, eds., *Handbook of Social Cognition*, vol. 3. Hillsdale, N.J.: Erlbaum.

Hogg, Michael A., and Dominic Abrams 1988 *Social Identifications*. London: Routledge.

——, Deborah J. Terry, and Katherine M. White 1995 "A Tale of Two Theories: A Critical Comparison of Identity Theory with Social Identity Theory." *Social Psychology Quarterly* 58:255–269.

Jones, Edward E., A. Flammer, A. Grob, R. Luthi, J. Rubin, and G. Fletcher 1989 "Attribution Theory." In J. Forgas and M. Innes, eds., *Recent Advances in Social Psychology: An International Perspective*. Amsterdam: North-Holland.

——, and Richard E. Nisbett 1972 "The Actor and the Observer: Divergent Perceptions of Causality." In Edward E. Jones, David E. Kanouse, Harold H. Kelley, Richard E. Nisbett, Stuart Valins, and Bernard Weiner, eds., *Attribution: Perceiving the Causes of Behavior*. Morristown, N.J.: General Learning Press.

Kahneman, Daniel, Paul Slovic, and Amos Tversky, eds. 1982 *Judgment under Uncertainty: Heuristics and Biases*. New York: Cambridge University Press.

Kenny, David A., and Linda Albright 1987 "Accuracy in Interpersonal Perception: A Social Relations Analysis." *Psychological Bulletin* 102:390–402.

Lodge, Milton 1981 *Magnitude Scaling*. Beverly Hills, Calif.: Sage.

Macy, Michael W., and John Skvoretz 1998 "The Evolution of Trust and Cooperation between Strangers: A

Computational Model." *American Sociological Review* 63:638–660.

Markovsky, Barry 1985 "Toward a Multilevel Distributive Justice Theory." *American Sociological Review* 50:822–839.

Mead, George Herbert 1934 *Mind, Self, and Society.* Chicago: University of Chicago Press.

Merton, Robert K., and Alice S. Rossi 1968 "Contributions to the Theory of Reference Group Behavior." In Robert K. Merton, *Social Theory and Social Structure*, enlarged ed. New York: Free Press.

Newcomb, Theodore M. 1943 *Personality and Social Change.* New York: Holt, Rinehart, and Winston.

Nisbett, Lee, and Timothy DeCamp Wilson 1977 "Telling More Than We Can Know: Verbal Reports on Mental Processes." *Psychological Review* 84:231–259.

Nisbett, Richard E., and Lee Ross 1980 *Human Inference: Strategies and Shortcomings of Social Judgment.* Englewood Cliffs, N.J.: Prentice-Hall.

Quattrone, George A. 1986 "On the Perception of a Groups' Variability." In Stephen Worchel and William G. Austin, eds., *Psychology of Intergroup Relations*, 2nd ed. Chicago: Nelson-Hall.

Read, Stephen J., and Lynn C. Miller, eds. 1998 *Connectionist Models of Social Reasoning and Social Behavior.* Mahwah, N.J.: Erlbaum.

Rosenberg, Morris 1979 *Conceiving of the Self.* New York: Basic Books.

Ross, Lee 1977 "The Intuitive Psychologist and His Shortcomings: Distortions in the Attribution Process." In Leonard Berkowitz, ed. *Advances in Experimental Social Psychology*, vol. 10. New York: Academic Press.

Schneider, David J., Albert H. Hastorf, and Phoebe C. Ellsworth 1979 *Person Perception*, 2nd ed. Reading, Mass.: Addison-Wesley.

Singer, Eleanor 1981 "Reference Groups and Social Evaluations." In Morris Rosenberg and Ralph H. Turner, eds., *Social Psychology: Sociological Perspectives*. New York: Basic Books.

Smith, Eliot R., and James DeCoster 1998 "Person Perception and Stereotyping: Simulation Using Distributed Representations in a Recurrent Connectionist Network." In Stephen J. Read and Lynn C. Miller, eds., *Connectionist Models of Social Reasoning and Social Behavior.* Mahwah, N.J.: Erlbaum.

Stangor, Charles, and J. E. Lange 1994 "Mental Representations of Social Groups: Advances in Understanding Stereotypes and Stereotyping." In Mark P. Zanna, ed., *Advances in Experimental Social Psychology*, vol. 26. San Diego: Academic Press.

Stevens, S. S. 1975 *Psychophysics: Introduction to its Perceptual, Neural, and Social Prospects.* Beverly Hills, Calif.: Sage.

Stryker, Sheldon 1980 *Symbolic Interactionism: A Social Structural Version.* Menlo Park, Calif.: Benjamin Cummings.

Suls, Jerry M., and Richard L. Miller, eds. 1977 *Social Comparison Processes.* Washington, D.C.: Halsted-Wiley.

Tajfel, Henri 1981 *Human Groups and Social Categories.* Cambridge, UK: Cambridge University Press

—— 1982 *Social Identity and Intergroup Relations.* London: Cambridge University Press.

Taylor, Shelley E., and J. Crocker 1981 "Schematic Bases of Social Information Processing." In E. T. Higgins, C. P. Herman, and M. P. Zanna, eds., *Social Cognition: The Ontario Symposium.* Hillsdale, N.J.: Erlbaum.

——, and Susan T. Fiske 1978 "Salience, Attention, and Attribution: Top of the Head Phenomena." In Leonard Berkowitz, ed., *Advances in Experimental Social Psychology*, vol. 11. New York: Academic Press.

——, Susan T. Fiske, Nancy L. Etcoff, and Audrey J. Ruderman 1978 "The Categorical and Contextual Bases of Person Memory and Stereotyping." *Journal of Personality and Social Psychology* 36:778–793.

Turner, John C. 1987 *Rediscovering the Social Group: A Self-Categorization Theory.* Oxford, UK: Basil Blackwell.

Webster, Murray, and Barbara Sobieszek 1974 *Sources of Self Evaluation.* New York: Wiley.

Wilder, David A. 1986 "Social Categorization: Implications for Creation and Reduction of Intergroup Bias." Pp. 291–355 In Leonard Berkowitz, ed., *Advances in Experimental Social Psychology*, vol. 19. New York: Academic Press.

Wilson, Timothy D., Jay G. Hull, and Jim Johnson 1981 "Awareness and Self-Perception: Verbal Reports on Internal States." *Journal of Personality and Social Psychology* 40:53–71.

Zebrowitz, Leslie A. 1990 *Social Perception.* Pacific Grove, Calif.: Brooks/Cole.

BARRY MARKOVSKY

SOCIAL PHILOSOPHY

American sociology, with the significant exception of symbolic interactionism, generally has turned to Europe for a philosophical grounding. The years after World War II, when Talcott Parsons at Harvard and Paul Lazarsfeld and Robert Merton at Columbia dominated the field, were no exception. Parsons had studied in Germany and had translated Weber; Lazarsfeld brought to the United States an Austrian philosophical heritage; Merton was a specialist in the philosophy and sociology of science. Under the guidance of these three men, American sociology was strongly influenced by the philosophers of the Vienna Circle, especially Carnap and Popper, and to a lesser degree by British logical positivism.

The common ingredient in this philosophical heritage was the notion that there were few obstacles to the creation of a science of human behavior modeled on the natural sciences. A great deal of attention was paid to hypothesis testing, criteria for evidence, and the nature of statistical proof. Most important, this way of thinking assumed that there was a social reality that would prove to have the same nature as physical reality. A predictive science of human behavior was possible because the social world was assumed to work in lawlike ways. The problems of the social sciences lay in discovering reality, not in the nature of reality.

This assumption would be shaken from two different directions. On the one hand, in many cases sociologists would lose their faith in the natural science model as the most appropriate way to think about society. In part as a result of the political upheavals of the 1960s, adherence to the patient accumulation of facts to verify what Merton called "middle level" theories about the world was difficult to maintain. On the other hand, philosophers increasingly came to question the epistemology associated with the natural science model. Kuhn's thesis that scientific insight resulted from a new paradigm had a stunning effect on social science, while Polanyi argued for a more "artistic" and "sociological" conception of scientific inquiry (Kuhn 1970; Polanyi 1968). As epistemological skepticism invaded the natural sciences, its implications for the social sciences became even more serious.

One of the first consequences of this increasing skepticism was the discovery in America that the European philosophical heritage was far broader than it first had appeared. Weber, for example, had been influenced strongly by Nietzsche, yet Parsons's interpretation of Weber downplayed the significance of heroism, irrationality, and cultural pessimism and presented Weber as an American

pluralist. The two philosophers who perhaps had the greatest influence in Europe during and after Parsons's visits to Germany were Heidegger and Husserl, and neither played a significant role in Parsons's outlook. The late Wittgenstein was discovered to be quite different from the earlier one, who had been convinced that pure logic would make philosophy unnecessary. French existentialism would become prominent in the 1960s, yet its dominance would not last, and its influence on American sociology was minimal. What had been a selective and partial reading of European philosophy by American sociologists could no longer last.

Even during the years when Parsons was the leading American sociologist, alternatives had existed. Husserl's phenomenology was one. As brought to the United States and applied to sociology in the work of Schutz (1967), phenomenology argued for the importance of the "life-world," the everyday events out of which people's understanding of the world around them becomes possible. Schutz was unable to convince Parsons of the importance of phenomenology (Schutz 1978), but he did influence one of Parsons's most brilliant students, Garfinkel (1967). Ethnomethodology became the most important alternative to structural functionalism in the 1960s and 1970s. The legacy of phenomenology also could be seen in the work of other sociologists, such as Berger and Luckman (1967). Other alternative traditions, such as the influence of Wittgenstein, also existed during this period, especially in Great Britain. Finally, among Marxists, the traditions of the Frankfurt School and the legacy of Lukacs constituted an important basis for social science theorizing (Arato and Gebhart 1977).

As the wide variety of ideas associated with European philosophy became increasingly known to sociologists, confidence in the natural sciences as a model for the social sciences gave way to far more nuanced approaches. No theorist in contemporary sociology was more aware than Habermas (1987) of the necessity of incorporating insights from a wide variety of philosophical traditions. Not only did Habermas bring to the task of sociological theorizing his background in Frankfurt School Marxism, plus a far more realistic reading of Weber than the one offered by Parsons, he also grounded his work in British linguistic philosophy, the Schutzian life-world, and American pragmatism. To read Habermas was to learn about those whom Habermas had read, bringing wide swaths of European philosophy to the attention of many American readers. Habemas was not alone in trying to synthesize philosophical traditions with the social sciences. Bourdieu (1984) in France was equally influential in sociology; his combination of theoretical insight, empirical investigation, and concern with how knowledge is produced made him a major figure in American sociology (Bourdieu and Waquant 1992; Lamont and Fournier 1992).

Habermas in particular argued for the importance of modernity, for the possibility of using rationality as a standard by which communicative utterances could be judged, thus making possible a social order held together by norms that lay outside the purely subjective preferences of the individuals who constituted that social order. This belief in reason would lead others to criticize Habermas as excessively rationalistic and therefore too close to the assumptions of a nonproblematic reality that had guided Parsons (Lyotard 1984). Postmodernism would become the most radical challenge imaginable to the earlier Parsons's faith in a scientific model for the social sciences.

With postmodernism, the philosophers once ignored by American social science became the most important ones to read. Foucault (1971), under the influence of Nietzsche, argued that knowledge is the product of a general *episteme* that in itself is not a reflection of a reality in the world but the product of a particular historical period and its self-understanding. Lyotard (1984), borrowing from Wittgenstein, viewed science as a "language game" preoccupied with strategy and tactics, anything but a dispassionate and objective search after truth. Derrida (1978), under the influence of Heidegger, argued for the indeterminacy of concepts such as truth, justice, and morality. Philosophers could not seek fixed universals; they were engaged in the practice of rhetoric, defending or attacking contingent, local, and socially constructed practices that defined truth, justice, and morality in the interests of certain groups and against the interests of others.

Postmodernism has not had the impact in sociology that it has had in literary criticism, history, and law. Numerous sociologists continue to study the empirical world by testing various hypotheses on the basis of evidence collected through surveys, demographic data, and other essentially quantitative methods. However, the postmodern challenge to normal science is likely to prove to be significant. Postmodernism is the culmination of all the challenges to the Parsonian consensus that once existed in the field; it represents what seems to be an end point to the process of questioning the existence of a nonproblematic social reality that can be understood by an observer standing outside that reality.

The question raised by the varieties of epistemological skepticism currently prevalent in the humanities is whether any science, let alone a social science, is possible. Just as some scientific fields seek to reduce the laws of one field, such as biology, to those of another, say, biochemistry, postmodernism argues that all fields of inquiry can be reduced to the study of rhetoric. In a perhaps unintended fashion, the implication of this argument is a hegemonic one: The rhetorical methods associated with literary criticism will become the model for all inquiry, just as science was once understood to be.

The rhetorical issues involved in social science theorizing have been analyzed in the case of economics by McCloskey (1985). In addition, some work in the sociology of science has made it clear that scientists have strategies by which they present themselves to the world and hope to gain acceptance (for an example, see Latour [1987]). However, does it follow that there is no grounding for social science, no Durkheimian facts in the world to which one can appeal to resolve disputes about knowledge? There is, of course, no way to answer such a large question satisfactorily in a brief article, but it is possible to offer the hope that both science and rhetoric can play a role in the sociological enterprise.

Sociology began, as Lepenies (1988) has argued, "between science and literature." Its most important theorists were attracted to positivistic understandings of knowledge, but they were also essayists dealing with some of the most significant issues in the moral philosophy of their time. One could argue that this "ambivalence" between fields has consistently characterized sociology at its best (Merton 1976). Merton, for example, though engaged in what he called the "systematics" of theory, was also a historian of science, wrote with reference to the entire Western tradition of philosophy and literature, and was very much part of the milieu of the New York intellectuals of his day (Merton 1967, pp. 1–37).

The fate of sociology may lie in finding a balance between a scientific grounding in fact and an appreciation of how rhetorical strategies affect the ways in which scholars argue about facts. Unlike earlier sociologists, sociologists today cannot be confident that there will exist a one-to-one relationship between social reality and its representations; we must always be skeptical about the likelihood that the indicators we use actually measure the real world. But this does not mean that sociologists should give up collecting evidence, testing hypotheses, or trying to establish facts. It means only that the truths uncovered by these methods are not universals that exist for all time but are contingent on historical periodization and location.

From this perspective, the question becomes one of the length of the historical periods and the width of the locations by which we can judge the truths we discover. If we could determine that it is possible to discover regularities in, for example, the way liberal democracies have organized themselves over the past 200 years, that would be a significant and important accomplishment. It would mean neither that we had discovered an unchanging reality nor that our discoveries are simply part of a rhetorical strategy. A sociology that modeled itself neither on physics nor on literary reading, but combined elements of both would be a sociology more chastened than Parsonianism but more hopeful than postmodernism.

(SEE ALSO: *Epistemology; Human Nature; Marxist Sociology; Postmodernism; Pragmatism*)

REFERENCES

Arato, Andrew, and Eike Gerhardt, eds. 1977 *The Frankfurt School Reader*. New York: Urizen Books.

Berger, Peter, and Thomas Luckmann 1967 *The Social Construction of Reality: A Treatise in the Sociology of Knowledge*. Garden City, N.Y.: Doubleday.

Bourdieu, Pierre. 1984 *Distinction: A Social Critique of the Judgement of Taste*. Richard Nice, trans. Cambridge, Mass.: Harvard University Press.

——, and Lois Wacquant 1992 *An Invitation to Reflexive Sociology*. Chicago: University of Chicago Press.

Derrida, Jacques 1978 *Writing and Difference*. Alan Bass, trans. Chicago: University of Chicago Press.

Foucault, Michel 1971 *The Order of Things: An Archeology of the Human Sciences*. New York: Pantheon.

Garfinkel, Harold 1967 *Studies in Ethnomethodology*. Englewood Cliffs, N.J.: Prentice-Hall.

Habermas, Jurgen 1987 *Lifeworld and System: A Critique of Functionalist Reason*, vol. 2 of *The Theory of Communicative Action*. Thomas McCarthy, trans. Boston: Beacon Press.

Kuhn, Thomas S. 1970 *The Structure of Scientific Revolutions*. Chicago: University of Chicago Press.

Lamont, Michele, and Marcel Fournier 1992 *Cultivating Differences: Symbolic Boundaries and the Making of Inequality*. Chicago: University of Chicago Press.

Latour, Bruno 1987 *Science in Action: How to Follow Scientists and Engineers through Society*. Cambridge, Mass.: Harvard University Press.

Lepenies, Wolf 1988 *Between Literature and Science: The Rise of Sociology*. R. J. Hollingdale, trans. Cambridge, UK: Cambridge University Press.

Lyotard, Jean-François 1984 *The Post-Modern Condition: A Report on Knowledge*. Geoff Bennington and Brian Massumi, trans. Minneapolis: University of Minnesota Press.

McCloskey, Donald 1985 *The Rhetoric of Economics*. Madison: University of Wisconsin Press.

Merton, Robert K. 1967 *On Theoretical Sociology: Five Ways, Old and New*. New York: Free Press.

—— 1976 *Sociological Ambivalence and Other Ways*. New York: Free Press.

Polanyi, Michael 1968 *Personal Knowledge: Towards a Post-Critical Philosophy*. Chicago: University of Chicago Press.

Schutz, Alfred 1967 *The Phenomenology of the Social World*. George Walsh and Frederick Lehnert, trans. Evanston, III.: Northwestern University Press.

—— 1978 *The Theory of Social Action: The Correspondence of Alfred Schutz and Talcott Parsons*. Richard Grathoff, ed. Bloomington: Indiana University Press.

ALAN WOLFE

SOCIAL POWER

See Social and Political Elites; Social Control.

SOCIAL PRESTIGE

See Occupational Prestige; Status Attainment; Social Mobility.

SOCIAL PROBLEMS

The discipline of sociology was born during a century of rapid social change attributable largely to the Industrial Revolution. Social theorists in nineteenth-century Europe devoted much of their attention to the institutional consequences of the erosion of the old social structure. American sociologists in the late nineteenth and early twentieth centuries, especially at the University of Chicago, added an intellectual orientation derived from the political idealism and meliorist pragmatism then fashionable in this country. "Social problems" generally were understood to be conditions that disrupted peaceful social life (e.g., crime) or produced obvious human misery (e.g., poverty) and that could be eliminated or alleviated by means of enlightened social policy and effective social engineering. Nearly all the conditions envisioned as social problems were associated with burgeoning cities and the dispossessed immigrants (foreign and domestic) they attracted. Few scholars doubted that these problems could be objectively diagnosed and treated, much like a malady in the human body.

By midcentury, however, American sociology was influenced increasingly by the functionalism and positivism of some of the earlier European intellectuals, whose major works had only recently been translated into English. Under this influence, sociologists assumed a more detached and value-neutral posture toward traditional social problems. While still acknowledging certain social conditions as problematic, most sociologists limited their responsibilities to scientific analysis of problems and their causes, leaving meliorist activism to politicians, social workers, and interest-group partisans. A split within the American Sociological Association between the more detached and the more activist visions of the discipline led to the formation in 1952 of the Society for the Study of Social Problems, which generally favors a more actively meliorist role for sociology. Since its inception, that society has published the quarterly *Social Problems*, the journal that most defines the content and direction of social problems theory and research in American sociology.

THE TRADITIONAL PARADIGM

Historically, the reigning paradigm in the sociology of social problems has properly been called an *objectivist* one. From this perspective, social problems are conditions that (1) are in some sense undesirable to any trained and objective observer and (2) are in one way or another amenable to alteration. Interest-group differences are acknowledged in regard to how the problems should be defined and corrected, but it is taken for granted that the problems themselves exist as objective realities in the form of structural arrangements, material conditions, institutional processes, interactional patterns, and the like. In much of the literature on social problems, especially textbooks, there is an implicit analogy to medical diagnosis; that is, a social problem is to society as a disease is to the body, an objective reality apart from popular opinion. Often conventional medical terms are even used, such as *pathology* (or *social pathology*), *epidemiology*, and *etiology*, not only for social problems that might be quasi-medical in nature (such as alcoholism and mental illness) but even for those which are entirely societal (such as poverty and juvenile delinquency). From this point of view, social problems require the investigation of diagnostic experts (social scientists) who can objectively discern the nature of a problem and the most effective way of addressing it and thus enhancing the welfare of people and society.

These diagnostic experts also come from different schools of thought, as is often the case in other disciplines. Two theoretical orientations have tended to dominate the diagnosis and analysis of social problems by sociologists who work within the traditional paradigm. The first is functionalism in one version or another. From a functionalist perspective, society is seen as a more or less organic entity made up of interdependent parts (i.e., institutions). Breakdowns occasionally occur, but the whole generally succeeds in maintaining its natural state of equilibrium. These breakdowns (also called *dysfunctions* or *social disorganization*) are social problems; once they are fixed, the social system can return to a normal state of functioning. This perspective has been criticized by activists as being informed by the conservative assumption that the existing social system is acceptable as it is, with only meliorative adjustments needed to deal with the occasional breakdown.

The second school of thought within the traditional paradigm, one generally preferred by activists and derived mainly from the Marxist heritage, is a more radical theoretical perspective sometimes called *critical theory*. From this perspective, social problems are the inevitable and endemic characteristics of a capitalist system. Efforts to deal with social problems in such a system can never produce more than temporary palliation, or, worse still, only co-op discontent and protest in the class interests of the dominant and oppressive establishment. Therefore, only the drastic overhaul or total overthrow of the capitalist system can produce a society free of social problems. This radical perspective shares with its more conservative functionalist counterpart the premise that social problems can in principle be objectively identified, diagnosed, analyzed, and corrected.

The belief that social problems have objective bases, which is the foundation of the traditional paradigm, continues to inform public policy at local, state, and federal levels of government in the United States and elsewhere. Accordingly, public funding for research on and amelioration of conditions officially designated as social problems has helped promote the objectivist paradigm in sociology. In the war on poverty of the 1960s, the war on drugs of the 1990s, and the war on violence at the beginning of the twenty-first century, billions of dollars in government support have gone into research on the prevention and/or correction of the social problems deemed most prevalent and consequential in a given era. Both the objectivist paradigm and the professional careers of its proponents, including sociologists with an applied orientation, have been strengthened in the process.

THE EMERGENT PARADIGM

While the objectivist approach continues to dominate textbooks and policy-oriented sociology, the academic literature on social problems in recent decades, including much that has appeared in *Social Problems*, has provided a robust alternative theoretical paradigm. Generally called *subjectivist*, in contrast to its traditional counterpart, this paradigm derives from different epistemological premises. With roots in phenomenology and symbolic interactionism rather than in the positivism of the objectivist paradigm, the subjectivist approach to social problems in its original formulation is akin to what is sometimes called the *labeling* perspective in the study of crime and deviance. Intimations of this subjectivist paradigm can be found in some nineteenth-century European theoretical literature and even in the work of some American sociologists earlier in the twentieth century (Fuller 1937; Fuller and Myers 1941a, 1941b; Mills 1943; Waller 1936). The emergence of this paradigm into the mainstream of the discipline, however, has occurred mainly since the 1960s in the work of Becker (1966), Blumer (1971), and the team of Kitsuse and Spector (Kitsuse and Spector 1973; Spector and Kitsuse 1973, 1977). More recently, the paradigm has been promoted in the works of Best (1989, 1990) and the team of Holstein and Miller (1993; Miller and Holstein 1993a).

In the simplest terms, the subjectivist paradigm holds that a social problem lies in the eye of the beholder, not in objective reality. Certain social *conditions* may be real (e.g., deviance, inequality, depletion of the ozone layer, and natural disasters), but to term them *problems* requires an evaluative judgment not inherent in the condition itself; thus, there is a distinction between a (real or imagined) social condition and its acquisition of the standing as a recognized social problem. In this formulation, social problems are best seen as projections of collective sentiments and representations rather than as mirrors of objective conditions (Best 1989; Holstein and Miller 1993; Mauss et al. 1975; Miller and Holstein 1993a; Spector and Kitsuse 1977). Collective sentiments and representations reflect judgments emanating from the political, economic, cultural, moral, religious, and other interests of the persons who allege the existence of a problem. Accordingly, the subjectivist paradigm denies the analogy to medical diagnosis on the grounds that there are no generally accepted scientific standards in sociology, as there are in medicine, for judging what is "pathological." For example, in the study of societies there is no counterpart to the medical standard that "normal" human body temperature is 98.6 degrees Fahrenheit (and that significant departures from that figure are symptomatic of pathology). Instead, the judgment that a social condition is undesirable or problematic in any sense is entirely relative to cultural (or subcultural), generational, and many other social variables.

As evidence of relativity and variability in the definition of the term "social problems," subjectivists make at least two historical observations. First, social conditions once regarded as serious problems in the United States are no longer so regarded, whether or not they are still extant. One example is witchcraft, which now is considered never to have existed "in reality" but nevertheless was recognized as a major social problem in seventeenth-century Massachusetts and elsewhere. Other, more recent examples include miscegenation, which gave rise to a powerful eugenics movement early in the twentieth century; prostitution, which is now legal in some jurisdictions, and illegal in others but nowhere regarded as the national social problem that it was at one time; and homosexuality, which once rated attention, along with prostitution, in most social problems textbooks and even a listing as a disorder in the official diagnostic manual of psychiatry but now often is considered a legitimate lifestyle and is protected by civil rights legislation. In none of these examples has there been any evidence of a reduction in the *actual incidence* of the condition, and so the erosion in their status as "real" social problems can be attributed only to changes in public *perception*.

The second observation, related to the first, is that no consistent relationship is apparent between the waxing and waning of given social *conditions*, on the one hand, and the official or public designation of those conditions as problems, on the other hand. For example, the official and professional recognition of racial discrimination as a social problem in the United States came not while the Jim Crow regime was at its worst (before World War II) but only after the lot of African-Americans had begun to improve significantly. Similarly, it is only since the 1980s that so-called hate crimes (crimes motivated by bias based on race, religion, ethnicity, sexual orientation, gender, etc.) have entered into national discourse despite the fact that this type of intergroup violence is as old as humankind. In the opposite direction, the war on poverty of the 1960s was effectively dropped from the national agenda of social problems with no change in the actual incidence of poverty. Similarly, the national war on drugs was officially declared after more than a decade of *decline* in the incidence of alcohol and drug use by both adults and youths in the United States.

This common and paradoxical lack of correspondence between *objective* social *conditions* and the ebb and flow of social *problems* means that the two phenomena can vary independently. From the subjectivist viewpoint, the traditional objectivist focus has made the mistake of studying not social problems but only certain social conditions. In evaluating these conditions as problems, objectivists have not assumed the positivist, value-neutral stance of science, as they have supposed; instead, they have unquestioningly accepted the transitory evaluative definitions of interest groups, government funding agencies, and a fickle public. If the objectivists have been studying the wrong thing, what *should* the focus be for sociologists of social problems?

From the subjectivist viewpoint, the sociological study of social problems, properly understood, is the study of the process by which putative social conditions come to be defined as social problems by governments and publics (Spector and Kitsuse 1977). In this formulation, social problems are reconceptualized in terms of discourse, interactions, and institutional practices by which only some social conditions are defined as social problems and given a place in the social problems marketplace (Best 1990; Hilgartner and Bosk 1988). The social conditions themselves can be left to sociologists with other specialities: Criminologists can and should study crime; family sociologists can and should study divorce, spousal conflict, and child-rearing stresses; environmental sociologists can and should study the ways in which the physical environment and the organization of social life interact; specialists in stratification can and should study inequality; and so on. None of this other work, however important, constitutes the sociology of social problems per se, for social problems do not originate in social conditions. They originate in *claims-making activities* of interest groups and partisans who undertake to gain political acceptance for their perceptions of certain conditions as "problems," after which those perceptions reflect the evolution of social problems construction (Spector and Kitsuse 1977; Jenness 1993). It is those claims-making activities, then, that should constitute the focus of study in the sociology of social problems. Put another way, the study of social problems is a study of the social construction of reality (Berger and Luckman 1966).

Thus, subjectivists who study social problems in this way also are called *social constructionists* (or simply *constructionists*).

To understand how social problems are constructed, Kitsuse, Spector, and their disciples focus primarily on claims-making activities. These activities consist of the usual tactics of interest groups in asserting claims and grievances, including boycotts, demonstrations, and lawsuits, as well as the strategic use of terms, labels, semantics, and other rhetorical devices, to win political and public support for definitions of certain putative social conditions as problems (Spector and Kitsuse 1977, pp. 9–21, 72–79; Schneider 1985, pp. 213–218, 224). The particular arena within which claims-making activities occur can be as large as American society or as small as a college campus, a corporation, or even a professional society. Whatever the arena, it is claims-making activities or "social problems work" that constitutes the appropriate focus of research in social problems (Miller and Holstein 1989).

While the subjectivist or social constructionist paradigm is relatively recent as a theoretical alternative to the positivist or objectivist tradition in the study of social problems, it is actually cognate to several other well-established lines of inquiry in sociology. One of these fields is *cultural analysis*, represented especially in the work of Douglas (1966; Douglas and Wildavsky 1982). Broadly defined, cultural analysis is the study of the production and distribution of culture (including popular culture). As applied to social problems, cultural analysis includes the assessment of risk as a cultural product, much like a religious ideology (Stallings 1990). Miller and Holstein (1989) see a parallel here to the early Durkheimian concept of *collective representations*, which they understand as a cultural product of social problems work (see also Gusfield 1981).

A second theoretical link can be made between the social constructionist approach to social problems and *conflict theory* (Pong 1989). Inspired partly by Marxism, conflict theory, like critical theory, rejects the functionalist assumption that the natural condition of society is a state of equilibrium among interdependent parts (institutions). Instead, it emphasizes the naturally conflicting tendencies in society among economic, political, religious, and other interest groups (Eitzen and Zinn 1988; Skolnick and Currie 1985). While the objectivist tendency in the way conflict theory *defines* social problems does not accord well with the social constructionist paradigm, the claims-making activities that are so important in that paradigm are classical examples of the political struggle and agitation that constitute the typical focus of conflict theorists and, more recently, of the critical theorists working in the deconstructionist (Michaelowksi 1993; Pfohl 1993), feminist (Gordon 1993), postmodernist (Agger 1993), and poststructuralist (Miller 1993) traditions. These recent critical challenges "represent promising opportunities to reconsider assumptions, distinctions, and categories on which social constructionism and social problems theory rests" (Miller and Holstein 1993c, p. 536).

The social constructionist perspective converges perhaps even more closely with a third important preoccupation of sociology: *social movement theory*. The claims-making activities that are the principal focus of the constructionist approach are also the classical tactics and strategies of social movement activists. This would include both rhetorical products, such as ideology and propaganda, and mobilizing activities, such as demonstrations, agitation, and political organization (Hilgartner and Bosk 1988; Mauss et al. 1975; Mauss 1989). The "resource mobilization" approach to social movements that has gained currency in recent years seems especially close to the claims-making focus of the subjectivist or constructionist perspective on social problems (Zald and McCarthy 1987; Turner 1981).

At least in part because of the many ways in which the subjectivist approach to social problems has converged with other literatures in the social sciences, it has come to dominate scholarly approaches to social problems theory. Indeed, by the mid-1980s Schneider, a former editor of *Social Problems*, concluded in the *Annual Review of Sociology* that "over the last two decades the constructionist approach to social problems has constituted the only serious and sustained recent discussion of social problems theory" (Schneider 1985, p. 210). By the mid-1990s, it had produced "a torrent of empirical studies" (Miller and Holstein 1993b, p. 3) that focus on diverse social conditions and activities, including alcohol and driving (Gusfield 1981), hyperactivity (Conrad 1975), child abuse (Best 1990), AIDS (Albert 1989), alcoholism

(Schneider 1978), cigarette smoking (Markle and Troyer 1979), crime (Fishman 1978), rape (Rose 1977), homosexuality (Spector 1977), hate crime (Jenness and Broad 1997), premenstrual syndrome (Rittenhouse 1992), chemical contamination (Aronoff and Gunter 1992), drugs (Orcutt and Turner 1993), satanism (Richardson et al. 1991), prostitution (Jenness 1993), and even earthquakes (Stallings 1995). True to the constructionist perspective, this work has been sustained by research questions and procedures focused not on social conditions but on the full range of political and claims-making activities that cause these activities to be understood as social problems.

As demonstrated by Mauss (Mauss et al. 1975; 1989) these are also the activities typically associated with social movements. Accordingly, an issue among subjectivists and their allies is the question of whether the constructionist approach to social problems is equivalent to the study of social movements. The 1985 and 1989 annual meetings of the Society for the Study of Social Problems featured the theme of social problems as social movements. At those meetings and in subsequent publications, proponents of the subjectivist perspective have not agreed on whether the study of social problems should be subsumed by social movement theory or, alternatively, should be approached as a theoretically distinct field of study. Some would say that the dominant way in which social conditions come to be seen as social problems is through the work of social movements (Gerhards and Rucht 1992; Mauss 1989; Troyer 1989; Holstein and Miller 1993; Miller and Holstein 1993a). As early as 1975, Mauss (p. 38) presented the case for considering "social *problems* as simply a special kind of *movement*." This case rests largely on the proposition that the characteristics of social problems are typically those of social movements and that social problems are always outcomes of social movements. In this formulation, the study of social movements and the study of social problems are rendered compatible through an examination of the genesis of social problems movements, the organization and mobilization of social movements, the natural history of social movements, and the decline and legacy of a social problem. More recently, Bash (1995, pp. xiii–xiv) argued "that what is addressed as the Social Movement, in the one instance, and what is targeted as a host of social problems, in the other, may not reflect *distinctive*

sociohistorical phenomena at all." In contrast, Troyer (1989) has noted the similarities *and* differences between the definitional approach, the standard structural approach, and the more recent resource mobilization approach to social movements (Zald and McCarthy 1987). More recently, Klandermans (1992, p. 77) has observed that "many situations that could be considered a social problem never become an issue, even though they may be no less troublesome than situations that do become a rallying point. Further, a social problem does not inevitably generate a social movement" (he does not cite any examples).

A more vigorous debate among subjectivists began with the provocative critique offered by Woolgar and Pawluch (1985) of the "ontological gerrymandering" they attributed to the constructionist analysis of social problems. A successful constructionist explanation for social problems, they argued, "depends on making problematic the truth status of certain states of affairs selected for analysis and the explanation, while backgrounding or minimizing the possibility that the same problems apply to assumptions upon which the analysis rests" (Woolgar and Pawluch 1985, p. 216). Since constructionist analysis is itself a claims-making activity, these authors observe, it involves selective relativism and theoretical inconsistency: Constructionists invoke subjectivist assumptions about the phenomena under study but at the same time present their claims as objective facts.

In an attempt to rescue the constructionist paradigm from this apparent inconsistency, Ibarra and Kitsuse (1993, p. 26) have proposed replacing the term "putative condition" with the term "condition-category" as the appropriate focus of study. Mauss (1989, pp. 36–37, notes 1 and 2), however, implicitly rejects the entire issue raised by Woolgar and Pawluch by insisting that constructionists need not question the objective reality of "putative conditions" any more than that of any of the other elements in the construction of social problems but should focus only on the process by which those conditions come to be defined as problems. Yet if the issue of "ontological gerrymandering" has stalled the theoretical development of the constructionist perspective, as is feared by Ibarra and Kitsuse (1993), at least that argument has required of subjectivists more awareness of their own potential biases.

The position advocated by Mauss might be called "strict constructionist," an example of which can be found in the work of Jennes and Broad (1997) on the anti–hate crime movement in the United States. In this work, the authors do not attempt to evaluate the accuracy or "objective" reality of the claims made by the women's movement or gay/lesbian movement in the efforts of those movements to define violence as a social problem. In contrast, a somewhat nuanced approach, that might be called a "contextual constructionist approach" includes the evaluation of claims by interest groups as an important part of the analysis of the development of a social problem. For example, Best (1993), in his work on threats to children, relies on statistical and other data to assess the claims he describes. Calling a statement a "claim" does not discredit it, according to Best, who calls for social scientists to "worry a little less about how we know what we know, and worry a little more about what, if anything, we do know about the construction of social problems" (Best 1993, p. 144).

THE CURRENT INTELLECTUAL STATE OF AFFAIRS

In effect, two paradigms for understanding and explaining social problems have historically defined the sociological study of social problems. The traditional objectivist paradigm, which dominates textbooks and anchors policy-relevant research, evaluates certain social conditions as problems by definition. In this conceptualization, there is an implicit analogy to a cancer or another disease in the human body. That is, a social problem is understood as an objectively real and undesirable condition in society that should be diagnosed and treated by experts (especially sociologists). The more recently developed subjectivist paradigm, in contrast, denies that any social condition can be defined objectively as a social problem, for such a definition depends on the evaluation and claims-making activities of interest groups. Those groups organize and mobilize social movements in an attempt to gain general political acceptance of certain "undesirable" conditions as "social problems."

Despite the growing prominence of the subjectivist approach in academic debates, at the level of social policy and undergraduate teaching the objectivist paradigm is likely to remain dominant.

One reason for this dominance in the public policy arena is the objectivist bias in the political culture of North America, in which public opinion has traditionally taken for granted the amenability of social ills to objective diagnosis and the responsibility of the political system to ameliorate those ills. As for undergraduate teaching, the lack of intellectual sophistication typically found at the freshman and sophomore levels of college education, where most courses in social problems are taught, makes teaching the subjectivist position difficult. The phenomenological epistemology of the subjectivist paradigm may be too abstract for most college students. Thus, the overwhelming majority of social problems textbooks continue to be organized around one or both versions of the traditional objectivist paradigm insofar as they assume that select social conditions—most frequently things such as crime, mental illness, poverty, environmental degradation, and suicide—are inherently social problems. It is rare to find a textbook that is organized around subjectivist concerns (but see Best 1995).

The emergent subjectivist paradigm is likely, however, to continue to provide the basis for the most novel and creative scholarly and professional literature on social problems. This is the case because its epistemology and methodology leave much room for development, in comparison with objectivism and positivism. Some scholars have even attempted to reconcile the objectivist and the subjectivist paradigms (e.g., Jones et al. 1989), but such attempts are most often made in textbooks, which are notorious for their sacrificing of theoretical focus in favor of eclecticism. Ultimately, the two paradigms probably cannot be reconciled, since they proceed from different epistemologies and study different topics. Objectivism focuses on certain social conditions, such as inequality and deviant behavior, taking for granted the evaluation of those conditions as problems. Subjectivism focuses on the *political players and processes* by which those conditions come to be defined as problems.

REFERENCES

Agger, Ben 1993 "The Problem with Social Problems: From Social Constructionism to Critical Theory." In James A. Holstein and Gale Miller, eds., *Reconsidering Social Constructionism: Debates in Social Problems Theory.* New York: Aldine de Gruyter.

Albert, Edward 1989 "AIDS and the Press: The Creation and Transformation of a Social Problem." In Joel Best, ed., *Images of Issues: Typifying Contemporary Social Problems*. Hawthorne, N.Y.: Aldine de Gruyter.

Aronoff, Marilyn, and Valerie Gunter 1992 "Defining Disaster: Local Constructions for Recovery in the Aftermath of Chemical Contamination." *Social Problems* 39:345–365.

Bash, Harry 1995 *Social Problems and Social Movements*. Atlantic Highlands, N.J.: Humanities Press.

Becker, Howard 1966 *Social Problems: A Modern Approach*. New York: Wiley.

Berger, Peter L., and Thomas Luckmann 1966 *The Social Construction of Reality*. New York: Doubleday.

Best, Joel 1989 "Afterword." In Joel Best, ed., *Images of Issues*. New York: Aldine de Gruyter.

—— 1990 *Threatened Children: Rhetoric and Concern about Child Victims*. Chicago: University of Chicago Press.

—— 1993 "But Seriously Folks: The Limitations of the Strict Constructionist Interpretation of Social Problems." In James A. Holstein and Gale Miller, eds., *Reconsidering Social Constructionism: Debates in Social Problems Theory*. New York: Aldine de Gruyter.

—— 1995 *Images and Issues: Typifying Contemporary Social Problems*. New York: Aldine de Gruyter.

Blumer, Herbert 1971 "Social Problems as Collective Behavior." *Social Problems* 18:298–306.

Conrad, Peter 1975 "The Discovery of Hyperkenesis: Notes on the Medicalization of Deviant Behavior." *Social Problems* 23:12–21.

Douglas, Mary L. 1966 *Purity and Danger: An Analysis of Concepts of Pollution and Taboo*. New York: Praeger.

——, and Aaron Wildavsky 1982 *Risk and Culture*. Berkeley: University of California Press.

Eitzen, D. Stanley, and Maxine B. Zinn 1988 *Social Problems*, 4th ed. Boston: Allyn and Bacon.

Fishman, Mark 1978 "Crime Waves as Ideology." *Social Problems* 25:531–543.

Fuller, Richard C. 1937 "Sociological Theory and Social Problems." *Social Forces* 4:496–502.

——, and Richard R. Myers 1941a "Some Aspects of a Theory of Social Problems." *American Sociological Review* 6:24–32.

——, and Richard R. Myers 1941b "The Natural History of a Social Problem." *American Sociological Review* 6:320–328.

Gerhards, Jürgen, and Dieter Rucht 1992 "Mesomobilization: Organizing and Framing in Two Protest Campaigns in West Germany." *American Journal of Sociology* 98:555–595.

Gordon, Avery 1993 "Twenty-Two Theses on Social Constructionism: A Feminist Response to Ibarra and Kitsuse's 'Proposal for the Study of Social Problems." In James A. Holstein and Gale Miller, eds., *Reconsidering Social Constructionism: Debates in Social Problems Theory*. New York: Aldine de Gruyter.

Gusfield, Joseph R. 1981 *The Culture of Public Problems: Drinking-Driving and the Symbolic Order*. Chicago: University of Chicago Press.

Hilgartner, Stephen, and Charles L. Bosk 1988 "The Rise and Fall of Social Problems: A Public Arenas Model." *American Journal of Sociology* 943:53–78.

Holstein, James A., and Gale Miller, eds. 1993 *Reconsidering Social Constructionism: Debates in Social Problems Theory*. New York: Aldine de Gruyter.

Ibarra, Peter R., and John I. Kitsuse 1993 "Vernacular Constituents of Moral Discourse: An Interactionist Proposal for the Study of Social Problems." In James A. Holstein and Gale Miller, eds., *Reconsidering Social Constructionism: Debates in Social Problems Theory*. New York: Aldine de Gruyter.

Jenness, Valerie 1993 *Making It Work: The Prostitutes' Rights Movement in Perspective*. New York: Aldine de Gruyter.

——, and Kendal Broad 1997 *Hate Crimes: New Social Movements and the Politics of Violence*. New York: Aldine de Gruyter.

Jones, Brian J., Joseph A. McFalls, Jr., and Bernard J. Gallagher III 1989 "Toward a Unified Model for Social Problems Theory." *Journal for the Theory of Social Behavior* 19:337–356.

Kitsuse, John I., and Malcolm Spector 1973 "Toward a Sociology of Social Problems: Social Conditions, Value Judgments, and Social Problems." *Social Problems* 20:407–419.

Klandermans, Bert 1992 "The Social Construction of Protest and Multiorganizational Fields." In Aldon D. Morris and Carol McBurg Miller, eds., *Frontiers in Social Movement Theory*. New Haven, Conn.: Yale University Press.

Markle, Gerald E., and Ronald Troyer 1979 "Smoke Gets in Your Eyes: Cigarette Smoking as Deviant Behavior." *Social Problems* 26:611–625.

Mauss, Armand L. 1989 "Beyond the Illusion of Social Problems Theory." In James A. Holstein and Gale Miller, eds., *Perspectives on Social Problems*, vol. 1. Greenwich, Conn.: JAI Press.

——, and associates 1975 *Social Problems as Social Movements*. Philadelphia: Lippincott.

Michaelowski, Raymond 1993 "(De)Construction, Postmodernism, and Social Problems: Facts, Fiction, and Fantasies at the 'End of History.'" In James A. Holstein and Gale Miller, eds., *Reconsidering Social Constructionism: Debates in Social Problems Theory*. New York: Aldine de Gruyter.

Miller, Gale 1993 "New Challenges to Social Constructionism: Alternative Perspectives on Social Problems Theory" In James A. Holstein and Gale Miller, eds., *Reconsidering Social Constructionism: Debates in Social Problems Theory*. New York: Aldine de Gruyter

——, and James A. Holstein 1989 "On the Sociology of Social Problems." In James A. Holstein and Gale Miller, eds., *Perspectives on Social Problems*, vol. 1 Greenwich, Conn.: JAI Press.

—— 1993a *Constructionist Controversies: Issues in Social Problems Theory*. New York: Aldine de Gruyer.

—— 1993b "Constructing Social Problems: Context and Legacy." In Gale Miller and James A. Holstein, eds., *Constructionist Controversies: Issues in Social Problems Theory*. New York: Aldine de Gruyter.

—— 1993c "Social Constructionism and Its Critics: Assessing Recent Challenges." In James A. Holstein and Gale Miller, eds., *Reconsidering Social Constructionism: Debates in Social Problems Theory*. New York: Aldine de Gruyter.

Mills, C. Wright 1943 "The Professional Ideology of Social Pathologists." *American Journal of Sociology* 49:165–180.

Orcutt, James, and J. Blake Turner 1993 "Shocking Numbers and Graphic Accounts: Quantified Images of Drug Problems in the Print Media." *Social Problems* 40:190–206.

Pfohl, Stephen 1993 "Revenge of the Parasites: Feeding Off the Ruins of Sociological (De)Construction." In James A. Holstein and Gale Miller, eds., *Reconsidering Social Constructionism: Debates in Social Problems Theory*. New York: Aldine de Gruyter.

Pong, Raymond W. 1989 "Social Problems as a Conflict Process." In James A. Holstein and Gale Miller, eds., *Perspectives on Social Problems*, vol. 1. Greenwich, Conn.: JAI Press.

Richardson, James T., Joel Best, and David Bromley 1991 "Satanism as a Social Problem." In James T. Richardson, Joel Best, and David Bromley, eds., *The Satanism Scare*. Hawthorne, N.Y.: Aldine de Gruyter.

Rittenhouse, C. Amanda 1992 "The Emergence of Premenstrual Syndrome as a Social Problem." *Social Problems* 38:412–425.

Rose, V. M. 1977 "Rape as a Social Problem: A By-product of the Feminist Movement." *Social Problems* 25:75–89.

Schneider, Joseph 1978 "Deviant Drinking as Disease: Alcoholism as Social Accomplishment." *Social Problems* 25:361–372.

—— 1985 "Social Problems Theory: The Constructionist View." *Annual Review of Sociology* 11:209–229.

Skolnick, Jerome H., and Elliott Currie, eds. 1985 *Crisis in American Institutions*, 6th ed. Boston: Little, Brown.

Spector, Malcolm 1977 "Legitimizing Homosexuality." *Society* 14:20–24.

——, and John I. Kitsuse 1973 "Social Problems: A Reformulation." *Social Problems* 21:145–159.

—— 1977 *Constructing Social Problems*. Menlo Park, Calif.: Cummings.

Stallings, Robert A. 1990. "Media Discourse and the Social Construction of Risk." *Social Problems* 37:80–95.

—— 1995 *Promoting Risk: Constructing the Earthquake Threat*. New York: Aldine de Gruyter.

Troyer, Ronald J. 1989 "Are Social Problems and Social Movements the Same Thing?" In James A. Holstein and Gale Miller, eds., *Perspectives on Social Problems*. vol A. Greenwich, Conn.: JAI Press.

Turner, Ralph H. 1981 "Collective Behavior and Resource Mobilization as Approaches to Social Movements: Issues and Continuities." In Louis Kreisberg, ed., *Research in Social Movements, Conflicts, and Change*, vol. 4 Greenwich, Conn.: JAI Press.

Waller, Willard 1936 "Social Problems and the Mores." *American Sociological Review* 1:922–933.

Woolgar, Steve,w and Dorothy Pawluch 1985 "Ontological Gerrymandering." *Social Problems* 32:214–227.

Zald, Mayer N., and John D. McCarthy 1987 *Social Movements in an Organizational Society: Collected Essays*. New Brunswick, N.J.: Transaction.

ARMAND L. MAUSS
VALERIE JENNESS

SOCIAL PSYCHOLOGY

Social psychology is the study of individual behavior and psychological structures and processes as both outcomes of and influences on interpersonal relationships, the functioning of groups and other collective forms, and culturally define macrosocial structures and processes. Social psychologists vary in the theoretical orientations and methods they use, the conceptual distinctions they draw, and the substantive causal linkages they study. Much of the variability in these areas is accounted for by the academic tradition in which a social psychologist has been trained.

Contemporary social psychology has intellectual roots in both psychology and sociology. Psychological social psychologists are guided by social learning theory as well as by orientations such as exchange and role theories. For the most part, their methods consist of laboratory and field experiments, and data analysis is accomplished with quantitative techniques. They discriminate between individual behavior and psychological structures and processes and interpersonal settings. The primary interest of psychological social psychology is the influence of the perceived social environment on individual cognitive, affective, and behavioral responses (Gilbert et al. 1998).

Contemporary sociological social psychology encompasses two major perspectives: symbolic interactionism and personality and social structure. Within symbolic interactionism, other distinctions are drawn according to the degree to which the proponents emphasize consistencies in human behavior as opposed to creative and emergent aspects of behavior, the influence of social structure in placing constraints on social interaction through which concepts of the self and others are formed, and the relative merits of qualitative and quantitative research methods. Considering these perspectives together, sociological social psychologists are influenced most frequently by symbolic interactionism, role theory, and exchange theory. They employ a range of research methods, including social surveys, unstructured interviews, observational techniques, and archival research methods; laboratory and field experiments also are used on occasion. Data analysis is accomplished with both qualitative and quantitative techniques. Distinctions are drawn between individual behaviors, psychological structures, groups and other interpersonal systems, and culturally defined macrosocial structures and processes. Sociological social psychologists focus on the reciprocal causal influences between individual psychological structures and macrosocial structures and processes or those between psychological processes and ongoing interpersonal systems (Cook et al. 1995; Michener and DeLamater 1994).

Implicit in the explanatory constructs sociologists use in investigating patterns of social behavior are individual-level psychological constructs.

The concept of culture, for example, frequently is defined in terms of shared normative expectations that are learned and transmitted in the course of social interaction. This definition implies subjective probabilities, evaluative judgments, and processes of symbolic communication through which normative expectations are transmitted and shared. Further, the substantive referents of culture relate to individual-level phenomena such as systems of values, beliefs, and perceptual orientations. In short, definitions of sociological explanatory constructs and the substantive referents of those constructs tend to be abstractions from individual-level psychological responses and systems, including those relating to cognition, affect, and goal orientation. A full understanding of most, if not all, sociological constructs depends on comprehension of the psychological responses and systems that the sociological constructs connote and from which the soiological concepts can be generalized.

The current state of social psychology is best understood through a description of the range of theoretical orientations and research methods used, the conceptual distinctions that are drawn, and the causal linkages that are investigated by representatives of the two social psychological traditions.

THEORY AND METHOD

Social psychologists use a broad range of theoretical perspectives and research methods to study the reciprocal causal linkages between individual-level and social-level variables.

Theoretical Perspectives. Among the more frequently used theoretical perspectives are symbolic interactionism, role theory, exchange theory, and social learning theory.

Symbolic interactionism. From this perspective, people are perceived as acting toward others on the basis of the meaning those others and their behaviors have for the actors. Those meanings are derived and modified during social interaction in which people communicate with one another through the use of shared symbols. Symbolic interactionism encompasses the notion that people's ability to respond to themselves as objects permits them to communicate to themselves, through the use of symbols, the meanings that are given to people and objects by the persons who perceive them. Thus, people interpret the world to themselves and respond according to that interpretation. The interpretation of a situation occurs in the course of ongoing social interaction. In short, persons become objects to themselves, interact with themselves, and interpret to themselves ongoing events and objects in the environment.

Proponents of symbolic interactionism vary in the extent to which they focus on the influence of a stable social structure on these processes. Those who deny the significance of a social structure concentrate on the process of cognitive interpretation and the creative construction of behavior that grows out of a person's interpretation of the ongoing interactive situation. Appropriate to this emphasis, empirical investigations employ observation and in-depth interviewing to the exclusion of experimental and quantitative, nonexperimental methods (the Chicago School). Derivatives of this approach to symbolic interactionism include the dramaturgical school, in which the metaphor of the theater is used to study how people create impressions of themselves during face-to-face interaction, and ethnomethodology, in which theoretical perspective students study the implicit rules governing interaction in particular situation to understand how people construct reality through social interaction.

For those who focus on the significance of social structures to symbolic interaction, the meanings of the behaviors in social interaction depend on the relevance of those behaviors for the social-identity-related standards by which people evaluate themselves. Individuals interact within a framework that defines the social identities of the interacting parties and the normative expectations that are applicable to each identity as it relates to the other identities in that situation. The behaviors that have the most meaning are relevant for highly placed standards in a person's hierarchy of values. The more a behavior of a person or the others with whom he or she is interacting validates or contradicts the social identity (male, father) that is important to that person, the more meaningful that behavior will be to him or her. To the extent that the behaviors of others toward a person signify evaluatively significant aspects of the self, it is important to anticipate responses from others. The others whose responses are more likely to signify evaluatively relevant information about the self are significant others (Charon 1998; Couse

1977 Kaplan 1986; Michener and DeLamater 1994; Stephan and Stephan 1990).

Role theory. From this perspective, human social behavior is viewed in the context of people playing roles (that is, conforming to normative expectations) that apply to people who occupy various social positions and interact with people in complementary social positions. As individuals change from one social position to another in the course of a day, they play different roles (as a father, for example, and then as an employer). The roles individuals play also change as they interact with people in different positions (a professor interacting with a colleague, with the dean, and with a student). As people shift roles, they also change the ways in which they view the world, the attitudes they hold toward different phenomena, and their behaviors. Although people identify more with some roles than with others, their ability to play their preferred roles is limited by the contradictory demands made on them by the other roles they are called on to play (Biddle 1986; Turner, 1990).

Exchange theory. This perspective is relevant to the investigation of the conditions under which individuals enter into and maintain stable relationships. One is most likely to do this when the rewards gained from the relationship are perceived as high, the costs are low, and the reward–cost differential is favorable compared with the perceived alternatives. Rewards (power, prestige, material goods) and costs (interpersonal hostility, great expenditures of money, long hours of work) are defined by personal values. Attraction to relationships is also a function of the extent to which the participants perceive each other as receiving outcomes (rewards) that are appropriate to their inputs (costs). In the absence of such equity, the participants adjust their behavior or way of thinking in an attempt to restore the fact or appearance of equity in a relationship (Molm and Cook 1995; Stephan and Stephan 1990).

Social learning theory. This orientation addresses how individuals learn new responses that are appropriate in various social situations. The primary processes through which social learning occurs include conditioning, by which one acquires new responses through reinforcement (that is, the association of rewards and punishments with particular behaviors), and imitation, by which one observes the reinforcement elicited by another person's behavior (Bandura 1986; Taylor 1998).

Methods. Social psychological research employs a variety of methods, including social surveys, naturalistic observation, experiments, and analysis of archival data. Social surveys may be conducted by personal or telephone interviews or by self-administered questionnaires. For the most part, naturalistic observation involves observing ongoing activity in everyday settings (that is, field studies); in participant observation, the investigator plays an active role in the interaction. Experimental research involves the manipulation of independent variables to assess their effects on outcomes. Subjects are assigned at random to the independent conditions. The experiments may be conducted in the laboratory or in natural settings; in the latter case, the experimenter has less control over theoretically irrelevant variables but the experimental conditions are more realistic for the subjects. Archival research involves the use of existing data to test hypotheses. In some instances, the data can be used exactly as they appear, as with some statistical data. In other instances, such as newspaper stories, the data must be converted into another form, for example, for use in content analysis, which involves categorizing and counting particular occurrences (Cook et al. 1995; Gilbert et al. 1998; Michener and DeLamater 1994).

CONCEPTUAL DISCRIMINATIONS

The pursuit of the goals of social psychology by scientists from psychological and sociological traditions has entailed the differentiation between concepts at the individual level and the social level.

Individual-Level Concepts. Social psychologists have focused on dynamic psychological structures, intrapsychic responses, and individual behaviors as outcomes of or influences on social structures and processes.

Psychological structures. At the individual level, psychological structures have been represented as dynamic organizations of dispositions to respond at the intrapsychic level or the behavioral level. More inclusive concepts, such as the personality, reflect the organization of psychological dispositions in terms of a structure of relatively stable cognitive, evaluative, affective, and behavioral tendencies. The concept of the person has been understood in terms of a structure of predispositions to respond at the intrapsychic or behavioral level that are organized around a hierarchically related system of situationally defined social identities. The self has been treated as an inclusive structure of dispositions to respond reflexively at the cognitive, evaluative, affective, and behavioral levels. Less inclusive structures refer to organizations of particular psychological dispositions, such as personal value systems, treated as the hierarchy of situationally applicable criteria for self-evaluation; the structure of attitudes or generalized evaluative responses; and the system of concepts and schemas (structures of related concepts) a person uses to order stimuli (Kaplan 1986).

These structures are treated as components that are related to one another in a stable dynamic equilibrium and at the same time as having the potential to change. The structures of predispositions, when stimulated by internal or external cues, respond at the intrapsychic level or the behavioral level. The predispositions are inferred from the observed behaviors and self-reports of intrapsychic responses to recurrent stimuli in particular situations.

Intrapsychic responses. These are cognitive (including awareness and conceptual structuring), evaluative, and affective (or emotional) responses to contemporary stimuli, including one's own or others' behaviors in particular situational contexts. The current situation may stimulate one to attend to particular aspects of oneself, classify others in terms of group-membership concepts, attribute others' failures to external rather than internal causes, evaluate oneself as a failure, or experience attraction to other people. Intrapsychic responses are inferred from one's perceptible behaviors or self-reports of percepts, beliefs, attitudes, and feelings relating to the current situation.

Behavior. Individual behavior refers to the class of responses that are perceptible to others as well as to oneself. Behavior is distinguished from intrapsychic responses and the stable organization of dispositions to respond (person or personality) that are perceptible only to the self. Behavior includes purposive or unintended communications about oneself or others, helping and hurtful responses, affiliation and disaffiliation with other individuals or groups, conformity to or deviation from one's own or others' expectations, cooperation and competition, positive and negative sanctioning of one's own or others' behaviors, and the myriad other perceptible responses one may make to oneself, others, or other aspects of one's environment (Kaplan 1986; Michener and DeLamater 1994; Stephan and Stephan 1990). Behavior is conceptualized as the outcome of socially influenced psychological structures and intrapsychic processes and as influencing social-level variables.

Social-Level Concepts. These concepts include interpersonal systems and culturally defined macrosocial structures.

Interpersonal systems. Interpersonal systems are defined as those in which two or more individuals interact with each other or otherwise influence each other over a brief or extended period. The interaction or mutual influence is governed by shared normative expectations that define appropriate behavior for individuals who occupy complementary or common social positions in the course of the interaction or mutual influence. The shared expectations may exist before participation in the interpersonal system and reflect the common culturally defined macrosocial structure or may be refined or emerge during the ongoing social interaction or mutual influence in response to the unique characteristics of the interacting individuals or other situational demands. The social positions a person occupies and the interpersonal systems in which a person participates as a consequence may be given at birth or may be adopted later in life according to stage in the life cycle and current situational demands. Interpersonal systems include interpersonal relationships, groups, and collective forms.

Interpersonal relationships are those in which two individuals have an ongoing interaction that is governed by their shared normative expectations. These expectations are derived from social definitions that delineate appropriate behavior for people occupying the social positions that characterize the individuals and emerge in the course of the ongoing social interaction. For example, a married couple's shared expectations depend on a common understanding of the obligations and rights of a husband and a wife in relation to each other, and the same is true of friends; in addition, in the course of social interaction, specific evaluative expectations regarding what each person in the relationship will and should do in various

circumstances develop. Individuals may interact with one another in the capacity of having the same status (such as group member or friend) or complementary statuses (such as husband and wife) or in the capacity of representing conflicting or cooperating groups. Relationships develop through predictable stages. Intimate relationships develop from the awareness of available partners, to contact with those who are thought to be desirable, to various stages of emotional involvement. The accompanying increases in emotional involvement represent increases in self-disclosure, trust, and mutual dependence (Berscheid and Reis 1998; Michener and DeLamater 1994).

A group consists of a number of individuals in ongoing interaction who share a set of normative expectations that govern the behavior of the members in relation to one another. Normative expectations may refer uniformly to all group members as they interact with one another and with nongroup members or to different individuals in their various social relational contexts. Individuals share an identity as members of a group as well as common goals; these goals may include the personal satisfaction gained from the intrinsically or instrumentally satisfying intragroup relationship or from a group identity that evokes favorable responses from extragroup systems. Group members may share norms from the outset and refine or change their expectations over time, or the norms may emerge in the course of member interaction. Groups include friendship networks, work groups, schools, families, voluntary associations, and other naturally occurring or purposively formed ad hoc associations. Groups vary in size, stability, the degree to which interaction among the members is regulated by preexisting role definitions, and complexity of role differentiation as well as the extent to which a group is embedded in more inclusive groups. Groups also vary according to whether the gratifications achieved from participation in a group are intrinsic to the social relationships and are diffuse as opposed to instrumental to the achievement of other ends and delimited.

Over the course of time, groups develop structures characterized by status hierarchies and functional role differentiation, or those structures may be predefined for new members. Status hierarchies reflect the values placed by group members on positions within the group. The individuals who occupy those positions are more or less esteemed depending on the valuation (status) of a position. Individuals who have higher-status positions and are consequently more highly esteemed ordinarily receive greater rewards (as these are defined by group members) and exercise greater influence over group decisions. In formal groups, functional differentiation is indicated by the formal role definitions associated with the various social positions that make up a group. In informal groups, over time some individuals come to be expected to perform certain functions, such as leading the group toward solving a problem (the task leader) or accepting responsibility for relieving tensions and maintaining group solidarity (the social-emotional leader) (Levine and Moreland 1998; Ridgeway and Walker 1995).

Collective forms include publics, audiences, crowds, and social movements. Collective forms are characterized by the mutual influence of individuals in responding cognitively, affectively, and behaviorally to a common focus. Individuals are undifferentiated according to social position: They share the social position defined by their common attention to an idea, person, object, or behavior. The common stimulus, previously learned dispositions to respond to that stimulus, and mutual influences through social contagion, social observation, and emergent norms that govern mood, action, and imagery lead to collective behaviors. Collective behaviors by large numbers of individuals who are not physically proximate in response to mass media and interpersonal stimulation include mass expressions of attitudes (public opinion), attraction (fads, fashions, crazes), and anxiety (panics). Crowd behaviors are collective responses by large numbers of physically proximate individuals who are influenced by social contagion, observation, and the resultant emergent norms. Social movements are expressions of dispositions to behave similarly with regard to a social issue (Michener and DeLamater 1994).

Culturally defined macrosocial structures. The inclusive sociocultural structure provides shared meanings and defines relationships among individuals depending on their social positions or identities in a situation. The social structure is made up of the stable relationships between social positions or identities that are culturally defined in terms of the rights and obligations people who occupy one position have in interacting with people who occupy another position. In the course of

the socialization process, individuals learn the rights and obligations that apply to those who occupy the various social positions, and those rights and obligations constitute the role that defines a social position. The inclusive social structure is a system consisting of components that are related to one another in a relatively stable dynamic equilibrium but may change over time as changes in structural positions and their role definitions become prevalent in interpersonal settings throughout the society. The culturally defined inclusive macrosocial structure encompasses systems of stratification, social differentiation according to race or ethnicity, and major social institutions as well as other consensually defined social structures (Kerckhoff 1995).

CAUSAL RELATIONSHIPS

Within a social psychological framework, a person's psychological structure, intrapsychic responses, and behaviors are viewed in terms of the profound influence exerted on that person by his or her past and continuing participation in interpersonal and social systems. In turn, the person behaves in ways that have consequences for the interpersonal systems and social structures in which he or she participates. Implicit in this framework is a general causal model. Social structural arrangements define systems of shared meanings that in turn define the role expectations that govern behavior in interpersonal systems. A person is born into functioning interpersonal systems and throughout the life cycle participates in other interpersonal systems that together reflect culturally defined macrosocial structures and processes. In the course of a person's life in the context of dynamically evolving interlocking interpersonal systems, biogenetically given capabilities are actualized; the person learns to view the world through a system of concepts, internalizes needs, symbolizes those needs as values, accepts social identities, and develops emotional cognitive and behavioral dispositions to respond. These relatively stable psychological structures are stimulated by contemporary social situations that have symbolic significance for the individual and thus evoke predictable personal responses. Over time, the same social situations stimulate personal change.

The development of language skills, along with a person's experiences as the object of others' responses to him or her in the course of the socialization process, influences the development of a person's tendencies to become aware of, conceive of, evaluate, and have feelings about herself or himself as well as dispositions to behave in ways that are motivated by the need to protect or enhance the self. The nature of a person's responses to herself or himself are influenced by past and present social experiences. Those responses in turn influence the relationships and groups in which a person participates and indirectly influence the more inclusive social system, thus intervening between social influences on the person and her or his influence on interpersonal systems and the culturally defined social structure (Corsaro and Eder 1995; Fiske et al. 1998; Elder and O'Rand 1995; Kaplan 1995; Kerckhoff 1995; Krauss and Chiu 1998; Maynard and Whalen 1995; Miller-Loessi 1995).

The substantive concerns of social psychological theory and research reflect detailed consideration of these general processes. These concerns address (1) the influence of culturally defined macrosocial structures and processes or interpersonal systems on psychological structures, intrapsychic responses, and individual behaviors or (2) the influence of psychological structures, intrapsychic responses, and individual behaviors on interpersonal systems and culturally defined macrosocial structures and processes.

Social Influences on Psychological Structures. Substantive concerns with social influences on individual psychological structures, intrapsychic responses, and behaviors have focused on long-term social structural influences through socialization processes and contemporary interpersonal influences in interpersonal settings.

Social structural effects. Social structural arrangements define the content, effectiveness, and style of the socialization experience and thus influence a person's psychological structures. Individuals occupy social positions by being born into them or achieving them later in life. Each social position is defined in terms of role expectations that specify appropriate behavior for people who occupy that position in the context of particular relationships. As a result of occupying positions, people become part of interpersonal systems that consist of themselves and those who occupy complementary positions. In these relationships and groups people

become socialized. Socialization is the lifelong process through which an individual learns and becomes motivated to conform to the norms defining the social roles that are played or might be played in the future that individual and those with whom she or he interacts. Socialization occurs in a variety of social contexts, including the family, school, play groups, and work groups, through the experience of rewards and punishment consequent to performing behaviors, observation of the consequences of behaviors for others, direct and intended instruction by others, and self-reinforcement. The acquisition of language skills permits one to be rewarded and punished through the use of symbolic responses, communicate with others about the appropriateness of different responses, and reinforce responses through the process of becoming an object to oneself and disapproving or approving of one's past or anticipated behaviors. The cognitive structures used in coding and processing information about one's own behavior and the hierarchy of self-evaluative criteria also are learned in the course of socialization.

The content of role definitions and the centrality of particular roles for a person's identity structure depend on stage in the life cycle, role definitions associated with other social positions, and the historical era. The roles that are most central to a person's identity and contribute most to self-esteem depend on that person's position in the social structure, including age and gender. During a particular historical period, for example, men may base their self-esteem more on success in the occupational sphere whereas women in the same stage of life base theirs on adequate performance of family roles.

The effectiveness of the socialization process is influenced by more or less invariant developmental stages of cognitive and emotional development in interaction with the varying demands made on the individual at various stages in life as well as by discrepancies between the demands made on a person and the resources that would permit her or him to meet those demands (Corsaro and Eder 1995; Elder and O'Rand 1995; Miller-Loessi 1995).

The social structure affects the style of the socialization process as well. Higher-socioeconomic-status parents are more likely than are lower-class parents to base rewards and punishment on a child's intentions than on actual behavior and to rely on reasoning and the induction of shame and guilt rather than physical punishment. As a family becomes larger, parents are more likely to exercise autocratic parenting styles, while children elicit less attention from parents and develop more independence (Michener and DeLamater 1994).

The end result of the social-structure-influenced socialization process is the development of psychological structures that are stimulated by social-identity-related situations or are evoked more generally in the course of social interaction. Depending on whether persons are born into male or female social positions, they develop different achievement orientations and evaluate themselves in accordance with the success their in approximating the standards of achievement they set for themselves. Individuals in higher socioeconomic classes tend to value a sense of accomplishment and family security more highly than do those with lower socioeconomic status, who tend to put more emphasis on a comfortable life and hope of salvation. More specifically, individuals who are born into a higher social class are more likely to be socialized to value educational achievement and aspire to higher levels of education. Those who achieve at higher levels in school are more likely to interact with others who respond to them in ways that reinforce academically oriented self-images and values that reflect an achievement orientation. Individuals whose occupational status involves self-direction tend to develop a high valuation of responsibility, curiosity, and good sense, while those in occupational positions characterized by close supervision, routine activities, and low levels of complexity in work tasks tend to develop a high valuation of conformity (Heiss 1981; House 1981; Kohn et al. 1983; Rokeach 1973; Sewell and Hauser 1980).

In general, in the course of socialization people become disposed to identify others in their environment, anticipate their responses, imagine aspects of themselves as eliciting those responses, behave in ways calculated to elicit those responses, and value the responses of others and the aspects of the self that elicit those responses. Radical resocialization, by which an individual unlearns lifelong patterns and learns new attitudes, values, and behaviors, may occur in circumstances in which the agents of socialization have uniform and total control over the individual's outcomes, as in some psychiatric hospitals, penal institutions, traditional military academies, and prisoner-of-war camps (Goffman 1961).

Interpersonal effects. The contemporary interpersonal context stimulates self-conceptions and self-evaluative, affective, and behavioral responses. Each social situation provides participants with physical cues that allow them to make inferences about the social identities of the other participants, the role expectations each person holds of the others, and the perceived causes of the behaviors of the interacting parties. These conceptions regarding the situated identities are in part responses to the demand characteristics of the situation and in part the outcomes of the need of one party to project a particular social identity on the other person so that the first party can play a desired complementary role (Alexander and Wiley 1981). The situational context provides symbolic cues that specify the relevance of particular traits, behaviors, or experiences for one's current situation; it also provides a basis for comparing one's characteristics with those of other people.

The current social situation defines the relevance of some self-evaluative standards rather than others. The presence of other people, cameras, or mirrors makes people more self-aware and thus stimulates their disposition to evaluate themselves. Certain responses of others (sanctions), in addition to constituting intrinsically value-relevant responses, communicate to persons the degree to which they have approximated self-evaluative standards. In the early stages of development of a group, individuals may be assigned higher-status positions on the basis of status characteristics (such as those relating to age, sex, ethnicity, and physical attractiveness) that have evaluative significance in the more inclusive society. Although these characteristics may not be relevant to the ability to perform the functions for which the group exists, the high valuation of these status characteristics may lead to the assignment of individuals to high-status positions in the group through a process of status generalization (Berger et al. 1989; Ridgeway and Walker 1995). As a consequence of culturally defined preconceptions regarding the merits of various status characteristics, persons with those characteristics are expected to perform better on a group task.

With regard to affective responses, social stimuli evoke physiological reactions that are labeled as specific emotional states, depending on the cues provided by social circumstances (Kelley and Michela 1980). In turn, individuals who label an experience as a particular emotional state selectively perceive bodily sensations as cues that validate that experience (Leventhal 1980; Pennebaker 1980). Social stimuli that evoke psychological distress include contexts in which a person is unable to fulfill role requirements because of the absence of personal and interpersonal resources and the presence of situational barriers to fulfilling the obligations associated with the social positions that person occupies. Other such stimuli are represented by intrinsically distressing aspects of social positions. People may be distressed not only because they cannot do their jobs well but also because of the absence of meaning that their jobs have for them and because of other noxious circumstances correlated with the position (time pressures, noise, lack of autonomy, conflicting expectations) (Kaplan 1996).

Situational contexts define expectations regarding appropriate and otherwise attractive behavior and thus stimulate behavior that anticipates fulfillment of the expectations and achievement of the goals (including avoidance of noxious states such as social reception). In collective forms of interpersonal systems, emergent norms govern actions as well as moods and imagery for publics and crowds and so lead to mass behaviors such as crazes and panics and crowd behaviors such as rioting. The motivation for participation in social movements is influenced by expectations regarding the value and likelihood of the success of a movement (Michener and DeLamater 1994).

In interpersonal relationships as well, shared expectations govern attraction to others, helping behavior, and aggressive behavior. An individual tends to be attracted to those with whom interaction is facilitated, those who are characterized by socially appropriate and desirable traits (including physical attributes), those who share tastes with and are otherwise like that individual, those who manifest liking for him or her, and in general those who may be expected to occasion rewarding outcomes. Helping behavior is evoked by situational demand characteristics, such as role definitions that define helping behavior as appropriate for people who occupy particular social positions, or

by interpersonal expectations that helping behavior by the other person should be reciprocated. The likelihood of conforming to these situational demand characteristics increases when a person perceives that the rewards for doing so will be forthcoming (including personal satisfaction in helping others, a sense of fulfillment in doing what one is called on to do, and approval by others) and that failure to do so will bring negative sanctions (social disapproval, a self-evaluation of having failed to do the right thing). Conformity to demand characteristics that require helping behavior may be impeded if a person perceives that it would involve costs, such as hindering the achievement of other goals. The awareness of potential rewards or costs for engaging or failing to engage in helping behavior is facilitated by situational characteristics such as the presence of observers and circumstances that produce self-awareness. The need to help others is increased by experiences that evoke negative self-evaluations. The resulting negative self-feelings motivate helping behavior as a way of improving one's self-evaluation (Michener and DeLamater 1994).

Aggressive behavior may arise in response to situational demand characteristics such as perceiving oneself as playing a role that requires aggressive behavior either as a response to intentional aggressive behavior directed toward one by others or simply as a communication of an aggressive stance. Reinforcement by rewards increases the frequency or continuity of aggressive patterns. Rewarding outcomes of aggression include the related rewards of social approval, an improved position in the prestige hierarchy of the group, self-approval, and material gain. Individuals are inhibited from engaging in aggressive behavior when they perceive the act as contrary to normatively proscribed roles or otherwise anticipate adverse consequences of the behavior. These inhibiting effects may be obviated by the reduced self-awareness that results from being part of a crowd, for example, or by the administration of psychotropic drugs (Bandura 1973; Baron 1977; Kaplan 1972; Singer 1971).

In group contexts, role definitions and influences on self-awareness affect individual behavior. The assignment of individuals to higher-status positions in a group and concomitant expectations of higher levels of performance or of the adoption of particular functional roles frequently motivate people to conform to those expectations or lead to the provision of resources that permit them to do so (Berger et al. 1989). When socially induced self-awareness causes people to attend to public aspects of themselves, they tend to be responsive to group influences. When self-awareness causes them to attend to their personal standards, they tend to direct their behavior to conform with those values even when they conflict with group standards. Thus, exposure to cameras induces public self-awareness and increases social conformity, while exposure to mirrors evokes private self-awareness and an increase in self-direction (Scheier and Carver 1983).

The effects of social stimuli on deviant, as opposed to conforming, behavior have been addressed from a variety of theoretical frameworks, including structured strain theory, differential association and deviant subculture theories, control theory, self-theory, and the labeling perspective. Attempts to integrate or elaborate any of these approaches encompass the following ideas (Gibbs 1981; Hollander 1975; Kaplan 1984; Messner et al. 1989; Moscovici 1985). First, individuals who experience rejection and failure in conventional social groups lose their motivation to conform to conventional norms and are motivated to deviate from those norms. At the same time, these individuals are disposed to seek alternative deviant patterns to attain or restore feelings of self-worth. Second, individuals who participate in groups that endorse behaviors that are be defined as deviant in other groups (whether because they seek alternative deviant patterns through which they can improve self-worth or because of long-term identification with a deviant subculture) positively value the "deviant" patterns and are provided with opportunities and the resources to engage in the deviant behavior. Third, individuals with the motivation and opportunity to engage in deviant behavior are deterred by anticipated negative responses from groups that define that behavior as deviant and to which they remain emotionally bonded. Individuals tend to conform to the normative expectations of a group to the extent that they are made aware of the deviant nature of their behavior or attributes, are attracted to the group and therefore are highly vulnerable to the sanctions the group may administer for deviant behavior, are prevented from leaving the group and so freeing themselves from vulnerability to the group's

negative sanctions, identify with the group and thus adopt its normative standards, and internalize the normative standards and regard conformity as intrinsically valuable. Fourth, individuals who evoke negative social sanctions in response to initial deviance continue or increase the level of deviant behavior as a result of the effects of the negative social sanctions on increased alienation from the conventional group, increased association with deviant peers, and increased motivation to justify the initial deviance by more highly evaluating a deviant act. Continuity or escalation of deviant behavior also is likely to occur if motives that ordinarily inhibit the performance of deviant acts are weakened and if a person perceives an association between the deviant behavior and satisfaction of preexisting needs (including the need to enhance one's self-esteem).

Psychological Influences on Social Systems. The consequences of socially influenced psychological processes may be observed at the interpersonal level and at the more inclusive, culturally defined macrosocial-structure level (Kaplan 1986).

Interpersonal systems. Intrapsychic responses and behaviors influence interpersonal systems in a wide variety of ways. Among the more salient consequences are those relating to the stability and functioning of groups, intragroup influences, group membership, and intergroup relationships.

Individuals affect both the *stability* and the *functioning* of their groups through their behavior. The stability of a group is enhanced to the extent that individuals conform to the expectations other people have of them and thus validate those expectations. An individual contributes to group functioning by playing the roles other people expect her or him to play in the group, permitting others to play their complementary roles. Conformity is influenced by the need for self-approval and the approval of others when the criteria for approval are the group standards. If personal and group standards reflect the value of scholarship, individuals may study hard; if approximation to the standards of a particular social identity (such as male) is a salient basis for self-evaluation, people strive to conform to what they perceive as the role expectations associated with that position. More generally, persons may evaluate themselves in terms of conforming to others' expectations. A salient value may be to evoke approving responses from others. To that end, a person may behave in number of ways, including conforming to others' expectations and presenting oneself to others in ways calculated to evoke approving responses. However, a person will strive to conform to group standards in order to approximate self-values only to the extent that success or failure is attributed to the degree of personal effort rather than to circumstances (Kaplan 1995). Conformity is also an outcome of the need for others' approval. In a group in which the members are highly attracted to the group, conformity to group norms, including those related to productivity, is high. In such cohesive groups, members have greater power over one another than they do in groups where the individuals are less attracted to and dependent on the group (Cartwright and Zander 1968; Cialdini and Frost 1998; Hare 1976). The need for others' approval is reflected in the use of disclaimers and excuses to mitigate others' responses to personal behaviors (Hewitt and Stokes 1975; Karp and Ybels 1986; Spencer 1987). A perceived threat to the group increases members' attraction to the group and conformity to shared norms while decreasing tolerance of deviance.

Interpersonal influence occurs through the use of both overt and covert behaviors. Overt methods of persuasion include the use of information or arguments, the offering of rewards, and the threat of punishment. Covert attempts to influence others are reflected in self-presentation in order to create the impression of oneself as likable or in other ways to manipulate the impression others have of one. Attempts at persuasion are more or less effective depending on the characteristics of the source of the communication, the message itself, and the target of the communication. For example, communications are more persuasive if they come from a number of independent sources each of which is perceived to be expert, trustworthy, or otherwise attractive to the target of the communication, than they are if they occur in mutually exclusive circumstances. The effectiveness of threats and promises in influencing others depends on the magnitude and certainty of the proffered rewards and punishments. When the parties involved in the influence process all have the capacity to reward or punish one another, changes in opinions or behaviors are influenced by bargaining and negotiation processes. Among the possible outcomes, depending

on a number of circumstances, are mutual influence, escalation of conflict, accommodation of one person to the demands of the other, and failure of the parties to agree (Michener and DeLamater 1994). In the course of group interaction, individuals develop more extreme attitudes than they held as individuals. This may be due to the pooling of arguments, which adds new reasons for the initially held attitude, or to the social support provided by other group members, which permits the person to be more extreme in his or her opinions with less fear of group rejection (Brandstatter et al. 1982).

Persons are motivated to present themselves in ways that evoke desired responses from others. This is accomplished through a variety of tactics. A significant feature of self-presentation is an individual's social identity in a situation. By projecting a particular identity, the individual effectively imposes complementary identities on others; if the other people perform the roles associated with those identities, they in effect endorse the identity that the individual wishes to project. This imposition of social identities on others (altercasting) has the desirable effect of affirming the social identity the individual wishes to project. For example, by complying with a reason's demands or following her or his lead, the others affirm that person's position of authority or leadership. In addition, people's favorable responses are intrinsically valued, other rewarding outcomes are contingent on them, and they indicate to a person that her of his public image reflects her or his personal ideals. Self-presentation may be used to create false as well as true images of oneself. The creation of false images (impression management) also is used to evoke responses from others that serve one's personal needs. Tactics involving the false presentation of self include pretenses that one admires other individuals or share their opinions and presenting oneself as if one had admirable qualities that one does not in fact possess (Baumeister 1982; Tedeschi 1981).

The attraction and maintenance of group membership are a function of the perception by members that group participation is intrinsically desirable or instrumental to the achievement of shared or individually defined goals (Evans and Jarvis 1980). Relationships, as well as larger groups, grow and become resistant to dissolution as the partners become increasingly dependent on each other for need satisfaction, which may lie in the relationship itself or in the role the partner plays in facilitating the satisfaction of other needs outside the relationship (that is, by providing social support). Primary relationships dissolve to the extent that the costs come to exceed the rewards—whether in absolute terms or relative to the cost-benefit ratio that may be obtained from alternative relationships—and to the extent that the costs of remaining in the relationship outweigh the costs (including social disapproval) associated with terminating it (Cialdini and Frost 1998; Kelley and Thibaut 1978; Kerckhoff 1974). Among the costs are perceptions of inequity. Group members tend to compare the relationship between their own contributions to the group and the rewards they receive with other members' contributions and rewards. Judgments of inequity are made when members perceive rewards to be out of proportion to contributions. Judgments that inequitable states exist stimulate responses to reduce the inequity or at least the perception of the inequity. The inability to redress or tolerate inequitable relationships may lead to eschewing membership in a group (Walster et al. 1978). In general, people select group memberships, when they have a choice, and maintain them in accordance with their value in facilitating self-approving responses. People maintain relationships by whose standards they may evaluate themselves positively and tend not to associate with groups by whose standards they would be considered failures (Kaplan 1986).

The nature of the responses *that groups evoke from nonmembers is* influenced by the nonmembers' perceptions, evaluations, and feelings toward themselves and others. Negative emotions, such as anger, and consequent aggressive behavior may be directed toward groups when individuals' interests cannot be served except at the cost of frustration of the objectives of another group or when individuals associate the other group with past experiences of failure. Among the benefits persons may experience at the cost of the other group's outcomes is increased self-esteem. Aggressive behavior directed toward others deflects anger that might have been directed toward oneself. When the basis of one's feelings of accomplishment are judged relative to the achievements of another group, aggressive behaviors that lead to the failure or destruction of the other group enhance feelings of pride in one's own group. Stronger levels of identification with one's group or social category increase the need to enhance one's group identity at the cost of adverse outcomes for other groups (Bobo 1983; LeVine and Campbell 1972; Worchel and Austin 1986). The tendency to devalue others as they deviate from one's own group's standards increases the justification for negative attitudes and hostile actions toward the other group. The need to justify aggressive attitudes toward another group also frequently leads to biased perceptions that reinforce or validate preexisting attitudes toward that group. Reversal of the process is impeded by the decreases in communication that accompany negative attitudes toward that group. Frequent experiences of observing aggressive responses desensitize a person to the effects of these responses and establish a normative judgment that they are within the expected range of responses.

Other individuals or groups may be the objects of helping behavior, depending on the actor's intrapsychic responses. Negative affect (particularly negative self-feelings) decreases helping behavior by focusing attention inward and away from the plight of other individuals. Thus, some individuals are less likely to empathize with or even be aware of others' needs. At the same time, distressful self-feelings motivate an individual to behave in ways that will earn self-approval. Helping behavior may serve this function by fulfilling others' expectation that helping behavior be offered, conforming to role definitions of helping behavior as appropriate for particular social identities, and conforming to self-values regarding altruistic behavior and thus compensating for feelings of rejection and failure (Dovidio 1984).

Macrosocial structures . Psychological structures, intrapsychic responses, and behaviors influence the substance of the social structure at any given time and social change over time. Dimensions of personality that reflect evaluative standards affect the positions an individual has in the social structure. High value placed on educational attainment and achievement orientation lead ultimately to educational achievement and high occupational status. Similarly, studies of the relationship between the occupational structure and personality suggest that workers may be selected into jobs because of the fit between their personality characteristics and the requirements of the work situation (Kerckhoff 1989). Individuals who value self-direction select occupations that permit the exercise of self-direction, that is, ones that involve less routine, more complex tasks, and low levels of supervision. Persons who place a high value on conformity tend to opt for occupations that are closely supervised, routine, and noncomplex.

The effects of persons as products of past socialization experiences and as stimulated by contemporary social situations on interpersonal social systems and the more inclusive social structure are mediated by the responses of those persons to themselves. An individual influences the current and future functioning of interpersonal systems by becoming self-aware and conceiving of the self in particular ways, evaluating the self as more or less closely approximating personal standards, and experiencing self-feelings that stimulate self-protective and self-enhancing responses, some of which directly and indirectly affect the functioning of the interpersonal or social systems in which that individual participates.

If a person fails to behave in ways that meet self-imposed demands, that person will experience negative self-feelings that motivate him or her to behave in ways that will reduce the self-rejecting feelings. If the person identifies the self-rejecting experiences with particular social identities, she or he may reject the group and define it as a negative reference group, overidentify with the group and reevaluate formerly denigrated attributes as desirable ones, or project undesirable characteristics onto other groups or social categories and act with hostility toward them. Negative self-feelings also may lead to reduced levels of socioeconomic aspirations, occupational change, withdrawal from political participation or association with political activism, and changes in patterns of religious affiliation and participation (Kaplan 1986; Rosenberg and Kaplan 1982). If the circumstances that hinder a person from behaving in ways that earn self-approval and the self-protective responses they stimulate are widespread, the inclusive social structure will be affected. The person's responses directly affect interpersonal systems, that is, individuals who interact in the context of social relationships and groups that are governed by shared situation-specific, identity-specific, or person-specific expectations. If the individual is motivated to withdraw from or otherwise disrupt the functioning of the interpersonal systems in which she or he participates, the functioning of the other individuals will be similarly disrupted, since others' performance is contingent on the individual's conformity to their expectations. However, the functioning of the interpersonal system willbe facilitated if the individual is motivated to conform to the normative expectations that the participants in the interaction situation view as applicable to the person in that particular situational context. If the disposition to deviate from normative expectations is prevalent, disruptions of social relationships will be widespread and the social structure will be less resistant to changes in patterns of response over time. While widespread conformity to shared expectations in particular social contexts has stabilizing influences on the broader social structure, widespread innovation or deviation from them influences the development of new social structural arrangements and definitions.

(SEE ALSO: *Affect Control Theory and Impression Formation; Aggression; Attitudes; Attribution Theory; Behaviorism; Cognitive Consistency Theories; Collective Behavior; Decision-Making Theory and Research; Extreme Influence; Field Theory; Game Theory and Strategic Interaction; Identity Theory; Intelligence; Interpersonal Attraction; Personality and Social Structure; Personality Theory; Persuasion; Prejudice; Role Theory; Self-Concept; Small Groups; Social Perception; Socialization; Symbolic Interaction Theory*)

REFERENCES

Alexander, C. Norman, Jr., and Mary Glenn Wiley 1981 "Situated Activity and Identity Formation." In M. Rosenberg and R. H. Turner, eds., *Social Psychology: Sociological Perspectives*, New York: Basic Books.

Bandura, Albert 1973 *Aggression: A Social Learning Analysis*. Englewood Cliffs, N.J.: Prentice-Hall.

——. 1986. *The Social Foundations of Thought and Action*. Englewood Cliffs, N.J.: Prentice-Hall.

Baron, Robert A. 1977 *Human Aggression*. New York: Plenum.

Baumeister, Roy F. 1982 "A Self-Presentational View of Social Phenomena." *Psychological Bulletin* 91:3–26.

Berger, Joseph, Morris Zelditch, Jr., and Bo Anderson, eds. 1989 *Sociological Theories in Progress*. Newbury Park, Calif.: Sage.

Berscheid, Ellen, and Harry T. Reis 1998 "Attraction and Close Relationships." In D. T. Gilbert, S. T. Fiske, and G. Lindzey, eds., *The Handbook of Social Psychology*, vol. 2, 4th ed. New York: McGraw-Hill.

Biddle, Bruce J. 1986 "Recent Developments in Role Theory." In A. Inkeles, J. Coleman, and N. Smelser, eds., *Annual Review of Sociology*, vol. 12. Palo Alto, Calif.: Annual Reviews.

Bobo, Lawrence 1983 "Whites' Opposition to Busing: Symbolic Racism or Realistic Group Conflict?" *Journal of Personality and Social Psychology* 45:1196–1210.

Brandstatter, Hermann, James H. Davis, and Gisela Stocker-Kreichgauer, eds. 1982 *Group Decision Making*. New York: Academic Press.

Cartwright, Dorwin, and Alvin Zander 1968 *Group Dynamics*. New York: Harper & Row.

Charon, Joel M. 1998 *Symbolic Interactionism: An Introduction, an Interpretation, an Integration*, 6th ed. Upper Saddle River, N.J.: Prentice Hall.

Cialdini, Robert B., and Melanie R. Frost 1998 "Social Influence: Social Norms, Conformity, and Compliance." In D. T. Gilbert, S. T. Fiske, and G. Lindzey, eds., *The Handbook of Social Psychology*, vol. 2, 4th ed. New York: McGraw-Hill.

Cook, Karen S., Gary Alan Fine, and James S. House, eds. 1995 *Sociological Perspectives on Social Psychology*. Needham Heights, Mass.: Allyn and Bacon.

Corsaro, William A., and Donna Eder 1995 "Development and Socialization of Children and Adolescents." In K. S. Cook, G. A. Fine, and J. S. House, eds., *Sociological Perspectives on Social Psychology*. Needham Heights, Mass.: Allyn and Bacon.

Dovidio, J. H. 1984 "Helping Behavior and Altruism: An Empirical and Conceptual Overview." In L. Berkowitz, ed., *Advances in Experimental Social Psychology*, vol. 17. New York: Academic Press.

Elder, Glen H. Jr., and Angela M. O'Rand 1995 "Adult Lives in a Changing Society." In K. S. Cook, G. A. Fine, and J. S. House, eds., *Sociological Perspectives on Social Psychology*, Needham Heights, Mass.: Allyn and Bacon.

Evans, N. J., and Patricia A. Jarvis 1980 "Group Cohesion, a Review and Reevaluation." *Small Group Behavior* 11:359–370.

Fiske, Alan P., Shinobu Kitayama, Hazel R. Markus, and Richard E. Nisbett 1998 "The Cultural Matrix of Social Psychology." In D. T. Gilbert, S. T. Fiske, and G. Lindzey, eds., *The Handbook of Social Psychology*, vol. 2, 4th ed. New York: McGraw-Hill.

Gibbs, Jack P. 1981 *Norms, Deviance, and Social Control*. New York: Elsevier.

Gilbert, Daniel T., Susan T. Fiske, and Gardner Lindzey, eds. 1998 *The Handbook of Social Psychology*, vols. 1 and 2, 4th ed. New York: McGraw-Hill.

Goffman, Erving 1961 *Asylums*. Garden City, N.Y.: Anchor.

Hare, A. Paul 1976 *Handbook of Small Group Research*. New York: Free Press.

Heiss, Jerold 1981 "Social Roles." In M. Rosenberg and R. H. Turner, eds., *Social Psychology: Sociological Perspectives*. New York: Basic Books.

Hewitt, John P., and R. Stokes 1975 "Disclaimers." *American Sociological Review* 40:1–11.

Hollander, Edwin P. 1975 "Independence, Conformity and Civil Liberties: Some Implications from Social Psychological Research." *Journal of Social Issues* 31:55–67.

—— 1981. "Social Structure and Personality." In M. Rosenberg and R. Turner, eds., *Social Psychology: Sociological Perspectives*. New York: Basic Books.

Kaplan, Howard B. 1972 "Toward a General Theory of Psychosocial Deviance: The Case of Aggressive Behavior." *Social Science and Medicine* 6:593–617.

—— 1984 *Patterns of Juvenile Delinquency*. Beverly Hills, Calif.: Sage.

—— 1986 *Social Psychology of Self-Referent Behavior*. New York: Plenum Press.

—— 1995 "Drugs, Crime, and Other Deviant Adaptations." In H. B. Kaplan, eds., *Drugs, Crime, and Other Deviant Adaptations: Longitudinal Studies*. New York: Plenum Press.

—— ed. 1996 *Psychosocial Stress: Trends in Theory and Research*. New York: Academic Press.

Karp, David Allen, and William C. Ybels 1986 *Sociology and Everyday Life*. Itasca, Ill.: Peacock.

Kelley, Harold H., and J. Michela 1980 "Attribution Theory and Research." *Annual Review of Psychology* 31:457–501.

——, and John W. Thibaut 1978 *Interpersonal Relations: A Theory of Interdependence*. New York: Wiley.

Kerckhoff, Alan C. 1974 "The Social Context of Interpersonal Attraction." In T. Huston, ed., *Foundations of Interpersonal Attraction*. New York: Academic Press.

—— 1989 "On the Social Psychology of Social Mobility Processes." *Social Forces* 68:17–25.

—— 1995 "Social Stratification and Mobility Processes: Interaction between Individuals and Social Structures." In K. S. Cook, G. A. Fine, and J. S. House, eds., *Sociological Perspectives on Social Psychology*. Needham Heights, Mass.: Allyn and Bacon.

Kohn, Melvin L., and Carmi Schooler, with the collaboration of Joanne Miller, K. Miller, S. Schoenbach, and R. Schoenberg 1983 *Work and Personality: An Inquiry into the Impact of Social Stratification*. Norwood, N.J.: Ablex.

Krauss, Robert M., and Chi-Yue Chiu 1998 "Language and Social Behavior." In D. T. Gilbert, S. T. Fiske, and G. Lindzey, eds., *The Handbook of Social Psychology*, vol. 2, 4th ed. New York: The McGraw-Hill.

Leventhal, Howard 1980 "Toward a Comprehensive Theory of Emotion." In L. Berkowitz, ed., *Advances in Experimental Social Psychology*. vol. 13. New York: Academic Press.

Levine, John M. and Richard L. Moreland 1998 "Small Groups." In D. T. Gilbert, S. T. Fiske, and G. Lindzey, eds., *The Handbook of Social Psychology*, vol. 2, 4th ed. New York: McGraw-Hill.

Levine, Robert A., and Donald T. Campbell 1972 *Ethnocentrism: Theories of Conflict, Ethnic Attitudes and Group Behavior*. New York: Wiley.

Maynard, Douglas W., and Marilyn R. Whalen 1995 "Language, Action, and Social Interaction." In K. S. Cook, G. A. Fine, and J. S. House, eds., *Sociological Perspectives on Social Psychology*. Needham Heights, Mass.: Allyn and Bacon.

Messner, Steven F., Marvin D. Krohn, and Allen E. Liska 1989 *Theoretical Integration in the Study of Deviance and Crime: Problems and Prospects*. Albany: State University of New York Press.

Michener, H. Andrew and John D. DeLamater 1994 *Social Psychology*, 3rd ed. New York: Harcourt Brace College Publishers.

Miller-Loessi, Karen 1995 "Comparative Social Psychology." In K. S. Cook, G. A. Fine, and J. S. House, eds., *Sociological Perspectives on Social Psychology*. Needham Heights, Mass.: Allyn and Bacon.

Molm, Linda D., and Karen S. Cook 1995 "Social Exchange and Exchange Networks." In K. S. Cook, G. A. Fine, and J. S. House, eds., *Sociological Perspectives on Social Psychology*. Needham Heights, Mass: Allyn and Bacon.

Moscovici, Serge 1985 "Social Influence and Conformity." In G. Lindzey and E. Aronson, eds., *Handbook of Social Psychology*, vol. 2, 3rd ed. Reading, Mass.: Addison-Wesley.

Pennebaker, James W. 1980 "Self-Perception of Emotion and Internal Sensation." In D. W. Wegner and R. R. Vallacher, eds., *The Self in Social Psychology*. New York: Oxford University Press.

Ridgeway, Cecilia L. and Henry A. Walker 1995 "Status Structures." In K. S. Cook, G. A. Fine, and J. S. House, eds., *Sociological Perspectives on Social Psychology*. Needham Heights, Mass.: Allyn and Bacon.

Rokeach, Milton 1973 *The Nature of Human Values*. New York: Free Press.

Rosenberg, Morris, and Howard B. Kaplan, eds. 1982 *The Social Psychology of the Self-Concept*. Arlington Heights, Ill.: Harlan Davidson.

Scheier, Michael F., and Charles Carver 1983 "Two Sides of the Self: One for You and One for Me." In J. Suls and A. G. Greenwald, eds., *Psychological Perspectives on the Self*, vol. 2. Hillsdale, N.J.: Erlbaum.

Sewell, William H., and Robert M. Hauser 1980 "The Wisconsin Longitudinal Study of Social and Psychological Factors in Aspirations and Achievements." *Research in Sociology of Education and Socialization* 1:59–99.

Singer, Jerome L., ed. 1971 *The Control of Aggression and Violence: Cognitive and Physiological Factors*. New York: Academic Press.

Spencer, J. William 1987 "Self-Work in Social Interaction: Negotiating Role-Identities." *Social Psychology Quarterly* 50:131–142.

Stephan, Cookie White, and Walter G. Stephan 1990 *Two Social Psychologies*, 2nd ed. Belmont, Calif.: Wadsworth.

Taylor, Shelley E. 1998. "The Social Being in Social Psychology." In D. T. Gilbert, S. T. Fiske, and G. Lindzey, eds., *The Handbook of Social Psychology*. vol. 1, 4th ed. New York: McGraw-Hill.

Tedeschi, James T. ed. 1981 *Impression Management Theory and Social Psychological Research*. New York: Academic Press.

Turner, Ralph H. 1990 "Role Change." In W. R. Scott and J. Blake, eds., *Annual Review of Sociology*, vol. 16. Palo Alto, Calif.: Annual Reviews.

Walster (Hatfield), Elaine, William Wolster, and Ellen Berscheid, eds. 1978 *Equity: Theory and Research*. Boston: Allyn and Bacon.

Worchel, Stephen, and William G. Austin, eds. 1986 *The Social Psychology of Intergroup Relations*. Monterey, Calif.: Brooks/Cole.

Zillman, Dolf 1979 *Hostility and Aggression*. Hillsdale, N.J.: Erlbaum.

HOWARD B. KAPLAN

SOCIAL PSYCHOLOGY OF STATUS ALLOCATION

The processes of status allocation are among the most important phenomena of societal stratification structures, along with the ways in which those structures vary over time and between societies and the causes and consequences of those variations (Haller 2000). Within these partly stable structures, these processes include the formation of individuals' status aspirations, the effect of those aspirations on attained statuses, and the causes of status aspirations (Haller 1982), including those describing a person's social origins (Alwin 1989). One's social status is defined in terms of both ascribed and achieved characteristics. Unless the value or meaning of ascribed characteristics changes, it is only through change in one's achieved characteristics that one's status in society can change. In modern society, occupation, income, and education are the most common achieved characteristics that are studied within the framework of status attainment.

People tend to see themselves and others as occupying positions along hierarchical continua, with evaluations being associated with a person's location in the hierarchy. One's plan, however vague, to strive for a particular place in a status hierarchy is defined as one's level of aspiration. As a mediator of achieved characteristics, and perhaps of ascribed characteristics as well, one's levels of aspiration affect one's levels of attainment (Haller 1982).

Status attainment research is concerned with the process by which people come to occupy their positions in life, some higher and some lower. Through social policy and social practice, the social system provides the opportunity structure for status attainment. The interface between sociology's study of stratification and psychology's study of individual motivation and achievement is dealt with by the field of the social psychology of status attainment.

HISTORY OF THE THEORETICAL FIELD

From the 1960s to the early 1980s, the theory of status allocation developed vigorously, increasing its theoretical comprehensiveness while maintaining its conceptual parsimony and explanatory power (Sewell et al. 1969, 1970; Haller and Woelfel 1972; Haller and Portes 1973; Haller 1982). These developments were matched by similar improvements in methods for testing the hypotheses of the theory (Duncan 1968; Duncan et al. 1968; Van De Geer 1971; Hauser et al. 1983). The social psychological theory of status attainment is both coherent and comprehensive by current standards of social science theory. The theory emerged from two traditions: one sociological, focusing on social

stratification research, and the other from social psychology, focusing on the self-concept and its formation.

The modern study of social stratification began with the work of Sorokin (1927) and was continued by Svaltastoga (1965), Duncan (1968), and Haller (1970), among others. Stratification theorists typically posit at least four classes of fundamental status variables, or status content dimensions. Those content dimensions reflect the societal rewards an individual receives and the means to obtain those rewards. Thus, they also may be seen as dimensions of power. Content dimensions are conceptualized as political status, economic status, social status, and informational status (Haller 2000). In status attainment research, educational attainment, occupational prestige, and income are examined as the main variables by which one can measure a person's positions on the content dimensions.

The social psychological tradition that influenced status attainment is based primarily on work by Mead (1934). Lewin (1939) and Heider (1958) influenced this tradition as well. This tradition suggests that status in open societies is earned as opposed to being bestowed by a person's lineage. Before persons assume their eventual statuses, they knowingly or unknowingly develop a level of aspiration for educational status, occupational status, income, and political influence. One's level of aspiration is formed in three ways: by the modeling of others who are present, by self-reflection, and by adopting the status expectations held for a person by others. One can model the behavior of another person whom one knows only through mediated communication (e.g., by learning about another person's behavior by reading about it in books, newspapers, or magazines or by observing that behavior on television or in movies). One also can learn about the status expectations that others hold for oneself through the media. There is evidence, however, that most sources of influence are not transmitted in this way but instead by the direct and indirect effects of "significant others" (Haller and Woelfel 1969, 1972; Haller et al. 1969).

Once formed, aspirations are difficult to change, and they guide the decisions one makes about life. Consequently, one's level of aspiration is a significant determinant of one's level of attainment (Haller 1982).

Since the early 1980s, much work on status attainment has not been systematic but instead directed by policy considerations (Haller 1982). Interestingly, in the last two decades, research on status attainment has grown more in other countries than it has in the United States. In the United States, approximately the same number of studies were conducted on status attainment in each year over the last two decades. However, studies in other countries have more than doubled, and for the first time since the inception of the field, more research is being conducted outside of the United States than within it.

STATUS ATTAINMENT MODELS

A complete model of the process of status attainment does not exist. However, many significant contributions to what is known about status attainment have come from just a few perspectives. The work of Blau and Duncan (1967) was significant for its careful operationalization of concepts and presentation of formal models subject to statistical analysis. Those authors presented an important model concerned with the effects of parents' status, one's own education, and one's first job, although their model had four flaws. First, it lacked indicators for wealth and power, two important status content dimensions. Second, it contained a relatively primitive theory of the mechanisms of status attainment. Third, it lacked a comprehensive set of exogenous variables, which were limited to the father's occupational and educational statuses. Fourth, much variance in educational and occupational statuses was not explained.

A more complete model of status attainment was introduced informally in 1967; a test of it appeared in Sewell et al. (1969). The conceptual system it embodied, however imperfectly, became known as the Wisconsin model. Path analyses emphasized the social psychological and social structural antecedents of educational and occupational attainment. This early form of the model assumes that all relationships between the key variables are linear and that social psychological variables mediate the process of status attainment. Status aspiration for education and occupation was found to be a powerful mediator of status attainment.

An important contribution of this research was the elaboration, both theoretical and methodological, of the concept of the significant other's influence. One's set of significant others is often larger than one's referent group of parents and peers. This set was defined to include all those who serve as definers and models. *Definers* are those who communicate their expectations, *whereas* models are those who provide illustrations of their statuses and related behaviors; an individual can serve in both capacities. The Wisconsin model changed the conception of social influence used in the study of status allocation from a list of individuals to a set of social processes by which the individuals in one's environment help determine one's status destination.

Sewell et al. (1969) found that the social structural and psychological factors of socioeconomic status and mental ability affect the academic performance of youths and that significant others have great influence in the status attainment process. However, the sample on which their original model was tested was limited, and this was a drawback for evaluating the internal and external validity of their model. The original sample consisted of 929 Wisconsin students who completed a survey as well as a follow-up group of males studied in 1964 whose fathers had been farmers in 1957 (Sewell et al. 1969).

The original form of the Wisconsin model was modified slightly in a study by Sewell et al. (1970), who proposed small changes that would make it applicable to boys with different residential backgrounds. As in the 1969 versions, one's ability and one's significant others were shown to affect one's educational and occupational aspirations. In turn, those aspirations affected one's educational and occupational status attainment (Sewell et al. 1970). Most significant was the finding that the Sewell et al. (1969) model could be used with minor modifications for young men from a variety of backgrounds.

The Wisconsin model was refined in two significant ways by Haller and Portes (1973). First, the model was modified by clarifying and completing the set of content dimensions of status. Second, it was shown that each content dimension of status also is manifested in both of two social psychological isomorphs (status "mirror" images): a status aspiration variable of each focal person and a corresponding variable describing the status orientation levels each of the focal person's significant others expects of him or her (definers) or illustrates to him or her (models). Third, the Wisconsin model incorporated structural dimensions of status. Two critical structural dimensions are status dispersion and status crystallization. Status attainment models were held to work best when status dispersion is wide, which means that inequality is great; there is little to learn about attainment in fairly homogeneous status systems. Status crystallization is the degree of correlation among status content dimensions (e.g., how one's wealth corresponds to one's power). When crystallization is high, a status attainment model is relatively simplified: It is as if the ultimate endogenous variable were an unobserved variable with many correlated indicators. In complex societies with moderate to high crystallization, status attainment models must be more complex, because the isomorphs of each status content dimension must be treated as separate endogenous variables in the model.

The Wisconsin model was retested in 1983 with more recently developed estimation procedures. It was found to be even more effective in explaining the process of educational and occupational attainment than it previously had been thought to be (Hauser et al. 1983). However, the model was not tested as a whole because not all the variables in the model were measured.

Concerns with Current Status Attainment Models. Research on status attainment models has not advanced much since the early 1980s, and flaws in the models of that time remain. More recent research has focused mostly on status inheritance, but the inheritance models are incomplete. None of these models has included measures drawn from the power dimension; indeed, none has seriously attempted to cover the entire range of variables implied by each of the four general status content dimensions (Haller 2000). In the models that have been tested, about 25 to 35 percent of the variance in attainment can be explained by parental status variables. The more nearly complete models explain much more than this.

The social psychological variables used in models today are virtually the same ones used twenty-five years ago. However, the world has changed drastically in the last twenty-five years, particularly with the advent of and pervasive use of communication technology. It is conceivable that mediated sources of influence play a greater role in status attainment process, but it is impossible to know whether this is true. More generally, it is quite possible that the relationship among status attainment variables has changed, and there may be additional variables to consider.

Concerns with Current Status Attainment Research. The initial fifteen years of research from 1967 through 1982 were significant in terms of formulating theory, defining variables, and enlarging the subject populations to which the attainment model applied. Haller (1982) described four avenues of study that would advance status attainment research greatly.

First, there has not been a longitudinal study that followed a cohort sample and observed the influence of the variables in the model on status attainments beyond mid-career. For example, what influences the selection of a second occupation? In addition, how do one's high school occupational, educational, and income aspirations affect one's position and income thirty years or more after those aspirations are formed? Second, most earlier attainment research was restricted to high school students and their first positions after school. The development of status orientations among young children needs to be explored. Third, it is important to understand how status definers emerge in young children. Fourth, the mechanisms that activate the status attainment process have to be explicated.

Above all, the full panoply of variables specified in Haller (1982) should be tested on today's youthful cohorts as they move through life.

THE STATE OF KNOWLEDGE

In status attainment research, the key variables that are feasible today are educational attainment, occupational prestige, and income. What is known about those variables?

Educational Status Attainment in the United States. *Young children and early teens.* The first longitudinal study of educational attainment conducted with young children spanned the period from fall 1985 to spring 1987. Achievement in the first grade was studied for minority groups, including African-Americans and Hispanics. Parental involvement, mobility, and motivation all had a direct influence on first-graders' outcomes. Interestingly, at least two of the three variables—parental involvement and mobility—are under the direct control of the parents. Additionally, the cognitive readiness of children entering kindergarten was found to have an indirect effect on first-graders' outcomes. All the variables examined had a significant direct or indirect effects on those outcomes, including motivation, peer environment, parental involvement, readiness, and mobility (Reynolds 1989).

The second longitudinal study of educational attainment spanned a one-year period from fall 1987 to fall 1988, using a national sample of 3,116 youths. Data from this study were used to assess science achievement, attitude toward mathematics, and science and mathematics achievement in grades seven and eight. For young teenagers, prior achievement played a large mediating role in future mathematics and science achievement, but classroom context and parental involvement influenced their achievement as well (Reynolds 1991). Science achievement was directly affected by prior achievement, peer environment, and the amount and quality of instruction; mathematics achievement was most strongly influenced by prior achievement and the home environment (Reynolds and Walberg 1991, 1992).

Teenagers. Intelligence is a factor in predicting educational and occupational aspirations, but other variables appear to have a greater effect. There is a relatively small effect of parents' statuses on their children's but a relatively large effect of status aspirations and significant others' expectations on one's educational and occupational attainment. Thus, if one has significant others who expect one to go to college, it is more likely that one believes that going to college is possible and one is more likely to go.

Using annual data collected since 1975 for the Monitoring the Future survey, Morgan (1998) found that the educational aspirations of high school seniors increased between the late 1970s and the early 1990s. This effect was greater for white students than for African-American students. Morgan (1998) viewed aspirations as part of a cognitive process of continually calculating the costs and benefits of one's educational aspirations; this variable may influence the effects of significant others. The finding is consistent with the results of many early studies (Haller and Miller, 1963, Hypothesis 4,– pp. 31, 41–45, 96), and is an expression of the

well-known Zeigarnik effect (Zeigarnik 1927, Lewin 1951).

The Wisconsin model from the 1970s worked well for the group of white males but not as well for others. With the addition of identity theory (Burke 1989) to the Wisconsin model, that model was found to work not only for white males but for African-American and white females as well. Identity theory suggests that one's identity originates from one's social interactions with others. When one's identity is established, one acts in ways that maintain and confirm that identity. White males and females and African-American females constructed an academic identity that directly influenced their college plans. In other words, if they constructed the meaning of going to college in terms of job-related reasons ("Going to college will help me get the kind of job I want"), they were more likely to go to college. However, the model's predictive ability for African-American males has been minimal. Preliminary research has indicated that one of the reasons for this may be that in that group there is insufficient correspondence between the constructs used in the modified Wisconsin model and the processes associated with African-American male attainment (Burke 1989; Burke and Hoelter 1988).

Education Outside the United States. *Australia.* In Australia, education is required for those aged 6–15. Thus, required education ends after the tenth year of school; however, students may elect to stay in the system for two more years. Students who left school after the tenth year earned less than did those who stayed the additional two years. Importantly, socioeconomic background, type of school attended, and career orientations appeared to be unrelated to the decision to leave school after the tenth year (Saha 1985).

Australian research sought to determine whether attending a private Catholic high school influenced attendance at college and the receipt of a college degree. Approximately two-thirds of those from public schools and two-thirds of those from private schools eventually obtain a college degree. However, only approximately 58 percent of those who receive a secondary degree from a Catholic school obtain a college degree (Williams and Carpenter 1990). Thus, receiving a private education results in the same chance of obtaining a college degree as does receiving a public school education, but receiving a Catholic school education gives one a relatively lesser chance to obtain a college degree.

Young adult unemployment in Australia varied between 27 percent and 52 percent from the mid-1960s to the early 1980s. One might assume that most youths were encouraged to obtain further education, but that was not always the case. A revision of the Ajzen–Fishbein model of attitude–behavior relations (Carpenter et al. 1989) was used to assess youths' intentions toward entering the workforce immediately after high school; the influence of economic conditions also was considered in this model. Parental and peer influence played a powerful role in molding a youth's intentions; however, the youth's decision to transform the intention into action was mediated by his or her self-perception of past academic performance.

Greece. A Greek study (Kostakis 1992) examined information and occupational demands in terms of the specific sources Greek students might use to influence their decisions about the future. How and from whom one gains information was considered a socially determined process. An individual's significant others, consisting of friends and relatives, appeared to be the most important source of information for all groups; however, significant others were more available to higher-status individuals. Considered as an information source for vocational occupations, schooling was relied on by lower-status youths, rural youths, and girls.

Israel. In many studies, teachers were viewed as significant others, but their influence on status attainment did not appear to be large. However, little was known about a teacher's long-term influence on status attainment. A national representative sample of 834 Israeli adults aged 21–65 was studied to ascertain the effect of the influence of a former teacher (Enoch et al. 1992). The group was divided into two cohort groups: older (ages 40–65) and younger (ages 21–39). Perceived teacher influence was found to be a determining factor in respect to occupation only for the older group. Furthermore, it was found that the Oriental (Sephardic) older group perceived teacher influence as being greater than did any of the other groups in terms of occupational attainment, whereas the older Ashkenazic group identified perceived

teacher influence as a significant variable in educational attainment.

Occupational Status Attainment in the United States: The Role of Gender. Typical status attainment models account for more variance in male occupational attainment than in female occupational attainment. A possible reason is that typical occupational status attainment models view occupations as discrete categorical variables as opposed to preferences along a continuum. When occupational titles were measured as a continuous variable, as was done by the Wisconsin researchers, it was found that a student's gender and a family's socioeconomic status were related to occupational choice. Additionally, significant others' expectations for a student played a role in determining aspirations. Significant others' expectations appeared to be affected most by gender as opposed to aptitude or ability. Thus, males and females may have their aspirations influenced by significant others who seem to choose traditional gender occupations for them (Saltiel 1988).

After the 1960s and 1970s, occupational status attainment research in the United States focused on gender differences in attainment, perhaps because changes in gender roles accelerated at that time. More women have chosen to pursue higher education and enter male-dominated careers than ever before. How will the increasing diversity of occupations open to women affect women's aspirations and eventual occupational attainment?

There were no significant differences in levels of occupational aspiration between boys and girls and in different high school grades in the early 1960s (Haller et al. 1974). However, little research examining gender differences was conducted in the 1970s and the early to middle 1980s to determine whether aspirations affected occupational attainment.

Consistent with the Wisconsin model, women in the 1980s who pursued male-dominated careers such as business, engineering, and law were found to be subjected to a network of influences, as opposed to a single influence. Parents' educational level was acknowledged as an influence in typical status attainment research, but until the late 1980s, the specific effect of parents' possession of a college degree on their children was not considered. For both African-American and white women, parental income was found to have a significant indirect effect on women's educational attainment. Furthermore, for white women only, the father's and mother's education proved to have significant indirect effects (Gruca et al. 1988).

Women recently have been receiving approximately 50 percent of the bachelor's degrees in life sciences and mathematics, but they are significantly underrepresented in science and mathematics occupations (National Research Council 1991). If women are attaining initial degrees in the same numbers as men, why are they not represented equally in the fields to which those degrees lead?

For women, significant factors associated with persistence in scientific and mathematical careers after college include receiving encouragement from teachers and parents, particularly the mother (Rayman and Brett 1995). Those who stay in science and mathematics careers after graduation do not necessarily believe that their current occupation is compatible with family life; however, the majority of these women have not been affected by family needs. Those who changed careers from a mathematics- or science-related occupation to one not oriented in those directions were more likely to believe that family need plays a role in occupational attainment. Over 50 percent of this group had taken time off from work, refused promotions, reduced their work schedules to part-time, or changed location because of family need. Grades in science and mathematics courses did not significantly affect attitude and achievement in science and mathematics. Additionally, self-esteem and perceived self-confidence did not play a role in deciding who stayed with scientific and mathematical careers and who did not (Rayman and Brett 1995).

Occupational Status Attainment outside the United States. *Canada.* The Canadian Mobility Study (Boyd et al. 1995) was directly influenced by the 1962 Occupational Change in a Generation Study in the United States. Using data from the early 1970s, this study showed that great inequalities exist in income, assets, and educational attainment between genders and among those with various ethnic origins (Porter 1995, p. 61). Preliminary research indicated that motherhood, as opposed to or in addition to being married, was the most significant variable determining the occupational status attainment of native-born Canadian

women (Boyd 1995a, p. 284). This finding makes sense, as motherhood, as opposed to marriage, generally requires time off from work. Some women choose to stay at home to raise a child; even if this time off from work is brief, by affecting continuity of employment, it affects one's advancement potential.

Interestingly, occupation and status seem to be consistent from generation to generation (McRoberts 1995, p. 98). One of the reasons for this is that the advantages of background often are passed on to children. For example, wealthy parents are more likely to have received higher education and are better able to afford to have their children receive higher education. Although it is not impossible for a child from a lower-income family to attend an institution of higher education, it is not as likely. This conclusion comes from a study of Canadian-born males in 1973 whose occupations were compared with those of their fathers.

Also of interest is the role of immigrants in status attainment levels in Canada. Native-born Canadian men have an average occupational status lower than that of American-born, German-born, and United Kingdom–born male immigrants and an average occupational status higher than that of immigrants from Poland, Italy, Greece, and Portugal (Boyd 1995b, p. 440). Much of the inequality between the Canadian-born and non-Canadian-born men results from differences in family origin and education.

Similarly, non-Canadian-born women tend to have an average occupational status lower than that of Canadian-born women, but non-Canadian status seems to have less of an impact on female immigrants from the Unites States and the United Kingdom. As in the United States, females have a lower average occupational status than do males (Boyd 1995b, p. 441).

Taiwan. Taiwan consists primarily of three ethnic groups: the aborigines, the Taiwanese, and the mainlanders. Although the Taiwanese account for slightly more than 85 percent of the population, the mainlanders, who account for approximately 12 percent, hold the political power. A study involving 3,924 men from the three ethnic groups determined that the mainlanders had an average occupational status higher than that of the Taiwanese or the aborigines (Tsai 1992).

The father's occupation was found to be the determining factor for first occupation among aborigines over 35 years old. However, for those under 35 years of age, residence and educational attainment were found to be significant influences on the first occupation. This result was different for the Taiwanese and the mainlanders, for whom the most important determinant of first occupation was their level of educational attainment (Tsai 1992).

Israel. In Israel, a better education does not necessarily predict better occupational attainment (Semyonov and Yuchtmahn-Yaar 1992). It once was believed that as Arabs became increasingly integrated into the general Jewish population in Israel, educational attainment and status attainment would become more equal between those two groups. From 1972 through 1983, the Arab population increased its average educational attainment level; however, its average occupational attainment declined. Market discrimination was estimated to account for 6.5 percent of the occupational gap between Jews and Arabs in the highest age group (ages 54–65), but its effect increased to nearly 25 percent in the youngest age group (ages 25–36). Clearly, there are social variables at work here that are not included in traditional status attainment models.

Political and Economic Status. Little research has been conducted in the areas of political and economic status. The link of economic status to the prior generation is much weaker than are educational and occupational links that generation. There are a number of reasons why economic status is much more difficult to study than are the educational or occupational variables. Many studies rely on participants to report information for their parents, and although occupational and educational attainments generally are known to family members, specific income information, particularly over a life span, is not. Also, the fluctuating rate of inflation makes it difficult to compare incomes directly across generations. Additionally, an economy's supplies and demands vacillate and ultimately determine an occupation's worth at a given moment. Thus, although the prestige of occupations may not change much, the income associated with those positions may change a great deal, in part as a result of market forces. Finally, the range of incomes today is greater than ever before. Chief executive officers, entertainment performers, and professional athletes command high incomes. With more income "outliers" today, reliably measuring income and incorporating it into status attainment models are difficult. As a result of these factors, less is known about income status attainment than about educational or occupational attainment.

Similarly, little is known about political status attainment. Political status originally was defined as influence, authority, coercion, and power. Unlike occupational and educational achievement, which have been relatively well defined, there is little agreement on a person's political status.

In a study involving sports teams across cultures, age, experience, and performance were deemed to be the most significant factors in defining status in Canada and India (Jacob and Carron 1996). Both cultures gave more importance to achieved sources of status, such as experience and performance level, than to ascribed status, such as religion, race, and parental occupation. Surprisingly, age was found to be a significant determinant of status, apparently because it serves as an indicator of experience.

CONCLUSION

Some analysts, including Breiger (1995) and Ganzeboom et al. (1991), believe that theory formulation has become very narrow in social attainment research. However, there are several directions future research can take. First, status allocation research can increasingly feature the systematic incorporation of societal factors considered from the perspective of the individual. For example, advances in network analysis will allow measurement of extended networks and the influences of their members (Wasserman and Faust 1994). Similarly, simulation can provide a method to test models of social influence posited in status allocation models, allowing the investigation of the stability, equilibrium, rate of change, and other qualitative features of status dynamics in a social group (see Gilbert and Doran 1994; Jacobsen and Bronson 1995; Latané 1996). Finally, more extensive measurement of the multidimensional features of occupations and the related variables will allow the creation of models of greater complexity, for example, reflecting nonprestige or nonhierarchical features of status allocation (see Woelfel and Fink 1980).

This article makes it evident that researchers need to focus anew on conceptual clarity and theoretical parsimony. In the future, it is important that new research be executed with variables that include all that have been specified as crucial, along with the causal lines that were so specified, as elements of the theory referred to as the Wisconsin model (Haller 1982). As implied here, this should be done for both males and females in different decades and in societies with differing stratification structures.

REFERENCES

Alwin, D. F. 1989 "William H. Sewell: Recipient of the 1988 Cooley-Mead Award." *Social Psychology Quarterly* 52(2):85–87.

Blau, P. M., and O. D. Duncan, 1967 *The American Occupational Structure*. New York: Wiley.

Boyd, M. 1995a "Educational and Occupational Attainments of Native-Born Canadian Men and Women." In M. Boyd, J. Goyder, F. E. Jones, H. A. McRoberts, P. C. Pineo, and J. Porter, eds., *Ascription and Achievement: Studies in Mobility and Status Attainment in Canada*. Ottawa, Canada: Carleton University Press.

—— 1995b "Immigration and Occupational Attainment in Canada." In M. Boyd, J. Goyder, F. E. Jones, H. A. McRoberts, P. C. Pineo, and J. Porter, eds., *Ascription and Achievement: Studies in Mobility and Status Attainment in Canada*. Ottawa, Canada: Carleton University Press.

——, J. Goyder, F. E. Jones, H. A. McRoberts, P. C. Pineo, and J. Porter 1995 *Ascription and Achievement: Studies in Mobility and Status Attainment in Canada*. Ottawa, Canada: Carleton University Press.

Breiger, R. L. 1995 "Social-Structure and the Phenomenology of Attainment." *Annual Review of Sociology* 21:115–136.

Burke, P. J. 1989 "Academic Identity and Race Differences in Educational Aspirations." *Social Science Research* 18:136–150.

——, and J. W. Hoelter 1988 "Identity and Sex-Related Differences in Educational and Occupational Aspirations Formation." *Social Science Research* 17:29–47.

Carpenter, P. G., J. A. Gleishman, and J. S. Western 1989 "Job Intentions and Job Attainment: Young People's Career Beginnings." *Australian Journal of Education* 33(3):299–319.

Duncan, O. D. 1968 "Social Stratification and Mobility: Problems in the Measurement of Trend." In E. B. Sheldon and W. E. Moore, eds., *Indicators of Social Change*. New York: Russell Sage Foundation.

Enoch, Y. R. Shapira, and A. Yogev 1992 "Teachers as Significant Others in the Status Attainment of Israeli Adults." In A. Yougev, ed., *International Perspectives on Education and Society*, vol. 2. Greenwich, Conn.: JAI Press.

Ganzeboom, H. B. G., D. J. Treiman, and W. C. Ultee 1991 "Comparative Intergenerational Stratification Research: Three Generations and Beyond." *Annual Review of Sociology* 17:277–302.

Gilbert, N., and J. Doran, eds. 1994 *Simulating Society: The Computer Simulation of Social Phenomena*. London: UCL Press.

Gruca, J. M., C. A. Ethington, and E. T. Pascarella 1988 "Intergenerational Effects of College Graduation on Career Sex Atypicality in Women." *Research in Higher Education* 29(2):99–124.

Haller, A. O. 1970 "Changes in the Structure of Status Systems." *Rural Sociology* 35:469–487.

—— 1982 "Reflections on the Social Psychology of Status Attainment." In R. M. Hauser, D. Mechanic, A. O. Haller, and T. S. Hauser, eds., *Social Structure and Behavior*. New York: Academic Press.

—— 2000 "Societal Stratification." In E. A. Borgatta and Rhonda V. J. Montgomery, eds., *Encyclopdia of Sociology*, 2nd ed. New York: Macmillan.

Haller, A. O., and Miller, I. W. 1971 *The Occupational Aspiration Scale*. Cambridge, MA: Schenkman.

——, L. B. Otto, R. F. Meier, and G. W. Ohlendorf 1974 "Level of Occupational Aspiration: An Empirical Analysis." *American Sociological Review* 39:113–121.

——, and A. Portes 1973 "Status Attainment Processes." *Sociology of Education* 46:51–91.

——, and J. Woelfel 1969 "Identifying Significant Others and Measuring Their Expectations for a Person." *Revue Internationale de Sociologie* 5:395–429.

—— 1972 "Significant Others and their Expectations: Concepts and Instruments to Measure Interpersonal Influence on Status Aspirations." *Rural Sociology* 37:591–622.

——, ——, and E. L. Fink 1969 *The Wisconsin Significant Other Battery*. Arlington Heights, Va.: Educational Resources Information Document Center.

Hauser, R. M., S. Tsai, and W. H. Sewell 1983 "A Model of Stratification with Response Error in Social and Psychological Variables." *Sociology of Education* 56:20–46.

Heider, F. 1958 *The Psychology of Interpersonal Relations*. New York: Wiley.

Jacob, C. S., and A. V. Carron 1996 "Sources of Status in Sport Teams." *International Journal of Sport Psychology* 27(4):369–382.

Jacobsen, C., and R. Bronson 1995 "Computer Simulations and Empirical Testing of Sociological Theory." *Sociological Methods and Research* 23:479–506.

Kostakis. A. 1992 "Social Determinations of the Use of Information as It Relates to Occupational Choices of Greek Youth." In A. Yougev, ed., *International Perspectives on Education and Society*, vol. 2. Greenwich, Conn.: JAI Press.

Latané, B. 1996 "Dynamic Social Impact Theory: The Creation of Culture by Communication." *Journal of Communication* 46(4):13–25.

Lewin, K. 1939 "Field Theory and Experiment in Social Psychology." *American Journal of Sociology* 44:868–897.

Lewin, K. 1951 *Field Theory in Social Science*. D. Cartwright, ed. New York: Harper.

McRoberts, H. A. 1995 "Mobility and Attainment in Canada: The Effects of Origin." In M. Boyd, J. Goyder, F. E. Jones, H. A. McRoberts, P. C. Pineo, and J. Porter, eds., *Ascription and Achievement: Studies in Mobility and Status Attainment in Canada*. Ottawa, Canada: Carleton University Press.

Mead, G. H. 1934 *Mind, Self, and Society*. Chicago: University of Chicago Press.

Morgan, S. L. 1998 "Adolescent Educational Expectations." *Rationality and Society* 10:131–162.

National Research Council 1991 *Women in Science and Engineering: Increasing Their Numbers in the 1990's*. Washington, D.C.: National Academy Press.

Porter, J. 1995 "Canada: The Societal Content of Occupational Allocation." In M. Boyd, J. Goyder, F. E. Jones, H. A. McRoberts, P. C. Pineo, and J. Porter, eds., *Ascription and Achievement: Studies in Mobility and Status Attainment in Canada*. Ottawa, Canada: Carleton University Press.

Rayman, P., and B. Brett 1995 "Women Science Majors—What Makes a Difference in Persistence after Graduation?" *Journal of Higher Education* 66(4):388–414.

Reynolds, A. J. 1989 "A Structural Model of First Grade Outcomes for an Urban, Low Socioeconomic Status, Minority Population." *Journal of Educational Psychology* 81(4):594–603.

—— 1991 "The Middle Schooling Process: Influences on Science and Mathematics Achievement from the Longitudinal Study of American Youth." *Adolescence* 26(101):133–158.

——, and H. J. Walberg, 1991 "A Structural Model of Science Achievement." *Journal of Educational Psychology* 83(1):97–107.

—— 1992 "A Process Model of Mathematics Achievement and Attitude." *Journal for Research in Mathematics Education* 23(4):306–328.

Saha, L. J. 1985 "The Legitimacy of Early School Leaving: Occupational Orientations, Vocational Training Plans, and Educational Attainment among Urban Australian Youth." *Sociology of Education* 58:228–240.

Saltiel, J. 1988 "The Wisconsin Model of Status Attainment and the Occupational Choice Process." *Work and Occupations* 15(3):334–355.

Semyonov, M., and E. Yuchtman-Yaar 1992 "Ethnicity, Education, and Occupational Inequality: Jews and Arabs in Israel." In A. Yougev, ed., *International Perspectives on Education and Society*, vol. 2. Greenwich, Conn.: JAI Press.

Sewell, W. H., A. O. Haller, and G. W. Ohlendorf 1970 "The Educational and Early Occupational Status Attainment Process: Replication and Revision." *American Sociological Review* 35(16):1014–1027.

——, ——, and A. P. Portes 1969 "The Educational and Early Occupational Attainment Process." *American Sociological Review* 34(1):82–92.

Sorokin, P. A. 1927 *Social Mobility*. New York: Harper and Row.

Svalastoga, K. 1965 *Social Differentiation*. New York: David McKay.

Tsai, S. 1992 "Social Change and Status Attainment in Taiwan: Comparisons of Ethnic Groups." In A. Yougev, ed., *International Perspectives on Education and Society*, vol. 2. Greenwich, Conn.: JAI Press.

Van de Geer, J. P. (1971). *Introduction to Multivariate Analysis for the Social Sciences*. San Francisco: W. H. Freeman.

Wasserman, S., and K. Faust 1994 *Social Network Analysis: Methods and Applications*. Cambridge, UK: Cambridge University Press.

Williams, T., and P. G. Carpenter 1990 "Private Schooling and Public Education." *Australian Journal of Education* 34(1):3–24.

Woelfel, J. D., and E. L. Fink 1980 *The Measurement of Communication Processes: Galileo Theory and Method*. New York: Academic Press.

Zeigarnik, B. 1927, Über das behalten von erledigten und unerledigten Handlungen. *Psycholigisch Forschung* 9:1–85.

Archibald O. Haller
Edward L. Fink
Laura Janusik

SOCIAL RESOURCES THEORY

NOTE: *Although the following article has not been revised for this edition of the Encyclopedia, the substantive coverage is currently appropriate. The editors have provided a list of recent works at the end of the article to facilitate research and exploration of the topic.*

This article introduces the theory of social resources (Lin 1982, 1983). It describes the fundamental propositions of the theory and reviews empirical research programs and results pertaining to the theory. It concludes with a discussion of some issues regarding extensions and modifications of the theory.

Resources are goods, material as well as symbolic, that can be accessed and used in social actions. Of particular interest are the valued resources—resources consensually considered as important for maintaining and improving individuals' chances of survival as they interact with the external environment. In general, valued resources are identified with indicators of class, status, and power in most societies. In the following discussion, resources refer to valued resources.

Resources can be classified in two categories: personal resources and social resources. *Personal resources* are resources belonging to an individual; they include such ascribed and achieved characteristics as gender, race, age, religion, education, occupation, and income as well as familial resources. These resources are in the possession of the individual and at the disposal of the individual. *Social resources*, on the other hand, are resources embedded in one's social network and social ties. These are the resources in the possession of the other individuals to whom ego has either direct or indirect ties. A friend's car, for example, may be ego's social resources. Ego may borrow it for use and return it to the friend. Ego does not possess the car, and accesses and uses it only if the friend is willing to lend it. The friend retains the ownership. Similarly, a friend's social, economic, or political position may be seen as ego's social resources. Ego may seek the friend's help in exercising that resource in order for ego to obtain or achieve a specific goal.

Much of sociological research focuses on personal resources. While social network analysis has been a long-standing research tradition in sociology and psychology, attention had been given to the structure and patterns of ties and relations. Only recently, in the past two decades, sociologists and anthropologists have explored the theoretical significance of the resources brought to bear in the context of social networks and social ties. The theory of social resources makes explicit the assumption that resources embedded in social connections play important roles in the interaction between social structure and individuals. More specifically, the theory explores how individuals access and use social resources to maintain or promote self-interests in a social structure that consists of social positions hierarchically related and organized in terms of valued resources. It has been argued that social resources are accessed and mobilized in a variety of actions by an individual to achieve instrumental and/or expressive goals.

Two terms need some clarifications here. I assume that a social structure consists of different levels, each of which can include a set of structurally equivalent positions. They are equivalent primarily on the basis of levels of similar valued resources, and secondarily, similar life-styles, attitudes, and other cultural and psychological factors. For the purposes here, the terms, "levels" and "positions," are used interchangeably. Also, status attainment is assumed to refer to the voluntary aspect of social mobility. Involuntary social mobility, due to job dissatisfaction, lack of alternatives, or other "pushing" or forced factors, is excluded from consideration. As Granovetter (1986) pointed out, voluntary social mobility generally results in wage growth. Likewise, it is argued that voluntary social mobility accounts for the majority of occurrences in status attainment.

THEORY OF SOCIAL RESOURCES AND SOCIAL ACTIONS

Attention in this article will be given to the theory of social resources as it is applied to the context of instrumental actions. Instrumental actions are a class of actions motivated by the intent to gain valued resources (e.g., seeking a better occupational position). In contrast, expressive actions are a class of actions motivated by the intent to maintain valued resources (e.g., seeking to maintain a marital relationship). Social resources have broad implications for both types of social actions (Lin 1986). However, for the present discussion, social resources will be considered in the perspective of instrumental actions only. To carry the discussion at a more concrete level, attention will be given to the status attainment process, which can be seen as a typical process focusing on an instrumental goal. In the following material, the propositions of the theory of social resources will be presented in the specific framework of the status attainment process, to illuminate clearly and concretely the theoretical implications in a specific research tradition.

I have specified three hypotheses (Lin 1982): the social resources hypothesis, the strength-of-position hypothesis, and the strength-of-ties hypothesis. The *social resources hypothesis*, the primary proposition of the theory, states that *access to and use of better social resources leads to more successful instrumental action*. In the case of status attainment, it predicts that job-seekers are more likely to find a better job (in terms of prestige, power, and/or income) when they are able to contact a source with better resources (in terms of occupation, industry, income, etc.).

The other two hypotheses identify factors that determine the likelihood of access to and use of better social resources. The *strength-of-position hypothesis* stipulates that *the level of original position* is positively *associated with access to and use of social resources*. For the process of status attainment, it suggests that the original social position of a job-seeker is positively related to the likelihood of contacting a source of better resources. Position of origin can be represented by characteristics of ego's parents or previous jobs.

The *strength-of-ties hypothesis* proposes that *use of weaker ties is positively related to access to and use of social resources*. For status attainment, it states that there is a positive relationship between the use of weaker ties and the likelihood of contacting a source of better resources. For the formulation of the strength of weak ties argument, see Granovetter (1973, 1974).

Thus, the theory contains one proposition postulating the effect of social resources and two propositions postulating causes of social resources. The strength-of-position hypothesis implies an inheritance effect. A given position of origin in the hierarchical structure in part decides how well one may get access to better social resources embedded in the social structure. It is a *structural* factor and independent of individuals in the structure, although individuals may benefit. On the other

hand, the strength-of-ties hypothesis suggests the need for *individual action*. Normal interactions are dictated by the homophily principle, the tendency to engage in interaction with others of similar characteristics and life-styles. Going beyond the routine set of frequent interactants and seeking out weaker ties represent action choices beyond most of the normative expectations of the macrostructure (see Granovetter 1973, 1974).

It is true that the beginning of a job search often is unplanned. Many job leads become available through casual occasions (e.g., parties) and through interactions with casual acquaintances. It is not necessarily the case that a job search always begins with the individual actively seeking out contacts for this purpose. However, this does not negate the basic premise that individuals are situated at different levels of positions in the structure and have, therefore, access to "casual" occasions involving participants of certain types and amounts of resources, including social resources. In fact, it has been empirically demonstrated (Campbell, Marsden, and Hulbert 1986; Lin and Dumin 1986) that higher-level positions have greater access to more diverse and heterogenous levels of positions in the hierarchical structure than lower-level positions, therefore having greater command of social resources. Thus, it can be expected that "casual" occasions for the higher-level positions are structurally richer in job and other types of information and influence. Such structural advantage, deducible from the pyramidal assumption of the theory, has distinct effect when a job search is eventually launched by the individual. *In relative terms, the strength of position should have stronger effects on social resources than the strength of ties*. This statement recognizes the significance of structural constraints everywhere in the social structure. In empirical systems, both factors are expected to operate, even though their relative effects may vary.

EMPIRICAL RESEARCH AND THEORETICAL EXTENSIONS

Research programs examining the theory of social resources in the context of socioeconomic attainment have been carried out in North America (Ensel 1979; Lin, Ensel, and Vaughn 1981; Lin, Vaughn, and Ensel 1981; Marsden and Hulbert 1988), in West Germany and the Netherlands (Flap and De Graaf 1988; De Graaf and Flap 1988;

Sprengers, Tazelaar and Flap 1988; Boxman, Flap, and De Graaf 1989; Wegener 1991), in Taiwan (Sun and Hsiong 1988), and in China (Lin and Bian 1990). Thus far, evidence strongly supports two of the three hypotheses: the social-resource hypothesis and the strength-of-positions hypothesis. Those with better origins tend to find sources for better resources in job-seeking, while contacting a source of better resources increases the likelihood of finding a better job. These relations hold even after the usual status attainment variables (e.g., education and first-job status) are taken into account. These results, as Marsden and Hulbert showed, are not biased by the fact that only those contacting interpersonal sources in job-seeking are selected for study.

However, evidence is equivocal on the strength-of-(weak) ties hypothesis. For example, Lin and associates have found evidence that weaker ties linked job-seekers to contacts with better resources, whereas Marsden and Hulbert (1988) did not. The different findings may be due to the interaction between the two exogenous variables: the strength of position and the strength of ties. Lin and others have found that the advantage of using weaker ties over the use of stronger ties decreases as the position of origin approaches the top of the levels. Lin, Ensel, and Vaughn (1981) hypothesized a ceiling effect for weak ties. At the top of the hierarchical structure there is no advantage to using weak ties, since such ties are likely to lead to inferior positions and therefore inferior resources. They did not anticipate similar ineffectiveness of weaker ties toward the bottom of the structure. Marsden and Hulbert (1988), however, also found that those with the lowest origins did not benefit more from contacts with weaker ties in gaining access to better resources than from contacts with stronger ties. One speculation is that those at the lower positions have more restricted range of contacts (Campbell, Marsden and Hulbert 1986; Lin and Dumin 1986), rendering the weaker ties accessible less effective. Thus, a nonlinear relationship (interaction) between strength of ties and social resources may be involved (Wegener 1991).

Another elaboration concerns the distinction between two types of social resources: network resources and contact resources. Network resources refer to resources embedded in one's ongoing social networks and ties. In this conceptualization, the researcher is interested in identifying the on-going social ties, and from these identified ties, exploring resources they have. These resources are seen as social resources to ego (Campbell, Marsden, and Hulbert 1986; Lin and Dumin 1986; Boxman and Flap 1990). Contact resources, on the other hand, refer to resources associated specifically with a tie or ties accessed and mobilized in a particular action. For example, the researcher is interested in identifying the contact ego used in a particular job-seeking situation and specifying the social resources in terms of what resources the contact possessed (Lin, Ensel, and Vaughn 1981; Marsden and Hulbert 1988; Sun and Hsiong 1988; Lin and Bian 1990). Recent research (Lai, Leung, and Lin 1990) shows that network resources and contact resources are two conceptually distinctive and causally related components of social resources. Network resources, reflecting resources in ego's social network, contribute to the access of contact resources in the context of a particular action (e.g., seeking a job). Each in turn contributes to the ultimate success of the action (e.g., getting a high-status occupation).

FURTHER RESEARCH ISSUE

Some theoretical and methodological issues remain in the extension and application of the social resources theory.

One issue concerns the cost of social resources. Unlike personal resources, which ego may use and dispose of relatively free of constraints, social resources are "borrowed" from one's social ties. Thus, there should be a cost attached to such access. In most cases there is an implied obligation of reciprocity—that is, ego is committed to offer his or her resources as social resources to the alter from whom resources have been borrowed. The problem arises when ego and the alter do not occupy similar social positions, thus possessing dissimilar resources. In the case of ego seeking help from the alter, in fact, the better the social position the alter occupies, the more effective it provides social resources to ego. It is conceivable that ego possesses other resources, which may provide to be useful to the alter in the reciprocity process. For example, a banker (ego) may seek political influence from a politician (the alter), who in turn may secure financial benefit with ego's help. Fair exchange of different valued resources occurs. There will also be situations where ego with inferior resources gains as a result of help from an alter with superior resources (e.g., a graduate student getting a desirable job with the help of a professor), the reciprocity becomes more intricate. One way of reciprocity requires quantity in compensation of quality (e.g., willingness to put more effort into a research or writing collaboration). Another form of reciprocity requires efforts to increase the value of the alter's resources (e.g., citations to the professor's work in one's publications). Variations in such reciprocal uses of social resources and, therefore, in cost deserve further conceptualization and research.

Another area worthy of research attention is the use of social resources for expressive actions. It has been hypothesized that, in contrast to instrumental actions, expressive actions would be more effective if ego and the alter share similar traits and experiences. The argument is that homophily (sharing similar characteristics and life-styles) increases the likelihood of the alter understanding the emotional stress experienced by ego (Lin 1986). Thus, the expectation is that strong ties, rather than weak ties, may provide the more desirable social resources for expressive actions. However, reality is much less tidy than this conceptualization. In some expressive actions (e.g., seeking support in time of a divorce), both emotional and instrumental support are needed. Further complicating the situation is that often the strong ties (e.g., spouse) are the sources of stress, and expressive actions must by definition be provided by either weaker ties or surrogate strong ties (e.g., relatives or a friend or professional helper) (Lin and Westcott forthcoming). Much more conceptual and empirical work is needed to tease out these issues.

Finally, there is the intriguing question of whether the theory of social resources can help conceptualizing the interplays between social structure and social action. I argue that the theory of social resources makes two kinds of contributions toward an understanding of social structure and social action (Lin 1990a, 1990b). First, research on social resources has offered the plausibility that under structural constraints, individual choices (in terms of social ties and social contacts) may yield different and meaningful consequences. It has been shown that given two individuals with similar personal resources (including original social positions), they might experience different outcomes in instrumental actions, depending on social re-

sources they access and use. To an extent such different access is dictated by structural constraints. As mentioned earlier, original position affects the range of social ties in the social hierarchy and therefore the likelihood of accessing better social resources. However, after such structural constraints have been taken into account, there is evidence that some flexibility remains in the choice of social ties and use of social resources, and such choice and use yield meaningful and different results.

Second, much of past research on social structure as well as social resources has assumed that social structure has a priori existence and imposes constraints within which individuals conduct meaningful actions. The theoretical possibility that individual actions and choices may constitute fundamental driving forces in the formation and functioning of social structures has gained currency in sociology (Coleman 1986, 1988, 1990). Social resources, it is argued, may also contribute to this theoretical formulation.

One may assume that individuals strive to gain resources for the promotion and maintenance of one's survival and well-being. Personal resources may be preferred to social resources in this striving, since the former incur less cost and are more manipulable. However, the speed of cumulation may differ for the two types of resources. Acquisition and cumulation of personal resources may be additive. On the other hand, acquisition and cumulation of social resources may be exponential, in that once a social tie is established, not only the tie's personal resources become social resources to ego, but the tie's social resources (through its ties) also become social resources. Thus, social ties, through their networking patterns and dynamics, accelerate one's social resources. While social resources come at a cost, as discussed earlier, it is to the benefit of ego to acquire as much social resources as possible. Thus, social resources constitute the fundamental motivation to networking in the promotion and maintenance of one's self-interest and well-being. Such networking constitutes the elementary blocks in the emergence of social structure. Subsequently, the management and manipulation of the constructed and extended network that contains increasingly heterogeneous participants with varying demands for secondary resources (e.g., quality of life considerations) dictate the development of hierarchical positions and role expectations, which in turn reduce the range of possible individual action choices. Further theoretical work along these lines promises to contribute to the current interest and debate in the interrelationships between social actions and social structure.

(SEE ALSO: *Exchange Theory; Social Network Theory; Social Support*)

REFERENCES

Barbieri, Paolo 1997 "The Hidden Treasure. A Map of the Social Capital in a Metropolitan Area" (Il Tesoro nascosto. La mappa del capitale sociate in un'area metropolitana) *Rassegna Italiana di Sociologia* 38:343–370.

Beggs, John J., and Jeanne S. Hurlbert 1997 "The Social Context of Men's and Women's Job Search Ties: Membership in Voluntary Organization, Social Resources, and Job Search Ourcomes." *Sociologcial Perspectives* 40:601–622.

Boxman, E. A. W., Hendrik D. Flap, and P.M. De Graaf 1990 "Social Capital, Human Capital, and Income Attainment: the Impact of Social Capital and Human Capital on the Income Attainment of Dutch Managers in 1986." Paper presented at the European Conference on Social Network Analysis, June, Groningen, Netherlands.

Boxman, E. A. W., and Hendrik D. Flap 1990 "Social Capital and Occupational Chances." Paper presented at the International Sociological Association, XIIth World Congress of Sociology, July, Madrid.

Breiger, Ronald L. 1990 *Social Mobility and Social Structure*. New York: Cambridge University Press.

Campbell, Karen E., Peter V. Marsden and Jeanne S. Hulbert, 1986 "Social Resources and Socioeconomic Status," *Social Networks*, 8(1):97–116.

Coleman, James S 1986 *Individual Interests and Collective Action*. Cambridge: Cambridge University Press.

—— 1988. "Social Capital in the Creation of Human Capital," *American Journal of Sociology* 94(Supplement):S95–S120.

—— 1990. *Foundations of Social Theory*. Cambridge, Mass.: Harvard University Press.

De Graaf, Nan Dirk, and Hendrik Derk Flap 1988 "With a Little Help from My Friends," *Social Forces* 67-2:452–472.

Ensel, Walter M 1979 "Sex, Social Ties, and Status Attainment." Ph.D. diss., Department of Sociology, State University of New York at Albany.

Flap, Hendrik D. and Nan Dirk DeGraaf 1988 "Social Capital and Attained Occupational Status," *Netherlands Journal of Sociology*.

Green, Gary P., Leann M. Tigges, and Irene Browne 1995 "Social Resources, Job Search, and Poverty in Atlanta." *Research in Community Sociology* 5:161–182.

Granovetter, Mark 1973 "The Strength of Weak Ties." *American Journal of Sociology* 78:1360–1380.

—— 1974 *Getting a Job*. Cambridge, Mass.: Harvard University Press.

—— 1982 "The Strength of Weak Ties: A Network Theory Revisited." In Peter V. Marsden and Nan Lin, eds., *Social Structure and Network Analysis*. Beverly Hills: Sage.

Kulik, Liat 1997 "Anticipated Dependence: A Determinant in an Integrative Model of Power Relations among Elderly Couples." *Journal of Aging Studies* 11:363–377.

Lai, Gina Wan-foon, Shu-yin Leung, and Nan Lin 1990 "Network Resources, Contact Resources, and Status Attainment: Structural and Action Effects of Social Resources." Paper presented at the annual meeting of the American Sociological Association, August, Washington, D.C.

—— 1998. "Network Resources, Contact Resources, and Status Attainment." *Social Networks* 20:159–178.

Lin, Nan 1982 "Social Resources and Instrumental Action." In Peter V. Marsden and Nan Lin, eds., *Social Structure and Network Analysis*. Beverly Hills: Sage.

—— 1983 "Social Resources and Social Actions: A Progress Report." *Connections* 6:10–16.

—— 1986 "Conceptualizing Social Support." In Nan Lin, Alfred Dean, and Walter M. Ensel, eds., *Social Support, Life Events, and Depression*. Orlando, Fla.: Academic Press.

—— 1990a "Social Resources and Social Mobility: A Structural Theory of Status Attainment," In Ronald Breiger, ed., *Social Mobility and Social Structure*. New York: Cambridge University Press.

—— 1990b "Social Resources and the Emergence of Social Structure," Paper presented at the XII World Congress of Sociology, July, Madrid.

—— and Yan-jie Bian 1990 "Getting Ahead in Urban China: Differential Effects of Social Connections (Guanxi)." Paper presented at the Sunbelt Network Conference, February, San Diego.

——, and Mary Dumin 1986 "Access to Occupations through Social Ties." *Social Networks* 8:365–385.

——, Walter M. Ensel, and John C. Vaughn 1981 "Social Resources and Strength of Ties: Structural

Factors in Occupational Status Attainment." *American Sociological Review* 46:393–405.

——, John C. Vaughn, and Walter Ensel 1981 "Social Resources and Occupational Status Attainment." *Social Forces* 59:1163–1181.

——, and Jeanne Westcott (Forthcoming) "Marital Engagement/Disengagement, Social Networks, and Mental Health." In John Eckenrode, ed., *The Social Context of Stress and Coping*. New York: Plenum.

Marsden, Peter, and Jeanne Hulbert 1988 "Social Resources and Mobility Outcomes: A Replication and Extension," *Social Forces* 66(4):1038–1059.

Sprengers, Maarten, Frits Tazelaar, and Hendrik D. Flap 1988 "Social Resources, Situational Constraints, and Reemployment." *Netherlands Journal of Sociology* 24.

Sun, Chingshan, and Ruimei Hsiong 1988 *Social Resources and Social Mobility*. Taiwan: Tunghai University.

Tausig, Mark 1990 "Microsocial Implications of the Macrostructural Distribution of Social Resources." *Sociological Focus* 23:333–340.

Tigges, Leann M., Irene Browne, and Gary P. Green 1998 "Social Isolation of the Urban Poor: Race, Class, and Neighborhood Effects on Social Resources." *Sociological Quarterly* 39:53–77.

Wegener, Bernd 1991a "Job Mobility and Social Ties: Social Resources, Prior Job and Status Attainment." *American Sociological Review* 56(February)1–12.

—— 1991b "Job Mobility and Social Ties: Social Resources, Prior Job, and Status Attainment." *American Sociological Review* 56:60–71.

NAN LIN

SOCIAL SECURITY SYSTEMS

In the United States, Social Security refers to a set of programs, including old-age, survivors, and disability insurance, for the elderly and their dependents. This particular use of the term "social security" relates as much to the special and delimited character of the welfare state in the United States as it does to the generally accepted meaning of the term. For organizations such as the International Labour Office and the International Social Security Association and for scholars concerned with comparative studies, the term refers to a wider variety of programs. For instance, in its volume *Social Security throughout the World*, the Social Security Administration states:

The term "social security" in the context of this report refers to programs established by government statutes which insure individuals against interruption or loss of earning power, and for certain special expenditures arising from marriage, birth, or death. (1985, p. ix)

The concept of social protection that underlies this definition includes unemployment programs to cover involuntary temporary loss of work, sickness programs to cover loss of income from sickness and the cost of medical care, disability or occupational injury programs to cover physical limitations on working, family allowances to cover loss of economic status from the addition of members to the family, and social assistance to cover circumstances such as family disruption that cause income to fall below specified levels. Protection of earning power from loss of work or health conditions associated with old age also remains crucial. Still, many of the other programs, more common in the advanced welfare systems of western European nations than in the United States, must be considered part of social security systems.

The relative size of programs devoted to the elderly perhaps warrants the special attention paid to old age in social security systems. Among all expenditures for education and social security programs, those for old-age pensions represent the largest component, averaging 36 percent across high-income nations in 1985 (Organization for Economic Cooperation and Development 1988, Tables 1 and 3). The next largest component, 22 percent, is devoted to health care, which also disproportionately benefits the elderly. Furthermore, the growth rate of programs for the aged has exceeded that for other programs, and in the future, expenditures for those programs will account for an even greater proportion of the total. Spending for unemployment, family allowances, and social assistance represents a relatively small part of social security programs. As Myles (1984) notes, the welfare state is primarily a welfare state for the elderly.

The need for collective protection for the aged or others stems from the existence of economic insecurity. Loss of earning power as a result of poor health, old age, or unemployment remains a possibility for nearly all the participants in a market economy but is uncertain enough to make it difficult to predict loss of income or future savings potential. Traditional protection against such risk in preindustrial societies developed informally through the family. Under ideal circumstances, children and relatives could support parents who were unable to provide for themselves or wanted to step down from their economic role of provider. In premodern societies, social security thus took the form of an intergenerational contract, based on norms of filial piety and parental control over wealth, between children or other relatives and parents (Simmons 1960). Never a guaranteed source of protection, however, other family members became an even less reliable source of support with the decrease in family size, the increase in mobility, and the industrialization of labor that accompanied the demographic and industrial transitions. With the development of large-scale corporate capitalism in the late nineteenth and early twentieth centuries, the risks of forced retirement and unemployment grew. Systems of social security collectivized and formalized the relationship between young workers and elderly, unemployed, or disabled nonworkers. Workers would contribute support to certain categories of non workers in return for the expectation that they would be covered if they became unable to work. The state has always played a crucial role in this collectivized contract by making participation in the systemcompulsory for most workers. Voluntary programs of saving for unexpected contingencies are insufficient because many people are not rational in saving for events that may not occur or occur only in the far future. Private compulsory systems industries, unions, and businesses similarly face problems of incomplete coverage, financial insolvency, and job movement. In contrast, collectivizing social security provides for reliable funding, and it is easier to predict events for a group than it is for individuals.

Most nations provide for more than social security alone. The broader welfare state in capitalist societies also supports education, retraining, full employment, business regulation, price supports, infrastructure, and legal rights. In the former socialist societies of Eastern Europe, social security systems involved broader social protection through guaranteed employment; subsidized food, housing, and energy prices; and the reduced importance of market performance as the criterion for economic support. Recent market-oriented reforms in eastern Europe may expand the emphasis on social security systems as they are typically and more narrowly defined in capitalist societies.

If motives of social protection are common to social security systems, the coverage of the population and the distribution of benefits vary widely. Benefits may be distributed on the basis of at least four criteria, each of which may be emphasized or deemphasized in particular systems. First, citizenship entitlement provides basic benefits—usually in the form of flat-rate cash payments—to individuals or families as a right of citizenship regardless of work history, contributions, or income. Second, employment-related criteria base eligibility on wage or payroll contributions made before the contingency that causes earnings to cease. As a form of public or social insurance, these benefits reinforce market criteria of income determination. Third, need-based criteria provide benefits by comparing resources with a standard that typically is based on subsistence needs. Means-tested or social assistance programs target benefits at the most needy, usually those not covered by citizenship or insurance programs. Fourth, entitlement sometimes is granted on the basis of marital or family status, usually to women and homemakers or families with young children.

To a large extent, nations mix their degrees of reliance on the different criteria. Nations that began with universal systems added earnings-based supplements (e.g., Sweden), and those which originally enacted earnings-based benefits have added universal benefits (e.g., Great Britain) or some form of minimum benefit (e.g., the United States). Similar claims have been made about the mix of public and private systems. To limit inequality, nations that traditionally relied on private systems (e.g., the United States) have increasingly expanded public system benefits, while nations that traditionally relied on public systems (e.g., West Germany) have increasingly expanded private benefits for high-income workers who want a higher return on their contributions.

Some argue that social citizenship remains the most important component of social protection because security is not complete until the state grants alternative means to economic welfare to the market (Esping-Andersen 1989; Korpi 1989). Because meager means-tested benefits are structured to avert work disincentive effects, they fail to emancipate individuals from dependence on the market. Because social insurance benefits stem from labor-based contributions—that is, qualification based on previous contributions defines the right to receive benefits—they maintain links to the market. Because family benefits depend on the qualification of others by virtue of need or contribution, they also fail to detach distribution from the market mechanism. A definition of social security would thus require decommodifying labor or insulating workers from dependence on the market for economic support. According to Esping-Anderson, in decommodifying welfare states,

> *citizens can freely, and without potential losses of job, income or general welfare, opt out of work under conditions when they themselves consider it necessary for reasons of health, family, age or even educational self-improvement; when, in short, they deem it necessary for participating in the social community.* (1989, p. 22)

Few, if any, nations meet the high standards defined by citizenship rights or decommodification. Nearly all nations rely at least partially on earnings-related benefits to supplement universal benefits; flat-rate benefits available to all are too expensive to provide generously for all elderly persons. Still, the trend is toward expanded social rights. Recent efforts to gain the right to protection from economic insecurity follow efforts in previous centuries to gain civil rights such as freedom of speech and equality before the courts and the political right to universal voting (Marshall 1964). This process highlights the dynamic meaning of social security and the continuing evolution of its definition.

Political debate over how far governments should extend definitions of social security to include citizenship rights reflects larger tensions between the relative roles in the market and the state in public policy (Myles 1984). On the one hand, inequality in earnings and contributions during work life means that the market retains a strong influence on social security benefits and the financial circumstances of nonworkers. On the other hand, equality of participation in the democratic political system provides impetus for equality in benefits unrelated to the market. The underlying dynamics of market and democracy—differentiation versus equality—both show in varying degrees in the benefit structures of different systems and debates over the definition of what social security should provide.

HISTORICAL BACKGROUND

A formal social security system was slow to come to the United States. The first public social security system (although limited in coverage and generosity) emerged in Bismarckian Germany in 1889 and was followed by systems in Denmark in 1891, New Zealand in 1898, Austria in 1906, and Australia and Great Britain in 1908 (Social Security Administration 1985). Legislation at the national level was not passed in the United States until 1935, and the first old-age pension was not paid until 1940. In part, the expansion of disability benefits to Civil War veterans (even if they had not been injured or seen combat) in 1890 provided a de facto pension system for northern whites but did not promote the implementation of a more general national pension system for nonveterans (Orloff and Skocpol 1984).

The reasons why Civil War pensions did not lead to a more comprehensive social security system have been examined extensively. The historical persistence of individualist, laissez-faire values obstructed public support for public programs (Rimlinger 1971). Big business preferred private negotiations with labor, and small business wanted to avoid the cost of social security provisions. Relative to a powerful business community, weak, decentralized labor unions were unable to agree on a common approach or push redistributive public programs as they did in several European nations (Stephens 1979). Relatedly, the United States did not have a socialist or social democratic party committed to labor goals, because regional, ethnic, and racial divisions split clearly defined class interests in support of social legislation. Southern congressional representatives, who wanted to maintain cheap agricultural (particularly black) labor in their region, used their power in a committee-dominated federal government to block legislation (Quadagno 1988). Finally, the lack of a professional civil service bureaucracy to administer the program and the existence of often corrupt patronage politics at the local level might have limited public support for a large public social security system (Skocpol and Ikenberry 1983). All these forces played a role in blocking attempts in the first several decades of the twentieth century to expand protection beyond the veterans' pension and partial state-based programs for mothers' pensions or industrial accident insurance.

The impetus for the passage of old-age and unemployment social security came from the Great Depression. The rapidly expanding costs of private pensions and a crisis of capitalist growth lessened opposition of big business to federal pension legislation and a more general role of the government in the capitalist economy (Jenkins and Brents 1989). Southern congressmen were persuaded to support legislation that excluded agricultural and domestic workers and insisted that means-tested levels for old-age assistance be set at the state level; both factors would limit the disruption of the low-wage southern economy. Popular demands in the early 1930s by several hundred thousand supporters of the Townsend movement for a federal government pension for every citizen over age 60 may have hastened enactment (Williamson et al. 1982). Ultimately, the goal of reducing unemployment by removing older workers from the labor force and supporting at least temporarily those who were unemployed proved crucial in passing the initial legislation in 1935 (Schulz 1988; Graebner 1980).

The original 1935 Social Security Act mandated only limited coverage and benefit levels for old-age retirement. Only 60 percent of the workforce was covered: Agricultural, domestic, and self-employed workers; military personnel; federal, state, and local employees; and employees of nonprofit, tax-exempt organizations were all excluded. Moreover, benefit levels were quite low: Policymakers intended not to replace work income fully or assure the maintenance of workers' preretirement standard of living but instead to supplement private sources of retirement income with minimal public benefits (Achenbaum 1986). Social Security benefits alone would hardly meet what would be considered poverty levels in many states at the time (Quadagno 1984).

The initial structure of the social security system, along with the incremental changes made in the following decades, was for the most part market-conforming. Early debates about the degree to which the program should redistribute income across classes were settled in favor of those who wanted to maintain the connection between contributions and benefits (Cates 1983). Funding from general revenues was rejected in favor of contribution-based financing, reinforcing the view of the system as an insurance system. Flat-rate benefits were rejected as unsuitable for a nation with such regional and social heterogeneity; instead, benefits would reflect preretirement income levels. A cap placed on taxable wages, which ostensibly concentrated both contributions and benefits for ordinary middle-income wage workers, introduced some regressiveness into the formula. The major exception to this strategy was that benefits for low-wage workers were higher relative to contributions than were those for high-wage workers (Myers 1981). Also, provisions for unemployment benefits, aid to dependent children, and relief for the blind targeted modest benefits for needy groups (Achenbaum 1989). The system thus began as and remains a mixture of social insurance based on contributions and social adequacy based on social need (Munnell 1977).

Expansion of the system began before the first benefits were paid out and continued for several more decades. In 1939, dependents and survivors were made eligible for benefits. Coverage was extended in the 1950s to include most self-employed, domestic, and agricultural workers, and the participation of state and local employees was made elective (federal employees kept their own system until 1984). In 1956, actuarially reduced benefits were made available at ages 62–64 for women, and in 1961 the same option for early retirement was made available to men, an option now exercised by a majority of new beneficiaries. Also in the 1950s, benefits equal to those for retirees were added for disabled persons aged 50–64 and later for disabled workers of all ages. In 1965, Medicare for the elderly and Medicaid for the poor were added to provide protection against the high costs of medical care. Benefit and contribution levels also rose with extensions of coverage and disability. Ad hoc adjustments to benefit levels, which well exceeded inflation (Tomasson 1984), were common until 1972, when benefits were linked to yearly increases in the consumer price index. Payroll taxes and the maximum taxable wage also increased.

The growth of benefits and coverage nonetheless proceeded more quickly than did that of contributions, and by the late 1970s this situation resulted in funding problems. The concept of the accumulation of a reserve was replaced quickly by a pay-as-you-go system in which current workers paid for current retirees (with enough of a surplus to cover year-to-year fluctuations). In the early years of the system, the ratio of one retiree to 120 workers made this system of funding workable. By the 1970s, the ratio of retirees to workers was one to five. Combined with increasingly high benefit levels, the growing dependency ratio resulted in payments that exceeded contributions. Amendments in 1977 "deliberalized" benefits for the first time by, among other things, freezing minimum benefits and making the earnings test more stringent (Tomasson 1984). Far from sufficient to deal with the implications of higher benefits and an older age structure, these changes only delayed a more serious restructuring. A $17 billion deficit in 1983 made further deliberalization necessary. In 1981, a Reagan administration proposal to lower benefits, change the retirement age, delay cost-of-living increases, and reduce family benefits for dependents and survivors was met with nearly universal opposition. To move the negotiations out of the public eye, where painful and politically unpopular choices could be agreed on, a bipartisan commission was appointed to develop proposals to deal with both short-term and long-term funding problems (Light 1985). The commission offered a compromise plan that was quickly passed by Congress and signed by President Reagan.

To summarize a complex 1983 amendment, a number of major changes were made in the direction the system was to take compared with previous decades. For the first time, Social Security benefits above specified levels were to be taxed. The age of eligibility for full retirement benefits would be extended gradually to 67 beginning in 1999, and payroll taxes would be increased along with the maximum taxable wage base. All these changes have had the desired effect: Contributions now exceed benefits paid. The long-run projection is that the surplus accrued during the next thirty years probably will balance the expected deficit when large baby boom cohorts reach retirement age (Social Security Administration 1989). The surplus, however, is by law used to purchase Treasury bonds, which fund deficits in general revenue spending. Since the bonds will have to be paid off by taxpayers through general income taxes later on, funding problems will not disappear.

The cumulative changes in the system now result in the coverage of over 90 percent of workers, who qualify for benefits by accumulating forty quarters, or ten years, of covered employment. Besides the basic benefit, a minimum benefit is available for those with long-term covered employment at low wages, a dependent's benefit at 50 percent of the spouse's benefits is available to spouses, and a survivor's benefit is available at 100 percent of the deceased spouse's benefits. Supplemental Security Income (SSI) provides cash assistance—unrelated to contributions and funded from general revenues—for needy aged, disabled, and blind persons who meet the means test. Among the elderly, 38 percent of all income comes from Social Security, and a majority of elderly persons depend on Social Security for more than half their income (Sherman 1987).

The position of the U.S. Social Security system relative to those of other nations depends on how generosity is measured. As a percentage of gross domestic product (GDP), the U.S. systems ranks quite low. Considering pensions alone, however, a measure of the benefit of a new retiree as a percentage of the wage of the average manufacturing worker ranks the United States higher. The United States falls slightly below average for single workers and slightly above average for married workers (Aldrich 1982). Part of the discrepancy stems from the concentration of public spending on pensions in the United States to the neglect of other programs. The family allowance spending and free health care for the nonaged that are common in other advanced industrial democracies are absent altogether in the United States except for need-based public assistance such as Aid to Families with Dependent Children and Medicaid. The United States provides well for those whose contributions during their work lives are high—the average retiree, in other words—but spends less in the aggregate for those who are not covered. Finally, the low percentage of the aged in the United States relative to other advanced industrial nations makes it possible to replace an above-average proportion of preretirement wages while spending a below-average fraction of GDP.

COMPARATIVE PERSPECTIVES

Many developing nations have begun to implement more formal social security systems, primarily for the benefit of urban workers and civil servants, but few of those countries have the economic resources needed to provide more than minimal coverage or protection from economic contingencies (Midgley 1984). Comparative studies have concentrated on the historical emergence and current policies of mature welfare states in advanced industrial nations.

Among the high-income democracies, substantial variation exists in spending levels and the structure of benefit distribution. Including pension, health care, occupational injury, unemployment, family allowance, public assistance, and related programs for civil servants and veterans, mean spending as a percentage of GDP in 1980 was 19 percent (International Labour Organization 1985). Nations that spend the most include Sweden (31.2 percent), the Netherlands (27.6 percent), Denmark (26.2 percent), and France (25.5 percent), and the nations that spend the least are Japan (9.8 percent), Italy (11.3 percent), Australia (11.6 percent), and the United States (12.2 percent). As was discussed above, countries also vary in the extent to which they rely on universal benefits relative to insurance or need-based benefits. According to Esping-Andersen (1989), Sweden and Norway in particular have the most equalizing social security programs; Finland, Denmark, Belgium, and the Netherlands also structure benefits on the basis of citizenship rights. The English-speaking nations and Switzerland tend to base their systems most on market-related criteria.

A comparison of the maximum and minimum benefit levels of pensions during the 1980s further illustrates important intercountry differences. In the United States, the difference between the maximum and minimum benefit is $9,900; in West Germany, it is $11,000 (Social Security Administration 1985). These figures contrast with those for nations with primarily flat-rate systems, such as Canada ($500), Denmark ($1,300), and the Netherlands ($0). Nations also differ in the frequency of adjustment for the cost of living, the ages of eligibility for early or normal retirement, the degree of retirement required for the receipt of benefits on reaching retirement age (i.e., the existence of a retirement test), and the wage ceiling for social security taxation. Scales summarizing national differences on all these dimensions provide an overview of the divergence in pensions (Day 1978; Myles 1984).

In the 1950s and 1960s, scholars predicted convergence in social security systems as advanced industrial technology spread: The standardizing effects of technology would reduce preexisting cultural and political differences among the economically developed nations. The need for a recently trained, highly educated, and geographically mobile labor force in industrial economies would make older workers superfluous to the production process. Without means of employment, the elderly would depend on government programs for economic support. In this functionalist framework, the state meets the needs of business for a differentiated labor force while simultaneously meeting the financial needs of surplus workers unable to find employment (Wilensky 1975). Hence, retirement and social security grew rapidly among all developed nations, especially in the decades after World War II.

Similar convergence in social security systems is predicted by neo-Marxist theories of monopoly capitalism. Here the focus is on the requirements of the capitalist mode of production and the power of the capitalist elite. State-sponsored insurance subsidizes the costs of the production of capital, and state-sponsored social assistance helps maintain the legitimacy of the political and economic system in the face of discontent among the superfluous population (O'Connor 1973). The standardizing force is therefore the needs of increasingly monopolized capital to maintain high profit and investment, but the consequence is still the expansion of the state in similar forms among advanced industrial nations. Partisan democratic politics play a minimal role in either the industrialist or the capitalist logic.

The fact that in contrast to the predictions of convergence theories, expenditure levels have continued to diverge across nations over the last several decades has led more recently to a number of political explanations of variation in social security. The most common explanations focus on the differential political power of labor unions across the advanced industrial democracies. In places where labor is centralized and unions have high membership, labor gains power in negotiation with capital and also can contribute to the election of socialist, social democratic, and labor parties that represent its interests. As a result, social legislation decreasing the scope of the market and emphasizing distribution based on political power emerges in areas where labor is strong and leftist parties have ruled for significant periods. In places where labor is weaker and more fragmented, rightist parties are more powerful and market-reinforcing programs with low benefits are common. Relatedly, the emergence of corporatist bargaining structures in which officially designated representatives of labor and capital negotiate economic policy with state managers has emerged in some nations—usually small nations with a strong political representation of labor. The corporatist bargain has been for labor to hold down wage demands in return for full employment and generous, redistributive welfare spending (Goldthorpe 1984).

Other theories agree with the importance of political forces in generating divergence but focus on the political activity of the aged as well as on classes (Pampel and Williamson 1989). Even among the advanced industrial nations, substantial differences in the percentage of the aged exist and appear to be related to welfare spending through both demographic and political channels. Given the same benefit level in 1980 as in 1960, aging of the population can account for only some of the observed increase in pension spending. However, the size of benefit increases over time correlates closely with the size of the elderly population. Beyond demographic effects, then, the elderly appear, at least in some countries, to be an influential political interest group in supporting higher pension and health care spending.

Others have emphasized the role of the state in divergent social security policies. Beginning with the assumption that public policies cannot be reduced to the demands and preferences of any single social group, state-based theories have examined how the structure of relatively autonomous state agencies and the interests of state managers can shape the way in which demands are expressed and translated into legislation. Qualitative studies have identified, within specific historical and national contexts, the state characteristics important for particular policy outcomes. The quantitative literature, however, has had less success relating state characteristics such as size and centralization to measures of social security spending or citizenship rights.

Any resolution of the theoretical debates and mixed empirical results will come from synthetic efforts at theory building and statistical analysis.

Class, status-demographic, political, productive, and state factors all may prove important for understanding social security system development once theories and models more clearly specify how one set of factors varies with the levels of the others. Efforts to estimate nonlinear, interactive models are under way and should prove crucial for future research (Hicks et al. 1989; Pampel et al. 1990).

CONSEQUENCES

The huge literature on the consequences of social security spending for social equality and social behavior is beyond the scope of this article. Controversy exists not so much on whether spending has an effect but on the kinds of social phenomena it most affects.

One view is that social security spending directly reduces economic inequality without substantially changing social behavior such as labor force participation, living arrangements, and savings. The major evidence in favor of redistributive consequences comes from studies that subtract transfers from total income and compare inequality with and without those transfers (Smeeding, et al. 1988). In the United States and a number of European nations, pretransfer inequality and poverty are higher than they are for posttransfer income distribution. According to the results of this methodology, expenditures for pensions are particularly egalitarian. However, advocates of this view have been less willing to accept the claim that transfers promote inequality by providing incentives to leave the labor force, in other words, by inducing behavior that indirectly contributes to higher rates of poverty and inequality. Implicitly, unemployment and low income are seen as the result of discrimination and lack of opportunities, situations that do not change with the receipt of benefits.

Other views weigh the behavioral responses to transfers as important relative to the redistributive consequences. If transfers induce labor force and living arrangement changes that make pretransfer income distribution less egalitarian than it would be if transfers were not present, the evidence of redistribution cited above would have to be seen as flawed (Danziger et al. 1981). For instance, pensions have the largest effect in reducing pretransfer inequality but also induce voluntary retirement that lowers earnings relative to what they would be without pensions or retirement benefits. Similarly, transfers increase an individual's ability to afford independent living arrangements, and this makes pretransfer income figures misleading.

Trends in poverty and inequality do not provide unambiguous evidence for either view. Certainly, the absolute income of the elderly in the United States has risen with the growth of Social Security benefits. As Social Security benefits rose dramatically in the last several decades, poverty among the aged declined from 35 percent (compared with 22 percent for the general population) in 1960 to 12 percent (compared with 13 percent for the general population) by 1987 (U.S. Bureau of the Census 1989). However, the improved economic position of the elderly also stems from the fact that recent cohorts entering old age have been better off financially and more likely to have accumulated private pensions and savings to support themselves than were previous cohorts. For overall income inequality, the trend shows little change (at least until 1980) despite the massive growth of transfers (Levy 1987). Either transfers were not redistributive or pretransfer inequality increased. Perhaps household changes, in part an indirect response to transfers, balanced the direct effects of transfers on inequality (Treas 1983). After 1980, inequality grew, but again, it is difficult to separate the effects of changes in the occupational structure from changes in real Social Security benefits for the poor and unemployed.

Comparative evidence on the relationship between social security spending and inequality across advanced industrial nations is also mixed (compare Pampel and Williamson 1989 with Esping-Andersen 1985). Nations with high spending levels and benefit structures based on citizenship rights, such as those in Scandinavia, have always had lower levels of income inequality among both the aged and the general population. However, it is difficult to establish a causal association between those levels and social security benefits across nations that differ in so many other social and economic characteristics.

Given the mixed empirical evidence, views on the redistributive consequences of the welfare state reflect theoretical assumptions about the determinants of the levels and structure of social security spending. Neo-Marxist theories of monopoly capitalism, which assume that high inequality is an inherent and necessary feature of advanced capitalism, argue that social security systems help maintain that structure rather than change it. Interest-group and neopluralist theories see middle-class, politically powerful groups as the primary recipients of most spending, which limits the extent of redistribution to the poor. Other theories claim the opposite. In industrialism theories, spending is directed at the surplus workers who are most in need. In social democratic theories, spending is directed to the working class and the poor represented by leftist parties and unions. Still others claim that the state and institutional context shapes the ability of spending to reduce inequality. As in the study of the determinants of spending, interactive or contextual studies probably will be needed to make sense of the comparative experience.

ISSUES

A number of issues or problems face policymakers who deal with social security systems. A few of these issues are reviewed briefly below. Some apply especially or primarily to the United States, while others apply to all advanced industrial nations and third world nations.

First, concern has been expressed over the inequitable treatment of women in earnings-related social security systems. When receipt of benefits for women in old age depends on the benefits of their spouses, high rates of marital breakup and widowhood make reliance on this source of financial security risky. When receipt of benefits of women in old age depends on wage contributions, discontinuous labor force participation during the childbearing years penalizes women. Universal benefits provide some support for older women, but other policy options are emerging to deal more directly with the gender-based problems. Some nations give social security contribution credits to women who leave the labor force to raise children or split the earned credits of a couple equally between the spouses. Classification of welfare state regimes needs to consider gender as a component of social rights (Orloff 1993).

Second, the improved economic position of the elderly, declining poverty rates, and higher public benefits in the 1970s and the 1980s stand in contrast to the declining real level of benefits and increasing poverty among children in the United States. The improved position of the elderly relative to children may stem from the increasing size and political power of elderly cohorts compared to the smaller cohorts of children (Preston 1984). The fact that benefits for children take the form of means-tested social assistance—a type of program that receives weak public support relative to pensions because it is not shared by large parts of the population—also contributes to this inequality. Other nations that have family allowance systems that provide cash benefits to all or nearly all parents have experienced little concern over generational equity.

Third, after decades of expansion, policymakers must face problems in balancing continued demands for more spending with limits on taxation. On the one hand, with the problems of support that still exist among vulnerable groups such as the oldest old, minority group members, and widowed women, more spending is needed. Increasingly expensive health and long-term care for the elderly and disabled add to the cost of social security systems. Despite the cost, support for pension and health care continues to be strong (Coughlin 1980). On the other hand, critics have argued that the rising costs of social security contribute to inflation and unemployment by reducing savings and productivity. Those who are more sociologically oriented suggest that high expenditures tend to weaken community and family bonds, which ultimately are the source of protection for those in need (Glazer 1988). Certainly, concern with high tax levels has led politicians to attempt to control spending and reduce taxes in nearly all advanced industrial democracies. Balancing these goals without resorting to deficit spending will remain the task of governments in the decades to come.

Fourth, concern over population aging relates to debates about controlling the cost of social security. The difficulties in meeting funding demands are likely to worsen in the next century with the entrance of large baby boom cohorts into old age. In part, this is a problem of declining fertility, which reduces the size of younger, working cohorts relative to older, retired cohorts. In the recent past, when the relative sizes of working and elderly cohorts were reversed, social security recipients were treated generously, receiving benefits worth five to six times their contributions and the accrued interest (Wolff 1987). Future retiring cohorts are not likely to experience such high returns on their contributions and are sometimes skeptical of receiving any at all. Still, funding problems for aging populations are not insurmountable. Many European nations, whose fertility levels fell faster than those of the United States, already have aged populations as large as 17 percent of the total—levels that will not be reached for thirty years in the United States. Through appropriate political and economic policies, the United States can meet the needs of its elderly population (Aaron et al. 1989).

Finally, these issues are emerging as important in third-world nations. Although the percentage of the aged in those nations is small and social security remains primarily a family rather than a state responsibility, that situation can change quickly. Rapid declines in fertility sharply increase the percentage of the aged, make family care for the elderly difficult, and generate demands for public support. With scare resources, the state may risk being overwhelmed by these demands. Public understanding of the process of building social security systems in those nations remains meager.

RECENT TRENDS

If they follow the trends of recent years, the first decades of the twenty-first century will see demands for both stability and change in social security programs in the United States. In terms of stability, major changes in the system have been difficult to legislate. In the late 1980s, Congress passed legislation to add coverage for catastrophic health care and prescriptions to Medicare by increasing taxes on the affluent elderly. The funding mechanism avoided cross-generational taxes on workers but concentrated the costs of the new benefits on a relatively small part of the aged population that already had supplemental private health care coverage. The vocal opposition of those paying the higher taxes for the new provisions led Congress to rescind the legislation shortly after the new program began. Concentrating the costs of expanded social security programs on a small group of beneficiaries did not prove successful; sharing the costs among persons of all ages and among all the recipients appears crucial to the success of any changes in social security programs.

Another major social security initiative to improve health care in the early 1990s also failed. After entering office in 1993, President William Clinton proposed a form of national health care that represented the most substantial change in American social security protection since the 1960s. The proposal did not advance a single-payer model of national health care such as those used in Canada, the United Kingdom, and many other European nations but aimed to provide universal coverage through a complex system of public and private health care delivery. Reflecting in part the suspicions of citizens of a huge change in government's role in health care as well as resistance to the change from the health and medical care professions, Congress rejected the proposed legislation.

Just as efforts to expand social security programs have failed, so have efforts to cut benefits substantially. Proposals by Republicans to control Medicare, Medicaid, and Social Security costs have met with acute resistance that has essentially blocked legislation. These examples indicate the desires of citizens for stability in most social insurance programs. Social assistance programs have, however, undergone major changes. With bipartisan political support, Aid to Families with Dependent Children has been renamed Temporary Assistance to Needy Families and now contains a work requirement for the continued receipt of benefits. The lack of change in social insurance programs and the major change in social assistance programs reflect the broad-based support for the former relative to the latter. Means-tested programs have never had the public approval enjoyed by insurance programs (Marmor et al. 1990).

In terms of demands for change, much concern remains about the long-term future of social security programs even as citizens resist short-term changes. As the baby boom generation approaches retirement age and the expected future deficit in the Social Security Fund comes closer, worries about funding have reemerged. Some economists predict serious problems. Thurow (1996, p. 46) states, "Already the needs and demands of the elderly have shaken the social welfare state, causing it for all practical purposes to go broke." Even if it is not broke, Social Security probably will provide returns on contributions to future generations of retirees that do not reach today's high levels. According to Kotlikoff (1992), those age 25 in 1989 will pay $193,000 more in taxes than they will receive in government benefits over their lifetimes; in contrast, those age 75 in 1989 will receive $42,00 more in benefits than they pay in taxes. Despite the uncertain assumptions about the future contained in these forecasts, they present a disconcerting picture. As a result of these sorts of claims, polls show that young workers doubt that Social Security will even exist when they retire (Kingson and Berkowitz 1993, p. 87).

Given future funding concerns, recent federal budget surpluses have generated a desire to "save" Social Security. Ironically, the surplus results in large part from Social Security revenues that exceed current payments and thus mask deficit spending in other parts of the government, yet the surplus has produced debate about how to proceed. Some want to return the surplus to taxpayers in the form of tax cuts that, under the assumptions of supply-side economics, will generate economic growth and make it easier to support the large baby boom population of retirees in the decades to come. Others want to use the surplus to invest in Social Security by paying off current government debt that in future decades would aggravate the problem of funding retirement benefits. No legislation has passed yet, and policies change quickly with economic and political circumstances. The consensus seems to be to use part of the federal surplus for debt reduction toward the goal of Social Security solvency. However, unexpected military costs, such as those for the Serbian–Kosovar conflict, can reduce the surplus and eliminate its use for Social Security.

An alternative approach to improving Social Security solvency in the twenty-first century is to privatize contributions. An extreme version of privatization would follow the lead of Chile in allowing individual workers to invest their contributions in private accounts that fund their own retirement. The shift from a pay-as-you-go program to a funded program would involve an enormous change in the nature of old-age benefits that would create numerous risks (Williamson 1997). A less extreme version recommended by a recent commission on Social Security would allow the government to invest some contributions in stock funds. The stunning upward movement in the stock market in the mid-1990s brought enormous returns to those with private pension investments and highlighted the low returns provided by the current system of using surplus contributions to buy government bonds. Controversy over government involvement in the stock market has, however, slowed action on the commission's recommendations.

Economists have taken the initiative in making policy recommendations for social security, while sociologists have aimed more to defend the current system against attacks. More than sociologists, economists tend to view the low rates of return on old-age contributions and the work disincentive effects of social assistance with alarm. Sociologists, in contrast, highlight the threats of privatization to social equality and universalism in public benefits (Minkler and Estes 1991), the government's role in social protection (Quadagno 1996), and the widespread sense of generational solidarity that citizens share in their attitude toward Social Security (Bengtson and Achenbaum 1993). Their contribution will continue to come from studies of the consequences of varied social security policies across the high-income nations for social equality (Esping-Andersen 1990; Korpi and Palme 1998), generational relations (Cohen 1993; Marmor et al. 1994; Myles and Quadagno 1991; Pampel 1994), and economic well-being (Rainwater and Rein 1993; Crystal and Waehrer 1996).

(SEE ALSO: *Government Regulation; Public Policy Analysis; Retirement; Social Gerontology*)

REFERENCES

Aaron, Henry J., Barry P. Bosworth, and Gary Burtless 1989 *Can America Afford to Grow Old? Paying for Social Security*. Washington D.C.: Brookings Institution.

Achenbaum, W. Andrew 1986 *Social Security: Visions and Revisions*. Cambridge, UK: Cambridge University Press.

—— 1989 "Public Pensions as Intergenerational Transfers in the United States." In Paul Johnson, Christoph Conrad, and David Thomson, eds., *Workers versus Pensioners: Intergenerational Justice in an Aging World*. Manchester, UK: Manchester University Press.

Aldrich, Jonathan 1982 "The Earnings Replacement Rate of Old-Age Benefits in Twelve Countries, 1969–80." *Social Security Bulletin* 445(12):3–11.

Bengtson, Vern L., and W. Andrew Achenbaum, eds. 1993 *The Changing Contract across Generations*. New York: Aldine de Gruyter.

Cates, Jerry R. 1983 *Insuring Inequality: Administrative Leadership in Social Security, 1935–53*. Ann Arbor: University of Michigan Press.

Cohen, Lee M., ed. 1993 *Justice across Generations: What Does it Mean?* Washington DC: Public Policy Institute, American Association of Retired Persons.

Coughlin, Richard M. 1980 *Ideology, Public Opinion, and Welfare Policy*. Berkeley: Institute of International Studies, University of California.

Crystal, Steven, and K. Waehrer, 1996 "Later-Life Economic Inequality in Longitudinal Perspective." *Journal of Gerontology: Social Sciences* 51B:S307–S318.

Danziger, Sheldon, Robert H. Haverman, and Robert Plotnick 1981 "How Income Transfer Programs Affect Work, Savings, and the Income Distribution: A Critical Review." *Journal of Economic Literature* 19:975–1028.

Day, Lincoln 1978 "Government Pensions for the Aged in Nineteen Industrialized Countries." *Comparative Studies in Sociology* 1:217–234.

Esping-Andersen, Gosta 1985 "Power and Distributional Regimes." *Politics and Society* 14:222–255.

—— 1989 "The Three Political Economies of the Welfare State." *Canadian Review of Sociology and Anthropology* 26:10–35.

—— 1990 *The Three Worlds of Welfare Capitalism*. Princeton, N.J. Princeton University Press.

Glazer, Nathan 1988 *The Limits of Social Policy*. Cambridge, Mass.: Harvard University Press.

Goldthorpe. John H. 1984 "The End of Convergence: Corporatist and Dualist Tendencies in Modern Western Societies." In John H. Goldthorpe, ed., *Order and Conflict in Contemporary Capitalism*. Oxford, UK: Clarendon.

Graebner, William 1980 *A History of Retirement*. New Haven, Conn: Yale University Press.

Hicks, Alexander, Duane Swank, and Martin Ambuhl 1989 "Welfare Expansion Revisited: Policy Routines and Their Mediation by Party, Class, and Crisis, 1959–1982." *European Journal of Political Research* 4:401–430.

International Labour Organization 1985 *The Cost of Social Security*. Geneva: International Labour Organization.

Jenkins, J. Craig, and Barbara G. Brents 1989 "Social Protest, Hegemonic Competition, and Social Reform: A Political Struggle Interpretation of the Origins of the American Welfare State." *American Sociological Review* 54:891–909.

Kingson, Eric R., and Edward D. Berkowitz 1993 *Social Security and Medicare: A Policy Primer*. Westport, Conn.: Auburn House.

Korpi, Walter 1989 "Power, Politics, and State Autonomy in the Development of Social Citizenship: Social Rights during Sickness in Eighteen Countries since 1930." *American Sociological Review* 54:309–328.

——, and Joachim Palme 1998 "The Paradox of Redistribution and Strategies of Equality: Welfare State Institutions, Inequality, and Poverty in the Western Countries." *American Sociological Review* 63:661–687.

Kotlikoff, Laurence J. 1992 *Generational Accounting: Knowing Who Pays, and When, for What We Spend*. New York: Free Press.

Levy, Frank 1987 *Dollars and Dreams: The Changing American Income Distribution*. New York: Russell Sage Foundation.

Light, Paul 1985 *Artful Work: The Politics of Social Security Reform*. New York: Random House.

Marmor, Theodore R., Jerry L. Mashaw, and Philip L. Harvey 1990 *America's Misunderstood Welfare State: Persistent Myths, Enduring Realities*. New York: Basic Books.

——, Timothy M. Smeeding, and Vernon L. Greene, eds. 1994 *Economic Security and Intergenerational Justice: A Look at North America*. Washington D.C.: Urban Institute.

Marshall, T. H. 1964 *Class, Citizenship, and Social Development*. Chicago: University of Chicago Press.

Midgley, James 1984 *Social Security, Inequality, and the Third World*. New York: Wiley.

Minkler, Meredith, and Carroll L. Estes, eds. 1991 *Critical Perspectives on Aging: The Political and Moral Economy of Growing Old*. Amityville N.Y.: Baywood.

Munnell, Alice H. 1977 *The Future of Social Security*. Washington D.C.: Brookings Institution.

Myers, Robert J. 1981 *Social Security*, Rev. ed. Homewood, Ill.: Irwin.

Myles, John 1984 *Old Age in the Welfare State: The Political Economy of Public Pensions*. Boston: Little, Brown.

——, and Jill Quadagno, eds. 1991. *States, Labor Markets, and the Future of Old Age Policy*. Philadelphia: Temple University Press.

O'Connor, James 1973 *The Fiscal Crisis of State*. New York: St. Martin's.

Organization for Economic Cooperation and Development 1988 *The Future of Social Protection*. OECD Social Policy Studies No. 6. Paris: Organization for Economic Cooperation and Development.

Orloff, Ann Shola 1993 "Gender and the Social Rights of Citizenship: The Comparative Analysis of Gender Relations and Welfare States." *American Sociological Review* 58:303–328.

——, and Theda Skocpol 1984 "Why Not Equal Protection? Explaining the Politics of Public Social Spending in Britain, 1900–1911, and the United States, 1880–1920s." *American Sociological Review* 49:725–750.

Pampel, Fred C. 1994 "Population Aging, Class Context, and Age Inequality in Public Spending." *American Journal of Sociology* 100:153–195.

——, and John B. Williamson 1989 *Age, Class, Politics, and the Welfare State*. Cambridge, UK: Cambridge University Press.

——, ——, and Robin Stryker 1990 "Class Context and Pension Response to Demographic Structure." *Social Problems* 37:535–550.

Preston, Samuel H. 1984 "Children and the Elderly: Divergent Paths for America's Dependents." *Demography* 21:435–457.

Quadagno, Jill S. 1984 "Welfare Capitalism and the Social Security Act of 1935." *American Sociological Review* 49:632–647.

—— 1988 *The Transformation of Old Age Security: Class and Politics in the American Welfare State*. Chicago: University of Chicago Press.

—— 1996 "Social Security and the Myth of the Entitlement Crisis." *The Gerontologist* 36:391–399.

Rainwater, Lee, and Martin Rein 1993 "Comparing Economic Well-Being of Older Men in Six Countries." In A. B. Atkinson and Martin Rein, eds., *Age, Work and Social Security*. New York: St. Martins.

Rimlinger, Gaston 1971 *Welfare Policy and Industrialization in Europe, America, and Russia*. Toronto: Wiley.

Schulz, James 1988 *The Economics of Aging*. Dover, Mass.: Auburn House.

Sherman, Sally R. 1987 "Fast Facts and Figures about Social Security." *Social Security Bulletin* 50(5):5–25

Simmons, Leo 1960 "Aging in Preindustrial Societies." In Clark Tibbits, ed., *Handbook of Social Gerontology*. Chicago: University of Chicago Press.

Skocpol, Theda, and John Ikenberry 1983 "The Political Formation of the American Welfare State in Historical and Comparative Perspective." *Comparative Social Research* 6:87–148.

Smeeding, Timothy, Barbara Boyle Torrey, and Martin Rein 1988 "Patterns of Income and Poverty: The Economic Status of Children and the Elderly in Eight Countries." In John L. Palmer, Timothy Smeeding, and Barbara Boyle Torrey, eds., *The Vulnerable*. Washington D.C.: Brookings Institution.

Stephens, John D. 1979 *The Transformation from Capitalism to Socialism*. London: Macmillan.

Social Security Administration 1985 *Social Security throughout the World*. Washington D.C. U.S. Government Printing Office.

——— 1989 "Actuarial Status of the OASI and DI Trust Funds." *Social Security Bulletin* 52(6):2–7.

Thurow, Lester C. 1996 *The Future of Capitalism*. New York: William Morrow.

Tomasson, Richard F. 1984 "Government Old Age Pensions under Affluence and Austerity: West Germany, Sweden, the Netherlands, and the United States." *Research in Social Problems and Public Policy* 3:217–272.

Treas, Judith 1983 "Trickle-Down or Transfers? Postwar Determinants of Family Income Inequality." *American Sociological Review* 48:546–559.

U.S. Bureau of the Census 1989 *Statistical Abstract*. Washington D.C.: U.S. Government Printing Office.

Wilensky, Harold 1975 *The Welfare State and Equality*. Berkeley: University of California Press.

Williamson, John B. 1997 "A Critique of the Case for Privatizing Social Security." *The Gerontologist* 37:561–571.

———, Linda Evans, and Lawrence Powell 1982 *The Politics of Aging*. Springfield, Ill.: Charles C Thomas.

Wolff, Nancy 1987 *Income Redistribution and the Social Security Program*. Ann Arbor: University of Michigan Press.

FRED C. PAMPEL

SOCIAL STRATIFICATION

In all complex societies, the total stock of valued resources is distributed unequally, with the most privileged individuals and families receiving a disproportionate share of power, prestige, and other valued resources. The term "stratification system" refers to the constellation of social institutions that generate observed inequalities of this sort. The key components of such systems are (1) the institutional processes that define certain types of goods as valuable and desirable, (2) the rules of allocation that distribute those goods across various positions or occupations (e.g., doctor, farmer, "housewife"), and (3) the mobility mechanisms that link individuals to positions and generate unequal control over valued resources. The inequality of modern systems is thus produced by two conceptually distinct types of "matching" processes: The jobs, occupations, and social roles in society are first matched to "reward packages" of unequal value, and the individual members of society then are allocated to the positions defined and rewarded in that manner.

There are, of course, many types of rewards that come to be attached to social roles (see Table 1). The very complexity of modern reward systems arguably suggests a multidimensional approach to understanding stratification in which analysts specify the distribution of each of the valued goods listed in Table 1. Although some scholars have advocated a multidimensional approach of this sort, most have opted to characterize stratification systems in terms of discrete classes or strata whose members are similarly advantaged or disadvantaged with respect to various assets (e.g., property and prestige) that are deemed fundamental. In the most extreme versions of this approach, the resulting classes are assumed to be real entities that predate the distribution of rewards, and many scholars therefore refer to the "effects" of class on the rewards that class members control (see the following section for details).

The goal of stratification research has thus devolved to describing the structure of these social classes and specifying the processes by which they are generated and maintained. The following types of questions are central to the field:

1. What are the major forms of class inequality in human history? Is such inequality an inevitable feature of human life?

2. How many social classes are there? What are the principal "fault lines" or social cleavages that define the class structure? Are those cleavages strengthening or weakening with the transition to advanced industrialism?

3. How frequently do individuals cross occupational or class boundaries? Are educational degrees, social contacts, and "individual luck" important forces in matching individuals to jobs and class positions? What other types of social or institutional forces underlie occupational attainment and allocation?

Types of Assets, Resources, and Valued Goods Underlying Stratification Systems

Asset Group	Selected Examples	Relevant
1. Economic	Ownership of land, farms, factories, professional practices, businesses, liquid assets, humans (i.e., slaves), labor power (e.g., serfs)	Karl Marx, Erik Wright
2. Political	Household authority (e.g., head of household); workplace authority (e.g., manager); party and societal authority (e.g., legislator); charismatic leader	Max Weber, Ralf Dahrendorf
3. Cultural	High-status consumption practices; "good manners"; privileged lifestyle	Pierre Bourdieu, Paul DiMaggio
4. Social	Access to high-status social networks, social ties, associations and clubs, union memberships	W. Lloyd Warner, James Coleman
5. Honorific	Prestige; "good reputation"; fame; deference and derogation; ethnic and religious purity	Edward Shils, Donald Treiman
6. Civil	Rights of property, contract, franchise, and membership in elective assemblies; freedom of association and speech	T H. Marshall, Rogers Brubaker
7. Human	Skills; expertise; on-the-job training; experience; formal education; knowledge	Kaare Svalastoga, Gary Becker

Table 1

4. What types of social processes and state policies maintain or alter racial, ethnic, and sex discrimination in labor markets? Have these forms of discrimination been weakened or strengthened in the transition to advanced industrialism?

5. Will stratification systems take on new and distinctive forms in the future? Are the stratification systems of modern societies gradually shedding their distinctive features and converging toward a common (i.e., postindustrial) regime?

These questions all adopt a critical orientation to human stratification systems that is distinctively modern in its underpinnings. For the greater part of history, the existing stratification order was regarded as an immutable feature of society, and the implicit objective of commentators was to explain or justify that order in terms of religious or quasi-religious doctrines. During with the Enlightenment, critical "rhetoric of equality" gradually emerged and took hold, and the civil and legal advantages of the aristocracy and other privileged status groupings were accordingly challenged. After these advantages were largely eliminated in the eighteenth and nineteenth centuries, that egalitarian ideal was extended and recast to encompass not only such civil assets voting rights but also economic assets in the form of land, property, and the means of production. In its most radical form, this economic egalitarianism led to Marxist interpretations of human history, and it ultimately provided the intellectual underpinnings for socialism. While much of stratification theory has been formulated in reaction against these early forms of Marxist scholarship, the field shares with Marxism a distinctively modern (i.e., Enlightenment) orientation that is based on the premise that individuals are "ultimately morally equal" (see Meyer 1994, p. 733; see also Tawney 1931). This premise implies that issues of inequality are critical in evaluating the legitimacy of modern social systems.

BASIC CONCEPTS

The five questions outlined above cannot be addressed adequately without first defining some of the core concepts in the field. The following definitions are especially relevant:

1. The degree of *inequality* in a given reward or asset (e.g., civil rights) depends on its dispersion or concentration across the individuals in the population. Although many scholars attempt to capture the overall level of societal inequality in a single parameter, such attempts obviously are compromised insofar as some types of rewards are distributed more equally than others are.

2. The *rigidity* of a stratification system is characterized by the continuity over time in the social standing of its members. If the current wealth, power, or prestige of individuals can be predicted accurately on the basis of their prior statuses or those of their parents, then there is much class reproduction and the stratification system is accordingly said to be rigid.

3. The process of stratification is *ascriptive* to the extent that traits present at birth (e.g., sex, race, ethnicity, parental wealth, nationality) influence the subsequent social standing of individuals. In modern societies, ascription of all kinds usually is seen as undesirable or "discriminatory," and much state policy is therefore directed toward fashioning a stratification system in which individuals acquire resources solely by means of their own achievements.

4. The degree of *status crystallization* is characterized by the correlations among the assets listed in Table 1. If these correlations are strong, the same individuals (i.e., the "upper class") will consistently appear at the top of all status hierarchies, while other individuals (i.e., the "lower class") will consistently appear at the bottom of the stratification system.

These four variables can be used to characterize differences across societies in the underlying structure of stratification. As the discussion below reveals, there is great cross-societal variability not only in the types of inequality that serve as the dominant stratifying forces but also in the extent of such inequality and the processes by which it is generated, maintained, and reduced.

FORMS OF STRATIFICATION

It is useful to begin with the purely descriptive task of classifying the various types of stratification systems that have appeared in past and present societies. Although the staple of modern classification efforts has been the tripartite distinction between class, caste, and estate (e.g., Svalastoga 1965), there is also a long tradition of Marxian typological work that introduces the additional categories of primitive communism, slave society, and socialism (Marx [1939] 1971; Wright 1985). As is shown in

Table 2, these conventional approaches are largely but not entirely complementary, and it is therefore possible to fashion a hybrid classification that incorporates most of the standard distinctions (see Kerbo 1991 for related work).

For each of the stratification forms listed in Table 2, it is conventionally assumed that certain types of assets emerge as the dominant stratifying forces (see column 2) constitute the major axis around which social classes, strata, or status groupings are organized (see column 3). If this assumption holds, the rigidity of stratification systems can be indexed by the amount of class persistence (see column 5) and the degree of crystallization can be indexed by the correlation between class membership and each of the assets listed in Table 1 (see column 6). The final column in Table 2 rests on the further assumption that stratification systems have reasonably coherent ideologies that legitimate the rules and criteria by which individuals are allocated to positions in the class structure (see column 7).

The first panel in Table 2 pertains to the "primitive" tribal systems that dominated human society from the beginning of human evolution until the Neolithic revolution of 10,000 years ago. Although tribal societies assumed various forms, the total size of the distributable surplus was in all cases limited, and this cap on the surplus placed corresponding limits on the overall level of economic inequality. Also, customs such as gift exchange, food sharing, and exogamy were practiced commonly in tribal societies and had some redistributive effects. In fact, many observers (e.g., Marx [1939] 1971) treated these societies as examples of "primitive communism," since the means of production (e.g., tools and land) were owned collectively and other types of property were distributed evenly among tribal members. This does not mean that a perfect equality prevailed; after all, the more powerful medicine men (i.e., shamans) often secured a disproportionate share of resources, and the tribal chief could exert considerable influence on political decisions. However, these residual forms of power and privilege were never inherited directly and typically were not allocated in accordance with such simple ascriptive traits as ethnicity, race, or clan. The main pathway to political office or high status and prestige was through superior skills in hunting, magic, or leadership (see Lenski 1966 for further details). While

Basic Parameters of Stratification for Eight Ideal-Typical Systems

System (1)	Principal Assets (2)	Major Strata or Classes (3)	Inequality (4)	Rigidity (5)	Crystallization (6)	Justifying Ideology (7)
A. Hunting and gathering society 1. Tribalism	Human (hunting and magic skills)	Chiefs, shamans, and other tribe members	Low	Low	High	Meritocratic selection
B. Horticultural and agrarian society 2. Asiatic mode	Political (i.e., incumbency of state office)	Officeholders and peasants	High	Medium	High	Tradition and religious doctrine
3. Feudalism	Economic (land and labor power)	Nobility, clergy, and commoners	High	Medium-high	High	Tradition and Roman Catholic doctrine
4. Slavery	Economic (human property)	Slave owners, slaves, "free men"	High	Medium-high	High	Doctrine of natural and social inferiority (of slaves)
5. Caste society	Honorific and cultural (ethnic purity and "pure" lifestyles)	Castes and subcastes	High	High	High	Tradition and Hindu religious doctrine

C. Industrial society
  6. Class
     system
	Economic
	(means of production)
		Capitlaists and
		workers
			Medium-high	Medium	High	Classical
						liberalism

7. State socialism	Political (party and workplace authority)	Managers and managed	Low-medium	Low-medium	High	Marxism and Leninism
8. "Advanced" industrialism	Human (i.e., education, expertise)	Skill-based occupational groupings	Medium	Low-medium	Medium	Classical liberalism

Table 2

meritocratic forms of allocation often are seen as prototypically modern, they were present in an incipient form at very early stages of societal development.

With the emergence of agrarian forms of production, the economic surplus became large enough to support more complex systems of stratification. The "Asiatic mode," which some commentators regard as a precursor of advanced agrarianism, is characterized by (1) the absence of strong legal institutions recognizing private property rights (with village life taking on a correspondingly communal character), (2) a state elite that extracts the surplus agricultural production through rents or taxes and expends it on "defense, opulent living, and the construction of public works" (Shaw 1978, p. 127), and (3) a constant flux in elite personnel

resulting from "wars of dynastic succession and wars of conquest by nomadic warrior tribes" (O'Leary 1989, p. 18). This mode thus provides the conventional example of how a "dictatorship of officialdom" can flourish in the absence of private property and a well-developed proprietary class. The parallel with modern socialism looms so large that various scholars have suggested that Marx downplayed the Asian case for fear of exposing it as a "parable for socialism" (Gouldner 1980, pp. 324–352).

Whereas the institution of private property was underdeveloped in the East, the ruling class under Western feudalism was very much a propertied one. The distinctive feature of feudalism was the institution of personal bondage; that is, the nobility not only owned large estates, farms, or manors but also held legal title to the labor power of its serfs (Table 2, line B3). If a serf fled to the city, this was considered a form of theft: the serf was stealing the portion of his or her labor power owned by the lord (Wright 1985, p. 78). As such, the statuses of serf and slave differ only in degree, with slavery constituting the "limiting case" in which workers lose all control over their own labor power (line B4). At the same time, it would be a mistake to reify this distinction, since the history of agrarian Europe reveals "almost infinite gradations of subordination" (Bloch 1961, p. 256) that blur the conventional dividing lines between slavery, serfdom, and freedom. While the slavery of Roman society provides the best example of complete subordination, some slaves in the early feudal period were bestowed with "rights" of real consequence (e.g., the right to sell surplus product), and some nominally free men were obliged to provide rents or services to a manorial lord. The social classes that emerged under European agrarianism thus were structured in quite diverse ways, but in all cases rights of property ownership were firmly established and the life chances of individuals were defined largely by their control over property in its differing forms. Unlike the ideal-typical Asiatic case, the nation-state was peripheral to the feudal stratification system, since the means of production (i.e., land and humans) were controlled by a proprietary class that emerged independently of the state.

The historical record shows that agrarian stratification systems were not always based on strictly hereditary forms of inequality (Table 2, panel B, column 5). The case of European feudalism is especially instructive in this regard, since it suggests that stratification systems often become more rigid as the underlying institutional forms mature and take shape (Mosca 1939; Kelley 1981). Although it is well known that feudalism after the twelfth century (i.e., "classical feudalism") was characterized by a "rigid stratification of social classes" (Bloch 1961, p. 325), the feudal structure appears to have been more permeable in the period before the institutionalization of the manorial system and the associated transformation of the nobility into a legal class. In this transitionary period, access to the nobility was not legally restricted to the offspring of nobility and marriage across classes or estates was not prohibited, at least not formally. The case of ancient Greece provides a complementary example of a relatively open agrarian society. As Finley (1960) and others have noted, the condition of slavery was heritable under Greek law, yet manumission (the freeing of slaves) was so common that the slave class had to be replenished constantly with new captives secured through war or piracy.

The most extreme examples of hereditary closure are found in caste societies (Table 2, line B5). While some scholars have argued that American slavery had "caste-like features" (Berreman 1981), it is Hindu India which clearly provides the defining case of caste organization. The Indian caste system is based on (1) a hierarchy of status groupings (i.e., castes) that are ranked by ethnic purity, wealth, and access to goods or services, (2) a corresponding set of "closure rules" that forbid all forms of intercaste marriage or mobility and thus make caste membership both hereditary and permanent, (3) a high degree of physical and occupational segregation enforced by elaborate rules and rituals governing intercaste contact, and (4) a justifying ideology (Hinduism) that successfully induces the population to regard such extreme forms of inequality as legitimate and appropriate. What makes this system distinctive is not only its well-developed closure rules but also the fundamentally honorific (and noneconomic) character of the underlying social hierarchy. As is indicated in Table 2, the castes of India are ranked on a continuum of ethnic and ritual purity, with the highest positions in the system reserved for castes that prohibit behaviors that are seen as dishonorable or "polluting." In some circumstances, castes that acquired political and economic power eventually advanced in the status hierarchy, yet they usually did so after mimicking the behaviors and lifestyles of higher castes.

The defining feature of the industrial era (Table 2, panel C) has been the emergence of egalitarian ideologies and the consequent "delegitimation" of the extreme forms of stratification found in caste, feudal, and slave systems. This can be seen in the European revolutions of the eighteenth and nineteenth centuries that pitted the egalitarian ideals of the Enlightenment against the privileges of rank and the political power of the nobility. In the end, these struggles eliminated the last residue of feudal privilege, but they also made new types of inequality and stratification possible. Under the class system that ultimately emerged (line C6), the estates of the feudal era were replaced by purely economic groups (i.e., "classes") and the old closure rules based on hereditary principles were supplanted by formally meritocratic processes. The resulting classes were neither legal entities nor closed status groupings; consequently, the emergent class-based inequalities could be represented and justified as the natural outcome of economic competition among individuals with differing abilities, motivation, or moral character (i.e., "classical liberalism"). This class structure had such a clear "economic base" (Kerbo 1991, p. 23) that Marx ([1894] 1972) of course defined classes in terms of their relationship to the means of economic production. The precise contours of the industrial class structure are nonetheless a matter of continuing debate; for example, a simple ("vulgar") Marxian model focuses on the cleavage between capitalists and workers, whereas more refined Marxian and neo-Marxian models identify additional intervening or "contradictory" classes (Wright 1985) and other (non-Marxian) approaches represent the class structure as a continuous gradation of socioeconomic status or "monetary wealth and income" (Mayer and Buckley 1970, p. 15).

Regardless of the relative merits of these models, the ideology underlying the socialist revolutions of the nineteenth and twentieth centuries was explicitly Marxist. The intellectual heritage of these revolutions and their legitimating ideologies ultimately can be traced to the Enlightenment; that is, the egalitarianism of the Enlightenment was still very much in force, but now it was deployed against the economic power of the capitalist class rather than against the status and honorific privileges of the nobility. The evidence from eastern Europe and elsewhere suggests that these egalitarian ideals were only partially realized. In the immediate postrevolutionary period, factories and farms were collectivized or socialized and fiscal and economic reforms were instituted expressly to reduce income inequality and wage differentials among manual and nonmanual workers. Although these egalitarian policies subsequently were weakened or reversed through the reform efforts of Stalin and others, this does not mean that inequality on the scale of prerevolutionary society was ever reestablished among rank-and-file workers. At the same time, it has long been argued that the socialization of productive forces did not have the intended effect of empowering workers,

since the capitalist class was replaced by a "new class" of party officials and managers who continued to control the means of production and allocate the resulting social surplus. This class has been variously identified with intellectuals or the intelligentsia (e.g., Gouldner 1979), bureaucrats or managers (e.g., Rizzi 1985), and party officials or appointees (e.g., Djilas 1965). Whatever the formulation adopted, the assumption is that the working class ultimately lost out in contemporary socialist revolutions, just as it did in the so-called bourgeois revolutions of the eighteenth and nineteenth centuries.

Whereas the means of production were socialized in the revolutions in eastern Europe and the former Soviet Union, the capitalist class remained largely intact throughout the process of industrialization in the West. The old propertied class may, however, be weakening in the West and the East alike as a postindustrial service economy diffuses and technical expertise emerges as a "new form of property" (Berg 1973, p. 183). It follows that human and cultural capital may be replacing economic capital as the principal stratifying force in advanced industrial society (Table 2, line C8). According to Gouldner (1979) and others (e.g., Galbraith 1967), a dominant class of cultural elites is emerging in the West, much as the transition to state socialism allegedly generated a new class of intellectuals in the East. This does not mean that all theorists of advanced industrialism posit a grand divide between the cultural elite and a working mass. In fact, some commentators (e.g., Dahrendorf 1959, pp. 48–57) have argued that skill-based cleavages are crystallizing throughout the occupational structure, resulting in a continuous gradation or hierarchy of socioeconomic classes. In nearly all models of advanced industrial society, it is further assumed that education is the principal mechanism by which individuals are sorted into such classes, and educational institutions thus serve in this context to "license" human capital and convert it to cultural currency.

SOURCES OF STRATIFICATION

Although the preceding sketch indicates that a wide range of stratification systems emerged over the course of human history, it remains unclear whether some form of stratification or inequality is an inevitable feature of human society. In addressing this question, it is useful to consider the functionalist theory of Davis and Moore (1945), which is the best-known attempt to understand "the universal necessity which calls forth stratification in any system" (p. 242). The starting point for any functionalist approach is the premise that all societies must devise some means to motivate the best workers to fill the most important and difficult occupations. This "motivational problem" can be addressed in a variety of ways, but the simplest solution may be to construct a hierarchy of rewards (e.g., prestige, property, power) that privileges the incumbents of functionally significant positions. As noted by Davis and Moore (1945, p. 243), this amounts to setting up a system of institutionalized inequality (i.e., a "stratification system"), with the occupational structure serving as a conduit through which unequal rewards and perquisites are disbursed. The stratification system therefore may be seen as an "unconsciously evolved device by which societies insure that the important positions are conscientiously filled by the most qualified persons" (Davis and Moore 1945, p. 243). Under the Davis–Moore formulation, it is claimed that some form of inequality is needed to allocate labor efficiently, but no effort is made to specify how much inequality is sufficient for this purpose. The extreme forms of stratification found in existing societies may well exceed the "minimum . . . necessary to maintain a complex division of labor" (Wrong 1959, p. 774).

The Davis–Moore hypothesis has come under criticism from several quarters. The prevailing view among postwar commentators is that the original hypothesis cannot adequately account for inequalities in "stabilized societies where statuses are ascribed" (Wesolowski 1962, p. 31). Whenever vacancies in the occupational structure are allocated on purely hereditary grounds, there is no need to attend to the "motivational problems" that Davis and Moore (1945) emphasized, and one cannot reasonably argue that the reward system is serving its putative function of matching qualified workers to important positions. It must be recognized, however, that a purely hereditary system is rarely achieved in practice; in fact, even in the most rigid caste societies, talented and qualified individuals typically have some opportunities for upward mobility. Under the Davis–Moore formulation (1945), this slow trickle of mobility is regarded as so essential to the functioning of the social system that elaborate systems of inequality have evidently been devised to ensure that the trickle continues. Although the Davis–Moore hypothesis therefore can be used to explain stratification in societies with some mobility, the original hypothesis becomes wholly untenable in societies with complete closure (if such societies could be found).

The functionalist approach also has been criticized for neglecting the "power element" in stratification systems. It has long been argued that Davis and Moore (1945) failed "to observe that incumbents [of functionally important positions] have the power not only to insist on payment of expected rewards but to demand even larger ones" (Wrong 1959, p. 774). In this regard, the stratification system may be seen as self-reproducing: The holders of important positions can use their power to influence the distribution of resources and preserve or extend their own privileges. It would be difficult, for instance, to account fully for the advantages of feudal lords without referring to their ability to enforce their claims through moral, legal, and economic sanctions. The distribution of rewards thus reflects not only the "latent needs" of the larger society but also the balance of power among competing groups and their members.

Whereas the early debates addressed conceptual issues of this kind, subsequent researchers shifted their emphasis to constructing "critical tests" of the Davis–Moore hypothesis. This research effort continued throughout the 1970s, with some commentators reporting evidence consistent with functionalist theorizing (e.g., Cullen and Novick 1979) and others providing less sympathetic assessments (e.g., Broom and Cushing 1977). The 1980s was a period of relative quiescence, but Lenski (1994) recently reopened the debate by suggesting that "many of the internal, systemic problems of Marxist societies were the result of inadequate motivational arrangements" (p. 57). That is, Lenski argues that the socialist commitment to wage leveling made it difficult to recruit and motivate highly skilled workers, while the "visible hand" of the socialist economy could never be calibrated to mimic adequately the natural incentive of capitalist profit taking. These results lead Lenski to conclude that "successful incentive systems involve . . . motivating the best qualified people to seek the most important positions" (p. 59). It remains to be seen whether this reading of the socialist "experiments in destratification" (Lenski 1978) will generate a new round of functionalist theorizing and debate.

THE STRUCTURE OF MODERN STRATIFICATION

The recent history of stratification theory is in large part a history of debates about the contours of class, status, and prestige hierarchies in advanced industrial societies. These debates may appear to be nothing more than academic infighting, but among the participants they are treated as a "necessary prelude to the conduct of political strategy" (Parkin 1979, p. 16). For instance, considerable energy has been devoted to drawing the correct dividing line between the working class and the bourgeoisie, since the task of identifying the oppressed class is seen as a prerequisite to devising a political strategy that might appeal to it. In such mapmaking efforts, political and intellectual goals are often conflated and debates in the field are accordingly infused with more than the usual amount of scholarly contention. While these debates are complex and wide-ranging, it will suffice here to distinguish between four major schools of thought.

Marxists and Post-Marxists. The debates within the Marxist and neo-Marxist camps have been especially contentious not only as a result of such political motivations but also because the discussion of class in *Capital* (Marx [1894] 1972) is too fragmentary and unsystematic to adjudicate between competing interpretations. At the end of the third volume of *Capital*, one finds the famous fragment on "the classes" (Marx [1894] 1972, pp. 862–863), but this discussion breaks off at the point where Marx appeared to be ready to advance a formal definition of the term. It is clear, nonetheless, that his abstract model of capitalism was resolutely dichotomous, with the conflict between capitalists and workers constituting the driving force behind further social development. This simple two-class model should be viewed as an ideal type designed to capture the developmental tendencies of capitalism; after all, whenever Marx carried out concrete analyses of existing capitalist systems, he acknowledged that the class structure was complicated by the persistence of transitional classes (i.e., landowners), quasi-class groupings (e.g., peasants), and class fragments (e.g., the lumpen

proletariat). It was only with the progressive maturation of capitalism that Marx expected these complications to disappear as the "centrifugal forces of class struggle and crisis flung all *dritte Personen* [third persons] to one camp or the other" (Parkin 1979, p. 16).

The recent history of modern capitalism suggests that the class structure has not evolved in such a precise and tidy fashion. As Dahrendorf (1959) points out, the old middle class of artisans and shopkeepers has declined in relative size, yet a new middle class of managers, professionals, and nonmanual workers has expanded to occupy the vacated space. The last fifty years of neo-Marxist theorizing can be seen as the intellectual fallout from this development, with some commentators attempting to minimize its implications and others putting forward a revised mapping of the class structure that explicitly accommodates the new middle class. In the former camp, the principal tendency is to claim that the lower sectors of the new middle class are in the process of being proletarianized, since "capital subjects [nonmanual labor] . . . to the forms of rationalization characteristic of the capitalist mode of production" (Braverman 1974, p. 408). This line of reasoning suggests that the working class may gradually expand in relative size and therefore regain its earlier power.

At the other end of the continuum, Poulantzas (1974) has argued that most members of the new intermediate stratum fall outside the working class proper, since they are not exploited in the classical Marxian sense (i.e., surplus value is not extracted). This approach may have the merit of keeping the working class conceptually pure, but it reduces its size to "pygmy proportions" (see Parkin 1979, p. 19), and hence dashes the hopes of those who see workers as a viable political force in advanced industrial society. There is, then, much interest in developing class models that fall between the extremes advocated by Braverman (1974) and Poulantzas (1974). For example, the neo-Marxist model proposed by Wright (1978) describes an American working class that is acceptably large (approximately 46 percent of the labor force), yet the class mappings in this model still pay tribute to the various cleavages and divisions among workers who sell their labor power. That is, professionals are placed in a distinct "semi-autonomous class" by virtue of their control over the work process, while upper-level supervisors are located in a "managerial class" by virtue of their authority over workers (Wright 1978). The dividing lines proposed in this model thus rest on concepts (e.g., autonomy and authority relations) that once were purely the province of Weberian or neo-Weberian sociology. As Parkin (1979) puts it, "inside every neo-Marxist there seems to be a Weberian struggling to get out" (p. 25).

These early class models, which once were quite popular, have been superseded by various second-generation models that rely more explicitly on the concept of exploitation. In effect, Roemer (1988) and others (Wright 1997; Sørensen 1996) have redefined exploitation as the extraction of "rent," which refers to the excess earnings that are secured by limiting access to positions and thus artificially restricting the supply of qualified labor. If an approach of this sort is adopted, one can test for skill-based exploitation by calculating whether the cumulated lifetime earnings of skilled laborers exceed those of unskilled laborers by an amount larger than the implied training costs (e.g., school tuition and forgone earnings). In a perfectly competitive market, labor will flow to the most rewarding occupations, equalizing the lifetime earnings of workers and eliminating exploitative returns. However, when opportunities are limited by the imposition of restrictions on entry (e.g., qualifying examinations), the equilibrating flow of labor is disrupted and the potential for exploitation emerges. By implication, the working class can no longer be viewed as a wholly cohesive and unitary force, as some workers presumably have an interest in preserving and extending the institutional mechanisms (e.g., schools) that allow them to reap exploitative returns.

Weberians and Post-Weberians The rise of the "new middle class" has proved less problematic for scholars working within a Weberian framework. Indeed, the class model advanced by Weber suggests a multiplicity of class cleavages, since it equates the economic class of workers with their "market situation" in the competition for jobs and valued goods (Weber [1922] 1968, pp. 926–40). In this formulation, the class of skilled workers is privileged because its incumbents are in high demand on the labor market and because its economic power can be parlayed into high wages, job security, and an advantaged position in commodity markets (Weber [1922] 1968, pp. 927–928). At the same time, the stratification system is compli-

cated by the existence of "status groupings," which Weber saw as forms of social affiliation that can compete, coexist, or overlap with class-based groupings. Although an economic class is merely an aggregate of individuals in a similar market situation, a status grouping is defined as a community of individuals who share a style of life and interact as status equals (e.g., the nobility, an ethnic caste). In some circumstances, the boundaries of a status grouping are determined by purely economic criteria, yet Weber notes that "status honor normally stands in sharp opposition to the pretensions of sheer property" (Weber [1922] 1968, p. 932).

The Weberian approach has been elaborated and extended by sociologists attempting to understand the "American form" of stratification. In the postwar decades, American sociologists typically dismissed the Marxist model of class as overly simplistic and one-dimensional, whereas they celebrated the Weberian model as properly distinguishing between the numerous variables Marx had conflated in his approach. These scholars often disaggregated the stratification dimensions identified by Weber into a multiplicity of variables (e.g., income, education, ethnicity) and then showed that the correlations between those variables were weak enough to generate various forms of "status inconsistency" (e.g., a poorly educated millionaire). The resulting picture suggested a "pluralistic model" of stratification; that is, the class system was represented as intrinsically multidimensional, with a host of cross-cutting affiliations producing a complex patchwork of internal class cleavages. While one critic has remarked that the multidimensionalists provided a "sociological portrait of America as drawn by Norman Rockwell" (Parkin 1979, p. 604), some post-Weberians also emphasized the "seamy side" of pluralism. In fact, Lenski (1954) and others (e.g., Lipset 1959) have argued that modern stratification systems can be seen as breeding grounds for personal stress and political radicalism, since individuals with contradictory statuses may feel relatively deprived and thus support "movements designed to alter the political status quo" (Lenski 1966, p. 88). This line of research died out in the early-1970s under the force of negative and inconclusive findings (Jackson and Curtis 1972). Althoughthere has been a resurgence of theorizing about issues of status disparity and relative deprivation (e.g., Baron 1994), much of this work focuses on the generic properties of all "post modern" stratification systems rather than the allegedly exceptional features of the American case.

In recent years, the standard multidimensionalist interpretation of "Class, Status, and Party" (Weber 1946, pp. 180–95) has fallen into disfavor, and an alternative version of neo-Weberian stratification theory has gradually taken shape. This revised reading of Weber draws on the concept of social closure as defined and discussed in the essay "Open and Closed Relationships" (Weber [1922] 1968, pp. 43–46; 341–348). By social closure, Weber is referring to the processes by which groups devise and enforce rules of membership, typically with the objective of improving the position [of the group] by monopolistic tactics" (Weber [1922] 1968, p. 43). While Weber does not directly link this discussion with his other contributions to stratification theory, later commentators pointed out that social classes and status groupings are generated by simple exclusionary processes operating at the macro-structural level (e.g., Giddens 1973). Under modern industrialism, there are obviously no formal sanctions that prevent labor from crossing class boundaries, yet various institutional forces (e.g., private property, union shops) are quite effective in limiting the amount of class mobility over the life course and between generations. These exclusionary mechanisms not only "maximize claims to rewards and opportunities" among the members of closed classes (Parkin 1979, p. 44), but also provide the demographic continuity needed to generate distinctive class cultures and "reproduce common life experience over the generations" (Giddens 1973, p. 107). As is noted by Giddens (1973, pp. 107–12), barriers of this sort are not the only source of "class structuration," yet they clearly play a contributing role in the formation of identifiable classes under modern industrialism. This revisionist interpretation of Weber has reoriented the discipline toward examining the causes and sources of class formation rather than the potentially fragmenting effects of cross-cutting affiliations and cleavages.

Gradational Status Groupings The theorists discussed above have all proceeded by mapping individuals or families into mutually exclusive and exhaustive categories ("classes"). As this review indicates, there continues to be much debate about the location of the boundaries separating these categories, yet the shared assumption is that fundamental class boundaries of some kind are present, if only in a latent or incipient form. By contrast, the implicit claim underlying gradational approaches is that such "dividing lines" are largely the construction of overzealous sociologists and that the underlying structure of modern stratification can be more closely approximated with gradational measures of income, status, or prestige. The standard concepts of class action and consciousness are similarly discarded; that is, whereas most categorical models are based on the (realist) assumption that the constituent categories are "structures of interest that provide the basis for collective action" (Wright 1979, p. 7), gradational models usually are represented as taxonomic or statistical classifications of purely heuristic interest.

This approach has been pursued in various ways, but typically not by operationalizing social standing in terms of income alone. It does not follow that distinctions of income are sociologically uninteresting; in fact, if one is intent on assessing the "market situation" of workers (Weber [1922] 1968), there is much to recommend a direct measurement of their income and wealth. The preferred approach has nonetheless been to define classes as "groups of persons who are members of effective kinship units which, as units, are approximately equally valued" (Parsons 1954, p. 77). This formulation was first operationalized in postwar community studies (e.g., Warner 1949) by constructing broadly defined categories of reputational equals ("upper upper class," "upper middle class," etc.). However, when the disciplinary focus shifted to the national stratification system, the measure of choice soon became occupational scales of prestige (e.g., Treiman 1977), socioeconomic status (e.g., Blau and Duncan 1967), or global "success in the labor market" (Jencks et al. 1988). Although there is much debate about the usefulness of such scales, they continue to serve as standard measures of class background in sociological research of all kinds.

GENERATING STRATIFICATION

The language of stratification theory makes a sharp distinction between the distribution of social rewards (e.g., the income distribution) and the distribution of opportunities for securing those rewards. As sociologists have noted, it is the latter distribution that governs popular judgments about the legitimacy of stratification: the typical American, for example, is willing to tolerate substantial inequalities in power, wealth, or prestige if the opportunities for securing those social goods are distributed equally across all individuals. Whatever the wisdom of this popular logic, stratification researchers have long explored its factual underpinnings by describing and explaining the structure of mobility chances.

The study of social mobility is, then, a major sociological industry. The relevant literature is vast, yet much of this work can be classified into one of three traditions of scholarship.

1. The conventional starting point has been to analyze bivariate "mobility tables" formed by cross-classifying the occupational origins and destinations of individuals. These tables can be used to estimate the densities of occupational inheritance, describe patterns of mobility and exchange between occupations, and map the social distances between classes and their constituent occupations. Moreover, when comparable mobility tables are assembled for several countries, it becomes possible to address long-standing debates about the underlying contours of cross-national variation in stratification systems (e.g., Erikson and Goldthorpe 1992).

2. It is a sociological truism that Blau and Duncan (1967) and their colleagues (e.g., Sewell et al. 1969) revolutionized the field with their formal "path models" of stratification. These models were intended to represent, if only partially, the process by which background advantages can be converted into socioeconomic status through the mediating variables of schooling, aspirations, and parental encouragement. Under formulations of this kind, the main sociological objective was to show that socioeconomic outcomes are structured not only by "native ability" and family origins but also by various intervening variables (e.g., schooling) that are themselves only partly determined by origins, race and gender, and other ascriptive forces (Blau and Duncan 1967, pp. 199–205). This line of research, which

had fallen out of favor by the mid-1980s, has been rediscovered and revived as stratification scholars react to the now-fashionable argument (i.e., Herrnstein and Murray 1994) that inherited intelligence is increasingly determinative of stratification outcomes.

3. These "status attainment" models have been criticized for failing to attend to the social structural constraints that operate on the stratification process independently of individual-level traits. The structuralist accounts that ultimately emerged from these critiques amounted in most cases to refurbished versions of the dual economy and market segmentation models that were introduced and popularized several decades ago by institutional economists. When these models were redeployed by sociologists in the early 1980s, the usual objective was to demonstrate that women and minorities were disadvantaged not only because of deficient investments in human capital (e.g., inadequate schooling and experience) but also by their consignment to "secondary" labor markets that on average paid lower wages and offered fewer opportunities for promotion or advancement.

These three approaches to stratification analysis typically are implemented with quantitative models of the most sophisticated sort. In a classic critique, Coser (1975) suggested that stratification researchers were so entranced by quantitative models of mobility, attainment, and dissimination that "the methodological tail was wagging the substantive dog" (p. 652). This latter argument can no longer be taken exclusively in the intended pejorative sense because new models and methods have raised important substantive questions that previously had been overlooked. In this sense, The development of structural equation, log-linear, and event history models are properly viewed as watershed events in the history of mobility research.

ASCRIPTIVE PROCESSES

The forces of race and gender have long been relegated to the sociological sidelines by class theorists of both Marxist and non-Marxist persuasions. In most versions of class-analytic theory, status groups are treated as secondary forms of affiliation, whereas class-based ties are seen as more fundamental and decisive determinants of social and political action. Although Race and gender have not been ignored altogether in such treatments, they typically are represented as vestiges of traditional loyalties that will wither away under the rationalizing influence of socialism, industrialism, or modernization.

The first step in the intellectual breakdown of this model was the fashioning of a multidimensional approach to stratification. Whereas many class theorists gave theoretical or conceptual priority to the economic dimension of stratification, the early multidimensionalists emphasized that social behavior could be understood only by taking into account all status group memberships (e.g., race, gender) and the complex ways in which they interact with one another and with class outcomes. The class-analytic approach was further undermined by the apparent reemergence of racial, ethnic, and nationalist conflicts in the late postwar period. Far from withering away under the force of industrialism, the bonds of race and ethnicity seemed to be alive and well: The modern world was witnessing a "sudden increase in tendencies by people in many countries and many circumstances to insist on the significance of their group distinctiveness" (Glazer and Moynihan 1975, p. 3). This resurgence of status politics continues today. In one last several decades, ethnic and regional solidarities have intensified with the decline of conventional class politics in central Europe and elsewhere, and gender-based affiliations and loyalties have strengthened as feminist movements diffuse throughout much of the modern world.

This turn of events has led some commentators to proclaim that the factors of race, ethnicity, and gender are now the driving force behind the evolution of stratification systems. In one such formulation, Glazer and Moynihan (1975) conclude that "property relations [formerly] obscured ethnic ones" (p. 16), but now it is "property that begins to seem derivative, and ethnicity that becomes a more fundamental source of stratification" (p. 17). The analogous position favored by some feminists is that "men's dominance over women is the cornerstone on which all other oppression (class, age, race) rests" (Hartmann 1981, p. 12; see also Firestone 1972). This formulation

begs the question of timing; that is, if the forces of gender or ethnicity are truly primordial, it is natural to ask why they began expressing themselves with real vigor in more recent history. In addressing this issue, Bell (1975) suggests that a trade-off exists between class-based and ethnic forms of solidarity, with the latter strengthening whenever the former weaken. As the conflict between labor and capital is institutionalized (via "trade unionism"), Bell argues, class-based affiliations typically lose their affective content and workers must turn to racial or ethnic ties to provide them with a renewed sense of identification and commitment. It could be argued that gender politics often fill the same "moral vacuum" that this decline in class politics has allegedly generated.

It may be misleading to treat the competition between ascriptive and class-based forces as a sociological horse race that only one of the two principles can ultimately win. In a pluralist society of the American kind, workers can choose an identity appropriate to the situational context; a modern-day worker may behave as "an industrial laborer in the morning, a black in the afternoon, and an American in the evening" (Parkin 1979, p. 34). Although this situational model of status has not been adopted widely in contemporary research, there is some evidence of renewed interest in conceptualizing the diverse affiliations of individuals and the "multiple oppressions" (see Wright 1989, pp. 5–6) that those affiliations engender. It is now fashionable, for example, to assume that the major status groupings in contemporary stratification systems are defined by the intersection of ethnic, gender, and class affiliations (e.g., black working-class women, white middle-class men). The theoretical framework for this approach is not always well articulated, but the implicit claim seems to be that these subgroupings shape the "life chances and experiences" of individuals (Ransford and Miller 1983, p. 46) and thus define the social settings in which subcultures typically emerge. The obvious effect is to invert the traditional post-Weberian perspective on status groupings; that is, whereas orthodox multidimensionalists described the stress experienced by individuals with inconsistent statuses (e.g., poorly educated doctors), the new multidimensionalists emphasize the shared interests and cultures generated within commonly encountered status sets (e.g., black working-class women).

The sociological study of gender, race, and ethnicity has thus burgeoned. As is noted by Lieberson (1994, p. 649), there has been a certain faddishness in the types of research topics that scholars of gender and race have chosen for study, with the resulting body of literature having a correspondingly haphazard and scattered feel. The following research questions have nonetheless emerged as relatively central ones in the field:

1. How are class relations affected by ascriptive forms of stratification? Can capitalists exploit ethnic antagonisms and patriarchy to their advantage? Do male and majority group workers also benefit from stratification by gender and race?

2. What accounts for variability across time and space in ethnic conflict and solidarity? Will ethnic loyalties weaken as modernization diffuses across ethnically diverse populations? Does modernization instead produce a "cultural division of labor" that strengthens communal ties by making ethnicity the principal arbiter of life chances? Is ethnic conflict further intensified when ethnic groups compete for the same niche in the occupational structure?

3. What are the generative forces underlying ethnic, racial, and gender differentials in income and other socioeconomic outcomes? Do those differentials proceed from supply-side variability in the occupational aspirations or the human capital workers bring to the market? Alternatively, are they produced by demand-side forces such as market segmentation, statistical or institutional discrimination, and the seemingly irrational tastes and preferences of employers?

4. Is the underlying structure of ascriptive stratification changing with the transition to advanced industrialism? Does the "logic" of industrialism require universalistic personnel practices and consequent declines in overt discrimination? Can this logic be reconciled with the rise of a modern ghetto underclass, the persistence of massive segregation by sex and race, and the emergence of new forms of poverty and hardship among women and recent immigrants?

These questions make it clear that ethnic, racial, and gender inequalities often are classed together and treated as analytically equivalent forms of ascription. Although Parsons (1951) and others (e.g., Tilly 1998) have emphasized the shared features of "communal ties," such ties can be maintained (or subverted) in very different ways. It has long been argued, for example, that some forms of inequality can be rendered more palatable by the practice of pooling resources (e.g., income) across family members. As Lieberson (1994) points out, the family operates to bind males and females together in a single unit of consumption, whereas extrafamilial institutions (schools, labor markets, etc.) must be relied on to provide the same integrative functions for ethnic groups. If these functions are left wholly unfilled, one might expect ethnic separatist and nationalist movements to emerge. The same "nationalist" option is obviously less viable for single-sex groups; indeed, barring any revolutionary changes in family structure or kinship relations, it seems unlikely that separatist solutions will ever garner much support among men or women. These considerations may account for the absence of a well-developed literature on overt conflict between single-sex groups.

CONCLUSIONS

In recent years, criticisms of the class-analytic framework have escalated, with many scholars arguing that the concept of class is "ceasing to do any useful work for sociology" (Pahl 1989, p. 710). Although such postmodern accounts have taken many forms, most proceed from the assumption that social classes no longer definitively structure lifestyles and life chances and that "new theories, perhaps more cultural than structural, [are] in order" (Davis 1982, p. 585). In accounts of this sort, the labor movement is represented as a fading enterprise rooted in the old conflicts of the workplace and industrial capitalism, whereas new social movements (e.g., environmentalism) are assumed to provide a more appealing call for collective action by virtue of their emphasis on issues of lifestyle, personal identity, and normative change.

This argument has not been subjected to convincing empirical tests and may prove to be premature. However, even if lifestyles and life chances are truly "decoupling" from economic class, this should not be misunderstood as a more general decline in stratification per se. The massive facts of economic, political, and honorific inequality will still be operative even if conventional models of class ultimately are found deficient in characterizing the postmodern condition. As is well known, some forms of inequality have increased in recent years (e.g., income inequality), while others show no signs of disappearing or withering away (e.g., political inequality).

This persistence and in some cases deepening of inequality is coupled with the continuing diffusion of antistratification values and a correspondingly heightened sensitivity to all things unequal. As egalitarianism spreads, the postmodern public becomes heavily involved in monitoring and exposing illegitimate (i.e., nonmeritocratic) forms of stratification, and even small departures from equality are increasingly viewed as problematic and intolerable (Meyer 1994). Moreover, because stratification systems are deeply institutionalized, there is good reason to anticipate that demands for egalitarian change will outpace actual changes in stratification practices. These dynamics imply that issues of stratification will continue to generate discord and conflict even in the unlikely event of a long-term trend toward diminishing inequality.

REFERENCES

Baron, James N. 1994 "Reflections on Recent Generations of Mobility Research." In David B. Grusk, ed., *Social Stratification: Class, Race, and Gender in Sociological Perspective*. Boulder, Colo.: Westview.

Bell, Daniel 1975 "Ethnicity and Social Change." In Nathan Glazer and Daniel P. Moynihan, eds., *Ethnicity: Theory and Experience*. Cambridge, Mass.: Harvard University Press.

Berg, Ivar 1973 *Education and Jobs: The Great Training Robbery*. Harmondsworth, UK: Penguin.

Berreman, Gerald 1981 *Caste and Other Inequities*. Delhi: Manohar.

Blau, Peter M., and Otis Dudley Duncan 1967 *The American Occupational Structure*. New York: Wiley.

Bloch, Marc 1961 *Feudal Society*. London: Routledge and Kegan Paul.

Braverman, Harry 1974 *Labor and Monopoly Capital*. New York and London: Monthly Review Press.

Broom, Leonard, and Robert G. Cushing 1977 "A Modest Test of an Immodest Theory: The Functional Theory of Stratification." *American Sociological Review* 42:157–169.

Coser, Lewis A. 1975 "Presidential Address: Two Methods in Search of a Substance." *American Sociological Review* 40:691–700.

Cullen, John B., and Shelley M. Novick 1979 "The Davis-Moore Theory of Stratification: A Further Examination and Extension." *American Journal of Sociology* 84:1424–1437.

Dahrendorf, Ralf 1959 *Class and Class Conflict in Industrial Society*. Stanford, Calif.: Stanford University Press.

Davis, James 1982 "Achievement Variables and Class Cultures: Family, Schooling, Job, and Forty-Nine Dependent Variables in the Cumulative GSS." *American Sociological Review* 47:69–86.

Davis, Kingsley, and Wilbert E. Moore 1945 "Some Principles of Stratification." *American Sociological Review* 10:242–249.

Djilas, Milovan 1965 *The New Class*. New York: Praeger.

Erikson, Robert, and John H. Goldthorpe 1992 *The Constant Flux: A Study of Class Mobility in Industrial Societies*. Oxford, UK: Clarendon Press.

Finley, Moses J. 1960 *Slavery in Classical Antiquity*. Cambridge, UK: W. Heffer and Sons.

Firestone, Shulamith 1972 *The Dialectic of Sex*. New York: Bantam.

Galbraith, John K. 1967 *The New Industrial State*. Boston: Houghton Mifflin.

Giddens, Anthony 1973 *The Class Structure of the Advanced Societies*. London: Hutchinson.

Glazer, Nathan, and Daniel P. Moynihan 1975 "Introduction." In Nathan Glazer and Daniel P. Moynihan, eds., *Ethnicity: Theory and Experience*. Cambridge, Mass.: Harvard University Press.

Gouldner, Alvin 1979 *The Future of Intellectuals and the Rise of the New Class*. New York: Seabury.

—— 1980 *The Two Marxisms: Contradictions and Anomalies in the Development of Theory*. New York: Seabury Press.

Hartmann, Heidi 1981 "The Unhappy Marriage of Marxism and Feminism: Towards a More Progressive Union." In Lydia Sargent, ed., *Women and Revolution*. Boston: South End Press.

Herrnstein, Richard J., and Charles Murray 1994 *The Bell Curve: Intelligence and Class Structure in American Life*. New York: Free Press.

Jackson, Elton F., and Richard. F. Curtis 1972 "Effects of Vertical Mobility and Status Inconsistency: A Body of Negative Evidence." *American Sociological Review* 37:701–13.

Jencks, Christopher, Lauri Perman, and Lee Rainwater 1988 "What Is a Good Job? A New Measure of Labor-

Market Success." *American Journal of Sociology* 93:1322–1357.

Kelley, Jonathan 1981 *Revolution and the Rebirth of Inequality*. Berkeley: University of California Press.

Kerbo, Harold R. 1991 *Social Stratification and Inequality: Class Conflict in Historical and Comparative Perspective*. New York: McGraw-Hill.

Lenski, Gerhard E. 1954 "Status Crystallization: A Non-Vertical Dimension of Social Status." *American Sociological Review* 19:405–413.

—— 1966 *Power and Privilege*. New York: McGraw-Hill.

—— 1978 "Marxist Experiments in Destratification: An Appraisal." *Social Forces* 57:364–383.

—— 1994 "New Light on Old Issues: The Relevance of 'Really Existing Socialist Societies' for Stratification Theory." In David B. Grusky, ed., *Social Stratification: Class, Race, and Gender in Sociological Perspective*. Boulder, Colo.: Westview.

Lieberson, Stanley 1994 "Understanding Ascriptive Stratification: Some Issues and Principles." In David B. Grusky, ed., *Social Stratification: Class, Race, and Gender in Sociological Perspective*. Boulder, Colo.: Westview Press.

Lipset, Seymour M. 1959 *Political Man: The Social Bases of Politics*. Baltimore: Johns Hopkins University Press.

Marx, Karl (1939) 1971 *The Grundrisse*. New York: Harper & Row.

—— (1894) 1972 *Capital*, 3 vols. London: Lawrence and Wishart.

Mayer, Kurt B., and Walter Buckley 1970 *Class and Society*. New York: Random House.

Meyer, John W. 1994 "The Evolution of Modern Stratification Systems." In David B. Grusky, ed., *Social Stratification: Class, Race, and Gender in Sociological Perspective*. Boulder, Colo.: Westview Press.

Mosca, Gaetano 1939 *The Ruling Class*. New York: McGraw-Hill.

O'Leary, Brendan 1989 *The Asiatic Mode of Production*. Oxford, UK: Basil Blackwell.

Pahl, R. E. 1989 "Is the Emperor Naked? Some Questions on the Adequacy of Sociological Theory in Urban and Regional Research." *International Journal of Urban and Regional Research* 13:709–720.

Parkin, Frank 1979 *Marxism and Class Theory: A Bourgeois Critique*. New York: Columbia University Press.

Parsons, Talcott 1951 *The Social System*. Glencoe, Ill.: Free Press.

—— 1954 *Essays in Sociological Theory*. Glencoe, Ill.: Free Press.

Poulantzas, Nicos 1974 *Classes in Contemporary Capitalism*. London: Verso.

Ransford, H. Edward, and Jon Miller 1983 "Race, Sex, and Feminist Outlooks." *American Sociological Review* 48:46–59.

Rizzi, Bruno 1985 *The Bureaucratization of the World*. London: Tavistock.

Roemer, John 1988 *Free to Lose*. Cambridge, Mass.: Harvard University Press.

Sewell, William H., Archibald O. Haller, and Alejandro Portes 1969 "The Educational and Early Occupational Attainment Process." *American Sociological Review* 34:82–92.

Shaw, William H. 1978 *Marx's Theory of History*. Stanford, Calif.: Stanford University Press.

Sørensen, Aage B. 1996 "The Structural Basis of Social Inequality." *American Journal of Sociology* 101:1333–1365.

Svalastoga, Kaare 1965 *Social Differentiation*. New York: D. McKay.

Tawney, R. H. 1931 *Equality*. London: George Allen and Unwin.

Tilly, Charles 1998 *Durable Inequality*. Berkeley: University of California Press.

Treiman, Donald J. 1977 *Occupational Prestige in Comparative Perspective*. New York: Academic Press.

Warner, W. Lloyd. 1949 *Social Class in America*. Chicago: Science Research Associates.

Weber, Max (1922) 1968 *Economy and Society*. Berkeley: University of California Press.

—— 1946 *From Max Weber: Essays in Sociology*, ed. and transl. by Hans Gerth and C. Wright Mills. New York: Oxford University Press.

Wesolowski, Wlodzimierz 1962 "Some Notes on the Functional Theory of Stratification." *Polish Sociological Bulletin* 3–4:28–38.

Wright, Erik O. 1978 *Class, Crisis, and the State*. London: New Left Books.

—— 1979 *Class Structure and Income Determination*. New York: Academic Press.

—— 1985 *Classes*. London: Verso.

—— 1989 *The Debate on Classes*. London: Verso.

—— 1997 *Class Counts: Comparative Studies in Class Analysis*. Cambridge, UK: Cambridge University Press.

Wrong, Dennis H. 1959 "The Functional Theory of Stratification: Some Neglected Considerations." *American Sociological Review* 24:772–782.

DAVID B. GRUSKY

SOCIAL STRUCTURE

"Social structure" is a general term for any collective social circumstance that cannot be altered by isolated actions and thus is fixed or given for the individual. It thus provides a context, environment, or fixed backdrop for action. The size of organizations, the distribution of activities in space, shared language, and the distribution of wealth all might be regarded as social structural circumstances that set limits on feasible activities for individuals.

Social structure is objective in the sense that it is the same for everyone and is beyond the capacity for alteration by any individual. Accordingly, social structure often is spoken of in the singular and as a thing apart, as if there were only one from whose effects no one can escape. This usage masks disagreement about the exact extension of the term but reflects the intention of authors to highlight abstract patterns as an inflexible collective circumstance to which individuals must adapt.

Social structure, or the weaker structural regularities, arises because of the prevalence of social routine. Many social patterns change very slowly either through unmotivated inertia, through willful efforts to renew or reproduce them, or as a collective consequence of individual efforts undertaken for independent reasons. An image or picture, such as a map colored by the linguistic practices of the inhabitants of geographic areas, will lose accuracy slowly and often would remain largely accurate after a century or more. Such substantial durability, along with the accompanying slow continuous change, suggests the possibility of regularities or even scientific laws governing the phenomena that underlie the description.

Routines endure and structural regularities persist for at least three general reasons. Social life is subject to physical constraints such as distance. Thus, most people live close to where they work or do both at one place. For related reasons, many persons maintain stable residences. Furthermore, many people need or desire the company or cooperation of representative social types, such as those who share their religious convictions, or particular work skills. Accordingly, one can associate social attributes with geographic maps. This was a central activity of the Chicago school of sociology (Park and Burgess 1924) and gave rise to the perspective of human ecology (Hawley 1986). The specialization of social types and activities in space is subject to powerful incentives that induce similarity in the face of turnover among individuals. For example, ethnic concentrations result in specialized facilities, such as food shops, that attract replacements that conserve the ethnic character. Such patterns often persist beyond the lifetimes of the people who initiated them.

A second source of routine is limited learning capacity or the complexity of many social activities. Linguistic rules, moral codes, and work skills illustrate social capacities whose acquisition requires considerable time and effort. This socialization often requires extended exposure to others who know the routines well, especially when the delicate skills of interpretation are involved.

The difficulties of acquiring capacity can confound individual wills. Bernstein (1975) described how linguistic conventions acquired in the home reflect the conditions of adult work and render individuals unsuited for occupations that are not similar to those of their parents. In the same way, a New Yorker who wished to speak in Latin would have to make a huge investment in learning a novel linguistic code. However, this would not undo the investment in English by other New Yorkers, and thus Latin would be impractical for directing taxi drivers. Similar reasons impel the adoption of the abrasive social style of New Yorkers by newcomers. The general principle is that most people must adapt to many surrounding ways of doing things because those ways change so slowly.

A third source of structural regularity is laws governing averages. An example is the suicide rates studied by Durkheim. People commit suicide for a variety of personal motives and the act is never repeated by anyone, yet the frequency of the act is fairly stable over time and thus is stably different among different populations. This is the case because variable causes tend to average into stable totals whenever many instances are drawn from constant underlying conditions. Many of the rates that result are sufficiently stable to sustain plans and projections, which in turn can be embedded in routines, even though the underlying activity is very complex in its detailed causation.

The several sources of stable routines underlie the properties that frequently are associated with proposed structural regularities. Structural regularities often are depicted as abstract, enduring, and operative across a large scale of units. These attributes reflect genesis, for many structural regularities ultimately stem from the long historical process of imposing routines that made a large scale feasible. For example, Tilly (1975) shows how the modern European state resulted from parallel decisions by state makers forced by military competition to pursue centralization by reordering the established routines of ordinary people. The history of collective contention (Tilly 1986) can be seen as the efforts of the victims to defend older patterns against intrusions by state agents such as tax collectors and against the vast reorganization of work and fortune implicit in the expansion of capitalism.

Mann (1986) argues that large-scale cooperation rests on enduring patterns of power. For example, shared religious ideology is a form of power because it makes people subject to claims on their activity. Rapid religious change is not infrequently the result of conquest. Once it has been established, religion is often compulsory. Coercion aside, religious conformity can provide insurance against the risks and pains of social isolation. Other large-scale patterns, such as the division of labor, are maintained in the face of considerable shifting by persons among different roles. This often is implemented by powerful actors who are motivated to induce (or coerce) approximate substitutes to fill in for those who withdraw (or die). In such terms, abstract stability, a large scale, and consequent duration often can be seen to be sustained through underlying causal regularities. In human terms, the reproduction of social structure consists of a myriad of modest efforts that sum to a stable result.

This interdependence underlies the transcendence of abstract structural regularity over individual will. Generally, one cannot learn more than locally applicable routines and must rely on others for critical needs. Thus, one assumes that the staff members in the emergency room will not all take the day off. This frees accountants from the necessity of acquiring medical skill to meet their own needs. As a result, the details of actual routines are known only locally, and the only possible knowledge of the overall pattern is coarse or abstract. Even accountants cannot count up the details they must count on. A further implication is that the alternatives to enacting the routines with which

one is familiar are often limited. It requires time on a historical scale to construct such a pattern. That history has happened, and if the conditions that made narrow, specialized learning practical suddenly came unglued most people would be in a terrible fix.

A special case of social routines consists of those worked out with others, who then are often hard to replace. Replacement is generally more troublesome as the duration is longer, such as many kinship bonds, which can be effectively irreplaceable for many adults. These social relations can be mapped as social networks describing the pattern of the links that surround individuals. The analysis of such patterns is not infrequently (or unreasonably) called "structural analysis," though it hardly exhausts the term.

Elaborate routines, especially social ties, are subject to pressures toward isomorphy, which is defined as a common anatomy or structure. An example is the formation of families, which are different in detail but share common features partly in response to common problems that must be solved within a shared environment. Goode (1970) analyzes the sources and consequences of such regularities. In modern societies, assumptions about such features often are written into administrative procedures such as tax codes, which provide further impetus for individuals to adopt a variant of the pattern defined as normal. Changing and varied individual desires are often in conflict with those pressures to cooperate in the reproduction of the supposedly "normal" pattern.

Emergent properties that apply to wholes but not to parts often are attributed to social structure. Some properties, such as size distributions and complexity, do not have direct individual analogues. Others arise because the net result of many partially independent actions can be different from the intentions of individuals. Thus, markets with many participants can experience crashes in value when many people try to sell in anticipation that others are about to do so, producing a result that no one desires. Kindleberger (1980) describes the recurrence of such crises. Routines are executed by fallible humans and are only locally adapted, somewhat independent, and imperfectly flexible. Many properties of the resulting averages or combinations do not follow from the components in any simple sense.

As the preceding analysis suggests, structural visions are various. One unifying theme is an appeal to abstract, extraindividual patterns that change slowly or not at all. A second unifying theme is that those regularities cause or condition many of the choices and behaviors of individuals. A final common theme is less unifying than divisive. Some structural visions are accompanied by claims of centrality. A particular array of simple elements is proclaimed, often on metatheoretical or philosophic grounds, to be the central deep structure whose inevitable unfolding underlies a vast array of surface appearances. Such comprehensive views have inspired competing, incompatible schools of thought on whose behalf a claim is sometimes made to *the* structural vision of society or the human condition.

Most of these structural visions are comprehensive worldviews that require detailed study in their own right. Among the most prominent are those of Marx and Freud, but there have been structuralist movements in nearly every field of social studies. Nearly all proceed from some highly abstract characterization of the human mind, laws of thought, or the human condition. All of social or mental life is viewed as a manifestation of the reproduction of such elements, often unfolding dialectically. This is presented as the inevitable underpinnings of individual or collective biographies. Piaget (1970) has provided an unusually concise description of an interdisciplinary structuralism based on mathematical progress; this description parallels his more famous theory of discontinuous advancement in human cognitive development. Originators and their descendants often delight in such subtle and insightful reductions of familiar patterns to the chosen central supports.

The term "structure" is most commonly employed in sociology without these all-encompassing ambitions. In empirical sociology, especially quantitative studies based on random samples of persons, the term is invoked for varied efforts to use the larger and often more durable features of social life as explanatory factors for individual conduct and outcomes. The most common contrast is with individual-level causes, including attitudes and aspirations. Sometimes attributes such as race, gender, and class are labeled structural to imply that the underlying mechanism is an external force imposed on individuals independently of their wills.

The reasoning behind this is not always explicit, but the usage is justifiable. Generally, the factors labeled structural are alternatives among a differentiated array of possibilities to which individuals are confined for substantial periods. "Structure" then refers to the differentiating average conditions in which people live their lives. At least implicitly, such differences correspond to differences in the routines employed to adapt to local conditions as well as to resources that render routines practical. Classifying people by indicators of the local conditions that surround them reflects the opportunities they have for association and hence for processes such as influence, cooperation, and victimization. Some characterizations also correspond to labels, most notably race and gender, and broadly indicate common tendencies in routines of others to which one is likely to be exposed. Such differences are quite stable, impersonal, and hard to evade. Taken together, these differences in conditions contribute to differences in average responses or individual behaviors.

There is some confusion about the nature of such structural causation, which often is framed as an alternative explanation to individual choice. Persuasive force often comes from stories in which the predominant outcome is made to feel inevitable. This is at odds with the normal empirical result of a difference in tendency or proportion. Rules that hold without exception are rare. This should be expected. Structural abstractions mask much detail that varies. The implicit reference is to averages over multiple executions of complex routines. To take an obvious example, racial discrimination involving job applicants is not invariant but occurs often enough to lead to considerable differences.

Structural causes are not literally the antithesis of individual choice. More precisely, they reflect patterns over which individuals have limited control. The binding force of structural regularity is intrinsically probabilistic. People almost invariably have options, and exceptions to regularities are somewhere in reach. However, established structure—ultimately routines acquired over time, bonds developed to particular others, and the meshed ways of doing that result—exerts a frictional tug. Friction is implicit in the pain of forgone routines and the time required to work out new ones. Such pains may be amplified when those who benefit from regularities exert their power to maintain them. On any large scale, the path of least resistance consists of acting today nearly the same way as one acted yesterday. By no means does this rule out individual exceptions, resistance, or willful alterations to parts of the overall web, but friction is cumulative. For example, the rupture and replacement of one bond are quite different from the rupturing of all bonds at once. Similarly, any single person may change jobs, although in practice only to a very limited range of alternatives, yet if all jobs were randomly reshuffled one day, nearly all would go undone, for every job would be subject to the incompetence of the "first day on the job." In summary, the frictional forces of social structure do not rule out rare and/or modest exceptions but generally ensure that wholesale, simultaneous exceptions are rare to the vanishing point.

Empirical applications generally draw on fragments of social structure that are taken as conditioning factors for particular outcomes. The larger challenge is to translate the impersonal, durable complexity of stable differences in condition into a formal calculus, or a theory of social structure. Parsons's (1951) extensive analysis of the logic of social systems was an early and seminal attempt. His student Merton, under the banner of "theories of the middle range," provided a more easily applied set of general tools for structural analysis. Several of Merton's students, including Boudon, Blau, and Coleman, further developed formal calculi for social structure that benefit from the use of mathematical tools.

Parsons's complex system begins with the conditions for stabilizing interaction or, in current terms, meshing routines. Parsons characterizes the routines that govern choice as extended chains of logic linking means to ends. At their most abstract, those chains are anchored in ultimate ends, or values. Durable stability results from consensus on the values that are installed in individuals by more or less extended socialization.

In Parsons's view, the logical chains governing decision making are morally potent norms, or rules governing social conduct. The durable web that shapes individual choice is therefore the complex of norms animated by the anchoring ultimate values. Parsons imposes on this a logical calculus of the different functions necessary for ensuring that the pattern is resistant to shocks that draw it away from equilibrium. A concomitant of this theme of differentiation is complementary specialization in distinct but interdependent expectations bundled into the social roles enacted by different players.

Parsons's calculus of the functional necessities of meshing differentiated normative specifications proved widely compelling but difficult to apply. His presentation is notoriously hard to read. Applications of the scheme usually consisted of classifying normative elements into taxonomies delimiting functional contributions. These qualitative operations were by no means mechanical or easily communicated as a stable procedure that would steer different investigators to identical results. This rendered moot the possibility of generating conclusions from initial conditions through the application of formal tools. In a similar way, while many were inclined to agree that Parsons's system illuminated how a social system governed by a logic over normative rules might work, it was less than evident that concrete social systems had such logical coherence.

Merton's (1968) "theories of the middle range" provided a more readily applicable set of tools. Like Parsons, Merton proposed that the enduring regularities that make up social structure are normatively defined. However, instead of attempting to calculate over extended normative webs, he drew attention to the implications of positions. Thus, he emphasized that roles place individuals in relations with concrete others or that membership in groups, both present and anticipated, provides reference points for calculating comparisons of expectations and outcomes. Unlike Parsons's more elaborate concerns, Merton's lent themselves to the construction and interpretation of surveys and other manageable research projects.

Merton did not assume, as Parsons did, that norms and roles can be divined from an overarching logic. More frequently, he treated contrasting norms as empirical counterparts of lay distinctions among different roles or group memberships. This can be viewed as a central motivation for the common use of the structural concepts outlined above. However, Merton more often used factual (or readily inferred) norms grounded in different stable positions to highlight dilemmas. Concrete people could be understood as facing practical problems of resolving competing and often contrary normative standards. This strategy of framing the practical problem as the resolution of contrary expectations frequently leads to insight into choices that at first seem senseless or even self-defeating.

Merton's analyses rested on qualitative inferences, often turning on the meaning of norms. One of Merton's students, Boudon (1982), provides formulations in which social structure refers to numerically definite distributions so that the implications of such extraindividual constraints emerge from formal calculations. For example, he posits an array of young persons committed to personal advancement who make investments in education. However, when all do what is individually sensible, the collective result illustrates Merton's unintended consequences. If there is a fixed and therefore scarce supply of desired positions that will go to those who have the most education, many of those who invest will discover that their efforts are frustrated by the simultaneous striving of others. Boudon provides many illustrations of the perverse effects that can obtain when individual motive operates against a backdrop of a fixed system of positions.

Another of Merton's students, Blau (1977), presents a deductive structural theory based on the notion that social structure consists of arrays of positions, which he calls parameters. Blau divides differentiation into two types: among unranked or nominal categories such as religion and among continuous arrays of ranked positions that differ in their amounts of a scarce and valued resource. The distribution of individuals over positions gives rise to numerical properties of whole social structures, including the heterogeneity of nominal differences, inequality among ranks, and consolidation intersection, or the degree of correlation independence of positions on separate dimensions.

Blau's concept of social structure leads to differences in the sizes of collections of individuals occupying different positions. Size in turn strongly conditions the rate of interaction, or social association. More differentiated structures result in higher rates of intergroup association, and Blau argues that this leads to the successful meshing of routines, or social integration. The intersection of different dimensions, which results in even smaller subgroups defined by multiple positions, also enhances social integration. Conversely, the consolidation of dimensions, homogeneity rather than heterogeneity, diminishes rates of intergroup contact and hence hinders social integration. Inequality emerges as a special case that illustrates Blau's taste for paradoxical results. Greater inequality leads to smaller strata and fosters intergroup relations, but those relations often take the form of interpersonal conflict, including crime (Blau and Blau 1982).

Blau's notions are particularly suitable for research application because his notion of structure more or less directly corresponds to widely used operationalizations such as gender, race, ethnicity, religion, occupational rank, and wealth. Of course, these are social constructs and in some final analysis are defined by norms and other ideal elements. At the same time, they are for most people most of the time subject to slow or even no change. This sustains the usefulness of a numerical calculus that rests on the notion that size is an objective, impersonal, and durable reality.

Coleman (1990) provides one of the most ambitious attempts to specify social structure as a mathematically tractable map of interdependence. He posits actors with rights of control over their own actions and over tangible things desired by others or resources. His actors maximize the achievement of their desires by exchanging their control in return for that which others control. The result in general is an equilibrium in which initial control in conjunction with the desires of others produces differential power. Within this apparatus, Coleman is able to provide a rigorous analysis of the emergence of larger-scale phenomena, including groups, norms, and corporate actors.

Although all these accounts lie along a single path of intellectual descent, there is a major divide with respect to the elemental nature of social structure. For Parsons, it is an interdependent complex of norms. Unfortunately, there does not exist at present any way to formalize or calculate the mutual implications in a web of symbolic elements. Later analysts who have gone much farther in rendering complexity calculable have done so from "hard" assumptions that take social structure from the outset as a set of objective positions (with objective properties) so that size, distribution, rates of exchange, and so forth, can be treated mathematically.

More recent treatments have built on the rich, although eclectic, tradition of taking relations or social ties that are knitted into networks as fundamental. One point of departure is Granovetter's (1973) observation that weak ties are surprisingly efficacious in securing resources, notably access to better jobs. Weak ties are most likely to form bridges between clusters of interconnected and thus redundant strong ties. Burt (1992) generalizes this, suggesting that "structural holes," or gaps spanned by positions whose ties unite the otherwise disconnected, are a potent source of advantage. He was able to display supporting evidence from contexts as diverse as executives competing for promotion and sectors of an industrial economy. Burt's concepts are derivative in the best sense; that is, they are a conceptual refinement that moves on to novel terrain, building on what he can take as an established view of social structure.

Tilly (1998) has distilled from network concerns a potent challenge to much received thinking about stratification. He proposes that "durable inequality" reverberates from underlying schemas governing how networks are formed. Categorical divisions such as race, gender, nationality, and citizenship are embedded in widely shared, deeply learned propensities for action, or routines. Recurrent organizational problems, such as assigning work and dividing rewards, are most easily and durably resolved when they are consonant with widely shared assumptions about categorical differences. Somewhat like Burt, Tilly focuses less on origins and more on implications. He examines how relational considerations secure inequalities through persistent configurations of exploitation and resource hoarding that are diffused by emulation and ultimately underpinned by adaptation. In this view, social structure is not globally coherent or uniform but is, somewhat like DNA, a complex melange constructed from varying combinations of a few very simple elements.

A noteworthy gap here is that the proponents of formal theory (and those proposing building blocks) tend to posit or assume "hard" properties, giving limited attention to how or why the hypothesized elementary patterns emerged or became predominant. This leaves open issues of variability and interpretive options (or meaning) that others see as fundamental. Indeed, some authors believe that human judgment is distinctive and that no mechanical analogue or simulation of human society (Habermas 1987) or human cognition, (Penrose 1989) will ever be possible.

In summary, there are no widely accepted sets of notions that capture all the properties that have been seen as fundamental to the concept of social structure. The huge catalogue of demonstrated effects of structural regularities cannot be organized in a tidy way. Enthusiasm for the different attempts to represent the concept in compact terms varies widely. Sufficiently close attention to the details of competing claims could convince one that no shared subject is really at issue. As in the analysis of social structure itself, it is necessary to carefully select the right degree of abstraction and appropriate pattern of highlighting to discern any common pattern in the competing pictures, but there is nevertheless a pattern to be found.

REFERENCES

Bernstein, Basil 1975 *Class, Codes, and Control*. New York: Schocken.

Blau, Peter 1977 *Inequality and Heterogeneity*. New York: Academic Press.

Blau, Judith, and Peter Blau 1982 "The Cost of Inequality: Metropolitan Structure and Violent Crime." *American Sociological Review* 47:114–129.

Boudon, Raymond 1982 *The Unintended Consequences of Social Action*. New York: St. Martin's.

Burt, Ronald S. 1992 *Structural Holes*. Cambridge, Mass.: Harvard University Press.

Coleman, James S. 1990 *Foundations of Social Theory*. Cambridge, Mass.: Harvard University Press.

Goode, William J. 1970 *World Revolution in Family Patterns*. New York: Free Press.

Granovetter, Mark 1973 "The Strength of Weak Ties." *American Journal of Sociology* 78:1360–1380.

Habermas, Jurgen 1987 *The Theory of Communicative Action*, vol. 2: *Lifeworld and System: A Critique of Functionalist Reason*. Boston: Beacon Press.

Hawley, Amos 1986 *Human Ecology*. Chicago: University of Chicago Press.

Kindleberger, Charles 1980 *Panics, Manias, and Crashes*. New York: Basic Books.

Mann, Michael 1986 *The Sources of Social Power*, vol. 1: *A History of Social Power from the Beginning to A.D. 1760*. New York: Cambridge University Press.

Merton, Robert 1968 *Social Theory and Social Structure.* New York: Free Press.

Park, Robert, and Ernest Burgess 1924 *Introduction to the Science of Sociology.* Chicago: University of Chicago Press.

Parsons, Talcott 1951 *The Social System.* New York: Free Press.

Penrose, Roger 1989 *The Emperor's New Mind.* New York: Oxford University Press.

Piaget, Jean 1970 *Structuralism.* New York: Basic Books.

Tilly, Charles 1975 *The Formation of Nation States in Western Europe.* Princeton, N.J.: Princeton University Press.

—— 1986 *The Contentious French.* Cambridge, Mass.: Harvard University Press.

—— 1998 *Durable Inequality.* Berkeley: University of California Press.

STEVEN L. RYTINA

SOCIAL VALUES AND NORMS

Values and norms are evaluative beliefs that synthesize affective and cognitive elements to orient people to the world in which they live. Their evaluative element makes them unlike existential beliefs, which focus primarily on matters of truth or falsehood, correctness or incorrectness. Their cognitive element makes them unlike motives that can derive from emotions or psychological drives. Values and norms involve cognitive beliefs of approval or disapproval. Although they tend to persist through time and therefore faster continuity in society and human personality, they also are susceptible to change (Moss and Susman 1980; Alwin 1994).

The evaluative criteria represented in values and norms influence the behavior of subject units at multiple levels (e.g., individuals, organizations, and societies) as well as judgments about the behavior of others, which also can influence behavior. For example, values and norms affect the evaluation of individuals as suitable marriage partners and in that way influence marital behavior. Values and norms also affect evaluation of the governing policies and practices of societies and thus have an impact on diplomatic relations and the policies of one society's government toward other societies.

CONCEPT OF A VALUE

A value is a belief about the desirability of a mode, means, or end of action (Kluckhohn 1951; Schwartz and Bilsky 1987). It indicates the degree to which something is regarded as good versus bad. A value tends to be general rather than specific, transcending particular types of action and situations. As a general evaluative criterion, it is used to assess specific behaviors in specific situations.

The evaluative criteria represented by values derive from conceptions of morality, aesthetics, and achievement. That is, a mode, means, or end of action can be regarded as good or bad for moral, aesthetic, or cognitive reasons and often for a combination of those reasons (Kluckhohn 1951; Parsons and Shils 1951). For example, being considerate of others may be valued positively (i.e., be viewed as desirable or good) for moral reasons, neatness may be valued positively for aesthetic reasons, and intelligence may be valued positively for cognitive reasons. Since the distinguishing characteristic of a value is evaluation as good or bad, a value that has a cognitive basis is a function of cognitive appraisal based on competency and achievement rather than on scientific or utilitarian grounds. For example, the choice of steel rather than iron to construct a building is a decision based on scientific or utilitarian criteria rather than on values.

The concept of a value must be differentiated from other concepts that appear to be similar. One of those concepts is a preference. A value may be thought of as a type of preference, but not all preferences are values. The distinctive characteristic of a value is that it is based on a belief about what is desirable rather than on mere liking. A preference for an equitable rather than inequitable distribution of rewards is a value, but a preference for vanilla rather than chocolate ice cream is not.

The concept of a value also bears some similarity to the concept of an attitude. Some analysts have suggested that a value is a type of attitude (Fishbein and Ajzen 1975; Glenn 1980), but there are differences between the two concepts. An attitude refers to an organization of several beliefs around a specific object or situation, whereas a value refers to a single belief of a specific kind: a belief about desirability that is based in conceptions of morality, aesthetics, or achievement and transcends specific behaviors and situations. Because of its generality, a value occupies a more central and hierarchically important place in human personality and cognitive structure than does an attitude. It is a determinant of attitudes as well as behavior. Thus, evaluations of numerous attitude objects and situations are based on a relatively small number of values. Not all attitudes, however, derive from values. For example, an attitude toward skiing may be based on the extent to which that sport is found to be enjoyable rather than on a value. The concept of a value also differs from the concept of an interest in much the same way that it differs from the concept of an attitude, since an interest is a type of attitude that results in the directing of one's attention and action toward a focal object or situation. As is true of attitudes more broadly, some interests derive from values but others do not.

The concept of a value also can be distinguished from the related concept of a motive. The basic property of a motive is the ability to induce valences (incentives) that may be positive or negative. A value has a motive property, involving a predisposition to act in a certain way, because it affects the evaluation of the expected consequences of an action and therefore the choice among possible alternatives; however, it is a less person-centered concept than a motive, which also encompasses emotions and drives. A value is a particular type of motive involving a belief about the desirability of an action that derives from an evaluation of that action's expected consequences in a situation. A value is a distinctively human motive, unlike motives that operate at both the human and the infrahuman levels.

A value also differs from a need. Although both function as motives because of their ability to induce valences, a need is distinctive in being a requirement for the continued performance of an activity and the attainment of other valued outcomes (Emerson 1987). Some needs have a biological basis; others are psychological, often deriving from the persistent frustration of important goals. Although a value may arise from a need, becoming a cognitive transformation of that need, not all needs are transformed into values and not all values derive from needs. Needs also may derive from the structure of a situation, having a social or economic basis rather than a person-centered biological or psychological basis. For example, a need for income may cause an actor to behave in ways that conflict with his or her values. A need differs from a value in that the continued functioning of the actor and the acquisitions of other valued outcomes are contingent on its being met. A need also differs from a value in that it implies a deficit that imposes a requirement, whereas a value implies motivation that is based on a belief about desirability.

Finally, a value can be differentiated from a goal. A value sometimes is thought of as a goal because goals are selected on the basis of values. However, some values focus on modes of action that are personal attributes, such as intelligence, rather than ends of action, or goals. Values are not goals of behavior. They are evaluative criteria that are used to select goals and appraise the implications of action.

CONCEPT OF A NORM

Like a value, a norm is an evaluative belief. Whereas a value is a belief about the *desirability* of behavior, a norm is a belief about the *acceptability* of behavior (Gibbs 1965; Marini 1984). A norm indicates the degree to which a behavior is regarded as right versus wrong, allowable versus unallowable. It is an evaluative criterion that specifies a rule of behavior, indicating what a behavior *ought* to be or *ought not* to be. A *prescriptive* norm indicates what should be done, and a *proscriptive* norm indicates what should not be done. Because a norm is a behavioral rule, it produces a feeling of obligation. A value, in contrast, produces a feeling of desirability, of attraction or repulsion.

A norm also differs from a value in its degree of specificity. A norm is less general than a value because it indicates what should or should not be done in particular behavioral contexts. Whereas a value is a general evaluative criterion that transcends particular types of action and situations, a norm is linked directly to particular types of action and situations. For example, there may be a norm proscribing the killing of other human beings that is generally applicable except in situations such as war, self-defense, capital punishment, and euthanasia. Situational variability of this type sometimes is referred to as the *conditionality* of a norm. A norm, like a value, is generally applicable to the *types* of action and situations on which it focuses, but it is less general than a value because it is less likely to transcend particular types of action and situations.

Because norms often derive from values, they have their basis in conceptions of morality, aesthetics, and achievement and often in a combination of those conceptions. The basis of a norm tends to affect its strength, or the importance attached to it. For example, a norm based in morality that differentiates right from wrong is likely to be considered more important than a norm based in aesthetics that differentiates the appropriate from the inappropriate, for example, in matters of dress or etiquette. A norm, however, differs from a custom in much the same way that a value differs from a preference. A norm involves an evaluation of what an actor *should* do, whereas a custom involves an expectation of what an actor *will* do. It may be expected, for example, that people will drink coffee, but it is usually a matter of indifference whether they do. Drinking coffee is therefore a custom, not a norm; it is not based on a belief about what people ought to do.

THE STRUCTURE OF VALUES AND NORMS

Multiple values and norms are organized and linked in the cultures of human social systems and also are linked when they are internalized by individuals. Cultural "value orientations" organize and link values and norms to existential beliefs in general views that also might be called worldviews or ideologies (Kluckhohn 1951). They are sets of linked propositions embracing evaluative and existential elements that describe preferred or obligatory states. Values and norms are linked to and buttressed by existential beliefs about human nature, the human condition, interpersonal relations, the functioning of social organizations and societies, and the nature of the world. Since existential beliefs focus on what is true versus untrue, they are to some degree empirically based and verifiable.

In most of the early conceptual and theoretical work on values, values and norms were not differentiated clearly. Later, particularly as attempts to measure values and norms were made, the two concepts were routinely considered distinct, and studies focusing on them have been carried out separately since that time. As a result, the relationship between values and norms rarely has been analyzed theoretically or empirically.

Values and norms are closely related because values usually provide the justification for norms. As beliefs about what is desirable and undesirable, values often are associated with normative beliefs that require or preclude certain behavior, establishing boundaries to indicate what is acceptable versus unacceptable. For example, the positive value attached to human safety and security is supported by norms that proscribe doing harm to other persons and their property. Not all values are supported by norms, however. Displaying personal competence in a variety of ways is positively valued, but norms do not always require it. Similarly, not all norms support values. For example, norms in regard to dress and etiquette can be quite arbitrary. Their existence may support values, but the specific rules of behavior they establish may not.

Many cultural value orientations organize and link the values and norms that operate as evaluative criteria in human social systems. These orientations are learned and internalized by individuals in unique ways that vary with an individual's personal characteristics and social history and the interaction between the two. Cultural value orientations and internalized individual value orientations are more comprehensive systems of values and norms than those activated as influences on particular types of behavior. The latent structure of values and norms that characterizes a social system or an individual can be thought of as a map or blueprint (Rokeach 1973). Only a portion of the map or blueprint that is immediately relevant to the behavioral choices being made is consulted, and the rest is ignored temporarily. Different subsets of values and norms that make up different portions of the map or blueprint are activated when different types of behavioral choices are made. For example, the values and norms relevant in choosing a mate differ from those relevant in deciding how to allocate one's time among various activities.

The Object Unit. A characteristic of values and norms that is important for understanding their structure is the type of *object unit* to which they pertain, such as an individual, an organization, or a society. Values and norms establish what is desirable or acceptable for particular types of object units. For example, physical and psychological health are positively valued ends of action for individuals, and norms that proscribe or prescribe action to maintain or promote health govern individual action. Democracy, distributive justice, and world peace are positively valued ends of action for societies, and norms, usually in the form of laws, proscribe and prescribe certain actions on the part of a society's institutions in support of those values. Individuals may value democracy, justice, and peace, but these are societal values, not individual values, since they pertain to the characteristics of societies, not to those of individuals. Differentiating values by their object units is important in conceptualizing and measuring values relevant to the explanation of behavior because correspondence between the actor, or subject unit, and the object unit determines the extent to which behavior by the actor is relevant to achieving a particular end. Individuals differentiate between personal and societal values because they do not have direct influence over social values, thus distinguishing their beliefs on the basis of whether they think those beliefs will lead to action (Braithwaite and Law 1985).

The Basis of Evaluation. As evaluative criteria, values and norms have the ability to induce valences (incentives). They affect evaluation of the behavior of others and involve a predisposition to act in a certain way because they affect the evaluation of the expected consequences of action. The evaluation that occurs on the basis of values and norms derives from two structural properties: the polarity, or directionality, of the value or norm and the standard of comparison that is used.

Polarity. The polarity of a value or norm is the direction of its valence, or motive force, which may be positive or negative. In the case of a value, something that is evaluated as desirable will have a positive valence, whereas something that is evaluated as undesirable will have a negative valence. In the case of a norm, something that should be done will have a positive valence, whereas something that should not be done will have a negative valence.

Standard of Comparison. A value or norm also is characterized by a standard, or level, of aspiration or expectation. This evaluative standard is a reference point with respect to which a behavior and its consequences are evaluated. A subject unit's own action and that of others, as well as the ends that result or may result from action, are evaluated on the basis of whether they are above or below an evaluative standard.

In the case of a value, the evaluative standard determines the neutral point on the value scale at or above which a behavior or its consequences will be evaluated as desirable and below which a behavior or its consequences will be evaluated as undesirable. In both economics and psychology, it has been recognized that there is a utility, or value, function that should be considered nonlinear (Marini [1992] provides a discussion of these developments), and there is empirical evidence that it generally is appropriate to assume the existence of a reference point on a utility, or value, scale. This reference point plays a critical role in producing a nonlinear relationship between the value scale and the objective continuum of behavior and its consequences. It has been observed that value functions change significantly at a certain point, which is often, although not always, zero. In the prospect theory of Kahneman and Tversky (1979), outcomes are expressed as positive or negative deviations from a neutral reference outcome that is assigned a value of zero. Kahneman and Tversky propose an S-shaped value function that is concave above the reference point and convex below it but less steep above than below. This function specifies that the effect of a marginal change decreases with the distance from the reference point in either direction but that the response to outcomes below the reference point is more extreme than is the response to outcomes above it. The asymmetry of the value function suggests a stronger aversion to what is evaluated as undesirable, an asymmetry that is consistent with an empirically observed aversion to loss.

In the case of a norm, the evaluative standard is set by what is defined to be acceptable versus unacceptable. It is a level of expectation that is determined by the specific behaviors that are regarded as right versus wrong, appropriate versus inappropriate. An important difference between a value and a norm is that whereas there is a continuous, nonlinear relationship between a value scale and the objective continuum of behavior or its consequences above the neutral point set by the evaluative standard, this relationship is not expected between the scale of evaluation based on a normative criterion and the objective continuum of behavior. Because a normative standard establishes a boundary of acceptability or requirement that applies to all those covered by the norm, compliance with a normative expectation is not evaluated as a continuous variable on the basis of variation in behavior above the reference point set by the normative expectation. However, violation of a normative standard is evaluated as a continuous variable on the basis of variation in behavior below the reference point set by the standard. Negative deviations from the standard are likely to be evaluated in much the same way as are negative evaluations from the reference point on a value scale, which is convex below the reference point. Because of the strong aversion to what is evaluated as being below the reference standard, behavior that violates a normative standard is likely to be eliminated from consideration as an option.

The level of aspiration or expectation that operates as an evaluative standard for an actor is socially determined to a large degree. It is a "comparison level" learned from others whom the actor takes as referents. As a result of variation in the characteristics of actors, the social environments to which they are exposed, and the interaction between those two factors, the evaluative standards associated with values and norms vary across actors. Even among actors in the same social environment, the evaluative standard is specific to the actor, although there may be a high degree of consensus about it in a social group.

The evaluative standards associated with values and norms are subject to change in an individual actor. An important source of change is experience that affects the level of ability, knowledge, or accomplishment of an actor. For example, the evaluative standard for achievement values is affected by an actor's level of achievement. There is evidence that people tend to raise their value standards with success and lower them with failure. Thus, as a worker learns a job, that worker's ability to perform the job increases, as does the worker's evaluative standard. A level of ability that once was aspired to and evaluated as "extremely good" may, after increases in the worker's ability, come to be viewed as "mediocre" and below the worker's current evaluative standard for expected performance. Experience also may affect the evaluative standard for norms. For example, there is evidence that the experience of divorce changes normative beliefs about divorce in the direction of increasing its acceptability (Thornton 1985). Another source of change in the evaluative standards associated with the values and norms of an actor is an increase in knowledge of the world that alters the existential beliefs connected with values and norms.

The evaluative standards associated with values and norms vary not only among actors and over time for the same actor but also with the characteristics of other actors whose behavior is the object of evaluation. These characteristics may differentiate among actors or among the circumstances of the same actor at different times. For example, the value standard used by an adult to evaluate a child's knowledge will vary for children who have completed different amounts of schooling, such as an elementary school student, a high school student, or a college student: The amount of knowledge evaluated as "very good" for an elementary school student will differ from that evaluated as "very good" for a student at a more advanced stage of schooling. Different value standards will be applied to different students and to the same student at different stages of schooling. Similarly, in a work organization, the value standard used to evaluate performance may vary for different categories of workers: Those with more experience may be evaluated according to a higher standard. Again, these different standards may be applied to different workers who are in different categories or to the same worker as he or she progresses from one category to another.

Like a value standard, a normative standard may vary with the characteristics of other actors whose behavior is an object of evaluation. However, there is a difference between a value and a norm in this regard. Because a value is a continuous variable, variation in the value standard with the characteristics of the other actors whose behavior is being evaluated need not have implications for whether the value applies to those actors. In contrast, because a norm is a discrete variable that differentiates what is acceptable from what is unacceptable, variation in the evaluative standard of a norm with the characteristics of other actors whose behavior is being evaluated determines whether the norm applies to other actors with particular characteristics. This variability—that is, variability in whether a value or norm *applies* based on the characteristics of the actors being evaluated—is a dimension of the importance of a value or norm and is labeled its conditionality.

Dimensions of Importance. It is commonly recognized that values and norms differ in their priority, or importance, and that those differences are another aspect of the structure of values and norms. Differences in priority produce a structure that is to some degree hierarchical. Recognition that not all values are of equal importance has led to the use of ranking procedures to measure values (Allport et al. 1960; Rokeach 1973). These procedures have been criticized for forcing respondents to represent their values in a ranked order that does not allow for the possibility that some values may be of equal importance (Alwin and Krosnick 1985; Braithwaite and Law 1985). Although there is a hierarchy among values, there may be sets of values that occupy the same position in the hierarchy. The priority of a value or norm not only has implications for its influence on behavior but also may have implications for the probability that it will change, since values and norms of high priority have been argued to be less likely to change than are those of low priority.

The priority, or importance, of a value or norm can be assessed on a number of dimensions: (1) strength, or intensity, (2) centrality, (3) range, (4) conditionally, and (5) intent. Although these dimensions are conceptually different, they are likely to overlap empirically to a considerable degree. The extent to which and ways in which they overlap in reflecting the importance of a value or norm are not known.

Strength. The *strength* of a value or norm can be defined as the maximum strength of the force field it can induce. The strength of the valence reflects its hierarchical position in the latent map or blueprint that characterizes the structure of values and norms for a social system or an individual. Although the strength of a value or norm is likely to display considerable stability, it is also subject to change. At the level of the social system, it may change as a result of long-term changes in social organization and aspects of culture as well as precipitating events. As the social system changes, socializing influences on individuals change. Changes in the values and norms of individuals occur both over the life course (Glenn 1980; Alwin 1994) and as a result of differences between those who are born and move through life in different historical periods. The motivational force of a value at a particular time, however, is not necessarily the maximum strength of its latent force field, because attaining a valued outcome may reduce the subjective utility of additional units of that outcome as a result of diminishing marginal utility, or satiation. In the case of either a value or a norm, whether one attains an outcome also may alter the maximum strength of its latent force field. For example, if attainment is problematic, the importance of a value or norm may decline as a way of reducing cognitive dissonance.

Centrality. The *centrality* of a value or norm can be defined as the number and variety of behaviors or ends to which it applies. Because a central value or norm contributes more than does a peripheral one to the coherent organization and functioning of the total system, the disappearance of a central value or norm would make a greater difference to the total system than would the disappearance of a peripheral value or norm. A central value or norm is more resistant to change than is a peripheral value or norm; however, if change occurs, the more central the value or norm changed, the more widespread its repercussions (Rokeach 1973, 1985).

For individuals and even for social groups, concern and responsibility for the well-being of others is a central value that pertains to a large number and variety of specific behaviors and ends. It is supported by a central proscriptive norm that one should not harm others and a central prescriptive norm that one should help others, particularly if they are in need. These norms pertain to a large number and variety of specific behaviors. In contrast, excitement and adventure are more peripheral values, affecting a smaller number and variety of specific behaviors and ends. In connection with these values, peripheral norms govern the carrying out of specific types of activities that may be sources of excitement and adventure, such as the rules governing sports and potentially dangerous recreational activities.

For individuals, life values that pertain to the overall ends, or goals, of life along with the norms that support them tend to be more central than are the values and norms that pertain to particular life domains or social roles. Part of the reason for this is that life values affect whether particular life domains or social roles are entered into and the amounts of time and energy a person spends in different domains and roles. They also affect an individual's domain- and role-specific values and norms. For example, life values include things such as attaining a high material standard of living, having meaningful family relationships and friendships, making the world a better place, and having a good time. Life values of this type are among the factors that influence entry into various life domains and roles, the activities in those domains and roles, and how much investment is made in each one (e.g., marriage, parenthood, employment, friendships, leisure activities and hobbies, community activities, religion). Values and norms pertaining to each of the domains and roles are to some degree a function of overall life values. For example, if an individual places a higher priority on making the world a better place than on material well-being, that individual's employment values will place a higher priority on the possible influence and significance of the work performed than on the earnings derived from the work. Similarly, if an individual places a higher priority on meaningful relationships than on material well-being, marital values will place a higher priority on love and mutual respect than on the shared material standard of living.

Range. The *range* of a value or norm can be defined as the number and variety of actors of a particular type of object unit (e.g., individuals, organizations, and societies) to which it applies. Whereas the dimension of centrality focuses on the characteristics of action and its ends (i.e., the number and variety of behaviors or ends to which a value or norm applies), the dimension of range focuses on the characteristics of actors (i.e., the number and variety of individuals or larger social units to which a value or norm applies). The characteristics of actors used to define the range of a value or norm tend to be ascriptive or group-defining characteristics of individuals or larger social units. In the case of individuals, these are characteristics such as age, sex, nationality, race, and ethnicity. A value or norm with a broad range applies to all actors of a particular type of object unit, whereas a value or norm with a narrow range applies to a very restricted category of actors of that type. For example, concern about and responsibility for the well-being of others is a value with a broad range that applies universally to individuals throughout the world. In contrast, wisdom is a value with a narrower range because although it applies throughout the world, it applies primarily to people of older ages. Similarly, the norm against incest has a broad range because it applies universally to individuals throughout the world. In contrast, the norm prescribing paid employment has a narrower range because it applies primarily to men in particular age categories.

Conditionality. The *conditionality* of a value or norm can be defined as the number and variety of situations to which it applies. Whereas the dimension of centrality focuses on the characteristics of action or its ends and the dimension of range focuses on the characteristics of actors, the dimension of conditionality focuses on the characteristics of situations, including a situation's actors. When conditionality pertains to the characteristics of a situation's actors, it usually refers to emergent or potentially changing characteristics of actors that define the situation rather than to ascriptive characteristics that define membership in social groups. Although values are less tied to specific types of situations than norms are, both values and norms vary in the degree to which they are conditioned on the characteristics of situations. For example, some values pertaining to modes of conduct, such as courtesy, cleanliness, and honesty, are applicable across most situations. Others are applicable in many fewer situations or may even be bipolar, with the polarity of the value being conditional on the situation. For example, aggressiveness is positively valued in some types of competitive situations, such as warfare and sports, but negatively valued in some types of cooperative situations, such as conversation and child rearing.

The conditionality of a value or norm is evident when a given subject actor who is evaluating a given type of action or end of action makes different evaluations in different types of situations, that is, when the evaluation varies with the characteristics of the situation. For example, friendliness is valued positively, but it is a value characterized by some conditionality, since it is valued negatively when exhibited toward strangers in dangerous environments. Killing other human beings is normatively proscribed in almost all situations, but the norm has some conditionality because killing is not proscribed in warfare, self-defense, capital punishment, and euthanasia. In capital punishment and some types of warfare, killing actually is prescribed. Abortion is believed by some people to be normatively proscribed, and whether it is normatively proscribed often depends on the characteristics of the situation, including how conception occurred, whether the mother's health is in danger, and whether the mother can care for the child. Opposition to abortion is therefore a norm of higher conditionality than is the proscription against killing other human beings. The conditionality of a value or norm is defined by the number and variety of situations to which it applies *consistently*, that is, with the same polarity. A value or norm that has the same polarity across many and varied types of situations is a value or norm of low conditionality and therefore of high priority. A value or norm that has the same polarity in only a few similar types of situations is a value or norm of high conditionality and low priority.

Intent. Whether a value applies to a mode, means, or end of action has been labeled its intent (Kluckhohn 1951). Mode values pertain to the manner or style in which an action is carried out and refer to both the action and the actor. They pertain to qualities manifested *in* the act, and if such qualities are observed consistently over time for a type of action or for an actor, they are applied not just to a single instance of action but to a type of action or to an actor more generally. Adjectives such as "intelligent," "independent," "creative," "responsible," "kind," and "generous" describe mode values. Instrumental values focus on necessary means to other ends. They refer to action that constitutes the means or from which the means are derived. For example, a job and the earnings it provides may be viewed as means to other ends such as acquiring the material resources necessary to sustain life. Goal values, in contrast, pertain to self-sufficient, or autonomous, ends of action. They are not subordinate to other values and are what an actor values most. Some analysts have argued that they can be defined as what an actor desires without limit. They focus on sources of intrinsic satisfaction or happiness but are distinguished from pleasures, which, except when elevated to become goal values, are satisfactions that are enjoyed incidentally and along the way. Pleasures are not necessarily based on beliefs about desirability, since they can be based on mere liking.

A norm may apply to a mode or means of action but not to an end of action. By requiring or prohibiting a way of acting or a type of action, norms limit the modes and means used in accomplishing ends. For example, the values of honesty and fairness govern modes and means of accomplishing ends, and associated with these values are norms that require honest and fair action.

Values and norms cannot always be identified as falling into a single category of intent. For some types of action, mode values and norms and instrumental or goal values and norms overlap; choosing an action as a means or to directly achieve an end actually defines the mode of action. For example, accomplishing a task by a means that shows concern for others defines a mode of acting that is kind, considerate, polite, and caring. Choosing to accomplish a task by honest means defines a mode of acting honestly. Acting to achieve an end that benefits others defines a mode of acting that is caring, giving, and generous. Mode values and norms and instrumental or goal values and norms do not always overlap, however. A given mode may be applied to a variety of means and ends, and choosing a means or acting to achieve an end does not necessarily imply or define a mode. For example, for modes that reflect ability or competence, as described by adjectives such as "intelligent", "creative," "efficient," "courageous," "organized," and "self-reliant," there may be no necessary connection or only a limited one between the values reflected in the mode and the values reflected in the acts undertaken as means or ends.

Differentiating between instrumental values and goal values is difficult because the two types are interdependent. Their relationship is not just one of sequence, since achieving particular ends may require the use of certain means (Kluckhohn 1951; Fallding 1965). Differentiating between instrumental values and goal values also requires reflection by the actor. An important concern of moral philosophy has been identifying the end or ends of action that ultimately bring satisfaction to human beings, that is, that have genuine, intrinsic value (Lovejoy 1950). The focus has been on identifying important goal values and distinguishing them from less important instrumental values. This means–end distinction is not as well developed in the category systems of all cultures as it is in Western culture (Kluckhohn 1951), and even among persons exposed to Western culture, it is not developed equally or similarly in all actors. Not all actors make the distinction or make it in the same way. What are instrumental values to some actors are goal values to others.

When mode, instrumental, and goal values are separable, they can all affect behavior. Sometimes they point to identical actions, and sometimes they do not. Similarly, when mode and instrumental norms are separable, both can affect behavior. Among values that can pertain to either means or ends, the distinction between instrumental and goal values is a dimension of importance, with goal values being of higher priority than instrumental values (Fallding 1965; Braithwaite and Law 1985). However, values that can pertain only to a mode or means are not necessarily of lower priority than are values that can pertain to ends.

Interrelationships. Because social structure, as defined both organizationally and culturally, links sets of values and norms, there are patterned relationships among the sets of values and norms held by actors. These relationships can be seen as being influenced by conceptual domain, dimensions of importance, behavioral context, and interdependence.

Conceptual Domain. Values and norms that are conceptually similar are thought of as falling within the same conceptual domain, and a conceptual domain is identified by the observation of strong empirical relationships among sets of values or norms. Domains that are conceptually distinct also can have relationships to one another. Compatible domains are positively related, and contradictory domains are negatively related. Empirical research provides some evidence of the existence of conceptual domains of values and norms and the relationships among them. For example, in Western societies, a value domain emphasizing pleasure, comfort, and enjoyment has a negative relationship to a prosocial value domain that emphasizes concern and responsibility for others. Similarly, a value domain emphasizing the extrinsic attainment of power, money, and position has a negative relationship to the prosocial value domain (Schwartz and Bilsky 1987). Values appear to be organized along at least three broad dimensions: (1) emphasis on the self versus others, (2) emphasis on achievement versus pleasure, and (3) emphasis on the external versus the internal. Although there has been less research on the pattern of interrelationships among norms, evidence indicates that norms fall into conceptual domains. Norms pertaining to honesty, for example, are conceptually separable from norms pertaining to personal freedom in family matters, sexuality, and mortality.

Dimensions of Importance. Interrelationships among values and norms also are affected by dimensions of importance, since these dimensions affect their application across object units, social institutions, social roles, and behavioral contexts. Dimensions of importance such as centrality, range, and conditionality are linked to variability in application across object units, social institutions, and social roles. Values and norms that have high importance because they are broadly applicable are more likely to be interrelated than are values and norms that have low importance, which apply more narrowly. Values and norms that apply narrowly are related to each other and to values and norms that apply more broadly only under the conditions in which they apply.

Behavioral Context. Interrelationships among values and norms are influenced not only by conceptual domains and dimensions of importance but also by the behavioral contexts to which they apply. Values and norms that are relevant to the same or related behavioral contexts tend to be interrelated. For example, the values and norms that play a role in interpersonal relationships differ in some respects from those which play a role in educational and occupational performance. The value of concern for others and the norms that support it are of high priority in interpersonal relationships but can be of low priority in the performance of educational and occupational tasks.

Interdependence. Socially structured or otherwise necessary links among modes, means, and ends of action are a source of interdependence among values and norms. Mode values and norms and instrumental or goal values and norms can overlap, and instrumental and goal values are interdependent when achieving particular ends requires the use of certain means. This interdependence constrains the extent to which the relative priority of values can affect action. For example, attaining a less highly valued means cannot be forgone to attain a more highly valued end if the end cannot be attained without the means.

THE ORIGIN OF VALUES AND NORMS

Multiple values and norms are organized and linked in the cultures of human social systems, which are linked when they are internalized by human actors or institutionalized by corporate actors. *Social* values and norms, in contrast to *personal*, or *internalized*, values and norms refer to the values and norms of a social unit that encompasses more than one person. These may refer to the officially stated or otherwise institutionalized values and norms of an organization or society, or to the collective, or shared, values and norms of the individuals who constitute a social unit such as an informal reference group, a formal organization, a society, or a societal subgroup defined by a shared characteristic. When a social value or norm refers to a collective property of the members of a social unit, it may be held with varying degrees of consensus by those who constitute that unit (Rossi and Berk 1985). An important difference between formal organizations and informal social groups or geographically defined social units is that formal organizations usually come into being for a specific purpose and are dedicated to particular types of activity and to achieving particular ends. As a result, their objectives are both narrower and more varied than those of other social units.

The Social Origin of Personal Values and Norms. The values and norms of individual persons derive from the social environments to which they are exposed. Through socialization, individuals become aware of and internalize social values and norms, which then become important internal determinants of action. An individual's internalized values and norms reflect the values and norms of the society and the various subgroups and organizations within that society to which that individual is exposed, particularly, although not exclusively, in the early stages of the life course. Once social values and norms are internalized, they can direct the behavior of individuals irrespective of external influences. Internalized values and norms are a source of *self-expectations* and a basis of *self-evaluation*, with the subjective response to an outcome ensuing from the self-concept. Adherence to self-expectations enhances self-esteem, producing a sense of pride and other favorable self-evaluations. Violation of self-expectations reduces self-esteem, producing guilt, self-depreciation, and other negative self-evaluations. To preserve a sense of self-worth and avoid negative self-evaluations, individuals try to behave in accordance with their internalized values and norms. Sociologists tend to see internalized values and norms as an important influence on human behavior, and this makes them see the social values and norms of society as governing and constraining the choices individuals make. Social values and norms also affect behavior because they are internalized by significant others and thus affect an actor's perception of other people's expectations. To the extent that actors are motivated to comply with what they perceive the views of others to be, social values and norms become a source of external pressure that exerts an influence that is independent of an individual's internalized values and norms.

Although change in personal values and norms occurs over the life course, there is some evidence that levels of stability are relatively high (Moss and Susman 1980; Sears 1983; Alwin 1994). It has been argued that values and norms that are more closely tied to the self-concept and considered more important are more resistant to change (Rokeach 1973; Glenn 1980). Those values and norms may undergo less change because they are internalized through conditioning-like processes that begin early in life and are strongly linked to existential beliefs. They tend to be tied to shared mental models that are used to construct reality and become embedded central elements of cognitive organization with a strong affective basis. Some types of values, norms, and attitudes (for example, political attitudes) are quite malleable into early adulthood and then become relatively stable. After this "impressionable," or "formative," period when change is greatest, they are relatively stable in midlife, and this stability either persists or declines in the later years (Alwin et al. 1991; Alwin 1994).

The pattern of life-course change and stability described above has been argued to be due to a number of influences. One is the process of biological and psychological maturation with age, which is most rapid in the early stages of life. As functional capacity develops, influences at that time have the advantage of primacy, and when they are consistent over a period of years, affective "mass" is built up. Nevertheless, some types of values, norms, and attitudes remain malleable into early adulthood, and strong pressure to change or weak earlier socialization can lead to resocialization in late adolescence or early adulthood (Sears 1981; Alwin et al. 1991). It is likely that change declines after early adulthood in part because individuals tend to act on previously formed values, norms, and attitudes as they seek new information and experiences. This selective structuring of new inputs enhances consistency over time, since new inputs tend to reinforce rather than call into question earlier ones.

Another influence on life-course change and stability in values and norms is change in social experiences and roles over the life course (Wells and Stryker 1988; Elder and Caspi 1990). These changes are extensive during the transitional years of early adulthood and may increase after retirement. They represent opportunities for change because they bring the individual into contact with new individuals, reference groups, and situations, and change in values and norms is likely to occur through both interaction with others and adaptation to situations. Role change can produce change as a role occupant engages in new behaviors, is exposed to new circumstances and information, and learns the norms governing role behavior. After early adulthood, a decline in the number of changes in social experiences and roles leads to greater stability in values and norms.

Sources of Change in Social Values and Norms. Change in social values and norms occurs through a variety of processes. One influence is historical change in the conditions of life that occurs through technological innovation, alterations in economic and social organization, and change in cultural ideas and forms. Historical change by definition involves "period effects," but because those effects tend to be experienced differently by different birth cohorts (i.e., those at different ages when a historical change occurs), the influence of historical change on social values and norms occurs to some degree through a process of cohort succession.

Change in social values and norms also occurs through change in the social values and norms of subgroups of social units. This change can be of several types. First, change in the presence and size of subgroups with different values and norms produces change in the collective values and norms of the group. For example, the presence of new immigrant groups with different values and norms or a change in the relative size of groups with different values and norms affects the values and norms of the collective unit. Second, change in the degree of similarity or difference in the values and norms of subgroups can produce change in overall values and norms. On the one hand, acculturation through intergroup contact and similar experiences will reduce the distinctiveness of subcultural groups; on the other hand, segregation and increasing divergence in the life experiences of subgroups will widen their cultural distinctiveness.

Third, some subcultural groups may be more subject to particular period influences than others are, and this differential responsiveness can increase or decrease differences in values and norms among subgroups.

Another source of change in social values and norms is change in exposure to social organizations that exert distinct socializing influences. For example, exposure to religious, educational, or work organizations may produce differences in values and norms between those with such exposure and those without it. The extent to which exposure to different organizational environments is likely to affect personal values and norms depends on the distinctiveness of those environments, which also is subject to change. Thus, social values and norms are affected by both changes in the exposure of the population to different organizations and changes in what is socialized by those organizations.

THE ROLE OF VALUES AND NORMS IN EXPLAINING BEHAVIOR

The ways in which values and norms influence behavior must be understood in a larger explanatory framework, and models of purposive action in all the social sciences provide that framework (Marini 1992). These models rest on the assumption that actors are purposive, acting in ways that tend to produce beneficial results. Although the models of purposive action that have emerged in various social sciences differ in the nature of the assumptions made about purposive action, they share the basic proposition that people are motivated to achieve pleasure and avoid pain and that this motivation leads them to act in ways that, at least within the limits of the information they possess and their ability to predict the future, can be expected to yield greater reward than cost. If reward and cost are defined subjectively and individuals are assumed to act in the service of subjective goals, this proposition links subjective utility, or value, to action. In sociology, a model of purposive action assumes the existence of actors who may be either persons or corporate actors. The usefulness of these models in sociology hinges on making appropriate connections between the characteristics of social systems and the behavior of actors (the macro–micro connection) and between the behavior of actors and the systemic outcomes that emerge from the combined actions of multiple actors (the micro–macro connection).

In a model of purposive action, an individual actor (person or corporate actor) is assumed to make choices among alternative actions structured by the social system. Choices among those actions are based on the outcomes expected to ensue from those actions, to which the actor attaches some utility, or value, and which the actor expects with some probability. The choices of the actor are governed by beliefs of three types: (1) the perceived alternatives for action available, (3) the perceived consequences expected to result from each alternative, and (3) the perceived probabilities with which those consequences are expected to result. The choices of the actor also are governed by the actor's preferences, or the subjective utility (rewards and costs) of the consequences expected to result from each alternative. Values and norms are among the preferences of an actor that influence action. As evaluative beliefs that synthesize affective and cognitive elements, they affect the utility of the outcomes expected to ensue from an action. Action often results not from a conscious weighing of the expected future benefits of alternatives but from a less deliberate response to internalized or institutionalized values and norms (Emerson 1987). The actor's finite resources—the human, cultural, social, and material capital available to the actor that enables or precludes action—operate as influences on the choices made by the actor.

The component of a model of purposive action that makes the macro–micro connection links the characteristics of the social system to the behavior of actors and models the effects of social structure (both organizational and cultural) on the beliefs and preferences of actors as well as on the available alternatives for action and actors' resources. In this component of the model, characteristics of the micro model are taken as problematic and to be explained. These characteristics include: (1) the beliefs and preferences on the basis of which an actor makes choices, (2) the alternatives available to an actor, and (3) the resources available to an actor. A third component of a model of purposive action makes the micro–macro connection, linking the behavior of individual actors to the systemic outcomes that emerge from the combined actions of multiple actors. This link may occur through a simple mechanism such as aggregation, but it is more likely that outcomes emerge through a complex interaction in which the whole is not just the sum of its parts. The action, or behavior, of the system is usually an emergent consequence of the interdependent actions of the actors that compose it.

REFERENCES

Allport, Gordon W., Philip E. Vernon, and Gardner Lindsey 1960 *Manual: Study of Values*, 3rd ed. Boston: Houghton Mifflin.

Alwin, Duane F. 1994 "Aging, Personality, and Social Change: The Stability of Individual Differences Cover the Adult Life Span." In D. I. Featherman, R. M. Lerner, and M. Perlmutter, eds., *Life Span Development and Behavior*, vol. 12. Hillsdale, N.J.: Erlbaum.

——, Ronald L. Cohen, and Theodore M. Newcomb 1991 *Political Attitudes over the Life-Span: The Bennington Women after Fifty Years*. Madison: University of Wisconsin Press.

——, and Jon A. Krosnick. 1985. "The Measurement of Values in Surveys: A Comparison of Ratings and Rankings." *Public Opinion Quarterly* 49:535–552.

Braithwaite, V. A., and H. G. Law 1985 "Structure of Human Values: Testing the Adequacy of the Rokeach Value Survey." *Journal of Personality and Social Psychology* 49:250–263.

Elder, Glen H., and Avshalom Caspi 1990 "Studying Lives in a Changing Society: Sociological and Personological Explorations." In A. I. Rabin, R. A. Zucker, R. A. Emmons, and S. Frank, eds., *Studying Persons and Lives*. New York: Springer.

Emerson, Richard M. 1987 "Toward a Theory of Value in Social Exchange." In K. S. Cook, eds., *Social Exchange Theory*. Newbury Park, Calif.: Sage.

Fallding, Harold 1965 "A Proposal for the Empirical Study of Values." *American Sociological Review* 30:223–233.

Fishbein, Martin and Icek Ajzen 1975 *Belief, Attitude, Intention and Behavior*. Reading, Mass.: Addison-Wesley.

Gibbs, Jack P. 1965 "Norms: The Problem of Definition and Classification." *American Journal of Sociology* 70:586–594.

Glenn, Noval D. 1980 "Values, Attitudes and Beliefs." In O. G. Brim, Jr., and J. Kagan, eds., *Constancy and Change in Human Development*. Cambridge, Mass.: Harvard University Press.

Kahneman, Daniel, and Amos Tversky 1979 "Prospect Theory: An Analysis of Decision Under Risk." *Econometrica* 47:263–291.

Kluckhohn, Clyde 1951 "Values and Value-Orientations in the Theory of Action: An Exploration in Definition and Classification." In T. Parsons and E. A. Shils, eds., *Toward a General Theory of Action.* New York: Harper & Row.

Lovejoy, Arthur O. 1950 "Terminal and Adjectival Values." *The Journal of Philosophy* 47:593–608.

Marini, Margaret Mooney 1984 "Age and Sequencing Norms in the Transition to Adulthood." *Social Forces* 63:229–244.

——, 1992 "The Role of Models of Purposive Action in Sociology." In J. S. Coleman and T. J. Fararo, eds., *Rational Choice Theory: Advocacy and Critique.* Newbury Park, Calif.: Sage.

Moss, Howard A., and Elizabeth J. Susman 1980 "Longitudinal Study of Personality Development." In O. G. Brim, Jr., and J. Kagan, eds., *Constancy and Change in Human Development.* Cambridge, Mass: Harvard University Press.

Parsons, Talcott, and Edward A. Shils 1951 "Values, Motives, and Systems of Action." In T. Parsons and E. A. Shils, eds., *Toward a General Theory of Action.* New York: Harper & Row.

Rokeach, Milton 1973 *The Nature of Human Values.* New York: Free Press.

—— 1985 "Inducing Change and Stability in Belief Systems and Personality Structures." *Journal of Social Issues* 41:153–171.

Rossi, Peter H., and Richard A. Berk 1985 "Varieties of Normative Consensus." *American Sociological Review* 50:333–347.

Schwartz, Shalom H., and Wolfgang Bilsky 1987 "Toward a Universal Psychological Structure of Human Values." *Journal of Personality and Social Psychology* 53:550–562.

Sears, David O. 1981 "Life-Stage Effects on Attitude Change, Especially among the Elderly." In S. B. Kiesler, J. N. Morgan, and V. K. Oppenheimer, eds., *Aging: Social Change.* New York: Academic Press.

—— 1983 "The Persistence of Early Political Predispositions: The Roles of Attitude Object and Life Stage." In L. Wheeler, eds., *Review of Personality and Social Psychology,* vol. 4. Beverly Hills, Calif.: Sage.

Thornton, Arland 1985 "Changing Attitudes toward Separation and Divorce: Causes and Consequences." *American Journal of Sociology* 90:856–872.

Wells, L. E., and Sheldon Stryker 1988 "Stability and Change in Self over the Life Course." In P. B. Baltes, D. L. Featherman, and R. M. Lerner, eds., *Life-Span Development and Behavior.* Hillsdale, N.J.: Erlbaum.

MARGARET MOONEY MARINI

SOCIAL WORK

Social work has been defined as being "concerned with the interactions between people and their social environment which affect the ability of people to accomplish life tasks, alleviate distress, and realize their aspirations and values. The purpose of social work therefore is to (1) enhance the problem-solving and coping capacities of people, (2) link people with systems that provide them with resources, services, and opportunities, (3) promote the effective and humane operation of these systems, and (4) contribute to the development and improvement of social policy" (Pincus and Minahan 1973, p. 9). A key difference between social work and sociology lies in the emphasis placed on intervention in social work. A social worker expects to be actively involved in the amelioration of social problems, while a sociologist typically focuses on understanding the nature and extent of social issues. Social workers establish a helping relationship with a client system (individual, family, small group, community), using their assessment skills and knowledge of helping resources to identify alternatives that may improve a situation.

PROFESSIONAL ROOTS

Professional social work is historically tied to the emergence of social welfare as a social institution. Social welfare as it has come to be known, can be traced to society's numerous attempts to accommodate changes in economic and social relationships over time. The beginning of institutionalized social welfare is frequently ascribed to the English Poor Law of 1601. As the most critical part of modern social welfare's foundation, the Elizabethan poor laws were characterized by the articulation and promulgation of the principle of public responsibility and obligation for the economic well-being of the people. However, "the Poor Laws in England and in American communities were not primarily concerned with poverty and how to eliminate it. Instead, they were concerned with pauperism and the potential claims on community funds, the danger that paupers might get by without working" (Dolgoff and Feldstein 1984, p. 80). This continuing tension between public obligation and social control is one of several dualities that characterize the context of professional social work practice. Institutionalized social welfare is the environment in which the profession of social work has developed. The history of social welfare is paralleled by and enmeshed with the increasing professionalism of those who administer social welfare programs.

Early social work was characterized by two streams of activity: social reform and direct assistance to individuals and families. The practice of friendly visiting and the development of both the Charity Organizations Societies and settlement houses illustrate both types of effort. Representatives of Charity Organization Socities, the so-called friendly visitors, engaged in social investigation and moral susasion improve the lives of the poor. The thrust of those encounters was to place responsibility on the persons or families for their economic and social status, what is known now as "blaming the victim." The work of the Charity Organization Societies formed the origins of the social work method later known as social casework.

Residents of settlement houses, Jane Adams included, were friendly visitors who came to stay. A group of middle-class or upper-class individuals moved into residence in a poor area in an effort to study neighborhood conditions firsthand and work with neighborhood residents on solving neighborhood problems. While some settlement house efforts focused on assimilation, later programs focused on improving conditions in immigrant communities. In cities across the nation, settlement houses helped acculturate vast numbers of immigrants in the early part of the twentieth century. Settlement house activities emphasized teaching English, health practices, occupational skills, and environmental changes through cooperative efforts. Settlement house staff developed social group work, community organization, social action, and environmental change efforts. Furthermore, settlement house workers were active in the legislative arena, gathering and promulgating facts in order to influence social policy and legislation.

An early and continuing cleavage in the profession has its origins in differing explanations of social dysfunction. Some early social workers espoused the theory of the social causation of social problems and sought governmental actions to meet needs as well as developing coalitions for reform and institutional change. The educational foundation came from sociology, economics, and political science. Others emphasized individual causation of social problems, promoting an individually focused therapeutic approach to helping. These social workers identified the need to draw on psychological theory but emphasized the individual interacting with a social environment. These two primary orientations would feed the development of professional social work and provide the basis for conflict within the practice community and in professional social work education

PROFESSIONALIZATION

An issue throughout the development of professional social work has been the nature of its professional status. In 1915 Abraham Flexner critiqued the professional status of social work at the National Conference of Charities and Corrections. Although Flexner criticized social work as lacking a specific skill for a specific function, he also recognized its professional spirit. The ideal-type model of a profession has been the conception against which social work has measured itself through much of its history. Greenwood's (1957) analysis examined the extent to which social work possessed five classic traits of a profession: systematic theory, authority, community sanction, an ethical code, and a professional culture. Characterizing social work as a less-developed profession, Greenwood concluded that it possessed these attributes to a moderate extent. The predominant direction of the field, however, has been to continue its professional development along all five dimensions. The recent emphasis on building the empirical base of practice coupled with more stringent licensure requirements by states are indicators of the continued progression of social work toward greater professional status. It would be incorrect to assume, however, that this direction is embraced by the profession as a whole. For those whose dominant professional identification is with the field's social action tradition, increasing professionalization means being co-opted. Achieving the public acceptance accorded to a profession can distance social workers from their constituencies and limit confrontational strategies that are central to advocacy for the oppressed.

In the 1920s the practice of social work emerged in so-called fields of practice or settings: family and child welfare and medical, psychiatric, and school social work. Social workers defined their central problems and responsibilities as being characteristic of their particular fields. The concept of method also emerged during this period. Method developed first around casework and later in relation to both group work and community organization. Methods were based on selected theories of human behavior drawn from psychology and sociology. Setting referred to the organizational context within which services were delivered.

This combination of method and field of practice or setting fragmented professional social work, slowing the development of an integrated theoretical base for practice across methods and settings. Social casework theory and method developed to a large extent in isolation from group work and community organization. The curricula for professional social work education followed the same pattern, with separate tracks for each method. It took until the 1970s for the development of a conceptual approach based on the essential components of professional practice regardless of where a social worker was employed. Pincus and Minahan (1970) articulated a conceptual framework for generalist practice, that is, for social work service delivery across practice settings. This approach encompassed three major components: the *social systems* in relation to which a social worker carries out his or her role, the stages of *planned change* or problem-solving processes, and interactional and analytic *skills* for data collection, analysis, and intervention.

VALUES, ETHICS, AND THE BUREAUCRATIC CONTEXT

Since social work as a profession is concerned with social change and the improvement of the conditions in which people live, its orientation cannot be value-free or purely theoretical. A defining characteristic of social work practice is a fundamental commitment to knowledge, skills, and a core set of professional values to enhance the well-being of people and ameliorate environmental conditions that affect people adversely. Among the values and principles that guide professional practice are respect for individual worth, dignity, the right to self-determination, and active partici-

pation in the helping process; helping clients obtain needed resources; demonstrating respect for and acceptance of the characteristics of diverse populations; a commitment to the promotion of social change to achieve social and economic justice; an understanding of the dynamics of oppression and discrimination, along with attention to populations at risk; and a holistic view of the interactions between people and the complex environment in which they live. These values are embedded in the *Code of Ethics* of the National Association of Social Workers (1994). The code focuses on the conduct and comportment of a social worker as well as ethical responsibilities to clients, colleagues, employers, the profession, and society.

A distinguishing characteristic of social work is that the majority of its practitioners are employed by a variety of public and private social welfare agencies. Some social workers are employed by agencies that are sanctioned to function as agents of social control, while others have the authority to determine eligibility for benefits and services. The bureaucratic environment, however manifested, dramatically shapes the practice of social workers. The process of professional socialization is designed to instill a culture, a set of values and expectations, that may conflict with the work environment.

Professionals' autonomy can be circumscribed by organizational commitments, policies, and procedures. In these circumstances, just whose agent is the professional social worker: the agency's, the client's, the community's, or his or her own as an autonomous professional? In an organizational context, what form can a social worker's social action efforts take? How far can an employed social worker go in challenging an agency's priorities, policies, and procedures before his or her services are no longer desired? How long does it take before a professional social worker starts to identify more as an agency employee than as an autonomous professional? Given the range of practice settings and the variety of roles of social workers, there are no easy answers to these questions. These realities can produce a conservatizing effect on social work, limiting many workers' willingness or ability to take risks as autonomous professionals in the name of social justice and reform. In these circumstances, one can see how theories of individual causation can prevail over explanations that invoke the influence of larger social forces in the creation and amelioration of social problems. This tension, with its roots in the origins of the profession, continues, as demonstrated by the overwhelming preference of students and professionals for work with individuals and families, mostly in the psychotherapeutic model.

THE KNOWLEDGE BASE AND EMPIRICALLY BASED PRACTICE

The creation of a systematic body of theory has been under development from the early days of the profession. Richmond's *Social Diagnosis* (1917) organized the contemporary theory and method of social work and formulated a data collection approach designed to serve as the foundation for diagnosis. Richmond organized and analyzed the naturalistic observations she made while working with individuals and families. Her work is the origin of psychosocial history taking and treatment plan development and perhaps the core of social casework practice methods. Richmond's contribution to the organization of what eventually would become social casework practice is legendary, forming the bedrock of clinical social work. Her approach, later to be known as empirically based practice, represents one of the two major streams of knowledge and theory development in social work. The other major focus has relied heavily on the application of social science (primarily sociological and psychological) theory to the explanation of social problems and the development of interventions to ameliorate those problems.

The breadth of social work practice (encompassing work with individuals, families, groups, and communities and including social work program administration, public policy development, and social planning) provides a rich and continually changing field for exploratory, descriptive, and explanatory empirical efforts. The early 1970s was a benchmark in the development of the profession's knowledge base. Along with the massive investment in social programs of the 1960s came the realization that good intentions and humane values are not enough. Funders focused increasingly on outcomes. Attention was shifted to the development of empirically based justifications for programs, services, and budgets. Program evaluation became the dominant focus of much of social work research during this period, including methodology, design, outcomes, and professional accountability. This direction came to be known as the practice effectiveness movement. As articulated by Fischer, the question became, "Is Casework Effective?" (Fischer 1973; Fischer and Hudson 1976).

During this period, a study of the effects of adult protective services by Blenkner et al. (1971) at the Benjamin Rose Institute in Cleveland created a furor. An early social experiment, this demonstration program, which employed skilled caseworkers, was reported to be associated with more negative effects than was the control program, which employed less highly trained workers. After one year, the findings were alarming. The experimental group manifested higher death rates, higher utilization of protective services, higher rates of institutionalization, a nonsignificant increase in contentment, and a nonsignificant decrease in symptoms of emotional disturbance. The authors concluded that the "effect of more skilled social workers on the clients was to 'overdose' them with help. This led to more concrete assistance, including institutionalization, which in turn was responsible for the higher death rate. . . . More highly trained social workers were apparently more lethal" (Tobin 1978). These findings could not demonstrate the effectiveness of professional social work intervention, illustrate accountability, or be used to justify program expenditures.

This study and the controversy it generated shifted attention from program description to research design, sampling, and data analysis. Investigators (Berger and Piliavin 1976; Fischer and Hudson 1976) reanalyzed the data in an attempt to discover alternative explanations for the findings. Berger and Piliavin argued that although randomization had been used to assign clients to groups, the experimental group was older and more mentally and physically impaired than were the controls. Fischer and Hudson (1976) challenged the sample size used in Berger and Piliavin's regression analysis and demonstrated that age, mental status, and physical status, although separate variables, produced an additive effect. The nature of the debate had shifted: Methodological issues had become the basis of discussion. Values and good intentions alone would no longer be sufficient grounds for justifying programs or demonstrating professional accountability.

THE PRACTITIONER-RESEARCHER

Concern with the outcomes of social work interventions led to the concept of the social worker as both practitioner and researcher. From this perspective, social workers are seen as having the opportunity and responsibility to develop methods and skills from an empirical base, from the experience provided in their own practice to develop, test, and refine practice innovations. Embedded in this movement toward practitioner-based empirical practice was the notion that evaluation and research were too critical to leave in the hands of a group of research "specialists." Perhaps more fundamental is the belief that social work research is too important to leave in the hands of those who are not social workers: "It is the practicing professional who encounters and struggles with current issues and who is most sensitive to the critical knowledge gaps in the field. Thus social workers are in the best position to formulate and conduct the needed research and evaluation and they must be committed to acquiring the understanding required to direct the helping effort" (Grinnell 1996, p. 5)

These developments coincided with the expansion of doctoral education in social work. While past doctoral preparation often focused on the development of advanced clinical skills, contemporary training at the doctoral level is almost exclusively research-based, designed to provide students with the skills needed to contribute to the empirically anchored knowledge base of the profession. As a result, a cohort of social work researchers has been trained over the last twenty years, and this group has developed a body of theory and knowledge that has been generated directly as social work research. Social work no longer defers to sociology for the methodological sophistication to evaluate its programs and practice outcomes.

SOCIOLOGY AND SOCIAL WORK

Over time the link between social work and sociology has been strong, although the two fields have grown increasingly distant. There can be little doubt, however, regarding the importance of sociological theory and research for the development of the knowledge and theoretical base of social work practice. For example, social stratification, conflict theory, deviance, organizational theory, community development and dynamics, family studies, occupational sociology, criminology, and life-span theories are only a few areas of sociological theory development and research that have informed and directly influenced both the theory and the practice of social work. Landmark social program evaluation studies were undertaken by sociologists, some of whom were members of faculties of social work, in the late 1950s and 1960s (Meyer and Borgatta 1959; Meyer et al. 1965).

Clearly, social work and sociology are related, although there are fundamental differences. Sociologists study and analyze social organizations and institutions. The emphasis has been on theory development, primarily through positivistic approaches, focusing on measurement and design issues. Although the development of grounded theory (Glaser and Strauss 1967) has been a major conceptual contribution in sociology, it has not been the dominant influence. Although there are reform-minded, "radical" sociologists, they are a minority. Sociologists are interested in understanding the "why" of human interaction. Sociology observes; it maintains a detached posture.

In contrast, social workers attempt to apply theories of social organization and interaction to improve social functioning. Social workers go beyond understanding social problems in their efforts to improve social functioning; social work intervenes. The goal is engendering progressive social change, improving social conditions, creating more humane delivery systems, and problem solving with individuals, families, groups, communities, and organizations and in public policy. Social workers develop and implement interventions in the form of programs, policies, and services in the context of public funding and demands for professional accountability. The orientation is toward outcomes, cost-effectiveness, and cost-benefit analyses.

There has been and continues to be tension in the relationship. Heraud notes that "the social worker may be able to participate actively in policy making through social science research; there is considerable need for research related to both intended and unintended consequences of social policy . . . there is considerable need in the initial stages of such research for intuition and speculation. Instead of only using the sociologist at this stage, who may be a distant figure, the social worker may have an important role to play" (1970, p. 287). Several years earlier, Halmos noted that social workers could function "as an intelligence agent of the sociologist and of the policy maker, and a trusty pilot of the sociological researcher" (1961, p. 9). Although these attitudes may be antiquated, elements of such elitism remain, particularly in sociology's limited interest in applied social research.

Some attention has been paid to the development of so-called applied sociology. While the main body of sociological thought focuses on exploratory, descriptive, and explanatory theory; modeling; and empirical testing, "applied sociology" briefly emerged in response to the increasing interest in social program evaluation and the limited supply of trained methodologists who could design and execute well-formulated evaluative studies. Thus, applied sociology could provide an alternative, public-policy-oriented career path for sociologists, since the preferred, higher-status university-based employment opportunities were limited.

Over the last twenty five years, however, social work researchers have become key players in the design, implementation, and analysis of applied social research, particularly through their involvement in federally funded demonstration projects. During this period, there has been a proliferation of journals of social work, including research journals (*Social Work Research and Abstracts, Research on Social Work Practice*), as well as a range of specialty journals (*Gerontological Social Work, Health and Social Work, Child Welfare, School Social Work*), which provide publication outlets for researchers and practitioners.

At one time, social work education occurred within the social sciences, frequently attached to sociology. More recently, social work has emerged as an independent professional discipline, forming alliances with a variety of other professions, such as law, education, business, and nursing. Increasing numbers of pragmatic students have been attracted to social work because of the ability of graduates to find employment.

The undergraduate degree (BSW) offers a generalist foundation that is built on a set of social science prerequisites. The graduate degree (MSW), the terminal educational degree for the profession, is based on specialized courses that offer advanced theoretical content in fields of practice and methodological approaches. The Council on Social Work Education (CSWE) has exercised a substantial influence in setting standards for social work education. Periodic accreditation reviews by the council assure uniformity and consistency in the required content. Particular attention has been paid to including content on minorities and oppressed populations. Accreditation by the CSWE is essential for the credibility of any social work education program in the United States.

Social work is an evolving profession, with its form and emphasis changing in response to the societal context within which social workers practice:

> "*Most social workers feel that although there are critical problems and pressures, numerous opportunities are available for the social work profession to move ahead on a sound basis, strengthening current delivery of services and innovating services that have been practically untouched to date. . . . Once thought of as a basket-on-the arm assistance for the poor, it is now a discipline, scientific in method and artful in manner, that takes remedial action on problems in several areas of society*" (Skidmore et al. 1997 pp. 376 to 3).

REFERENCES

Berger, Raymond, and Irving Piliavin 1976 "The Effect of Casework: A Research Note." *Social Work*: 21:205–208.

Blenkner, Margaret, Martin Bloom, and Margaret Nielson 1971 "A Research and Demonstration Project of Protective Services." *Social Casework* 52:483–499.

Dolgoff, Ralph, and Donald Feldstein 1984 *Undertanding Social Welfare*, 2nd ed. New York: Longman.

Fischer, Joel 1973 "Is Casework Effective? A Review." *Social Work* 18:5–20.

——, and Walter Hudson 1976 "An Effect of Casework? Back to the Drawing Board." Points and Viewpoints. *Social Work* 21:347–349.

Glaser, Barney, and Anselm Strauss 1967 *The Discovery of Grounded Theory: Strategies for Qualitative Research*. New York: Aldine de Gruyter.

Greenwood, Ernest 1957 "Attributes of a Profession." *Social Work* 2:45–55.

Grinnell, Richard 1996 *Social Work Research and Evaluation*. Itasca, Ill.: Peacock.

Halmos, Peter 1961 "Problems Arising in the Teaching of Sociology to Social Workers." *International Social Service Review* 8:122–130.

Heraud, Brian 1970 *Sociology and Social Work*. New York: Pergamon.

Meyer, Henry, and Edgar Borgatta 1959 *An Experiment in Mental Health Rehabilitation: Evaluating a Social Agency Program*. New York: Russell Sage Foundation.

——, ——, and Wyatt Jones 1965 *Girls at Vocational High: An Experiment in Social Work Intervention*. New York: Russell Sage Foundation. National Association of Social Workers 1994 *Code of Ethics*. Washington, D.C.: National Association of Social Workers.

Pincus, Allen, and Anne Minahan 1970 "Toward a Model for Teaching a Basic First Year Course in Methods for Social Work Practice." In Lillian Ripple, ed., *Teaching Social Work Practice*. New York: Council on Social Work Education.

—— 1973 *Social Work Practice: Model and Method*. Itasca, Ill.: Peacock.

Richmond, Mary 1917 *Social Diagnosis*. New York: Russell Sage Foundation.

Skidmore, Rex, Milton Thackeray, and William Farley 1997 *Introduction to Social Work*, 7th ed. Boston: Allyn and Bacon.

Tobin, Sheldon 1978 "Old People." In Henry Maas, ed., *Social Service Research: Reviews of Studies*. Washington, D.C.: National Association of Social Workers.

CAROL D. AUSTIN
ROBERT W. McCLELLAND

SOCIAL-AREA ANALYSIS

See Cities.

SOCIALISM AND COMMUNISM

What is socialism? According to a Hungarian joke made during the "gentle revolution" of 1989, it is the "longest and most painful road from capitalism to capitalism" (Garton Ash 1990). Although this biting definition was fashionably cynical about Soviet-type societies in the wake of their fall, it provides no substantive insights into one of the major social organizational forms of modern history.

The origins of socialism are obscure. Intellectual historians have traced its beginnings to the religious utopias of the Old Testament (Laidler 1968), the principles of Mosaic law (Gray 1963), the anti-individualism of the radical sects that emerged after the French Revolution (Lichtheim

1969), and the publication of the *Communist Manifesto* (Sweezy 1983). As well as can be determined, the term made its first appearance in Italian print in 1803, although its meaning at that time differed somewhat from the current interpretations (Cole 1959). For this reason, the origin of the term usually is attributed to the *London Co-Operative Magazine*, where it was used to designate followers of Robert Owen (Nuti 1981). The first French usage followed shortly thereafter when, in 1832, a French periodical, *Le Globe*, used it to characterize the writings of Saint-Simon (Bell 1968; Kolakowski 1978).

Despite its complicated origins, by 1840 the concept was used commonly throughout Europe and was making its way across the Atlantic to the United States. By the early 1920s, the Soviet Union had already claimed "socialism" as its overall organizing principle; ironically, at that time, over 260 definitions of the term were available in the social scientific literature (Griffith 1924), rendering its meaning somewhat ambiguous. Since then, further transformations of the concept have appeared; for instance, scholars now differentiate among Chinese socialism, corporatist socialism, democratic socialism, radical socialism, and Russian socialism.

The common core of socialist ideas is hard to define. To be sure, all socialists were critical of the competitive and unequal nature of capitalist society, and without fail, they championed a more egalitarian and just future. At the same time, their visions of the organization of a socialist future were sufficiently diverse to render a single definition of the term practically impossible. It is frequently assumed, for example, that all socialists wanted to establish communal ownership, yet many were content with the centralization of resources in the hands of the state (e.g., Bernstein 1961) and others actually protested the abolition of private property (e.g., Saint-Simon 1964). Battles also were waged over the role of the state: Some believed that centrally managed administrative organs would become superfluous under a socialist regime (Proudhon 1966), while others regarded those organs as essential for the management of community affairs (e.g., Cabet 1975). Many argued that the freedom of the individual must be guaranteed at all costs even under socialism (e.g., Fourier 1971), while others were willing to impose limitations on such freedom in the name of equality and efficient production (Mao 1971). Finally, some believed that socialism could be realized through gradual reforms (Bernstein 1961), while others thought that it was possible only through a major revolution (Lenin 1971).

Because of the nontrivial nature of these differences, a single definition of socialism is likely to conceal more than it illuminates. For this reason, it is more productive to highlight features of the concept by examining separately some of the best known schools of socialist thought.

THE IDEA OF SOCIALISM

In the view of utopian socialists, socialism was a romantic vision whose purpose was not necessarily to be realized but to serve as an ideal against which the evils of capitalism could be compared. The specific content of this vision varied from author to author, but two central themes can be identified.

The ideal of community was the first of those themes. From Fourier to Cabet, through Owen and Saint-Simon, all utopian theorists championed a new social order organized around small communities. In most sketches of socialism, this vision was realized in an agrarian setting (e.g., Cabet 1975), although some required advanced industrial development (e.g., Saint-Simon 1964). In either case, however, it was assumed that those communities would be based on fellowship, harmony, and altruism—virtues that utopian theorists favored on moral grounds over bourgeois individualism.

Nostalgia for the past is the second common theme in utopian socialist thought. It frequently appeared in utopian novels and usually assumed one of two forms. In some versions, the protagonists in those novels were returned to a romanticized preindustrialism, while in others, they returned to an even more distant past, such as the Middle Ages (e.g., Morris 1970). Despite such variation in the settings of those novels, the message they sought to convey was more or less the same: In the transition to industrial capitalism, people abandoned the "golden age" of social harmony and replaced it with a fragmented and competitive social order that is unable to provide for the full satisfaction of human needs.

In the hands of scientific socialists, the idea of socialism represented more than just an attractive

dream (Marx and Engels 1968). Karl Marx, for example, considered it a historically possible future for capitalism, as he assumed that the internal contradictions of capitalism would create some of the preconditions for socialism. According to his theory of historical materialism, the demands made by capitalist development will create increasingly grave crises for the ruling class. He maintained that with the mechanization of production and the concentration of capital in the hands of a few, there will be greater polarization in terms of class inequalities and an increase in the degree of exploitation of the working class. As capitalism enters its advanced stage, the condition of the working class will deteriorate and the struggle over the quality of its existence will intensify. At first, the war between the "two hostile camps" of capitalist society (the bourgeoisie and the proletariat) will be waged within the boundaries of particular nation-states. However, as capitalism expands into new markets internationally, workers across the world will be forced to unite in their effort to overthrow capitalist society. Socialism, according to Marx, will emerge out of this final instance of class struggle.

It is ironic that the "father of socialism" never provided a detailed blueprint for his model of the future. It is evident from a number of passages, however, that Marx envisioned two stages in the evolution of socialism. In the lower stage (which he referred to as *socialism*, or the "dictatorship of the proletariat"), he foreshadowed major improvements in the human condition. He predicted, for example, that private property would be abolished, the forces of production would be nationalized and placed in the hands of the state, rights of inheritance would be eliminated, universal suffrage would be introduced, state representatives would be elected from among the working people, and education would become accessible to all. At the same time, because Marx expected this to be a transitional stage, he believed that some elements of capitalist society would continue to prevail. Specifically, he mentioned that income inequalities would continue to exist in the lower stage because workers would still be paid according to the amount of work they contributed to the social good.

At some point, according to Marx, this transitional phase in the development of human history would evolve into the higher stage of socialism, a stage that he often referred to as *communism*, or the "realm of freedom." Under communism, work would no longer be an obligation but a free and creative activity, alienation would be transcended, the production process would be under the direct control of the producers, and rewards would be distributed in accordance with the principle of "to each according to his need" rather than "to each according to his ability."

Scientific socialism gained considerable popularity among French, German, and British socialists during the nineteenth century. Many agreed with Marx's assessment of bourgeois society and were attracted to his vision of the future. As the century progressed, however, and the Marxist scenario still appeared to be far away, some began to raise questions about the continued relevance of scientific socialism in the modern age. The main protagonist in this debate was Eduard Bernstein, a leading advocate of democratic socialism.

Bernstein and his followers called into question various elements of scientific socialism, but they were especially concerned about Marx's predictions concerning the development of industrial capitalism. On the basis of new empirical evidence, Bernstein (1961) noted that the standard of living at the turn of the century was improving rather than deteriorating, class inequalities were far from polarized, and the ownership of capital, rather than being concentrated in the hands of a few, was becoming diversified. In addition, he observed that general strikes were becoming less common and socialist parties were gaining considerable strength in the political organization of the state. In light of those findings, Bernstein called for a revision of the Marxist program and offered a new interpretation of socialism.

According to Bernstein, democracy was the most important feature of socialist society. He discouraged his confederates from describing socialism as a "dictatorship of the proletariat" and recommended that they acknowledge its fundamentally pluralist character. Of course, for Bernstein, the significance of democracy was not simply that it guaranteed the representation of minority rights under socialism; it was also that it assured a peaceful transition from capitalism through a series of parliamentary reforms. For many later socialists, this emphasis on reform came to represent the essence of democratic socialism; it was this idea, in fact, that earned the "revisionist" label for this school of socialist thought.

Needless to say, Bernstein was not the only theorist to revise Marx's ideas on socialism. In the early part of the twentieth century, Vladimir Ilyich Lenin (1971) also amended the concept by adding to it several new notions, some of which were derived from his experience with political organization in tsarist Russia. Taken together, these propositions constitute Russian socialism, also known as Bolshevik theory.

The best known contribution of this school of thought to socialist theory is the idea of the "vanguard party." According to Lenin, Marx was unduly optimistic in his belief that the proletariat could develop the necessary class consciousness to overthrow capitalism. If left to their own devices, Lenin claimed, workers would defend only their immediate (i.e., economic or trade union) interests and would not know how to translate them into revolutionary action. To assist them in this task, he suggested that a vanguard party of intellectuals must be formed, the task of which would be to develop a revolutionary theory, "go among the masses," and politically educate the proletariat. From the point of view of Bolshevik theory, therefore, the success of the socialist revolution depends not on the political maturity of the working class but on the strength of the vanguard party.

A second feature of Russian socialism that sets it apart from the Marxist scheme is grounded in its claim that the prospects of a proletarian revolution can arise not only in advanced industrial societies but also in precapitalist economic formations. Given the importance of the vanguard party in Lenin's version of socialism, this idea makes perfect sense: As long as a country is equipped with a group of willing, dedicated, and professional revolutionaries, it should be able to make the transition to socialism without the benefits of advanced technology or without having passed through the capitalist stage.

Last but not least, Lenin took from Marx the idea that socialism will come in two stages. In terms of his scheme, however, the lower stage (the "dictatorship of the proletariat") would not be a brief transitional period but would require a whole epoch in human history. During this time, the bourgeois state would be "smashed," the class rule of the proletariat would be institutionalized, and opponents of the socialist regime would be suppressed by the "special coercive force" of the proletarian state. The higher state of socialism ("communism") would be realized once the socialist state had "withered away" and democracy had become a "force of habit."

Russian socialism constitutes one of many indigenous graftings of the socialist vision. Another well-known attempt in this direction was made by Mao Zedong (1971), who accommodated the idea of socialism to the conditions of a peasant country. Those revisions led to the emergence of what is known as Chinese socialism or Maoism.

Unlike most interpretations of socialism, Mao's is famous for its glorification of the peasantry. Earlier socialists, among them Marx and Lenin, were skeptical about the revolutionary potential of agricultural laborers. For the most part, they regarded them as inherently petty bourgeois and, consequently, as unlikely allies of the proletariat. Mao argued, however, that in a peasant country such as China, traditionally conceived paths to socialism are not viable because they require the mass mobilization of something that his type of country does not have: an industrial proletariat. He insisted therefore that the socialist revolution in China was a peasant revolution and had no reservations about organizing agricultural workers into a revolutionary force.

Another trademark of Chinese socialism is its lack of confidence in the guaranteed future of socialism. According to Mao's writings, socialist victories are not everlasting; even as the dust from the revolution begins to settle, old inequalities can resurface and new ones may emerge. For this reason, the work of revolutionaries is never complete: They must be constantly on guard against opposition and be prepared to wage a permanent revolution.

THE REALITY OF SOCIALISM

During the nineteenth century, a number of communities were established to attempt the realization of the socialist vision, including Etienne Cabe's Icaria in Illinois, Charles Fourier's Brook Farm in Massachusetts, William Lane's New Australia in Paraguay, and Robert Owen's New Harmony in Indiana. In nearly all these cases, an attempt was made to isolate a small group of dedicated social-

ists from the rest of society and create a model environment for efficient production and egalitarian social exchange. The documented history of these communities suggests that they experienced varying amounts of success (Ross 1935). Some attracted a large number of followers (e.g., Icaria) and prospered for more than a decade (e.g., Brook Farm). Others were fraught with hardships from the beginning (e.g., New Australia), and some collapsed within a few years (e.g., New Harmony). In the end, however, all the utopian experiments failed: They suffered from lack of preparation and meager financial support, harsh living environments and a dearth of agricultural skills, heterogeneous membership, and a lack of long-term commitment to the socialist vision. The individuals who flocked to those communities were sufficiently adventuresome to embark on a project to build a new world but were not prepared for the trials of pioneering.

Experiments with socialism in the twentieth century were more successful and longer-lasting than their utopian counterparts. After the Russian Revolution, 1917–1923, the Soviet Union was the first country to call itself socialist. By the middle of the century, however, there were regimes in Europe, Asia, Latin America, Africa, and the Near East modeling themselves after the Soviet scheme (Hollander 1983). At the risk of oversimplifying, the following traits may be identified as the most important features of those "actually existing" (Bahro 1978) socialist societies: (1) They were characterized by a common ownership of the means of production and distribution. (2) Their economic activities were centrally planned by the state, and market forces played little or no role in the allocation of their resources. (3) One party ruled their political life and legitimated itself by reference to some version of Marxism and Leninism. (4) That party dominated their political culture with a unitary ideology and directed all their executive, legislative, and judiciary powers.

In their purest form, Soviet-type societies have secured a number of major achievements. Within decades of the revolution, they industrialized their outmoded economies (Berend and Ránki 1974), guaranteed full employment and attained price stability (Nove 1989), incorporated women into the labor force (Rueschemeyer and Szelényi 1989), developed their natural resources and advanced science and technology (Nuti 1981), strengthened their military power (Starr 1988), and improved their educational, health care, and welfare systems (Ferge 1979). Along with those changes, socialist societies made a strong commitment to reducing income, educational, and occupational differentials after World War II (Szelényi 1998). Empirically, a number of studies have shown that those formally egalitarian policies have had impressive results: In nearly all these countries, inequalities in income have decreased (Matthews 1972; Walder 1989), educational opportunities have expanded (Lane 1976), and distinctions of prestige between manual and nonmanual occupations have narrowed (Parkin 1971; Giddens 1973). Policies also were implemented by socialist states to reduce the intergenerational transmission of social inequalities: Inheritance of wealth was eliminated, and quotas were imposed on educational and occupational recruitment to favor children from the working class and from peasant families (Simkus and Andorka 1982; Szelényi and Aschaffenburg 1993). Perhaps in part as a result of these changes, socialist societies carved out for themselves a position of considerable importance in the world system in the twentieth century. In the 1960s, for example, the Soviet Union competed directly with the United States in space exploration, the race for military power, and the development of science, technology, athletics, and the arts.

The economic and social miracles achieved by these countries in the years after World War II could not be sustained, however. By the early 1970s, centrally managed economies began to exhibit multiple signs of strain. Bureaucratic blunders on the part of state officials resulted in poor investment decisions (Nove 1983b), frequent bottlenecks created breakdowns in production (Bauer 1978), chronic shortages of consumer items provoked anger and dissatisfaction among the citizens (Kornai 1986), and curious managerial techniques (in the form of bribing, hoarding, and informal networking) had to be developed to mitigate the ineffective relationship between economic units and the state (Stark 1986).

Problems with central management, of course, were not restricted to the economic sphere. With a growing number of empirical studies during the 1970s (see Hollander 1983), the social and political consequences of Soviet-type planning became evident, although most scholars continued to be impressed by the initially positive outcome of egalitarian state policies in socialist societies. At the same time, they soon began to realize that the quotas introduced after World War II were often applied inconsistently and in almost all circumstances disturbingly short-lived (Szelényi 1998). It is clear from these studies that the initial attempts to "build socialism" soon were overturned by a "second stage" in socialist development (Kelley and Klein 1986) that was marked by the crystallization of inequalities and the emergence of new privileges (Ossowski 1963; Nove 1983a). By the 1970s, many of those societies began to demonstrate substantial inequalities in their prestige hierarchies (Inkeles 1966), patterns of social mobility (Connor 1979), opportunities for educational attainment (Simkus and Andorka 1982), and distribution of monetary and nonmonetary rewards (Szelényi 1976; Walder 1986).

The political inequalities that characterized Soviet-type societies during their heyday are well documented in the literature. Many studies have shown, for example, that Communist Party functionaries and the so-called *nomenklatura* elite enjoyed definite social, political, and economic advantages: They attended party schools, shopped at special stores, vacationed at the most desirable holiday resorts, and had better access to decision-making posts (Szelényi 1987). In addition to those privileges, they were more likely to receive state-subsidized housing, purchase a car or vacation home, eat meat several times a week, and participate in cultural activities. Such differences in the allocation of goods and resources have led many to conclude that the political sphere was central to the stratification system of socialist societies (Goldthorpe 1966; Bauman 1974). Indeed, some scholars have suggested that the political elite may well have constituted a New (dominant) Class in socialist regimes (Djilas 1957; Konrád and Szelényi 1979).

In light of these problems as well as the apparent failure of the egalitarian experiment, socialist states made a number of attempts to reform their ailing economies. Yugoslavia began this trend by introducing a new economic program that combined free market principles with workers' self-management; in 1949, Yugoslav leaders abandoned central planning, tied wages to the financial success of firms, and liberalized foreign trade (Sirc 1979). Hungary followed suit in 1968 by introducing its own version of market socialism (Hare et al.

1981), and China joined the trend in the late 1970s with similar economic reforms (Nee 1989).

Partial reprivatization, however, was not the only way for centrally managed economies to embark on the road to recovery. East Germany, for example, refused to combine planning with market reforms and chose to strengthen the operation of its central management (Szelényi 1989). In an effort to "scienticize" economic planning, East German leaders purchased state-of-the-art computers and sophisticated econometric programs to model the behavior of thousands of firms and anticipate the needs of millions of consumers. Cuba also refrained from market reforms in the late 1960s (Leogrande 1981). Hoping to prevent the restoration of capitalism in his country, Fidel Castro argued against the implementation of profit incentives to motivate workers. Instead, he introduce a rigorous political education program, the main purpose of which was to convince workers that they needed to expend maximum effort at work not for personal financial benefit but out of a moral commitment to socialism.

Despite those efforts to revitalize their economies, socialist societies were unable to recover from their experiences with overcentralization. Paradoxically, perhaps, reform plans were applied inconsistently, market rules were not followed rigorously, and the state continued its paternalistic practice of bailing out unsuccessful firms. Meanwhile, political opposition to those regimes continued to grow: Peasants asked for market reforms (Lewis 1979), workers demanded a say in management (Pravda 1979; Kennedy 1991), and intellectuals called for expanded political democracy and protection of their civil rights (Harman 1983). In the spring of 1989, many of those conflicts came to a head as a "gentle revolution" began to unfold in those countries. With a few exceptions, Soviet-type societies formally accepted the principles of multiparty democracy and announced their intention to move in the direction of a market economy.

THE LEGACIES OF SOCIALISM

If attempts to establish the socialist vision during the twentieth century were fraught with social and economic problems, efforts to undo the structure of existing socialist societies have proved equally challenging. Perhaps the biggest task facing postcommunist societies is to conquer the eco-nomic legacies of socialism and make the transition to capitalism without the assistance of a capitalist class (Eyal et al. 1998). In this sense, the postcommunist revolution in Central Europe resembles the Russian Revolution. In 1917, a group of intellectuals constituted themselves as a political class in a peasant country to lead a "proletarian revolution" without a proletariat but with the express purpose of creating a proletariat. In 1989, a fraction of the intelligentsia seized power in Central Europe and sought to lead a "bourgeois revolution" without a bourgeoisie but with the objective of creating a bourgeoisie (Szelényi et al. 1995).

Needless to say, this objective was not an easy one. In all formerly socialist countries, the economic infrastructure was poorly developed and arguably deteriorating, the industrial firms of classical socialism were too large to be privatized easily, and the transition to a postindustrial service economy had not progressed very far (Böröcz and Róna-Tas 1995; Volgyes 1995). The distinctive feature of the transition is that despite such seeming homogeneity in the conditions of origin, there was great heterogeneity in the pathways to capitalism. For example, the East German model is one of centrally managed privatization in the context, of course, of West German "colonization." By contrast, the Czech reformers acquiesced entirely to the "invisible hand" of capitalism, by which all workers were granted vouchers that could be redeemed for shares in any company. Finally, in Hungary, the transformation is best described as a form of "political capitalism" (Hankiss 1990; Staniszkis 1991), by which former communist bureaucrats used their political position to accumulate wealth and buy state companies. Where these privatization strategies will lead remains unclear, but one thing is certain: There is no single plan for designing capitalism, just as there was no simple blueprint for establishing socialism (Stark 1992).

Although most discussions of the transition to postcommunism have focused on the economic legacies of socialism, the political legacies are no less problematic as some form of successful marketization is sought. There are two political legacies of particular interest here. First, after forty years of communist rule and rampant political deception, the reigning view among East European workers involved considerable cynicism toward political elites, and such deep-seated cynicism could not be overcome immediately even when new leaders were vying for power (Kovrig 1995). This cynicism undermined popular support for long-term sacrifices of the sort that all marketization strategies would necessarily entail. Second, the concept of marketization was not completely endorsed by the general population, as there was a long heritage of support for state paternalism in which basic needs, such as health care, education, and a living wage, were guaranteed (Szelényi et al. 1996). There was also widespread concern that marketization would increase inequality to levels that were unacceptably high. It has to borne in mind, then, that the transition to a market economy was undertaken simultaneously with a transition to political democracy. Democratic regimes, for all their possible virtues, are not necessarily well suited for revolutionary economic transformations and the popular sacrifice that such transformations typically imply (O'Donnell and Schmitter 1986).

Finally, the emergence of postcommunism is further complicated by the social legacies of communism. Most notably, the transition to the high-unemployment economy of postcommunism created special problems of legitimacy for a new market society, since Central Europeans had come to expect full employment from the state (Moskoff 1994). Similarly, one of the great successes of communism was its low levels of income inequality (relative to the capitalist alternative), and consequently, the sudden and visible increases in inequality in the postcommunist world were not readily accepted. It was all the more problematic that the prime beneficiaries of this growing wealth were in some instances the former communist elites themselves (Róna-Tas 1994; Fodor et al. 1995; Szelényi and Szelényi 1995). For all its economic failings and political repression, actually existing socialism was at least partially consistent with the original vision of social egalitarianism, and one cannot expect such success to be relinquished without a struggle.

THE FUTURE OF SOCIALISM

The question remains: Can the *idea* of socialism survive the *reality* of the past eighty years? For some, the answer to this question is in the negative, as the failings of socialism are so dramatic that the concept of socialism is inextricably associated with its particular realization, thus rendering it

effectively dead for all of history (Jowitt 1992). This is, then, a peculiar form of path dependency in which the possibly premature turn to socialism in the early twentieth century proved in the end to be its historical downfall. As a fallback position, one might argue that while socialism is perhaps dead in all the countries that experienced its "grief and shame" (Djilas 1998), it might nonetheless surface anew in countries that never underwent this premature experiment. Is there, in other words, a viable base for socialism in the Western world? The standard postmaterialist position on this score is that the base for socialism was at its strongest in the early twentieth century but has since dissipated with the decline in the size of the working class, the weakening of trade unions, and the associated rise of interest politics focusing on issues such as the environment, nuclear war, and gender politics (Inglehart 1983; Piven 1992). The implication is that socialism is dead not because of its tarnished history but because there is no longer a substantial base of working-class supporters.

This line of reasoning, for all its appeal, is not easily reconciled with the continuing support for social democratic policies and communist political leaders in formerly socialist countries. In many formerly communist societies, the initially extreme anticommunist sentiment weakened quickly, and the Communist Party was returned to power in the "second round" elections (Szelényi et al. 1996). Moreover, public opinion polls in those countries consistently reveal that the general population remains supportive of fundamentally social democratic policies even while disavowing support for highly repressive forms of communism of the sort that characterized Soviet-type societies. Under this formulation, a more mature civil society is in formation that probably will pursue a "Swedish form" of social democracy that maintains some elements of classical socialism (i.e., economic egalitarianism) yet abandons others (i.e., political inegalitarianism and repression).

REFERENCES

Bahro, Rudolf 1978 *The Alternative in Eastern Europe*. London: New Left Books.

Bauer, T. 1978 "Investment Cycles in Planned Economies." *Acta Oeconomica* 21(3):243–260.

Bauman, Zygmunt 1974 "Officialdom and Class: Basis of Inequality in Socialist Society." In Frank Parkin, ed., *The Social Analysis of Class Structure*. London: Tavistock.

Bell, Daniel. 1968. "Socialism." In David L. Sills, ed., *International Encyclopedia of the Social Sciences*, vol. 14. New York: Macmillan and Free Press.

Berend, Iván T., and György Ránki 1974 *Economic Development in East-Central Europe in the Nineteenth and Twentieth Centuries*. New York: Columbia University Press.

Bernstein, Eduard 1961 *Evolutionary Socialism*, Edith C. Harvey, trans. New York: Schocken.

Böröcz, József, and Ákos Róna-Tas 1995 "Small Leap Forward: Emergence of New Economic Elites." *Theory and Society* 24:751–781.

Cabet, Etienne 1975 *History and Constitution of the Icarian Community*, Thomas Teakle, trans. New York: AMS Press.

Cole, George D. H. 1959 *A History of Socialist Thought*, 5 vols. London: Macmillan.

Connor, Walter D. 1979 *Socialism, Politics, and Equality*. New York: Columbia University Press.

Djilas, Milovan 1957 *The New Class: An Analysis of the Communist System*. New York: Harcourt Brace Jovanovich.

—— 1998. *The Fall of the New Class: A History of Communism's Self-Destruction*. New York: Knopf.

Eyal, Gil, Iván Szelényi, and Eleonor Townsley 1998 *Making Capitalism Without Capitalists: The New Ruling Elites in Eastern Europe*. London: Verso.

Ferge, Zsuzsa 1979 *A Society in the Making*. New York: M. E. Sharpe.

Fodor, Éva, Edmund Wnuk-Lipinki, and Natasha Yershova 1995 "The New Political and Cultural Elites in Hungary, Poland, and Russia." *Theory and Society* 24:783–800.

Fourier, Charles 1971 *Harmonian Man: Selected Writings of Charles Fourier*, Mark Poster, ed.; Susan Hanson, trans. Garden City, N.Y.: Doubleday.

Garton Ash, Timothy 1990 *The Uses of Adversity: Essays on the Fate of Central Europe*. New York: Vintage.

Giddens, Anthony 1973 *The Class Structure of the Advanced Societies*. London: Hutchinson.

Goldthorpe, John H. 1966 "Social Stratification in Industrial Society." In Reinhard Bendix and Seymour Martin Lipset, eds., *Class, Status, and Power*. New York: Free Press.

Gray, Alexander 1963 *The Socialist Tradition: Moses to Lenin*. London: Longmans.

Griffith, D. F. 1924 *What Is Socialism? A Symposium*. London: Richards.

Hankiss, Elemér 1990 *East European Alternatives*. Oxford, UK: Clarendon Press.

Hare, P., P. Radice, and Nigel Swain 1981 *Hungary: A Decade of Economic Reform*. London: Allen and Unwin.

Harman, Chris 1983 *Class Struggles in Eastern Europe, 1945–1983*. London: Pluto Press.

Hollander, Paul 1983 *The Many Faces of Socialism*. New Brunswick, N.J.: Transaction.

Inglehart, Ronald 1983 "The Persistence of Materialist and Postmaterialist Value Orientations." *European Journal of Political Research* 11:81–91.

Inkeles, Alex 1966 "Social Stratification and Mobility in the Soviet Union." In Reinhard Bendix and Seymour Martin Lipset, eds., *Class, Status, and Power*. New York: Free Press.

Jowitt, Ken 1992 *New World Disorder*. Berkeley: University of California Press.

Kelley, Jonathan, and Herbert S. Klein 1986 "Revolution and the Rebirth of Inequality: Stratification in Post-Revolutionary Society." In Jack A. Goldstone, ed., *Revolutions*. San Diego, Calif.: Harcourt Brace Jovanovich.

Kennedy, Michael D. 1991 *Professionals, Power, and Solidarity in Poland*. Cambridge, UK: Cambridge University Press.

Kolakowski, Leszek 1978 *Main Currents of Marxism*, 3 vols., P. S. Falla, trans. Oxford, UK: Oxford University Press.

Konrád, György, and Iván Szelényi 1979 *The Intellectuals on the Road to Class Power*, Andrew Arato and Richard E. Allen, trans. New York: Harcourt Brace Jovanovich.

Kornai, János 1986 *Contradictions and Dilemmas: Studies on the Socialist Economy and Society*. I. Lukacs, J. Parti, B. McLean, and G. Hajdú, trans. Cambridge, Mass.: MIT Press.

Kovrig, Bennett 1995 "Marginality Reinforced." In Zoltan Barany and Ivan Volgyes, eds., *The Legacies of Communism in Eastern Europe*. Baltimore: Johns Hopkins University Press.

Laidler, Harry W. 1968 *History of Socialism*. New York: Crowell.

Lane, David 1976 *The Socialist Industrial State: Towards a Political Sociology of State Socialism*. London: Allen and Unwin.

Lenin, V. I. 1971 *Selected Works*. New York: International Publishers.

Leogrande, William 1981 "Republic of China." In Bogdan Szajkowski, ed., *Marxist Governments*, vol. 2. New York: St. Martin's.

Lewis, Paul G. 1979 "Potential Sources of Opposition in the East European Peasantry." In Rudolf Tökés, ed., *Opposition in Eastern Europe*. Baltimore: Johns Hopkins University Press.

Lichtheim, George 1969 *The Origins of Socialism*. New York: Praeger.

Mao Zedong 1971 *Selected Readings from the Works of Mao Zedong*. Peking: Foreign Language Press.

Marx, Karl, and Frederick Engels 1968 *Selected Works*. Moscow: Progress Publishers.

Matthews, Mervyn 1972 *Class and Society in Soviet Russia*. New York: Walker.

Morris, William 1970 *News from Nowhere*. London: Routledge and Kegan Paul.

Moskoff, William 1994 "Unemployment in the former Soviet Union." In James R. Millar and Sharon L. Wolchik, eds., *The Social Legacies of Communism*. Washington, DC: Woodrow Wilson Center Press.

Nee, Victor 1989 "A Theory of Market Transition: From Redistribution to Markets in State Socialism." *American Sociological Review* 54: 663–681.

Nove, Alec 1983a "The Class Nature of the Soviet Union Revisited." *Soviet Studies* 3:298–312.

—— 1983b *The Economics of Feasible Socialism*. London: Allen and Unwin.

—— 1989 *An Economic History of the USSR*, 2nd ed. Harmondsworth, UK: Penguin.

Nuti, Domenico Mario 1981 "Socialism on Earth." *Cambridge Journal of Economics* 5:391–403.

O'Donnell, Guillermo, and Phillippe C. Schmitter 1986 *Transitions from Authoritarian Rule: Tentative Conclusions about Uncertain Democracies*. Baltimore: Johns Hopkins University Press.

Ossowski, Stanislaw 1963 *Class Structure in the Social Consciousness*. London: Routledge and Kegan Paul.

Parkin, Frank 1971 *Class Inequality and Political Order*. New York: Praeger.

Piven, Frances Fox 1992 "The Decline of Labor Parties: An Overview." In F. F. Piven, ed., *Labor Parties in Postindustrial Societies*. New York: Oxford University Press.

Pravda, Alex 1979 "Industrial Workers: Patterns of Dissent, Opposition, and Accommodation." In Rudolf Tőkés, ed., *Opposition in Eastern Europe*. Baltimore: Johns Hopkins University Press.

Proudhon, Pierre Joseph 1966 *What Is Property? An Inquiry into the Principle of Right and of Government*, B. R. Tucker, trans. New York: H. Fertig.

Róna-Tas, Ákos 1994 "The First Shall Be Last? Entrepreneurship and Communist Cadres in the Transition from Socialism." *American Journal of Sociology* 10:40–69.

Ross, Lloyd 1935 *William Lane and the Australian Labor Movement*. Sydney, Australia: Forward Press.

Rueschemeyer, Marilyn, and Szonja Szelényi 1989 "Socialist Transformation and Gender Inequality: Women in the GDR and Hungary." In David Childs, Thomas A. Baylis, and Marilyn Rueschemeyer, eds., *East Germany in Comparative Perspective*. London: Routledge.

Saint-Simon, Claude H. 1964 *Social Organization, the Science of Man, and Other Writing*, Felix M. H. Markham, ed. and trans. London: Harper and Row.

Simkus, Albert A., and Rudolf Andorka 1982 "Inequalities in Educational Attainment in Hungary, 1923–1973." *American Sociological Review* 47:740–751.

Sirc, Ljubo 1979 *The Yugoslav Economy under Self-Management*. London: Macmillan.

Staniszkis, Jadwiga 1991 *The Dynamics of Breakthrough in Eastern Europe*. Berkeley: University of California Press.

Stark, David 1986 "Rethinking Internal Labor Markets: New Insights from a Comparative Perspective." *American Sociological Review* 51:492–504.

—— 1992 "Path Dependence and Privatization: Strategies in East Central Europe." *East European Politics and Societies* 6:17–54.

Starr, Richard F. 1988 *Communist Regimes in Eastern Europe*, fifth ed., Stanford, Calif.: Hoover Institution.

Sweezy, Paul M. 1983 "Socialism." In Tom Bottomore, ed., *A Dictionary of Marxist Thought*. Cambridge, Mass.: Harvard University Press.

Szelényi, Iván 1976 "The Housing System and Social Structure in Hungary." In Bernard Lewis Faber, ed., *The Social Structure of Eastern Europe*. New York: Praeger.

—— 1989 "Eastern Europe in an Epoch of Transition: Toward a Socialist Mixed Economy?" In Victor Nee and David Stark, eds., *Remaking the Economic Institutions of Socialism*. Stanford, Calif.: Stanford University Press.

——, and Szonja Szelényi 1995 "Circulation or Reproduction of Elites during Post-Communist Transformation in Eastern Europe: Introduction." *Theory and Society* 24:615–638.

Szelényi, Szonja 1987 "Social Inequality and Party Membership: Patterns of Recruitment into the Hungarian Socialist Workers' Party." *American Sociological Review* 52:559–573.

—— 1998 *Equality by Design: The Grand Experiment in Destratification in Socialist Hungary*. Stanford, Calif.: Stanford University Press.

——, and Karen E. Aschaffenburg 1993 "Inequalities in Educational Opportunity in Hungary." In Yossi Shavit and Hans-Peter Blossfeld, eds. *Persistent Inequality: Changing Educational Attainment in Thirteen Countries*. Boulder, Colo.: Westview.

——, Iván Szelényi, and Imre Kovách 1995 "The Making of the Hungarian Postcommunist Elite: Circulation in Politics, Reproduction in the Economy." *Theory and Society* 24:697–722.

——, ——, and Winifred R. Poster 1996 "Interests and Symbols in Post-Communist Political Culture: The Case of Hungary." *American Sociological Review* 61:466–477.

Volgyes, Ivan 1995 "The Economic Legacies of Communism." In Zoltan Barany and Ivan Volgyes, eds., *The Legacies of Communism in Eastern Europe*. Baltimore: Johns Hopkins University Press.

Walder, Andrew G. 1986 *Communist Neo-Traditionalism: Work and Authority in Chinese Industry*. Berkeley: University of California Press.

—— 1989 "Social Change in Post-Revolutionary China." *American Review of Sociology* 15:405–424.

SZONJA SZELÉNYI

SOCIALIZATION

Socialization has had diverse meanings in the social sciences, partly because a number of disciplines claim it as a central process. In its most common and general usage, the term "socialization" refers to the process of interaction through which an individual (a novice) acquires the norms, values, beliefs, attitudes, and language characteristic of his or her group. In the course of acquiring these cultural elements, the individual self and personality are created and shaped. Socialization therefore addresses two important problems in social life: societal continuity from one generation to the next and human development.

Different disciplines have emphasized different aspects of this process. Anthropologists tend to view socialization primarily as cultural transmission from one generation to the next, sometimes substituting the term "enculturation" for socialization (Herskovits 1948). Anthropological interest in socialization or enculturation coincided with the emergence of the "culture and personality" orientation of the late 1920s and 1930s, when the works of Mead (1928), Benedict (1934), and Malinowski (1927) focused on cultural practices affecting child rearing, value transmission, and personality development and helped shape the anthropological approach to socialization. Much of the work in the culture and personality field was influenced by psychoanalytic theory. Contemporary cultural anthropology is guided less by psychoanalytic theory and more by social constructionist theories (such as symbolic interactionism), which view socialization as a collective and interpretive process of reality construction involving the reproduction of culture. This orientation has been shaped largely by the work of Geertz (1973), whose influence is also evident in sociological work on socialization, such as that of Corsaro and Eder (1995).

Psychologists are less likely to emphasize the transmission of culture and more likely to emphasize various aspects of individual development (Goslin 1969). There is considerable diversity within psychology in regard to the aspect of socialization studied. For developmental psychologists, particularly those influenced by Piaget (1926), socialization is largely a matter of cognitive development, which typically is viewed as a combination of social influence and maturation. For behavioral psychologists, socialization is synonymous with learning patterns of behavior. For clinical psychologists and personality theorists, it is viewed as the establishment of character traits, usually within the context of early childhood experiences. The subfield of child development is most closely associated with the topic of socialization within psychology, where socialization is largely equated with child rearing (Clausen [1968] provides a historical overview of socialization in these disciplines).

Political science has shown some interest in socialization, but in a limited sense. Its studies have not gone much beyond political socialization: the process by which political attitudes and orientations are formed. However, a different and more esoteric use of the term occasionally appears in this literature: socialization as "collectivization," that is, the transformation of capitalism to socialism and/or communism.

Within sociology, there have been two main orientations toward socialization. One views socialization primarily as the learning of social roles. From this perspective, individuals become integrated members of society by learning and internalizing the relevant roles and statuses of the groups to which they belong (Brim 1966). This view has been present in some form from the beginnings of sociology as a discipline but has been most closely associated with structural-functionalist perspectives.

The other, more prevalent sociological orientation views socialization mainly as self-concept formation. The development of self and identity in the context of intimate and reciprocal relations is considered the core of socialization. This view is closely associated with the symbolic interactionist perspective, a synthesis of various strands of pragmatism, behaviorism, and idealism that emerged in the 1920s and 1930s in the writings of a number of scholars at the University of Chicago, especially Mead (1934). In Mead's writings, the self is a reflexive, thoroughly social phenomenon that develops through language or symbolic interaction. Language enables the development of role-taking, by which the individual is able to view himself or herself from the perspective of another person. This becomes the basis for selfhood and the interpenetration of self and society. Mead and other symbolic interactionists have argued that self and society are two sides of the same coin. The basis for their assertion is that the content of self-conceptions (e.g., identities) reflects the aspects of the social process with which the individual is involved through the internalization of role identities, values, and meanings. This internalization in turn reproduces society. From the interactionist perspective, both self and society depend on the same process of social interaction by which "realities" are created and constantly negotiated (Gecas 1982).

For contemporary interactionists as well, socialization is distinguished from other types of learning and other forms of social influence by its relevance for self-conceptions, that is, for people's thoughts and feelings about themselves. As such, socialization is not merely the process of learning rules or norms or behavior patterns; it is a matter of learning these things only to the extent to which they become part of the way people think of themselves. The mark of successful socialization is the transformation of social control into self-control. This is accomplished largely through the development of identities, the various labels and characteristics attributed to the self. Commitment to identities (such as son, mother, professor, honest person) is a source of motivation for individuals to act in accordance with the values and norms implied by those identities (Foote 1951; Stryker

1980; Gecas 1986). The focus on identity also emphasizes the membership component of socialization: To be socialized is to belong to a social group.

Socialization as identity formation occurs through a number of more specific processes associated with self-concept development: reflected appraisals, social comparisons, self-attributions, and identification (Gecas and Burke [1995] and Rosenberg [1979] discuss these processes). Reflected appraisals, based on Cooley's (1902) "looking-glass self" metaphor, refer to people's perceptions of how others see and evaluate them. To some extent people come to see themselves as they think others (particularly significant others) see them. People also develop conceptions of themselves with regard to specific attributes by comparing themselves to others (social comparisons) and making self-inferences from observing their own actions and their consequences (self-attributions). Particularly important to socialization as identity formation is the process of identification. Initially used by Sigmund Freud, this concept refers to the child's emotional attachment to the parent and desire to be like the parent; as a consequence, the child internalizes and adopts the parent's values, beliefs, and other characteristics. Among other things, through identification with the parent, the child becomes more receptive to parental influence.

Identification also is used to refer to the imputation or ascription of identities. Here the focus is on the establishment of identities in social interaction, which is an important aspect of defining situations and constructing realities. This also has important socializing consequences, as much of the literature on labeling, stereotyping, and expectancy effects attests.

CONTENT AND CONTEXTS OF SOCIALIZATION

Much research on socialization has been concerned with identifying the aspects of the socializee's development that are affected by particular agents and contexts of socialization and through particular processes. The focus has been primarily on the family context, in which the initial or *primary* socialization of the individual takes place. Studies of child rearing in "normal" as well as "abnormal" situations (e.g., institutionalized children, "closet children"' feral, children") have identified a number of conditions that must be present for primary socialization to take place, that is, for the child to become a person. These conditions include the use of symbolic interaction (language) in the context of an intimate, nurturant relationship between an adult and a child. These conditions are necessary for the initial sense of self to emerge and for normal cognitive and even physical development to take place. The claim that the family (in some form) is a universal feature of human societies is based in large part on this important socialization function.

Parental support continues to be important in the socialization of offspring through childhood, adolescence, and beyond. It is one of the most robust variables in the literature on child rearing. Parental support has been found to be positively related to a child's cognitive development, moral behavior, conformity to adult standards, self-esteem, academic achievement, and social competence. Conversely, lack of parental support is associated with negative socialization outcomes for children and adolescents: low self-esteem, delinquency, deviance, drug use, and various other problem behaviors (Rollins and Thomas 1979; Peterson and Hann 1999).

Parental control is almost as prominent as support in the socialization literature. "Control" refers to the degree to and the manner in which parents attempt to place constraints on a child's behavior. Other terms used for this dimension of parenting are punishment, discipline, restrictiveness, permissiveness, protectiveness, supervision, strictness, and monitoring. Parental control is a more complicated variable than is parental support. It is necessary to distinguish different types or styles of control because they frequently have opposite socialization consequences. An important distinction is that between "authoritarian" and "authoritative" control (Baumrind 1978) or "coercion" and "induction" (Rollins and Thomas 1979). Authoritarian or coercive control (control based on force, threat, or physical punishment) is associated with negative or unfavorable socialization outcomes, whereas authoritative or inductive control (control based on reason and explanation) has positive outcomes.

The most powerful models of parental influence in the socialization of children are those which combine the dimensions of support and control. Parents are most effective as agents of socialization when they express a high level of support and exercise inductive control. In these conditions, children are most likely to identify with their parents, internalize parental values and expectations, use parents as their models, and become receptive to attempts at parental influence. Conversely, low parental support and reliance on coercive control are associated with unfavorable socialization outcomes (for reviews of this literature, see Peterson and Rollins 1987; Maccoby and Martin 1983; and Rollins and Thomas 1979).

Parental support and control cover much of the ground in the research on child rearing but not all of it. Other important socialization variables here are extent of parental involvement with the child (e.g., time spent), level of performance expectations, extent to which political or religious beliefs and value systems are taught to the child by the parent, and various characteristics of the parent, such as patience, tolerance, honesty, integrity, competence, and age and sex (of parent and child). Many factors affect the process and outcomes of family socialization.

Much of the socialization that takes place in the family involves learning appropriate role behavior associated with the various family positions. For the child, the most significant of these behaviors involve sex and age roles. Through processes of reinforcement from parents and others, identification with various role models, and parental admonitions and instructions, a child is socialized into the behavioral expectations associated with these roles. Of the two, sex roles have received more of the research attention on role learning in the family (Block [1983] provides a review). This research suggests that sex-role socialization is extensive (usually starting at birth with differential treatment of male and female infants), pervasive (various agents and contexts of socialization), and consequential for a wide range of other individual and social outcomes. A prominent theme in much contemporary research on sex-role socialization is that the differential treatment that emphasizes "masculine" characteristics for boys and "feminine" characteristics for girls is detrimental to the development of both girls and boys and to the relationship between the sexes (Bem [1974] discusses the virtues of androgyny). This research reflects the ethos of equality between the sexes in most modern societies.

Most studies of socialization within the family assume a unidirectional influence from parent to child. Parents typically are viewed as agents of socialization (part of the job description of a parent), and children as objects of socialization. Given the disparities in power, status, and competence between parent and child, it is justifiably assumed that the direction of influence is mainly from parent to child. However, it has become increasingly evident that socialization is a reciprocal process, with children influencing parents as well. Over the past few decades, the thinking with regard to socialization processes has shifted from unidirectional to bidirectional and reciprocal models (Corsaro and Eder 1995; Gecas 1981). For example, in considering the association between parental punishment and a child's deviant behavior, which is one of the most consistent findings in socialization research, it can be argued that the child's behavior is both a consequence and a cause of the parental behavior. That is, a child's aggressive or deviant behavior may *elicit* more punitive parental behavior as well as being affected by the parental behavior. Socialization increasingly is viewed as reciprocal, even though the degree of influence is typically not equal.

Besides parents and other adult kin, siblings serve as agents of socialization within the family context. As family size increases, more of the socialization of the younger children is taken on by their older siblings, either by default or because the parents delegate this responsibility to the older children. Some have argued that this puts younger children in large families at a disadvantage with regard to cognitive development, since they have relatively less contact with the most competent and committed family members, the parents (Zajonc 1976). However, these findings, based mostly on cross-sectional data, have not gone unchallenged (Galbraith 1982; Blake 1989).

An increasingly pervasive agent of socialization in contemporary families is television. Children spend more time watching television than at any other activity except school and sleep (Bronfenbrenner 1970). The purpose of most television programs children watch is typically not to socialize or educate but to entertain and sell products. However, a good deal of unintended socialization is likely to occur, from shaping conceptions of reality (e.g., sex roles and ethnic stereotypes) to styles of behavior and tastes. In general, television

is perceived as having a negative influence on children, with the exception of a few educational programs on public television. Much of the concern has focused on the extensive violence and sexual themes and situations in television programs. Bandura et al.'s (1963) work on modeling has persuasively shown that exposure to aggressive behavior tends to increase aggression in the viewer. Along with its undesirable consequences for child socialization, Bronfenbrenner (1970) observes that television is detrimental to child development with regard to the behavior it prevents, that is, the human interaction that is forgone in the course of being a passive viewer. The role of television as an agent of socialization in families seems to be increasing by default as the amount of contact between parents and their children decreases. Various social forces (such as increasing numbers of working mothers, single-parent families, dual-career families, and the professionalization of child care) have decreased the amount of parent-child interaction and thus parents' role as a socializing agent. This vacuum has been filled increasingly by the child's involvement with television and with peers. For children in American society, television, peer groups, and school are increasingly important agents of socialization.

Like the family, the school is an institution whose mandate is to socialize children. The school's mission, however, is more narrowly defined than is that of the family and is concerned primarily with the formal instruction and the development of children's cognitive skills. In this sense, the school context is less involved in *primary* socialization (i.e., the development of basic values, beliefs, motivations, and conceptions of the self) and more involved in *secondary* socialization (i.e., the development of knowledge and skills). This is not a very precise distinction, however. In the course of the socialization experienced in school, things other than skills and knowledge also are learned, such as norms, values, attitudes, and various aspects of a child's personality and self-concept. Much more is typically learned in school than what is explicitly taught.

Many activities associated with school (specifically in the classroom) have implications for a child's self-concept (Hewitt 1998). For example, one of the most important activities involves evaluation of the student's performance by the teacher:

performance on tests, class reports, presentations, assignments, and the like. Success in these activities, based on one's own efforts, is good for self-esteem and builds confidence in one's abilities. However, failure is not, and *public* failure is even worse. School provides numerous opportunities for public failure as well as public success. One of the consequences of performance evaluations may be the categorization or "labeling" of students, by teachers as well as others, as "smart," "dumb," "slow learner," "underachiever," and so on. Negative as well as positive labels affect the way in which others respond to a person and, through their responses, reinforce and shape that person in the labeled direction. This process is called "expectancy effects" (Jones 1977) or "self-fulfilling prophecy" (Merton 1957). Rosenthal and Jacobson (1968) found that teachers' expectations of students, even when based on erroneous information, had a significant effect on how students developed over the course of the school year: When the teacher was led to believe that a student would be a "slow learner," that student was more likely to do poorly in class. Labeling and expectancy effects occur in most socialization contexts and have important consequences for self-concept development.

However, students, like other socializees, are not passive recipients of the pressures they experience. Covington and Beery (1976) propose that two fundamentally different motivation patterns emerge in schools as a result of these pressures: One is oriented toward striving for success, and the other toward avoiding failure. Failure-avoiding strategies (such as nonparticipation, withdrawal, procrastination, and putting off work assignments until too late) are attempts to disassociate one's performance from one's ability and worth. Failure then can be attributed to lack of effort or to external circumstances (less damaging attributions for the self), not to lack of ability (a more damaging attribution). This is a form of role distancing, the separation of the self from the behavior required of a role occupant; it is also an obstacle to school achievement. As Covington and Beery (1976) point out, failure-avoiding strategies are self-defeating: In their attempts to avoid feelings of failure, these students increase the probability of actual failure. For some students this is one of the unintended and undesirable consequences of classroom socialization. In the process of socializing students toward achievement and mastery (desir-

able outcomes), pressures are generated that may result in undesirable adaptations.

The third most important context for the socialization of children and adolescents is the peer group. In terms of structure and function, the peer group is a very different context from family and school. Unlike those two contexts, it is not the "job" of peers to socialize each other, even though a great deal of childhood socialization occurs in this context, some of it in reaction against the socialization experienced in the family and school.

There are several important features of the peer group as a context of socialization. Most important, it is a *voluntary* association, and for most children it is the first. This permits greater freedom of choice regarding associations in the group. A second important feature is that association is between status equals. Consequently, interaction is more likely to be based on egalitarian norms. Status distinctions emerge, of course, but are more likely to be based on achievement and negotiation. However, the basic relationship within peer groups is not hierarchical; rather, it is the friendship bond, based on equality, mutual tolerance, and concern. Third, the peer group is an arena for the exercise of independence from adult control. As such, it is often the context for the development of values, norms, and behavior in opposition to those of adults (such as the subcultures described by Coleman [1961] and in much of the literature on juvenile delinquency). Fourth, children's peer groups, in contemporary American society at least, typically are segregated by sex and differ in organizational patterns: Girls' peer groups tend to feature closely knit and egalitarian friendships, whereas boys' peer groups tend to be loosely knit, larger groups with clear status hierarchies. An important socialization consequence of intensive association with same-sex peers and involvement in sex-typed activities is that this strongly reinforces identification and belongingness with members of the same sex and contributes to the development of stereotypical attitudes toward members of the opposite sex. Not only sex-role identity but also much of sexual socialization during childhood occur in the context of peer rather than parent-child associations, since parents are much less interested in discussing sexual matters with their children than are the children's peers (Fine 1987; Corsaro and Eder 1990). Peers provide an alternative reference group for children as well as an alternative source of self-esteem and identity. For these reasons, attachment to peers may be even stronger than attachment to family, especially for adolescents.

The socialization experienced by adults generally falls in the category of secondary socialization, building on the socialization experiences of childhood. Much of this is role-specific (Brim 1968), that is, learning the knowledge and skills required for the performance of specific adult roles, such as occupation, marriage, and parenthood. As individuals become committed to the roles they play, they come to identify themselves and think of themselves in terms of these role-identities (Stryker 1980).

Since work is a dominant activity and setting for most adult men and women, much of adult socialization involves either preparation for an occupation or career (which usually takes place specialized schools or training programs such as law school, medical school, and college) or on-the-job training. The work setting can have a substantial socializing effect on workers, affecting more than just their knowledge and skills. Kohn and Schooler (1983) have shown how certain occupational conditions affect the development of a worker's values and personality. Specifically, they found that work that is routine, closely supervised, and relatively uncomplicated gives rise to values of conformity, whereas work that is complex and encourages self-direction increases the value workers place on independence and autonomy. Kanter (1977) found that the nature of work relations, particularly the structure of opportunity on the job, affects workers' attitudes and behaviors as a consequence of their adaptations to the work situation. Workers' adaptations to their work situations do not necessarily lead to commitment to the job or self-investment in terms of the occupational role. On the contrary, a prevalent theme in much of the sociological literature on work and workers (especially that with a Marxist perspective) deals with the alienating consequences of work in capitalist societies.

Many other contexts have socializing consequences for adults: family, political and religious organizations, recreational settings, and voluntary associations. The socialization that takes place in these contexts can be considered "developmental" (Wheeler 1966) because it builds on previous socialization and is a continuation and expansion of past socialization experiences. *Resocialization* refers to socialization experiences that represent a more radical change in the person. Resocialization contexts (e.g., mental hospitals, some prisons, reform schools, therapy groups, political indoctrination camps. religious conversion settings) have as their explicit goal the transformation of the individual. An important feature of resocialization is the replacement of one's previous set of beliefs, values, and especially conceptions of the self with a new set grounded in the socializing group's ideology or world view. This has been described as a process of death and rebirth of the self (Lifton 1963). Typically, this is accomplished through intense small group interaction in which the physical and symbolic environments are highly controlled by the agents of socialization. It is an experience that usually involves considerable stress for the socializee.

SOCIALIZATION OVER THE LIFE COURSE

Socialization is a lifelong process of change. Even though the socialization experienced in the family is in some ways the most consequential, individuals typically have important socializing experiences throughout their lives. A central theme in the life-course literature is the degree of continuity and consistency in personality as an individual moves through the life course. Positions on this issue range from the claim that personality is shaped largely during early childhood (most evident in psychoanalytic theories) to the claim that people are thoroughly malleable, changing across situations and throughout their lives (characteristic of constructivist theories). The majority appear to argue for an intermediate position, maintaining that the "core" personality or self-concept develops in early socialization experiences, while various other characteristics are added to self through the acquisition of new roles, identities, and socializing experiences (Brim 1966). For example, Clausen (1993) found that the development of "planful competence" during the childhood and early adolescent years affected the life course of adults many years later, resulting in individual histories of cumulative advantage or disadvantage. The previous discussion suggests how contexts of socialization, which are typically age-graded, can contribute to the development of different aspects of individuals associated with different ages and stages of life.

Some important socializing experiences and changes are keyed to developmental or maturational considerations: There are differences between the concerns and capabilities of children and those of adolescents, those of young adults and those of people in middle age, and those of the middle-aged and those of older persons. Erikson's (1959) developmental scheme, building on the Freudian theory of psychosexual development but extending it beyond childhood, emphasizes the different developmental tasks associated with different stages of life. The challenges or developmental tasks proposed by Erikson are (1) trust versus mistrust, (2) autonomy versus shame, (3) initiative versus guilt, (4) industry versus inferiority, (5) identity versus identity confusion, (6) intimacy versus isolation, (7) generativity versus self-absorption, and (8) integrity versus despair. Most of the socialization research guided by Erikson's formulations has focused on stage 5, adolescence, and the developmental task highlighting identity concerns. In modern society adolescence has long been considered a time when self-concept concerns increase in prominence. Physiological changes and changes in social circumstances (e.g., high school, dating, career considerations) contribute to an increase in self-awareness and concern about how one is viewed by others. Research by developmental psychologists generally has found that good family relations (those high in parental support, communication, involvement, and inductive control) facilitate the development of ego identity in adolescence (Gecas and Seff [1990] and Steinmetz 1999 provide reviews). By adolescence, however, the influence of parents is substantially less than it was during childhood. Increasingly, other agents and contexts of socialization become important to the adolescent: peers, school, friends, coaches, and so forth. The adolescent's struggles with identity are worked out in a number of competing arenas.

Identity concerns are not limited to adolescence, of course. If one considers socialization a lifelong process of self-concept formation, matters of identity are important at various stages of the individual's development. Identity concerns are most likely to be accentuated during periods of transition, particularly those involving entrance into or exit from social statuses and roles. Some of these role transitions are institutionalized and highly ritualized. The rites of passage in various cultures marking the transition from childhood to adulthood can be elaborate and dramatic. Sometimes this involves acquiring a new name as well as a new status (as in many of the Plains Indian cultures). In contemporary Western societies, these status passages may be less dramatic but still quite consequential for the person: getting a driver's license, high school graduation, marriage, divorce, the first full-time job, retirement, widowhood. In general, each major transition initiates a new socializing experience or situation that has implications for the individual's self-concept.

Some theorists have focused on transitions in adulthood (Levinson 1978; Levinson and Crumpler 1996) and examined the circumstances that can lead to a "midlife crisis" an acute reexamination of the self. Evidence that such a crisis typically occurs at midlife is sparse. The adult years, especially in the later stages, are still relatively neglected by life-course scholars compared to studies of childhood and adolescence, but this may be changing. As longevity continues to increase in modern society, so will concern with socializing experiences in the later stages of life. We may be expanding some stages (e.g., postretirement and widowhood) as well as creating new ones, such as the "nursing home stage," as the life span increases.

In considering socialization over the life course, it is necessary to take history and culture into account. Not just the content of socialization during various "stages" of life but also the stages themselves vary with the culture and the historical context. For example, adolescence as an identifiable stage of life is a relatively recent historical construct in Western societies, closely associated with the extension of formal education to high school (Gecas and Seff 1990). Even childhood, as Aries (1960) documents, is not universally considered a distinct stage of life. The modern conception of childhood as an identifiably distinct stage emerged during the European Renaissance, partly as a consequence of the emergence of parochial schools. More recently, Elder (1974) has shown a historical consciousness in his life-course analyses by examining how specific historical events (e.g., the Great Depression; World War II) differentially affected two cohorts of children and their families. Whether there are eight stages of life, four stages, or seven stages (as Shakespeare observed) depends on the society and one's analytic purposes.

CONTEMPORARY ISSUES AND THEMES IN SOCIALIZATION RESEARCH

For much of its history, the concept of socialization has been heavily imbued with the notion of adaptation and conformity of the individual to societal expectations. The past few decades, however, have seen a marked shift to a more active view of the self, with an emphasis on self-socialization. Renewed interest in the self-concept as a source of motivation (Gecas 1986) and an agent in its environment has contributed to this shift, as has the increased interest in adult socialization (Levenson & Crumpler 1996). Even in studies of parent-child interaction, the child (even the infant) is increasingly viewed as an active partner in his or her socialization (Rheingold 1969). In short, the outcomes of socialization (whether conceptualized as values, self-conceptions, behavior patterns, or beliefs) are increasingly viewed as the products of reciprocal and negotiated interactions between agent and socializee.

A concern with social structure and its effects on the process and outcomes of socialization is still the hallmark of the sociological orientation to socialization, from social class influences (Gecas 1979) to the effects of family structure. Changes in family structure over the past few decades have increased interest in the effects of single-parent families, reconstituted families, and day care on child socialization (McLanahan and Sandefur 1994). Some of these changes have negative consequences for child socialization, some are benign, and some are ambiguous. It is evident that family trends and their consequences for child socialization will continue to generate a great deal of passionate debate in public and academic spheres because of their policy and value implications (Popenoe [1993] and Skolnick [1991] present contrasting views on the implications of these trends).

While most of socialization research has involved mainstream American populations, interest in cultural and subcultural variations in socialization experiences has been increasing. Socialization scholars have become sensitive to the criticism that our theories of socialization and self-conception are ethnocentric, reflecting a parochial, Western perspective. This cultural self-consciousness has generated some interesting comparative studies, especially comparisons of socialization experiences in individualistic cultures (such as most Western societies) with those in collectivistic cultures (such as most Asian and many African cultures). In general, the self in collectivistic cultures is experienced much more in relational terms, that is, as interdependent, socially situated, and lacking definition outside the group context. By contrast, in individualistic cultures the self is more likely to be experienced as autonomous and unique and much less as a part of the social context. The socialization experiences in the former cultures tend to emphasize the primacy of the group (e.g., one's family, clan, or society) over the individual, whereas in the later the emphasis is on the development of independence, individual uniqueness, the ego, and autonomy (Markus and Kitayama 1991; Neisser and Jopling 1997). Ethnic subcultures within American society, such as Mexican-Americans and Native Americans, also reflect a more collectivist ethos than does mainstream culture, with consequences for socialization patterns. Within American society the cultural influences of ethnic minorities on socialization patterns typically interact with and may be confounded by social class influences. For example, studies of African-American families and peer groups may reflect adaptations to economic deprivation as much as they reflect distinct subcultural elements.

What effect will rapidly evolving computer technology have on the socialization of children and adults? The ubiquity of computers in classrooms, homes, workplaces, and recreation centers is evident in American society. Children are becoming involved with this technology at a very early age; even preschoolers are becoming "computer-literate." Unlike television, computers are an interactive technology that is likely to engage and develop the user's cognitive and motor skills. Thus, there is reason to hope that the influence of computers on children's development will be beneficial or at least benign, as some scholars have suggested (Turkle 1984). Computers and information technologies are rapidly transforming modern societies, affecting most aspects of people's lives. Surely they also are affecting the processes and outcomes of socialization, but the nature of these processes and outcomes remains to be studied by socialization scholars.

In traditional, relatively stable societies (which are increasingly rare), socialization is relatively routine and unproblematic. By contrast, in modern societies characterized by rapid social and cultural change, the socialization of children and adults is increasingly problematic and more likely to be contentious but also more interesting.

REFERENCES

Aries, Phillip 1960 *Centuries of Childhood: A Social History of Family Life.* New York: Random House.

Bandura, Albert, Dorothea Ross, and Sheila A. Ross 1963 "Imitation of Film-Mediated Aggressive Models." *Journal of Abnormal and Social Psychology* 66:3–11.

Baumrind, Diana 1978 "Parental Disciplinary Patterns and Social Competence in Children." *Youth and Society* 9:239–276.

Bem, Sandra L. 1974 "The Measurement of Psychological Androgyny." *Journal of Consulting and Clinical Psychology* 42:155–162.

Benedict, Ruth 1934 *Patterns of Culture.* Boston: Houghton Mifflin.

Blake, Judith 1989 *Family Size and Achievement.* Berkeley: University of California Press.

Block, Jean H. 1983 "Differential Premises Arising from Differential Socialization of the Sexes: Some Conjectures." *Child Development* 54:1335–1354.

Brim, Orville G., Jr. 1966 "Socialization through the Life Cycle." In O. G. Brim, Jr., and S. Wheeler, eds., *Socialization after Childhood: Two Essays.* New York: Wiley.

—— 1968 "Adult Socialization." In J. A. Clausen, ed., *Socialization and Society.* Boston: Little, Brown.

Bronfenbrenner, Urie. 1970. *Two Worlds of Childhood: U.S. and U.S.S.R.* New York: Russell Sage Foundation.

Clausen, John A. 1968 "A Historical and Comparative View of Socialization Theory and Research." In J. A. Clausen, ed., *Socialization and Society.* Boston: Little, Brown.

—— 1993 *American Lives.* New York: Free Press.

Coleman, James S. 1961 *The Adolescent Society.* New York: Free Press.

Cooley, Charles H. 1902 (1964) *Human Nature and the Social Order.* New York: Scribner's.

Corsaro, William A., and Donna Eder 1990 "Children's Peer Cultures." *Annual Review of Sociology* 16:197–220.

—— 1995 "Development and Socialization of Children and Adolescents." In K. S. Cook, G. A. Fine, and J. S. House, eds., *Sociological Perspectives on Social Psychology.* Boston: Allyn and Bacon.

Covington, Martin V., and Richard G. Beery 1976 *Self-Worth and School Learning.* New York: Holt, Rinehart and Winston.

Elder, Glen H., Jr. 1974 *Children of the Great Depression.* Chicago: University of Chicago Press.

Erikson, Erik H. 1959 *Identity and the Life Cycle.* New York: International Universities Press.

Fine, Gary A. 1987 *With the Boys: Little League Baseball and Preadolescent Culture.* Chicago: University of Chicago Press.

Foote, Nelson N. 1951. "Identification as the Basis for a Theory of Motivation." *American Sociological Review* 16:14–21.

Galbraith, Robert C. 1982 "Sibling Spacing and Intellectual Development: A Closer Look at the Confluence Models." *Developmental Psychology* 18:151–173.

Gecas, Viktor 1979 "The Influence of Social Class on Socialization." In W. R. Burr, R. Hill, F. I. Nye, and I. L. Reiss, eds., *Contemporary Theories about the Family*, vol. 1. New York: Free Press.

—— 1981 "Contexts of Socialization." In M. Rosenberg and R. H. Turner, eds., *Social Psychology: Sociological Perspectives.* New York: Basic Books.

—— 1982 "The Self-Concept." In R. H. Turner and J. F. Short, Jr., eds., *Annual Review of Sociology.* vol. 8. Palo Alto, Calif.: Annual Reviews.

—— 1986 "The Motivational Significance of Self-Concept for Socialization Theory." In E. J. Lawler, ed., *Advances in Group Processes.* vol. 3. Greenwich, Conn.: JAI Press.

——, and Peter J. Burke 1995 "Self and Identity." In K. S. Cook, G. A. Fine, and J. S. House, eds., *Sociological Perspectives on Social Psychology.* Boston: Allyn and Bacon

——, and Monica Seff 1990 "Families and Adolescents: 1980s Decade Review." *Journal of Marriage and the Family* 52:941–958.

Geertz, Clifford 1973 *The Interpretation of Cultures.* New York: Basic Books.

Goslin, David A. 1969 *Handbook of Socialization Theory and Research.* Chicago: Rand McNally.

Herskovits, Melville J. 1948 *Man and His Works: The Science of Cultural Anthropology.* New York: Knopf.

Hewitt, John P. 1998 *The Myth of Self-Esteem.* New York: St. Martin's Press.

Jones, R. A. 1977 *Self-Fulfilling Prophecies: Social Psychological and Physiological Effects of Expectancies.* New York: Wiley.

Kanter, Rosabeth M. 1977 *Men and Women of the Corporation*. New York: Basic Books.

Kohn, Melvin L., and Carmi Schooler 1983 *Work and Personality: An Inquiry into the Impact of Social Stratification*. Norwood. N.J.: Ablex.

Levenson, Michael and Cheryl Crumpler. 1996 "The Models of Adult Development," Human Development 39:135–149.

Levinson, Daniel J. 1978 *The Seasons of a Man's Life*. New York: Knopf.

Lifton, Robert J. 1963 *Thought Reform and the Psychology of Totalism: A Study of Brainwashing in China*. New York: Norton.

Maccoby, Eleanor E., and John A. Martin 1983 "Socialization in the Context of the Family: Parent-Child Interaction." In P. H. Mussen, ed., *Handbook of Child Psychology*, vol. 4. New York: Wiley.

Malinowski, Bronislaw 1927 (1953) *Sex and Repression in Savage Society*, London: Routledge.

Markus, Hazel R., and Shinobu Kitayama 1991 "Culture and the Self: Implications for Cognition, Emotion, and Motivation." *Psychological Review* 98:224–253.

McLanahan, Sara S. and G. Sandefur. 1994 *Growing Up with a Single Parent*. Cambridge, MA: Harvard University Press.

Mead, George H. 1934 *Mind, Self, and Society*. Chicago: University of Chicago Press.

Mead, Margaret 1928 *Coming of Age in Samoa*. New York: Morrow.

Merton, Robert K. 1957 *Social Theory and Social Structure*. Glencoe, Ill.: Free Press.

Neisser, Ulric and David A. Jopling, eds. 1997 *The Conceptual Self in Context*. New York: Cambridge University Press.

Peterson, Gary W. and Della Hann 1999 "Socializing Children and Parents in Families." In M. B. Sussman, S. K Steinmetz, and G. W. Peterson, eds., *Handbook of Marriage and the Family*. 2nd Edition. New York: Plenum.

Piaget, Jean 1926 *The Language and Thought of the Child*. London: Kegan Paul.

Popenoe, David 1993 "American Family Decline, 1960–1990: A Review and Appraisal." *Journal of Marriage and the Family* 55:527–555.

Rheingold, Harriet L. 1969 "The Social and Socializing Infant." In D. A. Goslin, ed., *Handbook of Socialization Theory and Research*. Chicago: Rand McNally.

Rollins, Boyd C., and Darwin L. Thomas 1979 "Parental Support, Power, and Control Techniques in the Socialization of Children." In W. R. Burr, R. Hill, F. I. Nye, and I. L. Reiss, eds., *Contemporary Theories about the Family*, vol. 1. New York: Free Press.

Rosenberg, Morris 1979 *Conceiving the Self*. New York: Basic Books.

Rosenthal, Robert and L. Jacobson 1968 *Pygmalion in the Classroom*. New York: Holt, Rinehart, and Winston.

Skolnick, Arlene 1991 *Embattled Paradise: The American Family in an Age of Uncertainty*. New York: Basic Books.

Steinmetz, Suzanne K. 1999 "Adolescence in Contemporary Families." In M. B. Sussman, S. K. Steinmetz, and G. W. Peterson, eds., *Handbook of Marriage and the Family*, 2nd ed. New York: Plenum.

Stryker, Sheldon 1980 *Symbolic Interactionism: A Social Structural Version*. Menlo Park, Calif.: Benjamin/Cummings.

Turkle, Sherry 1984 *The Second Self: Computers and the Human Spirit*. New York: Simon and Schuster.

Wheeler, Stanton 1966 "The Structure of Formally Organized Socialization Settings." In O. G. Brim, Jr., and S. Wheeler, eds., *Socialization after Childhood: Two Essays*. New York: Wiley.

Zajonc, Robert B. 1976 "Family Configuration and Intelligence." *Science* 192:227–236.

Viktor Gecas

SOCIAL-POLICY ANALYSIS

See Public policy analysis.

SOCIETAL STRATIFICATION

Societal stratification phenomena are the relatively enduring, hierarchically ordered relationships of power among the units of which society is composed. The smallest units are adults, gainfully employed men and/or women, nuclear families, or sometimes extended families or households. Such units are ordered from highest to lowest in terms of power: political power, acquisitional power, the power of prestige, and the power of informational standing. Everybody experiences stratification every day, although a person often notices it only in the sense that some people seem better or worse off than he or she is. Social thinkers, powerful people, and revolutionaries have always been especially concerned with stratification.

Secure knowledge of the varying forms stratification structures may take is important because of the effects those structures have on many aspects of human experience, such as people's dreams of a better life, efforts to improve their situations, strivings for success, fear of failure, sympathy for the less fortunate, envy of others' good fortune, and even feelings about revolution.

A complete understanding of stratification requires several kinds of knowledge: first, what stratification structures consist of and how they vary; second, the individual and collective consequences of the different states of those structures; and third, the factors that make stratification structures change. This article reviews current thinking on the first of these elements.

HISTORY: CLASSICAL THEORY

Two different lines of thought inform modern theory on societal stratification. One is *classical* theory; concerned with political power and privilege, it employs historical evidence. The other is the *empirical tradition*, which deals with systematic data on stratification as it exists contemporarily. Present-day theory of the behavior of stratification phenomena can be traced to Karl Marx's challenge to the manufacturing and financial elites of his day. Behind his concerns and those of the working class for which he was Europe's chief spokesman for many years lay the great economic and political upheavals of the eighteenth and nineteenth centuries.

The American and French revolutions and their aftermath culminated in legislation that made adults in many countries equal before the law. The related wave of emancipation of slaves and serfs in Europe and the Americas was also part of the intellectual environment of that day. Of more direct relevance to Marx's thinking was the rise of trade and the factory system, along with the growth of cities and the expansion of wealth. Marx saw urban populations dividing into two opposed classes. The capitalist class employed the workers; owned the workplaces, machines, and tools; and had ready access to large amounts of money for investment. The capitalists were opposed by their employees, the working class, who had nothing to offer but their time and energy. In Marx's view,

these two classes differ in terms of power and privilege: power because capitalists give orders that workers must accept, privilege because capitalists take the surplus (whatever is left after paying the cost of production) for themselves and their investments, leaving for workers only the wages that the market for labor forces capitalists to pay. Actually, Marx was interested in how these classes came into being and the conflicting interests they expressed. He did not write specifically on societal stratification as it is understood today.

Later writers on stratification, attempting to elucidate or contradict Marx, spelled out more complex sets of stratification dimensions. Weber (1946, 1947) saw power as the general factor basic to the enduring inequalities referred to as stratification. Sometimes, like Marx, he used categories whose underlying dimensions had to be elucidated by others. Party, class, and status groups were his key concepts. When these concepts are dimensionalized (reconstituted as variables), "party" is seen to be legitimate political influence, "class" is seen to express a hierarchical order of economic status, and the variable underlying "status groups" is seen to be their hierarchical order according to the degree of social honor. In other writings, Weber saw education as a stratification variable. In still others, he often wrote about authority, or legitimate superordinate and subordinate relations of power. Weber said nothing about how people are distributed in these dimensions or, of course, about how and why such distributions vary.

More thoroughly and precisely than Marx or Weber, Sorokin (1927) crafted the bases of modern theories of societal stratification. He distinguished political stratification, economic stratification, and occupational stratification. The first is a dimension of political power, and the second a dimension of the power of income and wealth. He left the dimensionality of occupational status unclear, sometimes implying that it was authority, sometimes privilege, and sometimes intelligence. Much of Sorokin's theory of societal stratification remains intact. First, he noted that all societies are stratified to some degree, a position widely accepted today. Second, empirical researchers continue to refine and elucidate his concepts of occupational status and occupational mobility. Third, in this connection he asked why occupational stratification exists and concluded that organized communal life requires mechanisms and people to coordinate essential activities and that such coordination demands and rewards unusual ability. This view, now called *the functionalist hypothesis*, has been elaborated and disputed ever since. Fourth, he held that the degree of stratification varies from society to society and over time within given society: Stratification, he said, is in "ceaseless fluctuation." Sorokin specified several ways in which stratification structures may vary. The whole structure may rise or fall; the top may rise or fall, changing the degree of inequality; and the "profile," or the shape of the distribution, may vary. Similarly, the rate of individual upward or downward mobility may vary, and whole strata may rise or fall.

Sorokin thus presented a theory that specified (1) the general dimensions by which people are stratified within a society, (2) some ways in which the distributions of people on those dimensions may vary, and (3) why stratification exists. Also, he held such structures to be in ceaseless change.

The latest work in the classical tradition is that of Lenski (1966). His key dimensions are power, privilege, and prestige, in that order of importance. Beyond this, Lenski offers three main ideas. First, both functional theory and conflict theory, its opposite, are partly right. Society's needs demand coordination, implying the existence of strata based on power or authority and implying a degree of consent on the part of many of those whose activities are organized by others. However, conflict results from that control: Authority is often abused and, even when it is not, may be misunderstood. Second, inequalities are mostly those of power, with inequalities of privilege and prestige following mostly as consequences of them. Third, the degree of inequality, which is seen as a single phenomenon encompassing the rate of mobility and the distance between strata, increased with the growing comprehensiveness and complexity of society until the Industrial Revolution, after which it declined. According to Lenski, the main forces driving change in the degree of inequality are the size of the surplus of production and, undergirding this, the march of technological efficiency.

Lenski is clearly in the classical tradition in his concern with power and privilege and dependence on historical evidence. To some extent, he echoes

Sorokin's concern with variations in stratification structures through an emphasis on the degree of inequality. He provides a compelling treatment of the issue of conflict versus societal necessity in regard to the existence of stratification. He uses historical evidence effectively and systematically to mark variations of inequality in agrarian and horticultural societies. However, Lenski's emphasis on two main, all-encompassing aspects of stratification—power (his key criterion variable) and inequality (used to denote the way in which power and its concomitants are apportioned)—forces too many separately varying stratification phenomena into too few molds. This problem becomes critical in industrial societies, where stratification dimensions vary independently of one another.

HISTORY: THE EMPIRICAL TRADITION

As has been noted, this tradition of research on stratification is concerned with the here and now. This line of research has developed excellence in the measurement of the hierarchical positions of small demographic units within larger stratification structures. Although newer than the classical tradition, it has a long history. Several more or less independent status-measurement devices were formulated in the 1920s and 1930s. Most were concerned with either the prestige of the breadwinner's occupation or the quality of the home. They tended to share certain assumptions: that stratification consists of a single hierarchy, in the early days usually called *social class*; that one or two different scales are sufficient to test hypotheses concerning social class; that social class positions can be distinguished by direct observation and/or interviews with someone who knows the status holders; that routines can be devised that allow one to assign valid and reliable numerical scores to each status holder on each of the scales used to measure social class; that the unit to be scored is the household, which can be one person or several persons living in a single home; and that it is the whole unit that is to be scored, whether with data on the home or data on the head of the household. Many of these devices became obsolete because they had to be recalibrated for each new community or type of community to which they were applied. Those that survived—education and occupational status—did so because they provide comparable scores across large populations, such as nations.

Of the two main survivors, educational attainment is easy to measure: the exact number of school years successfully completed from none through sixteen, seventeen, eighteen, and so on. Measurement of occupational status is another matter. Two systems are currently in use. Occupational prestige ratings assume that each person in a given occupation shares the prestige most people attribute to that occupation. Occupational prestige scales have been constructed for many countries (Treiman 1977). Occupational socioeconomic status indices (SEI) are scales that use education and income to measure the status level of each occupation and then attribute to an individual the resulting score of her or his occupation. In the United States, Treiman's prestige scale and the SEI provide highly correlated occupational scores (Featherman and Hauser 1978).

Regardless of the original intent of such scales—to measure positions in what once was believed to be the only stratification hierarchy—the two variables educational attainment and occupational status are also appropriate for use with the classical theorists' multidimensional view of stratification.

A SYNTHESIS

The current synthesis was carried out by stratification theorists who were both sensitive to the concerns of classical theorists with power and privilege and steeped in the empirical tradition. Thus, they brought the classical theorists' concern with political power, economic power, and social honor (Weber), including Sorokin's occupational status and Lenski's prestige, together with the empiricists' concern with education and occupational status (overlapping Weber, Sorokin, and Lenski) and with quantitative measurement and analysis.

Svalastoga's *Social Differentiation* (1965) appears to be the first statement of the synthesis. Svalastoga indicates the centrality of four dimensions of status: political, economic, social (mostly occupational), and informational (mostly educational). He calls attention to structural variations through his "parameters": the degree of inequality, the correlation among dimensions, and the degree of permeability (intergenerational circulation mo-

bility or movement up and down the hierarchies). Duncan (1968) both accepted and clarified Svalastoga's synthesis. His list of "scales of reward or status" provides a good outline of the large number of variables that should be measured to achieve a full-scale determination of people's levels on each status dimension. Also, he divides three of Svalastoga's four dimensions into two categories each. He, like Svalastoga, then lists three ways in which the structure of stratification variable may vary. The first is the degree of inequality. The second is called "rigidity of inequality" or "status crystallization," which is the same as Svalastoga's "correlation." The third is "rigidity of stratification," which is Svalastoga's "permeability" turned upside down.

Like Sorokin's and others' positions, Haller's (1970) statement of the synthesis assumes that stratification to one degree or another exists in all societies at all times. Revised slightly in this article, this form of the synthesis holds that there are two classes of dimensions of stratification. The first are "content"— or *power*—dimensions, after Weber: the capability of a given unit to elicit from others behavior promoted by the first unit, with such power having been routinized by coercion or consent. Agreeing conceptually but not always terminologically with the classical writers, this expression of the synthesis posits political power, economic power, and the power of prestige as universal dimensions of power. For civilized societies, it adds the power of years of formal education.

This position thus posits legitimatized political influence (including authority) as the dimension underlying Weber's "party," Sorokin's "political stratification," Lenski's "power," and Svalastoga's "political status." It posits Weber's "class," Sorokin's "economic stratification," Lenski's "privilege," and Svalastoga's economic status as referring to the same set of hierarchical phenomena: access to goods and services—the *economic* dimension of a stratification structure. From Weber, it takes the variable of social honor; from Sorokin and modern occupational status researchers, that of occupational stratification; from Svalastoga, that of social status; and from Lenski, that of prestige. From the empirical tradition, it takes the measurement of occupational power ("status"). All these elements are seen as referring to a third homogeneous set of hierarchical phenomena: the power of respect or deference attributed to a unit because of that unit's participation in a social category (such as an occupation) that has a specific level of evaluation by a society—the *prestige* dimension of societal stratification. As has been indicated, from Svalastoga and Duncan, with much support from the empiricists and also some from Weber, it takes informational power as a content dimension of a stratification structure, with education as its main indicator.

At the general level, each power dimension is of course presumed to be applicable in some form to all human societies as far back as human communal life can be traced. It is the exact expression of each dimension and the relationship among the dimension that vary across time and place. For entire contemporary societies, the main expressions of each dimension seem to be the following: for the political power dimension, *political power*, a variable researchers cannot yet measure despite its centrality in classical theory; for the economic dimension, *income* (occasionally wealth), a variable of concern to those in the empirical tradition; for the *prestige dimension, occupational status* in either of its two main forms of occupational prestige ratings (Treiman 1977) and occupational socioeconomic index scores (Featherman and Hauser 1978); and for the informational power dimension, *educational attainment level* in terms of years of formal schooling successfully completed. Thus, in recent years it has become apparent that for today's societies, the main variables of the empirical tradition have central places among the content dimensions of the classical tradition. Income, occupational status, and education are the theoretically defensible variables most readily available to measure three of the four classical content dimensions.

Like Sorokin's, Svalastoga's, and Duncan's, Haller's formulation of the synthesis specifies several structural dimensions, with each one held to be applicable to every appropriate measure of each content dimension. The three structural dimensions of Svalastoga and Duncan are included: degree of inequality, status crystallization, and degree of status inheritance. Two others from Sorokin are included, although they are modified to fit today's understanding. One is the general level or central tendency, and the other is a division of Sorokin's concept of profile into two concepts: mode structure and skewness. Although calculated from data on small units, each structural dimension applies to the society as a whole. Although logically they are partly dependent on one another, each one makes a unique contribution to an understanding of stratification. Each appears to be amenable to statistical description. Each is applicable to every indicator of the standing of every small unit (say, family) in the society. Valid measures of each content dimension taken at one point in time on a generalizable sample of the population of small units of that society would provide a complete description of the stratification structure of that society at that time. Successive measures would provide a complete description of the evolution of that society's stratification structure over time, thus providing a general idea of the variations in the degree of stratification in that society. Each applies to comparisons over time or among societies.

General Level. As Sorokin realized, the levels of structural dimensions may rise and fall as wholes. That is, the average economic, political, prestige, and informational standing of small units changes over time. These rises and falls may be seen in changes in the central tendency—say, the arithmetic mean or the median value—of the standing of small units. The rises and falls of the central tendency of any one of these dimensions do not necessarily follow the same pattern as those of another. Average economic, prestige, and informational power may increase, for example, while average political influence falls. This could happen in a society where a development-oriented dictatorship reduces citizen political participation while increasing levels of income, raising prestige by upgrading the occupational structure, and increasing access to education. Indeed, the economic, prestige, and educational levels of the populations of the more developed democracies have increased almost consistently since World War II, though this may not always be said for dictatorships. Also, raising the level of the occupational structure is exactly what some researchers mean by *upward structural mobility*, the case in which almost everyone is carried upward by changes in the economy that eliminate low-skill jobs while adding specialized jobs.

Degree of Inequality. The distances among the small units of a society may increase or decrease over time. This, so to speak, stretches the positions on the power dimensions apart or squeezes them together. The statistical term for this is the *degree of dispersion.* A number of measures of dispersion exist, such as the standard deviation (or its square, the variance), the range, the semi-interquantile (or quintile, decile, etc.) range, the share distributions, and the Gini, Theil, and Kuznets coefficients. There are two basic types of inequality: absolute and relative. Absolute conceptions assume that the metric on which the degree of inequality is measured is fixed so that as, say, real income per capita grows, the dollar difference between the mean of the top 10 percent and the mean of the bottom 10 percent of the small units may increase while each is rising above its previous level, with the slope of the top rising faster than is the slope of the bottom. For income, a proper description of these phenomena would be "changes in the *size distribution* of income." Absolute inequality and its changes are sometimes published. Much more often published are the *share distributions* of income. For any society at any time, share distributions take the total amount of, say, income as a constant 100 percent (or 1.00) and determine the degree to which the whole amount, regardless of its absolute size, is evenly or unevenly divided among the population. These distributions include the percentage of all income held by the top X percent and the bottom Y percent of the population. Or, as in the case of the Gini, Theil, and Kuznets coefficients, they use values ranging from 1.0 to zero, in which 1.00 is the maximum degree of inequality and zero is complete equality. Viewed at one point in time in a single society, measures of relative inequality are useful, but for comparison among societies or across time in the same society, they may be misleading. In fact, for many years the share distribution measures of the income of the American people remained essentially unchanged while the size distribution inequality increased dramatically (U.S. Department of Commerce 1980). This was the case because real per capita income was increasing rapidly. The greater the degree of inequality, the greater the degree of stratification.

Crystallization. It has long been recognized that a stratification structure may tend toward or away from monolithicity, in which the different power dimensions merge into a single hierarchy or tend to be in partially separate hierarchies. At one extreme, the position of a small unit on any

one of the dimensions can be found by knowing its position on any other dimension. In other words, if the four content dimensions are perfectly correlated, those in lofty positions on one dimension also will be in lofty positions on all the other dimensions, while those in humble positions on one will be in similarly low positions on any other. At the opposite extreme, a unit's position on a given content dimension is irrelevant to its position on any other. In the real world, any two or three might be highly interrelated, all might be moderately intercorrelated, and so forth. For obvious reasons, Svalastoga called this structural dimension "correlation." Others have called it "status crystallization." Note that crystallization levels and forms may be summarized better by a method called *factor analysis* than by the correlations themselves. Factor analysis can show which sets of content variables tend to vary together in a population and which do not. It also can help determine which are the dominant dimensions and which are of lesser importance in a given stratification structure. For example, it appears that the former Soviet stratification structure was dominated by the political dimension; the American, by the economic dimension. Factor analysis of the correlations of the content dimensions could indicate whether these beliefs are true. The greater the degree of crystallization, the greater the degree of stratification.

Status Inheritance. Status inheritance is the degree to which people's level on a given content dimension is controlled by that of their parents. It is exactly the obverse of circulation mobility: A high degree of power position inheritance implies a low degree of circulation mobility. The basic statistical summary of this phenomenon is either the correlation coefficient (r) or the coefficient of determination (r^2) of the power dimension positions of offspring and their parents. (The r^2 tells how much one variable is determined by the others.) The greater the degree of status inheritance, the greater the degree of stratification.

Sorokin's Profile. Every variable has a so-called distribution, a shape that appears when the number of scores (the *frequency*) is plotted against the value of scores. Much statistical theory today assumes that real-world distributions conform to certain mathematical shapes. The bell-shaped "normal" curve is the one most often used. For distribution of income, the "log normal" curve, with which the distribution of the natural logarithm of the individual amounts forms a normal curve, is often employed. Stratification researchers often take it for granted that the distributions of power dimensions are either normal or log normal, but there is no sociological reason to assume this. The shape of the distribution of a content dimension is precisely what Sorokin meant by his term "profile." Lacking the data and concepts to proceed further, he simply called the real-world shapes of these distributions their profiles. Today we can see that there are two aspects of each profile: mode structure and skewness.

In strikingly underdeveloped societies, almost everyone is concentrated at the very lowest values of economic, political, occupational, and educational power: extremely poor, utterly uninfluential, of low prestige, and illiterate. Above those people, their "betters" are arranged in rank order, with a wide range in which the few people who are above the bottom dwindle up the line to a handful of individuals of lofty standing. Each such distribution would have a very low mode (or distinct cluster of cases) and median (where half of the cases are higher and half are lower) and a higher arithmetic mean, with a sharply skewed tail. In somewhat more developed societies, such distributions, instead of yielding bell-shaped or log normal curves, might show multiple modes, with many people concentrated around a fairly low point, quite a few concentrated around a point a bit higher, a few concentrated toward the top, and after that a sharp skewing up to the very few at the top. The consequences of such forms for the lives of the people involved are no doubt great. For example, if in a certain society almost everyone is destitute, the few who are more or less well to do are highly visible. Even if the wealthy were really not far above the others, everybody would think of that society as being highly stratified. If in another society people are bunched together at several points along a hierarchy, thus forming multiple modes, or discrete classes, those in each mode might come to consider themselves members of a special class in opposition to those concentrated at another mode. Thus, the exact forms of profiles are essential to a description of a society's stratification structure. Theoretically, these forms have substantial consequences for many stratification-dependent behaviors.

Profile: Mode Structure. Mode structure refers to the number, size, and location of distinct modes on the distribution of each content variable. In polymodal structures, the more pronounced the modes, the greater the degree of stratification.

Profile: Skewness. Several statistical devices exist to mark the degree of skewness. The greater the level of skewness, the greater the degree of stratification.

ILLUSTRATIONS

Data by which to measure and compare stratification structures are exceedingly difficult to obtain. A complete description at a specific point in time requires well-measured, valid indicators of four power dimensions, one or more for each dimension. For each indicator, several measurements must be made: The average level, the degree of absolute and relative inequality, the degree and factor-analytic forms of the crystallization of the whole set of indicators of the power dimension, the degree of power position inheritance, and the distributions of each one must be plotted to indicate its mode structure and measure its skewness. Describing such an overall structure requires the construction of 24 or more different indicators of structural dimensions. These indicators have to be based on representative, societywide samples large enough to permit the recording of small differences, as in the case of the few people at the upper end of a skewed distribution. The study of variations in the structure of stratification demands that comparable measurements be taken on the same variable at different times and in different places. In itself, the requirement of comparability is extremely severe when one is making comparisons among societies with different cultures or over long periods of time within the same society.

Exploratory work of this sort has been conducted on data provided by Brazil. The data were collected on a national probability sample of households in 1973 and are available for all employed men and women in the households sampled. These people are the "small units" of the descriptive analysis presented below. Brazil is a particularly good place in which to conduct such exploratory research for two reasons: It is a large country whose regions are markedly different from each other in terms of development, and it has only one language and culture. The first factor makes it feasible to test for structural variations of stratification associated with development levels, treating regions as societies; the second eases the problem of comparability.

As was indicated earlier, it is not currently feasible to obtain measures of the political power dimension in Brazil or anywhere else. However, there is widespread agreement that income is a proper measure of the economic status dimension, that occupational status instruments based on the average education and income of each occupation are proper measures of the prestige dimension, and that education is a similarly appropriate measure of the informational status dimension. These data are available for some of the parameters that would have to be assessed to obtain a complete description of the regional-development variations of the Brazilian stratification structure in 1973.

Here one is comparing sharply different development regions. The stratification structures of three of Brazil's socioeconomic development (SED) macroregions in 1970 were delineated by obtaining multiple-item, factor-weighted SED scores on that nation's 360 official continental microregions and plotting their levels on the map of Brazil (Haller 1983). This showed the following five macroregions: the Developed South (median SED = 78 on a scale of zero to 100), the South's Developing Periphery (median SED = 54), the Undeveloped Amazonia (median SED = 32.5), the Unevenly Developed Northeast (median SED = 31), and the Underdeveloped Middle North (median SED = 13).

Obviously, this article cannot reproduce each one of the structural dimensions for each SED macroregion for men and for women. Instead, it provides a few key illustrations for three of the regions: the Developed, the Developing, and the Underdeveloped.

Variables routinely used as indicators were formulated to measure three of the four stratification content dimensions: education in years successfully completed, occupational status scores (composed of canonically weighted scores based on the education and income of each occupation), and annual income in 1973 U.S. dollars.

The illustrations are based on regularly employed men and women 15 to 65 years of age. All such persons who lived in the three regions under comparison and were part of the sample have been included. The numbers of sample members vary sharply by region and by sex. The Developed South is much more populous than the other two regions, and about three times more men than women are employed. The largest of the six gender-by-region subsamples thus consists of men in the South: over 40,000 (see Table 1). The smallest consists of women in the South's Developing Periphery: over 2,500.

Let us begin with the profiles (see Figure 1), graphs that have been sketched to show the shape of the stratification structures for men and for women as they appear in the three regions. There are two reasons for paying close attention to these curves. First, they show power relations among the people. The presence of multiple modes shows the existence of discrete and potentially opposed classes. Both the mode structure and the marked skewing indicate a high degree of stratification for each sample. Second, the fact that these distributions diverge sharply from normal or log normal curves shows that the numbers, that is, the data presented in Tables 1 and 2, are at best approximate because the shapes of the distributions affect their meaning.

The curves show the following:

1. Multiple modes are exhibited by both men and women in 11 of the 12 graphs pertaining to the developed and developing regions. The exception is distribution of women's income in the developing region.

2. For the two most developed regions, comparable curves show just about the same mode structure. In these regions, education tends to be bi- or trimodal and occupational status tends to be at least trimodal. Among men and among women in the developing region, income also exhibits multiple modes. In the underdeveloped region, the shape of the curves is markedly different form that of the others. The curves in this region show a heavy concentration of both men and women at the bottom of each indicator variable,

Illustrative Variations of Brazilian Regional Stratification Structures by Development, Employed Persons Age 15–65, 1973.

	REGION					
	Men			Women		
STRATIFICATION CONTENT VARIABLE	Developed	Developing	Underdeveloped	Developed	Developing	Underdeveloped
Education						
General level (average)	4.9	4.2	1.7	5.3	5.1	1.6
Absolute inequality (Standard deviation)	3.9	3.8	2.3	4.3	4.5	2.7
Occupational Status						
General level (average)	19.4	16.8	6.7	20.3	21.1	8.6
Absolute inequality (Standard deviation)	18.9	18.0	10.8	19.7	20.4	14.6
Circulation mobility $(1-r^2)$	0.72	0.79	0.85	0.69	0.75	0.63
Income, Annual						
General level (average)	1,800	1,423	536	891	610	264
Absolute inequality (Standard deviation)	2,670	2,330	903	1,132	864	400
Number of Persons	1,578	7,686	5,841	15,711	2,581	2,777

Table 1

NOTE: *Education* is in estimated years. *Occupational status* is in canonical socioeconomic status units (0–100); *circulation mobility* is intergenerational. *Income* is in U.S. dollars.

though some of the region's six graphs show the formation of small second and sometimes third modes at high status levels. The apparent conclusion is that the underdeveloped area exhibits a relatively high degree of equality at the very bottom of the Brazilian stratification structure. This is precisely the opposite of the thinking among many observers of Brazil, who believe that inequality is greater in the underdeveloped region (perhaps because of the glaring visibility of the tiny stratum at the top).

3. Each curve shows a high degree of skewness. That is, the highest positions are held by a tiny proportion of the people, and on the whole, as the tail of the distribution lengthens, the higher the level, the tinier the percentage of the people.

4. In every case, the main modes are the one or two at the bottom, where most people tend to be concentrated.

5. Almost every graph shows a tendency for one or two smaller modes to appear toward the middle of the distribution. For education, this occurs at around grade 12. For occupational status it is about 50 units, or the level of office clerks, primary school teachers, and the like. For income, it is about $2,000 to $3,000 per year, or a monthly wage between $160 and $250.

6. There may be a tiny mode near the top of the educational and occupational status distribution in the more developed regions.

7. For occupational status and income, women are more concentrated toward the bottom than are men.

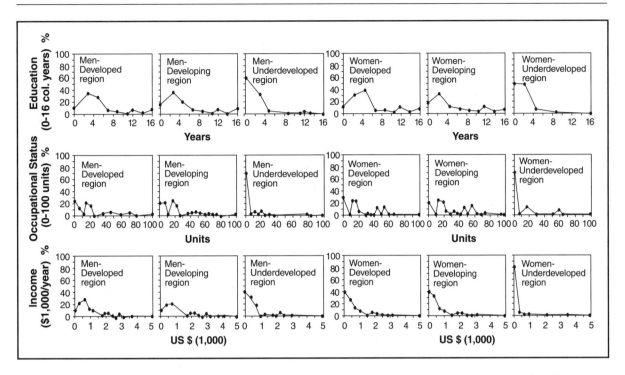

Figure 1. Illustrative Variations of Brazilian Regional Stratification Profiles, by Development, Employed Persons Age 15–65, 1973

SOURCE: See Table 1 for definitions and sample sizes.

8. Clearly, the main regional variations in profile are between the two more developed regions and the underdeveloped region.

9. In terms of mode structure, the more developed areas seem more stratified than does the underdeveloped area.

10. In terms of skewness, it appears that the underdeveloped area is more highly stratified.

Data on the general levels and absolute inequality levels of the three content dimensions are presented in Table 1. For occupational status, the degree of circulation mobility also is presented. The general level rises with development for all three variables, except for the occupational levels of women in the developing region, whose status is slightly higher than that of women in the developed region. Again, with two exceptions among women in the developing region, the higher the level of development, the greater the degree of absolute inequality. Echoing what was gleaned from the graphs, the general level and the absolute

inequality levels of the underdeveloped region are markedly lower than those in the other areas. Finally, among men, the higher the level of development, the lower the degree of circulation mobility. Women show no trend in this regard.

Evidence regarding structural crystallization is presented in Table 2. Among men, the higher the level of development, the higher the degree of crystallization. Among women, the same trend may be present in the data, but with one small inconsistency.

CONCLUSION

This article has attempted to describe the contemporary synthesis of classical and empirical traditions of sociological thought concerning societal stratification, with special emphasis on what may be learned about ways to describe variations in stratification structures. It also presents some illustrations showing how indicators of some of the structural dimensions vary across development regions among employed men and women in

Illustrative Variations in Structural Crystallization among Brazilian Development Regions, Employed Persons Age 15–65, 1973 (Correlation Coefficients).

	REGION					
	Men			Women		
STRATIFICATION CONTENT VARIABLE	Developed	Developing	Underdeveloped	Developed	Developing	Underdeveloped
Education by occupational status	0.52	0.51	0.35	0.65	0.67	0.52
Education by income	.27	.18	.16	.23	.20	.20
Occupational status by income	.23	.16	.13	.23	.17	.16

Table 2

Brazil. In general, these indicators show that the more highly developed a region is, the more stratified it is.

Measuring stratification variations among societies is an immense task because of the number of variables that must be studied and because of differences in culture, language, and social organization among peoples. Still, at both the individual and societal levels, the effects of structural differences of stratification are among the most perplexing of this age and perhaps of all ages. For this reason, understanding how and why stratification structures vary and specifying the consequences of such differences are worth the considerable effort required.

REFERENCES

Duncan, Otis Dudley 1968 "Social Stratification and Mobility: Problems in the Measurement of Trend." In Eleanor Bernert Sheldon and Wilbert E. Moore, eds., *Indicators of Social Change: Concepts and Measurements.* New York: Russell Sage Foundation.

Featherman, David L., and Robert M. Hauser 1978 *Opportunity and Change.* New York: Academic Press.

Ganzeboom, Harry B. G., Donald J. Treiman, and Wout C. Ultee 1991 "Comparative Intergenerational Stratification Research: Three Generations and Beyond." *Annual Review of Sociology* 17:277–302.

Grusky, David B. 1994 *Social Stratification: Class, Race, and Gender in Sociological Perspective.* Boulder, Colorado: Westview Press.

Haller, Archibald O. 1970 "Changes in the Structure of Status Systems." *Rural Sociology* 35:469–487.

—— 1983 *The Socioeconomic Macroregions of Brazil.* Lanham, Md.: Bernam-Unipub.

Lenski, Gerhardt 1966 *Power and Privilege: A Theory of Social Stratification.* New York: McGraw-Hill.

Sorokin, Pitrim A. 1927 *Social Mobility.* New York: Harper.

Svalastoga, Kaare 1965 *Social Differentiation.* New York: David McKay.

Treiman, Donald J. 1977 *Occupational Prestige in Comparative Perspective.* New York: Academic Press.

U.S. Department of Commerce 1980 *Social Indicators II.* Washington, D.C.: U.S. Government Printing Office.

Weber, Max 1946 "Class, Status, and Party." In Hans Gerth and C. Wright Mills, eds., *From Max Weber.* New York: Oxford University Press.

—— 1947 "Social Stratification and Class Structure." In A. M. Henderson and T. Parsons, eds., *The Theory of Social and Economic Organization.* New York: Free Press.

ARCHIBALD O. HALLER

SOCIETY AND TECHNOLOGICAL RISKS

If there is an organizing theme in sociology, it is social order: what it looks like, how to think about the various forms it takes, and how to explain it. Conversely, what happens when social order breaks down? What changes are wrought in how people see the world, and most important, what is altered in how they relate to one another when social order goes awry? The study of risk, danger, and catastrophe is a special case of the larger field of social breakdown.

Sociologists have long been interested in phenomena that harm people and what people value. Until recently, most of this work concentrated on harm from natural events such as earthquakes, floods, and tornadoes, but many researchers now write about "technical" or "technological" risks. In some ways the distinction between natural and technological risks or disasters is not helpful: There is no objective difference between a death caused by a fire and a death caused by an airplane crash. Yet in other ways those who have been fascinated by how modern technologies fail people have asked a broader set of questions than they could have if they did *not* see a difference between natural and technological risks. They have asked new questions about the functions of expertise and science in modern society, the roles of power and authority in the creation of danger, and the capacity of people to build systems they cannot control.

In this encyclopedia of sociology, risk and danger are treated mainly as a sociological problem, but this is not necessarily the case. Scholars writing about these issues come from economics, geography, psychology (Mellers et al. 1998), anthropology (Oliver-Smith 1996), and even engineering (Starr 1995) and physics. This is basically a good thing: Too much sociology is self-referential and inbred, and truly interdisciplinary work creates considerable intellectual, if not professional, excitement. No one can write about technological risks in an interesting way without reading and thinking in interdisciplinary terms.

Scholars concerned with technological risks have addressed a wide variety of topics that range from how individuals think about risks to how nation-states develop strategies to mitigate threats from failures of high technology. Some scholars even write about risks that might be faced by societies far in the future. Toxic threats have drawn particularly close scrutiny from scholars, and there are important sociological studies of Love Canal, Three Mile Island, Chernobyl, Bhopal, the *Challenger*, nuclear waste, and nuclear weapons. One reason for this is that toxic risks invert the way natural disasters do damage. Rather than assaulting people from the outside, as do other calamities, toxic hazards assault bodies from within. Toxic injuries also have no definable end, and so their victims can never know when they are safe from further damage. The point here is that the

meaning of toxic threats is fundamentally different from that of natural disasters (Couch and Kroll-Smith 1985; Erikson 1990, 1994). The disruption in social order thus can be largely internal, with psychological and emotional suffering caused by the breakdown of external social systems (Sorokin 1968).

In general, the sociology of risk is concerned with researching and explaining how interactions between technology and modes of social organization create hazards or the potential for hazards (Clarke and Short 1993). A hazard can be an actual threat to people's lives (toxic chemical contamination, for example) or the *perception* that there is a threat. Indeed, many analysts focus on risk perception: what people think is dangerous and why they think what they do (Freudenburg 1988). The word "technology" refers to the social and mechanical tools people use to accomplish something, such as the design of a nuclear power plant and the vocabularies used by experts when they talk about effectively evacuating an urban area after a major radiation release from a nuclear power plant. "Modes of social organization" refers to both social structure (e.g., hierarchies of power) and culture (e.g., the degree of legitimacy granted to experts). In the twenty-first century society will continue its march toward social and technical complexity. One expression of this complexity is a capacity to create machines and institutional arrangements that are at once grand and terrifying. With these developments, it seems, publics are increasingly aware of the potentially devastating consequences of system failures even as they enjoy the cornucopia engendered by modern social organization and modern technology.

This is an opportune place to identify an area of research that will be increasingly important for both intellectual and policy reasons. A lot of work in psychology and economics, which echoes the concerns of political and economic elites, concerns public perception of risk. Much of that work has shown that the general public does not make decisions in accordance with a hyperrational calculus in which its preferences and values are always consistent and, more to the point, agree with those of trained scientific researchers. Consonant with the concern with public irrationality is the notion that people panic when faced with risks they do not understand. It is easy to find this idea in media reports of high-level politicians' remarks after a large accident: Politicians worry that people will overreact in very unproductive ways. The image is one of people trampling each other to make for the exits of a burning building or escape from a sniper's random rifle shots. Translated to perception of risk regarding accidents and disasters, the image becomes one of individuals pursuing their self-interest to the exclusion of those of their neighbors and communities: to get out of Love Canal, to run away from Three Mile Island, or to flee a burning airplane that has barely managed to land.

In fact, research indicates that people *rarely* panic even when it might be rational to do so. I have reviewed scores of cases of natural and technological disasters—trains fall over and release toxic chemicals that endanger a town, earthquakes shake a city to its core, fires threaten to level an entire neighborhood—and have found very few instances of uncontrolled flight at the expense of others. After the Chernobyl catastrophe in 1986 there was some panic, though that response might have been highly sensible. The U.S. firebombing of Tokyo in World War II also elicited some cases of panic. With exceptions of that sort, it is hard to find widespread panic after any type of disaster. Even events such as the fire at the Beverly Hills Supper Club and the stampede at the Who concert, which are commonly thought of as examples of panic, were not (Johnson 1987). Rather than panic, the modal reaction is one of terror, followed by stunned reflection or sometimes anomie and ending with a fairly orderly response (e.g., reconstruction or evacuation). Even in the horrors chronicled by the U.S. Strategic Bombing Survey, cities burn, bodies explode, houses fall down, and still people do not panic (Janis 1951; Hersey 1985).

One way to classify research on risk is in terms of micro and macro perspectives. Both micro and macro studies have made important contributions to an understanding of the connections between risk, technology, and society. Micro-level research, generally speaking, is concerned with the personal, political, and social dilemmas posed by technology and activities that threaten the quality of people's lives. Macro-level work on risk does not deny the importance of micro-oriented research but asks different questions and seeks answers to those questions at an institutional level of analysis.

As some of the examples below illustrate, much macro work emphasizes the importance of the institutional context within which decisions about risk are made. Sociologists of risk are keen to distinguish between public and private decisions. Some people make choices that affect mainly themselves, while those in positions of authority make choices that have important implications for others. This is only one among many ways in which the sociology of risk is concerned with issues of power and the distribution of hazards and benefits.

THE MICRO LEVEL

As noted above, a substantial body of work has demonstrated that the public overestimates threats that are dramatic (e.g., from airplane accidents), particularly violent (e.g., from handguns), and potentially catastrophic (e.g., from nuclear power plants). Similarly, people tend to underestimate more prosaic chronic threats such as those from botulism and asthma. Several explanations for this phenomenon have been proposed; the one that is most convincing focuses on the mechanisms through which information about risks is channeled to people (Kahneman et al. 1982). Specifically, the media—especially newspapers and television—are more likely to feature dramatic, violent, or catastrophic calamities than less sensational threats. One reason the media find such risks more interesting is that they are easier to cover and hence more easily fit into tight deadlines. Covering prosaic risks is also more time-consuming than covering short, dramatic accidents. Thus, there are several good structural reasons why the media pay attention to high-drama risks and neglect low-drama risks. Scholars are able to explain why the public has biased estimates of risk by focusing on the structural connections between people and the media, specifically on the constraints that lead the media to be biased about certain types of information.

Another example at the micro level of analysis is found in the work of Heimer (1988, 1992; Heimer and Staffen 1998), who analyzed how information is used and transmitted in intensive care units for infants. Her study is cast at a micro level of analysis in the sense that one of her concerns is how parents think about information regarding terribly sick babies. However, like all good sociological studies, Heimer's connects what parents think with the social contexts in which they find themselves. For example, one of her findings is that when hospital personnel transmit information to parents about their infants, that process is structured to protect the hospital from lawsuits and only secondarily to apprise parents of the condition of their children. Thus, Heimer describes, much as a psychologist might, how parents think but also demonstrates that how they think is contingent on the organizational needs of hospitals.

THE MACRO LEVEL

Macro-level work on risk includes research on how professionals influence the behavior of regulatory agencies, how organizations blunder and break down (Vaughan 1999), how social movements arise to push issues into the public debate, and how national cultures influence which risks are considered acceptable (Douglas 1985). Many macro theorists are deeply concerned with how the institutional structure of society makes some risks more likely than others to gain political and intellectual attention (Clarke 1988). Consider motor vehicle risks. Nearly 40,000 people are killed on U.S. highways every year, and most people would agree that that is an appalling mortality rate. Although it is a commonplace that half those deaths are alcohol-related, it is not really known how much of the carnage is in fact due to alcohol (Gusfield 1981). Nevertheless, one probably can reasonably assume that a significant proportion is caused by drunk drivers (even 10 percent would be 4,000 people). Most people would agree that 4,000 deaths per year is grounds for concern, yet it also is known that high rates of fatal traffic accidents are associated with speeding, wrong turns, and improper passing. Objectively, there is no difference between a death caused by someone making a wrong turn and one caused by a drunk driver, yet most cultures say the two deaths are very different. In the United States there is even a small social movement galvanized around the issue of drunk drivers, an example of which is the organization called Mothers Against Drunk Driving. Why is there no organization called Mothers Against Improper Passers? A sociological answer is that most cultures frown on using drugs to alter one's degree of self-control and that a person who does so is defined as morally decadent and lacking social

responsibility. Thus the opprobrium unleashed on drunken drivers has less to do with the objective magnitude of the problem than with the apparent danger such drivers represent to the cultural value of self-control.

Another example of macro work on risk, this time concerning organizations and symbols, is the oil spill from the *Exxon-Valdez* tanker in March 1989. At the time, the Exxon spill was the worst ever to occur in U.S. waters, leaking at least eleven million gallons into Prince William Sound and the Gulf of Alaska. The spill caused massive loss of wildlife, and although no people died, it did disrupt social relationships, create a political crisis, and reorient debates about the safety of oil transportation systems in the United States. From a sociological point of view, one of the most interesting things about the spill is how corporations and regulatory agencies plan for large oil spills. Sound research shows that not much can be done about large amounts of spilled oil (Clarke 1990), yet organizations continue to create elaborate plans for what they will do to contain large spills and how they will clean the oil from beaches and shorelines. They do this even though there has never been a case of successful containment or recovery on the open seas. Organizations create plans that will never work because such plans are master metaphors for taming the wild, subjugating uncertainty, and proclaiming expertise. In modern societies, expert knowledge and rational organization are of paramount importance, and there now seems to be an institutionalized incapacity to admit that some things may be beyond people's control (Clarke 1999).

Another example is the 1984 tragedy in Bhopal, India. At least 2,600 people died when a complex accident in a Union Carbide plant released toxic chemicals into the environment. At the time, Bhopal was the worst single industrial accident in history (the nuclear meltdown at Chernobyl in 1986 eventually will lead to more deaths). The Bhopal tragedy was certainly an organizational failure, as studies have documented (Shrivastava 1987). However, what was most interesting about the Bhopal accident was that the risk created by the Union Carbide chemical plant had become institutionalized to the point where very few, if any, of the key players, were worried about a potential catastrophe. The poor people who lived next to the plant seemed to have accepted official assurances that they were safe and in any case had little choice in the matter. Government officials—the ones assuring those who lived near the plant of their safety—seemed to have accepted the disastrous potential of the plant as part of the price of having a large corporation in their country. For their part, corporate officials and experts seemed to have given insufficient thought to the possibility of killing several thousand Indians. One reason the Bhopal disaster is sociologically interesting is the degree to which groups and organizations come to accept risk as part of their everyday lives. The same observation might be made of automobile driving, nuclear power plants, and lead-contaminated water pipes (even brass pipes contain about 7 percent lead).

Anyone reading about how social organization and technology can break down must wonder whether it must always be so. Some people believe that it must, and although those scholars may be wrong (Clarke 1993), they cannot be ignored. High-reliability organizations (HROs), as they are called, are said to be possible. These organizations are alleged to be so safe that they are error-free. The claim is not that these organizations cannot fail but that they never do so in an important way (Roberts 1993). Somehow these organizations (a U.S. nuclear aircraft carrier is a good example) are able to maintain a strict hierarchy while enabling people low in the hierarchy to intervene in the functioning of the organization to prevent failure (contradicting how most organizations work). Moreover, rather than cover up their mistakes as most organizations do, HROs try hard to learn from theirs. Finally, these organizations have a lot of redundancy built into them, preventing small errors from escalating into complete system failure.

High-reliability theory is animated by a disagreement with what is called normal accident theory (NAT) (Perrow 1984). NAT views the complexity of high-technology systems as problematic. The components in complex systems, say, a nuclear power plant, can fail in ways that no one could have anticipated and that no one understands when a catastrophe unfolds. From this view, rather than safety, redundancies can add technical complexity and lead to the formation of political interest groups, both of which can interfere with safe operations (Sagan 1993). Rather than honest learning, NAT stresses that managers and experts often engage in *symbolic* representations of safety, trying to convince the public, regulators, and other organizations that they are on top of potential problems (Clarke and Perrow 1996). An important contribution of NAT lies in locating the source of risk in organizations per se. Its structural emphasis draws attention away from easy and familiar explanations such as human error.

The contrast between NAT and HRO theory goes beyond their assessments of the inevitability of organizational failure, for the two schools of thought exemplify the concern with social order and disorder that I mentioned above. High-reliability theory is optimistic about human perfectibility, highlighting society's tendency to create and maintain order; normal accident theory is pessimistic about human perfectibility, fundamentally viewing failure and disorder as inherent in the human condition.

An important work that emphasizes the imperfections of organization is Vaughan's book on the *Challenger* accident (1996). Vaughan argues that what looked like a highly risky decision—to send the *Challenger* up that day—was in fact normal given the routines and expectations that organized the thoughts of the officials and experts involved in that choice. An important reason for this "normalization of danger" was the high production pressures that the decision makers faced. It was not a matter of people deliberately taking chances they knew were unreasonable because of clear, external, imposing pressures. It was a more subtle process by which the very definition of "reasonable" shifted in a way that did not contravene those pressures. Vaughan's view stresses the commonality of error in all organizations. Some organizations make computer chips, some make space flights, but all fail. Vaughan details the mechanisms that produced a certain worldview of danger and safety that prevailed at NASA, and in so doing she connects micro and macro, structure and culture.

Every year the natural environment seems to be more polluted than it was the preceding year. Why? A commonsense explanation might claim that people do not care enough about the environment, perhaps attributing callous attitudes and personal greed to politicians and corporations. Such an explanation would focus on the motives of individual managers and politicians but from a sociological point of view would miss the all-important institutions in which such decision makers function. Sociologists know that those who occupy top positions in government and corporate organizations are not without intelligence and good sense. These decision makers may be individually quite concerned about environmental degradation, but because of their structural locations, they are subject to pressures that may be at odds with environmental health and welfare. These pressures originate in specific social structures that create institutional interests that may be contrary to individual preferences (Clarke 1988). A corporate executive seeks (and *must* seek) to remain in business, if necessary at the expense of others' well-being or the environment. A similar explanation accounts for why Ford's president, Lee Iacocca, in the 1970s marketed Pintos that had propensity to explode and burn. In other words, market institutions are arranged so that it is sensible for any individual or organization to force negative externalities on society. For its part, one of the key functions of government is to maintain a political and economic environment that is favorable to business. Thus, an explanation that centers on the institutional constraints and incentives that shape decisions about pollution can account for the behavior of organizations, experts, and officials far better than can an explanation that focuses on their personal characteristics.

FUTURE DIRECTIONS

Future developments in the sociology of risk probably will revolve around issues of social conflict: its bases, meaning, and role in spurring social change. Society—and sociology—will be confronted with fundamental dilemmas in the twenty-first century. Society will have to deal with issues of environmental justice and the likelihood that pollution and risk are unequally distributed. Modernity brings both fruits and poisons. In particular, people must come to grips with what may the primary dilemma of modern times: How can an industrial and democratic system that yields such a high standard of living also be involved in the creation of terrible hazards? Answering this question will require a recognition that many of the most frightening threats—nuclear meltdowns near large cities, toxic leachate in water tables, ozone destruction, explosions of liquefied natural gas from supertankers, failure to contain nuclear waste—almost seem

beyond control. It may be the case that before society can better control political and technological systems, people must admit that some aspects of the technical world are not within human control.

REFERENCES

Clarke, Lee 1988 "Explaining Choices among Technological Risks." *Social Problems* 35(1):501–514.

—— 1990. "Oil Spill Fantasies." *Atlantic Monthly*, November, pp. 65–77.

—— 1993 "Drs. Pangloss and Strangelove Meet Organizational Theory: High Reliability Organizations and Nuclear Weapons Accidents." *Sociological Forum* 8(4):675–689.

—— 1999 *Mission Improbable: Using Fantasy Documents to Tame Disaster*. Chicago: University of Chicago Press.

——, and Charles Perrow 1996 "Prosaic Organizational Failure." *American Behavioral Scientist* 39 (8):1040–1056.

——, and James F. Short, Jr. 1993 "Social Organization and Risk: Some Current Controversies." *Annual Review of Sociology* 19:375–399.

Couch, Stephen R., and J. Stephen Kroll-Smith 1985 "The Chronic Technical Disaster." *Social Science Quarterly* 66(3):564–575.

Douglas, Mary 1985 *Risk Acceptability According to the Social Sciences*. New York: Russell Sage Foundation.

Erikson, Kai 1990 "Toxic Reckoning: Business Faces a New Kind of Fear." *Harvard Business Review* 90(1):118–126.

—— 1994 *A New Species of Trouble: Explorations in Disaster, Trauma, and Community*. New York: Norton.

Freudenburg, William R. 1988 "Perceived Risk, Real Risk: Social Science and the Art of Probabilistic Risk Assessment." *Science.* 242:44–49.

Gusfield, Joseph 1981 *The Culture of Public Problems: Drinking-Driving and the Symbolic Order*. Chicago: University of Chicago Press.

Heimer, Carol A. 1988 "Social Structure, Psychology, and the Estimation of Risk." *Annual Review of Sociology* 14:491–519.

—— 1992 "Your Baby's Fine, Just Fine: Certification Procedures, Meetings, and the Supply of Information in Neonatal Intensive Case Units." In James F. Short, Jr., and Lee Clarke, eds., *Organizations, Uncertainties, and Risk*.

——, and Lisa R. Staffen 1998 *For the Sake of the Children: The Social Organization of Responsibility in the Hospital and the Home*. Chicago: University of Chicago Press.

Hersey, John 1985 *Hiroshima*. New York: Knopf.

Janis, Irving Lester 1951 *Air War And Emotional Stress*. New York: McGraw-Hill.

Johnson, Norris R. 1987 "Panic and the Breakdown of Social Order: Popular Myth, Social Theory, Empirical Evidence." *Sociological Focus* 20(3):171–183.

Kahneman, Daniel, Paul Slovic, and Amos Tversky 1982 *Judgment under Uncertainty: Heuristics and Biases*. Cambridge: Cambridge University Press.

Mellers, B. A., A. Schwartz, and A. D. J. Cooke 1998 "Judgment and Decision Making." *Annual Review of Psychology* 49:447–477.

Oliver-Smith, Anthony 1996 "Anthropological Perspectives on Hazards and Disasters." *Annual Review of Anthropology* 25:303–328.

Perrow, Charles 1984 *Normal Accidents: Living with High Risk Technologies*. New York: Basic Books.

Roberts, Karlene H., ed. 1993 *New Challenges to Understanding Organizations*. New York: Macmillan.

Sagan, Scott 1993 *The Limits of Safety: Organizations, Accidents, and Nuclear Weapons*. Princeton, N.J.: Princeton University Press.

Shrivastava, Paul 1987 *Bhopal: Anatomy of a Crisis*. Cambridge: Ballinger.

Sorokin, Pitirim A. 1968 [1942] *Man and Society in Calamity*. New York: Greenwood Press.

Starr, Chauncey 1995 "A Personal History: Technology to Energy Strategy." *Annual Review of Energy and the Environment* 20:31–44.

Vaughan, Diane 1996 *The Challenger Launch Decision: Risky Technology, Culture, and Deviance at NASA*. Chicago: University of Chicago Press.

—— 1999 "The Dark Side of Organizations." *Annual Review of Sociology* 25:271–305

LEE CLARKE

SOCIOBIOLOGY, HUMAN

THE DARWINIAN SETTING

Sociobiology is the term used to describe a relatively recent stage in the continuing development of evolutionary biology. It systematically brings the study of social behavior under the umbrella of the Synthetic Theory (or the Modern Synthesis) that, starting in the 1920s, arose from the marriage of Darwinian theory and Mendelian, or genetic, science (Huxley 1942). The most challenging aspect of the new elaboration concerns a decisive step into human behavior. Sociologists (and social scientists in general) have not responded with enthusiasm; the old anthropocentrism with its extreme stress on culture and socialization (environmentalism) is still dominant. Resistance, however, is slowly breaking down, and one may speak of a human sociobiology taking the form of "evolutionary anthropology," "evolutionary psychology," "evolutionary sociology", and so forth. It can even be stated that human sociobiology may represent the beginning of the long-desired synthesis of the social sciences. At the same time, the introduction of cultural parameters into evolutionary explanation may further enrich the modern synthesis.

The term "sociobiology" harks back to the mid-1940s, and the evolutionary study of behavior began to develop rapidly only in the 1960s. However, its roots can be traced back to Darwin's ([1859] 1958) theory of evolution by natural selection, still the cornerstone of evolutionary science. From today's perspective, Darwin's theory can be conveniently stated as follows:

1. The rate of reproduction in populations, such as species, tends to be faster than the growth of the resources needed to sustain all their members.

2. As a result, populations experience a real or potential scarcity of resources.

3. This scarcity stimulates the "struggle for existence": competition of various kinds both within and between populations.

4. Some individuals in any given population are more succeessful than others in the struggle and thus are more likely to survive long enough to reproduce.

5. This differential reproductive success is in the last analysis the result of "variations" between individuals: genetic differences. That is, some variations are better suited (adapted) than others for the competition.

6. The better adapted these variations are, the more likely they are to be inherited by one's descendants.

7. This generational preservation of favorable variations and the concomitant elimination of unfavorable ones are together referred to as "natural selection."

This theory either contains or fosters the basic elements of the theoretical program of sociobiology. Specifically, (1) it establishes natural selection as the basic mechanism in the evolution of behavior, (2) its stress on competition calls attention to the perennial question regarding the role of altruism and selfishness in social life, (3) its focus on heredity suggests that aspects of human behavior, including culture, may be at least partly the result of natural selection and thus of forces long at work in human evolution, (4) perhaps more important, it guides inquiry toward a systematic theory of human nature. The crucial question of this theory is: In the course of human evolutionary time, what *innate* behavioral tendencies (predispositions, psychological adaptations, epigenetic rules, etc.) have been forged by natural selection and environmental pressures acting on genetic matter? These adaptations are likely to be implicated to some degree in socialization processes, thus proposing a more complete explanation in social science.

ELEMENTS OF SOCIOBIOLOGICAL THEORY

The modern synthesis stimulated scientific activity in general and, through such disciplines as entomology, primatology, and ethology, paved the way to the evolutionary study of behavior. Then in 1975 a seminal work proclaimed the advent of a "new synthesis" (Wilson 1975). The master stroke of sociobiology is the revival of "the struggle for existence," that is, the *behavioral* aspect of evolution on which natural selection was clearly based in the work of Darwin. The ultimate consequence of this struggle, or competition for resources, is natural selection: the differential contribution of offspring to future generations. This differential is a rough measure of what Darwin, following the sociologist Herbert Spencer, called "fitness." Accordingly, we are already in a position to state that *in the last analysis* individuals (or simply organisms) may be productively viewed as being in competetion with one another for reproductive success, or genetic fitness. (Without the behavioral component, the statement would read, classical Darwinian logic: Organisms are the descendants of the more reproductively successful organisms.)

The Maximization Principle. This Darwinian-Mendelian idea is rendered more formally by what is considered the general law or principle of sociobiology. Sometimes referred to as the maximization (or fitness) principle, this law states that, while organisms engage in all sorts of behaviors, in the last analysis they tend to behave in ways that maximize their inclusive fitness, or the chance of conveying their genotype (genetic makeup) to future generations. This is a probability statement: That is, some individuals are more successful than others in the reproductive competition. This idea of variability reflects the logic of natural selection and accommodates many facts that may seem strange or contradictory of evolutionary theory. A case in point is the parental abuse of children. Clearly, if organisms differ in the degree to which they behave adaptively one effective way to show this is for them to differ in the way they treat their children. However, this statement is heuristically a bit "lazy": It stimulates research insufficiently. Like many other laws in science, it would be more useful if it took the form of a contingent proposition. A first approximation in this direction is available and the provisos proposed are "creature comforts," "self-deception," and "autonomization of behavior" (the tendency of means, such as wealth, to become ends in themselves), all of which appear to condition negatively the maximization tendency (Lopreato 1989; for incisive analyses of this argument, see Crippen 1994; Maryanski 1998, pp. 11–16; Maryanski and Turner 1998, pp. 128–131).

The use of the adjective "inclusive" is intended to underscore the fact, better understood in the post-Darwinian period (Hamilton 1964), that the fitness of organisms is measured in terms of their relatedness both to their offspring and to other members of their genetic kin, whom they typically favor in many fundamental ways over nonkin. Hence, family life issues are central foci of sociobiology. Also, the maximization principle does not fit neatly into the mold of individual experiences. Human beings are not overtly obsessed with the enhancement of their fitness, and some, as was noted above, actually behave maladaptively. It is necessary to keep in mind, therefore, that the principle does not assume consciousness of the fitness consequences of behavior.

The fitness principle performs various functions. The crucial one is to logically structure established discoveries and thus stimulate cumulative, systematic knowledge. Central in this undertaking is the discovery of the mental rules that may be said to constitute human nature. Are people, for example, constituted to facilitate the persistent prejudices and ethnic affiliations that periodically flare up in bloody conflicts across the globe? Surely, people grow up with such prejudices and absorb them, but why is this learning universal? Is it possible that it is an effect of evolutionary forces? To learn any given behavior, one must have a capacity for it in the brain. Try as humans might, they never can be socialized to behave like foxes, or like any other animal. Aristotle was correct in his metaphor of the oak acorn: If an acorn becomes anything, it can only become an oak, never, say, a fig tree.

The Law of Altruism. As fitness theory develops, the principle surrounds itself with auxiliary statements of theory that facilitate the quest for a theory of human nature. In what follows, this article touches on a few of these. Let us start by noting that central to sociobiological reasoning is the metaphor of "the selfish gene" (Dawkins 1976), which recalls the so-called Hobbesian question of order: For whose benefit does the individual behave? Selfishness is such a prevalent concept in evolutionary science that according to Wilson (1975, p. 3), the question of its opposite, what the sociologist Auguste Comte termed "altruism," constitutes "the central theoretical problem of sociobiology." Acts that benefit others are commonly observed in all behavioral disciplines. How to explain them? The social and moral disciplines have been of little help, largely because of the ambiguity of their concepts. What seems altruistic to scholar X is viewed as selfish by colleague Y.

Sociobiologists have taken a major step toward the solution of this problem. Countless observations coupled with the logic of the fitness principle have led to the position that altruism strictly viewed refers to genetically "self-destructive behavior performed for the benefit of others" (Wilson 1975, p. 578). In short, genuine altruism reduces the benefactor's fitness; hence, if it arises in a given population, natural selection may be expected to wipe it out fairly quickly. If, for example, Mary is driven by her genes to do good for John at the expense of her own reproductive interest (e.g., cohabit with him and then be abandoned childless at an age when her chances of marriage and/or reproduction are greatly reduced), her altruistic genes will not be represented in the next generation (unless they are conveyed by her blood kin). What is it, then, that people call altru-

ism? Typically, it is either favoritism toward kin (*nepotistic favoritism*) or favoritism accompanied by the expectation of reciprocation (*reciprocal altruism*). Both types benefit the "altruist," sometimes with interest. Evolutionists' venture into the topic of altruism has produced rich harvests, particularly the discovery of *kin selection and inclusive fitness* (Hamilton 1964) and the theory of *reciprocal altruism* (Trivers 1971), which together yield the law of altruism.

Kin selection and inclusive fitness are dramatically illustrated by the study of eusocial insects, such as ants. Approximately three-quarters of these animals are female ("workers"), and very few reproduce. It would be a mistake, however, to consider them genuine altruists. Workers are so named because they are very diligent in catering to the needs of the queen (typically their reproductive mother) and her prodigious brood. Furthermore, given their peculiar reproductive system (*haplodiploidy*, whereby females have both parents while males, hatched from unfertilized eggs, have only a mother), workers are more closely related to the future generations than are their counterparts in diploid species such as mammals. As a result, failure to reproduce results in little or no loss in fitness. In short, eusocial insects have evolved according to kin selection and inclusive fitness. Indeed, this strategy is widespread among social animals. In humans, this fact is underscored by last wills and testaments, according to which people rarely bequeath their (fitness-enhancing) resources to anyone except blood kin (Clignet 1992).

Kin Selection and Ethnic Conflict. The familism inherent in kin selection has numerous expressions. One is related to the widespread phenomenon of ethnic identification and the recurrent cases of ethnic violence that often take everyone but the participants by surprise. More than eighty years ago, Pareto applied the logic of kin selection to explain the formation of persistent groups such as ethnic groups. They are "natural formations," he argued (1916, section 1022), "growing up about a nucleus which is generally the family, with appendages of one sort or another, and the permanence of such groups in time engenders or strengthens certain sentiments that, in their turn, render the groups more compact, more stable, better able to endure." This evolutionary perspective on ethnicity and ethnocentrism had been foreshadowed by Sumner (1906) and was subsequently approximated by several sociologists (e.g., Park and Burgess 1921; Gordon 1964). More recently, van den Berghe (1981) produced a thoroughly evolutionary theory of ethnicity and ethnic conflict (see also Lopreato and Crippen 1999, chap. 9).

Sociologists continue to debate the causes of ethnic phenomena, typically focusing on cultural factors, such as differences in language or religion, that are specific to given times and places. Are such factors relevant? Very probably, but ethnic phenomena are persistent and universal; across the globe there are numberless mixtures of peoples who have an awfully hard time living together in peace. Any universal phenomenon requires first and foremost a universal explanation.

In brief, during nearly all of human evolutionary history people lived in small bands of about twenty-five to fifty individuals, often surrounded by neighbors who coveted their resources. Warfare or the threat of it was frequent. Benedict (1934, pp. 7–8) described "primitive man": "From the beginning he was a provincial who raised the barriers high. Whether it was a question of choosing a wife or taking a head, the first and important distinction was between his own group and those beyond the pale. His own group, and all its ways of behaving, was unique." Intense internal solidarity was a precondition of survival. To practice it was also to practice kin selection and kin favoritism. Since the modern human brain evolved in such circumstances, it can be concluded that the tendency to identify with one's own "clan"—to distinguish between "us" and "them"—is alive and well in human society. Ethnicity is an extension of the family. Nepotistic favoritism is wired in the brain, and at the *ultimate* or general level it and the kin selection to which it is inextricably associated are the cause of the persistence of ethnic identification and recurrent ethnic conflict. "Who am I?" "Who are mine?" These are enduring whispers in the human psyche.

Of course, it is difficult to answer such questions in the megasociety, and that is one reason why most of the time people live in a reasonably peaceful relationship with their neighbors. Still, people are attentive to markers of "weness" such as a common name, common historical experiences, distinctive cuisine and artistic expressions, and often a common language, in historical time if not now (van den Berghe 1981).

Reciprocal altruism. Reciprocal altruism refers to the fact that if and when people engage in actions that benefit others, they do so with the expectation, conscious or not, that the others will repay, especially if they are not related. This is the object of a much-tested and growing theory first stated by Trivers (1971). According to the basics of this theory, the evolution of reciprocal altruism was facilitated by three broad conditions: (1) repeated situations in which the value of altruism to beneficiaries was, in terms of fitness, greater than the cost incurred by the benefactors, (2) membership in a small group featuring little or no migration, thus enhancing the chances of reciprocity, (3) fairly equal ability between pairs of individuals to engage in mutual help. Trivers proceeds to argue that a system of reciprocal altruism is subject to "cheating": Some individuals do not reciprocate the benefits they receive. Indeed, an underlying assumption of Trivers's theory is that givers are motivated to receive more than they give. Accordingly, as reciprocal altruism was evolving, another set of adaptations, what Trivers terms a "psychological system," was arising fairly in step with it; their function was to regulate cheating. They include emotions such as friendship, sympathy, trust, suspicion, and moralistic aggression, along with hypocrisy and feelings of guilt.

Combining the logic of kin selection and reciprocal altruism, it is possible to state a *law of altruism* as follows: *In keeping with the fitness principle, social oganisms have evolved to favor others (1) in direct proportion to their degree of genetic relatedness to them and (2) to the extent that the benefit they derive from doing good to others is, in terms of fitness, equal to or greater than the cost of their altruism.*

The law is relevant to various human phenomena, and casts light on a number of puzzles. For instance, social scientists have noted that the exchange of gifts is a universal institution in human society (Mauss [1925] 1954). Moreover, a version of this tendency termed "potlatch" is in varying degrees "a universal mode of culture" (Lévi-Strauss [1949] 1969). In an extreme form of potlatch practiced by the "Indians" of Vancouver and Alaska, one gives with a view to crushing another and thus gaining "privileges, titles, rank, authority, and prestige" (Lévi-Strauss [1949] 1969, chap. 5). Specifically, gifts are given to a competitor with the shared understanding that the recipient will reciprocate with interest after a reasonable interval.

When such an obligation cannot be met, the recipient loses status, titles, and so forth. Social theorists have been eager to downplay the individual's selfish undercurrent and the social conflict it engenders. The law of altruism conversely predicts selfishness, competition, and precariousness of status in one's group.

Nevertheless, the extreme stress on selfishness cannot go unchallenged for the human species. The only known attempt of this sort avoids the genetic trap (altruists are by definition "selected out"). Using a biocultural perspective at the core of which is the evolution of *the idea of the soul* and *self-deception*, it concludes that behaviors intended to save the soul mimic fitness-enhancing behaviors (Lopreato 1984, pp. 207–235). Catholic nuns and Buddhist monks, for example, practice celibacy and other forms of ascetc behavior in view of immortal ends. Typically, they contribute little or nothing to the fitness-enhancing resources of their blood relatives. Yet their type manages somehow to "reproduce" itself. Genuine or "ascetic" altruism may be rare in human society, but it is a cultural fact.

The Law of Anisogamy. Human psychological adaptations may be divided into two major types. One is specieswide, referring to innate tendencies that in varying degrees cut across gender. Examples include tendencies toward kin favoritism, ethnic identification, reciprocal altruism, and cheating. The other major class accounts for the fact that throughout human society there have been some remarkable differences, as well as similarities, along sex lines (Trivers 1972; Kimura 1992; Lopreato and Crippen 1999). The differences are suggested by a basic diversity in physioanatomy. *Anisogamy*, the name given to it, refers to the difference in size and structure between male and female sex cells (gametes). Male gametes (sperm) are minuscule and contribute only genes to reproduction. They are produced in huge quantities almost continuously after the onset of sexual maturity. The reproductive potential of males is therefore huge, and some men have fathered thousands of children (Betzig 1986). By contrast, female gametes are much larger, are nutritious, and are produced *in utero* once in a lifetime. Then, beginning at menarche, they are released, typically one at a time, about once a month, so that on average women produce some 300 to 400 mature eggs in a lifetime, only a very small number of which are likely to result in offspring. Women are constitued to bear the cost of pregnancy, nursing, and much of the protection and guardianship, at least during the offspring's tender years. In short, each child represents a huge reproductive investment for the typical woman.

By contrast, males make a very small investment. They do not get pregnant or suffer nausea; nor do they risk their life at the birth of a child and for months or years afterward. If we consider such other facts as abandonment, divorce, and the refusal or failure to provide child support, the level of paternal investment is on average truly puny. There is no intention here to condemn men or glorify women. It is a matter of trying to grasp certain facts in order to understand certain others. Males and females have evolved under the pressure of significantly different, though partly complementary, reproductive strategies, and much of their behavior is an effect of this fact. It is now time to state what was earlier termed the *law of anisogamy* (Lopreato 1992, p. 1998): *The two sexes are endowed with differing reproductive strategies, and their behaviors reflect that difference in direct proportion to their relevance to it.* The closer one gets to the fundamental activities of life (sexual behavior, family life, and among endless others the conditions that recall the division of labor in the clan, the type of society in which the human species spent 99.5 percent of its history), the more likely one is to observe the effects of anisogamy. The basic implications of anisogamy have been drawn by Trivers (1972) in a seminal paper on "relative parental investment."

Differential Parental Investment and Sexual Selection. The law of anisogamy contains a number of corollaries. The two major ones noted briefly here are very closely related. Differential parental investment (DPI) states in effect that females make both a greater initial parental investment and greater subsequent parental investments than do males, so that their behavior is more finely adjusted to the well-being and reproductive success of the offspring. Supporting facts are legion. They are epitomized by the following widely noted findings, among others: On average females are more cautious than males in their sexual activity, and they tend to prefer as mates men who are in fact, or show promise of becoming, relatively rich in the resources needed to raise healthy and reproductively viable offspring. Mating has always been far riskier for women, and this fact is deeply rooted in the brain. As a consequence, it tends to express itself even in times and places where mating need not have reproductive consequences. For millions of years, and even today in much of the world, an unwanted pregnancy or a pregnancy with a partner who will contribute little or nothing to the well-being of the offspring may consume a large portion of a woman's reproductive potential. In summary, women go for quality; men, for the allure of quantity.

A study of 10,047 individuals living in various countries on six continents strongly suggests that culture has a notable influence on mate preferences and that the two sexes agree on some of the basic requirements of a good mate, such as honesty and dependability. However, the findings also reveal some marked universal differences that are predictable from the law of anisogamy. For instance, females are significantly more likely than males to emphasize ambition and industriousness. Conversely, males more than females prefer mates who are physically attractive, younger than themselves, and at the peak of their reproductive value even if they are of lower socioeconomic status (Buss 1989).

The sexual selection (SS) corollary may be stated in Trivers's (1972, p. 140) words as follows: "Individuals of the sex investing less will compete among themselves to breed with members of the sex investing more, since an individual of the former can increase its reproductive success by investing successfully in the offspring of several members of the limiting sex."

The idea of sexual selection is a remarkable example of great ideas that emerge out of creative confusion. Darwin understood that in the final analysis the measure of survival is reproductive success. Nevertheless, he tended to focus on survival as *longevity*. As a result, certain observations, both behavioral and physical, confronted him with a special challenge. Why the great horns, the displays, the mimicry, the special weapons, "the instrumental music," or, among other male characteristics, the huge tail of the peacock? Such unusual features tend to attract predators and thus reduce longevity. Darwin (1859, but especially 1871) concluded that if such "secondary sexual characters" enhance the bearers' ability to reproduce, they are likely to be favored by natural selection even if they act negatively on longevity. However, because

such characters were conspicuous in sexual competition, they suggested to him the label "sexual selection." There is some debate over the meaning of this term (see Mayr 1972 for a review), but it is safe to say that it refers not to a type of selection but instead to a major cause of natural selection. "After all," as Dobzhansky et al. (1977, p. 118) noted, "Darwinian fitness is reproductive fitness," whatever the cause. Sexual selection, or *competition for mates*, refers most explicitly to the struggle for genetic survival. It further suggests that much animal behavior and appearance are adapted not so much to the problem of daily survival as to the job of securing adequate mates.

Viewed as competition, sexual selection has become a valuable tool of research, especially in view of certain distinctions suggested by Darwin himself. In current language there are two major types of sexual selection. One, often termed "intrasexual selection," subsumes a female-female competition and a male-male one. The other refers to a form of male-male competition, too (the competition "to charm the females"), but Darwin viewed it as an effect of the females' response to "charm." Accordingly, it has come to be known as *female choice* (or "intersexual selection"). It is evident that differential parental investment and sexual selection are closely linked properties of anisogamy. In fact, one may combine the logic of DPI and SS to state what may be termed the DPI-SS corollary as follows: *Given anisogamy, females have been selected to engage in choosy behavior, while males have been selected to specialize in agonistic behavior.*

Female choosiness in human beings takes many forms. This article has mentioned the tendency to prefer resource-rich mates. As a group, even in a highly developed society like the United States, women pay less attention to looks, have and claim to want fewer sexual partners, are less likely to have their first sexual experience with a stranger, are more likely to expect a commitment before engaging in sex, and among many other differences, are less likely to cheat on their mates, whether husbands, cohabitors, or boyfriends (Laumann et al. 1994).

Competitiveness, too, takes many forms. One is reflected in the ancient and still fairly common practice of polygyny, especially if one considers the greater tendency of divorced men to remarry and have further children (Betzig 1986; Lenski and Lenski 1987). Another form is expressed in violent behavior. Killing, for example, is throughout the world a largely male behavior and is concentrated among young men during the peak years of their reproductive life. Prominent among the motives for homicide are sexual jealousy and rivalry as wall as dominance contests in various contexts (Daly and Wilson 1988). Death by trauma (murder and accidents) accounts for a relatively high percentage of male mortality and part of the lower life expectancy of men (Verbrugge 1989). Of course, there are many other forms of competitiveness, and women are not immune to the tendency to practice them.

Of Sex Roles. Sociological practice is almost entirely environmentalist and often clashes with an evolutionary perspective. For example, according to "feminist" authors, especially so-called *gender feminists*, men and women are born with identical potentials. The idea that, given anisogamy, the brain has been neuroendocrinally gendered (Kimura 1992) is extraneous if not altogether offensive to them. They argue conversely that society is ruled by a system of *patriarchy*, and socialization thus proceeds to produce differences that are detrimental to women. Girls are socialized to be passive and subordinate, while boys are trained to strive for success and dominance (Lerner 1986, p. 29). In short, so-called sex roles are the effect of culturally prescribed discrimination and must be explained in terms of cultural causes only. Some writers go so far as to argue that physiology is irrelevant or that "human physiology is *socially* constructed and gendered" (Lorber 1994, p. 46; emphasis added).

Sociobiologists do not deny that once an arrangement such as patriarchy is in place, the channels of socialization tend to develop in view of its mandates. However, science does not merely assert facts; it seeks to explain them. As Hrdy (1997, pp. 7–8; italics in the original) notes, "an evolutionary perspective pushes the search for patriarchy's origins back . . . by millions of years by asking an additional question: *Why* should males seek to control females?" That is, why patriarchy in the first place? Accordingly, it less superficially identifies sexual selection "rather than male desire for power as the engine driving the system" of patriarchy.

To understand patriarchal phenomena and have more than a wishful chance of bringing effective cultural forces to bear on them, one must begin by answering Hrdy's question. In the process, a very unpleasant irony will be uncovered. The dynamics that produced patriarchy include female complicity with domineering males. Male dominance has been achieved at least in part because of female preference (female choice) for dominant males. Indeed, males dominate females by dominating other males with female help. Thus, the pickle that many people find so distasteful "turns out to have been seasoned with only a sprinkle of culture at best, although once culture arose it made it even more tartish. It is also true that our female ancestors had a hand in the preparation" (Lopreato and Crippen 1999). Moreover, women throughout the world continue to support patriarchy through their persistent tendency to favor dominant males.

CONCLUSION

In order to advance, would-be sciences need to discover the value of a number of time-tested techniques. These techniques include especially the use of remote concepts and logical ways to operationalize them, the nomothetic derivation and testing of hypotheses, and the logical structuring of the hypotheses in a body of systematic, cumulative knowledge that facilitates further research and discovery. The history of science strongly suggests that to accomplish even these minimal feats, it is necessary to either discover one general principle or to borrow it in full or modified form from a cognate and more advanced science. At the start of the third millennium there is still no general principle in sociology, general in the sense that it would contain the logic for a large number of derivative statements linking discovery and explanation across the institutional framework. The fitness principle and the theoretical tools surrounding it constitute an invitation from sociology's most proximate natural science to embrace the fact that the human brain represents a tenacious link to a past that in part is still present. The potential payoff is likely to be far greater than even the most sanguine evolutionists can imagine. It may suffice to consider that just as Newtonian laws eliminated the old prejudice of geocentrism, thus freeing the mind to behold previously inconceivable wonders of nature, sociobiology offers a human perspective from a distance, thus freeing the mind from the still-oppressive assumptions of *anthropocentrism* and *temporecentrism*, benighting corollaries of geocentrism.

According to many critics of sociobiology, since certain behaviors are "natural," they are not subject to cultural intervention. This is an error that sociobiologists do not commit. Because they are evolutionists, their theorizing is subject to a systemic perspective: "Phenotype" (any feature of anatomy, physiology, or behavior) is a result of the interaction between genotype and environment, including culture. It is essential to have knowledge of both. To change the world, as many scholars are inclined to do, with knowledge (always imperfect) of one to the exclusion of the other is not only obscurantism; it is poor, perhaps dangerous, engineering as well.

REFERENCES

Benedict, R. 1934 *Patterns of Culture*. Boston: Houghton Mifflin.

Betzig, L. L. 1986 *Despotism and Differential Reproduction: A Darwinian View of History*. New York: Aldine.

Buss, D. M. 1989 "Sex Differences in Human Mate Preferences: Evolutionary Hypotheses Tested in 37 Cultures." *Behavioral and Brain Sciences* 12:1–49.

Clignet, R. 1992 *Death, Deeds, and Descendants*. New York: Aldine.

Crippen, T. 1994 "Toward a Neo-Darwinian Sociology: Its Nomological Principles and Some Illustrative Applications." *Sociological Perspectives* 37:309–335.

Daly, M., and M. Wilson 1988 *Homicide*. New York: Aldine.

Darwin, C. (1859) 1958 *The Origin of Species*. New York: Mentor.

—— 1871 *The Descent of Man and Selection in Relation to Sex*. New York: Appleton.

Dawkins, R. 1976 *The Selfish Gene*. Oxford: Oxford University Press.

Dobzhansky, T., F. J. Ayala, G. L. Stebbins, and J. W. Valentine 1977 *Evolution*. San Francisco: Freeman.

Gordon, M. M. 1964 *Assimilation in American Life*. New York: Oxford University Press.

Hamilton, W. D. 1964 "The Genetical Theory of Social Behaviour: I and II." *Journal of Theoretical Biology* 7:1–52.

Hrdy, S. B. 1997 "Raising Darwin's Consciousness: Female Sexuality and the Prehominid Origin of Patriarchy." *Human Nature* 8:1–49.

Huxley, J. 1942 *Evolution: The Modern Synthesis*. New York: Harper.

Kimura, D. 1992 "Sex Differences in the Brain." *Scientific American* 268:119–125.

Laumann, E., R. Michael, S. Michaels, and J. Gagnon 1994 *The Social Organization of Sexuality*. Chicago: University of Chicago Press.

Lenski, G., and J. Lenski 1987 *Human Societies*. New York: McGraw-Hill.

Lerner, G. 1986 *The Creation of Patriarchy*. Oxford: Oxford University Press.

Levi-Stauss, C. (1949) 1969 *The Elementary Structures of Kinship*. Boston: Beacon.

Lopreato, J. 1984 *Human Nature and Biocultural Evolution*. London: Unwin Hyman.

—— 1989 "The Maximization Principle: A Cause in Search of Conditions." In R. W. Bell and N. J. Bell, eds., *Sociobiology and the Social Sciences*. Lubbock: Texas Tech University Press.

—— 1992 "Sociobiology." In E. F. Borgatta, ed., *Encyclopedia of Sociology*. New York: Macmillan.

——, and T. Crippen 1999 *Crisis in Sociology: The Need for Darwin*. Rutgers, N.J.: Transaction.

Lorber, J. 1994 *The Paradoxes of Gender*. New Haven, Conn.: Yale University Press.

Mauss, M. (1925) 1954 *The Gift*. London: Cohen and West.

Maryanski, A. R. 1998 "Evolutionary Sociology." *Advances in Human Ecology* 7:1–56.

——, and J. H. Turner 1998 "New Evolutionary Theories." In J. H. Turner, ed., *The Structure of Sociological Theory*, 6th ed. New York: Wadsworth.

Mayr, E. 1972 "Sectual Selection and Natural Selection." In B. G. Campbell, ed., *Sexual Selection and the Descent of Man*. Chicago: Aldine.

Pareto, V. (1916) 1963 *A Treatise on General Sociology*. New York: Dover.

Park, R. E., and E.W. Burgess 1921 *Introduction to the Science of Sociology*. Chicago: University of Chicago Press.

Sumner, W. G. 1906 *Folkways*. New York: Ginn.

Trivers, R. L. 1971 "The Evolution of Reciprocal Altruism." *Quarterly Review of Biology* 46:35–47.

—— 1972 "Parental Investment and Sexual Selection." In B. H. Campbell, ed., *Sexual Selection and the Descent of Man, 1871–1971*. Chicago: Aldine.

van den Berghe, P. L. 1981 *The Ethnic Phenomenon*. New York: Elsevier.

Verbrugge, L. M. 1989 "The Twain Meet: Empirical Explanations of Sex Differences in Health and Mortality." *Journal of Health and Social Behavior* 30:282–304.

Wilson, E. O. 1975 *Sociobiology: The New Synthesis*. Cambridge, Mass.: Harvard University Press.

JOSEPH LOPREATO

SOCIOCULTURAL ANTHROPOLOGY

In the United States, anthropology usually is considered to consist of four subdisciplines, or "subfields": archaeology (describing and understanding past human behavior by examining material remains), physical or biological anthropology (describing the evolution and modern physical variation of the human species), anthropological linguistics, and sociocultural anthropology. Most university departments of anthropology have faculty in three or four of these subdisciplines. Sociocultural anthropology often is called simply cultural anthropology in the United States, although a few academic programs use the term "social anthropology," the common designation in Europe. Some anthropologists identify applied anthropology as a fifth subfield, while others consider it part of sociocultural anthropology.

Anthropology is defined as the study of human commonalities and differences and expressly includes the entire temporal and geographic range of humankind in its scope. The database of the discipline is large, including prehistoric populations as well as every variety of contemporary society. In distinguishing itself from other social sciences, anthropology emphasizes the holistic, comparative, culture-centered, and fieldwork-dependent nature of the discipline.

In Europe, social anthropology is more closely allied with economics, history, and political philosophy than it is with physical anthropology and archaeology, which often are taught in separate programs. As social anthropology evolved in Europe, it came to be associated with studies of the economy, ecology, polity, kinship patterns, and social organization of non-Western peoples, particularly in colonial Africa and Asia. The European approach to theory was associated with sociological (especially functionalist) and, more recently, historical approaches. In the United States, where research focused initially on Native Americans and was strongly influenced by the particularistic descriptive approach of Franz Boas's ethnography, anthropology came to be associated with culture, that "complex whole" (in Edward Tylor's words) encompassing customs, language, material culture, social order, philosophy, arts, and so on. European social anthropologists have not failed to address culture and Americans have not neglected social structure, yet the difference in terminology distinguishes an emphasis on social relations from an emphasis on shared meaning and behavior.

The heart of sociocultural anthropology is ethnography, the written description of a culture group. Ethnography has undergone many changes since it began with field reports by missionaries and colonial officials. The pace of change has increased since the 1960s, as recognition of global links has become standard, other social scientists have adopted ethnographic methods, and postmodernism has imposed stricter self-reflective criteria on writers. The methodological partner of ethnography is ethnology, the comparative study of societies. In its first decades, anthropology established the ideal that a complete ethnographic record of the world's cultures would allow comparative studies that would lead to generalizations about the evolution and functioning of all societies. Cross-cultural studies continue to be one of the distinctive contributions of anthropology to the social sciences.

HISTORY

Anthropology and sociology share common origins in the nineteenth-century European search for a science of society. Sociocultural anthropology and sociology also share a theoretical history in the ongoing struggle between the desire for a generalizing, rule-seeking science and that for a humanistic reflection of particular lives. Throughout the twentieth century, academic specialization and differences in research topics, geographic focus, and methodological emphasis separated the two disciplines. In the last several decades, globalization has fostered a partial reconvergence of methods and subjects, though not of worldviews, ethos, or academic bureaucracies.

Sociocultural anthropology often is contrasted with sociology: It is said that anthropologists study small-scale societies, assume that those societies are self-sufficient, and are usually outsiders (politically, ethnically, and economically) to the groups they study. These generalizations are partly true.

The methods of sociocultural anthropology have emphasized the usefulness of seeking "the large in the small" by becoming intimately acquainted with a single band, village, tribe, island, or neighborhood, and anthropology's early link to colonialism and its base of support in Europe, Japan, China, and the United States has privileged wealthy outsiders as observers of peasants, tribal peoples, and marginalized groups. However, anthropology has always kept the larger picture in mind, and for every study of an "isolated" population, there are ethnographies that reveal links at the regional, national, and global levels. The affiliation of sociocultural anthropology with archaeology and paleoanthropology ensures that the long term and the large scale are never far from sight. Ethnographies of industrialized societies, ranging from ethnic minorities to corporate cultures, begin with the microcosm but connect to larger questions. Sociology has been associated from its beginnings with studies of modernization and globalization in Western societies. In the postwar world, anthropologists became of necessity students of these processes in the same small communities that had been their prewar subjects of study. Anthropologists have sought ways to encompass urban life, regional processes, and global economic and political transformations in their work, leading them to develop skills in quantitative social research as well as their traditional qualitative methods.

Developments in method and theory in the twentieth century have led to a widely perceived split between sociocultural anthropologists who seek a "natural science of society" and those who emphasize anthropology's humanistic role as an interpreter of cultural worlds. These differences are reflected in the distinction between "emic" and "etic" strategies. Based on the linguistic concept of the phoneme, emic work calls for the researcher to understand the "inside" view, focus on meaning and interpretation, and "grasp the native's point of view . . . to realize *his* vision of *his* world," in Bronislaw Malinowski's words. A good ethnography enables readers to understand the motives, meanings, and emotions of a different cultural world. The etic (from "phonetic") approach seeks generalizations beyond the internal cultural worlds of actors, applying social science concepts to the particulars of a culture and often using cross-cultural comparisons to test hypotheses. A good ethnography presents data that can be compared with other cases. In recent years, the writing of ethnography has self-consciously struggled to develop a style that can evoke the sensibility of a culture while including descriptive information in a format that allows cross-cultural comparisons.

Sociocultural anthropology begins with description and usually intends that description (ethnography) to be a prelude to cross-cultural comparison that will lead to generalizations about types of societies or even about human universals. At the same time, anthropologists are as likely as other social scientists to be influenced by fashions in theory.

THEORY

The nineteenth-century origins of anthropology, like those of sociology, are rooted in the expanding inquiry into the nature of human society that characterizes the nineteenth and early twentieth centuries, but anthropology's roots also involve the questions of biological and social evolutionism characteristic of the era, as epitomized in the work of Charles Darwin and Herbert Spencer. Anthropology and sociology share origins in the foundational work of Durkheim, Weber, and Marx. However, cultural anthropology adds to its pantheon of ancestors Tylor, Morgan, and Frazer; it is in the work of these three men that one can see how anthropology was set on a different trajectory. The American Lewis Henry Morgan (*Ancient Society*, 1877) and the British Edward Burnett Tylor (*Primitive Culture*, 1871) and James Frazer (*The Golden Bough*, 1890) are counted among the founders of anthropology because they sought to establish general laws of human society through the comparative study of historical and contemporary peoples. Tylor, Morgan, and Frazer were unilineal evolutionists who believed that universal stages of evolution could be identified in the transition from simple to complex societies and that modern peoples could be ranked in this evolutionary scale. These two strands—the belief that comparison can produce scientific generalizations and the search for evolutionary processes—continue to characterize anthropology, though the racist evolutionism of these early approaches was discarded as anthropology was established as a discipline in the 1920s and 1930s.

While the work of the nineteenth-century social theorists presaged both anthropology and sociology, by the turn of the century, each field was established in separate academic departments and increasingly distinct research programs. In the United States, anthropology as a scholarly project emerged through the work of scholars drawn to the task of reconstructing Native American cultures and languages, especially under the auspices of the Bureau of American Ethnology and the formative political, administrative, and scientific work of Franz Boas. Boas responded to the prevailing ideas of unilineal evolutionism with a theory that came to be called historical particularism, rejecting broad generalizations about stages of evolution in favor of detailed studies of the environmental context and historical development of particular societies. Boas also trained the first generation of professional anthropologists in the United States, and his students, such as Alfred L. Kroeber, Robert Lowie, and Edward Sapir, pioneered new theories that could replace unilineal evolutionism. Sapir's and Benjamin Whorf's work on links between language and culture, Margaret Mead's on enculturation and psychological anthropology, Ruth Benedict's on ethos, Zora Neale Hurston's on folklore, and Kroeber's on the superorganic all fostered decades of theoretical development that pushed American anthropology in distinctive directions. Field studies with Native Americans and other North American minorities honed the skills of the first generations of American anthropologists in linguistic work, informant interviews, life histories, and historical reconstruction and established the holistic style of American anthropology, integrating archaeology, linguistics, and physical anthropology with the study of society and culture.

While Boas's students filled library shelves with detailed and impressive ethnographies, a new theoretical orientation developed in Great Britain that would have a great impact on the culture-centered world of American anthropology. This was functionalism, and its key proponents in anthropology were Bronislaw Malinowski (psychological functionalism) and A. R. Radcliffe-Brown (structural functionalism). The period of interest in the ways in which cultural institutions maintain social order—which affected the United States when Radcliffe-Brown and Malinowski spent time at American departments of anthropology in the

1930s—marks the point at which most texts officially distinguish British social anthropology from American cultural anthropology. Radcliffe-Brown countered Boasian particularism with an emphasis on the search for general laws of society and stimulated a generation of European and American students to do the same. British social anthropologists turned their analytic focus on the study of persons and relations in persisting social structures and pushed themselves and their students to develop the close observation, incisive analysis, and careful record keeping that marked the coming of age of long-term participant observation as a research method. Functionalist studies took place in the context of colonialism, with the limitations and power imbalance that that implies, yet remain impressive for the quality of detail and their capacity to integrate descriptions of political, economic, and kinship relations. Many ethnographic classics were produced by British social anthropologists of that era (e.g., Malinowski's *Argonauts of the Western Pacific* in 1922 and Evans-Pritchard's *Witchcraft, Oracles and Magic among the Azande* in 1937 and *The Nuer*, 1940) and their students, including Raymond Firth, Meyer Fortes, Audrey Richards, Lucy Mair, Edmund Leach, Max Gluckman, and Fred Eggan.

While American anthropologists added the study of social structure and function to their repertoire, they did not abandon their interest in historical developments, language, personality, and ethos and retained a "four-fields" orientation in the training of graduate students. While some social anthropologists found the idea of culture impossibly vague, American anthropologists reveled in the complexity of the concept, with Kroeber and Kluckhohn assembling a compendium of more than 150 definitions of "culture." Stimulated by the challenge of British social anthropology, the work of Kroeber, Mead, Benedict, and Sapir from the 1920s through the 1950s explored culture as a distinct level of analysis and a way to grasp the distinctive ethos and worldview of each culture, along with the active role of the individual's acts and words in shaping a culture.

In the 1940s and 1950s, the influence of materialist approaches in the social sciences, while limited by the anticommunism in American public life (explicitly Marxist approaches did not appear until the 1970s), was manifested in a new set of evolutionary and generalizing approaches in American anthropology. The work of Julian Steward and Leslie White laid the groundwork for a new approach to studies of adaptation and cultural change. White argued for an evolutionary scheme in which culture (the uniquely human capacity to manipulate symbols), as the superorganic human adaptive mechanism, develops through evolutionary stages marked by the increasing ability of human groups to capture energy through technological systems. Steward worked on a smaller scale, arguing for the analysis of structural similarities among cultures at a regional level, which can be understood by recognizing the hierarchical relations among three "levels of sociocultural integration": technoeconomics (infrastructure), sociopolitical organization, and ideology (superstructure). Steward's scheme allowed anthropologists to catalogue cultures as structural types and encouraged the study of change over time in a "multilineal evolutionary" process that he contrasted with White's more abstract global stages.

Materialist studies continued to develop and to shape archaeology as well as cultural anthropology. Marshall Sahlins and Elman R. Service merged White's and Steward's approaches in a neoevolutionist theory that encouraged both archaeologists and materialist-oriented sociocultural anthropologists to consider the regional and large-scale classification and development of societies. Marvin Harris, Eleanor Burke Leacock, and Morton Fried attempted to explain cultural diversity and change in the context of the causal primacy of production and reproduction. In the 1960s and 1970s, the new field of cultural ecology developed a "neofunctionalist" approach that allowed scientists to include cultural and social aspects of human behavior in natural science research. Roy Rappaport's 1967 *Pigs for the Ancestors* began with an effort to measure the energy intake and outflow of a highland new Guinea population; the 1984 edition included a lengthy discussion of criticisms of neofunctionalist theory and the applicability of adaptive and evolutionary concepts to human groups.

In France, Claude Levi-Strauss was developing ideas that would transform the world of social science through structuralism, which emerged in the 1960s and 1970s as a totalizing theory aiming at uncovering the common structures of the human mind. Structuralism, which was influenced by the linguistics theories of Saussure and Jakobson, treated the products of culture as symbolic systems and examined the formal patterns of those systems in order to envision discern universal structures and cognitive patterns of the human mind. Structuralism was applied to myths, kinship, relations to art, and every other aspect of culture. The work of Levi-Strauss, Edmund Leach, and other structuralists drew sharp rebuttals from theorists who sought explanations of human diversity in material and social conditions rather than in mental templates. Although the abstractness of structuralism eventually limited its interest to students of culture, it continues to be a useful technique, particularly in the analysis of the symbolic products of culture.

Ethnoscience, which emerged in the 1950s, also examined the mental categories underlying cultural products. Drawing heavily on linguistic theory and methodology, ethnoscience tried to develop fieldwork methods sufficiently rigorous to delineate the mental models that generate words and behavior and, in its emphasis on the emic approach, insisted on the necessity of fully accessing the native understanding of cultural domains. As ethnoscience faded in importance in the 1970s, it was succeeded by cognitive anthropology, the cross-cultural study of cognition.

Structuralism, ethnoscience, and responses to materialist neoevolutionist theory stimulated the emergence of symbolic anthropology and cultural analysis in the 1960s and 1970s, and this in turn led to the "interpretive turn" that has continued in cultural anthropology through the rest of the century. Again, linguistics proved influential, as David Schneider, Clifford Geertz, and Victor Turner explored new ways to study the cultural construction of meaning and the public representation of meaning in cultural elements. Most symbolic anthropologists focus on the description and interpretation of particular cultural cases, emphasizing the ethnographer's role in explicating cultural events or products, though a few symbolic anthropologists, such as Mary Douglas, have sought general models of symbol systems. Symbolic anthropology shifted in the 1980s toward interpretive anthropology, which in turn generated a decade of reflection on the writing of ethnography, seeking modes of representation that would represent the worldview, internal logic, and emotional sensibility of a culture. Emerging from interpretive approaches have been experiments in ethnography, renewed interest in life histories, and extensive critiques of an etic-oriented ethnography that relies on the authoritative voice of an "outside" observer and author. The 1980s also saw a new interest in history, spurred in part by the work of French scholars such as Braudel, Bourdieu, and Foucault and also playing a part in drawing some sociocultural anthropologists toward humanistic approaches.

American cultural anthropology has always taken an interest in evolutionary questions, and in the 1970s, the biologist E. O. Wilson used sociobiology to challenge social scientists to study the role of natural selection in human behavior. Anthropologists' immediate response was to criticize sociobiology as sociologically naive, culture-bound, and potentially racist and sexist. In the longer term, however, this challenge renewed anthropologists' interest in the holistic approach to culture, stimulating new approaches to the flexible and complex linkage of genetic inheritance and cultural malleability. Archaeologists, physical anthropologists, and cultural anthropologists share an interest in these long-term questions, which now are studied as "human behavioral ecology."

ORGANIZATION

While anthropological theory has participated in many of the trends in the social sciences in this century, anthropologists most often speak of themselves in terms of the topics they study and the geographic areas in which they are expert. A cultural anthropologist might say that she studies "gender issues in the Middle East," "political hierarchy in Polynesia," or "hunter-gatherer ecology in the Arctic," with the implication that her theoretical school is a less useful category or that one might include several different theoretical or methodological approaches to one's topic.

A review of textbooks in anthropology and courses offered in larger departments provides an indication of the overlap and the difference in range between sociological and anthropological topics. Traditional topics in anthropology include the categories of sociopolitical life (political anthropology, the anthropology of religion, social organization, patterns of subsistence, economic anthropology), cross-cultural approaches to all social science topics (ethnicity and identity, psychological anthropology, urban anthropology, ethnohistory, gender), theoretical approaches (sym-

bolic anthropology, cultural ecology), applied topics (legal anthropology, developmental anthropology, culture change, medical anthropology, education and culture), and topics reflecting the persistent holism of the anthropological enterprise (language and culture, genetics and behavior).

Anthropologists' regional focus traditionally has been small-scale non-Western societies, but this has changed dramatically in the last fifty years. While sociologists and other social scientists have become more active in non-Western contexts (particularly economic development and modernization), anthropologists have become more active in studying Western societies, using their traditional skills of small-community ethnography, cultural models, and comparison in these situations. However, as part of their postgraduate training, most American and European anthropologists do a lengthy period of participant observation research in a small-scale society, usually a foraging band or a tribal or peasant society.

One stimulus to anthropologists' willingness to become wholeheartedly involved in the study of Western, industrialized, and mass societies has been the growth in applied work. While sociology was committed to researching public policy issues from its beginning, anthropology has only intermittently taken on research directed at social problems and policy issues. Beginning with government work during World War II and the postwar Fox and Vicos projects in applied anthropology and as a result of globalization and limited academic job opportunities for anthropologists, there has been an increase in putting anthropological concepts and methods to the service of immediate outcomes rather than academic research. The greatest demand for applied anthropology is in economic and social development, medical anthropology, the anthropology of education, and international business.

METHODS

Anthropology was born in the theories of "armchair anthropologists" who based their theories about the evolution of human beliefs and societies on the reports of colonial officials, missionaries, and merchants. Since that time, the commitment of researchers such as Boas, Mead, and Malinowski to detailed, long-term field studies has generated the impulse that has sustained generations of anthropologists in an effort to produce detailed, fine-grained, firsthand descriptions of the world's cultures. Cultural anthropology has long held that long-term participant observation, including mastery of local languages, is the best way to produce valid ethnographic description. Participant observation is the source of anthropology's ethnographic database and the foundation on which controlled cross-cultural comparison is built.

The work of field research and the writing of ethnography have received much attention in recent decades. Participant observation is now an umbrella term for a research project that, while it extends over the long term (usually at least a year) and relies on the use of the local language, key informants, and living "close to the ground" with the people being studied, is likely to include a range of additional research techniques. Sociocultural anthropologists also are trained in kinship analysis, unstructured and structured interviews, questionnaires, scales, taxonomies, and direct and unobtrusive observation. In the past decade, there has been a growing expectation that researchers will combine qualitative and quantitative research methods, increasing both the validity and the reliability of ethnographic work. Applied anthropology has generated its own methods, some of them shaped by the time and cash restraints of nonacademic research, such as rapid rural assessment, participatory appraisal, and decision-tree modeling.

Cross-cultural comparison has been a goal of anthropology from the start. The first armchair anthropologists used sometimes unreliable secondhand information to generate categories and stages of social evolution, but researchers soon employed more scientific methods. Archaeologists' work on regional and chronological linkages encouraged ethnologists to trace the development, distribution, and diffusion of culture traits (especially in the United States, with Boas's encouragement). British social anthropologists and the neoevolutionists urged the use of regional and global comparisons to generate models of structural stability and change. George P. Murdock greatly facilitated large-scale comparison when he created the Human Relations Area Files, the physical form of the great database of human cultures anthropology had long sought. Cross-cultural studies in anthropology have allowed anthropologists to generate and test midlevel hypotheses about cultural patterns and allowed social scientists to test the broader validity of hypotheses generated in Western contexts.

CURRENT ISSUES

In surveying the history of anthropological theory, one often notices the persistent tension between materialist and idealist ways of studying culture. In the current environment, after a decade of postmodern critiques, this tension has actually split a few academic departments, severing archaeology and biological anthropology from cultural anthropology, or "scientific" from "humanistic" approaches. Research specialization and job-market pressures also interfere with the holistic four-fields approach that American anthropologists have long considered their hallmark. In addition, sociocultural anthropology has been pressed by the inroads of literary criticism, cultural studies, ethnic studies, and other related fields into its traditional preserve. Like other social sciences, anthropology feels that it is living through a "crisis" that represents both a point in a repeated cycle of theoretical change and a response to national and global contexts.

However, the end of the twentieth century has seen a wider range of research and applied work than had ever been done previously (see recent issues of *American Anthropologist, American Ethnologist, Current Anthropology*, and *Human Organization*). Current work in anthropology includes traditional detailed ethnographies that aim to increase the descriptive database of the world's cultures, problem-focused fieldwork aimed at elucidating theoretical puzzles, reflexive ethnography that attempts to find a moral and artistic center from which to write, analyses of organizations and evaluations of programs intended to guide policy decisions, and hypothesis-testing data crunching. The long-standing distinction between materialist and idealist approaches continues as interpretive, postmodern anthropology seeks new ways to do the job it has been critiquing for a decade and as ecological, evolutionist, and materialist approaches argue with renewed vigor for a scientific discipline.

Sociocultural anthropology and sociology share modern interests in agency; power; the relative role of social structures and individual action in culture change; the intersections of ethnicity, class, and gender; and the historical shaping of modern institutions and cultural representations. In all its interests, ongoing input from archaeology, biological anthropology, and linguistics has given sociocultural anthropology a uniquely broad and deep perspective on the human condition, and its stream of theory is fed from these other sources of knowledge about the human condition. In describing the commonalities that unite cultural anthropology, Rob Borofsky speaks of anthropologists' shared ethics: a desire to publicize "human commonalities" (especially in countering racism), the valuing of cultural diversity, and the use of cultural differences "as a form of cultural critique" of the anthropologist's home culture and in general of industrial mass society. Despite an explosion of variation in what sociocultural anthropologists do, anthropologists' holistic and comparative worldview remains distinctive.

REFERENCES

Bernard, H. Russell 1994 *Research Methods in Anthropology: Qualitative and Quantitative Approaches.* Thousand Oaks, Calif.: Sage.

Borofsky, Robert, ed. 1994 *Assessing Cultural Anthropology.* New York: McGraw-Hill.

Harris, Marvin 1968 *The Rise of Anthropological Theory: A History of Theories of Culture.* New York: Crowell.

Hatch, Elvin 1973 *Theories of Man and Culture.* New York: Columbia University Press.

Kaplan, David, and Robert A. Manners 1972 *Culture Theory.* Prospect Heights, Ill.: Waveland Press.

Kuper, Adam 1983 *Anthropology and Anthropologists: The Modern British School.* London: Routledge and Kegan Paul.

Kuznar, Lawrence 1997 *Reclaiming a Scientific Anthropology.* Walnut Creek, Calif.: AltaMira Press.

Marcus, George E., and Michael M. J. Fischer 1986 *Anthropology as Cultural Critique: An Experimental Moment in the Human Sciences.* Chicago: University of Chicago Press.

McGee, R. Jon, and Richard L. Warms 2000 *Anthropological Theory: An Introductory History.* 2nd ed. Mountain View, Calif.: Mayfield.

Moore, Jerry D. 1997 *Visions of Culture: An Introduction to Anthropological Theories and Theorists* Walnut Creek, Calif.: AltaMira Press.

LIN POYER

SOCIOLINGUISTICS

When Brown and Gilman published their classic work on pronouns of power and solidarity (1960; see also 1989), no one characterized that paper as a major contribution to "sociolinguistics." When Gumperz and Hymes published their updated *Directions in Sociolinguistics* in 1986 (the 1972 edition was based on a 1966 publication of the American Anthropological Association), they were providing a paradigmatic definition of recognizable enterprise; that book included contributions by many of the founders. A two-part survey of sociolinguistics written in 1973 (Grimshaw 1973b, 1974a) noted that more had been published on sociolinguistic topics in the early 1970s than in all previous years. That review commented on about fifty new titles; only a few sociologists (particularly Basil Bernstein and Joshua Fishman, each with several volumes) were represented. In the three decades since that time, interest in language *in use* (micro sociolinguistics) has continued to grow exponentially; while that interest still is not seen as part of mainstream sociology, it is moving in that direction (Lemert 1979). Interest in more macro dimensions of the sociology of language—for instance, language conflict, language maintenance, and language spread and decline—also has grown, though much more slowly.

SOME ACTIVITIES AND SOME LABELS

At least a dozen specialties investigate some aspect of language: its origins, structure, invariant and variant features, acquisition, use in social contexts, change, spread, and death, and so on. Among those specialties, there are at least five whose practitioners do not consider themselves sociolinguists or sociologists of language and whose research seldom is incorporated directly into sociolinguistics/sociology of language (SL/SOL) investigations:

1. Formal linguistics that focuses on languages as autonomous systems and investigates how those systems work independently of human and/or social agency. This activity often is referred to as "autonomous linguistics" and occasionally as "nonhyphenated linguistics."

2. Anthropological linguistics devoted to a "description" (writing of grammars and

dictionaries and audio and phonemic recording of phonological systems) of languages in specific, usually nonmodern societies.

3. Psycholinguistics, which covers a wide range of topics, including the acoustics of perception, cognitive constraints on the complexity of clausal embedding, theories of innateness and learning in language acquisition, and the physical location of language functions in the brain.

4. Social psychology of language (from psychological social psychology), wide-ranging specialty that includes research on message characteristics and influence, self-disclosure, relationships between personality and speech, and relationships among body movements, speech, and "meaning."

5. Conversation analysis/ethnomethodology (CA), an approach that views talk in muchthe same way formal linguists view language: as a system that is syntactically organized and has structure that can be discerned independently of the social attributes of participants in particular talk.

CA has identified devices such as "preinvitations" and "preclosings" as well as ways of constructing accusations without accusing anyone explicitly (Atkinson and Drew 1979); workers in the field are interested in how these devices are used in the course of the immediate talk, not in how they might be directed to more complex goals of conversational participants. Whalen (1991) notes that CA "examines talk as an object in its own right, as a fundamental type of social action, rather than primarily as a resource for documenting other social processes." None of the five activities listed above deals with language primarily as social resource.

In contrast, another handful of specialties focuses on the social dimensions of language/talk as interactional resource, a component of individual and group identity, and a social object. The ethnography of speaking and ethnolinguistics, like the anthropological practices from which they take their names, focus on the diversity of available linguistic resources and the uses to which those resources are put in individual speech communities and in human society at large, respectively.

There is a strong comparative dimension to these arenas of investigation.

Sociolinguistics manifests a different kind of comparative orientation. The micro variety usually focuses on interactional accomplishment through the medium of language in use in social contexts: (1) comparisons of means and ends, including attention both to how individual ends can be accomplished by different means (ways of talking) and to how different outcomes may simultaneously result (intentionally or otherwise) from the production of same or very similar bits of talk, and (2) comparisons of the different resources available to different participants in talk. The sociology of language, as the macro variety of sociolinguistics often is called (Grimshaw 1987a), tends to focus on distributional studies, such as the distribution of language varieties across individual repertoires and the distribution of repertoires across social aggregates, categories, and groups (nations or classes, genders or age groups, and families or friendship networks, respectively). At the most macro level, this implies studies of language maintenance, supersession and change, conflict, and so on.

The sociological social psychology of language is oriented to group effects on individual behaviors, including the acquisition of social-cultural competence through the medium of talk, the role of talk in the acquisition and organization of evaluative orientations, and uses of talk/written language in social control. At some point, the last activity shades off into symbolic interactionism; this boundary is not explored here. Finally, specialized studies of proxemics (social and interpersonal spacing) and kinesics (body movement, the organization of facial features, gesture, posture) have been done from both sociological and psychological perspectives (Hall 1966, 1974; Kendon, [1977] 1990).

SOME QUESTIONS OF ORIENTATION

Since later sections of this article illustrate how sociological theory can be enriched by empirical SL/SOL research in specific substantive areas, the comments here are limited to four questions of general orientation in theoretical work in SL/SOL: (1) What are causal and other relations between language/speech and other social behavior(s)? (2) Are grammars of social interaction possible, and is there a universal grammar? (3) What is the relevance of a micro–macro distinction for understanding the importance of language/speech in social life, and now are the two levels articulated in social behavior? (4) Is theoretical advance and/or understanding best sought by focusing on social processes or on specific substantive arenas of social behavior?

Causal Directionality/Covariation/Cotemporality/Mutuality. As in other varieties of social behavior, SL/SOL theory and research must deal with complex problems of cause and effect. There are four principal perspectives on the causal relationship between social structure and language (see Grimshaw 1974b; Hymes 1966):

1. That which sees language as fundamental (or as source, cause, independent variable, or set of independent variables), a position consonant both with an extreme Whorfian position (language *determines* how people think) and the commonsense observation that people sometimes do not know what is going on until they hear other people talking

2. That which sees social structure as a determinant or an independent variable or set of such variables, position consonant with people's awareness that they talk differently in different situations, with different interlocutors, and depending on the nature of their interactional goals

3. That which sees neither as prior to the other, with both being seen as co-occurring and codetermining

4. That which sees both as being determined by a third factor, whether innate features of the human mind—the view of Cartesian linguistics (Chomsky 1966, 1968)—*Weltanschauung*, or the intrinsic demands of an ordered universe

Most SL/SOL correlational studies focus on how the location of individuals or groups in the social structure is *reflected* in speech and/or other language behavior, as in the case of regional or class dialects, or *determines* it, as in the case of the section of a language variety in different situations and with different conversational partners (Blom and Gumperz 1972) or of pronominal forms or

other names (for a review of some of this literature, see Grimshaw 1980a). A smaller but substantial number of correlational studies attempt to discover how language use (spoken and written) is associated with interactional outcomes as varied as providing or not providing a requested favor, succeeding or not succeeding in school, and deciding whether to go to war (for a review, see Grimshaw 1981; for illustrations of claims about language use and the risks of war, see Chilton 1985; Wertsch and Mehan 1988). Although closer scrutiny often reveals that *ways of talking* are themselves resources that are differentially available to interactants with different social origins, some language resources appear to be available throughout social structures. Ways of talking in turn have been shown to have effects independent of structural relations.

Figure 1 is a simplified schematic representation of a mutual-embeddedness perspective. It is also a schematic showing how the processes of cultural reproduction would operate in a world without change. Bernstein (1975), Bourdieu (Bourdieu and Passeron 1977), Cicourel (1980a, 1980b, 1981), Collins (1981a, 1981b), and Habermas (1984–1987) all address the question of cultural reproduction and questions of change. All take essentially mutuality perspectives. All accord central importance to language in the reproduction process. Collins explicates ways in which language is simultaneously a resource in interaction and a source of change. Only Bernstein and Cicourel actually collect data on language in use, and only Cicourel directly investigates talk. None of these scholars would strongly disagree with this characterization; each would wish to "complete" the chart by incorporating neglected features (see Bernstein's diagram of the process [1975, p. 24], with its foregrounding of different transmission agencies, such as family and education; modes of social control; specific speech varieties; and context-dependent and -independent meanings).

In the mid-1960s, Fischer (1965, 1966) published perhaps the strongest version of the mutual-embeddedness position and, from the disciplinary perspective of sociology, perhaps the most esoterically documented. (The papers are reviewed extensively in Grimshaw 1974b.) Fischer argued nothing loss that phonological and syntactic differences between two related but mutually unintelligible languages (Trukese and Ponapean, separated for

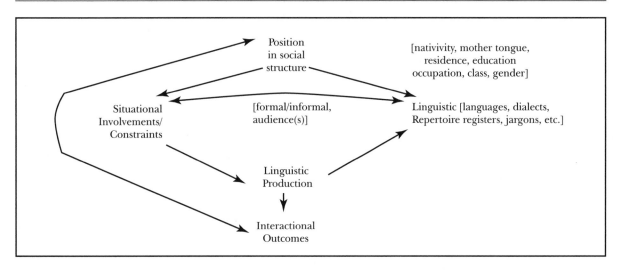

Figure 1. Sketch of a mutual-embeddedness perspective (cultural reproduction without change)

about eight centuries) are isomorphic to differences in the social structures of the two societies:

> As societies become more complex and social roles become more differentiated, the realized meaning of words in particular contexts becomes less important than the common or basic meaning. Speakers are forced to assume a greater cognitive gap between themselves and their listeners. At the same time, the basic meaning of the items of the lexicon tends to become more abstract and attenuated, since speakers have less need for words which can express much meaning in compact form to listeners who are conceived as being much like the self; they have more need, instead, for words which can be used in many different contexts with many different listeners who are conceived of as being very different from the self and from each other. (Fischer 1966, p. 178)

The mutuality perspective is a richly suggestive one.

Grammars of Social Interaction/A Grammar of Social Interaction. Linguists write grammars; that is, they describe and write "rules" for phonological and syntactic systems for individual languages. They are also committed to the goal of writing a grammar of language, that is, identifying in grammars of individual languages features and/or rules that hold for all languages: a universal grammar. They distinguish between absolute and quantitative universals (i.e., between features

of all languages that can be explained on theoretical grounds as required constituents and features that occur in all or most languages, such as terms for female derived from that for male [this kind of feature is known as marking], but for which no theoretically principled basis can be identified) and between weaker and stronger claims of universality (i.e., between a claim that all languages contain certain elements [nouns, verbs, prepositions] and a claim that those elements appear in the same order in utterances in every language).

An interest in the intrinsic ordering of the universe and a concern to avoid repeating old errors and rediscovering the already known are central in linguists' interest in both the regularities in individual languages and universal rules. Sociologists have similar concerns in seeking to discover the rules of interactional grammars for specific societies or groups and in seeking social interactional universals and the role of language in use in both grammars and the grammar. Although there are greetings in most, if not all, societies (this is more a quantitative than an absolute universal, and there are societies in which greeting is the marked case and nongreeting the unmarked), how they are done, to whom, and to what purpose may vary considerably (Firth 1972; Goffman 1971; Ibrahim et al. 1976; Kendon and Ferber 1973).

Similarly, there must be a need for information everywhere, but questions are not the appropriate manner for obtaining information in every society (see Goody 1978; sources cited in Grimshaw 1969). Again, it seems likely that interpersonal relations of power and affect and considerations of valence and cost are everywhere involved in requesting behavior (Brown and Levinson 1987; Grimshaw 1989); their relative importance and the consequent variety of modes of requesting behaviors vary considerably.

Ways of talking are everywhere critical resources in interaction; very little is known, however, about what features of *language in use in social contexts* may be universal or, for that matter, about which rules *within* speech communities (or social groups) are variant and which are invariant (Labov 1968; Grimshaw 1973a). Indeed, some sociologists find the notion of rule misleading on grounds that expectations and behaviors are always under negotiation (Berger and Luckmann 1966). Notions of rules and exceptions vary across disciplines (Edgerton 1985; Labov 1968; Grimshaw 1973a, 1981).

Micro–Macro, Conversation, and Interaction/ Official Languages and Language Policies, SL/ SOL. These distinctions, along with the familiar polarities of social psychology and social organization—or qualitative and quantitative methods— often appear in discussions of sociological interest in language and language in use. Three sorts of questions can be asked in this arena:

1. What are sociology's interests in what goes on in conversation/interaction, and what does a specific focus on talk teach sociologists that other modes of study do not?

2. What are sociology's interests in looking at language as an individual social attribute that, aggregated, has supraindividual importance in ways similar to ethnic group, class, religion, and other categorical attributes? What are sociology's interests in questions about how language is linked to life chances, why and how it becomes a focus of positive and negative attitudes, and how languages spread, change, contract, and die?

3. How do the things that go on in individual conversations on the micro level get articulated with, and aggregated into, processes of change in languages themselves, in their prestige, in policies re-

garding their use, and so on, on the macro level?

As was suggested above, the micro–macro question is closely related both to those about mutual embeddedness and to those about cultural reproduction. The dimension added by asking the articulation question is that of social change: If socializing/cultural transmission agencies operate to *reproduce* values, attitudes, behaviors, and so on, in new generations, how does change occur? A perspective offered by Collins (1981a, 1981b) is that participants bring to *everyday* conversations interactional resources that are enhanced or reduced in the course of interaction and that modest changes in interactional resources ultimately eventuate in changes in institutions and cultural systems—and languages. Related formulations are cited in Grimshaw (1987b). The macro–micro questions constrain one to think deeply both about processes of change and about how people try to get co-conversationalists to agree with them or to do what they want those them to do.

Substance or Process: "Top-Down" or "Bottom-Up." Two additional questions about the construction and use of theory have methodological as well as theory-building implications. The first question is whether when sociologists study the uses of language in specific contexts such as educational, military, or medical institutions, they are interested primarily in understanding (1) the institutions themselves, (2) social processes such as negotiation or socialization or, more broadly, conflict or cooperation, (3) a specific kind of situated interaction, such as an interview, as a representative of a species of situation, or (4) how talk works in interaction. There are, of course, no pure cases The second question has been put by Cicourel (1980a) as a distinction between "top-down" and "bottom-up" theorizing. By "top-down," Cicourel means approaching corpora of talk with sets of conceptual notions ranging from the generality of "cultural reproduction" or "role" and/or "conflict" to the specificity of "role conflict" or different "footings" in talk (Goffman 1981). By "bottom-up," he refers to researchers immersing themselves in their data and identifying regularities, then validating that identification, then discovering regularities in relations between previously observed regularities, and so on. All the investigators whose work is mentioned in this article—indeed, all sociologists—would like to believe that they let their data guide them to theory construction, and all are to some extent guided in their work by prior theoretical constructions.

DATA, DATA, EVERYWHERE

While sociologists sometimes are intimidated by the complex structure of formal linguistic theory, they may be equally envious of the easy access of linguists to their data, either in their own intuitions about the languages they speak or in the bath of talk and writing in which all people live (compare the ways of studying phonology in, for example, Chomsky and Halle 1968; W. Labov 1980). Students of SL/SOL share the advantage that many of the data in which they are interested are fairly accessible and, with modern technology, fairly easy to collect (denial of access and questions of ethics aside). They share the disadvantage that many of the sociological questions they want to study—matters as varied as (1) attitudes about different speech varieties, (2) the impact of stratification on the acquisition of those attitudes, and (3) the ways in which phonological variation *affects* stratification—can be considerably more difficult to identify, conceptualize, and measure. Just as there are fundamental questions about theoretical orientation in SL/SOL, there are fundamental questions about methods.

This brief discussion can comment on only a few of these methodological questions: (1) What constitutes optimal data for SL and SOL, or micro and macro, research? (2) How can the optimal data best be collected? (3) What need is there for modes of work, such as comprehensive discourse analysis (CDA), that differ from more familiar modes of sociological investigation? (4) What are the roles of collaborative and comparative studies in SL/SOL research?

What Constitutes Optimal Types of Data for SL/SOL? Labov (1972a) remarked that linguists work variously in library, bush, closet, laboratory, and street, where they collect and/or produce data that can be labeled texts, elicitations, intuitions, experimental results, and observations, respectively. Among the many sorts of data that can be useful in the investigation of SL/SOL issues, those associated with the following four "how" questions are central:

1. *How* do people actually talk/write? This has two dimensions: (a) What varieties of language (spoken and written are assumed in the following discussion) do individual members of speech communities control? (b) How do individuals employ their language resources in social interaction? The optimal data for such studies are extended texts.

2. *How* are language varieties and patterns of use distributed across categories of age, class, gender, occupation, nationality, religious affiliation, and residence? The optimal data here are a combination of sampled texts and observations.

3. *How* do members of social groups learn about language and its appropriate use, and how do they learn second (and higher-order) languages? The optimal data here are experimental results and observations and, to a lesser extent, texts.

4. *How* do people feel about language; that is, what are the attitudes of individuals and groups toward language varieties, repertoires, language change, and literacy? Data that have been employed in addressing these questions have included all five of the varieties listed by Labov (1972a), and each has proved useful.

What Are the Criteria for Optimal Data? There is no such thing as a "verbatim" record without electronic recording, and optimal records of conversation include both high-fidelity audio recording and possibly multiple sound-image recordings (for discussions of sound-image recording, including some of the controversies about such data collection, see Feld and Williams 1975; Grimshaw 1982, 1989). When one is working with written texts, optimal data include photographic copies of handwritten originals as well as printed versions. Whatever texts and observations are collected and used as data, however, those materials are valuable only to the extent that contexts of both "situation" and "text" (i.e., embedding talk and written material) are provided (the distinction is Halliday's following Malinowski). Two excellent articulations of the importance of context that suggest different boundaries for what must be taken into account are those of Corsaro (1981, 1985) and Cicourel (esp. 1994).

People are often skeptical of claims about what talk is actually like until they see it transcribed; they then are skeptical that the transcription is accurate until they hear electronically recorded audio while reading a transcript. Investigators who work with texts, elicitations, and observations must always take into account the effects of monitoring in most varieties of SL/SOL data; Labov (1972a) has referred to the Observer's Paradox; that is, "we want to observe how people talk when they are not being observed." One also should keep in mind, however, Sol Worth's observation that all behavior, however carefully monitored, is "natural" (personal communication). Labov has developed elicitation techniques that have the advantage of generating different levels of self-consciousness of, and thus monitoring of, talk (see, e.g., 1972b).

Other concerns with data in SL/SOL research are, like those just reviewed, quite similar to those in sociological research in general. Self-report data on language varieties employed by oneself or one's family or of uses of literacy are notoriously unreliable, and definitions and measurements of individual attributes such as literacy and bilingual fluency are often inconsistent.

The Need for Methods Specific to SL/SOL. Many of the data employed in SL/SOL research are the same as or very similar to those employed in other arenas of sociology, as are the methods employed in analysis. This similarity may be least evident in the case of the activities labeled "conversation analysis" (see Whalen 1991) and "comprehensive discourse analysis" (Labov and Fanshel 1977). Labov and Fanshel realize that the goal of comprehensiveness is chimerical: their pioneering study demonstrated the importance of such aspects of talk as prosodic and paralinguistic features. Lexical, syntactic, and even phonological selection are deeply involved in what is "actually said" (i.e., interactionally intended) in talk (for a discussion of the process of "disambiguation" of text, see Grimshaw 1987c). Sociologists have employed CDA and adaptations of it to ask more specifically sociological questions. Other students have developed similarly fine-grained approaches to written texts (Silverman and Torode 1980). Perhaps sociologists are now aware that questions about language as language have sociological significance and that talk and writing are no longer just media that contain answers to other questions.

Collaborative, Comparative, and Corroborative Research on SL/SOL. While SL and SOL research and publications have increased tremendously in the last few decades, their literatures continue to be diffuse. There have been few replications. Most research has been on English, and much of the material on other languages is published in English. While much of the early activity in SL was interdisciplinary, there have been few truly interdisciplinary studies (for a discussion of problems with such projects, see Grimshaw, Feld et al. 1994) or parallel studies of shared data (see, however, Chafe 1980; Dorval 1990; Grimshaw, Burke, et al. 1994). There have been few explicitly comparative studies in which the same or collaborating investigators have simultaneously studied the "same" phenomenon in different speech communities (see, however, Watson-Gegeo and White 1990) or in different institutional contexts in same societies (see, however, Grimshaw 1990). There is reason to believe that all three of these important kinds of research are on the increase. Scholars all over the world are trying out SL formulations largely generated in the United States and Europe in their own societies, more and more work is being done on related SL phenomena in societies and speech communities where earlier work followed more traditional courses in linguistics and anthropological linguistics, and researchers from an increasingly wide range of disciplinary backgrounds are finding in SL/SOL data and theory materials to use in addressing their own questions.

An Additional, Residual, Neglected Question. Claims about the relative validity, reliability, and general worth of quantitative and qualitative research appear in SL/SOL, as they do in most areas of sociological work. While the modes of work are loosely associated with the micro–macro distinction, there are representations of both modes in both arenas.

SL/SOL AS A RESOURCE IN SOCIOLOGICAL THEORY BUILDING

A diminishing number of sociologists remain unfamiliar with SL/SOL and therefore unaware of both substantive findings and theoretical developments that could be helpful in their work. It is possible here to mention only a few contributions to the understanding of (1) substantive areas, (2) social processes, and (3) relations among language, literature, identity, and so on. Let us begin with two instances of sociologically relevant contributions by the linguist best known to sociologists (possibly excepting Chomsky), William Labov, and then turn to research by sociologists and other nonlinguists that focuses from the outset on identifiably sociological concerns.

Suggestive Empirical Findings. Studies of classrooms, courtrooms, and clinics have generated findings that sometimes have resulted in changes in pedagogic, legal, and medical practice as well as contributed to our theoretical understanding of SL/SOL. Studies of a multitude of other settings, ranging from street, to dinner table, to backyard party, to workplace, also have produced important theoretical insights. Two of these findings come from Labov's quantitative studies of language use in urban areas of the eastern United States (New York City and Philadelphia); the first has important implications for understanding social stratification, the second for understanding ethnic (and possibly class) relations, and both for understanding processes of social change.

In studies of dialects associated with class, Labov and others have shown that linguistically insecure informants, more often than not women with aspirations for upward social mobility (or concerns about slipping), often hypercorrect their phonological production in the direction of what they perceive as prestige variants, thus producing the prestige variant with higher frequencies than do those at social levels above them—and sometimes produce it inappropriately (Labov gives as an example, "Hi, say, that's hawfully good of you"). Awareness of this phenomenon should alert sociologists to look for analogues in other behavioral arenas (there is a family relationship to anticipatory socialization; the roots of the labeled behaviors may differ quite considerably); Labov (1972b, 1986) has pointed out important implications of this research for studies of linguistic (and, one may add, social) change.

Labov's second finding is that the speech of urban blacks who have contact with whites continues to be modified in the direction of the grammar of the dominant group, while blacks in the increasingly segregated inner cities speak ever more divergent language varieties. This divergence co-occurs with concomitant differentiation in incomes and educational achievement, heightening

social distance and probably enhancing intergroup hostility (see Williams et al. 1964). Labov comments, "The linguistic situation correlates with the formation of what has been called a 'permanent underclass'" (1986, p. 278).

Some Little Concepts and Some Central Processes. Studies of actual talk that occurs in the course of everyday interaction have generated both (1) concepts that allow one to taxonomically identify previously unspecified regularities in that interaction (in a manner similar to Goffman's labeling of, among other things, front and back regions, side involvements, and the more specifically talk-related "footing") and (2) new understandings of the working of what might be called "master social processes," such as conflict and socialization. Instances of the former (all from Grimshaw 1989) are the identification of hyperinvolvement (a phenomenon in which interactants are so deeply involved in the ongoing that they miss the things they intend to monitor), defects of nerve (a situation in which interactants know how to do something but are reluctant to do it because they are concerned that it may generate injury to self or another party), and phenomena such as topic avoidance, topic exploitation, and topic truncation (the last occurring when it becomes obvious to an interactant that interactional goals are not going to be accomplished).

An instance of this is Corsaro's (1985) demonstration of the processes involved in children's learning how to recognize and construct the cultures and social structures in which they find themselves. Another is Grimshaw's (1990) distillation of the reported findings of a number of individual studies of conflict talk into propositions about the conflict process (see below).

Discourse in organizations: What can be learned from a language-oriented approach to social structure and social behavior depends on researchers' choices of an "entering wedge" (the term is John Useem's), that is, the selection of units of analysis, particulars of language in use to be attended, and questions to be asked. The paragraphs below will address things that have been learned from studies of language in use in (1) public bureaucracies in Sweden, focusing on *narratives* in the public domain, (2) organizations (primarily in the United States), employing a *conversation analytic* method, (3) a specific event within a university (a dissertation defense) examined by an interdisciplinary group employing a range of approaches and asking a number of different questions, and (4) a sampling of more narrowly focused studies of language in use.

Focus on narrative: Czarniawska is a student of management and organization who disclaims linguistic or sociolinguistic competences language in use is nonetheless central to her analyses of public administration in Sweden. In *Narrating the Organization* (1997), Czarniawska demonstrates for the study of organizations, a central descriptive and analytic role of stories/narratives and a dramaturgical perspective. Czarniawska asserts that stories rule people's lives and constitute the basis for the construction of society (p. 5); she seems to believe that the centrality of narrative as the main source of knowledge "in the practice of organizing . . . is not likely to generate much opposition" (pp. 5–6). I find this surprising if true. Her project is to apply the narrative perspective (for which she credits Jean-Francois Lyotard) to elucidate continuities and change in Swedish public institutions and/or organizations at various governmental levels. The argument is dense, and the examples unfamiliar; the demonstration is persuasive both for the organizations studied and for the application of this perspective to other arenas of social life.

Czarniawska conceptualizes organizational life as stories, and organizational theories as ways of reading stories (pp. 26–29). She invokes Burke and Goffman in identifying drama and autobiography as special kinds of narratives (p. 32), noting (following Merelman) how drama, for example, can simultaneously or alternatively generate catharsis, personification, identification, and suspense (p. 36). She observes that stories not only can be vehicles for identity claiming by their tellers but also can be contested by other stories, unsuccessfully performed, and turned into serials (and sagas); importantly, all descriptions favor the theories of their tellers (p. 71).

In her exposition of how she studied Swedish public organizations, Czarniawska reviews a number of methodological conundrums related to the logic of inquiry of interpretive studies, including (1) *interruption* of texts (p. 92, per Silverman and Torode 1980), (2) the advantages of "outsideness (p. 62), (3) issues of case studies versus "window" studies (pp. 64 ff), (4) the identification of action

"nets" in organizational "fields" (p. 66), and (5) the place of notions of institutionalization and norms in studies focusing on narratives (pp. 68 ff.).

Focusing on two specialized fields—municipal administration and social insurance—she shows how *stories, themes,* and *serials* can be employed to elucidate the role of "good" and "bad" friction in social change, how new and old ways of acting have been integrated, and how new processes of "companyization" and "computerization" change the workplaces of individuals as well as the larger bureaucratic landscape. Narratives are central to people's lives, and Czarniawska has shown the necessity of attending to them.

Conversation(al) analysis as a sociological method: CA is treated elsewhere in this encyclopedia; conversational analysis (CAs) do not consider themselves sociolinguists or sociologists of language. For many years, the author has told CAs that their work is highly original, exciting, and of great potential value to sociology and that that potential will be achieved only when they integrate CA methods and concepts into more traditional sociology, simultaneously showing how traditional sociological concepts and perspectives ranging from status and role, to social structure, to socioeconomic status (SES), to self-esteem could help in interpreting CA findings.

Increasing numbers of researchers across the social sciences and humanities have come to value CA as an approach to everyday talk; until recently, CA-trained sociologists did not undertake to *demonstrate* the value of talk as data for studying fundamental sociological questions such as how social organization is constituted, reproduced, and modified—and how members contribute to that constitution, reproduction, and modification through talk—in what may appear to be mundane and unremarkable interactions. (CA methods are increasingly being employed in sociological analyses. Atkinson and Drew [1979] on Court proceedings, Maynard [1984] on plea bargaining, and Goodwin [1990] on black children's play groups are impressive examples. These studies do not as directly as the work discussed here foreground the epistemological issues implied by the CA posture described above [see, for example, Boden pp. 214–215].)

Boden (1994) provides a demonstration that many readers will find convincing. Using audio-recorded talk from telephone calls and meetings of varying levels of formality collected in organizations ranging from a travel agency and a local television station to hospitals and a university administrative department to the Oval Office, Boden shares her understanding of the sometimes extraordinarily delicate but analytically identifiable ways in which talk is employed to "inform, amuse, update, gossip, review, reassess, reason, instruct, revise, argue, debate, contest, and actually *constitute* the moments, myths and, through time, the very *structuring* of [the] organization" (p. 8). The argument is often dense, and for readers unfamiliar with CA, it may be difficult to follow. The way in which an accountant comes to see that physicians in different departments may differently view policy change that could improve a hospital's overall revenue position but reduce "their" money (p. 58 ff) is a case in point.

Boden's goal is to use her collected talk to undertake two quite different but complementary projects:

(1) to examine a range of more specific aspects of the organization of talk in the work settings that make up the business day; and (2) to discover through *those materials how an apparently fragmentary process of information gathering, transmission, and very local assimilation is transformed into the goals, agendas, and decisions of organizations (p. 107).*

In the course of pursuing her projects, Boden shows how members of organizations can at the same time account for their behaviors in terms of a "rational actor" model and be unaware of how actual decision making is accomplished incrementally in fragments of unremembered and individually unremarkable chat rather than through a focused weighing of "rational" considerations. Boden simultaneously shows how concurrent and articulated employ of the previously segregated conceptual apparatuses of general sociology and CA (e.g., adjacency organization, agenda, bracketing, placement, sequence [centrally and critically], turn and so on) is mutually enhancing.

Boden argues that stages of (1) collection of actual talk, (2) identification of sequentiality in that talk, and (3) discovery in the talk and its sequentiality of the fundamental stuff and fundamentals of organization, (4) allow and/or contribute to sociological theory at levels of considerable abstractness (p. 206 ff). One may find in Boden's

study a convincing *demonstration* of Collins's "microfoundations of macrosociology" perspective.

Boden goes a step further and anticipates the result in offices of the future of today's incremental changes (p. 209 ff); they will be places with more talk (and reduced opportunities for reflection), sped-up expectations of productivity, increased scope of action for all personnel, a flattened hierarchy, and real downsizing. Careful study of Boden's book allows one to see how (1) she came to make such a projection and (2) one can evaluate a novel and productive application of CA to central sociological issues.

Collaborative work across disciplines: As early as the 1970s, concern was expressed about the increasingly disparate and noncumulative character of work on language in use in social contexts (Grimshaw 1973b, 1974a). In response to this concern, the Committee on Sociolinguistics of the Social Science Research Council initiated in the 1970s the Multiple Analysis Project (MAP), in which representatives of different disciplines and different theoretical and methodological approaches agreed to undertake analyses of a shared corpus of data, in this case a ten-minute fragment of a doctoral dissertation defense (Grimshaw 1989; Grimshaw, Burke, et al. 1994). The author has (Grimshaw 1994a) attempted to assess the success of this project in achieving its goals of theoretical cumulation, testing the comparative strengths and weaknesses of analytic approaches and methods, and an illumination of a shared corpus of data beyond that available from one or two studies by individual researchers. While it is not possible to conclude that one or another of the analytic modes employed is more comprehensive, a reading of the studies together conveys a sense of the complexity of language use in talk in its several contexts beyond the richness of most studies done from single analytic perspectives (but not all; see Labov and Fanshel [1977], who synthesized a variety of perspectives in their pioneering study of Rhoda and her therapist).

The anthropologists, linguists, and sociologists who investigated the dissertation segment variously focused on laminations of context (Cicourel 1994), formulaic talk (Wong Fillmore 1994), clause structure (Halliday 1994), humor (Fillmore 1994), [Who didn't find funny that which sociologists in the defense thought was.], speech acts, cohesive devices (Burke 1994; Hasan 1994), prosodic features and contextualization cues (Cook-Gumperz and Gumperz 1994), proforms (Grimshaw 1994b), and many other elements of the talk to study an equally wide range of behavioral outcomes. The outcomes included the reproduction and/or reshaping of social structure; control of the course of talk (and, by extension, interaction); creation of social relations; social and sociolinguistic constraints on discourse and interaction; negotiation of meaning; the notion of fluency, humor, laughter, and short-term social reorganization; membership-affiliation-identification processes and the structuring of group boundaries; and "face work" and political maneuvering. Each of these varieties of behavioral outcome is autonomously a sociological matter. In more macro directions, they are also deeply implicated in the search for answers to the following five interrelated questions; the answers to which require attending to particularities of language in use:

1. How is social structure generated, sustained, reproduced, and changed?

2. What is the role of social interaction/talk in the creation, realization, maintenance, and so on, of social structure?

3. How does interaction *work*? What permits it to continue and even flourish in social environments of competitiveness and aggressiveness?

4. What is the role of "meaning" in driving interaction and shaping social relations? How is "meaning" socially constrained and sociolinguistically/linguistically signaled?

5. What resources—social, sociolinguistic, and linguistic—are available to interactants for signaling meaning, sustaining interaction, and creating social relations?

What is going on, in short, when someone orders another person rather than asking or cajoling, or when someone says, "Don't include *me* in that you!" or when an interactant says, "Along those lines . . . " and then challenges something said by an interlocutor/conversational partner?

Other convergences: Ochs, Schegloff, et al. (1996), another volume of studies of language in use, provides additional evidence of the convergence of CA (and linguistic) concerns with those of both sociolinguists and more traditional sociologists. The book is innovative in that the collaboration it reports is among pioneers in articulating work in formal syntax, CA, paralinguistics (e.g., voice quality, intonation, and tempo), kinesics (e.g., facial expression, gesture, and "body language"), and proxemics (interpersonal distancing and arrangements of "things" in space) in investigating interactional accomplishment. It illustrates some of the range of autonomously syntactic (e.g., clausal organization and reorganization, employ of inflection and particles, movement of nouns or verbs), prosodic and paralinguistic, pragmatic, and other devices available in different languages and cultures (English, Finnish, Japanese, Kaluli) for the management of turns (including shifts of rights to the floor, acceptance or rejection of interruptions, and simultaneous speech), making credible claims, and making cautious characterizations of those not present or accomplishing a joint response to disruption. Fox et al. (1996) claim that English clause beginnings are richer than Japanese with information about "how clause is likely to continue," thus providing potential interrupters with valuable information. They also observe that repair (by the speaker or another person) extends the possibilities for how an utterance can be completed *in any language* (p. 220). They are talking about *syntactic resources for interaction*. Some of these resources and/or devices are both familiar and fun in a Goffmanesque manner, as when the reader is introduced to and immediately resonates to notions such as "trailoffs" and "rush-throughs" (Schegloff) and "outlastings" (Lerner 1996).

The book is informative because in addition to demonstrating the interinfluence of syntax and interaction, it provides windows to sociological understandings revealed when seldom exploited perspectives are applied to concerns at the core of sociology, including issues of symbolic interaction, the socialization of neophytes, and social change. Beyond this, it allows similarly (and seminally) novel views of specialties such as the sociology of science and that of occupations. Particularly instructive, for example, are Ochs, et al. (1996), on how scientists construct indeterminate referential identities—sometimes in the process blurring the distinction between themselves and the physical world under their scrutiny—and how meaning is built through routine interpretive activity involving talk, gesture, and graphic representation. Also engrossing is Goodwin's (1996) rich integration of different channels of behavior (syntactic production, intonation, body movement, display of awareness of a world beyond the immediate and ongoing) in a dynamic reconceptualization of Goffman's notion of participation framework as it operates in situations of disruption (of initially unknown magnitude) of routines—in an airport control tower.

Sociologists can profit from this book because of sociologically relevant questions posed, answers given, and because of passing observations. Lerner's (1996) thoughtful and suggestive work on how and why interlocutors complete utterances of speakers without being asked initially suggests as functions of such completion (1) agreement, (2) preemption of disagreement, (3) collaboration, and (4) heckling (p. 244). Lerner later argues that an early opportunistic completion may be intended to initiate or sustain a special alignment with a speaker such as affiliation (pp. 263–264). Sorjonen (1996) suggests that repeats and the Finnish particles *niin* and *joo* variously function as (1) interrogatives, (2) exclamations, (3) requests for confirmation (p. 279 ff.), (4) challenges, and (5) expressions of ritualized disbelief. There are obvious parallels to English. She also has some observations on sweetening recommendations of others when the recommender suspects that an unwanted invitation or request may be forthcoming. Schieffelin (1996, p. 442 ff.) shows how the invention and introduction of an evidential construction to refer to printed religious material, translatable as "known from this source/not known before," not only has granted authority to written text when there is no basis in fact for doing so but also has been associated with the introduction of higher status for a new role of interpreter of Christianity in a society where prior stratification rested on different bases (and, not incidentally, also to a lowering of the status of women in a previously more egalitarian society).

Social conflict as process: conflict talk as language in use in social context: Early studies of intragroup conflict were largely experimental (often involving researcher-instigated disputes in dyads), usually nonattentive to particulars of subjects' talk, and, in part because of these two features, likely to overestimate the proportion of disputes that are in some way "resolved" (Corsaro and Rizzo 1990; Goodwin 1996). These writers and others have suggested that many pioneer stu-

dents of conflict talk (and social conflict more generally; for an early modern commentary, see Bernard 1950) were concerned with the disruptive consequences of disputation and thus tended to underestimate more positively valued outcomes, such as the creation of social organization and socialization of conflict participants (long ago identified by Simmel and others). In recent years researchers have, with great profit, turned increasingly to texts of actual disputes.

Students of processes of social conflict have more frequently than most other social scientists sought to formalize the regularities they have discovered in this phenomenon in propositions (see Coser 1956; Mack and Snyder 1957; Williams 1947; Williams et al. 1964). Taking into account the interaction of the sociological variables (affect, power, valence) and considerations of continua such as intensity, hostility, and violence and matters of external threat and internal cohesion as manifested in a range of studies of conflict talk, the author has formulated preliminary propositions. Space limitations constrain discussion of various sorts of propositions or of how sets of propositions permit the forecasting of patterns of conflict talk. Consider, however, the following:

Many disputes include instances of assignment of blame or responsibility (see Fillmore 1971). A discourse rule for this behavior might look like the following:

1. *Rule for assigning blame (responsibility).* If A asserts that B should and could have performed a behavior X_1 but willfully did not or that B should and could have avoided performing a behavior X_2 but nonetheless wilfully performed it, A is heard as blaming B for the nonoccurrence or occurrence of X_1 or X_2, respectively (Grimshaw, 1992 p. 312).

The influence of power on the availability of aggressive, uncompromising, and sometimes hostile modes of talk in conflict is similar to its influence and constraint on other selection of ways of talking:

2. *Ceteris paribus*, selection of more "confrontational" modes of conflict talk (e.g., threats or insults and increased amplitude or physiological rage displays, threatening kinesic posture, or gestures)

is directly related to increasing relative power (Grimshaw 1992, p. 315).

It is interesting to note that in talk where the parties are proxy military representatives of superpowers discussing matters of very high valence, confrontational modes generally are avoided (Grimshaw 1992). A growing literature on conflict talk demonstrates that the behavior of interest is simultaneously immensely complicated and has a rich potential for new understandings both of social conflict itself and of discourse more generally. This is true even though records of critically important conflict-talk events on the group and international levels have not been available for study (Grimshaw 1992).

Language, Writing, Literacy, and Literature. Recent events have demonstrated the continuing importance of what Geertz (1963) labeled "primordial sentiments" and shown that feelings about language are central among those sentiments. The range of sociological and sociologically relevant ways in which both language in general and writing and literacy in particular permeate and/or pervade human cultural and social structures and relations, as well as conceptions of identity and of self on the individual level, defies easy summary or description. People go to court in defense of their mother tongue; people have also fought in the streets and burned themselves alive over language issues. Becoming literate in any language can be primarily an instrumental acquisition; in some instances, it can have profound effects on both individual personalities and social organization (see, particularly, J. Goody 1987). The "invention" and development of national languages can have reverberating effects through previously atomized collectivities (Anderson 1990); when printed material becomes available, it can have critical impacts both on change in general (Eisenstein 1979) and on the development of national communities and identities (Anderson 1983).

Sociologists of literature have shown how national literatures can reveal cultural and social values (e.g., Moore 1971); sociologists who study both contemporary life and that in past times are becoming increasingly aware of the rich data in personal documents from journals to correspondence. It is even possible to hear the question, "Who wants citizens to be literate, and to what

ends?" (the implication is that social control may be as much a goal as is the enrichment of individual lives [see Kress and Hodge 1979]). Related interests have drawn a number of investigators to study of *how* written materials affect their readers, a question that has been addressed both by methods that project the "interruption" or "interrogation" of written and/or spoken texts (Silverman and Torode 1980) and by those of psycholinguistics or cognitive science.

Language and personal and social identity: This introduction to matters of language in use in social contexts should not be closed without mention of a dimension of social life increasingly recognized by sociological social psychologists as well as sociolinguists. This section includes brief reviews of two studies that focus on this *use* of language in identity matters and closes with a listing of suggestive but previously unexamined questions.

Constitution of morally relevant categories of people: T. Labov (1980) has been concerned with specifying how ascriptions of morality are made in conversational discourse and about whom (i.e., which persons and collections of persons) they are made. She has concluded that a task prior to the location of evaluation and obligation in talk is the specification of how people are located in talk and how morally relevant categories of people are constituted.

According to Labov (1980), all types of "collections of people" (a term "used to designate any plurality of people which can be referred to in talk or systematically inferred from the talk") are potentially relevant in moral matters; since there is a potentially infinite number of such collections, it is imperative to develop procedures for reducing the number to be examined in any given investigation, that is, to discover principled bases for classifying collections. She does this by first developing discovery procedures for locating collections and then gathering the collections into sets bounded by common identifying dimensions.

Labov (1980) observes that references in talk to collections of people often occur in the form of common nouns, proper names, and pronouns. What people are often unaware of, she argues, are collections of "hidden people," that is, "those collections of people not immediately evident in the surface talk, but systematically retrievable." Collections are hidden in five ways:

1. In references to social organization(s), incidents, and specific categories (e.g., in the case of academic settings, belonging-to-department-people, participating-in-defense-people, and faculty people).

2. Social characterizations, that is, collections defined by verbs of activity or specific attributes (e.g., candidate-attacking-people or candidate-defending-people or identification by gender, academic rank, features of personal appearance, voice quality, etc.) She (p. 135) notes that some activities, such as guessing, telling, and thinking, since they are features of all people, are nondiscriminating and thus analytically without value.

3. Ellipsed individuals or collections (i.e., where there is shared knowledge of past characterizations).

4. Collections concealed in references to time or place.

5. Plurals hidden in singulars.

Collections can conveniently be labeled as "feature plus people," for instance, "doing research on language and identity people" or "reading encyclopedia articles people," to make *explicit in a standardized way what features of the people are being considered*" (emphasis added). It is precisely such explicitness that is needed for the specification of identities and their boundaries.

Labov realizes that the identification of collections used by individual speakers is not sufficient to permit an understanding of how discussion of moral matters is accomplished in talk, and she continues by raising several critical questions. The general question is, "How do analysts (and interlocutors) know that coconversationalists are talking about a 'same' collection?" There is no easy answer to this question; collections to which reference is being made change in the course of a single speaker's utterance, overlap across utterances, shift across utterances because the original speaker's identification was unclear or because a hearer-become-speaker misheard or deliberately Misunderstood (Grimshaw 1980b) the original identification, are layered, subsumed, expanded (Labov's

notion of layering is loosely akin to both the linguistic and Goffman's [1981] more specialized uses of the term "embedding"), and so on. Resolution of these complexities is a requirement for coherent and cohesive discourse. Labov proposes the "notion of 'category consensus' for a situation where the relevance of a given collection of people is shown interactional support" and "which occurs as co-interactants ratify the use of specific collections of people." Category consensus is not always achieved; like other varieties of consensus, it is often the subject of challenge, negotiation, and metadiscussion. This is, of course, what the study of identity(ies) is about.

Exploitation of referential ambiguity in pronominal usage: A complication is introduced by the use of definite or indefinite articles such as "reading-*the*-Borgatta-encyclopedia people" versus "reading-*an*-encyclopedia people." This introduces the possibility of the use of referential ambiguity in language as an interactional resource. The question of how collectivities (both categories and groups) are constituted and bounded and how that boundedness may be explicitly or implicitly signaled in spoken or written discourse provides a venue for additional demonstration of the value for sociology of examination of language in use. Personal and other pronouns are a useful resource in boundary work; their referential ambiguity also provides a resource exploitable for including and excluding both those present and those absent from relevant social collectivities (Grimshaw 1994a).

The fact that there are times when hearers or readers don't know to what person or set of persons reference is being made can be weighted with social implication when it is not clear, for example, *who* is being scolded or praised, positively or negatively or neutrally characterized, or invited or rejected. Uncertainty can persist even in the presence of apparently disambiguating specifications such as "you all," "all of you," "the n of us" (when the collection address includes n-plus persons), and "the four of them." Hearer-readers ordinarily are able to make inferences that are correct or close enough that they can sustain conversation (or reading) without continuously finding it necessary to stop to resolve ambiguities. It is also true, of course, that ambiguities may go unrecognized, be recognized but not resolved, or even be intentionally exploited. Unresolved ambiguities can be inconsequential, but they may occasionally have delayed consequences of considerable importance (e.g., when "uninvited" guests turn up or unintended "insults" are repaid with interest).

Most readers will be far more familiar with the language–identity connection in which people participate whenever they talk with others. Except under extreme circumstances (ongoing or pending disaster) or service situations in which interactants are treated more as part of the scene than as other humans, the first thing people do when a partner in interaction speaks (in person, on the telephone, or in writing) is to "place" that person in terms of background (in which one usually includes age, education, ethnicity and national origin, gender, occupation, regional provenance, social class, and, depending on situation, other achieved and ascribed attributes). This sensitivity to the link between how people speak and who they are is further demonstrated by the ways in which the speech of others is imitated in "poshing up" (Goffman 1979) and in the production, with varying degrees of friendliness, condescension, and hostility, of "mock" Spanish or black English or other real or imagined languages (Hill).

Note, for example, the insertion of foreign words and phrases (insertion of not-currently-in-use-code speech: (1) foreign words and phrases, e.g., āp kē bād, buenos dias, je ne sais pas, obrigado, paz, СПАСИ́БО, was gibts (2) technical terms and phrases, such as "deep structure," "diglossia," "dope," "gigabyte," "identity," "S and M," "solenoid," and (3) phonological variants and regional dialect lexical items or, more comprehensively, code switches in which a different language, dialect, or register is employed for an extensive stretch of talk. How are such insertions and switches to be interpreted? Readers will be able to construct scenarios in which the following are or are intended to be conveyed: "I am one of you," "I am not one of you, but I am attuned and sympathetic to you," "I and those of my auditors who understand what I have just said are different (superior to?) from those who did not understand," "I and those who understand my metaphorical use of a variant are different from (superior to) those who processes it nonmetaphorically" (e.g., "humorous" employ of socially disvalued variants).

Questions of language in use and matters of identity (and thus of stratification, life chances, social conflict, and so on) are inextricably interrelated and intertwined; neither can be fully comprehended without attention to the other.

APPLIED SOCIOLINGUISTICS, SOCIAL AMELIORATION, AND THEORY BUILDING

The increased interest in SL/SOL has been accompanied by and contributed to by growing public exposure to and interest in language as a social problem. Consider in the last decade of the twentieth century in the United States alone issues of free speech ("hate crime" versus political correctness, arrests for public "cursing") in both public discourse and on private computers, the "English as official language" movement and accompanying disputes about "rights" to non-English ballots or other government documents, and the public hue and cry about "Ebonics." Public concern about propriety in language use is not a new phenomenon (see Kamensky 1997).

Work on "real" problems in a variety of institutional areas has benefited from a growing body of theory, to which it has in turn contributed. Again a distinction can be made between micro and macro concerns. Micro sociolinguistic research has been done on how communication fails in classrooms, courtrooms, and clinics; macro studies have examined how the speaking of socially disvalued language varieties is associated with educational failure, differential treatment in the judicial system, and unsuccessful interaction with medical services delivery systems. Ameliorative programs have ranged from bilingualism in education to the English as official language movement, from the provision of interpreters in the courtroom to attempts to simplify legal language, and from attempts to teach prospective doctors to become better interviewers and listeners to trying to get doctors to use less technical language. Bitter controversies have raged over how the ways children talk are related to educational success and failure; the Ebonics dispute is one instance among many (see Labov 1982). Some investigators have argued that some language varieties are not suited for abstract, critical, logical, and propositional thought; others, that the success and failure of persons who speak in different ways are determined by the political preferences about language varieties of gatekeepers such as teachers and employers.

Recent years have seen the development of the role of the "language scientist" as an expert witness (e.g., Rieber and Stewart 1990); SL considerations are sometimes deeply involved in such testimony. Many of these programs and much of this work initially grew out of concerns with language varieties associated with ethnicity (in the United States, different varieties of Spanish and, particularly, Black Vernacular English (BVE]). There has also been more explicit attention paid to problems of communication across classes, age groups, and, particularly, gender; Tannen's (1990) book on gender differences in talk spent many months on best-seller lists.

On a more explicitly macro level, language planning and language policy have become more visible arenas of government activity in both rich countries, which must deal with visiting or immigrant workers who speak unfamiliar languages, and poor countries, which must make decisions about which competing languages are going to receive official status and support or about which orthography to employ for previously unwritten languages. (The latter is a decision that is likely to have political as well as economic implications.) They must in some cases decide whether high literacy (often seen as an index of modernism) will ultimately contribute to their economies (or other values) as much as or more than would other investments (on outcomes of increases in literacy in industrial [izing] and less developed countries, respectively, see Graff 1979; Goody 1987). Both rich and poor countries must deal with native multilingualism; they have done it with varying success in Belgium, Canada, Finland, India, Indonesia, the former Soviet Union, Spain, Switzerland, and a number of countries in Africa (see McRae 1983, 1986, 1997, for excellent studies on Switzerland, Belgium, and Finland, respectively).

REFERENCES

Anderson, Benedict R. O'G 1983 *Imagined Communities: Reflections an the Origin and Spread of Nationalism.* London: Verso.

—— 1990 *Language and Power: Exploring Political Cultures in Indonesia.* Ithaca, N.Y.: Cornell University Press.

Atkinson, J. Maxwell, and Paul Drew 1979 *Order in Court: The Organisation of Verbal Interaction in Judicial Settings.* Atlantic Highlands, N.J.: Humanities Press.

Berger, Peter L., and Thomas Luckmann 1966 *The Social Construction of Reality: A Treatise in the Sociology of Knowledge.* Garden City, N.Y.: Doubleday.

Bernard, Jessie 1950 "Where is the Modern Sociology of Conflict?" *American Journal of Sociology* 56:11–16.

Bernstein, Basil 1975 *Class, Codes, and Control.* vol. 3: *Towards a Theory of Educational Transmission.* London: Routledge and Kegan Paul.

Blom, Jan-Petter, and John J. Gumperz 1972 "Social Meaning in Linguistic Structure(s): Code-Switching in Norway." In J. J. Gumperz and D. Hymes, eds., *New Directions in Sociolinguistics: The Ethnography of Communication.* New York: Holt, Rinehart and Winston.

Boden, Deirdre 1994 *The Business of Talk: Organizations in Action.* Cambridge, UK: Polity.

Bourdieu, Pierre, and Jean-Claude Passeron 1977 *Reproduction in Education, Society, and Culture,* trans. Richard Nice. London: Sage.

Brown, Penelope, and Steven C. Levinson 1978 "Universals in Language Usage: Politeness Phenomena." In E. Goody, ed., *Questions and Politeness: Strategies in Social Interaction.* Cambridge, UK: Cambridge University Press.

Brown, Roger, and Albert Gilman 1960 "The Pronouns of Solidarity." In T. A. Sebeok, ed., *Style in Language.* Cambridge, Mass.: MIT Press.

—— 1989 "Politeness Theory and Shakespeare's Four Major Tragedies." *Language in Society* 18:159–212.

Burke, Peter J. 1994 "Segmentation and Control of a Dissertation defense." In A.D. Grimshaw et al., *What's Going on Here? Complementary Studies of Professional Talk.* Norwood, N.J.: Ablex.

Chafe, Wallace, ed. 1980 *The Pear Stories: Cognitive, Cultural, and Linguistic Aspects of Narrative Production.* Norwood, N.J.: Ablex.

Chilton, Paul, ed. 1985 *Language and the Nuclear Arms Debate: Newspeak Today.* London: Frances Pinter.

Chomsky, Noam 1966 *Cartesian Linguistics: A Chapter in the History of Rationalist Thought.* New York: Harper and Row.

—— 1968 *Language and Mind.* New York: Harcourt, Brace and World.

——, and Morris Halle 1968 *The Sound Pattern of English.* New York: Harper and Row.

Cicourel, Aaron V. 1980a "Three Models of Discourse Analysis: The Role of Social Structure." *Discourse Processes* 2:101–131.

—— 1980b "Language and Social Action: Philosophical and Empirical Issues." *Sociological Inquiry* 40:1–30.

—— 1981 "Notes on the Integration of Micro- and Macro-Levels of Analysis." In K. Knorr-Cetina and A. V. Cicourel, eds., *Advances in Social Theory and Methodology: Toward an Integration of Micro- and Macro-Sociologies.* Boston: Routledge and Kegan Paul.

—— 1994 "Theoretical and Methodological Suggestions for Using Discourse to Recreate Aspects of Social Structure." In A. D. Grimshaw et al., *What's Going on Here? Complementary Studies of Professional Talk.* Norwood, N.J.: Ablex.

Collins, Randall 1981a "On the Microfoundations of Macrosociology." *American Journal of Sociology* 86:984–1014.

—— 1981b "Micro-Translation as a Theory-Building Strategy." In K. Knorr-Cetina and A. V. Cicourel, eds., *Advances in Social Theory and Methodology: Toward an Integration of Micro- and Macro-Sociologies.* Boston: Routledge and Kegan Paul.

Cook-Gumperz, Jenny, and John J. Gumperz 1994 "The Politics of a Conversation: Conversational Inference in Discussion" In A. D. Grimshaw, et al., *What's Going on Here? Complementary Studies of Professional Talk.* Norwood, N.J.: Ablex.

Corsaro, William A. 1981 "Communicative Processes in Studies of Social Organization: Sociological Approaches to Discourse Analysis." *Text* 1:5–63.

—— 1985 *Friendship and Peer Culture in the Early Years.* Norwood, N.J.: Ablex.

——, and Thomas A. Rizzo 1990 "Disputes in the Peer Culture of American and Italian Nursery School Children." In A. D. Grimshaw, ed., *Conflict Talk: Sociolinguistic Investigations of Arguments in Conversations.* Cambridge, UK: Cambridge University Press.

Coser, Lewis A 1956 *The Functions of Social Conflict.* Glencoe, Ill.: Free Press.

Czarniawska, Barbara 1997 *Narrating the Organization: Dramas of Institutional Identity.* Chicago: University of Chicago Press.

Dorval, Bruce, ed. 1990 *Conversational Organization and Its Development.* Norwood, N.J.: Ablex.

Edgerton, Robert B. 1985 *Rules, Exceptions, and Social Order.* Berkeley: University of California Press.

Eisenstein, Elizabeth L. 1979 *The Printing Press as an Agent of Change: Communications and Cultural Transformations in Early Modern Europe.* Cambridge, UK: Cambridge University Press.

Feld, Steven, and Carroll Williams 1975 "Toward a Researchable Film Language." *Studies in the Anthropology of Visual Communication* 2:25–32.

Fillmore, Charles J. 1971 "Verbs of Judging: An Exercise in Semantic Description." In C. J. Fillmore and D. T. Langendoen, *Studies in Linguistic Semantics.* New York: Holt, Rinehart and Winston.

—— 1994 "Humor in Academic Discourse." In A. D. Grimshaw et al., eds., *What's Going on Here? Complementary Studies of Professional Talk.* Norwood, N.J.: Ablex.

Firth, Raymond 1972 "Verbal and Bodily Rituals of Greeting and Parting." In J. S. La Fontaine, ed., *The Interpretation of Ritual: Essays in Honour of A. L. Richards.* London: Tavistock.

Fischer, John L. 1965 "The Stylistic Significance of Consonantal Sandhi in Trukese and Ponapean." *American Anthropologist* 67:1495–1502.

—— 1966 "Syntax and Social Structure: Truk and Ponape." In W. Bright, ed., *Sociolinguistics: Proceedings of the UCLA Sociolinguistics Conference, 1964.* The Hague: Mouton.

Fox, Barbara A., Makoto Hayashi, and Robert Jasperson 1996 "Resources and Repair: A Cross-Linguistic Study of Syntax and Repair." In E. Ochs, et al., eds., *Interaction and Grammar.* Cambridge, UK: Cambridge University Press.

Geertz, Clifford 1963 "The Integrative Revolution: Primordial Sentiments and Civil Politics in the New States." In C. Geertz, ed., *Old Societies and New States: The Quest for Modernity in Asia and Africa.* New York: Free Press.

Goffman, Erving 1971 *Relations in Public: Microstudies of the Public Order.* New York: Basic Books.

—— 1981 *Forms of Talk.* Philadelphia: University of Pennsylvania Press.

Goody, Esther N. 1978 "Towards a Theory of Questions." In E. N. Goody, ed., *Questions and Politeness: Strategies in Social Interaction.* Cambridge, UK: Cambridge University Press.

Goody, Jack 1987 *The Interface between the Oral and the Written.* Cambridge, UK: Cambridge University Press.

Goodwin, Charles 1996 "Transparent Vision." In E. Ochs et al., eds., *Interaction and Grammar.* Cambridge, UK: Cambridge University Press.

Goodwin, Marjorie Harness 1990 *He-Said-She-Said: Talk as Social Organization among Black Children.* Bloomington: Indiana University Press.

Graff, Harvey J. 1979 *The Literacy Myth: Literacy and Social Structure in the Nineteenth-Century City.* New York: Academic Press.

Grimshaw, Allen D. 1969 "Language as Obstacle and as Data in Sociological Research." *Items* 23:17–21.

—— 1973a "Rules in Linguistic, Social and Sociolinguistic Systems and Possibilities for a Unified Theory." In R. S. Shuy, ed., *Twenty-Third Annual Round Table.*

Monograph Series on Language and Linguistics (1972). Washington, D.C.: Georgetown University Press.

—— 1973b "On Language in Society: Part I." *Contemporary Sociology* 2:575–585.

—— 1974a "On Language in Society: Part II." *Contemporary Sociology* 3:3–11.

—— 1974b "Sociolinguistics." In I. de Sola Pool and W. Schramm, eds., *Handbook of Communication*. Chicago: Rand McNally.

—— 1980a "Social Interactional and Sociolinguistic Rules." *Social Forces* 58:789–810.

—— 1980b "Mishearing, Misunderstandings and Other Nonsuccesses in Talk: A Plea for Redress of Speaker-Oriented Bias." *Sociological Inquiry* 40:31–74.

—— 1981 "Talk and Social Control." In M. Rosenberg et al., eds., *Sociological Perspectives on Social Psychology*. New York: Basic Books.

——, ed. 1982 *Sound-Image Records in Social Interaction Research*. Special issue of *Sociological Methods and Research* 11.

—— 1987a "Sociolinguistics versus Sociology of Language: Tempest in a Teapot or Profound Academic Conundrum?" In U. Ammon, N. Dittmar, and K. J. Mattheier, eds., *Sociolinguistics: An International Handbook of the Science of Language and Society*, vol. 1. Berlin: Walter de Gruyter.

—— 1987b "Micro-Macrolevels." In U. Ammon, N. Dittmar, and K. J. Mattheier, eds., *Sociolinguistics: An International Handbook of the Science of Language and Society*, vol. 1. Berlin: Walter de Gruyter.

—— 1987c "Disambiguating Discourse: Members' Skill and Analysts' Problem." *Social Psychology Quarterly* 50:186–204.

—— 1989 *Collegial Discourse: Professional Conversation among Peers*. Norwood, N.J.: Ablex.

——, ed. 1990 *Conflict Talk: Sociolinguistic Investigations of Arguments in Conversations*. Cambridge, UK: Cambridge University Press.

—— 1992 "Research on the Discourse of International Negotiations: A Path to Understanding International Conflict Processes?" *Sociological Forum* 7:87–119.

—— 1994a "Referential Ambiguity in Pronominal Inclusion: Social and Linguistic Boundary Marking" In A.D. Grimshaw et al., eds., *What's Going on Here? Complementary Studies of Professional Talk*. Norwood, N.J.: Ablex.

—— 1994b "What We Have Learned: Some Research Conclusions and Some Conclusions about Research." In A. Grimshaw et al., eds., *What's Going on Here?*

Complementary Studies of Professional Talk. Norwood, N.J.: Ablex

——, Peter J. Burke, Aaron V. Cicourel, Jenny Cook-Gumperz, Steven Feld, Charles J. Fillmore, Lily Wong Fillmore, John J. Gumperz, Michael A. K. Halliday, Ruqaiya Hasan, and David Jenness, eds., 1994 *What's Going on Here? Complementary Studies of Professional Talk*. Norwood, N.J.: Ablex.

——, Steven Feld, and David Jenness 1994 "The MAP: An Ethnographic History of the Project and a Description of the Data." In A. Grimshaw et al., eds., *What's Going on Here? Complementary Studies of Professional Talk*. Norwood, N.J.: Ablex.

Gumperz, John J., and Dell Hymes, eds. (1972 [1966]) 1986 *Directions in Sociolinguistics: The Ethnography of Communication*. Oxford, UK: Basil Blackwell.

Habermas, Jürgen 1981–1984 *The Theory of Communicative Action*, trans. Thomas McCarthy. Boston: Beacon Press.

Hall, Edward T. 1966 *The Hidden Dimension*. Garden City, N.Y.: Doubleday.

—— 1974 *Handbook for Proxemic Research*. Washington, D.C.: Society for the Anthropology of Visual Communication.

Halliday, Michael A. K. 1994 "So You Say 'Pass' . . . Thank You Three Muchly." In A. D. Grimshaw et al., *What's Going on Here? Complementary Studies of Professional Talk*. Norwood, N.J.: Ablex.

Hasan, Ruqaiya 1994 "Situation and the Definition of Genres." In A. D. Grimshaw et al., *What's Going on Here? Complementary Studies of Professional Talk*. Norwood, N.J.: Ablex.

Hill, Jane H. 1999 "Language, Race, and White Public Space." *American Anthropologist* 100: 680–689.

Hymes, Dell 1966 "Two Types of Linguistic Relativity (with Examples from Amerindian Ethnography)." In W. Bright, ed., *Sociolinguistics: Proceedings of the UCLA Sociolinguistics Conference, 1964*. The Hague: Mouton.

Ibrahim ag Youssouf, Allen D. Grimshaw, and Charles S. Bird 1976 "Greetings in the Desert." *American Ethnologist* 3:797–824.

Kamensky, Jane 1997 *Governing the Tongue: The Politics of Speech in Early New England*. New York: Oxford University Press.

Kendon, Adam 1977 1990 *Conducting Interaction: Patterns of Behavior in Focused Encounters*. Cambridge, UK: Cambridge University Press.

——, and Andrew Ferber 1973 "A Description of Some Human Greetings. In R. P. Michael and J. H. Crooks, eds., *Comparative Ecology and Behavior of Primates*. London: Academic Press.

Kress, Gunther, and Robert Hodge 1979 *Language as Ideology*. London: Routledge and Kegan Paul.

Labov, Teresa G. 1980 *The Communication of Morality: Cooperation and Commitment in a Food Cooperative*. Unpublished dissertation. New York: Columbia University.

Labov, William 1968 "A Proposed Program for Research and Training in the Study of Language in Its Social and Cultural Settings." New York: Columbia University (mimeograph).

—— 1972a "Some Principles of Linguistic Methodology." *Language in Society* 1:97–120.

—— 1972b *Sociolinguistic Patterns*. Philadelphia: University of Pennsylvania Press.

——, ed. 1980 *Locating Language in Time and Space*. New York: Academic Press.

—— 1982 "Objectivity and Commitment in Linguistic Science: The case of the Black English Trial in Ann Arbor." *Language in Society* 11:165–201.

—— 1986 "Language Structure and Social Structure." In S. Lindenberg, J. S. Coleman, and S. Nowak, eds., *Approaches to Social Theory*. New York: Russell Sage Foundation.

——, and David Fanshel 1977 *Therapeutic Discourse: Psychotherapy as Conversation*. New York: Academic Press.

Lemert, Charles C. 1979 *Sociology and the Twilight of Man: Homocentrism and Discourse in Sociological Theory*. Carbondale: Southern Illinois University Press.

Lerner, Gene H. 1996 "On the 'Semi-Permeable' Character of Grammatical Units in Conversation: Conditional Entry into the Turn Space of Another Speaker." In E. Ochs et al., eds., *Interaction and Grammar*. Cambridge, UK: Cambridge University Press.

Mack, Raymond W., and Richard C. Snyder 1957 "The Analysis of Social Conflict—Toward an Overview and Synthesis." *Journal of Conflict Resolution* 1:212–248.

Maynard, Douglas W. 1984. *Inside Plea Bargaining: The Language of Negotiation*. New York: Plenum.

McRae, Kenneth D. 1983 *Conflict and Compromise in Multilingual Societies: Switzerland*. Waterloo, Ontario, Canada: Wilfred Laurier University Press.

—— 1986 *Conflict and Compromise in Multilingual Societies: Belgium*. Waterloo, Ontario, Canada: Wilfred Laurier University Press.

—— 1997 *Conflict and Compromise in Multilingual Societies: Finland*. Waterloo, Ontario, Canada: Wilfred Laurier University Press.

Moore, T. Inglis 1971 *Social Patterns in Australian Literature*. Berkeley: University of California Press.

Ochs, Elinor, Patrick Gonzales, and Sally Jacoby 1996 "'When I Come Down I'm in the Domain State': Grammar and Graphic Representation in the Interpretive Activity of Physicists. In E. Ochs et al., eds., *Interaction and Grammar*. Cambridge, UK: Cambridge University Press.

——, Emmanuel A. Schegloff, and Sandra A. Thompson, eds. 1996 *Interaction and Grammar*. Cambridge, UK: Cambridge University Press.

Rieber, Robert W., and William A. Stewart, eds. 1990 *The Language Scientist as Expert in the Legal Setting: Issues in Forensic Linguistics*. Vol. 606 of *Annals of the New York Academy of Sciences*.

Schegloff, Emanuel A. 1996 "Turn Organization: One Intersection of Grammar and Interaction." In E. Ochs, et al. eds, *Interaction and Grammar*. Cambridge, U.K.: Cambridge University Press.

Schieffelin, Bambi B. 1996 "Creating Evidence: Making Sense of Written Words in Bosavi." In E. Ochs et al., eds., *Interaction and Grammar*. Cambridge, UK: Cambridge University Press.

Silverman, David, and Brian Torode 1980 *The Material Word: Some Theories of Language and Its Limits*. London: Routledge and Kegan Paul.

Sorjonen, Marja-Lenna 1996 "On Repeats and Responses in Finnish Conversations." In E. Ochs et al., eds., *Interaction and Grammar*. Cambridge, UK: Cambridge University Press.

Tannen, Deborah 1990 *You Just Don't Understand: Men and Women in Conversation*. New York: Morrow.

Watson-Gegeo, Karen A., and Geoffrey M. White, eds. 1990 *Disentangling: Conflict Discourse in Pacific Societies*. Stanford, Calif: Stanford University Press.

Wertsch, James, and Hugh Mehan, eds. 1988 *Discourse of the Nuclear Arms Debate*. Special issue of *Multilingua: Journal of Cross-Cultural and Interlanguage Communication* 7.

Whalen, Jack 1991 "Conversation Analysis." In E. Borgatta and M. Borgatta, eds., *Encyclopedia of Sociology*, vol. 4. New York: Macmillan.

Williams, Robin M., Jr. 1947 *The Reduction of Intergroup Tensions*. New YorK: Social Science Research Council.

——, John P. Dean, and Edward A. Suchman 1964 *Strangers Next Door: Ethnic Relations in American Communities*. Englewood Cliffs, N.J.: Prentice-Hall.

Wong Fillmore, Lily 1994 "The Role and Function of Formulaic Speech in Conversation." In A. D. Grimshaw et al., eds., *What's Going on Here? Complementary Studies of Professional Talk*. Norwood, N.J.: Ablex.

ALLEN D. GRIMSHAW

ISBN 0-02-864852-8

90000